AMERICA'S POLITICAL DYNASTIES
from Adams to Kennedy

Also by Stephen Hess
(with Malcolm Moos):
HATS IN THE RING

AMERICA'S POLITICAL DYNASTIES

from Adams to Kennedy

STEPHEN HESS

DOUBLEDAY & COMPANY, INC.
GARDEN CITY, NEW YORK
1966

Library of Congress Catalog Card Number 66–17414
Copyright © 1966 by Stephen Hess
All Rights Reserved
Printed in the United States of America
First Edition

For Elena

CONTENTS

ILLUSTRATIONS

The Best Butter

"'It was the *best* butter,' the March
Hare meekly replied."

—Alice in Wonderland

THE Constitution could not be more specific: "No title of nobility
shall be granted by the United States."

Yet, in the nearly two centuries since these words were written, the
American people, despite official disapproval, have chosen a political nobility. For generation after generation they have turned for leadership
to certain families. "People's Dukes," Stewart Alsop calls them.[1]

Nor are these political dynasties numerically insignificant. There have
been some 700 families in which two or more members have served in
Congress, and they account for nearly 1700 of the 10,000 men and
women who have been elected to the federal legislature since 1774.*

The scholarship of politics, however, pays little attention to this phenomenon. It is as if a native ethos—"all men are created equal"—prohibits
calling attention to the fact that there are some families who have more
talents or more appeal to the voters; who, in short, are far more equal
than others at the political starting gate. As John Fischer, one of the
few writers to devote himself to this equalitarian blind spot, has written, "The notion that exceptional people ought to get exceptional consideration—and that their abilities might be transmitted by heredity—is
felt to be shockingly undemocratic and un-American."[2]

Then in mid-twentieth century, suddenly, surprisingly, shockingly,
American political life seemed to be largely peopled by such unique
families. They were all around us; we could hardly avoid them—Kennedys, Lodges, Longs, Tafts, Roosevelts.[3] The current United States
Senate alone contains seventeen members who are in some manner dynastically connected.[4]

This trend may be because public service is becoming a family tradi-

* Appendix B lists all families who have produced three or more members of
Congress.

tion, as it has long been in Great Britain; or because politics is becoming a "rich man's game" and the dynasties can usually afford to play; or because Americans vote for a son under the impression that they are voting for the father—or grandfather; or because we feel assured that the "People's Dukes" will keep their hands out of the till; or because there is some ability which can be transmitted through the genes; or simply because the voters have a sneaking weakness for dynasties.

But as we ponder over the proliferation of dynasties it is also worth noting that America always has had a political elite. Since the colonial Winthrops of New England, Randolphs of Virginia, Livingstons and De Lanceys of New York, our history has been peppered with "royal families." Yet with the exception of the Adamses and Harrisons, whose members studded our list of presidents, how many of these ancient names come to mind? Perhaps today's dynastic shock waves would be tempered by the knowledge that Delaware once sent five Bayards to the United States Senate or that there were four New Jersey congressmen from the family of Stockton or that one generation of Lees contained seven prominent public figures.

This study, then, is in the nature of calling attention, taking note. Its purpose is to bring together for the first time the panorama of American political dynasties from colonial days to the present; to investigate their roles in shaping the nation; and to recount the lives of some two hundred often engaging, usually ambitious, sometimes brilliant, occasionally unscrupulous individuals.

Arthur M. Schlesinger, Jr., has stated, "As a democracy the U.S. ought presumably to be able to dispense with dynastic families."[5] But it hasn't. And this is their story.

The children of President Taft—Bob, Charlie, and Helen—were playing charades at the White House. The word to be acted out was "dynasty." They were dying nastily outside of the Emancipation Proclamation Room. Just then a group of distinguished foreigners was ushered in. The game ended abruptly.[6]

But the young Tafts' problem has lingered on. How does one define "dynasty"?

A simple, statistically provable definition has been chosen for this study: *A dynasty is any family that has had at least four members, in the same name, elected to federal office.*[7] (The word "elected" should be stressed, for this elite has not existed through "divine right" or nepotism. It has been freely chosen.)

Twenty-two families qualify under this definition; fourteen of whom are discussed in this book.† Two additional families—the Kennedys and

† Eight dynasties were excluded because, given space limitations, they were felt to be of less interest to the general reader. However, other factors, such as

the Lodges—are included for other reasons. Only by genealogical sleight of hand (such as counting the late President's maternal grandfather) can the Kennedys qualify as a dynasty. But to have left them out solely for reasons of rigid definition would have been to turn one's back on the most interesting family currently on the political scene. While to exclude the Lodges would be, quite literally, an attack on motherhood! For although there have been only three Lodges in national elective office, when George Cabot Lodge ran for the Senate against Teddy Kennedy in 1962 he could count *eight* congressional ancestors. To ignore such impressive maternal and collateral lineage would be to deny that it takes two to propagate the species.

American political dynasties are fluid, mercurial things. Some will die. Some will be born. Nothing illustrates this so well as the career of the Longs. A half century ago they were obscure central Louisiana farmers; today their ancestry includes two governors, three senators, and three congressmen.

When Napoleon was assuming imperial pretensions and had gathered his own royal court, one of the more noble courtiers, who looked down his nose at Bernadotte, was informed by the marshal: "Sir, you are only a descendant. *I* am an ancestor."[8] How right he was! For Bernadotte later became Charles XIV, founder of the present royal house of Sweden. But, without Bernadotte's foresight, this study can report only on dynasties at a particular moment of history.

From the sixteen political dynasties with which this book is primarily concerned have come eight presidents, three vice-presidents, thirty senators, twelve governors, fifty-six members of the United States House of Representatives or Continental Congress, and nine cabinet officers.

Who are these families of such impressive statistics?

Most frequently, as the March Hare said, they are the best butter: old stock, Anglo-Saxon, Protestant, professional, Eastern seaboard, well to do.

—At least eight of the dynasties had arrived in America by the end of the seventeenth century; only two came after the Revolution.

—Eleven of their Founding Fathers were English.

—All but one of the dynasties have been primarily Protestant.

—Of eighty-three dynasts elected to federal office, fifty-seven have been lawyers, although some never practiced and others eventually left the profession or had another occupation.

---

contemporaneousness and geography, were also considered. For example, the distinguished Hoar family was left out primarily because two more recent Massachusetts dynasties have now overshadowed its achievements. It should be noted that eleven of the sixteen families in this study have had at least one member run for federal office in this generation.

—Only five of the dynasties have made most or all of their political reputation outside of the original colonies.

—More than half have been in the millionaire class at some time.

But being poor or Celtic or Catholic or in some other way different from the norm had not necessarily been disqualifying. The Muhlenbergs —impecunious German ministers—sent six members to Congress. The Kennedys have been mavericks in every respect except wealth.

As might be expected of old families, their wealth has often come from the land. First they planted it; later they sold it. Some of the more acquisitive used this base to build a second fortune. The Livingstons, one of whom married Robert Fulton, held the earliest steamboat monopoly; the Stocktons had an exclusive railroad franchise between New York and Philadelphia.

While the dynasties have been wealthy, rarely have they been immensely wealthy. (Moreover, as a high birth rate has been a dynastic characteristic, their money is apt to be dissipated through dispersion.) There have been no Astors, Vanderbilts, or Goulds in Congress. One reason for this is the hardening of upper-class arteries—and political participation requires societal circulation. Yet if public office was beneath the ken of Mrs. Astor's "Four Hundred," it was equally beneath the contempt of Jay Gould, a firm believer in the proposition that political influence could be purchased when needed. (Some of the sons and grandsons of robber barons have turned to public service, but enough time has not yet elapsed for them to build political dynasties.) However, although the very rich steered clear of elective office, they were not averse to having their daughters marry politicians, thus suggesting the second great source of dynastic income.[9]

The story is told that when Dwight Eisenhower was propelled into politics in 1952 he sought to find a common trait among the breed of political men with whom he had been thrown. Some, he concluded, were bright—some were not; some were good conversationalists—some were not; some had senses of humor—some did not. But the one common denominator he found was that they had all married above themselves![10] American political dynasts have followed the "Eisenhower axiom."

At least five of these clans can trace the bulk of their wealth directly to advantageous marriages. The correspondence of Presidents John and John Quincy Adams is filled with tales of money miseries; then the latter's son married the daughter of Peter Chardon Brooks, Boston's first millionaire. Also bagged in the great fortune hunt have been such capitalistic game as an Astor, Beekman, Cabot, Du Pont, Havemeyer, Morgan, Sears, Stevens, and Van Rensselaer.

The dynasties have likewise received massive transfusions of political blood through the heirs of Henry Clay, John Witherspoon, Francis Preston Blair, George Mason, John Tyler, Charles Carroll of Carrollton, and others. Any *Almanach de Gotha* of American political royalty would also have to note the frequency of interdynasty matches—the cross-fertilization of Roosevelts and Livingstons, Livingstons and Lees, Bayards and Livingstons, Bayards and Carrolls, Carrolls and Lees, Lodges and Frelinghuysens, Muhlenbergs and Hiesters, Stocktons and Adamses. Such high-grade genealogical ore has inspired one writer to claim that Theodore Roosevelt and Franklin Delano Roosevelt were hereditarily joined to ten other presidents of the United States.[11]

The dynastic daughters were used as pawns in this chess game of political eugenics. Either through parental arrangement or because they were thrown together on the same circuit or because they were looking for husbands who resembled their fathers, they married a host of powerful politicians or sons of powerful politicians. Five Livingston girls were wed to congressmen in one generation. (If this helped to consolidate or expand the dynasties' positions, it was hardly a one-way street. As a Hollywood wag said when David O. Selznick married Louis B. Mayer's daughter, "The son-in-law also rises.")[12]

Yet despite such careful mating and other advantages, the dynasties have not escaped their share of insanity, suicide, alcoholism, mental retardation, financial reverses, acts of embezzlement, and sexual scandal.

They have been remarkably versatile in another way. It might be supposed that the quest for public office would be all-consuming. But the families of America's political elite have also managed to produce poets, novelists, scientists, inventors, clergymen, educators, and men of commerce. While the Roosevelts are known now for other talents, they can point with pride to the inventor of the electric organ, an early steamboat innovator, a pioneer conservationist, a New York philanthropist, a radical economist, and a connection with Mother Seton. Four other dynasties also claim important religious figures. The first Frelinghuysen in America was known as "The Apostle of the Raritan"; the first Muhlenberg was "The Patriarch of the German Lutheran Church in America." The Tucker family of Virginia is probably better remembered for legal scholars, novelists, and Episcopal bishops than for sending five sons to the United States Congress. And a well-known anthology of American poetry includes works by an Adams, a Tucker, a Lodge, and a Muhlenberg.[13]

Most surprising has been the high mobility of the dynasties. Since these families have been well to do and well connected, it might be assumed that the sons would choose to remain in their well-preserved compounds. But greener pastures do not only beckon to those whose grass is burned out. Perhaps reflecting the wanderlust of their nation, political dynasts have been a footloose lot. Only three of these sixteen families have never sought election outside the confines of their native states. There have even been four-state and five-state dynasties.

For more than a century and a half the Harrisons were Virginia aristocrats, rich, respected, and politically successful. They had served in the colony's legislature for five consecutive generations and had added the family's name to the Declaration of Independence. Then at the end of the eighteenth century they became political nomads. And in their second century and a half on the American continent they were elected to national office from Ohio, Indiana, Illinois, and Wyoming.

A bankrupt storekeeper named Washburn had five politically ambitious sons: son number one became a Maine congressman and governor; number two became a congressman from Illinois; number three became a Wisconsin congressman and governor; the fourth became a Minnesota congressman and senator; the fifth son went to California and later became U.S. minister to Paraguay. Possibly, as their proud mother said, no one state was big enough to hold them. Certainly, as the Kennedys were to conclude, there is a dynastic saturation point within a state's boundaries. It also may be that the same attributes of restlessness and ambition make a successful politician and a wanderer.

But if large families create dynastic problems, there appear to be outweighing advantages. A definite correlation exists between family size and political success. With the exception of those constitutional iconoclasts, the Adamses, a dynasty blooms when the birth rate is high and decays in direct proportion to its decline in numbers. In the case of the Livingstons, Washburns, Lees, Kennedys, and Muhlenbergs the most politically productive generation has been the largest. This may be merely a matter of probabilities—if there are five sons the chances are greater of one getting elected to office than if there is an only son.

It also suggests that these families have been the recipients of good luck and the grace of God. For it is a truism to say that they must reproduce to remain a dynasty. So they survive, in part, because they have not been unduly cursed with impotence, sterility, celibacy, homosexuality, or premature death.

These, then, are the general characteristics of the dynasties. But there must be a great many families who equally fit the description without having sent a member to Congress. What makes one family, generation after generation, run for political office, rather than go into the widget business or pursue no pronounced occupational pattern?

There are certain traits that are generally found in all politicians—no matter what their fathers' profession—for example, ambition, gregariousness, energy, often a physical attractiveness, tenacity. Given a "political personality," a man may be attracted to public life and the public may be attracted to him. Can such characteristics be inherited? Will a political personality, through genes and chromosomes, produce another political personality? The author is neither geneticist nor biologist and the riddle of nature-nurture is complex. But the latest studies agree that, while personality traits are not inherited in an absolute sense, certain potentials are inherited. "Biological inheritance," write Professors Kluckhohn and Murray, "provides the stuff from which personality is fashioned and, as manifested in the physique at a given time-point, determines trends and sets limits within which variation is constrained."[14]

This perhaps is what Dr. Oliver Wendell Holmes meant when he said that a child's education begins 250 years before it is born.[15]

Thus a dynasty may start with an inherited *tendency*, at which point environment comes into play. Many dynasties are founded, or greatly reinforced, by one dominant personality. This first politician, the political paterfamilias, whether old John Adams or old Joe Kennedy, Robert Livingston, First Lord of the Manor, or Alphonso Taft, instills in his young a sense of duty to family. The tribal sense, or dynastic instinct, is often what initially distinguishes the Kennedys and Adamses from their less motivated contemporaries.

Now politics becomes the home environment. Young John Quincy Adams eavesdrops on his father's conversations with Thomas Jefferson; young Charles Francis Adams eavesdrops on John Quincy Adams' conversations with Henry Clay. This can be an intoxicating brew.

Also by the second generation there is the "Daddy's business factor." The pressures and proclivities that operate on a young Du Pont or send successive generations of certain families to West Point can be seen at work on young Roosevelts, Lodges, and Tafts.[16]

Unlike young Du Pont, however, young Roosevelt or Lodge has no business that he automatically inherits. Daddy served at the will of the people and he must submit himself to that same will. Yet his legacy is far from worthless. It consists of two priceless commodities: connections and a brand name. As has been repeatedly shown, this is not a key to the White House, but if skillfully applied it can open the door to the state legislature or even Congress.

Two examples illustrate the value of the political brand name:

—Senator Albert Gore polled the citizens of Washington, D.C., in February 1960 on their preference for a Democratic presidential nominee. His list included all the leading candidates plus the names of John Eisenhower and Franklin D. Roosevelt, Jr.—sons of presidents, but hardly presidential contenders. More than twenty-five per cent chose Eisenhower or Roosevelt.[17]

—A deadlock over reapportionment in 1964 necessitated the at-large election of the entire Illinois House of Representatives. The ballot of 236 names resembled an orange bath towel. On the Democratic list was Adlai E. Stevenson III, thirty-three, son of the 1952 and 1956 Democratic presidential nominee; on the Republican list was Earl Eisenhower, sixty-six, brother of the 1952 and 1956 Republican presidential nominee. *Neither legislative candidate had ever sought office before.* When the votes were counted, first among the 118 Democrats was Adlai E. Stevenson III; first among the 118 Republicans was Earl Eisenhower.[18]

But dynasties could not exist by name alone. Jefferson felt that there was a natural aristocracy among men whose bases were "virtue and talents." While political virtue is a prickly nettle to grasp, the dynasties at least have usually lived by the Christian concept of "stewardship," a sense of obligation to use their wealth and position to improve society according to their convictions. They also have had a strong sense of country or patriotism and, in some cases, a highly developed sense of history.

As for the second half of the Jeffersonian equation, American political dynasties have generally earned high marks. They have produced mediocrity, of course; but by and large they have been men of talents. The American experience would have been far poorer without such dynasts as John and John Quincy Adams, Richard Henry Lee, Theodore and Franklin D. Roosevelt, William Howard Taft, Robert Taft, and John F. Kennedy.

In an era when the nation is producing more leaders of inherited social, economic, and political advantage than at any time since the American Revolution, the question of class leadership in a democracy deserves careful scrutiny.

"History," E. Digby Baltzell tells us, "is a graveyard of classes which have preferred caste privileges to leadership."[19] In countries where a decaying aristocracy retains some degree of governmental control this can create serious problems. But this has not been the American habit. Rather than polluting the political blood stream, the caste-conscious heirs of once potent political dynasties have proved to be harmless and somewhat pathetic. A century after a wise man of humble roots was elected President, one of Abraham Lincoln's last male descendants was quoted as saying with airy disdain, "I never take part in politics. None of the family does."[20]

Other great names, such as the Adamses, the Tuckers, the Virginia branch of the Lees, the Livingstons, and the Stocktons, have also left the field of combat. Some have retired to a form of American Shintoism—devoting their days to worship at the shrine of illustrious ancestors; some have simply changed direction and have subsequently done important work in other fields. All have left politics gracefully. And the political loss to society has been slight—except for the possible loss of talent. Thus the United States has suffered little when its dynasties decline.

On the other hand, the nation has benefited measurably from having an elected elite. For the voters have been selective even within the dynasties. After the initial dynastic boost, the sons of the famous have found their own level. Only one President's son has also become President; others have had to settle for lesser offices or even political rejection.

More than a half century ago Harvard's president, Charles W. Eliot, wrote, "If society as a whole is to gain by mobility and openness of structure, those who rise must stay up in successive generations, that the higher levels of society may be constantly enlarged. . . ." While he felt that the family, rather than the individual, was the important social unit, he was not preaching a doctrine of exclusivity. He was neither snob nor Brahmin apologist. Rather his ideal society envisioned all families as "free starting," with a fluid aristocracy that made room for "new-risen talent."[21]

This has been the American model.

The Adams Dynasty

"The Adams family was extraordinary not only
for the continuity of its achievements but also
its diversity. Among them were two Presidents, a
Secretary of the Navy, an industrialist, two authors, a diplomat. . . ."

—John F. Kennedy[1]

"It would be difficult to find in history another
case of four successive generations of intellectual
distinction and highest public service equal to
that shown by the Adams family during the past
century and a half."

—Henry Cabot Lodge, Sr.[2]

THE inheritance of an Adams includes a standard set of physical
characteristics. It is as if a die stamps out assembly-line face and body
parts. The Adams frame is short and stocky. (John Adams, when Vice-
President, was called "His Rotundity.") The Adams face, from top to
bottom, has a tendency to baldness, a broad forehead, finely arched
eyebrows, penetrating eyes, a slightly aquiline nose, and a bulldog jaw.

Each Adams has also inherited an uncommonly constant collection of
personality traits. To the observing public, the typical Adams has been
tactless, often beyond the point of rudeness; lacking in humor; introspective, sometimes morbidly so; preachy, scholarly, and moralistic;
austere, cold, and unsocial.

Tactlessness, an overwhelming political liability for most mortals, has
been a "prenatal manner" to an Adams—"congenital, hereditary and
in the blood," according to the second Charles Francis Adams.[3] In
1782 Sir John Temple said of John Adams, "He is the most ungracious
man I ever saw."[4] And James Russell Lowell later remarked, "The

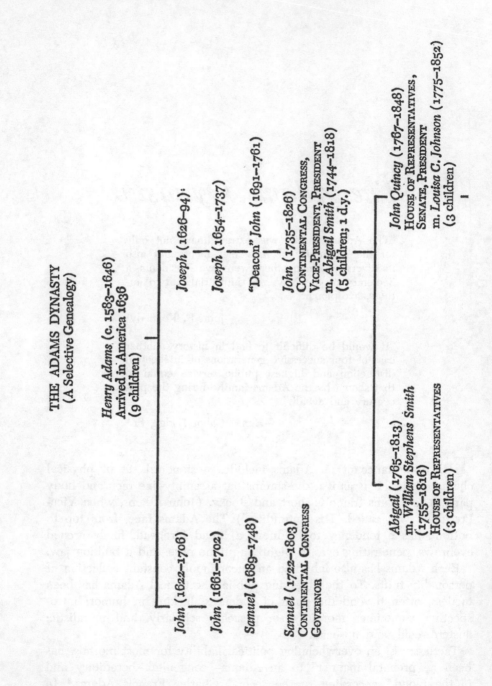

THE ADAMS DYNASTY
(A Selective Genealogy)

Henry Adams (c. 1583–1646)
Arrived in America 1636
(9 children)

Joseph (1626–94)

Joseph (1654–1737)

"Deacon" John (1691–1761)

John (1735–1826)
CONTINENTAL CONGRESS,
VICE-PRESIDENT, PRESIDENT
m. *Abigail Smith* (1744–1818)
(5 children; 1 d.y.)

John Quincy (1767–1848)
HOUSE OF REPRESENTATIVES,
SENATE, PRESIDENT
m. *Louisa C. Johnson* (1775–1852)
(3 children)

Abigail (1765–1813)
m. *William Stephens Smith*
(1755–1816)
HOUSE OF REPRESENTATIVES
(3 children)

John (1622–1706)

John (1661–1702)

Samuel (1689–1748)

Samuel (1722–1803)
CONTINENTAL CONGRESS
GOVERNOR

George Washington (1801–28)
(unmarried)

Charles Francis (1807–86)
HOUSE OF REPRESENTATIVES,
minister to Great Britain
m. Abigail Brooks (1808–1889)
(6 children; 1 d.y.)

Brooks (1848–1927)
Author
m. Evelyn Davis
(d. 1927)
(no issue)

Henry (1838–1918)
Author
m. Marian Hooper
(1843–85)
(no issue)

Charles Francis (1835–1915)
Author, railroad
president
m. Mary Ogden (1843–1935)
(5 children)

Catherine
m. Henry Sturgis Morgan
(5 children)

John Quincy (1833–94)
Democratic leader of
Massachusetts
m. Fanny Crowninshield
(6 children; 2 d.y.)

Charles Francis (1866–1954)
Secretary of Navy
m. Frances Lovering
(1869–1956)
(2 children)

Charles Francis (1910–   )
Business executive
m. Margaret Stockton
(3 children)

Adamses have a genius for saying even a gracious thing in an ungracious way!"*

No one has been more aware of an Adams failing than an Adams. Through diaries, autobiographies, and letters they practiced self-flagellation of the soul.† John Quincy Adams thought himself "a man of reserved, cold, austere, and forbidding manners; my political adversaries say, a gloomy misanthropist, and my personal enemies, an unsocial savage."[5] These were the same family traits that caused Governor Marcus Morton of Massachusetts to call Charles Francis Adams "The Greatest Iceberg in the Northern hemisphere."[6]

Yet, within his intimate circle, an Adams has often been able to display considerable conviviality. At a New York dinner party in the late 1830s the host served fourteen different madeiras, and John Quincy Adams surprised and delighted his companions by correctly identifying eleven of them.[7] While Henry Adams, an eccentric recluse to the world in general, was a devoted and cherished part of a particular social world that included John Hay, Theodore Roosevelt, and Henry Cabot Lodge, Sr. Hay was fond of calling Henry "Porcupinus Angelicus." And clearly, for four generations the Adams prickly exterior was a protective armor to cover a morbidly sensitive interior.

As politicians, the Adamses have stood before the people but have never been of the people. They haven't known how to be popular. When an inebriated voter said to President John Quincy Adams, "I hope the Constitution may never be broken," the President stiffly replied, "I concur heartily in that wish and hope that *your* constitution may never be broken."[8] It was not meant as a joke; he simply did not know how to cope with the intoxicating banter of the hustings. In New York in 1826, Charles Francis Adams was amazed to find among his father's supporters "an attachment to him amounting even to enthusiasm." But he quickly explained to himself: ". . . perhaps the wine produced as much of this as anything else."[9]

It has been long lives, not any deliberate acts on their part, that have brought the Adamses whatever public popularity they received from their contemporaries. In the public mind, old age bestows lovable-

---

* This faculty for tactlessness was apparently transmuted to the Adams wives. During the Great Secession Winter of 1860–61, Mrs. Charles Francis Adams managed to praise abolitionist John Brown at a Washington dinner party composed of Southern congressmen! See Arthur F. Beringause, *Brooks Adams* (New York: Knopf, 1955), p. 26.

† The inkstained hand is another Adams characteristic. The writings of the family total 400,000 pages, "and perhaps substantially more," in the estimation of the editors of *The Adams Papers* at Harvard. The papers, only through 1889, are reproduced on 27,464 feet of 35-millimeter film and will ultimately be published in 80 to 100 volumes.

ness on a politician. And longevity has been an Adams characteristic. The average life span of the seven most famous members of the dynasty is more than eighty-two years.

The Adamses rose to prominence over the strenuous objections of the leading citizens of Massachusetts, their home state, and without the necessary financial means to support the occupation of public servant in a republic.

Ironically, the dynasty, now synonymous with Proper Boston, spent its most productive years at odds with the Back Bay elite. The Adamses of Quincy started on "the wrong side of Boston's narrow-gauge social tracks," writes social arbiter Cleveland Amory.[10] When John Adams entered Harvard College in 1751 he was ranked socially as fifteenth in a class of twenty-four; he would have rated even lower had his mother not been a Boylston. Politically, he and Sam Adams were for independence, which was against the better judgment of State Street; John Quincy Adams was for union and against the Hartford Convention; Charles Francis Adams was for abolition. For three generations the Adamses were almost perversely opposed to whatever Boston's leading merchants felt was in their best interests. It would have been asking a saintly dose of charity to forgive the Adamses for their hundred years of being "right." Small wonder that Henry Adams, in the fourth generation, could write of his family's "inherited quarrel with State Street."[11] Or that his brother Charles Francis could write, "I have tried Boston socially on all sides; I have summered it and wintered it, tried it drunk and tried it sober; and, drunk or sober, there's nothing in it—save Boston!"[12]

The absence of financial underpinnings to support the very considerable Adams zest for public service has been a much greater liability. John Adams, a simple farmer's son, gave up a successful law practice at thirty-nine to enter the Continental Congress; and after that, with very minor exceptions, he had no private employment for the remaining fifty-two years of his life. His son John Quincy Adams, from his admission to the bar in his early twenties until his death at eighty-one, was outside government service for just seven years. During their combined appointive and elective careers of seventy-eight years they received little in the way of monetary satisfaction from a young nation that prided itself on meager public salaries. "A curiosity" is what John Adams called the $5000 he annually received for being Vice-President of the United States; as Secretary of State, John Quincy Adams was paid $3500 a year.[13]

The plight of the first two generations of Adamses was further complicated by the nature of the offices they held. As representatives of the United States in the diplomatic community their living and entertainment expenses were expected to be well above their government remunerations. Adams figured that while Secretary of State his expenses exceeded his salary by $4000 to $5000 a year. They were poor men playing in a rich man's league. As minister to Russia, John Quincy Adams' salary was second only to that of the President of the United States. Yet it was a paltry figure when compared to the $350,000 a year that the French government gave its ambassador for official expenses.[14] The immensely practical Abigail Adams was so worried about her son's financial position that she asked President Madison to recall him from Russia. Madison obliged, and even offered the young man a seat on the Supreme Court, which the Senate confirmed. But he declined the honor. The Adams men would always grumble and do their duty.

It was not until the death of Peter Chardon Brooks in 1849 that the Adams family was on firm financial footing. Brooks was the father-in-law of Charles Francis Adams, and Boston's first millionaire. His estate settled $300,000 on the third-generation Adamses. The generous bequest may have turned out to be a double-edged sword which contributed to the decline of the dynasty. For in the fourth generation the financially independent Brooks Adams would write to his financially independent brother Henry, "The greatest relief a man can have is a fixed occupation, which has become a second nature, and which absorbs his time. Our misfortune has been that this necessary application of our energy has been denied us. We live largely on ourselves."[15]

Given politically unpalatable personalities, which all the Adamses vigorously contended could not be altered, a collection of formidable enemies, and a lack of financial means, the Adamses built a great political dynasty. They succeeded, over mountainous odds, by sheer intellectual ability and an inherited capacity for hard work.

During his years in the Continental Congress, John Adams served on more than ninety committees and was chairman of twenty-five; his son John Quincy Adams was still working a twelve-, thirteen-, and even eighteen-hour day at seventy years of age. Nothing pleased John Adams more than when a Baltimore newspaper called him an "old fielder"— for, as he explained to Abigail, "An old fielder is a tough, hardy, laborious little horse that works very hard and lives upon very little."[16]

The Adamses established unsurpassed records for industry in every job they held. After his four colleagues had left Ghent, John Quincy Adams stayed on to complete the record of the negotiations that ended the War of 1812, although it meant that his wife and seven-year-old son had to travel alone across two thousand miles of war-torn Europe in midwinter. Later, when he was Secretary of State, Congress assigned him the task of preparing a report on weights and measures. This was the type of job that is traditionally sloughed off on subordinates. But not by Secretary Adams. He spent three years of his spare time writing a weighty tome that has become a scientific classic. John Quincy Adams also achieved the dubious distinction of being probably the only American foreign minister to have been locked in the State Department by a janitor while working long after the official closing hour.

This energy was a manifestation of the Adams ambition and will power. John Adams wrote to his son, a twenty-seven-year-old lawyer, "If you do not rise to the head not only of your profession but of your country, it will be owing to your own laziness, slovenliness, and obstinacy."[17] It has been said that only five presidents dreamed from boyhood of being in the White House, but this was the dream of almost every male Adams for three generations. John Quincy rose to the head of his country, as his father predicted; Charles Francis ran for Vice-President and narrowly missed a presidential nomination; John Quincy II also ran for Vice-President; Brooks Adams waited in vain for the vice-presidential nomination at the 1896 Democratic Convention; even Henry Adams, now remembered for his other-worldliness, had great if ill-defined ambitions during his early career. As a fledgling reporter he talked of making his political writing into "a power in the land," and while disclaiming ambition for political office, Henry added, "*except very high office* I would take none."[18]

Yet it was a strict Adams rule, only rarely broken, not to lift a finger to aid one's own political ambition. A frustrated supporter, waiting for John Quincy Adams to declare himself for the presidency in 1824, wrote his reluctant favorite, "Kings are made by politicians and newspapers; and the man who sits down waiting to be crowned either by chance or just right will go bare-headed all his life."[19] The Adams doctrine of "the office seeks the man" was carried to its ultimate application in 1833 when John Quincy was a candidate for governor of Massachusetts and his son Charles Francis was running for the state legislature: the younger Adams voted for neither his father nor himself!

While these industrious, intellectual Adamses were building a massive record of achievement, there were others in the family who fared less well. It was almost unconscionably difficult to be an Adams, and all who were so blessed could not live up to their inheritance. As Henry Cabot Lodge, Sr., said, "This remarkable heritage brought to those who received it burdens as well as honor."[20] As often as not, the burdens exceeded the honor.

Of the three sons of Abigail and John Adams, one became President of the United States but two dissolved in drink. Their daughter lived an equally unhappy life, although not of her own volition. John Quincy Adams also had three sons: one committed suicide in his late twenties, another died in his early thirties, which left Charles Francis, as he wrote in his diary, "the only one who remains to keep the name and the family in our branch at least from destruction."[21]

On the last day of 1798, President John Adams wrote his wife, "My children give me more pain than all my enemies."[22] His daughter and first-born, Abigail, had married Colonel William Stephens Smith when her father was minister to Great Britain and Smith was secretary to the legation. The tall, dark, and dashing officer, a former aide-de-camp to General Washington, was to spend the remainder of his years in pursuit of pleasures which he could not afford; in pursuit of land speculations which rarely materialized; in pursuit of public sinecures which were supplied by his father-in-law at considerable moral and political cost. (Ironically, the very odd young man whom John Adams' daughter jilted went on to become a famous playwright and chief justice of the Vermont Supreme Court.)[23]

The son for whom President John Adams grieved was Charles, three years younger than John Quincy. During the Revolution the father had taken the two boys with him to Europe, but while John Quincy went on to Russia as private secretary to American diplomat Francis Dana, Charles became homesick and returned to mother in Massachusetts. After Harvard and a legal training he married Sally Smith, the sister of William Stephens Smith, a "modest and composed" girl, in the opinion of her mother-in-law. Charles was to give the Smith family as much grief as his brother-in-law was to give the Adamses. He too was affected by the get-rich-quick lures of land speculation, and his ruinous losses were compounded by the guilt of having also lost the savings that John Quincy had entrusted to his care. Charles became an alcoholic and died at thirty. The father received the news at almost the same moment that he learned of his loss of the presidency to Jefferson.

John Adams' other unfortunate son was Thomas Boylston, the youngest child, who lived with his father in the ex-President's last years. Thomas also drank too much, and periodically deserted his family. His nephew Charles Francis, then at Harvard, unctuously decided that Thomas' fate "was necessary to check our pride."[24]

Most tragic was the fate of John Quincy's eldest child, George Washington Adams. When he was born in Berlin in 1801, the young father wrote, "I know not whether upon rigorous philosophical principles it is wise to give a great and venerable name to such a lottery-ticket as a new-born infant—but my logical scruples have in this case been overpowered by my instinctive sentiments."[25] George turned out to be a brilliant young man who beat Ralph Waldo Emerson in competition for the Boylston Prize at Harvard, studied law with Daniel Webster, and was elected to the Massachusetts legislature at twenty-five. Yet he was erratic, undisciplined, and irresponsible. Filled with his private romantic dreams, he left his personal and business affairs in a tatter. The Puritan sermons of his well-meaning and devoted father only added to his inability to cope with reality. Even in his dreams he heard his father admonishing, "Remember, George, who you are, what you are doing!"[26]

On April 29, 1828, George took a steamboat to Washington. The engines kept telling him, "Let it be, let it be, let it be, let it be." In the middle of the night he awakened a passenger to ask if the stranger had been spreading rumors against him. He asked the captain to stop the ship and put him ashore because "there is a combination among the passengers against me." The hallucinatory young man added, "I heard them talking and laughing at me."[27] In the morning George's hat was found on the upper deck; the former President claimed his son's body at the New York morgue.

George had left a note for his brother, asking him to look after a young girl he had made pregnant. Charles Francis destroyed the letter. "I shall do what I can in pursuit of the spirit of the request, though I confess the whole to be a foolish effusion of a thoughtless moment," wrote the brother in his diary.[28]

From 1636, when Henry Adams brought his nine children to Massachusetts from England, until the birth of Samuel Adams in 1722, the most exalted Adams was a village pastor in New Hampshire. The records of these early Adamses, according to the second Adams to be President of the United States, are "of humble life, but there is nothing in them of which a descendant need be ashamed."[29] They were typical New England yeomen. Deacon John Adams, the father of the first Adams President, was a farmer, cordwainer or shoemaker, tithingman, and village selectman.

Then suddenly, without explanation, this line of uninterrupted mediocrity was shattered by two signers of the Declaration of Independence.

Samuel and John Adams were third cousins, their great-grandfathers having been brothers. Sam, the elder by thirteen years, tutored his young relation in revolution. And "this brace of Adamses," as they were called by old Governor Shirley, teamed up with the Lees of Virginia to maneuver the separation from Great Britain. It was inevitable that peace would separate the cousins politically. As John wrote his wife, "Master Cleverly used to say thirty years ago, 'I pity Mr. Sam Adams, for he was born a rebel.'" John added, "I hope he will not die one."[30] But Sam, the greatest manager of the mob in American history, had little talent for constructive statesmanship and died a hard-shelled reactionary. Moreover, he had only daughters, and so the political dynasty would be carried forward through his cousin's line.‡

Deacon John Adams left the bulk of his estate to his sons Elihu and Peter Boylston. Elihu became a militia captain and died of dysentery early in the Revolution; Peter lived a long life as a Quincy farmer in the manner of his father. The eldest son, John Adams, received the greatest inheritance, an education.

After college and a brief try at teaching, he turned to the law. And while a struggling young lawyer he married Abigail, daughter of the Reverend William Smith. The marriage was objected to by Mrs. Smith, who was a Quincy, and whose father, the Honorable John Quincy, had been the Speaker of the Massachusetts House of Representatives for fourteen years. Mrs. Smith's daughter deserved better than the son of Deacon John Adams.§

The union of Abigail Smith and John Adams was a long and constant love affair. Thirty-one years later Abigail would write her husband, "Years subdue the ardor of passion, but in lieu thereof a friendship and affection, deep rooted, subsists which defies the ravages of time, and will survive whilst the flame exists. Our attachments . . . increase, I believe, with our years."[31]

She was more than a lover and the bearer of John's five children, one of whom died in infancy. For she had the "capacity to comprehend." Their letters are a blend of love *and* politics; and hers, as John admitted, "are much better worth preserving than mine." Her graceful comments and apt quotations were even raided by her husband for his own use in corresponding with the leaders of the nation. In truth, John Adams called his wife "My best, my dearest, my wisest friend in this world."[32]

Their marriage was marked by long separations. After thirteen years as Mrs. John Adams, Abigail wrote that "not more than half that time have we had the happiness of living together."[33] And the years apart increased as her husband served his country in congresses and diplo-

‡ However Samuel Adams was to have a nephew and a grandson in the Congress. The nephew, Joseph Allen (1749–1827), voted for John Adams as a Federalist presidential elector in 1797 and was a member of the House of Representatives in 1810 and 1811. Adams' grandson, Charles Allen (1797–1869), was elected to the House of Representatives in 1848 and 1850 on the Free Soil ticket. See *Biographical Directory of the American Congress 1774–1961* (Washington: Government Printing Office, 1961), pp. 472 and 469.

§ Abigail Adams' mother, Elizabeth Quincy Smith (1721–75), might have made less of social distinctions if she could have known that her only son, William Smith (1746–87), was to become an alcoholic, who was accused of counterfeiting and deserted his family to live with another woman. See Page Smith, *John Adams* (Garden City, New York: Doubleday, 1962), pp. 668 and 719.

matic posts. While John worked at revolution, Abigail was their children's protector, teacher, disciplinarian, and even breadwinner. She ran the farm and added to her meager earnings by selling the bits of linen and calico that John sent her from France.

John Adams came more slowly to a belief in American independence than his cousin Sam. He was first concerned with justice. (He and his heirs would always be first concerned with abstracts; they were more comfortable with generalities than with particulars.) In 1770 John Adams' abstract justice led him to defend British Captain Preston and his soldiers when they were tried for firing on the citizens of Boston. He knew the "Boston Massacre" had been incited; the mob was wrong. It was a made-to-order cause for Adams, who enjoyed playing the martyr and now felt he was sacrificing his political future. But Sam Adams could not afford his cousin's self-righteousness: independence was an end that necessitated some unholy means. John won his case and, quickly thereafter, a seat in the Massachusetts legislature as well.

When he was elected to the Continental Congress in 1774, John was a provincial lawyer who had only once been outside his own colony. Three years before he had gone to Connecticut to take a mineral-water cure. (Hypochondria was another Adams trait, though they quickly forgot their ailments when involved in a cause.) And so he rode off to Philadelphia to "see a little more of the world" and to enter "the theater of action."

The Puritan found Philadelphia to be a city of "sinful feasts" of "everything which could delight the eye or allure the taste; curds and creams, jellies, sweetmeats of various sorts, twenty sorts of tarts, fools, trifles, floating islands, whipped syllabubs . . . Parmesan cheese, punch, wine, porter, beer, etc."[34] For a man who would not allow his wife to read Lord Chesterfield's letters because they were "stained with libertine morals," it was a rude shock to find that he enjoyed these new sensations. It was the beginning of a lifelong struggle, wrote biographer Page Smith, "in which the hedonist had as ally Adams' passionate involvement in life, and the Puritan a conscience hammered out by four generations of forebears who had carried on an unending dialogue with God."[35]

"This assembly is like no other that ever existed," Adams wrote from Philadelphia. "Every man in it is a great man, an orator, a critic, a statesman; and therefore every man upon every question must show his oratory, his criticism, and his political abilities. The consequence of this is that business is drawn and spun out to an immeasurable length. I believe if it was moved and seconded that three and two make five, we should be entertained with logic and rhetoric, law, history, politics, and mathematics, and then—we should pass the resolution unanimously in the affirmative."[36] Yet during the long and tedious sessions Adams proposed George Washington as Commander-in-Chief, a masterful stroke of continental unity; he almost singlehandedly founded the American navy; and, as chairman of the Board of War and Ordnance, he began to build America's war machine. But the crowning achievement of his four years in the Congress was independence. Wrote Richard Stockton, a delegate from New Jersey, "I call him the Atlas of American independence. He it was who sustained the debate, and by the force of his reasoning demonstrated not only the justice but the expediency of the measure."[37]

In November 1777, Congress elected Adams to a three-man commission to France. The next February he left America with his eleven-year-old son John Quincy. And with the exception of four months in 1779, he remained abroad for a decade; for nearly six years without his wife.

His diplomatic career was checkered. Abigail proudly said that her husband was "made of the oak instead of the willow. He may be torn up by the roots, or break, but he will never bend."[38] This was hardly the stuff of which successful diplomats are made. On the ornamental level, a friend lamented of Adams, "He can't dance, drink, game, flatter, promise, dress, swear with the gentlemen, and small talk and flirt with the ladies—in short, he has none of the essential *arts* and *ornaments* which make a courtier."[39] And yet, unable to swim in the social whirl and unwilling to bend when principle was involved, John Adams participated in two amazing diplomatic accomplishments; one of which was solely on his own responsibility.

France was America's greatest ally. But, under Louis XVI and Foreign Minister Vergennes, it was also an absolute monarchy playing the time-honored game of balancing alliances for its own protection and advancement. The North American Revolution was a useful piece to manipulate on the board of world power. Benjamin Franklin, the senior American diplomat, understood this game; he would move in his country's best interests when the circumstances were right. Arthur Lee, the other commissioner in France, was a patriotic zealot, unwilling to play by these rules. By temperament and training, John Adams was to side with Lee, as he had sided with Lee's brothers in the Congress. His presence in France only compromised the delicate American position. Fortunately he realized that the tripartite American mission was unworkable and recommended to Congress a single representative, which by experience and prestige would have to be Franklin. Ten months after his arrival in Paris he was on his way home. His first mission abroad was a failure.

The three months that were allotted to Adams in America before he returned to Europe were spent in more productive pursuits. On his arrival in Massachusetts in August 1779 he was elected to a state convention to draft a constitution. This was an ideal assignment; nothing pleased an Adams so much as considering general principles of government. John Adams wrote the document, which became the model for the constitutions of other states and would influence the writing of the federal Constitution. The Adams constitution was built on "balanced" government: a two-house legislature, a strong executive, and an independent judiciary.

Adams then returned to Europe to negotiate treaties of peace and commerce with Great Britain at such time as the mother country might be ready to consider them. The thought of the unbending Bostonian as sole negotiator was not an especially pleasing one to Vergennes. So the French minister, working behind Adams' back, managed to get Congress to broaden the peace commission to five members. Adams was to be joined by Franklin, Jay, Jefferson, and Henry Laurens of South Carolina. The question now for Adams was what to do with his time until Britain was prepared to negotiate. Franklin typically suggested that he should relax and enjoy the pleasures of France—an idea that Adams was incapable of considering. It was at this point that Adams, acting without congressional mandate, want to Holland to see about a loan to relieve the serious financial pressures on his war-torn country. By the time he left Europe in 1788 he had successfully concluded four Dutch loans, thus saving the credit of the United States.

His second diplomatic triumph, in collaboration with his able colleagues, was the treaty of peace with Great Britain. The Americans were not in a strong bargaining position. The war had exhausted the insurgent nation and could not have been continued indefinitely. Yet the American negotiators received far more than they conceded; Adams' particular contribution being the securing of the Newfoundland fishery rights.

Now, after their long separation, Abigail and her daughter joined him in Europe, and John Quincy Adams made an important decision. The son had been eleven when he went to France. He was now eighteen. During the years abroad he had studied at a private school in France and at the University of Leyden; had spent two years in St. Petersburg as private secretary to the American representative to Russia; and had served as his father's secretary in Holland and during the peace negotiations in Paris. He read or spoke Greek, Latin, Dutch, French, and German. He had listened to and questioned the great men of the world. The temptation to remain in Europe was great, but he determined to return home and become a schoolboy again. (Perhaps the example of William Temple Franklin influenced him: Benjamin Franklin's grandson also went to France as a boy, and had turned into a dandy who could be seen leading a cat around by a ribbon.) So in 1785 John Quincy Adams sailed for Boston and Harvard.

It was to be the fate of successive generations of Adamses to serve their country in London during the three most strained periods of Anglo-American relations: after the War for Independence, after the War of 1812, and during the Civil War. In the year that John Quincy entered Harvard his father was appointed the first minister to Great Britain. There was a dramatic confrontation between the stocky ex-rebel and his former King. Had circumstances been different, John Adams might have stood before George III as a traitor in irons, rather than as the accredited representative of the United States of America. Despite a chilly reception from British society, and an incapacity to adapt to life at court, Adams' dogged determination and intense patriotism brought him diplomatic success.

In 1788 John Adams sailed for home and the third phase of an amazing career. As a legislator, he had helped to achieve independence; as a diplomat, he had helped secure it. Now, as an executive, he would see if he could make it work.

But before entering the White House he was to spend eight unhappy years as the Vice-President of the United States. It took unbearable self-control to be the silent presiding officer of the Senate—self-control which he did not always possess. He bitterly complained, "My country has in its wisdom contrived for me the most insignificant office that was the invention of man."[40]

Speaking with obvious pride and excitement, Vice-President Adams in 1794 announced to the Senate that George Washington had nominated his son to be minister resident to the Netherlands. The appointment of John Quincy Adams had been Washington's idea; the Vice-President had discreetly resisted pressuring his superior. Yet young Adams, with his knowledge of Holland and its language, was a natural choice. Besides, it was a most insignificant legation.

Once John Quincy Adams had been his father's diplomatic secretary; now he took his brother Thomas with him. This form of apprenticeship was to be an Adams tradition for three generations and an incomparable experience for the younger members of the family.[41] (With one exception, all the young assistants performed with credit.)

Because of the wars of the French Revolution the U. S. Embassy at The Hague was to become America's most important listening post in Europe, and the twenty-seven-year-old minister was to live up to the expectations of President Washington, who wrote the young man's proud father, "I shall be much mistaken if, in as short a period as can well be expected, he is not found at the head of the diplomatic corps."[42] Some, however, were not so pleased by the prospects of an Adams dynasty. On the eve of the 1796 presidential election Samuel Harrison Smith's Philadelphia *New World* urged readers to vote for Jefferson because "Adams has sons who might aim to succeed their father; Jefferson, like Washington, has no son."[43]

The question of nepotism also troubled the Adamses. John Quincy was much opposed to accepting an appointment from his father. After John became President, his son wrote Abigail, "Louis the 14th was one day expressing his astonishment at the stupidity of a certain ambassador at his court. 'He must be the relative of some minister.'" John Quincy added, "I have no desire to be the application for a similar reflection." Washington, however, urged his successor to keep John Quincy in the diplomatic corps because he "is the most valuable public character we have abroad," and the new President then named his son to be minister plenipotentiary to Prussia. "Merit in my family," he wrote John Quincy, "deserves as much of its Country as in another."[44] The decision was a relatively easy one. His son was a diplomat of obvious worth, and, in an Administration noted for disloyalty to its chief executive, Adams was at least assured of direct and reliable reporting from the European scene.[45]

Other relatives and in-laws gave the President a more uneasy time. During the four White House years Abigail was often sick. Their son Charles was sinking rapidly and would die before the end of the presidential term. John Quincy had married while overseas, and a federal job had to be found for his bankrupt father-in-law. (He was made Director of Stamps.) A son of Abigail's sister had also gone bankrupt, and turned to his uncle. (He was made an assistant judge in the District of Columbia.¶)

And there was the constant embarrassment of son-in-law William Stephens Smith. The President sent his name, along with a list of military appointments, to the Senate to be adjutant general of the army. Smith was the only man rejected. Adams then made him a lieutenant colonel in charge of a provisional regiment. But when the regiment was disbanded, another position had to be found. He was made surveyor of the District of New York and inspector of the revenue. Later Smith was dismissed when he became involved in a South American revolution. However, by this time John Adams had left office and could no longer help his lovely daughter's improvident husband.

Such minor acts of nepotism were politically irritating but hardly the cause of John Adams' fall. With the passing of George Washington, the last dike to hold back the party division was gone. Adams might be the head of the government, but Hamilton was head of his party. And Hamilton and the Federalists wanted war with France. Adams' one great act as President, perhaps the greatest act of his public life, was that he kept the peace. Hamilton and his party would not forgive him this wise course.

¶ The nephew, William Cranch (1769–1855), however, turned out to be a distinguished jurist. He was the first court reporter for the U. S. Supreme Court (then an unsalaried position), the first professor of law at Columbian College (now George Washington University), and chief judge of the U. S. Circuit Court for the District of Columbia from 1806 until his death. One of his sons, John Cranch (1807–91), was a portrait painter of considerable ability; and a son-in-law, William Greenleaf Eliot, became the grandfather of poet T. S. Eliot.

The President went into the election of 1800 with a united Jeffersonian party against him and a badly divided Hamiltonian party as his nominal ally. George Cabot, a high priest of Federalism, wrote, "We shall do as well with Jefferson for President . . . as with anything we can now expect."[46] Yet Adams ran far ahead of his own party and a change of 250 votes in New York City would have brought his re-election. Adams felt that the cause of his defeat was his peace mission to France. Abigail's analysis was probably more correct: "The defection of New York has been the source [of defeat]," she wrote. "That defection was produced by the intrigues of two men [Hamilton and Burr]."[47]

John Adams' public life was now ended. He returned to Quincy decidedly land-poor, having put most of his capital, over $50,000, into the purchase of 900 acres. If it had not been for the secret savings of Abigail, invested in securities, the former President might have been in dire distress. He would spend the quarter century still allotted to him as a farmer, prolific letter writer, and enthusiastic observer of his brilliant son's career.

Upon his defeat, John Adams immediately recalled his son from Berlin. The returning diplomat brought home a wife and infant son. In 1797 John Quincy had married Louisa Catherine Johnson, daughter of the American consul in London, and a niece of Thomas Johnson, the Revolutionary governor of Maryland. Her father had been sent to London by an Annapolis firm before the Revolution, married a middle-class Englishwoman, and spent the war years in France.

It was at first unclear to John Quincy's patriotic parents whether their son was contracting a union with an English girl. Abigail wrote her son, "I would hope for the love I bear my country that the Siren is at least half-blood." An opposition newspaper in Boston quickly sought to make political capital of the match: "Young John [Quincy] Adams' negotiations have terminated in a marriage with an English lady. . . . It is a happy circumstance that he had made no other Treaty." This misconception would remain a political albatross throughout John Quincy's career. As late as the presidential campaign of 1828, his opponents in western Pennsylvania passed stories about his "English" wife.[48]

When he brought his wife of four years home on a New England Thanksgiving in 1801, it was like stepping into "Noah's Ark" for the frail and poetical Louisa. Confronted by the rustic Yankees and her competent mother-in-law, she felt herself "literally and without knowing it a fine lady." To her grandson Henry she would be remembered as "an exotic, like her Sevres china." But she "could never be Bostonian, and it was her cross in life."[49]

Louisa was cultivated, retiring, romantic; her husband was an Adams —stiff, combative, restless. During their more than fifty years of marriage she would never feel at home with "the disgusting realities of a heartless political life." The official social calls were a torment. The long separations from her children, she felt, were partly to blame for their tragic lives. She called her attempt at autobiography *The Adventures of a Nobody*. Written during a period of physical ills and emotional stress, it is a pitiable tale, recounting how her father's bankruptcy, only two weeks after her wedding, "gave a colouring to my days, which could never be eradicated . . . [and] turned every sweet into gall."[50] Yet John Quincy never felt that he had been the unsuspecting suitor tricked into marriage by an impoverished family. In his own memoirs, probably more accurate than his wife's, he acknowledges that "our union has not been without its trials" but speaks of Louisa as "a faithful and affectionate wife, and a careful, tender, indulgent, and watchful mother to our children."[51]

The couple was back in Boston scarcely a year when the Massachusetts legislature sent John Quincy to the United States Senate. Jefferson, his father's Republican enemy, was President; the freshman legislator had been elected by the Federalists. Yet he promptly approved the President's Louisiana Purchase, earning the enmity of the Federalists, and opposed the Administration's plan for governing and taxing the territory, earning the enmity of the Republicans. The incapacity of an Adams to live under party government, begun by his father, was sharpened to an art by the son. In his long career John Quincy would break with every political party that elected him to office. "I have been styled a deserter from all parties because I truly never belonged to any party," he later wrote.[52]

The final break with the Federalists came with his support of the Embargo of 1807. It was a just retaliation, in his opinion, for the British firing on American ships and impressment of American sailors. But it was against the pro-British inclinations of his party and the commercial interests of his state. Recalling John Adams' unpopular peace mission to France, Federalist Theodore Lyman wrote, "Curse on the stripling, how he apes his sire!"[53] John Quincy prophetically predicted that his vote would cost him his Senate seat. Nine months before the end of his term the Massachusetts legislature elected a successor and instructed him to vote for the repeal of the embargo. Adams promptly resigned. (His five years in Washington made little contribution to the national good; but a century and a half later earned a "profile in courage" from another young Bay State senator, John F. Kennedy.)

His next assignment, as minister to Russia, was given him by President Madison, Jefferson's heir. On August 5, 1809, a little over a year after his hasty exit from the Senate, Mr. and Mrs. John Quincy Adams and two-year-old Charles Francis left for the imperial court at St. Petersburg.[54] The Adamses' two eldest sons remained in Quincy under the watchful supervision of their grandparents.

The Russia to which Adams was being sent, in his opinion, "has been thawed out of her eternal snow and has crawled or stalked over all Europe, a tremendous power whose future influence cannot be foreseen."[55] At court John Quincy got on well with Czar Alexander, with whom he took morning strolls. But this was still not a diplomatic assignment of the highest magnitude, nor were his five years in Russia of major importance in the shaping of American foreign policy. Yet as his minor post in Holland had proved to be an excellent vantage point for observing the wars of the French Revolution, so now was Russia a window on the Napoleonic Wars.[56] John Quincy had the good fortune to be in the right places at the right times.

In 1815 there was another parallel in the astonishingly similar careers of John Adams and John Quincy Adams. Just as the father had been the senior American representative on the commission that negotiated peace with Great Britain in 1783, so now was his son named the senior American representative on the commission to conclude the second treaty of peace with Great Britain. The first American commission had outmaneuvered the British and won a treaty well above the expectations of their situation. The second American commission was equally superior to their counterparts, and secured an equally favorable treaty.[57] The United States had taken a beating in the War of 1812. Even its greatest victory, Jackson's at New Orleans, came too late to be known to the American negotiators. Yet the peace treaty was concluded without the loss of any rights. Again the particular contribution of the Adams negotiator was the protection of the Newfoundland fisheries.

With the successful conclusion of the peace conference, John Quincy, still following in his father's footsteps, was rewarded with the English mission. As the second Adams envoy to Great Britain, he would feel the same cool breeze of society and the same pinch of economy. John Adams warned him, "The corps diplomatique will say 'Adams lives *dans la plus infame oeconomy.*' Their coachmen and footmen will look down on yours with the utmost scorn and contempt. . . . *Quid inde?* Your father has seen and felt all this before you."[58]

John Quincy brought his two eldest sons to London. Charles Francis and John were sent to a boarding school at Ealing, where their lives were complicated by the taunts of their classmates. One English boy asked John if he had ever been at Washington (a sly reference to the burning of the capital by the British troops). "No," replied the patriotic youth, "but I have been at New Orleans."[59] The Adams children would always be fighting their parents' battles. Years later young Henry Adams, son of Charles Francis of the Ealing school, would indignantly see his

Boston chums wearing black arm bands because of Charles Sumner's election to the Senate, and in defense of his father's abolitionist sentiments would put on a white arm band.

The office of Secretary of State was considered the steppingstone to the presidency. Of Washington's successors, only John Adams had not occupied it. In 1817 the new President, James Monroe, himself a former Secretary of State, had the choice of three qualified men for the position —Albert Gallatin, Henry Clay, and John Quincy Adams. But the first two had political liabilities, and Adams got the coveted assignment.[60]

Arriving in the United States after eight years abroad, the new Secretary of State hurried to his aged parents in Quincy—but first he had to bring his diary up to date—and while journalizing, he missed the steamboat to take him to the eagerly awaited reunion!

Henry Adams once wrote that his grandfather "was always on the outskirts,—a kind of free lance, following the march of forces which he never commanded."[61] There was considerable validity in the assessment. John Quincy's presidency was to be a failure. Even his great fight against slavery would only be a preliminary bout. But for eight years as Secretary of State he was a major force in molding American history. These were richly productive years: he settled the long-smoldering Florida question, with Spain ceding the territory to the United States; he settled the western boundary of Louisiana; he concluded a treaty with Russia that limited her claims to the Northwest; he was the architect of the Monroe Doctrine, defining United States interests in the Western Hemisphere.

Early in his career John Quincy told his father, "I have been accustomed all my life to plain dealing and candor, and am not sufficiently versed in the art of political swindling to be prepared for negotiating with an European Minister of State."[62] Yet as Henry Cabot Lodge, Sr., later said, an Adams "judged himself far more severely, far more harshly . . . than any dispassionate critic would think of doing."[63] Because of, or in spite of, his Puritan character, John Quincy Adams ranked among his nation's greatest foreign secretaries.

Now the vastly ambitious Adams was within striking distance of his goal. His one sadness was that his mother had not lived to see him elevated to the White House, in whose bare ballroom she had once hung the family wash. John Quincy had always been extremely close to his mother. Within minutes of signing the Treaty of Ghent he sent Abigail the important news; three days later he wrote his wife. On October 28, 1818, he told his diary:

Had she lived to the age of the Patriarchs every day of her life would have been filled with clouds of goodness and of love. There is not a virtue that can abide in the female heart but it was an ornament of hers. She had been fifty-four years the delight of my father's heart, the sweetener of all his toils, the comforter of all his sorrows, the sharer and heightener of all his joys. It was but the last time when I saw my father that he told me, with an ejaculation of gratitude to the Giver of every good and perfect gift, that in all the vicissitudes of his fortune, through all the good report and evil report of the world, in all his struggles and in all his sorrows, the affectionate participation and cheering encouragement of his wife had been his never-failing support, without which he was sure he should never have lived through them.[64]

There were four candidates for the presidency in 1824—Andrew Jackson, John Quincy Adams, William H. Crawford, and Henry Clay. None had a majority, and the election would be decided by the House of Representatives from among the top three contenders. Crawford had a stroke, and the contest narrowed to Jackson and Adams. The support of Clay would settle the contest.

Here was Adams, the unbending Puritan, the inheritor of a tradition that the office seeks the man, the candidate who had not aided his own cause during the canvass, now placed in a position where he must bargain to obtain the office that was his life's ambition. This he knew. He wrote, "There is in my prospects and anticipations a solemnity and moment never before experienced, and to which *unaided nature is inadequate*." Bargain he did, though he would not even admit it to his diary. Clay's emissaries came to him and he wrote, "*Incedo super ignes* [I am treading coals of fire]."[65] The House made Adams President, and Adams made Clay his Secretary of State. This was a topic for Washington wits; Margaret Bayard Smith reported: Prometheus had made a clay man and the United States now had a "Clay President."[66]

John Quincy told his son, "No person can ever be a thorough partisan for a long period without sacrifice of his moral identity. The skill consists in knowing exactly where to draw the line." John Quincy Adams drew the line *after* the presidency. ("The Puritan character," Henry Adams would write, "could be supple enough when it chose.")[67]

The "deal" that made Adams President was probably unspoken. Clay could never have supported Jackson under any circumstances, and he was also the logical choice for Secretary of State. Yet it would haunt and finally defeat Adams. He was a minority President. The Vice-President and the Congress were against him. He would not use the powers of the chief executive in his own behalf. During four years he removed only twelve persons from office, nor would he appoint his supporters. "The friends of the Administration have to contend not only against their enemies, but against the Administration itself," said Henry Clay, "which leaves its powers in the hands of its own enemies."[68] And on top of this the opposition was given a magnificent rallying cry: the supposed deal between Adams and Clay.

Immediately upon his election John Quincy Adams notified his father.

The old President replied, "My dear Son . . . Never did I feel so much solemnity as upon this occasion. The multitude of my thoughts, and the intensity of my feelings are too much for a mind like mine, in its nine-tieth year."[69] The ancient patriot did not live to see the full suffering of his son in the White House. On July 4, 1826, he died at the age of ninety-one. On the same day in Monticello death came to Thomas Jefferson. It was a remarkable coincidence. On the fiftieth anniversary of the Declaration of Independence, the man who wrote it and the man who secured its passage left this world together.[70] President John Adams was laid to rest at his beloved Quincy, while the pastor read from the First Book of Chronicles: "He died in a good old age, full of days, riches, and honor, and Solomon his son reigned in his stead."

The second Adams President had a first-rate design for America. He had worked hard to expand its continental boundaries, and now he wanted to span it with roads and canals. It was an ambitious program for "internal improvements." Yet Congress would have no part of it. Rejecting a systematic plan, the best Congress would do was an occasional purchase of stock in some enterprise, such as the Dismal Swamp Canal Company. John Adams had considered his presidency to be a failure; now his son drew the same conclusion of his: "I fell, and with me fell . . . the system of internal improvement by National means and National Energies. The great object of my Life therefore as applied to the Administration of the Government of the United States, has *failed*."[71]

Adams was overwhelmingly defeated by Jackson. During the nation's first fifty years the two Adamses were the only Presidents to be denied a second term.

Out of office John Quincy Adams faced the serious problem of what to do with the remainder of his life. By 1829 the precedent was well established: ex-Presidents were expected to lead sedate and rustic retirements. But John Quincy did not have John Adams' type of original mind, which could happily meditate over the state of nature. He was a combatant who loved combat for combat's sake. The former President understood this, writing in his diary, "More than sixty years of incessant active intercourse with the world has made political movement to me as much a necessary of life as atmospheric air. . . . And thus, while a remnant of physical power is left to me to write and speak, the world will retire from me before I shall retire from the world."[72]

An opportunity arose for him to run for the House of Representatives from the Old Plymouth district in 1830. Charles Francis was bitterly opposed to the move. At twenty-three he did not yet understand his father. Ralph Waldo Emerson better knew the chemistry of the elder Adams. "Mr. Adams chose wisely and according to his constitution, when, on leaving the Presidency, he went to Congress," the philosopher wrote in his *Journal.* "He is no literary old gentleman, but a bruiser, and loves the *melee.* When they talk about his age and venerableness and nearness to the grave, he knows better, he is like one of those old cardinals, who, as quick as he is chosen Pope, throws away his crutches and his crookedness, and is as straight as a boy. He is an old *rogue* who cannot live on slops, but must have sulphuric acid in his tea."[73]

Moreover, John Quincy Adams needed the eight dollars a day that a congressman received! He had invested heavily and unwisely in a Washington grist and flour mill. By 1832 he owed $42,000, some of it to his former valet.

As disgusting as politics was to Louisa, she was nevertheless happy to see her husband back in harness. She told her son, "Your father is in high spirits dabbling as usual in public affairs while *fancying he has nothing to do with them.* His mind must be occupied with something, and why not this?"[74]

Congressman John Quincy Adams would soon have a cause to match his high spirits.

His distaste for slavery was inherited from his mother. As far back as the Revolution, Abigail had written, "I wish most sincerely there was not a slave in the province! It always seemed a most iniquitous scheme to me to fight ourselves for what we are robbing the Negroes of, who have as good a right to freedom as we have!"[75] Yet John Quincy's last crusade began not as a fight for abolition but over the constitutional question of free speech and petition. The Southern slaveholders and their Northern allies made a serious tactical mistake when they joined the issues. In 1836 the House of Representatives passed the notorious gag rule; by 1840 it had become a standing rule of procedure. The House would receive no abolitionist petitions. If the majority could cut off discussion on slavery, why could it not outlaw debate on any other subject? This was a ready-made issue for an Adams.

For nine years John Quincy tried to present abolitionist petitions to the Congress. For nine years he was shouted down, threatened with assassination, brought before the House for censure, formally charged by the Southern representatives with perjury and treason. Julia Gardiner, later to be the wife of President John Tyler, recalled the scene from her vantage point in the congressional gallery: "Mr. Adams was excessively bald, and as he sat in the middle of the House, with his immense petition rolled around a kind of windlass to sustain it, his excitement was manifest in the flaming redness of his bald head, which acted as a chronometer to his audience."[76] At first the old man stood alone, then gradually he gained disciples. At long last he had captured the public imagination. He was now "The Old Man Eloquent." And on December 3, 1845, the gag rule was rescinded. John Quincy Adams, seventy-eight years of age, had won his greatest fight.

During these turbulent years Charles Francis Adams, the rather prig-
gish boy, had become a married man. His wife, Abigail Brooks, was the
least exceptional of the Adams women, yet proved to be an understanding and successful wife and mother. She was very Victorian; in fact, in
her later years she bore a striking resemblance to the English Queen.
While Adams at first found her temper to be "high," her education
"faulty," and her speech at times "unmeaning and loud nonsense," after
ten years of marriage he told himself, "Perhaps of all my good fortune
. . . the circumstance of my marriage was the greatest incident; For it
stimulated me in the right direction and prevented the preponderance
of my constitutional shyness and indolence. Of my wife I need not speak
as the passage of time has only contributed to make me prize her more
highly."[77] The advantages of marriage also included a wealthy father-in-
law, Peter Chardon Brooks. Coming from an almost destitute minister's
family, he built a fortune, reputedly four million dollars, as a marine insurance broker, and used it generously to promote the ambitions of his
two political sons-in-law, Adams and Edward Everett.*

The raising of a family and the deaths of his brothers helped to mature
Charles Francis. John Quincy had once written his eldest child, "My sons
have not only their own honor but that of two preceding generations to
sustain." Charles Francis now carried this burden alone. He records in
his diary, "Evening, A long conversation with my father. Family pride.
A strong instance in himself, much exceeding even what I suspected. I
feel at times depressed by it, for now the dependence upon me is perfectly prominent."[78]

He was elected to the Massachusetts House of Representatives in 1840.
After three years he was elevated to the state Senate. These five legislative years were important in his development and in his understanding of
his father. His slumbering Puritanism suddenly awoke. He became a passionate supporter of his father's fight against the gag rule and an anti-
slavery leader in his own right.

John Quincy Adams now could die at peace. For his great battle had
been won and his only living son had at last picked up the mantle of
leadership. The Adams dynasty would continue. The old man wrote to his
heir:

I have noticed with inexpressible pleasure your firm unwavering adherence
to honest principle, and feeling as I do that my own career of exertion for

* Edward Everett (1794–1865) was in many ways the opposite of Adams.
Handsome with glossy luxuriant hair and piercing eyes, he was considered the
most brilliant boy ever to have gone to Harvard and the finest classical scholar
in New England. Honors were showered on him—member of the House of
Representatives (1825–35), governor of Massachusetts (1836–40), minister
to Great Britain (1841–45), president of Harvard (1846–49), U. S. Secretary
of State, 1852–53, senator (1853–54)—yet either ambition or character kept
him from greatness, and his political reputation was as a compromiser.

the cause of my country and of human liberty, is at its close, at the approach of the most portentous crisis that it ever encountered, it is a consolation to me that you have engaged in it, with all your faculties, and such is my faith in the Justice and Mercy of God, that I will die in humble hope, that however severe your trial may be, your strength will be found equal to it, and will finally result in the glorious triumph of Freedom and of Truth.[79]

The ancient congressman took his seat as usual in the House of Representatives on February 21, 1848. Suddenly he slumped to the floor. He was taken to the Speaker's office, and two days later he died in the Capitol of the United States. John Quincy Adams' last words were, "This is the end of Earth, but I am composed."[80]

The year 1848 was significant in the annals of the Adams dynasty. The second generation passed on; the third generation moved onto the national scene for the first time, and the last member of the fourth generation entered the world.

The Free Soil Party, the new anti-slavery coalition, met in Buffalo to pick its candidates for the presidential election. In mourning for his father, Charles Francis Adams was wearing a black crepe band on his white hat. This symbolic link to the late anti-slavery champion did not escape the assembly. The delegates chose Martin Van Buren for President and Charles Francis Adams for Vice-President. The rallying cry would be, "Van Buren and Free Soil; Adams and Liberty."

Each Adams fervently prayed to be allowed by the public to stand or fall on his own worth. Yet each Adams, in his own mind as well as the people's, was so inextricably interwoven with his ancestors that it became increasingly difficult for public and Adams to separate them. Such was the dilemma of Charles Francis Adams. He and his brother were the only Americans ever to have had the burdens and honors of being both sons and grandsons of presidents.

Nowhere in his public career is this inheritance more perplexing than in the 1848 campaign. Charles Francis fully recognized that his nomination was in large part a tribute to the memory of John Quincy Adams. Still, he complained that "the apparent distinction of my name and family has been the thing most in my way."[81] A son would write of him:

Never claiming anything, or even seeking recognition, because of his father and his grandfather, constant reference to them in connection with himself annoyed, and at times irritated him. He could not habituate himself to it, nor learn to take it lightly and as a matter of course. . . . To have one's ancestors unceasingly flung in one's face is unpleasant, and listening to the charges incessantly rung upon them becomes indubitably monotonous. This, however, all through life, was to an unusual degree the fate of Mr. Adams, and never so much as in the campaign of 1848. . . .[82]

Yet he stood before the Worcester Free Soil Convention, with his striking resemblance to his forebears, and grossly exploited the words of John
Adams. "Sink or Swim, Live or Die, Survive or Perish, to go with the
liberties of my country, is my fixed determination"—his grandfather had
said when he signed the Declaration of Independence—and now he par-
roted this heritage for dramatic effect. To one observer, it was "as if old
John Adams had stepped down from Trumbull's picture . . . to give his
benediction."[83]

The Free Soil ticket received almost 300,000 votes, one tenth of the
total ballots cast. General Zachary Taylor was elected President. The
anti-slavery movement went into a decline until the Kansas-Nebraska Act
and the formation of the Republican Party.

Charles Francis used his politically enforced leisure to compile *The
Works of John Adams* in ten volumes. The time had come to start defending the reputation of the ancestors. Charles Francis, the politician-
antiquarian, balanced between past and present; by the end of his sons'
generation, the family balance would be almost totally tipped toward the
past.

With the revival of anti-slavery sentiment, a decade after the Free
Soil defeat, Republican candidate Charles Francis Adams was elected to
Congress from his father's old district. Henry Adams, like Charles Francis
before him, disapproved of his father's election. In 1860 Congressman
Adams was re-elected over Leverett Saltonstall, a Constitutional Union
leader, and young Henry, in the Adams tradition, went to Washington
as his father's secretary.

It was the Great Secession Winter of 1860–61. As the Southern states
dropped out of the Union, the big question was which would come first
—Lincoln's inauguration or war. It was imperative to the North that the
President-elect take over the reins of the federal government. That he
did was in part because of the efforts of Senator William Seward and Congressman Charles Francis Adams. Adams, the driving force behind the
Committee of Thirty-three, was determined to keep the Congress talking
until Lincoln arrived in the capital. Representative Reuben Davis of
Mississippi accurately called Adams' committee "a tub thrown out to the
whale, to amuse only, until the 4th of March next."[84] Young Henry Adams
listened to his father and Seward plot and maneuver. It was reminiscent
of his father's awe at overhearing conversations between John Quincy
Adams and Henry Clay, or his grandfather's boyhood recollections of
listening to John Adams and Thomas Jefferson. For three generations the
Adams children eavesdropped on greatness.

On March 4 Lincoln became President. March 5: Seward became Sec-
retary of State. On March 20 Adams was commissioned minister to Great
Britain. Yet Charles Francis did not sail for England until the first of
May, after Fort Sumter had been attacked. John Quincy Adams II was

to be married in April to Fanny Crowninshield of Boston, and his parents wished to attend the ceremony. The Confederate envoys, without equally pressing social obligations, beat Adams to London. By the time the American minister arrived the British government had issued a proclamation of neutrality. For the first time in more than a century an Adams had thought of family before country; the consequence was a serious diplomatic blow.

But once in London the third Adams to be United States minister to Great Britain made few errors. The English were cold and reserved as usual. But Charles Francis, in the words of a son, "was a little colder and a little more reserved." He beat the British at their own game "for the very good reason that the game was natural to him."[85] And when the British seized the Laird rams, which were being built in Liverpool for the Confederate navy, Adams scored a major diplomatic coup. The Union victories at Gettysburg and Vicksburg combined had depressed the price of Confederate bonds on the European market by thirteen points; the seizure of the deadly warships dropped the price by fourteen points.

During Charles Francis Adams' long tenure in England his eldest son began a career in politics. John Quincy Adams II, the political heir of the fourth generation, moved onto the national scene in August 1866 as a delegate to the National Union Convention. He went to Philadelphia to protest the harsh reconstruction policy of the Radical Republicans. This initial act of defiance sealed his political fate: when he was nominated to be collector of customs at Boston the next year, the Republican Senate rejected his name. Adamses had always been mavericks; now the day of the maverick had passed. John Quincy II promptly became a Democrat, which meant politically that he no longer expected his reward in this world. At the 1868 Democratic Convention he received one vote for President. Old John Quincy would have been proud of his namesake, and, had that anti-slavery firebrand had a sense of humor, he would have been amused that the vote had been cast by a South Carolinian.†

The dynasty's last chance for a serious presidential nomination came at the 1872 Liberal Republican Convention. Charles Francis Adams was

---

† As the young John Quincy Adams was becoming an anti-Grant leader, a distant cousin was performing yeoman service for the Union general. William Taylor Adams (1822–97) had made a fortune as a hack writer. During his lifetime he published 126 books, using such pseudonyms as "Oliver Optic" (for juvenile stories), "Irving Brown" (for tales of love), and "Clingham Hunter, M.D." (for travel sketches). In 1868 his campaign biography of Grant appeared as *Our Standard-Bearer; or, the Life of General Ulysses S. Grant: His Youth, His Manhood, His Campaigns, and His Eminent Services in the Reconstruction of the Nation His Sword Has Redeemed: As Seen and Related by Captain Bernard Galligasken, Cosmopolitan, and Written out by Oliver Optic.*

the front runner. But the "Great Iceberg" did nothing to cultivate the delegates, and actually wrote a letter that had rather the reverse effect. On the first ballot he received 203 votes to 147 for Horace Greeley. On the sixth ballot the publisher was nominated. He was then endorsed by the Democrats, but not before John Quincy Adams II had bolted the convention over the currency question. The Republicans, seeking to take advantage of the split in the opposition ranks, set up a "Straight-Out" Democratic Party, whose convention nominated young Adams for Vice-President. He immediately declined the "honor," which didn't discourage the decoy party from going ahead with its canvass. John Quincy II thus became the fourth of his dynasty to be on a ticket for national office. The unwilling candidate with the illustrious name received nearly 30,000 votes.

The news of his defeat for the presidential nomination was relayed to Charles Francis Adams while he was on his way to Geneva. His appointment as United States representative at the five-nation *Alabama* claims conference was a bitter pill to President Grant but had been insisted upon by Secretary of State Hamilton Fish. The British had failed to prevent the Confederacy from building the *Alabama*. Its guns had taken a considerable toll. The British agreed to arbitrate the question of reparations. Only Charles Francis' skill kept the commission from foundering and the United States was awarded $15,500,000.

This closed the public career of Charles Francis Adams. He had said, "Public life was a very fascinating occupation, but like drinking brandy. The more you indulge in it, the more uncomfortable it leaves you when you stop."[86] The heady brew was never offered again, although his name kept cropping up as a potential candidate for one office or another. In 1875, when he was proposed for the governorship of Massachusetts, Hamilton Fish wrote that it was the "annually returning periodical demand for a pure, an exemplary statesman in the person of Charles Francis Adams —Governor, President—Town Clerk or something."[87]

Returning to the family archives, Charles Francis published a twelve-volume edition of his father's diaries. (He had earlier edited the letters of his grandmother, two volumes of John Adams' letters to Abigail, and the ten-volume *Works of John Adams*.) This herculean task completed, he said, "My mission is ended, and I may rest."[88] He then sank into a mental decline and finally died in 1886, aged seventy-nine.

Each of his sons had a different appraisal of Charles Francis Adams. Brooks, the youngest, wrote, "My father impressed himself upon me as the most remarkable man I have ever known."[89] Charles Francis, Jr., in his autobiography, wrote of him with hardly disguised hatred. About the only good thing he could say was that his father hadn't forced him to go to a public school![90] Henry, the closest to his father, probably had the most unclouded judgment:

Charles Francis Adams was singular for mental poise—absence of self-assertion or self-consciousness—the faculty of standing apart without seeming aware that he was alone—a balance of mind and temper that neither challenged nor avoided notice, nor admitted question of superiority or inferiority, of jealousy, of personal motives, from any source, even under great pressure. This unusual poise of judgment and temper ripened by age, became the more striking to his son Henry as he learned to measure the mental faculties themselves, which were in no way exceptional either for depth or range. Charles Francis Adams's memory was hardly above the average; his mind was not bold like his grandfather's or restless like his father's, or imaginative or oratorical—still less mathematical; but it worked with singular perfection, admirable self-restraint, and instinctive mastery of form. Within its range it was a model.[91]

The Adams dynasty had flourished for over a century: from John Adams to John Quincy Adams to Charles Francis Adams. A fourth generation now reached maturity, and Mrs. James A. Garfield, while visiting at Quincy in 1869, marveled at their prospects. They "are showing even more marked ability" than their ancestors, she observed.[92] Indeed in the late 1860s and early 1870s the intellectual and reform circles in America seemed to be ablaze with young Adamses. John Quincy II was rebuilding the discredited Democratic Party; Charles Francis, Jr., was exposing the manipulations of the railroad barons; and Henry was shooting off sparks in every direction as a crusading journalist. Yet buried within the brilliance of this youthful foliage was the seed of dynastic destruction.

First of all, the eldest, John Quincy II, recognized by the family as the political heir apparent, was a most unlikely Adams. He was initially suspect as the only member of the dynasty ever to have been accused of having been "a good fellow."[93] Moreover, he didn't even preserve his letters, considering it a "vile family habit."[94] In short, he was everything an Adams is not supposed to be—easygoing, charming, a wit, inclined to indolence, discouraged by strong opposition. After having been twice burned by his opposition to Radical Republicanism and Grantism, he seemed happier fishing and sailing. He once even forgot to appear before the Massachusetts Supreme Court, when he was counsel in an important case, because "the smelts are biting like thunder."[95]

In 1868 he ran as a Democrat for governor of Massachusetts. Unlike his grandfather, he was destined to be in the wrong place at the wrong time. Losing the governorship was to be his lifetime avocation. But he really preferred being moderator of the Quincy town meeting. As his brother Henry pointed out, "He had all he wanted; wealth, children, society, consideration. . . ."[96] It was not until the Democrats returned to office in 1892 that he might have also had political power. Grover Cleveland, the first of his party to have been elected President in thirty-two years, tried to persuade John Quincy to enter his Cabinet as Secretary of the Navy. This would have been a fitting tribute to a man who had cheerfully sought political oblivion in the perennial minority party, and whose great-grandfather had founded the American navy. But he was in ill-health and declined the appointment. Defying family tradition to the end, he died at sixty, considerably short of the fourscore years that are allotted to every Adams.

The fatal flaw in the second son of the fourth generation was not that he lacked ambition. For Charles Francis Adams, Jr., the most Adamsesque of the four brothers, frankly admitted that he coveted power. After distinguished service in the Union Army—rising from lieutenant to brigadier general in command of a regiment of Negro cavalry—he sought out the best avenue to position in society, and settled on the railroads. Although he was to rise to titular leadership in his chosen profession, he had not chosen wisely. In the slippery world of Goulds, Fisks, and Vanderbilts he could not overcome being an Adams. He was the first in the family ever to have set out to make money. It was, in his words, "a rather low instinct."[97] And the fact that he was unsuited for it made it a poor vehicle for power.

When Jay Gould cornered the Erie Railroad, Charles Adams described him as "strongly marked by his disposition for silent intrigue. . . . There was a reminiscence of a spider in his nature."[98] Soon Gould would spin his web around the unsuspecting Adams. In 1884, while the Union Pacific was under congressional investigation, Gould suddenly stepped aside as president of the railroad and Adams took over its management. Appointment of the illustrious name with its inherited aura of incorruptibility was all the assurance Congress needed to drop its probe of Gould's illegal manipulations. But six years later, when Gould was ready to regain control of the line, Adams was the helpless fly. It was no contest; Adams' dream of power abruptly ended, and he retired to more scholarly pursuits.

Even while locked in unequal combat with Gould, Adams found time to write a two-volume biography of Richard Henry Dana. In retirement he devoted most of his leisure to research into early Massachusetts history. He also published a biography of his father, greatly to the displeasure of brothers Henry and Brooks. Charles had never liked Brooks, but in his early years his relationship with Henry had been intimate. However, as their paths diverged the closeness gave way to a tolerance that was maintained by studiously avoiding a collision course. After the Charles Francis Adams biography appeared, Henry wrote Brooks, "I have sinned myself and deeply, and am no more worthy to be called anything, but, thank my diseased and dyspeptic nervous wreck, I did not assassinate my father."[99] And yet, to the more dispassionate reader, Charles Adams, the son who displayed such deep hatred of his father in his own autobiography, was an objective, even sympathetic biographer.

When Henry Adams returned from London, where he had been his father's secretary during the Civil War, articles poured from his pen—attacks on the Grant Administration, Congress, political rings, monetary policies, the railroads. He even published a piece debunking the legend of Captain John Smith and Pocahontas. His style reminded the editor of the *Nation* of old John Quincy Adams' "peculiar powers as an assailant . . . an instinct for the jugular and carotid artery as unerring as that of any carnivorous animal."[100]

Life was exciting. He was named one of the three best dancers in Washington. He was appointed an assistant professor of history at Harvard and the editor of the *North American Review*, a journal of minuscule circulation and mighty influence. He was an idol-breaking editor: "Write thirty pages of abuse of people and houses in England"; "Put more energy into the literary notices"; "Stand on your head and spit at someone"; "Rake up a heap of old family scandals." He was an equally stimulating teacher. When asked how the Popes were elected in the eleventh century, he replied, "Pretty much as it pleased God." What is transubstantiation? "Good heavens! How should I know? Look it up." John Adams? "Gentlemen, John Adams was a demagogue."[101] Henry Cabot Lodge, Percy Belmont, and his other students idolized him.

And to add to life's joy, in 1872 he married Marian ("Clover") Hooper. To Henry, his Boston bride "is certainly not handsome; nor would she be quite called plain, I think. She is twenty-eight years old. She knows her own mind uncommon well. . . . Her manners are quiet. She reads German—also Latin—also, I fear, a little Greek, but very little. She talks garrulously, but on the whole pretty sensibly. . . . She dresses badly. She decidedly has humor. . . . She has enough money to be quite independent."[102] (When Charles heard that his brother might marry a Hooper, he exclaimed, "Heavens!—No!—they're all crazy as coots. She'll kill herself, just like her aunt!"[103])

The young couple spent their honeymoon on a barge on the Nile, and their years commuting between Boston, London, and Washington. They gathered a circle of fascinating friends: poet-statesman John Hay, geologist Clarence King, novelist Henry James, zoologist Alexander Agassiz. They started to build a town house on Lafayette Square next door to Hay. These were also productive years. Henry's brilliant biography of Albert Gallatin appeared in 1879, along with three volumes of Gallatin's writings, which he edited; a satirical novel of Washington life, *Democracy*, was anonymously published in 1880;[104] his biography of John Randolph appeared in 1882; in 1884 and 1885 he privately printed the first two volumes of his *History of the United States*. Then on December 6, 1885, Marian Adams, an accomplished photographer, after a long period of mental depression during which her mind dwelt on nothing but self-destruction, killed herself by swallowing photographic chemicals.

In response to a letter of sympathy, Henry wrote: ". . . I have found myself strengthened by two thoughts. One was that life could have no other experience so crushing. The other was that at least I had got out of life all the pleasure it had to give. I admit that fate at last has smashed the life out of me; but for twelve years I had everything I most wanted on earth."[105]

Henry Adams lived on. He even indulged in a relationship with the beautiful and fascinating Elizabeth Cameron, unhappy wife of a United States senator, which Henry's most thorough biographer feels may well have been ("after the passionate sighings"), for reasons of "Puritan scruple or diminishing ardor, that anomaly in nature, a Platonic one."[106] Yet except for one short period, when he became interested in the cause of Cuban independence, he was never again involved in the present. Later, during John Hay's incumbency as Secretary of State, Adams had a passive, yet valuable, function in American statecraft: the two friends took afternoon walks, and Henry's whimsical gloom braced the diplomat against the unalloyed optimism of President Theodore Roosevelt.

But he could never be pulled back into the main stream of his century. Instead he directed his passion to wandering. With the artist John La Farge he explored the Orient and the islands of the Pacific; he met Robert Louis Stevenson in Samoa and wrote a book on Tahiti; he explored Cuba with Clarence King and the American West with Hay. He spent long periods in France. With the Lodges and their poet son Bay he discovered the great Gothic cathedrals. And from these lonely years came his two masterpieces, *Mont-Saint-Michel and Chartres* and *The Education of Henry Adams*.

The life of the youngest of the fourth generation, Brooks Adams, was almost a parody of his imposing ancestors. He bent to the breaking point their theories of government, and he twisted their eccentricities into near madness. Yet there was still a rampaging genius somewhere in him. As philosophy, his *The Law of Civilization and Decay* was a significant development in seeking formula to explain history, and proved him one of the first to recognize the effect of geography on politics.

Brooks Adams was always strange. As an eleven-year-old, his mother wrote of him: "Papa reads aloud for an hour or two evenings, & poor Brooks screams, & laughs, & rants, & twists, & jumps, & worries about so, that we have been obliged to set him on a footstool, in the middle of the room. He wears the furniture out so badly. . . ."[107] In his freshman year at Harvard he was caught cheating on a Latin examination; later brother Charles caught him billing sizable quantities of wine to his account.

There is an apocryphal tale that when a young lady turned down his proposal of marriage Brooks could not believe that an Adams had been rejected. On repeating her decision, he promptly left, giving as his final opinion, "Why you perfect damn fool."[108] Brooks finally married Evelyn ("Daisy") Davis.[109] It is said that this union came about in an equally unreal fashion. He is supposed to have told Mrs. Henry Cabot Lodge, "If I could find a woman like you, I would marry her instantly." Mrs. Lodge suggested her sister and Brooks was true to his word. But first he warned Miss Davis that he "was an eccentric almost to the point of madness" and she would have to marry him "on her own responsibility and at her own risk."[110] He was to call his wife *affectionately,* "idiot from hell." But the gentle and gracious Daisy was pleased to escape from genteel poverty into such a distinguished family. She did as much as any woman could for Brooks, while managing to spend all but her last years outside of a mental institution.

With each passing year Brooks Adams became more gruff, irascible, and argumentative. His friend Theodore Roosevelt wrote to John Hay, "He [Brooks] is having a delightful time here, and simply revelling in gloom over the appalling social and civic disasters which he sees impending." It became a ritual for Brooks and Henry to predict the end of the world. Brooks said 1926. Henry said 1917. Brooks said 1911. Henry said 1913. Brooks said, "The world is done," Henry replied, "The world is done. Of course it is!" Brooks was perfectly serious; Henry only partly so, and then with a wink. Charles Francis, who never liked Brooks anyway, told Henry, "Though I do not share the fears and apprehensions of my brother Brooks, and though I do not think the world is going to come to an end,—I know I am."[111]

Brooks loved Henry. After his sainted father had passed on there was no one but Henry who could understand him. "You have been my good genius." Henry respected his brother's intellect and was powerfully influenced by his theory of history. "I have sought all my life those truths which this mighty infant, this seer unblest, has struck with the agony and bloody sweat of genius." Yet Henry could not stand to be with Brooks. The torrent of words, ideas, concepts left him exhausted. He wrote a friend, "My irritability has become so acute that I have to grind my teeth and bite my tongue whenever Brooks talks with me. He is my double, and you know how I exasperate myself."[112] He invented any excuse to flee from Brooks. Brooks got married; Henry went to Ottawa. Brooks came to Washington; Henry escaped to Paris.

If the world was "done," as Henry and Brooks agreed, they disagreed on what to do about it. Brooks was the activist. Henry had given up. Henry preferred to live in the twelfth century. Brooks was anxious to fight on in the twentieth. "I am morally certain," Brooks told Henry, "that men are losing energy—mental energy I mean—very fast—so fast that you can trace the shrinkage from year to year." But Henry wrote him, "I fear you must get some other help than mine for your efforts to protect mankind and ourselves."[113] And so, with the fabled Adams energy, Brooks would go it alone. He would pump the energy back into man—as a teacher at Boston Law School, as a writer of books and magazine articles, as an unsolicited adviser to his brother-in-law, Senator Lodge, and to President Teddy Roosevelt, even as a political candidate. Brooks ran for the Massachusetts legislature but lost by two votes—his uncles Chardon and Shephard Brooks voted against him.

There was a strong streak of mysticism in Brooks Adams. "What I produce I do not manufacture—I find." When he forwarded a manuscript to Henry he wrote, "What I send you is rough stone. It comes that way out of the ground. I can't control it."[114] What he dredged up was a pastiche of fascistic ideas: racist theories, the inferiority of the Orientals, hatred of the Jews; authoritarian concepts of government; schemes for dividing society by class.‡

In 1917, as the last public act of the fourth generation, Brooks was elected to the Massachusetts Constitutional Convention. It was one hundred and thirty-eight years after John Adams had written Massachusetts' first constitution. The delegates were silent in order to hear the words of his great-grandson:

To carry on anything great . . . we need to establish something close to dictatorship. The United States government cannot keep pace with the age. Mr. President . . . democracy ought to and must perish.[115]

The same convention that listened in amazement to Brooks's polemics also contained another Adams—his nephew Charles Francis, the son of the unsuccessful Democratic leader. The young Adams had been elected by the largest number of votes cast for a delegate at large. "One hates to believe that an Adams can be popular," commented the New York Times.[116]

The fifth-generation Adams looked like his forebears—short of stature, balding, with the large nose, narrow and severe mouth.[117] Yet he was unique in one sense: he was to be the end of America's greatest political dynasty.

After graduating from Harvard, where he was class president and earned the lifelong nickname "Deacon," Charles Francis Adams went to Europe for a year. Instead of using the time abroad to search his soul, as Uncle Henry had done, he went to study English yacht racing! (But this too was in his heritage, for an ancestor of his Crowninshield mother had built the first American yacht.[118]) The Deacon would become one

‡ Henry Adams shared his brother's anti-Semitism. Yet their adored sister Louisa (1831–70) married a Philadelphia Jew, Charles Kuhn (1821–99), and Henry was very close to art critic Bernard Berenson. For a sociological interpretation of Adams' anti-Semitism, see E. Digby Baltzell, The Protestant Establishment (New York: Random House, 1964), p. 93.

of the country's finest yachtsmen. Most of his boats were named with a double *o*—*Papoose, Baboon, Gossoon, Harpoon*. However it was in the *Resolute* that he won his greatest race by defeating Sir Thomas Lipton's *Shamrock IV* for the 1920 America's Cup.

Charles Francis became a lawyer, married Frances Lovering, a congressman's daughter, and, only six years out of Harvard, was named the university's treasurer. He served from 1898 to 1929, increasing the school's endowment fund from twelve million to a hundred million dollars. Twice he was also elected mayor of Quincy on the Democratic ticket. But he was no more devoted to party labels than his ancestors had been. When he was selected, without his knowledge, by the 1920 Democratic State Convention as a candidate for presidential elector, he asked to have his name withdrawn from the official ballot—he was going to vote for Harding! Later he advocated that presidents should be limited to a single six-year term and be required to renounce party affiliation.

On his appointment as Secretary of the Navy in 1929 he was so politically unknown that many mistook him for Charles Francis ("Pop") Adams, an improbably remote cousin who was an owner of the Boston Braves and Boston Bruins.[119] The nautical post was a natural for the "right" Adams; not only had Great-great-grandfather John Adams founded the American navy, but Great-grandfather Benjamin W. Crowninshield had been Madison's Secretary of the Navy, and his brother Jacob Crowninshield had been confirmed as Jefferson's Secretary of the Navy (although he never served). So Charles Francis Adams resigned from over forty corporate directorships and went to Washington, where each day he waited his turn in the cafeteria for navy beans. (In reality, he said, they were Boston beans.) Once a week, reported the New York *Times* on its front page, "Secretary Adams has a [cod] fish ball with his beans."[120]

If the menu pleased him, the persistence of reporters and photographers did not. Once when ordered by the photographers to sit at his desk and "write something," they discovered that what he was writing was "This is hell this is hell this is hell."[121] Yet reporters sometimes found that his wry humor made good copy. At the London Naval Conference of 1930 the "Topics of the Times" told how "he was seen, the other day, sailing a number of toy boats in the waters of Kensington Garden, in the heart of London! The implication is obvious. The Secretary of the American Navy, having had all his large ships torpedoed by insidious foreign diplomats, is forced to concentrate on toy models in an artificial lake. . . ."[122]

His regime at the Navy Department was a conservative one. He wished to bring the fleet up to the parity allowed by the 1930 conference, but President Hoover ordered retrenchment as the depression began, and the navy's strength fell far behind the quotas permitted by inter-

national agreement. If he had less influence on naval policy than he
desired, Secretary Adams at least influenced one question of state protocol. Mrs. Hoover decided that White House receptions would be concluded when the band played a certain tune. A meeting of the cabinet
wives was convened to choose the key number, and the matter was
promptly settled when Mrs. Adams announced that her husband was
familiar with only two pieces of music—"The Star-Spangled Banner" and
"The Blue Danube Waltz." Since the former would have brought the
guests to attention rather than to the exits, the latter was designated as
the official concluding melody.[123]

At one time it was reported that Adams' relations with the President
were almost at the breaking point. Hoover, however, professed profound
admiration for his Secretary of the Navy, and in his memoirs wrote,
"Had I known him better earlier, I should have made him Secretary of
State."[124]

When Franklin Roosevelt entered the White House, Adams returned
to corporate management and sailing. In 1939, at the age of seventy-
three, he won the King's, Astor, and Puritan Cups, the three most
coveted domestic racing trophies, in a single season. It was as if a
twelve-year-old horse had captured the triple crown. The next year,
while fishing vessels and freighters hugged port because of a roller-
coaster sea, he skippered his eight-meter yacht to victory over a six-mile
course off Marblehead. Not until 1951, when he declined to become
chairman of the New York, New Haven and Hartford Railroad, was
there any sign that the Deacon was slowing down. He died in 1954 at
the Adamsian age of eighty-seven.

His daughter Catherine married Henry Sturgis Morgan, younger of the
two sons of J. P. Morgan. The 1923 wedding on the lawn of the Adamses'
Concord estate was reported to be "as simple as possible in character."
The bridegroom, having just graduated from Harvard, joined his father's
firm, and on the elder Morgan's death in 1943, he inherited half of a
reputed sixty-million-dollar fortune.[125] The Deacon's son, Charles Francis
Adams, married Margaret Stockton, daughter of the president of the
First National Bank of Boston, and a direct descendant of the New
Jersey political dynasty. This fourth Charles Francis Adams is now
chairman of the board and chief executive officer of the Raytheon Company, a major defense and space equipment supplier. "To the best of
my knowledge," he writes, "no members of the family are active in
political life."[126]§

§ Two years after he made this statement, however, his second cousin,
Thomas Boylston Adams (1910–   ), announced his interest in becoming the
Democratic nominee for the U. S. Senate from Massachusetts. This Adams is
a grandson of Charles Francis Adams of the Union Pacific Railroad and a son
of John Adams (1875–1964), who was president of the Adams Securities

James Michael Curley, the Beau Sabreur of Boston Irish politics, was as usual locked in a life-or-death struggle for mayor in 1929. Night after night he turned his withering sarcasm on a former supporter who had gone over to the enemy. "You can imagine my astonishment last Thursday afternoon," he told rallies, "to see Billso Hickey strolling down the street with Abigail Homans."[127] Mrs. Homans¶ was the sister of Secretary of the Navy Charles Francis Adams; Mr. Hickey was of less exalted lineage. Clearly, thought Curley, who always kept his finger raised to test the political wind, the Adamses were ripe for ridicule; a breed of aristocratic fops, ideally suited to be campaigned against—even if they had long ago retired from the competition. Such had become the fate of America's most illustrious dynasty.

Part of the cause for his eldest brother's failure in politics, felt Henry Adams, was that he refused to "sacrifice" himself to "get cheers from an Irish mob."[128] Yet the Adamses could hardly blame their decline on demographic changes. Other Brahmins continued to have notable successes. Even Curley, the Adams-baiter, was himself defeated by Henry Cabot Lodge, Jr., who then went on to beat a Casey and a Walsh, before losing to a Kennedy. A Saltonstall has been equally successful. In fact, the Adams decline began with the rise of Andrew Jackson, a full generation before the great Irish immigration.

But Henry Adams was right if he meant that his family no longer made the effort to do and say those things which distinguish the man who asks his fellows for political power. Although the Adamses were never noted for currying favor, John Quincy Adams actually published an epic poem about Irish freedom, *Dermot MacMorrogh, or the Conquest of Ireland; an Historical Tale of the Twelfth Century,* in four cantos. (It did him little good with his Irish constituents.) After the great John Quincy, the Adamses never even tried. They survived politically for another three generations primarily on appointive office, a sure sign of dynastic decline.

The Adamses themselves put forth several explanations for their political demise. John Adams might even have contended that it was a *planned* exodus to higher forms of cultural expression. While serving as

---

Company and of the Massachusetts Historical Society (1950–57). Before 1966, Thomas never displayed an unseemly interest in elective office. His background is as an editorial writer for the Boston *Herald,* a faculty member of Harvard's Peabody Museum of Archaeology and Ethnology, a vice president of the Sheraton hotels, and successor to his father as president of the Massachusetts Historical Society.

¶ Abigail Adams married Robert Homans, an upper-caste lawyer with a Harvard degree. Of their four children, Helen Homans Gilbert, wife of the board chairman of the Gillette Safety Razor Company, is chairman of the board of Radcliffe College and was acting president in 1964–65; George Homans is professor of sociology at Harvard.

"militia diplomat" in France, he wrote Abigail, "I must study politics and war that my sons may have liberty to study mathematics and philosophy. My sons ought to study mathematics and philosophy . . . in order to give their children a right to study painting, poetry, music, architecture. . . ."[129] This theory of politics to poetry in three generations turned out to be a fairly accurate prediction. Yet how would the second President have explained that in the fourth generation his heirs "retrogressed" to commerce?

It was the opinion of Brooks Adams that "a single family can stay adjusted through three generations." He then added, "It is now full four generations since John Adams wrote the Constitution of Massachusetts. It is time that we perished. The world is tired of us."[130] This Darwinistic view was in part a rationalization for the failure of the fourth generation of Adamses. It also conveniently meshed with Brooks's "law" of civilization's decline; thus, in one broad brush stroke, he could blame the world for the failure of his family.[131] His argument, however, breaks down when one examines other political dynasties. Benjamin Harrison joined with John Adams in signing the Declaration of Independence; his great-grandson, in Brooks's generation, was President of the United States; his great-great-great-grandson, in the present generation, has been a member of Congress. Likewise the Bayards of Delaware were political contemporaries of John Adams and are still going strong after six consecutive generations in elective office.

This is not to say that Brooks had not correctly identified a factor that certainly played a role in the dynasty's downfall. The Adamses, to use the expression of Brooks's brother Charles, were always "otherwise-minded." As the American people tended to draw away from the pure Burkean philosophy of political representation, the iconoclastic Adamses became less acceptable as politicians. But to blame society hardly "excuses" the Adamses; there would continue to be great dissenters, though their names would not be Adams.

Other causes contributed to the family's fall as a political dynasty. Wealth—usually a distinct aid in dynasty-building—played a strange trick on the Adamses, and seemed to remove some of the spur to political involvement. The ever present eccentricities, accentuated in each successive generation, made them less appealing to the electorate. And they had just plain bad luck from a dynastic standpoint—Henry and Brooks were childless—although there were still enough Adamses to have carried on if they had wished to. But, most important, the dynasty simply lost its zest for public service. Even as early as the third generation, Charles Francis Adams referred to his distinguished career as minister to Great Britain as "my eight years of purgatory in public office."[132]

But rather than some general law of decline, which must stretch or overlook enough specifics to reach an all-inclusive theory, one should look at each Adams separately. In the fourth generation, John Quincy II, for some inexplicable reason, had neither the ambition nor the single-mindedness to be a successful politician; Charles deliberately chose another avenue to power, and chose unwisely; Henry had finer aesthetic than political antennae and, after the death of his wife, was emotionally unsuited for political life anyway; and Brooks always bordered on insanity. In the fifth generation, Secretary of the Navy Charles Francis Adams considered politics more an act of civic-mindedness, like giving to the Community Chest, and as a tithe to one's ancestors, than as an end in itself.

The Adamses' fight with State Street, on which they long seemed to thrive, was finally won by the Street. Charles Francis Adams III and Abigail Adams Homans became Proper Boston.

Yet for a century and a half the direct descendants of a simple Quincy farmer were prominently involved in the political fabric of their country. Through election and appointment they played a leading role in every major development in American history from the fight for independence through the fight to abolish slavery. John Adams, the farmer's son, became one of the most important members of the Continental Congress, first Secretary of Defense of his rebel government, a negotiator of the foreign loans that financed the Revolution and of the treaty that brought peace, his nation's first minister to Holland and Great Britain, the first Vice-President of the United States, and its second President. His son John Quincy Adams was also minister to Holland and Great Britain, as well as minister to Prussia and Russia, United States senator and congressman, a negotiator—like his father— of peace with Great Britain, Secretary of State, and sixth President of the United States. John Quincy's son Charles Francis Adams was a congressman and a minister to Great Britain—as his father and grandfather had been before him—and the United States representative on the *Alabama* Claims Commission. After this the Adamses would still produce brilliant historians, a Secretary of the Navy, and business leaders.

When Sir Francis Galton wrote his classic study of hereditary genius he rated the Adamses as the only American family worthy of inclusion.[133] Much later, John F. Kennedy also looked back on man's past achievements and said, "I feel that the Adams family intimidates us all."[134]

The Lee Dynasty

"The Family of Lee has more merit in it than
any other Family."

—John Adams[1]

"I always think of myself as a rediscoverer of
Stratford. . . . It is a shrine dedicated to a great
American family and especially to the memory of
that very great gentleman, Robert E. Lee. It is
equally a permanent memorial to a brave, young
civilization for which modern America will always
be grateful."

—Franklin D. Roosevelt[2]

FOUR years after the first Henry Adams brought his large family to
Massachusetts in 1636, Richard Lee, twenty-seven years old and unmarried, came to Virginia. The immigrant Adams had been a poor
farmer in England and died a poor farmer in America, leaving to his
heirs a house and barn, a cow and a calf, some pigs, furniture, untensils,
and three beds (one in the parlor, two in the chamber).[3] The immigrant Lee, on the other hand, left an estate of 13,000 acres, all rich
tobacco land, and died perhaps the wealthiest man in Virginia.[4]

While it had taken the Adamses another four generations to acquire a
taste for politics, the first Lee probably stepped off the boat with a
political appointment in his pocket. From the humble position of clerk
of the Quarter Court, he rose rapidly: Attorney General of Virginia,
High Sheriff of York County, House of Burgesses, Secretary of State,
Governor's Council. By the time of the American Revolution four generations of Lees had sat on the ruling council of their colony.

This first Lee was the poor relation of an ancient Shropshire family
whose coat of arms was topped by a squirrel thoughtfully nibbling an
acorn. Underneath was the motto *Non Incautus Futuri* (Not Unmindful
of the Future). A. E. Housman's *Shropshire Lad* would later muse, "In
my own shire, if I was sad,/Homely comforters I had." But the restless

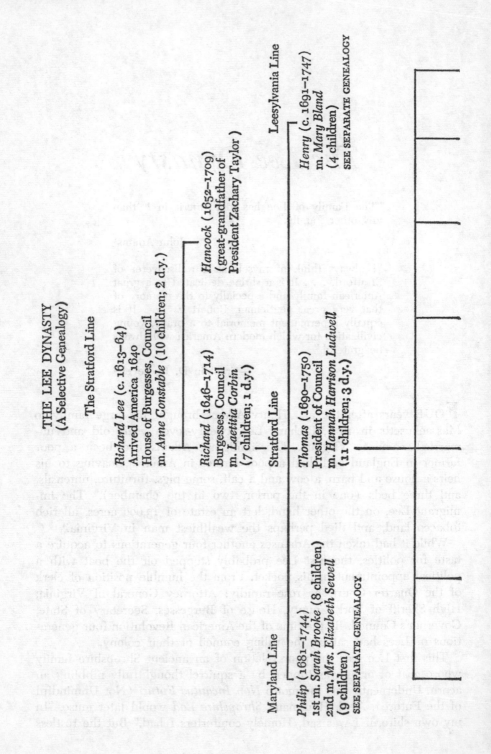

THE LEE DYNASTY
(A Selective Genealogy)

The Stratford Line

Richard Lee (c. 1613–64)
Arrived America 1640
House of Burgesses, Council
m. Anne Constable (10 children; 2 d.y.)

Richard (1646–1714)
Burgesses, Council
m. Laetitia Corbin
(7 children; 1 d.y.)

Hancock (1652–1709)
(great-grandfather of
President Zachary Taylor)

Stratford Line

Thomas (1690–1750)
President of Council
m. Hannah Harrison Ludwell
(11 children; 3 d.y.)

Henry (c. 1691–1747)
m. Mary Bland
(4 children)
SEE SEPARATE GENEALOGY

Leesylvania Line

Maryland Line

Philip (1681–1744)
1st m. Sarah Brooke (8 children)
2nd m. Mrs. Elizabeth Sewell
(9 children)
SEE SEPARATE GENEALOGY

Philip Ludwell
(1726–75)
Council
m. Elizabeth Steptoe
(3 children; 1 d.y.)

Hannah
(1728–82)
m. Gawen Corbin

Richard Henry
(1732–94)
CONTINENTAL CONGRESS,
SENATE
1st m. Ann Aylett
(d. 1768) (4 children)
2nd m. Anne Gaskins
Pinckard (5 children)

Francis Lightfoot
(1734–97)
CONTINENTAL
CONGRESS
m. Rebecca Tayloe
(no issue)

Alice
(1736–1818)
m. William
Shippen
(8 children;
6 d.y.)

William
(1739–95)
Diplomat
m. Hannah
Ludwell
(4 children;
1 d.y.)

Arthur
(1740–92)
CONTINENTAL
CONGRESS
(unmarried)

Matilda (d. 1790)
m. "Light Horse Harry" Lee
See Leesylvania Line

Anne (1770–1804)
m. Attorney General
Charles Lee
See Leesylvania Line

Francis Lightfoot (1782–1850)
m. Jane Fitzgerald

Anne Shippen (1761–1841) ("Nancy")
m. Henry Beekman Livingston
(1 child)

Samuel Phillips (1812–97)
Admiral
m. Elizabeth Blair (1 child)

[Francis Preston] Blair (1857–1944)
SENATE
m. Anne Clymer Brooke
(3 children; 1 d.y.)

THE LEE DYNASTY
(A Selective Genealogy)

The Leesylvania Line

Richard Lee (c. 1613–64) m. Anne Constable (10 children; 2 d.y.)

Richard (1646–1714) m. Laetitia Corbin (7 children; 1 d.y.)

Henry (c. 1691–1747) m. Mary Bland (4 children)

Henry (1729–87) m. Lucy Grymes (8 children)
House of Burgesses, Virginia Senate

Henry (1756–1818)
("Light Horse Harry")
CONTINENTAL CONGRESS,
GOVERNOR, HOUSE OF
REPRESENTATIVES
1st m. Matilda Lee (4 children; 2 d.y.); 2nd m. Ann Hill Carter (6 children; 1 d.y.)

Charles (1758–1815)
U.S. Attorney General
1st m. Anne Lee (6 children; 3 d.y.)
2nd m. Mrs. Margaret Peyton (3 children; 1 d.y.)

Richard Bland (1761–1827)
HOUSE OF REPRESENTATIVES
m. Elizabeth Collins
(5 children; 2 d.y.)

Lucy
(1786–1860)
m. Bernard Moore Carter

Henry (1787–1837)
("Black Horse Harry")
m. Anne McCarty
(1 child; 1 d.y.)

Ann Kinloch (1800–64)
m. Judge William Marshall
(2 children; 1 d.y.)

Sydney Smith (1802–69)
Naval commander,
m. Anna Maria Mason
(7 children; 1 d.y.)

Robert Edward (1807–70)
Confederate general,
college president,
m. Mary Anne Custis
(7 children)

Fitzhugh (1835–1905)
General, GOVERNOR
m. Ellen B. Fowle
(5 children)

George Washington Custis
(1832–1913)
Confederate general,
college president
(unmarried)

William Henry Fitzhugh
(1837–91) ("Rooney")
Confederate general,
HOUSE OF REPRESENTATIVES
1st m. Charlotte Wickham
(2 children; 2 d.y.);
2nd m. Mary T. Bolling
(2 children)

Robert Edward, Jr.
(1843–1914)
1st m. Charlotte Haxall
(no issue);
2nd m. Juliet Carter
(2 children)

George (1877–1934)
Army colonel
m. Kathro Burton
(2 children)

George Bolling (1872–1948)
Doctor
m. Helen Keeney
(2 children)

Fitzhugh (1905–   )
Admiral
m. Harriet F. Davis
(3 children)

Robert Edward IV (1924–   )
Newspaper executive
(2 children)

THE LEE DYNASTY
(A Selective Genealogy)

The Maryland Line

Richard Lee (c. 1613–64)
m. *Anne Constable*
(10 children; 2 d.y.)
|
Richard (1646–1714)
m. *Laetitia Corbin*
(7 children; 1 d.y.)
|
Philip (1681–1744)
Moved to Maryland, 1700.
1st m. *Sarah Brooke*
(8 children)
2nd m. *Mrs. Elizabeth Sewell*
(9 children)

Alice
2nd m. *Meriwether Smith*

Thomas (d. 1749)
m. *Christiana Sim*
(2 children)

George William Smith
(1762–1811)
GOVERNOR

Thomas Sim (1745–1819)
CONTINENTAL CONGRESS, GOVERNOR
m. *Mary Digges*
(8 children; 2 d.y.)

Eliza (1783–1862)
m. *Outerbridge Horsey*
(1777–1842)
SENATE
(4 children)

John (1788–1871)
HOUSE OF REPRESENTATIVES
m. *Harriet Carroll*
(4 children; 1 d.y.)

and ambitious Lee never looked back, and he found his comforts far from the shire of his youth. Shortly after his arrival in America he married Anne Constable, a young lady of quality, who apparently was a ward of the governor. Their progeny in the name of Lee would include three chief executives of Virginia, a governor of Maryland, two signers of the Declaration of Independence (the only brothers to affix their names to the document), several diplomats, an Attorney General under the Administrations of George Washington and John Adams, a Revolutionary general, four Confederate generals, one Union admiral, and nine members of Congress.

Quantitatively, it is an unmatched collection of public honors.

For a family whose rigid convictions would contribute to America's two revolutions, its founder ironically was a man of no firm political beliefs. He declared fealty to Charles II in 1650, swore allegiance to the Commonwealth in 1652, and hailed the Restoration in 1660. He was in public office first as a means of advancing his fortunes and later as a mark of the dignity he had achieved. Richard Lee was primarily an empire builder.

The Lee dynasty was not a direct result of its founder's economic purposefulness. While the eldest sons customarily inherited the money, it was the younger sons who made the political reputations. The Lees' wealth brought status, connections, and usually an excellent education—all advantageous commodities—but politically the dynasty was based on talent rather than position.

Although Robert E. Lee, best known of the dynasty, was of such saintly disposition that one almost longs for some transgression to relieve the monotony of his personal goodness, the political members of the family were often argumentative, suspicious, and vain. Not without cause could they be called "the Adamses of the South."

The son who most resembled the adventurous and pioneering founder was Hancock Lee, fifth of the eight children of Richard Lee to survive infancy.

Hancock married Sarah Allerton, granddaughter of a *Mayflower* passenger. It would become a habit for the Lees to unite with other illustrious lines, but never would they add to the family tree a more unique scoundrel than old Isaac Allerton. The tall and angular tailor, fifth man to sign the Mayflower Compact, was an unlikely Puritan. Perhaps his fellow Pilgrims realized that his talents were exclusively secular when they made him their business agent. In this capacity he took seven trips to London to borrow money and secure supplies. It soon became apparent, however, that Isaac was looking out for his own commercial interests first. Yet as the husband of Fear Brewster and the son-in-law of the revered elder William Brewster his sharp dealings were overlooked for a time—even after he had brought to Massachusetts the first proprietor of a bawdy house!

In his defense it can be said that his ability to borrow money at relatively low interest rates kept the colony from foundering. But finally Allerton was thrown out of Massachusetts. It took two or three years to audit his financial records, and then it was discovered that he had even "scrued up his poor old father-in-law's account to above two hundred pounds. . . ."[5] It was his granddaughter who married Hancock Lee. (Isaac Allerton's other distinction was that he was the first maternal ancestor in America of Franklin D. Roosevelt.)

Not content to seek their fortunes at home, Hancock Lee and his heirs set out for the banks of the Ohio, and played a part in the settlement of Kentucky. While the Virginia Lees were writing resolutions and signing declarations, these cousins were paddling canoes and getting scalped. No Lee of this line was ever elected to Congress, but Hancock Lee's great-grandson, Zachary Taylor, became President of the United States, and others of this branch married Confederate President Jefferson Davis and Senator John J. Crittenden.[6]

The Lee patriarch's principal heir, also named Richard, preferred scholarship to real estate, keeping his notes in Greek, Latin, and Hebrew. His landholdings remained intact, but as a grandson ruefully commented, "He neither improved nor diminished his paternal estate, though in that time he might with ease have acquired what would produce at this day a most princely revenue."[7] In politics, Richard II succeeded his father on the powerful twelve-man Council, which also sat as the highest court in the colony, and, as would be expected of a royal counselor, was a firm foe of anything that threatened the status quo. During Bacon's Rebellion he was imprisoned for seven weeks.

It was his sons who founded the lines of Stratford, Leesylvania, and Maryland, the three family tributaries that would produce leaders of the American Revolution.

The Maryland line began around 1700 when Philip Lee moved to an inherited plantation on the Patuxent.[8] He had seventeen children (eight by his first wife; nine by his second). His grandson* was towering, handsome Thomas Sim Lee, the Revolutionary War governor of Maryland, who labored tirelessly to raise and equip troops, and later,

---

* Another grandson, George William Smith (1762–1811), succeeded to the governorship of Virginia when James Monroe resigned. One month later, however, he was burned to death in the great Richmond Theatre fire, in which seventy persons were known to have perished. After having first reached safety, the governor fatally returned to rescue his little son. See Margaret Vowell Smith, *Virginia, 1492–1892, A History of the Executives* (Washington: Lowdermilk, 1893), Vol. II, pp. 318–19.

during a second term, helped to put down the Whiskey Rebellion. Then he declined a third term and retired from politics.[9] Although a son served briefly in Congress,† and a daughter married a United States senator,‡ these Lees virtually abandoned political life by the beginning of the nineteenth century, leaving the pursuit of public honors to their Stratford and Leesylvania cousins.

The founder of the Stratford line was Thomas Lee, a fifth son, who, having little education and a patrimony that consisted of a cow pasture, rose to become acting governor of Virginia and the largest landowner the dynasty ever produced.

Part of Thomas Lee's business success was the result of family connections. At the age of twenty-one an uncle secured for him an appointment as agent for Lady Fairfax's vast interests in Virginia. He capably handled the noble lady's accounts for four years, then put the information he had acquired to work for himself.

Yet combined with this ability to take advantage of opportunities was a vision of what later Americans would call their "manifest destiny." Two generations of Virginia Lees had remained rooted in the mother country, and the three thousand miles of water between their homes and their loyalties only attested to the strength of the roots. The Richard Lees had looked east; now Thomas' gaze was firmly fixed on the west.

With the driving force of the disinherited, a quality lacking in his studious parent, Thomas Lee took his quest for land over the mountains to the Ohio and the Mississippi. For this purpose he formed the Ohio Land Company. (He would not live to see his instrumentality touch off the French and Indian War.)

Westward expansion had been made possible by the Treaty of Lancaster, which Lee helped to negotiate in 1744. For a few hundred dollars

† John Lee (1788–1871) was a member of the U. S. House of Representatives from 1823 to 1825. But he was better known for pioneering the development of the Chesapeake and Ohio Canal and the Baltimore and Ohio Railroad. He was married to Harriet Carroll, a member of the richest and most distinguished Catholic family in America. (Her grandfather was Charles Carroll of Carrollton, signer of the Declaration of Independence.)

‡ Eliza Lee (1783–1862) was the wife of Outerbridge Horsey (1777–1842), U.S. senator from Delaware. This match inspired some ribald comment from James A. Bayard, who wrote Caesar Rodney: "Our friend Horsey is certainly about to suffer a great metamorphosis . . . the time is not known when the old Bachelor is to be merged. It can't well happen in Lent as the Lady is a Catholic, and not allowed to *taste flesh* during the quadragesimal fast." (Italics in original.) See Henry C. Conrad, editor, "Letters of James Asheton Bayard, 1802–1814," *Papers of the Historical Society of Delaware*, XXXI (Wilmington, 1901), pp. 15–16. A great-grandson of the couple, Outerbridge Horsey (1910–   ), was appointed U.S. ambassador to Czechoslovakia in 1962. See New York *Times*, November 15, 1962, p. 18.

the Iroquois gave up their lands west of the Alleghenies. Lee's bargain, transferring the Northwest Territory to England, made Peter Minuit look like a hopeless spendthrift.

Lee became acting governor of Virginia in September 1749 and served until his death fourteen months later. He died without knowing that his royal appointment as governor was then on its way from London. Had he lived, he would have been the first native-born American so honored.[10]

The Virginia of Thomas Lee's prosperity was quite different from the frontier that his grandfather had known a century before. The change sprang from one root, tobacco, on which now depended the entire economy of the colony. The crop exhausted the earth, forcing its planters constantly to expand their tillable acreage. The humbler landholders could not compete in this race for space. Labor had to be imported to keep pace.

The slaveholding plantation became a way of life, and the plantation turned Virginia into an oligarchy, with the Council ruled by the Tidewater barons, and the House of Burgesses serving as a forum for the second sons and lesser aristocrats.

The social character of the colony and the character of its social leaders was shaped by the plantation. From the halls and gardens of Stratford, which Thomas Lee built between 1725 and 1730, and the other great manors, finely attired Virginians lived a charmed existence. It was a life of fox hunting and gambling, but so too could it be a life of study and contemplation. Thus did America's most rigid class structure produce overbearing, domineering plutocrats and independent, public-spirited patriots, both strains often to be found in a single individual.

As befits a great landholder, Thomas Lee married the daughter of a great landholder. Hannah Ludwell's paternal grandfather was a governor of the Carolinas; her maternal grandfather was a Harrison. From this Harrison-Ludwell-Lee merger came eight children, including four sons who would be unequaled for collective political achievement until a poor Maine storekeeper named Washburn sent four sons to Congress from four different states.

When Thomas Lee died in 1750 only Philip Ludwell and Hannah of his eight had reached majority. Philip, of course, was the principal heir, and would become the fourth Lee to sit in the Virginia Council. He was first and last a royalist, although he was more interested in thoroughbred horses than in politics. Pompous and self-important, he treated his indentured servants with disgust and cruelty and the tradesmen with disdain and arrogance.[11] Nor was he less highhanded in dealing with his own brothers and sisters. Arthur, the youngest, was made to eat and work with the slaves. Under their father's will Philip was responsible for disbursing certain legacies to the younger children. They were never paid in full. William wrote bitterly to his eldest brother: "Certainly to be twelve years out of my pittance which my father left me, without even common interest for it, while you have been indulging in affluence and I, procuring my bread with the sweat of my brow, is surely bad enough and it is time to put an end to it."[12] The courts finally removed Philip as guardian.

Rather than continue the discord and years of incessant litigation with her brother, Alice Lee gave up her small inheritance and moved to England. But she was not to remain abroad permanently as she had planned. In London she met and married William Shippen, Jr., a young American medical student. He was from a distinguished Philadelphia family founded by Great-grandfather Edward Shippen, a Yorkshireman, who accumulated a large fortune as a merchant, converted to Quakerism, and became the acting governor of Pennsylvania.[13] Alice Lee Shippen would have a daughter whose marriage into the powerful Livingston dynasty of New York was to have tragic consequences for both families.§

Very different from Alice Lee, a conventional eighteenth-century wife who subordinated herself to her husband and became completely dependent on his will and decision, was her elder sister Hannah. If Hannah's traits of independence and courage were considered peculiar in a woman, in her Lee brothers they would produce patriots and statesmen.

Hannah left Stratford at twenty to marry Cawen Corbin and become mistress of Peckatone, where she took an unusually active part in the plantation's development. She also joined the Baptist Society, a sect that was looked upon with extreme disfavor by the Established Church in Virginia. When her husband died she was incensed to find that his will required her to forfeit two thirds of his estate if she remarried. (She was then only thirty-one years old.) Moreover, as one of America's first suffragists, she resented having to pay taxes without having a voice in government.

One of the witnesses of Corbin's will was his physician, Richard Lingan Hall, a man of high standing and integrity, with whom Hannah fell deeply in love. Two years after her husband's death she arranged for Dr. Hall to live with her at Peckatone. Their union, which lasted happily for nearly eighteen years, was without the aid of clergy. Possibly they would have got married, but Virginia required that this could only be by ritual of the Church of England, and to this the Baptist Hannah would never consent. Also, of course, taking the formal vows would have meant losing Peckatone. She had a son and a daughter by Dr. Hall, although she continued to live as "Mrs. Hannah Corbin, widow," and

§ See Livingston Dynasty, pp. 83ff.

the children went by the name of Corbin. Hannah's design for living apparently was accepted by her neighbors, and there is no indication that she ever lost the affection of the Lee family.[14]

Of the four remarkable younger sons of Thomas Lee,¶ the most significant was Richard Henry, in whom were fused the dominant traits of the preceding three generations: the aggressiveness of Richard the Emigrant; the bent for scholarship of the second Richard; the political aptitude of his father.

Richard Henry Lee was tall and lean, with reddish hair, deep-set cavernous eyes, and an aquiline nose, giving him something of the appearance of a Roman emperor. As a young man his one desire was to be engaged in politics, and he spent long hours in the library at Stratford learning his fundamentals from John Locke. Despite his flair for personal controversy there would always remain in him the remnants of a meditative student.

He would develop into a great orator, "the Cicero of America," with a unique ability to put his thoughts into the fewest possible words. His style, though spirited and rich in classical allusion, was never flamboyant. His harmonious voice sounded trained, and his enemies would accuse him of practicing in front of a mirror. His first great speech, upon entering the House of Burgesses in 1759, was for the emancipation of the slaves. Although he opposed the institution because of its effect on white society, rather than on the Negro, it was probably the severest indictment of slavery ever uttered by a Virginian.[15] This view was shared by his descendants, including Robert E. Lee.

In contrast to his brother Richard, Francis Lightfoot Lee had neither the habit of command nor the ability to make enemies. He was not a good speaker, being shy and reserved. In fact, he never liked politics; it was his duty, not his delight. Nancy Shippen wrote a sonnet to this favorite uncle, beginning, "Thou sweetest of all the Lee race." He was always chafing to return to his childless wife Becky. They lived for each other's company, and politics was the incessant intruder in their house. Yet the genial and gentle Frank was a valuable ally to his brother in the legislative halls of state and nation.

The two youngest brothers were also studies in contrast. William was

¶ Another son, Thomas Ludwell Lee (1730–78), served in the House of Burgesses but refused to step onto the national scene with his brothers. John Adams, quoting Chancellor Wythe, said of him, "Thomas Lee was the most popular man in Virginia, and the delight of the eyes of every Virginian, but . . . would not engage in public life." Best known of his descendants was Edward D. White (1845–1921), U.S. senator from Louisiana and Chief Justice of the Supreme Court. See Edmund Jennings Lee, *Lee of Virginia, 1642–1892* (Philadelphia: Franklin Printing, 1895), pp. 168–71.

painfully blunt and unsocial, with intelligence of a native, unschooled
variety. He was the most practical of the sons of Thomas Lee. Arthur, on
the other hand, was a great conversationalist, idealistic, impractical,
introspective, pensive—the most intellectual of the brothers. They both
went to England—William to enter business; Arthur to study medicine,
then law. While in London William married his first cousin, Hannah
Ludwell.[16] But Arthur remained a bachelor, although at one time he
commissioned niece Nancy Shippen to propose to a number of young
ladies on his behalf. When they rejected him he resigned himself to a
state of singleness.

So it was that on the eve of the American Revolution the family of Lee
was strategically placed on two continents. Arthur in London, where he
could pass on to his brothers, and other correspondents, the latest news
of British policy—"The most constant and certain intelligence," said John
Adams, "which was received from any individual within my knowledge"[17]; Alice Lee Shippen in Philadelphia, soon to become the seat of
the Continental Congress in which two of her brothers would represent
Virginia; Richard Henry and Francis Lightfoot in the House of Burgesses
at Williamsburg.

The two Lees in the Virginia legislature, together with Patrick Henry
and Thomas Jefferson, comprised the hard-core opposition to Great
Britain. When this insurgency was transferred to Philadelphia upon the
convening of the first Continental Congress in September 1774, the
Virginians made common cause with Samuel Adams, the "Grand Incendiary," and his cousin John. This Lee-Adams junto would remain in
the minority for the next year and a half, while the loyalists, who controlled the congressional machinery, tried to drive a wedge between
them. The two families were played off against each other in making
committee assignments, but the loyalists failed to reckon with the stubborn streaks in both clans, and their maneuvers only succeeded in bringing the Adamses and Lees closer together.

Then public sentiment began swinging over to the independence faction as America and Great Britain fought an undeclared war at Lexington, Concord, and Bunker Hill. On July 2, 1776, the greatest day in
the history of the Lee dynasty, Richard Henry Lee, his red hair now
graying, an injured left hand wrapped in a black handkerchief, introduced a resolution in the Congress: "That these united colonies are,
and of right ought to be, free and independent states; that they are
absolved from all allegiance to the British crown, and that all political
connection between them, and the state of Great Britain, is, and ought
to be, totally dissolved." The motion was seconded by John Adams. Its
passage marked the separation of the United States of America from
Great Britain.

The Declaration of Independence, adopted two days later, did not *declare* independence but, as it states, declared the *causes* compelling independence. It was Jefferson's magnificent language that turned the Fourth of July, rather than the Second, into a national holiday.

That the author of the Declaration of Independence was Thomas Jefferson and not Richard Henry Lee was primarily a matter of political accommodation. The conservatives wanted Benjamin Harrison to chair the drafting committee; Lee was the first choice of the Adams faction. But Lee, unlike Jefferson, was incapable of standing on principle without inciting enmity, so "Jefferson was [made] chairman," said John Adams, ". . . because we united on him to the exclusion of R. H. Lee, in order to keep out Harrison."[18]

While Richard Henry Lee and Francis Lightfoot Lee were maneuvering in Congress for American independence, their brothers Arthur and William were playing a role in the same struggle on the other side of the Atlantic.

Arthur, in London, was appointed secret agent by the Continental Congress in 1775, making him America's first foreign service officer. Besides his work as a one-man CIA, he was charged with seeking the support of the Bourbon kings of France and Spain. This assignment brought him in contact with an eccentric collection of Frenchmen, including Pierre Augustin Caron de Beaumarchais, author of *The Marriage of Figaro*, convicted forger, comptroller of the royal pantry and bearer of the King's meat. (Lee first met Beaumarchais when the *ersatz* aristocrat came to London to buy off a blackmailer of Madame du Barry.) Lee's negotiations resulted in the United States receiving $200,-000 each from France and Spain for the purchase of munitions. It was with these arms that the Americans won their first great victory of the war at Saratoga.[19]

In October 1776, Lee joined Benjamin Franklin and Silas Deane in Paris as a member of the tripartite American Commission to France. And when Franklin, now in his seventieth year, resigned the strenuous additional duties of American commissioner to Spain, Lee added Madrid to his portfolio. William Lee joined this band of "militia diplomats" in 1777 as commercial agent at Nantes, France, the home base for privateering operations against the British, and then became American commissioner to the courts of Vienna and Berlin.

In the years since his arrival in England William had become a man of means, in both the commercial and the political worlds. Besides being a successful tobacco merchant, he had been elected to the lifetime post of London alderman and, had he chosen to remain loyal to the Crown, would probably have become the city's lord mayor.

Before long a healthy feud had developed between Arthur Lee and his fellow commissioners. He accused Deane of using his official position for personal gain, a charge that touched off a congressional investigation. (Deane was eventually succeeded by John Adams.) His differences with Franklin, on the other hand, were primarily a great tin-pannic clash of personalities: Lee, supremely ambitious and egotistical, zealous and unbending; the ancient Franklin, as witty and gay as his youthful colleague was somber, as placid as Lee was volcanic, as accommodating to the world as he found it as Lee was unswerving in his crusade to change it.

It galled Lee that the practical inventor and philosopher of homely virtue was revered on two continents, while he went unrecognized and unappreciated. He was much like John Adams, who shared his opinion that Franklin was devious and overrated. Yet, as diplomats, neither could master the art, at which Franklin was supreme, of going roundabout to reach a goal that lay straight ahead. The Virginian was obsessed with replacing Franklin and becoming the sole minister to France. But Franklin got the appointment, and Lee's diplomatic career, more noteworthy for the dissension he caused than for solid achievements, was at an end.

"That band of brothers," as John Adams affectionately called the Lees, had a magnetic ability to draw controversy to themselves. Arthur Lee's conduct in Europe was just one of the matters that required defense by the Lees in Congress. There were also whispering campaigns, the product of Benjamin Harrison's imagination, to the effect that Richard Henry Lee was attempting to have Washington removed as head of the army and that he had ordered his overseer to accept only bullion in payment for rents. The latter was a serious accusation, for it meant that Lee was debasing the paper currency that Congress had issued for the conduct of the war. But the Lees were able to take care of themselves. Both charges were proved false.[20] And the brothers were not incapable of spreading malicious rumors of their own manufacture.[21] More substantial, however, was the indictment of the Lees' brother-in-law, Dr. William Shippen, Jr.

After marrying Alice Lee, the doctor returned to America and became professor of anatomy and surgery at the College of Philadelphia. Shippen's rival in the administration of the school was Dr. John Morgan, the other senior member of the faculty. Benjamin Rush was allied with the Morgan faction. This feud would become the basis for a bitter and protracted fight for the leadership of the Continental Army Medical Service, with Shippen ultimately becoming the director general. But in 1780 Rush accused him of selling hospital stores as his own property, speculating, failing to keep proper accounts, neglecting his duties, and other "Scandalous and infamous practices such as are unbecoming the Character of an Officer & Gentleman." A court-martial board, by a single vote, refused to convict, although Shippen was found guilty of speculating in and selling hospital stores. This record was transmitted to Congress, where for a month the Lees furiously upheld the honor of their brother-in-law. Finally Congress voted to take no further action against the doctor.[22]

The acquittal was a Pyrrhic victory. For Shippen's reputation was permanently tarnished. Moreover, because of economic pressures which resulted from a declining practice, he urged his daughter Nancy into a disastrous marriage with the wealthy Henry Beekman Livingston. Then, after the death in 1798 of his only son, Tom Shippen, a young man of great gifts and irresponsible character, the doctor seemed to lose interest in life. His health gradually declined, and he died in 1808, Dr. Rush attending.[23]

His wife survived him by a decade. Alice Lee's life had been difficult —early and bitter court fights with her eldest brother Philip, loss of six of her eight children in infancy, the scandal of her husband's trial, the death of her promising son Tom at thirty-three. She had been against Nancy's marriage to Livingston but was too weak to stand up to her husband. Then she helplessly watched her daughter's unhappiness.[24] In her last years, poor and totally blind, she was forced to give up her home and keep changing her place of habitation. Alice Lee Shippen died in her early eighties, in a state of religious melancholia.

While the Stratford Lees were first to bring national repute to the dynasty, their Leesylvania cousins were not far behind.

Charles Lee would become Attorney General of the United States under Presidents Washington and Adams. He was one of the few cabinet officers to remain loyal to John Adams, who, just before leaving office, tried to repay him with the chief judgeship of the fourth federal circuit. Lee declined the "midnight" appointment.[25] His brother, Richard Bland Lee, served in the House of Representatives for three terms and struck a notable bargain with Alexander Hamilton. In return for his vote on the Assumption Bill, which assured its passage, the capital of the United States was to be moved to Washington, D.C.[26] But most remarkable was a third brother, "Light Horse Harry" Lee.

These brothers were the children of Henry Lee, a member of the House of Burgesses, and Lucy Grymes, a lowland beauty whose sunny hair and blue eyes had been much admired by George Washington in his youth. Legend has it that the general later favored Light Horse Harry because of his tender memories of the young man's mother.

At the age of thirteen Harry was sent to Princeton, that hotbed of American independence, and came under the influence of President John Witherspoon and fellow student James Madison. With the coming of the war young Harry was put in command of a small, lightly equipped detachment of cavalry. The assignment appealed to his spirit of bravado and dream of glory. He loved to dash into combat astride a handsome horse. He loved to outfit himself in shining knee-length boots, white lambskin breeches, green jacket, and plumed helmet. He loved war.

Light Horse Harry Lee was tonic to the poorly trained, overmatched American army. He was its Jeb Stuart and its George Patton. And his heroics, which may have been militarily insignificant, were of psychological importance. He was ambushed with ten men by two hundred soldiers of the King and successfully fought them off. He made a daring raid on a British garrison of little value and escaped before the enemy could fire a shot. Yet the swashbuckling officer also is generally credited with devising the grand strategy of the war. While serving under Nathanael Greene, the twenty-six-year-old lieutenant colonel proposed the march into South Carolina that eventually trapped Cornwallis at Yorktown. But Lee felt he was not given proper recognition and left the army a bitter man.

In the spring of 1782 he married his cousin, eldest daughter of the despotic Philip Ludwell Lee. She was known as "the Divine Matilda" and was her father's favorite, in whose honor he founded a town named Matildaville. She inherited Stratford. When the lovely bride died in 1790 at the age of twenty-six, she left two high-strung, quick-tempered children, Lucy and Harry, neither of whom would be remembered with great affection in the annals of the dynasty. Light Horse Harry made a good husband, but it was already clear that the former cavalryman was ill suited for peacetime. His extravagant way of living and irresponsible business dealings so worried Matilda that she willed Stratford to her little son, by-passing her husband.

With the war successfully concluded, the nation turned its attention to how it proposed to govern itself. Richard Henry Lee, now almost an invalid from gout, had become president of the Congress. His brother Arthur had been elected to Congress after his return from France. Together they were instrumental in getting the Northwest Territory ceded to Congress. (This action, the first taken by the new nation that was federal in character, was in the nature of finishing family business, for it had been the Lees' father who secured the territory from the Indians.)

Richard Henry Lee declined election to the Constitutional Convention, feeling that it would be improper to help write a document which he would then have to act on as a congressman. What resulted was not to his liking. He proposed to Congress a series of safeguards, later to become the Bill of Rights. But Harry Lee argued that the sole duty of Congress was to transmit the Constitution to the states for action. He carried the day, and the battleground shifted.

Having lost the fight for amendments to his young cousin, Richard Henry changed his strategy and fought for the total rejection of the Constitution. Although he was not a member of the Virginia ratifying convention his hard-hitting volume, *Letters of the Federal Farmer*, had an impact on the delegates. However, the Federalists, led by Pendleton, Madison, Marshall, and Harry Lee, were victorious by ten votes. Richard Henry then pressed for constitutional revisions as a member of the new United States Senate. When the first ten amendments were adopted he retired from public life, but he died still unreconciled to the Constitution.

Success at the Virginia ratifying convention was Harry Lee's stepping-stone to the governor's office. He was elected in 1791. His three years in Richmond came at a crucial time for the nation. The federal Union had to prove itself and it fell to Lee to establish its supremacy. When the Western farmers, who had been heavily taxed by the new government, threatened to secede, President Washington called out 15,000 troops, a larger force than he had led in the Revolution. Governor Lee was made a major general and put in command. The mere presence of Lee's force was enough to disperse the insurgents, but the Whiskey Rebellion was in principle the same as that which would divide the nation in 1861.

Only as a soldier was Lee truly happy. He was bred to arms, it was his only profession, he said. While serving as governor he seriously toyed with the idea of joining the revolutionary French army. Becoming a Lafayette in reverse appealed to his vision of glory. George Washington, however, strongly urged him to forget the notion. There also was a second restraining influence. The widower had proposed to Ann Hill Carter, seventeen years his junior, and her father made his staying in Virginia a condition of the marriage. When Lee chose Ann, Washington wrote him that he was pleased he had "exchanged the rugged and dangerous field of Mars for the soft and pleasurable bed of Venus."[27]

The second Mrs. Harry Lee was a great-great-granddaughter of Alexander Spotswood, Virginia's greatest colonial governor, and a great-granddaughter of Robert ("King") Carter, whose estate of 300,000 acres was only slightly smaller than the state of Connecticut. The Lees and Carters had been feuding for nearly a century, ever since Thomas Lee replaced King Carter as Lady Fairfax's agent in Virginia. For the powerful and imperious Carter to be superseded by a mere lad of twenty-one was a blow to his ego and his pocketbook. Later Carter asked Lee for permission to cut a road through his property to facilitate the movement of copper ore to market. The request was refused. One ramification of this long-standing dispute was Benjamin Harrison's machinations against Richard Henry Lee when they were both in the Continental Congress—Harrison was King Carter's grandson. But now the families were uniting and from the union would come Robert E. Lee, who some contended was more Carter than Lee.

Harry Lee was to have one last shining moment. In 1799 he was elected to Congress by a vote of 233 to 47. The victory was primarily the result of Washington's influence. During the balloting he rode up to the Montrose courthouse square and announced, "I vote for General Lee." Washington died soon afterward, and Lee was chosen by Congress to deliver the official eulogy at the Muhlenbergs' church in Philadelphia. For the final time in the glow of public praise, Harry Lee described the President as "first in war, first in peace and first in the hearts of his countrymen."

But now the world of Light Horse Harry began to shatter.

He was left politically adrift when the pendulum of power swung over to the party of Jefferson. So bitter was his hatred of the "Sage of Monticello" that he even voted for Aaron Burr when the 1800 presidential election was thrown into the House of Representatives.

The politician without an office, the soldier without a war, now reaped what he had sowed. He had chased the rainbow's end, wildly, lavishly, grandly throwing his inheritance into worthless land speculations. There was no money left. His last tragic days are described by Burton J. Hendrick, the biographer of the Lee family: "Living on small loans, hiding from creditors, piling up debt wherever credit could be obtained, crossing to the other side of the street and disappearing down alleys to avoid pursuing tradesmen; yet all this time maintaining an optimistic temper, cheerfully lending to one friend the money he had extracted from another, full of engaging conversation, fertile in epigram and anecdote, always willing to entertain strangers with recollections of Washington and Lafayette, fond of making bombastic speeches, of parading the highway in his old military cape, his head topped by a gorgeous white high hat—an adornment which, as legal proceedings disclosed, had not been paid for."[28]

It became the fate of Ann Lee, spoiled child of the noble Carter family, to suffer the poverty that was her husband's final lot. She supported six children on an inheritance from her father that never brought in more than $1440 a year, and was as low as $605 in some years. In 1807 she had written to Mrs. Richard Bland Lee, who also was pregnant, "I do not envy your *prospect*, nor wish to *share in them* [sic]."[29] Her unwanted child was Robert E. Lee. Two years later the infant's father was sent to debtors' prison, where he could look out on the courthouse square in which George Washington had once voted for him. There he remained for two years. His wife could never bring herself to use the words "imprisonment" or "jail," instead she talked of "his present situation." Ann Lee, always frail, began a decline into the state of chronic invalidism. Her frequent fainting spells gave rise to the erroneous report that she had once been pronounced dead and buried alive.[30]

Harry Lee left Virginia when his son Robert was six years old. For the last five years of his life he wandered among the islands of the

West Indies, seeking to regain his shattered health. In February 1818, at Cumberland Island, off the coast of Florida, Light Horse Harry died at the estate of his old comrade in arms General Nathanael Greene.

In Harry's youngest son the glory that he had sought would be permanently achieved for the dynasty. But the lives of the two children by his marriage to Matilda Lee would comprise a different kind of chapter in the family's history.

Attractive, temperamental, and fond of excitement, Lucy Lee became the bride of Bernard Moore Carter, her stepmother's brother. They moved to Woodstock, his beautiful estate in Fauquier County. But Lucy longed to live in Philadelphia, the winter social capital. She finally got her wish, according to her great-grandson, by burning down the house at Woodstock. Her long-suffering husband left her. Lucy then moved to Philadelphia. "How could I stand Bernard Carter?" she once asked. "He is the handsomest man I ever saw, but such a fool!"[31]

Lucy's brother Harry, with his mealy mouth, would never be mistaken for handsome, but he was a brilliant conversationalist, though somewhat sarcastic, and had inherited his father's charm and his mother's Stratford estate. His entrance into the Virginia House of Delegates in 1810 was looked upon as the first step in a promising political career. He also made an advantageous marriage with Anne McCarty of the neighboring Pope's Creek plantation, and the next year, 1818, she gave birth to a daughter.

But two years later began a chain reaction of tragedy for Harry and his wife. Their little girl, while romping in the Great Hall at Stratford, ran out the door and tumbled fatally down the steep front steps. The grief-stricken mother took to morphine, soon becoming an addict. Her younger sister Elizabeth, plump, petite, and gentle, lived at Stratford. Harry had been made her guardian. And when his wife withdrew into the hazy world of drugs, he and his sister-in-law had an affair that became known throughout the state after Elizabeth bore a child—born dead, according to tradition. Anne left her husband. Elizabeth cut off her beautiful hair and put on mourning clothes. Her lover was thereafter known as "Black Horse Harry." The stigma of Lee's "seduction" was compounded by charges that he had misappropriated Elizabeth's inheritance. Thus forced to sell his estate to make restitution, Stratford, birthplace of two signers of the Declaration of Independence and the commander of the Army of Northern Virginia, passed out of the Lee dynasty forever. In 1828 it became the property of Elizabeth McCarty, now married, although the change of station didn't alter her habit of wearing heavy mourning in public as a permanent symbol of her contrition. She remained mistress of Stratford for a half century.

Ostracized by Virginia society, Black Horse Harry picked a meager living on the fringes of politics. He became a ghost writer for John C. Calhoun and Andrew Jackson, helping to compose the latter's first inaugural address. All agreed that he had a first-rate mind. Said John Quincy Adams, who appointed him Assistant Postmaster General: "Lee's reputation is bad with regard to private morals and his political course is unprincipled; but he writes with great force and elegance."[32] Jackson made him consul general at Algiers, a post that the President thought was beneath senatorial notice. He was wrong. The Senate overwhelmingly rejected the nomination. "Lee's own connections were the cause of his rejection," thought William Lewis, a member of Jackson's kitchen cabinet. ". . . it must deeply wound his feelings, and prove, I fear, greatly injurious to his future prospects in life."[33] In 1837 Lee died in Paris, where he was writing a biography of Napoleon. Anne McCarty Lee, cured of the drug habit, had returned to her husband. She lived three years longer, dying in a condition of abject poverty.

Robert E. Lee's recollections of the father who had spent two years in prison and had left Virginia when he was six must have been imprecise and hazy. But they were never bitter. Ann Carter had deeply loved her husband. She had married him gladly and eagerly despite the fact that he had just been rejected by her best friend. This love she passed on to Robert, while at the same time instilling in the boy a sense of self-control that had been totally absent in his reckless father. She also taught him the code she had learned from the Carters—a blend of religion and *noblesse oblige*. The relationship between mother and son in the household without a man was made even closer by Ann's invalidism. Robert would carry her in his arms to her carriage. He was her nurse, companion, and protector. When he left for West Point she said, "How can I live without Robert? He is both son and daughter to me."[34]

An army career was almost inevitable. Light Horse Harry Lee's legacy had been a distrust of politicians and a love of soldiering. Moreover, the life of an officer was an honorable escape hatch for sons of shabby gentility.

To young John Hood, Lee was later to say, "Never marry unless you can do so into a family that will enable your children to feel proud of both sides of the house."[35] This sense of family, amounting virtually to an Episcopal Shintoism, was always a powerful force in Lee. He knew his cousins to the third and fourth generations, and was happiest in their company. In 1831, following his own advice, he married into the family of the noblest Virginian of them all. In the famous mural by Edward Savage, *Family Group at Mount Vernon*, the little boy at the right on whose slim shoulders George Washington is resting his arm is George

Washington Parke Custis. He was Martha's grandson and the first President's adopted son. He now became Robert E. Lee's father-in-law.

Besides such illustrious antecedents, Custis was the builder of Arlington, an imposing estate high on the bank of the Potomac overlooking the capital, and a playwright of limited talent and popular acclaim. It was a strange profession for an aristocratic and religious Virginian. If dramatists were not considered wholly disreputable in his social circle, they were certainly viewed as little more than idlers. "I have made a great mental effort lately," he wrote his wife. "But I am sure you and the bishop will think my energies might have been better employed."[36] Between 1830 and 1837 his patriotic extravaganzas, such as *Pocahontas, or the Settlers of Virginia,* were popular entertainment in Philadelphia, Baltimore, Washington, and New York.

It took awhile for Custis to become resigned to the marriage of his only child to a poor second lieutenant of engineers. Mary was frail, hardly suited for the life of a camp follower. Furthermore, there was little room for advancement in a peacetime army. At the outset of the Mexican War, seventeen years after Lee's graduation from the Military Academy, he was still only a captain. But fighting was what Lee had been trained for, and once in combat he quickly proved himself. During the year in Mexico he was breveted three times.

In 1852 Lee became superintendent of West Point. One of his cadets was his oldest son Custis. At first somewhat indolent, the young man soon responded to his father's tactful prodding and graduated first in his class, having spent his four years at the Point without receiving a single demerit. Less happy were the experiences of the superintendent's nephew, Cadet Fitzhugh Lee.

This lighthearted student-soldier was the son of Lee's beloved brother, Sydney Smith. Considered by some to be less aloof than his younger brother, Smith Lee had chosen the navy as his branch of service. He commanded Perry's flagship when the commodore sailed to Japan, and would become commandant of the Naval Academy. He also had given his children a maternal family to be proud of. His wife Anna was a granddaughter of George Mason, author of the Virginia Bill of Rights, and a sister of powerful United States Senator James M. Mason, chairman of the Foreign Relations Committee, author of the Fugitive Slave Act of 1850, and later to be Charles Francis Adams' adversary as Confederate commissioner to Great Britain.

But the ghosts of distinguished ancestors could not prevent Fitz Lee from having a good time. Twice he was found guilty of being absent without leave, twice Robert E. Lee recommended his dismissal from the corps, and twice his fellow classmen petitioned to allow him to remain at the academy, pledging their best behavior as collateral for his retention. Secretary of War Jefferson Davis overruled Superintendent Lee and allowed the young man to continue his training.*

Lee's second son, "Rooney," was about to enter Harvard along with Henry Adams. Ancestral friendship, however, was not enough to draw John Quincy Adams' grandson to the grandson of Light Horse Harry Lee. Young Adams felt that the tall, handsome, genial Lee had "the Virginian habit of command" but "little else."[37] Rooney had no aspirations as a scholar and left college in his junior year to accept a commission as a second lieutenant, which had been secured for him by General Winfield Scott. "I make this application mainly on the extraordinary merits of the father, the very best soldier that I ever saw in the field," wrote "Old Fuss and Feathers."[38]

Thus were the last days of ante bellum being spent by four future Confederate generals—Robert E. Lee, Fitzhugh Lee, Custis Lee, and Rooney Lee.

The coming of the war had an unexpected effect on another member of the dynasty. Commander Samuel Phillips Lee was a serious-minded, usually solemn naval officer; an alert disciplinarian, who, in the opinion of some subordinates, never slept. The commander learned of the rebellion as he was rounding the Cape of Good Hope on the way to the East Indies. Acting against orders, he turned his ship about and returned to the United States. He was later made acting rear admiral and served creditably for more than two years as the head of the North Atlantic Blockading Squadron.[39]

The Union admiral was a grandson of Richard Henry Lee.

But perhaps a more significant relationship in its effect on the side he chose was his marriage to Elizabeth Blair. The witty and charming Betty entangled Lee in powerful Northern political connections. His father-in-law was Francis Preston Blair, Sr., of Andrew Jackson's kitchen cabinet; one brother-in-law was Montgomery Blair (named in honor of the Revolutionary hero), who would be Lincoln's Postmaster General; another brother-in-law was hard-drinking Congressman Francis Preston Blair, Jr., of Missouri, chairman of the House Committee on Military Affairs—later Union general and senator. Moreover, Montgomery Blair was married to a daughter of Levi Woodbury, a New Hampshireman who served as governor, senator, cabinet officer, and Justice of the Supreme Court. And

---

* Robert E. Lee had more success in dismissing another cadet. James McNeill Whistler, although first in his class in drawing, was so deficient in chemistry that on one examination he defined silicon as a gas. Years later the famous artist said, "Had silicon been a gas I would have been a major general." See Philip Van Doren Stern, *Robert E. Lee, the Man and the Soldier* (New York: McGraw-Hill, 1963), p. 92.

finally, Montgomery Blair's brother-in-law was Gustavus Vasa Fox, Assistant Secretary of the Navy during the Civil War.[40]

The senior Blair had been an obscure Kentucky editor until coming to Washington in 1830 to start an Administration newspaper for Jackson. He was an ugly little man who resembled a walking skeleton—his partner thought that when wearing thick winter clothing he weighed one hundred and seven pounds, of which eighty-five were bone, twenty-two gristle, nerve, and brain.[41] His bland manners and mild temper were camouflage for a writing machine that was bold, dogmatic, defiant, and dripping with sarcasm. Compared to his *Globe*, the rival *National Intelligencer* had the personality of a dignified maiden aunt.

The good, gray *National Intelligencer* had been founded by Samuel Harrison Smith at the beginning of the Jefferson Administration.† In 1807 Smith hired young Joseph Gales, Jr., to cover the proceedings of the Senate. Three years later he sold the paper to his reporter. The new proprietor was the husband of Sarah Lee, a niece of Light Horse Harry, and first cousin of Robert E. Lee.[42] The childless Sarah, brilliant and beautiful, was the leader of the most elegant salon in Washington. While her husband resented the new power of the Blairs, she opposed the upstarts in society.

But in the President the Blairs had both protector and friend. They built their home across the street from the Executive Mansion, and Jackson, fearing that its damp cellar might cause their delicate daughter to become ill, had the fair Betty moved into the White House. He loved her as if she were his own child, calling her "his Little Democrat" and restraining himself from smoking or cursing in her presence.

The Blairs' influence waned with the closing of the Jacksonian era. During the 1840 presidential election the Harrison forces, who had a song for every occasion, sang:

> King Matty he sat in his "big White House,"
> A curling his whiskers fine,
> And the *Globe* man, Blair, sat by his side,
> A drinking his champaigne wine.

The impending slavery struggle, however, revived their political fortunes. When abolitionist Charles Sumner was beaten on the floor of the Senate, the elder Blair took him to his country estate, Silver Spring, to recover.

Old Frank Blair may have influenced Samuel Phillips Lee's decision to fight for the Union, but he was notably unsuccessful with his son-in-law's third cousin. On April 18, 1861, he invited Colonel Robert E. Lee to Blair House and, at the request of President Lincoln, offered him com-

† For the career of Smith and his wife, Margaret Bayard, see Bayard Dynasty, pp. 280–81.

mand of the United States Army. Lee reportedly replied: "Mr. Blair, I look upon secession as anarchy. If I owned the four millions of slaves, I would cheerfully sacrifice them to the preservation of the Union, but to lift my hand against my own State and people is impossible."[43] The next day he learned that Virginia had seceded. At midnight Lee sat down to compose his resignation from the United States Army.

It was now one hundred and two years since Richard Henry Lee had denounced slavery in the Virginia House of Burgesses. Robert E. Lee shared that view. The will of his father-in-law, George Washington Parke Custis, manumitted his slaves, and Lee was willingly its executor.‡

It was now sixty-seven years since Light Horse Harry Lee had turned back the Whiskey Rebels to uphold the principle of Union. His son had devoted his adult life to the service of that Union.

Yet Lee would fight to uphold slavery and turn his back on the Union. He was, as he told Blair, a Virginian first. It was his primary allegiance, and for it he would bear arms in defense of a cause he found repugnant. For a Virginian of his class—a simple, religious man—this may have been a difficult time, but it was not a difficult decision. "When I speak of my country," John Randolph of Roanoke once said, "I mean the Commonwealth of Virginia." In this tradition, Robert E. Lee would lead the Army of Northern Virginia through the bloodiest days of America's costliest war—at Manassas and Fredericksburg, Chancellorsville and Gettysburg, the campaign of the Wilderness, Spotsylvania, Cold Harbor, the siege of Petersburg, the fall of Richmond, and, finally, Appomattox.

His sons entered the Confederacy in the same spirit of duty rather than principle. Custis first put his engineering skill to work on the fortifications around Richmond; then, contrary to his desire for field service, became aide-de-camp to Jefferson Davis. When Rooney was captured, his older brother, under flag of truce, asked to be allowed to take his place so that the prisoner could be with his desperately sick wife. The request was turned down; Rooney's wife died while he was in Yankee hands. Custis later became a division commander in the Army of Northern Virginia and was also taken prisoner of war. The youngest son, Robert E. Lee, Jr., was a student at the University of Virginia when the war began. Mary Custis Lee clung tenaciously to all her children, but toward "my dear little Rob" she was particularly possessive. The young man's father begged him to remain in school. It would be a long war, and there would be enough fighting for everyone. But the eager youth en-

‡ Custis also had at least one child by a slave. He gave this mulatto daughter, Maria Carter, fifteen acres when she married Charles Syphax. This property was confiscated along with the rest of the Arlington estate during the Civil War, but Congress passed a special bill that returned the small parcel of land to the heirs of Mrs. Robert E. Lee's half sister. See Sidney Hyman, "Washington's Negro Elite," *Look*, April 6, 1965, p. 63.

listed as a private in the artillery in March 1862, rising eventually to the rank of captain.

Since his days as the bad boy of West Point, Fitzhugh Lee had distinguished himself as an Indian fighter. As a cavalry lieutenant he had taken part in the Wichita expedition, the greatest confrontation between Comanches and U.S. troops that had ever taken place. Pressing forward in advance of his men, according to an account by his bugler, "Lee came face to face with an Indian brave. He raised his pistol, the Indian drew his bow, and both fired at the same instant. The lieutenant's bullet struck the Indian squarely between the eyes and the Indian's arrow entered his right side under his extended arm. . . ."[44] This daring he brought to his assignment as commander of the cavalry corps of the Army of Northern Virginia. At the battle of Winchester he had three horses shot from under him and was severely wounded. On another occasion he nearly captured his Union cousin, Colonel Louis Marshall.

The Marshalls were also an ancient Virginia family, arriving in the Old Dominion around 1650. Colonel Thomas Marshall married a Randolph and was an intimate school friend of George Washington, with whom he served during Braddock's ill-fated expedition. One of his sons was the Chief Justice of the Supreme Court, and a grandson married Ann Kinloch Lee, the sister of Robert E. Lee. The Confederate general's brother-in-law was a Baltimore judge, deeply committed to the Union cause. Torn between husband and brother, Ann Lee Marshall was driven to the brink of insanity. She rarely left her bed, first mouthing pieties to her husband's side, then recanting with such words as "But after all, they can't whip Robert."[45] Her only son, a West Point graduate, was on General Pope's staff. Robert E. Lee said that he could forgive his nephew's fighting against the South but not his joining Pope. "I am sorry he is in such bad company," Lee wrote his wife.[46] One night at Catlett's Station, where Pope was making his headquarters, Colonel Marshall was mixing a toddy in his tent when he heard the rebel yell of Stuart's cavalry. Leaving the drink intact, he made a hasty retreat. Then Fitzhugh Lee walked in and drank the waiting beverage. Later he said, "I can testify that . . . my cousin, Louis Marshall, knows how to make toddies!"[47]

The Civil War was never "the War Between the States" to Robert E. Lee—he thought of it as God's vengeance on a sinful nation. Lee entered it, and left it, without the righteous zeal of the Confederate politicians, whom, like their Northern counterparts, he instinctively distrusted. God's will having been done, he calmly accepted the results. He decided to surrender his troops when he saw no further military value in bearing arms, a decision that saved thousands of lives and harsher terms of capitulation. "All you boys who fought with me go home and help build up the shattered fortunes of our old state," he told his soldiers after Appomattox.[48]

His own chance to serve came in September 1865, when he started out for Lexington, Virginia, to assume the presidency of little Washington College. Through education the South would be rebuilt. Politics never tempted him. There was talk of his running for governor in 1867. Mrs. Lee was ambitious for him to end his career with the same honor that had been his father's, but he quickly vetoed the idea. In the summer of 1868 there was even an editorial in the New York *Herald* proposing him for President. The newspaper reasoned that if the nation must have a soldier—meaning Grant—it might as well have the best of all soldiers.

The college post offered Lee the opportunity to resume his much-interrupted duties as husband and father. Mrs. Lee had long suffered from chronic rheumatism. Although she remained cheerful and uncomplaining, she was now confined to a wheel chair. Just as it had been Lee's fate to spend his youth ministering to an invalid mother, so would his final years be centered around an invalid wife. Their son Custis was with them in Lexington, having been appointed professor of civil engineering and applied mechanics at Virginia Military Institute. The Arlington estate, which had been his inheritance from his maternal grandfather, had been confiscated by the government and was being used as the national military cemetery. (After an 1882 Supreme Court decision in his favor, Congress purchased the property for $150,000.) However, the other two plantations that Grandfather Custis had left to Rooney and Rob were still in their possession, and they turned to the soil for a livelihood.

Lee was anxious to see his sons married and was not above writing Rob that he had "the very girl for you. . . ."[49] Yet, as his son wrote, "With his daughters he was less pressing. Though apparently always willing to have another daughter, he did not seem to long for any more sons."[50] There had been four girls; Annie had died during the war. When suitors came to call on Mary, Agnes, and Mildred, the General and Mrs. Lee would retire to the dining room. But as the clock struck ten he would close the shutters, and, if that hint went unheeded, would say, "Good night, young gentlemen."[51] So the girls, their faces thin and tight-lipped, their eyes touched with melancholy, remained unwed. They spent their days at home—where the townspeople thought they were looking down their noses at Lexington society—or visiting cousins in Tidewater Virginia and the Eastern Shore of Maryland, or serving in such posts as Honorary President, Lee Chapter, United Daughters of the Confederacy.[52] Mrs. Josephus Daniels recalls Mary Lee, then eighty-two, at a Confederate reunion in 1917, where she was acting kittenish with the old soldiers and talking of the dangers of having words like "moonlight" whispered into her "youthful and innocent ears." Noting the absence of gray on her ancient head, Mrs. Daniels was asked by her grandchildren, "You don't mean it is dyed or that she wears a wig?" Mrs. Daniels then "indicated that such might be the case."[53]

Six months before his death in 1870 Robert E. Lee took a trip through Virginia, the Carolinas, Georgia, and Florida. Ostensibly it was for his health. But also he was paying his last respects at the grave of Light Horse Harry Lee, the father he had barely known but always venerated. All along the route he was mobbed by cheering crowds. The attitude of the South toward the man who had led it in defeat was expressed by a young Virginia girl: "We had heard of God, but here was General Lee!"[54]

Gradually the North also came to recognize the greatness of its former adversary. Foremost of his Yankee enthusiasts was Charles Francis Adams, the railroad president who had fought at Gettysburg. We owe a debt of gratitude to Lee, he said, for not prolonging the war, for burying animosities and working to reunite the nation, and, said the great-grandson of John Adams, if Lee made a mistake in choosing revolution over union, "in the throng of other offenders I am also gratified to observe certain of those from whom I not unproudly claim descent."[55]§

Custis Lee succeeded his father as president of Washington College. In the same year, 1871, the General Assembly of Virginia changed the school's name to Washington and Lee University. Rooney Lee served in the state senate for three years and was a member of the United States House of Representatives at the time of his death in 1891. Rob took time out from farming to write an excellent portrait of his father, *Recollections and Letters of General Robert E. Lee*. One of Rooney's sons, George Bolling Lee, became a noted New York gynecologist; his son, Robert E. Lee IV, is now national advertising manager of the San Francisco *Chronicle*.[56]

Ironically, it was Fitzhugh, the nephew whose dismissal from West Point had been recommended by Robert E. Lee, who best exemplified what the Confederate leader had tried to stand for in his last years. Fitz was elected governor of Virginia in 1885, serving until 1890, and was appointed consul general at Havana by President Cleveland in 1896. At the outbreak of the Spanish-American War President McKinley made him a brigadier general. A perhaps apocryphal story was then ascribed to an unreconstructed rebel, who, on hearing the news, is supposed to have said, "Do you know, sah, that they had the impudence to

§ Charles Francis Adams' brother Henry did not agree with him. "I think Lee should have been hanged," said Henry. "It was all the worse that he was a good man and a fine character and acted conscientiously. These facts have nothing to do with the case and should not have been allowed to interfere with just penalties." Jacob E. Cooke, "Chats with Henry Adams," *American Heritage*, December 1955, p. 44.

offer Fitz Lee a commission as brigadier in their Yankee ahmy when he was a majah general in ouah ahmy?" But to most Americans the appointment of Major General Fitzhugh Lee, C.S.A., as Brigadier General, U.S.A., was a symbolic act of considerable magnitude. As the New York *Times* commented upon his death in 1905, "There is no man in the South, and no man in the United States, who contributed more than Fitzhugh Lee to form, after the division of the Civil War, 'a more perfect union.' "[57]

The heirs of Fitzhugh Lee formed an unusual record of occupational consistency. His two sons became cavalry officers. (Fitzhugh II was an aide-de-camp to President Theodore Roosevelt; George Mason Lee fought in the Philippine Insurrection.) His three daughters married army officers (all generals).[58] Colonel George Mason Lee married a general's daughter and had two children. His daughter was twice wed, both times to naval officers. She had a son by each. Both are now naval aviators. And Colonel George Mason Lee's son is Vice Admiral Fitzhugh Lee, commandant, National War College, formerly deputy chief of the Atlantic Fleet, head of naval air technical training, and skipper of the carrier *Manila Bay* during the battle for Leyte Gulf. The admiral looks upon his family as a military dynasty, not a political one. For his ancestors, in a direct line, were: Colonel George Mason Lee (father); General Fitzhugh Lee (grandfather); Commander Smith Lee (great-grandfather); General Light Horse Harry Lee (great-great-grandfather).[59]

But some Lees have maintained the family's interest in politics. Significantly, the politicians have been in that branch of the dynasty which was victorious in the Civil War. Betty Blair and Admiral Samuel Phillips Lee had one child. In 1913 he became the first person to be directly elected by the people to the United States Senate.

Blair Lee graduated in 1880 from Princeton, where he had been one of the founders of the Ivy Club. He entered the Maryland State Senate in 1905, for the first of two terms, and distinguished himself as a progressive, introducing bills for a direct primary system and the creation of a Public Service Commission to regulate the utilities. At the 1912 Democratic Convention Lee swung the Maryland delegation to his old friend Woodrow Wilson, Princeton, Class of '79. The next year the President campaigned for Lee's election to the United States Senate. William Jennings Bryan also came into the state, telling a large crowd at Hagerstown that Blair Lee was the only man east of the Mississippi to have supported him against McKinley who was worth a hundred thousand dollars.[60]

This ninth Lee to serve in the Congress was married to Anne Clymer Brooke, whose great-great-uncle George Clymer of Pennsylvania joined her husband's great-grandfather in signing the Declaration of Independence. They had two sons—P. Blair Lee, now a prominent Philadelphia banker and chairman of the Philadelphia Housing Authority, and Colonel E. Brooke Lee, long-time political strong man of Montgomery County, Maryland, who quit Princeton to study politics in his father's Senate office.

In World War I copper-haired Brooke Lee gathered in a bevy of decorations, including two Croix de Guerre, the Distinguished Service Cross, Silver Star, and the Belgian Order of Leopold for leading a daring raid through enemy lines. The returning hero was elected comptroller of the state of Maryland in 1919, then became Maryland's Secretary of State (1922) and Speaker of the House of Delegates (1928).[61] His first wife was a daughter of the president of the state Senate and a first cousin of powerful Maryland Congressman Lansdale Sasscer. One of their sons would continue the name of Lee in politics; a daughter married David Scull, a chairman of the Maryland Republican Party. Colonel Lee's third wife has been vice-chairman of the Maryland Democratic Party.[62]

The colonel never sought national office. However, for nearly three decades he was considered one of the powers behind the throne in Maryland politics and was a delegate to six Democratic presidential conventions. (His father had been a delegate to eight.) In 1932, along with Senators Walsh and Bulkley, he wrote Repeal into the national party platform. He also helped to make Harry Truman the vice-presidential nominee in 1944.

Then in the 1950s the colonel stepped aside to make room for his son, Blair Lee III, who was to serve eight years in the state legislature and build a strong reputation for political independence.[63] By 1962 young Lee was considered ready for higher office. Governor J. Millard Tawes asked him to run on his ticket for congressman at large. But Lee declined, choosing instead to seek the senatorial nomination as the running mate of George P. Mahoney, a building contractor and perennial candidate. To many it appeared to be an unnatural alliance. Some said that Lee had been guided by his father's counsel. If so, it was bad advice.[64]

There were five entries in the 1962 Maryland primary for U. S. Senate, but only two, Lee and Congressman Daniel Brewster, were serious contenders. (One candidate was a clown who campaigned in an Uncle Sam suit.) Brewster and Lee had strikingly similar backgrounds, both had attended St. Paul's School and Princeton, both had been World War II officers, both claimed to be Kennedy democrats, although Lee claimed to have been on the Kennedy bandwagon longer. Stumping Prince Georges County, Lee told the voters that the Washington suburbs hadn't had a representative in the Senate since his grandfather retired in 1916. "That was the year I was born," he added.[65] Such were the marginal issues between the two gentlemanly, button-down candidates until the final days of the contest. Then Lee brought up some embarrassing connections of his rival's law partner. Brewster countered with charges of "bossism" (Lee was being supported by Jack Pollack of Baltimore) and said that Lee's father, "a discredited politician," was trying to stage a political comeback through his son.[66] But these were minor irritants compared to the donnybrook being staged by gubernatorial candidates Tawes and Mahoney. Lee was on Mahoney's ticket; Brewster was paired with Tawes. A national liberal organization, the Committee for an Effective Congress, endorsed Lee, calling him a person of "the highest calibre . . . a free society can offer."[67] Yet Governor Tawes won his fight and swept Congressman Brewster along with him. Lee carried just two of the state's twenty-three counties—both within his family's political suzerainty—and one of the six districts of Baltimore—Jack Pollack's.[68]

A happier moment for the Lees came in October 1964 when Blair House, now the President's guest house, was redecorated and the old colonel returned to the scene of his birth and the room in which his great-grandfather had offered command of the Union Army to Robert E. Lee.[69] His son Brooke, a Washington business executive and a Republican, was with him. But Blair Lee III was otherwise occupied as a regional director of President Johnson's campaign, an appointment that had been endorsed by Senator Brewster.[70]

There are great hazards in writing the obituary of a political dynasty. In May 1965 the Montgomery County Democratic Committee refused to endorse the last Lee to be actively engaged in politics for a relatively insignificant post. Blair Lee III wanted to fill a vacancy on the Maryland National Capital Park and Planning Commission, a job he had held from 1949 to 1951 and which had been his father's from 1942 to 1947. The anti-Lee forces in the county contended that his appointment would constitute a conflict of interests since the Lee family had major landholdings in the area.¶ The old colonel, clad in gray suit and battered work shoes, his hair now silver, came to the Democratic meeting to plead for his son. It was to no avail. Said one precinct chairman as he watched the Lees' defeat, "This is the last hurrah . . . the end of an era."[71] But the Republican-controlled County Council ignored the action of Lee's own party and elected him to the post, proving once again the resiliency of a political dynasty that has survived for three hundred and twenty-five years.

¶ Colonel E. Brooke Lee owns 2764 acres of farmland, of which 1048 acres are in Montgomery County, Maryland. See Washington *Post*, July 16, 1965, p. B8.

Yet with the exception of these "Northern" Lees, who carved their political domain out of a small corner of Maryland, the political dynasty expired in the waning days of the nineteenth century.

If death had a political cause, the exact year may have been 1893, when Fitzhugh Lee was defeated for the United States Senate by Thomas S. Martin, a shrewd railroad lawyer and Virginia's first political boss. (In 1911 another candidate with Lee connections would try to unseat Martin. But Congressman William Atkinson Jones—whose grandmother was a Lee and a first cousin of Light Horse Harry—only succeeded in undermining his health in the assault.)[72] The Organization, as Martin's edifice was named, permanently changed the nature of politics in the Old Dominion. And if there was anything left of the independent, free-wheeling spirit of Richard Henry Lee and his brothers in their heirs they could no longer be attracted to Virginia politics.

But the death of the Lees more probably had natural causes. Robert E. Lee had three sons; the three sons had two sons; the two sons had one son. And he lived far from the soil of his ancestors—in San Francisco.

Moreover, the sons of Fitzhugh Lee, and all who came after them, chose to make their careers in the armed services, a calling which, except in the case of the returning hero, is hardly conducive to political life. Besides the tradition of civil and military separateness, there is the overriding liability of never having a permanent home. As these Lees moved from post to post Virginia must have seemed as distant as the old country was to the immigrants on Ellis Island.

Qualitatively too, something was happening to the Lees. Judging from the four volumes of *Who Was Who in America*, which cover the years from 1607 to 1960, there appeared to be a steady hardening of those arteries that produce men who are remembered in history.

Years	(Number of Lee Entries)	Number of Lees Descended from Richard the Emigrant	Number of Lee Dynasts in Politics
1607–1896	(31)	14	12
1897–1942	(52)	3	1
1943–1950	(16)	2	1
1951–1960	(20)	0	0

Then some Lees began to realize the exploitative possibilities of their famous name. By 1963 a great-great-nephew of Robert E. Lee, who ran a furniture store in Elkton, Maryland, and sold rock 'n roll music, was presiding as master of ceremonies at public gatherings, where he performed a "Robert E. Lee dance," described as "sort of like the twist and sort of like flamenco, but wilder than either." He was known in the neighborhood as "The General."[73] And in 1964 a Washington lawyer by the name of Lee, who claimed descent from the Virginia line, had an artist airbrush a mural of Stratford Hall on his office wall. The "wall effect," as the artist called it, was in muted rust to complement the room's gold carpeting.[74]

Yet there were still enough Lees to have continued the political dynasty had there been the interest and aptitude. The Society of the Lees of Virginia was formed in 1922—membership open to those who could prove their descent from Richard the Emigrant. One hundred and three persons had joined by 1949, of whom forty-two were in the name of Lee. The geographical distribution of these proven Lees was Virginia, 12; Maryland, 8; Washington, D.C., 6; Pennsylvania, 4; others scattered in North Carolina, Delaware, Connecticut, Missouri, New Hampshire, New York, and Canada. Except for Senator Blair Lee, the society's first president, none indicated a political occupation on the application forms. Rather they were thinly spread through all the professions that one might expect to find in families of middle-class background: four doctors, five lawyers, three engineers, three insurance agents, two bankers, two small manufacturers, clergyman, social worker, dentist, real estate broker, farmer, scientist, writer.[75] They were obviously a respectable group. But were they, like those who had preceded them—the enterprising Richard the Emigrant, the westward-moving Hancock, Thomas Lee of the Treaty of Lancaster, the Revolutionary governor of Maryland, the brothers who signed the Declaration, the brothers who were militia diplomats, the dashing Light Horse Harry, the commander of the Army of the Potomac—were they, these professional, competent twentieth-century Lees, the sort who would become revolutionaries or build empires or lead armies?

The Livingston Dynasty

> "The great landed families, the Livingstons, Van Rens-
> selaers, Schuylers, Van Cortlandts, Phillipses, Morrises,
> with their huge manorial estates, their riches, their abso-
> lute social pre-eminence and their unquestioned political
> headship, formed a proud, polished, and powerful aristoc-
> racy, deep rooted in the soil; for over a century their sway
> was unbroken, save by contests between themselves or
> with the royal governor, and they furnished the colony
> with military, political and social leaders for generation
> after generation."
>
> —Theodore Roosevelt[1]

IN 1683, a decade after his arrival in America, Robert Livingston bought
2000 acres from the Mohican Indians, of which 200 acres faced the
Hudson River about forty miles south of Albany. The tract was purchased for a small quantity of blankets, shirts, stockings, caps, kettles,
axes, scissors, mirrors, fishhooks, bottles, rum, beer, knives, nails, and
other useful or amusing items.[2] Two years later Livingston bought another 600 acres along the Massachusetts border; the Indians received
a slightly better price. Now Livingston petitioned the colonial governor
of New York for a patent for his lands—the Hudson River tract "adjacent
unto" the Massachusetts border tract.[3] The request was granted; the
Lordship and Manor of Livingston was royally created. But there was
one thing wrong with this transaction: Livingston's two tracts were not
contiguous as he had stated; they were miles apart. And so when Livingston Manor was finally surveyed it was found to consist not of the expected 2600 acres but of 160,240 acres. Robert Livingston, First Lord
of the Manor, had secured title to 157,640 acres which he had not
purchased. The founder of the dynasty had pulled "one of the grossest
land frauds ever perpetrated in an age noted for unethical dealings."[4]
   Aside from family apologists, few can contemplate this first American Livingston without wincing. Historians have judged him: "The time-
serving, political turncoat, sinecurist and army contractor, Robert Liv-

THE LIVINGSTON DYNASTY
(A Selective Genealogy)

The Manor Line

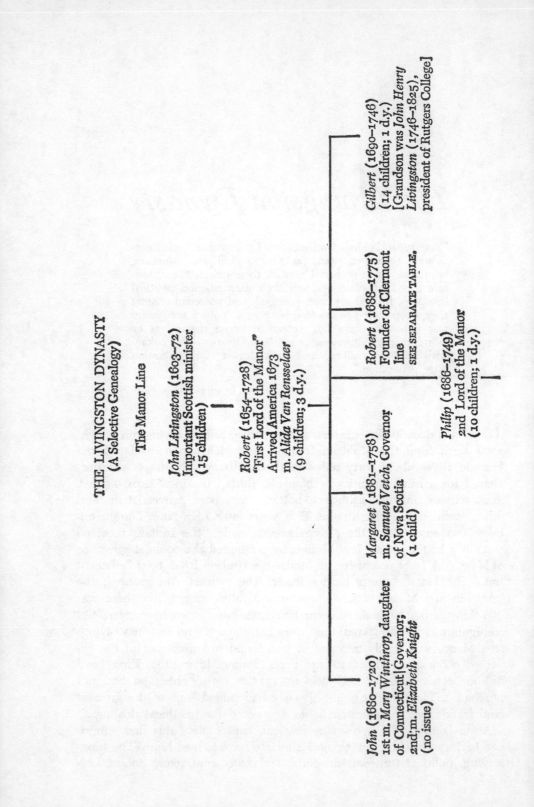

John Livingston (1603–72)
Important Scottish minister
(15 children)

Robert (1654–1728)
"First Lord of the Manor"
Arrived America 1673
m. *Alida Van Rensselaer*
(9 children; 3 d.y.)

John (1680–1720)
1st m. *Mary Winthrop*, daughter
of Connecticut Governor;
2nd; m. *Elizabeth Knight*
(no issue)

Margaret (1681–1758)
m. *Samuel Vetch*, Governor
of Nova Scotia
(1 child)

Philip (1686–1749)
2nd Lord of the Manor
(10 children; 1 d.y.)

Robert (1688–1775)
Founder of Clermont
line
SEE SEPARATE TABLE.

Gilbert (1690–1746)
(14 children; 1 d.y.)
[Grandson was *John Henry
Livingston* (1746–1825),
president of Rutgers College]

Robert (1708–90)
3rd Lord of the Manor
[13 children; 4 d.y.]
[Granddaughter Harriet
Livingston (1786–1824)
m. Robert Fulton,
steamboat inventor]

Philip (1716–78)
"The Signer"
CONTINENTAL CONGRESS
(9 children)

William (1723–90)
CONTINENTAL CONGRESS,
GOVERNOR
(13 children; 2 d.y.)

Sarah (1725–1804)
m. Lord Stirling,
American Revolutionary general
(2 children)

Peter Van Brugh (1710–92)
President, New York Provincial
Congress
(12 children; 4 d.y.)

Mary (1738–1821)
m. James Duane
CONTINENTAL CONGRESS

Catherine (1755–1826)
m. William Duer,
CONTINENTAL CONGRESS

Susan
(b. 1755)
m. John Kean
CONTINENTAL
CONGRESS

Elizabeth
(1761–87)
m. M. Otto
French
diplomat

Susan
(b. 1748)
m. John Cleves
Symmes
CONTINENTAL
CONGRESS
(no issue)

Catherine
(1751–1813)
1st m. Matthew Ridley
Diplomat
(no issue)

Sarah
(1756–1802)
m. John Jay
CONTINENTAL
CONGRESS
(4 children)

Henry Brockholst
(1757–1823)
Supreme Court
justice
(9 children)

THE LIVINGSTON DYNASTY
(A Selective Genealogy)

The Clermont Line

Robert Livingston (1654–1728)
"First Lord of the Manor"
Arrived America 1673
(9 children; 3 d.y.)

Robert (1688–1775)
Founder of Clermont line
(1 child)

Robert Robert (1718–75)
"The Judge"
m. *Margaret Beekman*
(11 children; 1 d.y.)

Janet
(1743–1828)
m. *General Richard Montgomery*
(no issue)

Henry Beekman
(1750–1831)
m. *Anne Shippen*,
niece of
Richard Henry Lee
(1 child)

Gertrude
(1757–1833)
m. *Morgan Lewis*,
General, GOVERNOR
(1 child)

Edward
(1764–1836)
HOUSE OF REPRESENTATIVES,
SENATE, Secretary of State
1st m. *Mary McEvers* (d. 1801)
(3 children)
2d m. *Louise D'Avezac Moreau*
(1 child)

Robert R.
(1746–1813)
"The Chancellor"
CONTINENTAL CONGRESS
m. Mary Stevens
(2 children)

Catharine
(1752–1849)
m. Reverend
Freeborn Garrettson
(2 children)

Alida
(1761–1822)
m. John Armstrong,
General, SENATOR
(1 child)

Margaret Beekman
(unmarried)

Elizabeth Stevens
(1780–1829)
(11 children; 6 d.y.)
[Great-great-grand-
mother of *Eleanor
Roosevelt*]

Cora
m. Thomas P. Barton
(no issue)

Margaret R. Armstrong
(1800–72)
m. William Backhouse Astor
(7 children)

ingston" (Gustavus Myers); "He could 'turn his coat' easier than any
man living" (George W. Schuyler); "In the pursuit of the one cherished
ambition of his life [the possession of a great fortune] this man spared
no friend or feared any foe, and in the perfection of his plans he did not
hesitate to take advantage of the various social and political conditions
which then existed in New York for the furtherance of his purpose"
(Thomas Allen Glenn).[5] His contemporaries thought no more highly of
him: The Earl of Bellomont charged that he "pinched an estate out of
the poor soldiers' bellies"; Governor Fletcher said, ". . . his beginning
being a little Book keeper, he has screwed himself into one of the most
considerable estates in the province," and then added, "he had rather be
called knave Livingston than poor Livingston."[6]

Who was this unloved man whose male heirs included a signer of the
Declaration of Independence, seven members of Congress, a signer of
the Constitution, two secretaries of state, a chancellor of New York, a
governor of New Jersey, a Supreme Court justice, a senator from Louisiana, two ministers to France, and whose female descendants married
two Revolutionary War generals, the inventor of the steamboat, five
congressmen, two Supreme Court justices, two governors of New York,
and two cabinet members?

Robert Livingston was descended from a younger son of the fourth
Lord of Callendar, a noble Scottish family related to Mary Queen of
Scots and Isabel Stuart, mistress of James IV. His father, grandfather,
and great-grandfather were ministers of the Scottish Church.[7] The Reverend John Livingston, his father, was called "the Godly Livingstone"
or, in a ballad of his day, "Mess John."[8] His union with Janet Fleming in
1635 was admittedly not fast-starting ("I may truly say it was above a
month after [the wedding] before I got marriage-affection to her . . .
and I got it not until I obtained it by prayer"). But it picked up momentum and "thereafter I had a great difficulty to moderate it"[9]: Robert
was their eighth son and fourteenth child in a family of fifteen.[10] John
was exiled from England in 1663 for his refusal to accept the Episcopal
settlement imposed upon Scotland, and fled to Holland with his young
son. And so when the nineteen-year-old Robert arrived in America in
1673 he had two assets—a good name and a knowledge of the Dutch
language.

Within five years after his arrival in Albany he acquired a third asset,
a wife who connected the young Scotsman with the three leading Dutch
families in the colony. Alida Livingston was a Schuyler, the widow of
a Van Rensselaer, and the sister-in-law of a Van Cortlandt.[11] With her
large, bulbous nose she could hardly qualify as a beauty, but for a
trader with his eye on the main chance there was beauty in the sudden
business solicitations which the nuptial brought.

Livingston shrewdly diversified his business risks, operating as whole-saler and retailer, importer and exporter, shipowner and land speculator. When it suited his purpose he could be charming and courtly; as an associate said, he could "put a fair Gloss upon the foulest Actions where his Interest is Concern'd."[12] He could also be bitter and self-righteous to those who were in his debt, a righteousness which did not extend to his own obligations to his creditors.[13] His godly father wrote in his auto-biography, "I chose rather to want sundry things than to be in debt."[14] Robert chose to want not and to operate on credit. As an article pub-lished by the Harvard Graduate School of Business Administration rather genteelly phrased it, "Livingston's greatest failing as a businessman was his habitual tardiness in meeting his financial obligations."[15]

As a colonial entrepreneur, Livingston's genius came in exploiting public service as a means to private gain. Yet since he was an expan-sionist in an age of colonial expansion his own interests generally coin-cided with those of the British Empire. His first step up the govern-mental ladder came within a year after his arrival in Albany when he secured appointment to the menial positions of town clerk and secretary to the board of commissioners for Indian affairs. "So successfully did he guide the deliberations of the commissioners," reports John A. Krout, "that he became the dictator of their policies rather than the registrar of their opinions."[16] He later became the colony's secretary of Indian affairs, a post which was particularly advantageous for a land speculator. Who better could know of available and desirable locations than the secretary of Indian affairs?

The consolidation of Robert's political power came in 1715 when he succeeded in turning Livingston Manor into a pocket borough. The royal patent gave the freeholders the right to send a representative to the General Assembly. Since the vote was not by secret ballot the effect was to insure the election of a member of the lord's family. For the next sixty years, until the Revolution abolished the pocket borough system, the First Lord of Livingston Manor, followed by his sons, grandsons, and a great-grandson, sat in the Assembly.[17]

By 1687 Robert Livingston's dual vocations of business and politics required an assistant and so he imported a nephew from Scotland, also named Robert. (Like most of the other American political dynasties, the Livingstons did not believe in novelty in family nomenclature.) Robert the Nephew served as his uncle's deputy town clerk until 1704, when the First Lord's son became old enough to replace him. The Nephew later became mayor of Albany for nine years, but he never really ac-quired his uncle's acquisitive nature, which was a disappointment to the older man. The uncle's family apparently held a low view of their poor relation. On one occasion the Lord's son-in-law, Samuel Vetch, wrote the Nephew: "Dear Cousin, . . . We entirely disobeyed my father and mother-in-law by putting our business in your hands, which he says will be very ill-managed." Signed, "your loving cousin, Saml Vetch."[18] Nor did the Nephew's heirs ever display the brilliance of the Manor line, although his female descendants married into some of New York's most illustrious families.[19]

Toward the close of the First Lord of the Manor's political career his son reported, ". . . it seems said here that you are the monarch of the whole Province."[20] He was then the powerful Speaker of the General Assembly. Yet his record was not an unbroken line of successes. Twice his enemies prematurely congratulated themselves on his political demise. The first time was when the democratic Jacob Leisler seized control of the New York government in the name of William of Orange. Nicholas Bayard was thrown in jail, but Livingston managed an escape to Connecticut. However, King William, who tolerated no revolution not of his own making, allowed Leisler to be hanged for treason, and Livingston returned to power.[21] The second political near fatality was the bizarre case of Captain William Kidd, pirate.

Unfortunately for Livingston and Kidd, they both happened to be in London at the same time in 1695; the former to press some claims against the home government. As a respectable New York merchant captain, Kidd had earlier endeared himself to the provincial government by taking part in the countermeasures against Leisler.[22] Livingston, always on the lookout for a profitable opportunity, now recruited his fellow New Yorker for a venture that in six years would lead to Kidd's death by hanging. Some of the most prominent members of the Whig ministry wished to outfit a privateering ship to operate against their twin enemies, pirates and Frenchmen. Lord Bellomont, the Earl of Orford, the Duke of Shrewsbury, and others, were to raise the money; Livingston was to be the middleman, or as Kidd later put it, "the projector and promoter and Chief Manager of the design"[23]; Kidd was to be captain of the *Adventure* galley, 287 tons, 30 mounted guns, crew of 154. There was no hint that the undertaking was to be anything but a legitimate business operation, the officially sanctioned looting of enemy vessels. Even the King was a silent partner, to receive a tenth of the profits. There are still those who believe that Kidd never turned pirate, that he was merely the victim of political intrigue.[24] But the more accepted view is that the captain did raise the skull and crossbones, probably pressed into it by a mutinous crew who were compensated for their services on the basis of "no plunder, no pay." The Whig-financed pirate delighted the Tories, who unsuccessfully tried to use his escapades to topple His Majesty's Government. The Lords of Trade also asked Livingston some embarrassing questions. But the political storm blew over, and Livingston even escaped forfeiting the £10,000 bond he had posted on Kidd's performance. (It was to be the fate of the noble Livingston family to be implicated with the two most notorious American pirates, Kidd and Jean Lafitte.) As for Kidd, the scaffold broke while he was swinging for his crimes; he was successfully hanged on the second try. His swag, including 1111 ounces of gold and 2353 ounces of silver, was recovered on Gardiner's Island in 1699, although this fact failed to deter generations of treasure hunters and the hero of Edgar Allan Poe's "The Gold Bug."

Marriages played an important role in the advancing and consolidating of the Livingstons' economic, political, and social fortunes. The First Lord of the Manor arrived at a rule which his heirs hewed to: what cannot be achieved by work and talent can often be got by marriage. John, his eldest son, was a case in point. His first wife was Mary Winthrop, only child of Governor Fitz-John Winthrop of Connecticut, the granddaughter of another governor of Connecticut, and great-granddaughter of the first governor of Massachusetts.[25] After the marriage the governor's son-in-law became a member of the Connecticut Assembly and later a member of the Council. However, Mary Winthrop Livingston died young and childless.

John's choice for a second wife was less acceptable to the Livingstons. After a disrespectfully short period of mourning he decided to marry Elizabeth Knight. The match was opposed by both of his sisters. Joanna described her prospective sister-in-law as being of "a very Staind Carrecter" and felt that John "desperrigs our family to make it Equall with Mrs. Kniets."[26] Elizabeth was the daughter of Madam Sarah Knight, who had earned her honorific title as a schoolmistress, and included Benjamin Franklin among her pupils. (She was later to earn further fame as a diarist when her record of a 1704 journey from Boston to New York City was published in 1846, and reprinted many times thereafter.[27]) There was little in this background to lead Joanna Livingston to her unequal estimation of the two families, although Madam Knight's father had had one encounter with the law. He was Thomas Kemble, an eminent Boston shipper, who had once spent two hours in the stocks for "lewd and unseemly behavior," which consisted of kissing his wife on the doorsteps of his home after he returned from a voyage of three years![28]

John's other sister was more specific in her complaints. Margaret was the wife of Colonel Samuel Vetch, the soldier-trader who first formulated a comprehensive plan for driving the French from North America and was subsequently rewarded with the governorship of Nova Scotia. Although he had the misfortune to die in a London debtor's prison, Vetch was considered a suitable match for a Livingston, and in the next generation Vetch's only heir was to link the Livingston dynasty with that branch of the Bayard dynasty which remained loyal to the Crown during the American Revolution.[29]

Margaret Livingston Vetch wrote her father that John had meant to marry Miss Knight even before his first wife's death, and, she felt, "a woman that will encourage a man in such a matter during the life of his wife is not to be looked on as one of very good principle!" Moreover, added the outspoken Mrs. Vetch, Elizabeth Knight had a "very indifferent reputation in the town either for honor or modesty . . ." and there had been "very odd" talk of "unlawful familiarities" between the Knight girl and her brother.[30] Yet, despite these protests, John Livingston and Elizabeth Knight were married by Dr. Increase Mather in 1713. The union was barren, John died seven years later, and the story of the Livingstons shifts to Philip, John's younger brother, who would now become the Second Lord of Livingston Manor.

Philip was one of the handsomer members of a family known more for the prominence of their noses than for physical attractiveness. A lady historian judged that he had "a winning way with women, and went about breaking hearts promiscuously."[31] But if he was unlike the First Lord in this respect, he was the only son to inherit his father's business acumen. Having assumed Robert's position for Indian affairs, he also was made a member of the Council, leaving Manor representation in the lower house to his two younger brothers, Gilbert and Robert of Clermont. Besides being one of the chief speculators in New York lands during the 1730s and 1740s, the Second Lord built the first New York ironworks in 1741; set up a second furnace in 1749; added a Schenectady store to the family's chain, which included stores in Albany and on the Manor; and was part owner of eight ships, some of them engaged in the slave trade.

The First Lord had operated on the principle that the family was an economic unit, employing or making use of his sons and sons-in-law to handle different aspects of his diversified and far-flung operations. The Second Lord now perfected this system. Five of Philip's sons, his brother Gilbert, and four of Gilbert's sons were directly engaged in his economic activities at one time or another. There were Livingstons deployed in New York to handle the family's buying and selling, as well as other Livingstons running the ironworks, collecting debts, on board the Lord's ships, bookkeeping, and minding the stores. Livingstons looked after the dynasty's interests in the Council, the Assembly, the Indian affairs commission and the surveyor's office. And if the Second Lord, this genius of family organization, was also accused of selling arms for use against the New England colonies or cheating the Mohawks out of their land—well, that too was part of his heritage.

The system of primogeniture and entail insured that the great Livingston fortune would be handed down virtually intact from eldest son to

eldest son. Yet with an estate the size of Robert Livingston's there was
enough left over to settle the younger children comfortably. The First
Lord had four sons: John had no children by either of his marriages;
Philip became the Second Lord and primary heir to his father's lands
and power; Gilbert, perpetually in financial difficulty, had his vast debts
paid by his father (and produced no heirs of note until his grandson
John Henry became an important Dutch Reform clergyman and president of Rutgers College); Robert was given a 13,000-acre tract which he
called Clermont.

There is a family tradition that Clermont was Robert's reward for the
discovery of an Indian plot, and one version of the story is that "the
bloody conspiracy was communicated to young Robert Livingston by a
pretty, young Mohawk squaw, who had fallen in love with the handsome
young Scotch trader, and that her life was a forfeit for her passionate
attachment."[32]

This second Robert Livingston married Margaret Howarden, of whom
little is recorded except that her maternal grandfather became pecuniar-
ily involved with Lord Cornbury, the transvestite governor of New York,
and lost the money, as did all others who had financial dealings with that
odd nobleman.[33] As for Robert of Clermont, he was remembered by his
grandchildren as a tall, ramrod-straight octogenarian, who learned to
speak German fluently in his eighty-sixth year and was passionately devoted to the cause of American independence. He spoke his last words
after the battle of Bunker Hill, and supposedly they were, "What news
from Boston?" At any rate, it was from the romantically originated
Clermont estate that sprang the second great Livingston line.

The Clermont branch was transformed into a major force by maritally
grafting onto it another great manorial estate. Robert of Clermont's only
child, Judge Robert Livingston (he was a member of the New York
Supreme Court), took for his bride in 1742 another only child, the sole
heir of Colonel Henry Beekman of Rhinebeck, whose predatory instincts were as finely attuned as any Livingston's. It was said of him that
"his greed for land was such that, if there were any land on the moon,
he would try to own the greater part of it."[34] Margaret Beekman (and
family anecdotes usually refer to her by her maiden name, as if her
money gave her male status) inherited her father's estate of 240,000
acres. The merger of the Beekman and Clermont estates justified this
estimation by the Judge: "I think not improbable that I may be absolutely
[the] Richest man in the whole Government."[35]

Yet in a society where love matches in marriage were more a statistical
possibility than a prime consideration, the devotion between Judge Robert Livingston and Margaret Beekman was especially noteworthy. After
thirteen years of marriage and seven children, the Judge wrote his wife,
"You are the cordial drop with which Heaven has graciously thought fit

to sweeten my cup. . . . My imagination paints you with all your loveliness—with all the charms my soul has for so many years doated on,—with
all the sweet endearments past and those which I flatter myself I shall
still experience." And Margaret's assessment of her husband was equal
to his regard for her.[36]

This Robert had little of the Livingstons' rage for riches; there is no
evidence that he engaged in business activity of any scope, and his
fellow jurist, William Smith, was fond of paying him this supreme compliment: "If I were placed on a desert island, with but one book and
one friend, that book should be the Bible and that friend Robert R.
Livingston."[37]

The Judge, who shared his father's fervor for the Revolutionary cause,
died in the first year of the war. Thomas Jones, the loyalist historian of
New York, writes that "when he found Great Britain in earnest he put
an end to his life by the use of a halter."[38] Actually, he died suddenly
of apoplexy.

The stage is now set for the Revolutionary War generation of Livingstons, perhaps the most remarkable single generation ever produced by
any American political dynasty; rivaling in brilliance, if not in effective-
ness, the contemporary Lee brothers; but clearly without peer if the
husbands of the Livingston women are included.

When John Adams went to Philadelphia for the opening of the first
Continental Congress he stopped in New York and was briefed on the
politics of the colony by Alexander McDougall, the radical leader. "The
two great families in this province, upon whose motion all their politics
turn," the Massachusetts man was told, "are the Delanceys and Livingstons . . . there is virtue and abilities as well as fortune in the Livingstons, but not much of either of the three in the Delanceys."[39]

Through its first and second generations the Livingstons had been
primarily an economic dynasty. While they were deeply engaged in
politics, it was as a means to an economic end. The man who turned
the family into a great political dynasty, and a republican one at that,
as Adams was told, was William Livingston, youngest son of the Second
Lord of the Manor. Under his leadership, during the three decades before
the Revolution, the Livingstons became more than a political force in
New York—they became a political party.

William Livingston was an unlikely leader of the people. A young lady,
alluding to his tall and graceless figure, called him "the whipping-
post."[40] His own description was "long-nosed, long-chinned, ugly-look-
ing." But although the nose was the subject of much political lampoon-
ing, he found in it a source of secret pride.[41] He was considered a bad
public speaker by such diverse authorities as John Witherspoon and

Thomas Jones.[42] He was irritable and uncomfortable at pretentious social gatherings and fashionable balls. The theater was an unnecessary extravagance. He was a dilettante who jumped from one absorbing passion to another; a rebel with a great many causes.

He was an equally unlikely Livingston. William once told a friend, "I do not set a proper value on money. . . . I dispair of ever attaining the Art of keeping it."[43] His business records were slovenly; his fees often went uncollected. The family blamed these unfortunate characteristics on the fact that he was raised by his maternal grandmother, who was too lenient with her young charge.[44]

The first major incident that distinguished William from other young men of his class occurred while he was an apprentice in the law office of James Alexander, a descendant of the Earls of Stirling.[45] A young fellow named Rice, who was employed as the organist at Trinity Church, sent a pair of gloves to Alexander's daughter as a valentine. Mrs. Alexander refused to allow the girl to accept the humble lad's gift. This so incensed William that he published an article, "Of Pride Arising from Riches and Prosperity," in which he attacked his employer's wife as "the haughtiest and most insolent woman in the city." William was promptly dismissed. He completed his legal training under William Smith, Sr.[46]

That William's behavior was not merely an isolated example of youthful rebellion was soon evidenced by his announced intention of marrying Susanna French. All the sons of the Second Lord had married well, generally daughters of the Dutch landed aristocracy in New York. But Susanna's family, although socially prominent, was bankrupt.[47] William's father finally consented to the match if the young couple agreed to wait three years. About a year later Susanna was pregnant. They were secretly married and went to live with an aunt of the bride. Significantly, the Second Lord of the Manor gave each of his sons except William a New York City town house.

However, William correctly judged that no matter how outraged his family might be by his behavior they would not abandon him. As a lawyer, most of his income came from representing various members of the clan. Nor did William's legal talents let them down. When Gilbert Livingston's youngest son, twenty-three-year-old Cornelius, was accused along with three other young men of raping a fourteen-year-old girl, Willam framed the girl's mother on the charge of stealing a petticoat. The woman was sentenced to a public whipping; the boys were acquitted. Cornelius was then sent to sea on one of Philip Livingston's ships.[48]

In 1752 William founded the *Independent Reflector*, a muckraking weekly whose proclaimed aim was "to proceed unawed and alike fearless of the humble scoundrel and the eminent villain."[49] As the organ for a brilliant and vitriolic pen, it has had few equals in American journalism.

Among William's targets was "The Extravagance of our Funerals," a colonial exposé of the American way of death, perhaps inspired by the £500 price tag on the burial ceremony of his father.[50] The crusading editor also took after some prominent merchants, including two Roosevelts, who were maneuvering to gain title to valuable shore-line property at no cost. "Too severe," was the judgment of his brother Robert, who was now the Third Lord.[51] The mayor recommended that the grand jury bring William to trial for libel. He was attacked from the pulpit, to which Livingston replied in print: "The author takes this opportunity for returning his thanks to the reverend gentleman who did him such signal honour, last Sunday, as to make him the subject of his sermon, and greatly admires his ingenuity in proving him to be the Gog and Magog of the Apocalypse, who have hitherto puzzled all the divines in the world."[52] Finally, the *Independent Reflector* was "tyrannically suppressed."[53] But it had already developed one political issue which would launch "the Livingston Party."

This issue was presented by the founding of King's College, now Columbia University. All the colleges in the colonies had strong sectarian ties, and now the Anglican Church made its bid for a New York school. Livingston and his newspaper fought for a non-sectarian institution. Toleration would end, he wrote, "should one Party obtain Sole Management of the Education of our Youth."[54] Columbia was finally established as an Anglican school, but Livingston won a partial victory. Half of the public funds that had been allotted to the college were diverted to a new city jail and pesthouse. Commented Livingston's old mentor, William Smith, Sr., this arrangement "rids us of a bone of contention by dividing it between the two pest houses."[55]

William had uncovered a popular cause: the Episcopalians controlled the government but were a minority of the population. The Livingstons would now be the champions of the masses, i.e., the non-Episcopalians. In the General Assembly elections of 1758 the Livingston (or Presbyterian) Party defeated the De Lancey (or Episcopalian) Party, and held control of the legislature for the next decade. Out of this contest, which soon became more personal than religious (for, indeed, some of the Livingstons were Episcopalians!), came the later division between Loyalists and Revolutionaries in New York State. In 1776, it was the Livingstons, of English origin, who declared for independence, while the French Huguenot De Lanceys remained loyal to the Crown. The ancient policies of James II and Charles II determined the battle lines a century later in New York. The fate of "the Godly Livingstone," banished by Charles II, was the legacy of William and his family. The mother country had left the Livingstons an inheritance of religious persecution, while the De Lanceys remembered England as their protector in another age.

The Livingstons however were far from being revolutionary hotheads.

The only one to join the Sons of Liberty was Peter R. Livingston, some-times called "Jew Peter," the eldest son of the Third Lord. But he was an unstable character, as we shall see, and joined the radicals more out of a sense of thrill-seeking than from a deep commitment to the cause of independence. The rest of the clan was ideologically somewhere be-tween the Sons of Liberty and the Loyalists. During the Stamp Act controversy they had favored the non-importation of English goods rather than open defiance of authority. And when the mobs took to the streets they were sincerely shocked. While the Livingstons could pic-ture themselves as being oppressed by the English Parliament, they were holding dictatorial rein over their tenant farmers. During the anti-rent rebellion of 1766 William Livingston appeared in court some fifty times in proceedings to eject defiant tenants. Such action gave the De Lanceys, who were more merchants than landowners, a powerful campaign slo-gan, "No Lawyers in the Assembly," with which they defeated the Livingstons in the election of 1769. The setback convinced William to move his family to Elizabeth Town, New Jersey, where he built Liberty Hall and contemplated embarking on the life of "Philosophic Solitude," about which he had once written a 684-line poem.[56]

It may have been the influence of their in-laws as much as any other factor that convinced the Livingstons they should play such a vital role in the fight for independence.

William Livingston, the ugly proprietor of Liberty Hall, was the father of three comely daughters, a contrast that was not lost on his enemies. Later, when he was the war governor of New Jersey, a writer in the *Royal Gazette*, a New York loyalist newspaper, remarked that the girls were "so amiable in appearance as to make it scarcely possible to suppose they are daughters of such an arch-fiend. . . ."[57]

The sedate Susannah, the eldest, was later to be the unhappy third wife of John Cleves Symmes, congressman-judge-land promoter, which also made her the stepmother of a First Lady, Mrs. William Henry Harrison.[58]

Catherine, "La Kitty," was the middle Livingston daughter and mad-cap of the family. Once when she brewed some forbidden China tea she fooled her stern father by coloring it with jam and passing it off as "strawberry tea."[59] She was also something of a heartbreaker. Gouver-neur Morris wrote her love poems. And on one occasion when she failed to reply to his passionate letters she gave him the lame excuse that she couldn't write because she had hurt her ankle! The statesman's most re-cent biographer comments, "Looking back over Morris' life for thirty years, one might well conclude that if he had married Kitty Livingston and 'settled down' with that enchanting girl he might have been the third President."[60] However, she waited until she was thirty-six to marry, and then chose Matthew Ridley, an American diplomat and trusted confidant of John Adams during the peace negotiations in Paris.[61]

But it was the husband of William Livingston's youngest daughter who had the most profound effect on him. Sally was the beauty. When she attended theater in Paris, the audience rose in tribute, mistaking her for Marie Antoinette.[62] At eighteen she became the bride of a well-connected, twenty-nine-year-old New York lawyer named John Jay.[63] The young man had proposed in succession to two De Lancey sisters and had been twice rejected. Tory pamphleteers blamed his Whigism on these refusals.[64] But no matter what motivated his strong attachment to the American cause, it undoubtedly reinforced William Livingston's predilections in that direction. The Reverend John Vardill, a loyalist who took refuge in England during the Revolution and supplied the British authorities with information about the American leaders, wrote that Livingston "is much . . . under the influence of his Son-in-Law Mr. Jay for whose talents he has the fondest partiality."[65]

Surveying a family dinner party at Clermont, Judge Robert Livingston's eldest daughter Janet observed, "Never was a table so surrounded."[66] For, indeed, the Judge's sons-in-law were as distinguished a group as any socially ambitious hostess could wish to assemble for a meal. There was Richard Montgomery, whom Washington Irving was to describe as "the beau ideal of a soldier"; Thomas Tillotson, physician and secretary of state of New York[67]; Reverend Freeborn Garrettson, one of the most important figures in the establishment of the Methodist Church in America—"all meekness and love, and yet all activity"[68]; Morgan Lewis, jurist-general-governor, as well as the son of a signer of the Declaration of Independence[69]; and finally John Armstrong, collector of high public offices, who was called "morose" by Napoleon, "pugnacious" by Van Buren, and "the devil" by Dallas.[70]

It was the handsome Montgomery who catalyzed the Clermont Livingstons' deep involvement in the American Revolutionary cause. The son of an Irish member of Parliament, a British officer by training, he married Janet Livingston in 1773 and became a New York farmer. After only three years in America he was appointed a brigadier general by the Continental Congress and left his young bride to take arms. On November 13, 1775, he captured Montreal, but six weeks later was killed while storming the west wall of Quebec. In the British Parliament, Edmund Burke paid glowing tribute to the hero who had conquered two thirds of Canada in a single campaign. Lord North replied, "I cannot join in lamenting the death of Montgomery as a public loss. He was brave, he was able, he was humane, he was generous; but still, he was only a brave, able, humane, and generous rebel."[71] The death of the generous rebel left the Clermont Livingstons no option but to pick up his sword.

Nor was Montgomery the only rebel general connected with the dynasty. Major General William Alexander was married to Sarah Livingston, daughter of the Second Lord of the Manor. However, while Montgomery was an unalloyed hero, Alexander was often something of a joke. He had spent a fortune lobbying for a peerage, a claim which was rejected by the House of Lords in 1762. Nevertheless, the Americans indulged his fancy by calling him "Lord Stirling," although secretly laughing at his social pretensions. An anecdote that made the rounds in the American army was that Stirling had witnessed the execution of a soldier for desertion at which the criminal repeatedly cried out, "The Lord have mercy on me." To which his lordship warmly exclaimed, "I won't, you rascal, I won't have mercy on you."[72] The British were equally amused by the self-styled peer. Reverend Jonathan Odell, the bitter Tory satirist, who wrote of William Livingston as having "Gall in thy heart, and malice on thy brow; Coward, yet cruel—zealous, yet profane," dismissed Livingston's brother-in-law in four contemptuous lines:

> What matters what of Stirling may become?
> The quintessence of whiskey, soul of rum;
> Fractious at nine, quite gay at twelve o'clock;
> From thence till bed-time stupid as a block.[73]

And yet, for all his weaknesses, Stirling was a useful, courageous, and unselfish officer. He was without personal military ambition during a time when his fellow generals often seemed more concerned with their own advancement than the good of the cause. Repeatedly allowing others to take commands to which he held greater claim, Stirling accepted, year after year, many of the army's more irksome duties. If his record was for the most part one of failures and misadventures, his devotion earned the sincere gratitude of his Commander-in-Chief.[74]

The Livingstons and their in-laws compiled an exemplary military record. There were seven or eight Livingstons at Saratoga with Gates, three commanding regiments; there were five Livingstons with Montgomery at Quebec; a Livingston foiled Benedict Arnold's plot by driving off the ship that was waiting to return John André to the British lines[75]; fourteen Livingstons served in the regular army, two in the navy. The family historian proudly contends: "It is doubtful whether any other family in the thirteen Colonies contributed so many of its members to the patriot army and navy."[76]

When the first Continental Congress convened in 1774, William Livingston was a representative from New Jersey, and the five-man New York delegation included his brother Philip and two Livingston in-laws, James Duane and John Jay. Duane was married to the daughter of the Third Lord of the Manor, who preferred to entrust his political interests to his son-in-law. It was a wise move; Duane was a shrewd manipulator. Vardill found him to be "a plodding lawyer, capable of any meanness," while John Adams' first impression was that Duane's eyes, which were a trifle cocked, hinted a certain artfulness.[77] There is no reason to believe that Adams adjusted his opinion after closer inspection. But Duane was a convivial fellow. Seeing him at a ball, the Marquis de Chastellux declared him to be "ten per cent more lively than all the other dancers."[78] A political opponent, however, thought it was "ludicrous" for "a man of his years and make, and a member of Congress too, to be labouring and sweating his fat sides in a public dance. . . ."[79] Here was a skillful politician, well able to look after the Manor's interests.

John Adams found Philip Livingston a very different sort, although no more to his taste. "Phil Livingston is a great, rough, rapid mortal. There is no holding any conversation with him. He blusters away. . . ." Benjamin Rush assessed him from a slightly higher elevation: "A blunt but honest man."[80] "Honest Phil" Livingston, a son of the Second Lord, had at least one skeleton in his closet. During the French and Indian War he had probably been involved in smuggling goods to enemy islands in the West Indies. He was one of the wealthiest merchants in New York City and a political conservative.[81] "If England should turn us adrift," he told Adams, "we should instantly go to civil wars among ourselves."[82] Although he later worked tirelessly for the American cause, it was ironic that he, among all the Livingstons, should gain immortality by signing the Declaration of Independence.

Philip was a signer for a very Livingston-like reason. In the second Continental Congress the New York delegation was enlarged and Robert R. Livingston, Jr., became the third of his dynasty to hold national office. He was Philip's cousin, of the Clermont line, and for purposes of identification is always referred to as "the Chancellor"—a title he later held in New York State for twenty-four years. The two Livingston congressmen were also members of the state legislature, and they arranged jointly to cover both bases. When Philip was in Philadelphia, Robert would represent the family in New York, and vice versa. Thus, when Richard Henry Lee's motion for independence was voted on in June, Robert was in attendance, Philip was in New York; and when the Declaration was signed, Philip was there and Robert was in New York. The Chancellor had cause to wonder at history's equity; for he, along with Jefferson, Adams, Franklin, and Sherman, comprised the committee to draft the Declaration—yet he was not one of the signers.

The third of the trio of Livingston congressmen also failed to sign the Declaration. Prior to the fateful Fourth of July, William Livingston had been appointed a militia general, and at the end of August, after only four years' residence in New Jersey, he was elected the state's first governor, defeating Richard Stockton on the second ballot.[83] (The infant state also adopted the Livingston coat of arms as its great seal "until another could be procured.") Livingston's salary was £500, with another £350 coming from such perquisites as the issuance of marriage licenses; it was less than a fourth of the compensation received by William Franklin, the last British governor. But if the pay was short, the title was long and munificent—"His Excellency William Livingston, Esquire, Governor, Captain General, and Commander-in-Chief in and over the State of New Jersey and Territories thereunto belonging, Chancellor and Ordinary of the same." To the loyalist press, however, he was known by a string of less exalted names, among them being "Don Quixote of the Jersies," "Mock Governor," "Knight of the Most Honourable Order of Starvation," "Spurious Governor," "Itinerant Dey of New Jersey," and "The Despot-in-Chief in and over the Rising State of New Jersey, Extraordinary Chancellor of the same, etc." The patriots preferred to call him "Doctor Flint," a tribute to his granite firmness during the years when New Jersey was a Tory-infested battlefield.

There was an odd twist to the enmity in which Livingston was held by the Tories. Major John André delighted a loyalist audience by reciting a sort of political parable, or what he called an "extempore dream." Each rebel leader was depicted as a wild beast, with Livingston being the wolf. "I beheld with surprise," concluded André, "that he retained the same gaunt, hollow, and ferocious appearance, and that his tongue still continued to be red with gore. Just at this time Mercury touched me with his wand, and thereby bestowed an insight into futurity, when I saw this very wolf hung up at the door of his fold, by a shepherd whose innocent flock had been from time to time thinned by the murdering jaws of this savage animal."[84] It was a forecast from one whose own fate was to be death by hanging in less than two years.

As the price on Governor Livingston's head mounted, he wrote Henry Laurens, "They certainly overrate my merit, and I cannot conceive what induces them to bid so extravagant a sum, having now raised my price from 500 to 2000 guineas. . . ."[85] But Livingston was elusive game. On one foraging expedition, led by a British Colonel Stirling, the enemy troops found that the sole occupant of Liberty Hall was Kitty, whose flirtations had given her valuable training in artful dodging. She relates the encounter:

There were, I knew, some valuable letters in a little escritoire that father kept in one corner of the bedroom,—I was afraid that these might be the papers that Colonel Stirling sought. So when he came there to look, I playacted. Oh, but I was most confused, I'm sure, for Colonel Stirling stopped and looked at me and asked politely if these were personal papers. So I told him that they were most private letters and I blushed, and he supposed that some young gentleman was writing to me and that he ought not to intrude upon a maiden's romance.

So, I thought, that I would give him a reward for his consideration. I told him that I just remembered that there were most important writings in the attic. 'Ho, ho,' he said, 'so the broomstick governor thought that we would never look among the rubbish! Let's go up and see.' And we climbed the ladder—he was a gentleman and he went first—and, sure enough, there were great bundles of letters there. Stirling never stopped to look at them. He grabbed them up, crammed them in his pockets, and he called down to his men to come and get the rest.

I stood there, filled with laughter that I didn't dare show, while Colonel Stirling threw down bundle after bundle of the papers to his men below. There must have been hundreds of them and the Colonel was sure now that he had found the inner secrets of the whole United States. Then when he had taken all of them, he thanked me most politely for my help and said that rebel ladies were attractive wenches.

What he thought when he got back to Staten Island and found out that he had carried off legal briefs, copies of ancient laws, and old proclamations, every one of which is printed in the books, I'll never know. But it was fun while it lasted.[86]

The British officer failed to mention the coup in his official report. But the young lady's maneuver leaked out and caused him considerable embarrassment.

Across the Hudson another Livingston was being cast as a heroine by the advancing British army. New York had been organized as an independent state, and while a Clinton was named governor, all the other high officials seemed to be Livingstons: Philip "the Signer" was a state senator, Walter was Speaker of the Assembly, Gilbert was representative for Dutchess County, Robert R. was made Chancellor, and John Jay was the chief justice. Now Margaret Beekman was alone at Clermont with her small children. A family story, which correctly conveys her fortitude, though it may not have happened, claims that she was nursing a wounded British officer, a relative of Richard Montgomery, when the enemy troops appeared. He offered to protect her home, but she replied that she preferred sharing the fate of her friends and her neighbors.[87] Margaret Beekman Livingston then escaped with her children, her servants, and a few belongings. Clermont was burned to the ground. As soon as the British moved on she returned and rebuilt her home.

On September 27, 1779, John Jay was appointed minister plenipotentiary to Spain. "Adieu, my dear John, may you be as happy as I wish you," wrote Chancellor Livingston.[88] Their friendship dated back to college days at Columbia; Jay had been a year ahead of Livingston. Later they had been law partners and, most recently, congressmen together (both having been elected at twenty-nine years of age). Once, in a mood of youthful introspection, Jay had sent Livingston an assessment of their characters:

I took it into my head that our dispositions were in many respects similar. Afterwards I conceived a different opinion. It appeared to me that yours had more vivacity. Bashfulness and pride rendered me more staid. Both equally ambitious, but pursuing it in different roads. You flexible, I pertinaceous. Both equally sensible of indignities, you less prone to sudden resentments. Both possessed of warm passions, but you of more self-possession. You formed for a citizen of the world, I for a College or a Village. You fond of a large acquaintance, I careless of all but a few. You understood men *and women* early, I knew them not. You had talents and inclination for intrigue, I had neither. Your mind (and body) received pleasure from a variety of objects, mine from few. You were naturally easy of access, and in advances, I in neither.[89]

Now affairs of state had reversed their roles: Jay, who imagined himself fitted "for a College or a Village," was off to join America's militia diplomats in Europe; Livingston, "a citizen of the world," was to stay at home.

While Abigail Adams had been forced to remain in Quincy and coax sustenance for her family out of the barren earth during most of her husband's tenure in Europe, the wealthy minister to Madrid was accompanied to his post by his lovely wife. Those two great war widows, Mrs. Richard Montgomery and Mrs. Joseph Warren, discussed Mrs. Jay's departure: "She is very handsome, which will secure her a welcome with the unthinking," wrote Janet Montgomery to Mercy Warren, "whilst her understanding will gain her the hearts of the most worthy. Her manners will do honor to our countrywomen, and I really believe will please, even at the Court of Madrid."[90] But Sarah Livingston Jay was not merely a charming ornament; she was her husband's trusted confidante. And at least one diplomatic observer thought her something more: Don Diego Gardoqui told his government, "This woman, whom he loves blindly, dominates him and nothing is done without her consent, so that her opinion prevails, though her husband at first may disagree; from which I infer that a little management in dealing with her and a few timely gifts will secure the friendship of both. . . ."[91]

Minister Jay also took his brother-in-law to Spain as his private secretary. Brockholst Livingston would someday sit on the Supreme Court of the United States, at which time Joseph Story would thus describe him: "A fine Roman face; an aquiline nose, high forehead, bold head and projecting chin, indicating deep research, strength and quickness of mind. . . . He evidently thinks with great solidity and seizes on the strong points of argument. He is luminous, decisive, earnest and impressive on the bench."[92] But one gets an entirely different opinion of his character from his behavior in Spain. He acted like a spoiled, selfish brat. He was petulant, sulky, sullen, and captious. At the Jays' table he told a Frenchman that he had seen the entire American Congress drunk at one time. Another day he told a foreigner that Congress was far worse than a monarchy. And when his sister advised him to be "careful to do nothing that might lessen the respectability of the representatives of our country," he announced that "he prefer'd going to America to remaining like a slave here."[93] When he finally left in 1782, Sally Jay thought it necessary to write her sister Kitty of his behavior, with instructions to turn the letter over to their father if Brockholst should try to slander the Jays. However, this step was unnecessary because he was captured by the British on the way home.

Congress established a Department of Foreign Affairs in 1781. In selecting its head, the Adams-Lee faction supported Arthur Lee, the Francophobic former diplomat; Luzerne, the powerful French minister, countered by throwing his influence to Chancellor Livingston. On the third day of balloting Livingston defeated Lee, eight states to four. Livingston thus became the first American Secretary of State, and the nominal boss of John Jay, Benjamin Franklin, and John Adams. The latter wrote from Amsterdam, "It is with great pleasure I learn, that a Minister is appointed for foreign affairs, who is so capable of introducing into that department an order, a constancy, and an activity, which could never be expected from a Committee of Congress. . . ."[94] Livingston was indeed an administrative genius who could turn chaos into order. But his judgment and ability to affect policy were severely limited by three thousand miles of water, and, despite his attempts, policy formulation was most often the ad hoc arrangement of the American ministers abroad. The Chancellor strongly opposed the peace negotiators' decision to treat with Great Britain behind the back of France—a precaution devised by Jay, who reached Paris before Adams could get there from Amsterdam. The move guaranteed superior terms for the Americans and had the wholehearted support of Adams, who commented, "The principal merit of the negotiations was Mr. Jay's. . . . A man and his office were never better united than Mr. Jay and the commission for peace. Had he been detained in Madrid, as I was in Holland, and all left to Franklin as was wished, all would have been lost."[95]

Chancellor Livingston resigned in December 1782 and, twice being persuaded by Congress to extend his service, finally left for Clermont in June. As the first American Secretary of State, he estimated that running the office had cost him $3000 a year more than his salary. The post remained vacant for a year, and then the Chancellor's best friend, John Jay, returned home and assumed the duties.

The Chancellor was thirty-six years old and already growing deaf. An eminent doctor had tired to cure him by passing an electric current through both ears; the treatment left him deafer than before. He now returned home to find Clermont in the midst of one crisis for which the British could not be blamed.

His brother Henry Beekman Livingston, four years his junior, was arrogant, strong-willed, self-indulgent, and pathologically quarrelsome. He had fought bravely alongside Montgomery at Montreal, but when his brother-in-law found that he could not get along with the other officers, whom he considered his social inferiors, the general tactfully dismissed Henry by sending him home with dispatches. His subsequent army career was a repetitious combination of front-line courage and campsite tantrums. On one occasion he was court-martialed and reprimanded for making unflattering remarks about his commanding officer, General Alexander McDougall, who was too plebeian for Livingston's taste. Finally, in 1778, he resigned his commission, informing the president of Congress that he was "not yet so callous to the Impression of Insult as to be insensible of the repeated Indignities offered me in the Promotion of Officers my inferior."[96]

About this time Henry began courting a pretty Philadelphia belle, Nancy Shippen, the daughter of Benjamin Rush's perennial antagonist, Dr. William Shippen, and his wife Alice Lee, of the Stratford Lees. Henry threw himself at the young lady: at half past three in the morning he wrote, "My Dearest Girl . . . to divert myself will Scrall a few Lines; the writing, which at Best [is] Bad, is now worse, from the Dimness of a Lonesome Taper, emblematical of your Lovers Situation with this Difference that it Burns at one End, I all over. . . ."[97] But he had competition from a young French diplomat, Louis Otto. Nancy was torn between her two suitors. The Frenchman was handsome; the American was rich. Her father finally helped her make up her mind. Although Dr. Shippen had been officially exonerated of any wrongdoing in his administration of the Army Medical Department, his practice had been badly damaged by Rush's charges. It would be a great relief to him if his daughter could make a match with a Livingston of New York. "Your P[appa] knows that my Fortune cannot be compared with that of [Livingston]," wrote Otto, "therefore he prefers him; perhaps true wisdom would distinguish happiness and riches. . . ."[98]

Nine months and two weeks after the wedding Nancy Shippen Livingston had a daughter who was named Margaret Beekman, after the grand dame of Clermont. But, as she was soon to discover, her husband was also the father of a number of other children, born to his collection of mistresses. Moreover, he had a plan to gather all these offspring, including her own Peggy, under one roof. This was the last straw in the bundle of gross indignities to which Henry Livingston had subjected his teen-age bride. On a spring day in 1783 she took little Peggy and fled her husband's house.

She had considered the Livingstons to be "charming people & the family altogether, (except my unfortunate husband) delightful."[99] Now she would find that they were Livingstons first; charming people second. In any family conflict, right or wrong was a secondary consideration to blood. Henry was "blood"; Nancy was not. The one exception was Margaret Beekman—the old lady stubbornly fought for her wronged daughter-in-law.

Divorce in eighteenth-century America was a prima facie case against a woman's moral reputation. And the case of Nancy Shippen Livingston vs. Henry Livingston was muddied by the husband's malicious charges of an affair between his wife and a French diplomat. Opposing Nancy was the powerful Livingston dynasty and her own father, whose concern was to avoid further scandal. For active defenders she could count only two, Margaret Beekman and her uncle Arthur Lee. Fearful of losing her child, Nancy dropped the proceedings.

After this Nancy's zestful promise blurred into religious melancholia. Louis Otto married another Livingston, who died in childbirth.[100] He then returned to France, where he was to become the Comte de Mosloy, maker of the Peace of Amiens and negotiator of Napoleon's marriage to Marie Louise. Margaret Beekman died in 1800, regally seated at the head of her dining table at Clermont. She left her granddaughter and namesake the fortune which had once seemed so important to the Shippens. It brought no happiness, as Otto had tried to suggest. Nancy and her daughter lived as recluses. Nancy Shippen Livingston died in her eightieth year, having spent her last four decades composing epitaphs, hymns, and long letters of condolence, which were chiefly accounts of her dreams of the dead. Her spinster daughter, Margaret Beekman Livingston, died in her eighty-second year, also a religious fanatic, who had lost her fortune to swindlers posing as clergymen. The two Livingstons, mother and daughter, were buried in a single grave.

The war affected the Livingston fortune as it did most of the great landed estates. The Third Lord of the Manor complained that he was being "taxed $43,890, which is a twenty-third part of the whole state of New York."[101] This burden had left him with so little ready cash that he asked a brother not to send letters by post because he didn't have money to pay the postman. However, he put the dynasty's economic plight into proper perspective when he chided a complaining brother: ". . . allow me to remind you that you still enjoy the necessaries, and many of the conveniences of life, which, under the present circumstances of the country, is no ordinary blessing. Moreover, you enjoy a large landed property, of which perhaps you receive at present but little, as is the case here, and everywhere else. But it will come after a little while, and we must be thankful to kind Providence and patiently wait his time."[102] Besides, the family still hadn't completely lost its eye for the main chance. John R. Livingston found that the Revolution, like all wars, presented many opportunities for morally dubious but profitable ventures; and at least three Livingstons were investing heavily in the confiscated lands of loyalists, which gave them a major holding in urban real estate for the first time, as well as the satisfaction of taking over the property of their old political enemies, the De Lanceys, at bargain-basement prices.[103]

But the changes wrought on the dynasty's economic position were minor compared to those on its political structure. The war transferred leadership from the Manor Livingstons to the Clermont Livingstons.

Of the Manor line, only William Livingston survived the Revolution as a political force. His tenure as war governor of New Jersey had been a conspicuous success. A study of the forty-eight men who served as chief executives during this period rated him among the top eight.[104] He had once said, "Man vested with boundless Authority to preserve his Integrity for three years, is taking human nature in the gross as much as can reasonably be expected."[105] Yet the "Don Quixote of the Jersies" continued to serve as governor for fourteen successive one-year terms. He bitterly regretted not having been a signer of the Declaration, but, as his last significant act, he put his signature to the new Constitution of the United States.

His sons, however, were a major disappointment. Young William drank heavily, was badly in debt, and became involved in an unsavory affair with a village barmaid. Brockholst married his landlady's daughter and killed a man who made a remark about his prominent nose. John Lawrence, a midshipman, had been lost at sea during the war, and his father became an easy mark for any confidence man who could concoct a story of the youth's survival.

The governor died in 1790, as did his brother Robert, Third Lord of the Manor, who had broken the entail on his estate. To have done otherwise would have meant the succession of Peter R. Livingston as the head of the line, and that would have been disastrous. The eldest son was tempestuous, unstable, and egocentric. At Harvard (where he didn't graduate), his room was remembered for its bounty of liquor and absence of books. Life at the Manor he found dull; one winter he complained that he had only had "one frolic," during which he was "obliged to go home with one shoe." The prewar agitation had proved Peter to be politically reckless; later he proved equally irresponsible in money matters. By 1771 he was so deeply in debt that it was necessary for his father to assume the support of his family. The other brothers eventually petitioned the Third Lord to stop paying Peter's bills.[106]

The Manor estate was left to the Third Lord's eight children and within a month of the father's death the heirs were fighting over how to divide the spoils—five slaves, 170 needles, nine fishhooks, ten empty bottles, one pound of dried codfish, one dried chop, and some considerably more valuable property. One daughter charged in court that the others were conspiring to withhold her share of the estate.[107] Moreover, internecine warfare had also broken out between the Manor and Clermont families. The dispute involved the right to erect a gristmill on Roeliff Jansen Kill. Before peace again reigned in the dynasty such high-powered legal talent as Alexander Hamilton, John Morin Scott, James Duane, and Brockholst Livingston had been employed.[108]

When the power of the dynasty passed to the Clermont branch it came to rest first in the hands of the able and ambitious, imaginative and impulsive Chancellor Robert R. Livingston. Together with Hamilton and Jay he had been instrumental in securing the ratification of the federal Constitution in New York State against seemingly overwhelming odds. As Chancellor it had been his honor to administer the oath of office to George Washington. And under the Administration of the first President it was to be expected that he would be rewarded for his ability and past services to the nation and federalism. But such was not to be the case. It was said in New York that "the Clintons had *power*, the Livingstons had *numbers*, the Schuylers had *Hamilton*."[109] When choosing sides in postwar politics, one would have been justified in declaring, "Give me Hamilton and you can have the field." Of all the great factions, only the Livingstons were frozen out of national office. The Chancellor soon surmised that "pains have been taken to prejudice me in the presidents opinion. . . ."[110] The position of Chief Justice of the Supreme Court, which he secretly coveted, went to John Jay. The preferment of Jay was another wedge in the parting of the two patriots. Livingston had always been the more affectionate; Jay had always seemed to deny a part of himself to their friendship. When Jay returned from Europe in 1784 Livingston figuratively ran to greet him with open arms; Jay withdrew from the embrace. Perhaps too much had changed in the twenty years since they had been together at college. Perhaps it was expecting the impossible to ask Jay to return to the schoolboy basis on which their friendship had been founded.

The result of Jay's coolness, Hamilton's hostility, and Washington's indifference was that Robert R. Livingston became a Republican—and he carried the whole dynasty into Jefferson's camp. Issues or rationalizations would follow; the initial move was motivated by pique. Once again this most aristocratic of the Northern dynasties was thrown into the "liberal" party.

In 1792 Jay was the Federalist candidate for governor against George Clinton, the incumbent, who controlled the election machinery. Clearly Jay was counted out, and the Livingstons supported the fraud. Mrs. Jay, deeply wounded by her family's actions, cried out, "Oh, how is the name of Livingston to be disgraced! . . . those shameless men, blinded by malice, ambition and interest. . . ."[111] The Chancellor's part in the campaign was unfortunate. This was an era of violent press tirades, always delivered anonymously. A correspondent in the *Daily Advertiser* wrote on hearing that the Chancellor was about to support Clinton: "My dear friend, I know that thou art a wag and readest merry books—thou rememberest it is written in *Rabelais,* that when Pantagruel f——ted, he shook the earth three leagues around. Dost thou seriously believe that the C****r's influence will extend over as many acres in any county?"[112] Perhaps the C****r appreciated this joke against himself. But when it was followed by a particularly personal attack, signed "Timothy Tickler," Livingston exploded in a rage. His published answer accused Jay of being "Timothy Tickler," of being a monarchist, of sacrificing "the earliest friendship of your youth to the cause of avarice and ambition," and of having a "cold heart, graduated like a thermometer, [which] finds the freezing point nearest the bulb." Jay replied with dignity and moderation: he had not been "Timothy Tickler," nor had he written any other political paper that year; he did not know the author of the attack on Livingston and had not been consulted as to its publication. Besides that, he met Livingston's loss of temper with stony silence. His revenge, if such he felt it was, came three years later when he again ran for governor, this time against the Chancellor, and soundly defeated his former friend.[113]

The upturn in the public fortunes of the Livingstons coincided with the appearance on the political scene of the Chancellor's youngest brother Edward. He was to be the intellectual star of the dynasty; remembered by Sir Henry Maine as "the first legal genius of modern times."[114] "The life of Edward Livingston," wrote William Howard Taft, "is one of the most romantic and checkered that I know."[115]

Edward was eighteen years younger than the Chancellor. Just eleven when his father died and his brother was first elected to the Continental Congress, his childhood recollections were of Montgomery going off to war and his mother fleeing with him from Clermont as the British troops advanced.

When in 1795 Edward Livingston became the fourth member of his dynasty to serve in Congress, he was a likable and dashing young man of thirty. He had his father's sweet disposition, that flair for dress which distinguished many of the family, and typically Livingston features that were best described as "a most engaging ugliness."[116] The Chancellor treated this much younger brother like a son, and freely criticized him for his own good: Edward "has genius enough to make a great figure," he said, but suffers from an "habitual indolence."[117] Edward's political opponents asked how a fashionable man about town, who even drove a chariot, could be in sympathy with the people. But when it was discovered that the Federalist candidate also drove a chariot the issue was considerably diluted. "Beau Ned" was to recall these days as a constant struggle between duty and pleasure. In verse, his conscience told him, "Remember you're a lawyer!" But—

> Alas! unheeded cries, its voice is drown'd
> By frolic's pleasure's more attractive sound;
> She bids her roses in his fancy blow,
> And laughing cries, "Remember you're a beau."[118]

Yet in Washington the inner struggle turned and his superior intellect raised him to a position of Republican leadership in the House following the retirement of Madison in 1797. He played a prominent part in the congressional fight against the Jay Treaty. And his finely reasoned speech in opposition to the Alien and Sedition Laws was "printed in satin and hung up in thousands of the taverns and parlours of the Democratic States."[119] But after three terms Edward declined renomination and returned to New York, leaving behind a cloud of accusations about his role in the Jefferson-Burr presidential contest.

When the presidential election of 1800 was thrown into the House of Representatives, Livingston was a lame-duck congressman. Still his influence was considerable. James Bayard, who was himself to determine the outcome of the canvass, said, "Livingston's means were not limited to his own state; nay, I always considered more than the vote of New York within his power."[120] Bayard surmised that a Livingston switch to Burr could start a bandwagon. And there were high-level rumors that this was exactly what the strategy of the Burr forces would be. Hamilton wrote Gouverneur Morris that Burr "perfectly understands himself with Edward Livingston, who will be his *agent* at the seat of Government" and that Livingston had "declared among his friends that his first ballot" would "be for Jefferson—his second for Burr."[121] But Livingston's vote remained in Jefferson's column, and the Virginian was victorious on the thirty-sixth ballot. ". . . if Livingston had not betrayed his trust," wrote a Hamilton lieutenant, "Burr would certainly have been President."[122]

The question remains whether Jefferson paid a price for this wavering

New York vote. If he did, the price was considerable. For seven members of the dynasty, three Livingstons and four in-laws, were shortly given federal, state, or municipal posts. Jefferson made Edward the district attorney for New York, and he was also appointed mayor of New York. The latter position was estimated to be worth $10,000 to $15,000 a year in fees. (Indeed, it was so lucrative that De Witt Clinton resigned his Senate seat to become mayor in 1803.) The Chancellor was made minister to France. Brockholst became a state Supreme Court justice, as did Smith Thompson, who was married to a Livingston.[123] Edward's three brothers-in-law, Thomas Tillotson, John Armstrong, and Morgan Lewis, respectively became secretary of state of New York, United States senator, and Republican candidate for governor.

But for Edward his dual positions, district attorney-mayor, were to be his undoing. While conscientiously tending to his municipal duties during the yellow fever epidemic of 1803, he fell victim to the disease; when he recovered the federal treasury in the city had been embezzled of $43,666.21. At that time the district attorney's functions included the collection of customhouse revenues. Livingston, always unable to manage financial matters, had left this detail to a subordinate. When the assistant's theft was discovered, Livingston immediately resigned and agreed to make good on the defalcation. The Treasury Department finally closed its account against Livingston in 1830, by which time he had paid the government $102,017.20, including accumulated interest. His brilliant career in New York politics was finished. He wrote Mrs. Montgomery that he would "begin the world anew" in New Orleans.[124]

Robert Troup, a New York politician whose distaste for Chancellor Livingston was only equaled by his distaste for France, wrote Rufus King in 1801: "The Chancellor expects soon to embark for France. . . . His quitting the Court of Chancery is a comfortable relief to us! He is now so deaf, as a judge, he may be truly said to be deaf to the voice of justice! With all my bawling I could hardly make him hear me. At Buonaparte's table his situation must be delightful to himself and the company. One of his sons will be obliged constantly to sit alongside of him and cry out, Mr. Livingston—Mr. Livingston—Mr. Livingston! Citizen sans culottes speaks to you!"[125] Troup may have been happy to see Livingston removed to France, but Napoleon apparently didn't share his joy. Gouverneur Morris wrote the Chancellor that "the French thought it very extraordinary, that, to succeed a minister who could not *speak* their language, we have sent one who could not *hear* it."[126]

The new minister's entourage included his wife, his two daughters, and their husbands, who served as his secretaries. Not having any male heirs, the Chancellor did the next best thing: he married his daughters to Livingstons. The dynasty had found that such intra-family marriages were an excellent substitute for entail. Since it was no longer permitted to hand down the great estates intact to the eldest sons, the best way to keep the lands within the family was to marry within the family. So in the fifth and sixth generations there were ten marriages between or within the Clermont Livingstons and the Manor Livingstons. The Chancellor employed his two children in this consolidation process. Elizabeth Stevens Livingston, the eldest, was betrothed to Edward Philip Livingston, a grandson of Philip the Signer, and the son of Philip Philip, who had moved to the West Indies, built a sizable estate there, and become a member of the Jamaican Parliament. Edward Philip was to be a New York State senator and lieutenant governor but, being foreign-born, was ineligible for the office of governor.[127] The Chancellor's second daughter, Margaret Maria, was the beauty of the family. The German dramatic poet, Kotzebue, called her the youngest sister of Venus. She was married to Robert L. Livingston, a grandson of the Third Lord of the Manor.[128] The Chancellor's sons-in-law were to carry on his vast steamboat enterprises after his death, and he would have been proud of their close dealings and illiberal policies.

The culmination of the Chancellor's tenure as American minister to France was the Louisiana Purchase, that huge ceding of territory which embraces the present states of Arkansas, Missouri, Iowa, Nebraska, South Dakota, almost all of Oklahoma and Kansas, and large portions of North Dakota, Montana, Wyoming, Minnesota, Colorado, and Louisiana. "Other treaties of immense consequence have been signed by American representatives," wrote Henry Adams, ". . . but in none of those did the United States Government get so much for so little. The annexation of Louisiana was an event so portentous as to defy measurement; it gave a new face to politics, and ranked in historical importance next to the Declaration of Independence and the adoption of the Constitution—events of which it was the logical outcome; but as a matter of diplomacy it was unparalleled, because it cost almost nothing."[129] How much credit does Chancellor Livingston deserve for this action? The plan was Jefferson's. The decision was Napoleon's—born of necessity, for had he not sold the land to the United States, the British could have wrested it from him. Supporters of Monroe, who was sent to France at the last minute, give him some credit. But the hard work was Livingston's. It was he who knocked on Talleyrand's door day after day. He was "the American protagonist in the history of the Purchase."[130] And perhaps he was something more, thought John Quincy Adams. "The credit of the acquisition of Louisiana," said the Old Man Eloquent, "whether to be considered as a source of good or evil, is perhaps due to Robert R. Livingston more than to any other man."[131] "We have lived long," said Livingston after signing the treaty, "but this is the noblest work of our lives."[132] Thus ended the Chancellor's political career. (But he was still to be engaged in one more activity of immense consequence.) He was replaced in Paris by his brother-in-law John Armstrong, whose nomination had been saved from Senate rejection by the vote of the Vice-President. Armstrong's ministry was marked by "idleness and pique."[133]

The story of the steamboat in America is a tangled web of political, technical, and personal relationships among four men: Chancellor Robert R. Livingston, Robert Fulton, John Stevens, and Nicholas Roosevelt. A fifth man, Benjamin Latrobe, played a secondary role. Popular history, in sorting out the credit, has made Fulton the "inventor" of the steamboat; while Livingston's money, said Henry Adams, "gave immortality to Fulton."[134] Of the others, Stevens is remembered primarily for his work as a railroad pioneer; Latrobe as a great architect and designer of the United States Capitol; and Roosevelt is largely forgotten.

The five had a great deal in common: soaring imaginations, a capacity for great enthusiasms, the ability to leapfrog from one endeavor to another. As for mechanical and creative aptitudes, Fulton and Latrobe were clearly geniuses; Roosevelt was a competent professional; Stevens was an inspired amateur; Livingston was an experimenting dilettante.

Here were five men, goaded by the goddess of invention, who were seeking fame more than fortune. This alone should have assured their inability to resolve their differences. But their shifting associations and antagonisms were further complicated by family alliances: Fulton was to marry Livingston's cousin; Roosevelt was married to Latrobe's daughter; Livingston was married to Stevens' sister.

John Stevens was the third of his name and line in America.[135] His grandfather, the first John Stevens, was a quick-witted and personable real estate speculator who accumulated a fortune in landholdings, particularly in the Perth Amboy area. The second John Stevens married a daughter of James Alexander and became a Revolutionary politician, member of the Continental Congress, president of the New Jersey convention which ratified the federal Constitution, and the man primarily responsible for the first election of William Livingston as governor. The third John Stevens also tried his hand at politics. He was treasurer of New Jersey from 1777 to 1782, and as a result of his bookkeeping techniques it took years to unravel the finances of the state.[136] He also bought Hoboken, all 564 acres, for about $9000 when the land was confiscated from loyalist William Bayard. (The property was valued at more than a million dollars when Stevens died in 1838.) But he had too many interesting ideas to worry about developing his holdings. There was, for example, his proposal to build a tunnel of heavy waterproof leather between Manhattan and Long Island.[137] So he floated "through the world on a cloud of his own promissory notes."[138] He became intrigued with the steamboat experiments of Fitch and Rumsey, and turned to his brother-in-law for financial aid in entering this novel field. His sister Mary had married Chancellor Livingston. She was "a polite, sensible, well-bred woman," who had little interest in the flighty musings of her husband and brother, but who tried to keep them as amicably disposed toward each other as possible.[139]

The brothers-in-law brought Nicholas Roosevelt into the partnership. He was the son of a prosperous goldsmith and was acknowledged as the master engine builder in the United States. As a young man Roosevelt had experimented with paddle wheels for steamboat navigation. He now tried to interest Stevens and Livingston in the principle. But Livingston vetoed Roosevelt's idea. He considered himself more than merely the project's financier; as he had once told Joseph Priestley, "Mechanicks is my hobby horse."[140] Roosevelt let it be known that he detested know-it-all amateurs. Yet despite this friction the trio managed to constuct a craft that was capable of doing three miles an hour in still water. This wasn't good enough. Livingston had managed to lobby a bill through the New York legislature giving his combine a monopoly of the Hudson River if they were able to build a vessel that could go upstream at four miles an hour. The politicians had been amused by the Chancellor's science-fiction presumption and had gladly given in to his whim, for as Latrobe wrote, "the navigation by steam was thought to be on footing as to practicability as the navigation by Reindeer in the Chancellor's park."[141] At this point the Chancellor considered that the Livingston-Stevens-Roosevelt monopoly was ended (an interpretation open to legal question) and went off to Paris as the American minister.

In Paris Livingston made the acquaintance of Robert Fulton, son of an impoverished Pennsylvania farmer, who had come to Europe to study painting but had turned to less pacific pursuits—the invention of a submarine and torpedo. The diplomat was fascinated by Fulton's submarine, then considered inhuman by professional soldiers. When Sir Charles Blagden, secretary of the Royal Society in London, argued that "no civilized nation would consent to use it," Livingston replied that since modern wars were commercial wars the mass destruction of shipping by "plunging boats" would put an end to warfare.[142]

A new Hudson River monopoly was passed by the legislature under the prodding of the Chancellor's brother-in-law Thomas Tillotson. This time the exclusive rights were granted to Livingston and Fulton. John Stevens was given an opportunity to buy into the partnership but declined. He had his own steamboat plans and didn't wish to share the inventor's credit with Fulton. Moreover, he now felt that a state monopoly was unconstitutional. (It was an opinion that the Stevens family later altered when they formed a railroad monopoly in New Jersey with the Stocktons.) On August 17 and 18, 1807, the *Steamboat*—later rechristened the *Clermont*—successfully made its maiden voyage from New

York to Albany. The ungainly craft looked like a sawmill mounted on a scow and set on fire.

When the boat reached the Clermont landing, carrying a fashionable contingent of Livingston relatives, the Chancellor announced the engagement of Robert Fulton to his cousin Harriet, daughter of Walter Livingston of the Manor line. The Chancellor had prudently waited until Fulton's steamboat was a success; presumably it would have been inappropriate to give the hand of a Livingston to a failure. Fulton's biographer saw it as "a union influenced without doubt" by the fact that the bride-to-be was a Livingston.[143] But Latrobe found Harriet to be "a very learned lady, somewhat stricken . . . rich, elegant, spirited & able to manage any man."[144]

Fulton's steamboat was propelled by the paddle wheels that Livingston had once rejected. Those supporting Roosevelt's claim to the invention contend that the Chancellor recalled the suggestion and passed it on to Fulton. However, the historian of the steamboat, James Thomas Flexner, should have ended such speculation for all time. Fulton's role was not as an original thinker but as one who could weave all past work into a harmonious and successful conclusion. Others, including Roosevelt and Stevens, had made important contributions, but "popular history is correct: Robert Fulton was the inventor of the steamboat."[145]

The Chancellor set about to get monopoly rights for the steamboat in Ohio, Kentucky, Indiana, Tennessee, and Louisiana. He was only successful in Louisiana, where his brother Edward had become a political power. Meanwhile in New York the monopoly was being challenged on all sides, including attacks by John Stevens. The relations between the brothers-in-law were now "an odd mixture of personal affection and professional animosity."[146] A bitterness had also developed between Stevens and Fulton. Fulton accused Stevens of luring away the mechanics he had trained. If "one man moves from my shop, even by his own voluntary act," he wrote, "I shall instantly insist on all rights to which I am entitled in law and justice. . . ." Stevens promptly replied, "Your letter of this date is couched in terms so very offensive that I shall not have deemed it incumbent upon me to have returned an answer. . . ."[147] At the same time Roosevelt was pressing his claims through his father-in-law. Latrobe wrote his daughter, "Fulton I respect & love & believe him to be honest, tho' devoted to his interest. Of the Chancellor I have no good opinion."[148] Roosevelt was finally given the right to build a vessel for the Natchez–New Orleans trade, which was under the supervision of Edward Livingston. Latrobe also became involved as a steamboat builder at Pittsburgh. But Roosevelt and Latrobe soon found that they couldn't get along with Fulton. The Chancellor died in 1813, which effectively ended any chance of compromise between the Livingstons and Stevenses. John Stevens turned his steamboat interests over to his sons, for he now had a more pressing enthusiasm—the development of a steam engine for railroads. Fulton sold his share of the steamboat patent to the Chancellor's sons-in-law, who then refused his request for navigation rights on particular rivers. Fulton's bitterness ran over: ". . . till now [I] never requested a favor for my own relations. Now that I have requested it, it is refused for the reason that it is profitable. I did not make that a reason when I consented to the above grants to the Livingston family. . . ."[149] The issue of who controlled the steamboat was ultimately decided by the United States Supreme Court. It was an invention, said Napoleon, which "may change the face of the world." Yet for its developers this great breakthrough of the Industrial Revolution ended in squabbling and rancor.

The Livingstons' control of New York State ended in 1808 when the Chancellor's brother-in-law, Morgan Lewis, failed to win re-election as governor. Lewis had proved incapable of holding together a political force; the Chancellor had retired from politics; Edward was in exile; Brockholst Livingston, the only member of the family left with the toughness and stamina to become an effective leader, was removed from the scene by appointment to the United States Supreme Court. The final act of New York's first great political dynasty would be played far away in Louisiana.

Edward Livingston, the former New York mayor and district attorney, quickly established himself as a leading lawyer in New Orleans. One of his more interesting clients was Jean Lafitte, the handsome and ruthless pirate, who ran a smuggling enterprise of considerable size from the secluded islands of Barataria Bay. It was rumored that Livingston and John Grymes each received fees of $20,000 to defend Lafitte's brother Pierre, but that Grymes gambled away the entire $40,000 on his way back to New Orleans from Barataria.[150]

This unsavory association was to stand the United States in good stead when Jackson defended New Orleans in the War of 1812. Livingston's connections with the Lafitte brothers helped to convince the pirates that they should throw their support to the Americans, despite a lucrative offer from the British. Jackson had been a colleague of Livingston's in Congress, and he now appointed the attorney as his aide-de-camp. Livingston knew little of soldiering, but then Jackson knew little of composition. Livingston's task was to draft the general's orders and proclamations.

When Edward was twenty-four he had married Mary McEvers, the daughter of a New York merchant. The most vivid recollection of this "most distinguished belle" was when her ostrich-feather headdress caught fire at one of Martha Washington's Friday evening soirees, and the flames were extinguished by the President's aide-de-camp.[151] Mary died in 1801. In New Orleans Edward took as his second wife a lovely dark-eyed, oval-faced, nineteen-year-old widow, Louise D'Avezac Moreau. She was the daughter of a Santo Domingo planter who had been forced to flee the island during the Negro insurrection. At the time of their marriage Louise spoke no English.

At the battle of New Orleans Livingston secured the appointment of his brother-in-law, Auguste Genevieve Valentin D'Avezac, as judge advocate. D'Avezac was to become Livingston's trusted lieutenant in Louisiana politics, as well as one of New Orleans' greatest criminal lawyers, of whom it was said that "no client of his ever suffered capital punishment."[152]

Livingston never felt himself a Louisianan; he was always a displaced New Yorker who was simply in temporary residence at the place which provided him with the best opportunity to pay his vast debts. Yet it was Louisiana that gave him an opportunity for immortality. He was commissioned to write the penal code of the state. The result brought him immediate international fame, yet, ironically, the legislature refused to adopt the reforms. If it had done so, said a distinguished sociologist, Louisiana "would have been at least a century in advance of the rest of the world."[153] The proposed system, according to Victor Hugo, classed Livingston "among the men of this age who have deserved most and best of mankind." Jeremy Bentham urged Parliament to print the Livingstonian code for the guidance of the English nation. And the work of the lawgiver was hailed by the crowned heads of Russia, Sweden, and the Netherlands.[154]

Through his years in Louisiana, Livingston was a perennial and unsuccessful office-seeker. He was defeated for Congress in 1812, 1818, and 1820. Finally in 1823, now a slightly stoop-shouldered man of fifty-nine, Edward returned to Congress after a lapse of more than twenty-two years. Of those who had once been his colleagues, only John Randolph of Roanoke was left. They had been bitter antagonists. (Randolph once said of Livingston, "He shines and stinks like rotten mackerel by moonlight!"[155]) Yet they would share the distinction of being the only men to vote in both presidential elections that were thrown into the House of Representatives. Livingston had been a powerful figure in the 1801 election of Jefferson; in 1824, when the race was between John Quincy Adams and Jackson, he remained loyal to his old friend and general. But his figure hardly cast a shadow; Adams was elected on the first ballot.

During Livingston's next six years in the House and two in the Senate he was a devout Jacksonian. Only once did he veer from the party line. When President Jackson nominated "Black Horse Harry" Lee to be consul general to Algiers, Livingston refused to support the immoral Virginian. This almost perfect voting record was viewed with favor by the

President when it became necessary to reorganize the Cabinet in 1831. A surprised Livingston was picked to be the new Secretary of State. He wrote his devoted wife: "Here I am, in the second place in the United States—some say the first; in the place filled by Jefferson and Madison and Monroe, and by him who filled it before any of them, my brother; in the place gained by Clay at so great a sacrifice; in the very easy-chair of Adams; in the office which every politician looks to as the last step but one in the ladder of his ambition; in the very cell where the great magician [Van Buren], they say, brewed his spells. Here I am, without an effort, uncontrolled by any engagements, unfettered by any promise to party or to man; here I am!"[156]

But once there the old man had little effect on the Administration. His memory was beginning to fail; Jackson looked elsewhere for advice. "He is a polished scholar, an able writer, and a most excellent man," said the President, "but he knows nothing of mankind."[157] Only once did Livingston rise above his infirmities; Jackson called on his old ghostwriter of New Orleans to draft the Nullification Proclamation. "Let it receive your best flight of eloquence," demanded the President.[158] And Livingston composed for Jackson a hard-hitting warning to the secessionists of South Carolina; a message of eloquence.

In 1833 Livingston left the State Department to head the mission to France. His career would now exactly parallel his older brother's: congressman, Secretary of State, minister to France. John Randolph of Roanoke was delighted for Edward's "most able coadjutor," Louise: "*Dowdies,* dowdies won't do for European Courts—Paris especially," he wrote his former congressional colleague. "There and at London the character of the Minister's lady is almost as important as his own. It is the very place for her. There she would dazzle and charm; and surely the *salons* of Paris must have far greater attractions for her than the Yahoos of Washington."[159] Louise, with her charming French accent, had been able to blend successfully her worldly heritage with the tenets of the Methodist Church, to which she had been converted by her sister-in-law, Mrs. Freeborn Garrettson. In his old age Edward wrote his wife: "What have you done for thirty years past but direct me by your prudence from rash undertakings, and encourage me in every honorable and useful pursuit, and console me under afflictions that would have overwhelmed me, and made me relinquish every effort, if you had not been at my side to teach me to bear them? What I am, my dear Louise, I owe chiefly to you. . . ."[160]

Livingston was going to be united in Europe with his brother-in-law, Auguste D'Avezac, whom Jackson had appointed chargé d'affaires to the Netherlands in 1829, and who would hold the post under four presidents for a total of fifteen years. The thoughtful Jackson also gave an appointment as secretary to the French legation to Thomas Pennant Barton,

husband of the Livingstons' only child. The young man was a Philadel-
phian of excellent lineage and fastidious tastes, later to become one of
the nation's greatest bibliophiles.[161] Barton had had stiff competition for
the hand of the lovely Cora.* Josiah Quincy, reporting on a Washington
ball in 1826, wrote: "I was introduced to Miss Cora Livingston; and I
must be able to paint the rose to describe a lady who undoubtedly is the
greatest belle in the United States. In the first place, she is not handsome,—I mean not *transcendentally* handsome. She has a fine figure, a
pretty face, dances well, and dressed to admiration. It is the height of
the *ton* to be her admirer. . . ."[162]

The French mission had one paramount purpose—to secure payment
of a twenty-five-million-franc claim for depredations upon American shipping during the Napoleonic wars. Minister Livingston was tactful, firm,
persistent, and unavailing. Finally Jackson lost patience and sent a blunt
message to Congress urging reprisals. Now the Gallic pride was offended,
and Livingston's usefulness came to an end. He left the legation in the
care of his son-in-law and retired to Montgomery Place, the estate that his
sister had willed him. The widow of Richard Montgomery had spent a
long and lonely lifetime building a show place of waterfalls, glens, groves,
and ornamental gardens. But Edward had less than a year to enjoy his
retreat; he died in 1836.

The childless Bartons then moved into the house overlooking the Hudson, where Thomas spent his remaining thirty-three years personally
dusting his 16,000 books. In 1856 Josiah Quincy happened by Montgomery Place and was reintroduced to Cora after three decades. "I will not
describe the old lady, in cap and dress of studied simplicity," wrote the
gallant Bostonian. "My nap had lasted ten years longer than Rip Van
Winkle's and this was the penalty. . . . 'You would not have known me!'
said Mrs. Barton. I could only be silent."[163]

From the time that the brothers William and Philip went off to
Philadelphia in 1774 until Edward left the Senate in 1831 to become
Secretary of State, there had been seven Livingstons in the Congress.
This comprised the record of the dynasty. Thereafter there would be an
occasional officeholder in the family: a Livingston served two years as

---

* In 1825 Cora Livingston had been engaged to William Clarke Somerville
(1790–1826), a dashing and aristocratic Marylander. As a soldier of fortune
he had permanently impaired his health while fighting for Venezuelan independence. Returning to the United States, he purchased Stratford Hall, the
ancestral home of the hard-pressed Virginia Lees, from "Black Horse Harry"
Lee. Before he could make Cora its mistress, however, President John Quincy
Adams asked him to assume a delicate diplomatic assignment in Greece. The
wedding was postponed. Somerville died on the way to his post and was
buried in France by Lafayette. See Ethel Armes, *Stratford Hall, the Great
House of the Lees* (Richmond: Garrett & Massie, 1936), pp. 411–21.

Speaker of the New York Assembly; another was U.S. minister to Ecuador for a year.[164] But these were now hereditary sports. A great-grandson of the Chancellor, who kept a villa in Italy and passed his days studying genealogy and colonial history, decided to run for Congress in 1898—he was defeated by twenty-five votes.[165]

In the Revolutionary War generation there had been twenty-two Livingstons in New York—fifteen of whom held political office. Two generations later just five offices were held by the dynasty, although there were now forty-five Livingstons. By mid-nineteenth century there was only one Livingston in office.

Through the female lines alone—primarily by marrying into the Fish dynasty of New York and the Kean dynasty of New Jersey—did Livingston genes remain in the body politic.[166] As the family entered ante bellum America, to the extent that they participated in politics at all, it was merely to make pro forma contributions to the "right" party so as to assure that government would be safe for aristocracy.

The death of the dynasty was self-inflicted. They were not retired by the people; they retired from the people. As historian George Dangerfield put it, they did not wish "to condescend to the demands of popular politics." When Chancellor Livingston was asked why he left the political scene he replied, "I should find myself ill-calculated to take a lead among men rendered fastidious by too much courtship, to intrigue with little men, to carry measures & to hold out lures for the ambition of every scoundrel that had smoked & drank himself into the honorable station of village chieftain."[167] One by one the old safeguards had been removed: first their pocket borough was abolished; then property qualifications for voting were removed by the New York Constitution of 1821; a constitutional amendment in 1844 eliminated property qualifications for holding office; finally the state constitution of 1846 made all offices elective, including judgeships. Politics was no longer the game the Livingstons had played and loved.

So they retired to their country estates. (One hundred and fifty years after the founding of the Manor, one fourth of the dynasty lived in its shadow.) They married other Livingstons. (One fourth of the men of the Manor and Clermont lines in the fifth generation married within the family.) They had fewer children. (The median number of children per Livingston family dropped from nine in the third generation to two in the sixth generation.) Their income now came from investments rather than from entrepreneurial activities.[168] And from the high banks of the Hudson they looked down their noses at the rest of the world.

The dynasty had fought to reach the peak. The Livingstons may have forgotten the fight, or wished to forget some of the details. But of this they were sure: they were the aristocracy, and this was as it was meant to be. Gustavus Myers wrote that the family's motto was: "The Family

Should Always Derive Benefit."[169] Now, in the social and economic sense, the benefits had been derived and the job at hand was to maintain them. Once it had been necessary to have a large family to deploy in the economic and political wars. Now it was no longer necessary to place sons in strategic government positions. How many children were needed to clip coupons? Or perhaps, as one scholar suggests, "fewer children meant less danger of marriage outside the small approved circle."[170]

And besides—maintaining the status quo could be a full-time occupation. There was always some new group with social pretensions. In New York in the 1820s and 1830s it was the New Englanders. Wrote one Livingston to another, "You can abuse RC as much as you please for as soon as I discovered he was a Yankee I cut his acquaintance therefore you cannot say too much against him for I detest Yankees."[171] John P. Marquand, that chronicler of the elite Yankees' inhumanity to the world, would have smiled sardonically.

When the Union, the first gentlemen's club in New York, was founded in 1836, there were fourteen Livingstons among its charter members. When the Knickerbocker was founded in 1871, because the Union was not select enough, there were four Livingstons as charter members.

The Proper Livingston Male belonged to these clubs, as well as to the St. Nicholas Society (membership limited to those whose ancestors resided in New York prior to 1785) and the New York Genealogical and Biographical Society. He was married to a Livingston or, if one didn't happen to be available, to a member of one of the older New York families, most often the De Peysters. In rare cases he might have to go as far afield as the gentry of Baltimore or Philadelphia. He had two children. His money was invested in ancestral land and sound railroad stocks. He might not be a millionaire but was certainly worth half a million. He kept three homes: one in New York (Fifth Avenue); another in Dutchess County; and the third probably at Bar Harbor. He took no part in politics, neither was he a director of any eleemosynary institutions. The closest the dynasty came to producing another national political figure was Secretary of the Treasury Ogden Mills, whose mother was a Livingston.

The Proper Livingston Female had a profile very much like her brother. However, she was permitted to marry a minister or a doctor or a military officer—professions which her brother wouldn't think of entering; nor would he have married into such families.[172]

As the dynasty withdrew more and more into its own social shell, a typical Livingston, read an 1867 obituary, was one whose "ample fortune, derived from his ancestors, placed him beyond the necessity of labor of any kind, and his life was passed in pursuits, rural and agricultural, congenial to his tastes. . . ."[173] Each successive Livingston seemed to become more studied in his avoidance of productive activity, a trend which was finally carried to its ultimate conclusion in 1889, when on the death of one Robert E. Livingston the Poughkeepsie *Daily Eagle* announced that he had "never entered into any pursuits."[174] The obituary of a dynasty.

The Washburn Dynasty

> "Aim at the stars. If you don't hit any-
> thing, you'll have the satisfaction of see-
> ing your arrow go up and come back
> again."
>
> —Martha Washburn to her sons.[1]

THEY were the only family ever to send four brothers to the United
States Congress.

Even more amazingly, they represented four different states—Maine,
Illinois, Wisconsin, and Minnesota—and three of them served together in
the House of Representatives for a period of five years.*

For one long generation, from 1851 to 1895, it seemed to be true, as
their political enemy, Ignatius Donnelly, said, that in the remarkable
Washburn family "every young male . . . is born into the world with
'M.C.' franked across his broadest part."[2]

Yet this is only part of the saga of the seven sons of a bankrupt
Maine storekeeper who warned them that the only way to break a bundle
of sticks was to separate it. The sons lived by the axiom. While in Congress, Israel, Elihu (who spelled his surname with a final *e*) and Cadwallader shared the same house, and, in the words of able reporter
George Alfred Townsend, "They loved and strengthened each other
up."[3] It was generally felt that a district that was lucky enough to have
a Washburn congressman virtually got three representatives for the price
of one.[4]

When tight-pursed Elihu Washburne, who was known as "the Watch-

---

* On two other occasions there were three brothers in Congress at the same
time. Between 1825 and 1827 James Findlay (1770–1835) was a member
of the House of Representatives from Ohio, while his brother John (1766–
1838) served in the House from Pennsylvania and his brother William (1768–
1840) was a Pennsylvania senator. Then for four months in 1862–63 Maine
was represented by Samuel C. (1815–82) and Thomas A. D. Fessenden
(1826–68) in the House and William Pitt Fessenden (1806–69) in the Senate.

THE WASHBURN DYNASTY
(A Selective Genealogy)

Israel Washburn, Sr. (1784–1876)
Maine State legislator
m. Martha Benjamin (1792–1861)
(11 children; 1 d.y.)

Israel, Jr.
(1813–83)
HOUSE OF
REPRESENTATIVES
(Maine), GOVERNOR
(4 children)

Algernon Sidney
(1814–79)
Maine banker
(4 children; 2 d.y.)

Elihu Benjamin
(1816–87)
HOUSE OF
REPRESENTATIVES, (Illinois),
Secretary of State,
minister to France
(7 children; 2 d.y.)

Cadwallader Colden
(1818–82)
HOUSE OF REPRESENTATIVES
(Wisconsin), general,
GOVERNOR; millionaire
(2 children)

Charles Ames
(1822–89)
Minister to Paraguay
(3 children)

Samuel Benjamin
(1824–90)
Naval captain
(5 children; 3 d.y.)

William Drew
(1831–1912)
HOUSE OF REPRESENTATIVES
(Minnesota), SENATE,
millionaire
(9 children; 2 d.y.)

Stanley (1878-1950) Journalist

Cadwallader (1866-1965) Artist

William Drew (1863-1929) Minnesota legislator

Fanny (1852-1925) m. Charles Payson, minister to Denmark

Hempstead (1851-1918) Mayor of Chicago

Robert Charles (b. 1861) Washington State legislator

Charles Fox (1849-84) Minnesota legislator

John (1858-1919) Business executive

dog of the Treasury," let one of brother Cadwallader's appropriations bills slip through without objection, an observer noted, "The watchdog don't bark when one of the family goes by."[5]

Fiercely proud of each other, they were also fiercely united against an enemy. During a hassle on the floor of the House of Representatives in February 1858 Washburn of Wisconsin rushed to the defense of Washburne of Illinois. He grabbed his brother's attacker by the hair, but the hair turned out to be a wig and came off in Cadwallader's hands. "This incident was so funny," reported an eyewitness, "that they all stopped to laugh and the pause put an end to the riot. Cadwallader restored Barksdale's wig to him and in his excitement, Barksdale put it on wrongside foremost."[†] *Punch* of London commemorated the melee in verse,[6] and the incident was later much enlarged by a Washburn nephew who said, "They had several fights on the floor with ambitious cavaliers who wished to lick them, but as they were all giants, they generally got by."[7]

These "giants" ranged in height from five and a half feet upwards to five feet ten. But their achievements were of more herculean proportions: *Israel,* after ten years in Congress, became the two-term governor of Maine; *Algernon Sidney* was a Maine bank president; *Elihu* served in the House for eighteen years and then became Secretary of State and United States minister to France; *Cadwallader Colden* was a congressman for five terms, major general in the Union Army, governor of Wisconsin, and the first millionaire in the family; *Charles* was a gold miner, novelist, newspaper editor, inventor, and United States minister to Paraguay; *Samuel* was a merchant marine captain at twenty, and seriously wounded while commanding a Union gunboat during the battle at Fort Darling; *William Drew* spent six years in the House of Representatives, six years in the Senate, and became the dynasty's second millionaire.

It was not sufficient to say that the large family of Israel Washburn, Sr., was "poor." In recounting his early life for the benefit of his children, Elihu B. Washburne, then United States minister to France, wrote, "Our family was very, very poor."[8]

Father's country store had been attached by the sheriff in 1829 and everything that the law allowed was sold. A debt of twenty-five dollars

† The congressional rumble began when Laurence M. Keitt, a hot-tempered and often inebriated representative from South Carolina, called Grow of Pennsylvania a "black Republican puppy." Keitt was then knocked down; Barksdale of Tennessee grabbed Grow; Pottle of New York struck Barksdale, who believed he had been hit by Washburne of Illinois. For differing accounts of the fight, see O. O. Stealey, editor, *Twenty Years in the Press Gallery* (New York: Publishers Printing Co., 1906), p. viii, and Neil MacNeil, *Forge of Democracy, the House of Representatives* (New York: McKay, 1963), p. 309.

to one "Uncle Lovewell" was repaid by Elihu's working as a farm hand for five months. Father Washburn turned to farming on a Livermore, Maine, site that has been described as "so rocky it was difficult to find the soil."[9]

All the brothers were able to say, as Elihu did, "Witnessing the poverty and struggles of my parents, I determined to shift for myself. From the time I was fourteen I was not only not an expense to them, but my various little earnings went to help support the family."[10] The boys worked as store clerks, hired hands, and teachers. Elihu, after reading the autobiography of Ben Franklin, became an apprentice printer. In later years, when running for Congress, he would go into the offices of the county newspapers, pick up a composing stick, and set a few lines of type.

Among the sons there was usually only one good coat to go around, made from their own sheep and woven by their mother. This family coat was made tailless so as to get as much as possible out of a web of cloth. While an embarrassment to the boys, their mother reminded them, "It is far better to have brains in your head than tails in your coat."[11]

Poverty, however, was not a badge of dishonor. The Washburns were eminently respectable New Englanders, descended from John Washburn, who had come to the Plymouth Colony in 1631. Great-grandfather Washburn had been a member of the convention that wrote Massachusetts' first constitution in 1780; Grandfather Washburn had served in the Revolutionary Army. Even Father Washburn, the impoverished storekeeper, was considered a leading citizen of his town, a cheerful storyteller, who was four times elected to the state legislature. His brother Reuel had been a judge of probate, state senator, and had lost a contested election to Congress by five votes, although the family never conceded the defeat.[12]

But it was the mother who was the driving force of the family. Martha ("Patty") Benjamin, also of hearty New England stock, was a woman of courage and limitless ambition for her sons. Despite their straitened finances, she had a large house built; the old one, she determined, would not be good enough for her sons. Then as they reached manhood and left home, Mrs. Washburn instituted a simple ceremony: on the third finger of the left hand of the one who was leaving the homestead she placed a plain gold band.

The sons—as legislators, governors, and diplomats—wore Mother's ring all their lives.

When asked why her sons moved to different states, the proud mother answered, "No one state is big enough to hold them."[13]

The first to go west was Cadwallader. In 1839 he took the Erie Canal to Buffalo, boarded the steamer *Great Western* for Chicago, and then rode a horse to Davenport, Iowa. The voyage was financed by Sidney, who, the next year, made the same "traveling" loan to Elihu. Sidney had been selling goods over the counter in a Boston general store. He returned to Maine as a cashier in the Hallowell bank, and eventually rose to its presidency. Hallowell was then the principal port of entry and export for much of inland Maine; the head of its financial institution was a person of some importance in the state.[14] But in comparison to his brothers Sidney's was a modest success: he was the one who stayed in the background, helped the others along, and took satisfaction in their achievements.

On Cadwallader's advice, Elihu settled in Galena, Illinois, population 4000. The men from the Fever River lead mines lived in the surrounding villages of Blackleg, Red Dog, Bunkum, Hard Scrabble, Fair Play, Dog Town, and New Diggings. It was a profitable place for a young lawyer. "The people are a litigious set," said Elihu.[15]

Meanwhile, Cadwallader had moved on to Mineral Point, Wisconsin, to become a timberlands speculator and co-owner of the bank. By 1856 his holdings were valued at half a million dollars. The pace was too fast for his partner, Cyrus Woodman, who took his profits and went off to Europe so that his children could learn foreign languages. But Cadwallader plunged on, weathering one financial crisis after another, often with a timely loan from Elihu, who insisted on high interest rates for the good of his brother's soul. "I don't believe you would be happy," wrote Elihu to Cadwallader, "unless you could buy the whole world and give your note for it."[16] Cadwallader's investments reached across into Minnesota. At the falls of St. Anthony he became an owner of the Minneapolis Mill Company, which controlled the water power on the west side of the falls. William Drew, the youngest brother, arrived in Minneapolis in 1857 and was made secretary of the company.

Samuel had gone to sea in 1842 and was now sailing the Boston–Liverpool and Boston–New Orleans routes. Israel entered the Maine legislature the same year. And in 1844, with aid from his brothers, Charles entered Bowdoin College. After graduation he took the three months' trip around Cape Horn to California. The new forty-niner, together with another young man named Leland Stanford, headed for the mother lode.

By mid-century the Washburn brothers spanned the continent.

In December of the Great Secession Winter, Congressman Israel Washburn Jr., was in Washington. He was packing to return to Maine, having been elected governor, and his close friend Senator Seward was staying with him. The house guest invited Congressman Charles Francis Adams and his son Henry to dinner at Washburn's. "Israel was as usual," reported Henry Adams, "ugly as the very devil, but good-humored and nervous and kindhearted as ever. . . ."[17]

At the time Israel was forty-seven, the eldest of seven sons and three daughters.‡ He was born, as were all the Washburn children, at the house in Livermore that had been built by the father of Hannibal Hamlin, the Vice-President-elect. (Years later Hamlin told a Livermore audience that "this probably accounts for the distinction of the [Washburn] sons." The remark was received with "great laughter" by the home-town crowd.[18])

Being short, nearsighted, and with a body too large for his legs, young Israel was ill suited for manual labor. In the struggling Washburn family it fell to his lot to work as a store clerk. Later, unable to afford a college education, he studied law with Reuel Washburn, and undoubtedly also learned a great deal about politics from his uncle, who was to die at age eighty-five after delivering a vigorous speech at the town meeting.§

Now, after ten years, Israel was closing a distinguished congressional career. When he entered the House in 1851 he proclaimed himself "fiercely liberal and 'conscience.'" A few hours after the passage of the Kansas-Nebraska Bill in 1854 the dedicated anti-slavery congressman called thirty of his colleagues to a meeting to discuss the formation of a new political party. The session did not stake a claim for Israel as the founder of the Republican Party—earlier meetings had been held at Ripon, Jackson, and elsewhere—but the Washburn meeting was the first attended by important national leaders. As such, Israel Washburn earned a place as one of the major organizers of the new party.

His two one-year terms as governor of Maine were measurably successful. He was in office during the early stages of the Civil War, and his main task was to raise, equip, and transport troops. Nearly 50,000 enlisted.

Shortly after his term expired in 1863, President Lincoln appointed him collector of the port of Portland. As governor he had received $1500 a year; his new part-time federal post paid $6000, as well as certain collection fees and considerable patronage. Israel held the lucrative position until 1877 when he openly considered starting a newspaper in

‡ The three Washburn sisters were: *Martha Benjamin Washburn* (b. 1820), married Captain Charles L. Stephenson, five children; *Mary Benjamin Washburn* (1825–67), married Gustavus A. Buffum, five children, lived in Missouri; *Caroline Washburn* (b. 1833), married Dr. Freeland S. Holmes, who died while serving as a Union surgeon during the Civil War, two children. The widow Holmes then looked after her blind father in Livermore and later kept house for her brother Cadwallader.

§ Reuel Washburn had a son Ganem who served in the Wisconsin State Senate, 1859–60, and a granddaughter Clara who married Charles Henry Morgan (1842–1912), a five-term congressman from Missouri.

opposition to James G. Blaine, with whom he had been sparring for years.¶ The contemplation of such a venture ended his service with the federal government.

He was then offered the presidency of Tufts College, but declined. Tufts had been founded in 1847 as a means of educating the sons of Universalists without danger of other denominational influences, and away from the worldly temptations of Boston. As a devout Universalist, Israel had been active in the college's management.

Israel chose instead to become president of the Rumford Falls Railroad, a line of thirty miles running from Mechanic Falls to Canton. He had long been interested in railroading, and while in Congress his pet project was a proposed line from New York to White Haven, Nova Scotia. As early as 1873 he had urged a direct railroad from Minneapolis to the East via Sault Sainte Marie. William Drew Washburn would start to build it in 1885, two years after his brother Israel's death.

Three years younger than Israel, Elihu Benjamin Washburne was the political sparkplug of the dynasty. His eighteen years in Congress earned him the honorific, "Father of the House." And the power deriving from his congressional seniority was only exceeded by that power whose source was his intimacy with two presidents, Lincoln and Grant. Washburne had been Lincoln's campaign biographer as well as Grant's sponsor during the Civil War. As President, Grant gave to Washburne the highest tribute that was his to confer—the office of Secretary of State. Yet it was friendship for Grant that may have denied Washburne the Republican presidential nomination in 1880.

While the brothers probably most honored Israel, the eldest, it was from Elihu that most political favors flowed. When Cadwallader left Congress to organize a regiment of cavalry, it was Elihu, chairman of the House Appropriations Committee, who assured that it would be the best equipped in the Union Army. Then Elihu asked Grant to put Cadwallader on his staff; the general promptly complied.[19] Lincoln first announced his candidacy for a second term in a letter to Elihu, and, not without significance, the President tendered the collectorship of Portland to Israel at the same time.[20] Elihu also got Charles a job in the Federal Land Office when he graduated from college, and may have later influenced Lincoln's decision to make him minister to Paraguay.[21]

¶ Blaine, who generally avoids unkind personal remarks in his autobiography, twice pays glowing tributes to Elihu B. Washburne ("courageous, faithful representative, intelligent in all his actions . . ."), but dismisses Israel as "impulsive, energetic, devoted to the cause of the Union. . . ." See James G. Blaine, *Twenty Years of Congress* (Norwich, Conn.: Henry Bill Publishing Co., 1884), Vol. I, pp. 305 and 329; Vol. II, p. 424.

There were also brothers-in-law to be taken care of—his sisters' husbands and his wife's brothers. One instance of Elihu's generosity, to the husband of his sister Martha, shows that the recipient had no idea of what he had been offered. Wrote Charles L. Stephenson, "I am obliged to you in offering to procure for me the office of supervising inspector for this district. . . . In the meantime I wish you would send me the law and instructions upon the subject that I may learn something of the duties of the office."[22]

In the Washburn family, Elihu was always running political interference. When William Drew considered opposing Congressman Ignatius Donnelly in 1868, it was Elihu who attempted to soften the opposition by charging that Donnelly had left Philadelphia "under suspicious circumstances," had changed his name, was a political turncoat, an "office-beggar," a coward, and a liar.[23]

Washburne's influence with Lincoln and Grant was partly good luck: all three were from Illinois. But most credit goes to Elihu's political instincts—his ability to spot a winner. He had known Lincoln well since the winter of 1843; by 1847 he was calling him "Old Abe," although Lincoln was then only thirty-six. He was a fervent Lincoln supporter at the 1860 convention,* and later wrote his campaign biography, which one scholar feels did much to assure the presidential victory.[24] When the President-elect was smuggled into Washington in March, Washburne was the only one waiting at the station to meet him; when Lincoln died, Washburne was a pallbearer.

Lincoln and Washburne had fought the political wars together; they were mutually indebted, although once Lincoln reached the White House the obligations fell more to the congressman. But with Grant and Washburne the obligations were differently distributed.

When Elihu first met Grant in May 1861 the future President was a clerk in his father's Galena leather store. It was Congressman Washburne who got Grant an appointment as a colonel in the 21st Illinois Volunteers; who lobbied him through the grades of brigadier general, major general, and lieutenant general, and who was his defender after Shiloh.[25] An anonymous letter to the President complaining about Grant's drinking habits was automatically bucked to his congressional sponsor, with the marginal notation, "General Grant was appointed chiefly on the recommendation of Hon. E. B. Washburne—Perhaps we should consult him."[26] (No disciplinary action was taken.)

* The 1860 Republican Convention caused a fleeting disarray among the Washburn brothers. Elihu was for Lincoln, Cadwallader and Israel were for Seward, although Israel was ready to accept William Pitt Fessenden as a compromise candidate. When Lincoln finally captured the nomination Elihu wrote Cadwallader: "You made a fool of yourself." Joseph Schafer, "Washburniana," *Wisconsin Magazine of History*, XIV, No. 3 (March 1931), p. 315.

These obligations were gratefully recorded in the general's letters to Washburne.[27] The congressman was not unaware that he had hitched his wagon to a star and that he would one day recoup his political investment with interest compounded.†

At Appomattox Washburne placed himself strategically at Grant's side. (And the inkstand that Grant and Lee dipped their pens into was presented to Israel Washburn, Sr.)[28] On election night 1868, Grant waited in the library of the Washburne home for the returns that would make him President.

The nation wondered what manner of man was this Washburne, the kingmaker.

"The model is Yankee," wrote a newspaperman, "but the cargo is Western. He is broad-shouldered, good-bellied. . . . He leaves a plump impression upon your mind." Added the New York *Tribune*, "His hair was iron gray, worn long, half rolled under at the ends like a Southerner's. . . ."[29]

He was a politician first and foremost. (Eighteen years after his first election to Congress he could recall from memory the vote in all eight counties of his district.) And as a politician Washburne was a Radical Republican. (He gave as his opinion of Andrew Johnson: "In my judgment the safety of the country, the cause of good government, the preservation of Constitutional right and public liberty, depend upon the prompt impeachment of the President of the United States."[30]) But his major reputation had been made as the zealous guardian of the public's money, the ever alert foe of government waste and extravagance. To some, such as Secretary of the Navy Gideon Welles, his was a "mock economy."[31] And Ignatius Donnelly, no friend of the Washburns, said that if Elihu ever reached heaven "he would harangue the assembled hosts, cherubim and seraphim, angels and archangels, with insinuations of dishonesty, would plead for economy, and would have the wheels of the universe stopped because they consumed too much grease."[32]

† Grant and Washburne also engaged in some joint financial investments through the good offices of Jay Cooke, which were apparently profitable for all concerned. Grant writes Washburne, October 8, 1865: "On arrival I found your letter relative to our Jay Cook [sic] . . . speculation. I saw Cook. He says that he took advantage of our confidence in him and changed our speculation so that we will make about $25,000 to close out now. I said close." Another letter from Grant on October 28, 1865, indicates that there were also some minor losses. Both letters are in the Hempstead Washburne II Collection (transcripts in the possession of Thomas D. Washburne of Baltimore). Most of the Grant-Washburne correspondence was published by James Grant Wilson, editor, *General Grant's Letters to a Friend, 1861–1880* (New York & Boston: T. Y. Crowell, 1897). However the two letters referring to the Jay Cooke speculations are omitted.

Grant's reward to Washburne was the office of Secretary of State. Regardless of politics, it was hailed as an atrocious appointment. Elihu may have had qualifications for Treasury or Interior, but he had neither experience nor interest in foreign affairs. Gideon Welles shook his head in disbelief and wrote in his diary: "Jefferson is the first; Washburne is the last."[33] But Elihu lasted only five days. He was sworn in on March 5 and resigned on March 10. Grant then made him U.S. minister to France.

The most authoritative version of the quick shift was that Washburne's plan had been to go to France with the prestige which a nomination as Secretary of State would give him. Wrote Senator Fessenden: "Whoever heard before of a man nominated Secretary of State merely as a compliment?"[34] Washburne's choice of posts was motivated by two factors: his wife's desires (she being of French descent‡) and his precarious health. However even this diplomatic demotion came as cold comfort to many. He "goes as Minister to France, a post for which he may have some qualifications," commented the *Nation*, "but what they are it would be difficult to say."[35] Yet Washburne remained at his post for eight and a half years, longer than any other American in history, and was to be universally hailed as his country's greatest diplomat in France since Benjamin Franklin.

Instead of finding "quiet and repose," as he had hoped, he was "plunged into the most terrible events of the century."[36] For Washburne's years in France coincided with the Franco-Prussian War, the siege of Paris, and the Commune. He was to be the only diplomat to remain in Paris throughout the hostilities (a precedent he established for American ambassadors in 1916 and 1940); he became the only channel of communications between Bismarck and the French government; he would assume diplomatic responsibility for "half of the nationalities of the earth," while supervising relief to 30,000 persons and successfully protecting millions of dollars of abandoned American property. Even his strongest supporters were amazed by his skill and courage; his numerous detractors were flabbergasted. By the time Washburne returned home he was considered a potential presidential nominee.

Minister Washburne's tour of duty began serenely enough with an imperial dinner in his honor at the Tuileries. It was to be the last state dinner for Napoleon III and Eugénie. The French were about to lose a devastating war; Paris would be under siege for a hundred and thirty-

‡ In 1845 Washburne married Adele Gratiot (1826–87), "the first white child born in Galena." She was the granddaughter of Charles Gratiot (1752–1817), a Frenchman who came to the Illinois region in 1777, became a famous fur trader and associate of the first John Jacob Astor, and performed important services for General George Rogers Clark during the American Revolution. Her maternal uncle was Edward Hampstead (1780–1817), first delegate from the Territory of Missouri to the U. S. Congress.

two days, and under bombardment for twenty-two days. Washburne was the only diplomat from a major power to remain at his post in the capital. On the thirty-fourth day of the siege fresh meat was rationed to one-sixteenth of a pound per day, but was not available. "The magnificent blooded steed of the Rothschilds by the side of the old plug of the cabman" went to the slaughterhouse. Mule meat, at two dollars a pound in gold, was considered superior to horse meat. Washburne assured the Swiss minister that he would not starve; the Swiss, who apparently had a sense of humor, answered, "*Neigh.*" Butcher shops were stocked with cats, rats, and dogs. On the sixty-sixth day of the siege Washburne wrote in his diary: "The new quotations for today . . . for cats: a common cat, eight francs; a Thomas cat, ten francs; for rats, a common rat, two francs; a long-tailed rat, two francs and a half; for dogs, a cur of low degree, two francs a pound; for a fat dog, two and a half francs." A newspaper cartoonist, illustrating the danger of eating rodents, pictured a cat jumping down a man's throat after a rat.[37]

But Elihu had concerns other than diet. At the request of Count Bismarck he assumed responsibility for the Prussian property and lives in the enemy capital. He worked twelve to eighteen hours a day issuing visas to those who wished to return home, giving money to starving refugees, and getting them out of prison. The South American republics asked the same favor of him. Even Rumanian students were put in his charge. On some mornings three thousand persons waited to see him; Paris police held back the crowd.

In the beleaguered city Washburne's diplomatic bag was the only contact with the outside world. The French Foreign Minister got what news he could via pigeon, while Elihu received English and American newspapers. The legation was filled with news-hungry reporters, but, by agreement with Bismarck, Washburne could give no information. A London correspondent in Paris wrote, "His very looks are commented on. 'We saw him today,' says an evening paper. 'He smiled. Good sign. Our victory must be overwhelming.'" When his porter was offered a thousand-franc bribe for the latest London paper, Washburne concluded that "it is too much for me to have the news for two millions of people, and I don't care to bear the burden. . . . I have therefore written Bismarck that I will have no more London newspapers sent to me."[38]

During the Commune, which followed the Franco-Prussian War, Washburne again remained in Paris, the only member of the diplomatic corps to do so. He once more protected American property, and unsuccessfully negotiated with the Reds to spare the life of the Archbishop of Paris. On one occasion his own life was in danger when a shell struck the embassy, missing him by twenty feet.

By the end of the two wars the "good-bellied" diplomat was seventeen pounds lighter and had earned the respect of the world. Said Secretary of State Hamilton Fish, "Washburne is entitled to all the honor his friends may wish to confer upon him. . . . No compliment can be paid him that I would not join in."[39]

There was some reason to believe that the honor would be the 1880 Republican presidential nomination. Hayes had stated at the outset of term that he would not be a candidate for re-election. The office was up for grabs. As a candidate Washburne would have several advantages: he had avoided the scandals of the Grant Administration, having declined the Secretary of Treasury portfolio in 1874 to remain in France, and his work in Paris had made him immensely popular with German-Americans and Catholics. But Grant wanted a third term and Washburne would not announce his candidacy in opposition to his old friend. Without having an avowed candidate, Elihu's supporters were helpless. On the thirty-sixth ballot the nomination went to James Garfield.§ Grant held that Washburne's support had been halfhearted and had cost him the nomination. The former President never spoke to Elihu again, and his son was reported to have called Washburne a liar and a fraud.[40]

Elihu Washburne then retired to Chicago to write his recollections of eight and a half years in France.

Charles Washburn, the brother who went to California with the forty-niners, was the writer in the family. He stayed in the mother lode only long enough to stake himself to a San Francisco newspaper.

As proprietor of the *Alta California* and then the *Daily Times*, he followed the political line set down by his brothers in Washington—strongly Republican and opposed to slavery. For his efforts he received a harmless flesh wound from a Southerner who challenged his opinions and his right to hold them.

He also wrote less dangerous stuff for a small monthly magazine, the *Pioneer*, under such pen names as Oliver Outcast, Peregrine Pilgrim, and Peter Plunkett. In 1861 his first novel, *Philip Thaxter*, was published. It tells the story of an upstanding New Englander who goes to California where he embarks "on the sea of dissipation and sin" as he rushes "headlong into anything that promises gold and excitement."[41] The book ends when his faithful wife finds him and they live happily ever after on a ranch that he won at faro from a Mexican.

A second novel, *Gomery of Montgomery*, in two volumes, appeared in 1865. It chronicles three generations of a New England family, the Gomerys, also ending happily when Randolph Gault, alias Joe Pumagin, proves that Freeborn Gomery was cheated out of his property by the

§ Although the nomination for the vice-presidency was a mere formality, with Chester Arthur having been decided upon as the candidate as a means of healing the Republican split in New York, Washburne still received 193 complimentary votes.

wily Seth Mettlar and his attorney Mr. Dextrous, and Freeborn's son
Walter is peacefully interred in native soil after having been lynched
by a Southern mob for engineering the escape of "more'n a hundred of
our niggers."[42] (Neither *Gomery* nor *Philip Thaxter* sold very well; both
barely paying for their expenses.)

The editor-novelist was a Republican presidential elector in 1860, and
while carrying California's returns to Washington he also brought along
his own application for collector of the port of San Francisco. Lincoln
did not favorably consider the office-seeker, because, in the opinion of
Charles's daughter, "he feared another Washburn appointed to what was
then a very important post would cause disapproval."[43] Instead the
President gave Charles a consolation prize: the post of American minister to Paraguay.

Charles's experience in Paraguay reads like the plot of one of his
novels. For various reasons he was continually in a wrangle with the
United States Navy. The natives were no more friendly. Paraguayan
dictator Francisco Salano Lopez was under the influence of his mistress,
the Irish-born Parisian courtesan Madame Lynch, who took an instant
dislike to Washburn. But Lopez also wished to wed the second daughter
of the Emperor of Brazil, was rejected, and declared war on his neighbor. Charges were trumped up against Washburn, including an alleged
plot "to kill off the soldiers of the Republic by poisoning the wine in
the public storehouses."[44] (There was no wine in the public storehouses.)
A U.S. gunboat finally got Charles out of the country, but two members
of his legation were captured and tortured. One of them, Porter Bliss,
saved his life by writing a biography of Washburn which was sufficiently
libelous to please Lopez. Like Penelope—weaving by day, unweaving by
night—Bliss made deliberate errors in his manuscript and prolonged his
life while correcting the proofs. His scheme worked and he was rescued
as "the last sheet of manuscript had but just passed from his hands."[45]

The lifesaving book, *Historia Secreta de la Misión del Cuidadano
Norte Americano Charles A. Washburn cerca del Gobierno de la Repúb-
lica del Paraguay*, contained such imaginative nonsense as that Washburn
suffered from "an organic infirmity known in the profession by the
scientific name of Kleptomania," and had been kicked out of college for
stealing silver spoons from the table of the academic commons.[46] Charles
was very amused, but some people took it at face value. On returning
to the United States his conduct was investigated by the House Committee on Foreign Affairs. Then, according to his daughter, "his influential brothers came up like a phalanx of protection at his back," and
Washburn was completely exonerated.[47]

There were similarities between the assignments of the two Washburn
envoys. Charles in Asunción and Elihu in Paris shared the common experiences of neutralist diplomats in wartime—safeguarding property,

protecting refugees, maintaining lines of communication, personal dangers. Yet their tours abroad were vastly different. Charles's memoirs, in two volumes, *The History of Paraguay, with Notes of Personal Observations, and Reminiscences of Diplomacy under Difficulties,* could be a comic opera version of Elihu's memoirs, in two volumes, *Recollections of a Minister to France.* There is the difference between *la belle France* and Paraguay, "an insignificant little state, scarcely known beyond South America"; the difference between the Prussian military might and the Brazilians, who had attained "perfection . . . in the art of carrying on war without exposing themselves to danger"; and the difference between European statesmen and the dictator Lopez, "a wretch so vile, cowardly, and cruel that all history could not show his parallel."[48] In the end Elihu returned home with highest honor; Charles barely escaped with his life, and returned to a congressional investigation.

After his seven unhappy years as a diplomat Charles went back to writing—publishing his book on Paraguay and volumes on electoral reforms and graduated taxation. He also invented a typewriter, "Washburn's Typeograph," which was sold to the Remington Company. The machine had no capital letters and no margin lock, so that, as his daughter explained, "You could go on hammering the keys, and the effort of the mechanism to pass an impassable point would bend the type badly."[49]

It was proposed that Washburn, Crosby and Company, the giant flour-milling concern in Minneapolis, should adopt a new logotype. The designer brought Crosby his idea—a crescent with the first and last letters smaller than those in the middle. "It will never do," said Crosby. "You might as well spell God with a small g, as Washburn with a small w."[50] The Washburn that he referred to was Cadwallader Colden.

This Washburn brother, who had been the first to go west, made a fortune in Wisconsin timber speculations and increased it manyfold in Minnesota flour milling. His character was brusque and unbending. He would never be called representative of the people, nor did he ever make an effort to curry political favor. Yet he served five terms in the House of Representatives and was governor of Wisconsin for two years.

Two years younger than Elihu, and the best looking of the brothers, with deep-set, penetrating eyes and a firm jaw, Cadwallader was part of the prewar complement of Washburns in Congress. He left Washington in 1861, with the blessings of his brothers, to recruit a cavalry regiment. While Elihu's influence hardly retarded his rapid rise to major general, he was nevertheless a brave officer whom Grant credits with his success in getting into the Yazoo Pass.[51] And on November 29, 1863, with 2800 troops, Cadwallader compelled the Confederates to evacuate

Fort Esperanza, Texas, in an engagement that "gave the union forces control of the entire coast of Texas from Matagorda Bay to the Rio Grande."[52]

Returning to Congress for another two terms after the war, Cadwallader left little impact on national affairs. He led the opposition to the purchase of Alaska and championed state ownership of the postal telegraph system.¶ The latter proposal was opposed by the newspaper industry, which feared it would mean a rate increase.

His two years as governor, from 1872 to 1874, further proved that he lacked the politician's instinct for survival. By putting through a liquor control law, with a heavy bond for saloonkeepers and stiff penalties for drunkenness, he assured the disaffection of Wisconsin's large German population and defeat at the polls. "While his public career may not have been especially brilliant," said his friend General Atwood, "it was able, practical and substantially useful to the country."[53]

But Cadwallader did make a major contribution to the country, although it was not political. In Belgium he found machinery that was capable of taking the hard spring wheat, easily raised in Wisconsin and Minnesota, and turning it into a flour that was acceptable to the American consumer. His product was awarded the first gold medal ever given to a non-European country—thus inspiring his brand name, "Gold Medal Flour." Washburn's vision was followed by broad prairies of wheat.

When he died in 1882 he was the largest single owner of mill property in the world. His estate was valued at between two and three million dollars. Large bequests went to charity, and a fund of nearly $200,000 was left for the care of his insane wife, but there was still some $850,000 to be divided among his two daughters and his brothers and sisters. The daughters contested the will in the Wisconsin courts, charging that their father had been unduly influenced by his brothers.[54] There was also litigation between the C. C. Washburn Flouring Mills and the Washburn, Crosby Company—the Washburn who owned the mills having different interests from the Washburns who leased them. Cadwallader's legacy turned out to be a bitter conclusion to the lifelong story of seven brothers who "loved and strengthened each other up."

¶ Announced Cadwallader to the House of Representatives: "Let the government buy out the lines, transfer the management to the post office department, and reduce at once the cost of telegraphing to a uniform rate, for any distance to twenty cents for twenty words, and you will bring blessings and benefits to millions of our people who have hitherto been deprived of the use of the telegraph." Quoted in David Atwood, *Memorial Addresses on the Life and Character of Hon. C. C. Washburn* (Madison, Wis.: D. Atwood, 1883), pp. 12–13.

The youngest brother, William Drew Washburn, was in temperament and achievement very much like Cadwallader. He would carry forward the industrial empire that his brother had begun, building the railroads that would take the wheat to the markets of the world—the Minneapolis and St. Louis to the South; the Minneapolis, Sault Sainte Marie to the East. Their accomplishments, taken together, comprised a notable chapter in the Northwest expansion.

He too would have a long career in politics—eight years in the Minnesota legislature, six in the U. S. House of Representatives, six in the Senate—but it was not particularly productive. "Washburn was no politician," said a friend. "He did not like to travel from town to town, sleep and eat in dirty hotels and hob-nob with local bosses."[55] The one word that best described him was "aristocrat." And this image was heightened when he built an enormous home in Minneapolis, situated in the middle of ten manicured acres. (He made just one mistake in its construction, reminisced a son. He installed an elevator run by water which emptied all the tanks after a trip to the top floor.)[56]

Twenty-eight years after his oldest brother's first election to the House of Representatives, William Drew Washburn followed him to Washington. It was the famous "brass kettle" campaign of 1878—the brass kettle being the object with which the monopolistic Minneapolis Millers Association graded wheat. In the hands of demagogic Ignatius Donnelly, the Greenback Party candidate, this small cylindrical vessel became the symbol of the farmers' discontent. Moreover, Washburn, his Republican opponent, was both miller and railroad owner. (Later the Washington Gridiron Club would call him "the Flour of the Senate.")[57]

Washburn's election was contested by Donnelly, who charged bribery, illegal voting, and intimidation of voters. The investigation of the allegations was complicated by a mysterious letter to the congressional committee chairman. "If you will keep Washburn in his seat, in spite of the Democrats," read the anonymous note, "we will pay Mrs. S. [the chairman's wife] $5,000. Get the thing squashed." After extensive hearings, the committee's unanimous opinion was that the bribe had been authored by one of Donnelly's own counsel.[58] Washburn did keep his seat, and was twice re-elected.* In Washington he moved his large family into a house on Eye Street that had been formerly occupied by Secretary of State Frelinghuysen, and fought tenaciously for appropriations to arrest the spring flooding of the Mississippi.

Election to the United States Senate had been a long-cherished ambition in the Washburn family. Israel had failed in three attempts, Elihu

* Donnelly then temporarily retired to literary pursuits, publishing a 998-page volume, *The Great Cryptogram*, in which, by decoding Shakespeare's plays, he concluded that they had been written by Francis Bacon.

and Cadwallader twice each. Finally in 1889, as the last national act
of the dynasty, William Drew was elected to a full six-year term. As a
senator his one major act was to cast the deciding vote against Henry
Cabot Lodge's Force Bill. This so angered President Harrison that he
cut off Washburn's patronage for two years.[59]

It was expected that Washburn would be re-elected in 1895, since
he had received the endorsement of the Republican Convention. But
five days before the state legislature met, popular Knute Nelson repudiated his pledge to the senator and announced his own candidacy.
The Norwegian-born governor was easily elected, while Washburn
charged his defeat was "honeycombed with treachery," brought about
by "a shameless use of money . . . [and] the outrageous manipulation
of state patronage."[60]

At the 1900 Republican Convention Washburn was chosen by his
state as its favorite son for the vice-presidential nomination. However,
after learning of efforts to draft Theodore Roosevelt, whom he greatly
admired, he withdrew in favor of the Rough Rider.[61]

Of the fourth Washburn congressman's career, the state historian of
Minnesota commented, "He had been loyal to his party, but not ser-
vile."[62]

The next generation of Washburns, the ninth in America, produced
some interesting characters: a dashing war correspondent, a well-known
artist, a business leader, several capable local politicians. But it was
chiefly notable for failing to approach the achievements of its remarkable
fathers.

The seven famous Washburn brothers had thirty-four children, nine
of whom died at an early age. Of those who reached adulthood, fourteen were males.

One of Cadwallader's daughters married Charles Payson, a U.S. minister to Denmark and an exceptionally able Assistant Secretary of State,
who was removed from office by James G. Blaine to make room for
his son.[63]

Algernon Sidney, the Maine bank president who had staked his
brothers to their starts in the Middle West, had a son John who went
to Minnesota in 1880 and, at the time of his death in 1919, was chairman
of the board of Washburn, Crosby, and director of a host of other
milling, railroad, and financial institutions.[64]

Most flamboyant of the generation was Stanley, youngest of Senator
William Drew Washburn's nine children. Between 1904 and 1917 he
reported on a hundred battles and three wars for the Chicago *Daily
News, Collier's Weekly,* and *The Times* of London. He was with Baron
Nogi when the old Samurai captured Port Arthur in the Russo-Japanese

War; he covered the Russian Revolution of 1905; he was with the French at Verdun, on the Russian front in 1914 and 1915, and attached to the Rumanian army in 1916. True to the daredevil tradition of Richard Harding Davis, young Washburn traveled the world with his saddle, for "on a hurry call that may mean days of riding . . . [it could make] all the difference between success and failure."[65] He wrote five books on his war experiences and two on his explorations in western Canada.[66]†

Stanley's older brother Cadwallader was stricken with spinal meningitis at the age of five, which deprived him of hearing and speech, and later prompted the *Art Digest* to write, "It is a recognized fact, physiologically, that when one of the senses is impaired the others become keener in perception as a compensation."[67] One critic would call him "the world's greatest etcher."[68]

After graduating from Gallaudet College in Washington, Cadwallader studied architecture at M.I.T., painting at the New York Art Students' League, and in Madrid and Paris. His work, which turned from purely architectural pictorialization to impressionism, is remarkable for its varied subject matter. During his long life he literally traveled the seven seas in search of material to capture on his copper plates. His etchings include the gardens of Kyoto, death in a Mexican bull ring, the breezes of the Riviera, herdsmen of Tunisia, South Pacific cannibals, Siamese temples, Mallorcan smugglers, insects of the Marquesas Islands, and the Maine scenes that have been familiar to generations of Washburns.[69]

The highest this generation rose politically was mayor of Chicago. Hempstead Washburne, a son of the U.S. minister to France, won election in 1891 by 369 votes. He owed his victory to Carter Harrison, who split the Democratic ranks by running as an independent.‡ Washburne's two years at City Hall, according to one objective historian, comprised "a record of uniformly high achievement."[70] He reorganized the police department, taxed the gas companies, reduced utility rates, and established better building standards. But he declined to run again, and Carter Harrison was swept back into office. Later, when Harrison's

† Stanley Washburn married Alice Belle Langhorne of Virginia, a second cousin of Lady Astor. They had a daughter and two sons. Stanley Washburn, Jr., is now sales promotion director of Pan American World Airways; C. Langhorne Washburn is the top professional Republican fund raiser in the country. He served as Nelson Rockefeller's finance director during his campaign for the presidential nomination in 1964, and is now finance director of the Republican National Finance Committee and finance director of the Republican Congressional Campaign Committee. Interview with C. Langhorne Washburn, October 21, 1965.

‡ See Harrison Dynasty, pp. 234–35.

son became mayor, Hempstead was appointed to the Civil Service Commission.§

There were three Washburns in the state legislature: Charles Fox, a son of the Maine governor, was in the Minnesota House and Senate; Robert Charles, the Maine banker's son, was in both branches of the Washington State legislature; and William Drew Washburn, Jr., represented a Minneapolis district for eight terms in the state House of Representatives.

The latter tried his hand at newspaper reporting (on the Minneapolis *Tribune* and Chicago *Tribune*) before turning to land and mineral development. He also considered himself something of a poet, publishing a slim volume entitled *Some Rejected Verse*. Politically his liberal views were often a shock to his friends. The second William Drew Washburn's greatest coup came in the 1901 session of the legislature, when, as a freshman representative, it was expected that he would follow in the footsteps of his father. The main issue before the Assembly was a bill to raise the railroad tax. As a son of a railroad president he was taken into the confidence of the bill's foes, and thus learned of the railroads' scheme to distribute funds to corruptible legislators. He then exposed the bribe attempt, after which the opposition collapsed and the increased tax was passed.[71] William Drew Washburn spent his last fourteen years living at the Minneapolis Athletic Club, where he is remembered as a bookish, absent-minded gentleman whose lighted pipes were always setting him on fire.[72]

Yet there was still a glimmer of national aspirations in the Washburns. Three made efforts to follow their fathers to Congress. Hempstead sought a seat in 1888, but when he found that the local organization planned to stick with the incumbent, he withdrew from the race; William Drew ran in a 1918 Republican primary, and lost; Stanley ran as the Republican candidate in the Third District of New Jersey in 1934, and lost. A political dynasty ground to a halt.

Once when the sons of Israel Washburn, Sr., gathered at The Norlands, the great home they built for their father, a dispute arose over who among them was the most distinguished. The question was put to a secret ballot. And when the result was counted, each had received one

§ A daughter of Hempstead Washburne, Dr. Annette Washburne, became a noted neuropsychiatrist, and first woman to be named a full professor at the University of Wisconsin Medical School. See *Wisconsin State Journal*, April 13, 1958, Section 6, p. 5. The mayor's grandson, Thomas D. Washburne, has been a reformist member of the Baltimore County (Maryland) Board of Election Supervisors. See Edwin Hirschmann, "An Outspoken Minority of One," Baltimore *Evening Sun*, February 1, 1965, p. B2; interview with Thomas D. Washburne, February 10, 1965.

vote—his own. These men of Maine were proud of their achievements and gave no ground, even to their brothers. Their record has remained unequaled in American politics—four brothers in Congress from four different states, two governors, and two heads of foreign missions. They served an aggregate of fifty years in the United States House of Representatives and Senate yet were unable to pass on their stature to their sons. They formed a unique dynasty; a dynasty that died in a generation.

The Muhlenberg Dynasty

> "Clergymen, soldiers, scholars, statesmen, the Muhlenbergs have represented the best in our national life since the earliest days of the Republic."
>
> —Franklin D. Roosevelt[1]

A GERMAN named Tyrker sailed from Iceland with Leif Ericson in the year 1000, thus becoming one of the first white men to set foot on the North American continent.

It was not, however, until after the Thirty Years' War, when economic collapse, religious bigotry, and the tyranny of autocratic rulers swept the petty Teuton principalities, that any considerable number of Germans emigrated to the New World.

Most of the Germans arriving in the eighteenth century came to Pennsylvania. Partly this was because they were attracted to the Quakers' advocacy of peace and religious tolerance; partly this was because William Penn was a skillful advertising man who knew the value of catchy slogans and a saturation campaign.

They would be known as the "Pennsylvania Dutch"—a corruption of the word *Deutsch*, meaning "folk." By 1752 Henry Melchior Muhlenberg estimated their number at over 100,000; fourteen years later Benjamin Franklin believed that they comprised a third of the population; by the time of the Revolutionary War some authorities place their number as high as one half of Pennsylvania's population.

Yet even with such a potential power base the Germans were inconspicuous in American political life during the colonial period. It was not until 1764 that a German was even elected to the Pennsylvania legislature. They were well satisfied to entrust the colony's politics to the Quakers. Their only demand was exemption from military service; a small price to pay, thought the Quakers, for so many votes.

Unlike his English neighbor, the eighteenth-century German in Pennsylvania brought to America no meaningful heritage of political action.

THE MUHLENBERG DYNASTY
(A Selective Genealogy)

Henry Melchior Muhlenberg (1711–87)
Arrived America 1742.
"Patriarch of Lutheran Church in America"
m. *Anna Maria Weiser*, daughter of
famous Indian agent
(11 children; 4 d.y.)

Frederick Augustus (1750–1801)
1st Speaker, HOUSE OF
REPRESENTATIVES
(6 children)

Eve Elizabeth (1748–1808)
m. C. E. Schulze
(6 children)

Maria Salome (1766–1827)
m. *Matthias Richards*,
HOUSE OF REPRESENTATIVES
(9 children)

Henry E. (1753–1815)
Minister, botanist,
college president
(8 children)

J. Peter G. (1746–1807)
General, HOUSE OF
REPRESENTATIVES, SENATE
(7 children)

Henry William
(1772–1805)
(3 children)

Henry Augustus (1782–1844)
HOUSE OF REPRESENTATIVES,
Minister to Austria.
m. 2 daughters
of Gov. Joseph Hiester.
(7 children)

Frederick Hall
(1795–1867)
(5 children)

Francis Swaine (1795–1831)
HOUSE OF REPRESENTATIVES
(no issue)

John A. Schulze (1775–1852)
GOVERNOR

William Augustus (1796–1877)
Minister, founder of
St. Luke's Hospital
(New York)
(unmarried)

Henry Augustus
(1823–54)
HOUSE OF
REPRESENTATIVES

Frederick Augustus
(1818–1901)
College president
(6 children)

William Frederick
(1851–1915)
M.D.

Frederick A. (1887–   )
HOUSE OF REPRESENTATIVES
(4 children; 1 d.y.)

His heritage, on the contrary, left him not only inexperienced but deeply suspicious: government he associated with war, ravage, and persecution. He came to America, in many cases, to practice a religious separatism, and some of his sects actually directed him to stand clear of secular fallout. Let the Englishman render unto Caesar that which was Caesar's; he would render unto God that which was His.

This separatism was accentuated by difference in language. Until the German immigrant became conversant in English he would remain at a distant political disadvantage.

Moreover, the German considered politics to be an impractical profession, and, above all, he was a practical man. Politics was both unsafe and unprofitable; when a political party was ousted the professional politician lost his job. What kind of an occupation was this for an honest, frugal, industrious German boy?

The eventual politicalization of the Germans was a derivative of their Americanization. Only as they became assimilated, only as they became Americans, did they significantly enter into political life. Later, of course, they would learn the tricks of appealing to the electorate as German-Americans, just as other ethnic groups would play at bloc voting. But this was an American game.

The one family most responsible for the Americanization of the Germans was the Muhlenbergs. They would lead—often drag—their fellow Germans across the cultural, political, and language barriers that separated them from the rest of the society in which they lived. Ironically, their success foredoomed their demise as a political dynasty.[2]

Most of the pious early German settlers came from the peasant class. Although the estimate was probably high, a pamphlet published in London in 1754 asserted that half of them were illiterates.[3] Into such a society came a minister, an educated man, a man of vision, spiritual power, and the ability to be ruthless when it served his God. It was not unexpected that Henry Melchior Muhlenberg emerged as the most important German in eighteenth-century America.

His father was a shoemaker in Einbeck, but Henry's ability had always found important aristocratic and clerical patronage. He was a graduate of the University of Göttingen and the great citadel of Pietism at Halle. When he came to America in 1742, at the age of thirty-one, it was not because he was hungry or displaced but because his church fathers had sent him.

Muhlenberg's patron, the twenty-fourth Count Reuss of Kostritz, once said, "Our Lord Jesus, the Head Shepherd, needs not only under-shepherds, but also sheep-dogs, which must by their barking round up the sheep and goats on the pasture into one flock."[4] Such was to be Muhlenberg's role. He was not an outstanding theological thinker, but he was a great church administrator.

Flying the banner *Ecclesia Plantanda* (The Church Must Be Planted), within six years after his arrival in Philadelphia he had organized the first Lutheran Synod in America.[5] Within ten years he had gathered together twenty congregations. His tireless efforts took him not only across Pennsylvania but also into New York, New Jersey, Maryland, Delaware, South Carolina, and Georgia. He standardized the German Lutheran liturgy and drafted a church constitution that was to become the model for all new congregations in the colonies.

In the ecclesiastical wars some of the vanquished called him "the old fox," but later generations gave him the honorific, "Patriarch of the Lutheran Church in America."[6]

In 1745 Muhlenberg married a daughter of Conrad Weiser, the famous Indian agent. When Weiser was fourteen his family became part of a large Palatinate migration to Livingston Manor, where the First Lord of the Manor, as was his habit, lined his pockets as the official purveyor to the settlers. Livingston's treatment of the refugees was so wretched that after three years they fled into the Schoharie Valley.[7] From there young Weiser went to live with an Iroquois chief, learned the Mohawk language, and earned the name *Tarachiawagon* (He Who Holds the Heavens). For the next three decades the adventurous German was to play a large part in formulating colonial Indian policy. In 1844, through his influence, his friend Thomas Lee signed the Treaty of Lancaster.

Muhlenberg first met his father-in-law, according to one fanciful writer, while the old Indian agent was "sitting by the roadside in full panoply of an Onondaga chief."[8] Romantic tradition also has it that Weiser was married to an Indian girl. In fact, a later Muhlenberg, the founder of St. Luke's Hospital in New York, was fond of saying, "I like to think there is a drop of genuine American blood in my veins."[9] Unfortunately, as Henry Melchior Muhlenberg himself attested, his mother-in-law was "a German Christian person of evangelical parentage."[10]

This dashing spirit of the Weisers would occasionally bubble to the surface in future generations of Muhlenbergs, as when one of Conrad Weiser's Muhlenberg grandsons cast off his ministerial robe to become a Revolutionary general.

Of Henry Melchior Muhlenberg's seven children, his three sons—Peter, Frederick, and Henry Ernst—became clergymen, and two of his daughters married clergymen. This was as the Patriarch had planned. The sons had been sent back to Germany for a sound church education. His calling would be theirs.

That the old sheep dog failed to keep his own flock in the ministry was not his fault. Revolutionary times always undermine the patterns of the past.

The time was January 1776. Young Pastor Peter Muhlenberg, eldest of the Patriarch's sons, stood before the Sunday worshipers at his church in Woodstock, Virginia. His sermon recounted the wrongs inflicted on the colonists by the British. He quoted from Holy Writ—"There is a time for all things . . . a time to preach and a time to pray." Then, rising to a trumpet blast of indignation, he said that those times had passed. "There is also a time to fight! And that time has now come!"

The sermon finished, the benediction pronounced, Pastor Muhlenberg threw off his gown of black and stood before the assemblage in the buff and blue of a Continental Army colonel, while the drums at the church door beat a tattoo calling recruits to follow him to battle.[11]

The story of the fighting parson's farewell to his parishioners grew into legend, handed down from generation to generation. Congressman John Bubenheim Bayard often repeated it to his children as "one of the most thrilling [incidents] of the war"; his son-in-law, Chief Justice Kirkpatrick of New Jersey, told the tale he had heard from Bayard to his children[12]; Thomas Buchanan Read reconstructed the scene in verse, and a century of school children memorized the lines from their *McGuffey's Readers:*

> The pastor rose; the prayer was strong;
> The psalm was warrior David's song;
> The text, a few short words of might—
> "The Lord of Hosts should arm the right!"
>
> When suddenly his mantle wide
> His hands impatient flung aside,
> And lo! he met their wondering eyes
> Complete in all a warrior's guise.[13]

Peter, who was to become a brigadier general, was in the midst of the fighting at Brandywine and Germantown. He was with Washington at Valley Forge, with Greene at Monmouth Court House, and with Wayne at Stony Point. Later he was sent back to Virginia to recruit an army for the defense of the state, and concluded his military career by commanding the brigade that stormed the key British redoubt at Yorktown. The Muhlenbergs, even the old Patriarch, proudly followed the exploits of "Our General."

When the war broke out Frederick, the second son, was serving a congregation in New York. At first he didn't approve of his elder brother's decision. "I think you are wrong in trying to be both soldier and preacher together," he wrote. "No man can serve two masters."[14] But his sympathies were so clearly with the revolutionaries that before long he was forced to flee from the British.

Back in Philadelphia he was elected to the Continental Congress—the "Rump Parliament," as his father called it. Complained the Patriarch, he is "now in the Hurle burle till his waxen wings are melted."[15] No man can serve two masters; Frederick would never return to the ministry. His unhappy father, who took his dreams seriously, had a nightmare in which Frederick, dressed in rags, suddenly fell into a heap. The father was powerless to help him; his son was lost in "the political dungheap."[16]

The Patriarch's attitude toward the war was ambivalent. On the one hand were his family loyalties and personal sympathies—his sons were American patriots and the burden of guilt for this "unnatural and inhuman war" was on the British. On the other hand were his sense of obligation to George III and his view of authority. "Fear God, honor the King and those in authority, and love thy neighbor," was his personal philosophy.[17] Moreover, Muhlenberg felt doubly bound to the House of Hanover: he had been born its subject in Germany and was now a subject of the Hanoverian King of England who had given protection to the Lutheran Church in America.[18] But in taking sides his most overriding consideration must be to protect the Church—*his* Church—from possible postwar reprisals. It was unclear which side would wield the victor's justice. Muhlenberg therefore chose the most difficult course of all in wartime—to remain neutral.

The war, like a rampaging river, had etched new patterns into the landscape. Now Peter was a general, Frederick a politician. But the most unpredictable new path was taken by the youngest son, Henry Ernst, whom war had turned into a botanist!

He most resembled his father, being heavy set, of medium height, with a florid complexion. Henry Ernst Muhlenberg, the most intellectual of the brothers, had been ordained at seventeen, which was partly an act of confidence in the family name, but also an indication of the youth's scholarship. Before the war he had been an assistant to his father in Philadelphia. But when the British occupied the city he found himself without a church. It was during this period of enforced leisure that he began the study of botany. Within three years he had compiled a list of 1100 plants in the Lancaster area. Considering the restrictiveness of his personal explorations, his contribution to descriptive botany was remarkable. He named nearly one hundred plants, about half of them reeds and grasses. Because his works were extensively plagiarized by European and American scientists proper recognition was belated. But over the years his achievements have been honored with the naming of a goldenrod (*Solidago Muhlenbergii*), a willow (*Salix Muhlenbergii*), a yellow oak (*Quercus Muhlenbergii*), a reed, two mosses, two lichens, a fungus, even a turtle (*Clemmys Muhlengerii*), and a short-lived journal of botany

(*Muhlengeria*).[19] Although Muhlenberg stayed in the clergy and followed his father as president of the Pennsylvania Ministerium, he would be best remembered as a scientist and educator.

For the Germans in Pennsylvania education was viewed as a function of the Church rather than the State. It was natural then that the Muhlenbergs, as the church leaders, would also play a dominant role in education.

When the University of Pennsylvania was incorporated in 1779 a member of each religious denomination was put on the board of trustees. A son-in-law of the Muhlenberg Patriarch, the Reverend John Christopher Kunze, was chosen to represent the German Lutherans.* At an early meeting Kunze told his fellow trustees, "There are entire counties which are occupied entirely by Germans whose children cannot speak a single word of English."[20] As a result of his pleas he was appointed to head a German department, which was really a secondary school to prepare German students for the university. This experiment failed, but it led to the founding of a separate German institution, Franklin College, with Henry Ernst Muhlenberg as its first president.

The versatile Benjamin Rush, one of the few Englishmen who sincerely respected the Germans (although he was also aware of the political utility of his friendship), was on the board of directors, and journeyed to Lancaster for the inaugural ceremony in 1787. He reported to his mother-in-law, Annis Boudinot Stockton, that it was "one of the highest entertainments I ever enjoyed in my life." He also used the opportunity to tell the assemblage that "by means of this seminary . . . the partition wall which has long separated the English and German inhabitants of the state will be broken down . . . and in the course of a few years by means of this College the names of German, Irishman, and Englishman will be lost in the general name of Pennsylvanian."[21]

In 1849 a son of the botanist-college president, Dr. Frederick Augustus Hall Muhlenberg (who had studied medicine under Benjamin Rush), was a trustee of the college, and his son, Frederick Augustus Muhlenberg, was on the faculty. The two Muhlenbergs proposed and put through the merger that created the present Franklin and Marshall College.

Then in 1867, when the German Lutheran Church took over another

---

* John Christopher Kunze (1744–1807), the son of a Saxony innkeeper, arrived in America in 1770, and the following year married Muhlenberg's second daughter, Margaretta Henrietta (1751–1831). He replaced the Patriarch as pastor of St. Michael's Church in Philadelphia after a bitter struggle with Henry Ernst Muhlenberg. He was also a noted scholar of Greek, Latin, Hebrew, Arabic, and Italian literature; and professor of oriental languages at Columbia College, 1784–87 and 1792–99. The Kunzes had a son and four daughters, one of whom married into the P. Lorillard tobacco family.

college, Allentown Collegiate and Military Academy, Professor Muhlenberg was asked to become its first president. The new institution was named Muhlenberg College, although its historian recounts that "the well-known modesty of President Muhlenberg led him to express his deep regret that the College had received the name of his family."[22]†

The Muhlenbergs' educational efforts accelerated the process of assimilation. But equally important to the Americanization of the Pennsylvania Germans was the family's long and acrimonious battle to introduce English into the church service.

This problem was squarely faced by the Patriarch, who urged his colleagues and sons to master the language of the country in order to spread the gospel more widely. Within twelve years after his arrival in America Muhlenberg was preaching in both English and German.[23] And in 1747 the farsighted pastor wrote an English constitution for a church in Frederick, Maryland, although few of the congregants could speak the language—thus forestalling any church-state problems that might arise with the English government in Annapolis.[24] His son-in-law Kunze, while unable to preach in English himself, succeeded in training the first English-speaking German Lutheran clergymen in America. General Peter Muhlenberg, after his father's death, became the leader of the English movement. And although German was the language of the Muhlenberg home, so successful was the Patriarch's indoctrination of his sons that Frederick, then a member of the Continental Congress, wrote brother Henry: "I confess on the subject of politics English comes easier to me than German."[25]

Yet it was an uphill fight; the majority of the Church wished to retain German exclusively. In 1798, when a newly organized English Lutheran Church in New York sought recognition by the Ministerium, it was bluntly told that it could join the Episcopalians, which the pastor, officers, and entire congregation promptly did. There was even a court case in Philadelphia in which the defendants were charged with conspiracy to prevent the introduction of English into the congregation. They were found guilty, but pardoned by a German governor. The most militant were fighting more than a rear-guard action to preserve a cherished heritage. "What would be the result throughout Pennsylvania and northern Maryland in 40 or 50 years [if the German language is retained]?" asked one pamphlet. The answer: "An entirely German

† Frederick Augustus Muhlenberg (1818–1901) was a member of the faculty of Franklin College, 1840–50; professor of ancient languages at Pennsylvania College (now Gettysburg College), 1850–67; president of Muhlenberg College, 1867–76; professor of Greek, University of Pennsylvania, 1876–88; president of Thiel College, Greenville, Pennsylvania, 1891–93. He was married to Catherine Anna Muhlenberg (1827–94), a granddaughter of General Peter Muhlenberg.

State, where, as formerly in Germantown, the beautiful German language would be used in the legislative halls and the courts of justice."[26]

The Muhlenbergs eventually won the language fight, but, as a byplay of the struggle, the most creative member of the dynasty became an Episcopalian.

When the second generation of Muhlenbergs left the ministry it was predictable that they would gravitate toward politics. Frederick and Peter were men of proven ability, nurtured on public service, dedicated to the American cause (which was not the universal sentiment in the German community), and with a name that had commanded respect for a generation.

Like the Adamses, they could not afford the luxury of public life. While in Congress Frederick wrote his brother that he could not even afford a horse; and he tried to supplement his income with several commercial ventures but was not a notably successful businessman.[27] On two occasions this would deter Muhlenbergs from serving in important national offices.

Frederick was not a leading spirit in the Continental Congress. However, he served diligently for a term as chairman of the Medical Committee, performing duties comparable to those of a director general for military hospitals. He often vacillated on public questions but apparently had the knack of resolving the differences of others, for he was often chosen to be the presiding officer—a job he held for three years in the Pennsylvania Assembly, and later in the state convention that ratified the federal Constitution.

In the deeply rancorous battles over a state constitution that rocked Pennsylvania from 1776 to 1789, he was a leader of the faction which wanted a stronger government.[28] This fight he lost, yet by maneuvering Pennsylvania's acceptance of the federal Constitution he won the larger issue of strong national government.

The elections of 1788, to choose members to the first Congress under the new Constitution, saw both Frederick and Peter standing for the House of Representatives. Although the Anti-Federalists hoped to split the German vote by putting Peter on its ballot, the Germans chose familiar names and both Muhlenbergs were victorious. After the war the former general concluded that he could not "mount the parson after the soldier," and went west to survey the lands that had been given to him and other officers in recognition of their military service. Later, returning to Pennsylvania, he was elected vice-president of the state, under the ailing Benjamin Franklin, and performed many of the duties of chief executive.

Meeting in New York, the first Congress elected Frederick as its

Speaker without dissent. (The wealthy Elias Boudinot, who was never really in the running, wrote his wife that he was happy to have been passed over because of the "very large expense" attached to the position.[29]) The speakership was to be an office of high honor and responsibility, modeled after the presiding officer of the English House of Commons. A troop of cavalry escorted Muhlenberg into the city; both houses of Congress in a body paid their respects to him on New Year's Day; he would receive twelve dollars a day—twice the salary of the other congressmen.

The Pennsylvania Germans were ecstatic that one of their number had been chosen. A letter to the *Philadelphische Correspondenz* by an anonymous writer said that "the blood of the grandchildren of our grandchildren will proudly well up in their hearts when they will read in the histories of America that the first Speaker of the House of Representatives of the United States of America under the new Constitution was a German, born of German parents in Pennsylvania."[30]

But the honor had in no sense gone to Muhlenberg as a tribute to his German ancestry. He was selected primarily for geographic considerations. The first President was from the South; the first Vice-President was a New Englander; the first Speaker should be from the middle states.[31]

Here was the unassailable proof of the Americanization of the Germans. Henry Melchior Muhlenberg had come from Germany; his son was an American. And as an American, a representative of the middle states, he had been elected Speaker of the House.

This was the political high-water mark of the dynasty. It had performed the amazing feat of pushing the Germans into the mainstream of their adopted country in less than two generations. And as their constituents became assimilated they had less need for such unique spokesmen. Successive generations of Muhlenbergs would be elected to national office, a remarkable total of six would serve in Congress, but never for long or with very great influence. The symbolic elevation of Frederick Muhlenberg to the speakership ended their primary *raison d'état* as a political dynasty.

The Muhlenbergs were uneasy in the Federalist Party. They supported its strong nationalist aims but were discomforted by its aristocratic strain. The question of an official title for the President was a case in point. With strong urging from John Adams the Senate was leaning toward "High Mightiness." At a presidential dinner party Washington asked Peter Muhlenberg for his opinion. "Why, General," replied Peter, "if we were certain the office would always be held by men as large as yourself or my friend Mr. Wynkoop [the tallest member of the House of

Representatives], it would be appropriate enough; but if by chance a President as small as my opposite neighbor [John Adams] should be elected, it would become ridiculous."[32] Washington and Adams weren't amused.‡

Peter soon joined the Jeffersonian Republicans; Frederick remained a nominal Federalist and was soundly beaten as his party's candidate for governor of Pennsylvania in 1792 and 1796. But his record in Congress was becoming more and more Republican. In the 2nd Congress this tendency defeated him for re-election as Speaker. The Federalists' suspicions were justified: during the First Session of the 2nd Congress (1791–92) he sided with Republican leader James Madison on twenty-one of thirty-two key votes. Only two other members outside of the South had a more Anti-Federalist voting record. And in the 3rd Congress, when the Republicans had gained a majority, he was again elected Speaker.

Once more, in 1796, Frederick sided with the Federalists, and it ended his career on the national level. When the question of whether to appropriate money to carry out the Jay Treaty was before the House, Muhlenberg cast the tie-breaking vote in favor of the treaty and peace with England. The *Gazette of the United States* reported that he acted "after some hesitation," as well he should have, since the vote was vastly unpopular in his constituency. John Berkeley, one of Jefferson's political organizers, wrote, "It is necessary at the same time to aid the common object by getting all our friends . . . to throw out Muhlenberg, who gave the casting vote for the British treaty, and elect Blair McClenachan in his room, who recommended to kick the treaty to hell."[33] Muhlenberg declined to seek a fifth term.

The crucial vote also had two unexpected repercussions. At the time Frederick's son was courting a young lady from Philadelphia whose father was an ardent Federalist. The prospective father-in-law told Frederick, "If you do not give us your vote, your Henry shall not have my Polly." Frederick's grandson, when telling the story, usually added, "But the vote went the right way, peace was secured, and here I am."[34]

The other by-product of Muhlenberg's vote also concerned in-laws. On hearing of his action, Frederick's brother-in-law, a fanatical Republican, stabbed him with intent to kill. Nor was this the first difficulty with his wife's family. John Schaeffer, another brother-in-law, had earlier imperiled Muhlenberg's political career by trying to get the French to buy a worthless hull as a privateer during the American Revolution. The

‡ Frederick Muhlenberg shared his brother's joke, referring to six-foot-three Senator William Maclay as "Your Highness of the Senate." See *The Journal of William Maclay* (New York: D. Appleton, 1890), pp. 32–33.

scheme was exposed and Schaeffer pleaded with Ambassador Benjamin Franklin to "do Every thing that Lais in your Power to relive me of my Distrest Situation."[35] The perceptive Franklin, who knew a con man when he saw one, let Schaeffer cool his heels in a French prison.

While his vote on the Jay Treaty virtually ended Frederick's career, Peter Muhlenberg was just starting to ride the crest of Republican popularity. He had been three times elected to the House of Representatives and served as a Jeffersonian presidential elector in 1796. He again campaigned vigorously for the Virginian in 1800, this time with the aid of his brother. When Pennsylvania went Republican, John Adams blamed his defeat on the Muhlenbergs. "Those two Germans," he wrote, "who had been long in public affairs and in high office, were the great leaders and oracles of the whole German interest in Pennsylvania and the neighboring states. . . . The Muhlenbergs turned the whole body of the Germans, great numbers of the Irish, and many of the English, and in this manner introduced the total change that followed in the Houses of the legislature, and in all the executive departments of the national government." Then the former President mused, "Upon such slender threads did our elections then depend!"§

During the ensuing fight in the House of Representatives over whether the presidency should go to Jefferson or Burr, some Republicans feared that the Federalists would seize control of the government, and a plan was formulated to have Peter Muhlenberg lead a military march on the capital to restore order. The precaution was unnecessary.

On the day Jefferson was inaugurated, March 4, 1801, Peter Muhlenberg was sworn in as United States senator from Pennsylvania. It was a special session that ended the next day, and he resigned before the Senate reconvened. In six years in the House of Representatives and two days in the Senate Peter Muhlenberg never made a single speech.

He left the Senate to become supervisor of internal revenue for Pennsylvania; the job paid more and allowed him to spend more time at home. Peter died in 1807, Dr. Rush attending. Frederick, who became receiver-general of the Pennsylvania Land Office, died in 1801.

Before charting the third generation, there is another durable Pennsylvania German family that deserves attention. The paths of the Hiesters and Muhlenbergs continually crossed. Like the Muhlenbergs,

§ Benjamin Rush agreed that the Muhlenbergs had tipped the scale against Adams, calling Peter "the most popular and powerful German in Pennsylvania." He wrote Adams that Peter had turned against him because he had been overlooked in the distribution of military commissions. Rush to Adams, November 21, 1805. L. H. Butterfield, editor, *Letters of Benjamin Rush* (Princeton: Princeton University Press, 1951), Vol. II, p. 908.

six Hiesters were to serve in Congress¶; four times the dynasties inter-married.*

The first Hiesters in America were three brothers who emigrated from Westphalia to Pennsylvania a few years before the arrival of the Muhlenberg Patriarch.† They were a family of some means, with a hereditary coat of arms, and immediately purchased a tract of between 2000 and

¶ Hiesters in the U. S. House of Representatives: *Daniel Hiester* (1747–1804), 1789–96, 1801–4; *John Hiester* (1745–1821), 1807–9; *Joseph Hiester* (1752–1832), 1797–1805, 1815–20; *Daniel Hiester* (1774–1834), 1809–11; *William Hiester* (1790–1853), 1831–37; *Isaac Ellmaker Hiester* (1824–71), 1853–55.

* Intermarriages: *John Sylvanus Hiester* (1774–1849) m. *Mary Catharine Muhlenberg* (1774–1846), a daughter of Speaker Frederick Muhlenberg, 6 children; *Mary Elizabeth Hiester* (1784–1806) m. *Henry A. Muhlenberg* (1782–1844), a son of botanist Henry Ernst Muhlenberg, 1 daughter; *Rebecca Hiester* (1781–1841) m. *Henry A. Muhlenberg* (see above), 6 children; *Isaac Hiester* (1785–1855) m. *Hester Muhlenberg* (1785–1872), a daughter of General Peter Muhlenberg, 4 children. See Henry Melchior Muhlenberg Richards, "The Hiester Family," *The Pennsylvania-German Society, Proceedings and Addresses*, XVI (Lancaster, Pa., 1907).

† THE HIESTERS (A Selective Genealogy)

Johannas Hiester

John (1707–57)
Arrived America 1732
(4 children; 2 d.y.)

Joseph (c. 1710–77)
Arrived America 1737
(7 children)

Daniel (1713–95)
Arrived America 1737
(7 children; 1 d.y.)

Joseph (1752–1832)
CONGRESS, GOVERNOR
(6 children; 3 m.
Muhlenbergs)

John (1745–1821)
CONGRESS
(7 children)

Daniel (1747–1804)
CONGRESS
m. *Rosanna Hager*
(no issue)

William
(1757–1822)
(5 children)

Daniel (1774–
1834) CONGRESS

Isaac (1785–1855)
m. a Muhlenberg
(4 children)

William (1790–
1853) CONGRESS

William Muhlenberg
(1818–71)
State Senate
(2 children; 1 d.y.)

Isaac Ellmaker
(1824–71)
CONGRESS

3000 acres in Berks County. Their continuing prosperity can be measured by the estate of Joseph Hiester, the most famous of their sons, who left $468,000 when he died in 1832—as compared with the wealthiest of the contemporary Muhlenbergs, whose net worth was estimated at $80,000.[36]

In all, the Hiesters were elected nineteen times to national office, serving in Congress for an aggregate of thirty-five years and five months. But three of the six Hiester congressmen were one-termers, and only two were of particular interest.

Daniel Hiester was son and son-in-law of two of the wealthiest German colonists, and his accounts show that he spent lavishly to maintain his handsome appearance. Like all of his family of arms-bearing age, he served with distinction in the Revolutionary War, rising to the rank of militia brigadier general. The returning veteran was elected to the first three Congresses. He finally resigned in 1796 and moved to Hagerstown, Maryland, having married the daughter of Jonathan Hager, whose foresight and ability had built the prosperous settlement.‡ He was then elected to Congress from his new home. When Hager died intestate his property settled on his only son, who deeded 1400 choice acres to his sister. Claimants to the confused estate contended that Hiester not only blackmailed his brother-in-law into making the settlement but used a ruse to get his wife to convey the property to him. Hiester died childless in 1804, but the case dragged on for generations, much to the benefit of the legal profession.[37]

When Daniel moved to Hagerstown his place in Congress was taken by his first cousin Joseph Hiester, a man of very different nature. Frank and simple—although he was also a wealthy man—totally free from guile, the tall and powerfully built Joseph had been an ardent Whig before the Revolution. During the war he was captured at the battle of Long Island, badly treated as a prisoner of war, and later slightly wounded at Germantown. Although not brilliant, he was fearless in expressing his

‡ Jonathan Hager (1714-75) arrived in Philadelphia in 1736 and laid out Hagerstown in 1762. An English traveler in 1772 observed: "About 30 miles west of Frederick-town, I passed through a settlement which is making quick advances to perfection. A German adventurer, whose name is Hager, purchased a considerable tract of land in this neighborhood, and with much discernment and foresight determined to give encouragement to traders, and to erect proper habitations for the stowage of goods, for the supply of the adjacent country. His plan succeeded; he has lived to behold a multitude of inhabitants on lands, which he remembered unoccupied; and he has seen erected in places, appropriated by him for that purpose, more than a hundred comfortable edifices, to which the name of Hager's Town is given, in honor of the intelligent founder." Quoted in Daniel Wunderlich Nead, *The Pennsylvania-Germans in the Settlement of Maryland* (Lancaster, Pa.: Press of the New Era Publishing Co., 1914), pp. 55-56.

views, and possessed of more than a normal share of shrewd horse sense. In 1820, running against an indifferent incumbent, he was elected governor of Pennsylvania. The campaign was among the most vitriolic in the state's history, and Hiester was accused, among other things, of being pro-slavery, aristocratic, ignorant, senile, voluntarily having surrendered to the British, and having been shot by his own general.

Once in office, much to the misfortune of many of the political leaders who had supported him, Hiester proved to be what they had claimed he was—honest. At sixty-eight years of age, and viewing the governorship as the summit of his career, he pledged to serve only one term. In his inaugural address he put forth a program of reform which included merit appointments, a restriction of the governor's patronage, reduced public salaries, a more humane penal system, and expanded aid to education. By the end of his four years in office, even if he had wished it, Hiester stood not a chance of renomination.[38]

He was succeeded as governor by a little-known state senator named John Andrew Schulze, a grandson of Patriarch Muhlenberg.

John Andrew Schulze was the son of Henry Melchoir Muhlenberg's oldest daughter, who had married one of his ministerial protégés. The future governor had also been ordained as a Lutheran clergyman, but after six years he turned to mercantile pursuits, thus earning the less than flattering sobriquet of "stickit minister." His five years in the state legislature left him as undistinguished as when he entered politics, which was probably the reason he was chosen to run for governor. But while the political bosses rightly thought him to be a man of no great intellectual power, they misjudged his independence and decisiveness.[39]

His two terms in office were not unlike his predecessor's. The Schulze program included expanded suffrage, judicial reform, an elaborate system of roads and canals, and the enlargement of free public education. He was not, however, above distributing largess to his relatives: an uncle was given a judgeship,§ and his sister's brother-in-law, Simon Cameron, was made adjutant general of the state.¶

§ Matthias Richards (1758–1830) married Patriarch Muhlenberg's third daughter, Maria Salome (1766–1827). He was a prosperous saddler whose surname had been anglicized from Reichert by his Scotch-Irish schoolmasters. Also from a prominent political family, he served two terms in Congress (1807–11); his brother John (1753–1822) served a single term (1795–97); and their uncle Michael Hillegas (1729–1804), a wealthy sugar refiner, was the first Treasurer of the United States (1775–89). See Emma St. Clair Whitney, *Michael Hillegas and His Descendants* (Pottsville, Pa.: Press of M. E. Miller, 1891).

¶ Mary Magdalena Schulze (1787–1876) married John Cameron (1797–1841), whose brother Simon (1799–1889) and his son Donald (1833–1918) dominated Pennsylvania politics for four decades, and served an aggregate of

In 1828 John Quincy Adams asked Schulze to join his ticket as the candidate for Vice-President; the governor refused, and the nomination went to Richard Rush. At the end of his second term Cameron tried to get his patron another nomination but failed.

The governor then retired to gentleman farming on 500 acres in Lycoming County, which the neighbors called "Schulze's Folly."[40] Surprisingly enough for a man who reputedly saved two thirds of his $5000 annual salary as governor, Schulze went bankrupt in 1844 and all his possessions were sold at a debtor's auction.

There were two other politicians in the third generation. Francis Swaine Muhlenberg,* a son of the Revolutionary general, served as private secretary to Governor Hiester and then moved to Ohio where he lived on land given to his father for his military service. After a year in the Ohio legislature he was elected to the House of Representatives. But the third Muhlenberg congressman was in office for only seventy-five days. He died at thirty-six, leaving no descendants.

The last of the dynasty to achieve a national political reputation was Henry Augustus Muhlenberg, son of the famous botanist and son-in-law of Governor Joseph Hiester. He had been trained for the clergy by his father and his uncle Kunze, and for twenty-four years served as pastor of Trinity Church in Reading. He was also the third Muhlenberg to become president of the Lutheran Ministerium of Pennsylvania.

Forced by ill-health to resign from the ministry in 1828, Muhlenberg was promptly drafted by the Democrats of Berks County to run for Congress. The former pastor quickly discovered that the talents of the pulpit were not unsuited for the political stump. Elected five times to the House of Representatives, he became a forceful advocate of Andrew Jackson and his good friend Martin Van Buren. For his role as one of Jackson's commanders in the war against the United States Bank the President liked to call him *General* Muhlenberg. When James Buchanan

---

thirty-four years in the U. S. Senate. Simon Cameron's grandfather, a farmer, came to Pennsylvania from Scotland in 1755 and married Martha Pfoutz of a Palatine German family; his father was a poor tailor with eight children. See Lee F. Crippen, *Simon Cameron, Ante-Bellum Years* (Oxford, Ohio: Mississippi Valley Press, 1942), pp. 2–3.

* He was named after Francis Swaine (1754–1820), husband of Patriarch Muhlenberg's youngest daughter, Mary Catharine (1775–1812). Swaine was a good-natured and kindhearted Irishman who was generally helped along by the Muhlenbergs. General Peter appointed him as his aide during the war, but Swaine was formally reprimanded for "repeated neglect of duty." Then he became clothier to the state of Pennsylvania, possibly through Frederick's influence, but he lost this position too; and finally after the war he was made a general in the militia, again with the assistance of Peter. All the Swaines' children died in infancy.

told Jackson "that Mr. Muhlenberg was no General," the President replied, "No matter, he ought to have been!"[41]

A schism developed in the Pennsylvania Democratic Party in 1835
when Governor George Wolf refused to step down after serving two
terms. In a three-way contest, Muhlenberg and Wolf split the Democratic vote and caused the election of the Anti-Mason candidate. The
bitterness of the campaign necessitated Muhlenberg's removal from the
state for the good of the party. President Van Buren offered to make
him Secretary of the Navy or minister to Russia, but he declined—either
position, Muhlenberg felt, would have severely strained his modest financial resources.

However, the temptation to be the first American minister to Austria
was so great that Muhlenberg resigned from Congress in 1838. Old John
Quincy Adams commented to his diary: "This appointment is a pure
electioneering expedient to pacify the party schism in Pennsylvania and
to tickle the catastrophe of the Pennsylvania Germans. As German is
Muhlenberg's native tongue, he will find himself at home in Vienna."[42]
The new diplomat enjoyed the society of Prince Metternich and the
opportunity to travel, but the position was too much for his pocketbook
and he resigned after two years.

Back in Pennsylvania he again sought the governorship in 1844, this
time with the support of a united party. His victory seemed assured
when, in the midst of the campaign, he died of apoplexy, a disease that
took the lives of many of the Muhlenbergs.

Another Pennsylvania German replaced Henry Augustus Muhlenberg
on the Democratic ticket and was elected. However, this virtually ended
the long reign of the so-called "Dutch governors." While the Scotch-
Irish had furnished most of the state's political leadership, from the
precincts to the Senate, the Germans had a near monopoly on Pennsylvania's Executive Mansion. Six of the state's first ten governors were
German.[43]† But by mid-nineteenth century the Pennsylvania Germans,
and the Muhlenbergs, were turning to other pursuits.

They were not destined to continue as a political dynasty. Henry
Augustus Muhlenberg had a son and namesake who was elected to

---

† After the state constitution of 1790 the first ten governors of Pennsylvania:
Thomas Mifflin (1788–99), English, defeated Frederick Muhlenberg in 1792
and 1796; Thomas McKean (1799–1808), Irish, elected in large part because
of the support of Peter and Frederick Muhlenberg; Simon Snyder (1808–17),
German; William Findlay (1817–20), Irish, defeated Joseph Hiester; Joseph
Hiester (1820–23), German; John Andrew Schulze (1823–29), German;
George Wolf (1829–35), German; Joseph Ritner (1835–39), German, de-
feated Wolf and Henry A. Muhlenberg; David Rittenhouse Potter (1839–45),
Irish; Francis R. Shunk (1845–58), German, replaced Henry A. Muhlenberg
on the ticket.

Congress in 1852, but he died ten months after being seated—aged thirty-one.

The main thrust of the fourth generation would be in religion and education. One Muhlenberg, as already noted, planned the merger that created Franklin and Marshall College and became the first president of Muhlenberg College. Another Muhlenberg had an even more profound effect on American intellectual life.

The grandson of the first Speaker of the House of Representatives, William Augustus Muhlenberg was the heir of the marriage that had been consummated by the Jay Treaty. This descendant of a long line of German Lutheran clergymen became the most renowned Episcopal minister of his day. One biographer credits the denominational change to the fact that "when his widowed mother sold a lot to St. James' Episcopal Church the vestry gave her a pew, which she was too thrifty to leave unoccupied. . . ."[44] But it is more plausible to suspect that the English-speaking youth joined the church in which he felt most comfortable.

Muhlenberg's influence affected nearly every aspect of his adopted religion. His money, passed down from his maternal grandfather, built the Church of the Holy Communion in New York, in which he established the principle of equality of worship without the renting of pews; he founded the first church sisterhood; he founded the first church hospital, St. Luke's in New York; he experimented with Christian communal living; he founded the Memorial Movement, out of which grew the World Council of Churches; he founded an educational institution which became the model for Episcopal secondary schooling; he was one of the foremost composers of hymns.‡

As an educator, Bishop Henry Codman Potter compared him favorably with the great Thomas Arnold of Rugby: Muhlenberg's "mind possessed the magnetism of Arnold without his impatience; the religious earnestness of Arnold without his tendency to speculation. And the boys caught and reflected the master's spirit. . . ."[45] On Muhlenberg's eightieth birthday in 1877 William Cullen Bryant published "From Tweed to Dr. Muhlenberg." To the poet, New York's political boss and the kindly minister epitomized the two extremes of human character.

For nearly a century after the fifth Muhlenberg congressman died in office the dynasty turned its back on Washington. They were professional people—doctors, lawyers, clergymen, bankers, teachers. On occasion they did a little political moonlighting, such as serving as local revenue collector. When their country was at war they donned uni-

‡ Muhlenberg wrote "I Would Not Live Alway" and "Saviour, Who Thy Flock Art Feeding." He also wrote, with Lincoln's consent, a "metrical version" of the Emancipator's Thanksgiving Proclamation of 1863.

forms.§ But usually they could be found at home in the Pennsylvania Dutch country—the region where they had lived since the eighteenth century—respected pillars of a small corner of America.

Then in 1946 a Muhlenberg, who was an architect by profession, decided to "find out if the family was going downhill politically."[46] Frederick Augustus Muhlenberg of Reading, heir to the name of the first Speaker of the House of Representatives and great-great-grandson of the noted botanist, ran for Congress. He was elected, served one term, and returned to the business of designing buildings.¶

The Muhlenbergs were unique in the annals of American political dynasties—they were Germanic. (While the first American Frelinghuysen came from Prussia, that family so quickly and successfully melded with the rest of society that the only lasting part of their Old World heritage is the name.)

The power base of the Muhlenbergs was narrow, generally the tri-counties of Berks, Lancaster, and Montgomery, so that they rarely rose above the House of Representatives. But quantitatively their record was remarkable. Only three families have sent more members to Congress. Taken together with the Hiesters—who represented the economic wealth of the Pennsylvania Germans, while the Muhlenbergs represented the intellectual—their achievement was unsurpassed: twenty-seven national election victories, sixty-five years in the Congress.

Yet the two families were rarely in the main stream of American political life. There were no presidents as in the Adams, Harrison, Roosevelt, Taft, and Kennedy dynasties; no secretaries of state, such as graced the Livingstons, Washburns, Bayards, and Frelinghuysens; no Senate leaders as are found among the Breckinridges, Lodges, and Tafts. There was a Muhlenberg Speaker of the House of Representatives, but he sacrificed his political career after a relatively short period of national service; there was a Muhlenberg senator, but he served only two days; there was a Muhlenberg diplomat, but he headed a minor legation.

Indeed, the Muhlenbergs' greatest accomplishments lie outside of the

§ Major Peter Muhlenberg (1787–1844), a son of the Revolutionary general, was wounded in the War of 1812 while serving with General Pike in the Canadian campaign and later fought under Jackson at New Orleans; his son, Brevet Lieutenant Colonel Francis Peter Muhlenberg (b. 1840), entered Vicksburg with Grant; Lieutenant Charles Philip Muhlenberg (b. 1872), a grandson of the botanist, fought at Antietam; Frederick Augustus Muhlenberg (1887–   ) was a captain in the First World War and a colonel in World War II.

¶ Speaking as the only architect in Congress, Muhlenberg was highly critical of President Truman for adding a balcony to the South Portico of the White House. He called the action "illegal." See Edward T. Folliard, "Why Mr. Truman Built the Balcony," Washington *Post*, May 25, 1965, p. A18.

political arena. Other dynasts have contributed their names to institutions of higher learning, but only the Muhlenbergs have had a college named in honor of their *family,* in recognition of their collective achievements in education. Other political dynasties have produced notable churchmen, but none has made the lasting impression of Henry Melchior Muhlenberg. It was in the churches and colleges of their area that they established a reputation.

Politics was the by-product; election to office the result of a community's confidence. Once the Germans accepted themselves as Americans, the Muhlenbergs seemed to lose interest in politics as a vocation.

But if their impact on national politics was negligible, their political influence among the German element was not. Political action was one avenue (though not as significant a one as the pulpit or the classroom) by which the Muhlenbergs transported a minority group—speaking a different language, following different customs, suspicious of outsiders, prone to stand apart—into full participation in American life. This was no mean achievement.

The Roosevelt Dynasty

"One reason,—perhaps the chief—of the virility of the
Roosevelts is this very democratic spirit. They have
never felt that because they were born in a good
position they could put their hands in their pockets
and succeed."

—Franklin Delano Roosevelt[1]

SINCE the President of the United States had to be in New York City
in order to march in the annual St. Patrick's Day parade, he agreed to
give away the bride in a wedding that was to be held at a brownstone
house just off Fifth Avenue. Even without the presence of a President
the wedding was considered of some social importance: the guest list
included Astors, Livingstons, Vanderbilts, and other pillars of society.

Yet on this one day each year fashionable Fifth Avenue is reserved
for the sons of Erin and those who feel emotional or political kinship.
The close proximity of society was bound to create confusion. The avenue
was a sea of marchers. The side streets were blocked off. Add a President
of the United States to this combustible equation and the result is chaos.

Some of the guests, thwarted on all sides, failed to arrive until after
the Reverend Endicott Peabody had performed the ceremony. But this
was only the beginning of the young couple's trials on their wedding day.
From the street the lusty strains of "Wearin' o' the Green" drowned out
the traditional "Oh, Promise Me." And the newly united pair discovered,
when they turned to receive the congratulations of the assembled, that
they were standing alone. The President, playing a piper's tune of amusing stories, had led the guests to the library, where he was holding
court.[2]

The President of the United States on this March Friday in 1905 was
Theodore Roosevelt, of whom his youngest son later said, "Father always
wants to be the bride at every wedding and the corpse at every funeral."[3] The bride was his niece Eleanor, orphaned daughter of his unfortunate brother Elliott; the bridegroom, a twenty-three-year-old Columbia
Law School student, was Franklin Delano Roosevelt.

THE ROOSEVELT DYNASTY
(A Selective Genealogy)

Claes Martenszen van Rosenvelt
Arrived before 1649
(6 children)

Nicholas (1658–1742)
(8 children)

Oyster Bay Line

Hyde Park Line

Johannes (b. 1689)
(5 children)

Jacobus (1692–1776)
(11 children)

Jacobus (b. 1724)
(10 children)

Isaac (1726–94) "The Patriot"
(10 children, 3 d.y.)

James J. (1759–1840)
(6 children)

Nicholas I. (1767–1854)
Steamboat inventor

James (1760–1847)
(10 children)

Cornelius V. S. (1794–1871)
(6 children, 1 d.y.)

James I. (1795–1875)
HOUSE OF REPRESENTATIVES

Isaac (1790–1863)
(2 children)

Theodore (1831–78)
m. Martha Bulloch
(1834–84)

Robert B. (1829–1906)
HOUSE OF REPRESENTATIVES

James (1828–1900)
1st m. Rebecca Howland (d. 1873)
2d m. Sara Delano (1854–1941)

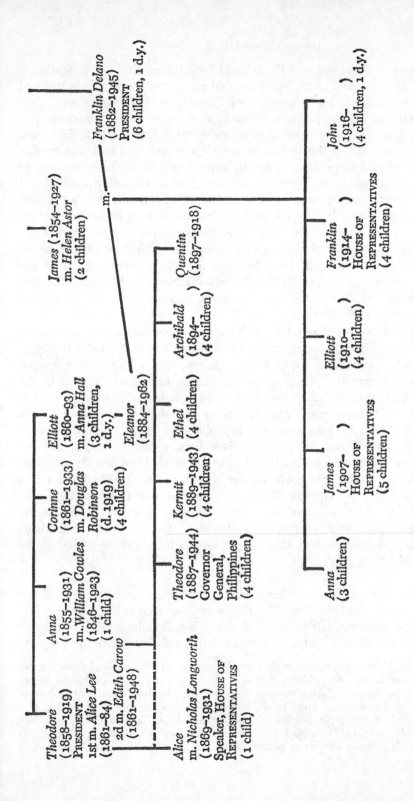

Theodore Roosevelt and Franklin Delano Roosevelt were distantly related, fifth cousins. Later, when people compared the dynamic traits of these two chief executives, they spoke loosely of "Roosevelt genes." Few recalled that Ulysses S. Grant, a President not commonly pointed to with pride, bore the same genetic relationship to F.D.R. as did T.R.[4] And during the reign of the second Roosevelt a writer who took the trouble computed that there were no less than seventeen thousand living persons whose relationship to Theodore was as close as that of Franklin.[5]

Twentieth-century Americans were fascinated that one family tree had grown two such illustrious branches. In adoration or in anger they referred to the Roosevelts as "the Royal Family," and by adroit genealogical juggling, including such blood connections as ninth cousins twice removed, it was "proved" that the two Roosevelts were related to ten other presidents of the United States—Washington, Madison, the two Adamses, Van Buren, the two Harrisons, Taylor, and Taft—as well as the President of the Confederacy.[6]

Conveniently overlooked in such royalist calculations was that, rather than being American aristocracy, the Roosevelts were in fact a family of moderately successful shopkeepers, bankers, and minor landed gentry. Through longevity, advantageous marriages, and some success in the more genteel trades, they had broken into society without capturing it.

For eight generations, until the smug quietude of the family circle was shattered by two consummate politicians, the Roosevelts were a prosaic, self-satisfied lot, generally free from genius, public service, or almost any creative spark. After the nation entered the first Rooseveltian era the best archivists could do for the name was to dig up a minor Revolutionary patriot, one Tammany politician, one anti-Tammany politician, an early steamboat innovator, and the inventor of the electric organ. Then, after centuries in America, two Roosevelts suddenly emerged who seemed to have been born to lead, although lacking the antecedents of leadership.

Claes Martenszen van Rosenvelt, a Dutchman, was the first of the line to reach the New World.* (Theodore Roosevelt called him his "very common ancestor.") It is recorded that Claes bought a farm in 1649 on Manhattan Island, south of Murray Hill, and just north of property

---

* F.D.R.'s daughter reports that her father, in all his study of family genealogy, had never been able to find out what Claes did for a livelihood before coming to America. "As a consequence, he said, he had come to the conclusion that our ancestor must have been a horse thief or some other kind of a thief and, therefore, a fugitive from justice." F.D.R.'s conclusion, however, was only designed to tease his aristocratic mother. See Anna Roosevelt, "My Life with F.D.R.: The Road to the White House," *The Woman,* August 1949, p. 50.

owned by Governor Peter Stuyvesant. The background of the humble man who was to become one of the most distinguished of American ancestors-to-be received front-page attention in 1935 when his great-great-great-great-great-grandson was President of the United States. It was then widely rumored that F.D.R.'s forebears were Jewish. As one anti-Roosevelt tract stated, "Strangely enough, there is no record whatever of Martenszen's marriage to Jannetje Samuels, or of either of them having been members of the Reformed Dutch Church, although their children were baptized there. This has led some people to suppose that they were of the Jewish religion, for baptism in the Reformed Dutch Church was the only practical way of registering births and the names of some of the people who had their children baptized there would seem to indicate that they were Jewish."[7]† F.D.R. recognized this sudden interest in his ancestry in a letter to the Detroit *Jewish Chronicle*. "All I know about the origin of the Roosevelt family in this country is that all branches bearing the name are apparently descended from Claes Martenssen van Roosevelt [sic]." Continued the presidential descendant, "Where he came from in Holland I do not know, nor do I know who his parents were. . . . In the dim distant past they may have been Jews or Catholics or Protestants—what I am more interested in is whether they were good citizens and believers in God; I hope they were both."[8]

It was Claes's son Nicholas, a fur trader and shopkeeper, who adopted the present spelling of the family name. He also had a lively wife who was brought to trial for exposing her ankles "in unseemly fashion, to the scandal of the community."[9] More important, he was the first Roosevelt to hold public office, serving as a New York alderman in 1700. From his sons Johannes and Jacobus are descended the Oyster Bay and Hyde Park Roosevelts respectively. The brothers, unlike their heirs, worked in harmony, being partners in a very shady real estate venture which was exposed by William Livingston in his *Independent Reflector*.

The fortune of the Hyde Park Roosevelts, amounting to approximately one million dollars on the death of F.D.R., was founded by Jacobus' son Isaac.[10] Although the Bayards had introduced sugar refining to New York, and the Livingstons were in the business before him, Isaac Roosevelt became one of the first large-scale sugar refiners. His heirs invested their inheritance wisely, primarily in coal and railroads, and augmented it through judicious marriages, but thereafter they were content to live as country gentlemen, and never again was there another real money-maker in this branch of the dynasty.

Isaac was also the only one of F.D.R.'s ancestors who sought in any way to mold the society in which he lived. He was a passionate, though

† More probably no marriage was recorded in America because they were married in Holland.

minor, actor during the Revolutionary period—serving in the New York Provincial Congress in 1775; as a member of the convention that drafted the first constitution of New York in 1777; subsequently as a member of the first state Senate; and as an ardent Federalist in the New York convention that ratified the federal Constitution. F.D.R. was to recall his patriotic forebear during the 1936 canvass. When he reached Poughkeepsie on the day before the election, the President invoked the name of Isaac Roosevelt as a rejoinder to those who charged that he was less than devoted to the Constitution. "About a block from where I stand up there on the corner of Main Street," said candidate Roosevelt, "there was a little old stone building and in the year 1788 there was held there the constitutional convention of the State of New York. My great-great-grandfather was a member of that convention. . . . And so you will see that not only in my own person but also by inheritance I know something not only about the Constitution of the United States, but also about the Bill of Rights."[11] (Although the kinship was less direct, Theodore Roosevelt also used old Isaac to establish his patriotism-by-inheritance.[12]) Yet, while Isaac served well the cause of American independence at a time when it was not fashionable in New York, his place in history was more properly defined by a non-Roosevelt President, George Washington, who wrote in his diary in 1788: "Received an invitation to attend the funeral of Mrs. Roosevelt (the wife of a Senator in this State), but declined complying with it, first, because the propriety of accepting an invitation of this sort appeared to be very questionable, and secondly, (though to do so in this instance might not be improper), because it might be difficult to discriminate in cases which might thereafter happen."[13] Despite the historical recollections of T.R. and F.D.R., the Roosevelt family had still not quite earned presidential recognition.

It took another two generations for the Oyster Bay Roosevelts to establish their fortune, but when they did so it far eclipsed the wealth of their Hudson River cousins. The acquisitive Roosevelt was T.R.'s grandfather, known in the family as C.V.S., for Cornelius Van Schaaick. A little man with a large head, a high brow, and a thick nose, C.V.S. knew from the start that making money would be his ruling passion. In 1821 he wrote his fiancée, "Economy is my doctrine at all times—at all events till I become, if it is to be so, a *man of fortune*."[14] (The italics are his.) He waited until the Panic of 1837; then, as property values toppled, he plunged into Manhattan real estate. By 1842 the New York *Sun* listed his worth at $250,000; by 1845, $500,000; by 1868, $1,346,000 in taxable property alone; at his death in 1871 he was known to be one of the five richest men in New York.

Grandson Theodore, whose knowledge of economics was meager, was to turn his back on mere wealth-gathering, but the main thrust of the Oyster Bay clan would always be toward Wall Street rather than Washington. In 1797 C.V.S.'s father had started a Maiden Lane hardware shop which specialized in imported plate glass; C.V.S.'s son switched from plate glass to banking; and C.V.S.'s great-grandson switched from banking to trust fund management after distant cousin Franklin signed the Federal Banking Act of 1934.

The firm of Roosevelt & Son, 48 Wall Street, celebrated its hundred and fiftieth anniversary in 1947. The senior partner was then George Emlen Roosevelt, fifth member of his family in direct succession to head the firm which was believed to manage funds in excess of a hundred million dollars.[15] While T.R.'s immediate family had political reasons to feud with the F.D.R. clan, the enmity of the Wall Street Roosevelts was primarily economic. In 1934 an apocryphal tale made the rounds on "The Street." George Emlen Roosevelt, it was said, had written the White House about the disposition of some funds held for the President's mother. "Dear Cousin Franklin: In view of the Administration's attitude toward the utility industry, what do you suggest that we do with Mrs. Roosevelt's utility investment?" The reply supposedly ran: "Dear Cousin George: I have nothing to suggest. Investments are your business, not mine." Whereupon, the legend concluded, came the retort: "Dear Cousin Franklin: We have liquidated the utility holdings in question and have invested the proceeds in Government bonds. Now it's your business."[16]

While most of the Hyde Park Roosevelts led pleasant, unimportant lives on their Hudson River estates, and most of the Oyster Bay Roosevelts concentrated on making money, an occasional Roosevelt took off in unexpected directions, thus adding some diversity to the family's otherwise bland diet.

From the Hyde Park branch came two distinguished religious figures and a philanthropist.[17] The sister of Isaac "the Patriot" had a granddaughter, known as Mother Seton, who founded the Sisters of Charity in 1809 and will probably become the first American-born saint of the Roman Catholic Church (F.D.R. told an aide that his great-grandfather had been in love with her);[18] her nephew, John Roosevelt Bayley, was Cardinal Gibbons' predecessor as Archbishop of Baltimore; and James H. Roosevelt, an invalid bachelor, left his estate of one million dollars to found Roosevelt Hospital in New York. But there were no politicians in this branch of the dynasty between Isaac the Patriot and Franklin the President.

The Oyster Bay Roosevelts were more daring, more political, and, on rare occasions, even naughty![19]

T.R.'s first cousin Cornelius married a French actress (". . . a disgrace to the family—the vulgar brute," commented the future President, then a student at Harvard[20]). The wayward Roosevelt lived the rest of his life in Paris, joyously and handsomely, on borrowed money which he never repaid. His son André followed in his sire's footsteps, flying over erupting Andean volcanoes, popularizing Bali as a tourist attraction, and (according to Cousin Nicholas) having "extramarital relations [which] added to the population of four continents" and "business ventures [which] were largely at the expense of new acquaintances hypnotized by his name. . . ."[21] When André died in 1962, at the age of eighty-three, the New York *Times* listed his occupation as "adventurer."[22]

Others, though hardly in the black sheep category, displayed a type of *joie de vivre* that was wholly absent in the history of their Hyde Park cousins:

—Nicholas Roosevelt claimed that Chancellor Livingston and Robert Fulton pirated his side-wheel principle when they built the *Clermont*. His wife (the daughter of the great architect Benjamin Henry Latrobe) had the first child to be born on a steamboat in the Mississippi. He was the first creative Roosevelt and died a poor man.‡

—Hilborne Roosevelt, T.R.'s first cousin, was an organ maker, much to the dismay of the family. He patented the first electric organ in the United States and escaped disgracing the dynasty by becoming rich.

—Clinton Roosevelt, a radical member of the New York Assembly in 1835, advocated a form of national socialism and branded bankers as oppressors of the people.

—James I. ("it stands for I—me!") Roosevelt served as a Tammany congressman and judge, of whom Philip Hone wrote: "Roosevelt, the leader of the blackguards, in whose person, as its representative, our poor city is disgraced, takes the lead in opposition to the law and resorts to every species of vile, disgraceful conduct and language. . . ." He got his comeuppance when he married the daughter of Governor Van Ness of Vermont, a buxom beauty, who had an arrangement with a department store by which her requests for petty cash were added to her unsuspecting husband's bills. In this way she supposedly acquired $30,000 for her private needs.

—And T.R.'s uncle, Robert Barnwell Roosevelt, a luxuriantly whiskered gentleman, was a pioneer conservationist and long-time fish commissioner of New York State. As a municipal reformer he helped replace the Tweed Ring with respectable and ineffectual Mayor William Havemeyer. He was also a one-term congressman, U.S. minister to the Netherlands, and treasurer of the Democratic National Committee during Grover

‡ See Livingston Dynasty, pp. 113–16.

Cleveland's successful race against Benjamin Harrison. Uncle Bob was as close as the Oyster Bay Roosevelts came to producing a national figure until his nephew rode up San Juan Hill.

The two Roosevelt presidents were the same number of generations removed from their "very common ancestor." Their fathers were contemporaries. But T.R. was a child of his father's youth, and F.D.R. of his father's fifty-fifth year.

The courteous, fastidious country squire who was F.D.R.'s father was established enough in wealth to look down on the Vanderbilts, whose dinner invitations he refused (". . . if we accept," he told his wife, "we shall have to have them to our house."[23]) James Roosevelt's manorial existence in Dutchess County irritated some relatives, one of whom later said, "He tried to pattern himself on Lord Landsdowne, sideburns and all, but what he really looked like was Landsdowne's coachman."[24] Yet behind this dignified exterior must have burned some flame of the romantic. For while on a post-college tour of Europe he enlisted in Garibaldi's red-shirted legion. However, after a month of waiting around to battle for Italian independence, he returned to the greater excitement of being an American tourist.§

While he considered the Vanderbilts' money too new or ill gotten, James Roosevelt was not above dabbling in the world of commerce. At various times he was president of the Louisville, New Albany and Chicago Railroad; a holder of large real estate interests in West Superior, Wisconsin; and president of the Champlain Transportation Company, which ran paddle-wheelers on Lake Champlain and Lake George. Several times he tried and failed to make large financial killings, once in a Nicaraguan canal venture. Politics, however, he felt was definitely not a respectable vocation. For some inexplicable reason this very patrician gentleman was a Democrat, but when President Cleveland offered him a diplomatic post, probably as minister to Holland, it never entered his mind to accept.[25]

By his first wife, Rebecca Howland, of the ancient Pilgrim family, he had a son, James Roosevelt Roosevelt, called "Rosy." Mrs. Roosevelt died in 1873, and seven years later James married again. The bride was tall, gracious Sara Delano; half her husband's age, the age of her stepson. In 1882 she bore an only child, Franklin Delano Roosevelt.

§ Politically, the time was not ill spent—at least from one descendant's point of view. Said Franklin D. Roosevelt, Jr., when dedicating a plaque in Verrazano Park, New York City: "I feel a rather close affinity to all Italians here and in Italy because my grandfather, James Roosevelt, fought as a member of Garibaldi's army in his fight for the unification and independence of Italy." See New York *Times*, April 11, 1965, p. 77.

The Delanos liked to trace their ancestry to William the Conqueror. With even more authority they could find in their lineage three signers of the Mayflower Compact, including Isaac Allerton, a scoundrel who was ordered to leave Massachusetts in 1635 when it was discovered that while acting as the business agent for the Plymouth Colony some of the Pilgrims' money had stuck to his fingers.¶ But the Delano of whom F.D.R. liked most to boast was one Thomas, who married the daughter of Priscilla Alden of "speak for yourself, John" fame. The historian of the Delano clan calls this match "the first shot-gun wedding in American history." His evidence is the court record of Plymouth Colony for October 30, 1667, which shows that Thomas was fined ten pounds "for having carnall copulation with his *now* wife before marriage." (John Alden was one of the tribunal who sat in judgment of his son-in-law.)[26]

The lovely Sara's family had been long associated with the sea. Her father was a retired China trader, having made two fortunes (and lost one) as a merchant in opium and other oriental commodities. He shared the Delanos' staunch Republicanism and enjoyed saying that, while all Democrats weren't horse thieves, all horse thieves were Democrats.*

In her ghost-written account of F.D.R., Sara Delano Roosevelt inadvertently allows a picture to be painted of a lonely, "sequestered" boyhood.[27] He was breast-fed for a year and dressed in frilly outfits until he was five. In the company of his elderly father he had made eight trips to the health spas of Europe by the time he was fourteen. Then he was sent to Groton, and from there to Harvard. James Roosevelt died when his son was a college freshman, leaving a will that appointed "my wife sole guardian of my son Franklin Delano Roosevelt, and I wish him to be under the influence of his mother."[28] Sara promptly moved to Boston to carry out her late husband's wish.

The childhood of T.R. was a very different matter. His father, the elder Theodore Roosevelt, of the firm of Roosevelt & Son, had married a beautiful Southern belle, Martha Bulloch. Her youngest daughter recalled her black hair, "fine of texture and with a glow that sometimes seemed to have a slightly russet shade . . . her skin was the purest and most delicate white, more moonlight-white than cream-white, and in the

¶ See Lee Dynasty, pp. 49–81.
* He was overlooking his Republican relation, Columbus Delano, who as Grant's Internal Revenue Commissioner and Secretary of the Interior left for posterity a record of unusual corruption in his agencies. A contemporary called him a "dry, baldish, clerical-looking man with a sly, contriving air. . . . His appointment marked a sad step in the deliquescence of the [Grant] Administration." See Daniel W. Delano, Jr., *Franklin Roosevelt and the Delano Influence* (Pittsburgh: James W. Nudi, 1946), pp. 115–16.

cheeks there was a coral, rather than a rose, tint."[29] This lovely young lady grew up on a Georgia plantation, the great-granddaughter of the state's first governor, and the child of a confusing marriage that rather shocked polite Savannah society.†

Martha Bulloch Roosevelt was an adored wife but an ineffectual mother and housekeeper. She was incapable of either keeping an appointment on time or managing routine money matters; so, after giving birth to four children, the transplanted Southern flower began a decorative decline. She discovered that headaches were an ideal excuse to retire from the perpetual motion of the Roosevelt household, and her eldest daughter Anna, fourteen years of age, assumed efficient management of the family. Known as Bamie or Bye, Anna Roosevelt was not exactly a hunchback. She suffered from a spinal ailment that badly crippled her but which with amazing courage she refused to let interfere with a whirlwind of activities. To sister Corinne and brothers Theodore and Elliott she was more mother than peer. Elliott was the leader of the younger children, Theodore was the sickly one, suffering, as he said, from "asmer." (Never being much of a speller, T.R. later tried to make the English language conform to his own orthography.) Under the supervision of his father, whom he considered "his best and most intimate friend," Teddy adopted a rigorous routine to build his frail body.[30]

The one dark cloud over this closely knit family was the Civil War. The children's maternal uncles were deeply involved in the cause of the South: James Dunwody Bulloch ("Uncle Jimmy") was the Confederate agent who played such a skillful cat-and-mouse game with Charles Francis Adams over the building of war vessels in England; his brother, Irvine Bulloch, as a midshipman on the *Alabama*, fired the last guns in the fight with the *Kearsarge*.‡ To save his wife's feelings, the elder Theodore Roosevelt, although only twenty-nine, stayed out of the Union Army. Instead he became an allotment commissioner, making the rounds

† As a young man her father had courted, and been rejected by, Martha Stewart of Savannah. He then married Hester Elliott, daughter of United States Senator John Elliott, and subsequently Martha Stewart married the senator. After Senator Elliott and Hester Elliott Bulloch died, the widow and widower were wed, Bulloch thus marrying his former stepmother-in-law! President Theodore Roosevelt's mother was the child of this second round of matrimony. See Carleton Putnam, *Theodore Roosevelt, the Formative Years* (New York: Scribner's, 1958), p. 1 n.

‡ Theodore Roosevelt was to turn this into a political asset. While traveling through the South in 1905, a Washington *Star* reporter wrote, "One would suppose that the President himself fired the last two shots from the *Alabama* instead of his uncle. Mr. Roosevelt's relationship with a Confederate officer is accepted as practically equal with having fought for the cause himself." See Henry F. Pringle, *Theodore Roosevelt* (New York: Harcourt, Brace, 1931), p. 371.

of military camps to induce troops to send part of their pay home to their families. (At least one Roosevelt, sister Corinne, felt that T.R.'s later passion for military heroics could be traced to his unspoken disappointment over his father's failure to fight on the Northern side.)[31]

The senior Theodore Roosevelt was an important member of the community. Besides being a successful businessman, he helped found the New York Orthopaedic Hospital (motivated by Bamie's illness), the Metropolitan Museum of Art, and the Museum of Natural History, as well as being a major force in the administration of the Children's Aid Society and the Newsboys' Lodging House. In the opinion of a close friend, "He literally 'went about doing good.' "[32] Yet, though to a lesser degree than F.D.R.'s father, he found politics to be distasteful. Only once was he involved in political life, and then more as a symbol than an active participant. President Hayes appointed him as collector of customs for the port of New York, a patronage-rich office then held by Chester A. Arthur of Senator Conkling's organization. In this fight between the reformers and the machine, Roosevelt's role was to represent civic virtue. But the machine had the votes, and the nomination was rejected by the Senate. The nominee had made no effort on his own behalf.[33] In two months he was dead. Each of the Roosevelt children inherited $125,000; they would each get another $62,500 when their mother died six years later.[34] Teddy continued at Harvard, where he was a sophomore; Elliott dug into his inheritance to go around the world hunting big game.

Elliott Roosevelt was handsome and charming; not at all like his brother Teddy, who had a queer voice, enormous teeth, and wore thick glasses. There was an impulsive, appealing quality about Elliott. As a child of seven he gave his new overcoat to a ragged urchin who looked cold. "He never could learn to control his heart by his head," said his daughter Eleanor, the future First Lady. "With him the heart always dominated."[35] When Franklin Delano Roosevelt was born his parents asked Elliott to be a godparent. He replied that while unworthy of the distinction, "My dear little mother has persuaded me that I should accept the high honor you offer me."[36] Elliott was amusing. Not long after returning from his world safari he married Anna Hall, granddaughter of a Livingston and great-great-granddaughter of the powerful Chancellor.[37] With her blue eyes and sunny hair, all agreed that Anna was "a singularly beautiful and gracious woman, a queen of the world in which she moved."[38] The young couple, wrote their daughter, joined the "fun-loving younger set on Long Island in summer, with hunting and polo and gay evening parties."[39] Elliott also took up serious drinking.

Although Theodore Roosevelt made Phi Beta Kappa and Porcellian, his heart was not on studies or clubs. He was in love. He met the young lady when he spent a weekend at the Chestnut Hill home of Harvard friend Richard Saltonstall (father of U. S. Senator Leverett Saltonstall). Next door was Saltonstall's first cousin Alice Lee, whose ancient family tree bore a profusion of Cabots, Jacksons, Higginsons, and other distinguished Massachusetts names.[40] She was tall, yet exceedingly feminine, with light brown hair, a slightly tilted nose, and blue eyes.[41] Friends called her "Sunshine." They were married in 1880; three years later she gave birth to a daughter. It was St. Valentine's Day and the new father joyfully rushed home from Albany, where he was serving in the state Assembly. He was met in the doorway by Elliott. "There is a curse on this house." Wife and mother lay dying. Martha Bulloch Roosevelt and Alice Lee Roosevelt were buried the next day. The infant, named Alice, was taken in by Bamie; Theodore returned to Albany, and later to the Bad Lands of Dakota. Like Henry Adams, he couldn't bring himself to mention his first wife's name in his autobiography.

Almost exactly eight months after Theodore Roosevelt's daughter Alice was born, his brother Elliott's wife also gave birth to a girl, christened Anna Eleanor, but always known as plain Eleanor. While little Alice seemed to have inherited her mother's grace and looks, little Eleanor had not. She was the shy, awkward daughter of a beautiful mother; turned inward, she lived in a dream world populated exclusively by herself and her idealized father. She was eight when her mother died. By then Elliott was a confirmed alcoholic, living in Virginia, where he had been given a job by brother-in-law Douglas Robinson, Corinne's husband. His daughter lived only for his enchanting letters, which she always carried with her. He died in 1893—thirty-three years of age. Eleanor continued to stay with Grandmother Hall, eventually moving to Tivoli, part of the original Livingston estate on the Hudson. But the large house was more a prison for an alcoholic uncle. Watching her uncle lose his power of self-control, Eleanor wrote that "it began to develop in me an almost exaggerated idea of the necessity of keeping all of one's desires under complete subjugation."[42]§

When she was two, Alice Roosevelt got a stepmother. After taking a devastating drubbing in a race for mayor of New York City, T.R. went

§ Eleanor also had an alcoholic brother, G. Hall Roosevelt (1891–1941). Like their father, he was generous, handsome, and talented, but, as his sister wrote, "You could never convince him that it is very hard to shake a habit you have once let get hold of you." By the time he realized he had a serious drinking problem "he no longer wanted to stop." He was at one time city controller and chairman of the Detroit Unemployment Bureau. His second wife, Dorothy Kemp, was a concert pianist and unsuccessful candidate for Congress in 1942.

off to London to marry Edith Carow, a childhood sweetheart. The
Carows had lost their money and were now living in Europe where it
was cheaper to keep up appearances. The family, however, had not always known hard times. (Her maternal grandfather was Union General
Daniel Tyler, whose leadership bears some of the blame for the disaster
at Bull Run, but who later became a successful iron manufacturer and
railroad president.[43]) Bamie's offer to keep little Alice was politely rejected by the new Mrs. Roosevelt. Edith, having watched the marriage
ceremony of T.R. and Alice Lee, felt she had waited long enough to take
full possession of her husband's life. In an unassuming, efficient, sometimes ruthless way she demanded complete control of the household.
Corinne warned Bamie to cease and desist or they might lose Theodore
altogether.

But Bamie did not have to wait long to display again her maternal instincts. The call came from "Rosy" Roosevelt, F.D.R.'s half brother. He
had married Helen Astor, whose mother was *the* Mrs. Astor of Ward
McAllister's glittering Four Hundred. Backed by his wife's money, Rosy
dabbled in Democratic politics, and a $10,000 contribution to Cleveland's
war chest in 1892 landed him the post of first secretary of the American
Embassy in London. When Rosy's wife died, leaving her two small
children an estate of $1,500,000, Bamie went over to take charge.¶ "You
are an angel, as usual," wrote Mrs. Henry Cabot Lodge, "to go & take
care of all the poor forlorn things of the world."[44]

It was hardly a sacrifice. Ambassador Thomas Francis Bayard's wife
was a rather shy hostess, and before long Bamie had taken over not only
the Roosevelt household but the supervision of all social functions at the
embassy as well. Soon it became evident that she had also taken over
Commander William Sheffield Cowles, the naval attaché, a somewhat
portly gentleman of forty-nine with a great walrus mustache. They were
married in 1895 and went off to the Continent on a wedding trip. Unfortunately, sister Corinne was in Paris, and deposited her children with
the honeymooners! "There was something so funny about this that we
could hardly bear it," wrote Bamie.[45] When the newlyweds finally left
Europe, *The Times* of London had nothing to say about the departure

¶ James Roosevelt Roosevelt's daughter Helen was to marry Theodore Douglas Robinson, son of Corinne Roosevelt, and an Assistant Secretary of the
Navy. Rosy's son James made a less respectable match. He took as his bride
one Sadie Meisinger, known as "Dutch Sadie" at the Haymarket Dance Hall,
New York City's most notorious house of assignation. The couple left for Florida under assumed names, but later the unhappy and chastened young man
returned to New York and devoted his energies to the Salvation Army. See
Allen Churchill, *The Roosevelts: American Aristocrats* (New York: Harper
& Row, 1965), p. 230.

of the naval officer, remembered primarily as a pleasant clothes horse, but wrote with "dismay" of losing Bamie, who had become "almost indispensable."[46]

"[Theodore] Roosevelt, more than any other man living within the range of notoriety," wrote Henry Adams, "showed the singular primitive quality that belongs to ultimate matter—the quality that medieval theology assigned to God—he was pure act."[47] The amazing political career of this "interesting combination of St. Vitus and St. Paul" (as Lord Morley called him) began when T.R. was elected to the New York legislature at the age of twenty-three.[48] He reached Albany because an Irish Catholic named Joe Murray wanted to wrest control of the Twenty-first Assembly District from a German Jew named Jake Hess. While T.R. had neither experience nor accomplishment to recommend him, he did have a good name. An endorsing editorial in the New York *Post* said, "Mr. Roosevelt has hereditary claims to the confidence and hopefulness of the voters of this city, for his father was in his day one of the most useful and public-spirited men in the community. . . ."[49] Uncle Robert Barnwell Roosevelt, whom the newly elected legislator resembled in energy and interests, helped him get choice committee assignments. From then on Teddy was on his own, and for two years proved to be a zealous crusader who instinctively knew how to strike dramatic chords.

During Teddy's undergraduate years at Harvard, Henry Cabot Lodge had been an instructor there. But Lodge was known as a hard marker and a boring lecturer, and so T.R. avoided his courses. The deep friendship between these patrician politicians did not begin until the 1884 Republican Presidential Convention, when the two young delegates teamed up in a futile effort to block the nomination of James G. Blaine. Lodge, more than any other man, would mastermind T.R.'s rise to the presidency.

After the Blaine convention Roosevelt left for his ranch in Dakota Territory; returning to New York would only have renewed memories of his pretty young wife, so recently dead. He sought therapy in riding the range. Life to Theodore Roosevelt was always a grand play to be performed in costume. Donning an outrageous outfit—silk neckerchief, fringed buckskin shirt, sealskin chaparajos, alligator-hide boots—he proceeded to have some outrageous adventures. (Once he shared a hotel bed with a gentleman who was arrested during the night for robbing a Northern Pacific train.[50]) But when not playing cowboy T.R. turned out a prodigious number of books—biography, American history, Western stories. He wrote as much for income as for enjoyment, since he had sunk a great deal of his inheritance into ranching ventures that were wiped out by the blizzards of 1886. In common with his friend Lodge,

Roosevelt shared a capacity for sound scholarship—a capacity, however, which they rarely indulged after entering politics, although this never stilled their constantly moving pens.

Coming back to New York in 1886, Teddy finished last in a three-way race for mayor, and *Puck* composed his political obituary: "Be happy, Mr. Roosevelt, be happy while you may. You are young—yours is the time of roses—the time of illusions. . . . Bright visions float before your eyes of what the Party can and may do for you. . . . We fear the Party cannot do much for you. You are not the timber of which Presidents are made."[51]

Thus dismissed, Roosevelt did not return to public life until 1889, when pressure from Lodge, now a senator, got him appointed to the U. S. Civil Service Commission, a job whose importance was measured by its salary—$3500 a year. Working under Benjamin Harrison was "horribly disheartening," Roosevelt discovered. "Oh, Heaven, if the President had a little backbone," he wrote Lodge.[52] On another occasion he reported to his mentor that he had told Harrison the parable of the backwoodsman and the bear: "Oh Lord, help me kill that bar, [prayed the backwoodsman] and if you don't help me, oh Lord, don't help the bar."[53] The "backwoodsman" finally got some non-divine assistance in his crusade against the spoilsmen when Grover Cleveland succeeded to the presidency. However, after six years in Washington Teddy began to get restless. A reform mayor had been elected in New York and offered to make him the sanitation commissioner, which he considered infra dig for a Roosevelt. But when the police commissionership was tendered, he promptly accepted.

Being top cop of the nation's largest city was a glorious job for the ebullient Teddy. He pedaled to headquarters each morning on a bicycle, and wandered the streets late at night looking for crime or a patrolman who was indulging in a schooner of beer at the side door of a saloon. Later, an Irish policeman, tears streaming down his face, would ask T.R.'s sister, "Do you remember the fun of him, Mrs. Robinson?" Time may have lent enchantment. During his reign at Mulberry Street a reporter was able to frighten the constabulary badly by merely chattering a pair of gleaming false teeth. Vendors started to sell small whistles shaped like "Teddy's Teeth."[54] It all made grand newspaper copy, even if the commissioner was less than a success as he rode off in all directions in the hot pursuit of vice. Theodore Roosevelt's destiny was to capture the imagination of the American people; he first succeeded as head of the New York police force. Henry Cabot Lodge even began to suggest that the presidency was a distinct possibility.

Wirepulling by Lodge, William Howard Taft, and others got T.R. the position of Assistant Secretary of the Navy in 1897, a post from which he was able to observe with gusto the coming of war with Spain. Roosevelt had always wanted to lead his countrymen in battle. He now sent to Brooks Brothers for a soldier suit (blue "without yellow on the collar and with leggings") and recruited his band of "Rough Riders."* The nation had never before, and would never again, see the likes of the 1st United States Volunteer Cavalry. Lieutenant Colonel Roosevelt found his troopers in the Ivy League, the Somerset and Knickerbocker clubs, the New York police force, the Texas Rangers. There were polo players, Indians and Indian fighters, broncobusters and steeplechase riders. "It was the society page, financial column, and Wild West Show all wrapped up in one," wrote a reporter.[55]

The Spanish-American War, to those who were in it, was a "splendid little war." But it really wasn't much. The American people, however, would have settled for almost anything, as long as the outcome was victorious. Teddy's capture of San Juan Hill was hardly more than a skirmish. His cavalry had left its horses at home and scrambled up the slope on foot. Later, when Edith saw the site of her husband's heroics, she was amused to find that it was hardly as steep as he had led her to believe. Still, for T.R. it was *the* time of my life," as he confided to Lodge.[56] Less than three months later Roosevelt was back at home, a national hero, and the Republican candidate for governor of New York.

For Thomas Platt, the "Easy Boss" of New York politics, the thought of having to make Roosevelt his gubernatorial candidate was not pleasing. Yet he liked less the prospects of losing an election, and the incumbent Republican Administration was in the midst of a scandal. The uncontrollable T.R. was the lesser of two evils. As the Roosevelt campaign train steamed through the state a bugler would appear at each stop to play the cavalry charge. Then the candidate emerged, surrounded by his faithful Rough Riders. "You have heard the trumpet that sounded to bring you here," he intoned. "I have heard it tear the tropic dawn when it summoned us to fight at Santiago."[57] Poor Mr. Van Wyck, the Democratic candidate, never had a chance.

It may be too machiavellian to suppose that Tom Platt spent the full two years of Theodore Roosevelt's governorship plotting ways to get rid of him, but the thought certainly entered his mind. By the 1900 Republican Convention he had devised a scheme: kick T.R. upstairs to the vice-presidency. The outmaneuvered national chairman, Mark Hanna,

---

* Roosevelt used the phrase casually in a conversation with Washington correspondent Richard V. Oulahan of the New York *Evening Sun*, whose story was published under the headline, "Roosevelt's Rough Riders." T.R. didn't like the term and asked Oulahan to use "mounted riflemen" as better expressing the character of the regiment. Only the reporter's ear for alliteration saved "Rough Riders" for its ultimate place in American history. From an unpublished manuscript, "How the Rough Riders Were Named," shown to the author by the late Mrs. Richard V. Oulahan.

could only gasp, "Don't any of you realize that there's only one life between this madman and the White House?"[58] On Inauguration Day Platt boasted that he had come to Washington "to see Theodore take the veil." Another spectator, Alice Roosevelt, now a grown-up seventeen, watched the parade from a window over Mme. Payne's Manicure Shop on Pennsylvania Avenue, and wondered to herself "what sort of a 'risk'" President McKinley was.[59]

Less than seven months later McKinley was assassinated and Theodore Roosevelt was President of the United States. "His Accidency," quipped Henry Adams.[60]

Every President introduces a new cast of characters on the American scene. The Roosevelt players resembled a three-ring circus. Forty-two-year-old Teddy was the youngest chief executive in history, and he brought to the White House a pride of children, six in number, ranging from the lovely Alice to four-year-old Quentin. In between there were Theodore, Jr., fourteen; Kermit, twelve; Ethel, ten; and Archibald, seven.

And the children brought their pets. The stately White House was turned into a menagerie. Alice had a lizard, "Emily Spinach" ("Spinach" for its color; "Emily" for a very thin aunt); the boys had ponies, rabbits, guinea pigs, dogs, squirrels, raccoons, and badgers, called by such spiritual and secular names as "Bishop Doane," "Admiral Dewey," "The Prodigal Son," "Dr. Johnson" (after their Dutch Reformed pastor), "Caesar," "Father Grady" (in honor of an Oyster Bay priest), and "Fighting Bob Evans." Kermit was known to come to breakfast with a kangaroo rat in his pocket; Quentin once used the White House elevator to bring a pony to visit Archie, who was sick in bed upstairs; "Loretta," a parrot, was taught to say, "Hurrah for Roosevelt," and there was even a bear christened "Jonathan Edwards" (the great divine being distantly related to the President's wife.)[61]

"I don't think that any family has ever enjoyed the White House more than we have," the President wrote to son Kermit.[62] When Quentin started to go to school he brought "the gang" back to his house for baseball on the South Lawn or a pillow fight with Father. "Nothing was too sacred to be used for their amusement, and no place too good for a playroom," lamented the chief usher.[63] In this they were encouraged by the President. When he stopped to think about decorum, which was rarely, T.R. said, ". . . really it seems, to put it mildly, rather odd for a stout, elderly President to be bouncing over hay-ricks in a wild effort to get to goal before an active midget of a competitor, aged nine years." But then he added, more in character, "However, it was really great fun." Ethel was a perfect little lady, even a Sunday school teacher, and Edith tried her best to maintain order. Yet she fought against overwhelming odds. As Sir Cecil Spring-Rice, the British ambassador, put it, "You must always remember that the President is about six."[64]

It was blue-eyed Alice, however, who most fascinated the American public. Songs were written in her honor and national fads emulated her bizarre behavior. "I can do one of two things," T.R. told novelist Owen Wister, "I can be President of the United States, or I can control Alice. I cannot possibly do both." The *Journal des Debats* of the French Chamber of Deputies tabulated that in a fifteen-month period Alice had attended 407 dinners, 350 balls, 300 parties, 685 teas, and made 1706 calls. *Town Topics*, a New York society journal, cattily commented, ". . . if the young woman knew some of the tales that are told at the clubs in Newport she would be more careful in the future about what she does and how she does it."[65] Instead she was seen at the race track, smoked cigarettes in public, and fell in love with bald-headed Congressman Nicholas Longworth, scion of a distinguished Cincinnati family.

When Nick, the son of a federal judge, first arrived in Washington in 1903, wearing the brightest waistcoats the capital had ever seen, he was immediately recognized as a charming and entertaining fellow. He could play the violin well enough to draw fulsome praise from Zimbalist, Reiner, and Stokowski; he could also perform with the fiddle behind his back and the bow between his knees.[66]

On February 17, 1906, the "national bridegroom," as Nick was dubbed by the Washington *Times*, drove up to 1600 Pennsylvania Avenue in his new red motorcar. In the East Room five hundred guests were assembled for the most important marriage of the young century, the tenth wedding in the history of the White House. Alice waited, lovely in ancestral lace and a train five yards long. Cousin Franklin Delano Roosevelt gallantly arranged the bride's veil for the photographers. Later Alice would recall, "I remember looking up and seeing Nick and thinking how hopelessly Middle West he did seem."[67] But she was the only one who saw anything provincial about the ceremony. Gifts poured in from all over the world—a necklace of aquamarines with 120 diamonds in the pendant, a dog with an Alice-blue blanket, a $25,000 Gobelin tapestry from the French government, a dower chest from the Dowager Empress of China, antique jewelry from the King of Spain, a mosaic table from the King of Italy. The President finally announced that it would not be proper for official presents to be received from other nations. "So like him," said Cabot Lodge, "to come to that decision after the gifts were on the way." Bamie replied, "At least Theodore didn't issue his awful ban before the string of [sixty-three matched] pearls from Cuba arrived."[68] (There was a report that the Cubans had first considered presenting Alice with San Juan Hill!) Finally Major McCawley handed the bride his sword to cut the cake, and the newlyweds boarded the Elysian, a private railroad car, for the honeymoon trip to Florida.

Lincoln Steffens said that T.R. "thought with his hips." Yet after the assassination of McKinley the nation, and especially the business community, was relieved to find that no precipitous actions were forthcoming from the new President. Roosevelt was content to wait for his own mandate. It came with his overwhelming victory in 1904. On March 4, 1905, while little Quentin was being boosted onto the platform by two black-robed justices of the Supreme Court so that he might have a better view, Theodore Roosevelt took the oath of office in his own right, and the real Rooseveltian era began.

Living under the reign of "Theodorus I, Czar Rooseveltoff" (a Henry Adams designation) was an exhausting yet exhilarating experience for a nation grown used to a long line of fossilized chief executives. Suddenly there was a President who believed that he was empowered to do anything that was not specifically prohibited in the Constitution. It was a shocking concept. Once in the New York Assembly a Tammany politician named Tim Campbell had asked Roosevelt to vote for a measure which T.R. told him was plainly unconstitutional. To this, Tim replied, "What the divil is the Constitution between frinds?"[69] As President, thought the conservatives, Roosevelt was a Tim Campbell constitutionalist. He had the Interstate Commerce Act strengthened, got sweeping laws passed in the field of pure food and drugs, made memorable efforts to protect the national forest and land reserves, and took after the "malefactors of great wealth." He was the first President to control the trusts (although he instituted only twenty indictments, compared to forty-five under Taft). It was T.R.'s role to broach important questions rather than to solve them. What was wrong with our industrial society? What could be done about it? Because of Roosevelt the nation, rather than the fringe reformers, for the first time demanded answers.[70]

Here was an American President who thought of his country as a world power, and morally entitled to be one. But if there was any doubt of America's moral sanctity, he modernized the fleet and sent it around the world for all to see. The Monroe Doctrine, he felt, ranked with the Ten Commandments—maybe higher. He took over the financial management of the Dominican Republic, got Great Britain to settle the old Alaska boundary dispute on his terms, brought about settlement of a European intervention in Venezuela, and, for good measure, "took Panama" so that he could build the canal. As a crowning achievement, this most militant of all American chief executives was awarded the Nobel Peace Prize.

After seven and a half years of Theodore Roosevelt the nation was emotionally exhausted. "He's a darlin' man, but so distressin'," said an Irish policeman in Boston. So T.R. waited until his friend Taft was moved into the White House and then left for Africa with Kermit. "Wall Street," said some wag, "hopes every lion will do its duty."

But the former President was never far from the thoughts of his countrymen. At the 1910 Gridiron Dinner most of the nation's dignitaries were totally ignored, while the reporters acted skit after skit devoted to the distant Roosevelt. To the tune of "I Wonder Who's Kissing Her Now," a bold hunter in an African jungle sang:

> I wonder who's wielding the stick;
> I wonder if Taft's learned the trick;
> Malefactors of wealth who do business by stealth—
> I wonder who's cussing them now![71]

The "Square Deal" was in a shamble by the time T.R. returned to the United States—or so he wanted to believe. And Theodore Roosevelt, who was too young to be an ex-President, once again threw his hat in the presidential ring. The 1912 Republican Convention, as the barkeep philosopher Mr. Dooley predicted, was a "combination iv th' Chicago fire, Saint Bartholomew's massacree, the battle iv th' Boyne, the life iv Jessie James, an' th' night iv th' big wind." Taft, the incumbent President with the full weight of the organization behind him, won an expected renomination. In November, Wilson was elected president; yet Roosevelt, the man without a party, finished substantially ahead of Taft in the three-way race.

Thus ended the political career of Theodore Roosevelt. There had been considerable speculation that he would be the Republican presidential nominee in 1920, but he died the year before at the age of sixty-one. "My last vision of fun and gaiety will vanish when my Theodore goes," Henry Adams once said. "Never can we replace him." His faults, added the sardonic sage, "are but trifles like the warty growths on a magnificent oak tree."[72]

One day in 1907 Franklin Delano Roosevelt told his fellow law clerks how he expected to spend the rest of his life: first the New York legislature, then Assistant Secretary of the Navy, followed by the governorship of New York, and finally—the presidency.[73] This was a remarkable statement from a young man who had shown neither brilliance nor unseemly ambition at Groton, Harvard, and Columbia Law School. It was, of course, a perfectly accurate prediction. But equally interesting, it was the outline of a career that exactly paralleled his fifth cousin Theodore's. It can hardly be allowed that this was unintentional, for T.R. was a hero to his distant relation. F.D.R. had even crossed party lines to cast his first vote in 1904 for the Republican Roosevelt.

When F.D.R. married Eleanor in 1905, the President told his new nephew-in-law, "Well, Franklin, there's nothing like keeping the name in the family."[74] While the bridegroom's mother was fond of Teddy, it is unlikely that she shared this enthusiasm. On being informed of the engagement, Sara Delano Roosevelt wrote in her diary, "Franklin gave me quite a startling announcement."[75] She then proceeded to take her son on a cruise of the West Indies. But the trip did not have the desired effect, and in her book, *My Boy Franklin,* she fails to mention this attempt to set the ship of love off course, preferring to have history record that "Franklin, unknown to any of us, had become engaged to his distant cousin, Anna Eleanor Roosevelt, a delightful child of nineteen, whom I had known and loved since babyhood."[76] It was not that the senior Mrs. Roosevelt objected to Eleanor, it was just that she would have liked to have Franklin to herself. Her daughter-in-law was to write that "she never accepted the fact of his independence and continued to the last to try to guide his life."[77] And she held a potent weapon over the newly-weds—the purse strings. It was the mother-in-law who chose the location of Eleanor's home (near to her own), paid for it, and picked out the furnishings.

F.D.R. started his ascent up the predicted political ladder in 1910. Running as the Democratic candidate for the state Senate in strongly Republican Dutchess County, he won a narrow and surprising victory. His name had helped. The young candidate didn't bother to correct any mistaken impressions that he was a son or nephew of the Roosevelt President. He managed adroitly to work T.R. into his speeches. "A little shaver said to me the other day that he knew I wasn't Teddy," he told one meeting. "I asked him 'why' and he replied: 'Because you don't show your teeth.'"[78] His election, however, was primarily the result of intensive campaigning and a nationwide backlash against the Taft Administration.

As a legislator F.D.R. followed in the T.R. pattern of being a reformer who was better at dramatizing issues than getting meaningful results. His most notable achievement in Albany was to block the election of "Blue-eyed Billy" Sheehan to the U. S. Senate; yet the man chosen was no more savory.†

† If F.D.R.'s failures could be charged off to inexperience, the same could not be said for his legislative contemporary, Theodore Douglas Robinson. Assemblyman Robinson was T.R.'s nephew, the son of Corinne Roosevelt and her wealthy realtor husband. He reached the legislature by defeating the regular Republican organization in Herkimer County, and later served three terms in the state Senate. The highlights of his achievements were proposals to license cats, train hunting dogs, make it a penal offense to use another person's laundry mark, and build a movable sidewalk between the Senate and Assembly chambers.

By climbing on board the Woodrow Wilson bandwagon early enough, F.D.R. was able to assure presidential gratitude after the 1912 election. Wrote Cousin Theodore: "Dear Franklin: I was very much pleased to see that you were appointed as Assistant Secretary of the Navy. It is interesting to see that you are in another place which I myself once held. . . . When I see Eleanor I shall say to her that I do hope she will be particularly nice to the naval officers' wives. . . ."[79] The young Assistant Secretary's record was again similar to his Roosevelt predecessor's. He too preached military preparedness to the point of insubordination. He also tried unsuccessfully to get an army command for T.R. after the nation entered World War I.

F.D.R.'s jump from second-echelon bureaucrat to presidential running mate in 1920 resulted mainly from this coattail connection with T.R. For the former President had died in 1919, and the nation was again feeling sympathetic toward the name. When venerable Henry Cabot Lodge heard that young Roosevelt was to be the Democratic vice-presidential candidate he said, "He is a well-meaning, nice young fellow, but light."[80] Added William Howard Taft, "He will not add any particular strength anywhere but he will give the ticket a good social flavor."[81] As the Democratic Roosevelt toured the country, people shouted, "I voted for your father" and "You're just like the Old Man."[82] This was the moment, if one can be pinpointed, when the Oyster Bay Roosevelts fell out with the Hyde Park Roosevelts.

The main issue of 1920 was the League of Nations. F.D.R. was running as the heir of Wilson, father of the League; but the heirs of T.R., Alice Roosevelt Longworth in particular, were "irreconcilables." They resented the connection of their name with the hated League; they deeply resented a Democratic Roosevelt; and they most deeply resented what they felt was the exploitation of their name—for what were the Roosevelts before Teddy?

Moreover, the Oyster Bay branch had its own political plans for the family—and they centered around Theodore Roosevelt, Jr.—not F.D.R. Young Teddy was sent out by the Republican National Committee to try to untangle the political orientation of the Roosevelts. He charged that Franklin was a "maverick" who "doesn't have the brand of our family!" Later Nick Longworth called F.D.R. a "denatured Roosevelt," and Alice, most viper-tongued of them all, is said to have called him "80% Eleanor and 20% mush."[83] The Hyde Park matriarch, Sara Delano Roosevelt, grew fiercely resentful of these intra-family snipings. When asked why the T.R. branch was so antagonistic to the F.D.R. branch, she replied, "I can't imagine, unless it's because we're better looking than they are."[84]

It is an oft-told story—recounted in book, play, and film—of how F.D.R. was stricken with polio in the summer of 1921; of how his mother wished

him to retire to Hyde Park, but an Albany newspaperman, Louis Mc-
Henry Howe, kept his elective hopes alive and trained Eleanor Roosevelt
to carry part of the political burden; and of how F.D.R. fought back until
he rose at the 1924 convention to place Al Smith's name in nomination
for the presidency. James Roosevelt recalls that famous "Happy Warrior" speech. As the crowd at Madison Square Garden was swept with
emotion his sister Anna whispered to him: "Jimmy, do you think Father
may become President?" The son looked up at the speaker, his legs in
steel braces, his hands tightly grasping the rostrum, and answered, "Unfortunately, it's out of the question."[85]

Yet four years later he was elected governor of New York; in eight
years he was the Democratic nominee for President. Wrote Walter
Lippmann:

His mind is not very clear, his purpose is not simple, and his methods are
not direct. . . . Mr. Roosevelt does not ring true. . . . He is no enemy of entrenched privilege. He is a pleasant man who, without any important qualifi-
cation for the office, would very much like to be President.[86]

But any Democrat could have been elected in 1932.

Along with Walter Lippmann, the American people had little reason
to suspect what was about to start on March 4, 1933. The nation was at
the trough of its greatest depression, and it had just elected a man who
had never known want. The vast crowd in front of the Capital had come
to be convinced, not to reaffirm its faith. The new Roosevelt President,
his chin outthrust, announced: "First of all, let me assert my firm belief
that the only thing we have to fear is fear itself." The people, he said,
had asked for direct, vigorous action. He would give it to them. And
then, like a chain of popping firecrackers, the New Deal closed the
banks, an Agricultural Adjustment Act became law, the Civilian Con-
servation Corps was authorized, federal grants were made for unemployment relief, the securities business was controlled, Tennessee Valley
Authority was created, legislation was enacted to save small home
mortgages from foreclosure, the railroads were regulated.

As the exuberant voice took his "fireside chats" directly into the American home, the unemployed, the minority groups, those lowest on the
economic scale, knew that this man, this Hudson River aristocrat with the
trace of Boston in his speech, was talking about their problems, that he
was going to do something about them, that he cared. One writer called
it the "West Bronx FDR Mystique." Out in Kansas the old Progressive
Republican, William Allen White, was fascinated. "The Constitution is
straining and cracking. But, after all, the Constitution was made for
people. . . . It is bewildering—this new deal—the new world. How much

is false, how much is true . . . only time will tell. In the meantime, the wizard in the White House works his weird spell upon a changing world."[87]

What was this bewildering New Deal? Primarily it was a collection of governmental attempts to meet current problems. It was perpetual motion striking out in all directions. Its key was "Answers, not Philosophy." It sought to give relief, not a grand design for the ages. For the New Deal President was no theorist but a pragmatic politician who was concerned with relieving suffering and getting elected. He surrounded himself with ideas and he left all the idea-givers with the impression that he agreed with them. There were the social thinkers like Tugwell, the social workers like Hopkins, the conservative businessmen like Lewis Douglas. He played them like a majestic organ, harmoniously and discordantly. And from the sparks generated by rubbing two ideas together emerged policy. If the ideas didn't always work, if they were sometimes unconstitutional, if recovery turned into recession, at least the people knew that F.D.R. was trying.

Everyone, however, did not share the "West Bronx FDR Mystique." The President had woven a Democratic coalition of labor, liberals, and minorities, powerful enough to keep him in office for four terms. But there were some who were not in the fabric. This was especially true around the economic fringes on top and bottom. The dispossessed, who for the first time had tasted government largess, wanted a headier brew. They turned to the Father Coughlins, the Francis Townsends, and the Huey Longs. The well-born, who considered F.D.R. a "traitor to his class," turned to the Liberty League. Perhaps not realizing the consequences, Roosevelt was hardening the political arteries of the country. Then world events cut across class lines.

As war darkened the European continent, the American President confined himself to righteous protests against Nazi Germany and Fascist Italy. He repeatedly paused to let his people catch up, but he never got too far out front. This dilemma was finally solved for him. The New Deal ended in an avalanche of Japanese bombs. On December 7, 1941, the New Deal President became the War President. Politics was suspended for the duration, and F.D.R. died shortly before V-J Day lifted the moratorium.

Looking back over her life, Eleanor Roosevelt saw certain distinct patterns. The pattern of her early married years had been largely determined by her mother-in-law; the pattern of her middle years by her children and husband; the pattern of her latter years was her own. She seemed to pick up momentum as more and more she became a public person, throwing her phenomenal energy and moral earnestness into issues, problems, policy. After her husband's death she could have been nominated for the Senate, but she turned her back on elective politics and applied herself to the Democratic reform movement in New York. She continued her daily column, appearing in seventy-five newspapers, and her monthly magazine articles. Then there were books to be written, lectures to deliver, people to see, mail to answer, charities to be supported. So many things to do, so little time, as she spread her deep sympathies over mankind. President Truman appointed her to the American delegation to the United Nations. The new world organization was a natural canvas for her broad-gauge humanitarianism. At the UN she displayed a toughness that had not been apparent before. Diplomats discovered that she was no figurehead; the Soviets that she was no pushover. These were her shining years, just as the UN Declaration of Human Rights is her lasting monument. Once long ago a young girl paid a visit to Sagamore Hill, and Mrs. Theodore Roosevelt—her aunt Edith—wrote Bamie: "Poor little soul, she is very plain. Her mouth and teeth have no future, but the ugly duckling may turn out to a swan."[88] As if recalling this prediction of another century, Adlai Stevenson rose to pay tribute to the memory of Eleanor Roosevelt at the 1964 Democratic Convention. "She thought of herself as an 'ugly duckling,'" he told the delegates, "but she walked in beauty in the ghettos of the world, bringing with her the reminder of her beloved St. Francis, '. . . it is in the giving that we receive.' And wherever she walked, beauty was forever there."[89]

Honors, often undeserved, come to presidents' sons. But an immense burden often comes too. There is a merciless spotlight of publicity on all their activities; the most minor indiscretions are blown up to major proportions when committed by children of the famous. Life can be a series of pitfalls which are not in the paths of those with less recognizable names; the unscrupulous are there to exploit their inherited distinction; the well-meaning are there to hold temptations before them. There is always that fragile commodity, the reputation, to be lived up to or revolted against.

On a battlefield, however, a man can lose his ancestors. War, the great equalizer, was to play an important role in the lives of the sons of the two Roosevelt presidents. Teddy's four boys fought first in World War I; Franklin's four in World War II. All eight had distinguished records. In other pursuits, in peaceful times, they were to know varying degrees of failure; some aspired, all failed, to duplicate the political success of their fathers. But in wartime, when raw courage is a most highly prized human quality, all were successful. Quentin, having been praised for his fighting conduct, replied for all the Roosevelts. "Well you know," he said, "it's rather up to us to practice what father preaches."[90]

The Oyster Bay Roosevelts looked upon the First World War as a personal contest. Even before America entered the war Kermit had enlisted in the British army and was fighting in Mesopotamia; Ethel and her husband, Dr. Richard Derby, were serving at the American Ambulance Hospital in Paris; Ted, Archie, and Quentin were training at Plattsburg. All of them saw action later in France, as did Ted's wife, Eleanor, who was the first woman sent to the war area by the Y.M.C.A. All, including the women, were to receive a bevy of decorations, including the Military Cross of Great Britain, the War Cross of Montenegro, the French Legion of Honor, the Distinguished Service Medal, and the Distinguished Service Cross. Archie was wounded so badly that he was judged to be one hundred per cent disabled; Ted was both gassed and wounded; Quentin, the baby of the family, lost his life.

The "Peck's Bad Boy" of the White House days had grown up to be an impish-looking young man with his father's gift for unlimited enthusiasms. He was engaged to Flora Payne Whitney, granddaughter of the traction magnate who had been Cleveland's Secretary of the Navy. They wanted to get married in France, but the War Department refused to waive its ban against fiancées going overseas. On July 11, 1918, flying in a Nieuport, Quentin shot down his first German plane. Three days later, on Bastille Day, he was shot down. The German communiqué read: "Lieutenant Roosevelt, who had shown conspicuous bravery during the fight by attacking again and again without regard to danger, was shot in the head by his more experienced opponent and fell at Chamery."[91] Wrote his father: "Only those are fit to live who do not fear to die; and none are fit to die who have shrunk from the joy of life. Both life and death are part of the same Great Adventure. . . ."[92]

If Theodore Roosevelt failed to pass on to his sons the full bundle of traits that made him such a skillful politician, he did instill in them his devouring restlessness. The former President took Kermit with him to Africa in 1909, and wrote home with obvious pride that the boy's "keenness, cool nerve, horsemanship, hardihood, endurance, and good eyesight make him a really good wilderness hunter."[93]‡ The adventurous father and son also explored the Brazilian jungles, where they discovered the "River of Doubt."

In 1914 Kermit married Belle Willard, daughter of the American ambassador to Spain. The bride came from an interesting family. Her grandmother was Antonia Ford of Fairfax Court House, Virginia, whose dark

‡ T.R. was also pleased by a cartoon in *Punch* which showed the two hunters stalking the Sphinx. "Steady, Kermit," read the caption. "We must have one of these!" See Carleton B. Case, *Good Stories About Roosevelt* (Chicago: Shrewesburg, 1920), p. 105.

hair, long eyelashes, slightly tilted nose, and full lips gave her a provocative prettiness which she was to employ to advantage as a Confederate
spy. Jeb Stuart thought so highly of her daring that he commissioned
her an "honorary aide-de-camp." And the leader of Mosby's Rangers,
probably acting on information supplied by Antonia, was able to capture
Union General Edwin Stoughton from his peaceful bed in Yankee-held
Fairfax. Antonia was finally trapped by a woman counterspy. The Union
officer who then came to arrest her was Major Joseph C. Willard. The
ingenious Miss Ford married him![94]

Kermit Roosevelt and his Willard wife lived in New York, where he
entered the steamship business, eventually becoming a vice-president of
the United States Line and an explorer of some note. But his lifetime
interest in politics was nil.

The politician was to be his brother, Theodore Roosevelt, Jr. A reporter for the St. Louis *Globe-Democrat* wrote in 1898, "There is a
popular impression at Oyster Bay that little Teddy was close to forty
when he was born."[95] In physical traits and mannerisms the serious
youth closely resembled his father, who expected more from the eldest
son than from the other children—an added burden which almost caused
a nervous breakdown at one time. When he was fourteen Ted solemnly
told an old man at Oyster Bay, "I will always be honest and upright,
and I hope some day to be a great soldier, but I will always be spoken
of as Theodore Roosevelt's son."[96] In the trenches of France Ted first
proved himself to be a great soldier. As the former President lay dying,
Ted's wife told him, "You know, Father, Ted has always worried for
fear he would not be worthy of you." "Worthy of me?" replied the old
warrior. "Darling, I'm so very proud of him. He has won high honor
not only for his children but, like the Chinese, he has ennobled his
ancestors . . . my war was a bow-and-arrow affair compared to Ted's,
and no one knows this better than I do."[97]

There was a possibility that the Republican candidate for governor of
New York in 1918 would be Theodore Roosevelt, Jr., and that his Democratic opponent would be Franklin Delano Roosevelt. The contest never
materialized, but it marked the opening skirmish in the jockeying between these two men with but a single name to give to their country.
Ted ran for the state Assembly from Nassau County in 1919. His opponent, a tailor's son, sarcastically recalling T.R.'s famous phrase, said,
"My hat's in the ring too—and it isn't my father's."[98] Roosevelt was overwhelmingly elected; his only election victory in a lifetime of politics.
As a freshman legislator his most courageous act was to oppose the
expulsion of five Socialist assemblymen. His speech was followed by
Speaker Sweet, reading passages from the writings of the senior T.R. in
order to contrast the Americanism of the father with the un-Americanism
of the son.[99]

President Harding appointed young Ted to the position of Assistant Secretary of the Navy, the family's proving ground. One admiral groaned, "I have had to stand two Roosevelts—I cannot stand another!"[100] But the post was not a steppingstone to greater glory for Ted as it had been for T.R. and F.D.R. During his tenure control over the Teapot Dome oil reserves was transferred from the Navy Department to the Department of the Interior. Roosevelt opposed the action but faithfully carried the executive order to the White House. A conservationist watchdog named Harry Slattery had warned him that Interior Secretary Fall would turn over the oil to private interests. Roosevelt threw Slattery out of his office. Didn't he know that Fall had been one of his father's Rough Riders, hence sanctified? Fall gave Harry Sinclair the exclusive right to extract oil and gas from Teapot Dome. In the meantime Archie Roosevelt, for whom Ted had got a vice-presidency in one of the Sinclair companies, heard that the oilman had paid Fall $68,000. Archie resigned his position and came to Washington to testify before a congressional committee. He was followed as a witness by Sinclair's secretary, who said that his boss had sent Fall "six or eight cows." Perhaps Archie had mistakenly heard "$68 thou."[101] (In 1929 Fall was imprisoned for having received a $100,000 payoff from oilmen Sinclair and Doheny.) Assistant Secretary of the Navy Roosevelt's honesty was never in question, but, said the New York *World*, "he was too dull or too lazy to accept responsibility of high office. He went about the routine of his work asking no questions that were impolite, 'getting people to bring the answers,' and signing when and where they told him the document still needed ink."[102]

Somewhat tarnished, young Ted continued to plod along his father's political path. He had now been assemblyman and Assistant Secretary of the Navy. Next step would be governor of New York. (He was succeeded in the Navy Department by his first cousin, Theodore Douglas Robinson.) But Ted's opponent in 1924 was popular incumbent Alfred E. Smith, and Eleanor Roosevelt, the "maverick's" wife, seconded the governor's renomination. "Of course he will win!" she told the cheering delegates. "How could he help it, when the Republican convention yesterday [by choosing T.R., Jr.] did all it could to help him?" With her husband now a cripple, Eleanor was fast learning to do the politicking for the family. She had a frame built to resemble a teapot mounted on her car—it spouted real steam—and with her daughter Anna at her side she set out to remind the voters of the recent scandal that had implicated her first cousin. "In the thick of political fights one always feels that all methods of campaigning that are honest are fair," she later wrote, "but I do think now that this was a rough stunt and I never blamed my cousin when he retaliated in later campaigns against my husband."[103] Roosevelt lost by 108,000, running nearly one million votes behind his party's presidential candidate, Calvin Coolidge. The defeat marked the end of Ted's chances for an elective career; it also laid the groundwork for the reappearance of Franklin D. Roosevelt four years later.

Ted, however, continued in politics by presidential appointment. Hoover named him governor of Puerto Rico and then governor general of the Philippine Islands. In both posts he proved himself an able administrator. He was in the Philippines when the news arrived that F.D.R. had been elected President. A reporter wanted to know what relation he was to the new chief executive. Ted answered: "Fifth cousin about to be removed."[104] (Another who bore the same relationship, Nicholas Roosevelt, submitted his resignation as U.S. minister to Hungary; it was promptly accepted by Cousin Franklin.[105])

The Oyster Bay Roosevelts had been nearly unanimous in opposition to F.D.R. Alice even broke her lifelong rule against campaigning in order to alert the nation to the danger of electing her cousin. The one exception was Corinne Robinson, T.R.'s sister. She was a minor poet, the author of five volumes,§ and something of a politician in her own right, having made a seconding speech for Leonard Wood at the 1920 Republican Convention. She alone refused to oppose Franklin. Since her niece Eleanor was so deeply involved in the outcome, she said she would have to remain silent.

After F.D.R.'s election the Oyster Bay family became the "out-of-season Roosevelts," as humorist Frank Sullivan put it. When he wasn't working for a publishing firm, Ted, often accompanied by Kermit, was off on big-game expeditions. Their most successful trip was to Asia where they shot the rare *Ovis poli*. "You don't know what an *Ovis poli* is?" asked Will Rogers. "It's a political sheep. You hunt it between elections."[106] But there were no more elections for Ted. In 1936 he announced that he would run again for governor "if the people wish it."[107] *Vox populi* wasn't even a whisper.

"Princess Alice" also faded from the news after her husband Nick died in 1931.¶ Occasionally some isolated voice called for her election or

§ Corinne Roosevelt Robinson's verse often attempted to deify her brother. In "Theodore Roosevelt, a Woman Speaks to His Sister," she wrote:

> I pressed amid the crowd
> To touch his garment's hem,
> As one of old once touched
> The Man of Bethlehem.

Also see "To My Brother," *Service and Sacrifice* (New York: Scribner's, 1919), pp. 24–27.

¶ Being a son-in-law of Theodore Roosevelt had not always been easy for Nicholas Longworth. In 1912 he refused to join T.R.'s bolt of the Republican Party and remained loyal to his fellow Cincinnatian, William Howard Taft.

appointment to office. A weekly paper in the Philippines suggested that she would make a good governor general of the islands; some North Dakotans boosted her as a GOP vice-presidential candidate in 1932; a group named Pioneer Association of Independent Voters, Inc., urged her to run for senator from Ohio in 1934. But the only post she ever accepted was as a delegate pledged to Robert Taft at the 1936 convention. Alice was an excellent hater, but she had long ago forgiven William Howard Taft, and became rhapsodic over the ability of his eldest son. Being for Bob Taft she equated with being against Franklin D. Roosevelt. In a 1940 magazine article, she wrote, "I am for Bob Taft because I do not yearn any longer for the man who is always on his toes, waving his hat, raising his voice, 'raring' to go here, there, anywhere."[108] Her fame rested on her quick wit; correctly or not, she was credited with almost every great political *bon mot* of the twentieth century. Calvin Coolidge: "He must have been weaned on a pickle." Wendell Willkie: "He sprang from the grassroots of the country clubs of America." Thomas Dewey: "How can anyone vote for a man who looks like a bridegroom on a wedding cake?" After Cousin Eleanor started "My Day," Alice also became a newspaper columnist. But somehow her sparkling sayings evaporated like cotton candy when set down in type; the venture died in a few months.

After years of being the pace-setters, the Oyster Bay Roosevelts now seemed to have been left behind. In 1936, when F.D.R. was winning the

---

The result was that he lost his seat in Congress. Later he told a Boston audience, "May I suggest to any of you who may have ambitions to go to Congress, to see to it that, in the same campaign your most eminent constituent is not contesting the Presidency with your father-in-law." See *Reception and Dinner in Honor of the Fifty-sixth Birthday of Augustus Peabody Gardner, a Pioneer for Preparedness, by the Roosevelt Club, Hotel Westminster, Boston, November 5, 1921* (Boston, 1921), pp. 23–24.

Longworth was again elected to the House of Representatives in 1914 and served until his death. He was made Majority Leader in 1923 and Speaker in 1925.

In 1928 Longworth told the Hamilton County Republican Committee that he was a candidate for the presidential nomination. The strategy he outlined was to kill off Herbert Hoover's chances with favorite son candidates. But Hoover's strength, even in Ohio, was too great, and he was easily nominated. See Charles P. Taft, *City Management, the Cincinnati Experiment* (New York: Farrar & Rinehart, 1933), p. 162.

The Longworths' only child, Paulina (1926–57), married Alexander McCormick Sturm in 1944. The bridegroom had written and illustrated two childrens' books by the time he entered college—one, *The Problem Fox* (New York: Scribner's, 1941), tells a charming tale of an intellectual named August, who also happens to be a fox. Sturm died after a long illness at the age of twenty-eight; his widow committed suicide six years later. They had one child. See New York *Times*, August 27, 1944, p. 30, and January 28, 1957, p. 23.

greatest electoral victory in modern American history, T.R.'s wife came out of retirement to announce that the New Deal was "incompatible with our American democracy and liberty."[109] And Archie, in recent years, has added the family name to many ultra-rightist causes. As a trustee of the Veritas Foundation he is a leader among those seeking to root out subversion at Harvard.[110] He also sent a letter to every U.S. senator, stating, ". . . modern technical civilization does not seem to be as well handled by the black man as by the white man in the United States." Present civil rights difficulties he blamed on "socialistic plotters."[111]

Only the apolitical Kermit remained on good terms with F.D.R., and they were often seen yachting together. His wife and daughter were the only members of the Oyster Bay clan ever to have given election endorsements to their Hyde Park cousin.* In 1964, as if in answer to her brother-in-law's activities, Mrs. Kermit Roosevelt signed a full-page ad which appeared in leading newspapers. It was entitled, "Six Reasons Why You Should Worry About Extremism."[112]

But F.D.R. didn't have to worry about jibes from T.R.'s children—he had enough problems with his own.

In her autobiography Eleanor Roosevelt gives an almost embarrassingly frank account of life within the Hyde Park dynasty. Above the five children in the family hierarchy there were three potential sources of authority—father, mother, and grandmother.

F.D.R. thought his children should make their own decisions and their own mistakes; an attitude, his wife felt, which "came very largely from the fact that his mother had wanted to direct his every thought and deed and that he had had to fight for independence."[113] He was also a preoccupied man. During his children's formative years it was a private preoccupation; he was fighting for his health and was away from the family for long periods. Later it was a public preoccupation. "As Franklin became busier in his public life," his wife records, "he found it impossible to take time for the boys' interests, which kept them from asking for advice they might have sought quite naturally had he been freer to give it."[114] The Roosevelt boys deeply resented having to make appointments to see their presidential father. Later, when they had political careers of their own, the sons went to great lengths to paint a much closer, more filial picture of life with Father.[115] Yet in an unguarded mo-

---

* Kermit and Belle Roosevelt voted for F.D.R. in 1940 but were not active in the campaign. Four years later Mrs. Roosevelt joined the Women's Division of the Democratic National Committee, and her daughter Clochette, the wife of John G. Palfrey, became the head of Service Men's Wives to Re-elect Roosevelt. Interview with Mrs. John G. Palfrey, October 21, 1964.

ment Franklin, Jr., told an interviewer: "It might strike you as strange, but I spent relatively little time with father. The longest period I spent with him was an unforgettable five weeks in July, 1934. It was on a cruise. . . . I think that was the only time in my life that I was ever with father for such a long period."[116]

Eleanor Roosevelt shared her husband's problem of not being able to spend as much time with her children as she might have desired. For she too was a major public figure. Besides writing a daily newspaper column, a weekly radio program, and a monthly magazine column, the indefatigable Eleanor was serving as White House hostess, conducting a voluminous correspondence, making frequent lecture tours, partly running a furniture factory, and acting as the President's eyes and ears on fact-finding trips at home and abroad. Where the First Lady would turn up next became a question of some amusement to the American people. One of the most famous cartoons ever published by *The New Yorker* pictured the bottom of a coal mine: Says one grimy miner to another, "For gosh sakes, here comes Mrs. Roosevelt!" Eleanor had waged a valiant fight for this emancipation, not only against the domination of her mother-in-law, but also against the painfully shy defenses she had erected during an unhappy childhood. Her personal independence had a sanctity that comes only when it is earned in combat. She was determined that her children should have it by right, and she went to extremes to assure them that she was "not in any way trying to control or interfere with their lives. . . ." "I probably carried this theory too far," she later admitted.[117]

And then there was Grandmother. Sara Delano Roosevelt was too much the lady to show her distaste for politics. All those disagreeable people that Franklin kept bringing to Hyde Park! However, when Huey Long came to lunch she could not resist saying in a stage whisper, "Who is that dreadful person sitting next to my son?"[118] Political life had caused her son to grow apart from her, but it renewed her determination to keep her grandchildren under her influence. She spoiled them with gifts, expensive cars, and other lavish tokens of her affection. The boys, who had the Roosevelt charm and cunning, quickly realized that Grandmother was the exploitable avenue to anything that might otherwise be denied them. Only John, the youngest, a quieter and more conservative child, made few demands.

The Roosevelt boys seemed to drift through the White House years on a steady stream of deplorable publicity. There were innumerable speeding tickets, traffic accidents, divorces, and smashed photographers' cameras. The mayor of Cannes, France, even claimed that a young Roosevelt had dumped the contents of a champagne bottle on his head. After one night club ruckus the New York *Times*, with tongue in cheek, editorialized that what this really showed was that F.D.R. had no dictatorial ambitions. For if he had, "Instead of offering to punch his father's critic on the nose, Elliott Roosevelt would coldly bide his time and then have the offender interred or shot as soon as Elliott's father had made himself dictator of America."[119] The young men complained bitterly to their mother of the unfairness of it all. She spent hours trying to explain that being sons of a President also had compensations. "Even as I talked," she was to recall, "I knew I might as well 'save my breath to cool my porridge.' . . ."[120]

The business careers of F.D.R.'s children during their father's years as President also showed a marked insensitivity to their position or the family reputation. They were offered lucrative jobs, far above normal expectations, and they accepted without question. Elliott and Anna went to work for William Randolph Hearst, the vitriolic critic of their father. Jimmy, a tyro insurance broker in Boston, was soon a specialist in life, fire, marine, air, and group insurance. "The insurance fraternity," wrote Alva Johnston in 1938 "is as startled . . . as the medical fraternity would be if a youngster who had never attended a medical school suddenly turned out to be America's greatest specialist in the eye, ear, nose and throat, in abdominal and pulmonary surgery, in obstetrics, pediatrics, and chiropody."[121] Johnston also claimed that Jimmy's income was between $250,000 and $2,000,000 a year, and that the President's son had got Joseph P. Kennedy appointed as ambassador to Great Britain in return for help in soliciting insurance. (Kennedy told the press, ". . . it is a complete, unadulterated lie."[122]) Jimmy's answer was contained in an interview with Walter Davenport. He told how, right out of Harvard, he had been paid $15,000 a year by an insurance firm. "I wasn't being kidded," he admitted, "I knew perfectly well that they were paying me for the name and any value the name might have." Later he went into business for himself. "Sure I got into places I never would have if I wasn't the son of the President." But photostats of his tax returns for the five preceding years showed that his total taxable income was only $170,000.[123] The public was left with the impression that, while Johnston had grossly exaggerated, young Jimmy had still done exceedingly well during the depth of a national depression. The St. Louis *Post-Dispatch*, in a four-line editorial, summed up: "Advice to Young Men: To make a sure-fire success in the insurance business, and thereby gain a competence on which to enter public life and serve your fellow men, get your father elected President of the United States."[124]

The President was relatively scrupulous about giving public positions to relatives, although he couldn't resist appointing a Roosevelt as Assistant Secretary of the Navy—a "family tradition," he said.[125] The fifth member of the dynasty to hold the post was Henry Latrobe Roosevelt,

European representative for RCA and a great-grandson of the steamboat inventor.†

The only member of the President's immediate family to be put on the public payroll (at $10,000 a year) was son Jimmy, who was made a White House aide over strong protests from Eleanor. The maternal objections were stilled when F.D.R. asked her, "Why should I be deprived of my eldest son's help and of the pleasure of having him with me just because I am the President?"[126] Jimmy was active in Massachusetts politics where he had formed an alliance with James Curley. The New York *Times* said "it was no secret that he wanted to enter the race for governor of Massachusetts in 1936," although at that time he would have been only twenty-eight years old.[127] Two years later 100,000 persons signed a petition urging him to run for lieutenant governor. Clearly, as the press proclaimed, Jimmy was the "Crown Prince." How well he performed as a presidential aide is open to question. Arthur Krock thought him a success; James MacGregor Burns thought him a failure who was undermining congressional relations.[128] After less than a year his health broke. When the "insurance scandal" hit the headlines, Jimmy was at Mayo Clinic being operated on for a bleeding ulcer. He never returned to his White House post. Instead he went to Hollywood to become the producer of a film called *Pot o' Gold;* perhaps the worst movie ever made, he later claimed.

Elliott's political career was no less stormy. He dabbled in Texas politics after Hearst sent him to the Lone Star State as manager of his radio interests. He was made vice-chairman of the Young Democrats but resigned after protests that he had not earned the honor; he was appointed to the board of Texas A & M by a governor who then received a federal judgeship, causing some reporters to believe that Elliott was being groomed for lieutenant governor or governor. Before long he was in the thick of anti-New Deal plots. He told a radio audience that he hoped F.D.R. wouldn't run for a third term, and was promptly taken to task in an open letter by his brother-in-law John Boettiger (Anna's second husband). As a member of the Texas delegation to the 1940 convention, Elliott voted under the unit rule against his father's renomination.

All of the Roosevelt children married young. This, thought their mother, was "largely because they were not really rooted in any particu-

† Other relatives who received appointments: David Gray, Eleanor's uncle by marriage, was named minister to Ireland; First Cousin Warren Delano Robbins, who had been Hoover's chief of protocol, was made minister to Canada; Cousin Preston Delano, comptroller of the currency; and former minister to Hungary Nicholas Roosevelt came back into government for a short time as deputy director of the Office of War Information. All were well qualified.

lar home and were seeking to establish homes of their own."[129] All except one were also divorced young. Among F.D.R.'s four sons and a daughter there have been fifteen marriages, ten divorces—four while their father was President—and twenty children.‡ All their first marriages were into equally upper-crust families. (They were not always as pedigree-conscious in their subsequent matches.) Anna first married Curtis Dall, a Philadelphia stockbroker; Jimmy's initial wife was Betsey Cushing, daughter of an internationally famous brain surgeon; Elliott started his many walks to the altar with Elizabeth Donner, whose industrialist father developed the National Tinplate Works and the Union Steel Company; John wed Anne Clark of Nahant, Massachusetts, whose father is considered the founder of the investment counseling business in America. But it was the wedding of June 30, 1937, that bore the hallmark of Montague and Capulet. For Franklin Delano Roosevelt, Jr., third son of a President who thundered against the "economic royalists," was marrying Ethel Du Pont, "a slim princess in gossamer white," whose great industrial family had contributed at least $364,630 to defeat the President the year before.

At the door to the Du Ponts' quaint stone church at Christiana Hundred, their principal social secretary inspected the invitation cards of social reformers and robber barons. Inside, the household servants looked down from the choir stall. Posted around the church were units of Delaware police, secret service, and 350 regular army troopers. Army engineers set up a field kitchen; a tent was turned into a press headquarters with forty telegraph circuits and fifty operators. The Du Ponts' publicity man, hired to "assure authenticity," briefed the 150 reporters and photographers. After the ceremony, the newsmen were told, a reception for 1300 was held at the Tudor residence of the bride's parents. Eleanor Roosevelt left the receiving line to deliver her weekly radio broadcast. "I don't know whether to be happy or sad," the First Lady told her national audience. "I can only give my impression that it was a very lovely wedding. I, for one, always am torn between the realization of the adventure that two young things are starting on and its possibilities for good and bad."[130]

‡ A sociologist considers the high divorce rate among the Roosevelt children to be in part due to the fact that "old stock" (upper-class) Democrats "are still sociologically marginal; and sociological marginality often has to be paid for in various amounts of personal pathology." See E. Digby Baltzell, *The Protestant Establishment* (New York: Random House, 1964), pp. 308–9 n.

James Roosevelt believes that the high divorce rate has been a factor of their devotion to politics, which has centered their lives outside the home. Only in more recent years, he says, have F.D.R.'s children realized the importance of home values. Interview with James Roosevelt, May 12, 1965. (This explanation, however, implies a high divorce rate among politicians as an occupational class, which is not the case.)

The Second World War didn't completely push the Roosevelt sons out of the limelight. In the case of Elliott, in fact, the reverse was often the case.

Elliott's military career began with his usual dogged determination to lead with his chin. In 1940 he was given a captaincy in the Army Air Corps. Huge buttons immediately sprouted all over the country bearing the slogan, "Poppa, I wanta be a captain." William Allen White expressed his indignation in the Emporia *Gazette:* ". . . watch carefully during the enlistment period and see if the son of any other citizen of this United States, without military training, goes in as a captain."[131] In 1945 Elliott was again in the news when it was revealed that three GIs had been bumped off a military plane to make room for his English bull mastiff, named Blaze. "We would not go so far as to say that the story of Elliott Roosevelt's dog has blanketed the news of the great Russian offensive," wrote the New York *Herald Tribune,* "but we venture to guess that as a subject of discussion from coast to coast it is a strong rival."[132]

The Blaze incident caught fire at a most unfortunate time for Colonel Roosevelt; his promotion to the rank of brigadier general had just been submitted to the Senate. Republican Senator Bushfield reminded his colleagues that before becoming a brigadier general Robert E. Lee had been in the army for thirty-six years, George Marshall for thirty-five, and Dwight Eisenhower for thirty. Democratic Senator Thomas, who had also done some homework, replied that General Forrest had risen from lieutenant to lieutenant general in two years and General Sheridan from second lieutenant to lieutenant general in three years. With historical precedent on both sides, and with the Senate on the side of the Democrats, thirty-four-year-old Elliott Roosevelt, with four years of military experience, was made a brigadier general by a vote of fifty-three to eleven, thirty-one members abstaining.[133]

The young general was a brave officer. As a photographic pilot from the tropics to the arctic, his was often the dangerous mission of flying as low as one hundred feet over enemy targets in order to bring back close-up pictures. He was awarded the Distinguished Flying Cross for "heroism and extraordinary achievement." Jimmy, still suffering from gastric ulcers, became a marine lieutenant colonel, second in command of the proud Carlson's Raiders. For separate assaults on Makin Island he was given the Silver Star and the navy's second highest decoration, the Navy Cross. Franklin, Jr., became a navy lieutenant commander, in command of a destroyer escort, and won a Purple Heart and the Silver Star for exposing himself under fire in order to carry a critically wounded sailor to safety. John also became a lieutenant commander and received a Bronze Star for service as logistics officer for a carrier task group in the Pacific. Their combined service was a remarkable record of courage.[134]

The World War II record of the three living sons of Theodore Roosevelt, however, was something more than remarkable—it was amazing, for they were now well into their middle years.

Just as in the First World War, Kermit couldn't wait for America to enter combat. In 1939 he went to England and again became a British officer. A year later he resigned his commission to organize an international brigade against the Russians in Finland. But the Finns capitulated before he could get his 5000 volunteers into the field. Rejoining the British, he was sent to Norway and later to Cairo. After the U.S. declaration of war he became an American army major, took part in the first action against the Japanese in the Aleutians, and died there of natural causes in 1943.[135]

Declared totally disabled after his service in World War I, Archie Roosevelt was again back in the army as a lieutenant colonel. His men considered him to have been largely responsible for the capture of Salamaua. Technician (fifth grade) John Bertor of Coal City, Illinois, told a newspaper reporter of Roosevelt's daring tactics: "On the previous Wednesday, Colonel Roosevelt, with two officers and three enlisted men, made a reconnaissance tour of Salamaua Harbor. Under his orders we went close to the isthmus until Jap guns started firing at us. . . . Colonel Roosevelt stood up with a map in his hand and every time a gun fired jotted down its position. They fired at us for a half hour, barely missing us several times. The colonel noticed I was scared and said: 'You're safe with me. I was wounded three times in the last war and that's a lucky charm.' . . . The next day our artillery landed squarely in those guns and the Japs never fired them again." The enlisted man added, "Roosevelt's a good officer, but he's got too damn much guts." A year later, during the fighting on Biak Island, Archie was wounded by shrapnel. He may be the only American to have been discharged from both World Wars as one hundred per cent disabled in each case.[136]

Theodore Roosevelt, Jr., the unsuccessful politician, was also in uniform before the Pearl Harbor attack as a brigadier general with his old World War I outfit, the 1st Infantry Division. Drew Middleton, recounting the division's exploits, said of its assistant commander: "He was a little man whose bravery had to be seen to be believed. He had an antique disregard for his personal safety and a great gift for holding men together. He never said, 'Go!' He said, 'Come!' . . . he sometimes scared orthodox West Pointers who are suspicious of anything not included in the Academy's curriculum, but he was a great field officer."[137] Ted and his son, Captain Quentin Roosevelt, fought side by side in North Africa, where they were both given the Silver Star for gallantry in action and the Croix de Guerre. The father died of a heart attack on the Normandy battlefield without knowing that Eisenhower had just signed an order placing him in command of a division. He was posthumously awarded the Congressional Medal of Honor (for heroism on D-Day) and a Bronze Star (for heroic action in Algeria), making him the recipient of every U.S. combat medal. On his death the New York Times wrote: "When he went about his division in England, no sooner would a band catch sight of him than it would strike up an American song called 'Old Soldiers Never Die.' That was his piece, he used to say. . . . He will live in that collective memory that is history. Quentin, Kermit, Theodore dead; Archibald wounded . . . here is a tradition of honor that cannot die."[138]§

President Theodore Roosevelt had seventeen grandchildren, nine girls and eight boys. Four are now dead. Four have been divorced. The girls all married professional people—lawyers, doctors, architects, artists, writers, professors, government officials. One granddaughter is a novelist, another writes a newspaper column. The grandsons became business executives, engineers, government officials, musicians. Their lives form no discernible pattern. Rather they have gone off in all the directions that might be expected of any randomly selected seventeen well-educated Americans, although they have shown a greater than average interest in the arts. None, however, has ever sought election to public office, and only one has displayed more than a casual interest in politics.

The only one of T.R.'s grandchildren to hold political office has been Theodore Roosevelt III, the general's son. He is an investment executive who served for several years as Pennsylvania's secretary of commerce.[139] But Ethel Roosevelt Derby's daughter Edith, the wife of a Seattle attorney, has been very active in Washington State politics. She ran unsuccessfully for Republican national committeewoman and was co-chairman of the state's Scranton for President organization in 1964. At the 1960 Republican Convention she gave a seconding speech for Richard Nixon (along with F.D.R.'s son John and Bob Taft, Jr.).[140] Her sister is married to Robert T. Gannett, a member of the Vermont House of Representatives for four terms, who was defeated for the Republican congressional nomination in 1960.[141]

Most adventurous of the presidential grandchildren is Kermit Roose-

§ T.R.'s grandsons also served with distinction. Willard Roosevelt, Kermit's son, was in command of a destroyer in the Pacific; his brother Dirck (1925–53) was an ambulance driver with the British Eighth Army in Italy. Archibald's son and namesake was an army officer in Africa and the Middle East. Quentin Roosevelt (1918–48), who fought alongside his father in North Africa and on the Normandy beach, later became vice-president of the Chinese National Airline Corporation. In this capacity he participated in hazardous air drops to beleaguered Nationalist troops and died in a plane crash ten miles east of Hong Kong.

velt, Jr., called "Kim." A soft voice and mild manner belie his cloak-and-dagger career. As a Central Intelligence Agency operative, he directed the spectacular 1953 coup that overthrew Premier Mossadegh of Iran. There is even a legend that Roosevelt led the revolt with his gun at the head of an Iranian tank commander.[142] (Shades, perhaps, of his great-grandmother, the Confederate spy!) In another respect he has followed in the footloose steps of the old Rough Rider. Kim Roosevelt went to East Africa in 1960 to retrace the hunting expedition that father and grandfather had taken fifty-one years before.[143]

In contrast, his brother Willard Roosevelt composes avant-garde chamber music. Meyer Berger of the New York *Times*, perhaps recalling T.R.'s famous injunction about speaking softly and carrying a big stick, interviewed this grandson in 1958 and reported, "He speaks softly, has dreamer's eyes, and seems shy."[144]

Meg, a first novel, made its appearance in 1950. The author was Theodora Keogh, the daughter of Archie Roosevelt. (She was then married to Tom Keogh, an artist.) It tells the story of a twelve-year-old girl who attends a fancy private school while at the same time she joins a gang of East Side slum boys. Before T.R.'s granddaughter turned to storytelling she had a short fling as a professional dancer. In 1942 and 1943 she toured South America with her partner, Alexander Iolas. Their repertoire included a satire on the conjugal life of the Greeks, with costumes designed by Salvador Dali. The only problem was that Dali's creations were so weighty that it was difficult for the dancers to leave the ground. Mrs. Keogh's second novel, *Street Music*, concerns a music critic who becomes attached to a Parisian child criminal. Many of her early works center around young girls, but there ends the similarity to *Little Women*. She is more often compared to Colette, though not always favorably. Says the London *Times Literary Supplement*, "It is a little difficult to determine whether Miss Keogh is out to shock or whether she is a detached observer of the vagaries of sex."[145] The Roosevelt authoress is prolific; her books appear regularly at two-year intervals, and with time have become less concerned with the sex life of the very young and more with the mounting tensions of introspective women.

Theodora's sister is also a writer. Her specialty, however, is defense and foreign policy. When she was twenty, Edith Kermit Roosevelt married a middle-aged former Soviet diplomat, Alexander Barmine,[146] who had defected to the West in 1937. (He later became head of the Russian section of the Voice of America.) The bride's parents did not attend the wedding. The couple had one child during their four-year marriage. Edith became a Hollywood columnist, then a reporter for the Newark *Star-Ledger*, and now writes a weekly Washington column that appears in fifty newspapers.[147]

The two Roosevelt authoresses have a brother, Archie, Jr., a foreign service officer. Until 1950 he was known primarily as an expert on the Arab world, but he has more recently served in Spain under Ambassador John Davis Lodge, and has been special assistant to the American ambassador in London since 1962.

While the burning desire for political office has nearly been extinguished in the grandchildren of the Oyster Bay President, it still glows among the heirs of T.R.'s sister Corinne. Her son Theodore Douglas Robinson, the former New York State legislator and Assistant Secretary of the Navy, announced his candidacy for Congress shortly before his death in 1934.[148] And Corinne's son-in-law, Joseph Wright Alsop, served in both houses of the Connecticut legislature, chaired the 1912 Bull Moose campaign in his state (T.R. called him a "big, brave, strong, good man of sound common sense . . ."), and was Connecticut public utilities commissioner for twenty-six years. Two of the Alsop boys, Joseph and Stewart, became leading commentators on public affairs; a third son is a major figure in Connecticut Republican circles.

John Alsop, president of the Mutual Insurance Company of Hartford, was chairman of the Connecticut Citizens for Eisenhower Committee in 1952. He was credited with pinning the amiable political epithet "egghead" on Adlai Stevenson. Six years later he was an unsuccessful candidate for the gubernatorial nomination. As leader of old-line New England Republicanism in the state—"Brahmin" yet liberal in outlook, with a greater concern for issues and programs than for party organization and expansion—he captured the nomination for governor in 1962 in one of the narrowest contests in Connecticut Republican annals. Then the convention rose in rebellion and defeated John Davis Lodge's bid for a senatorial nomination. (Some delegates were already wearing "Lodge-Alsop" buttons.) In the general election Alsop was defeated by incumbent Governor Dempsey.

F.D.R.'s children seemed to settle down after World War II; they claimed it was a maturing experience. Jimmy was back in the insurance business, and as California Democratic chairman was trying to rebuild his political fortune. While at Mayo Clinic he had fallen in love with his nurse, Romelle Schneider, whom he wished to marry. The President sent Harry Hopkins to dissuade him from getting a divorce; the son resented the intrusion. Now he and his second wife were living in Los Angeles with their three children. Franklin, Jr., was a lawyer in New York and was making a political reputation through his activities in the American Veterans' Committee. John, who had begun his merchandising career as an $18.50-a-week stock boy at Filene's in Boston, was a top executive of a women's wear chain. Anna and her husband had moved to Phoenix to start a daily newspaper. Looking over the dynasty two years after F.D.R.'s death, Arthur Schlesinger, Jr., observed: "The Roosevelt family is obviously not a spent force in American political life. In ten years—maybe sooner—two of the most important states might have Roosevelts as governors. In a third state a Roosevelt-owned newspaper might become a big political factor."[149]¶

Only Elliott hadn't yet found himself. He was living at Hyde Park with his third wife, actress Faye Emerson, and was trying to "make Christians out of Christmas tree dealers" by underselling them in the Manhattan market. "Let him sell his shrunk spruce," snorted a competitor, "but the buyers will be getting stung—unless they like their needles on the floor instead of on the tree."[150] He also published a book about F.D.R., *As He Saw It*. Although printed in seventeen languages, and a best seller in the United States and Europe, its revelations left the family amazed. It was full of imaginary quotations (for the sake of readability, he explained), and was so methodically pro-Russian and anti-British that some believed it had been rewritten by a Communist editor. *Pravda* singled Elliott out as a "sincere friend of the Soviet Union." But the London *Daily Mirror* contended, "The book proves nothing except that great men often have silly sons."[151]

The first step toward the realization of Schlesinger's prediction took place in 1949 when Franklin, Jr., ran for Congress. New York's Twentieth District was an ideal launching pad for a son of F.D.R. It covered the upper West Side of Manhattan and was largely Jewish in population. The young candidate, however, had several liabilities: in the middle of the campaign his wife, the former Ethel Du Pont, flew to Reno for a divorce*; Tammany, feeling that the second F.D.R. hadn't earned the nomination, put up its own "Regular Democratic" candidate; and Roosevelt was a "carpetbagger," living on an estate in fashionable Woodbury, Long Island. "Do you want a congressman," asked his opponents, "or a Master of the Foxhounds?" On the other hand, he had one considerable asset—a striking physical resemblance to his father. All the sons were inches above six feet, but Frank also had the famous toothy smile, with deep clefts in his rounded cheeks, and the blue-gray eyes. His features were somewhat heavier than his father's had been at the same age, and his jaw was not quite as determined, but there could be no doubt of his

¶ The New York *Daily News* went one step further and began to worry that F.D.R., Jr., might someday become President. *The New Yorker* (April 27, 1946, p. 18), which wasn't particularly concerned, commented, ". . . it's as plain as the nose on Captain Patterson's face that young Roosevelt was named Franklin D., Jr., in order to give him the jump in the Electoral College."

* The Roosevelts had two sons, Christopher and Franklin III. In 1950 Ethel Du Pont Roosevelt married Benjamin S. Warren, Jr., a socially prominent Detroit lawyer. She committed suicide in 1965. See New York *Times*, May 26, 1965, pp. 1 and 26.

Franklin, Jr.'s second wife is tall, blond Suzanne Perrin of an upper-crust New York family. They were married in 1949 and now have two daughters.

ancestry. He even smoked cigarettes with the same cheek-sucking grimace. Both Frank and Jimmy spoke like their father, to the degree that detractors claimed they had studied recordings of F.D.R.'s inflection and mannerisms; Frank, however, was apt to spice his talk with New York City slang. On May 17, 1949, the assets far outweighed the liabilities. Frank received almost as many votes as his three opponents combined. When the results came into his headquarters at the Greystone Hotel, voices in the jubilant crowd were heard to shout: "Next stop, Albany!" "The next governor of New York!" And even, "White House, there's a knock on yo' door." The first of F.D.R.'s sons to seek elective office was on his way.[152]

But as the dynasty took one step forward it slipped two to the rear. First Anna's Arizona paper went bankrupt†; then Jimmy took on Earl Warren, California's all-time champion vote-getter, for the governorship in 1950. Jimmy had a sufficiency of his father's charm but little of his sense of political timing. In 1948, as Democratic National Committeeman, he had not only omitted Truman's name from a Jackson Day speech but had actually given a boost to Eisenhower for the presidency. With some fast running, however, he managed to get back on the Truman bandwagon. Jimmy was also discovering that there was a "Roosevelt backlash" in California. Some felt he was being propelled too much by the steam of another generation. A comedian at a San Francisco night club gave an imitation of Jimmy making a speech that began: "My fr-r-iends—I mean my *father's* fr-r-iends . . ." And Eleanor Roosevelt didn't help matters by campaigning for her son. In one speech she said that Jimmy's fine education and White House ex-

---

† Anna Roosevelt's first marriage to Curtis Dall ended in divorce in 1934. (He is now an ultra-rightist spokesman and president of the Liberty Lobby, a self-styled "pressure group for patriotism," which opposes foreign aid, wishes to abolish the income tax, and would like to get the U.S. out of the UN. See Arnold Forster and Benjamin R. Epstein, *Danger on the Right* [New York: Random House, 1964], p. 226.)

She then moved into the White House with her two small children. For their entertainment she wrote *Scamper, the Bunny Who Went to the White House* (New York: Macmillan, 1934) and *Scamper's Christmas, More About the White House Bunny* (New York: Macmillan, 1934). In 1935 she married John Boettiger, White House correspondent for the Chicago *Tribune*. They moved to Seattle when he became publisher of the *Post Intelligencer* and she was made editor of its woman's page. While he was in the army Anna again lived in the White House. After the war they founded a newspaper in Phoenix, the *Arizona Times*.

The Boettigers had one child. They were divorced in 1949, and the next year he leaped to his death from the seventh floor of a New York hotel. A brother said he was depressed over the failure of his newspaper.

F.D.R.'s only daughter is now married to James Halsted, a doctor with the Veterans' Administration. They presently live in Washington, D.C.

perience fitted him admirably "to lead California in the ways of democracy." Not feeling that it needed civics instruction, California re-elected Warren by over a million votes. Despite his grueling campaign schedule, Jimmy had taken the worst drubbing ever given to a major nominee for governor in the state, and had had to borrow $100,000 from his mother to pay his electioneering obligations.[153]

A Roosevelt who was not calculated in the dynasty's political equation unexpectedly entered the whirl in 1952 by campaigning across the country for Dwight Eisenhower. John Roosevelt was the youngest son, the tallest son, the quietest son, and the Republican son. He and his first wife lived in the social milieu that Roosevelts had always known before Teddy dramatically changed the course of the family's history. They had a cottage on the Hyde Park estate, and apartments in Manhattan, "partly for business," on Park Avenue and Sutton Place.‡ Over the years John had proved himself to be an entrepreneur of some scope. He was president of 4711, Ltd., distributor of colognes, soaps, and a hair lacquer; vice-president of Lee Pharmacal Company, producers of a home permanent called Shadow Wave; president of McKay-Davis Chemical Corporation, packager of pills and powders in cellophane; vice-president of a Pasadena construction company; and a partner in a company that packages automotive parts. In 1953 President Eisenhower put him on a committee to fight discrimination in plants working on government contracts, and in 1957 there was some talk of him as Republican candidate for mayor of New York. But public service as a vocation never tempted him, and he preferred to remain the amateur in politics.[154]

When Jimmy ran for governor, after Frank's election to Congress, some gagster observed that the brothers were harmonizing on the old ballad, "You take the high road and I'll take the low road, and I'll be in the White House before you." Although Jimmy met an impasse, by 1954 he was back again in high gear. A congressman was vacating a safe Democratic seat and Jimmy announced his candidacy. It was a lower-class district extending from central Los Angeles to the ocean and inhabited largely by minority groups. Jimmy lived in upper-class Pasadena, but this wasn't a problem since neither of the two preceding representatives had resided among their constituents. The problem was that Romelle Roosevelt chose this time to seek a divorce. The proceedings, rather than involving an unsoiled separation, were salacious enough to

‡ John and Anne Clark Roosevelt got a Mexican divorce in 1965 after twenty-eight years of marriage. They had four children, one of whom, a thirteen-year-old daughter, died in 1960 as the result of a horseback-riding accident. He subsequently married Mrs. Irene Boyd McAlpin, daughter of the president of the Commercial Chemical Company of Memphis and a great-granddaughter of the founder of Chattanooga. Mr. Roosevelt is now a senior vice-president of Bache & Company.

create national headlines. Then when the divorce was granted Roosevelt married his secretary.§ Despite the scandal, Jimmy won the primary and general election overwhelmingly.[155]

Yet it was not fated for Representative James Roosevelt (D, Cal.) to serve in the Congress with Representative Franklin Roosevelt, Jr. (D, NY). The New York congressman had other plans in 1954. He wished to be governor. During his five years in the House, F.D.R., Jr., compiled a deplorable absentee record and an almost perfect liberal-labor voting record. Still the liberals remained uneasy about the strength of his convictions. To this, Roosevelt replied, "I've never been an egghead liberal. The trouble with the doctrinaire liberals is that they mistake dogma for conviction." His congressional colleagues found him to be smart and charming, but slipshod on his homework and often not around when they needed him. Frank was determined to change this image as he set out to become the Democratic gubernatorial candidate. He lost weight, gathered a team of skilled brain trusters, applied himself to mastering the issues, and put on a strenuous campaign. By early September his Alsop cousins, Joseph and Stewart, reported, ". . . it is generally believed that Roosevelt is an odds-on bet for the nomination." But the convention turned instead to Averell Harriman and, as a consolation prize, gave Frank the nomination for state attorney general. Just as Jimmy had had the misfortune of being matched against Earl Warren, so had circumstances now put Frank in the same drawing with Jacob K. Javits. The combination of Tammany's enmity and Javits' popularity produced a sizable defeat for Roosevelt at the same time that Harriman was winning by a razor-thin margin. "As of November 1954," Frank said later, "I considered my political career to have been terminated by the success of my friend, Senator Javits. . . ."[156]

He was unduly pessimistic. For, as the Alsops wrote, "The fact is that Roosevelt takes to politics as easily as the offspring of the European families of acrobats take to the high wires." Frank's years in political limbo were spent as a Washington-based distributor for Fiat automobiles and as a representative for Dictator Trujillo of the Dominican Republic. Then in 1960 he found that the presidential candidacy of John F. Kennedy provided an opportunity to re-enter politics. Nearly a half century before, when Franklin D. Roosevelt was Assistant Secretary of the Navy and Joseph P. Kennedy was an assistant general manager of Bethlehem Ship, an alliance had been struck between the two dynasties. Though a sometimes stormy relationship, both families had reaped profits. Now young Roosevelt came to the aid of young Kennedy in the critical West Vir-

§ James Roosevelt first married (1930) Betsey Cushing, divorced 1940, two daughters; married second (1941) Romelle Schneider, divorced 1955, three children; married third (1956) Gladys Irene Owens, no issue.

ginia primary.¶ He implied that J.F.K.'s opponent, Hubert Humphrey, had an unsatisfactory World War II record which perhaps reflected on his willingness to fight for his country. The Washington *Star* called Frank's statement "a new low in dirty politics." Also shocked was Eleanor Roosevelt, a Humphrey advocate who had been uneasy about Kennedy since his equivocation over Senator McCarthy.* But Kennedy won the primary and his Roosevelt supporter was clearly marked for a place of honor in a future administration.

It took two years for Kennedy to repay the campaign debt. There was talk that a proposed Roosevelt appointment as Secretary of the Navy had been vetoed by Secretary of Defense McNamara, and that Roosevelt had rejected the ambassadorship to Italy. Finally, in February 1963, he was named Under Secretary of Commerce amidst howls from the political left and right. "Franklin D. Roosevelt, Jr., is an amiable politician who happened to help President Kennedy win the Democratic nomination in 1960," wrote the Washington *Post*. "If he has other qualifications . . . they are indeed hard to discover." The next day the *Post's* cartoonist, Herblock, pictured Roosevelt sitting on a pile of Trujillo money. The caption had him saying, "I'm broadminded—I'm just as willing to work for a democracy." Before approving the nomination, Republicans on the Senate Commerce Committee put the appointee through three grueling days of cross-examination. His services for Trujillo came in for careful scrutiny, as did charges by his former partner in the automobile agency that Roosevelt had conspired to force him out of the business. He was also questioned about a recent suspension of his driving license. ". . . does it not suggest a pattern," asked Senator Prouty, "or perhaps a public-be-damned attitude with respect to your use of city streets and highways?"[157]

The Roosevelts kept bobbing up in politics throughout 1964. In February, after losing the endorsement of the California Democratic Council,

¶ The Kennedy forces had a letter from F.D.R., Jr., to the voters of West Virginia shipped to Hyde Park for posting, although young Roosevelt had not lived there in years. Presumably, it was felt, the Hyde Park address would underline the Roosevelt endorsement. The cost of the mailing was $12,880. See Stewart Alsop, "Kennedy's Magic Formula," *Saturday Evening Post*, August 13, 1960, p. 60.

* Mrs. Roosevelt also opposed Kennedy's bid for the 1956 vice-presidential nomination. In 1958 she described Jack Kennedy as "someone who understands what courage is and admires it, but has not quite the independence to have it." Even after he became the presidential candidate of the Democratic Party Mrs. Roosevelt's endorsement was halfhearted and patronizing. She suggested that he lean on Adlai Stevenson's "more judicial and reflective type of mind." See Richard J. Whalen, *The Founding Father: The Story of Joseph P. Kennedy* (New York: New American Library, 1964), p. 449; Victor Lasky, *J.F.K., the Man and the Myth* (New York: Macmillan, 1963), pp. 415–16.

Jimmy announced that he would not be a candidate for the Senate; the New York *Times* reported in March that F.D.R., Jr., was weighing the possibility of a race for governor of New York in 1966; in May Elliott was elected Democratic National Committeeman from Florida; an Illinois congressman proposed in June that Franklin should be President Johnson's running mate ("Roosevelt," wrote United Press International, "appeared to agree with the suggestion"); also in June Jimmy's son-in-law was defeated in a New York congressional primary.† By the fall Jimmy could be found campaigning in central Alaska, Elliott was making speeches in Kentucky, Frank followed Barry Goldwater around the country as a one-man "truth squad." Even John, the Republican, had his hand in politics; an advertisement in the New York *Times* proclaimed, "'I resent Robert Kennedy's using my mother's name for his selfish ends.' —John Roosevelt."

If the 1964 pace was brisk, 1965's was of whirlwind proportions.

Jimmy, bald and fifty-seven, ran for mayor of Los Angeles. His opponents charged that he was merely trying to position himself for another assault on the Governor's Mansion. Jimmy answered that this was not so and pledged to serve a full four-year term. The issue became highly hypothetical when the voters soundly rejected Roosevelt in April. The mayoralty race, however, may have had something to do with his subsequent appointment as U.S. representative to the Economic and Social Council of the United Nations. Wrote columnist Joseph Kraft, "Congressman James Roosevelt . . . seems to be in the [UN] delegation as the price exacted by a political rival, Mayor Samuel Yorty of Los Angeles, in return for accepting Federal mediation between the rebellious Negro community of Watts and the Los Angeles authorities." The official ex-

---

† William Haddad is the husband of Kate Roosevelt. (She is the child of Jimmy's first marriage to Betsey Cushing, who subsequently became the wife of John Hay Whitney, owner of the New York *Herald Tribune*.) Haddad, a former reporter and associate director of the Peace Corps, ran as a reform Democrat against Congressman Leonard Farbstein in Manhattan's Nineteenth District, where the population is half Jewish. Some of his opponents called him "El Haddad" and circulated the story that he was an Arab. His father was a Syrian Jew. Jimmy Roosevelt came into the district to deny that he had repudiated his daughter for marrying a Jew. "She and I have always had a close relationship. I value it very much." Despite Roosevelt's endorsement, the son-in-law was defeated by a heavy vote from the Lower East Side. Haddad, after working as a top aide in Robert Kennedy's successful campaign for the Senate, joined the Office of Economic Opportunity as head of the inspector general's office (known as "the fink shop" to poverty warriors), and was subsequently accused by Farbstein of using his post as a staging ground for another congressional race. Haddad resigned in late summer, 1965; later Mayor-elect Lindsay appointed him to head a study of the poverty program in New York. Says a friend who has known him since college days, "Bill likes to be where the action is."

planation was that Roosevelt's familiarity with Capitol Hill would be useful in winning congressional support for the UN. At any rate, in September Jimmy resigned his seat in Congress to take up duties that his mother had once performed so well.[158]

Elliott also had a hat in the ring during 1965. He announced his candidacy for the part-time, $3000-a-year post of mayor of Miami Beach, the sunny city of 70,000 permanent residents and 32,000 hotel rooms. The peripatetic Roosevelt had formerly been a resident of New York, Texas, Colorado, and Minnesota. In 1963 he moved to Florida and started an import-export business. Now at fifty-four, tall and crew-cut, he aimed his mayoralty campaign at Miami Beach's large population of retired people, many of whom lived on the Social Security initiated by his father. Moreover, there was little chance that the voters could forget his antecedents. His slogan proclaimed him "a man with a name Miami Beach can be proud of." Opponent Melvin Richard, the incumbent, was also distressed by Elliott's use of Eleanor Roosevelt commemorative stamps on his campaign mailings (plus a sticker which read, "In a great tradition, elect Elliott Roosevelt"). Commented Rolfe Neill of the Miami Beach *Sun,* "The Richard forces can bellyache all they want, but if I had a mother with a postage stamp issued in her honor I'd use it on all my mail too."[159] Richard had some more things to say about Elliott's five marriages.‡ But after Roosevelt's election Drew Pearson wrote, "Elliott Roosevelt has had bad luck with some of his marriages, but his recent victory in winning the tough race to be Mayor of Miami Beach was due in part to the loyalty, devotion and hard work of the present Mrs. Roosevelt."[160] Two weeks after he took office in June, a Washington reporter found Mayor Elliott at an all-day meeting of the City Council, ruling with "a firm hand, a loud voice and a ready gavel."[161]

Although Frank was still Under Secretary of Commerce, he spent much of winter, 1965, making speeches in New York State. When asked if this activity had anything to do with a race for governor, he replied, "I'd be rather silly not to be interested."[162] Meanwhile, President Johnson named him chairman of the new Equal Employment Opportunities Commission, which was empowered to enforce the controversial fair employment practices section of the 1964 Civil Rights Act. Later he weighed the

---

‡ Elliott Roosevelt first married (1932) Elizabeth Donner, divorced 1933, one son; married second (1933) Ruth Googins, divorced 1944, three children; married third (1944) Faye Emerson, divorced 1950, no issue; married fourth (1951) Mrs. Minnewa Bell Ross, divorced 1960, no issue; married fifth (1960) Mrs. Patricia Peabody Whitehead, no issue. Roosevelt's fourth wife was the daughter of a Southern California oil millionaire and real estate developer, after whom Bell, California, is named. (Her brother, Alphonso Bell, is now a Republican congressman from Los Angeles County.) The fifth Mrs. Roosevelt is related to Mrs. Marietta Peabody Tree, formerly of the U.S. delegation to the UN.

possibilities of entering the contest for mayor of New York City. But he finally told a press conference that his "greater obligation" was to remain in his present job. He declined to predict whether this would also prevent him from seeking the governorship in 1966. This prompted columnist Jack Wilson to write, "Franklin D. Roosevelt, Jr. says he won't run for mayor of New York. He hasn't decided yet what else he won't run for."[163]

The Roosevelt dynasty bears some hallmarks of a political variant of "shirt sleeves to shirt sleeves in three generations." (Though the shirt sleeves have always had French cuffs.)

The early Roosevelts, as Gerald Johnson points out, were "intelligent without genius, decent without saintliness, educated without erudition, not slothful in business, but not titans of industry." If they escaped mediocrity, neither were they especially inspiring.

Then suddenly, unexpectedly, the dynasty produced the two most personally exciting figures in the history of American politics.

The next generation suffered from the Famous Father Complex. Marked for the limelight too early, they lived in the long shadows cast by their presidential sires. Except on the battlefield, they seemed to view life as an unfortunate paradox: if they succeeded, it was because of their parentage; if they failed, it was their own fault.

Particularly in the case of F.D.R.'s sons, some of their problems may have been just plain bad luck. (John F. Kennedy thought that if Franklin Roosevelt, Jr., had only secured the support of Tammany boss De Sapio in 1954 he would have become the Democratic gubernatorial candidate, he would have won, and he would have been the 1960 presidential nominee.[164]) Some of their problems began back in the childhood of their parents, creating attitudes over which they had no control. And some of their problems came from being "poor little rich boys." For the Roosevelts, accustomed to the trappings of wealth, are not a notably affluent lot, and there always has been a desperation about the sons' search for income. (As late as 1962, Congressman James Roosevelt was innocently implicated in a Maryland savings and loan scandal because he accepted the honorary presidency of an organization—a post that paid a mere $6000 a year.[165])

Yet if there have been problems not of their own making, they also have not been above exploiting the name that they considered an encumbrance; thus, through their own actions, adding to the ancestral load that weighed them down. Others in the same category, notably the Tafts, bided their time, slowly built their reputations, and managed, to a large degree, to emerge as political figures in their own right. But the Roosevelt sons, even after they reached the United States Congress and other high offices, never cleanly cut the umbilical cord.

The heirs of T.R. have solved this problem by leaving politics, though not public service. It is still too early to tell whether F.D.R.'s grand-children will follow the same course. They now range in age from early teens through early thirties.§

By any standard other than that set by their father and great-uncle, F.D.R.'s sons would be judged successful politicians. At present, one holds ambassadorial rank, one heads an important federal commission, and one is mayor of the seventh largest city in his state. Harold Ickes once accused Jimmy of having "no political ideals" and not being "a liberal."[166] But time has proved him wrong. The Democratic sons have tried to perpetuate their father's philosophy as they interpret it. Above all, and despite repeated setbacks, they have persevered. F.D.R.'s children, now in middle age, feel they have grown up.[167]

§ The only one to have so far opted for public service is the son of Anna Roosevelt's first marriage to Curtis Dall. He is now chief of the non-governmental organizations liaison section of the United Nations Public Information Department. Buzzie, as he was called around the White House in the thirties, is now known as Curtis Roosevelt, having legally changed his name in 1950. According to a friend, Curtis "tries to project the Roosevelt charm. He's conscious and conscientious about having a Roosevelt background." He has been married three times.

The Harrison Dynasty

Yes, grandfather's hat fits Ben—fits Ben;
　He wears it with dignified grace, Oh yes!
So rally again and we'll put Uncle Ben
　Right back in his grandfather's place.

—Presidential campaign song, 1888

THE private road bisects Berkeley Hundred, cutting through tobacco fields, passing slave quarters and workshops. After a mile and a half one comes to a gateway and straight ahead is the handsome mansion of red brick, rising three stories. On its first floor, off the center hall, are two "Great Rooms," paneled in wood, connected by doors on either side of a massive fireplace. Facing the James River, on the other side of the house, is the formal dining room. This was once the home of the Harrisons, a family of Tidewater Virginia aristocrats, and in it was born William Henry Harrison, "Log Cabin" President of the United States.

The apparent paradox between the elegant birthplace of "Old Tippecanoe" and his reputation as the favorite son of the pioneer West underlines one of the Harrisons' most notable political assets—adaptability. For from Virginia's coastal plain to the rugged mountains of Wyoming the dynasty has successfully quested after the American voter for ten generations.

A decade after the first Harrison arrived in Virginia, probably in 1632, he was elected to the House of Burgesses, thus founding the longest unbroken line of politicians in American history.

In each generation a Harrison would be elected to public office. The first five Benjamin Harrisons were part of their colony's ruling elite: all were elected to the House of Burgesses, one was its Speaker, another sat on the Governor's Council. The fifth Benjamin Harrison signed the Declaration of Independence; his son and great-grandson were presidents; his great-great-great-grandson left the United States Congress in 1965.

The colonial Harrisons accepted political office in the same spirit that they accepted management of their twenty thousand acres. It was a

THE HARRISON DYNASTY
(A Selective Genealogy)

Benjamin Harrison I (d. 1645)
Arrived America c. 1632
Virginia House of Burgesses
(2 children)

Benjamin II (1645–1712)
Burgesses, Council
(6 children)

Benjamin III (1673–1710)
Speaker of Burgesses
(2 children)

Hannah (1678–1731)[1]
m. *Philip Ludwell*
Burgesses, Council

Sarah (1670–1713)
m. *James Blair*
Founder, William
and Mary College

Benjamin IV (1700–44)
Burgesses
m. *Anne Carter*
(9 children; 1 d.y.)

Carter Henry
(1736–96)
m. *Susannah Randolph*
(6 children)

Benjamin V
(1726–91)
CONTINENTAL CONGRESS,
GOVERNOR
(8 children; 1 d.y.)

Charles
(1742–96)
General
(8 children)

Elizabeth
m. *Peyton Randolph*
CONTINENTAL CONGRESS

Robert Carter (1765–1840)
m. Ann Cabell
(10 children)

Carter Bassett (d. 1808)
HOUSE OF REPRESENTATIVES
(2 children)

William Henry (1773–1841)
HOUSE OF REPRESENTATIVES,
SENATE, PRESIDENT
m. Anna Symmes
(10 children; 1 d.y.)

Carter Henry (1796–1825)
(1 child)

John Cleves Symmes (1798–1830)
m. Clarissa Pike

William Henry (1802–38)
m. Jane Findlay Irwin

John Scott (1804–78)
HOUSE OF REPRESENTATIVES
1st m. Lucretia Johnson (d. 1830)
(3 children);
2nd m. Elizabeth Irwin
(10 children)

Carter Henry (1825–93)
HOUSE OF REPRESENTATIVES,
mayor of Chicago
(10 children; 6 d.y.)

Benjamin (1833–1901)
SENATE, PRESIDENT
1st m. Caroline Scott (2 children)
2nd m. Mary Scott Lord Dimmick (1 child)

Elizabeth (1897–1955)
m. James Blaine Walker, Jr.
(2 children)

Mary (d. 1930)
m. James McKee
(2 children)

Russell (1854–1936)
State Senate
m. Mary Saunders
(2 children)

William Henry (1896–)
HOUSE OF REPRESENTATIVES
(2 children)

Carter Henry (1860–1953)
Mayor of Chicago
(2 children)

responsibility of station. Benjamin Harrison V was to become a revolutionary, but he was hardly a born rebel. His place in society was doubly assured as master of the Berkeley Hundred plantation and grandson of "King" Carter, the richest man in America. Moreover, he was related by blood or marriage to every leading family in the Old Dominion. The Lees were cousins.[1] The Randolphs were cousins.[2] The Byrds were cousins. His brother-in-law was married to the sister of Martha Washington. He had attended William and Mary College, which was founded by a great-uncle.[3] He was a rich man who enjoyed his riches, entertained lavishly, and wore only the latest fashions—blue-tinted wigs and silver-buttoned silk coats in brilliant shades of yellow, blue, and purple.

At the end of 1780 two thousand British troops, under the command of Benedict Arnold, landed at the mouth of the James River and began a campaign of ravagement. When they reached Berkeley Hundred the turncoat general ordered the mansion's ancestral portraits thrown on a bonfire, thereby destroying for future historians the opportunity to describe the likenesses of the early Harrisons. But accounts of the imposing figure of Benjamin Harrison V remain. He was six feet four inches, weighed 249 pounds, and was renowned for his love of good food. (In later years he tried dieting by giving up "good old Madeira for light French wines."[4]) He was also a convivial companion and a notorious joker whose humor was of the earthy stag party variety. No occasion, he felt, was too solemn for a good laugh. On John Hancock's election as president of the Continental Congress, the delegate from Virginia picked him up bodily and deposited him in the presiding officer's chair. Even at the signing of the Declaration of Independence, Big Ben had a quip. "Do you recollect the pensive and awful silence which pervaded the house when we were called up, one after another, to the table of the president of Congress to subscribe what was believed by many at that time to be our own death warrants?" asked Benjamin Rush of John Adams. "The silence and the gloom of the morning was interrupted, I well recollect, only for a moment by Colonel Harrison of Virginia, who said to Mr. Gerry at the table: 'I shall have a great advantage over you, Mr. Gerry, when we are all hung for what we are now doing. From the size and weight of my body I shall die in a few minutes, but from the lightness of your body you will dance in the air an hour or two before you are dead.' This speech produced a transient smile. . . ."[5] (The only time that Harrison was ever reported to have been "out of humor" was when Samuel Adams, the perpetual manipulator, engineered the cancellation of a ball in honor of Martha Washington.[6])

In pre-Revolutionary politics, Harrison was an enlightened conservative, holding the middle ground between the older members of the Virginia oligarchy and the Young Turks like Jefferson and the Lees. To the Adamses, however, Harrison, who did not immediately fall into line for independence, was a reactionary. But then so were the majority of Americans.

Yet when he finally cast his lot for independence he became a valuable and unwavering patriot. While neither orator nor thinker, he did bring to Philadelphia the experience of twenty-six years in the House of Burgesses, and it was as a seasoned legislator that he made his contribution to the founding of the Republic. During many strained moments in the committee rooms Benjamin Harrison could be counted on to break the tension with a bit of bawdy humor, a talent that no Adams ever possessed. Even John Adams, who wrote that Harrison was "of no use in Congress," had later to admit that the Virginian had contributed "many pleasantries" that steadied rough sessions.[7]

Harrison left Congress in 1778 to re-enter Virginia politics. Many political leaders felt that the more important work of waging the war was being done on the state level. Clinton had returned to New York; Rutledge to South Carolina. Harrison defeated Jefferson for Speaker of the House of Delegates, and at the conclusion of the war he became Virginia's first peacetime governor. After serving three one-year terms, the constitutional limit, he attempted to recapture his old seat in the state legislature but was defeated by John Tyler of Greenway. (Fifty-five years later the two rivals' sons would form the ticket of "Tippecanoe and Tyler too.")

As a member of the Virginia convention that was called to vote on the new federal Constitution, Harrison, along with Richard Henry Lee and Patrick Henry, vigorously opposed the proposed scheme of government. But while Lee was philosophically against strong central government, Harrison's arguments were primarily commercial. Virginia's surrender of her right to regulate commerce would be greatly to her disadvantage, he contended.

With a joke on his lips, death came to Benjamin Harrison in 1791 after holding elective office almost continuously for forty-two years. His political activities had kept him from managing Berkeley Hundred effectively and a great plantation cannot prosper with an absentee landlord. Perhaps the index of his devotion to country was that Harrison died a relatively poor man.[*]

Of his three sons, the first became involved in some scandal that is lost to history,[†] the second had a brief political career,[‡] and the third became President of the United States.

[*] The Signer had a younger brother, Charles Harrison (1742–96), who was a Revolutionary brigadier general and Nathanael Greene's chief of artillery.

[†] The first wife of Benjamin Harrison VI (1755–99) died eight days after the birth of a son, and within weeks of her death he married Susanna Randolph of the neighboring Curles Neck plantation. She left him almost im-

William Henry Harrison, tall and slender with sallow complexion and dark eyes, was studying medicine under Dr. Benjamin Rush in Philadelphia when his father died. Apparently Benjamin Harrison had chosen this profession for his youngest son because the youth promptly switched to soldiering upon hearing of his father's death. Through the influence of Richard Henry Lee, he became an ensign, the lowest commissioned rank in the army.

In November 1791 the eighteen-year-old recruit arrived at the present site of Cincinnati to fight the Indians. During seven years in the army Harrison rose to captain, was cited for bravery, and married Anna Symmes.

The young bride's father was John Cleves Symmes, former delegate to the Continental Congress from New Jersey and judge of the Northwest Territory, who had recently wed Susan Livingston. (But the daughter of New Jersey Governor William Livingston never became adjusted to frontier life and left her husband in 1808.)

On hearing of his daughter's marriage, Symmes wrote that she "made rather a run away match of it, though she was married at my house in my absence."[8] The influential judge considered his new son-in-law to be a man of limited prospects. "If I knew what to make of Capt. Harrison, I could easily take proper arrangements for his family," wrote Symmes to Robert Morris, the young soldier's former guardian. "He can neither bleed, plead, nor preach, and if he could plow I should be satisfied."[9] The story is told that the next time he met Harrison, Symmes said the fatherly thing: "How, sir, do you expect to support my daughter in the style to which she is accustomed?" To which the proud Virginian replied, "By my sword, sir, and my good right arm."[10] This winning answer, according to legend, was enough to sweep aside all objections. Unfortunately the facts indicate that the two were partially estranged for fifteen years.

Ironically, in his last years Symmes was impoverished and only too happy to accept the charity of his son-in-law. Among the judge's many setbacks, not the least was the failure of Symmes City. Being himself unsuccessful in love, he saw his real estate venture also doomed by an affair of the heart. According to his grandson, the development was de-

---

mediately, taking his son with her. Benjamin's will states, "I do not decline mentioning my wife Susanna and my baby at Curles because my affection for them is lessened, but from some things which have passed between myself and some of her family, I expect I should not be a welcome guest among them. . . ." He does, however, make bequests to his wife's sister, and the biographer of the early Harrisons suggests that "perhaps he married the wrong sister." See Clifford Dowdey, *The Great Plantation* (New York: Holt, Rinehart & Winston, 1957), pp. 279–81.

‡ Carter Bassett Harrison (died 1808) studied law at William and Mary, served five years in the state legislature, and was a member of the U. S. House of Representatives, 1793–99.

stroyed "by the whimsical caprice of a black-eyed girl." When the un-named siren left Symmes City for Cincinnati, the lieutenant in charge of the army garrison followed her, and, since the settlers felt they would be safest where the troops were, they too departed for the Queen City.[11] Love, however, was probably the least important cause of Symmes's failure as a land promoter. In partnership with Elias Boudinot he pur-chased a tract of one million acres between the Great and Little Miami rivers. But Symmes was impulsive and careless. He parceled out land to which he had no title, and was finally sued by his associate. The verdict was in Boudinot's favor, and Symmes was forced to sell his property at a sheriff's auction to satisfy this and other judgments against him.[12]

Captain William Henry Harrison agreed with his father-in-law that the army was not the most productive way to support a growing family, and in 1798 he secured a $1200-a-year appointment as secretary of the North-west Territory. Then, when the Territory's population qualified it for a seat in Congress, Harrison was elected to the House of Representatives, where he engineered passage of a bill to create the Indiana Territory out of the western half of his constituency. President Adams appointed him its first governor in 1800. Having just turned twenty-seven, Governor Harrison took over the administration of what is now Indiana, Illinois, Wisconsin, most of Michigan, and some of Minnesota—population 5641, and the Indian tribes of Potawatomi, Miami, Sauk, Fox, Kickapoo, Shaw-nee, Piankashaw, Delaware, Wea, Eel River, Wyandot, and Chippewa.

As governor of a "first grade" territory under the Northwest Ordinance, Harrison held all executive, legislative, and administrative power in his hands. John Randolph of Roanoke, who saved some of his best blasts for relatives, called his cousin "a satrap who never forgets that he has been a satrap."[13] But it was not in Harrison's nature to be a dictator.

Although leaner and several inches shorter than his father, he had the Signer's easygoing, hail-fellow disposition. Moreover, Harrison needed the job and this meant following the policies of the national Administration in office. He received appointments from Adams, Jefferson, and Madison and was loyal to each although their aims were not always consistent. Always aiming to please, he sent little gifts to his benefactors—a bag of pecans, some Indian curiosities, the naming of a town and a species of bear after Jefferson. In return his commission was renewed in 1803, 1806, and 1809. On the occasion of one of these extensions he wrote Jefferson, "I beg you to receive my warmest thanks for this additional proof of your confidence and friendship. The emoluments of my office afford me a decent support and will I hope . . . enable me to lay up a small fund for the education of my children. I have hitherto found that my nursery grows faster than my strongbox."[14] (The Harrisons were to have ten children, four girls and six boys, one of whom died in infancy.)

During four terms as governor of the Indiana Territory, Harrison's most important work was in acquiring Indian land. This was in keeping with President Jefferson's instructions, though at times he followed orders with more enthusiasm than was called for. His primary problems were created by the brothers Tecumseh and Tenskwatawa, leaders of the proud Shawnee, and practitioners of a form of Red Muslimism. It was to humble them that Harrison, with a large ostrich feather in his beaver hat, marched 1020 men to Tippecanoe in November 1811. When the smoke had cleared, 37 Americans were killed and 151 wounded. The Indians had been routed, although they lost only 36 men. While the legendary battle accomplished little, it did create a new hero—William Henry Harrison, the hero of Tippecanoe.

The War of 1812 came at an opportune time in the hero's career. A governor can make an uncomfortable number of enemies during twelve years, and a military command would conveniently remove him from these malcontents. Harrison was made a general, primarily as a result of massive lobbying by Henry Clay.[15]

In a war more noted for its politicking than its fighting, Harrison won a victory at the battle of the Thames. Actually the British were retreating so fast that the Americans never did catch up to them, but the encounter was among the best the nation had to cheer about. Harrison made triumphal appearances in Washington, New York, and Philadelphia and then retired to his "log cabin."

The Harrison home on the banks of the Ohio River, sixteen miles below Cincinnati, had indeed been a humble log cabin when William Henry purchased it from his father-in-law. But he had expanded it into a spacious sixteen-room mansion, with the original cabin serving as a large living room.

Somehow Harrison's three thousand acres never seemed to provide adequately for his large and hospitable family, and William Henry always had an eye out for supplemental income from public office. He served in the House of Representatives from 1816 to 1819. From 1819 to 1821 he was in the Ohio Senate. And from 1825 to 1828 he was a United States senator. His legislative role, as he saw it, was not to lead public opinion but to reflect the will of those who elected him. "Upon this floor I stand as a Representative, or the agent, of my constituents; bound, I think, by every moral obligation to execute their will."[16] His special interests were veterans and military affairs—pensions for war widows and orphans, private bills for back pay, recommendations for new arsenals and forts. While in Congress he proposed a naval academy and a system of military training in every school in the country.

When not in office, Harrison was seeking office. He was defeated three times for United States Senate, once for governor, and twice for the House of Representatives. In 1823 and 1824 he tried in vain to get appointed as minister to Mexico. He hoped to be chosen as the vice-presidential candidate on the ticket with John Quincy Adams in 1828 but was passed over in favor of Richard Rush. Secretary of State Clay proposed him for minister to Colombia in 1827 and 1828. Finally an exasperated President wrote, "Vice-President, Major-General, Minister to Colombia—for each of these places he has been this very session as hot in pursuit as a hound on the scent of a hare." In John Quincy Adams' opinion, Harrison had "a lively and active, but shallow mind, a political adventurer, not without talents, but self-sufficient, vain, and indiscreet. He has, withal, a faculty of making friends, and is incessantly importuning them for their influence in his favor."[17] Harrison thought no higher of Adams: ". . . he is a disgusting man to do business [with] . . . stiff and abstracted in his opinions, which are drawn from books exclusively."[18] Yet Adams owed Harrison a favor. For in a legislature that took its pleasure by thwarting the President, Senator Harrison had been a firm supporter of Adams' program for internal improvements. So the gruff and cantankerous Adams appointed the genial and informal Harrison as minister to Colombia.

Harrison made no secret of his reason for desiring the diplomatic post. He was thousands of dollars in debt. "My great object is to save a little money."[19] His salary as minister would be $9000 with an equal amount for "outfit." In February 1829 the new minister, with his seventeen-year-old son Carter Bassett as attaché, arrived at the remote mountain-perched capital of Bogotá. But a month later Andrew Jackson became President and appointed a Kentucky congressman to succeed Harrison. This was strictly a matter of patronage, and the new Secretary of State, Martin Van Buren, instructed the lame-duck minister to continue in office until his replacement arrived, which was not until late September.

In Colombia, Harrison spent a great deal of time cultivating a vegetable garden. He had seeds imported from his Ohio farm, and the exotic produce was in constant demand at legation dinners. However, he was less successful as a diplomat. Simon Bolívar, having assumed dictatorial powers, found himself holding the tail of a tiger. Worn out at forty-five from his military and sexual exploits, the Liberator was secretly negotiating for a European prince to rule Colombia and give the country stability through dynastic succession. This scheme was alien to Harrison's republican principles, and he made his opinion explicit in a letter to Bolivar. Former President Adams wrote in his diary, "His [Bolivar's] principles of government have been always monarchical. . . . Harrison was but a short time there, but long enough to get involved in some of their party divisions. It was perhaps impossible to avoid it. . . . [His letter] must have nettled the liberator beyond measure. . . ."[20] Harrison was then officially kicked out of Colombia.

If Adams had little respect for Harrison the diplomat, from his own experience he could only feel sympathy for Harrison the father. For on Harrison's homecoming he was confronted with the tangled affairs of two of his sons.

His oldest boy, John Cleves Symmes Harrison, had been removed from his job in the Vincennes Land Office and accused of embezzling government funds. The claim against him came to $12,803.63 with interest charges. In November 1830, before the debt could be settled, Symmes Harrison died at the age of thirty-two. He left a wife, Clarissa, the daughter of General Zebulon Pike, and six children. William Henry took the fatherless family into his home and then turned to the charges against his son. He got congressional agreement for a substantial credit on disputed items and payment over eighteen years without interest. Finally, by selling part of his own land, he closed the account.

Harrison now turned his attention to the affairs of his other prodigal child, William Henry, Jr. Following a script that John Quincy Adams might have written, Harrison told his lawyer son, "I must again exhort you to abandon the lounging and procrastinating mode of life which for some time you have followed. In the morning go to your office and stay there until dinner and if you have no other business read professional books and never open any other book in those hours devoted to business."[21] The young man solemnly promised to reform, then got drunk. He gave up his law practice and tried farming. But an alcoholic farmer was as doomed to fail as an alcoholic attorney. The prohibitionist father realized that there would be no reformation. William Henry Harrison, Jr., died in 1838 at thirty-six years of age. His father now had three families to support.

Personal problems beset Harrison from all quarters. Another son, Benjamin, was reported to have been slain by the Mexicans in 1836. The report proved false; the young soldier of fortune had been only slightly wounded. He died of natural causes in 1840, a year after death came to his brother Carter Bassett Harrison, the former attaché. By the time William Henry entered the White House only John Scott Harrison of his six sons was still alive.

To his good friend Congressman James Findlay, whose niece had been the wife of his intemperate son, Harrison wrote, "To the distress produced by the destruction of my hopes in relation to two of my sons, is added that of increasingly embarrassing circumstances."[22] He was so deeply in debt that when he was appointed to the West Point Board of Visitors he had to borrow $220 at three per cent monthly interest in order to make the trip east. At this low ebb Harrison was grateful for the position of clerk of the Court of Common Pleas of Hamilton County. (Much of the work was handled by a son-in-law.)

Yet suddenly the court clerk was being proposed for President of the United States. In amazement, Beverley Tucker wrote in the Richmond *Whig*, "Why was he dragged from obscurity and disturbed in his slumber by this unreasonable dawn of glory? . . . Harrison should be allowed to go to sleep again . . . and awake sober as the clerk of a county court."[23]

The circumstances of the presidential boom were as unexpected as the choice of candidate. Richard M. Johnson of Kentucky was being promoted for the Democratic nomination, and his propagandists were trying to turn him into the real hero of the battle of the Thames. If Johnson was to be up, Harrison would have to be down. To Harrison the contentions of Johnson's camp were as ridiculous as crediting the victory at New Orleans to some colonel on Andy Jackson's staff. However, this gave Harrison a chance to defend himself, revive his war record, and become a presidential candidate.

The Democratic nomination went to Martin Van Buren, with Johnson as his running mate. But no matter how bravely he had fought at the Thames, Johnson was politically handicapped by a Negro mistress and two mulatto daughters. The Whig press dubbed Van Buren and Johnson as the "black ticket" and made every imaginable play on the word "color." Yet the Democrats were a united party, while the badly fragmented Whigs went into the canvass with four candidates—Senator Hugh L. White of Tennessee, Senator Willie P. Mangum of North Carolina, Senator Daniel Webster of Massachusetts, and Court Clerk William Henry Harrison. Although Van Buren was elected, Harrison received more popular and electoral votes than the three senators combined. A shift of two thousand votes in Pennsylvania would have thrown the race into the Whig-controlled House of Representatives and elected Harrison.

Four years later Harrison was made the Whigs' sole nominee, and John Tyler, a Virginia Democrat, became the vice-presidential candidate in an effort to win over disgruntled Southerners. The Whigs didn't bother to write a platform—there was nothing they could agree upon.

The election was handed to the Whigs when a Baltimore newspaper disparagingly suggested that Harrison should be given "a barrel of hard cider and a pension of two thousand a year, and, our word for it, he will sit the remainder of his days in a log cabin by the side of a 'sea coal' fire and study moral philosophy."[24] No other issue was needed; the "log cabin and hard cider" campaign was on. Pompous, aristocratic Congressman Hugh S. Legaré of South Carolina donned a coonskin cap. Even Daniel Webster uncovered a log cabin in his ancestry. A Philadelphia distillery marketed a bottle in the shape of a log cabin labeled "E. C. Booz Old Cabin Whiskey." A Richmond pickpocket on his way to jail urged the election of "Tippecanoe and Tyler, too." Harrison rallies were measured in acres—ten thousand men to the acre. There were ten acres at Dayton. The Whigs sang themselves to victory. (Even Beverley

Tucker, who liked the addition of Tyler to the ticket, composed a campaign song.) A newspaper editor recalled, "Men, women and children did nothing but sing. It worried, annoyed, dumbfounded, crushed the Democrats, but there was no use trying to escape. It was a ceaseless torrent of music, still beginning, never ending. If a Democrat tried to speak, argue, or answer anything that was said or done, he was only saluted with a fresh deluge of music."[25]

> What has caused this great commotion, motion, motion,
>   Our country through?
>   It is the ball a-rolling on,
> For Tippecanoe and Tyler too—Tippecanoe and Tyler too!

> Old Tip he wears a homespun coat,
> He has no ruffled shirt-wirt-wirt;
> But Mat he has the golden plate,
> And he's a little squirt-wirt-wirt.[26]

The recipient of all the enthusiasm made twenty-three speeches without saying anything. All requests for Harrison's views were handled by a three-man committee, prompting the Democrats to label him "General Mum." His victory over Van Buren, however, was overwhelming, and in December the President-elect resigned as clerk of the Court of Common Pleas of Hamilton County.

After picking his Cabinet, he chose a grand-nephew, Henry Harrison of Berkeley Hundred, to be his secretary[27] and then retired to his Virginia birthplace to write the inaugural address.§ The result was mostly patriotic rhetoric, full of classical allusions and generally devoid of solutions for the vexing issues of the day. Webster tried to edit the draft but confessed that all he managed to do was to "kill seventeen Roman proconsuls as dead as smelts."[28]

Once in the White House, President Harrison did his own marketing in the early morning, just as he had done when minister to Colombia. On March 28 he contracted a chill, which rapidly turned into pneumonia. On April 4 he was dead. The nation was stunned. Chancellor Theodore Frelinghuysen of New York University, in a memorial address, declared: ". . . while the messenger of death has thrown his darts among all other

§ Berkeley Hundred was to figure in American history once more before its final demise as a great plantation and its reconstruction as a tourist attraction. At the end of the first year of the Civil War, General McClellan, having been turned back at the gates of Richmond, camped his hundred thousand troops on its grounds. The manor house was turned into a temporary hospital, and the big poplars were cut down for campfires. On the great lawn, which served as the army's headquarters, General Dan Butterfield's bugler composed a simple melodic substitute for "lights out." Thus Berkeley Hundred first heard "Taps."

departments of society, never, until now, have we been called to render funeral honors to a deceased President. All around him, in the House of Representatives, the Senate and the Seat of Justice, victims had fallen, but the executive mansion had been spared. Perhaps the thought was rising into a measure of confidence that this exalted station was invested with peculiar immunities—That a mark so lofty would not range with the aim of the arrow. To-day, that illusion has vanished, and the charm is broken."[29] John Tyler proclaimed May 14 as a day of fasting and prayer for the first President to die in office. At the First Presbyterian Church in Louisville, its minister, William Lewis Breckinridge, told his congregants: "There is something not only impressive, but I think truly great, in the conception of national grief—a whole people mourning. The tears of a single individual are affecting. We cannot witness, without deep emotion, the sorrow of a family, all its members mingling their sighs and tears together. The heart could scarce bear to behold the grief of a whole city, and hear the lamentations of every citizen and every family rising in one groan to Heaven. But when these swell into the wailing of a nation, the sound is like the voice of God's thunder."[30]

The continuation of the Harrisons as a political dynasty now rested on the broad shoulders of John Scott Harrison, only surviving son of the late President. Quiet and meditative, he had been trained as a lawyer but preferred the life of a farmer. When his father went to Colombia he assumed management of the family lands.

Later he served two terms as a Whig congressman. But from Washington he wrote, "My thoughts are continually wandering from the hall of legislation to my children and my home."[31] Yet he served diligently and was rarely absent. Unlike his father, he believed that his conscience, not the opinion of his district, should determine his vote. He fought the Nebraska Bill, which reopened the slavery question, and when Representative Brooks assaulted Charles Sumner on the floor of the Senate, he told the Congress, "It has been said, Mr. Speaker, that no Northern man dare vote against the expulsion of the gentleman from South Carolina. . . . Sir, I dare do anything I think right; and when my constituents seek to deprive me of that privilege, I will say to them: 'Take back this bauble of office which I did not seek. . . .'"[32] Congressman Harrison was defeated in the next election. He never ran for office again.

Some old-line Whigs wanted to make John Scott a presidential candidate in 1856. He quickly scotched the suggestion, commenting that his supporters "calculated too largely on the potency of a *name*."[33] In 1861 the Democrats nominated him for lieutenant governor of Ohio. He declined. "I have no inclination to be a candidate for any office. If I ever cherished ambition for such distinction, I have been cured of it. . . ."[34]

However, John Scott Harrison has an unusual place in history. He is the only man to have been the son and father of presidents of the United States.

He also has a second claim to notoriety. Twenty-four hours after his death in 1878 his body was found hanging by the neck in a shaft at the Ohio Medical College.

The goulish mystery of who robbed the grave became a national sensation. "The Harrison Horror," as the case was called, uncovered a nationwide commerce in cadavers with Cincinnati as a shipping center for the dead traffic. The dean of the college in which the body was found revealed that most American medical colleges made annual contracts with grave robbers, who guaranteed to furnish them with a specified number of bodies. Legislation was then passed to eliminate the practice. On first learning of John Scott Harrison's passing, the Cincinnati *Daily Enquirer* wrote, "Most of those who will hear of his death did not know that he was living." But after the body was resurrected, the same paper wrote of him as an "honored citizen of the Ohio Valley and beloved member of society."[35]

Only one of John Scott Harrison's thirteen children became a public figure. And he was the most unlikely Harrison in the long history of the family. Coming from a tribe of giants, Benjamin Harrison was barely five and a half feet. "Perhaps for this reason, he wore a silk hat," opined Colonel Crook, the perennial White House aide.[36] Coming from a tribe of congenital hail-fellows, he was curt to the point of uncivility. Senator Hoar remarked that "Harrison would grant a request in a way which seemed as if he were denying it."[37] He was almost an Adams!

In one of the word pictures for which he was famous, Kansas editor William Allen White described Benjamin Harrison:

. . . bearded, soft-voiced, small-boned, gentle-eyed, meticulous of dress and in manners, in speech, in thought. He always spoke in complete sentences and often in rounded paragraphs. He finished his thought. He left nothing in the air. His desk was cleared at night, not as the desk of a captain of industry, for there was nothing brusque, vigorous or overwhelming about him. His desk was cleared as a gentleman's desk is cleared, with a certain deference to tomorrow. Personally, he was shy, most diffident and unassertive in his personal relations.[38]

After graduating from Miami University at Oxford, Ohio, and studying law in a Cincinnati office, Harrison married Caroline Scott, daughter of a pioneer in higher education for women, whose ancestors qualified her to become later the first president of the Daughters of the American Revolution.

The young couple settled in Indianapolis, where Ben became city attorney and cast his lot with a new political party, although his father warned him, "I do not believe that there is anything in the future of the Republican Party that would justify a man in making very great sacrifices to sustain its falling fortunes."[39]

In 1860, when Lincoln was the candidate for President, Harrison made his first race for state office. He was elected reporter of the Supreme Court of Indiana, a post which gave him the right to publish the Court's decisions and keep the profits. Hoosiers, listening to the stump speeches of Old Tippecanoe's grandson, were enchanted by his style, delivery, and quick responses. During one appearance he hunted in vain for a damaging statement by the democratic candidate for governor. "Gentlemen," he said, "I carefully pasted that extract from Mr. Hendricks' speech in my notebook, but it has disappeared. It simply goes to show that not a thing Thomas A. Hendricks says will stick."[40] Here was an odd phenomenon, indeed, for as Senator Depew later noted, if Harrison "spoke to an audience of 10,000 people he would make every one of them his friend, but if he was introduced to each of them afterward each would depart his enemy."[41]

Harrison joined the Union Army as a second lieutenant in 1862 and left it three years later as a brevet brigadier general. His success as a soldier was founded on careful preparation and meticulous attention to detail. War was like a gigantic lawsuit, and the counselor who best mastered the essentials would emerge victorious. But once on the field of battle he also displayed a bravery that was beyond courage; it was fearless. During one month, on the march with Sherman to Atlanta, he engaged in more battles than either William Henry Harrison or Andrew Jackson had fought in a lifetime. At Peach Tree Creek his boldness broke the back of Hood's assault, and Joe Hooker supposedly told him, "By God, I'll make you a brigadier general for this fight."[42]

When the era of the Union veteran in politics began, few stars were brighter than "Little Ben" Harrison's, the thirty-two-year-old former general.

Yet he preferred to bide his time. It would be more than a decade before he again became a candidate, although his name was constantly proposed for office. The Chicago *Times* felt that he was "a kind of Charles Francis Adams of Indiana."[43]

Instead, Harrison returned to the courtroom, handling the biggest and most sensational cases in the state. In one particularly notorious trial he defended the superintendent of the Indianapolis Deaf and Dumb Institute against a charge of mismanagement. A young student had accused one of her teachers of seduction, and to clear the name of the school and his client, Harrison proved that the girl had had relations with her uncle, not the teacher. The Indianapolis *Sentinel* spread the lawyer's fame in the case of "A Dumb Innocent That Could Not Say Him Nay."[44]

Finally, in 1876, came the political call that he could not refuse. The

Republican candidate for governor had been implicated in a scandal, and Harrison was nominated as the replacement. Indiana became the scene of a bitter battle between "Kid Gloves" Harrison and "Blue Jeans" Williams. The Democratic candidate was a six-foot-four-inch congressman, who was famous for homely quips and humble trousers, which marked him as a man of the people. Harrison's political symbol, marking him as a snobbish aristocrat, resulted from his having been poisoned during the Atlanta campaign; he now wore gloves as a protection against infection. As a campaigner, Harrison specialized in "waving the bloody shirt," the technique of pinning the label of Southern treason on the Democratic Party. But despite the enthusiasm of Indiana's war veterans, he went down to defeat, although he led the Republican ticket by several thousand votes.

Four years later, when the Republicans gained control of the state legislature, he was sent to Washington as a United States senator.

Except for Carrie Harrison's illnesses, the first years in the Senate were happy ones. His two children were about to be married. Mary, now in her twenties, was engaged to James McKee of Indianapolis.¶ And Russell had fallen in love with Mary Saunders, the blond daughter of Senator Alvin Saunders of Nebraska. This would be a useful alliance, for Saunders was an old political pro who would help Harrison win the Republican presidential nomination in 1888. Lincoln had made him territorial governor of Nebraska in 1861, and it was said that the President's last official act, as he was about to leave for Ford's Theatre, was to sign Saunders' commission for a second term.

The wedding took place in Omaha on January 9, 1884. The bride's ring was made from the gold of Russell's own mine. He was employed by the U. S. Assay Office in Helena, Territory of Montana, and was doing some mining on the side. The couple then left for their honeymoon in the palatial railroad car of the director of the Union Pacific.

The opulence showered on this union of two powerful senators' children may have suggested to Russell that there were quicker ways to get rich than as a minor government employee. He was soon involved in a financial tangle that was kept out of the nation's press by the proprietor of the Helena *Independent*. Russell had devised a scheme to get his capital out of the Montana Cattle Company while retaining control of the enterprise. To facilitate his manipulations he opened an office in New York and

¶ James R. McKee started in business as a shoe and boot jobber. In 1893 he was one of the principal figures in the formation of the General Electric Company, from which he retired as a vice-president in 1913. His wife died in 1930, leaving an estate of one and a half million dollars to McKee and their two children. He committed suicide at the age of eighty-four in 1942. See New York *Times*, November 21, 1930, p. 2, and October 22, 1942, p. 23.

enlisted the help of Stephen B. Elkins, a second-echelon robber baron.
Senator Harrison sent pleading letters to his son and got Elkins to promise
to help straighten out the young man's affairs.

There was no very good reason for making Benjamin Harrison the
Republican candidate for President in 1888. He had been just another
high-tariff senator and had not even been re-elected. The nomination
should have gone to James G. Blaine, who had made a strong race
against Grover Cleveland. But Blaine was ill and removed himself from
contention. However, his would still be the most powerful voice in the
convention. In a letter to Elkins, his chief political lieutenant, he outlined
the reasons for ruling out nine potential candidates, and concluded, "The
one more remaining, who in my judgment can make the best run, is Ben
Harrison."[45] So by a process of elimination Indiana's favorite son was
placed in nomination by Governor Albert G. Porter, who reminded the
delegates that the name of Harrison was "woven into the very fabric
of American History."[46] He was chosen on the eighth ballot.

The Republican nominee conducted a "front porch" campaign, although
at that time there was no porch on Harrison's Indianapolis home. Lew
Wallace wrote the official biography. As one wit said, "He did so well on
Ben Hur that we can trust him with *Ben Him*."[47] Besides the tariff, the
principal issue was William Henry Harrison's clothing. The Democrats
sang, "Grandpa's pants won't fit Benny," while the Republicans replied,
"Yes, Grandfather's hat fits Ben—fits Ben."

It was to be a close election, and Philadelphia merchant John Wana-
maker made sure that Harrison would not be defeated for lack of money.
As the first Indiana returns came in the New York *Times* reported that
"there seems to be no good reason to doubt that boodle and bulldozing
have carried the State for Harrison. . . ." The final results gave Cleveland
a majority of the popular vote, but it was cold comfort. Harrison was
elected, 233 electoral votes to 168.

As usual, the nation demanded intimate news of the occupants of the
White House.

President and Mrs. Harrison shared their new home with the First
Lady's ninety-year-old father; her elder sister, Mrs. Scott Lord; Mrs.
Lord's widowed daughter, Mrs. Dimmick; the Harrisons' daughter, Mrs.
McKee, and Mrs. McKee's two infants.

Have you heard the latest story of Baby McKee? A roll of important
papers has disappeared from the President's desk, and after a frantic
search, Baby McKee has been found "stirring the contents of a huge
spittoon with the precious roll."[48] Frank G. Carpenter of the Cleveland
Leader finally reported that word has gone out "to let up lest the
people of this country should come to believe the tales about this child's

having more influence than the members of the Cabinet."[49] (Later, White House aide Ike Hoover revealed that the President and his grandson were rarely together and their supposed intimacy was greatly exaggerated.[50])

Mrs. Harrison made equally good copy. She had electricity put in the White House, although the family was afraid to turn the lights on and off for fear of getting a shock. She held classes in china painting and conversational French for the fashionable ladies of Washington. She had the plumbing repaired. She inventoried the furniture. She searched the country for valuable White House treasures that had got into private hands.

Only the President was hard to humanize. Harrison was simply not destined to have popular appeal. Instead of going to the people, he counted on the congressional leaders to get his program enacted. And during the first half of his term, when his party controlled Congress, there were major successes—the Sherman Anti-Trust Act, the Silver Purchase Act, the McKinley Tariff Act, generous pensions for Civil War veterans. The only serious defeat was Henry Cabot Lodge's Force Bill to safeguard Negro voting rights in the South. Administratively, his performance on civil service left the reformers disappointed. He had brought in young Theodore Roosevelt as a Civil Service commissioner, but the two had violent arguments. After one session the President told a friend, "We got warmed up some. I am going to have my way about it, too." Then he added, "But you want to keep your eye on that young man. He'll be President someday, and then he'll have his way."[51] (Later, when Roosevelt was governor of New York, Harrison said, "The only trouble I ever had with managing him was that he wanted to put an end to all the evil in the world between sunrise and sunset."[52]) Harrison also brought to Washington another young man, William Howard Taft, as his Solicitor General.

The First Lady died in the fall of 1892. James Whitcomb Riley, the Hoosier bard, composed a poem to her memory—"All that was pure and good/And sweet in womanhood"[53]—and the mourning Chief Executive abandoned his campaign schedule. Out of respect, Grover Cleveland also canceled his political speeches.

Recalling the second Harrison-Cleveland contest, Henry Adams wrote, "The two candidates were singular persons, of whom it was the common saying that one of them had no friends; the other, only enemies."[54] Given this choice, the nation agreed that "we love him for the enemies he made," and elected Cleveland.

Yet there was one Harrison who was pleased by the outcome of the election. Carter Henry Harrison, former Democratic congressman, owner of the Chicago *Times,* and former mayor, was a third cousin of the defeated President.

The Democratic Harrison and the Republican Harrison shared a great-great-grandfather, Benjamin IV, the Virginia gentleman who had married "King" Carter's daughter. While the President's ancestor had signed the Declaration of Independence, his younger brother, ancestor of the Chicago Harrison, had also been something of a patriot as the chairman of a committee in Cumberland County, Virginia, that drafted the first publicly expressed demand for separation from Great Britain. His son moved to Kentucky in 1806, probably at the insistence of U. S. Attorney General John Breckinridge, who was his brother-in-law, and his grandson founded another Harrison political dynasty.[55]

The Chicago Harrisons, father and son, would be ten times elected mayor of Chicago, and together would govern the Windy City for a third of its first seventy-two years as a municipality.

President Benjamin Harrison might be called "the White House Iceberg," but his Democratic cousin's veins still pulsed with the hot sun of Virginia and Kentucky. He rode through the streets of his adopted Chicago on a handsome mare, waving his trade mark, a black slouch hat. A magnetic figure, skilled at creating dramatic situations, he was so flamboyant on the stump that he earned the nickname "The Eagle," a tribute to his spreadeagle style of oratory. "Let the eagle loose," his partisans would shout.

While personally incorruptible, Carter Harrison took his allies where he found them, which was generally among the saloon interests. Church forces and reformers accused him of winking at vice; one minister charged that he allowed thirty thousand prostitutes to have free run of the city. In 1893, while making a national reputation as the World's Fair mayor, he was assassinated by a crazed office-seeker in the doorway of his home. It is said that Grover Cleveland expected him to be a candidate for the Democratic presidential nomination in 1896.[56]

His son, also named Carter Harrison, was as handsome as a matinee idol. When he first ran for mayor in 1897 campaign posters showed him riding a bicycle, his chest covered with sporting medals. Two years later his campaign portrait was posed with his hands in his pockets. The legend underneath read: "Chicago is fortunate in having a mayor who keeps his hands in his own pockets." This was no idle boast. Once he refused his wife three postage stamps. If she really wanted to steal from the city, he told her, why stop with six cents? He could get her a million dollars just as easily!

Although sharing his father's view that vice could not be legislated out of existence, he was finally forced to take action against the city's spreading red-light district. During his fifth term in 1911 he closed the Everleigh Club, an establishment run by two genteel sisters, which was considered the highest-priced brothel in the world.[57] The second Harrison mayor also felt that with the right break he might have been President, but the closest he ever came to influencing a national election was when he arranged the defeat of Woodrow Wilson in the 1912 Illinois primary.[58]

When Benjamin Harrison left the presidency he again became an Indianapolis lawyer, reportedly earning $100,000 a year.

On April 6, 1896, he married Mary Scott Lord Dimmick, the niece of his late wife, who had lived in the White House with the Harrisons. He was then sixty-three; the bride was thirty-eight, a childless widow whose first husband had died while on their honeymoon. The second Mrs. Harrison was to give birth to a daughter, but the marriage also produced an estrangement between the former President and his son Russell. On Harrison's death in 1901 the bulk of his estate went to his second wife; Russell was left out of the will.

The widow of the twenty-third President moved to New York. She stayed active in Republican politics, although her vote went to Al Smith in 1928. (She was convinced that prohibition was a national evil and this was a way to register her convictions.[59]) Her daughter Elizabeth graduated from New York University Law School in 1919, three years later married a grandnephew of James G. Blaine, and went on to found a monthly news service for women investors that was distributed by banks throughout the country.[60]

Russell Harrison had been his father's secretary during the White House years, while his wife helped the First Lady with her social obligations. The young Harrisons were a gay and attractive couple whose apparent prosperity was the cause of a number of newspaper exposés. It was written that Russell received stock valued at a half million dollars in the Aransas Harbor City & Improvement Company, a Texas land promotion venture, although he had made no substantial investment, and that, without his knowledge, the manager of the Yellowstone Park Association had put 5000 shares of stock in trust for him.[61] The Brooklyn *Eagle* commented, "For the last three years young Mr. Harrison had a succession of these demoralizing surprises. His embarrassment must be like the setting hen that found so many nests full of eggs she didn't know which to cover."[62] But Harrison's fortunes were less dramatic after his father left office. He became the president of a street railway company in Terre Haute.

With the outbreak of war in 1898 Harrison went to Cuba, where he raised the first American flag over Morro Castle, an act that was in violation of an agreement with Spain, and for which he was severely reprimanded by his commanding officer, Major General Fitzhugh Lee. However, he was later promoted to lieutenant colonel, made inspector general of the Santiago Territory and then provost marshal in Puerto Rico. But in 1900 he was suddenly discharged from the army. The War Department denied that the dismissal had anything to do with the fact that ex-President Harrison refused to support McKinley's bid for re-election.

Returning to Indiana, Russell was admitted to the bar, and for many years represented the Mexican government. He also entered politics, first as a member of the Indiana House of Representatives and later as a state senator.

While Russell was serving in the Indiana Senate in 1927, his son won election to the Indiana House of Representatives. William Henry Harrison, age thirty-one, was the great-great-great-great-great-great-great-grandson of Benjamin Harrison I, who was elected to the Virginia House of Burgesses in 1642.

The latest Harrison in politics bears little resemblance to his presidential namesake or to the ancestor who joked at the signing of the Declaration of Independence. The genes that produced these giant men with great, bluff personalities seem to have become recessive. He is more in the mold of Little Ben, his presidential grandfather, and one sees in his face a fleeting reminder of H. T. Webster's cartoon character, "The Timid Soul."

He chose 1932, a bad year for Republicans, to try to become the seventh Harrison in Congress. He lost, as did his father, who was running for the state legislature on the same ticket.[63] Four years later William Henry Harrison moved to Wyoming and bought a cattle ranch. He was elected to the Wyoming House of Representatives in 1945 for the first of three terms, graduated to the United States Congress in 1950, won re-election, and then ran unsuccessfully for the Senate in 1954 against Joseph C. O'Mahoney. He was again elected to Congress in 1960 and 1962.

Regarded as an ultraconservative, Harrison was an early backer of Barry Goldwater for President, and voted against the 1964 Civil Rights Act, believing its public accommodations and fair employment sections to be unconstitutional.

Harrison's Democratic opponent in 1964 was Teno Roncalio, and the fight between the descendant of presidents and the son of an Italian immigrant was waged as a straight-out contest between liberalism and conservatism. All things being equal, it was expected that the conservative would win in Wyoming. Early predictions were that Harrison would be safe if Goldwater did even half as well as Nixon had done in 1960. But in a state where a thousand-vote margin is considered a landslide, Goldwater was defeated by over 17,000 votes, and Harrison, while running far ahead of his party's presidential candidate, nevertheless lost by 2000 votes.[64]

Over the course of ten generations, for three hundred and twenty-two years in America, the Harrisons sought public office with the tenacity of a Jason in search of the Golden Fleece.

They were not men of major talent, and, even though numbering two presidents and a signer of the Declaration, they were neither molders of public opinion nor shapers of history. Yet they made honorable contributions and have continually displayed amazing resourcefulness as politicians. They bounded back from defeat, regrouped, and stormed again the bastions of elective office. Their ambition knew no geographic boundaries. Unlike most political families, they refused to stay put and let the voters come to them; and for their efforts they were rewarded by the electorates of five states—Virginia, Ohio, Indiana, Illinois, and Wyoming. In this continuing quest, adaptability was their primary armor.

The present William Henry Harrison, defeated in 1964, will be seventy years old when there is another congressional election. His only son, an accountant, has no interest in running for office.[65] It is therefore quite possible that the longest continuous American political dynasty will end in this generation.

The Breckinridge Dynasty

"I haven't made up my mind. But when
I do, you can count on it, we'll be damn
bitter about it!"

—Desha Breckinridge[1]

THE issue on which the editor of the Lexington *Herald* hadn't made
up his mind may have been the League of Nations or it may have been
parimutuel betting at Kentucky race tracks. It really didn't make any
difference—the Breckinridges acted with equal fervor on questions both
monumental and fleeting. And this was a Breckinridge response.

Presbyterian minister Robert Jefferson Breckinridge felt so strongly
against the use of instrumental music in religious services that when
his brother, William Lewis Breckinridge, another Presbyterian minister,
introduced an organ into his church Robert preferred charges against
him in the synod.[2] He did not want to hurt his brother, but this was a
question of *principle*.

It was this ability to be "damn bitter" about almost any issues that
struck their fancy which made them one of the most colorful American
political dynasties. "An extraordinary family is this of Breckinridge,"
commented the Washington *Daily Chronicle* during the Civil War when
they were fighting with equal ferocity on both sides.[3]

Besides their rigidly held convictions, there were two other family
characteristics that contemporaries invariably commented upon.

First, the Breckinridge appearance: the men were generally over six
feet; handsome with auburn or chestnut hair, which turned prematurely
silver or iron gray; eyes piercing and deep set; shoulders broad; car-
riages straight and muscular. "The bearing of a Scottish Chieftain" was
the way one observer described John C. Breckinridge.[4]

Second, the Breckinridge ability as public speakers: no one who heard
them could ever resist reliving the experience. "Uncle" Boone Bradley
listened to John C. Breckinridge in 1856, and years later took a local

THE BRECKINRIDGE DYNASTY
(A Selective Genealogy)

Alexander Breckinridge (d. 1747)
Arrived America 1728; m. *Jane Preston*
(8 children)

Robert (c. 1720–72)
Judge, Botetourt County, Virginia

1st m. *Sarah Poage*
(2 children?)

2d m. *Letitia Preston*
(5 children)

Robert (1754–1833)
1st Speaker of Kentucky
House of Representatives
(unmarried)

John (1760–1806)
SENATE; U. S. Attorney General
m. *Mary H. Cabell*
(8 children; 2 d.y.)

James (1763–1833)
HOUSE OF REPRESENTATIVES
(10 children)

Alexander
m. *Jane Buchanan Floyd,*
whose son John Floyd was
GOVERNOR of Virginia
(4 children)

Letitia Preston
(1786–1831)
1st m. *Alfred Grayson*
(3 children)
2nd m. *Peter Porter*
HOUSE OF REPRESENTATIVES;
Secretary of War
(2 children)

Joseph Cabell
(1788–1823)
Speaker of Kentucky
House of Representatives
m. *Mary C. Smith,* granddaughter of John
Witherspoon
(6 children; 1 d.y.)

John
(1797–1841)
Minister;
college president
(4 children; 1 d.y.)

William Lewis
(1803–76)
Minister; college
president (12
children; 4 d.y.)

James Douglas
(d. 1849)
HOUSE OF REPRESENTATIVES
(1 child)

John Breckinridge
Grayson (1806–61)
Confederate general

John Cabell (1821–75)
HOUSE OF REPRESENTATIVES
SENATE, VICE-PRESIDENT
(5 children)

Robert Jefferson
(1800–71)
Minister; college
president; Union
leader in Kentucky
(14 children, 5 d.y.)

Clifton Rodes
(1846–1932)
HOUSE OF REPRESENTATIVES,
minister to Russia
(4 children)

Mary
(1881–1965)
Founder, Frontier
Nursing Service
(2 children: both d.y.)

Joseph Cabell
(1842–1920)
General, Spanish-American
War (13 children; 4 d.y.)

Henry
(1886–1960)
Assistant
Secretary of War
(3 children; 1 d.y.)

Elizabeth
m. John S. Graham,
Assistant Secretary
of Treasury
(4 children)

Scott D.
(1882–1941)
M.D. (3 children)

John Bayne
(1913–)
Kentucky Attorney
General
(2 children)

William Campbell Preston
(1837–1904)
HOUSE OF REPRESENTATIVES
1st m. granddaughter of Henry Clay;
2nd m. granddaughter of GOVERNOR
Joseph Desha of Kentucky
(7 children; 3 d.y.)

Desha
(1867–1935)
Editor and
publisher

Sophonisba P.
(1866–1948)
Educator, author
(unmarried)

Marie L.P.
(b. 1836)
m. William C. Handy
(8 children)

Levin Irving Handy
(1861–1921)
HOUSE OF REPRESENTATIVES

poet to the spot to recreate the scene. The resulting verse ends with the old man's eternal wish:

> If there be orators in heaven
> When I git thar and I am given
> A chance to hear them speak,
> I'm goin' to say to old John C.,
> "Jest say agin that speech for me
> You made on Eagle Creek."[5]

In the opinion of one feminine fan, it was worth a trip of a hundred miles just to hear William C. P. Breckinridge pronounce "watah." And he could put more into three words, "The Democratic Pahty," said another admirer, than most orators could put into an hour's speech. Eulogies were ideal vehicles for his tearful tones. One day, so the story goes, "Czar" Thomas Reed, the crusty Speaker of the House of Representatives, came into the hall while William was speaking. He listened for a moment, then snapped, "Who's dead now?"[6]

The Breckinridges, who arrived in Virginia in 1728, had little in common with the Lees, the Harrisons, and the rest of the Tidewater aristocracy. There is an old Virginia adage, "Gentleman and clams end at the fall line." The Breckinridges, living far inland, away from the massive slaveholding plantations, fell into neither category. They were more interested in survival than luxury. And so when they moved to Kentucky it was not out of love for adventure, Indian fighting, and pioneer life, but to make a better living and provide their children with a legacy of good land.[7]

Soon after their release from a British prison ship in 1781, two third-generation Breckinridges, Robert and Alexander, crossed the mountains into bluegrass country.* The brothers had one thing in common—they both sought the hand of the widow Floyd.[8] The retiring Alexander married the desirable lady and apparently spent his remaining years resting on his laurels. The bachelor Robert, unencumbered by further romantic interests, went on to become a militia general, a ratifier of the federal Constitution, one of the writers of Kentucky's first constitution, and first Speaker of the state House of Representatives.†

---

* Alexander Breckinridge, the founder of the American dynasty, died in 1747. His son Robert (1720–72) was a captain during the French and Indian War and a judge of the first court in Botecourt County, Virginia. Robert and Alexander, the first Breckinridges in Kentucky, were born to his first wife, Sarah Poage.

† Alexander had a son, James Douglas Breckinridge (d. 1849), a member of the Kentucky House of Representatives (1809–11) and the U. S. Congress (1821–23). He was married four times but had only one child, Eliza, who inherited the considerable estate of her bachelor great-uncle Robert Breckinridge.

Two half brothers, James and John, remained behind in Virginia.‡ Considering the Breckinridges' subsequent history of intradynasty squabbling, it is not surprising that one became a leading Federalist and the other a leading Republican. James, the Federalist, served thirteen sessions in the House of Delegates, lost the governorship to James Monroe, and was a four-term congressman. Despite his political hostility to Jefferson, he became a strong advocate of the President's plans for the University of Virginia, helped to select its site, and served on the first Board of Visitors.[9] John, the Republican brother, moved to Kentucky in 1793 and founded a political dynasty.

Going to Kentucky was not a difficult decision for brothers Robert and Alexander. Before the war they had been carpenters.[10] Virginia held little promise. But when John Breckinridge left his native state he was a congressman-elect. He had been a member of the state legislature for four years, first elected when he was nineteen. There is a persistent legend that he was denied his seat because he was under age, and only admitted after his stubborn constituents elected him for a third time. While this story has only recently been proved wrong, there is no doubt that the youthful legislator had a remarkable career in a body that included such seasoned veterans as Benjamin Harrison and Patrick Henry.[11] Breckinridge was part of the wartime legislature that was generally one step ahead of the enemy troops, participated in the debates that established postwar Virginia policy, and held several important committee assignments.[12]

Political success, however, did not assure financial well-being. John's law practice was comfortable but not lucrative, and his four-hundred-acre farm in Albemarle County barely paid its way. Moreover, by the time he left for Kentucky he had a wife and four children.§

So in March 1793, having sent most of their slaves ahead, the Breckinridge family went overland for a hundred and fifty miles to Red Stone, the embarkation point for the Monongahela River, and joined a caravan of flatboats to carry them downward toward Pittsburgh and the Ohio. John confided that his wife had not smiled once since they left home. Indian attack was still a real danger. (A favorite Indian trick was to force a white captive to stand on the bank and lure boatmen into

‡ They were the sons of Robert Breckinridge by his second wife, Letitia Preston (1728–98). (The Preston family has produced four members of Congress and a governor of Virginia.) James spelled his surname "Breckenridge." For the most part the family name was changed to its present spelling in this generation.

§ In 1785 he married Mary Hopkins Cabell, a daughter of Joseph Cabell (1732–98), a member of the Virginia House of Delegates (1776–81, 1788–90) and the state Senate (1781–85).

ambush.) But the Breckinridges saw no Indians; what would become Kentucky's greatest political family arrived safely in Lexington by the end of April.

Before the end of the first year in his adopted state John Breckinridge was appointed attorney general of Kentucky. His official duties were "not arduous and interfered little with his private practice."[13] He prospered, primarily because of the numerous conflicting claims over title to the virgin land; and his own landholdings rose to 30,000 acres.¶

John Breckinridge was elected to the state House of Representatives in 1797, served for four years, and was Speaker for half that time. It was there that he introduced the famous Kentucky Resolutions of 1798. President John Adams and the Federalists had passed the Alien and Sedition Laws; Jefferson and the Republicans were looking for a means to counter the repressive measures and turn them into a campaign issue. Breckinridge's Resolutions declared that the United States was a compact among the states, that "each party has an equal right to judge [congressional acts] for itself," and that the state of Kentucky judged the Alien and Sedition Laws to be "altogether void and of no force."[14] The Resolutions did not mention "nullification," but from the floor debate it was clear that this is what Breckinridge meant.*

For most of the nineteenth century historians chose to argue over whether Breckinridge really wrote the Kentucky Resolutions. Now that the smoke has cleared, it is obvious that he did not. Their author was Jefferson. But the Vice-President of the United States had to be protected: avowed authorship would have been sedition and grounds for impeachment.[15] So Breckinridge took his draft, made a number of modifications, and secured their passage.

In this way John Breckinridge introduced the doctrine of States' Rights into American politics. Sixty-two years later his grandson would

¶ The glowing letters he sent back to Virginia led his brother-in-law to make the move. Robert Carter Harrison (a nephew of Benjamin Harrison the Signer) was married to Ann Cabell, whose sister was Mrs. John Breckinridge. In 1806 Harrison brought his family to Kentucky, settling on land that Breckinridge had probably purchased for him. A half century later a grandson, Carter Henry Harrison, would spend his honeymoon in Chicago and stay to become one of the most dynamic mayors in the history of the Windy City. See John Wilson Townsend, "Carter Henry Harrison, Kentuckian," *Register of the Kentucky State Historical Society*, XXIV, No. 71 (1926), pp. 150–51.

* Breckinridge told the Kentucky legislature: "If, upon representations of the States from whom they derive their powers, they [Congress] should nevertheless attempt to enforce them [the Alien and Sedition Laws], I hesitate not to declare it as my opinion that it is the right and duty of the several states to *nullify* those acts, and to protect their citizens from their operation." See Nathan Schachner, *Thomas Jefferson* (New York: T. Yoseloff, 1957), p. 616. Italics added.

lead the slaveholding states out of the Democratic Party and run for President as the champion of the States' Rights doctrine.

At the time of his death Breckinridge owned fifty-seven slaves. And in the second constitution of Kentucky, which was largely his work, he protected the slavery interests. Twenty-two-year-old Henry Clay fought vainly for an emancipation clause, but he was no match for the experienced Breckinridge.

The most important work of Breckinridge's brief career began with his election to the United States Senate in 1801. He was quickly made Jefferson's floor leader and proved to be an expert at welding his temperamental troops into a unified majority. Henry Adams called him "the ablest of the Republican Senators."[16] His two biggest accomplishments were securing the repeal of the Judiciary Act in 1802 and getting approval of the Louisiana Purchase. On the latter, after Breckinridge fueled the engine of his steamroller, Federalist Senator Plumer complained that the Republicans took "less time to deliberate on this important treaty, than they allowed themselves on the most trivial Indian contract."[17]

Then in 1805 he became Attorney General of the United States. The West, which considered him its representative, was pleased with the cabinet recognition. But Jefferson had made a mistake in removing Breckinridge from the Congress; the President was never again to have so effective a senatorial leader. Breckinridge's new job paid $3000 a year, out of which he had to provide his own staff and office. His duties called for him to present the government's cases before the Supreme Court. Of his six cases, he lost four, none of them important. His tenure as Attorney General was too brief for him to have had any effect on the development of that office.

A later Breckinridge said that there is a family tradition that it was Jefferson's wish to have had Madison succeed him as President and then to have had Breckinridge succeed Madison.[18] But in 1806 a higher authority intervened. John Breckinridge died suddenly at forty-six years of age. Like most of the early Breckinridges, he left this earth in his prime.

The fatherless sons of the late Attorney General would always be known in Kentucky as "the Breckinridge brothers."[19] Their ages ranged from three to eighteen when their father died. Three of them grew up to become noted ministers and college presidents; the fourth was a local political leader.

There was also a daughter, Letitia, who first married Alfred Grayson of Kentucky and bore him a son, John Breckinridge Grayson. After her husband's death she married Peter B. Porter, a distinguished general in the War of 1812, by whom she had another son, Peter Augustus Porter.

President John Quincy Adams appointed General Porter as Secretary of War in 1828 and Letitia quickly became the belle of the capital. Margaret Bayard Smith considered her the most popular woman in Washington society since Dolley Madison. The *National Intelligencer* "puffed her at a great rate." And rightly so, thought Mrs. Smith, who called her "Gay, frank, communicative, kind. She is a universal favourite and it seems like no party at all, if she is not present."[20] At the end of the Adams Administration the Porters returned to Niagara Falls, where the general had a vision of a great water power development.

(Many years after Letitia's death her two sons would fight and die on different sides in a great war. Her Southern son, a West Pointer who had fought the Seminoles and the Mexicans, resigned his U. S. Army commission to become Confederate brigadier general in command of the Department of Middle and Eastern Florida. At Tallahassee he contracted a lung disease and died in October 1861. Her Northern son was a New York State legislator, who became a Union colonel and was killed leading his regiment at Cold Harbor in August 1862.)

Next in age to Letitia of Attorney General Breckinridge's children was Joseph Cabell Breckinridge. Sent north to Princeton College, he acquired both education and wife. The bride was Mary Clay Smith, daughter and granddaughter of two illustrious Princeton presidents. Her grandfather was that fiery Scot John Witherspoon, signer of the Declaration of Independence, who claimed that on his mother's side he could trace his ancestry back in a direct line to John Knox; her father was Witherspoon's successor at Princeton, "the most elegant" Samuel Stanhope Smith.[21]†

† Samuel Stanhope Smith (1750–1819) was the son of Robert Smith, an Irish immigrant, who became the second Moderator of the General Assembly of the Presbyterian Church in America. Two of his sons became eminent doctors and three became Presbyterian ministers. Samuel Stanhope Smith was president of Hampden-Sydney College before going to Princeton. He was succeeded at Hampden-Sydney by his brother, John Blair Smith, later president of Union College. Samuel Stanhope married Witherspoon's daughter Anna in 1774. They had nine children. Besides Mary, who married Joseph Cabell Breckinridge, another daughter became the mother of Mrs. William Lewis Breckinridge.

At Princeton Samuel Stanhope Smith was not always kindly thought of by his students. William Paterson, a future New Jersey governor, put his feelings into verse:

> Tutor Smith, so wond'rous civil
> Compound odd of Saint and Devil.
> This Smith a parson too, alas!
> He more resembles for an ass.

See William Paterson, *Glimpses of Colonial Society and the Life at Princeton College, 1766–1773* (Philadelphia: Lippincott, 1903), p. 121.

Yet he proved to be one of Princeton's greatest presidents and was respon-

With his Princeton bride, young Breckinridge returned to Kentucky, where, in his first try for the state legislature, he was elected by the largest majority in Fayette County up to that time. The personable and attractive Joseph was promptly made Speaker, and then secretary of state of Kentucky. This promising career was cut short when he died at thirty-four. (His son was John Cabell Breckinridge, Vice-President of the United States.)[22]

There is considerable difference of opinion over whether there was anything in the family background to lead three of Attorney General Breckinridge's sons into the ministry. One writer contends that there were no church members in the family and that they entered the clergy over considerable opposition from home[23]; another contends that the boys' mother was a devout Christian, and they grew up in an atmosphere of almost continuous religious revivals.[24] Whether by upbringing or revolt, the first of the Breckinridge ministers was John, whom Margaret Bayard Smith found to be a "zealous, saint-like man."[25] Besides serving a term in Washington as chaplain of the House of Representatives, his most important years were spent as pastor of the Second Presbyterian Church in Baltimore. Here he gained a reputation as an outstanding pulpit orator, becoming "as universally known . . . as any minister of the gospel in America had ever been."[26] Just before his death in 1841, at forty-four years of age, John had been chosen president of Oglethorpe University in Georgia.

His greatest fame came as an acrimonious critic of the Catholic Church. Yet five years after his death a false rumor circulated about the country that he had made a deathbed conversion to Catholicism. He would probably not have seen the irony, for the minister's final words, a summation of his life, were: "I am a poor sinner, who has worked hard, and had constantly before my mind one great object—the conversion of the world."[27]

Of the three Breckinridge ministers, the only one who has not been classified as a "controversialist" is William Lewis. He led a relatively quiet pastoral life, spending most of his years at the First Presbyterian Church of Louisville, and later becoming president of Centre College at Danville.[28] On the few occasions that he found himself in the midst

---

sible for introducing chemistry as a separate subject into the American college curriculum. As a disciplinarian, however, he earned a poor mark. During the "Great Rebellion" of 1807 the students twice attempted to burn down the college. Trustee Elias Boudinot reported that they were "shouting like drunken Indians" and Richard Stockton unsuccessfully tried to calm them. This was the beginning of the end for President Smith. After another student riot the trustees voted to appoint a vice-president to maintain order. Smith took the hint and resigned. See George Adams Boyd, *Elias Boudinot, Patriot and Statesman* (Princeton: Princeton University Press, 1952), pp. 267–69.

of controversy it was usually because he had been pushed there by his brother Robert Jefferson, the most fiery of all Breckinridges.

Robert Jefferson Breckinridge has been called "the flower of the great men of that name" and "a counterfeit and a hypocrite, not only a disgrace to his church but to his species."[29] He was not a neutral person; his loves and hatreds were deep-rooted and violent. Few, in turn, could remain indifferent toward him. With his flowing beard, iron gray at the sides, snow white beneath the chin, he looked like an Old Testament prophet. Yet he was a churchman who split his church; a family man who divided his family.

He also ranked with Horace Mann as a developer of state education, and was primarily responsible for keeping Kentucky in the Union. His broad intellectual interests were reflected in "books, debates, articles, and pamphlets, upon slavery, temperance, Popery, Universalism, Presbyterianism, education, agriculture, and politics, [which] would form a five-foot shelf."[30]

Although trained for the law, Robert Jefferson's first love was politics. He entered the Kentucky legislature in 1825 and ended his elective career when he proposed the gradual emancipation of the slaves. The defeat, said Cassius Marcellus Clay, "drove him into the Church."[31] It also had a profound effect on Henry Clay. Thirty years before he had fought the battle of emancipation against Robert Jefferson's father. However, now when abolitionist James G. Birney asked him for support, Clay declined, citing the example of Robert Jefferson, who "put himself down in popular estimation by having advocated emancipation" and had thus "disqualified" himself "for political usefulness."[32] It was not a fate that ambitious Henry Clay desired.

Breckinridge was not an abolitionist in the technical sense. What he believed in was gradual emancipation. When in 1833 ninety-six Negroes were sent to Liberia from Kentucky, eleven were slaves whom he had freed. For this support of the Colonization Society, William Lloyd Garrison showered typical abuse on him, and the mayor of Boston warned that he would be mobbed if he spoke there. To the abolitionists, Breckinridge was an ally of the slaveholders; to the slaveholders, he was a traitor to his class; to the general public, he was a disturber of the peace.

As an anti-slavery candidate, Robert Jefferson Breckinridge tried to make a political comeback in 1849, when he ran as a candidate for delegate to the Kentucky Constitutional Convention. He was opposed by his eloquent twenty-eight-year-old nephew, John Cabell Breckinridge, who was making his first race for the state legislature. It was a bloody campaign. At the Paducah courthouse one candidate pulled a pistol and shot his opponent. At a rally in Foxtown abolitionist "Cash" Clay was stabbed in the chest and beaten over the head. As he was about to be stabbed again, Clay grabbed the bowie knife and plunged it up to the hilt into his tormentor's body. The slavery man died a few hours later, but his party scored a sweeping victory at the polls. John Cabell Breckinridge was elected; Robert Jefferson Breckinridge was defeated.

The minister's position on slavery also split the Presbyterian Church. When the Synod of Kentucky would not agree to emancipation, Robert Jefferson Breckinridge stormed out of the meeting. "God has left you," he announced, "and I also will now leave you."[33]

Soon after he entered the ministry he went to Baltimore to succeed his brother John. In Maryland Robert continued his fight against slavery, carried on a campaign for temperance, and found time to assume his brother's anti-Catholic crusade. In fact he crusaded with a vehemence that far exceeded John's, who was of somewhat gentler nature. His supporters feared for his life. The Catholics brought him to trial for libel, but with John J. Crittenden as his counsel, Breckinridge was acquitted.

In 1845 he moved to Pennsylvania to become president of Jefferson College. The fringe benefits brought his salary up to $1600 a year. The trustees also agreed to build him a house, which he insisted should not have panels in the doors. Panels, he felt, were "symbolic of the Cross and, therefore, of Catholicism."[34] The trustees respected his wish.

On the eve of his move to Canonsburg, Robert Jefferson's wife died. Sophonisba Preston, the daughter of a Virginia congressman, left an inheritance of $128,000 and eight children, who went to live with relatives. But it was a difficult separation and after two years Breckinridge returned to Kentucky to unite his family and begin a new romance with Virginia Hart Shelby.[35] They were finally married after a checkered courtship. The second Mrs. Breckinridge brought $25,000 to the union and gave Robert three more children.

The most productive six years of Robert J. Breckinridge's life began in 1847 with his appointment as state superintendent of public instruction. When he took over the post the Frankfort *Commonwealth* commented that "the Common School System is a mockery."[36] Only one out of eight children between the ages of five and sixteen was in school. Kentucky had defaulted on its school bonds. Here was a cause to match his Irish fire and Scottish persistence. Despite opposition from the governor, he got the legislature to make interest due to the schools the first charge upon the state treasury. He got the voters to tax themselves two cents on each one hundred dollars of property. He had the constitution changed so that the state could never again default on its school bonds. He saw to it that the old bondholders were repaid with interest. He increased annual expenditures for education from $6.3 million to $137.3 million, and increased school attendance from 20,000 to 201,000.[37]

The political struggle between Robert Jefferson Breckinridge and John Cabell Breckinridge began in 1849, the year the nephew won his first elective office and the uncle suffered his final elective defeat. Despite their differences there was a deep affection between them. Robert took pride in John Cabell's meteoric rise—an ascent unequaled in American politics (1849, first elected to the state legislature; 1856, elected Vice-President of the United States). But he never confused pride with support—he fought his nephew all the way. John Cabell was a Democrat; Robert Jefferson was a Whig, then a Know-Nothing, and finally a Republican.[38]

John C. Breckinridge burst onto the national scene in 1851 when the Democrats nominated him for Congress in Ashland, Henry Clay's old district. In an amazing reversal of form, the handsome young Democrat won a 500-vote victory in the state's Whig stronghold.

Two years later, and out for revenge, the Whigs put up a former governor, Robert P. Letcher, to bring the freshman congressman to earth. But Letcher was past his prime. Cassius Clay described a memorable debate between the candidates: Letcher "had grown so corpulent by age and heavy eating, that he seemed at times on the very verge of suffocation, or apoplexy. The weather was very warm. Breckinridge went at him with the coolness of a skilled swordsman; making home-thrusts, and coolly observing the effect of each. Letcher was very much confused, greatly angry, and fought as one who had lost all muscular power, and even eye-sight. The perspiration poured off him; and he literally 'larded the earth.' His voice was guttural and ejected from his lungs a badly-charged fuse of wet and dry powder. The boys shouted: 'Cut the halter, and give him air!' It was a pitiable sight!" The Breckinridge supporters gleefully retired to Boon Creek to celebrate the inevitable election victory with old bourbon and mint slings.[39]

The congressman conducted himself with charm and courtesy in Washington. Yet these were times that severely strained good manners. In January 1854 Senator Stephen B. Douglas introduced the Kansas-Nebraska Bill, opening the floodgates that had contained the slavery question. Congress was racked by four months of bitter debate, in the midst of which Representative Frank B. Cutting of New York stated that Breckinridge "skulks behind the Senate Bill." These were not courteous words. The inevitable duel was arranged. Breckinridge chose rifles at sixty paces! But the seconds wisely argued about technicalities until the lawmakers cooled down, and thus the combat of honor was averted.[40]

Breckinridge decided to retire at the end of his second term. Fate and geography decided otherwise. The Democratic Convention of 1856 named as its standard-bearer James Buchanan, the "Old Public Functionary" from Pennsylvania. A Southerner was needed to balance the ticket. The delegates turned to the tall handsome Kentuckian, who on March 4, 1857, became the youngest Vice-President in American history.

Since he was only thirty-nine, and there was plenty of time, Breckinridge did not want the presidential nomination in 1860. Moreover, he never had the driving ambition of a Clay or a Webster. But there is a momentum that builds up to a presidential nomination that can assume its own velocity and character, regardless of the wishes of the party's acknowledged leaders. Stephen B. Douglas had split the Democratic Party and the Charleston convention adjourned without making a nomination. The delegates would try again in Baltimore, but the results were inevitable. There would have to be separate presidential tickets for the North and the South. Douglas would head the former; the rump convention of Southerners countered by choosing Breckinridge. Immediately after the nomination the Southern candidate turned to Mrs. Jefferson Davis. "I trust," he said, "I have the courage to lead a forlorn hope."[41]

The candidate received support from an unexpected source. Robert Jefferson Breckinridge wrote that he would vote for his nephew, "not approving of all his opinions—but thoroughly satisfied it was the only course open to me. . . ."[42] The volatile minister knew John Cabell to be pro-slavery, but he also felt him to be pro-Union. In this time of crisis one must weigh principles. He probably felt that in supporting his nephew he was choosing the principle of union over the principle of emancipation.

This endorsement gave the candidate a lot of explaining to do. Arriving in Lexington after a triumphant tour of the Southern states, John Cabell was scheduled to address a barbecue for 15,000. When the crowd had finished feasting on roast beef, mutton, and burgoo, the young candidate proclaimed his esteem and affection for his uncle, and then stoutly denied that he had ever sympathized with Robert Jefferson Breckinridge's anti-slavery doctrines. The enthusiastic audience shouted back, "That's so, John C."[43]

It was a four-cornered race: Breckinridge, Southern Democrat; Douglas, Northern Democrat; John Bell, Constitutional Unionist; Lincoln, Republican. The Negro slaves sang a little campaign ditty:

John C.
Breckinridge, he
Beat de Bell of Tennessee.[44]

This was correct as far as it went. He carried his precinct, ward, city, and district. But lost Kentucky to Bell and the nation to Lincoln. Breckinridge placed third in popular vote, second in electoral vote.

By eight on the morning of February 13, 1861, the day the electoral votes were to be counted, a crowd had already gathered at the Capitol. Rumors had circulated for weeks that Southerners would use this occasion to try to block Lincoln's election. Armed guards were stationed at every entrance to the House of Representatives. At noon the senators entered the chamber and took seats in a semicircle in front of the Speaker's desk. Vice-President Breckinridge then declared, "It is my duty to open the certificates of election in the presence of the two Houses."

A Southern member shouted, "Is the count of the electoral vote to proceed under menace? Shall members be required to perform a constitutional duty before the Janizaries of General Scott are withdrawn from the hall?" "The point of order is not sustained," Breckinridge shot back. The former presidential candidate of the South allowed no interference. When the last of the sealed envelopes had been opened and read, the Vice-President, standing erect, announced, "Abraham Lincoln, having received a majority of the whole number of electoral votes, is duly elected President of the United States."[45] Not for another hundred years would a Vice-President again be called upon to proclaim officially his own defeat for President.

When the Civil War began John C. Breckinridge was a United States senator, a position to which the Kentucky legislature had elected him in December 1859, a year and a half before the end of his term as Vice-President. There were still two outstanding senators from the slave states in Washington—Andrew Johnson of Tennessee and Breckinridge of Kentucky. Tennessee had seceded, but there was no doubt of Johnson's strong adherence to the Union; Kentucky had not seceded, and the North waited to see if Breckinridge would remain loyal.

On the last day of the congressional session, August 6, 1861, Breckinridge said good-by to his friend John W. Forney, editor of the Washington *Daily Chronicle*. "No," said Forney, "not goodbye, Breckinridge, but farewell. You will never again take your seat in the United States Senate."

The Kentuckian seemed surprised. "What do you mean? I will undoubtedly return to my post in December."

"No, my dear sir," replied the Union editor, "you will follow your doctrine into the Confederate Army."

"If I go over the lines," Breckinridge answered, "it will be to bring back with me my runaway son, Cabell, who has gone into the other army wholly against my will. But we shall meet, if we live, in the winter."[46]

But by December John C. Breckinridge was a general in the Confederate Army, and the United States Senate formally expelled him as a traitor. Lincoln was saddened by Breckinridge's decision. The Kentuckian had been a childhood friend of Mary Todd Lincoln. When one of Breckinridge's nephews visited the White House, the President told him, "I was fond of John and I regret that he sided with the South." Lincoln paused, a faraway look came into his eyes. "It was a mistake," he said slowly.[47]

Yet Breckinridge had honestly answered Forney in August. The decision to join the Confederacy had not been easy. And while he was to serve his "lost cause" courageously, there is evidence that he was never sure he had made the right decision. Years later, after defeat and exile, Breckinridge sat on the porch of a resort hotel in New Jersey and ruminated over things past. It is "far better," he concluded, "that we still live as one people. . . . Many a lonely hour I have spent in midnight moments on the streets of London and Paris awaiting the time that I could once again catch a glimpse of the Stars and Stripes, the flag of my fathers, and all I now wish is to sleep forever beneath its God-given folds."[48]‡

Of the political generals in the Confederate Army, Breckinridge proved to be one of the best.[49] He fought bravely and skillfully at Shiloh, Murfreesboro, Chickamauga, and Missionary Ridge. For a while in 1864 he commanded the Department of Southwest Virginia. He was with Jubal Early during the raids on the outskirts of Washington that vandalized Silver Spring, the estate of his distant kinsman, Francis Preston Blair, Sr. He had a natural flair that his men loved. Seeing Breckinridge on the battlefield at Shiloh, General Jordan said, "As he sat in his saddle he seemed to me altogether the most impressive-looking man I ever had seen."[50]

As if to atone for the sin of having supported John C. Breckinridge for President, his uncle applied every ounce of his enormous energy to the cause of Lincoln. While Kentucky hovered on the brink between Union and Confederacy, the Rev. Robert Jefferson Breckinridge flooded the state with his words. He spoke everywhere and turned his church magazine into the chief Union organ in Kentucky. Southern sympathizers destroyed his mailing list, threatened to kidnap his young son John, and heaped vituperation upon him. One newspaper called him "your reverend adviser-general in Kentucky, whose ambition [it is] to play at

‡ Judge J. W. Cammack of Kentucky also states that "older men who knew General Breckinridge personally had expressed to him the opinion that Breckinridge regretted, during his last years, that he had ever espoused the cause of the Confederacy." See Jonathan Truman Dorris, *Pardon and Amnesty Under Lincoln and Johnson* (Chapel Hill: University of North Carolina Press, 1953), p. 275 n.

once Cardinal Wolsey and Bloody Jeffries"; another wrote, "The abolitionists talk about 'the venerable Dr. Breckinridge.' What makes him venerable? His age? What's that compared with the Devil's?"[51]

But by September 1861 Robert Jefferson Breckinridge had won the first round. Kentucky ended its uneasy neutrality and announced that it would fight on the Union side. John Cabell Breckinridge was forced to flee the state to escape arrest.

The Union Breckinridge became the chief civilian adviser of General Stephen Burbridge, the U.S. commander in Kentucky. One of the President's in-laws intimated that Breckinridge was in line to become Secretary of War.§ Others suggested that he was Lincoln's first choice for Vice-President in 1864. But the only official honor he was given was appointment as temporary chairman of the National Union Convention.

The perspiring delegates who had come to Baltimore in June 1864 to nominate Lincoln for a second term cheered wildly when their national chairman introduced the "old War Horse of Kentucky." Unlike John C. Breckinridge, whose voice was deep and mellow, Robert Jefferson had a certain asperity of speech, the result of an early illness. But he shared his nephew's sense of showmanship. He quickly gained his listeners' sympathy by stooping his tall frame, then dramatically springing erect as he reached a climax. The convention was fascinated when the Southern gentleman told them:

[By] every blow you strike, *and every rebel you kill*, every battle you win, dreadful as it is to do it, you are adding, it may be a year, it may be ten years, it may be a century, it may be ten centuries, to the life of the Government and freedom of your children.[52]

"The speech of Dr. Breckinridge," recalled James G. Blaine, "was the most inspiring utterance of the convention"[53]—for the delegates knew that among the rebels he commanded them to kill were two of his own sons and a son-in-law.

The Civil War has been called "the Brothers War." In Kentucky it was meant literally. The state's three great political families—the Breckinridges, Clays, and Crittendens—were torn down the middle. President Lincoln's Kentucky in-laws, the Todds, were also on both sides of the conflict, though most were with the South.

Of Robert Jefferson Breckinridge's four sons of military age, the two

§ Dr. L. B. Todd wrote to Breckinridge, November 23, 1861, "I am perfectly satisfied, yes *I feel assured* that there must *very shortly* be a vacancy in the Cabinet—that Secretary Cameron must be removed and that a good Providence indicates yourself as the most suitable, worthy and exactly the Statesman and Patriot to become his successor." Quoted in William H. Townsend, *Lincoln and the Bluegrass* (Lexington: University of Kentucky Press, 1955), p. 286. Italics in original.

oldest joined the Confederate Army; the two youngest joined the Union Army. Of his sons-in-law, one fought with the South; another with the North. Three sons and a son-in-law were taken prisoner by the enemy.

The first to take arms was Robert Jr., the eldest. He had been city attorney of Lexington and an active campaigner for his cousin John Cabell in 1860. Without saying good-by to his father, he recruited one of the first Kentucky companies to join the Confederacy. Be as "lenient as possible," he asked his father in a letter.[54] The fiery old man responded by paying his son's debts and inviting his Confederate daughter-in-law into his home. After a year of fighting, young Robert's troops elected him to the Confederate Congress. But a year later he chose to return to active duty, and on Washington's Birthday, 1865, while in Kentucky on a secret mission, he was taken prisoner. A woman friend tried to prevent his arrest by pulling a pistol on his capturer; Colonel Breckinridge gallantly stepped between the lady and the Union officer and surrendered.[55]

The second son, William Campbell Preston Breckinridge,[56] deeply sympathized with the Southern cause. But out of respect for his father he remained "aloof" from the war. His wife Issa was sharply hostile to her father-in-law. Willie rebuked her: she should be grateful for Robert Jefferson's "love & kindness & influence." Then in July 1862 General John Morgan invaded Kentucky, and young Breckinridge made the "terrible but unavoidable" decision to take up arms against his father. Willie rose to colonel and in the final hours of the war became part of the bodyguard that accompanied Jefferson Davis and his Cabinet on its retreat southward.[57]

During October 1864 Robert Jefferson Breckinridge fell from his horse and was seriously injured. The old man continued to direct Lincoln's re-election campaign in Kentucky from his bed. One morning an unexpected visitor burst into his bedroom. "Father," exclaimed Confederate Colonel Robert Jefferson Breckinridge, Jr., "I heard you were fatally injured. I have ridden eighty miles without drawing bridle to embrace you once more." The Union leader and his rebel son embraced after nearly four years apart.

There was another visitor. Confederate Major Theophilus Steele had come to see his wife Sophonisba Breckinridge. A few minutes after his departure he was captured by Union troops. Sophie pleaded with her father to get Steele released. "The distress of my daughter breaks my heavy heart," he said, "but the fact that Major Steele is my son-in-law, to whom I am personally devoted, entitles him to no more consideration than any other rebel soldier."[58]

Only a month before Breckinridge had told a Lexington audience, "When Simon de Montfort was slaughtering the Protestants in the South of France, he was appealed to by certain persons, declaring that his men were mistaken, that they were killing many who were good Catholics. To which he replied: 'Kill them all; God knows his own.' And this is the way we should deal with these fellows; treat them all alike, and if there are any among them who are not rebels at heart God will take care of them and save them at last."[59]

The Union commander in charge of the Louisville prison put Major Steele in irons, locked in solitary confinement. He would be tried as a spy and hanged. Robert Jefferson Breckinridge was put to the test. Would he choose the way of Montfort or his daughter?

His answer was contained in a letter to the President. Major Steele was captured in uniform, he contended, and should be treated as an ordinary prisoner of war. Lincoln acted at once; the charges against Breckinridge's son-in-law were dropped.

Robert Jefferson's two sons on the Union side were Charles, a West Point captain, and Joseph Cabell, a volunteer, once cited for bravery and twice breveted. In July 1864 the twenty-one-year-old Joseph was taken prisoner in Georgia. His brother Willie rode through the night to assist him. When Robert Jefferson heard of the kindness of his Confederate son toward his Union son, he wrote Willie: "I thank God for preserving your life amid so many dangers and for His care of Joseph; and if my poor prayers avail anything, you will both survive these horrible times. . . . And now my son if anything befalls you, wherein a loving father may be of use to you personally, in life or death—let me know. . . . I have written this almost without tears. What then is too hard for your loving father?"[60]

The Rev. Mr. Breckinridge prayed to a God of vengeance for his country; to a God of love he prayed for his sons.

After a distinguished record in the field, President Jefferson Davis called John C. Breckinridge to Richmond in February 1865 to be the Confederacy's final Secretary of War. He tried to convince Davis that further fighting could only prolong the war, it could no longer win it. "This has been a magnificent epic," Breckinridge told Senator George Vest. "In God's name, let it not terminate in a farce."[61]

The Confederate Cabinet began their flight from Richmond on April 2, 1865. For the Secretary of War it was the beginning of a two-month adventure that "reads more like a Viking romance than a reality."[62]

By Southern "underground" the party successfully eluded federal troops in Virginia and the Carolinas. At Charlotte news reached them of the assassination of Lincoln. The Confederate leaders immediately saw it as a calamity for the South. The fact that Andrew Johnson had supported Breckinridge in 1860 was no comfort. On May 10, at Irwinville, Georgia, President Davis was taken. On the same day, eleven miles below Macon, Breckinridge's son Clifton was also captured. The

John Adams

1735-1826

Descended from four generations of unexceptional Massachusetts farmers, he became the first Vice President of the United States and the nation's second President.

Abigail Smith Adams
1744-1818
Her grandfather was speaker of the Massachusetts House of Representatives, and her mother thought she married beneath her station when she became the wife of John Adams.

Charles Francis Adams
1807-1886
This caricature appeared in *Vanity Fair*, London, 1872, at the time of the *Alabama* Claims Tribunal. Following in the footsteps of father and grandfather, he served as U. S. envoy to Great Britain.

John Quincy Adams
1767-1848
Carefully tutored in statecraft, he was the only President's son to become President, and, like his father, he was unable to win reelection.

Robert E. Lee
1807-1870
Although his father and, later, his son "Rooney" served in Congress, he distrusted
politicians and declined political office.

Fitzhugh Lee
1835-1905

Despite efforts by his uncle, Robert E. Lee, to have him expelled from West Point, he became a distinguished Confederate cavalry officer and a governor of Virginia.

Fitzhugh Lee
1905-

Grandson of the Confederate general of the same name, he is now commandant of the National War College and a fifth generation military officer. *(Official U.S. Navy photograph.)*

William Livingston
1723-1790
The Revolutionary War governor of
New Jersey was secretly proud of his
prominent Livingston nose.

Edward Livingston
1764-1836
His adopted state of Louisiana sent
him to the U.S. Senate. President
Jackson appointed him Secretary of
State.

Harriet Livingston
Fulton
1786-1824

She continued the Livingston tradition of making brilliant matches. Her husband, Robert Fulton, was the steamboat inventor.

Sarah Livingston Jay
1756-1802

One of the three high-spirited daughters of Governor William Livingston, she became the wife of John Jay, first Chief Justice of the U. S. Supreme Court.

William Augustus Muhlenberg
1796-1877
He influenced nearly every aspect of the Episcopal Church in America. Among his achievements was the founding of St. Luke's Hospital in New York City.

Frederick Augustus Muhlenberg
1887-
This Reading, Pennsylvania, architect became the sixth member of his family to serve in the U.S. House of Representatives.

John Randolph Tucker
1823-1897
His reputation in Congress was as a strict Constitutionalist, but he was equally famous as a Washington wit.

Henry St. George Tucker
1853-1932
Son of John Randolph Tucker, he was the fourth member of his dynasty in Congress, and, like his father, was a president of the American Bar Association.

James Asheton Bayard, Jr.

1797-1880

Besides serving as a U. S. senator from Delaware, he was the son, brother, father, and grandfather of U. S. senators from Delaware.

Thomas Francis Bayard, Sr.
1828-1898
While the presidency eluded him, his public career included service as U.S. senator, Secretary of State, and Ambassador to the Court of St. James's.

Alexis I. duPont Bayard
1918-
The current representative of the Bayard dynasty was the youngest lieutenant governor in Delaware history. *(Photo by Lubitsh & Bungarz.)*

Theodore Roosevelt
1858-1919
Clifford Berryman of the Washington *Star* pictured the "Rough Rider" corralling delegates to the 1912 Republican Convention. Note the "Teddy Bear" (lower left), which was this cartoonist's invention.

Franklin Delano Roosevelt

1882-1945

Cartoonist Berryman called this "A New Deal Version of David and Goliath" (July 15, 1940), but Vice President Garner proved no match for the ebullient F.D.R.

Eleanor Roosevelt
1884-1962
This photograph of President Theodore Roosevelt's niece was probably taken shortly after she became First Lady in 1933.

Alice Roosevelt Longworth
A year after this 1905 portrait the President's daughter married Ohio congressman Nicholas Longworth.

Elliott Roosevelt

1910-

This picture, with the portrait of his presidential father in the background, was used in Elliott's successful race for mayor of Miami Beach in 1965.

James Roosevelt

1907-

F.D.R.'s oldest son left Congress to join the U. S. Mission to the United Nations —a position his mother once held.

Franklin Delano Roosevelt, Jr.

1914-

The former New York congressman got a second political life by campaigning for John F. Kennedy in the 1960 West Virginia presidential primary.

Kermit Roosevelt
1916-
When this grandson of T.R. was a Central Intelligence Agency operative he reputedly engineered the 1953 coup that overthrew Premier Mossadegh of Iran. *(Photo by Chase, Ltd., Washington.)*

Edith Kermit Roosevelt
A syndicated column written by this granddaughter of T.R. appears in nearly fifty newspapers.

Secretary of War, on learning of Davis' fate, dismissed his forty-five-man guard. "I will not have one of these young men to encounter one hazard more for my sake," he was reported to have said.[63]

The fleeing Breckinridge, now the most "wanted" man in the Confederacy, crossed into Florida with his aide, Colonel James Wilson, and a Negro servant. They were soon joined by Colonel John Taylor Wood, a grandson of President Zachary Taylor and a cousin of Robert E. Lee. A graduate of the United States Naval Academy, Wood was one of the boldest and most skillful sailors in the Confederate Navy. The party grew to seven when Breckinridge was joined by three enlisted men—Sergeant Jerry O'Toole, Corporal Dick Russell, and Private Pat Murphy.

Now began the "Viking romance." As they passed through the high saw grass of the Everglades it struck Breckinridge that if a man had his arms tied and his face exposed he would be killed by insects in two nights. By the time they reached the present site of Palm Beach the bread was gone and they lived on the eggs of huge green turtles, which they dug out of the sand. Once they were spotted by a Union steamer, but they bluffed their way out of capture by pretending to be hunters and "wreckers." Early on the morning of June 6 the hungry Confederates met a party of Seminole Indians and were given some *koonti*. (Breckinridge said it was like thick pancakes, only "ten times as tough.") They also scrounged a few bits of fish that were left over from the Indians' breakfast. At the site of Delray the Confederate Secretary of War and his aides turned pirate and took over a sloop at gunpoint. On June 8 they left the Keys for Cuba. The waves on the open sea were twenty feet high; their feet and legs became blistered and swollen from the heat and salt water. Finally, on June 11, 1865, the former Vice-President of the United States arrived at Cardenas, seventy-five miles east of Havana.[64]

Only two Confederate cabinet officers successfully escaped from the United States. The other was Judah P. Benjamin, the brilliant Secretary of State, who arrived at Bimini Island in the Bahamas on July 10 and left for England in August. In London, fifty-four years old and without his once considerable fortune, Benjamin started a new life as a law student. When he died in 1884 he was an acknowledged leader of the bar and one of the highest-paid lawyers in England. He never again returned to the United States.

But Breckinridge did not desire an expatriate's life. His wife and two of their children joined him in exile. He owned some Minnesota land, which he turned over to a non-secessionist friend, who gradually sold pieces of the property to finance Breckinridge's wanderings through England, France, Greece, Egypt, the Holy Land, and Canada. His friends and even some of his former enemies urged him to return.

Horace Greeley, the editor of the New York *Tribune,* wrote that it was a "pity that the presence and counsel of General Breckinridge were wanting. We need him . . . in his own Kentucky, where a most unfortunate attempt to perpetuate class distinction . . . threatens to cause a feud and a struggle. . . ."[65] Finally, after an absence of almost eight years, Breckinridge started for home. He received an ovation all the way from the Ohio River, at Covington, to his native Fayette County.

The man who had gone from state legislator to Vice-President in six years never entered public life again, although Cassius Clay said that he was responsible for effectively killing the Ku Klux Klan in Kentucky.[66] In Lexington he practiced law and served as vice-president of the Elizabethtown, Lexington and Big Sand Railroad.

John C. Breckinridge died in 1875 at the age of fifty-four, the most beloved man of his time in Kentucky. Yet his great promise had been largely unfulfilled.

As for the Rev. Robert Jefferson Breckinridge, he resigned his position at the Danville Theological Seminary in 1869. His title had been professor of exegetic, polemic and didactic theology, but in effect he had been its president. The Presbyterian Church had once had great expectations for Danville. It was to have been the Princeton Theological Seminary of the West. But the Civil War, and Robert Jefferson's partisan role in it, successfully finished the school. There were so few students that no regular terms were held from 1867 to 1870, and there were only brief summer sessions in 1868 and 1869. The belligerent old man died in 1871. Although he had once been pastor of the First Presbyterian Church of Lexington, he left instructions to be buried at the Second Presbyterian Church. The First Church had been pro-Southern; the Second Church, pro-Union. Robert Jefferson Breckinridge made no concessions, even in death.

Robert Jefferson Breckinridge was survived by eight children. Of his two Confederate sons, Robert Jefferson, Jr., became a local judge and a state senator, whose election in 1900 as attorney general of Kentucky was successfully contested; William Campbell Preston became a distinguished congressman with a complex sex life.

Of his Union sons: Charles died in 1867; Joseph Cabell stayed in the army, rose to the rank of major general, became the inspector general, and had a horse shot from under him at Santiago during the Spanish-American War. His stern and imposing aura left no doubt about his profession or conviction. One day in Denver a passing stranger asked him, "What is the chief end of man?" Without a moment's hesitation Breckinridge snapped, "Man's chief end is to glorify God and enjoy

Him forever." The questioner held out his hand. "I knew by your look and carriage that you were an army officer and a Presbyterian."[67]

The fifth son and only surviving child of Robert Jefferson's second marriage was killed while trying to break up a tavern brawl.¶

Confederate Secretary of War John C. Breckinridge sent his young cousin, William Campbell Preston Breckinridge, back to Lexington before he made his dash for Cuba. Robert Jefferson greeted the son with open arms. But Willie's wife, Issa Desha Breckinridge, still had not forgiven her father-in-law for his espousal of the Union cause.* It was not until after the birth of their third child in 1867, a son Desha, that she relented and allowed her father-in-law to see his grandchildren.

In 1869 Willie made his first race for public office. He was defeated for county attorney because he favored admitting Negro testimony in courts. But people were beginning to talk about his amazing powers as an orator. The Rev. William Eliot Knight asked, "Did you ever hear him speak? He is the Cicero of his day. . . . To say that he is a genius is too inexpressive. . . . He can sway his audience like magic. Now he seems to be an easy and quiet brooklet, gliding along through fertile fields and meadows. . . . Now he is a mighty cataract, he plunges, he rushes, he drives. . . . Now he is like a gentle summer wind, blowing softly from some verdant garden laden with the perfumes of the mag-

¶ Of Robert Jefferson Breckinridge's daughters:

Mary Cabell Breckinridge married William Warfield, a Union Army captain. He became a noted breeder of thoroughbred cattle, and author of two books on the subject (*A History of Short Horn Cattle in America* and *The Theory and Practice of Cattle Breeding.*) A son, Ethelbert Dudley Warfield (1861–1936), became the president of three schools—Miami University at Oxford, Ohio, Lafayette College, and Wilson College.

Sophonisba Breckinridge and her husband, Dr. Theophilus Steele, the former Confederate major, moved to New York.

Marie Lettice Preston Breckinridge married the Rev. William Collins Handy. One of their eight children, Levin Irving Handy (1861–1921), became a one-term congressman from Delaware, 1897–99. See Alexander Brown, *The Cabells and Their Kin* (Boston and New York: Houghton Mifflin, 1895), pp. 502–3, 506, 508–9.

* Issa Breckinridge was the granddaughter of Joseph Desha (1768–1842), governor of Kentucky from 1824 to 1828. As a member of Congress he introduced the bill that authorized the design of the American flag as thirteen stripes and a star for each state. Governor Desha's sister Phoebe was a great-great-grandmother of President Lyndon Baines Johnson. See Edna Talbott Whitley, *Kentucky Ante-Bellum Portraiture* (no place of publication listed, 1956), p. 126; Washington *Post*, April 24, 1965, p. E1.

Issa was William C. P. Breckinridge's second wife. In 1859 he had married Lucretia Hart Clay, who died the next year in childbirth. She was a granddaughter of Henry Clay and a daughter of Lincoln's minister to Nicaragua. See Zachary F. Smith and Mary Rogers Clay, *The Clay Family* (Louisville: J. P. Morton, 1899), pp. 176–77.

nolia, the jasmine and the orange. Now he comes like a maddened and terrorizing hurricane. . . ."[68]†

The golden-tongued Willie was elected to Congress in 1884. For ten years he was a leading advocate of free trade, even when it was against the interests of his district, and a determined foe of the trusts.[69] A brilliant parliamentarian, according to a contemporary Washington reporter, "his equal for the conduct of a great annual appropriation bill through the House, and through the Committee of the Whole, has [not] appeared in either House of Congress in a generation."[70] "Keen and energetic," wrote the editor of the *North American Review*, "in the very prime of life, he is doubtless destined to achieve a more than brilliant success."[71]

Then suddenly his career was ruined. William Campbell Preston Breckinridge had been leading a double life. For ten years the statesman-orator had been keeping a young woman who claimed she had been three times pregnant by him. When Issa died in 1892, the mistress, Madeline Pollard, said that Willie had promised to marry her. Instead he had secretly wed another woman.‡ Miss Pollard countered by filing a $50,000 breach of promise suit. The trial lasted for more than a month, and the nation enjoyed a scandal worthy of the most salacious. One paperback book, which claimed that "it has not been our intention to pander to the tastes of the depraved and vicious," gave as its title page:

The Celebrated Trial

MADELINE POLLARD

vs.

BRECKINRIDGE

The Most Noted Breach of Promise Suit in
The History of Court Records

Containing

A Graphic Story of the Sensational Incidents
in the Joint Lives of the Now Famous Litigants,
as Given in Their Own Words

† A student of public speaking recalls hearing Breckinridge hold forth for two hours on the Constitution. "He pronounced it 'constichution,' with the emphasis on the 'chu.'" The memorable address ended: "As for myself I en-vy the boys and girls playing in the streets of Lex-ing-ton, for they will see gr-eat-er and gr-an-der things than their forefathers ever dr-eam-ed of—mar-ve-lous triumphs, un-pre-dictable achievements, not even the e-ter-nal God has set limits to the bound-a-ries of our mi-igh-ty republic." See Edgar Dewitt Jones, *Lords of Speech* (Chicago and New York: Willett, Clark, 1937), pp. 175–76.

‡ His third wife, Louise Scott, was the widow of E. Rumsey Wing, U.S. minister to Ecuador.

The two stories differ widely as to the material facts
in the case. Testimony of the Kentucky schoolgirl
directly contradicts the story of the silver-
tongued orator and statesman—Testimony
of prominent witnesses from various
states uncovering startling incidents in the lives of
plaintiff and de-
fendant.

The surprising disclosures and dramatic scenes that
filled the courtroom with a throng of excited
spectators fully described—The most
sensational testimony ever produced in court.

The trial began on March 8, 1894, in the Circuit Court of Washington.
The olive-drab courtroom had changed little since Mary Surratt had
been tried there for complicity in the Lincoln assassination. Breckinridge
entered, smiling and laughing, accompanied by his son Desha and a
retinue of seven attorneys. His chief counsel was former Ohio Congressman Benjamin Butterworth. Miss Pollard entered, solemn and clad
completely in black, accompanied by a matron from the House of
Mercy and her battery of attorneys. Her chief counsel was former Indiana Congressman Jeremiah Wilson.

The bailiffs held back the crowd. Judge Bradley had given orders
to keep out the many women who wished to hear the lurid testimony.
The old men, looking like church elders, came early and got good seats
on the hard benches and cane chairs. Those who were not so fortunate
stood at the windows looking in, although they could not see the witness
stand.

What was the charm of Madeline Pollard? Breckinridge's lawyers
planted a spy in the House of Mercy, an Episcopal home for unwed
mothers, where Miss Pollard lived. After the trial, a publishing firm
that specialized in "popular novels" (*A Mad Marriage, A Wronged Wife*)
brought out a fifty-cent edition of the Breckinridge spy's story, entitled,
*A Diary of Ten Weeks' Intimate Association with the Real Madeline
Pollard by Agnes Parker*. This is the author's first impression of Miss
Pollard:

. . . what a homely, common-looking woman! Her face is almost repulsive
in its coarseness; her eyes are too far apart, gray in color, with heavy black
brows. Her nose, which is particularly ugly, is turned up, with very large,
round nostrils; her cheeks are fat and round, giving her a doughy, expression-
less profile; while her mouth is decidedly coarse, her upper lip being very
thick and extending over the under. When she smiles, her face loses much of

its hardness. Her voice is decidedly soft and musical. There is a peculiar, indescribable something in it that is attractive. She speaks with marked affectation, with that labored care in the pronounciation of every word that suggests the "school-marm" giving out a dictation exercise.[72]

Other witnesses agreed: Madeline Pollard was no beauty.

The defense's strategy was to show that Miss Pollard was a woman of extremely loose morals, obviously not the type that a distinguished congressman would take in marriage.

"Miss Pollard," asked Butterworth, "did you ever at any time or place, prior to meeting Colonel Breckinridge, have any sexual relations with any man?"

"No! Never, never."

"Miss Pollard, have you at any time or place, after meeting Colonel Breckinridge, had sexual relations with any other man?"

"No! Never, never." Her words came out with an aspirated eloquence.[73]

She made a convincing witness. She even fainted at just the right moment to impress the twelve-man jury. Moreover, she produced two key witnesses who had heard Breckinridge announce his marital intentions.

The trial was further enlivened on the third day by a fist fight between the teams of opposing lawyers. The only casualty was Jere Wilson's silk hat, smashed beyond repair. The next day Breckinridge's lawyers had to deny formally to the judge that they were carrying concealed weapons.

The defense began on the ninth day. Colonel Breckinridge took the stand on the fifteenth day. He was now forced to change his strategy. There was no longer time for mirth and smiles. He would be frank and serious. He would tell all.

"I was a man of passion. She was a woman of passion," Breckinridge began.

"There was no seduction," he said, "no seduction on either side. It was simply a case of human passion."[74] But the affair had cooled, and any talk of marriage was under duress. Twice Miss Pollard had pulled a pistol on him.

The jury went out at 3:07 P.M. on the twenty-eighth day and returned one hour and twenty-three minutes later. The verdict was for the plaintiff. Miss Pollard was awarded $15,000.

William Campbell Preston Breckinridge ran for re-election in 1894. The congressman pleaded with his constituents. "I have sinned," he said, as only he could say it, "and I repent in sackcloth and ashes."[75] Madeline Pollard told Agnes Parker that she thought he would win. But her talents were not as a political prognosticator. He was defeated.

Two years later he broke with the national Democrats when the 1896 convention nominated William Jennings Bryan. He ran for Congress as a Gold Democrat and was beaten again.

When Willie's son Desha became publisher of the Lexington *Herald*, a struggling Democratic paper, in 1897, he made the former congressman his chief editorial writer. Desha had stood by his father during the trial and had given up his own legal career to promote his father's political aspirations. Now he gave him a job.

The postwar generation was also represented in Congress by Clifton Rodes Breckinridge, son of the illustrious John Cabell Breckinridge.[76]§ The two Breckinridge congressmen, Willie and Clifton, were remembered for being "passionately devoted to the interests of the common man."[77] While Willie held the ancestral Ashland seat in Kentucky, Clifton was elected from Arkansas.

Clifton had been only fifteen when he joined the Confederate Army. After the war he went to Washington College to study under Robert E. Lee. The general further instilled in him a love for his defeated region. And when he left school because of poor eyesight, he decided to settle in the Deep South rather than Kentucky, which was less harshly affected by Reconstruction. He first worked in New Orleans, then joined his brother Cabell as an Arkansas planter. With the close of Reconstruction, Arkansas sent Clifton to the House of Representatives.

He was elected six times. But his 1888 victory was contested by his Republican opponent, John M. Clayton, who claimed that the returns had been tampered with. Clayton was assassinated while taking testimony. The murderer was never discovered. A congressional committee, after examining 1200 witnesses, ruled that Breckinridge was not entitled to his seat. When the vote came before the whole House, many of the Democratic minority tried to block a decision by staying away, thus preventing a quorum. Clifton opposed this parliamentary skirmish and was unseated by a party-line vote. His constituents quickly re-elected him.

Resigning his House seat in 1894 to become United States minister to Russia, he held the diplomatic post for three years. In 1900 President

§ John C. Breckinridge had two other sons, Cabell and John Witherspoon. Cabell Breckinridge became a cotton planter in eastern Arkansas and married a daughter of Robert W. Johnson, who left the U. S. Senate in 1861 to enter the Confederate Senate.

John Witherspoon Breckinridge, known as "Owen" in appreciation of the heavy vote his father received in Owen County, moved to California, where a promising career as a lawyer and state senator was brought to a premature close by his death at age forty-two.

McKinley appointed him a commissioner to the Five Civilized Tribes, where he ended his public career mediating Indian affairs in what is now Oklahoma.

As the dynasty entered the twentieth century, there had been five Breckinridges in the House of Representatives, two senators, a cabinet member, and a Vice-President. There had been college presidents, ministers, soldiers, and numerous local officials.

The new century seemed to snuff out their desire for national office. One would make the attempt and fail.

In the post-Civil War era a number of Breckinridges turned to the military as a career. This took them and their children far from Kentucky. Others left the state because of the better opportunities available outside of the war-torn South. Kentucky's greatest political dynasty became rootless.

The family had never been a solitary force, flowing through time in a single unbroken line. There had always been wandering tributaries. The main current had first been John Breckinridge, Jefferson's Attorney General; by mid-century there had been a division as Robert Jefferson and John Cabell cut deep paths running north and south; now in the twentieth century the line trifurcated as three branches swept into the present.

There were the children of William Campbell Preston Breckinridge, the children of Clifton Rodes Breckinridge, and the children of Joseph Cabell Breckinridge, the bemedaled inspector general of the Spanish-American War.

Although no longer primarily political, they would continue, as Cassius Clay said, "remarkable for talent and character."[78]

The two remarkable children of William Campbell Preston Breckinridge were Desha and Sophonisba.

"Nisba" graduated from Wellesley in 1888, although it was not in the Breckinridge tradition to send their young ladies to college. Mrs. Clifton Breckinridge said that college would not be detrimental in itself, but Nisba would not want to live at home afterward.[79] She was right, of course. Nisba went on to study law, becoming the first woman admitted to the Lexington bar and the first woman admitted to practice before the Kentucky Court of Appeals.

She also received a Ph.D. from the University of Chicago, and became dean of the Chicago School of Civics and Philanthropy, later incorporated into the University of Chicago. Under her direction it became one of the outstanding schools of social service in the world.

Her ninety pounds were a study in energy. She never took vacations, she wrote or edited dozens of books, including the first casebooks on social work, and attended meetings all over the world. When President Franklin Roosevelt sent her to the Pan American Conference at Montevideo in 1933, she became the first woman to represent the United States at an international conference. The pioneer social worker, lawyer, educator, author died in 1948, at eighty-two. She had earned a place, according to Katharine Lenroot of the United States Children's Bureau, as "one of America's great women."[80]

Brother Desha became publisher of the Lexington *Herald* in 1897 and editor-publisher in 1904. With the exception of one brief period during the Spanish-American War, when he was aide-de-camp to his uncle, Major General Joseph Cabell Breckinridge, Desha guided the *Herald* until his death in 1935.

His life and newspaper were inalterably changed by his marriage to Madeline McDowell, a great-granddaughter of Henry Clay. "Of the

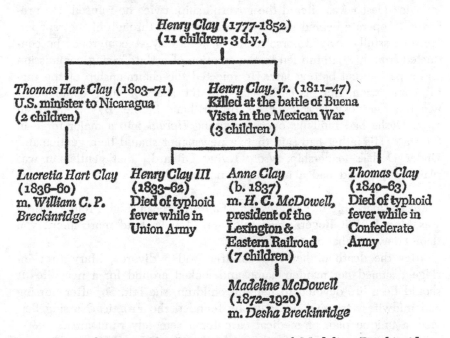

Henry Clay (1777-1852)
(11 children; 3 d.y.)

Thomas Hart Clay (1803-71)
U.S. minister to Nicaragua
(2 children)

Henry Clay, Jr. (1811-47)
Killed at the battle of Buena Vista in the Mexican War
(3 children)

Lucretia Hart Clay (1836-60)
m. William C. P. Breckinridge

Henry Clay III (1833-62)
Died of typhoid fever while in Union Army

Anne Clay (b. 1837)
m. H. C. McDowell, president of the Lexington & Eastern Railroad (7 children)

Thomas Clay (1840-63)
Died of typhoid fever while in Confederate Army

Madeline McDowell (1872-1920)
m. Desha Breckinridge

descendants of Henry Clay," a cousin wrote of Madeline Breckinridge, "she alone inherited his command of language, his power to sway and convince; as a thinker she was the most profound."[81] When Oswald G. Villard, the hard-boiled editor of the New York *Evening Post*, heard her speak in 1911, he commented, "At one time she fairly brought tears to the eyes of her auditors, and her plea for the ballot for women . . . is said to have shaken the faith even of an anti-suffrage editor of the *Outlook*. . . ."[82]

"Madge" Breckinridge, like her sister-in-law Sophonisba, who later wrote her biography, was in the vanguard of all the movements for social legislation during the first two decades of the century. Being afflicted with tuberculosis, she was especially active in programs for treatment of the disease. She founded the Kentucky Tuberculosis Association and the Blue Grass Sanitorium at Lexington, and was an organizer of the State Tuberculosis Commission.

Under her prodding Desha turned the *Herald* into the leading voice of the South for reform and social legislation. The paper actively supported her crusades for a child labor amendment and the League of Nations. Between October 18 and 23, 1920, Madge Breckinridge toured the state, giving twelve speeches for U.S. participation in the League. Two days after this herculean effort, on Thanksgiving morning, she died. Desha wrote a moving editorial—"She is Dead." It was unnecessary for him to mention her name. Lexington knew.

Twice Desha was offered the governorship; twice he refused. He preferred to operate behind the scenes and to speak through his newspaper. He successfully revived horse racing in Kentucky. A conference he conducted from his bathtub led to the creation of a state racing commission and a parimutuel betting law. He rejected the chairmanship of the racing commission. But his enthusiasm for the sport of kings could never win the Kentucky Derby for his Braedalbane Stable. By his death in 1935, Desha had built his once struggling *Herald* into a major force in the state. His father had said that "a newspaper should be a gentleman." Under Desha's leadership, wrote Irving Dilliard, "that gentleman was plain spoken and had a mission to perform."[83]

Most remarkable of Congressman Clifton Breckinridge's four children was Mary.¶ Will Rogers once told her, "I have read more about you than I have Mahatma Gandhi."[84]

After the death of her two children and a divorce, Mary Breckinridge resumed her maiden name and looked around for a new life. It should be a life devoted to helping children, she felt. So, after nursing and midwifery training, in 1925 she founded the Frontier Nursing Service, a unique plan of medical care for a remotely rural area.

The territory she chose for her experiment was seven hundred square miles in the mountains of Kentucky, most of it inaccessible by car. There she found ten thousand people, of whom few had ever been visited by doctor or nurse, with a typical family income in 1930 of $85.70.

She proceeded to raise money, train a staff, and build a small hos-

¶ Another of his children, James Carson Breckinridge (1877–1942), joined the Marine Corps during the Spanish-American War, became a major general in 1935, and was commander of Quantico (Virginia) Marine Barracks at the time of his death.

pital and five nursing centers. Her pattern of decentralization called for each nursing center to cover a five-mile radius, two nurses to a center, with the farthest patient not more than an hour away by horseback. In its first four decades the achievements of Mary Breckinridge's Frontier Nursing Service include the delivery of 10,000 babies.[85]

Major General Joseph Cabell Breckinridge had thirteen children, four of whom died in infancy.

Twenty-six-year-old Joseph Cabell Breckinridge, Jr., was killed when he was swept off a torpedo boat in Havana Harbor just before the outbreak of the Spanish-American War. Novelist Winston Churchill said of him: "Could the short life be written of Ensign Breckinridge . . . many a gilt-edged biography would pale in comparison. But three years out of the Academy, he had taken six drowning men from the sea. Once, when he was standing on the deck of the *Texas,* the ammunition hoist gave way and the shot began falling into the powder. From the edge of the hatch Mr. Breckinridge threw himself at the running bunch of strands and was carried around and around until his clothes were torn from his body and his hands and arms were stripped and bleeding. But there was no explosion."[86]

Captain Ethelbert Breckinridge was seriously wounded in the Philippines Insurrection. (His son, Major General William Mattingly Breckinridge, was chief of the U. S. Army Security Agency at the time of his retirement in 1962.)

Scott Dudley Breckinridge was an Olympic fencer and noted Lexington gynecologist.*

But the most unusual was Henry Breckinridge.

At twenty-seven, Henry was appointed the Assistant Secretary of War by President Wilson. With the outbreak of World War I in August 1914, the President sent Breckinridge, with two cruisers and nearly eight million dollars in gold, to supervise the "relief, protection and transportation of American citizens" in Europe.[87]

Secretary of War Garrison and his first assistant wanted Wilson to increase the size of the army. But Wilson's re-election slogan had been "He Kept Us Out of War." Garrison and Breckinridge resigned in protest. "These resignations created a sensation," recalled Secretary of the Navy Daniels. "Nothing else was talked about for days."

"Have you heard the sad news about Henry Breckinridge?" asked Senator Ollie James. "He is suffering from a terrible cold . . . caused by the fact that he hung his head out the window all night expecting

* Dr. Breckinridge (1882–1941) was co-author of *Surgical and Gynecological Nursing* (Philadelphia: Lippincott, 1916), and co-author, with his son Scott, Jr., of *Sword Play* (New York: A. S. Barnes, 1941). The latter was written while he was coach of the fencing team at the University of Kentucky.

to hear the newsboy shout 'Henry Breckinridge has resigned as Assistant Secretary of War and the Government is in peril.'"[88]

The former Assistant Secretary went back to France. This time as a soldier. He didn't re-enter politics until the 1932 Democratic Convention when he managed Harry F. Byrd's campaign for the presidential nomination. However, as Arthur Krock said, "Colonel Breckinridge is not much of a politician." He couldn't even identify Senator Carter Glass, who was to nominate his candidate.[89] Byrd received 25 votes on the first ballot—the entire Virginia delegation and a stray vote from Indiana. On the third ballot his total dropped to 24.96—the 96/100ths of a vote coming from North Carolina. F.D.R. was nominated despite Breckinridge's efforts.

In 1927 Breckinridge married Aida de Acosta Root. It was the second marriage for both.† As a young society girl in Paris the adventurous Aida de Acosta made a solo flight in a powered balloon dirigible. When she returned to earth her instructor informed her, "Mademoiselle, you are the world's first woman pilot." It was not an exploit in which her family took pride, and she kept the secret from 1903 until 1932.[90]

Breckinridge shared his second wife's love of flying.[91] In 1931, at forty-four, he qualified for his pilot's license. Two years later he went to Washington to become counsel for the Joint Committee to Investigate Dirigible Disasters. The U.S.S. *Akron* had crashed in the Atlantic with a loss of seventy-four crew members. After twelve days of hearings Breckinridge was unable to determine the exact cause of the crash—

† His first wife was Ruth Bradley Woodman of Concord, New Hampshire. They were married in 1910 and divorced in 1925. In 1941 she was reported missing from a ship said to have been sunk by a German submarine. See New York *Times*, February 18, 1947, p. 27. They had two daughters: Louisa Dudley died young; Elizabeth Foster married John S. Graham, an Assistant Secretary of the Treasury under President Truman, and a Democratic member of the Atomic Energy Commission appointed by President Eisenhower. See *Who's Who in America*, Vol. 31, p. 1123.

Her first husband was Oren Root, president of the Hudson and Manhattan Railroad, and a nephew of Secretary of State Elihu Root. Their son, Oren Root, Jr., was the leading organizer of the "Draft Willkie" movement in 1940. He later served as special assistant to Governor Nelson Rockefeller for two years and as New York superintendent of banking for nearly three years. He is now practicing law and serving as a trustee of the State University of New York.

The dynamic Aida Breckinridge lost the sight of one eye in 1922. Operations by Dr. William H. Wilmer saved some of her vision in the other eye, and, in appreciation, she raised five million dollars to build the Wilmer Ophthalmological Institute at Johns Hopkins. Then in 1945 she founded and became the executive director of the Eye Bank for Sight Restoration, an organization that collects tissue from the eyes of the dead for use in corneal graft operations. See Daniel Schwarz, "Builder of the Eye Bank," New York *Times Magazine*, November 2, 1947, pp. 18, 52–53.

probably bad weather. He recommended an expansion of the program.[92]

On March 1, 1932, when Charles A. Lindbergh discovered that his infant son was missing, he immediately made two phone calls. The first was to the New Jersey State Police. The second was to his close friend Henry Breckinridge. Breckinridge was intimately involved in the Lindbergh kidnaping case; the third ransom note was sent to his office. And when the child was found murdered, he was made a trustee of the foundation established in the baby's memory.[93]

Lindbergh piloted his friend around New York State when Breckinridge made his first race for political office. Never having held F.D.R. in high regard, his Roosevelt phobia reached the boiling point by 1934. He then announced that he would run for the Senate in order to "resist the Tammanyizing of the United States," and, for this purpose, he was forming the Constitutional Party with the "Pine Tree of Liberty" as its emblem.[94] The New York *Times* editorialized, "Colonel Breckinridge is an able man, experienced in public affairs as well as the law. But he must perceive that in this matter he is undertaking to lead a forlorn hope. . . ."[95] ("A Forlorn Hope"—can the *Times* have known that it had chosen the words with which John Cabell Breckinridge accepted the 1860 presidential nomination?)

The right-wing candidate took his campaign seriously. But his name sat forlornly on the seventh line of the voting machines. And when the machines in New York City were opened even Norman Thomas, the perennial Socialist office-seeker, received more than nine times the votes of the Pine Tree's Breckinridge.

He was not discouraged. Two years later he announced that he would enter the Democratic presidential primaries in Maryland, New Jersey, Ohio, and Pennsylvania "as a means of continuing the discussion for the defence of Constitutional liberty."[96] His platform did not differ markedly from the ultrarightest groups of today—with one exception. The Supreme Court was then striking down New Deal measures; Breckinridge promised to give it his "uncompromising support."[97] Though a Breckinridge was again championing a lost cause, for a brief moment he may have had the President worried. In the Maryland primary the confident Roosevelt made no noticeable effort, and Breckinridge, the candidate who was "not much of a politician," received sixteen per cent of the vote. Columnist Arthur Krock thought that the vote "does not presage the President's defeat. But it indicates that there is a chance to defeat him. . . ." In November Breckinridge helped Alf Landon carry Maine and Vermont.

Although he had been an early supporter of Woodrow Wilson, Henry did not hesitate to break with his President over America's state of defense preparedness. With war again in Europe, Breckinridge now cut his ties with his close friend Lindbergh, the America Firster who was leading the fight for isolation. Throughout 1939 Breckinridge took to the stump on behalf of a war effort against Germany, Italy, and Japan. In 1940 he intensified his efforts. His speaking schedule took him to Boston, Burlington, Morristown, Lexington, Trenton, New York City, Cleveland, Washington. He wrote a book, articles, letters to the editors. He sent out press releases and appeared on radio. On "The American Forum of the Air," he amazed two members of Congress:

REP. ANDREW MAY OF KENTUCKY: "You don't mean to say that there is anybody here favoring our going to war?"
REP. JAMES VAN ZANDT OF PENNSYLVANIA: "Breckinridge said we should declare war on Hitler immediately."
BRECKINRIDGE: "Most assuredly."[98]

It was Henry Breckinridge's last public fight, and his best.

The present.
The Louisville *Courier-Journal* of August 20, 1961, contained a three-column editorial cartoon. The artist shows a Western lawman in a firing stance, pistol in his right hand, briefcase in his left. It is John Bayne Breckinridge, attorney general of Kentucky. The caption reads, "Have (Legal) Gun—Will Travel."

This Breckinridge is six generations removed from the first of his name to arrive in America in 1728. In direct line, there have been Alexander the Founder (died in 1747); Robert (1720–72), a French and Indian War captain; John (1760–1806), senator and Attorney General of the United States; Robert Jefferson (1800–71), the turbulent pastor who kept Kentucky in the Union; Joseph Cabell (1842–1920), Spanish-American War general; Scott Dudley (1882–1941), Lexington doctor; and now, John Bayne Breckinridge, born 1913.

The most recent Breckinridge has battled the entrenched political powers in Kentucky since his graduation from the state university in 1937. During World War II he was an army officer in Albania. He entered the Kentucky House of Representatives in 1956, where he campaigned for clean election laws, an effective merit system for state employees, and home rule.

In the constantly shifting sands of Kentucky politics, Breckinridge, the leader of the Young Turks, was elected attorney general in 1959,‡ and proceeded to convert the Kentucky Department of Law from a strictly advice-giving organ into an arm of government to ferret out crime. He scored his greatest success by cleaning up vice, gambling,

‡ His nomination was part of a deal between Wilson Wyatt and Bert Combs. Both wanted to run for governor. Wyatt agreed to step down and be a candidate for lieutenant governor if Breckinridge was also put on the ticket. The Combs-Wyatt-Breckinridge combination was then elected.

and prostitution in Newport, Kentucky. Yet a newspaper editor, while admitting that Breckinridge was the best attorney general in his lifetime, felt that he had a serious political liability—no sense of humor.

In 1963 Breckinridge ran as an independent for lieutenant governor. Said the *Courier-Journal* when endorsing him, "Without the manpower or financial help that organizational support could offer him, Mr. Breckinridge has refused to engage in the colorful or irresponsible tactics that might bring his name more forcefully to public attention . . . he insists on talking to the voters as mature, intelligent people." He ran a strong race and was defeated.[99]

But still, say some who are familiar with the state's intricate political patterns, Kentucky has not seen the last of the Breckinridges.

The Bayard Dynasty

"It is pleasant and I think a source of just pride that in so many generations our family have been represented in the Senate with neither fortune, landed interest or solicitation to obtain the position. It is equally indicative . . . of the sound tone of feeling which pervades our State."

—James A. Bayard to his son, 1869[1]

SENATOR James A. Bayard, who took "just pride" in his family, was the son, brother, father, and grandfather of United States senators from Delaware. Six weeks after this letter to his son the Delaware legislature sent them both to the United States Senate. It was the only time in American history that father and son have been elected to the Senate on the same day, and the first time that a senator was succeeded in office by his son.

"In Delaware," writes a most thorough student of the state, "the historian must also be a genealogist."[2] Its political history has largely been the history of a few reigning dynasties—the Claytons, Rodneys, Saulsburys, Du Ponts, and Bayards. For more than fifty-three years, spread over four generations, the Bayards represented Delaware in the Senate. There was a Senator Bayard of Delaware in Washington for nearly half of the time between 1804 and 1929.

The first of the family to reach the New World were Anna Stuyvesant Bayard and her four children, who arrived at New Amsterdam aboard the *Great Crow* in 1647. She was the widow of Samuel Bayard, a wealthy French Huguenot merchant. The dynasty liked to think that they were descended from Pierre du Ferrail, Seigneur de Bayard, the famous fifteenth-century French knight *"sans peur et sans reproche."* In fact the first Senator Bayard of Delaware was dubbed "The Chevalier." But it

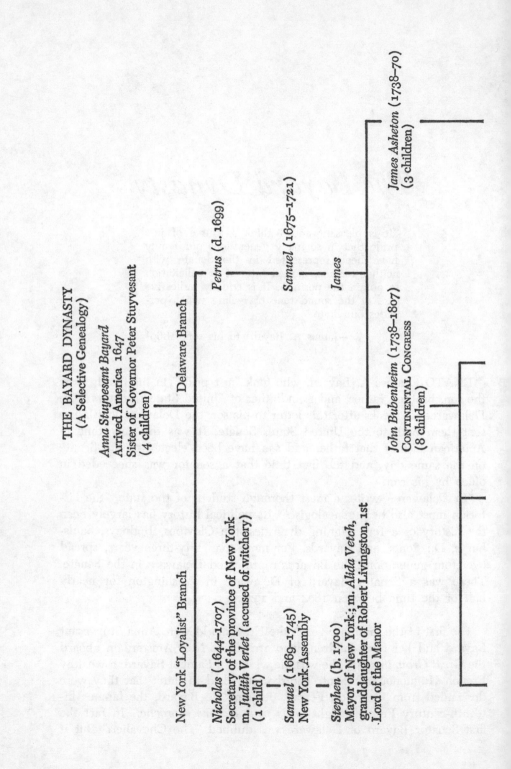

THE BAYARD DYNASTY
(A Selective Genealogy)

Anna Stuyvesant Bayard
Arrived America 1647
Sister of Governor Peter Stuyvesant
(4 children)

New York "Loyalist" Branch

Delaware Branch

Petrus (d. 1699)

Samuel (1675–1721)

James

James Asheton (1738–70)
(3 children)

John Bubenheim (1738–1807)
CONTINENTAL CONGRESS
(8 children)

Nicholas (1644–1707)
Secretary of the province of New York
m. *Judith Verlet* (accused of witchery)
(1 child)

Samuel (1669–1745)
New York Assembly

Stephen (b. 1700)
Mayor of New York; m. *Alida Vetch*,
granddaughter of Robert Livingston, 1st
Lord of the Manor

Samuel (1767–1840) Judge; m. *Martha Pintard*, niece of Richard ("the Signer") Stockton

Jane (1772–1851) Writer; m. *Andrew Kirkpatrick*, Chief Justice of New Jersey

Margaret (1778–1844) Novelist; m. *Samuel Harrison Smith*, newspaper publisher

James Asheton (1767–1815) SENATE ; m. *Ann Bassett*, daughter of Senator Richard Bassett

Littleton (1797–1859) HOUSE OF REPRESENTATIVES

Richard Henry (1796–1868) SENATE ; m. *Mary Carroll*, granddaughter of Charles Carroll of Carrollton ("the Signer") (8 children)

James Asheton (1799–1880) SENATE (3 children)

Florence (1865–1954) Suffrage leader m. *William S. Hilles*

Thomas Francis (1828–98) SENATE , Secretary of State

Thomas Francis (1868–1942) SENATE ; m. *Elizabeth Du Pont* (5 children)

Alexis I. Du Pont (1918–) Lieutenant Governor (6 children)

was in dubious recognition of his taste for fancy clothes, fine wines, and games of chance, rather than in honor of his supposed lineage.*

The reason Mrs. Bayard came to America was that her brother, Peter Stuyvesant, had been appointed director general of New Netherland. Stuyvesant, who was married to Bayard's sister, was a stern and stubborn colonial administrator. As governor of Curaçao he had had his right leg shot off, and his wooden substitute was decorated with a silver band. This was one of his few worldly affectations. His motto was "Trust in God rather than man." If the Dutch settlers had any question of where they stood with him, it was soon dispelled: "We derive our authority from God and the West India Company," he told them, "not from the pleasure of a few ignorant subjects."[3] This was hardly the lovable character whom Walter Huston portrayed in Knickerbocker Holiday. In the annals of colonial America he was remembered as "our great Muscovy Duke."[4]

Mrs. Bayard had many of her brother's characteristics. She was an imposing woman, religious, highly educated, with a sharp business mind and an imperious temper. However, she was apparently less inclined to deal harshly with those of dissenting views. When Stuyvesant had the Quaker Robert Hodgson tortured, she interceded with her brother and secured his release.[5]

The first Bayard politician was Nicholas, one of Anna's three sons. He was also the only Bayard to marry a woman who had been imprisoned for being a witch! The beautiful sorcerer was Judith Verlet. The charge filed against her in 1662 was that "Ann, the daughter of John Cole, who lived near a Dutch family, was seized in a strange manner with Fits, wherein her tongue was improved by a Demon . . . who confounded her language so that she made Utterances in Dutch, of which language she knew Nothing."[6] Since Judith spoke Dutch she was obviously the Demon who improved Ann Cole's speech. Her brother Nicholas Verlet, one of the richest merchants in New Amsterdam and the second husband of Anna Stuyvesant Bayard, rushed to his sister's defense. He brought with him a letter from Governor Stuyvesant to Governor Winthrop of Connecticut: "By this occasion of my brother-in-law being necessitated to make a second voyage to ayd his distressed sister, Judith Verlet, imprisoned, as we are informed, upon pretended accusation of Witchery, we really believe, and, out of faith, we dare assure, that she is innocent of such a crime. . . ."[7] Judith was then released.

Nicholas Bayard's stormy career in politics included thrice being imprisoned and once being sentenced to death. Starting as his uncle's pri-

* The French knight is pronounced Bá yàr'; the American family calls itself Bī'ērd.

vate secretary, he later managed to become mayor of New York and a member of the Governor's Council after Stuyvesant lost the colony to the English. When Jacob Leisler took over the government in the name of William of Orange, Bayard was heavily ironed and thrown into the dungeon. "Occasionally, to give him an airing, he was taken out, paraded through the fort and on the ramparts, as a spectacle to the scoffing mob."[8] Upon Leisler's downfall, Bayard had his chain "put on Leisler's leg" and was instrumental in getting him hanged for treason.[9]

This branch of the Bayard family was doing very well for itself until it chose the wrong side during the Revolutionary War. Nicholas' son married a Van Cortlandt; his grandson, a mayor of New York, married a granddaughter of Robert Livingston; and his great-grandson William owned all of Hoboken, New Jersey. This gentleman, who is usually called "Weeping Billy" Bayard, also had the ferrying monopoly between New York City and Hoboken.[10] It was his design to turn Hoboken into a tourist's delight. He had a thousand fruit trees planted on his property and advertised that New Yorkers would find there "every convenience for the entertainment of travellers."[11] Unfortunately for him, he preferred to retire to England when the shooting began. His vast estate was confiscated and sold to John Stevens for about $9000. (Where his home once stood is now located Stevens Institute of Technology.) After the peace negotiations John Jay, a cousin, saw Bayard on the street in London. "We passed each other as perfect strangers," records the American diplomat.[12]

These New York Bayards did not quite expire with American independence. A son of "Weeping Billy" amassed a sizable fortune (partly by judicious privateering during the War of 1812)†; a Bayard married General Arthur St. Clair (who managed to go bankrupt despite his wife's considerable dowry); and another married Stephen Van Rensselaer, the last patroon of central New York State.‡ But as America moved from colony to nation, it was the heirs of another son of Anna Stuyvesant Bayard who would make the family into a great political dynasty.[13]

† William Bayard, Jr. (1764–1826), was the first president of a savings bank in New York, organized in 1819; president, New York Chamber of Commerce, 1810–27; owner of the house on Greenwich Street to which Alexander Hamilton was brought after his fatal duel with Aaron Burr.

‡ Stephen Van Rensselaer (1789–1868), the husband of Harriet Elizabeth Bayard (1799–1875), was the son of General Stephen Van Rensselaer (1764–1839), who had been disastrously defeated at the battle of Queenstown Heights in the War of 1812, and had founded Rensselaer Polytechnic Institute. The general left an estate of 3000 farms comprising 436,000 acres in Rensselaer and Albany counties. These farms were rented in perpetuity, an arrangement that led to the bloody "anti-rent" war of upstate New York in the 1840s and forced Stephen Van Rensselaer the Younger to sell his vast holdings. With his death, even the manor passed out of the family.

One of the most outspoken opponents of the dictatorial Peter Stuyvesant was Augustin Herrman, agent for a big Dutch merchant house. He was born in Prague in 1621, emigrated to New Amsterdam by 1644, and married a sister of Judith Verlet, "the witch." Despite political differences, Stuyvesant esteemed Herrman's diplomatic talents and sent him on a number of delicate missions, including one to settle a land dispute in Maryland. The envoy was so enthralled by what he saw around the Chesapeake Bay that he proposed to map the entire province in return for 5000 acres of the desirable land. Lord Baltimore accepted the offer. Herrman's holdings eventually encompassed 25,000 acres, and, by a quirk of fate, he became indirectly responsible for the founding of the Bayard political dynasty.[14]

This great landlord had an unbalanced son, Ephraim, who became fiercely attached to a mystical religious sect called the Labadists. Founded by one Jean de Labadie, a Frenchman and sometime Jesuit, who lived entirely on herbs, his followers put much emphasis on the "inward light" and spartan rules of conduct. In 1680, after having been persecuted in most of the countries of Europe, the Labadists sent two emissaries to America to look for appropriate land.[15] In Ephraim Herrman they found both patron and convert, and he introduced them to a son of Anna Stuyvesant Bayard.

Although a deacon of the Dutch church, Petrus Bayard was in the midst of considerable religious turmoil, which was compounded by his dislike for urban living. How could one serve God in New Amsterdam, a city of traders?[16]

Much against his better judgment, Augustin Herrman deeded 3750 acres to his son's co-religionists, with Petrus Bayard acting as one of the trustees. The Labadists then proceeded to establish the first communistic settlement in the New World. The sect also practiced the separation of believer from unbeliever. Petrus the communist promptly left his wife.§ (Fortunately for the dynasty, he later returned to her.) The colony existed for only a half century and never included more than a hundred persons. But it brought the Bayards to the banks of the Delaware River.[17]

The heirs of Petrus Bayard were not as well connected socially or financially as their New York cousins, although they managed to accumulate comfortable landholdings. Petrus had twin great-grandsons, John Bubenheim Bayard and James Asheton Bayard, who married sisters.

§ Petrus Bayard married Blandian Kierstede, a granddaughter of Anneke Jans, whose claim to fame was that her estate on Manhattan Island was litigated by her heirs in a court fight that lasted over two hundred years. See George W. Schuyler, *Colonial New York, Philip Schuyler and His Family* (New York: Scribner's, 1885), Vol. II, pp. 337–62.

When James and his wife died at an early age, John adopted their three children, one of whom, James Asheton Bayard, became the first Bayard senator from Delaware.¶

John Bubenheim Bayard was one of the commercial leaders of Philadelphia, an early advocate of American independence, a member of the Sons of Liberty, the first of his dynasty to serve in Congress, and a militia colonel during the Revolution whose gallantry at the battle of Princeton was noted by Washington. After the Revolutionary War he lived in New Jersey, a move necessitated by financial reverses that were the result partly of his considerable contribution to the American cause and partly of business mismanagement by a son. He became mayor of New Brunswick and joined with his friend Alexander Hamilton in founding the city of Paterson, a financially disastrous venture, which was named in honor of Bayard's brother-in-law.[18]*

Bayard's contribution to his country was unique. He was neither an original thinker, an outstanding legislator, nor a great soldier. But he was a brilliant host. During his years in Philadelphia his home became a rallying place for Revolutionary leaders. John Adams wrote Abigail of his hospitality; his wines and choice meats were equally appreciated by Hancock, Sam Adams, Gerry, Lafayette, the Livingstons, Stockton, Hopkinson, Witherspoon, and James Wilson. Providing a pleasant common ground for patriots to discuss their disagreements or simply to forget them was a minor yet distinct achievement.

Of his five sons, two were of more than average ability: Andrew was the president of the Commercial Bank of Philadelphia for many years; Samuel married a niece of Richard ("The Signer") Stockton and was

¶ James Asheton Bayard, Sr. (1738–70), was a doctor. His other two children were John Hodge Bayard, who led an obscure life in western Maryland, and Jane Bayard, who died unmarried and insane.

* William Paterson (1745–1806) and John Bubenheim Bayard married daughters of Judge Anthony White of the Somerset County (N.J.) courts. They were brothers-in-law of General Anthony Walton White (1750–1803), adjutant general of New Jersey from 1793 until his death. See Somerset County Historical Quarterly, Vol. I, pp. 177 and 253; Vol. II, p. 5; Vol. VII, p. 111.

Paterson was the son of an Irish immigrant peddler who settled in Princeton in 1750. He studied law under Richard Stockton and was later the law teacher of Frederick Frelinghuysen. A member of the convention that wrote the U. S. Constitution, Paterson was considered by his fellow signer, William Pierce of Georgia, to be "one of those kind of men whose powers break in upon you, and create wonder and astonishment." Subsequently he was a U.S. senator, governor, and justice of the U. S. Supreme Court. He died in Albany, N.Y., while on a visit to his daughter, who was the second wife of General Stephen Van Rensselaer. See Willard Thorp, editor, The Lives of Eighteen from Princeton (Princeton: Princeton University Press, 1948), pp. 1–23.

sent to London by President Washington to prosecute American war claims as provided for in the Jay Treaty. He later became a local judge in New York and New Jersey, treasurer of Princeton College, and one of the founders of the Princeton Theological Seminary.[19]

But Bayard's exceptional children were his daughters Jane and Margaret. "I met with Miss Jane Bayard, who is a most charming girl," wrote Benjamin Rush to his wife in 1791. "Her reading, her eloquence, and her piety struck me very agreeably, and I have seldom been more delighted with a first interview with anyone. She seems to be intended both to adorn and enrich society by her talents and virtues."[20] This charming lady spent her long life ministering to the needs of her handsome and vain husband, Andrew Kirkpatrick, who was chief justice of New Jersey for nearly two decades.[21]† She refused to have any of her writing published while she was alive, but a posthumous volume reveals a sinewy style remarkably free of the literary curlicues of that day. It showed, said her daughter, a mind "bearing perhaps a tinge of melancholy."[22] A son of Jane Bayard Kirkpatrick served a single term in the Congress as a Democratic representative from New Jersey.

Margaret, John Bayard's other talented daughter, was the most gifted writer the dynasty produced. At eighteen, this fun-loving and fiery girl fell in love with Samuel Harrison Smith, a bookish newspaper editor. Despite the fact that his mother and Margaret's father were first cousins, and that his father had served with Margaret's father in Congress and on the Princeton board of trustees, there was strong parental opposition to a marriage.[23] Father Bayard's objections were probably threefold: the young man was not in a financial position to support his daughter; he was an impassioned Jeffersonian; and he was an "unbeliever" who rejected Christianity as a "fable." Being cast in the role of Juliet must have appealed to the romantic Margaret. She wrote her lover, "While I listen to a father whom I respect as equally as I love, and to the nearest friends I have, and discover all their sentiments and political principles directly opposed to you, my heart sickens within me. . . . How dare I hope that *you* alone are capable of rising superior to the prejudices of *family interest*, of education and party?"[24] Thomas Jefferson was inadvertently to become the matchmaker for the star-crossed couple.

Young Smith displayed a remarkably calm and judicious approach to

† Andrew Kirkpatrick (1756–1831) was the son of a member of the New Jersey legislature; a Princeton contemporary of James Madison and Richard Stockton; a law student of William Paterson; a member of the state Assembly (1797); and a justice of the state Supreme Court (1797–1824). His nephew, D. K. Este of Cincinnati, was a son-in-law of President William Henry Harrison. When the young man went west, Kirkpatrick gave him the following advice: "Never accept of an office till you are able to live without it." See James Grant Wilson, "Andrew Kirkpatrick," *Proceedings of the New Jersey Historical Society*, 2d Series, II (1872), pp. 79–97.

the news in an era when most newspapers were merely collections of gossip and partisan polemics. Moreover, he was an imaginative innovator and founder of the first newspaper in America to appear both morning and evening on the same day. (By printing two editions on one sheet, which was then cut in half, subscribers to his *New World* received two entirely different newspapers daily.) Such promise had not escaped Jefferson's notice; on the eve of the 1800 presidential election he offered Smith the financial backing to start a newspaper in Washington. Now in a position to support a wife, Samuel and Margaret were married, and left for the fledgling capital to found the *National Intelligencer*.

As the wife of an important editor, Margaret Bayard Smith became one of the pillars of Washington society. Her closest friends included the leading political figures of the first four decades of the nineteenth century—Jefferson, James and Dolley Madison, Henry Clay, cabinet members, senators, and congressmen. The Smiths were house guests at the famous plantations at Monticello and Montpelier. Margaret's letters to her sisters present a charming picture of life among the greats and their courtiers,[25] and many of the anecdotes that she first confided to them were later incorporated into a two-volume novel, *A Winter in Washington; or, Memoirs of the Seymour Family*, which was a decided literary success in 1824. Four years later she published her second novel, *What is Gentility? A Moral Tale*, in which she wrote, "Europeans have stigmatised us as a money-making people. If there is justice in the reproach, it is owing to the circumstance that *wealth* bestows distinction: take from it this power and infer it on *education*, and we shall then be a knowledge-seeking, and not a money-making people. . . ."[26]

When John B. Bayard adopted his brother's children he also became the stepfather of the first of four generations of Bayard senators. James Asheton Bayard graduated from Princeton in 1784. Three years later, now a lawyer, the future senator settled in Delaware. The move may have been caused by an estrangement from his foster father. A recent biographer could not find a single letter that James wrote to the old colonel over the next twenty years. And shortly after his arrival in Delaware, he wrote an uncle, "I would indulge myself in the pleasing expectation of seeing you at Christmas and the rest of my friends, if I thought they would approve and allow it."[27] Yet there is no explanation for cutting ties with the man who raised him and paid for his education. A possible cause of friction may have been James's religious beliefs, which cannot have been acceptable to the deeply devout Bayards of Philadelphia and New Brunswick. A Senate colleague, William Plumer of New Hampshire, later wrote of Bayard, "Having critically investigated the Christian theology, he became a deist—openly avowed and frankly maintained his opinion on that subject. . . ."[28]

Eight years after he moved to Wilmington, James A. Bayard took a step that firmly rooted him in the political life of his adopted state—he married Ann Bassett, the only child of Richard Bassett, a man of considerable wealth and a signer of the United States Constitution.‡ Another Founding Father said of Bassett, "He . . . has modesty enough to hold his Tongue."[29] It was a polite way of saying that he had contributed little to the important deliberations. However, Bassett was a leading force in making his state the first to ratify the Constitution, and later served as one of the first pair of senators from Delaware, and as a governor of the state. There was always a close relationship between Bayard and Bassett. The younger man acquired much legal knowledge from his wife's father. And at times Bassett would try to deflate his aspiring son-in-law by telling him, "All you know I taught you." To which Bayard's reply was, "You taught me all you knew, and all I know besides I taught myself."[30]

The tall, fair, well-proportioned Bayard was a man of considerable charm. "But," thought the puritanical Senator Plumer, "he lived too freely; he loved the pleasures of the table and of wine. . . . He was fond of cards." The best that Plumer could say of these addictions was that Bayard never appeared intoxicated "in the smallest degree," and though "he often remained at the card table all night," it never prevented him from attending to his duties in the Senate. Another of Bayard's often-mentioned characteristics was his remarkable ability as a public speaker.§ The French chargé d'affaires told him that, while most men are "great" on only one subject, "You Monsieur Bayard are *great* in debate in the halls of Congress, *great* at the dining table, *great* at wine and *great* at cards."[31]

With his gentleman's vices, it was fitting that Bayard also had a gentlemen's sense of honor. In 1800, after having been a member of the House of Representatives for three years, he fought a duel with a con-

‡ Bassett also had an adopted daughter Rachel, who married Joshua Clayton (1744–98), president of Delaware (1789–93), first governor of the state (1793–98), U.S. senator (1798); father and uncle of U.S. senators.

§ After Bayard delivered a six-and-a-half-hour speech in the Senate, Congressman-Manasseh Cutler commented: ". . . as a parliamentary speaker, perfectly at his ease—so careless, that he does not appear to have the least exercise of mind, and hardly to know, himself, that he is speaking, I doubt whether his equal can be found. And though his speaking seems to be as easy and as involuntary as his breathing, yet in the sublime, in pathos, in solemnity, as occasion requires, he arrests, he astonishes his auditory, but seems to know nothing about it himself." Quoted in John A. Munroe, editor, "William Plumer's Biographical Sketches of James A. Bayard, Caesar A. Rodney, and Samuel White," *Delaware History*, IV, No. 4 (September 1951), p. 360.

gressman from Rhode Island. Representative Champlin proposed that the salary of the collector of the port of Wilmington should be lowered. Representative Bayard considered this a personal insult, and the two repaired to a saw-pit shed because it was raining. In the exchange of shots, Bayard was wounded in the thigh and Champlin in the cheek. Honor now restored, the two fugitive congressmen went into hiding. "A prosecution is set on foot," wrote Speaker of the House Sedgwick. Bayard escaped to Wilmington; his second, John Rutledge, Jr., of South Carolina, reported that Mrs. Champlin, "at a dead hour of the Night, when men of quiet consciences were wrapped in sweet sleep, wrapped up her husband and stole him unheeded from the City." Two months later Bayard still feared to return to Philadelphia, and wrote his cousin Andrew, "I should have probably paid a visit to the city before this time if I had been entirely exempt from personal apprehensions. But as I have a great aversion from hard labour I have preferred renouncing the pleasure to running any risks. If the Governor would say that at all events a *nolle prosequi* should be granted I should feel myself restored to my ancient privilege of locomotion."[32] Bayard was soon back in circulation.

Although only thirty years old when he entered the Congress, Bayard quickly became one of the chief Federalist spokesmen in the House. While exhibiting some independence, he generally supported the policies of President John Adams. "The old man loves to be tickled now and then," Bayard wrote his father-in-law.[33] The congressman knew how to tickle. But as Adams made overtures to the French, Bayard, as a good Federalist, became disillusioned. In August 1800 he wrote Hamilton, "We must vote for him I suppose and therefore cannot safely say to every one what we think of him. But he has palsied the sinews of the party and if I relied on forebodings as ominous, I should believe that before another Presidential cycle had completed itself, he would give it its death wound."[34] Bayard prophesied correctly. The 1800 election would be the "death wound" of the Federalist Party. And Bayard's role in choosing the next President would have long-range ramifications for himself and his country.

Adams was defeated. But until Inauguration Day he still had the power of appointment, and there were deserving Federalists to be rewarded. Bayard secured one of the new federal District Court judgeships for his father-in-law. "2,000 dollars are better than any thing Delaware can give you," he reminded Bassett, "and not an unpleasant provision for life."[35] He was less successful in getting a judgeship for his cousin Samuel. Although he personally took the case to the President, it was vetoed by the New York congressional delegation, who had its own candidate. President Adams also considered making Bayard his Secretary of War, but then nominated him as United States minister to France. Reasons soon arose to cause the Delaware congressman to decline the honor.

Adams was defeated. But Jefferson was not yet elected. He and Aaron Burr had received the same number of electoral votes, since the ballots did not specify which vote was meant for President and which for Vice-President. This constitutional flaw would soon be corrected; in the meantime the election of a President would have to be settled by the House of Representatives, where each state would cast a single vote. As Delaware's lone congressman, Bayard's vote would be equal to that of the thirteen-man delegation from Pennsylvania. When the balloting began on February 11, 1801, Jefferson had eight states—nine were needed for election. Bayard's vote could decide the presidency, but he would vote with his party, and the Federalists were determined to vote for Burr. Jefferson, their archenemy, was too bitter a pill to swallow.

After eight ballots, Representative John Randolph sent a hurried note to his stepfather, St. George Tucker: "Eight states for Jefferson—six for Burr—two, Maryland and Vermont, divided. . . ."[36] In the divided states the Federalist congressmen had agreed to follow Bayard's lead; the representative from tiny Delaware now controlled three crucial votes.

The balloting droned on without change through Wednesday, Thursday, Friday, Saturday, and Monday.

Bayard became convinced that there would not be a breakthrough for Burr. He was also convinced that the nation must have a President on March 4. Bayard could make Jefferson President, but, as a practical politician, he hoped that "instead of being obliged to surrender at discretion, we might obtain terms of capitulation."[37] Bayard wanted Jefferson to agree to continue the Federalist fiscal system, to maintain a neutrality between England and France, to preserve the size of the navy, and to keep minor officials in office. He particularly feared for the job of Allen McLane, the Wilmington port collector over whose salary he had fought a duel. The emissary between Bayard and Jefferson was General Samuel Smith, a congressman from Maryland, who, after talking to Jefferson, assured Bayard that his terms were acceptable. The Federalist congressman then announced his decision to his party's caucus. "It has produced great clamour," Bayard told his father-in-law, "and the violent spirits of the Party denounced me as a Deserter of the Party."[38]

As soon as the results of the thirty-sixth ballot were announced, Bayard wrote Collector McLane, "Mr. Jefferson is our President. . . . I have taken good care of you, and think, if prudent, you are safe."[39] Editor Samuel Harrison Smith told his readers, "The voice of the people has prevailed."[40]

Bayard wrote his cousin Andrew, "We have made a President. . . ."[41]

More accurately and less modestly, he might have said, "I have made a President." And his action had quick repercussions for himself, his father-in-law, and his cousin Margaret's husband, Samuel Harrison Smith. Having been nominated and confirmed as minister to France, Bayard now declined the post. "As I had given the *turn* to the election," he wrote, "it was impossible for me to accept an office which would be held on the tenure of Mr. Jefferson's pleasure. My ambition shall never be gratified at the expense of a suspicion."[42] Richard Bassett also lost his job when the Republicans repealed the Judiciary Act, despite the arguments of Bayard, which John Adams called "comprehensive, masterly and compleat."[43] Jefferson's election was more satisfactory for Samuel Harrison Smith. The new Administration gave his newspaper the government's printing, and later President Madison made him commissioner of revenue.¶

As a Federalist, Bayard now became a member of a permanent minority. He wrote his good friend Caesar A. Rodney that "being only a Looker-on I amuse myself with the scene as it passes by."[44] But while complaining about his passive role, he did not take his work in Congress too seriously, and generally arrived in Washington two or three months after a session began. "It was an understanding between him and the people of Delaware," said Senator Plumer.[45] But all Delawareans were not enchanted with the arrangements. "A poor Farmer" complained in the *American Watchman*, a Wilmington publication, that Bayard was making fifteen or twenty dollars a day by "petty-fogging at New Castle" instead of attending Congress at six dollars a day."[46] Then in 1802 the casual congressman lost his seat to Rodney by fifteen votes. When the results were announced in Wilmington "a multitude" paraded and fired cannons, including one loaded with potatoes and herring.[47] Returning to Delaware, however, was not a disagreeable task for Bayard. After a few months he wrote Rodney:

I have been employed in the homely drudgery of making money, and you in the refined and elegant pursuits of attaining honour and reputation. I perceive plainly by the papers that you have not failed (as I knew you could not) in acquiring your object, and I have been as little disappointed as to mine. We are strange beings my friend, we contend for objects without knowing their value or insignificancy. The course of things forced us into a competition in which the successful party was to be the loser.[48]

¶ Smith sold the *National Intelligencer* in 1810. He later served as president of the Branch Bank of the United States, located in the District of Columbia. The Smiths had one son, Jonathan Bayard H. Smith (1810–89), who married a grandniece of Martha Washington. He was a lawyer in the capital until the Civil War, when, being a Southern sympathizer, he left the city. He died in California.

(Theirs was a strange rivalry indeed, for Bayard and Rodney were deeply devoted to each other. They loved to share wine, terrapin, snipe shooting, and off-color jokes about their friend Senator Outerbridge Horsey, who was first getting married at a late age. Bayard firmly believed, as he wrote Rodney, that "Political opinion need not have an influence on personal sentiment. That we are of different political Parties, and so likely to remain is very certain. . . . I believe you are a little more *peopleick* than myself, but that will wear off after carrying your share of government for awhile."[49])

No matter how much Bayard preferred making money to serving in Congress, he found himself back in Washington in 1804, having been elected to the United States Senate. He would remain in the Senate until 1813, becoming more and more frustrated as he helplessly watched the Administration move toward war with Great Britain. But the Senate was not all bad; it did provide him with the pleasure of annoying Senator John Quincy Adams of Massachusetts. The two men heartily despised each other. They continually accused one another of betraying Federalism, which was often true since they both displayed personal independence. On one occasion, after having been attacked by Bayard, Adams confided to his diary, "I believe my talents . . . greater than his, excepting that of unpremeditated eloquence. Of that I have very little, and he more than any man I ever heard in Congress." John Quincy also satisfied himself by adding, "I know my moral and political principles to be more pure than his; and this is saying little, for his are very loose."[50]

It was therefore ironic that James Asheton Bayard and John Quincy Adams should serve compatibly on the commission that ended the War of 1812. For Bayard, his work at Ghent was the premature close of a distinguished public career. For Adams, it was the virtual beginning of a career that would take him to the presidency. The appointment of Bayard was designed to give the peace negotiations a bipartisan character. He was expected to represent the Federalist point of view. Feeling that he could not with propriety retain his Senate seat and serve on the commission, Bayard resigned from the Senate. At Ghent Adams found his old adversary to be "entirely *another man*, with good health, good spirits, good humour, always reasonable," and "an American to the quick."[51] Without the brilliance of Albert Gallatin, Henry Clay, or Adams, Bayard was nonetheless highly competent and the most even-tempered of a volatile group. He was particularly adept at cooling down Adams and Clay when New England and Western interests were in conflict. And he was the only commissioner with whom the others were always sociable. Bayard significantly contributed to extracting his country with honor from a war he wished it had never entered. When peace was finally concluded, President Madison moved Adams from the Russian

legation to London and asked Bayard to become minister to Russia. But
Bayard was deathly ill and declined the post. Within a week of his
triumphant return to Delaware in August 1815, Bayard was dead. He
was forty-eight years old. His father-in-law, Richard Bassett, died a week
later, and a joint funeral service was held for the two statesmen.*

Matriculation at Princeton had become a tradition with the Bayards.
But family ties alone were not enough to keep the high-spirited Richard
Henry Bayard out of trouble. In 1812 Senator James A. Bayard wrote of
his oldest son, "The intelligence from Princeton has caused me some
anxiety. . . . I have written a feeling and a pretty sharp letter to Richard and most positively interdicted the use of any ardent spirits or
segars."[52] Liquor and tobacco were not the only temptations in Richard's path. A year after the senator's warning letter, an angry faculty
"collected at three oclock in the morning, in consequence of an unwar-
rantable ringing of the bell."[53] The professors traced a cord tied to the
bell clapper to Richard's room. It was grounds for expulsion. However,
several months later he was reinstated and graduated with his class in
1814.

A Bayard was next expected to study law. But there was a war on,
and Richard could not keep his mind on *Tucker's Commentaries on
Blackstone*. So, while his father was settling the peace, Ann Bassett
Bayard got her son an army commission. Richard was finally admitted
to the bar in 1818 with two distinct advantages over other young attorneys: first, he inherited many of his late father's clients; second, he
had married Mary Sophia Carroll, a noted beauty and the granddaughter
of Charles Carroll of Carrollton, the richest man to sign the Declaration
of Independence.† The young couple purchased the Wilmington mansion
of John Dickinson, the "Pennsylvania farmer" of Stamp Act days, and
assumed their rightful place as lions of society.

Richard Henry Bayard's introduction to the United States Senate was
not as an elected member but as a defender of his father. In 1830 the
memoirs of Jefferson were published, in which the Sage of Monticello
strongly denied that he and Bayard had made a deal for the presidency
in 1801. The son rushed to Washington with documents to clear the
family name. The disposition of General Smith, the intermediary,
strongly supported Bayard's claims. The case boiled down to whether
Jefferson actually knew that Smith was speaking for Bayard or was

---

* Bayard's estate provided an assured annuity of $3000 a year for his wife,
lump sums of $10,000 each to his four sons, $8000 each to his two daughters,
and considerable land in Maryland and Delaware divided among his heirs.
See Morton Borden, *The Federalism of James A. Bayard* (New York: Columbia University Press, 1955), p. 201.

† See Kennedy Dynasty, pp. 481, 484.

merely quizzing the presidential candidate for his own edification. Bayard certainly *thought* that Smith had arranged the deal; Jefferson's later denial was less tenable. Years later Albert Gallatin wrote of Bayard to Henry A. Muhlenberg: "Although he was one of the principal and warmest leaders of the Federal party and had a personal dislike for Mr. Jefferson, it was he who took the lead and from pure patriotism directed all those movements of the sounder and wiser part of the Federal party which terminated in the peaceable election of Mr. Jefferson."[54]

In 1832 Wilmington was chartered as a city, and Richard Henry Bayard was elected its first mayor, with power to hold court and perform marriages. It was the beginning of a public career that would span two decades. He was elected to the Senate in 1836 and resigned three years later to become chief justice of the Delaware Supreme Court. Then in 1841, largely because of John M. Clayton's support, Bayard was again elected to the Senate. But when his term expired in 1845 Clayton wanted the seat for himself. Richard put up a fight, but he was no match for Clayton's political machine. He was never elected to office again, although he served as American chargé d'affaires to Belgium from 1850 to 1853. The second of the Delaware dynasty was a good Whig but an insignificant statesman.

The main thrust of the Delaware dynasty in the second generation was provided by Richard Henry's younger brother, James Asheton Bayard, Jr. While Richard was a Whig, James was a Democrat. And since Delaware has always been a strongly conservative state, James's success had to wait until his party assumed the conservative position. As long as the Democrats were the party of Jackson and Van Buren, James A. Bayard was bound to fail in Delaware. (He was defeated for the House of Representatives in 1828, 1832, and 1834.) Jackson appointed him as one of five government directors of the United States Bank in 1834. However, when the other four failed to be confirmed by the Senate, Bayard asked the President to withdraw his name. He might have become a senator in 1838, but the Whig state Senate preferred to leave the seat vacant than to elect a Democrat. Only when the Democrats became the party of Pierce and Buchanan was the political success of Bayard assured.

The third of his family to be a United States senator, he was elected in 1851, re-elected in 1857 and 1863, and served until his resignation in 1864. He represented a slave state, although in 1860 Delaware only had 1798 slaves in a population of 112,216. In the growing controversy over slavery, the people of Delaware preferred not to rock the boat. The second James A. Bayard spoke for their interests: "All I care about is to see that the State does not become abolitionist or squatter sovereignized."[55]

When the Democratic Party met at Charleston to choose a candidate for the 1860 presidential election, Bayard's one interest was to stop Stephen B. Douglas. This proving impossible, the senator from Delaware bolted the convention along with the delegations from Alabama, Mississippi, Florida, Texas, South Carolina, Louisiana, and Georgia, and nominated John Breckinridge of Kentucky.[56] He then succeeded in having Breckinridge endorsed by the Democratic Party of Delaware. Actually this ticklish job was left to his able young lieutenant, Thomas F. Bayard, his son, while he vacationed at Saratoga Springs and Newport.[57]

Looking ahead to the fall election, Captain Samuel Francis Du Pont, a naval officer with Republican sympathies, predicted that in Delaware "the Douglas vote will be confined to the Paddies, but this will not draw enough from the Regular Democratic ticket to defeat it."[58] He was correct: Breckinridge carried the state; Douglas finished a poor fourth.

As the powder keg was about to explode in April 1861, Senator Bayard naïvely took a business and pleasure trip through the South. At Montgomery he heard the news that Fort Sumter had been fired upon. He opposed Lincoln's proclamation for troops and wrote that a Northern invasion would be "a costly experiment and utterly impracticable." If Delaware submitted to Northern despotism, he said, then it was not the state for him to live in. His son replied that "the abolitionists are rampant," he should carry a revolver at all times, and should change his rail route home in order to evade possible violence. A few days later in Philadelphia an angry mob did threaten his life.[59]

Senator Bayard was forced to amplify his position in a public statement. There were only two alternatives in his opinion: war or peaceful separation and recognition of Southern independence. Peaceful disunion, he said, was preferable to war. Thomas F. Bayard echoed his father's sentiments in a speech at Dover that would plague him for the rest of his political career.

The Bayards clung to their convictions throughout the war. In the Senate, James opposed all of the anti-slavery measures. Emancipation in the District of Columbia he declared to be an outrageous invasion of property rights and likely to cause disloyalty in the border states. He was the only senator who would not take the "ironclad" oath of allegiance to the federal government. Then in January 1864 the Senate adopted a resolution requiring all of its members to take the oath. Bayard complied, and resigned. After thirteen years in the Senate, he told his colleagues, he had "lost the hope" of being of service "to my country or to my state."[60] With tears in his eyes the old senator said good-by. (In 1960 Senator John F. Kennedy used Bayard's action as an argument against college loyalty oaths.[61])

In Delaware the senator's son was the unofficial head of the state's Southern sympathizers. Thomas F. Bayard was a first lieutenant in the Delaware Guard, a state militia organization that was feared by the federal government to have disloyal companies. But when General Henry Du Pont, who was later to win the Congressional Medal of Honor for heroism at the battle of Cedar Creek, gave the order to disarm such units, young Bayard refused to surrender his equipment and was arrested. His father took the case to the Secretary of War and a parole was arranged. Mrs. Sophie Du Pont wrote to her naval captain husband that Thomas wished to be made a martyr until he found that he might be imprisoned "in the interesting deserts of Accomac[k] county, Virginia," then he changed his mind.[62]‡

Yet James and Thomas Bayard, more accurately than the Du Ponts, reflected the feelings of the state of Delaware. In 1867 Governor Gove Saulsbury appointed James to the United States Senate. And in January 1869 the Delaware legislature elected him to the unexpired portion of the term he had resigned five years before. On the same day the legislature elected his son Thomas to succeed him for a full six-year term. On March 4, 1869, the elective career of James A. Bayard, Jr., ended, and the elective career of Thomas F. Bayard began. The fourth Bayard senator from Delaware would rise higher and shine brighter than any of his illustrious ancestors.

The new senator, in the opinion of the New York *World,* had "the unconscious grace of a pure Bayard."[63] Eugene Field, the poet and journalist, first saw and described Thomas in 1872: "The exceeding pallor of his face, the luster of his eyes, and the weird carelessness with which his long, black, bushy hair was tossed about his head, gave the man a certain distinct fascination."[64] While his Senate colleague, George Hoar, saw in him another Bayard characteristic—the ability to announce "a familiar moral principle as if it were something the people

‡ Yet there was one Bayard whose faith in the Union cause never wavered. He was George Dashiell Bayard (1835–62), a great-grandson of John Bubenheim Bayard. He graduated from West Point in 1856 and went to serve on the frontier, where he was badly wounded in an engagment with the Kiowa Indians. When the Civil War broke out George was a second lieutenant and cavalry instructor at West Point. In thirteen months he rose to the rank of brigadier general, becoming known as one of the most dashing officers in the Army of the Potomac. At the battle of Fredericksburg, on December 13, 1862, he was mortally wounded by a cannon ball. The twenty-seven-year-old hero was buried with military honors at Princeton. See *National Cyclopaedia of American Biography*, Vol. IX, p. 224

who listened to him were hearing for the first time, and of which he in his youth had been the original discoverer."[65]

Thomas F. Bayard became a fixture in the Senate. He remained there for sixteen years. And later, when he was Secretary of State, he told a Washington newspaperman "that he had made a great mistake in accepting the [cabinet] post, that his sphere was in the Senate and he should have remained there."[66] Yet like his father and his grandfather before him, Senator Bayard was rarely on the winning side of an issue.

During a high tariff era he stood for freer trade—as long as the interests of the Du Ponts were not adversely affected. (He opposed a reduction of duty on gunpowder and on matches for those who "were not a light unto themselves."[67])

During the Reconstruction era he stood firmly for States' Rights. When Senator Sumner introduced a civil rights bill, including provision for equal accommodations, Bayard replied:

What powers under the Constitution can be found to authorize the Congress of the United States to enter the States and take into their hands every domestic institution which is covered by this bill? The school, the house of public entertainment, the means of common carriage, the place of amusement, even Sir, the grave itself is not kept sacred for independent wish. . . . You are seizing into the hands of the Federal power the entire police control of the States.[68]

Only on the issue of corruption in the Grant Administration did Bayard have a limited success. His investigation of fraud in the New York Custom House resulted in the removal of Collector Murphy, who was replaced by Chester A. Arthur.

As the articulate voice of conservatism, Bayard became a three-time candidate for the presidential nomination. His cause was supported by the men holding "healthy financial views," as the Walla Walla *Statesman* put it,[69] including such illustrious names as Fitzhugh Lee, August Belmont, Maryland's Governor Carroll, Saltonstall of Massachusetts, Stockton of New Jersey, Hampton of South Carolina, and in Baltimore what Montgomery Blair called "the Maryland Club and the city aristocratic circles."[70] At Harvard, with Theodore Roosevelt as presiding officer, the student body voted overwhelmingly for Bayard.

Yet Bayard's presidential aspirations were destined to be frustrated. At the 1876 Democratic Convention he received only 33 votes; in 1880 he came closer, getting 153½ on the first ballot, but was then swept aside by the bandwagon for General Winfield Hancock. He showed his greatest strength in 1884, when he received 168 votes, only to lose to Grover Cleveland on the second ballot. Bayard simply had too many handicaps. Delaware carried no weight on the national scales. His Civil

War record made him an unattractive choice in the North, where Ohio newsman Frank Carpenter spoke for his section: "Living on the line between the North and the South, he [Bayard] was too lukewarm to be a Rebel and too timorous to be a Union man. He ended up by being the worst cross known in American politics, a Copperhead. . . ."[71] Yet Bayard's sympathies were not rewarded by full Southern support. Dixie politicians had their own problems. They were under increasing pressure from the inflationary Greenbackers, and Bayard's "hard currency" position would not do.

Moreover, Bayard would not actively seek the office. In 1880 he went so far as to authorize a Baltimore *Sun* editorial writer to put together a campaign biography, but even this appeared too late to have an influence on the delegates.[72] The paraphernalia of his candidacy in 1884—some white hats with tiny blue feathers, and some satin badges imprinted with blue hens—were no match for Cleveland's well-oiled machine. As the San Francisco *Call* commented, "Bayard . . . is somewhat too much of the Charles Francis Adams type of politician to achieve success in any party as party machinery now exists. . . ."[73] The delegates were devoted to Bayard, the man who had fearlessly spoken out for the party during the lean years. But make him their presidential candidate? Their first obligation was to pick a winner. As Congressman Stevens told the New York *Tribune,* "No man has a higher admiration for Bayard than I . . . but it would be a suicidal attempt to nominate him."[74] The chairman of the Massachusetts delegation in 1876 spoke for the party professionals when he said, "If this was a body to select a *President,* and not to nominate a *candidate,* I believe that Mr. Bayard would be the unanimous choice of the Convention."[75] (In the next century another senator, Robert A. Taft, would share the same fate.)

When the Democrats finally captured the White House, Grover Cleveland made Bayard his Secretary of State. Socially he was well qualified for the post—charming, cultivated, dignified.[76] "Carp" of the Cleveland *Leader* wrote that he "never sits down to dinner in anything less formal than a swallowtail coat and a white necktie. His family has the bluest of blue blood in their veins, and I doubt not that the English *Book of Heraldry* has a place on their parlor table."[77] Substantively, Bayard was a less appropriate choice. He had been chairman of the Senate Finance Committee, not the Committee on Foreign Relations. His main venture in external affairs had been to advise Secretary of State Hamilton Fish, a distant relative, on the American brief in the *Alabama* claims case.

Despite party clamor for patronage after twenty-four years in the wilderness, Secretary Bayard generally made creditable diplomatic appointments. The Austro-Hungarian government refused to accept his choice of Anthony M. Keiley as American minister because he was married to a Jew. The imperial court found "that his domestic relations preclude that reception of him by Vienna society which we judge desirable for the representative of the United States. . . ." Bayard promptly informed the Austro-Hungarian minister at Washington that "religious liberty is the bedrock of the American system."[78] He then appointed Keiley to an international tribunal at Alexandria, Egypt, and deliberately left the Vienna post vacant for two years.

With one exception—getting Bismarck to retreat from his imperialistic demands in Samoa—Bayard passed on to his successor the major problems of foreign relations. Such issues as the proposed isthmus canal, the Alaskan boundary, regulation of the fur-seal fisheries, relations with the Hawaiian Islands, and a Venezuelan boundary dispute were left unresolved. His treaty with Great Britain to settle the long-standing controversy over Northeast fishery rights was rejected by the Senate. It was a presidential year, and, as one Republican senator said, "We cannot allow the Democrats to take credit for settling so important a dispute."[79]

There was also some diplomatic unpleasantness in the 1888 presidential election. The British minister had been tricked into supporting Cleveland, which brought forth gleeful howls from the Republicans and forced Bayard to ask London for his recall. The New York *Tribune* imagined Bayard bursting into doggerel:

> Believe me that I made him go
>   for nothing that he wrote,
> But just because, as well you know,
>   I fear the Irish vote.[80]

Four years later when Cleveland was once more back in the White House, Bayard was not offered the chief cabinet portfolio. Perhaps to lessen the disappointment, the President raised the English mission to ambassadorial rank and made his former Secretary of State the first American ambassador to the Court of St. James's. Bayard was given James Roosevelt, Franklin Delano Roosevelt's half brother, as his first secretary. "Rosy," as the young man was called, had married the great-granddaughter of John Jacob Astor and a daughter of *the* Mrs. Astor. Having contributed $10,000 to the Cleveland campaign fund, he received the London post as the return on his money. Bayard was not pleased with his assistant. He wrote to a friend, "Mr. Roosevelt has suddenly put off to the United States and I believe intends to go to Egypt before he returns here. In the strictest confidence I may say that his absence is not to be regretted. . . . Happily there are no serious questions now which threaten the peace of the two countries, and if there were, Mr. Roosevelt would probably array himself against me. . . ."[81]

When Bayard reached England the United States was entering the era of the "big stick." As the noted international lawyer John Bassett Moore remarked, "We had been so long without a war that our people were growing nervous and irritable lest the world might think us not worth insulting."[82] Bayard was out of step with the times. He believed his job was to cement good relations between his country and the country to which he was accredited. This hardly fitted into the plans of Theodore Roosevelt and Henry Cabot Lodge, who had their own reasons for attacking the "Anglomaniacs." While vacationing in London, Lodge wrote home: "Did you ever hear of such an ass? You have no idea of what a cipher Bayard is here. None of the important men know him or notice him and he goes about making speeches at school festivals and other second rate things and eulogizes Cleveland and the Queen."[83] Republicans in the House of Representatives also looked for excuses to attack the ambassador. When Bayard equated "protection" with "state socialism," the high tariff advocates introduced a resolution of censure, and, despite an able defense by Congressman Henry St. George Tucker, the motion passed by a vote of 182 to 72.

Bayard retired at the end of the second Cleveland Administration in 1897. The English people presented him with a massive silver loving cup, nineteen and a half inches high, with figures of Britannia and Columbia clasping hands and holding olive branches over a bust of Thomas F. Bayard. He was sixty-nine and, according to the New York *World*, had a fortune estimated at $300,000.[84] But he had only a year to enjoy it. He died on September 28, 1898. A graceful opponent, John Hay, who had replaced him as ambassador to the Court of St. James's, issued a eulogy:

His scorn of everything mean or base; his disregard of consequences in the pursuit of what he thought right; his frank expectation of that sympathy which he was so ready to give; his belief in the sincerity of others, being himself absolutely sincere—all these qualities, even more than his good looks and gallant bearing, gave the impression not only of a young man, but of one who would always be young.[85]

The late ambassador had two politically oriented children to carry the family tradition into the twentieth century.

The outspoken Florence Bayard Hilles, his daughter, became an important suffragist, who led the first votes-for-women parade through the streets of Wilmington in 1915, was jailed in 1917 for leading a march around the White House, and was chairman of the National Woman's Party from 1933 to 1938. During the First World War she also shocked polite Wilmington by going to work in a munitions plant; she said it was the patriotic duty of physically fit women to replace men in industry during the emergency.[86]

Her brother Thomas F. Bayard, Jr., who would become the fifth of his name to be United States senator from Delaware, was married to a great-granddaughter of the founder of E. I. Du Pont de Nemours and Company. Bayard's father-in-law, Alexis Irenee Du Pont, had been vice-president and twenty per cent owner of the family business at the time of his elder brother Eugene's death in 1901. The passing of Eugene, the firm's president, left a leadership vacuum in the immediate family, and the surviving relatives sold out to Coleman Du Pont, a second cousin, who immediately made over four million dollars on the transaction without investing any of his own money.

But Coleman, a Rabelaisian character, was not content with merely being immensely rich. From his twenty-first-floor suite at the Hotel McAlpin in New York City, which he had built in partnership with Charles P. Taft, Coleman threw parties for "half the chorus of a Broadway show."[87] He also had political ambitions. At one point he even considered himself a potential President. This money could not buy. But he did get himself appointed to the United States Senate when an incumbent resigned in 1921.

The people of Delaware had been expecting a direct confrontation between Bayards and Du Ponts for nearly a century. In 1922 there were two senatorial contests on the Delaware ballot. One was for the remainder of the unexpired term held by Senator Coleman Du Pont; the other for a full six-year term to begin on March 4, 1923. The Republicans nominated Du Pont for both terms; the Democrats chose Thomas F. Bayard, Jr.—also for both terms.

Tom Bayard was a little too blunt to be fully appreciated by the professional politicians. And the people didn't know quite what to make of a fellow who shunned the conventional four-in-hand necktie in favor of a flowing black silk affair that overlapped his lapels. But as he told a reporter, "I've lived and breathed politics all my life." And he knew how to wage a clever campaign. There were two things going for him— a strong Democratic trend in the country, and the vote of Delaware's Republican congressman against an anti-lynching bill which pushed the Negroes into the Democratic camp. Another important factor was of his own making. Coleman Du Pont had built Delaware's highway and given it as a gift to the state. As each section of the road was completed a motion picture camera recorded its donor strutting by the roadside. These films, which became an integral part of the Du Pont campaign, gave Bayard the opportunity to drive home an effective point: My opponent, he charged, is "bribing you with the road in order to remind you, when driving over it, to vote for him." By election day Du Pont was forced to declare vehemently, "I don't want your votes if you only give them to me because I built that road!"[88]

The election proved that, while the Du Ponts may own the state, the Bayards run it—even if Tom Bayard's campaign was primarily paid for by Mrs. Elizabeth Bradford Du Pont, his mother-in-law.[89] He won the short term by 60 votes and the long term by 325.

In Washington Senator Bayard continued the States' Rights, conservative tradition that had become synonymous with the family name. He told a New York audience in 1925, "I am an old-fashioned Democrat. I may even say that I am a reactionary Democrat, for I follow the principles of Thomas Jefferson."[90] The fifth Bayard senator served only one term. He was badly defeated in the Hoover landslide of 1928. Said a New York *Times* editorial, "Tidal waves can't be expected to be discriminating. Indifferently they sweep in and sweep out; and are as likely to damage as to improve. Delaware is entitled to as much free choice as she is allowed to exercise in the matter of Senators, but in substituting a sometime Republican Governor [John G. Townsend, Jr.] for Thomas Francis Bayard, the advantage to her is not evident. The loss to the Senate and to the public is plain and great. . . . More than once he has refused to follow the majority of his party in its hankering after isms, worship of strange gods and neglect of the merits for political purposes."[91]

In 1952 a Bayard made an attempt to become the sixth of his family elected to the U. S. Senate. Alexis I. Du Pont Bayard, son of the fifth senator, was the Democratic opponent of incumbent John J. Williams. Lex Bayard had an impressive record: he went from Princeton into the marines in 1941, rose from private to captain, was in the regiment that placed the flag atop Mount Suribachi on Iwo Jima, and was wounded in the leg during that engagement. After the war he got a law degree at the University of Virginia and plunged into Delaware politics. A Wilmington *Journal-Every Evening* reporter wrote in 1948 that "Mr. Bayard admits it has been in his mind for as long as he can remember, some day to enter politics."[92] In that year he was elected lieutenant governor, at thirty the youngest in Delaware history.

But Senator Williams, the Millsboro chicken feed dealer and relentless exposer of government misfeasance, nonfeasance, and malfeasance, was an immovable object in the path of the ambitious young man. In 1952 Williams was riding a wave of popularity that had come to him as a result of uncovering graft and influence peddling in the Reconstruction Finance Corporation and the Internal Revenue Bureau. What Bayard was up against was evident from the wording of the *Delaware State News*'s endorsement of his opponent: "Senator Williams has done a brilliant job in the United States Senate. His investigations and subsequent airing of scandal and bribery and tax evasion has earned him a national reputation. More than any one man in our entire government,

Williams has demonstrated the inner rottenness of the Truman Administration."[93]

The youthful Democratic candidate hit hard at Williams' "isolationist" record, calling him one of the "greatest political ostriches of our times."[94] Breaking with his political ancestors, he went down the line for liberal policies. He plugged for civil rights, foreign aid, and against the McCarran Immigration Act. He told the farmers they never had it so good and had the full backing of organized labor, both nationally and in the state. The AFL's League for Political Education gave him one of his largest contributions.[95] Williams replied: "Mr. Bayard, who does not know what it means to earn his own living, cannot possibly understand the problems of working people."[96] Harry Truman whistle-stopped through Delaware and told a small early morning crowd at the Wilmington railroad station "that the grandfathers of Bayard and Governor Stevenson had served under President Cleveland."[97] It was a fact that apparently impressed the history-buff President but made little impact on the voters. General Eisenhower easily carried the state and Senator Williams led the ticket.

Since his defeat for the Senate, Bayard has become a senior partner in a Wilmington law firm that represents such blue-chip corporations as the United States Fidelity and Guaranty Company, Travelers Insurance Company, United States Time Corporation, the Pennsylvania Railroad, the Baltimore and Ohio, and the Reading Company.[98] He was also the owner of the Wilmington *Sunday Star*, which folded in 1954; ran for presidential elector in 1956; served as chairman of the Delaware Citizens for Kennedy Committee in 1960; and at the moment is a member of the Delaware River and Bay Authority.[99]

By breeding and tradition the Bayards have been part of "the class of gentry who looked upon themselves less as the representatives of the people than as their guardians and protectors"—as General James G. Wilson said of the first of this dynasty to serve in Congress.[100] As members of the American aristocracy, over the years they have linked fortunes through marriage with the Washingtons of Virginia; the Carrolls, Howards, and Wirts of Maryland; the Bassetts and Du Ponts of Delaware; the Kembles, Kirkpatricks, Stevenses, and Stocktons of New Jersey; the Stuyvesants, De Lanceys, Jays, Livingstons, Pintards, and Schuylers of New York; the Bowdoins and Winthrops of Massachusetts.

In tiny Delaware the Bayards have now thrived for five generations. One might have expected to find more political dynasties nurtured by the smaller states with relatively stable populations, where lines of loyalty could be firmly fixed over the years. Yet this has not generally been the case. Some of the smaller states are without national dynasties, while others have flourished in the larger states. It would appear that dynasts, a remarkably restless breed, have often been attracted to those areas where the political stakes are high. Some have even been known to pull up sturdy roots to seek greener pastures.

Yet Delaware has been fertile soil for the Bayards' brand of conservatism. Whether Federalist, Whig, or Democrat—the Diamond State and its leading political family have hewed to the right. Convinced of their own rightness and having the political constituency to support their convictions, the Bayards never raised expedience above conviction. The first James A. Bayard opposed the solid phalanx of his party by supporting Jefferson in 1801; the second James A. Bayard opposed the full force of the Senate during the Civil War; the first Thomas F. Bayard pitted himself against the might of a new American imperialism.

But the United States was moving too quickly to look back; the time to conserve was always in the future. So the Bayards since the close of the Federalist period have been interesting without being important, dissenters rather than movers. Perhaps the present generation signals a shift to the vital center where American policy is made. But through a century and a quarter in the Senate the Bayards never knew the luxury of being in the majority.

The Taft Dynasty

"No Taft, to my knowledge, has ever neglected a public duty for the sake of gratifying a private desire."

—Mrs. Alphonso Taft[1]

CINCINNATI has a certain rhythm that must be sensed if the city is to be understood," writes George Sessions Perry. "It is calm and has a kind of simple poise which its most circumspect elements describe as serenity, and which the progressive forces call complacency. Though quietly merry, it is somehow deliberate and legalistic, instead of being either intuitive or impulsive. . . ."[2] The Tafts of Cincinnati equally fit this description. For the association between the city of Cincinnati and the family of Taft, like other long marriages, has given to each the characteristics of the other. Their years together have made the resemblance so complete that it is now difficult to tell which takes after the other.

The city today seems to stand as a sprawling monument to its First Family. Streets, buildings, and institutions memorialize three generations of Tafts: Alphonso Taft Hall at the Law School of the University of Cincinnati; William Howard Taft Road, a main street that runs through suburbs into Walnut Hills; the Taft Museum, honoring Charles Phelps and Annie Sinton Taft; the Robert A. Taft High School; the Anna Louise Inn, a working girl's hotel named after a daughter of the elder Charles Tafts; Taft Drive, near Taft Field; Taft Theater and Taft Auditorium; Taft Field Tavern and Taft Road Tavern; Taft Sanitary Engineering Company; Taft Elementary School and Taft Branch Post Office.

The Tafts traveled far afield, gathering in the highest political and judicial honors in the land, and their city basked in the reflected glory; while at home, from Alphonso Taft's tenure on the City Council in the 1840s to his great-grandson Charles's fight for charter government since the 1920s, they fought to build Queen City in their image—neat, orderly, open-minded.

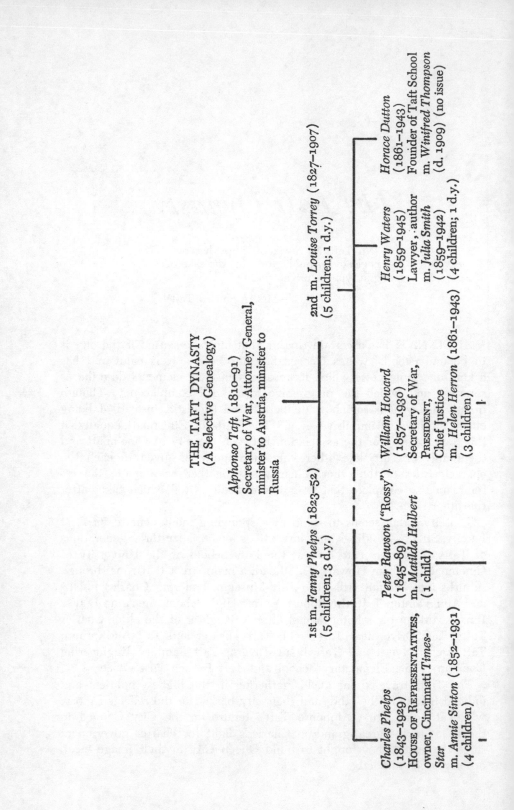

THE TAFT DYNASTY
(A Selective Genealogy)

Alphonso Taft (1810–91)
Secretary of War, Attorney General,
minister to Austria, minister to
Russia

1st m. Fanny Phelps (1823–52)
(5 children; 3 d.y.)

2nd m. Louise Torrey (1827–1907)
(5 children; 1 d.y.)

Charles Phelps
(1843–1929)
HOUSE OF REPRESENTATIVES,
owner, Cincinnati Times-
Star
m. Annie Sinton (1852–1931)
(4 children)

Peter Rawson ("Rossy")
(1845–89)
m. Matilda Hulbert
(1 child)

William Howard
(1857–1930)
Secretary of War,
PRESIDENT,
Chief Justice
m. Helen Herron (1861–1943)
(3 children)

Henry Waters
(1859–1945)
Lawyer, author
m. Julia Smith
(1859–1942)
(4 children; 1 d.y.)

Horace Dutton
(1861–1943)
Founder of Taft School
m. Winifred Thompson
(d. 1909) (no issue)

Jane (1874–1962)
m. Albert Ingalls
(1874–1943)
(3 children)

Hulbert (1877–1959)
Publisher, Times-Star
married 3 times
(4 children)

Robert Alphonso
(1889–1953)
SENATE
m. Martha Bowers
(1889–1958)
(4 children)

Helen
Professor
m. Frederick
Manning
(2 children)

Charles Phelps II
(1897–ㅤ)
Mayor of Cincinnati
m. Eleanor Chase
(1894–1961)
(7 children)

David Sinton Ingalls
(1899–ㅤ)
Assistant Secretary of
the Navy,
publisher, Times-Star
m. Louise Harkness
(5 children)

William Howard III
(1915–ㅤ)
Ambassador to Ireland
m. Barbara Bradfield
(4 children)

Robert, Jr.
(1917–ㅤ)
HOUSE OF REPRESENTATIVES
m. Blanca Noel
(4 children)

Seth Chase (1923–ㅤ)
m. Frances Prindle
(4 children)

Peter Rawson (1936–ㅤ)
(unmarried)

Yet they have lived in Cincinnati for only four generations. Five earlier generations of Tafts were rock-ribbed New Englanders. Much of their character was quarried from the granite of Vermont, and even today, when their name is synonymous with the Middle West, they retain a hard-core Yankeeism.

About four decades after the first American Adams came to Braintree, Massachusetts, in 1636, the first American Taft arrived there. He was Robert Taft, a Scotsman and a carpenter; also a cautious man who left his estate to his wife Sarah for as long as she remained unmarried, a remarkable proviso considering that she was past eighty when he wrote his will.[3] Later, when a Taft had become President, the industrious antiquarians of the Mayflower Society discovered that the family was eligible for membership, but the Tafts continue to maintain otherwise.[4]

Robert and Sarah had five sons who lived to ripe ages and had 45 children. Robert's son Robert had 12 children, 54 grandchildren, 128 great-grandchildren, and 320 great-great-grandchildren, all born in the name of Taft. Most of them remained on the soil or in humble occupations. When the present Charles P. Taft addressed a family reunion in 1960, he told his 260 assembled kinsmen: "The Tafts were not big shots or tycoons; they were carpenters, innkeepers, farmers—in other words, plain ordinary people."[5]

At the first family reunion, in 1874, Alphonso Taft said, "The American branch of our family tree does not flatter our vanity with many brilliant public careers. . . . Our family have not embarked much on National politics. . . ."[6]

Yet less than a century later the family archivist could point to a President of the United States, a Chief Justice of the Supreme Court, three cabinet appointments, three members of the U. S. House of Representatives, a Senate leader, heads of three foreign missions, and a large assortment of lesser municipal, state, and national officials.

The Alphonso Taft who came to Cincinnati in 1839 and founded a political dynasty is most generally described as "dour," "industrious," and "abstemious"—in that order. In personality he more closely resembled his mother, a grim, humorless Baptist, than his father, who was a good-natured and unsuccessful farmer with a keen interest in public affairs.[7] (Taft marriages have usually been unions of opposites, which have operated well on the constitutional principle of checks and balances.) Alphonso was the first of his family to graduate from college; being big and powerful, he often walked from his home in Vermont to New Haven. A founder of family traditions, he was followed at Yale by at least twenty Tafts.[8]

Once he was established in the practice of law Alphonso returned to New England to choose a wife of good solid stock. His choice was Fanny Phelps; they had two sons, Charles Phelps Taft and Peter Rawson Taft, before she died of tuberculosis in her twenty-ninth year. He then went back to New England again for matrimonial purposes.

Louise Torrey, the second Mrs. Alphonso Taft, had a strong-willed mother who was known to have battered down a door with an ax in defiance of her husband's wishes and to have exchanged notes on spiritualism with Horace Greeley. Her Boston merchant father, at the age of forty, moved to the small village of Millbury, Massachusetts, after a physician advised him that he had only a short time to live. With characteristic stubbornness, he remained in vigorous good health for the next forty-nine years.[9]

The mother of William Howard Taft, Henry Waters Taft, and Horace Dutton Taft was a woman of rare executive ability. Her presidential son once wrote, "When woman's field widens, Mother, you must become President of a Railroad Company."[10] As an example of her vitality, in her seventy-fourth year, with only twenty-four hours' notice, she rushed to Rome to be her son's official hostess when he was sent on a diplomatic mission to the Vatican. She was a serene, happy person who cared equally for her four children, her two stepsons, and her in-laws.* (Her husband's parents spent their last twenty years under her roof in Cincinnati.)

The Taft boys often spent their summers at Millbury with Grandfather Torrey, whose house was presided over by his maiden daughter Delia, a believer in the dubious proposition that "ladies of strong minds seldom marry."† Delia's sense of humor was later to receive national attention when her nephew entered the White House and the press gleefully reported the opinions of "Aunt Delia." At one time, when people were adopting fancy place names, such as Manchester by the Sea and Tivoli on Hudson, Aunt Delia chose to protest the befouled Blackstone River by dating her letters, "Millbury by the Sewer."[11] Grandfather Torrey, however, was of sterner stuff, believing that the best way to bring up boys was by "the Puritanical maxim that it is good for the soul to take one's pleasures sadly." A typical dinner table conversation at Grandfather's went:

"Henry, will you have mince pie or apple pie?"

"Oh, I don't care, Grandpa."

---

* Besides their famous sons, the Alphonso Tafts had a daughter Frances, born in 1865, who married Dr. William Edwards, a San Diego surgeon. They had no children.

† Mrs. Taft's other sister married Edward F. B. Orton (1829–99), a distinguished scientist and conservationist, who was state geologist of Ohio and president of Ohio State University.

"If you don't care, we won't cut the pie."[12]

While the boys were listening to the lectures of their elders, reading the books of Oliver Optic, and attending Sunday school at the Unitarian Church, Alphonso Taft was making his reputation as an independent city councilman and a three-term judge of the Cincinnati Superior Court. His most important decision upheld the right of the city Board of Education to ban the use of the King James Bible in public instruction. Taft's position was hailed by the Catholics but offended his political party, which tended to equate Catholicism with the Democrats, and this was to cost him the nomination for governor in 1875.[13]

Politically he was a Republican. He helped found the party in Cincinnati, served as a delegate to its first presidential convention, ran unsuccessfully for Congress in 1856, and was an alternate delegate when Lincoln was nominated. This was the beginning of a love affair between the Taft family and the Republican Party. Of all the American political dynasties, the Tafts would be the most party-oriented. And when a Taft supported a Democrat, as when Horace Dutton Taft voted for Grover Cleveland, it was cause for much head shaking within the tribe. Later there would be Taft Republicans, the adjective standing for "orthodox"; but to many it was a redundancy—Taft meant Republican, and vice versa.

In March of 1876, when Judge Taft was sixty-five years old, President Grant appointed him Secretary of War. The former Secretary had resigned, one step ahead of impeachment proceedings. The Washington *Chronicle* commented on the incoming cabinet member: "His acceptance of the Secretaryship inspires renewed confidence wherever he is known."[14] In a scandal-ridden Administration, this was exactly what the appointment was designed to inspire. Besides, Washington liked the tall, dark-haired Mrs. Taft. Three months later Taft left the War Department to become the Attorney General, where his main accomplishment was to engineer the acceptance of an electoral commission to resolve the disputed Tilden-Hayes presidential contest.

At the age of seventy-two, without any diplomatic experience, without knowing a word of a foreign language, and with a firsthand knowledge of European affairs that consisted of one summer abroad, Alphonso Taft was chosen U.S. envoy extraordinary and minister plenipotentiary to Austria-Hungary.[15] "You're off on a lark," wrote his son William Howard Taft.[16]

Fortunately the diplomatic issues were slight, primarily minor trade frictions, and the envoy and his wife busied themselves learning the etiquette of life at the most aristocratic court in Europe. Mrs. Taft caught on quickly, but Alphonso had a difficult time learning that a minister plenipotentiary does not buy fruit on a street corner and carry it home in a bag. He never did learn to be overly impressed by Austrian nobility. "A baron here ranks, I judge, about with a justice of the peace in Vermont," he wrote home from Vienna.[17] But the family managed to enjoy itself. Aunt Delia came to stay; William Howard Taft stopped by while on a summer trip to Europe; Horace Dutton Taft spent a year after his graduation from Yale, and proudly reported that at the court ball he only once addressed the Empress as "Your Majesty."[18]

Then in 1884 Alphonso was promoted to the St. Petersburg embassy. However, it would take more than the vast domain of the Czar to impress the dour Yankee from Cincinnati. "The great plains remind me of Iowa," he wrote.[19] Besides the usual problem of court manners, he was now confronted with a sticky diplomatic question: the right of Russian Jews who became naturalized American citizens to return to Russia to engage in trade. The Russians felt that U.S. citizenship was being used to circumvent their internal laws against the Jews; the American government felt that its citizens should not be discriminated against. The issue was still unresolved when Minister Taft's health broke after a severe Russian winter and he was forced to return home. He died in 1891.

The man who had brought the first great honor to the family left an estate consisting of a house and $482.80.‡

"To be the founders of a family," wrote Alphonso, "is a great matter."[20] He and his wife took their responsibility seriously; they loved their sons deeply, yet they were also stern disciplinarians. Encouragement was spiced with criticism. When the boys were not at the top of their classes, the parents wanted to know why. The sons were bombarded with Adamsesque letters; letter writing, explained William Howard to his Yale classmates, was his father's recreation. "I do not think you have accomplished as much this past year as you ought with your opportunities," the future President was informed by his father. "Our anxiety for your success is very great and I know that there is but one way to attain it, & that is by self-denial and enthusiastic hard work. . . ."[21]

The paternal spur produced four remarkable leaders in the fields of publishing, politics, law, and education. But, as in the case of one of John Quincy Adams' sons, it also produced an unfortunate result.

Peter Rawson Taft (called "Rossy") and Charles Phelps Taft were the children of Alphonso's first wife; they had each inherited $50,000 from their Phelps grandfather. Rossy had been first in his class at Yale; later, with Charles, he edited the Cincinnati Superior Court Reports. Rossy married pretty Matilda Hulbert, daughter of a brusque and dom-

‡ Alphonso's widow sold the Cincinnati house in 1899 for $18,000.

ineering capitalist. They had a son Hulbert. Then Rossy's health broke. At first he complained of headaches and eye trouble. He was obsessed with a sense of guilt that he was not living up to his father's expectations. He wrote William Howard, "We expect you younger boys, who have the benefit of our experience in education, to do great things. Never be content until you have done the very best you could have done. . . . Work hard, and do your part in building up the reputation of the family."[22] Finally, soon after the birth of Hulbert, he had a total breakdown and was confined in a sanitarium. His wife divorced him, with the understanding of the Tafts. In 1889, at the age of forty-three, Rossy died.

With the same parents, a common environment, education, and opportunities, even wives of a similar background, Rossy Taft went insane and Charlie Taft went on to become a great publisher, financier, and philanthropist.

Charles Phelps Taft was elected to the state legislature in 1871, where he secured the first codification of the Ohio schools. Two years later he married fun-loving, witty Annie Sinton. "She was one of the great heiresses of Ohio," Archie Butt was to write, "but is so natural and kindly that one would never suspect her of either great wealth or high position."[23] She once dropped a suitor because he tried to dazzle her by lighting a cigar with a new dollar bill. Her father was reputedly the richest man in Cincinnati. Sinton money fused with Taft ambition, intelligence, and sense of public service would build a political dynasty; William Howard Taft's rise to the presidency would be bankrolled by his brother Charles.

The Sinton money was made by an Irish immigrant of irregular education. Rugged, close-fisted David Sinton went to Ironton, Ohio, at the age of eighteen to work at a blast furnace. Soon he had a furnace of his own. With every cent of his own capital, and every cent he could borrow, he shrewdly built up a stockpile of pig iron, waited for the Civil War, and sold out at inflated prices. He then moved to Cincinnati and bought the Longworth house on Pike Street, a miniature White House designed by Hoban. Annie was his only child; her mother died when she was an infant, and her father guarded her as his most valuable possession. She was everything he was not—warm, spontaneous, generous, romantic.

Yet the autocratic Sinton approved his daughter's choice for a husband, although he thought the Tafts extravagant. The newlyweds moved into his Cincinnati White House, and Charlie bought an afternoon newspaper, the *Times*, originally known as *The Spirit of the Times*. The next year, 1880, he took over the *Evening Star* and merged the two. On Sinton's death, his entire estate, possibly fifteen million dollars, went to Annie; not wanting to make her husband subservient, she turned over to him her interest in the newspaper. When the *Times-Star* left the Taft family, after seventy-eight years of proprietorship, it could boast an unbroken record of never having supported a Democrat for state or national office. Charlie Taft's other contribution to journalism was to conceive the idea of leasing telegraph wires for the collection and distribution of news, an innovation he installed between New York and Cincinnati.

Charlie became the first rich man in the history of the Taft family. His business interests eventually encompassed the Cincinnati & Suburban Bell Telephone Company, the Cincinnati Gas & Electric Company, the Columbia Gas & Electric Company, and the Cincinnati Railway Company. He took over management of the 197,000 acres his father-in-law owned in Texas. There he built the town of Taft and started the Taft Oil and Gin Company, the Taft Packing House, and Taft's Crystal Shortening. He bought the Chicago Cubs, and they rewarded him with three National League championships, two World Series victories, and handsome dividends.

He and his wife threw their considerable energies into art collecting and philanthropy. They stocked their home with the paintings of Corot, Millet, Turner, Gainsborough, Rembrandt, Van Dyck, Hals, Rousseau; with Chinese porcelains and sixteenth-century crystals and Limoges enamels. They then turned over their collection, their home, and $2,700,000 to the city for a museum. The University of Cincinnati and the Cincinnati Symphony got millions; hundreds of thousands went to the Cincinnati Zoo.

These were the "rich Tafts." To them Cincinnati is indebted for part of its civic and cultural heritage. The "poor Tafts"—William Howard Taft and his heirs—left home to seek fame rather than fortune. They too succeeded—with the wholehearted support, moral and financial, of their Cincinnati relations. But at times they found it embarrassing that the public confused the two branches of the family. (For example, John L. Lewis said that Bob Taft was "born in velvet pants"—a statement which was hardly designed to thaw the senator's frosty political image.[24])

At the time of Alphonso Taft's death his four surviving sons were well on their way to success. The father had always felt his boys were destined for the law, and all had got law degrees. Henry Waters Taft was practicing in New York, a partner in Cadwalader, Wickersham & Taft, and a rising light at the nation's most competitive bar. William Howard Taft had already served as a judge of the Superior Court of Ohio for three years, and, much to the pleasure of his dying father, had just been named Solicitor General of the United States. Charlie, of course, was a millionaire.

While Alphonso never cared much about making money, Charlie's career was at least explainable. But Horace Dutton Taft, his youngest son, was an enigma. "I cannot comprehend Horace's idea of founding a private school or what in the world he can hope from it," Alphonso wrote. "The law is his proper field. His plans are fanciful. . . . It seems to us a singular perversion of mind and opportunities. . . ."[25]

But Horace went ahead and founded a school. He wanted to teach boys. It was to be the "singular perversion" of a lifetime. And he had his own ideas of how to teach them. One of his associates said, "Taft School has stood always for public service and basically an old-fashioned disciplinary course. We believe that education does not come by artificial means, and we have been cursed as old-fashioned by some progressive schools."[26] His students called him "The King." Williams College, when granting him one of his many honorary degrees, called him "Headmaster of headmasters." And in 1936, on his retirement, Yale acknowledged that "his plans are fanciful"—but with a difference:

In 1890 he made a dream come true; by a manner analogous to the divine creation of the world, he created out of his will the TAFT SCHOOL of which he has been Headmaster for 46 years. It rose like an exhalation. The School is one of the great schools of the country, and it might well have as its motto, "Here we learn not only scholarship but life."[27]

He had never seen brothers more devoted to each other than these Tafts, said Archie Butt, a skillful celebrity-watcher.[28] Even when the President of the United States asked Will Taft to head the civil government of the Philippines, the young judge told McKinley that he would just have to wait a week for an answer—first he would have to consult with his brothers.[29]

The Tafts called a family meeting in 1903. William Howard Taft was not there, but Mrs. Alphonso Taft, Aunt Delia Torrey, Mr. and Mrs. Charles P. Taft, and Henry W. Taft were present. After due deliberation they drafted a report: William Howard Taft was to be President of the United States.[30] It was a remarkable decision for two reasons: Taft was still more than six years away from entering the White House and he did not want to be President. But from the time Will was a child the Tafts never had any doubt that the honor and destiny of the family were bound up in him.

Equally determined that Taft would be President was his wife, the former Helen Herron, "the fascinating Nellie." She was not a beauty. She had a stubborn mouth. Nor did she make friends easily; reserved and literary—perhaps too intellectual for the young men who found her five sisters more flirtatious.§ Yet, though Will Taft was considered a ladies' man, no woman would ever rival Nellie for his love. "I have a

§ Her sister Lucy married Henry Frederick Lippitt (1856–1933), of an old Rhode Island family that pioneered the manufacture of cotton in the state. He was a U.S. senator (1911–17), the son and brother of Rhode Island governors, and the great uncle of the present governor, John H. Chafee.

treasure," he wrote when they became engaged—and to the last breath he never revised his judgment.

Nellie's ambition for her husband was not arrived at frivolously. She knew the White House well. Her father had been a classmate of Benjamin Harrison and a law partner of Rutherford B. Hayes; her mother, an intimate of Mrs. Hayes, was also the daughter and sister of congressmen.¶ At seventeen, when a house guest of President and Mrs. Hayes, Nellie announced that she was so taken with the White House that she would marry someone destined to be President.[31]

William Howard Taft—the man on whom all family ambition centered —was tall and round, his weight climbing to over 325 pounds when he was under stress; his legs seemed too short for his torso; his face was ruddy with a blondish mustache and dark hair. Despite his great bulk he was light on his feet and a nimble dancer. He was quick to joke about his generous proportions. When offered the Kent Chair of Law at Yale, he replied that it would be inadequate but that "a Sofa of Law" might be all right.[32] Then Taft probably chuckled a rapturous, subterranean, incomparable chuckle, "the most infectious chuckle in the history of politics."[33] Ellen Slayden, wife of a Texas congressman, said, "It reminded me of the cluck a whippoorwill gives, a laugh to himself, when he has been whistling with special vim and mischief."[34] The president of Western Reserve University felt he was always a playful and friendly boy.[35]

The stereotype of the jolly fat man fooled many into believing that his core was of jelly rather than tempered steel. The perceptive knew otherwise. He combined gentleness with toughness. When William Allen White crossed him, the Kansas editor saw Taft's "eye behind his smile veiling with almost the hint of a serpentine glitter."[36] And Teddy Roosevelt, while they were still friends, said that Taft was "one of the best haters" he had ever known.[37]

On the day that young Will Taft came to Washington to be sworn in as Solicitor General he was visited by Senator William M. Evarts of New York, the leader of the American bar. "Mr. Taft," said the senator, "I knew your father, and I valued his friendship very highly." He then came straight to the point. Evarts was presuming on this friendship to ask him to a dinner party that night at which he was short one man. And so on his first evening in Washington William Howard Taft dined between Mrs. Henry Cabot Lodge and Mrs. John Hay, neither of whom had the faintest clue to his identity.[38]

After he became Secretary of War, Taft was asked to explain his re-

¶ Mrs. Taft's maternal grandfather was Eli Collins (1786–1848), a member of the House of Representatives from New York, 1823–25; her uncle was William Collins (1818–78), congressman from the same district, 1847–49.

markable political ascent. He replied, "I got my political pull, first, through father's prominence. . . ."[39] Years later his senatorial son Robert would tell an interviewer, "The fact that father was President and Chief Justice of the United States was a tremendous help and inspiration in my public career."[40] The Tafts were displaying their usual candor: Father's name did open doors. However, as Robert pointed out when he was first elected to the Senate, this great asset "supplies the impetus which gives a man his start, but that impetus does not last forever. After the start is made, it is only by his own effort that a man can keep going, and one with a family name has a lot to live up to."[41]

If one were to plot on a graph the career of William Howard Taft the line would rise sharply and steeply, without a single dip, until he had reached the summit of American political life. He became assistant prosecutor of Hamilton County at twenty-three, collector of internal revenue for Cincinnati at twenty-five, judge of the Superior Court of Ohio at twenty-nine, Solicitor General of the United States at thirty-two, federal Circuit Court judge at thirty-four, president of the Philippine Commission at forty-two, civil governor of the Philippines at forty-three, Secretary of War at forty-six, and President of the United States at fifty-two. Each job seemed to be the logical outgrowth of the one before; each new opportunity seemed only to await the successful conclusion of the one preceding it.

In 1901, when Vice-President Theodore Roosevelt had a great deal of time on his hands, he wrote an article for the *Outlook* entitled "Governor William H. Taft." It began: "A year ago a man of wide acquaintance both with American public life and American public men remarked that the first Governor of the Philippines ought to combine the qualities which would make a first-class President of the United States with the qualities which would make a first-class Chief Justice of the United States, and that the only man he knew who possessed all these qualities was Judge William H. Taft of Ohio. The statement was entirely correct."[42] By the time the article was published McKinley had been assassinated and its author was President of the United States.

There is something especially appealing about a friendship between two great men; just as there is something tragic when such a friendship disintegrates. In bloom the friendship between Roosevelt and Taft was more elevating than that of Adams and Jefferson, for neither held in reserve a part of himself; in decay it was more personally corrupting, for the early presidents split over conflicting ideologies, while the later presidents were to split primarily over conflicting ambitions.

The two young men who were brought together in subordinate positions during the Harrison Administration were so attractively different: Roosevelt so combustible, creative, so divinely illogical; Taft so harmonious, solid, so thoroughly logical. Their aspirations would carry them forward together. If ever a man conceived himself to be destined to be President of the United States it was Roosevelt; if ever a man felt chosen for Chief Justice of the United States it was Taft. They could serve each other well. Taft helped get the Assistant Secretaryship of the Navy for Roosevelt, and later encouraged his White House ambitions when they looked most remote to the Rough Rider. When Roosevelt became President he preferred Taft over all others, making him in fact, if not title, "Assistant President." He twice offered him a place on the Supreme Court, which duty and his wife's ambition forced Taft to decline. Then Roosevelt committed the mistake that was bound to end their friendship: he made Taft President.

Taft's road to the White House was paved with greater public service than any President since Van Buren. His work marked him as the most brilliant jurist on a lower federal court. He went to the Philippines to rule a conquered nation; he left, according to Carlos Romulo, "enshrined in the Filipino heart."[43] He established a policy that would eventually lead to self-government and independence, but in the meantime would at least be benevolent and responsive. In this he was opposed by General Arthur MacArthur, the American military commander, who had a different idea of the place of "our little brown brothers." A song of his soldiers ended: "He may be a brother of William H. Taft, but he ain't no friend of mine!"[44] Back in Washington as Secretary of War he served as Roosevelt's principal trouble-shooter. Editorial page cartoonists, who loved to draw his massive dimensions, usually pictured him with a suitcase, rushing off to put out some far-off fire—to Panama to get "the dirt flying," to Cuba to bring an uneasy peace, to the Western states to campaign for a Roosevelt Congress.

This was also the formative period for Taft's three children, who were seeing more of the world than any future President's children since John Quincy Adams went off to Europe with his father. Visiting Japan, Bob kept a log of earthquakes, recording thirteen in one day; at the Vatican he told the Pope that he wanted to be Chief Justice of the United States when he grew up; in Manila the children turned the tennis court at Malacañan Palace into a deer park and kept a monkey until he broke loose and smashed every champagne glass in the palace. Baby Charlie, when he wasn't standing in front of a mirror saying, "I am the Governor of the Philippine Islands,"[45] was bossing the gardener's sons and learning a language that his mother thought "will be fearfully and wonderfully made of Tagalog, Spanish and English."[46]

Robert Alphonso Taft had been born in 1889 when his father was a state judge in Cincinnati; Helen was born two years later in Washington while Will was serving as Solicitor General; Charles Phelps arrived in 1897 after President Harrison had appointed Will to a newly created federal judgeship.

As a small boy Bob was orderly and precise, with an inexhaustible ability to entertain himself. He resembled his mother—a broad mouth that made him look very serious, slightly protruding teeth, and large eyes. At age six, when living across from a firehouse in Cincinnati, he accumulated data on how many miles each engine traveled and presented the firemen with a twelve-month report. He also made an elaborate chart to show every call box in the district. At seven he produced an epic Civil War poem, with a couplet about each Union general, including the memorable line: "General Pope,/Who washed his hands with Ivory soap."[47] Before he was ten he had taught himself to play chess and bridge, and was a mathematical prodigy. His uncle Louis More, a mathematician, later said, "Bob is the greatest man with figures I ever saw."[48]* There was also a gentleness to young Bob's character. When he was about four his father felt that he had earned a disciplinary action for some misbehavior.

"Papa," asked the child, "are you going to spank me?"

"Yes," said William Howard Taft. "It is for your own good and will hurt me more than it will you."

"Then," replied Bob, "can I kiss you first?"[49]

Brother Charlie was an entirely different kind of boy. He had inherited his father's dimple and chuckle. He was the extrovert and general mischief-maker. He had traveled twice around the world with his parents before he was eight, and, according to his sister, "gave interviews to the newspapers and posed for photographers at every stop!"[50] Later he would join that Peck's Bad Boy of the White House, Quentin Roosevelt, in such Executive Mansion diversions as pasting spitballs that looked like warts on the portrait of Andrew Jackson.[51]

From the Philippines Bob was shipped off alone across the Pacific to Uncle Horace's school at Watertown, Connecticut. After thirteen years the Taft School still had less than one hundred students, but it was already attracting boys from some of the better families, including the sons of Mark Hanna. Robert had no difficulty ranking first scholastically. The yearbook in 1904 said of him:

> He Greek and Latin speaks
> With greater ease
> Than hogs eat acorns and
> Tame pigeons peas.[52]

---

* Louis More, the husband of Nellie Taft's sister Eleanor, was the dean of the University of Cincinnati's Graduate School, and brother of the archconservative Princeton philosopher Paul Elmer More (1864–1937).

On the playing fields his prowess was less remarkable. He played second-string guard on the football team in his senior year, and Uncle Horace wrote his parents, "Bob will never make a good football player, but he throws himself into the game so hard he raises the morale of the team."[53] Charlie would be the natural athlete in the family.

Bob's classmates admired him, but they could not understand how he remained so indifferent to their high jinks. They had a special reason for trying to rope him into their plots. Recalls a fellow student: "Whenever we tried anything particularly outrageous, such as stealing up to the 'cupola' after hours to smoke, drink ginger ale and other 'daring' deeds, we always tried to seduce Bob into going with us, figuring that if we got caught it might help ease the punishment if we had H.D.'s nephew along with us. Sometimes it worked."[54] When Charlie, seven years behind his brother, entered the Taft School, their headmaster uncle tried to compare them. Charlie, he thought, "has a delight in every kind of fun that is simple and healthy. . . . At the same time he is steady and attends to business. Whether he has as strong a mind as Bob is doubtful. . . . He will find it easier, however, to take part in everything that comes up than Bob did. He is more facile in most ways."[55]

A year before the 1908 presidential election Will Taft's brother Charlie set up campaign headquarters for him in Ohio and Washington. Charlie had served the 1895–97 term in Congress. His motivation for wanting a House seat seems to have been primarily to show independence of his father-in-law, who opposed the move to Washington. Charlie had always arranged his life to suit David Sinton; now he wrote Will, ". . . the race is begun and Old Man Sinton will have to stomach it."[56] However he did not seek re-election. Only once again did Charlie attempt to win elective office. After his brother was elected President he announced that he would be a candidate for the United States Senate. The move was politically embarrassing to the President-elect. There were many reports that Will tried to remove from the race his brother's chief opponent, Congressman Theodore Burton, by offering him a cabinet appointment. Charlie finally withdrew and Burton was easily elected.[57] Yet these were only brief flare-ups of personal ambition; Charlie deeply held his father's pride in family, and cheerfully subordinated his own political aspirations to promote his younger brother's career. Since Will's days as Solicitor General, Charlie had been subsidizing him in amounts ranging from $6000 to $10,000 a year.

It was said that his brother's drive for the presidency cost Charlie $800,000. The reporters at the Washington Gridiron dinner in 1909 poked fun at such lavish spending. In one skit a customer in a diner ordered "breast of chicken with wings attached and boiled dumplings."

"*Angel with dough,*" called the waiter.

"Charles P. Taft, for one," echoed the chef.[58]

The financier was equal to the joke. Later he told Captain Butt, "Huntington [of the Southern Pacific Railroad] thought it came high to get a prince in the family. He ought to have tried getting a President into one!"[59]

When the 1908 Republican Convention opened at Chicago in June, Bob Taft, a Yale sophomore, reported, "I never have seen so many of our family together before."[60] Bob was sleeping on a folding bed in Uncle Charlie's office at the Auditorium. The candidate and his wife listened to the proceedings by telephone in his office at the War Department. Mrs. Taft was still unconvinced that Roosevelt did not plan to grab the nomination for himself; she winced as she heard the delegates cheer the President's name. But Roosevelt had chosen Taft without reservation and his man Lodge was in firm control of the convention. Will was easily nominated on the first ballot. From the Taft School, Horace wired the nominee, "We are jubilant. Discipline gone to smash."[61]

Before the inauguration Horace called a faculty meeting to change the school's rules so that nephew Charlie could watch his father become President. (The action prompted a news magazine nearly fifty years later to wrote of the Taft School: ". . . rules are still so strict that one of the few valid excuses for a student's absence is attendance at his father's inauguration for President."[62]) Uncle Horace need not have been so solicitous. For on the way to the ceremony Helen noticed that her little brother was carrying a copy of *Treasure Island*. "This affair is going to be pretty dry, and I want something to read," he said.[63] Robert, on the other hand, watched every detail with rapt attention. In the procession back to the White House, Mrs. Taft broke all precedent by insisting on riding in the open car with the President. "Some of the Inaugural Committee expressed their disapproval," she wrote, "but I had my way and in spite of protests took my place at my husband's side."[64]

The President's office during Roosevelt's occupancy had been a cluttered reflection of a cultured man with a craving for the strenuous life. There were a riding crop and a tennis racket in the corner, and piles of books—history, fiction, even poetry. But when reporter Ray Stannard Baker went to interview the new President he discovered a transformation had taken place. "Now the office had become, and not without significance, a law-office. On all sides of the room were cases filled with law-books, nothing but law-books."[65] And the new Cabinet, of which Taft was extraordinarily proud, contained five "good, first-class lawyers," including Henry Taft's partner George Wickersham. "The law to Presi-

dent Taft," thought his military aide, "is the same support as some zeal-
ots get from great religious faith."[66]

It soon became apparent that Roosevelt and the man he had chosen
as his successor held diametrically opposite views of the presidency. Taft
felt that the Chief Executive had no power that was not specifically
spelled out in the Constitution or an act of Congress. "There is no re-
siduum of power which he can exercise because it seems to him to be
in the public interest. . . ."[67] "I declined to adopt this view," said
Roosevelt. "My belief was that it was not only his right but his duty to
do anything that the needs of the nation demanded unless such action
was forbidden by the Constitution or by the laws."[68] There were two
categories of presidents, Roosevelt later wrote, the "Lincoln presidents"
and the "Buchanan presidents." He declared himself to be in the former
group; Taft he lumped with James Buchanan. If Roosevelt had not
classed himself with Lincoln, said Taft, "the identification . . . might
otherwise have escaped notice. . . ." It reminded him of the little girl
who told her father that she was the best scholar in the class. Had her
teacher told her so? "Oh no," she replied, "the teacher didn't tell me—I
just noticed it myself."[69]

Yet Taft, despite his strict interpretation of presidential functions,
proposed and, in some areas, achieved even greater reforms than Roosevelt. He secured a tariff revision, which on balance was a slight liberali-
zation of existing schedules; put through the postal savings bank system;
became "the father of the Federal Budget"; got the Senate to approve a
reciprocity treaty with Canada, later defeated by the Canadian legislature; brought more prosecutions under the Anti-Trust Act than ever before; and tried to get nations to settle disputes through international
arbitration.

But as a politician Taft was all thumbs. "The honest greenhorn at the
poker table" is what New York *Times* reporter Charles Thompson called
him.[70] Said Speaker Cannon in disgust: "If Taft were pope he'd want to
appoint some Protestants to the College of Cardinals."[71]

Roosevelt's chief claim to greatness, Taft thought, was his power to
rouse the public conscience—an ability in which he was totally lacking.
Roosevelt was the master of press relations; Taft's relations with the
press were atrocious. Any action that might bring him popularity he
considered demagogic. Roosevelt was the master of phrasemaking, it
was the birthright of his dynasty; Taft's public statements were stodgy
and soggy, his family's inheritance. The Rough Rider had once told
Stimson, "Darn it, Harry, a campaign speech is a poster, not an etch-
ing!"[72] Taft, like Stimson, was an etcher. He justified his programs in
long, legalistic pronouncements; and then, having said all there was to
say on a subject, he felt he need say no more. He didn't know how to
humor the insurgents in his own ranks, and midway in his term he

lost control of the Congress altogether. The new Democratic Congress had no intention of making life comfortable for the Republican President. One congressional committee even sought to embarrass him by digging up a minor scandal that had taken place ten years before in the State Department. Taft said it reminded him of the man who was asked by the waiter whether he wanted oxtail soup, which, he explained, was merely soup made from the tail of the ox. "Neighbor," the patron replied, "don't you think that's going a hell of a long ways back for soup?"[73]

His presidential years, Taft's daughter concluded, "were the only unhappy years of his entire life."[74]

The salary of the President had just been raised from $75,000 to $100,000; at last Taft would make enough to support his family luxuriously. He took to motoring with a passion. "Well, children," he would say, "enjoy this all you can, for in four years more you may have to begin to walk over again."[75] He playfully told Nellie that after the White House they would go back to the "lower middle class," and insisted that she not scrimp on her wardrobe, a dictum which, to his surprise, she followed. Mrs. Taft filled the Executive Mansion with furniture, tapestries, and screens from the Orient. She covered the floors with *petates* and filled the rooms to overflowing with plants, ferns, and exotic flowers, so that the servants, in concealed rebellion, were soon referring to the White House as "Malacañan Palace."[76]

The Tafts entertained lavishly. The lawn party they gave on their silver wedding anniversary was one of the largest affairs ever held at the White House. When Aunt Delia arrived, the Washington *Star* editorialized that now the party was "an assured success," since she would superintend the making of her famous apple pies. The old lady enjoyed the notoriety but confessed to the family that "she had not made an apple pie for forty years and never did know how to make one properly."[77] The President and his First Lady greeted the crush of guests under a blazing sign, "1886–1911," while searchlights from the Treasury and State Department buildings made the lawn as bright as noon. The effect, commented Mrs. Slayden, was "crude like a fair or a circus," which surprised her since "the Tafts have such excellent taste usually. . . ."[78]

But Mrs. William Howard Taft, who had felt destined to be First Lady since she was seventeen, was not destined to enjoy her reign. Three months after the inauguration she had a stroke. The President lovingly taught her to speak again, but, though she was to live until a week short of her eighty-second birthday and was to survive her husband by thirteen years, after her slow recovery she had a speech impairment for the rest of her life.

Helen Taft dropped out of Bryn Mawr College to replace her mother as the official White House hostess. The President thought she was very much like him. Frank and intelligent, with an outlook more liberal than her parents', she once made headlines by speaking in favor of the aggrieved shirtmakers. Usually, however, she remained quiet and discreet. The newspapers tried to whip up enthusiasm for "Helen pink," but the public would not let go of "Alice blue," and at the end of her father's Administration Helen returned without regret to the groves of academe and the beginning of a distinguished career as an educator.

While Helen was thrown uneasily into the limelight, and little Charlie had long grown to enjoy its glare, Bob Taft continued to try desperately to remain a face in the crowd. He graduated from Yale (first in his class, Berkeley Premium for excellence in Latin composition, Woolsey Scholarship for best examination in Latin and Greek composition, the Barge Prize for solution of an original mathematical problem, a second Ten Eyck Prize for debating, and a Philosophical Oration for general academic standing), and then went to the Harvard Law School (first in his class, editor of the *Law Review*). A young lady at a Boston party who had failed to catch his name had an impossible time trying to detect his identity by adroit questioning: *Where did he live?* His family home was in Ohio. *Did he go back there for holidays?* No, the family was now in Washington and he spent his holidays there. *What did the family do in Washington?* His father had a government job. *And where did they live in Washington?* "On Pennsylvania Avenue," answered Bob.[79] He did not mean to be coy, it was just that he would rather not be known as the President's son if he could help it.

During his vacations Bob brought some of his friends home, and Helen got them dates. Here within his intimate circle could be seen a person who friends always contended was "the real" Bob Taft. He had a sense of humor that was mildly merry and somewhat whimsical. (Much later a hotel doorman was marshaling chauffeured cars when he saw Taft. "Senator, may I call your car for you?" "It's an awfully good little car," replied Bob, "but I don't think it will come if you call it."[80])

At the White House the young Tafts and their friends were particularly fond of charades, and the leader of the charade set was Martha Bowers. She was the daughter of Lloyd Wheaton Bowers, Solicitor General of the United States, a striking figure with a dark seamed face and beetling brows, whom Felix Frankfurter considered the most brilliant American lawyer of his generation.[81] Martha was also the great-great-great-great-granddaughter of Yale President Timothy Dwight, and a granddaughter of Thomas Wilson, an Irish immigrant and a celebrated wit, who had been chief justice of the Minnesota Supreme Court. She would soon become Mrs. Robert A. Taft, and would one day be called "the brightest star in the [Taft] family. . . ."[82]

The trouble with Roosevelt was that he was too young. He was only fifty-one when he vacated the White House, in the prime of life, still in command of the most legendary mainspring of energy in American history. So he went big-game hunting in Africa to unwind. As he left Washington some congressmen lifted their glasses in a toast: "To the lions!"

Roosevelt sincerely wished Taft well and determined to allow him to run his own show. But it was hard; his rightful place would always be at the head of the charge. Then there were so many old friends who would hurry to Oyster Bay with tales of personal or ideological slights by the President. Others were running to Taft with the same sort of self-serving gossip. Minor incidents were blown up into major differences. Immediately after his election Taft wrote Roosevelt a letter of glowing thanks: "You and my brother Charlie" made me President.[83] It was now reported that 'Roosevelt was furious that Taft had lumped him with his brother as the kingmaker. So the separation began. "It is hard, very hard, Archie, to see a devoted friendship going to pieces like a rope of sand," said Taft.[84] Henry L. Stimson declared, "It was not principle but personality, not purpose but method, that divided Mr. Taft and Mr. Roosevelt."[85] Many, like Stimson, were torn between their loyalties to the two. The daughter of Maggie, the second maid at the White House, reported that "half the servants were for Taft; half were for T.R."[86] Archie Butt, devoted to them both, felt he just had to get away for a little while. He left for a European vacation, booking return passage on the *Titanic*. He never returned.

There was a grand irony in charging the two Tafts, William Howard and his son Robert, both with trying to *steal* presidential nominations. Bob had been called "Mr. Integrity," and it was certainly an inherited characteristic. Yet at the 1912 convention and forty years later their opponents contended that the Tafts had secured Southern delegates by foul means. "Thou Shalt Not Steal!" cried Teddy Roosevelt, and the refrain would be picked up by the Eisenhower forces in 1952. The Tafts were perplexed by the charge, for they had only been playing by the long-established rules. However, the outcomes of the two contests would be different. The elder Taft, unpopular as he might be, was still the incumbent President, and as such in control of the party machinery. With Taft's renomination assured, Roosevelt bolted the convention, announcing that he would "stand at Armageddon" and run on a third party ticket. The cynical politician-industrialist Chauncey Depew pronounced: "The only question now is which corpse gets the most flowers."[87]

Taft received the electoral vote of just two tiny states. "I regard this as something of an achievement," commented a reporter, "and should be disposed to compliment Utah and Vermont if it were not that the Mormon machine pulled Utah through and that it's a capital offense to vote a third party ticket in Vermont."[88]

At a "school of journalism" conducted by Washington's Gridiron Club in February 1913, the "professor" was asked:

"What is a remarkable coincidence?"

"The most remarkable coincidence of the year 1913," came the reply, "is that at the very moment Professor Wilson becomes President Wilson, President Taft becomes Professor Taft."[89]

The years at Yale would be happy and productive for the ex-President. Taft had saved $100,000 during his term as President, and its income, along with a $5000 salary as professor of law, would be enough, he felt, "to keep the wolf from the door, especially in view of the fact that I do not expect to eat as much after leaving the White House."[90] He also supplemented his income by public speaking. His secretary set up "a one-man lecture bureau," and anyone requesting his services was sent a list of thirty subjects to choose from—ranging from "Duties of Citizenship" to "The Initiative and Referendum." Taft's fees ran from $150 to $1000, averaging $400 an appearance.[91]

Yale gave a royal welcome to its only alumnus to have been President. "Second to no triumphal procession of any Caesar and surpassing any such celebration in the history of the college of the bulldog," wrote the New Haven *Journal-Courier*.[92] The school provided oversized chairs, with twenty-five-inch seats, for its distinguished faculty member, who set up an office at his brother's hotel, the Taft. Soon he was coaching the freshman debating team, which lost to Harvard and Princeton, and was enjoying himself at junior proms, student banquets, smokers, and ball games.

Helen Taft received an M.A. and a Ph.D. from Yale. Her dissertation was later published as *British Colonial Government After the American Revolution, 1782–1820*. When she was twenty-five, in 1917, Bryn Mawr made her its dean, and the next year its acting president. In 1920 she married Frederick J. Manning, an instructor at Yale, later professor of history at Swarthmore, who was to shock his father-in-law by voting for Al Smith.†

The baby of the family was now six feet one, broad-shouldered, by far the handsomest of the Tafts. It was to be expected that Charlie would be a scholar, but he was also an athlete, varsity tackle on the Yale football team and captain of the basketball team. Then after his junior year, with a war raging in Europe, he left college and enlisted

† The Mannings have two daughters: Helen, now married to Holland Hunter, professor of economics at Haverford College; and Caroline, now married to Frederic Cunningham, professor of mathematics at Swarthmore College.

in the army as a buck private. A few weeks later he married fluffy-haired, blue-eyed Eleanor Chase, daughter of the president of the Ingersoll Watch Company, whose family fortune was founded in brass and copper.‡ Charlie's father was pleased because "an association of that sort strengthens a boy against temptations which crowd on him in the army." In 1918 twenty-year-old Sergeant Major Taft sailed for France. "And now, Charlie my loving son, good-bye till we meet again. You are knight *sans peur et sans reproche*. God bless you and keep you."[93]

Bob and Martha Bowers were now married and the parents of two boys. William Howard Taft III,§ born in 1915, was small at birth, but, according to his proud grandfather, "he has shown a family trait in increasing his weight quite rapidly."[94] Robert arrived two years later. (He was not given his father's middle name but later adopted "Jr.")

The future senator tried to enlist in the army when the war came but was repeatedly rejected because of poor eyesight. So Bob went to Washington to join Herbert Hoover, the mining engineer who was making an international reputation as a food and relief administrator. Six days after the armistice, with Taft as his legal adviser and Lewis Strauss as his private secretary, Hoover sailed for Europe to set up headquarters in Paris.[95] Martha later joined her husband, and almost once every week managed to entice Bob and young Strauss away from the problems of feeding a starving continent for an evening at the Opéra Comique. After eleven months Bob Taft returned home, now being entitled to wear decorations from the governments of Poland, Belgium, and Finland. (He never did.)

After a lifetime of deferring to family wishes and his sense of duty, in 1921 William Howard Taft finally realized his ambition. He was appointed Chief Justice of the United States. "At last Mr. Taft has come to his journey's end," wrote a Washington correspondent. "He has been a long time on the way."[96]

Taft found his days on the Supreme Court to be everything he always

‡ Eleanor Chase Taft's sister is Lucia Chase, the ballerina. In 1926 she married Thomas Ewing, a great-grandson of the founder of the Alexander Smith & Sons Carpet Company. He died in 1933. Seven years later she was a founder of the Ballet Theatre, and has since been its principal financial supporter. It has been estimated that she spent two million dollars on the ballet company between 1940 and 1947 alone. See *Current Biography 1947*, pp. 103–4.

§ He was the third of the name because Henry W. Taft had a son William Howard Taft II (1888–1952), who was subscription-circulation manager of the New York *Times*, and later assistant vice-president and Secretary of the Bank of Savings, New York City. See New York *Times*, February 11, 1952, p. 25.

dreamed they would be. The bitter polemics of politics were behind him. "The truth is," he wrote in 1925, "that in my present life I don't remember that I ever was president." An apocryphal tale was told of a little boy who stopped him during his daily walk to the Court and said, "I know who you are. You used to be President Coolidge!"[97]

He proved to be a conservative, just as expected.[98] Jurisprudentially he wasn't able to win over Holmes, Brandeis, and Stone, but his affable nature won them as friends, and he was particularly surprised to discover how much he liked Brandeis, whose court appointment he had strongly opposed.

As the years passed, the aging Chief Justice decided that he would have to celebrate his birthday on "the Aunt Delia principle." (The old lady who lived to be ninety-two gave a dinner on her eightieth birthday in order that people might not think she was ninety.)

Finally, in early 1930, his health failed, and Bob Taft delivered his father's resignation to President Hoover. The Court, speaking through the eloquent pen of Oliver Wendell Holmes, then wrote him: "We call you Chief Justice still—for we cannot give up the title by which we have known you all these later years and which you have made dear to us. We cannot let you leave us without trying to tell you how dear you have made it. You came to us from achievement in other fields and with the prestige of the illustrious place that you lately had held and you showed us in new form your voluminous capacity for getting work done, your humor that smoothed the tough places, your golden heart that brought you love from every side and most of all from your brethren whose tasks you have made happy and light. We grieve at your illness, but your spirit has given life an impulse that will abide whether you are with us or away."[99]

He died on March 8, 1930, the only man to have served as both President and Chief Justice of the United States.

Another tribute that would have pleased him greatly came from humorist Will Rogers:

Mr. Taft, what a lovely soul! Just as a man and a real honest-to-God fellow, Mr. Taft will go to his grave with more real downright affection and less enemies of any of our Presidents.

It's great to be great but it's greater to be human. He was our great human fellow because there was more of him to be human. We are parting with three hundred pounds of solid charity to everybody, and love and affection for all his fellow men.[100]

The 1920s shaped the political future for Bob and Charlie Taft. They were now law partners, specializing in representing the diverse interests of Uncle Charlie and Aunt Annie.

In 1921 Bob was elected to the Ohio House of Representatives; in

1925 he was made majority leader; in 1926 he became Speaker; in 1930 he was elected to the state Senate. His political style was emerging. Like his voice, it was flat and tuneless. As for back patting, handshaking, and other tools of vote-seeking, Taft summarily dismissed them: "It is not honest to be tactful."[101] It was said of Taft that the only deceitful thing about him was the way he combed his hair. (Having inherited the Taft tendency toward baldness, he was what his friend Senator Millikin called "a slicker-overer.")

But he had an infinite capacity for hard work, and, as Alice Roosevelt Longworth put it, he was a man always willing "to grasp a political nettle."[102] As a state legislator he rewrote Ohio's tax system and fought the powerful Ku Klux Klan over the required reading of the Bible in public schools. He was also growing to dislike political disorder, just as he disliked disorder in his personal life. Politics was ordered through political parties. To work outside the party, no matter how grand the objective, was to be a maverick and a mutineer.

His brother held a different view. Cincinnati was then in the grasp of a Republican machine run by Rudolph Hynick, a remote-control boss, who was a New York burlesque impresario. Bob believed in "reform from within"; Charlie believed in "reform from outside." He became the leader of the Charter movement, a local third party, and, running against the organization, was elected prosecuting attorney in 1926.

Unfortunately for Charlie, he picked the wrong office for his political debut. As one veteran Cincinnati lawyer observed, "To be a good prosecutor, you've got to believe in punishment; you've got to be a killer. Charlie isn't a killer."[103] Taft's career as prosecutor ended in two complete fiascos—the trials of bootleggers Fat Wrassman and George Remus. Wrassman was acquitted of a murder charge when the witnesses suddenly left town. Remus admitted killing his wife, who was planning to marry a Department of Justice operative, but was declared insane. The jury then helped him celebrate the verdict at a champagne party. Six months later the Ohio Supreme Court decided that Remus had made a miraculous recovery and he was freed.[104]

The Republican organization, headed by Bob Taft, easily defeated Charlie Taft for renomination in 1928.

The political difference between his sons, thought the Chief Justice, was between "the practical good" and "the ideally good." William Howard Taft left no doubt that he felt Bob was following the path of greater wisdom.[105]

On New Year's Eve, 1929, Charles Phelps Taft died; Annie Sinton Taft died two years later. In old age the couple had grown quite deaf; Annie had also become rather eccentric. Their lives, so rich and full, were not without sadness: only son Howard had gone insane and been placed in an institution.

The "rich Tafts" left nephews Bob and Charlie each a five per cent interest in the Cincinnati *Times-Star*¶; ten per cent went to nephew Hulbert, the only child of the unfortunate Rossy Taft; the rest of the stock was passed on to their two daughters, Jane Ingalls, wife of a vice-president of the New York Central Railroad, and Anna Louise Semple, whose husband was a Latin professor at the University of Cincinnati.

Lean and unassuming Hulbert Taft became the paper's new editor and publisher. He had started as a reporter and during his long career scored two notable "beats," a 1929 interview with Mussolini at Chigi Palace and a later interview with Trotsky in Mexico. Under his leadership there would be no change in the complexion of the paper. John Gunther called him "the most conservative man I met in forty-eight states." He thought Dewey was a "radical" and the nomination of Willkie "treasonable."[106] In local politics he opposed Charlie Taft's Charter Party, while often giving qualified support to his cousin as a candidate. "Though I may have been prejudiced in favor of the Republican Party," said the wry, dapper editor when he celebrated his fiftieth year with the *Times-Star*, "I made the interesting discovery as a newspaperman that there are a lot of nice people in the Democratic Party."[107]

On Taft's retirement in 1954, David S. Ingalls became the new publisher, and four years later the *Times-Star* was sold to the Scripps-Howard chain. Old Hulbert objected strenuously; journalism was in his blood, and even during the depression he could not bring himself to lay off a single newsman. But Ingalls, speaking for the rest of the family, saw the paper primarily as a frightfully unprofitable business venture. Hulbert's sons then took over the family's radio and television interests and built them into a highly lucrative enterprise.* Their father, the unreconstructed newspaperman, died six months after the *Times-Star* was sold, leaving an estate of $3,409,122.[108]

The year 1936 marked the entrance on the national political scene of Bob and Charlie Taft. Charlie wrote a book, *You and I—and Roosevelt*, a plea for Republicans to adopt a "forward-looking program . . . addressed to the 10 million moderates who voted last time for Roosevelt."[109] It was a prescription for exactly the kind of "me too" campaign

¶ Robert A. Taft's 1000 shares were valued at $160,310—almost a third of his estate—when his will was probated in 1954. See New York *Times*, January 23, 1954, p. 15.

* Hulbert Taft was married three times and had four children by his first wife, Nellie Leaman, who died in 1927. Of his two sons, David died in 1962 at the age of forty-six; Hulbert, Jr. ("Hub"), is head of the Taft Broadcasting Company.

that Bob detested. The role of the opposition was to oppose, he felt, and his virulent anti-New Deal statements were making him the darling of the Ohio Republican organization. On the other hand, Charlie was denied an invitation to address a Republican dinner after his views became known. "They wanted someone who would damn F.D.R. and all his works," said Charlie. "I can't and won't, and some of the Republican orators and candidates who do, give me an acute pain in the neck."[110] Bob was made Ohio's favorite-son candidate for President that year, an unusual honor for a state legislator who had lost his seat in the Roosevelt landslide of 1932.

The chances of Bob Taft defeating incumbent Democratic Senator Robert Bulkley in 1938 were slim. He had a secret weapon, however— his wife. Joseph Alsop and Robert Kintner later wrote, "In the gigantic vaudeville of American politics, the family act is a new kind of turn, popularized as a sideline by Franklin Delano Roosevelt and Anna Eleanor Roosevelt, but brought to its real perfection by Robert Alphonso Taft and Martha Bowers Taft."[111] Columnist Doris Fleeson added: "Martha is the closest thing to an Eleanor Roosevelt that the party has produced."[112] (It was an often heard comparison that annoyed Taft.) Martha's speeches across the state, and later across the nation, were an antidote to Bob's learned, fact-crammed, often elliptical statements. He specialized in complexities; she grossly oversimplified. His voice was harsh and nasal; hers was a warm mezzo-soprano. His appearance was almost clerical; she looked like a friendly, dumpy housewife. He moaned, "I never can remember any funny stories," while her talks sparkled with humor—"the sort that tickles without scratching," said Alice Roosevelt Longworth.[113] ("The torch of Liberty is like your husband or your furnace. If you don't do something about it, it will go out." "To err is Truman." "We've got a highboy government in Washington. One bureau on top of another. And there are termites in the drawers."[114])

After Senator Bulkley's wife told a group of coal miners to vote for her husband because he was a humble man of simple tastes, not highly educated, Mrs. Taft rose and said, "My husband is not a simple man. He did not start from humble beginnings. My husband is a very brilliant man. He had a fine education at Yale. He has been well trained for his job. Isn't that what you prefer when you pick leaders to work for you?" She "wowed the miners," according to *Time* magazine.[115] When the votes came in, a Cleveland paper headlined the results: BOB AND MARTHA TAFT ELECTED TO THE SENATE.[116]

The senator-elect, in a derby hat and wearing rimless glasses, got off the train in Washington to find that he could almost have caucused with his Republican colleagues in a Union Station telephone booth. For in 1939 there were seventy-three Democrats in the ninety-six-man Senate. The dispirited minority was only too willing to give Taft key committee assignments and all the national leadership he wished to assume. Within a year the freshman senator from Ohio was the leading candidate for his party's presidential nomination. Harold Ickes asked President Roosevelt who he thought would be his opponent. He answered, "Taft."[117] "Bob Taft of Ohio is . . . today the No. 1 Republican Presidential possibility," reported *Time*. "Only a miracle could give the nomination to . . . Wendell Willkie."[118] The Taft camp was so confident of victory that its candidate's Washington telephone number was changed to "ME-1940."[119] Bob's cousin David Sinton Ingalls was his campaign manager and personal pilot. An unpretentious millionaire, grandson of the "rich Tafts" and husband of a Harkness of Standard Oil, Ingalls was the first aviator to win the Navy Cross for his exploits in World War I. Later President Hoover appointed him Assistant Secretary of the Navy, a job usually reserved for a Roosevelt.

Brother Charlie, now a Cincinnati city councilman, enthusiastically pitched in, as he would in all Bob's attempts to be President. The candidate's mother and sister went to the convention to see another Taft on his way to the presidency, although the former First Lady, who had wanted so much to live in the White House and had been so unhappy there, never wished her son to be President.

Bob's votes rose steadily for five ballots, but so did those of a "barefoot boy from Wall Street" named Willkie. On the sixth ballot Taft was denied the first of the three presidential nominations he sought.

Except for an abortive attempt to help Landon in 1936, and his work for his brother's candidacy in 1940, Charlie Taft confined his activities to Cincinnati. It seemed almost inconceivable that there could be a drive for any worth-while cause without him as chairman, fund raiser, or legal counselor. He taught Sunday school, settled strikes, organized campaigns for the Community Chest, built low-cost housing. Some called him a crusader; others said that "if his name wasn't Taft, he'd be a YMCA secretary."[120]

The Democratic Administration brought him to Washington in 1941 for wartime service. In a variety of second-echelon jobs he helped run health and recreation programs in areas swollen by army camps and defense industries, consolidated fund raising for overseas relief, advised the State Department of economic, transportation and communications problems. He was adviser to the American delegation at the San Francisco Conference, during which Senator Vandenberg wrote in his diary, "Charles Taft made his first appearance recommending a change in the language setting up the [United Nations] Social and Economic Council. He wanted to spell out a do-gooder program for the whole world. . . . The Delegation unanimously threw out the new proposals. . . . We are *not* going to try to make over the whole world in one document or at one sitting."[121]

Charlie was also given the job of pushing through Congress a renewal of the Reciprocal Trade Agreements Act. The leading opponent was Senator Robert Taft, who thoughtfully absented himself from committee when Charlie was testifying. "I'm still the little brother," Charlie told a reporter, "and he doesn't pay any attention to me. When I want to get a point over to him I send somebody who has his confidence; I don't tackle him myself any more." The next day Bob replied, "The trouble with Charlie is that he takes the opinions of any group of people with whom he is thrown. He seems to be sold on the beliefs of the present State Department staff. I'm not."[122] But generally they avoided areas of friction and remained close companions. Charlie steadfastly maintained that they were not as far apart ideologically as the press made them appear.

If, as most people said, Bob was more like his mother and Charlie took after his father, the differences between them were accentuated by the women they married. Again, in the Taft tradition, there was the blending of opposites; it was what made the Robert Tafts such a re-markable political team. Martha, the born campaigner and extrovert, was a public person. While the gentle Eleanor was a very private person, who never involved herself in politics, and kept busy with church work, humanitarian causes, and her seven children. The sisters-in-law intensified the political separateness of the two families.

"Taft failed to win the Presidency for the same reasons that he suc-ceeded in becoming the most influential senator of his time," wrote Elmo Roper, who polled the nation's feelings about Bob Taft from 1939 through 1952.[123] The astute pollster meant that the Senate, as meeting ground for minority views, could open its heart, and sometimes its mind, to a man of great integrity and logic, even if most people rejected his philosophy as irrelevant to their experiences. At a time when the nation was edging toward the greatest international struggle in history, the Ohio senator saw its destiny as distinct from that of the rest of the world; as the nation was stumbling through its greatest depression, he clung to the ideals of laissez-faire economics. Taft's view of life and government was flawlessly coherent, and the people four times chose Franklin D. Roose-velt, who rarely concerned himself with coherency. For Taft, the rational man, the idol of the Senate, was proceeding down a lonesome road, while America marched off in another direction with Roosevelt.

But besides their ideological differences, almost all Roosevelts offended the sense of order of almost all Tafts. "He proposes scheme after scheme intended for the ultimate benefit of the people," said Bob of Franklin, "but he has no interest in the manner in which each scheme is worked out. . . ."[124] Roosevelts were traditionally concerned with ends; Tafts with means. Then too, Franklin had his fifth cousin's habit of creating organized frenzy. And it was infuriating. "The New Deal had discovered the secret of perpetual emotion," said Bob, though the quip bore the mint mark of Martha.[125]

Yet Taft was a man of continuing paradoxes. The man who was so conservative on most public questions was an outstanding liberal in two important fields—low-cost public housing, an area that he believed was not being adequately served by the private enterprise system, and federal aid to education. Education, thought Taft, was the birthright of the young, who needed the special benefits of government in a way that would be unthinkable for adults. Moreover, education was "constitutionally socialistic," much as was the U. S. Post Office.[126]

John F. Kennedy saw another paradox: "The late Senator Robert A. Taft of Ohio was never President of the United States. Therein lies his personal tragedy. And therein lies his national greatness."[127] Taft never wavered in his presidential ambition, yet he would never make the compromises necessary to attain that ambition. Politicians might consider it a form of foot-in-the-mouth disease, but Taft persisted in saying things that could only alienate him from the majority of his countrymen. Kennedy's "Profile in Courage" of Taft was based on a speech he made on the eve of the 1946 congressional elections and ten days before the Nazi leaders were to be hanged, in which he denounced the Nuremberg war crimes trials as perversion of equal justice under law. Politically the Republican leader had chosen the wrong text at the wrong time. "But as a piece of sheer candor in a period when candor was out of favor, as a bold plea for justice in a time of intolerance and hostility," wrote Kennedy, "it is worth remembering here."[128]

The 1940s opened and closed with a Taft defeat for a presidential nomination. In between, the obituary columns tolled the passing of an earlier generation. The old schoolmaster, Horace Dutton Taft, eighty-one years of age, died in January 1943. Since his retirement in 1936 he had kept busy as an inveterate writer of letters to the editor and worker for liberal causes—a League of Nations, civil service reform, birth control. William Howard Taft had once said that he had the political views of "a theoretical pedant"; he was the least hidebound of the four famous brothers.[129] Mrs. William Howard Taft passed away in May 1943. Henry Waters Taft died in 1945, age eighty-six. The distinguished New York lawyer once wrote, "My excursions into the literary field are fitful; and the exactions of professional life leave little time for authorship."[130] Yet he had managed to write eight books—several on the law, one of family reminiscences, two on Japan, and two on the art of conversation.[131] He might have had a political career but declined a Republican nomination for governor of New York. His wife Julia enjoyed luxurious living, which corporation law rather than public office was more likely to gratify. (The rest of the family considered her a difficult person, and her conversion to Catholicism did not make her easier to accept.)†

Bob Taft's four sons were off at war. Bill, the oldest, was in military intelligence; Bob, Jr., who looked most like his mother, had left Harvard Law School to enlist in the navy and was a junior officer during the landings at Guadalcanal, Sicily, Salerno, Normandy, and Okinawa; Lloyd was also a naval officer on board the U.S.S. *Iowa;* and Horace ("Hoz"), who looked most like his father, was a master sergeant, seeing action in the Philippines.

At home Senator Taft decided to duck another campaign for the Republican presidential nomination in 1944. "I felt an obligation to permit John Bricker to run," he wrote, "and did not desire to give up my seat in the Senate. I was up for re-election."[132] His opponents called him "Our Illustrious Dunderhead," an "isolationist Tory" whose thinking had not advanced "beyond the middle of the last century."[133] Yet he managed to squeak through by 17,000 votes.

The next year Charlie Taft returned from Washington and was defeated for his old seat on the Cincinnati City Council. The loss was ascribed to various causes: peculiarities of proportional-representation voting, his late entry in the campaign, or simply that Cincinnati was getting a bit fed up with Tafts.

However, the dynasty's fortunes began to improve when the Republicans captured Congress in 1946. Bob preferred to let old Wallace White of Maine be the majority leader, but he so obviously ran the Senate that one newsman suggested that White should "install a rear view mirror at his desk in order to get Taft's signals instantly."[134] It was during the 80th Congress that Taft put through his most important piece of legislation, the Taft-Hartley Act, an attempt to restore balance to labor-management relations. The unions called it the "Slave Labor Act" and marked its principal author for oblivion. A week after it became law his son Lloyd was married at St. Joseph, Michigan. Local 931 of the United Electrical, Radio and Machine Workers Union, CIO, announced that it would picket the church. Signs were prepared: *Taft Married the N.A.M. Taft Divorced Himself from the American People.* Police were called out from six surrounding towns. But only fifteen pickets showed up and they were lost in the crowd of well-wishers.[135] The senator seemed undisturbed by the commotion. Lloyd was his second son to marry a Michigan girl, and

---

† Henry W. Taft was survived by three children: a daughter Louise; William Howard Taft II, the New York banker; and Walbridge S. Taft (1885–1951), who was a prominent yachtsman and succeeded his father in the firm of Cadwalader, Wickersham & Taft. He ran for Congress on the Republican Progressive ticket in 1916, losing to the Tammany incumbent. See New York *Times,* January 3, 1951, p. 27.

he quipped to Senator Vandenberg at the reception, "Well, Van, you may be Michigan's favorite son, but you can see I am Michigan's favorite father-in-law."[136]

The Republicans rejected Bob again in 1948. With victory in the air the delegates gave their hearts to Taft and their votes to Dewey. They were duty-bound to pick a winner; Taft, they always convinced themselves, could not win. William Howard Taft III was at the convention, where he met the chief of the Marshall Plan mission to Ireland. He told the chief that he had learned Gaelic as a hobby, and was offered a job in Dublin. It became a family joke that Bill was the only Taft to get anything out of that Republican Convention.[137] Young Bob was also there—"an errand boy, confidential messenger, and handler of details," he later said.[138] He was now an associate in his father's Cincinnati law firm. Lloyd was a reporter on the *Times-Star;* Horace was at Yale, studying physics.

When Congress convened in 1949 a small group of liberal Republican senators, led by Henry Cabot Lodge, tried to remove Taft from the chairmanship of the Republican Policy Committee. Taft beat back the thrust with little difficulty. Later that year Martha suffered a stroke. She returned from the hospital a permanent invalid, only her right arm free from paralysis. "Bob Taft, however, treated her as if she were the same full partner in his life she had always been," recalled Darrah Dunham Wunder, an old family friend, who then came to live with the Tafts.[139] Each night he wheeled Martha in to dinner, read to her until ten o'clock, then carried her to bed. Columnist Holmes Alexander remembered a party at the Tafts' Georgetown home: "The Senator stood, huge and hearty, in the informal receiving line. Beside him in a wheel chair sat Mrs. Martha Taft, her once alert face sagging with paralysis. She was a pitiable sight, but Taft did not know this. Martha was his personal treasure. He presented her to the company as the most charming hostess who ever received."[140]

The team of "Taft and Taft" had to go on as a solo in 1950. Bob was being opposed for re-election by the full force of organized labor and a spectacularly unlettered man called "Jumpin' Joe" Ferguson, the state auditor. The unions distributed one million copies of a comic book which portrayed Taft's career in possibly libelous strokes. (One union dared the senator to sue, but the gauntlet was never picked up.) Many leading Democrats, including Vice-President Barkley, came to Ohio to aid the crusade against Taft. His response was to work harder than ever, making as many as fourteen speeches a day and exhausting whole platoons of assistants and reporters. The result was his greatest victory, carrying every major industrial stronghold—Cleveland, Akron, Youngstown, Dayton, Toledo, Canton—and piling up a 430,000-vote margin.[141] It was his answer to the argument "Taft can't win," and the opening shot in his last campaign for the presidency.

As Bob set out to win the 1952 Republican presidential nomination, Charlie Taft made his own plans to become the Republican gubernatorial nominee in Ohio. The two candidates were received with varying degrees of enthusiasm by the party regulars. While a Gallup poll showed Bob to be the favorite of 1027 out of 1727 county chairmen, the Ohio Republican organization said of Charlie, "His political background has been and is a continuous association with Democrats."[142] The regulars were particularly bitter over Charlie's 1948 vote in the City Council that had made a Democrat mayor of Cincinnati. At that time a Republican councilman had shouted at him, "You are giving comfort to the enemy! . . . Your brother is one of the principal contenders for the office of President. Yet today, by your vote, you will elect as mayor one of the foremost supporters in this community of the Roosevelt New Deal machine." Charlie replied, "It has been my conviction for some time that one detriment to my brother's candidacy is the total inadequacy of his hometown Republican organization in its contribution to good government."[143] Charlie missed no opportunity to applaud his brother as he campaigned across the state, but Bob said, "I'm not going to take any part in behalf of or against my brother."[144] In May, without the support of the senior United States senator and with the opposition of the state organization, Charles Taft handily defeated a former governor and a state senator to become the Republican gubernatorial nominee.

The key to the 1952 Republican presidential convention, which was held at Chicago in July, was the seating of three Southern delegations. In 1912 Teddy Roosevelt had built his case around seventy-two disputed votes; Eisenhower now singled out sixty-eight votes from Georgia, Louisiana, and Texas. The fifty-year-old anti-Taft slogan, "Thou Shalt Not Steal," was dusted off by Henry Cabot Lodge, Eisenhower's political chief of staff. When Bob offered to split the votes, Lodge replied with finality, "General Eisenhower is a no deal man."[145] The issue may have been manufactured in the back room, but in the cold light of day it had a clean, clear ring of morality. The Eisenhower victory on the seating of the contested delegations was the push that started a bandwagon. When Harry S. Truman heard the news he said with a broad smile, "I am afraid that my favorite candidate is going to be beaten."[146] The old pro from Missouri was right; Taft went down to defeat on the first ballot.

Bob's defeat was a blow to Charlie's gubernatorial hopes in Ohio. "Had Bob been nominated, money would have poured in, and Charlie would have benefited," wrote Richard L. Maher of the Cleveland *Press*. "Republicans who dislike Charlie as much as they love his brother would have gone along out of loyalty to Bob. Today Bob's henchmen in Ohio are refusing to help Charlie. So there will be queer doings in Ohio this fall: some Democrats will support Taft for Governor and some Republicans, irked by his 'New Dealism,' will oppose him."[147] Taft was defeated for governor, even losing his own Hamilton County by almost 20,000 votes.

Although Charlie was to be mayor of Cincinnati in 1956 and 1957, the loss of the governorship ended his higher political aspirations.‡ If one were merely to weigh the political assets of the two brothers, it is startling that Bob became the political leader, while Charlie remained on the fringes of power, always on the verge, never quite grasping it. Both had the name, the courage, the ability, the energy. But it was Charlie who had the looks, the personality, the platform ability, and the war record. There was in him, wrote *Fortune* magazine, "a faint suggestion of St. George and St. Paul, with a dash of Frank Merriwell."[148] It was a statement that would never have been made of Bob. Yet three factors were at work against the younger son of President Taft. First, his brother was always ahead of him. ("There can be only one Senator Taft from Ohio," he once said.[149]) Second, he chose to operate outside of party channels in a Republican state that is noted for its cohesive party organization. Third, he was a dilettante, a brilliant Roman candle whose shafts of light scattered across the landscape, while his brother brought to politics a single-mindedness that is often the hallmark of the successful politician.

Only a year was left to Bob Taft after his defeat in 1952 for the presidential nomination. It was to be the most brilliant year of his life. It was a year in which he brought to bear his remarkable parliamentary knowledge to push through the program of the man who had taken from him the dream of a lifetime. After shaking off the bitterness of his defeat he became Eisenhower's leader in the Senate. No twentieth-century President has had a more effective legislative leader.[150] And it was a year in which the courage with which he faced death inspired a nation, and even became the theme of a book. On April 19, while playing golf with President Eisenhower at Augusta, Georgia, Taft first felt a pain in his hip. It was cancer. On July 31, 1953, he died. One of his doctors said, "He was about the best loser I have ever seen. He gave us all a lesson in how to die."[151]

Remarkable tributes came to Robert A. Taft in death. His body lay in a bronze coffin in the rotunda of the Capitol, just as had his father's twenty-three years before. A poll of senators chose him as the most outstanding man ever to have served in the Senate. A committee headed by Senator

‡ However, he made a halfhearted race for the Republican gubernatorial nomination in 1958. After Republican Governor O'Neill had a mild heart attack, Charlie filed as a "standby candidate," in case O'Neill's health forced his withdrawal. Taft claimed he would "not lift a finger" to advance his cause, but obviously some fingers were raised, for the "noncandidate" received thirty-six per cent of the vote. See James Reichley, *States in Crisis* (Chapel Hill: University of North Carolina Press, 1964), p. 134.

John F. Kennedy picked Taft, Clay, Webster, Calhoun, and La Follette
as Senate "immortals," whose portraits would hang in the Senate Reception Room.§ A marble monument, topped by twenty-seven bells, was
placed across from the Capitol in his memory. Washington, Jefferson, and Lincoln had been so honored, but never before had so massive a memorial been erected to a senator. Said Walter Lippmann, who
had usually crossed swords with him during his lifetime:

> The nation came to rely upon his character as something apart from his
> politics, and upon the quality of his mind rather than upon his political
> opinions.
> He was the very opposite of the hollow men with their fabricated person-
> alities. The inner man was the solidest part of Taft, and at the core he was
> so genuine and so just, so rational and so compassionate that he commanded
> the confidence of men when he could never convince them.[152]

Young Bob Taft might have succeeded his father in the Senate—at
least there was a great deal of sentimental enthusiasm for such a move
—but he preferred to bide his time and learn the political trade. The
Tafts, unlike the younger generation of Roosevelts, for example, have
never believed in capitalizing on the short-term advantages that are
offered to sons of distinguished fathers. There are foundation stones in
politics, they feel, and without cementing them firmly in place even the
most elaborate edifice will topple. There was precedent for Bob's de-

§ The degree to which John F. Kennedy's respect for Robert A. Taft was
politically motivated has been the subject of some discussion. Kennedy's
citation of Taft in *Profiles in Courage* may have been for purposes of "balance."
For Taft's act—speaking out against the Nuremberg trials—was clearly not comparable in magnitude to the other senatorial deeds on which the book was
based. If this was designed as a sop to the conservatives, then Kennedy was
successful. Wrote one right-winger of *Profiles in Courage*: "Kennedy's open
admiration for the great Ohioan [Taft] came as something of a shock to leftists
who have been seeking to portray him as a full-fledged liberal." See Russell
Turner, "Senator Kennedy: The Perfect Politician," *American Mercury*, March
1957, pp. 38–39.
It must also be recalled that Kennedy went to considerable lengths to woo
the Taft supporters in Massachusetts when he ran for the Senate against
Henry Cabot Lodge in 1952. A letter from the director of Independents for
Kennedy began: "Ambassador [Joseph] Kennedy, who by the way is a very
close friend of Senator Taft's, has supported the Senator during the Campaign
[for the Republican Presidential nomination]. . . ." See Ralph M. Blagden,
"Cabot Lodge's Toughest Fight," *Reporter*, September 30, 1952, p. 12.
And of his decision to include Taft among the five Senate "immortals,"
Professor Burns writes, "Actually, he [Kennedy] was glad from a political
standpoint to support Taft. At a time when his voting was becoming increasingly down-the-line liberal, he still wanted to keep some ties with the conservative camp." See James MacGregor Burns, *John Kennedy: A Political Profile*
(New York: Harcourt, Brace, 1960), p. 209.

clining national office. His father could have had a major appointment in his friend Hoover's Administration but remained instead in the Ohio legislature.

So in 1954 Bob ran for a seat in the state assembly. While the other candidates talked about local problems, he emphasized national issues. To reporters he explained, "That's what I know most about. After all, I've heard them discussed by experts in the living room of my own home ever since I was a child."[153] He served four terms in the legislature, the last as its majority leader, and sponsored nearly forty successful bills, covering a wide range of matters from securing higher interest on public funds deposited in banks to giving epileptics the right to get driver's licenses.

Unlike the usual procedure in dynasties—firmly adhered to by the Kennedys—that the oldest shall be the first, the Tafts preferred to follow a rule of natural political selection. Thus Charles Phelps Taft deferred to William Howard Taft, and now Robert Taft, Jr., rather than William Howard Taft III, was chosen to carry on the family tradition.¶

Bill Taft—the oldest of the senator's four sons—had prepared for a career as an English teacher. He wrote his Ph.D. thesis at Princeton on *Lytton as a Literary Critic,* and later taught at Maryland, Haverford, and Yale.* But he did not completely turn his back on politics. When Senator Taft ran for the presidential nomination in 1952, his son spent three weeks campaigning in South Dakota. His main reason for leaving the classroom, he says, was to see if he would like a political career. The senator won the primary by an 816-vote margin, but Bill concluded, "I didn't like constantly smiling—at least not professionally."[154]

However, Bill was still less than committed to the academic life. Having been a student of Celtic culture, whose interest in the Irish was reinforced by a tour of duty as a Marshall Plan official in Dublin, he determined, after Eisenhower was elected President, that he would seek the post of ambassador to Ireland. He waged what amounted to a full-scale political campaign in his own behalf. There were about fifty candidates for the job, including a number of wealthy political contributors. But Taft, then thirty-seven, got the jump on his competitors and never let up. He lined up endorsements from the Connecticut senators (he was a resident of New Haven) and got the backing of

¶ The senator's two youngest sons have never been involved in politics. Lloyd Bowers Taft was assistant publisher of the Cincinnati *Times-Star* at the time of its sale to Scripps-Howard, then became general manager of the Taft radio station in Birmingham, Alabama, and is now a New York stockbroker. Horace Dwight Taft is a professor of physics at Yale.

* While at Haverford College, Aunt Helen Taft Manning introduced him to his future wife, a student of hers named Barbara Bradfield from Grand Rapids, Michigan. Like her husband, she also earned a Ph.D. The William Howard Tafts have two sons and two daughters.

important Irish-American organizations. His father was amused and proud of his ambition but did not actively support him. Yet the name helped, as did his experience, and the "fat cats" tended to cancel each other out. In March 1953 William Howard Taft III won appointment as the first Gaelic-speaking U.S. ambassador to Ireland.

The towering new diplomat was a popular figure in Ireland. The life was pleasant and the people were flattered that the American could speak their ancient language—often better than they could speak it themselves. When Eisenhower was re-elected, Secretary of State Dulles asked him to stay on in Dublin, but the Taft conscience feared excessive comfort. Dulles then offered him the Ceylon embassy. He declined, feeling that his knowledge of Asia was inadequate. (The post went to a merchant who didn't know the Prime Minister's name.) However, Bill had made a positive decision: he would make diplomacy his career. He joined the policy planning staff at the State Department, later went to Mozambique as consul general, and is now in the Office of International Scientific Affairs. He is probably the only person ever to have become a foreign service officer after having served as a politically appointed ambassador. The odds are that he will one day become an ambassador again.

Bob, Jr., the fourth-generation Taft in politics, made his first race for a federal office in 1962, running for Ohio congressman at large against Richard D. Kennedy. His Democratic opponent had won his party's nomination in an eleven-man contest. The voters had simply chosen a familiar name; there could be no other explanation for selecting Kennedy, an unknown, inarticulate, and inept segregationist from Cleveland, who was no kin to the Massachusetts dynasty.[155] But though Taft was elected virtually by default (his winning margin was over 620,000 votes), he proved himself to be an effective campaigner. While not handsome, he was tall, powerfully built, with a big grin and a cheerful, outgoing personality. The contrast with his father could hardly escape notice. "I guess it's true when they say I meet people more easily," young Bob said. "It's not that my father was not a warm person—he was. But he was preoccupied and a little shy."[156] In contrast, too, were the first and second Mrs. Robert Tafts. Martha had been the political counterbalance to the senator's shyness; young Bob's wife, Blanca Noel, the daughter of a New York investment banker, detests public speaking and the notoriety that comes with political life. She has been known to disappear suddenly after sighting a television camera.†

† Mr. and Mrs. Robert Taft, Jr., have four children: Robert A. Taft II, a graduate of Yale, who served two years with the Peace Corps in Tanzania; Sarah, the wife of Winfield P. Jones II; Deborah, a college student; and Jonathan, born in 1955.

In Washington, where freshman legislators, like Victorian children, are expected to be seen but not heard, Bob Taft was a notable exception. In 1963 and 1964 his speaking schedule took him to Michigan, Indiana, Illinois, Maryland, Maine, New York, Connecticut, Virginia, and California. Clearly it was the name that was in demand. While many dynasts have gone to great pain to emphasize the great pain of wearing a distinguished label, the Tafts, including the present generation, admit without embarrassment that the name is a "definite advantage."

Young Taft's statements and votes on domestic issues proved him to be not very unlike his father ideologically; he called himself "a thinking conservative," and was outspoken in opposition to moves, including a tax cut, that would further unbalance the federal budget.[157] He was also a strong advocate of civil rights measures, having introduced a bill that was broader in scope than the original Kennedy proposal. If the press termed him a "Moderate Republican," it was in contrast to Barry Goldwater rather than his father. On foreign policy, however, he was more internationally oriented than the late senator.

When, in May 1964, he ran for the Republican senatorial nomination, his opponent, Ohio Secretary of State Ted Brown, a strong Goldwater supporter, told audiences, "Speaking bluntly, young Taft's record is more compatible with that of his uncle Charles than that of his distinguished father."[158] But Taft, backed by the state organization, ignored Brown's charges and won the right to challenge Democratic Senator Stephen Young by a four-to-one margin.

Old Senator Young was too easily dismissed by many observers. The seventy-five-year-old politician had won his first elective office in 1912, when Bob's grandfather occupied the White House. An expert in abrasive, and often abusive, stump speaking, Young, with utter scorn, referred to his opponent merely as "Junior," and attempted to wrap Bob in the views of his party's presidential candidate. "Junior has not repudiated them [the John Birch Society] and will not repudiate them," he asserted. "Goldwater extremism and Taft Juniorism in Ohio are really one and the same thing."[159] Charlie Taft, chairman of the Committee to Support Moderate Republicans, attempted to raise money for his nephew's campaign, but Bob's political problems were other than financial. Lyndon Johnson carried Ohio by the largest plurality ever achieved by a presidential candidate, over one million votes, and Young was firmly attached to his coattails. Out of 3.8 million votes cast for senator, Taft lost by 16,000. Despite a population increase, 175,000 fewer voters went to the polls than in 1960. The stay-at-homes were largely in rural and small-town Ohio where Republicans refused to vote for either Johnson or Goldwater. Taft was the innocent victim.

The defeat probably did little more than upset the political timetable that some columnists and friends had set for Bob. ("Elected to the Senate in 1964 and kept ever-increasingly before the national public," wrote pundit Marquis Childs in February 1963, "Taft could be the presidential nominee in 1968 when he is 50 years old."[160]) The circumstances of his 1964 loss—running so far ahead of the top of his ticket—and the apparent commitment that so many have made to his future could make Bob Taft a force in national political life for the next decade.

Charlie Taft's two sons may also have political futures.‡ Seth is a Cleveland lawyer who was a candidate for the Ohio State Senate in 1962. Running in a Democratic district, he lost by less than one vote per precinct. Many close to him feel that if he pursues politics it will be on the state, rather than national, level. Peter, the younger son, however, talks of broader horizons. Handsome and articulate, he is now a Washington attorney—the assistant to noted trial lawyer Edward Bennett Williams—after having served as clerk for Chief Justice Earl Warren. He is considering putting down his political roots outside of Ohio, although the Tafts, like the once famous Catawba wine of Cincinnati, may not travel well.

The diaspora of the Tafts could eventually spell their demise as a dynasty. While an American political dynasty usually depends on a high birth rate, and there are certainly enough Tafts to carry on, today only two make their political base in Cincinnati—the aging Charles, still on the City Council, and Bob, Jr., candidate for a congressional seat in 1966. Three of Senator Taft's sons no longer live in Ohio; one of Charles Taft's two sons is not now planning to make his residence there. Although the Harrisons and the Washburns have proved that a dynasty need not be firmly fixed in a single state, and the Kennedys may be proving that a dynasty can be national in character, the prevailing trend, reinforced by the federal nature of our system, has been to rely on the continuing loyalties of a relatively small electorate to build national power. The

‡ The Charles P. Tafts (she died in 1961) also had five daughters: Rosalyn died of polio in 1941; Lucia, a graduate of Vassar and a teacher, took her life in 1955, after a history of medical illnesses and depression; Sylvia is married to William Lotspeich, professor of medicine at the University of Rochester; Eleanor is married to Dr. Donald Hall, a Seattle physician; Cynthia is married to Donald Morris, a foreign service officer. Although paralyzed from the waist down by polio, Mrs. Morris earned a M.Sc. at the London School of Economics in 1951 and a Ph.D. in economics at Yale in 1959. She is now the mother of a son, a consultant to the Agency for International Development (AID), teaches a course at American University, and is the recipient of a three-year grant from the National Science Foundation to do research on the economics of underdeveloped nations. (Interview with Mrs. Morris, February 4, 1965, Washington.)

Breckinridges, for example, virtually died out politically after war, mobile occupations, and appointive office took them from Kentucky.

Even if this were to be the case, a great name has its own political currency and can often linger on for a generation or more after leaving its native soil. This usually occurs by appointment to office. But since American political power in the long run is always built on election, it is a sure sign of dynastic decay.

However, there is no doubt that the Tafts, individually and as a family, have always been deeply committed to public service. Without the flamboyancy of the Roosevelts or the great sustaining wealth of the Kennedys, they have plodded along for four generations in politics. They have been a kind of model of the unheroic leader, steady, sturdy, dedicated. Moreover, they have been more ideologically oriented than many other dynasties, which is apt to give them added staying power. It would be foolhardy indeed to count them out. Especially at a time when a relatively young dynast is a political leader of Ohio. And after Bob Taft, Jr.—time will tell.

The Frelinghuysen Dynasty

"Come hither, ye careless, at ease in sin, yet
carnal and earthly minded, ye unchaste whoremongers, adulterers, ye proud, haughty men
and women, ye devotees of pleasure, drunkards, gamblers, ye disobedient, ye wicked re-
jectors of the Gospel, ye hypocrites and dis-
semblers, how suppose ye it will go with you?"

—Rev. Theodorus Jacobus Frelinghuysen
to his congregants.[1]

THESE were words of the Great Awakening, the religious revival that
swept the country in the mid-eighteenth century and became the first
spontaneous mass movement in American history. Its leaders were
George Whitfield, Methodist; Jonathan Edwards, Congregationalist; William and Gilbert Tennent, Presbyterians; and Theodorus Jacobus Frelinghuysen of the Dutch Reformed Church. They preached an evangelical
piety, a denunciation of formalism, and a reformation of morals.

Another young man who reached America at the height of the movement was Henry Melchior Muhlenberg, who thoroughly agreed with the
aims of this new guard. It is probable that Muhlenberg met Frelinghuysen, for the German Lutheran minister twice visited Raritan during
Frelinghuysen's lifetime.[2] The ecclesiastical founders of these two great
political dynasties had much in common. Muhlenberg, "The Patriarch of
the German Lutheran Church in America," and Frelinghuysen, "The
Apostle of the Raritan," had both been trained in the doctrine of German
pietism. But Muhlenberg was to make his mark as a church administrator,
while Frelinghuysen was primarily an evangelist.

Frelinghuysen preceded Muhlenberg to America by eighteen years.
The Frelinghuysens were also from Germany, living in Westphalia on the
Dutch border, but they were purely Dutch in culture and religion, and
it was the Dutch Reformed Church that sent the first Frelinghuysen to
America to take charge of four congregations in the Raritan Valley of

THE FRELINGHUYSEN DYNASTY
(A Selective Genealogy)

Reverend Theodorus Jacobus Frelinghuysen (1691–1748)
"The Apostle of the Raritan"
Arrived America 1720
(7 children)

Reverend Theodore (1724–61)

Reverend John (1727–54)
m. Dinah Van Bergh (1725–1807) (2 children)

Margaret (1737–57)
m. Reverend Thomas Romeyn

Ann (1738–1810)
m. Reverend William Jackson

Frederick (1753–1804)
General, SENATE (7 children)

John (1776–1833)
Militia general (10 children)

Maria (1778–1832)
Temperance pioneer
m. Reverend John Cornell

Theodore (1787–1862)
SENATE, university president (no issue)

Frederick (1788–1820)
(5 children)

Frederick J. (1818–91)
(6 children)

Frederick Theodore (1817–85)
SENATE, Secretary of State (6 children)

Joseph Sherman
(1869–1948)
SENATE

Frederick (1848–1924)
Insurance company
president
(5 children)

George Griswold (1851–1936)
m. Sarah Ballantine (1858–1940),
brewery heiress
(2 children)

Sarah Helen
(c. 1854–1939)
1st m. John Davis,
Assistant
Secretary of State

Suzy
Opera singer
m. George Morris

Peter Hood Ballantine
(1882–1959) Cattle breeder
m. Adaline Havemeyer (1884–
1963), sugar heiress
(4 children)

Matilda E. Davis
m. George Cabot Lodge
(1873–1909), poet son
of Senator
Henry Cabot Lodge
(3 children)

Peter Hood Ballantine (1916–   )
HOUSE OF REPRESENTATIVES
m. Beatrice Procter
(5 children)

New Jersey.* Theodorus Jacobus settled in January 1720 at what is now Somerville, and is today in the district represented by Congressman Peter Frelinghuysen, his great-great-great-great-great-grandson.

Young minister Frelinghuysen, twenty-nine years old, had barely stepped off the boat when he found himself in trouble with his congregants. The orthodox Dutch farmers were not grateful to the zealous Frelinghuysen for his suggestion that they were whoremongers, adulterers, drunkards, and gamblers. In 1725 they sent a formal complaint to the mother church in Amsterdam. Among other charges, they accused their pastor of leaving a Jew lying in a mire contrary to the lesson of the Good Samaritan, of encouraging children to defy their parents, and of beckoning his friends to take better seats during church services. (The 146 pages of grievances were published in New York, the first book printed by John Peter Zenger.)[3]

Having no doubt of who was on God's side, Frelinghuysen excommunicated his enemies from the Church; constructed a strong parsonage to protect himself from an attack, complete with a smokehouse in the attic, so that he could cure his own meat in the event of a siege by his congregants; and painted a defiant jingle on the back of his sleigh:

> No man's tongue and no one's pen
> Can make me other than I am.
> Speak, evil speaker, without end,
> In vain you all your slanders spend.[4]

"The Apostle of the Raritan" eventually vanquished his foes, but at a considerable price. He had opened a schism in the Dutch Reformed Church that would not be healed until 1771, when John Henry Livingston united the warring factions.

Frelinghuysen had five sons and two daughters, all of whom either became ministers or married ministers. All the sons died within thirteen years of Theodorus Jacobus' death in 1748, two while returning from Holland where they had been ordained. Yet in their short lives, two of these second-generation ministers, Theodore and John, were to take giant steps toward one of their father's most cherished ideals—the education of the Dutch Reformed clergy in America.

Higher education in colonial America was begot by religion. Harvard and Yale were sired by the Congregationalists; Hampden-Sydney and Princeton by the Presbyterians; William and Mary and Columbia by the

* The Frelinghuysens should be considered primarily Dutch in antecedents, although they are still claimed by the German-Americans. See Albert Bernhardt Faust, *The German Element in the United States* (Boston and New York: Houghton Mifflin, 1927), Vol. I, pp. 153–54, 182.

Anglicans; Brown by the Baptists. Rutgers is the child of the Dutch Reformed Church. And the founding of Rutgers, originally named Queen's College, is the story of the Frelinghuysens.

The career of Theodore Frelinghuysen, eldest son of "The Apostle of the Raritan," is told by Anne MacVicar Grant as it must have appeared to the citizens of Albany, New York, at that time. In 1746 young Frelinghuysen became a parson at Albany where Mrs. Grant, the Highland poetess, spent her childhood. She recalls him as "a martyr to levity and innovation." At the time a troop of gay British soldiers threatened to set a rakish style for his parishioners; Theodore was especially incensed when the British gave a performance of *The Beaux Stratagem.* "This bode fair soon to undo all the good pastor's labors," said Mrs. Grant. "The evil was daily growing; and what, alas, could Domine [Minister] Frelinghuysen do but preach! This he did earnestly, and even angrily, but in vain."[5]

On a Monday morning, after Frelinghuysen had made a particularly zealous attack on theatrical amusements, he found on his doorstep a stick, a pair of old shoes, a crust of black bread, and a dollar. "The worthy pastor was puzzled to think what this could mean; but had it too soon explained to him. It was an emblematic message, to signify the desire entertained of his departure. The stick was to push him away, the shoes to wear on the road, and the bread and money a provision for his journey."[6]

One tradition declares that the minister took this message so much to heart that he committed suicide—a belief fictionalized in an 1875 London novel.[7] Actually, as Mrs. Grant explains, he left for an ocean voyage and fell overboard.

The people of Albany built his disappearance into a legend. Some said he had landed on an island and became a hermit; others contended that he had been picked up by another ship and would someday return. It was the type of romance that appealed greatly to a little girl with poetic instincts, and Mrs. Grant writes, "I remember some of my earliest reveries to have been occupied by the mysterious disappearance of this hard-fated pastor."[8]

But the death of Theodore Frelinghuysen had nothing to do with the "emblematic message" left on his doorstep. Six years before his death he had aggressively lobbied for an American college. In the winter of 1755 he traveled on horseback down the Hudson Valley to rally the ministers and congregations to his cause. His fellow ministers appointed him to carry the case to the mother church in Amsterdam. While in New York City in 1759 an opportunity arose to make the voyage. Without first returning to Albany he set sail for Holland, and it was on his return home that he mysteriously disappeared.

While Theodore worked within the Church for the principle of an

American college, his brother John set up a seminary in his home, which was the precursor of Rutgers as surely as the Tennents' "Log College" had given birth to the Princeton Theological Seminary.

The second son of Theodorus Jacobus, John Frelinghuysen, went to Holland to train for the ministry and returned home to take over three of his deceased father's congregations. The text of his first sermon in the Raritan church: "Instead of thy fathers shall be thy children." He also brought back to America a Dutch wife, Dinah Van Bergh. The pious Dinah would give birth to the first Frelinghuysen senator; strongly influence the life of her grandson, the second Frelinghuysen senator; and play a major role in the Frelinghuysen dream of an American college.

"Every incident in the daily life of this remarkable woman produced a religious influence," wrote Andrew D. Mellick, "and it would seem no experience could be hers without resulting in an individual blessing. Throughout her life she had implicit confidence in special providences, and many instances are related in which she claimed to have experienced undoubted proofs of direct answer to prayer. It was her constant habit to make affairs of either great or minor importance a matter of personal appeal to the Almighty."[9]

Probably the most astonishing example of divine intercession on her behalf occurred on her honeymoon trip to America. The ship sprang a leak; the captain abandoned hope. Dinah "retired to her cabin and submitted the case to her Heavenly Father." She then awaited the result with composure. And miraculously the water stopped rushing into the ship. On close examination, it is related, a swordfish was found to have become wedged into the open seam, thus effectively closing the leak!

When John Frelinghuysen died in 1754, Dinah decided to take her two infants, Eve and Frederick, back to Holland. Then she received a most unexpected proposal of marriage from one of her husband's students, Jacob Rutsen Hardenbergh. The story goes that when this eighteen-year-old mustered courage to approach the widow of his late preceptor, she replied, "My child, what are you thinking about!" (Mrs. Frelinghuysen was then approaching thirty.) However, she had her own second thoughts and accepted—taking her children to the home of her fiancé's father until the young man reached majority and was ready for marriage.

Jacob Rutsen Hardenbergh was part of what has been called "the Dutch aristocracy of New York." He was the grandson of the recipient of the Hardenbergh Patent, one of the largest land grants of the colonial period, which embraced most of Ulster, Delaware, Sullivan, and Greene counties on the west side of the Hudson River, a tract of over a million acres.[10] Young Hardenbergh took over John Frelinghuysen's ministry, raised his children, and realized his dream of a Dutch Reformed school in America. He became the actual founder and first president of Rutgers College.

The college at New Brunswick was finally opened in a former tavern, the Sign of the Red Lion. In 1771 the trustees appointed a faculty of one, who was expected "to teach the English Language grammatically," as well as "The learned Languages, liberal Arts and Sciences." The versatile scholar chosen was Frederick Frelinghuysen, son of John Frelinghuysen and Dinah Van Bergh Frelinghuysen Hardenbergh. He was eighteen years old, having graduated from Princeton the year before. On April 30, 1772, "Frederick Frelinghuysen, Tutor," placed the following advertisement in a New York newspaper:

The Respectable Public is hereby informed that agreeable to a former advertisement, a Seminary of Learning was opened at New Brunswick, last November, by the name of QUEEN'S COLLEGE. . . . Any Parents or Guardians who may be inclined to send their Children to this Institution, may depend upon having them instructed with the greatest Care and Diligence in all the Arts and Sciences usually taught in public Schools; the strictest Regard will be paid to their moral Conduct, (and in a word) to every Thing which may tend to render them a Pleasure to their Friends, and an Ornament to their Species.[11]

Frederick Frelinghuysen stayed at Rutgers only a short time. Jacob Rutsen Hardenbergh became the college's first president in 1786 but died four years later.† The school limped along through the next thirty years, half of the time under the presidency of John Henry Livingston, a great-grandson of the First Lord of the Manor. While a member of a very worldly dynasty (although from a "poor" branch), he became the most important Dutch Reformed minister of his generation. Acting as "an Ambassador of peace," the tall, dignified Livingston managed to reunite the church that the battling Frelinghuysens had torn into factions.[12] But at Rutgers his primary interest was the theological school, and his inattention to secular matters forced the college to close down for several years.

In 1793 a joint committee from the war-racked colleges of Princeton and Rutgers proposed a merger of the two schools, but the Rutgers trustees rejected the plan.[13] By 1824, under a charter from the state legislature, Rutgers had to resort to a lottery to raise funds.[14] The trustees turned the operation of the lottery over to professional managers, who

† The Hardenberghs continued to play an important role in Rutgers affairs after Jacob's death. His son, Jacob, Jr., was a trustee from 1792 to 1841; his grandson, Cornelius L. Hardenbergh, was appointed professor of law in 1835; and his great-great-grandson, Henry Janeway Hardenbergh (1847–1918), designed the college's Kirkpatrick Chapel. This noted architect was primarily known for hotel design; his work includes the Plaza in New York, the Copley Plaza in Boston, and the Willard in Washington.

kept what they raised in return for a guarantee of $25,000 to the college. The operators sold $336,977 worth of tickets in April 1825. (The highest prize, $15,000, went to the holder of ticket number 14-15-28). However the state soon charged the operators with irregularities, and the lottery was stopped. It is doubtful that the college received its full $25,000 from the venture. The school revived shortly after the lottery episode and was a going concern by 1850 when another Frelinghuysen became its president.

The American Revolution proved the ministers of the Dutch Reformed Church to be forceful advocates of independence. Governor William Livingston of New Jersey wrote that "the low Dutch clergy, both in this and in the state of New York, are almost universally friends of these United States." The three patriotic leaders of the Dutch clergy were Jacob Rutsen Hardenbergh and two sons-in-law of Theodorus Jacobus Frelinghuysen, William Jackson and Thomas Romeyn.[15]

Hardenbergh, a delegate to the New Jersey Provisional Congress which ratified the Declaration of Independence, slept with a musket at his bedside, for the British had put a price on his head. Several times he was forced to flee his home, and his church at Raritan was burned by the Queen's Rangers.

But unlike William Jackson, Ann Frelinghuysen's husband, he escaped capture. Jackson was taken prisoner by Lord Howe in New York, and charged with giving violently rebellious sermons. He successfully pleaded that he must act in accordance with the dictates of his conscience. After his release a congregant complained of his continued attacks upon the Crown. "Lord Howe has forgiven me," replied Jackson. "Why not you?"[16]

Another Dutch patriot was Frederick Frelinghuysen, the young Rutgers tutor and Princeton graduate. Under John Witherspoon, Princeton had become the hotbed of radicalism. As William Howard Taft, himself a Yale man, said, "Not one of her sister universities . . . can make itself as Princeton can so much a part of the history of the struggle for independence. . . ."[17] The students carried their principles to the point of dressing only in American-made cloth at commencement—a trying policy, for such cloth was hard to find. In Frederick's senior year they publicly burned a copy of a letter from New York merchants announcing that they planned to order goods from Great Britain. (These eighteenth-century Princeton men would compile a remarkable record: 27 delegates to the Continental Congress; 30 United States senators; 55 members of the House of Representatives; 17 governors; 14 cabinet officers. Of the writers of the Constitution, nine were from Princeton; Yale claimed four; Harvard three.[18]) Frederick Frelinghuysen, who was to become a senator and a general, said that he had learned patriotism as well as Greek from Witherspoon at Princeton.

It was the wish of Frederick's mother, the pious Dinah, that he would become a minister in the tradition of his father and grandfather. But the rigidity and strictness, particularly in regard to Sabbath observances, in the household of his Hardenbergh stepfather repelled the young man. He chose to study law. He probably began his law studies under Richard Stockton and, when Stockton became a member of the Legislative Council, switched to the office of William Paterson.[19]‡

At twenty-two years of age, Frederick was chosen with Witherspoon, Paterson, and Jonathan D. Sergeant to serve in the Provincial Congress. His votes during 1775 and 1776 showed him to be one of the most uncompromising supporters of American independence. Then in 1778 he was named to the Continental Congress. A few months later another New Jersey delegate, John Fell, sent Governor Livingston a whining letter: "I cannot help complaining to your Excellency of the behavior of some of the delegates from our state, which is not only disgraceful to the state, but in my humble opinion, treating me with the greatest impoliteness; they take upon them to leave Congress when they please and without leave, by which the state in course is not represented. Last Saturday Dr. Witherspoon went home without ever saying a word to me on the occasion, and this day Colonel Frelinghuysen went away in the same manner."[20] After only eight months in Congress Frelinghuysen resigned. In a curious letter to the Speaker of the state Assembly, he gave as his reasons: 1) his youth; 2) the pressing duties of "the other appointment with which the legislature of New Jersey has been pleased to honor me in the county of Somerset"; 3) "the amazing expense of attending at Congress, and my inability to support it"; 4) the opposition of Fell, who has "expressed himself with warmth and temper"; and 5) "some other circumstances which render my situation here peculiarly disagreeable, but I fear the evils which might arise from opening myself on this subject, would more than counterbalance any good it might probably answer. I trust, however, the representatives from New Jersey will not think it impertinent . . . to declare to them that the interests of America call on them for extraordinary vigilance."[21]

It is clear that Frelinghuysen did not have the stomach for legislative

‡ There was a close relationship between Frelinghuysen and the Stocktons. In 1788 Frederick tried in vain to secure the clerkship of the state Supreme Court for Samuel Witham Stockton; in the same year he joined with Samuel Whitham and Richard ("The Duke") Stockton in an unsuccessful venture called the New Jersey Land Society; and when Frederick resigned his Senate seat in 1796 he was replaced by Richard Stockton. See Richard P. McCormick, *Experiment in Independence, New Jersey in the Critical Period, 1781–1789* (New Brunswick: Rutgers University Press, 1950), pp. 97–98, 232.

intrigues, although we may never know exactly which intrigue turned his stomach. As for his other duties, since the only "Civil List" of Somerset County makes no reference to any position, Frederick was probably referring to his commission in the county militia. For a young man of twenty-six a soldier's life was far more agreeable than a legislator's. He served with distinction at the battles of Trenton, Princeton, and Monmouth. It is an accepted tradition that at the Trenton victory he fired the shot that killed the commander of the Hessian troops.

By the end of the war Frederick was recognized as the nation's leading Dutch-American. In New Jersey this was not an inconsequential distinction since the Dutch comprised over one sixth of the population. When the minister from the Netherlands arrived in the United States it was only to be expected that Congress asked Frelinghuysen to read his credentials in Dutch at the ceremony.§ In 1793 Frederick was elected to the United States Senate.

In each generation there would be a Frelinghuysen in Congress. In four of the five generations from Frederick to the present, there would be a Senator Frelinghuysen of New Jersey. Yet no major legislation would bear the family name, and only one member of the dynasty would serve more than a single senatorial term.

The first Senator Frelinghuysen, a loyal Federalist, was strictly a "back-bencher." Only once is there evidence that he was out of sorts with his party's policy. When President Adams moved to placate the French, Frelinghuysen wrote to Jonathan Dayton, "I entertain a strong Hope that the *terrible nation* [France] will be so much exasperated by the Impudent conduct of our Sea-Warriors in the West-Indies, as to declare war. . . ." But then thinking perhaps that his humble role was not to second-guess the President, he added, "But I forbear; I will submit to the powers that *be*, and not rail at the Lord's annointed."[22]

While in the Senate, Washington appointed Frelinghuysen a brigadier general in the campaign against the Western Indians. During the Whiskey Rebellion he was made a major general of the New Jersey militia. As his last act of public note he went off to fight the poor farmers of western Pennsylvania, possibly singing the marching song that Governor Richard Howell had personally composed for the New Jersey troops:

§ "Colonel Frederick Frelinghuysen spoke Dutch with such unusual facility that it was remarked by Mr. Van Solaner, Ambassador from the Netherlands, he excelled all in the use of that tongue that the Ambassador had met in this country." Andrew D. Mellick, Jr., "The Pious Dinah Van Bergh," *Somerset County Historical Quarterly*, Vol. III, p. 275; also see J. J. Boudinot, editor, *The Life, Public Services, Addresses and Letters of Elias Boudinot* (Boston and New York: Houghton Mifflin, 1896), Vol. I, pp. 402–3.

> To arms once more, our hero cries,
> Sedition lives and order dies;
> To peace and ease then bid adieu
> And dash to the mountains, Jersey Blue.
>
> Dash to the mountains, Jersey Blue,
> Jersey Blue, Jersey Blue,
> And dash to the mountains, Jersey Blue.[23]

When Frederick Frelinghuysen died on his fifty-first birthday, as he had always predicted he would, he left six children. His two daughters married ministers, and Maria Frelinghuysen Cornell founded one of the earliest American temperance organizations, the Sober Society of Allentown, Pennsylvania. John became an imperious militia general in the War of 1812; Frederick became a lawyer and the father of the third Frelinghuysen senator; Theodore became the second Frelinghuysen senator.

If the pious Dinah had been disappointed when her son Frederick turned his back on the ministry, she had no cause to lament the religiosity of her grandson Theodore. The ancient matriarch, who died in 1807 at age eighty-two, had the strongest influence on his development and, indeed, when Theodore died in 1862, the minister who delivered his memorial service told of how he loved "to speak of his grandmother . . . and how much he owed to her prayers and counsels." Added Dr. Campbell, "He must have received them in no stinted measure."[24]

Theodore Frelinghuysen became known as "The Christian Statesman." Even the viper-tongued John Randolph of Roanoke said of him, "This man does not boast of religion, but he has it, he *has* it!" Theodore kept a book of Scriptures by his razor, and a member of his household said, "I don't believe he would have considered the shaving properly done without the morning's text to meditate upon." In the middle of the day, for forty years without interruption, he put aside fifteen minutes for devotion, during which time he prayed aloud because, as he said, he found it "the best way to prevent wandering thoughts." Every evening after dinner he spent a half hour reading the Bible.[25]

He studied law under Richard Stockton, as his father had studied under Stockton's father, built a lucrative practice in Newark, and became attorney general of New Jersey. After twelve years as the state's legal officer he was elevated to the United States Senate in 1829. It was a time of legislative giants—Webster, Clay, Calhoun—and giant legislative questions. But Frelinghuysen confined his activities to a few intensely personal issues of a religious and moral character, such as his hopeless fight to prevent delivery of mail on the Sabbath. Jeremiah Evarts, the secretary of the American Board of Commissioners for Foreign Missions, was in Washington at the time and reported that Theodore "spoke an hour and a half, or more, and very much to the purpose. Mr. [Edward] Livingston replied, in a speech of three quarters of an hour in which he gained no credit. It was a low piece of bar-room talk about church and state, the blue laws of Connecticut, hanging witches at Salem, etc. etc. Mr. F., in a short reply, made Mr. L. rather ashamed of his tirade."[26]

Yet on the strength of one issue Frelinghuysen rose to national prominence. In a speech of five hours, spread over three days in April 1830, he fought in vain to prevent the state of Georgia from expelling the Cherokee Indians from their land. It was a memorable address which ended, "I had rather receive the blessing of one poor Cherokee . . . than sleep beneath the marble of all the Caesars."[27] Senator Thomas Hart Benton thought him a "pseudo-philanthropic intermeddler."[28] But young William Lloyd Garrison composed a poem entitled, "To the Hon. Theodore Frelinghuysen, On Reading His Eloquent Speech in Defense of Indian Rights." Wrote the future abolitionist leader:

> Yet, Frelinghuysen, gratitude is due thee,
>   And loftier praise than language can supply;
> Guilt may denounce and Calumny pursue thee,
>   And pensioned Impudence thy worth decry;
> Brilliant and pure, posterity shall view thee
>   As a fair planet in a troublous sky.[29]

"The Christian Statesman" was not returned to the Senate in 1834, probably because of his role as counsel in "The Great Quaker Case"—a dispute over the possession of church property between the orthodox Quakers and a splinter group, the followers of Elias Hicks. Frelinghuysen won the case for the orthodox faction, and in return the Hicksites voted against his party. Wrote the diarist Philip Hone, ". . . these Hicksites, in a spirit unworthy of their possessions of meekness and disregard of worldly politics, have deprived the State of the services of one of the most virtuous and enlightened statesmen. . . ."[30]

Returning to Newark, the ex-senator again practiced law, became mayor, and busied himself with his many philanthropic and religious interests, which over the years included: president, American Board of Commissioners for Foreign Missions; president, American Bible Society; vice-president, American Colonization Society; president, American Tract Society; vice-president, American Sunday School Union; vice-president and chairman of the Executive Committee, American Temperance Union.

The only unresolved business of the 1844 Whig Convention was the selection of a vice-presidential candidate. It was a foregone conclusion that the nomination for the presidency would go to Henry Clay. Four names were proposed for the running mate: Theodore Frelinghuysen; Governor John Davis of Massachusetts, known as "Honest John," a foe of slavery and a strong supporter of labor; New York's Millard Fillmore, the protectionist chairman of the House Ways and Means Committee; and little John Sergeant, the Philadelphia lawyer who had run with Clay in 1832, and whose high sense of public morals even rivaled Frelinghuysen's. (Sergeant had once introduced a bill in the Pennsylvania legislature to outlaw masquerades, which he felt led to wrongdoings.) All the candidates were considered able, none outstanding. On the third ballot the convention chose Frelinghuysen. His family name may have influenced the delegates: the Whig platform reminded the voters that its vice-presidential candidate had inherited "the principles as well as the name of a father who, with Washington on the fields of Trenton and Monmouth, perilled life in the contest for liberty and afterward, as a Senator of the United States, acted with Washington establishing and perpetuating that liberty."[31]

Presidential nominee Clay wrote to Thurlow Weed, the boss of New York: "The nomination of Mr. Frelinghuysen was no doubt unexpected by you as it was by me. I think, nevertheless, that it is a most judicious selection, and if he does not add any strength, which however, I think he will do, he will take away none from the ticket."[32] Wall Street lawyer George Templeton Strong held a higher opinion of Frelinghuysen's vote-getting power. "Good nomination was Frelinghuysen's, astute decidedly," he wrote in his diary. "Clay, being by the admission of his friends a good deal of a runner, will run none the worse for having a deacon to ride him."[33]

While most conventions seek balances of geography or ideology, the Whigs had made a balance of morality. Clay, well known for his delight in gambling and dueling, was paired with the president of the American Bible Society. Democratic cartoonists were quick to point out this wholly unholy alliance. One example shows the Devil whispering into Clay's ear, "That's right Harry! take a good Cover; we have 'all the talents' on our side, and if we get Frelinghuysen we will have considerable of the 'decency.'" To which Clay replies, " 'The Righteous shall be my defense' —as the scripture says."[34]

Clay found, however, that running with Frelinghuysen had its drawbacks—"The Christian Statesman" took a deep and nagging interest in the possibility of the Kentuckian's reformation, and for the next eight years bombarded him with notes of moral uplift. The high-living Clay accepted Frelinghuysen's concern with good humor and answered his letters with an unvarying sentence: "I am greatly obliged, my dear friend, by the kind interest you take in my spiritual welfare."[35]

Whig publicists had another problem with Frelinghuysen—his name!

It was particularly unsuitable for campaign songs and jingles. The party finally went into battle against James K. Polk chanting:

> Hurah! Hurah! The country's risin'
> For Henry Clay & Frelinghuysen.

It was an extremely close election. James Birney, the Abolitionist candidate, polled 15,812 votes in New York. Had a third of these gone to Clay he would have been elected President. In his post-mortem analysis, Frelinghuysen wrote Clay, "The alliance of the foreign votes and that most impracticable of all organizations, the Abolitionists, have defeated us."[36] Frelinghuysen's activities in behalf of the American Colonization Society had weakened the Whig appeal to anti-slavery men, while his activities in behalf of Protestant evangelical movements had weakened the Whig appeal to the Irish Catholics. The Catholic archbishop of New York said he would vote for Clay but not for Frelinghuysen. When told that this was impossible, he replied that then he would not vote for Clay.[37] The Frelinghuysen righteousness turned out to be a political liability.

"Theodore Frelinghuysen once told me," said the Rev. William Blauvelt, "that he never liked the practice of law, and intended gradually to get out of it."[38] In 1839 he was named chancellor of New York University. But his administration was not to be a success. He failed to provide the strong leadership that the young school needed. As one of his professors said, "It was, indeed, a fault in this great man and this pure Christian that he had a way of so constantly deferring to others. It was the carrying to excess the apostle's precept: 'Let each man esteem others better than himself.'"[39] During his eleven years at N.Y.U. the chairman of the Board of Trustees resigned with a particularly censorious blast, several of the top professors went to other schools, and the state reduced its financial aid. The historian of the university wrote that by 1850 Frelinghuysen "would gladly then have welcomed an open door to depart . . . the call to Rutgers was that open door; the chancellor withdrew from the institution. . . ."[40] Frelinghuysen served as president of Rutgers until his death in 1862.

Theodore Frelinghuysen had no children. But when his brother Frederick died he adopted his three-year-old son.[41] The boy, Frederick Theodore, studied law in his uncle's office and took over the ready-made practice when his uncle became chancellor of New York University. He also followed his foster father's footsteps when he was named attorney general of New Jersey in 1861 and United States senator in 1866.

Politically, however, Frederick T. Frelinghuysen broke with family tradition. For two generations in the Senate the Frelinghuysens had represented the conservative position. The first Frederick had been a

Federalist; his son Theodore had been a Whig who supported the Constitutional Unionists in 1860. But Theodore's adopted son joined the new Republican Party, and during his two terms in the Senate was part of the radical majority. He favored the impeachment of Andrew Johnson, although he told former Senator Ira Harris that "there was nothing against the President which could be called a crime or misdemeanor, but the President was a troublesome man" and "the majority would be justified in availing themselves of a technical advantage in getting rid of him."[42] Frelinghuysen also took over the management of the Civil Rights Bill when Charles Sumner became incapacitated and successfully shepherded it through the Senate.¶

A Democratic legislature in New Jersey replaced Frelinghuysen when his term expired in 1869. President Grant then appointed him minister to Great Britain, the Senate confirmed the nomination, but Frederick declined the honor—his public reason being that Mrs. Frelinghuysen did not wish to expose their children to the influence of life at the Court of St. James's.[43] It is more likely, however, that he preferred to remain in New Jersey with his eye firmly fixed on the next Senate opening in 1871.

At the Republican legislative caucus Frelinghuysen was opposed for the Senate nomination by Cornelius Walsh, a millionaire self-made from the manufacture of trucks. A Trenton observer reported that Walsh was "bought out of the competition by the promise of the nomination for Governorship."[44] Frelinghuysen was then elected United States senator. (Walsh was defeated in the general election for governor.)

When Frelinghuysen sought re-election in 1877 the Democrats held a one-vote majority in the legislature. However, he might still have pulled through. The nation was in the throes of the Tilden-Hayes election controversy. Republican Frelinghuysen might have given his support to Tilden in return for the one Democratic vote needed to keep him in the Senate. He could even have argued that since Tilden carried New Jersey he was morally bound to support him when the presidential election was thrown into the Congress. In this atmosphere the Republican caucus nominated Frelinghuysen; the Democrats chose John R. McPherson, the inventor of the cattle car.

Between the nomination and the election, Frelinghuysen took a strong

¶ This action earned for him the gratitude of the Negroes of Washington, who gave his name to a school for working adults in 1917. Frelinghuysen University (with its school song, "Hail, Frelinghuysen, Hail") valiantly limped along without accreditation for forty-four years. In 1947 it had a faculty of seven, a student body of fifteen, and a graduating class of one. See Washington *Afro-American,* June 7, 1947, p. 17; also *Course of Study in the Frelinghuysen University of Washington, D.C., 1920–1921* (copy in Main Branch, District of Columbia Public Library).

public stand in favor of Rutherford B. Hayes. He was made a member of the Electoral Commission, which would determine the contest, and he voted down the line for his party. The commission was made up of ten Democrats, ten Republicans, and Justice of the Supreme Court Joseph Bradley, who would break the tie. Unbeknownst to the New Jersey legislature, Frelinghuysen and Secretary of the Navy George M. Robeson probably settled the election in favor of Hayes. The night before the first crucial vote they visited Bradley's home and talked him out of supporting Tilden's claims.[45]

Although Frelinghuysen was now as good as beaten, the New Jersey Senate contest took an unexpected twist. The day before the state legislature was to meet, Robeson appeared in Trenton and announced "with a great flourish of trumpets" that he could get the necessary Democratic vote if the Republicans would make him their candidate. The Republican caucus reconvened and unceremoniously dumped Senator Frelinghuysen. Word was then spread that $60,000 awaited the Democrat who would vote for Robeson. But party lines held. The vote on the first ballot was 41 Democrats for McPherson, 40 Republicans for Robeson.

Within five years after his final defeat for the Senate, Frederick T. Frelinghuysen was named Secretary of State in the Cabinet of President Chester A. Arthur. It was an appointment based on Frelinghuysen's loyalties within the factionized Republican Party, rather than on his experience and ability in foreign affairs.

Fortunately the nation did not demand strong diplomatic leadership. The American people were too engrossed with internal problems arising from the settlement of the Far West and the change-over from an agrarian to an industrial society. The Springfield (Massachusetts) *Republican* was delighted to note, "Mr. Frelinghuysen is understood to hold that the American eagle should not strain his naturally fine voice by shrill and prolonged screaming on small occasions."[46] Others felt that Frelinghuysen looked on the eagle as "a mere hen—past middle age."[47]

His diplomatic appointments were creditable. He retained James Russell Lowell and Lew Wallace as ministers to Great Britain and Turkey respectively; appointed two millionaires, William Waldorf Astor to Rome and Levi P. Morton to Paris; and named former Secretary of War Alphonso Taft as minister to Austria-Hungary. At home the department was run with a staff of ninety-six, including messengers, watchmen, clerks, and "a conductor for elevator."[48] Frelinghuysen's Assistant Secretary was a young man named John Davis, who was also his son-in-law.

Socially, the Secretary of State maintained the honor of his country. His wife, a gracious hostess, was the former Matilda E. Griswold, daughter of a wealthy merchant who had been on the New York University Board of Trustees during Theodore Frelinghuysen's administration as chancellor.* The Frelinghuysens' home at 1731 Eye Street became the scene of many brilliant diplomatic receptions and was especially popular with President Arthur.

During his three and a half years as Secretary, Frelinghuysen negotiated for a naval base at Pearl Harbor, opened treaty relations with Korea, mediated a boundary dispute between Mexico and Guatemala, and participated in the Berlin Conference on the Congo, where, with the assistance of explorer Henry Stanley, the American representatives helped secure the acceptance of such principles as the abolition of the slave trade, freedom of trade, and the neutralization of the area in time of war.

The Arthur Administration ended on March 4, 1885. Frederick T. Frelinghuysen died less than three months after turning over the reins of the State Department to his successor, Thomas F. Bayard.

John Davis, Frederick T. Frelinghuysen's Assistant Secretary of State, deserves special notice. He formed the link between two great political dynasties, the Frelinghuysens and the Lodges.

The husband of Sarah Helen (Sally) Frelinghuysen was from an illustrious family. His grandfather was "Honest John" Davis, the shaggy-haired Massachusetts governor, senator, and congressman who had been defeated for the vice-presidential nomination in 1844 by Theodore Frelinghuysen. Moreover, he was doubly joined to noted historian-diplomat George Bancroft, each having married the other's sister. (Such ties, however, did not prevent the political rivals from exchanging harsh charges. Bancroft accused his brother-in-law of outright graft and even of cheering when the British burned the Capitol in 1814. Davis took the accusations with remarkably good grace.[49])

"Honest John" Davis had four outstanding sons: Bancroft Davis, Assistant Secretary of State under Grant, and successor to Uncle George Bancroft as minister to Berlin; Horace Davis, flour manufacturer and president of the University of California; Andrew McFarland Davis, author of important works on the history of currency and banking; and Hasbrouck Davis, who was brevetted brigadier general in the closing days of the Civil War. Sally Frelinghuysen married the Union general's son. After his State Department service he would be a federal judge in Washington from 1885 until his death in 1902.

* George Griswold (1777–1859) was from a family that emigrated from England to Connecticut in 1635. He started as a store clerk in Hartford, but at nineteen formed a partnership in New York with his brother that expanded into a world-wide commercial operation. He then served on the boards of insurance companies, banks, and railroads. His only political position was as a presidential elector for Zachary Taylor in 1848. See Joshua L. Chamberlain, "Founders and Benefactors," *New York University* (Boston: R. Herndon, 1901), pp. 8–9.

Sally Frelinghuysen Davis, daughter of the Secretary of State, was one of the belles of the Arthur Administration. It was even claimed that the President was hopelessly infatuated with her.[50] Four years after her husband's death she married Charles McCawley, a marine major fifteen years her junior. The ceremony took place in Providence Hospital, Washington, where the bridegroom was recovering from typhoid fever. Although her second husband had a commendable military record and would later serve as the Corps quartermaster general during World War I, he was primarily known to the public as the Beau Brummell of the McKinley and Theodore Roosevelt administrations. He was part of Roosevelt's "tennis cabinet," but the Rough Rider only took him on when he was feeling in particularly good form.[51] As a presidential aide Mc-Cawley often acted as the major-domo at White House receptions, and gallantly offered his sword to Alice Roosevelt Longworth to cut her wedding cake.[52]

The union between the Frelinghuysens and the Lodges occurred in 1900 when "Bessie" Davis, Sally Frelinghuysen's daughter, married the poet son of Senator Henry Cabot Lodge. She would give birth to two future politicians. And thus, through dynastic intermarriage, former Senator Henry Cabot Lodge, Jr., former Governor John Davis Lodge, and Congressman Peter Frelinghuysen would all be great-grandsons of Secretary of State Frederick T. Frelinghuysen.

The first Frelinghuysen senator may have ridden to the Capitol on horseback; the second probably rode in a carriage; the third most likely came by train. The fourth Frelinghuysen senator, and the first directly elected by the people, campaigned for office in an automobile, wearing goggles and duster, and averaging a dizzy twenty miles per hour along the deeply rutted dirt roads of New Jersey. He was Joseph Sherman Frelinghuysen, a grandson of militia General John Frelinghuysen of the War of 1812, and a son of Frederick J. Frelinghuysen, a lawyer who studied under Richard Stockton Field.

"In 1916," recalls Walter E. Edge, who was then running on the Republican ticket for governor along with senatorial candidate Joe Frelinghuysen, "patriotic eloquence was still admired and cynicism had not yet relegated it to the limbo of flag-waving. In fact, even actual waving of a flag was looked upon with approval. . . ." Each night as Edge and Frelinghuysen stumped the state, Joe would warm up the audience with a dramatic recitation of the poem "Your Flag and My Flag," climaxed by his waving an American flag that had just been handed to him by Edge's secretary. One evening the secretary failed to appear and "Joe, left flagless, waved his hands instead but the dramatic appeal was lacking." A "flag boy" was then added to the traveling company.[53]

Having substantially defeated the incumbent, James E. ("Farmer

Jim") Martine, Joe Frelinghuysen found the Senate to be a convivial place to work and play. Whenever possible he went out to the Chevy Chase Club with three of his colleagues, Senators Warren G. Harding, Stephen B. Elkins, and Eugene Hale. In the golf foursome Harding, a small-town publisher, and Elkins, a railroads and mining magnate, were paired against Hale and Frelinghuysen. On Christmas morning, 1919, Frelinghuysen made an amazing prediction to Russian diplomat Boris Bakhmeteff: Harding would be the next President of the United States![54] It was therefore with some satisfaction that he viewed the dark-horse nomination of his friend at the 1920 Republican Convention. "Thank God the country can look forward to a leader and not an autocrat," said Frelinghuysen, contrasting the Ohio senator with Woodrow Wilson.[55]

After Harding's victory the President-elect went to Florida for twelve days of cruising on Senator Frelinghuysen's 88-foot houseboat, the *Victoria*—a pleasure jaunt that was to inspire such New York *Times* headlines as "Harding Boat Sticks All Day on Mudbank," "Houseboat Mishaps Again Delay Harding," and "Harding Will Quit Stranded Victoria."[56]

Apparently the President did not hold the *Victoria*'s misfortunes against its owner, for Frelinghuysen became a regular member of Harding's twice-a-week poker games. Secretary of the Treasury Andrew W. Mellon occasionally sat in, and, while he always protested ignorance of the game's finer points, usually came out a winner.[57]

The most momentous event to occur at Raritan since the Great Awakening took place on Saturday afternoon, July 2, 1921. President Harding was visiting the Frelinghuysens for the weekend. Host and guest were on the golf links when "Doc" Smithers, a White House aide, arrived from Washington with an official pouch. He waited an hour and forty-three minutes for the President. Harding finally appeared in a Palm Beach suit, a white shirt buttoned by removable gold studs, and a green and red bow tie. He sat down to read the document Smithers had brought while Patsy, the Frelinghuysens' wire-haired terrier, sniffed the white presidential shoes. Then the President went into the living room and Mrs. Frelinghuysen cleared a small mahogany table. Harding signed at the bottom of the broad vellum document; a drop of ink fell on the "G" in his signature. "That's all," said the President of the United States on his way back to the golf course. The text he had just signed began, "Joint resolution terminating the state of war between the Imperial German Government and the United States of America . . ." Commented the New York *Times*, "More ceremony has been connected with making an entry in the family Bible or a debutante's memory book than that accompanying the signature that ended a war that called to the colors 4,800,000 Americans."[58]

Senator Joe Frelinghuysen had stood for a high tariff and against the League of Nations. He was for women's suffrage and against the soldiers' bonus. He was for universal military training and against the United Mineworkers Union. But when he came up for re-election in 1921 there was one overriding issue—Prohibition. Frelinghuysen was a "Dry"; Governor Edward I. Edwards, his opponent, was a "Wet." It was a dirty campaign. As early as June, Frelinghuysen's manager denied his candidate "has $30,000 worth of liquor in his cellar." Edwards denied he was a "rum hound," and invited his audience to inspect his countenance. "When Senator Frelinghuysen comes here," he added, "I want you to look at his face. Don't let Frelinghuysen tell you that color came from the golf links. That color cost money!"[59]

Said a New York *Times* editorial:

He [Frelinghuysen] is an amiable and a prosperous person who has never had any incendiary designs on the Raritan or the Potomac . . . with all respect, he is a mediocrity inflicted upon his State. His statesmanship is derived very largely by radiation and consists largely in devotion to golf. . . . He is likewise a great Dry. . . . He has an ample wine cellar, but he has promised not to refill it when his stock is exhausted.

Governor Edwards . . . is a frank and consistent Wet. . . . He doesn't drink himself, but is willing that other people should. So there will be a fair and square set-to between the Wets and the Drys. One might wish that the latter had a representative more rigorous in faith and practice than Mr. Frelinghuysen.[60]

The odds at first favored Frelinghuysen. Then they changed to even money. By election eve the two leading Broad Street bookmakers were giving six to five on Edwards. They estimated that three million dollars had been waged on New York and New Jersey contests. Betting was particularly lively in Brooklyn, they reported.[61]

The gambling men were overly cautious. Frelinghuysen was defeated by a smashing plurality of 89,133.

In 1928 Joe Frelinghuysen tried to make a comeback. He ran in the Senate primary against Hamilton Fish Kean, a long-time Republican National Committeeman, and ex-Governor Edward C. Stokes, who had most of the organization support. By now the state's governor and both senators were "Wets." Frelinghuysen modified his stand and supported a national referendum. This satisfied neither Wets nor Drys. Kean won, but the former senator ran a remarkably strong race. Frelinghuysen charged that there had been a deal between GOP leaders and Jersey City Mayor Frank Hague, with 30,000 Democrats voting in the Republican primary. He would not support Kean until the Republicans cleaned house. In the opinion of the New York *Times*, "Mr. Frelinghuysen has everything to gain and nothing to lose by assuming the role of reformer. But will the electorate take him seriously in that character?"[62] Frelinghuysen and Kean testified before a Senate committee, both stating they had spent $50,000 of their own money in the primary—the legal maximum. Frelinghuysen added that he had returned all other contributions. He also made one appearance before a state legislative committee. This completed his activities as a reformer, and he dutifully supported Kean.

Frelinghuysen made one last bid for public office. In the 1930 Republican primary he ran for the Senate against Dwight Morrow, ambassador to Mexico, and Congressman Franklin Fort, son of a New Jersey governor and candidate of the Anti-Saloon League. This time he campaigned actively as a "Wet," and also attacked the "power and light monopoly" controlled by the "leading international banking house of America, J. P. Morgan & Co. . . ." (Dwight Morrow was a former J. P. Morgan partner.) It rained on Election Day. "Well, this is Frelinghuysen weather," said Frelinghuysen. When he conceded the election the vote stood—Morrow, 222,674; Fort, 67,233; Frelinghuysen, 25,525.[63]

The current Frelinghuysen dynasty was introduced to the 1964 Republican Convention as "a delegate whose great-grandfather was a delegate to the 1860 convention that nominated Lincoln." He is Peter Hood Ballantine Frelinghuysen, Jr., a member of the House of Representatives since 1953 from the New Jersey district in which his family has lived for nearly two and a half centuries.

The patrician congressman is a self-styled "moderate, middle-of-the-road" Republican, a believer in liberalized foreign trade, an internationalist member of the House Foreign Affairs Committee, and a supporter of the 1964 Civil Rights Act.[64]

But there are those who contend he has grown more conservative with the accummulation of congressional seniority. As the ranking Republican on the Education and Labor Committee he led the fight against President Johnson's "anti-poverty" program, which he felt would "spawn its own bureaucracy" and "duplicate established Federal programs."[65] During the committee hearings he displayed a toughness bordering on ruthlessness that had not been previously evident in his soft-spoken, colorless manner and which earned him the title of "Petulant Peter" from Drew Pearson.[66]

At the opening of the 89th Congress, Frelinghuysen made two attempts at improving his lot in the House hierarchy. When Congressman Gerald Ford vacated the chairmanship of the Republican Conference Committee to become Minority Leader, Frelinghuysen was entered as a last-minute candidate. He lost by 75 to 62, which his sponsors regarded as a moral victory. But his subsequent race for Assistant Minority Leader was an unqualified disaster. Even with the full support of Ford he was defeated, 70 to 59. Some of the post-mortems felt his loss was primarily a slap at the moderates. A Southern Republican pointed out that Frelinghuysen was rated thirty-seven per cent "right" by the right-wing Americans for Constitutional Action. Columnists Evans and Novak wrote that he was the victim of a "whispering campaign describing him as a member of the liberal Eastern establishment. . . ."[67] But perhaps more important was the "popularity contest" feature. Running against a genial, well-liked party war horse, Frelinghuysen was variously described as "a blue blood," having "an abrasive manner," and displaying an "aloofness in personal relations."[68]

There is a strong sense of "family" in this eighth-generation Freling-huysen, the fifth of his name to serve in Congress. As a senior at Princeton he wrote a remarkably sophisticated biography of the first Frelinghuy-sen in America, the Reverend Theodorus Jacobus. His Washington office is cluttered with the fond mementos of the dynasty's campaigns—a letter from Colonel Frederick Frelinghuysen to his Revolutionary commander-in-chief, George Washington; a photograph of Chancellor Frelinghuysen with his New York University faculty; a Whig banner for the 1844 national candidates, Henry Clay and Theodore Frelinghuysen (looking at its slogan in early 1964, he commented, "Some say the Republican motto this year will be 'The nation's risin' for Lucius Clay and Freling-huysen'"—this was as close as he came to humor during two interviews)†; a passport signed by Frederick T. Frelinghuysen, Secretary of State; a placard urging votes for Joseph S. Frelinghuysen in the Republican senatorial primary, June 17, 1930. He talked knowledgeably and with feeling about these ancestors, in marked contrast to former Representa-tive William Henry Harrison of Wyoming, sixth of his dynasty in Con-gress, whose Washington office was almost bare of things past, and whose investigation into his background is limited and diffident.

The financial history of the Frelinghuysens tells much about the evolu-tion of their character. It breaks down into three stages: two generations of humble pastors; three generations of successful lawyer-politicians; two generations of multimillionaires' sons-in-law.

The present congressman's grandfather married the granddaughter of Peter Ballantine, a thrifty Scotsman who came to America in 1820, saved enough in ten years as a brewery worker to start his own company, and by his death in 1883 owned personal property alone estimated at five million dollars. Grandfather Frelinghuysen occupied himself looking

† In his introductory remarks at a Yale alumni dinner on April 24, 1964, the congressman said: ". . . if Bill [Scranton] should be looking for a running mate, it just happens that some one has dusted off a slogan from Henry Clay's campaign for president in 1844. It wouldn't be difficult to adjust it to 1964. 'Hurray, hurray, the country's risin',/For Bill Scranton and Frelinghuysen.' You will note that almost any name, short or long, can be fitted into the presidential slot in the jingle. It could even be Lucius Clay—or Cassius." *Yale Law Report*, Summer 1964, p. 8.

after the Ballantine fortune. (The Frelinghuysens sold their interest in P. Ballantine & Co. at the end of the Prohibition era.)

But the Ballantines had hardly a pittance compared to the in-laws of the congressman's father, the first Peter Hood Ballantine Frelinghuysen. In 1907, with Franklin Delano Roosevelt as an usher, he married the oldest daughter of Henry Osborne Havemeyer, the gruff, hot-tempered founder of the "sugar trust," whose plants manufactured half of the sugar consumed in the United States.‡ "To know when to plunge the knife deeply and when to stop," wrote an admiring 1903 biographer, "is an attainment with which few men are gifted. Mr. Havemeyer's career shows that he possessed it to a very great degree. . . ."[69]

The Ballantine millions were reinforced by Harry Havemeyer's many millions, and the early militancy of the Frelinghuysens was reinforced by Havemeyer's wife, Louisine. Congressman Frelinghuysen's maternal grandmother was a delightful mixture of self-assurance and naïveté. She helped her husband build one of the great private art collections, most of which is now in New York's Metropolitan Museum, and after his death became a leading suffragette. In 1919 she led a march down the middle of Pennsylvania Avenue and was jailed for burning an effigy of President Wilson in front of the White House. This was the only way she could qualify for the Prison Special, a transcontinental proselytizing tour. Captain Flathers, the Washington police chief, begged the plump little grandmother not to light the fire. "He almost wrung his hands." But she had her heart set on being a martyr. So they hauled her off in a Black Maria and the judge sentenced her to five dollars' fine or five days in jail. "Of course," she wrote, "no one thought of paying the fine." The other prisoners gave preferential treatment to their *grande dame* cell mate, such as first chance at the toilet. "Are you all right, Mrs. Havemeyer?" asked another suffragette. "Yes, fine," she replied, "but isn't it too funny?" However after one night in the "pestilential jail" she changed her mind and paid up. By now she had qualified for the suffrage train anyway. Recalling her prison confinement, she said, "The gas vapors from the sewers escaped; the fumes from the furnace escaped; the water escaped. . . . Everything escaped but the prisoners." The main reason she decided to leave jail was pressure from the "family tree." She

‡ The Havemeyers have been identified with the American sugar industry since the end of the eighteenth century. Henry Osborne Havemeyer's grandfather, who died in 1861, left an estate of three million dollars. His father continued the business with a cousin, William Frederick Havemeyer (1804–74), who retired at the age of thirty-eight to devote himself to local politics. He was three times mayor of New York, but after sweeping out the Tweed Ring in 1872 he proved to be an unsatifactory replacement. Henry Osborne Havemeyer (1847–1907) put together the "sugar trust" in 1887, which the government succeeded in dissolving three years later. It was a hollow victory, for Havemeyer reorganized his vast interests the next year.

received frantic telegrams informing her that she was casting a shadow on the dynastic escutcheon. Back home she reminded timid relations that she was not the first to be imprisoned for standing firm for convictions. There were John Bunyan, Galileo, Martin Luther, Joan of Arc! She was a hard woman to keep down.[70]

Mrs. Havemeyer determined that her first daughter, Adaline (the future Mrs. Frelinghuysen), would be educated to prove that women could be more intelligent than men, and that her second daughter would continue her interest in art. The younger daughter, Electra Havemeyer Webb, did become a great collector, though her 125,000 objects shocked her mother. She went in for Americana, gathering such choice items as a real covered bridge, a lighthouse, a stone jail, and the S.S. *Ticonderoga*, the last side-wheeler in the world. (They are now on display at her Shelburne Museum in Vermont.) But Adaline rebelled against her mother's intellectual determinism, choosing instead an early marriage and four children.

Her Frelinghuysen husband devoted his talents to cattle breeding on his Twin Oak Farm near Morristown. For nine consecutive years he held the national championship, and one of his bulls, Fern's Wexford Noble, was the grand champion at the National Dairy Show for three years. He also maintained a stable of race horses, as well as membership in a large assortment of the best golf, tennis, turf, and town clubs.[71]

The sportsman's son Peter, the present congressman, married a Procter, of the Procter & Gamble family.

The Frelinghuysens are very rich. Like the Kennedys, the family maintains its own philanthrophic foundation and a business office in New York to look after its interests. The congressman describes his two brothers as "unemployed," i.e., they work at such causes as the New Jersey Horsebreeding Association and the New Jersey Historical Society.

They are so firmly in society that they can afford to ridicule it. A cousin, Suzy Frelinghuysen Morris,§ listed her four-year-old Pekinese

§ Mrs. Morris is the granddaughter of Secretary of State Frederick T. Frelinghuysen. Her maternal grandfather was Thomas Talmadge Kinney (1821–1900), who, as editor of the Newark *Daily Advertiser*, played an important role in establishing what is now the Associated Press, and was a founder of the Society for the Prevention of Cruelty to Animals. See Francis Bazley Lee, *Genealogical and Memorial History of the State of New Jersey* (New York: Lewis Historical Publishing Co., 1910), Vol. I, pp. 321–22.

Her father, Frederick Frelinghuysen (1848–1924), was the long-time president of the Mutual Benefit Life Insurance Company. Once when asked by his employees if life was worth living, he shot back, "That answer depends upon the amount of service that you are able to render." William Rankin Ward, *Down the Years, a History of the Mutual Benefit Life Insurance Company, 1845 to 1932* (Camden: Haddon Craftsmen, 1932), p. 100.

dog Rose in the 1936 *Social Register*. "There was no particular reason," she said, "I was just filling out the thing and I did it."[72] The impulsive Suzy is also a devotee of Hindu philosophy, an abstract artist, and a critically acclaimed operatic soprano. Her painter husband told *The New Yorker* in 1948, "She is descended from a long line of blue-nosed Dutch clergymen who would jointly turn in their graves at the spectacle of their scion portraying ladies of such dubious reputation as Salome, Tosca and Santuzza."[73]

Other than the current congressman, the family is no longer political.¶ And he claims that he reached Congress quite by accident. Despite the energy and determination with which he now pursues public office, if there had been a different set of circumstances in 1952 he too might now be fashionably unemployed.

But talking with Congressman Frelinghuysen today, one gets the feeling, more than with any other contemporary dynast, that he wishes to be in public life less because of what he is than because of who his ancestors were. His sense of American history, and the Frelinghuysens' role in it, appears to have strongly motivated his career. Without detracting from the seriousness with which he does his job, it might be said that he is in Congress because he feels it is proper for some Frelinghuysen to be in Congress.

The Frelinghuysens were initially sustained in politics by an excess of religious and moral zeal. This quality, always difficult to maintain for an extended period, lost its potency after several generations. The loss coincided with the social acceptance of the family through longevity, accumulated wealth, and advantageous marriages. Perhaps zeal was then replaced by noblesse oblige: as part of the best butter, the dynasty felt an obligation to pay its tithe to the body politic. But without talent a sense of social obligation has little long-term political buoyancy. And the Frelinghuysens have always been capable rather than brilliant. What will this mean in the next generation? The congressman's three sons have not yet reached the age of decision.

Will membership in the social establishment, as in the case of the Livingstons, mean the death of a long and honorable political dynasty?

¶ The congressman has a twin brother, Henry Osborne Havemeyer Frelinghuysen, who has dabbled in politics from time to time. In 1938 he was elected coroner of Morris County, New Jersey—an office without duties other than to take charge of the bodies of "shipwreck victims." From 1956 to 1959 he was vice-chairman of the Republican Finance Committee of New Jersey, and in 1964 he headed the Scranton for President drive in his state. Letter to the author from H. O. H. Frelinghuysen, February 18, 1965.

The Tucker Dynasty

> "... one of the most sentimental
> and accomplished families our coun-
> try can boast."
>
> —John Adams to Richard Rush[1]

A NORMAN yeoman named Tucker crossed the Channel with William the Conqueror and founded a line of sturdy, respectable middle-class Englishmen. In the early seventeenth century a branch of the family moved to Bermuda, where one of its number became the second governor, and is now primarily remembered for his ability to outswear any of his constituents. From this line descended five United States congressmen, a profusion of notable American jurists, religious leaders, educators, and men of letters.

Colonel Henry Tucker—the military title stemmed perhaps from a militia command, for the colonelcy was then as much in vogue in Bermuda as later in Kentucky—represented the island's interests in London for five years beginning in 1779, where the record shows his love of the animated court life. He remained a man of youthful fire, elastic step, and erect carriage even into his seventieth year. In fact his bearing, thought a grandson, suggested "a descendant of the Great Mogul, or at least of the Plantagenets."[2]

He was, however, completely unsuccessful at business.[3] While fiercely ambitious for his four sons, and wishing to give each the advantages of a European education, his money ran out after he had sent Thomas Tudor Tucker to Edinburgh to study medicine. Thomas wrote his brother St. George: "We have the most indulgent of Fathers. . . . It is his great misfortune that his Abilities are not equal to his Desire of promoting his children's Interest."[4] But fortunately a school at Williamsburg, Virginia, recommended itself for cheapness.[5] And so in 1771 St. George Tucker was sent to William and Mary College. He would become the founding father of an American political dynasty.

These Tuckers have had one maddening trait—a fanatical devotion to certain given names. Eventually in America there would be three

THE TUCKER DYNASTY
(A Selective Genealogy)

Colonel Henry Tucker (1713–87)
Bermuda agent in London
(6 children)

Henry (1742–1808)
Acting governor of Bermuda
m. daughter of a governor
of Bermuda
(12 children; 3 d.y.)

Dr. Thomas Tudor (1745–1828)
Arrived in America, 1770
HOUSE OF REPRESENTATIVES
(2 children; both d.y.)

Dr. Nathaniel (1750–1807)
Poet, lived mostly in England
(7 children; all d.y.)

St. George (1752–1827)
Arrived in America, 1771
Federal judge; author,
Tucker on Blackstone
1st m. *Frances Bland Randolph,*
mother of Senator John
Randolph of Roanoke
(3 children)

Henry St. George ("India Henry")
(1771–1851)
Chairman, East India Company

Thomas Tudor
(1775–1852)
British admiral

Henry St. George
(1780–1848)
HOUSE OF REPRESENTATIVES
Judge; author, *Tucker on Laws
of Virginia*
m. *Anne E. Hunter*, 1st cousin
of Union General David Hunter
(13 children; 5 d.y.)

Nathaniel Beverley
(1784–1851)
Judge; novelist, *The
Partisan Leader*
(6 children)

Charlotte Maria
(1821–93)
Prolific author of
children's books
(unmarried)

[Nathaniel] Beverley
(1820–90)
Confederate agent
(8 children)

John Randolph ("Ran")
(1823–97)
HOUSE OF REPRESENTATIVES
Author, Tucker on the
Constitution
(6 children)

[Henry] St. George ("Sainty")
(1828–63)
Novelist, The Devoted Bride
m. Elizabeth Gilmer, daughter of
Virginia governor
(2 children)

Anne
m. Lyon G. Tyler, son of U.S.
President

Henry St. George ("Harry")
(1853–1932) HOUSE OF REPRESENTATIVES
Author, Tucker on Treaty-Making Power
1st m. Henrietta P. Johnston, granddaughter
of Confederate general Albert Sydney Johnston
(6 children)

Beverley Dandridge
(1846–1930) Episcopal
bishop; m. Maria
Washington, great-great-
grandniece of George
Washington (13 children)

Beverley Dandridge
(1882–)
Episcopal bishop
(5 children)

Henry St. George
(1874–1959)
Episcopal bishop
(2 children)

St. George Tuckers, five Henry St. George Tuckers, five John Randolph Tuckers, four Nathaniel Beverley Tuckers, and six Beverley Tuckers (males). There were also female Beverley Tuckers, and even one female Henry Tucker.

The chaos is further compounded by the fertility of the clan. A young lady who spurned the attention of a Tucker is reported to have said, "I would not marry him if he were the best man in the world and every hair on his head were strung with diamonds." When asked why she felt so strongly, her reply was, "Because his great-grandfather had fourteen children, his grandfather ten, and his father thirteen."[6]

Colonel Henry Tucker's family was relatively modest: four sons and two daughters. Daughter Eliza remained unmarried and was distinguished as the doting aunt. Daughter Frances, of striking beauty, with large dark eyes and a high forehead, married a cousin, another Henry Tucker, whose dominant traits were venality and a complete lack of scruples. He rose high in the affairs of Bermuda. Theirs was an unhappy marriage, but Frances had the satisfaction of outliving her husband by more than thirty years. Of their seven children, four married other Tuckers.

One of the colonel's sons remained in Bermuda. He, too, was named Henry, and he married the eldest daughter (also named Frances) of Governor George Bruere, a crusty old soldier who ruled the island for nearly twenty years and was noted for his rendition, after copious libations, of his success at the battle of Culloden, complete with marches, countermarches, shouts of victory, and a lusty rendition of "The British Grenadiers." In Bermuda's history it would be easy to find better governors than this irascible gentleman, but also worse.

The Brueres and the Tuckers were political enemies—the Tuckers being deeply involved in the cause of the American revolutionaries, while one of the governor's sons lost his life fighting the insurgents at Bunker Hill. Yet Henry Tucker, practical, even-tempered, conciliatory, managed to get on with his father-in-law, and, under the old man's patronage, rose to be president of the island's Council. Among the offspring of the happy Bruere-Tucker union were a daughter whose immortality was assured by Henry Raeburn's lovely portrait, which hangs in London's National Gallery*; a son who became a British admiral, severely wounded by the Americans in the War of 1812†; and another

---

* Anne Neale Tucker (1776–1861) was the wife of an English soldier, Henry William Lauzun. It was she who named one of her four daughters Henry, in honor of her father. See Mrs. George P. (Mary H.) Coleman, *Story of a Portrait* (Richmond: Dietz Press, 1935).

† Thomas Tudor Tucker (1775–1852) was wounded on March 28, 1814, when his ship *Cherub* assisted in the capture of the U.S. frigate *Essex* near Valparaiso. Tucker's part in the sea battle was inconsequential. See *Dictionary of National Biography*, Vol. XIX, p. 1211.

son, Henry St. George Tucker, accountant general of Bengal and chairman of the East India Company.‡

"India Henry" was also sentenced to six months' imprisonment for attempted rape, which did not noticeably slow down his rise in the Indian service. He and his wife, Jane Boswell, a relative of Johnson's biographer, had a large family, most of whom were murdered in the Sepoy Mutiny. However, a surviving daughter became a successful writer of children's stories under the pseudonym of "A.L.O.E." (A Lady of England). She published 142 books between 1854 and 1893, of which her best known were *Wings and Strings* and *The Rambles of a Rat.*§

Another of Colonel Tucker's sons settled in England and does not figure in the story of the political dynasty except that his sympathies were with the American revolutionists in whose praise he wrote a muddy allegorical play entitled *Columbinus.* Nathaniel was a doctor by vocation, a poet by avocation, although even his biographer rates him "a very minor eighteenth-century man of literary ambition . . . without great originality."[7] While lacking the rudder of practicality that guided his brothers to success, toward the end of his life he did achieve a degree of fame by translating the transcendental revelations of Emanuel Swedenborg from Latin into English. They were avidly read by William Blake and Samuel Taylor Coleridge, but only left Tucker's brothers confused. Wrote Thomas Tudor: "What do you make of Natty?" Replied Henry: "Poor Natty seems to have taken a religious turn—he affects to persuade us of his contentment, but in doing so he speaks (in my opinion) the language rather of dissatisfaction and disgust."[8]

The first of the Tuckers to settle in America was Thomas Tudor, who arrived in Charleston, South Carolina, soon after receiving a medical degree from the University of Edinburgh in 1770. (Strangely for a native of sunny Bermuda, he wrote his Latin dissertation on the effect of cold on the human body—*Dissertatio . . . de frigoris in corpus humanum viribus.*)

The people of Charleston did not take warmly to the new physician. In 1773 he was brought to trial by a wealthy lawyer on charges of having

‡ Henry St. George Tucker (1771–1851), a colonialist who opposed the "over-education" of Indian civil servants and the freedom of the Indian press ("a boon which could not fail to excite new feelings among them"), also wrote a book of charming riddles for his children, *The Sphinx* (London: Cox and Wyman, 1850?). See John William Kaye, *The Life and Correspondence of Henry St. George Tucker* (London: R. Bentley, 1854).

§ Charlotte Maria Tucker (1821–93) learned Hindustani when she was fifty-four years old and became a church missionary in northern India, where she was buried "in accordance with the terms of her will, without a coffin, at a cost not exceeding five rupees." See Agnes Giberne, *A Lady of England, the Life and Letters of Charlotte Maria Tucker* (New York: A. C. Armstrong, 1895).

failed to take proper precautions in a smallpox case. The young doctor, with more pride than patients, immediately challenged his detractor to a duel. When lawyer Williams declined, Tucker promptly posted the following notice "in the most public part" of a coffeehouse:

> Robt. Williams Junr. Atty. at law is a Liar,
> a Rascal & a Coward—whoever takes this down
> is desir'd to fix his own Name in its place.

Tucker was found guilty of sending a challenge to a duel and publishing a libel.[9]

After service as a Revolutionary Army surgeon, and a year as a prisoner of war, Tucker ran for a seat in the first Congress under the new Constitution. He was elected, but not before he had been severely wounded in the left thigh during a duel with his opponent's nephew. The congressman-elect was doubly pleased to get out of Charleston, for his medical practice was "so inconsiderable" as barely to offer him subsistence.[10] During his four years in Congress he proved himself a steadfast anti-Federalist. So when Jefferson became President he rewarded Tucker with appointment as Treasurer of the United States, a post he held until his death in 1828. His investments prospered after his entrance into public life. Since his wife and two children had died before him, he willed his estate, some $100,000, to be divided among all his relatives.

Despite the modest success of Thomas Tudor Tucker, the actual founder of the American political dynasty was his brother St. George. In this there is a certain irony, for, unlike the tempestuous Charleston congressman, St. George tried to avoid politics and warned his sons to do likewise. Being of judicial temperament, he advised against becoming "a target to be shot at with a thousand poisoned arrows." "I would not give a kiss . . . to be Pope," he said, "and much less to be Emperor."[11]

Only once did he ignore his better judgment and enter upon the political scene. As a member of the Virginia delegation (with James Madison, Edmund Randolph, and George Mason), he journeyed to Annapolis to set the stage for the convention which would write the U. S. Constitution.[12] Yet he led a remarkable life as "The American Blackstone"—judge, professor, legal scholar. And his fame was such that his obituary in 1828 was a news item in faraway London.

In St. George were merged many of the attractive qualities of his brothers: the practical sense of Henry; the generosity of Thomas Tudor; the poetic imagination of Nathaniel. It was not long after he arrived at Williamsburg to enter William and Mary that his engaging manners, ready wit, and good sense won him a place among the better element in Virginia's capital.

Like all the Tuckers, he had the facility of versifying. One of his poems was quoted by Benjamin Franklin in his autobiography[13]; another brought forth these extravagant lines from John Adams: "I know not which to admire most, its Simplicity, its Beauty, its Pathos, its Philosophy, its Morality, its Religion, or its Sublimity—Is there in Homer, in Virgil, in Milton, in Shakespeare, or in Pope, an equal number of lines which deserve to be engraven on the memory of Youth and Age in more indelible Characters?"[14] The verse which sent the second President into such a tizzy of delight was called "Resignation" or "Days of My Youth," and can still be found in some American anthologies.[15]¶

During the Revolutionary War St. George had a number of unusual assignments. He organized a successful plot to steal the gunpowder stored at Bermuda, which did not further endear the Tuckers to Governor Bruere. He was then sent on a special trade mission to the West Indies. But instead of earning Patrick Henry's thanks, the Virginia governor told him, "I think you paid too much for indigo."[16] (Patrick Henry might have been more appreciative if he could have known that St. George was to guarantee him a place in history. For the famous "Give me liberty or give me death" speech in 1775 was extemporaneous and has been reconstructed primarily from the notes of Tucker, then a young student listening from the gallery.[17])

As a militia lieutenant colonel he saw action at the battle of Guilford Court House, where he received a slight bayonet wound in the leg while blocking the path of a deserting American soldier. Whether it was "from design or accident" Tucker said he was unable to tell. Later he took part in the siege of Yorktown.[18]

But his most unique assignment was as a French interpreter, for the needs of Rochambeau's young adventurers were diverse. On one occasion, when the Vicomte de Pontevés Gien wished to court a Miss Nelson of Yorktown, but could speak no English, it was Tucker's duty to coach him in conversational seduction. The record of this Franco-American alliance, complete with the vicomte's translations in his own phonetic spelling, shows that the Frenchman's technique was to increase his passion in slow stages:

"Ai em go-en tou Boston bot hélas mai hairte rimens at York."
(*Je vais à Boston, mais, hélas! mon coeur reste à York.*)
"Your äis have perst mai harte."
(*Vos yeux m'ont percé le coeur.*)
"Ai yam verimottse in love offiou."
(*Je suis véritablement amoureux de vous.*)
"Ai love you tou mottse tou bi eble tou consil mai pashun."
(*Je vous aime trop, pour pouvoir cacher l'excès de mon amour.*)[19]

¶ Adams was apparently unaware of Tucker's satiric poems that appeared in Philip Freneau's *Gazette* in the summer of 1793, in which he lampooned the Federalists and dubbed Adams "Daddy Vice." See Percy Winfield Turrentine, *Life and Works of Nathaniel Beverley Tucker* (Unpublished Ph.D. dissertation, Harvard University, 1952), Vol. I, p. 193.

St. George had also known an affair of the heart. In 1778 he married twenty-five-year-old Frances Bland, the beautiful widow of John Randolph of Matoax.

Near the tower entrance of Bruton Parish Church in Williamsburg is a tall marble shaft marking the grave of one of the sons of this union. On its south side is written, "Descended from Virginia's best blood." The best blood comes from the Blands. For the impoverished Tucker married into one of the Old Dominion's most ancient and distinguished families. The first Bland is said to have voyaged to Virginia in 1635 to purchase large tracts of land. Light Horse Harry Lee had a Bland grandmother. Frances Bland's father was an American patriot who sold some of his slaves to buy gunpowder for the revolutionaries; her uncle Richard was a member of the Continental Congress, and her brother Theodoric would be elected to the first Congress under the new Constitution.

Frances had first wed a Randolph, with whom she was related by blood on both sides. This eugenistic couple produced three delicate, high-strung boys—Richard, Theodorick, and John (later to be known as John Randolph of Roanoke). When their mother remarried they were eight, seven, and five, respectively. St. George would give to these stepsons a generous love, though he could be stern when occasion required it; they, in turn, would bring into his serene life the only tragedy he was to know.

Not only was the lovely Frances rich, the inheritor of her first husband's Matoax estate of 1305 acres on the Appomattox River, but she was a humane and gifted supervisor of the plantation while St. George was away at war. Once, when far advanced in pregnancy, she journeyed fifty miles to protect a runaway slave from the brutality of his overseer.[20]

She gave her second husband a daughter and two sons who would reach maturity; then she died, age thirty-five.

Three years later St. George Tucker married another attractive young widow of aristocratic family and ample fortune.* Lelia Skipwith had been the wife of George Carter, master of Corrotoman, a plantation of 7000 acres, and a great-grandson of "King" Carter, the greatest landholder in Virginia history. Her own antecedents were equally impressive: Sir Peyton Skipwith, her father, held Virginia's only baronetcy of that period; her mother, a peppery Scottish woman, is reputed to be

---

* The second Mrs. St. George Tucker (1767–1837) had a son and a daughter by her first marriage. The girl, Mary Walker (Polly) Carter (died 1863), married Joseph C. Cabell (1778–1856), a Virginia legislator for all but two years between 1808 and 1835, and one of the most powerful political leaders on the state level, who consistently declined high national office. See Philip Alexander Bruce, *History of the University of Virginia* (New York: Macmillan, 1920), Vol. I, pp. 145–57; Alexander Brown, *The Cabells and Their Kin* (Boston and New York: Houghton Mifflin, 1895), pp. 263–67.

the ghost that still walks the steps of the Wythe House in Williamsburg.†

The judicial career of St. George Tucker began in 1788 and lasted, with a two-year interruption, for the remaining thirty-nine years of his life.[21] During eight years he held the highest judgeship in the state, president of the Virginia Supreme Court of Appeals, and for nearly fifteen years he served on the federal bench. At the same time he was professor of law at William and Mary College, succeeding his own great preceptor George Wythe in 1800.

This tradition of judge-professor would be handed down to both his sons, a grandson, and a great-grandson. Politics was a natural by-product of their legal competence. But they rarely sought elective office; it was only that they could rarely resist the call to public service. Yet it was in the courtroom and classroom, rather than the legislative hall, that they made their greatest impact. For over a century the Tuckers of Virginia would train the finest legal minds of the South, including Confederate Secretary of State R. M. T. Hunter, Virginia Governor Henry A. Wise, West Virginia Governor William A. MacCorkle, Senator Thomas Hart Benton of Missouri, Senator John S. Barbour of Virginia, Newton D. Baker, Wilson's Secretary of War, and John W. Davis, Democratic candidate for President in 1924.

St. George, just like all the Tuckers who would follow him, was a prolific writer. His best-known work was the five-volume annotated edition of *Blackstone's Commentaries* (popularly called *Tucker on Blackstone*), which contained one of the earliest legal interpretations of the United States Constitution and became the standard text for all law students in Virginia. He also submitted to the state legislature a *Dissertation on Slavery: With a Proposal for Its Gradual Abolition.* As the farsighted jurist noted, this is a subject of "first importance, not only to our moral character and domestic peace, but even to our political salvation."[22]‡

There was a saying in Virginia that only a Randolph was good enough for a Randolph.[23] Few families figured more prominently in

---

† Leaving a ball after some slight offense, Lady Skipwith broke a shoe strap while crossing Palace Street and entered Wythe House with one foot clad only in a silken stocking. "And now a watcher in the old house will hear at midnight, the click of one high heeled slipper on the shallow steps of the broad stairway, alternating with the soft tread of a bare foot. . . ." See Mrs. George P. (Mary H.) Coleman, editor, *A Williamsburg Scrap Book* (Richmond: Dietz Press, 1932), p. 34.

‡ John Adams wrote Richard Rush: "I have read the [Tucker] dissertation upon slavery and known of nothing better said, upon the most difficult subject and the most intricate problem the U.S. has had to solve." See Mrs. George P. (Mary H.) Coleman, editor, "Randolph and Tucker Letters," *Virginia Magazine of History and Biography,* XLII, No. 3 (July 1934), p. 222.

the early history of the colony and the nation. Thomas Jefferson had a Randolph mother. John Marshall had a Randolph grandmother. The first president of the Continental Congress was a Randolph, as was the first Attorney General of the United States.

And St. George Tucker had three Randolph stepsons, one of whom, John Randolph of Roanoke, was one of the strangest, perhaps most brilliant, characters in American history.§

For a short period as Jefferson's floor leader in the House of Representatives, John Randolph was a powerful and positive force in national politics. However, after breaking with his presidential cousin, his influence was never more than that of a dangerous gadfly whose sharp sting could inflict mortal harm. To Benjamin Rush he seemed "a mischievous boy with a squirt in his hands, throwing its dirty contents into the eyes of everybody that looked at him."[24] Among his targets were the two Adams presidents, and his destructive aim was uncannily accurate.¶

During his more than a quarter century in Congress, Randolph, aided by liquor and narcotics, grew more and more eccentric. Some attributed his weird behavior to sexual impotence.* He brought his dogs into Congress; he fought needless duels with Henry Clay and others; he became so fussy about the proper use of English that he rose in wrath from his deathbed to correct his doctor's pronunciation—"OmnIPotent, sir, read it *always* omnIPotent, sir!" were virtually his last words.[25] (This

§ He added "of Roanoke" to distinguish himself from a cousin of the same name whom he described as an infamous character and a homeless vagabond. See William Cabell Bruce, *John Randolph of Roanoke* (New York: Putnam's, 1922), Vol. II, p. 737.

¶ Said Randolph, "I bore some humble part in putting down the dynasty of John the First, and, by the grace of God, I hope to aid in putting down the dynasty of John the Second." Ibid., Vol. II, p. 507.

It was therefore surprising that John Quincy Adams' grandson Henry, who was not historically vindictive, should have chosen to write a biography of Randolph. See Henry Adams, *John Randolph* (Boston and New York: Houghton Mifflin, 1882). This distorted work was the eminent historian's least successful undertaking. Commented Lyon G. Tyler, the college president son of U. S. President John Tyler, "No one suffered more from the political opposition of Randolph than John Quincy Adams, and it is impossible to understand how a man of apparent culture and refinement as his grandson, Henry Adams, was, could have showed so little taste in becoming Randolph's biographer." *Tyler's Quarterly Historical and Genealogical Magazine*, IV, No. 4 (April 1923), p. 449.

* In his shrill, flutelike voice, Randolph once said, "Why should a man take pride in a quality in which a jackass is infinitely his superior?" Quoted in Francis Biddle, *A Casual Past* (Garden City, N.Y.: Doubleday, 1961), p. 32; also see Robert D. Meade, "John Randolph of Roanoke, Some New Information," *William and Mary Quarterly*, 2d Series, XIII, No. 4 (October 1933), pp. 256–64.

was a far cry from the Tuckers, who had the unusual habit of almost always dying with a joke on their lips.)

The relationship between Randolph and St. George Tucker was at first a close one. The boy's mother died when he was fourteen, and the stepfather tried to fill the void. He was unquestionably more indulgent of John than of his own sons, even advancing him money to pay gambling debts. (Tucker, on the other hand, exploded in indignation when he heard that one of his sons had been in a friendly card game, even though he had won.)

At twenty-three John Randolph wrote Tucker: "God bless you my father, my ever beloved friend. Whilst this heart has motion, it shall ever feel for you the liveliest affection."[26] Yet a decade later he would be viciously and publicly accusing Tucker of misappropriating slaves who had been left to him by his father, and angling to get his estate for the Tucker children. The charges were patently absurd. One theory for Randolph's behavior was that he resented his stepfather's remarriage—he was to call the second Mrs. Tucker "a shrew and a vixen," but this was long after his break with St. George, and his earlier letters speak of her with affection; another theory is that the bitterness was politically motivated—Randolph having been a leading supporter of Monroe for the presidency, while Tucker was for Madison—but this too is disproved by Randolph's letters of high regard for his stepfather after the 1808 presidential contest. The most straightforward explanation is that Randolph was insane and his behavior toward Tucker was pathological.

Carrying his accusations beyond the grave, Randolph's will repeated the false charges against St. George, and, to protect their father's reputation, the Tucker sons fought it through the courts. After twelve years of litigation the estate was settled and John Randolph of Roanoke was posthumously declared legally insane.

The oldest of St. George's stepsons was also to be an embarrassment. Richard Randolph, sweet-tempered and weak-willed, became the apex of the most scandalous triangle of eighteenth-century America. In a public letter to Judge Tucker, Richard announced that as the result of vicious rumors that he was guilty of "crimes at which humanity revolts," he would appear before the Cumberland County Court to answer any charges that his accusers wished to prefer against him.

On April 29, 1793, he was formally charged with infanticide and held without bail. Richard was married to a cousin, Judith Randolph, and her younger sister Nancy lived with them.[27]† The case that the state tried to prove was that he had had an affair with his sixteen-year-old sister-in-

† Richard Randolph (1770–96) married Judith Randolph (1772–1816) in 1789. They were distantly but doubly related. He and her father were third cousins, and her maternal grandmother was his father's sister.

law, she had given birth, and he had disposed of the child. The facts were unquestionably correct, though the child was probably stillborn. Randolph retained John Marshall and Patrick Henry as his counsel. And after a salacious trial he was acquitted, primarily because of the perjury of Judith (who swore that her sister had not given birth), and because the testimony of the Negro slave who had found the foetus was inadmissible in a Virginia court.

Three years later Richard died suddenly. A carefully researched novel contends that he was poisoned. The murder, so the story goes, was plotted by his wife and inadvertently executed by his mistress. Judith changed a medicinal recipe from a half grain of tartar emetic to read ten grains, a lethal dose, and then told Nancy to mix it and give it to him. As he writhed in agony Judith delayed sending for a doctor.[28]

Richard's will, influenced by the abolitionist views of Judge Tucker, was one of the most eloquent anti-slavery documents ever written. His Negroes were freed and settled on land across the river from his plantation. But the community, known as Israel Hill, soon became synonymous with poverty and degradation. Randolph's only noble act ironically was later used by proponents of slavery as a prime example of the evils of emancipation.[29]

Two children resulted from the marriage of Richard and Judith Randolph. The oldest, St. George, was born a deaf mute. In his twenty-third year he became violently insane and was institutionalized. Yet he lived to a ripe age, spending his last years as a harmless lunatic at Charlotte Court House, Virginia, where, with his flowing beard and long snowy white hair, he acquired a certain romantic aura in the neighborhood. The younger son, tall and swarthy Tudor Randolph, went to Harvard and was remembered by Jared Sparks, later a Harvard president, as "perhaps the most promising young man who has been at Cambridge within my knowledge of the institution."[30] In his senior year, however, he died of tuberculosis.

After his untimely death his uncle John Randolph of Roanoke wrote, "But it pleased God that my pride should be mortified . . . that, except in the veins of a maniac, and he too possessed 'of a deaf and dumb spirit,' there should not run one drop of my father's blood in any living creature besides myself."[31]

Judith Randolph died in 1816. Once a suitor had said that the whiteness of her skin was "not much inferior to that which is exhibited in the eastern sky just at the moment when aurora is about to disperse the beams of her effulgence to the whole animate world."[32] But even her face turned plain as her days were passed in bitterness and frustration.

Of these star-crossed Randolphs only the wayward and fiery Nancy salvaged some measure of happiness. But first she spent fifteen years in her sister's home, where she was kept in a constant state of humiliation —eating alone in the kitchen, cleaning the chamber pots. Then in April

1809 she was employed as housekeeper by wealthy Gouverneur Morris. And on Christmas Day she married the old Federalist diplomat. The marriage was tested and strengthened by the demented accusations of John Randolph, who wrote Morris that she had killed his brother and had an affair with a slave. Nancy gave her husband the one thing his full life lacked—a son and heir. And on his death the worldly patrician not only left his widow with a comfortable income but provided in his will that it should be increased in the event she remarried.

Before turning from the stepsons of St. George Tucker to his natural children, there is a distant cousin who added to the reputation of the dynasty.

George Tucker, related to St. George through both his parents, came to Virginia from Bermuda about 1790 when in his mid-teens, and was sponsored and introduced into society by his successful cousin. George was to become a congressman, member of Jefferson's first faculty at the University of Virginia, and prolific writer of history, philosophy, economics, and fiction.

For a future professor of "moral philosophy," George's early life was not noted for its high tone. Judge Tucker was constantly bailing him out of debt; a loan company once even had him arrested. He managed to dissipate a sizable inheritance from his first wife.‡ And in Washington, where he served in Congress from 1819 to 1825, most of his time was spent gambling. (At one sitting he lost $1000 to a professional card-sharp.)

Few people were indifferent to this Tucker. Attorney General William Wirt called him "a very good fellow."[33] But a young man who spent a day with him at the University of Virginia reported that Tucker was "vain and selfish." Moreover, he added, the professor and his wife "have no genuine hospitality in a single vein from the crowns of the heads to the sole of the feet, malgré their affected display of silver plate and fashion."[34]

‡ George Tucker (1775–1861) was married three times, first to Mary Byrd Farly, granddaughter of Colonel William Byrd III. She died in 1797, two years after their marriage, and left him a large part of a sugar plantation in Antigua, a share in 13,000 acres on the Dan River in North Carolina, and stock in the Dismal Swamp Canal Company. In 1802 he married Maria Ball Carter, seventeen-year-old daughter of the Blenheim branch of that distinguished family, and a granddaughter of George Washington's sister. She died in 1823. Five years later Tucker wed Louisa Thompson, a Baltimore widow.

His only son, Daniel, was judged insane and committed to a Philadelphia institution, where he died in 1838; his oldest daughter, Eliza, married Gessner Harrison, professor of ancient languages at the University of Virginia; and his second daughter, Maria, became the wife of George Rives (1802–74), wealthy planter and brother of William Cabell Rives (1792–1868), Virginia congressman, senator, and twice U.S. minister to France.

No matter what may have been his personal faults, George Tucker's writing displayed a lively, imaginative mind and a rather bizarre sense of humor. His more than twenty books and hundreds of articles included the first biography of Jefferson, in two volumes; a novel, *The Valley of Shenandoah*, an early attempt to depict Virginia life in fiction; *A Voyage to the Moon: With Some Account of the Manners and Customs, Science and Philosophy, of the People of Morosofia, and Other Lunarians*, a satire on certain contemporary institutions now long forgotten.§ In another piece of science fiction, "A Century Hence: Or a Romance of 1941," unpublished, Tucker predicts such future marvels as flying cars hurtling through space, the harnessing of the sun's rays for radiant heating, ways of making food from waste material, gaslights illuminating New York City, and a great competition between the United States, Russia, and England to build the first gigantic telescope to view the moon.[35]

The three children of St. George Tucker—Henry, Nathaniel Beverley (called Beverley), and Frances—were tutored by the son of a thrifty Scotch-Irish farmer who came to live with them in Williamsburg. At first Tucker paid John Coalter thirty pounds a year, but later they worked out an exchange of services, with the judge giving the young man instruction in the law. Coalter learned his lessons well and eventually succeeded his mentor on the Virginia Supreme Court of Appeals. He also was to become the husband of Frances Tucker.¶

Judge Tucker's two sons were poles apart in outlook and temperament. Henry, the elder by four years, was much like his father—gentle, humorous, open-minded. Beverley, quick-tempered, morose, eccentric, seemed to take after his idealized stepbrother, John Randolph of Roanoke. While Beverley was to become a leading States' Rights theoretician, who, in the words of Vernon Parrington, "tucked the horizon of Virginia about him like a Hudson Bay blanket and defied the cold winds of the North," his brother Henry took a broader constitutional view, supporting Jackson's national system of internal improvements and opposing the nullification doctrine.[36]

Sharing his father's distaste for politics, Henry's entire political career

§ Vernon Louis Parrington, Jr., describes *A Voyage to the Moon* as "a satirical romance, [which] contains some convincing satire on manners, and, mixed in with the pseudoscience, a superficial discussion of a utopian community." See *American Dreams, a Study of American Utopias* (Providence: Brown University Press, 1947), pp. 13–16.

¶ One of their three children, Elizabeth, rejected the marriage proposal of Francis Walker Gilmer (1790–1826), the brilliant protégé of Jefferson, who played an important part in establishing the University of Virginia. She subsequently became the bride of John Randolph Bryan, a namesake and former ward of John Randolph of Roanoke. Their son, John Coalter Bryan, was the principal heir of the Randolph will that was contested by his great-uncles.

was contained in a decade—two years in the Virginia House of Delegates, four in Congress, and four in the state Senate. On the local level he proposed a gradual emancipation of the slaves, as his father had done before him, which was defeated in the state legislature by a single vote.

He was elected to Congress in 1815 by a three-to-one margin, although he was sick in bed and didn't bother to campaign. In Washington, Henry opposed the raising of congressional salaries, a stand that put him at odds with John Randolph of Roanoke, who sharply asked their colleagues, "Was it wonderful that they should be considered by the people at large in the light of day laborers who worked here for something less than a dollar an hour?"[37] The pay raise went through, but Henry refused to accept the increase in his own salary.

Randolph's feud with Henry's father further strained their relationship, even though St. George advised his son "not to take part in my suffering." However, Henry wrote in 1819 that his stepbrother's presence in Congress "makes me rejoice the more at my retirement."[38]

But in the close confines of Virginia politics it was not easy to avoid conflicting paths. When the legislature voted for a new United States senator in 1825 the stepbrothers were opponents. Tucker led on the first two ballots; Randolph was elected on the third. Before the final ballot had been counted a spokesman for Tucker tried to withdraw his name, stating that he was acting on strict instruction from his candidate. There is some ground to believe that the legislators knew of Tucker's desire not to engage in a free-for-all with his stepbrother, and that this may have influenced the outcome.[39] But even if Henry did not actually throw the contest, his generous sentiments are well documented. On learning of Randolph's election, he wrote, "I could wish, indeed, that my name had been withheld, yet hope that its withdrawal, even at the time it took place, was not too late to manifest my deference to him. God preserve him as an honor to his station and the Old Dominion."[40]

Henry gladly gave up elective office for a place on the bench, serving for seventeen years as a state judge.* Part of the time he was

---

* In a satirical verse, Tucker expressed his disdain for the gamesmanship of politics:

> Hence, if you have a son, I would advise;
>   Lest his fair prospects you perchance may spoil;
> If you would have him in the State to rise,
>   Instead of Grotius let him study Hoyle.
> And if his native genius should betray
>   A turn for petty tricks, indulge the bent;
> It may do service at some future day,
>   A dexterous cut may rule a great event;
>   And a stacked pack may make a President!

Quoted in John Randolph Tucker, "The Judges Tucker of the Court of Appeals of Virginia, *Virginia Law Register*, I, No. 11 (March 1896), p. 809.

president of the Virginia Supreme Court of Appeals, the post St. George once held. (There was even a continuity between the legal decisions of father and son.[41]) His reputation was such that his three colleagues cheerfully received him as their presiding officer, even though he was the youngest member of the court.

This was also his most productive period as a writer. Working each day from four in the morning until breakfast, he completed the notable two-volume *Commentaries on the Laws of Virginia*, as well as his *Lectures on Constitutional Law*.

President Jackson wanted to make him the Attorney General of the United States, but Tucker declined. He said he was happy where he was.[42] (Roger Taney then took the federal post, and within a few years he succeeded John Marshall as Chief Justice of the United States.)

St. George Tucker once wrote of his second son, Beverley: "Some malignant star surely presided over his birth!"[43]

He had been a temperamental and precocious child, often a disciplinary problem. He longed for the affection of his father, yet felt unfairly that St. George was indifferent to him. This, perhaps, brought him closer to John Randolph of Roanoke. But any relationship between two such stormy individuals was bound to be a series of peaks and valleys. After one altercation Tucker moved to Missouri.

In St. Louis Beverley set up his law office in a hollow tree. However, despite such eccentricities, the distance between him and Randolph seemed to clear his head, and he served successfully on various state courts for nearly thirteen years.

Beverley's first wife was Polly Coalter, the redheaded sister of his childhood tutor and brother-in-law.† When she died in 1827, after eighteen years of marriage, he married her young niece, Eliza Naylor. The match was bitterly opposed by the Naylor family as a violation of church ordinances and divine law. The bride died of tuberculosis four months after the wedding, but the smoldering feud between the Naylors and Tucker went on for years and led to the suspension of Eliza's father and brothers from the Presbyterian Church.

For his third wife, Tucker took Lucy Ann Smith, the beautiful eighteen-year-old daughter of General Thomas Adams Smith, an outstanding soldier after whom Fort Smith, Arkansas, is named. Lucy was also the niece of Hugh Lawson White, the prominent senator from Tennessee, whom Tucker supported for President in 1836.

† John and Polly Coalter also had an older brother David (1764–1821), whose five daughters married important men of affairs. Among their husbands were William Campbell Preston (1794–1860), U.S. senator from South Carolina and brother-in-law of Robert Jefferson Breckinridge; Hamilton Rowan Gamble (1798–1864), Civil War governor of Missouri; and Edward Bates (1793–1869), Missouri congressman and Lincoln's Attorney General.

There were six children by this union, three boys and three girls, and all were given Beverley as a middle name. "I have been always treated as an alien to my family," wrote Beverley, "and hence I have taken care to designate all my children by a name that shall distinguish my branch of it."[44]

It was John Randolph who finally lured Beverley back to Virginia. Randolph had once written him, "You seem to be unconscious how much I had built upon you as the chief foundation of my happiness."[45] Now, in 1833, as he lay dying, Randolph begged Beverley to take care of him. As Beverley was moving his family to Roanoke, his stepbrother died. The suggestion was made that Nathaniel Hawthorne should write Randolph's biography. Beverley vetoed the idea, however, feeling it would be like having one of Byron's grandest, gloomiest poems "sung by a little girl in pantalettes accompanied by her small brother on the flageolet."[46] A more fitting memorial, he felt, was for him to continue Randolph's work in Congress. But Beverley was defeated by a vote of 1038 to 737, a loss he attributed to President Jackson's popularity among the "lower classes."[47]

He was then offered his father's old post as professor of law at William and Mary College. The position paid $600 and a fee of $30 for each student in his course. He began in 1834 with only three students but proved to be a highly popular teacher, and enrollment jumped to thirty-six by 1840. However, the next year Beverley's competition sharply increased when his brother Henry resigned from the Court of Appeals to to become law professor at the University of Virginia.

Henry's move was based on the growing needs of a large family. His sons were now of college age, and his expenses would be considerably less if he moved to Charlottesville. The university made generous provisions to attract the prestigious jurist, for its reputation was at a low point. Its law professor had just been murdered during a student riot. (The assassin apparently bore no personal grudge but "had been heard to say that he intended to shoot the first member of the Faculty who should attempt to tear off his mask during a riot."[48])

The Tucker brothers, using their father's textbook, now had a near monopoly on the teaching of law in Virginia. Beverley, on hearing of the loss of two prospective students to Henry, wrote, "I hope I shall be always capable of rejoicing in his success, tho at my own expense, in some small degree. . . ."[49] But the competition was not to be for long. Henry's poor health compelled him to retire in 1845. In his short career at the university he inaugurated an honor system, the first of its kind in the United States, and played a significant part in abolishing outmoded rules requiring the wearing of a uniform and early rising, which must have made him popular with the students.

The lasting reputation of Beverley was not to be as teacher or judge but as writer. In political tracts and novels he expounded a philosophy that was part John Randolph, part Professor Thomas R. Dew, a colleague at William and Mary. From his stepbrother he acquired a zeal for States' Rights. (As Randolph put it, "Asking one of the States to surrender part of her sovereignty is like asking a lady to surrender part of her chastity.") From Dew came the belief that slavery was "an absolute good."[50] This doctrinal combination was unrelieved by the slightest pause to take himself less than absolutely seriously, and was compounded by a complete absence of the Tucker sense of humor.

His almost pathological hatred of the North was illustrated by a clause he wished to insert in the Missouri constitution banning all Yankees from the new state. When asked how he could prevent them from crossing the Mississippi, Beverley replied that "he would have every ferryman stationed on either side of the river instructed, when a passenger came and wanted to cross, to ask the applicant for ferriage to pronounce the word 'cow,' and if he said 'keow' he would not be permitted to let him pass."[51]

However, what made Beverley into more than a mere crank was his considerable talent as a writer. Edgar Allan Poe called a Tucker novel "one of the very noblest fictions ever written by an American."[52]

His most famous work was *The Partisan Leader,* a novel, which was planned as a piece of anti-Van Buren propaganda in the 1836 presidential contest. (It appeared too late to have any effect.) Although written twenty-five years before the firing on Fort Sumter, he predicts secession and Civil War. The book also contained thinly veiled sketches of Beverley and Henry: the fictional older brother, successful in public life and well to do, acquiesces to federal encroachment on the states, believing union on any terms is better than disunion; the younger brother, less prosperous and respected, is rash, hot-tempered, and strong in his States' Rights convictions. Henry was deeply hurt by the characterization, and Beverley was deeply hurt by Henry's lack of approval.

Henry died in 1848, one of the last of the moderate Southern leaders; Beverley died three years later, one of the first of the Southern fireeaters.

Henry, as a young man, had thought himself passionately in love with Polly Carter, his stepsister. Fortunately for the political dynasty, she rebuffed him. For her marriage was childless, while Henry and his wife, Anne Evelina Hunter,‡ were to have thirteen children.

Besides her fertility, Henry's wife owned a strong character and a

‡ She was the daughter of Moses Hunter, a member of the Virginia House of Delegates (1779–86), and a maternal grandaughter of Revolutionay War General Adam Stephens. See Mary S. Kennedy, *The Seldens of Virginia and Allied Families* (New York: Frank Allaben Genealogical Co., 1911), Vol. II, pp. 135–36.

green umbrella—the latter was used as a rapier to keep her offspring from dozing during church services.[53]

Qualitatively as well, Henry had a remarkable family. His children included:

David Hunter Tucker (1815–71), professor at the Medical College of Virginia, who told his students that a stethoscope was "simply a tube with a patient at one end and a damned fool at the other," and attended Stonewall Jackson in his last illness; author, *Elements of the Principles and Practices of Midwifery* (Philadelphia, 1848); son-in-law of George Dallas, Vice-President of the United States.

Henry St. George Tucker (1828–63)—called "Sainty"—lawyer; clerk of the Virginia Senate and House of Delegates; author, *Hansford: A Tale of Bacon's Rebellion* (later reissued as *The Devoted Bride*), a milestone in the use of realism in the American historical novel; son-in-law of a Virginia governor; Confederate lieutenant colonel, who died of consumption contracted during the Peninsula campaign.[54]

Nathaniel Beverley Tucker (1820–90)—called Beverley—newspaper editor, diplomat, Washington lobbyist, Confederate agent, falsely accused of complicity in the assassination of Lincoln.

John Randolph Tucker (1823–97)—called "Ran"—Virginia attorney general, U.S. congressman, law professor, president of the American Bar Association, author.

The second Beverley Tucker was a massive, jolly fellow, in every way unlike the uncle for whom he was named. His giant figure in long black cape and beaver hat was well known in Washington, where he was editor of the *Sentinel,* and his effervescent spirit and good humor made him one of the capital's most popular men about town. As a reward for his editorial support, President Buchanan sent him to Liverpool to replace Nathaniel Hawthorne as the American consul.

When the Civil War broke out Beverley rushed home to Virginia, but Jefferson Davis sent him right back to Europe as a purchasing agent. Later he was transferred to Canada to arrange a cotton-for-bacon trade.[55] While in Canada he heard that the South had surrendered and that the U. S. Government was offering $25,000 for his apprehension, dead or alive.

On the morning of May 10, 1865, Major General David Hunter read the formal indictment charging that Jefferson Davis, Beverley Tucker, and others had "combined, confederated and conspired" with John Wilkes Booth to murder President Lincoln. Four of those named, including Tucker, were part of the so-called "Canadian Cabinet," the pseudo-diplomatic group of Confederate agents in Montreal. The case linking them with the assassination rested primarily on the testimony of an unreliable double spy and an unscrupulous quack doctor.[56] It could not have stood up in an ordinary court of law, and Tucker was never brought to trial.

In Tucker's reply to the absurd charges against him he argued that Andrew Johnson "is the only solitary individual . . . who could possibly realize any interest or benefit from the perpetration of this deed. . . ."[57] Such loose talk was eagerly seized upon by the President's enemies and subsequently figured in his impeachment trial.[58]

But Beverley reserved his full wrath for the president of the accusing tribunal, David Hunter. The stern and dedicated Union general had earned the lasting hatred of every Virginian by burning V.M.I.—"the West Point of the South." As Annie Broun, a native of Lexington, said: "Can I say 'God forgive'? Were it possible for human lips to raise his name heavenward, angels would thrust the foul thing back again. The curses of thousands will follow him through all time, and brand upon the name Hunter infamy, infamy."[59] Tucker now added that the general was childless because of "God's wise provision that monsters should not propagate their species. . . ." Furthermore, he charged that Hunter had "blackened his soul and charred his hands with the burning ruins of the homes of his own unoffending kindred, where, and among whom, he had in youth and manhood enjoyed the most elegant and lavish hospitalities."[60] What unquestionably rankled Tucker was that he and Hunter were indeed "kindred," as the term has always been used in the South, and the following genealogy must have been salt in the exiled Virginian's wounds:

Moses Hunter ———— (brothers) ———— *Andrew Hunter*
Married Mary Stockton, daughter of Richard ("the Signer")

Anne Evelina Hunter
m. *Henry St. George Tucker*

David Hunter
Chief judge at the trial of Lincoln's alleged murderers

[Nathaniel] Beverley Tucker
Accused of complicity in Lincoln's murder

For the next seven years Tucker was a wanderer. He tried his hand at managing a ranch in Mexico but was thwarted by the overthrow of Maximilian; he ran a hotel in Canada but was pressed to the wall by free-loading Southern exiles. Finally, in 1872, he returned to Washington to become a lobbyist, or, as his wife nicely phrased it, "an advocate of claims before the departments and before Congress."[61] (His main client was Thomas Scott, president of the Pennsylvania Railroad.)

Washington opened its heart to its long-absent friend. His many intimates included Grover Cleveland, and the story made the rounds that the President-elect told Tucker, "Well, Bev, tomorrow when I am inaugurated what can I do for you?" "Grover," replied the lobbyist, "I shall be on the Capitol steps, a humble onlooker, when you take oath as the President of the United States, and all I ask you to do when you have taken the oath is to beckon to me. I shall step right up. Then put your arms around me and call me Bev before that great assembled multitude, just as you have done tonight. This is all I ask!"[62]

But the only presidential favor he received was short-lived. A year before Tucker's death in 1890, Benjamin Harrison asked him to serve on a diplomatic delegation to Haiti. However, when an enterprising reporter revived the old story of his "complicity" in the Lincoln assassination, the President quickly withdrew the offer.

Beverley's brother Ran was also a friend of Grover Cleveland's. In fact it is generally accepted that the President would have appointed him to the Supreme Court except for an uneasy feeling that too much levity would be out of place on that august tribunal.

For Ran Tucker was a very funny fellow, although there was sometimes an unpleasant cutting edge to his wit. When he was first elected to Congress in 1875 a sober-minded constituent warned, "If you expect to do anything for your own reputation, or for this grand old Commonwealth, Sir, I hope when you get to Washington you will never tell an anecdote."[63] This well-meaning advice went unheeded. Tucker soon complained that the demand for his stories was so great that to accept all the invitations "to dine and be funny" would leave no time for his congressional duties.

During one dinner party, at which Paderewski was the guest of honor, Ran wagered ten dollars that he could get the dour Pole to laugh. But he refused to be amused. Finally Tucker asked the pianist if he would listen to his rendition of a difficult piece. Then he proceeded to give an exact and ridiculous imitation of Paderewski—hands flying, head shaking, hair falling over his face. The great musician exploded with gales of laughter and the mimic won his bet.[64]

James G. Blaine was among the many who found it impossible to top a Tucker performance. After a heated congressional debate between them, the Maine congressman concluded, "Oh, well, Mr. Speaker, I am not a lawyer." To which Ran replied, "Mr. Speaker, to the lawyers in this

House, the information imparted by the gentleman from Maine must come as entirely superfluous."[65]

On the other hand, Tucker was not only an attorney but possibly the supreme trial lawyer of his time.[66] He was attorney general of Virginia for eight years, including the period of the Civil War. Even the staid American Bar Association, of which he had been a president, conceded that Tucker "charmed jurors into forgetfulness of their enforced contribution to the cause of justice."[67]§

Like all his ancestors, Ran was a strict constitutionalist, a breed that was already considered "old-fashioned" by the time he entered the House of Representatives. His first congressional speech set the tone for his twelve years in Washington. The House was considering a $1.5 million appropriation for the Centennial Exposition at Philadelphia. Patriotic proponents of the measure were having an oratorical orgy. Carter Harrison of Illinois had just announced that the anniversary celebration would hatch a new brood of American eagles under "yonder magnificent dome cutting the blue field of Heaven with its rounded brow." (The Capitol building, presumably.) Tucker's answer was more earthbound. "Show me the granted power," he said, "or how this bill is necessary and proper to carry into effect an expressly granted power, or before God and under my oath I cannot vote for it."[68] A Fourth of July celebration was not called for in the Constitution, ergo it was unconstitutional. Such reasoning fascinated and infuriated James A. Garfield. Yet the two men, despite glorious battles in Congress, became devoted friends, and the President left Tucker as guardian of his children.[69]

Tucker arrived in Congress by accident. There had been a deadlock in his district, and Ran was given the nomination as a compromise, without having lifted a finger for the job. He was renominated five times without opposition. And through seniority and mental dexterity became a powerful member of the House: chairman, at different times, of the Ways and Means Committee and the Judiciary Committee; co-author of the Tucker-Edmunds Act, which outlawed polygamy in the Territory of Utah, and of the Tucker Act to regulate the counting of electoral votes. His floor speeches were among the most sparkling of his day, although dotted with Latin phrases and classical references, of which he was particularly vain. One colleague, in a teasing mood, once remarked, "*Nulla vestigia retrorsa,* exclaimed the gentleman in the lan-

§ Yet Tucker had some notable and historic failures. He represented Tilden before the 1877 Electoral Commission, and defended the Chicago Haymarket anarchists before the Supreme Court. When asked why he took the latter case, he replied, "I do not defend anarchy; I defend the Constitution." See Alexander Hamilton, *Memorial of Hon. John Randolph Tucker* (Richmond: James E. Goode Printing Co., 1897), and *Ex parte Spies, 123 U.S. 131.*

guage of Pocahontas, his ancestress." Tucker, whose veins held no Indian blood, dryly replied, "The descendant of Pocahontas never said
retrorsa instead of *retrorsum*."[70]

Finally, in 1887, Tucker relinquished his congressional seat. He had
been a strong free-trader ("Protection is privilege") in a strong protectionist district. It was time, he felt, for his constituents to have a representative more in tune with their thinking. He spent his last decade as
professor of law at Washington and Lee University, where he had
taught before entering Congress, and working on his two-volume *The
Constitution of the United States* (known as *Tucker on the Constitution*),
which was edited and posthumously published by his son Harry.

Two years after Ran Tucker left Congress, Harry Tucker was elected
to his old seat. The change-over from father to son was imperceptible.
When Congress wished to pass a minor vocational rehabilitation program, Harry dissented: "There is no power in the Constitution of which
we are aware under which such a bill can be passed."[71] Old-timers
thought they were hearing the echo of Ran's lonely fight against the
Centennial Exposition. Nor was Harry any better equipped to bend his
views to those of his constituents. In 1896, at the height of Bryanism,
Tucker opposed the strong sentiment of his district for easy money. He
feared physical violence when he went before the people; former supporters shook their fists in his face. "The nomination was Mr. Tucker's
if he would accept it upon the terms of voting for free silver," said a
fellow Virginia congressman. "Mr. Tucker refused to accept upon those
terms and lost the nomination."[72]

He retired to Washington and Lee University, as his father had done
before him, and for a short time in 1900 and 1901 he served as its acting
president. Later he became dean of the Law Department at George
Washington University, president of the American Bar Association, and
president of the Jamestown Tercentennial Exposition, where his duties
were primarily those of "chief publicity agent and good will ambassador."[73] This task pleased the urbane and courtly Harry, who maintained the Tucker tradition for good humor and high jinks. (On hearing
of the election of Grover Cleveland, Harry set out to present him with
a bottle of fine wine but was jostled in the milling crowd. As the bottle
crashed to the ground, Tucker loudly announced, "Grover Cleveland, I
christen you President of the United States!"[74])

Harry also found time for the dynasty's principal avocation, book
writing. His *Limitations on the Treaty-Making Power under the Constitution of the United States,* published in 1915, marked a milestone in
family jurisprudence. Probably never before was a legal scholar able to
rely almost exclusively on authorities from his own ancestors—from his

great-grandfather's *Tucker on Blackstone* to his father's *Tucker on the Constitution.*

Twice Tucker sought the Democratic nomination for governor of Virginia. But as an unrelenting foe of the machine he never had a chance. Senator Thomas S. Martin, the political boss of the state, gave him the kiss of death: "I would expect nothing from Tucker except bitter antagonism. He is, in my judgement, narrow and bigotted, as well as intensely hostile to me and my friends." In 1909 Tucker was defeated by a coalition between Martin and Bishop James Cannon, "The Dry Messiah," who was then superintendent of the Virginia Anti-Saloon League.[75]

But in 1922 he was again elected to the Congress, where he served until his death. His colleagues showed their respect by taking the unusual step of enlarging the House Judiciary Committee in order to make room for him. As a legislator he is best remembered as the author of the Seventeenth Amendment to the Constitution, providing for the direct election of United States senators, and for refusing to accept a congressional pay increase, a precedent established by his grandfather.

When he was seventy-six years old, in 1929, Tucker married for the third time.¶ A friend remarked that he had courage to marry at his age, to which Harry answered, "It takes courage to marry at any age. But remember, it was the spirit of '76 that made these United States!"[76] He died three years later. Riding back from the cemetery, Carter Glass, Willis Robertson, and other Virginia politicians started to recall Harry's many stories. Before long they were all laughing. "No one," said Senator Glass, wiping a happy tear from his eye, "would have enjoyed his own funeral more than Harry Tucker."[77]

Three years after St. George Tucker arrived in America the young man visited Princeton College. He attended the commencement exercise and then had dinner at Dr. Witherspoon's house. Briefly he recorded the event: "Psalms, Bible, and Prayers before supper. Never pay'd so dear for my Entertainment before."[78] A half century later Tucker's son Beverley was brought before the Missouri Presbytery on three counts of *dancing*—"Hereby bringing reproach on the church, injuring the cause of Christ and shewing contempt for the discipline of the church."[79] The

¶ His first wife was Henrietta Preston Johnston (1858–1900), whom he married in 1877. She was the daughter of William Preston Johnston, president of Tulane University, and the granddaughter of Confederate General Albert Sydney Johnston. Tucker's second wife was Martha Sharpe of Wilkes-Barre, Pennsylvania; his third wife was Mary Jane Williams of Culpeper, Virginia. See George Norbury Mackenzie, *Colonial Families of the United States of America* (New York and Boston: Grafton, 1915), Vol. V, p. 509; also Janie P. B. Lamb, "'Smithfield,' Home of the Prestons, in Montgomery County, Virginia," *Virginia Magazine of History and Biography*, XLVII, No. 2 (April 1939), p. 117.

dancer's nephew, Sainty Tucker, while a student at William and Mary, is supposed to have performed the cakewalk down the aisle of Bruton Church during a morning service. He pleaded intoxication and was let off with a reprimand.[80] Then, in the fourth generation, a new and unexpected development changed the course of the dynasty. The Tuckers got religion!

The Tuckers had been churchgoers, but for a hundred years they were more noted for dancing than for religiosity. Two of the Tucker judges had upheld the most severely anti-ecclesiastical laws ever enacted in the United States. But in 1875 Beverley Dandridge Tucker became a priest in the Protestant Episcopal Church. (He was a son of the Beverley Tucker who was accused of complicity in the assassination of Lincoln.) Why young Beverley chose this new calling is not clear, but that he gave a new direction to the previously secular dynasty cannot be questioned.

The wearing of the cloth, however, did not seem otherwise to change the sharply defined Tucker personality. In fact Beverley, who became bishop of Southern Virginia, frequently chose not to wear clerical clothes. Once while on a train the stout and florid bishop began to recite French poetry. Finally the lady sitting next to him got up and announced to the other passengers, "I cannot sit by that drunken foreigner any longer!"[81]

The bishop also liked to write poetry, and published two slim volumes, one of which contained some of his youthful love poems. The following verse, "*Ad Puerum:* The Dinner, after She Left!" illustrates his limited talent but worldly outlook:

> I care not for sherry a cent, Sir,—
> I call for my *Chérie* in vain,—
> My heart is with real pain rent, Sir,
> I scarcely have need of champagne.
> No fig would I give for a raisin,—
> Such reasons you only would waste,—
> The desert my sad heart now stays in
> Is dessert enough for my taste!
> But lo! as the ev'ning grows later,
> And the night is chasing the day,
> I'll order a pony, O Waiter,
> And drive all my sorrows away.[82]

After such youthful flings Beverley married the tall, angular, intelligent Maria Washington. Once at a church convention the wife of another bishop asked Maria the occupation of her father and was told farmer. Later the inquisitive lady said to her husband, "I can't understand how that charming Bishop Tucker happened to marry a farmer's daughter."

"Did she tell you what farm her father owned?" asked the husband.

"No, what difference does that make?"

"Well," he replied, "her father was John Augustine Washington, great-great-nephew of George Washington, and the farm was Mount Vernon."[83]* Maria was the last Washington born at Mount Vernon.

The Tuckers had thirteen children, nine of whom were boys; four became ordained clergymen, and two others lay missionaries in China. Two sons were made bishops; a third declined a bishopric. Beverley Dandridge Tucker, Jr., was bishop of Ohio. Henry St. George Tucker was bishop of Kyoto, where he preached only in Japanese, then bishop of Virginia, and finally presiding bishop of the Protestant Episcopal Church.[84]

For four generations each Tucker was dealt an almost identical hand. Successively, he became a lawyer, judge, law professor, and author of a learned treatise on the law. Together they compiled a remarkable record of homogeneity, an unbroken line of legal scholarship combined with public service.

From time to time a Tucker was expected to leave the classroom or the courtroom to serve in the federal legislature. Yet it was the issues of government, not the techniques of politics, that fascinated them. Politics was not the art of the possible, it was the avenue along which they fought for the absolute good as they saw it. A half loaf, rather than being better than no loaf, was unpalatable. If their constituents did not agree with their views, then they willingly retired, or accepted defeat gladly. For they could truthfully say that they had no hunger for power or aspirations for higher office. Although their combined service in the United States Congress totaled forty-four years, elective office was never an end in itself, the heady brew was never difficult to put down, and each left Washington with a certain feeling of relief.

St. George Tucker set a pattern for his dynasty. While too young to be

---

* Colonel John Augustine Washington, aide-de-camp to Robert E. Lee, was killed while reconnoitering an enemy position on September 13, 1861. In a poem entitled, "John Augustine Washington of Mount Vernon," his son-in-law wrote:

> He lay where he fell, with the light on his face,
> Untouched by dishonor and shame,
> Defeated, yet true to the pride of his race,
> The home where he'd dwelt and his name.

See Beverley Dandridge Tucker, *My Three Loves* (New York and Washington: Neagle, 1910), pp. 52–53.

Maria Washington also gave the Tuckers a connection with the Lee Dynasty, for she was the great-grandchild of Corbin Washington (the President's nephew) and his wife Hannah Lee (Richard Henry Lee's daughter). See Walter W. Spooner, editor, *Historic Families of America* (New York: Historic Families Publishing Association, 1907), p. 348.

a major force in the Revolutionary War movement, and too isolated in the declining city of Williamsburg to attract wide public notice, he nevertheless, by sheer intellectual ability, succeeded in becoming a highly influential voice in Virginia. This brilliant provincialism clung to his heirs. Although consistently elected to Congress, they remained largely local in reputation, and, despite the national legislation that bears their name, they have always been little known outside of the Old Dominion. Moreover, the legal legacy of St. George—a strict interpretation of the Constitution—made future Tuckers less and less fashionable as national politicians.

The temperament of the founder, which his heirs inherited in varying degrees, was more scholarly than activistic, and his love of family further acted as a check on overextending the public sector of his life. Succeeding generations would also struggle between the conflicting pulls of home and public service. And more often than in any other American political dynasty, family duty won out, as the Tuckers consistently rejected the sacrifices that total dedication to public life entails.

When St. George, the impoverished young Bermudian, married Frances Bland Randolph, he was making only the first of a long series of matches that would tie the Tuckers to patrician Virginia. Yet while the Tuckers would almost immediately become part of the oligarchy, they would never be part of the aristocracy, which derived its position from plantation life. They arrived too late and had neither the vast wealth necessary to go into the tobacco-growing business with its incessant demands for more land and more labor, nor the interest in things agricultural and commercial.

Their place in society, then and since, has been in the professional class, the intelligentsia. It was computed in 1942 that, of the forty-nine male Tuckers in America who were descended from Colonel Henry Tucker of Bermuda, thirty have been lawyers, doctors, clergymen, or engineers. Some measure of their ability can be judged from the fact that, of the eleven lawyers, eight have been jurists or professors of law or both; of the ten doctors, five have been heads of hospitals or professors of medicine or both; of the six clergymen, three have been bishops. Twelve Tuckers have published books or been editors; four were also poets.

As long as the primary profession was the law, the Tuckers were naturally a part of the political whirl. But since it was interest in the law, not politics, that brought them into public life and elective office, it is not surprising that when the family's primary profession shifted to the ministry the Tuckers lost the political impetus. There is no indication, as with the early Muhlenbergs or Frelinghuysens, that the pulpit will become a vehicle for public office. The Tucker political dynasty, perhaps second only to the Adams for intellectual ability, has now ended.

In 1801, when the first Beverley Tucker was a student at William and Mary, he wrote a short account of his family's history. In the preface he stated, "At this day it is deemed arrogant to remember one's ancestors. But the fashion may change, and should any one of my family ever do honor to his race, the world may be curious to trace it."[85] Nearly a century and a half later his foresight was acknowledged by an Attorney General of the United States. When dedicating a new Tucker law building at Washington and Lee University, Homer S. Cummings said, "There are few American families with such an illustrious history."[86]

The Stockton Dynasty

If I my Stockton should forget,
It would be sheer depravity. . . .

—Robert Louis Stevenson[1]

THE marriage of Annis Boudinot and Richard Stockton, probably in 1755, was not a match of social equals. The bride, in a poem of courtship, had written her lover, "I found me all thy own in spite of those/Whose cold unfeeling minds would bid us part."[2]

Although the Boudinots had arrived in America before 1700 and had achieved a degree of prosperity, their landholdings could not compare with those of the Stocktons, who had come from England in 1656 and had owned the better part of what is now Princeton, New Jersey, for three generations. Sedate, well bred, well connected, somewhat imperious, they already displayed aristocratic sensibilities.[3] Richard Stockton's father and grandfather had been judges, and he had been a member of Princeton College's first graduating class in 1748.* Later he would become the first of four generations of Stocktons in Congress.

Although Richard Stockton was to be a signer of the Declaration of Independence, it was his wife's talent for versifying that occasionally rates historical mention, thus illustrating what would often be the case in this dynasty—that the Stocktons were more noteworthy for whom they married.

The poems of Annis Boudinot Stockton at first captivated George

---

* Richard Stockton I (d. 1707), the immigrant, settled in Flushing, Long Island, but after becoming a Quaker he moved to New Jersey where there was a more substantial Quaker community. Richard Stockton II (d. 1709) moved to Princeton in 1696 and five years later bought 4450 acres from William Penn. His son, John Stockton (1701–58), was a judge of Somerset Common Pleas and a benefactor of Princeton University (then the College of New Jersey).

THE STOCKTON DYNASTY
(A Selective Genealogy)

Richard Stockton (d. 1707)
Arrived America 1656
(8 children)

Richard (d. 1709)
Owned most of Princeton, New Jersey
(6 children)

John (1701–58)
Judge of Somerset Common Pleas
(10 children)

Richard ("The Signer")
(1730–81)
CONTINENTAL CONGRESS
m. Annis Boudinot
(6 children)

Hannah
(1736–1808)
m. Elias Boudinot
CONTINENTAL CONGRESS
(1 child)

Susanna
(b. 1742)
m. Lewis Pintard;
their daughter
married a Bayard

Rebecca
(b. 1748)
m. William Tennent,
of family of famous
Presbyterian ministers

Samuel Witham
(1751–95)
Secretary of
New Jersey
convention that
ratified Constitution

Susan
(1764–1854)
m. William Bradford
U. S. Attorney General
(no issue)

Julia
(1758–1848)
m. Dr. Benjamin Rush,
CONTINENTAL CONGRESS
(13 children)

Richard ("The Duke")
(1764–1828)
SENATE
(9 children)

Lucius Horatio
(d. 1835)
Nominated for
Secretary of War

Mary
(d. 1846)
m. Andrew Hunter
(3 children)

Abigail
m. Robert Field
(6 children)

Richard Rush
(1786–1859)
U. S. Attorney General,
Secretary of Treasury

Richard
(1791–1827)
Attorney
General of
Mississippi

Robert Field
(1795–1866)
("Fighting Bob")
SENATE
(9 children)

Annis
(b. 1804)
m. John R.
Thomson,
SENATE

David Hunter
(1802–1886)
Union Army
general

Richard Stockton Field
(1803–70)
SENATE, federal
judge (3 children)

John Potter
(1826–1900)
SENATE
m. Sarah Marks
(3 children)

Mary
(b. 1830)
m. Admiral John C.
Howell, Secretary of
Navy

Robert Field
(1832–98)
Comptroller and
adjutant-general
of New Jersey

Washington, who called her "the elegant muse of Morven."† According to historian L. H. Butterfield, the Revolutionary commander sent her "probably the longest passage of literary criticism he ever wrote, and in elegance of style and gallantry of tone it would have done credit to the fourth Earl of Chesterfield."[4] But Washington was undoubtedly more taken with Mrs. Stockton's patriotic sentiments than her literary achievement. Many of her efforts commemorated Revolutionary events, such as Warren's death at Bunker Hill ("Ill-fated hand that sent the cruel dart/ That pierc'd brave Warren's generous human heart . . .").[5] However, as the lovely poetess continued to bombard Washington with her pseudo-classical odes, she evidently became something of a pest, and his notes of thanks became shorter and chillier.[6]

Sharing his wife's refined tastes, in 1766 Richard Stockton took a letter of introduction to a London publisher requesting that he be given "a sight of Samuel Johnson . . . for we Americans, when we go to England have as much curiosity to see a live author, as Englishmen have to see a live Ostrich or a Cherokee Sachem."[7] While abroad Stockton also tried to convince John Witherspoon that he should accept the presidency of Princeton. The Scottish preacher was agreeable, but Mrs. Witherspoon was not, and it was left to Benjamin Rush, a medical student at Edinburgh, to win over the reluctant wife.

At the outset of the American Revolution, Stockton was a prominent lawyer and a member of the colony's ruling elite—a justice of the New Jersey Supreme Court and a Provincial Councilman.‡ He was elected to the Continental Congress just in time to participate in the closing debate on the Declaration of Independence; John Adams recording that he made a "short but energetic speech" in its favor. Stockton, nearly six feet tall, signed the historic parchment and probably shared Benjamin Harrison's belief that he would hang quickly.

The New Jersey legislature met in August 1776 to choose its first governor. Stockton and William Livingston were tied on the first ballot. Had

† Morven was the Stocktons' home in Princeton, named by Annis Boudinot Stockton after the home of the hero in a sensational 1762 literary hoax, *Fingal, an Ancient Epic Poem in Six Books,* which was supposed to have been the recounting of the exploits of the king of northwestern Caledonia by his son Ossian, but turned out to have been the invention of a Scotsman, James Macpherson.

In 1951 Morven was given to the state of New Jersey and is now the Governor's Mansion.

‡ His law students included William Paterson and Elias Boudinot. The former, later to be called "the forerunner of John Marshall," apparently was not always an attentive pupil. Among Stockton's law briefs can be found poems that Paterson composed when his mind should have been filled with more mundane matters. One verse begins, "Hail, beauteous maid! thy charms inspire." See W. Jay Mills, editor, *Glimpses of Colonial Society and the Life at Princeton College, 1766–1773* (Philadelphia: Lippincott, 1903), pp. 19–20. For Paterson's subsequent career, see Bayard Dynasty, p. 279.

not the legislature taken the unusual procedure of allowing its presiding officer to vote, Stockton would have been elected. John Stevens, the chairman of the legislature, visited Stockton that night and asked him to withdraw in favor of Livingston. He suggested that Stockton would then be made chief justice of the state. Stockton's reply was an ambiguous no, which Stevens interpreted as meaning that he was not averse to being governor. Stockton afterward contended that he told Stevens he "had not the least inclination to serve in the office of Governor," and expected to be summoned by the legislature to make his self-sacrificing declination. The call never came. Livingston was elected governor and Stockton was elected chief justice. Stockton then accused Stevens of misrepresenting his position and denying him the opportunity to be magnanimous. Stevens replied that "had it been in his Power to acquaint [Stockton] . . . that he was Elected Governor . . . he had probably not been so greatly chagrined." The result of the squabble was that Stockton refused the chief justiceship and remained in Congress.[8]

The next month Congress sent him to inspect the Northern Army. At Saratoga, seeing the barefooted troops, he wrote, "My heart melts with compassion for my brave countrymen who are thus venturing their lives in the public service, and yet are so distressed."[9] By the time he returned home in November the British were marching through New Jersey. The Stocktons would have to abandon Morven and move fast to escape the enemy. Annis buried some of the family's most valuable possessions. And just before leaving Princeton she also hid the record of the college's American Whig Cliosophic Society—an act which earned for her an honorary membership in the world's oldest collegiate debating club.

The Stocktons fled to a friend's house in Monmouth County where Richard was captured by a band of Tories, some say through the treachery of a relative.§ He was the first of four signers of the Declaration to be taken prisoner by the British.

§ Most famous of the Tory Stocktons was Major Richard Witham Stockton of the Crown's forces. The British respectfully called him "Stockton, the famous land pilot." Among the rebels he was known as "Double Dick." Captured by the Americans in 1777, Washington decided to treat him as a prisoner of war rather than a traitor. After Stockton complained about conditions in Carlisle jail, the Continental Congress passed a resolution to have it made "as comfortable as circumstances will admit." See Thomas Coates Stockton, *The Stockton Family of New Jersey and Other Stocktons* (Washington: Carnahan Press, 1911), pp. 27–28, and Edward Alfred Jones, *The Loyalists of New Jersey* (Newark: New Jersey Historical Society, 1927), pp. 211–12.

After the war Stockton moved to Canada and, with others who had remained loyal to the King, founded St. John, New Brunswick, in 1782. Most of his heirs led productive lives in their new country and contributed at least one member to the Canadian Parliament. One of his granddaughters married Erastus Root (1773–1846), a four-term member of the U. S. House of Representatives from New York; a great-granddaughter married New York Congressman Selah Reeve Hobbie (1797–1854).

He was marched in freezing weather from Perth Amboy to a New York jail and severely treated. The extent of the brutality is not known. But Elias Boudinot, who went to New York under a flag of truce in the fall of 1777 to bring Washington a firsthand report on the conditions of American prisoners, wrote that the British provost marshal was a tyrant, known to have kept prisoners for up to fourteen weeks "locked up in the Dungeon on the most trifling Pretence, such as asking for more Water for Drink on a hotter Day than usual."[10] Benjamin Rush was incensed; he wrote of Stockton's treatment to Richard Henry Lee: "Every particle of my blood is electrified with revenge, and if justice cannot be done him in any other way, I declare I will, in defiance of the authority of the Congress and the power of the army, drive the first rascally tory I meet with a hundred miles, barefooted, through the first deep snow that falls in our country."[11] Congress threatened reprisals if Stockton was not treated befitting his rank, and the British then sent him home.[12]

But while in prison he signed an oath of adjuration and allegiance to the Crown. Whether acting under duress or out of fear for his family, Stockton swore to "remain in a peaceful Obedience to His Majesty and not take up arms, nor encourage Others to take up arms in Opposition to his Authority."[13] The act ended his political career, and he was forced to resign from Congress.

At Morven, according to Rush, "The whole of Mr. Stockton's furniture, apparel, and even valuable writings have been burnt. All his cattle, horses, and hogs, sheep, grain and forage have been carried away by them. His losses cannot amount to less than five thousand pounds."[14] Two of the three chests of buried valuables had been revealed to the British by a servant and looted. Yet amidst the wreckage the mistress of Morven found one faint cause for cheer. Mrs. Elizabeth Ellet, that indefatigable chronicler of Revolutionary women, wrote, "When Mrs. Stockton heard of the destruction of her noble library, she is said to have remarked that there were two books in it which she particularly valued—the Bible and Young's *Night Thoughts*, and that if these had escaped the burning she would not grieve for the loss of the rest. Tradition relates that when she returned to her desolated house, those very books were the only ones left."[15]

Stockton slowly regained his health, only to be afflicted with cancer in 1781. He died at fifty-one years of age. How well had he fulfilled his pledge to his fellow Declaration signers of life, fortune, and sacred honor? One opinion was given by his son-in-law and co-signer, Dr. Rush:¶

¶ Although Richard "the Signer" was the first major politician in the dynasty, his brother Samuel Witham Stockton (1751–95) held a series of minor diplomatic and political appointments. He went to Europe in 1774 as secretary to William Lee, the American agent in Germany and Austria; later became secretary to the New Jersey convention that ratified the federal Constitution;

RICHARD STOCKTON. An enlightened politician and a correct and graceful speaker. He was timid where bold measures were required, but was at all times sincerely devoted to the liberties of his country.[16]

Annis Boudinot Stockton lived another twenty years after the death of her husband. Each year she wrote an elegiac poem to his memory.

In 1789 old President John Witherspoon of Princeton lost his wife and decided to try his luck at courting the attractive widow Stockton. It became something of a family joke. A friend sent a little verse to Annis' daughter Mary:

> This little God of Love is a roguish elf:
> He makes old age look foolish as himself.
>   'Gainst sixty-two—
>   Oh, luckless lot—
>   His bow he drew
>   And true he shot
> Twang—went the string
> Whiz—flew the dart
>   On a *gray* goose quill
>   To an old man's heart.

The affair, however, was short-lived. The learned pedagogue-patriot married a twenty-four-year-old belle from Philadelphia. Another friend wrote Mary Stockton, "I hear that your Mama has lost her young gallant, Dr. Witherspoon."[17]

As was often the case with this dynasty, the marriages of the women were more noteworthy than the careers of the men. Of Richard the Signer Stockton's sisters, Rebecca married William Tennent, Susanna married Lewis Pintard, and Hannah married Elias Boudinot.

The Tennents were one of the most important clerical families in American history.[18] The first William Tennent came from Ireland around 1716 and founded the "Log College" at Neshaminy, Pennsylvania, the seed from which sprang the Princeton Theological Seminary and the first Presbyterian college in the United States. He had four sons, all notable Presbyterian clergymen, among them William, who late in life married Rebecca Stockton.[19]

Rebecca's husband, so say eyewitnesses, returned to life after having displayed every indication of death for four days, and having been resurrected, he gave an account of heaven as he had seen it.

According to Elias Boudinot, Tennent's biographer, the young minister

---

unsuccessfully ran for secretary of the House of Representatives when the first Congress was organized in 1789; and was secretary of state of New Jersey at the time he was thrown from his carriage and killed.

was conversing in Latin with his brother Gilbert when he became unconscious. All efforts to revive him failed; he was "cold and stiff as a
stake," in the words of Gilbert. Arrangements had been made for the
funeral when suddenly he gave signs of life. While apparently dead,
Tennent reported, he heard a heavenly host sing "songs and hallelujahs,
of thanksgiving and praise, with unspeakable rapture. I felt joy unutter-
able and full of glory. I then applied to my conductor, and requested
leave to join the happy throng; on which he tapped me on the shoulder,
and said, 'You must return to the earth.' This seemed like a sword
through my heart. In an instant I recollected to have seen my brother
standing before me disputing with the doctor. The three days during
which I have appeared lifeless, seemed to me not more than ten or
twenty minutes."[20]

Susanna Stockton's husband, Lewis Pintard, was not the sort to hear
celestial voices. He was a substantial New York merchant and at one
time the chief importer of madeira wines into the United States. (It was
the Pintards' daughter Martha who married Samuel J. Bayard, the member of that dynasty who prosecuted the American claims against Great
Britain under the Jay Treaty.)[21]* During the Revolutionary War Lewis
Pintard served under Elias Boudinot as deputy commissary of prisoners in New York, and was probably a member of General Washington's
espionage network behind enemy lines.

Elias Boudinot, the third of the notable Stockton in-laws, wrote that
without his wife he felt "like a Pelican in the Wilderness." The wife,
Hannah Stockton, could be a trifle hard of hearing when it suited her
purpose.[22] Boudinot studied law under Richard Stockton, with whom
he was doubly joined since Annis, the poetess, was his sister. After a
successful legal career Boudinot was elected to the Continental Congress
in 1777, and five years later was made its president. The honor came his
way mostly because of the system of rotating the post among the
states; he was known as a hard worker, rather than a statesman of the
first magnitude. This he readily admitted. "I did not choose myself, nor
ever did solicit the choice from any other Person," he wrote his wife,
"and therefore while I remain in this important Station, will make up by
Integrity & Application my want of those other Qualifications necessary

* The Pintards also had an adopted son John (1759–1844) who is considered "The Father of Historical Societies in America" because of his part in
organizing the New-York and Massachusetts Historical Societies; was one of
the founders of the free public school system in New York; advised Secretary
of the Treasury Gallatin on the purchase of the Louisiana Territory; served as
a New York City alderman (1788–89) and as a member of the New York
State Assembly (1790). Of Susanna Stockton Pintard, he said, "She always
treated me as her own child and I am certain I loved her as if she had been
my own mother."

for this important Trust."[23] Boudinot ended his political career as director of the Mint.

Having made a fortune, partly through Western land dealings in partnership with John Cleves Symmes (from which Symmes emerged a poor man),† Boudinot devoted his last sixteen years to philanthropic and literary pursuits. Among his many books was *A Star in the West,* written in his seventy-fifth year, in which he attempts to prove that the North American Indians are the descendants of the lost tribes of Israel.‡

But his most unique service to his country came as one of America's earliest intelligence officers. In 1777 Congress appointed him commissary general of prisoners with the rank of colonel. As the liaison between the British and Americans, Boudinot had a convenient "cover" for spying. He planted misleading information with the enemy, interrogated prisoners of war, sifted information that came from agents behind the lines, and warned civil and military authorities of the movements of British spies. It was through Boudinot that Washington probably recruited Lewis Pintard for espionage work. On May 3, 1779, the general wrote Boudinot, "It is a matter of great Importance to have early and good intelligence of the Enemy's strength and motions and, as far as possible, designs, and to obtain them through different channels. Do you think it practical to come at these by Means of Mr. P——d?" George Washington, the man "who couldn't tell a lie," then gives some insight into Revolutionary War intelligence operations: "If Mr. P——d is inclined to engage in a business of this kind, I shall leave it to you and him to fix upon such a Mode of corresponding, as will convey intelligence, in the Most Speedy, safe and efficacious Manner to guard against possible evils. Your correspondence might be under fictitious names, by numbers (representing Men and things) in character or other wise, as you shall agree. It is in my power, I believe, to procure a Liquid, which nothing but a counter Liquor (rubbed over the Paper afterwards) can make legible. Fire, which will bring lime juice, Milk and other things of this kind to light, has no

† See Harrison Dynasty, pp. 222–23.

‡ This was the heart of Boudinot's analogy between the Indians and the Jews: "They [the Indians] believed in one Supreme Being, and considered themselves his chosen people— They reckoned time after the manner of the Hebrews— Many words of their language are identical or similar, while repeatedly the construction is the same—certain tribes possessed a sacred ark carried by men sanctified and purified for the office, the ceremonial of which was like that of the Jews—up to a certain epoch some of the tribes practised circumcision, their feasts and fasts corresponding in great degree with those of the lost Tribes— They abstained from eating the Mexican hog—the sea cow or turtle and many animals & birds which they held as unclean— They had also their 'cities of Refuge' called 'old,' 'beloved,' 'holy' or 'white towns.'" See J. J. Boudinot, editor, *The Life, Public Services, Addresses and Letters of Elias Boudinot* (Boston and New York: Houghton Mifflin, 1896), Vol. II, p. 378.

effect on it. A letter upon trivial Matters of business, written in common Ink, may be filled with important Intelligence which cannot be discovered without the counter part, or Liquid here mentoned."[24]

The Boudinots had an only child, a daughter Susan.§ When she was nine, her parents took her to a social gathering at the home of William Franklin, the Tory governor of New Jersey, where she threw her cup of tea out the window—patriots didn't drink tea.[25] The little patriot later married William Bradford, the second Attorney General of the United States and a member of the country's leading newspaper publishing dynasty.[26] A granddaughter of John Bubenheim Bayard recalls how Mrs. Bradford, when traveling between Philadelphia and New York, would stop at their New Brunswick home "followed by her trunks and boxes" and "then the finery she condescended to show us."[27] When her husband died at forty of yellow fever, after having refused Dr. Rush's "mode of relief," the Bradfords and the Boudinots tangled in a long and bitter court fight over his estate, which also caused a lasting feud between Elias Boudinot and Benjamin Rush.

The most remarkable addition to the Stockton family circle was Benjamin Rush—husband of Julia Stockton, the first-born of Richard the Signer and Annis Boudinot Stockton. His energy, imagination, and range of interests have rarely been matched in the annals of the country. Over five decades, wherever American history was made, Dr. Rush could generally be found somewhere in the background. It was Rush who persuaded Witherspoon to come to America; it was Rush who convinced Tom Paine to write a tract for independence and gave it the title *Common Sense* (Paine wanted to call it *Plain Truth*); it was Rush who recorded Benjamin Harrison's jest on signing the Declaration; it was Rush who described Henry Muhlenberg's inauguration as president of Franklin College and was a charter trustee of the new school; it was Rush who brought John Adams and Thomas Jefferson together in their last years.

Rush met his future wife on the day of his graduation from Princeton. On leaving the commencement exercise he saw "a little creature" of four

§ Yet even without a male heir, Elias Boudinot's name continued to live through its adoption by a young Georgia Cherokee. Galagina (pronounced Kill-ke-nah) had been educated at a mission school at Cornwall, Connecticut, which was endowed by Boudinot. Out of gratitude to his benefactor, the Indian took his name. This Elias Boudinot (c. 1803–39) became the famous editor of the *Cherokee Phoenix*, a weekly newspaper printed partly in the Cherokee language. An involvement in Indian politics led to his murder. His son, Elias Cornelius Boudinot (1835–90), was chairman of the Democratic Party of Arkansas in 1860, the recruiter of an Indian regiment for the Confederate Army, and a delegate from the Indian Territory to the Confederate Congress.

"in danger of being trodden down by the crowd." He picked her up and carried her home, "listening with great pleasure to her prattling all the way."[28] The child grew into a lovely young lady with "brown hair, dark eyes, a complexion composed of white and red, a countenance at the same time soft and animated, a voice mild and musical, and a pronunciation accompanied with a little lisp."[29] Twelve years later, when Julia was sixteen and Rush was thirty, they were married by Dr. Witherspoon. Within six months the groom, the bride's father, and their minister signed the Declaration of Independence.

In a career crammed into sixty-eight years, Benjamin Rush was congressman, signer of the Declaration, physician general of the Revolutionary Army, a leading proponent of the federal Constitution, founder of the Pennsylvania Hospital in Philadelphia, president of the Philadelphia Medical Society, a founder of Dickinson College at Carlisle, a founder of the first free medical clinic in the country, a founder of the first Negro church in America, treasurer of the United States Mint, significant figure in the temperance and abolitionist movements, prison reformer, educational innovator, psychiatrist, prolific author, intimate friend of presidents and philosophers. And, throughout, a scrapper who loved a good fight.

His need to be in the center of controversy was almost pathological. At different times he took on George Washington, Elias Boudinot, William Cobbett, and Dr. William Shippen, brother-in-law of the famous Lees of Virginia, whom he accused of mismanaging the Revolutionary Army medical department.¶

A turning point in Rush's career resulted from his feud with William Cobbett, known as "Peter Porcupine," who was one of the early purveyors of yellow journalism in America. During the yellow fever epidemics that swept Philadelphia in the mid-1790s, Cobbett's paper, *Porcupine's Gazette*, viciously attacked Rush's bloodletting method of treatment. Rush's medical theory was that using the lancet was like emptying the pockets of a man who is struggling to raise himself. Cobbett showed the misguided Rush no mercy. A typical article, captioned "Rush and his Patients," read: "Wanted, by a physician, an entire new set of patients, his old ones having given him the slip; also a slower method of dispatching them than that of phlebotomy, the celerity of which does not give time *for making out the bill*."[30] Rush sued the publisher for libel and was awarded $5000. (He finally settled for $4250.) However, it was a hollow victory. Based on the trial's publicity, Cobbett started *Rush-Light*, a newspaper devoted to attacking the doctor. Its success made Cobbett a rich man and he returned to his native England. But for Rush the controversy with Cobbett had a disastrous effect on his practice and left him in serious financial straits.

¶ See Lee Dynasty, pp. 63–64.

At this point President John Adams stepped in. The friendship between Adams and Rush was a long and intimate one dating back to 1774 when the Quincy lawyer came to Philadelphia to attend the first meeting of the Continental Congress and Rush rode out to escort him into the city. Yet after the Revolution the two patriots drifted into rival political camps. By 1789 Rush had to write Adams, "I find you and I must agree not to disagree, or we must cease to discuss political questions."[31] Rush supported Jefferson for the presidency in 1796. But now he needed a job. And President Adams named him treasurer of the Mint, a political sinecure paying $1200 a year and requiring only a few minutes three or four times a week.[32] Years later Rush wrote Adams, "Had it not been for the emoluments of the office you gave me . . . I must have retired from the city and ended my days upon a farm. . . ." And in 1812, when Rush gratefully sent the ex-President a quarter cask of wine, he wrote, "I will say of the wine . . . what you said to me when I called to thank you for the appointment you gave me at the Mint: 'You have not more pleasure in receiving it than I had in giving it to a faithful old Revolutionary Whig.'" To which Adams characteristically replied, "When you thanked me [for the appointment], in strict propriety you were in error. You did wrong. I gave you nothing. I was trustee for our Country. Had I known a Man more fit, more deserving, you would not have been selected. You have given me your own. I have accepted your own. I ought therefore to give you ten thousand, thousand Thanks, and you ought to have given me none at all."[33]

The bitter quarrel between Rush and Elias Boudinot had tragic overtones, for the two patriots had been genuinely devoted to each other. This relationship was far more than familial pride in both having married Stocktons. When their home was threatened by the British during the war, Elias and Hannah Stockton Boudinot sent their only child to live with the Rushes for five months. Rush loved little Susan, calling her "the Dauphina," in affectionate recognition of her father's position as president of the Congress. Later when Philadelphia was engulfed by yellow fever, Benjamin and Julia Stockton Rush sent two of their children to live with the Boudinots. As late as 1797 Rush spoke of Boudinot as "my excellent friend."

The controversy was caused by the will of William Bradford, Susan Boudinot's husband and Benjamin Rush's patient. The principal legatee was to have been his wife. But on his deathbed he declared his intention of dying intestate, which would have left a good part of his money to his brother Thomas, whom he knew to be in financial trouble. However, he also made out large last-minute promissory notes to his sisters and a Miss Read, as well as a $1000 note to Rush, with the understanding that the income from it was to be used for charitable purposes. Why Bradford turned in death against his wife is not known. Miss Read has never been identified. Possibly Bradford felt his wife would be well provided for as the heir to her father's fortune.

William Bradford, the Attorney General of the United States, left behind a legal tangle that took sixteen years and at least three court trials to unsnarl. The case of Boudinot vs. T. Bradford turned on whether the deceased was sane at the time of his death. As physician in the case, Rush's testimony was crucial. He stated that William Bradford was sane; the court found in favor of Thomas Bradford.

The bitterness between Boudinot and Rush was compounded by their working relationship. For, as director of the Mint, Boudinot was Rush's superior. Rush accused his former friend of covetousness, lying, depravity, graft in the handling of Mint funds, and fraud in the handling of the Bradford estate. One of his specific charges was that Boudinot "has taken all the Dung of the Stable of the Mint, for his own use for several years, without crediting the Mint for it."[34] (In fact the dung had formerly been hauled away at the expense of the Mint, and Boudinot's arrangement saved the government money.) Boudinot thought Rush to be a madman, but his exact charges against the doctor have not come down to us in detail. Rush died in 1813; Boudinot in 1821. For the last thirteen years of Rush's life the two families didn't speak to each other. This time there was no happy ending; no President of the United States rescued Rush from the consequences of his disputatious nature.

Benjamin and Julia Stockton Rush had thirteen children whose careers ranged from brilliant to deranged. John, their eldest, was first sent to Princeton, but when the faculty censured him for playing cards on the Sabbath, his father promptly withdrew him for such scandalous conduct. John later received a medical degree and joined the navy. However, after killing a fellow officer in a duel and attempting to take his own life, he was judged to be insane and sent home. Dr. Rush reported the son's return to his confidant, John Adams: "In the month of February last [1810] he arrived in Philadelphia in a state of deep melancholy and considerable derangement. His appearance when he entered his father's house was that of the King of Babylon described in the Old Testament. His long and uncombed hair and his long nails and beard rendered him an object of horror to his afflicted parents and family. No entreaties could induce him to say a word to any of us. After three days spent in unsuccessful attempts to alter his appearance, we sent him to the Pennsylvania Hospital, where he has been ever since."[35] John Rush remained in the hospital's care for almost thirty years. The tragedy accelerated Benjamin Rush's work in the development of psychiatry as a science.

The second son, Richard, named after his grandfather Richard Stockton, was the special pet of Grandmother Annis Boudinot Stockton. In

1811 Richard was appointed Comptroller of the Treasury despite his father's pleas. Benjamin immediately cut off his son's inheritance. Why Dr. Rush felt so strongly is not clear, but he gives a clue in his autobiography when he writes, "To my sons, I bequeath a father's experience, and I entreat them to take no public or active part in the disputes of their country beyond a vote at an election. If no scruples of conscience forbid them to bear arms, I would recommend to them rather to be soldiers than politicians, should they ever be so unfortunate as to live in a country distracted by a civil war. In battle men kill, without hating each other; in political contests men hate without killing, but in that hatred they commit murder every hour of their lives."[36]

Richard Rush had a meteoric rise in politics. Madison made him Attorney General of the United States, Monroe named him minister to Great Britain, John Quincy Adams chose him Secretary of the Treasury, and Polk appointed him minister to France. John Randolph of Roanoke, however, thought less of his talents. "Never were abilities so much below mediocrity so well rewarded," said the acid-tongued Virginian. "No, not when Caligula's horse was made consul."[37] Yet despite an occasional detractor, he negotiated the Rush-Bagot Convention with Great Britain to limit armament on the Great Lakes, and was an important influence in writing the Monroe Doctrine. The ticket of John Quincy Adams and Richard Rush went down to defeat in the 1828 presidential election. The running mates shared a warm friendship that paralleled the intimacy that existed between their fathers. And, although he would not admit it, Benjamin Rush took a keen interest in his brilliant son's career.

James Rush, the third son, practiced medicine until he married millionairess Phoebe Ridgway, daughter of the second richest American of that era. Madam Rush, as she was called, built a great mansion with a dining room of twenty-five tables, and her husband retired into her corpulent and socially pretentious shadow.[38] Mrs. Ellet in *The Queens of American Society* states that seldom is social leadership gained "without beauty or attractive personal qualities, and without association with any great social event or institution"—except in the case of Madam Rush.[39]

Once a year this "acknowledged queen of Philadelphia fashionable society" gave a crashing ball, during which her husband "often sat alone in his library." She rarely gave small parties—"except to gentlemen." But every Saturday morning she held a reception at which she amused her guests with some curiosity of the day, such as a band of Aztec Indians. "Notwithstanding the endless gossip about her with the stronger sex," Mrs. Ellet hastens to add, "those who knew anything of her were constrained to admit that her intimacy never bordered in the least on flirtation. She had no personal attractions and never desired admiration."[40]

In his social isolation, James Rush wrote two books: *The Philosophy of the Human Voice*, a treatise on elocution, which was very popular in that age of declamation; and *A Brief Outline of an Analysis of the Human Intellect*, in two volumes, an important early work in the scientific development of psychology. After his wife's death James became an embittered recluse, willing his estate for the establishment of a branch library in Philadelphia, with the stipulation, "Let it not keep cushioned seats for time-wasting and lounging readers, nor places for everyday novels, mind-tainting reviews, controversial politics, scribblings of poetry and prose, biographies of unknown names, nor for those teachers of disjointed thinking, the daily newspapers."[41]

While Julia Stockton was caring for her volatile flock of Rushes, her sister Mary married Andrew Hunter, a minister and Princeton professor, whom Dr. Rush unsuccessfully tried to persuade to become president of Dickinson College (their son David became a Union Army general during the Civil War[*]); her sister Abigail married Robert Field, a descendant of the introducer of Copernican astronomy into England, which earned the family a crest showing a red arm issuing from the clouds and supporting a golden sphere (their son Richard Stockton Field became a United States senator); and brother Lucius Horatio Stockton was briefly in the limelight when John Adams made him Secretary of War during the closing days of his Administration, an appointment which was not confirmed by the Senate when Jefferson took office.

The mainstay of the dynasty's second political generation, however, was the second Richard Stockton.[42] He was known as Richard "the Duke," a sobriquet given to him by the younger members of the bar, which accurately characterized his stern integrity; his dignity, bordering on haughtiness; his formal attitude toward those of lower social rank; and his tall, stout, commanding appearance. This son of Richard the Signer combined a brilliant legal mind with high Federalist principles and fierce loyalty to his family. For twenty years he supported the credit of his financially troubled brother Lucius Horatio. When his daughter Mary was expelled from boarding school for impishly telling the other girls that she was secretly married and pregnant, the Duke took the headmistress and her husband to court and so mercilessly hounded them for years that they finally complained of his persecution in a newspaper advertisement.[†]

[*] See Tucker Dynasty, p. 384.
[†] Mary Stockton, the mischievous daughter, later married William Harrison of New York. John Pintard called him "an inflated bladder in prosperity," who took to drink in adversity and became "a wet Quaker . . . a *bon vivant* and debauchee." Mary left him and returned to her father's house. See Alfred Hoyt Bill, *A House Called Morven* (Princeton: Princeton University Press, 1954), p. 84.

Richard the Duke was elected to the United States Senate in 1796 to succeed Frederick Frelinghuysen, and served for two and a half years. In 1801 President Adams offered him one of the "midnight" appointments to the Circuit Court, but he declined, preferring to run for governor of New Jersey. He was defeated, just as his father had been. He was four times a gubernatorial candidate, but the closest he came to winning was in 1802 when the voting ended in a tie. His Republican opponents refused to negotiate or call a new election.[43]

When Federalist fortunes momentarily rose in 1812, Richard was elected to the House of Representatives. His single term in the lower house coincided with the second war against Great Britain, a conflict that he felt was "political insanity." The peace treaty he liked no better, calling it "a mere tub to the great whale." His sympathies really were with George Cabot, the Essex Junto, and "the doings at Hartford."[44] His last political notice was in 1820 when he received a complimentary eight electoral votes for Vice-President from the Massachusetts Federalists.

The mantle of political leadership should have passed from Richard the Signer to Richard the Duke to Richard Stockton III, the Duke's eldest son. But the young man, though charming and able, was beset by weaknesses. Gambling was one. After a bitter argument with his father Richard moved to Mississippi. Life in Natchez, away from the Duke, seemed to have worked wonders. Young Stockton was elected a justice of the state Supreme Court and was subsequently named attorney general of Mississippi. Then in 1827 word reached Morven that he had been killed in a duel. Moreover, as Samuel Bayard reported, Richard had been "grossly in the wrong."[45] There may have been some consolation in Richard's honorable behavior in his last moments. He had not fired his pistol and had left a note stating that this had been his intention.

Thus the fame and fortune of the dynasty were left in the hands of the Duke's second son, Commodore Robert Field Stockton, United States Navy, variously known as "Fighting Bob," "The Navy's Problem Child," and "Robert the Magnificent."

The high spirits, high living, ambition, initiative, and courage of Robert Field Stockton completely captivated Josiah Quincy of Boston when the two stayed at the same Washington boardinghouse in 1826. In the last year of his life Quincy recalled how the young men (he was twenty-four, Stockton was thirty-one) "would sit long into the night, gently sipping a medicine which the doctors of the capital thought destructive of the influenza germs . . . [which] I am obliged to give the bald English translation of whisky punch."[46] While "the medicine contributed a little to the easy flow of the narratives," the sailor told his companion of how in the War of 1812, when a mere midshipman, he was cited for bravery during the defense of Baltimore; how he stood up to the Algerian pirates; how he had fought three duels, wounding two of his adversaries[47]; how with pistol to the head of an African chieftain he had secured for the American Colonization Society all the land that is now Liberia; and how he helped suppress the slave traders in the West Indies. Thought the wide-eyed Quincy: "Had Sinbad the Sailor been a man of unimpeachable veracity, I am willing to allow that those who listened to the story of his voyages, as it fell from his own lips, might have been more astonished and interested than was the companion of Captain Stockton; but with this notable exception, surely no mariner of thirty ever had adventures more remarkable. . . ."[48]

Later Stockton battled the navy brass for the construction of steam warships. And when he succeeded in getting the steamer *Princeton* built, Stockton commanding, one of his guns exploded, killing the Secretary of State, the Secretary of the Navy, and President Tyler's future father-in-law.[49] Fortunately the President was detained below deck.

During the Mexican War, with Frémont and Kearny, Stockton captured California and assumed for himself the title of governor and commander-in-chief. (And winning for his family the honor of a city's name in the San Joaquin Valley.) Then in 1850 he quit the navy to enter politics.

Politically, the commodore was known to be consistently inconsistent. His gyrating allegiance swung from John Quincy Adams to Andrew Jackson to William Henry Harrison to John Tyler to the Know-Nothing Party to the Constitutional Unionists.‡ But Stockton's political power came neither from party loyalty, nor military exploits, nor distinguished lineage. It came from the Camden and Amboy Railroad.

When John Stevens (son of the man who blocked Richard the Signer from becoming the first governor of New Jersey) was pushed out of the Hudson River steamboat trade by Robert Fulton and Chancellor Livingston, he turned his steamboat interests over to his sons and set his inventive mind on building the first steam railroad in the United States. The sons—Robert Livingston Stevens, who inherited his father's mechanical genius, and Edwin Augustus Stevens, who was considered a "financial and organizational genius"—emerged as the dominant force in steamboating in the northeast after the Supreme Court voided the Ful-

‡ At one point he bought a newspaper, the *New Jersey Patriot*, to support the John Quincy Adams Administration. This act, felt Stockton, deserved a federal judgeship for his father, Richard the Duke. But President Adams rejected the suggestion, saying, "Such a system [of political rewards] would be repugnant to every feeling of my soul." The commodore promptly transferred his loyalty to Andrew Jackson. See Samuel Flagg Bemis, *John Quincy Adams and the Union* (New York: Knopf, 1956), pp. 138–39.

ton-Livingston monopoly. Now in 1828, armed with considerable resources, they joined their father in promoting a railroad empire in New Jersey.

Unfortunately their plan ran counter to the interests of Commodore Stockton's pet project, which was to dominate the state's transportation through a canal system. In 1823 the young naval officer married Harriet Maria Potter, a beautiful heiress from Charleston, South Carolina. He brought her back to Princeton and a home on the corner of Stockton Street and Bayard Lane, where they were soon joined by the bride's father, John Potter. The old man was persuaded to invest a half million dollars in his son-in-law's proposed Delaware and Raritan Canal Company. And so a battle of financial giants was joined.

At the 1829–30 session of the New Jersey legislature the two powerful lobbies clashed. "During that winter," writes J. E. Watkins, "the prominent friends of both companies thought it necessary to go armed about the streets of Trenton at night."[50] As reasonable men, it did not take long for the Stevenses and Stockton to agree that there should be profit for both. It is commonly assumed that they met in the lobby of the Park Theater, New York, and decided that railroad and canal should go forward together as a joint company.[51] Stockton had clearly outmaneuvered the Stevens brothers, since the railroad was the more valuable property in the merger. When the legislature approved the "act of union," the Princeton *Courier* announced: "Married in Trenton, on the 15th inst. by the Honorable the Legislature of New Jersey, Mr. Magnus Fluvius Canal to Miss Agilis Rail Road." The paper then burst into verse:

> The peerless pair their jealousies forego,
> Unite their stocks, and thus their wisdom show;
> Embrace the state within their circling arms,
> And teach the world the magic of their charms.[52]

The next year the legislature gave the Camden and Amboy a monopoly between New York and Philadelphia. The Stevenses had fought the Fulton-Livingston steamboat monopoly as unconstitutional. But this was different; *they* were monopolists. And as long as they controlled the New Jersey legislature they controlled the southern and western gateways to and from America's two major metropolises. A grandiosely named Newark newspaper, *Sentinel of Freedom*, quickly warned its readers of the railroad's political power: "We cannot forbear adverting to the horde of Lobby Members which throng the avenues and the halls of our state house, who boast of having formed a 'Third House' at our seat of government, more numerous and powerful than the other two combined, and the expenses of whose maintenance is said to cost more than that of the whole legislature. The operatives of the now united mammoth corporation are to be observed in all places and this influence

is more powerful and lasting than that of the hirelings of other interests."[53] For the next four decades New Jersey was said to be run from
Apartment 10, Snowden's Hotel, Trenton—the headquarters of the
railroad lobby. At a "midnight orgy" thrown by the C & A in honor of the
closing of the 1860 legislative session, the assemblymen joined voices in a
rousing rendition of a song whose chorus was:

> We are all a band of robbers
> We are all a band of robbers
> From the Camden and Amboy State.[54]

In 1851 the legislature of the Camden and Amboy State elected the
railroad's prime mover, Commodore Robert Field Stockton, to the United
States Senate. His one notable achievement in Washington was to introduce a bill to abolish flogging in the navy. Less than two years later he
resigned to get an early start in his race for the 1856 presidential nomination. But the Democratic Party wanted nothing to do with him, and he
turned to the American or Know-Nothing Party. "Whatever may be the
present aspect of the American Party," said Stockton's campaign biography, "its ultimate success admits of no doubt. It is absurd to suppose
that the people of the United States will much longer tolerate the
participation of their sovereignty with those hordes of incompetent aliens
annually swarming to our shores."[55] But even these lowly nativists rejected Stockton in favor of ex-President Fillmore. The commodore was
finally nominated for President by a rump convention whose platform
was the restoration of the Missouri Compromise. He thanked his few
supporters and gracefully withdrew in favor of Fillmore, who received
only the eight electoral votes of Maryland.

The commodore's last outburst on the national scene was in favor
of the Constitutional Union Party. On December 11, 1861, he told a
convention of its supporters that the North should yield and the South
should wait. He said, in effect, "that the African race was not worth
fighting over or for, slaves were being benefited by slavery and Christianity. . . . God meant that they should be returned home [Africa]
through the instrumentalities of the American Colonization Society;
Negroes were the most cowardly, most brutal, the most abandoned of
God's creations."[56]

Stockton's seat in the Senate was taken by John Renshaw Thomson,
his brother-in-law and a perennial official of the Camden and Amboy
Railroad. This fun-loving sportsman, the son of a great Philadelphia tea
merchant, had been the family's representative at Canton in his younger
days. But just before he was to marry Annis Stockton, his father tried to
skip the country ahead of his creditors. Thereafter Thomson worked for
his in-laws.

Thomson made a state-wide reputation as a supporter of the 1844 New Jersey constitution, a liberal document which also looked after the interests of the Camden and Amboy. That year he was the Democratic candidate for governor. The *State Gazette,* a Whig paper, pointed out: "Everyone knows the imperious character of Captain Stockton, and that he would treat any demur of Thomson as the revolt of a slave against his master."[57] Thomson lost. But getting into the United States Senate via the C & A-controlled legislature was an easier matter. He was elected in 1853, re-elected in 1857, and served until his death in 1862, after which his seat was filled by the commodore's first cousin, Richard Stockton Field.

The new senator was only half Stockton, his mother being Richard the Signer's daughter. In upbringing, however, he was more Stockton than Field, since his father died when he was a small child and his mother immediately returned to the Stockton compound at Princeton. There he studied law under his uncle, Richard the Duke. And as a lawyer most of his practice came from the Stockton business interests.

Yet Richard Stockton Field had a vastly different outlook from his mother's family. During three terms in the state Assembly, as a member of the New Jersey Constitutional Convention and as attorney general of the state, he proved to be something of a reformer and a scholar. His pet project was the creation of a state normal school, which was realized in 1835 with Field serving as president of the board until his death. He was also a founder and president of the New Jersey Historical Society and contributed a number of learned papers to its journal.

Moreover, while Richard the Signer and Richard the Duke had been slaveowners, Richard Stockton Field was a Republican and a firm believer in bringing the South back into the Union by force. It was because of his labors on behalf of the Republican Party that Field was appointed to the Senate in November 1862 by a Republican governor. The state legislature was in the hands of the Democrats and it was known that Field would be turned out in January. Yet during his short service in Washington, Field gained national prominence by making a powerful speech in support of the President's right to suspend the writ of *habeas corpus.* Also before he left the Senate, Lincoln appointed him to the federal District Court for New Jersey, where he served until he was stricken with paralysis in 1870.

The Stockton political dynasty ended with the fourth generation—the sons of the commodore. Robert Field Stockton was adjutant general of New Jersey and then state comptroller; John Potter Stockton was the fourth of his family to serve in Congress.

The commodore named his second son after his father-in-law, who had bankrolled him in his railroad and canal ventures. Young John Potter Stockton studied law in the office of Cousin Richard Stockton Field. But even with these impressive credentials he soon scandalized his social circle by marrying a seventeen-year-old Jew, Sarah Marks of New Orleans. One well-connected Princetonian, believing Miss Marks's father was a caterer, said that the Stockton coat of arms should be changed to a fork impaling an oyster. The new Mrs. Stockton was never completely accepted by her husband's family.

When the commodore's influence was at its height he had his son shipped off to Italy as minister resident to the Papal States. And in 1865 the New Jersey legislature sent John Potter Stockton to the United States Senate. James W. Wall, a rival of the Stocktons, wrote former President Buchanan, "The Camden & Amboy RR. Company paid as high as $40,000 to elect the Commodore's son." A month later Wall had second thoughts about the price and wrote Buchanan, "The Commodore boasted that he would have the office for his son if it cost $50,000."[58]

The election was contested in a complicated case that boiled down to whether a state legislature had the right to elect a senator by a plurality vote instead of a majority. Under normal circumstances the Senate would not have concerned itself with such fine points and would quickly have ruled in favor of Stockton, who had the greatest claim to the seat. But President Andrew Johnson's veto of the Freedman's Bureau Bill had just been sustained by a single vote in the Senate. For the radical Congress, itching to block the Executive's Reconstruction program, these were not normal times. One vote would have to be manufactured, and what better way than to unseat Stockton, a supporter of the President? As Maine's William Pitt Fessenden said, "It is all important now that we should have two-thirds in each branch."[59]

Stockton's colleague from New Jersey, Senator William Wright, was sick and wished to return home. But before leaving Washington he made a gentleman's agreement with Senator Lot Myrick Morrill—for as long as Democrat Wright was absent, Republican Morrill would refrain from voting. When the roll was called on the John Potter Stockton case, the vote stood 21 to 20 in favor of Stockton, with Stockton not voting. The radicals implored Morrill to vote. Hesitant and pale, Morrill asked the clerk to expel Stockton from the Senate. The vote was now tied 21 to 21. Stockton, in a fury, shouted for the clerk to call his name; denouncing Morrill, he voted for his own cause.

He had made a tactical error. If Stockton had let the tie vote stand he would have retained his seat. By breaking the rules of propriety and voting for himself he gave his enemies the opportunity to reopen the issue. The next day the chamber voted to expel Stockton from the Senate. Senator Fessenden wrote his brother, "It was a hard fight over Stockton, but we killed him at last. . . ."[60]§

The Stockton case had an immediate effect on Reconstruction. The next month, when Johnson vetoed the Civil Rights Bill, the Senate had the votes to override the President. The nation was thrown into a pamphlet war with opposing party scribes attacking Stockton or the Senate with equal vehemence. The New Jersey legislature, its sovereignty dishonored, unsuccessfully attempted to withdraw its ratification of the Fourteenth Amendment. The Senate passed its first law regulating the election of senators; James G. Blaine declared that it was "the direct fruit of the Stockton case."[61] The new law remained in effect until the Seventeenth Amendment took the election of senators out of the hands of the state legislatures in 1913.

The New Jersey legislature returned Stockton to the Senate in 1869. This time there was no question of his right to membership. Stockton took his seat on the Democratic side of the aisle immediately behind Thomas F. Bayard of Delaware. From this vantage point, in the opinion of Bayard's biographer, "He looked, dressed, and had the manners of a high-bred man of the world, was a clever debater, and never missed the chance to make a point against his political opponents."[62] But Stockton was not re-elected to the Senate. He settled for the position of New Jersey attorney general, where he remained for fifteen years with little if any influence on the state's politics.

The end of the political dynasty coincided with the end of Camden and Amboy rule in New Jersey. In 1871 the Pennsylvania Railroad, desperately needing an outlet to New York Harbor, leased the C & A for 999 years on extremely advantageous terms to the smaller company. The New York *Herald,* always a foe of the C & A, commented, "The halo of New Jersey's glory has left her. Her Ichabod hath departed. The Camden and Amboy road, the pride of the State and ruler of Legislatures has been ceded to the Pennsylvania; and Tom Scott [president of the Pennsylvania] like Commodore Stockton of old, carries the little borough in his breeches pocket."[63]

By the time John Potter Stockton died in 1900 his family's name was hardly known in the political world.[64] Historians would record the dynasty only in footnotes—a signer of the Declaration of Independence whose repudiation of the American cause was rarely commented upon,[65]

§ Commenting on the expulsion, James G. Blaine wrote: "Mr. Stockton has good ground for declaring that the Senate had not treated him with magnanimity or generosity. It is due to Mr. Stockton to say that under very trying circumstances he bore himself with moderation and dignity." See *Twenty Years of Congress* (Norwich, Conn.: Henry Bill Publishing Co., 1886), Vol. II, p. 159.

an adventurer who had helped to take California for the Union, a senator whose expulsion from the upper chamber may have altered the
course of Reconstruction. The collateral branches, particularly the dynamic Rushes, overshadowed the Stocktons, who at least had the knack
of marrying interesting characters.

During four generations in Congress the Stocktons' combined elective
service was less than fourteen years, and if the name was recognized by
the average American at the turn of the century, it was only as that of
the author of an intriguing tale about a princess and her lover.

"The Lady or the Tiger?"—a short story by a distant cousin, Frank R.
Stockton—was then stirring a national debate.¶ As the last of the Stockton political dynasty was being lowered into the ground the nation was
preoccupied with a more immediate concern—would the princess choose
to have her lover destroyed by the tiger rather than give him up to
another woman?

¶ It was this Stockton who was the subject of Robert Louis Stevenson's poem
("If I my Stockton should forget . . ."). But Frank R. Stockton (1834–1902)
was placed by his biographer "in the second rank of those who were carrying
the standard of American literary achievement during the last quarter of the
nineteenth century." See Martin I. J. Griffin, *Frank R. Stockton: A Critical
Biography* (Philadelphia: University of Pennsylvania Press, 1939), p. 144. His
complete works were brought out between 1899 and 1904 in a twenty-three-
volume edition. Besides "The Lady or the Tiger?" his best-known fiction is
The Casting Away of Mrs. Lecks and Mrs. Aleshine (1886).

This branch of the Stockton family was something of a literary dynasty.
Frank R. Stockton's half brother, John Drean Stockton, was owner and editor
of the Philadelphia *Post*, and drama and music critic of the New York *Herald;*
a half sister, Marie Louise Stockton, was a novelist and critic; and another
half brother, Thomas Hewlings Stockton (1808–68), published a collection of
poems, *Floating Flowers from a Hidden Brook* (Philadelphia: W. S. Young,
1844). However, the last named made his reputation as a clergyman, being
twice chaplain of the House of Representatives and once of the Senate. Radical Congressman Thaddeus Stevens called him "the most eloquent man in the
United States since the fall of Henry Ward Beecher." See Milton Lomask, *Andrew Johnson: President on Trial* (New York: Farrar, Straus, 1960), p. 121.

The Long Dynasty

"I have let Huey Long lie enough, and if it is
the last thing I do on earth, I am not going to
let him ruin the Long family."

—Julius Long[1]

"Julius . . . he stayed the sorehead all his life."

—Earl Long[2]

"Earl Long is getting as bitter toward me as he
was toward my father."

—Russell Long[3]

"The attacks of my blood brothers and sisters are
printed about me in every city. I cannot help
it. They are my blood."

—Huey P. Long[4]

To THE state of Louisiana and the parish of Winn, John M. Long
brought his family from Mississippi in 1859. In Louisiana counties are
called parishes, and Winn Parish, in the north central part of the state,
was destined by incorporation to be the poorest of the poor: when the
land was divided, Winn got what nobody else wanted.[5] It is hill country. (President Coolidge, visiting Louisiana in 1930, asked Huey Long
what part of the state he came from. Replied Huey, "I'm a hillbilly—
like yourself."[6]) It is Baptist country. (Huey recalled that a Methodist
preacher moved to Winn and would have starved to death had it not been
for the charity of the Long family.[7]) It is a parish of small farms and
cutover timberlands. The people there have said that they make a living
by taking in each other's washing.[8] Winn Parish . . . "where a man would
skin a flea for the hide and tallow."[9]

The major crop in Winn has always been dissent. At the convention
of 1861, called to decide whether Louisiana should join the Confederacy,
the delegate from Winn voted against secession: "Who wants to fight to

THE LONG DYNASTY
(A Selective Genealogy)

John M. Long (d. 1900)
Moved to Louisiana 1859
m. *Mary Wingate* (d. 1900)
(15 children)

|

Huey Pierce (1852–1937)
m. *Caledonia Tyson* (d. 1913)
(9 children)

George Shannon	*Huey Pierce*	*Earl Kemp*
(1883–1958)	(1893–1935)	(1895–1960)
HOUSE OF REPRESENTATIVES	GOVERNOR, SENATE	GOVERNOR
1st m. *Mary K. Shindel* (d. 1950)	m. *Rose McConnell*	m. *Blanche Revere*
2nd m. *Jewell I. Tyson*	SENATE	Louisiana
(no issue)	(3 children)	tax commissioner
		(no issue)

Russell Billiu
(1918–   )
SENATE
m. *Katherine Hattic*
(2 children)

keep the Negroes for the wealthy planters?" he asked.[10] John M. Long did not join the Confederate Army. His son, Huey P. Long, Sr., had strong Union sympathies. After the war Winn became a populist enclave. The Socialists elected half of the parish officials in 1908; Eugene Debs received almost thirty-six per cent of Winn's vote when he ran for President in 1912.

"There wants to be a revolution, I tell you," said Huey P. Long, Sr., his six-foot frame still erect and powerful after eighty-three years. "I seen the domination of capital, seen it for seventy years. What do these rich folks care for the poor man? They care nothing—not for his pain, nor his sickness, nor his death. . . . Maybe you're surprised to hear talk like that. Well, it was just such talk that my boy was raised under, and that I was raised under."[11]

By Winn standards Huey, Sr., was lucky. The railroad bought his farm and he was able to send six of his nine children to college. Julius, the oldest, became a lawyer; George became a dentist. But the money ran out before the two youngest, Huey and Earl, had their turn. They became traveling salesmen. Huey peddled a product called Cottolene, a vegetable shortening; Earl, two years his junior, sold baking powder.

Huey Long was designed for writers and cartoonists. A. J. Liebling, a reporter for a New York evening paper in the early 1930s, interviewed him at the Waldorf. "A chubby man, he had ginger hair and tight skin that was the color of a sunburn coming on. It was an uneasy color combination, like an orange tie on a pink shirt. His face faintly suggested mumps. . . ."[12] Below the unruly hair with its natural spit curl there were the deep-set brown eyes; the snub nose, turned up at an impudent angle; a wide mouth, heavy lips, dimpled chin. And farther down, the unwitting habit of scratching himself regularly on the left buttock.[13]

It was Huey Long who made a revolution in Louisiana politics and who, before he was cut down, constituted "the greatest individual challenge to Franklin Delano Roosevelt and to his New Deal policies."[14] Never has an American been called a dictator by so many responsible commentators. Carleton Beals considered him "the pole-cat, wild ass, Messiah and enigma of American politics."[15] John Gunther viewed him as "an engaging monster" and compared him to Hitler, Mussolini, Goering, Goebbels, Salazar, Franco, Dollfuss, Kemal, Metaxas, Stalin, and Pilsudski.[16] On the other hand, a new school of academic opinion is now going to the opposite extreme, even comparing Long to Jacques Maritain's image of the prophet leader, whose mission is "to awaken the people, to awaken them to something better than everyone's daily business, to the sense of a supra-individual task to be performed."[17]

The Long phenomenon grew out of the pathology of Louisiana politics.[18] Before Huey, the state was controlled by a coalition of the rich and corrupt, the great planters of the Black Belt and the machine bosses of New Orleans. The city was ruled by Mayor Martin Behrman, whose classic remark on vice was, "You can make it illegal, but you can't make it unpopular."[19] The poor, white and Negro, got little from government and expected less. Of those who ran the state, said Huey, "One of 'em skinned you from the ankles up, the other from the neck down."[20] Standing beneath the fabled Evangeline oak, inspiration of Longfellow, Huey told the rawboned, leather-faced Cajuns:

And it is here under this oak where Evangeline waited for her lover, Gabriel. This oak is immortal, but Evangeline is not the only one who waited here in disappointment. Where are the schools, the roads and highways, the institutions for the disabled you sent your money to build? Evangeline's tears last through one lifetime—yours through generations. Give me the chance to dry the eyes of those who still weep here.[21]

It was Huey's revolution to weld the poor into a viable political force; to make the poor redneck, the poor Cajun, and the poor Negro see that their political common denominator was "poor"—and that they must make common cause in the voting booth. He became the first major Southern leader to put aside appeals to race baiting and ante-bellum myths and address himself to social and economic ills. And when he was finished Louisiana had new schools and free textbooks and roads and mental hospitals and bridges. And when he was finished Louisiana had a secret police and a rubber-stamp legislature and a subservient judiciary. "Never before in American history," wrote Hamilton Basso, had the people "been so plainly asked to jettison the democratic system and consent to the erection of a totalitarian society in its place." They had been asked to "exchange political freedom for economic security."[22] To those who had nothing, it seemed like a good bargain.

Huey Pierce Long was born on August 30, 1893.* He maintained his blood was a mixture of English, Dutch, Welsh, Scottish, and French (although the last claim was more an appeal to the voters of southern Louisiana than a hereditary fact).

His first full-time job as a seller of a cooking compound introduced him to the hill folk of the upper parishes, who would be his political backbone, and to Rose McConnell, who would be his wife. The future Mrs. Long was pretty and plump, a dark-haired little belle from Shreveport with pale blue eyes. They met during a baking contest that Huey was conducting; Rose won. After they were married she convinced him that he should give up his peddler's pack for lawbooks. Huey entered Tulane, took eight months of the three-year course (as much as his money allowed), and then talked his way into a special bar examination, which he passed.

"I was born into politics, a wedded man, with a storm for my bride," said Huey.[23] Almost as soon as he had "lawyer" painted on a fifty-cent tin sign, he was searching the state constitution for a public office which did not prescribe a minimum age limit. The only post open to the twenty-four-year-old Huey was the Railroad Commission (later renamed the Public Service Commission). So in 1918 he ran and was elected from the northern Louisiana district. His financial angel ($500) was Oscar Kelly ("O. K.") Allen, a Winnfield storekeeper whom Huey had got out of a jam when he mixed up two corpses, one white and the other Negro. (Oscar was not too bright; later Huey made him governor of Louisiana.) Commissioner Long promptly forced giant Standard Oil to increase its tax payments and got the utilities to reduce their rates.

On his thirtieth birthday Huey announced that he was a candidate for governor. It rained hard on the day of the Democratic primary in 1924.

* Forty-three years later the voters of Louisiana approved a constitutional amendment to make this date a state legal holiday.

When the first ballot box was opened the vote was sixty to one for Long. "I'm beat," said Huey. "There should have been 100 for me and one against me. Forty per cent of my country vote is lost in that box."[24] He finished a strong third, but his country vote was washed out.[25] The returns showed that Huey was still a sectional candidate. To win the next time he would have to increase his strength among the French Catholics in the southern parishes. So in 1926 he campaigned for United States Senator Edwin Broussard ("Couzain Ed," he called him), and then claimed credit for his narrow victory. When he ran again for governor in 1928 he received 43.9 per cent of the primary vote. In Louisiana, where the Democratic nomination is tantamount to election, if a candidate doesn't receive a majority, a second primary is held between the two top contenders. But Huey managed to force his opponent to withdraw from the runoff primary, and, unopposed, he became the youngest governor in Louisiana history.

There would never be another state administration like Huey's. To his opponents it was something like gallows humor—if it wasn't so serious, it might be funny. But the majority of the people had no reservations. He called himself "the Kingfish of the Lodge," after a character on the "Amos 'n Andy" radio program. He led the Louisiana State University band, composed its songs, gave the football team pep talks between halves ("What the hell do you care if you break your legs while you're breaking their necks?"). And when LSU lost a game, seven to six, he introduced a bill in the legislature to outlaw the point after touchdown.[26] "Most of the people would rather laugh than weep," said Huey. "I don't see any harm in lightening up the tragedy of politics for the people."[27]

He caused an international incident by wearing green silk pajamas during a formal audience with the commander of a German cruiser. So to correct the faux pas, the Kingfish borrowed pin-striped pants from a hotel manager, boiled shirt from a waiter, coat from a preacher, collar "so high I had to stand on a stool to spit over it" and went to call on the mortified German officer.[28] Huey's speech was a masterpiece of tongue-in-cheek apology: "You see, I come from Winnfield up in the hills of Winn parish, in this State. I know little of diplomacy and much less of the international courtesies and exchanges that are indulged in by nations. In fact, I only happened to be governor of the State by accident, anyway. There was no royal heritage but simply by chance I happened to receive more votes than the other men aspiring to the same office."[29] The people loved it. Huey was showered with pajamas from admirers; later, pajamas even adorned his campaign posters. Shortly afterward the Kingfish, clad exclusively in his underwear, received a United States general and his aides. The Baton Rouge State-Times commented, "If General McCoy is loath to believe that he had a narrow escape, and that the governor does not receive visitors in the nude, he is just not acquainted with our governor."[30]

Only Huey could start a national debate over pot liquor, the juice that remains in a pot after turnip greens are boiled with a piece of salt pork. "The delicious, invigorating, soul- and body-sustaining pot likker," Huey called the brew. The Kingfish urged that corn pone should be "crumbled" in the pot liquor, rather than "dunked." Governor Franklin D. Roosevelt of New York wired the Atlanta *Constitution* that he sided with the "crumblers." Governor Pollard of Virginia declined to be drawn into another "liquor" question. Oklahoma's "Alfalfa Bill" Murray asked for a truce so that hog jowl and poke salad could be investigated. Finally Emily Post handed down a Solomon-like edict: "When in Rome, do as the Romans do."[31]

The New York *Times* editorialized that Huey was merely "a worthy competitor in the field of light political farce."[32] The assessment clearly underrated the man. For usually the Kingfish's farce was deliberately directed. "I like to cut around the opposition with a joke."[33]

Those who were not misled by the comedian's mask discovered a man of surprising intellectual ability. Edward J. Flynn, who heard Huey speak before the Committee on Credentials at the 1932 Democratic National Convention, concluded, "Never in all my experience have I listened to a finer or more logical argument. . . ."[34] When Huey pleaded a case before the United States Supreme Court, Chief Justice William Howard Taft "was reported to have said that Long was the most brilliant lawyer who had appeared before the Court."[35] And Professor Raymond Moley, the Roosevelt brain truster assigned to act as "a friendly contact" with Huey during the early New Deal days, wrote that the Kingfish "had, combined with a remarkable capacity for hard, intellectual labor, an extraordinarily powerful, resourceful, clear and retentive mind, an instrument such as is given to very few men."[36]

A redneck farmer summed up his devotion to the Kingfish. "At least we got *something*. Before him, we got nothing."[37] One of Huey's first acts as governor was to distribute free textbooks to all students in public, private, and parochial schools. His opponents argued that it was unconstitutional, a violation of the separation of church and state. Huey took the case to the Supreme Court. The books were furnished to the children, not the schools, he successfully contended. (Many of the state's large Catholic population suddenly saw in Huey a beauty which had not been evident to them before.) He started to pave Louisiana's roads—but in scattered patches of five, ten, or fifteen miles to a parish. "When the people once knew the pleasure of traveling over paved highways," explained Huey, "their support for a program to connect up the links was certain."[38] (His scheme also allowed a maximum of voters to see quickly the fruits of Longism.) But when he tried to impose a heavy tax on the Standard Oil Company the legislature felt the state had had enough of Huey. He was impeached on nineteen counts ranging from the serious to the ridiculous. Among the charges were misusing state funds, demolishing the Executive Mansion without authority, carrying concealed weapons, cursing, attempting to intimidate the press, appearing on the floor of the legislature without permission, and trying to hire a man named Battling Bozeman to assassinate a legislator.[39]

Huey avoided conviction by getting fifteen state senators to sign a round robin stating that they would not vote against the Kingfish *no matter what the evidence.* "Anti-Longs have never ceased to belabor the climax of the impeachment trial as a deliberate mockery of justice," wrote Professor Allan Sindler. "That view conveniently overlooked the fact that 'justice' was not present, hence could not be mocked. The impeachment was politically inspired from start to finish and, therefore, the round robin was of a piece with the rest of the play."[40] The roundrobineers were well rewarded for their loyalty. Newspapers proclaimed, "Theirs is the earth and the fullness thereof." When one of the faithful fifteen asked for another road for his district, Huey claimed that he replied, "My gracious, Hugo! Won't you ever get through asking for roads for that country? There isn't room to plow there now, we've got so much pavement and gravel in that country."[41]

He next sought to solidify his political position by running for the United States Senate against ancient incumbent Joseph Ransdell, whose goatee inspired Huey to call him "Feather Duster" and "Old Trashy Mouth." Long promised that if elected he would remain as governor; if defeated, he would resign. The only fireworks in the campaign came when one Sam Irby contended that he had been kidnaped by the Kingfish. (Irby was the uncle by marriage of Alice Lee Grosjean, a sparkling baby-doll brunette whom Huey had raised from his private secretary to be Louisiana's Secretary of State.) However, right before Election Day Uncle Sam turned up and said it was all a misunderstanding.†

It was also charged by a citizens' reform group, the Constitutional League, that Huey had appointed twenty-three relatives to the state payroll.[42] The Kingfish dubbed his attacker "the Constipational League." Considering the number of cousins he had, Huey told reporters, the per-

---

† Irby later wrote a book in which he claimed, "I was kidnapped by armed thugs; taken by force from the Gardner Hotel in Shreveport, Louisiana; rushed about the state by car and plane; manacled to a tree in a marsh [on Grand Isle], almost devoured by mosquitoes, starved, and threatened with assassination." Sam Irby, *Kidnapped by the Kingfish* (New Orleans: Orleans Publishing Co., 1932), p. 6.

centage working for the state was pretty low. "Of course, I gave my wife's brother a job. I have to live with his sister! You would do it too."[43]

The Constitutional League disbanded the day after the senatorial primary. Huey was now governor *and* senator-elect, and would soon also become Democratic National Committeeman and Democratic state chairman. There was no longer any doubt of who was Louisiana's Kingfish.

Having been attacked by the good-government element for doing too much for his family, Huey was now to be publicly attacked by his family for not doing enough. He had appointed Brother Earl as inheritance tax collector of New Orleans, a post that could pay as much as $15,000 in good years. (Huey had earlier promised to abolish the job and use the money to build a new hospital for tuberculars on Lake Pontchartrain, which prompted a newspaper to print a picture of Earl captioned, "New Lakefront TB Hospital."[44]) In 1932 Earl felt it was his turn to hold higher office. Huey argued that it would be politically disastrous to have brother succeed brother. But Earl disregarded the warning and filed for lieutenant governor. A tall, lean scrapper, he had sunk his teeth so deeply into the neck of a state representative during the impeachment fight that the legislator took a shot of lockjaw serum.[45]

The Long family, sisters and Brother Julius, rushed to Earl's support. Fourteen years Huey's senior, Julius had once been Winn district attorney, the first Long to hold public office. He had also practiced law with Huey, until Huey kicked him out. Earl would later say of Julius, "He was older and he thought we should have waited for him to blaze the trail. But we'd still be waiting for him to blaze. Back before Huey was elected railroad commissioner, Julius ran for judge in Winnfield. As fast as me and Huey went around making friends for him, he'd go around making enemies."[46] In the 1932 campaign Julius attacked Huey across the state. ("I told him how he had acted, how he had forgotten not only his own mother and daddy, but every sister and brother he had, and I want to say something along that line right here, since he wants to pretend he has some milk of human kindness in his heart for his family. I swear that I do not know of a man, any human being, that has less feeling for his family than Huey P. Long has."[47]) Huey answered with silence; he had the votes. O. K. Allen was elected governor, and Earl Long was badly defeated for lieutenant governor.

The year 1932 also marked Huey's entrance on the national scene. At the presidential convention the Kingfish whipped Arkansas and Mississippi into line for F.D.R. Said Senator Wheeler of Montana: "Roosevelt would never have won the Democratic nomination in 1932, in my opinion but for Huey Long." (Boss Flynn of the Bronx agreed.)[48]

However, in the United States Senate the Kingfish was somewhat less effective. After Long had broken every rule of decorum of that august chamber, Tennessee's Kenneth McKellar summed up Huey's status with his fellow legislators: "I don't believe he could get the Lord's Prayer endorsed in this body."[49] Still the people loved him. Alice Roosevelt Longworth described the scene in the galleries as Huey entered the Senate chamber. "All heads are immediately turned in his direction, and a veritable hum becomes audible. As he moves across the floor at his curious, rolling, loose-jointed gait, every eye follows him with an expression made up of interest, amusement and expectancy." Observed the sharp-tongued Princess Alice, "I have seen the same sort of look in the eyes of children as they pore over the comic strip following the adventures of the mischievous cartoon kids and their puppy dogs, goats and other attractively uncouth animals."[50] The spectators didn't go away disappointed. Huey conducted massive one-man filibusters (one lasting more than fifteen hours); he dictated recipes for fried oysters and Roquefort dressing; he announced, "I will accommodate any senator tonight on any point on which he needs advice"; he proposed to enact a law making it mandatory to play the jew's-harp with outward instead of inward strokes; in a blaze of headlines, he resigned from all his committee appointments, which didn't matter since his assignments involved interoceanic canals and other minor matters. And when he sat down the galleries emptied. "Yes, you can go now!" called Vice-President Garner to the departing spectators. "The show's over!"[51]

The Kingfish was off the Roosevelt bandwagon almost before he had climbed aboard. The split between F.D.R. and Huey was inevitable: one occupied the White House, the other wanted to. The junior senator from Louisiana now turned his scathing invective on the President and those around him. Long dubbed Roosevelt "Prince Franklin, Knight of the *Nourmahal*" (after Vincent Astor's yacht); New Dealers Henry Wallace, Harold Ickes, and Hugh Johnson he called, respectively, "Lord Corn," "the Chicago Chinch Bug," and "Sitting Bull." The National Recovery Administration was renamed "Nuts Running America."[52] Only Ickes could match Huey's colorful abuse; the Secretary of the Interior shot back, "The emperor of Louisiana has halitosis of the intellect."[53]

It was more than a war of invective, however. Huey skillfully concocted a simple formula of immense appeal to the one third of the nation whom F.D.R. had labeled ill clothed, ill housed, and ill fed. The "Share Our Wealth" program had been germinating in Huey's head as far back as 1918. While he kept juggling the figures, the general outline was this: all fortunes over $5,000,000 (or $3,000,000) would be liquidated; from this fund, every family would get $4000 (or $5000) to purchase a home, automobile, and radio; the minimum annual wage would be $2500; the maximum allowable income per year would be

$1,800,000; there would be free education from kindergarten through college, plenty of food from government surpluses, and cash bonuses for veterans. Over 27,000 Share Our Wealth clubs sprang up all over the United States and even in Canada, with a claimed membership of 7,682,768 (no dues required). Huey had to hire a staff of forty-eight stenographers to handle the mail, which reached a high of 37,000 pieces a day. The movement's own newspaper carried more advertisements than the *Saturday Evening Post*. Its catchy theme song, inspired by William Jennings Bryan's "Cross of Gold" speech, was composed by Huey himself. ("In the wintertime or spring:/There'll be peace without end,/Every neighbor a friend,/With every man a king."[54])

Huey later put his utopian outline into a book, *My First Days in the White House*, published posthumously in 1935.‡ Written in the past tense, it starts with the Kingfish delivering his inaugural address at the Capitol. He then chooses his Cabinet: Herbert Hoover as Secretary of Commerce, Al Smith as Director of the Budget, Franklin Roosevelt as Secretary of the Navy—F.D.R.: "What in the world do you mean by offering me a cabinet post, after all the things you have said about me as President?" Huey: "I only offered you a position which I thought you were qualified to fill."[55] President Huey proceeds to call the Mayo brothers to Washington to supervise free medical care for every American, and gets John D. Rockefeller, with Andrew Mellon as his assistant, cheerfully to direct the redistribution of the wealth. Today it reads like satire, often wildly funny.§

The President and James A. Farley, Democratic National Chairman, were not amused by the Kingfish, his antics, or his program. Roosevelt wrote Colonel House that the Republicans were probably financing Huey, and Farley ordered a secret poll to determine Long's strength. Much to Farley's surprise, the poll showed that Huey might get three to four million votes if he ran for President on a third-party ticket in 1936. "His support was not confined to Louisiana and near-by states," said Farley, "but his 'share the wealth' program was attracting strength in industrial and farm areas of the north."[56]

Then fate stepped in. Huey had always had a morbid fear of assassination and surrounded himself with gunmen. In July 1935 he told the Senate that his enemies had gathered in a New Orleans hotel to

---

‡ It has been claimed that the book was ghost-written by Huey's secretary, Earle Christenberry, and Raymond Daniell of the New York *Times*. See Hermann B. Deutsch, *The Huey Long Murder Case* (Garden City, N.Y.: Doubleday, 1963), p. 8.

§ In his study of American utopian literature, Vernon Louis Parrington, Jr., calls it "pretty poor fiction" but admits that Long "had a facile imagination." See *American Dreams, a Study of American Utopias* (Providence: Brown University Press, 1947), p. 198.

plan his death with "one man, one gun, and one bullet."¶ Roosevelt would then give the slayer a presidential pardon. The same month an unimportant anti-Long representative said to the Louisiana legislature:

I am not gifted with second sight. Nor did I see a spot of blood on the moon last night. But I can see blood on the polished floor of this Capitol. For if you ride this thing through, you will travel with the white horse of death.[57]

On the night of Sunday, September 8, Senator Long was in Baton Rouge to direct personally a special session of the legislature. O. K. Allen was governor, but Huey restricted his function to signing what was put before him. ("A leaf blew in the window of Allen's office, and fell on his desk," said Earl Long. "He signed it."[58]) As Huey hurried along the polished floor of the Capitol, trailed by his gunmen, twenty-nine-year-old Dr. Carl Austin Weiss walked up to the Kingfish, pressed a .22-caliber Belgian automatic pistol into his stomach, and fired a single bullet. Huey P. Long died on the morning of the second day after the shooting.*

Word of the assassination was relayed to Hyde Park where F.D.R. was having lunch with Joseph P. Kennedy. Twenty-eight years later Russell Long would rise in the United States Senate and say, "The news of the events that happened in Dallas that fateful Friday last month swept back all the crushing memories of another day—in 1935—when Baton Rouge was the scene of murder of a top Governmental official. The Kennedy family would mourn the death of John F. Kennedy in 1963. How well I know that special grief."[59]

Huey was buried in the shadow of the thirty-four-story state Capitol which he had had built for five million dollars. ("Only one building compares with it in architecture," he then said. "That's St. Peter's Cathedral in Rome, Italy." Earl called it a "silo."[60])

The poor people who loved him, from Dry Prong and Napoleonville

¶ Hodding Carter, then the editor of a small daily newspaper in Hammond, Louisiana, attended this meeting. Later he said that "the 'plotting' was limited to such hopefully expressed comments as 'Good God, I wish somebody would kill the son of a bitch.'" See Isabel Leighton, editor, *The Aspirin Age, 1919–1941* (New York: Simon & Schuster, 1949), p. 355.

* The legend and mystery encasing Long's death have inspired three books: Hermann B. Deutsch, *The Huey Long Murder Case;* David H. Zinman, *The Day Huey Long Was Shot* (New York: Obolensky, 1963); and Richard Briley III, *Death of the Kingfish! Who Did Kill Huey Long?* (Dallas: Triangle, 1960). Briley adds more heat than light; Deutsch and Zinman contend there is no doubt that Dr. Weiss was the assassin. As for his motive, Deutsch believes he acted to shield his family from a racial slur that he believed Huey was about to make against his father-in-law, Benjamin Pavy, an anti-Long judge; Zinman leans to a combination of factors—the alleged racial slur, the doctor's dislike of Long, and Long's action to gerrymander Pavy out of his judgeship.

and Winnfield, 150,000 of them, watched his coffin lowered into a hastily dug grave, and heard the Rev. Gerald L. K. Smith, a Share Our Wealth organizer, give a self-serving funeral oration:

I was with him when he died [intoned Smith]. I said "Amen" as he breathed his last. His final prayer was this: "O God, don't let me die; I have a few things more to do." The work which he left undone we must complete. As one with no political ambition and who seeks no gratuities at the hand of the State, I challenge you, my comrades, to complete the task.[61]

A biographer corrected the record: "Senator Long died, reluctantly and in a sort of childish hysteria, murmuring words which an ignoramus at the bedside translated into a bit of heroics about the Kingfish's unfulfilled mission for America."[62]

To the hill people of northern Louisiana Huey P. Long remains a kind of back-parish Robin Hood. In southern Louisiana the Cajuns still sing of him in ballad: "O they say he was a crook/But he gave us free school book/Now tell me why is it they kill Huey Long?"[63] At least four novels have been inspired by his career.† And from the myth of Huey Long a great political dynasty was built.

What would have been Huey's future had he not been murdered at forty-two? Louisiana Senator Allen Ellender feels that legal obstacles would have kept him from starting a third-party movement in 1936, and had he not been able to block Roosevelt's renomination, he would have supported a progressive Republican for President.[64] This is what may have prompted Forrest Davis to write that "the superstitious might be justified in regarding Long's death as another example of 'Roosevelt luck.'"[65] Earle Christenberry, Huey's friend and secretary, feels that he would have run for President in 1940.[66] Probably by that time war and prosperity would have eroded the Kingfish's political influence. Another school of thought contends that he would have gone to jail. The chief of the U.S. secret service and the head of the Treasury Department's Intelligence and Enforcement Division contend that they had a clear case of tax evasion against Huey.[67] (Yet, as Hermann Deutsch points out, after Huey's death the government lost its strongest tax-evasion case against a Long underling.[68]) President or prisoner? It is the sort of choice that Huey would have liked.

Probably the best assessment of the Kingfish, possibly the only fair one that can be made, was not surprisingly spoken by Huey Long himself: "Just say I'm *sui generis*, and let it go at that."[69]

† The novels: Hamilton Basso, *Sun on Capricorn* (New York: Scribner's, 1942); John Dos Passos, *Number One* (Boston and New York: Houghton Mifflin, 1943); Adria Locke Langley, *A Lion in the Streets* (New York: McGraw-Hill, 1945); Robert Penn Warren, *All the King's Men* (New York: Harcourt, Brace, 1946).

The immediate successor to the Kingfish's position, if not his power, was none other than quiet, housewifely Mrs. Huey P. Long. The governor quickly appointed her to complete the remaining year of her late husband's Senate term.

There was a kind of retribution in the honor. As her brother-in-law Julius wrote in a national magazine, "Huey Long personally deserves the condemnation of every self-respecting citizen of the United States of America for his immorality and debauchery . . . his private life these past eight years has been one of the greatest blots on honor and decency in public life in the history of America."[70] Rose and the kids had been packed off to Shreveport shortly after Huey became governor, and they had stayed behind when he went to Washington. Only after he got designs on the White House did Huey emerge as a family man on a well-publicized "second honeymoon" in New York. There Rose told reporters that the Kingfish was a loving and kindly mate who liked to chop wood for exercise, and with whom she never talked politics.[71]

Now she was United States Senator Rose Long. "I am 100 percent for labor and the farmer and will vote for everything to help them," she announced. "In my mind, I have a hazy idea about the things I want to do but I am not yet ready to announce them."[72] However, Rose was not to be the type of political wallflower who only needs the humid climate of Washington to blossom forth. She made just one speech in the Senate, a four-hundred-word appeal for enlarging Chalmette Park in New Orleans, during which her tongue played strange tricks—"delightful party on the patio" came out as "delightful patty in the partio."

Thus ended the career of the second Long senator. As they said in Louisiana, at least it gave Rose a "nice change of scenery."[73]

Those contending for Huey's mantle in the Long organization finally settled on a ticket for the 1936 election: Gerald L. K. Smith was squeezed out (and left Louisiana to re-emerge as the nation's leading anti-Semite); portly Richard Leche, a state judge, became candidate for governor; Earl Long was named for lieutenant governor. There had been a reconciliation between the brothers shortly before Huey's death—or, as the Kingfish put it, Earl was placed "on probation."[74]

To show further that Dick Leche was the true heir of the Kingfish, Huey's seventeen-year-old son Russell, a freshman at LSU, was paraded around the state at political meetings. (Huey's eldest son Palmer was never interested in politics, though his first wife, movie actress Cleo Moore, once considered running for governor of Louisiana as "the White Goddess."‡) Young Russell, who everyone said was the "spit 'n' image" of his father, had been born while Huey was out campaigning, and had

‡ Palmer is now in the oil business in Shreveport. Huey also had a daughter Rose, the wife of Dr. Oswynn McFarland (once director of the Huey P. Long Memorial Hospital), who lives in Boulder, Colorado.

been taught to fold and mail political literature by the time he could walk. His first state-wide appearances proved him to be a real comer, and he drew generous applause for a short, pat speech: "I'd like to meet all of you and shake hands with you, but I really came just to thank you for your friendship to my father."[75]

There was only one issue in the campaign—Huey's martyrdom. Gerald L. K. Smith had correctly seen that "the martyr's blood is the seed of victory."[76] Speakers for the Long ticket carried basins of red dye, and while the fluid trickled through their fingers, they declaimed: "Here it is, like the blood Huey Long shed for you, the blood that stained the floor as it poured from his body. Are you going to vote for those who planned this deed and carried it into execution?"[77] Leche received a resounding 67.1 per cent of the vote. Earl Long got 12,000 fewer votes, an indication that not everyone had forgiven him for his quarrel with his late brother. The ghost of the Kingfish proved to be a greater vote getter than Huey Long in the flesh.

Huey had been at his prophetic best when he said of his henchmen, "If those fellows ever try to use the powers I've given them without me to hold them down, they'll all land in the penitentiary."[78] And after Huey came Leche, who declared, "When I took the oath as governor, I didn't take any vows of poverty."[79] Now that Huey was gone, Roosevelt wanted an end to his political war with Louisiana, and so called off the income tax prosecutions pending against the Long leaders—an arrangement dubbed the "Second Louisiana Purchase." This was immediately followed by an orgy that clearly overstepped "the fuzzy limits of allowable graft."[80]

Finally Washington was forced to send in a young Assistant Attorney General, O. John Rogge, to clean up the mess. Leche was found to have an income of $282,000 in 1938 on a governor's salary of $7500. The state had been constructing buildings and paying for them twice, a practice called the "double dip." James Monroe Smith, the president of LSU, had been secretly printing state bonds to cover his wild stock speculations. Governor Leche was given ten years in the federal penitentiary; the Democratic National Committeeman was sentenced to four years; "Doc" Smith of LSU got two and a half. Others were found guilty of conducting illegal business by check, thus violating federal postal laws. "Major criminals should not commit minor crimes," announced the righteous Rogge.[81]

And in the wake of the scandals, as Leche was marched off to jail, Lieutenant Governor Earl Long became the new governor of Louisiana.

Later *Time* magazine would say of the second Long governor: "Earl has aped his brother with the beetle-browed assiduousness of a vaudeville baboon learning to roller-skate; he rubs himself with the legend of

Huey's greatness like a voodoo worshiper using 'Fast Dice Oil.' "[82] There
was no doubt that Earl lived in the shadow of his brother. Even when
he reached the exalted position of governor, the zenith of his ambition,
there was Huey right below his office window, perpetual lighting beam-
ing down on the huge bronze statue of the Kingfish in a double-breasted
suit that the state had erected over his grave. But Huey was more
than a magic charm to be rubbed smooth; he was also the rivaled sib-
ling. When Earl became the only three-time governor of the state, his
first thought was "Huey never done that." Huey was Earl's yardstick,
always there for comparison. "I ain't like Huey. He could go a-chomp-
ing around and get away with it. I've gotta go slower—I might get my
head knocked off. Maybe I ain't as much a genius. But I got more
horse sense." "Huey used to buy the Legislature like a sack of potatoes.
Hell, I never bought one in my life. I just rent 'em. It's cheaper that
way." "I've done more for the poor people of this state than any other
governor. The only other governor who came close was my brother,
Huey, and he was just starting out. I've got his experience and I've
got my experience, and you'll see that I can make a better governor."[83]

As lieutenant governor, Earl was never part of the inner circle. He
didn't like Leche. "The office of Lieutenant Governor is a part-time job
paying $200 a month," said Earl. "While I was Lieutenant Governor I
spent twenty per cent of my time in Baton Rouge. The rest of my time I
spent on a pea patch farm in Winnfield or practicing law in New Orleans."[84] He was never implicated in the scandals. "I ain't against stealing," Earl joked, "but it takes two of us to steal and the other might
squeal."[85] The Longs have always been more interested in power than
money, anyway.§

When Earl inherited Leche's scandal-ridden administration he announced that his motto would be "Better a little with righteousness,
than a great revenue without right."[86] But it was soon clear that the
new governor would not be a reformer. He needed the organization to
get elected in 1940, and the last thing the organization needed was a
new broom. After the president of LSU changed his academic gown
for horizontal stripes, Earl remarked, "Don't blame everyone. Look at
Jesus Christ. He picked twelve. And one of 'em was a sonofagun!"[87]

The 1940 gubernatorial race proved two things: Louisiana had momentarily had enough of Huey's heirs, although Earl received 40.9 per
cent of the vote in the first primary; and Earl Long was a worthy successor to the Kingfish in invective. As for his opponent, a successful small
city lawyer named Sam Jones, "He's High Hat Sam," said Earl, "the

§ Huey left an estate of $115,000, including insurance policies and oil stock.
Through 1947 Earl's taxable annual income never exceeded $14,000 and was
as low as $3600 in some years. See Harnett T. Kane, *Louisiana Hayride* (New
York: Morrow, 1941), p. 176; Allan P. Sindler, *Huey Long's Louisiana* (Baltimore: Johns Hopkins Press, 1956), p. 204n.

High Society Kid, the High-Kicking, High and Mighty Snide Sam, the
guy that pumps perfume under his arms."[88] The governor told the hill
farmers, "You vote for a good old country boy from over here in Winn
parish that thinks and smells like you on Saturday."[89] Replied his opponents, "Earl Long posing as a leader of the Huey Long people! That's
like Judas Iscariot running on the platform of Jesus Christ." A hostile
cartoonist pictured a disreputable bunch in a café plastered with signs,
"Vote for Honest Earl; He Ain't Like Us Burglars." And there was Earl
at the piano saying, "I just work here. I eat out."[90] Earl lost by slightly
more than 19,000 votes in the runoff primary. Immediately after the
election he tried unsuccessfully to get himself appointed secretary of
state. Then there was nothing he could do but go back to his pea patch in
Winnfield. For the first time since 1912, when Julius was elected district
attorney of Winn Parish, no member of the Long dynasty held public
office.

By 1948 the people of Louisiana were fed up with the good-government element. Sam Jones had been succeeded as governor by Jimmie
Davis, composer of "You Are My Sunshine." If the reformers had the
virtue of honesty, they also committed the political sin of being in-
credibly dull. (Moreover, Davis proved to be an absentee governor,
spending 108 days out of the state in 1946–47 while making a movie in
Hollywood.)

So Earl ran again for governor, determined that he would not be defeated for lack of promises. His something-for-everyone platform offered bonuses for veterans, hot lunches for school children, higher salaries for teachers, increased old-age pensions, wider highways, improved
mental institutions, more and better hospitals and prisons.

He also recruited an impressive array of familial support. Rose came
out of retirement to say a few nice words about her brother-in-law;
Brother George campaigned briefly; Nephew Russell, now a naval veteran of World War II, was back on the stump; and a new face, Cousin
Gillis Long, pitched in too. In the runoff primary Earl carried sixty-two
of the state's sixty-four parishes; all but thirty-three of 539 wards.

To celebrate the Longs' return to power after eight years on the pea
patch, Earl staged a jumbo inauguration in the LSU football stadium.
There were cowboys, clowns, a baseball game, a two-hour parade, 140
high school bands, refreshments, 16,000 gallons of buttermilk, 240,000
bottles of soda pop, 200,000 hot dogs. And one embarrassing incident:
Russell Long received a greater ovation than the new governor.

It was not easy to be Huey P. Long's son. The young man whose
bulbous nose, cleft chin, and unruly hair were traced from his father's
image had more than his share of schoolboy fights in defense of the
family name. At the age of thirteen, when most youths consider news-

papers as the conveyors of the comic strips, Russell Long granted his first press interview. "I miss my father a lot since he went to Washington." As he escorted the reporter to the door he added, "When I get big and run for office I want you to remember the promise you made to vote for me."[91] By 1938 he was a candidate—for president of the LSU student body. Russell hired airplanes to shower the campus with literature, imported Ted ("Is Everybody Happy?") Lewis' dance band, painted L-O-N-G on the bare backs of a bevy of bathing beauties. His victory was followed by a law degree, also at LSU, and navy service as a landing-boat officer in North Africa, Sicily, Anzio, and southern France.

Uncle-Governor Earl made him his executive counsel, in which post he helped draft the promised new programs and the unpromised $80,000,000 request for additional taxes to pay for them. Two months later United States Senator John Overton died, and Russell was soon campaigning in shirt sleeves, tie loosened, arms windmilling in rank imitation of his father. He compared his opponent to a "mosquito dodging through a barrage of Flit"—though his humor generally lacked Huey's steel edge.[92] He was a city boy and a college graduate masquerading as a Winn Parish bumpkin. Liebling found him "a toned-down" Long, "which is the equivalent of a Samson with a store haircut."[93] But if he didn't have quite the right smell on Saturday, he at least had the right name and physiognomy.

On November 2, 1948, Russell B. Long was elected to the United States Senate; the next day he celebrated his thirtieth birthday. He became the first American to have been preceded in the Senate by both his father and mother. In Washington young Senator Long took a seat behind the desk that had once been occupied by Huey P. Long.¶

In 1952, when Earl Long was prevented by law from succeeding himself as governor, a split developed between Earl and Russell that was reminiscent of the great intradynasty battle of 1932. Earl supported Judge Carlos Spaht as his replacement; his nephew was for Congressman Hale Boggs. The fight between Long and Long, as usual, overshadowed the main-rounder. Earl: "Russell Long was picked too green on the vine." Russell: "If I was picked too green on the vine, then Uncle Earl is too ripe on the vine and should be picked at once."[94]

The result was that neither Long-backed candidate won. Historically a Long gets forty per cent of the first primary vote. In the runoff he

¶ The desk had also been used by John C. Calhoun and Henry Cabot Lodge, Jr. In 1964 Russell Long agreed to give up the desk to Olin D. Johnston, a South Carolinian who wished to place himself in the seat of Calhoun; in turn, Russell Long was given a desk that had once been occupied by his mother, Senator Rose Long. See Washington *Post*, September 25, 1964, p. A16.

needs to pick up only another ten per cent, which is assured if his opponents cannot unite against him. In 1952 the Longs' forty per cent was divided in half: Earl's man getting 22.8 per cent; Russell's man getting 18.7 per cent. Robert Kennon, who had lost to Russell when the Longs were united in 1948, became governor.

It was not, however, a completely disastrous year for the Longs. George, the brother who fitted in between Julius and Huey, was elected to Congress from the Eighth District, which included the family homestead. He had been out of the state during the turbulent Huey Long days, practicing dentistry in Oklahoma and serving a term in the Oklahoma legislature (during which two governors were impeached). After returning to Louisiana George twice tried to get elected to Congress, each time without Brother Earl's support. When Earl was elected governor in 1948 he made George the superintendent of the Pineville State Colony and Training School, then fired him after a squabble over food-buying practices. (It was contended that George was buying unusually large quantities of canned goods from a crony.) George also had his own business, having invented a patent medicine called Vitalong that bore an uncanny resemblance to sherry. Finally in 1952 Earl agreed to support his brother, and George went off to Washington as the fourth representative of the Long dynasty. "There is no question that my election represents a comeback for the Longs in Louisiana," announced George.[95]

Most observers agreed that George, called "Doc" by his colleagues in the House, was the most easygoing and amiable member of the Long family.[96] He served in Congress until his death in 1958 at age seventy-three. Each year he gave a quail dinner at his home for the Louisiana delegation; interested himself in the Capitol's Prayer Room; sat on the House Administration and Veterans' Affairs committees; even sponsored a bill that became a public law (liberalizing requirements for outpatient dental care for veterans). When he was eulogized in Congress, Barratt O'Hara of Illinois said, "I shall miss hearing him speak from the well of the House, his arms flailing the depth of his feeling and giving a dramatic emphasis to words that often were blunt but came thundering from his lips, with intonations of real oratory, as bullets from a machine gun." Speaker Sam Rayburn, who wasted few words, merely noted, "Dr. George Long was a man of high character, of splendid ability, and was an all-round good man."[97]

In 1956 the Longs were in the embarrassing position of a baseball team with three runners on one base. Earl wanted to run for governor. So did Russell. So did George. After they exchanged a few mutually unkind words, Earl emerged as the dynasty's candidate and went on to win a stunning victory over New Orleans Mayor deLesseps S. Morrison ("Dellasoups" to Earl). Said George at the inauguration, "We always seem to get together at this time of year, particularly every four years."[98]

Earl Long, three times governor of Louisiana ("Huey never done that"), then had his wife elected Democratic National Committeewoman. There had even been a story that he wanted George to resign so that he could give "Miz Blanche" a congressional seat. Earl met pretty, dark-haired Blanche Revere when he was at law school and she worked behind the cigar counter at Monteleone Hotel, New Orleans. Unlike Rose Long, who claimed she never talked politics with Huey, Blanche became her husband's trusted political confidante. "I guess all the Longs just naturally take to politics," said Blanche, "and even though I'm a Long by marriage, I guess I take to it too."[99] In 1948 she ran Earl's state campaign headquarters and during his middle term as governor there was a rash of editorials about "petticoat politics."

The spring of 1959 closed in around Earl Long. He was a sick man, having already suffered one thrombosis; he was an aging man, barred by law from the lifeblood of running for governor again; he was a childless man, with "the pressures [said one psychiatrist] of being the childless branch of a dynasty"[100]; and he was a man suddenly standing alone against the terrible specter of mass hatred.

An explosion of fears and forces in the South, which followed the Supreme Court decision on desegregation of the schools, produced the White Citizens Councils, and in Louisiana a racist state senator named Willie Rainach sought to translate their bigotry into local law. The Longs had always paid lip service to segregation, but it had never been one of the tenets of their faith. ("My father and my mother favored the Union," said old Huey Long, Sr. "Why not? They didn't have slaves. They didn't even have decent land."[101]) Now as Rainach steamrolled his anti-Negro bills through the legislature the governor threw his once impressive body in their path. "A lot of people are following you, not because they agree with you but because they're scared of you," Earl shouted at Rainach. "I'm for segregation one hundred per cent, but I don't believe you should run for office on it."[102]

His voice rising and cracking under the strain, Earl Long hurled obscenities at the legislators over state-wide television. He shed the personal characteristics of a lifetime before the eyes of his terrified wife. He started chain smoking, carried a soda pop bottle filled with grape juice and gin ("one hundred proof Coke," said a reporter), and had well-publicized trysts with a redheaded stripper named Blaze Starr. Here were all the elements of an international news story. "Le Gouverneur Terrible," headlined a French journal.[103] A governor was dying, and attention must be paid.

After consulting with Russell, Blanche arranged to have a National Guard plane fly Earl to a mental institution across the state border in Galveston. She gave her story of the governor's crack-up to Life magazine: "They say that when Earl gets out of the hospital he will take his certificate of health and take it out on the campaign trail with him. Then he can say he is the only man in the race who can actually prove he is sane. The people will laugh and be happy again because they know he is the only man in the state who really knows their wants and needs. And I'll be happy again, too. I will know in my heart of hearts that he is well again. I've lived with this turbulent character for 27 years and I love him very much."[104] But the story didn't have a "they-lived-happily-ever-after" ending. What followed was more like a tragic performance of the Keystone Cops. Earl wangled his release from Galveston on the promise of entering Ochsner Clinic at New Orleans; then promptly walked out of Ochsner. Blanche countered by getting him committed to a state hospital for the insane; Earl immediately fired the superintendent and replaced him with a doctor who signed his release.

Earl Long's final race for state-wide office was as a candidate for lieutenant governor. He could manage to place no better than third in a six-man field. But there was still one last effort to be made.

In the Eighth Congressional District young Harold B. McSween had been elected to the seat left vacant by the death of George Long. In 1959, after his defeat for lieutenant governor, Earl decided to take on McSween. On the night before the primary election Earl suffered another heart attack but refused to enter a hospital for fear that it would deter people from voting for him. As the voters went to the polls on August 27 Earl Long gasped in pain on a bed in the Hotel Bentley, Alexandria. Finally, after the polls had closed and the news could no longer affect his chances, Earl went to the hospital. He won the primary for Congress by some 6000 votes. Earlier that year he had announced, "I won't quit running until I die."[105] It was a prophecy that no one doubted. On September 5 he died.

The Eighth District, heartland of the Longs, was not to be without a Long representative for long. In 1962 Gillis Long, a third cousin of Senator Russell Long,* defeated Harold McSween to become the fifth of the dynasty to serve in Congress.

```
    *  John Long ——————— (brothers) ——————— James Long
           |                                      |
       Huey, Sr.                               Thomas
           |                                      |
    Huey ("Kingfish")                           Floyd
           |                                      |
    Russell (SENATOR)                    Gillis (CONGRESSMAN)
```

The father of the new congressman had been a night counterman in a café that went bankrupt during the depression; he then moved his family to a forty-acre farm that was considered unworkable even by Winn Parish standards. He worked on it until Earl gave him a job as an attendant in a mental hospital. In 1940 Gillis started to work his way through LSU. When the war interrupted his education he became an infantry officer in Europe, was wounded, and served at the Nuremberg trials. Returning home, he finished college and got a law degree. He also was elected president of the LSU student body, worked in Earl's 1948 campaign, and went to Washington as a staff member of a Senate committee on which Cousin Russell served.

Still boyish in his early forties, his hair crew-cut, his jaw squared, his chin slightly cleft, his eyes deep-set and piercing brown, Gillis Long bears a pixie resemblance to Earl, whom he also "favors" on the stump with a voice that rises and cracks when making a point, while his hands instinctively come to rest on his buttocks when they're not flailing the air. Also like Earl, he gets along with little sleep and sees that his campaign associates do likewise by his compulsive use of the telephone at any hour of the day or night. Reporter Earl Mazo related a Gillis Long call at five-thirty one morning:

"Marshall," hollered Gillis, "Time to get up . . . daylight is a-comin'."

"Lordamighty," said the half-asleep Mr. Marshall to his wife, "it's Earl Long, returned from the dead!"[106]

Never far removed from either peak or nadir in their roller-coaster ride through Louisiana politics, the Longs were again threatened with an intradynasty slugfest in 1963. Part of the organization, with Blanche Long as campaign manager, supported the gubernatorial candidacy of John J. McKeithen, who was unacceptable to Russell.

Russell toyed with the idea of running himself. It had always been his ambition to follow his father and uncle into the Executive Mansion at Baton Rouge. But he had now gone too far along another road; he had been in the Senate for thirteen years and had become both captor and captive of its seniority system. With only the ancient Harry Byrd ahead of him, Russell could expect one day to become chairman of the powerful Finance Committee. Nineteen sixty-three was a turning point in his career: he turned his back on state elective office and announced his support of freshman Congressman Gillis Long for governor.

Nine men entered the contest. Besides Long and McKeithen, the principal contenders were former Governor Robert Kennon and former New Orleans Mayor Morrison. Pandering to frayed nerves in the race-troubled state, McKeithen attacked Morrison and Long as "the Kennedy Twins."[107] Long refrained from using the President as a political football. "Politically I should have," said Gillis, "but I just couldn't see a Democratic candidate for governor attacking a Democratic President."[108] President Kennedy was assassinated two weeks before the primary. Gillis reasons that the bullet in Texas defeated him in Louisiana. He contends that his expected Catholic and Negro vote swung over to Morrison, who was both a Catholic and a former official in the Kennedy Administration. Gillis Long finished third.

As McKeithen's campaign manager, Blanche Long toured the state, occasionally making speeches, more often just talking to the politicians. "When Earl went out [campaigning], he knew who to call in every precinct in Louisiana," she said. "Not very many politicians could do that. But I could."[109] Her candidate defeated Morrison in the runoff. The new governor quickly rewarded Blanche with a $10,000-a-year appointment to the State Tax Commission, the assessor of all residential and industrial property in the state of Louisiana. At the 1964 Democratic National Convention she represented her state on the Credentials Committee. As the year ended, a New Orleans politician told a reporter, "Some say Miss Blanche is the most powerful Long in Louisiana right now."[110]

The proliferation of Longs produced its own form of political population explosion. The dynasty seemed to have an almost infinite number of ambitions hungering for a finite number of public offices. It was like a game of musical chairs, and when the music stopped, by the rules of the game, someone would have to be seatless.

While Gillis, supported by Russell, was running for governor against a candidate backed by Blanche, another Long was making his first bid for state-wide office. He was Speedy O. Long, another of Russell's third cousins.†

When he was born in June 1928, two and a half months early and weighing two and a half pounds, his grandmother wrapped him in a blanket and left him overnight in the still warm stove. The premature baby was named Speedy. (His first schoolteacher was to send him home every day for a week before she could be convinced that her new pupil had truthfully given his Christian name.)

| † John Long ——— (brothers) ——— Charles William Long |
Huey, Sr.	Charles Felix
Huey ("Kingfish")	Felix
Russell (SENATOR)	Speedy (CONGRESSMAN)

His father was a barber in Tulles and dabbled in politics, serving on the town council and as mayor.‡ There were nine children (one of whom is now state director of a 95,000-member union of government employees). "Politics is all we ever had for breakfast," says Speedy.[111] "I was brought up to think that Huey Long was God Almighty, Earl was Jesus Christ and George was St. Peter."[112] When he was seven George Long took him campaigning; at eleven he spent two weeks on the stump with George; for a semester in college he lived at George's home in Pinesville.

In 1951 he graduated from Northwestern State College, having worked in the oil fields to support himself; in 1955 he married Florence Marie Theriot and spent his honeymoon campaigning successfully for the state Senate§; three years later he was defeated for Congress; the following year he won re-election to the state Senate and graduated from LSU Law School. Earl Long opposed him in 1955, opposed him in 1958, and supported him in 1959. When Earl's widow ran McKeithen's campaign in 1963, Speedy joined her ticket as candidate for state insurance commissioner, made as many as seventy speeches a week, and was defeated. But within the parishes that comprise the Eighth Congressional District he ran ahead of gubernatorial candidate Gillis Long. This set the stage for the first face-to-face confrontation of Longs at the ballot box.

The all-important Democratic congressional primary in 1964 came three weeks after the passage of the Civil Rights Act. Emotionalism was at its height. Both Long candidates were segregationists; but Speedy was outspoken, and Gillis, by central Louisiana standards, hadn't spoken loudly enough. Congressman Long had voted against the measure (". . . this act will create an alien force in the lives of communities all across our land"[113]), but opponent Long charged that he had indirectly aided the passage of the bill by voting to "pack" the House Rules Committee —i.e., enlarging its size from twelve to fifteen members—thus, according to Speedy, diluting the influence of the South. His slogan proclaimed: "Vote Against the Man Who Voted Against the South." Rhymed the "Original Knights of the Ku Klux Klan, Realm of Louisiana":

LET GILLIS GO.
ELECT SPEEDY O.[114]

‡ Felix Long (1899–   ) was appointed by Earl Long in 1956 to the state barbers' board. He was removed in 1963 by Governor Jimmie Davis (a political enemy of Speedy's), and reinstalled in 1964 after John McKeithen (a political ally of Speedy's) was elected governor. He is now secretary to the board, a full-time job, though he still keeps his barbershop and cuts hair on Saturdays.

§ His wife's uncle, Lee Theriot, is now chairman of the Louisiana Tax Commission, on which Blanche Long also serves.

During most of the eleven years before his election to Congress, Gillis had served in Washington as staff member on various Senate and House committees. Within a year after his election to Congress he was running for governor. During all this time Speedy was traveling the gravel and dirt roads of central Louisiana. A New Orleans state senator summed up the difference between the two Longs: "Speedy is a redneck. He thinks regionally. Gillis is a cosmopolitan."[115]

There aren't many cosmopolitans in the Eighth Congressional District of Louisiana. When the returns from the back country came in Speedy Long had defeated Gillis Long by 4900 votes. In the general election Speedy limited his campaigning to one two-and-a-half-minute television appearance. Although Republican Goldwater carried the district by two and a half to one, Democrat Long was easily elected.

President Johnson then appointed Gillis Long an assistant director of the Office of Economic Opportunity (a job he resigned in late summer of 1965); and Speedy Long became the sixth member of his dynasty to serve in the United States Congress.

When Russell Long, at the age of thirty, became a United States senator in 1948, he entered a legislative body whose rules of civilized procedure had been bent and burlesqued by his father. Some of his older colleagues had been witness to Huey's tirades. And here was a young man who arrived in Washington with the announced intention of vindicating the Kingfish's name. It was a deeply felt theme; to Cabell Phillips of the New York *Times* he said, "I think my father was one of the greatest men of his time. He was certainly the greatest man I ever knew."[116]

But Russell was a second-generation legislator who, like other sons of self-made men, worked hard to maintain a newly won respectability.¶ If his father was the shirt-sleeved laborer, he was the man in the gray flannel suit—Louisiana style. "I guess the main difference between me and my father is that the only way he knew to get the things he wanted was to fight and raise hell for them. He wanted all these good things to happen right now—fast," said Russell. "I know you can't get things that fast, and I'm satisfied to take my time. And if I do that, and make a good Senator, then I figure people will be bound to say, 'Well, Huey Long must not have been so bad after all.'"[117]

By his third term in the Senate, Russell had outgrown his compulsion

¶ The generational difference can also be seen in the careers of Eugene and Herman Talmadge of Georgia. "Ole Gene," the four-time governor, was noted for his snapping red galluses and his demogogic appeals to race and class. His son is now far removed from this boondocks style and "is credited with having one of the ablest minds in the Senate." See Joseph A. Loftus, "Talmadge Adopts a Yankee's Theme," New York *Times*, February 22, 1965, p. 34.

to be the "Princefish," merely Huey's boy. "I have a fond and warm recollection of my father," he said in 1963, "but I have my job to do, and for a long time now I have been working for Russell Long, not Huey Long."[118] When he steered the President's tax program through the Senate in 1964, Proxmire of Wisconsin, an opponent of the measure, called him a "legislative artist in action."[119]

After Hubert Humphrey became the Democratic nominee for Vice-President in August 1964, Russell Long quietly began lining up votes to succeed him as majority whip of the Senate.[120] While his chief opponent, Pastore of Rhode Island, campaigned by sending a belated form letter to his fellow senators, Russell made a point of asking his colleagues personally for their support. He was assured of a sizable bloc of Southern votes, but newspapermen were surprised at his strength among Northern and Western liberals. Clinton Anderson, the most outspoken foe of the filibuster, agreed to become his campaign manager; Paul Douglas, torchbearer for economic liberalism, announced that he was for Long because "he has a warm heart and a compassion for the poor."[121]

Long had the worst record of support for the Kennedy-Johnson program of any of the contenders for the post. *Congressional Quarterly* tabulated that out of thirty-seven key votes he had supported his party's presidents only eighteen times, and had opposed them nineteen times. He had been against the Civil Rights Bill, the nuclear test ban treaty, medical care for the aged under Social Security, and increased foreign aid. Yet there were clearly other factors at work. The election was something of a popularity contest, and Long was well liked; as the ranking member of the Finance Committee he had been in a position to bestow favors, and bestow them he had; moreover, he had put together a strange coalition of supporters—Southerners who were for him as a matter of course and Northerners who felt that he was in the agrarian populist tradition.

On the first day of the 89th Congress he was elected Democratic whip. He was following in powerful footsteps: of the last three whips, one was now President, one was Vice-President, and the third was majority leader.

Moreover, Finance Chairman Harry Byrd retired within a year. The ancient Virginian was able to turn his Senate seat over to his son, but not his seniority, and so Russell took over his chairmanship. The Louisiana senator announced defiantly that he would also retain his position as whip, and, despite minor senatorial grousing, his right to hold two powerful offices at the same time was not challenged. Russell Long, whose father could not have got the Lord's Prayer endorsed by the Senate, was now hailed (by William S. White) as "a genuine Senator's Senator."[122] Said a colleague, "Unless he overplays his hand, Russell Long is about to become the most powerful man in the Senate."[123]

Long concedes readily that he would like to be the Senate majority leader. But is this the ultimate goal of his ambition? Tom Wicker, the astute Washington bureau chief of the New York *Times*, believes that under certain circumstances the Democrats could tap Russell for a future vice-presidential nomination.* Yet there are others who paint a less promising picture of the senator's future. They see his present position of national leadership in the Democratic Party as basically inconsistent with the views of the party and people in Louisiana, especially on civil rights issues. And those who walk a tightrope must be aware of the risks of a fall.

The Longs of Louisiana: Huey, Earl, George, Rose, Blanche, Russell, Gillis, and Speedy—two governors; a lieutenant governor; three United States senators, elected five times; three congressmen, elected five times. All in two generations!

Huey, of course, was the colossus; without him there could have been no dynasty. Some dynasts are the driving force within the family, instilling the desire for office and the sense of public service in their heirs, but leaving little mark on their times; some become dynasts because of the marks they have left. Their flamboyant personalities or records of achievement create a demand for those who bear their name. Huey Long was of the latter variety. There is no record that he set out to create a dynasty; the dynasty was created because there was Huey. His name became a passport to public office in Louisiana.

This is not to say that there is no pride of family in the Longs. However, it was not the force that initially propelled the dynasty. And as often as not family pride was blunted by competing ambitions. Like a child's kaleidoscope whose loose fragments form an endless variety of patterns, political relationships within the dynasty have been in a constant process of change, of grouping and regrouping, as Longs fought one another, united, and fought again.

Yet through it all there has been a steadfastness to the populist legacy of Huey. The differences have not been ideological. Beneath the comic antics and political cynicism of Huey and Earl, there was a genuine desire to better the poor and disinherited. It was the root of their strength. And by and large it has been passed on to the second generation.

The generational differences, then, have been more of style than sub-

* "Given the shift, moreover, of Southern conservatism toward the Republican party . . . it is not too far-fetched to imagine a future election in which the Democratic party might want to reach out to the South for a moderate Vice-Presidential candidate who could help hold that region's 128 electoral votes." Tom Wicker, "The Son of the Kingfish," *New York Times Magazine,* April 4, 1965, p. 90.

stance. Though columnist Russell Baker sees in Russell Long "a tempestuous, moody, unpredictable charmer," who reminds him of a minor Labour Party official in the Welsh coal country, this only contrasts him with today's I.B.M. Senate, not with his galluses-snapping, buttock-slapping father.[124] Even Speedy O. Long, with his redneck appeal, dresses conservatively in dark suit and rep tie; speaks softly and displays a worldly vocabulary. It is difficult to imagine Russell or Gillis or Speedy spreading a newspaper on the floor of the Governor's Mansion and spending an evening spitting on it, as Earl once did to keep his disgust fresh for "them lyin' newspapers."

The new Longs have been housebroken. Compared to their forebears, they are tame, professional, homogenized. Huey said, "I don't see any harm in lightening up the tragedy of politics. . . ." But in his heirs some of that electricity is gone, a sacrificial offering to the gods of respectability.

It is hard to believe that it is less than a half century since the first Long arose as a political force. They are a young dynasty. The members of the second generation are only in their thirties and forties. And in a state where third cousins can claim political kinship there are plenty of Longs for every occasion. At the opening session of a recent state legislature Speedy Long held up his infant son in diapers for all to see. He just wanted Louisiana to know that the dynasty is "going to be around awhile."

The Lodge Dynasty

And this is good old Boston,
The home of the bean and the cod,
Where the Lowells talk only to Cabots,
And the Cabots talk only to God.

—John Collins Bossidy[1]

WHEN the first Henry Cabot Lodge ran for the Massachusetts legislature in 1879 his opponents called him "Lah-de-dah" Lodge, the "silver spoon young man" who "parted his hair and his name in the middle."[2] When the second Henry Cabot Lodge ran for the United States Senate in 1936 his opponent called him "Little Boy Blue . . . a sweet boy with an illustrious name."[3] Both Cabot Lodges were elected, showing perhaps that their ancestry, wealth, and social position were not so serious liabilities as their opponents imagined.

Yet, despite the aura of past generations that hangs over the Lodges, they are primarily a twentieth-century political dynasty. No Lodge was elected to national office until 1886, and since that time there have been just twelve years in which there was not a Lodge in elective or appointive office. During one period, at the close of the Eisenhower Administration, there was a trio of Lodge appointees—Henry Cabot Lodge, ambassador to the United Nations; Brother John Davis Lodge, ambassador to Spain; and Cabot's son, George Lodge, Assistant Secretary of Labor for International Affairs. Nevertheless, the Lodges seem somehow to be visitors to this century. Part of this impression comes from their half-century rivalry with the Kennedys, who, like the Duke of Plaza-Toro, appear to be a step ahead of next year's fashions. By comparison, there is about the Lodges the salt spray of clipper ships, the slight must of the gentleman's club, and the ingrained sense of duty of the Pilgrim fathers.

Ironically, however, the Lodges are not an old family by Bay State standards; and the Cabots, who *are* an old family, have not an illustrious name outside of Boston in the manner of Adamses and Lowells. The

THE LODGE DYNASTY
(A Selective Genealogy)

Giles Lodge (1770–1852)
Arrived in America, 1791
m. Mary Langdon

John Ellerton Lodge (1807–62)
Wealthy merchant

George Cabot (1752–1823)
SENATE
m. Elizabeth Higginson (1756–1826)
(9 children; 6 d.y.)

Henry Cabot (1783–1864)
m. Anna Sophie Blake (1796–1845)
(3 children; 1 d.y.)

Anna Sophie Cabot (1821–1900)

m.

Henry Cabot Lodge (1850–1924)
HOUSE OF REPRESENTATIVES, SENATE
m. Anna Cabot Mills Davis (1850–1915) ("Nannie")
(3 children)

Constance (1872–1941)
1st m. Augustus Peabody
Gardner (1865–1918), House
of Representatives (1 child)
2nd. m. Charles C. Williams,
General

George Cabot (1873–1909)
("Bay"), poet
m. Mathilda Frelinghuysen
Davis (c. 1877–1960) ("Bessie")
(3 children)

John Ellerton (1878–1942)
Oriental art scholar
m. Mary Connally
(no issue)

Helena
m. Edouard de Streel,
Belgian diplomat
(3 children)

Henry Cabot (1902–)
SENATE, ambassador
m. Emily Sears
(2 children)

John Davis (1903–)
HOUSE OF REPRESENTATIVES,
GOVERNOR, ambassador
m. Francesca Braggiotti
(2 children)

George Cabot (1927–)
Assistant Secretary of Labor
m. Nancy Kunhardt
(6 children)

first Lodge did not arrive in this country until after the American Revolution; the Cabot family came in 1700 but have since produced only one son of political note.* Yet it has been written that "almost at once the Cabots established the habit of making good marriages, a habit in which they have continued to this day."[4] The same applies to the Lodges. By the time George Cabot Lodge ran for the United States Senate in 1962 he could number eight members of Congress among his direct ancestors, of whom only three were Lodges and another a Cabot.

The first Lodge forebear to sit in the Senate was George Cabot, a third-generation American who managed to turn the American Revolution into a good thing financially by engaging in the "profitable patriotism of the privateer." Loyalist Judge Curwen wrote from London in 1779: "The Cabots of Beverly who . . . had not but five years ago a very moderate share of property are now said to be by far the most wealthy in the country."[5]

An imposing figure, standing over six feet in height, George Cabot was seen by a contemporary "as the traveler in Switzerland sees Mont Blanc towering above other mountains around him, wherever he may be." Just as all the Adamses were short and portly, the Cabots and Lodges have tended to be tall and lean. George Cabot also looked very much like George Washington, "as if the great man, as painted by Stuart, had walked out of the canvas. . . ." His manner was gracious and calm. When he spoke "all eyes and ears turned toward him, as if eager to catch the music of his voice and the light of his mind."[6]

This impressive gentleman had a curious career in politics. In the Senate he established himself as a national leader, as well as a man who knew how to look after his constituents' interests.[7] He became a close friend and trusted adviser of Hamilton and Washington. When Lafayette sent his son to America, Washington asked Cabot to take charge of him. "Next to Hamilton, and side by side with Rufus King," wrote Henry Adams, "he was revered in his time as the oracle of Federalism."[8] Then at the age of forty-four, after serving only five years of his term, Cabot

---

* However, in recent years the Cabots have increasingly turned their attention toward national affairs. John Moors Cabot (1901–   ), a career diplomat, has served as United States ambassador to Poland, Finland, Sweden, Colombia, and Brazil; his brother, Thomas Dudley Cabot (1897–   ), who is chairman of the Cabot Corporation of Boston, the world's largest producer of carbon black, was co-ordinator of the United States foreign aid program in 1950–51; Louis Wellington Cabot (1921–   ), son of Thomas Dudley Cabot and president of the Cabot Corporation, was chairman of the United States delegation to the United Nations Economic and Social Council at Geneva in 1961. See George F. W. Telfer, "Living Up to a Famous Name," *Christian Science Monitor*, January 30, 1963, p. 9c.

resigned from the Senate to become "a complete recluse." He disliked "the jarrings of the outer world" and could afford to have no more of it.[9] John Adams thought his retirement was a ploy: "It seems the mode of becoming great is to retire," he said, probably thinking of Jefferson at Monticello. "Mr. Cabot, I suppose, after aggrandizing his character in the shade a few years, is to be some great thing. . . . It is marvelous how a political plant grows in the shade—continued daylight and sunshine show our faults and record them."[10]

Adams tried to lure him back into public life with an appointment as the first Secretary of the Navy; the Senate confirmed the nomination without opposition, but he declined.

Only once were his friends able to shake his natural indolence. Strong in opposition to the War of 1812, he was stirred out of retirement to be president of the Hartford Convention, that ill-timed meeting which was unjustly thought of as the hotbed of secessionism. "George Cabot's close-buttoned ambition has broke out at last," proclaimed John Adams, "he wants to be President of New England, sir!"[11] But Adams was wrong again. Cabot proved to be a moderating influence who, when asked by a friend what he was going to do at Hartford, replied, "We are going to keep you young hot-heads from getting into mischief."[12] He then retired again, this time permanently.

George Cabot was survived by two children, Elizabeth and Henry. The daughter married John Thornton Kirkland, whose eighteen years as president of Harvard were marked by the founding of the law and divinity schools, and marred by student riots, which culminated in the "Great Rebellion" of 1823, when over half the senior class was expelled shortly before graduation.† (One of John Quincy Adams' sons was among those involved in the caper, but not even the President's influence could get Kirkland to reinstate the boy.[13]) Henry Cabot had also been thrown out of Harvard for participating in a student disorder, though not during his brother-in-law's reign. Young Cabot was to spend most of his life in comfortable retirement on his considerable inheritance, with his claim to fame being that as a child he had hidden under a table when George Washington paid a call on his father. It was his daughter who married a Lodge, and his grandson who was to become the most unlikely "boss" to grace American politics.

† John Thornton Kirkland (1770–1840) was an educationalist by inheritance. His father, Samuel Kirkland (1741–1808), was a missionary among the Indians of western New York and founder of Hamilton College. The young Kirkland, though not a great scholar, was an outstanding president of Harvard, 1810–28, primarily because of his ability to inspire others to greatness. See Russel B. Nye, *George Bancroft, Brahmin Rebel* (New York: Knopf, 1944), pp. 19–22.

At the time George Cabot was elected to the Senate in 1791, the first Lodge unexpectedly arrived in Boston. The immigrant was making a hasty escape from Santo Domingo, where the Negroes were rising against their masters. His stubborn and high-tempered son, John Ellerton Lodge, devoted his substantial energy to building one of the fastest and most successful fleets of clipper ships on the China run. He also married Anna Cabot. And they were the parents of Henry Cabot Lodge, Sr.

Of the future Senate leader, a journalist wrote, "Henry Cabot Lodge always creates the impression that it is a condescension on his part to God to have allowed Him to create a world which is not exclusively possessed by the Cabots and the Lodges and their connections."[14] Even his closest friends spoke of his "aloofness" and "socially undemocratic" demeanor.[15] It was an attitude bred and encouraged by his mother. Left a widow when her son was twelve, Anna Cabot Lodge spent the rest of her life pampering and indulging the boy whose exceptional talents she never doubted. By the time of her death in 1900, according to Lodge's most exacting biographer, he had become the "spoiled child of American politics."[16]

The second great influence on Cabot Lodge was his wife, Anna Cabot Mills Davis. Theirs was an impeccable social match. The Davis family had settled in New England as early as 1630; her father was Rear Admiral Charles Henry Davis, scientist, Civil War hero, head of the Naval Observatory at Washington; her mother was the daughter of an inconspicuous Federalist senator‡; her brother would also be an admiral (irreverently known as "Shakey" Davis); and a sister would become Mrs. Brooks Adams.[17]§

But in her own right the beautiful Nannie Lodge, with her blond hair and violet-blue eyes, was a most remarkable woman. John Singer Sargent longed to paint her portrait. Theodore Roosevelt, Lord Bryce, and Henry Adams were among the many who extolled her sweetness, gentle nature, and grace. Added Mrs. Winthrop Chanler: "Forget any praises I may have bestowed on others. She was the most charming woman I have ever known; an exquisite presence in this workaday world. She had unusual beauty, a pale face with regular features, and dark eyes the color of the sky when stars begin to twinkle. She had great wit; it was the only weapon she ever used in self-defense, and Cabot was a little afraid of its winged shafts. Daughter and sister to Admirals, she had perhaps caught from them a certain sense of discipline, some secret code of high behavior that guided her action but was never imposed on others. Gay and hospitable, she took delight in

‡ Elijah Hunt Mills (1776–1829), a Massachusetts lawyer, served in the House of Representatives, 1815–19, and in the Senate, 1820–27.

§ See Adams Dynasty, p. 42.

all that was delightful, yet never lost her bearings in fogs of enthusiasm. She combined the usually contrasting qualities of keen intelligence and warm-heartedness. I never found another human instrument so delicately tuned to understand and sympathize."[18]

It was no simple task to be Mrs. Senator Lodge. At one Gridiron dinner the question was asked: "Did you find out why Senator Lodge is the only Senator in the Academy of Immortals?" "Yes, sir," came the reply, "Senator Lodge got up the list."[19] Yet Nannie Lodge never feared bringing her husband back among the mortals. Once, after she had made him rewrite a speech for the third time, she said, "I suppose it is as good as you can do, my poor boy."[20] And as if to bring him further to earth, she called him "Pinky," a highly unlikely appellation for this tall, sententious grandee with the pointed beard, of whom it was said, "Throw a cloak over Lodge's left shoulder and he would step into a Velasquez group in the Prado and be authentic."[21]

They were married the day after his graduation from Harvard in 1871 and immediately went off to Europe for the grand tour. Cabot had no occupation and no notion of how to find one. This troubled him, particularly after the birth of his first child, Constance. He had no need of more money. But he had a driving, undirected ambition and the capacity for hard work. At this point he wrote for advice to Henry Adams, whose course in medieval history had been his only real educational experience at Harvard. Adams suggested that he become a Boston "literary lion" and offered to make him his assistant editor on the *North American Review*. Lodge recalled, "I trod on air as I walked, and the whole world was changed."[22]

Adams prodded and badgered his protégé—vary your construction, put the predicate first, strike out every superfluous word, condense your sentences. A Puritan Pygmalion intent on breathing life into his Yankee Aphrodite. And Lodge emerged from the cold stone: scholar, editor, teacher, author. He earned a Ph.D. in political science, the first granted by Harvard; he took over his mentor's courses, for which Adams paid him out of his own pocket; he produced a prodigious amount of historical writing, including biographies of Washington, Hamilton, Webster, and Great-grandfather George Cabot. Then Lodge discovered politics. The more political he became, the more polemical was his scholarship. Adams mourned the loss of his creation. Even after Lodge had reached the heights of the Senate he would write, "He ought to have been Professor at Harvard College, as I meant him to be when I educated him."[23] Adams went out of his way to expose the cant of Lodge's politics, which the latter took with good nature. They remained friends, partly because of Adams' respect for Mrs. Lodge.[24] But the feeling of the Harvard days was gone; and as the years passed Adams transferred his love to Lodge's eldest son.

There was nothing casual or occasional about Lodge the politician. He brought to the public arena the same powers of concentration and dedication he had once applied to the study of Germanic and Anglo-Saxon law. True, his personality made him an unlikely candidate for popular approval. "I wonder why these writers persist in calling me cold, and reserved, and a Brahmin," he once said to Theodore Roosevelt. "I can tell you, Cabot," replied the President. "It's because you are!"[25] Yet he would ballast his hauteur by working harder than his opponents and leaving nothing to chance. At twenty-nine, Lodge was elected to the Massachusetts legislature; he became Republican state chairman at thirty-three.

It can be said that Henry Cabot Lodge, Sr., started in politics as a liberal and grew more conservative with each passing year; while Henry Cabot Lodge, Jr., took off where his grandfather ended, and ended where his grandfather began. For as the younger Lodge closed his political career in opposition to Goldwater at the 1964 convention, the first Henry Cabot Lodge came to national prominence by opposing Blaine at the 1884 Republican Convention. Both Lodges lost. But the nineteenth-century defeat was more crucial, coming as it did at the opening of a promising career.

The presidential nomination of James G. Blaine, the tainted "Man from Maine," presented Lodge with his first significant political decision: should he oppose the Republican candidate in the general election, as the others in his social milieu were doing, or stick with his party? He chose the latter course, thus cutting himself off from Proper Boston.

Though the outside world considered him the epitome of Back Bay, inside the citadel Somerset Club members crossed the street to avoid meeting him for years afterward. Hurt deeply, Lodge offered neither apology nor excuse. "He held himself so aloof, and was apparently so well satisfied that this decision was the right one," wrote Bishop Lawrence, "that he seemed to assess us as ignorant and short-sighted. . . ."[26] Of course it was of no consequence to the Gentleman Independent that if Lodge had bolted his party he would have been ending his political career. For there were real and apparent reasons for Lodge's stand: outwardly he contended that, having fought the good fight as a convention delegate and lost, he was morally committed to support the nominee; actually, he was probably motivated by ambition to go to Congress. He was then a candidate for the House of Representatives from the Sixth Massachusetts District. In November he lost to the incumbent Democrat by 225 votes.

If Lodge ended the year 1884 by being in Boston, but no longer of it, he had also acquired a remarkable new friend; a friend who would bring into his life a sense of excitement and adventure that he had never imagined possible. At the convention he had fought side by side with a twenty-five-year-old New Yorker, Theodore Roosevelt. More important, after the convention they had made the same decision to support the party's nominee. Roosevelt, at first, was the more dependent; Lodge was older, more practical, capable of leveling off the massive Rooseveltian peaks and valleys of exaltation and depression. It was Lodge who was primarily responsible for Roosevelt's appointment as civil service commissioner and Assistant Secretary of the Navy. As early as 1895, when Roosevelt was far down the political pecking order as New York City police commissioner, Lodge wrote him, "I am no dreamer. . . . I do not say you are to be President tomorrow. I do say you will be—I am sure that it may and can be."[27] It was a vision constantly held before his friend. All the smart politicians told Roosevelt to refuse the vice-presidency; Lodge alone urged him to accept. And with McKinley's assassination Roosevelt became President. They had come a long way together—from the losing side in the Blaine convention to the White House.

Naturally Roosevelt then became the dominant figure. Lodge, who desired no office from his presidential friend, accepted the reversal of roles with good grace. He loyally supported the Administration. And even Roosevelt's break from Republican ranks in 1912, which Lodge could not endorse, failed to dampen their devotion to each other. The epitaph of the friendship was written in a memorandum by Roosevelt: "From that time on [the Blaine nomination of 1884], he was my closest friend, personally, politically, and in every other way, and occupied toward me a relationship that no other man has ever occupied or ever will occupy."[28]

After 1884 Lodge never lost another election. He fulfilled his ambition to go to Congress two years later, served for three terms, and then moved over to the Senate, where he remained for thirty-one years.¶ He was majority leader for his last six years, and chairman of the Foreign Relations Committee from 1919 until his death in 1924.

Lodge was not a man who cherished political consistency. He was the Senate's leading expansionist, thus an internationalist; the Senate's prime intriguer against Wilson's League of Nations, thus a nationalist; the main champion of civil service reform in the House, a drafter of the Sherman Anti-Trust Act and the Pure Food and Drugs Act, thus a liberal; a rock-ribbed protectionist, an opponent of women's suffrage

¶ In 1890 and 1892 Lodge successfully defended his House seat against Henry Adams' first cousin, William Everett, the son of sometime United States Senator Edward Everett. The younger Everett, an eccentric Harvard professor known as "Piggy," didn't live in the congressional district. Like his father, he was a long-winded orator, who never said "put in a hole" when he could say "deposited in a cavity." See John A. Garraty, *Henry Cabot Lodge* (New York: Knopf, 1953), p. 122.

and the direct election of senators, thus a conservative. But, above all, he was a partisan—often ruthless, often vindictive. Without serious political opposition in his home state throughout most of his career, and with the highest social, financial, and educational credit ratings, he might have sought greatness; yet he seemed almost deliberately to duck it.

For in the final analysis he was a man of neither lofty mind nor wide vision. "It is rather a pity," wrote a not unsympathetic journalist, "that Mr. Lodge never made anything of, never exploited or employed, the franchise for development that his State gave him so many years ago."[29] Henry Adams, who always seemed to have the last word, summed up the career of his former student: ". . . he could never feel perfectly at ease whatever leg he stood on, but shifted, sometimes with painful strain of temper, from one sensitive muscle to another, uncertain whether to pose as an uncompromising Yankee; or a pure American; or a patriot in the still purer atmosphere of Irish, Germans, or Jews; or a scholar and historian of Harvard College."[30]*

In 1892 another politician entered the family circle when the senator's daughter Constance married Augustus Peabody Gardner. "Gussie" Gardner was of the bluest blood, a descendant in the tenth generation of Thomas Gardner, the first overseer of the plantation at Cape Ann; a great-great-grandson of Timothy Pickering, John Adams' disloyal Secretary of State, and a grandson of John Lowell Gardner, a businessman of such acquisitive power that it was said "if you had started him at the foot of State Street with nothing on, by the time he had reached the Old State House he would have a new suit of clothes, spats, cane, a tall hat, and money in his pockets."[31] (His estate, estimated at fifteen million dollars, was divided between his two sons.)

Moreover, Gussie Gardner had the most fascinating foster mother who ever shocked Boston's society. Having been left an orphan in 1875, ten-year-old Gussie and his two brothers went to live with their uncle Jack and his wife, the fabulous Isabella Stewart Gardner. Short, plain-faced, red-haired, with a magnificent figure and incomparable grace, Aunt Isabella had a strange effect on even the most phlegmatic male. "The effect of an hour with you," wrote Henry Adams, "is that of the Absolute,—vertigo,—loss of relation, absence in space, time and thought. It is peace, repose or dream, rather like opium; but the return to air and dust is painful."[32] She was to build a Venetian palace in Boston, appear at the symphony with a Red Sox banner on her hat, drink

---

* This appraisal in *The Education of Henry Adams* caused Mrs. Lodge to inquire of its author, "Brother, why are you so hard on poor Pinky? You didn't mean all you said, did you?" Quoted in Ernest Samuels, *Henry Adams, the Major Phase* (Cambridge: Harvard University Press, 1964), p. 334.

beer at pop concerts, sit in the front row at a Jim Corbett boxing exhibition, parade a lion on a leash, and don sackclothes and ashes to scrub the steps of the Church of the Advent during Lent. This was the bizarre lady who dressed little Gussie for church, listened to his exploits at sports, and read him the novels of Dickens.[33]

Far from giving a sign that he would one day be a respected congressman, Gussie as a young man was "opinionated and argumentative, and was not always easy to get along with" (his wife's appraisal).[34] After Harvard, where his classmates thought him conceited, he devoted himself to gentleman farming, playing polo, and riding to hounds.[35] Distinguished army service during the Spanish-American War, however, turned Gussie to more productive pursuits. And after two terms in the Massachusetts Senate he was elected to Congress in 1902. Henry Adams gossiped to Mrs. Cameron, ". . . Hay tells me that Gussy's seat is said to have been the most expensive ever bought in the House."[36]

A newspaper editor, who knew the Gardners well, considered him "somewhat rollicking, somewhat of a playboy," and his wife "quite a character" who "wrote with all the perkiness of her father, and with all the indiscretion, or more than he had." Constance and Gussie were not happy together, though they remained married and had a daughter.[37]

Yet Cabot Lodge observed Gussie's career "with a very evident thrill of pride," although the relationship cannot always have been comfortable for the younger man.[38] As Congressman Nicholas Longworth, the husband of Alice Roosevelt, remarked: "Poor old Gussie, it is our fate never to be known as anything but sons-in-law."[39]

Reporting on a conversation with Henry Cabot Lodge's mother in 1895, Roosevelt wrote him: "I told her I was so glad you were going abroad, for the recreation, whereupon she answered, 'Yes, my dear, and for his education; he is *very* young. . . .'"[40] (The senator was then a grandfather.) The group that was leaving for a summer of European edification consisted of Cabot and Nannie Lodge, their two sons, and Henry Adams. In London their reception at the American Embassy was less than enthusiastic—Lodge cordially detested Thomas F. Bayard, and the sentiment was returned in kind by the ambassador. But the English aristocracy entertained Cabot royally, a fitting tribute to the former colony's most rabid Anglophobe. With the mentality of a tour guide, the senator led his party on a frenzied round of museums and churches. For Henry Adams it was the beginning of the explorations that would culminate in his monumental *Mont-Saint-Michel*.

It was in such an atmosphere, an intense hothouse of culture, that the two Lodge boys had lived since birth.

The younger son, John Ellerton Lodge, then nineteen, was to become an outstanding expert on oriental art and languages, a man of impeccable, limpid taste, and the first curator of the Freer Gallery in Washington. (The art critic for the Boston *Herald* felt he "would have gone much higher than the Freer Gallery if he hadn't been a son of Henry Cabot Lodge. People dismissed him as a Senator's son, when he was a man of great scholarly ability."[41]) During an illness he married his nurse, Mary Connally, an Irish Catholic from Canada, whose brother was a noted theologian. This Lodge lived as something of a hermit, spending his days in a basement office poring over ancient Chinese histories and novels, and spinning tales of emperors and yogis to his childless wife, a "woman of gracious silences."[42]

But it was on his brother, twenty-two-year-old George Lodge, called "Bay," that the parents and their intimate circle lavished attention and admiration. "[He] was one of the most complete examples I have ever known of a young genius before whom an adoring family unites in smoothing the way," judged Edith Wharton.[43] Adolescence for Bay Lodge had meant hunting antelope with Teddy Roosevelt on his Elkhorn Ranch in the Dakotas; splendid isolations on Tuckernuck Island with Sturgis Bigelow, the Boston Buddhist; advice from Uncle Brooks Adams —"Fall in love with married women!"—and founding with Henry Adams a private political party, the Conservative Christian Anarchists. He lived in a world peopled exclusively by his father's famous, often eccentric friends; he breathed a rarefied air.

Yet Bay grew up to be a handsome, athletic creature, charming of manner, delightful, even brilliant in conversation, with a probing mind and a philosophic soul. After his father had helped goad the nation into war with Spain, Bay went off to fight on his uncle Charles Henry Davis' ship; then met his brother-in-law, Gussie Gardner, for an invasion of Ponce, Puerto Rico. (Unfortunately the natives were happy to see them, making a battle superfluous.) Like Teddy Roosevelt, he had the time of his life. On returning home he became his father's secretary; then eloped with beautiful heiress "Bessie" Davis, the granddaughter of Secretary of State Frederick Frelinghuysen.† The Lodges had notched another dynasty on their political gun handle.

Poetry, felt Bay, was to be his profession. He published several volumes, including *Cain*, a verse drama, in which the crusty Adam and the sympathetic Eve are recognizable as Senator and Mrs. Henry Cabot Lodge. (A friend asked how he was treating Adam. Answered Bay, "I am whitewashing him."[44]) But his work, though extravagantly praised by his father's friends, and sometimes marked by a grave rhetorical beauty, was generally muddy and imitative. Today it is unremembered. Edmund Wilson writes, "One cannot say that he was a bad poet: he was hardly a poet at all. . . ." Van Wyck Brooks was more generous.[45]

† See Frelinghuysen Dynasty, pp. 355–56.

Whether he might have developed into a first-rate talent is a moot question. At thirty-six, alone with his father on Sturgis Bigelow's island off Nantucket, Bay Lodge was seized with a heart attack. "So he died," wrote the stunned senator to Bigelow, "perfectly quietly, without a gasp or a struggle, in my arms, sitting in your big chair in the parlor by the dining table. So he died in my arms." In verse, his uncertain calling, Bay had composed what could stand as his autobiography:

> . . . This is the song of the wave, that died in the fullness of life.
> The prodigal this, that lavished its largeness of strength
> In the lust of achievement.
> Aiming at things for Heaven too high,
> Sure in the pride of life, in the richness of strength,
> So tried it the impossible height, till the end was found. . . .[46]

The surer hand of Henry James described him as "a great and abundant social luxury." Agreed, thought Margaret Chanler, "Bay himself was the poem."[47]

His family carried on, or tried to. The young widow (of whom Bay had written, "She moves in the dusk of my mind, like a bell with the sweetness of singing") had three small children to look after: Helena and two sons, Henry Cabot Lodge and John Davis Lodge, ages seven and six respectively.[48] But Nannie Lodge, Bay's mother, never recovered, and died within a few years, while Bay's father called on Henry Adams to establish his son's immortality. Adams failed: *The Life of George Cabot Lodge*, his last published work, had none of the starry presence of his young friend, which he himself had captured in letters, and which Edith Wharton was to put into her memoirs. Instead Adams used Bay's form to express his own fears of a world he looked upon as an unwelcome stranger. The love he had given Bay in life he could not (or would not) restore to him in death.[49] Adams turned rather to Bay's sons. "Saint Thomas" he called little Cabot, imagining in him a strikingly physical resemblance to Aquinas. "Your grandchildren are enough to atone for all my failures," he wrote the senator. "They are kind to me, but I feel how poor a wretch I am. What a world this must be for such giants."[50] The little boys, future senators and governors, found Great-uncle Brooks Adams to be rather menacing but adored honorary Uncle Henry Adams, whom they called "Dordy" for no apparent reason.[51]

If Bay Lodge's life was unfulfilled, Gussie Gardner's death was unnecessary. The congressman had made a name as the leader of the insurgents in their fight against the heavy hand of Speaker Cannon.[52] But his real mission was to awaken the American people to the need to arm. As early as 1914 he was preaching preparedness with the evangelical fervor of a Billy Sunday. British Ambassador Cecil Spring-Rice wrote some doggerel poking fun at his militant congressional friend:

> What does Gussie Gardner say,
> In his nest at break of day?
> "Wake up, every mother's son,
> Buy a double-barrelled gun,
> Shoot a Dutchman or a Jap,
> Or some other foreign Chap."[53]

A month after Wilson's declaration of war in 1917, Gussie resigned his seat in Congress to go on active duty. Colonel Gardner was sent to Camp Wheeler, six miles outside of Macon, Georgia, as adjutant of the "Dixie" Division. After a few months he had himself demoted to major in order to get a line assignment. "If I go abroad as a Staff Colonel," he wrote his wife, "I shall probably pass my time sitting at a desk in an office in Chalons, and see nothing."[54]

It was one of the coldest winters that Georgians could remember. On January 8, while in the field as commander of the 121st Infantry Battalion, Gussie contracted pneumonia. Six days later he died. He was fifty-three years old, and was known to have had a weak heart. From another hero who still looked upon war as a gallop up San Juan Hill came a message to the widow: ". . . to my own children's children it will be a matter of pride that I was his friend," signed "Theodore Roosevelt."[55]

The first of the great battles between the clans of Lodge and Kennedy took place in 1916 when the senator was challenged by John F. Fitzgerald, whose daughter Rose had married Joseph P. Kennedy. The odds against "Honey Fitz" were so long that as late as mid-October he was trying to withdraw from the contest. Fitz could not even count on the united support of the Boston Irish, for "Hinnery Cabin Lodge" (as "Mr. Dooley" called him) had led many a St. Patrick's Day parade and was the nation's chief puller of the British lion's tail. Michael E. Hennessy of the Boston *Globe* quoted a Democrat as predicting, ". . . he'll bury Fitzgerald so deep that the entire membership of the Shovelers Union will have to be called upon to dig him out."[56] Fitzgerald ran against Lodge's pedigree, telling rallies that his foe had once "stumbled into a course in medieval history and had never emerged. . . ."[57] But Lodge ignored his opponent and ran instead against Woodrow Wilson.

While riding on a train, one Dr. Bailey of Tufts Medical School had picked up a juicy political morsel from Henry C. Breckinridge. The former Assistant Secretary of War, in club-car conviviality, had confided that Wilson's Cabinet threatened to resign over a secret modifying postscript the President tagged on his strong note of protest to Germany over the sinking of the *Lusitania*. When this information was relayed to Lodge he promptly converted it into a campaign issue. In a statement to the press Breckinridge then charged that such "mongering of back-stairs gossip is beneath contempt," and Wilson branded the accusation "untrue" (though it was false in detail, not in substance).[58] The charge and countercharges had little effect on the election outcome. Lodge and Wilson won narrow victories. Fitzgerald, surprisingly, had lost by only 33,000 votes.

The "Breckinridge incident" was only one skirmish in the long war between Lodge and Wilson. And when the two "scholars in politics" finally fired their last shot, Wilson lay dying and the League of Nations was dead. The immediate verdict on who killed the League was awarded to Lodge, though later judgment is more apt to divide the honor. The League had been Wilson's dream, and Lodge in principle claimed to support it. Yet these two stubborn men hugged it to death. Henry Cabot Lodge, Jr., in later years defended his grandfather's action with the same ferocity that the senior Lodge had employed in defense of George Cabot's participation in the Hartford Convention. The future American ambassador to the United Nations blamed the failure of the United States to enter the League on the breakdown of Wilson's health —a circumstance conveniently beyond the power of man, even Henry Cabot Lodge, Sr.[59] If the President had not had a stroke, it can be reasoned, presumably he would have accepted the Lodge Reservations. But when Senator Watson told the President, before his stroke, that the only way the Senate would approve the League was with the Lodge Reservations, Wilson shot back, "*Lodge* reservations? Never! I'll never consent to adopt any policy with which that impossible name is so prominently identified."[60]

True, the acceptance of the Lodge Reservations would have insured American entrance into the League. But in assessing the blame for the debacle, one must also look to the motives of the Senate leader. Lodge fought, he honestly felt, for American honor. Yet his narrow partisanship and vindictiveness made his actions suspect. Some friends, notably Elihu Root, contended that had Nannie Lodge been alive he would have acted differently. His daughter Constance said: "My father hated and feared the Wilson League and his heart was really with the irreconcilables. But it was uncertain whether this League could be beaten straight out this way, and the object of his reservations was so to emasculate the Wilson League that if it did pass it would be valueless and the United States would be honorably safeguarded. My father never wanted the Wilson League, and when it was finally defeated he was like a man from whom a great burden was lifted."[61]

Lodge's action had its supporters, of course, but they were not apparently among the Cabots, the ancient family whose kinship he so highly regarded. When the official Cabot history was written, the senator was dismissed as unfortunately "not a man of a large and more generous nature," whose fight with Wilson was motivated by "a petty and jealous nature." This opinion was not the author's alone, he said, "but the carefully considered judgment of the family."[62]

Except for the battle royal with Wilson, Lodge's political life was spent on the steps of the throne. He had been Roosevelt's courtier, not his heir apparent. In 1908, as chairman of the convention, he had dutifully officiated at the coronation of William Howard Taft. Once, in 1916, Roosevelt actually proposed Lodge for the presidential nomination, but the delegates thought it a joke and there is reason to doubt that even Teddy took his suggestion seriously.

Lodge was a kingmaker, not a king. In 1920 he was again chairman of the Republican Convention. As the gathering wilted through five steamy days in Chicago, Chairman Lodge coolly looked down from the rostrum. Though he put on a fresh collar every morning, H. L. Mencken thought it "a sentimental concession to the Harvard tradition. He might have worn the same one all week."[63] Humidity and humility left him untroubled. Then after the delegates had thoroughly confused matters, Lodge was part of the senatorial cabal that stepped in. In an act of selfless devotion to party, "Cabot the palladium of correctness, the super-grammarian" (again the choice of words is Mencken's), anointed Warren Gamaliel Harding, a quasi-illiterate with a fondness for corrupting the English language.[64] This was Cabot Lodge's last major political act.

By the time of the next Republican Convention there was a new President, Calvin Coolidge, who had also supplanted the senator as boss of Massachusetts.[65] Lodge—nine times a national delegate, three times permanent chairman, twice chairman of the platform committee, once temporary chairman—was ignored by his party. At Cleveland he sat in the hotel room he shared with his grandson and calmly read a volume of Shakespeare. Immediately after the polls closed in November he died, leaving an estate of $1,249,825.[66]

It was Bessie Lodge who had to be both mother and father to Cabot, John, and Helena, who laughed at their jokes, gathered them around the piano to sing the patter songs of Gilbert and Sullivan, read them a section daily from the Old Testament, and took them away to Paris for two years. Yet the old senator had a more than grandfatherly role in the raising of Bay Lodge's children. And toward his namesake he bore special ambition. When Cabot was ten the grandfather wrote him: "You know how at Nahant in autumn we see those long lines of birds flying South. Well one of those migratory birds as they are called came over the ocean the other day and whispered in my ear that you were lazy at school."[67] The boy was given a lecture for using "will" instead of "shall." But the senior Lodge could also be approving when Cabot measured up to expected standards. At Harvard he presented him with a mink-lined raccoon coat! The embarrassed undergraduate suggested that this glamorous garment should be exchanged for two of the conventional model, one for himself and one for John.[68]

A classmate, theatrical critic John Mason Brown, remembers Cabot at college as an extroverted, cocksure youth, whose "assurance was often mistaken for arrogance. . . ."[69] His grandfather's fight over the League made him a center of controversy in the Yard. While Bob Taft at Harvard had done everything possible to duck the notoriety of his name, young Lodge was less reticent. When Cabot and two friends, returning from a dance, were arrested for speeding, the policeman asked the driver's name.

"I am Henry Cabot Lodge, sir."

Then he asked the others for their names.

"Alexander Hamilton."

"Paul Revere."

"That's enough out of all of you," said the officer, and took them to the station house.[70]

As a boy Cabot had written a half-column article for the Boston *Herald* on how to fight the mosquito. (The editor wanted to title it, "Diversity of Intellectual Interests of the Lodge Family."[71]) After graduation from college Cabot continued his newspaper career as a reporter for the *Transcript,* that now defunct organ of gentility which arrived daily except Sunday, just at teatime, on the doorstep of every Proper Bostonian. (The story was untrue, but appropriate, that a Back Bay butler once announced, "Two reporters from the papers, sir, and a gentleman from the *Transcript.*") The other writers recall that the new gentleman swung his weight around and worked as he pleased.[72] But Lodge was also inventive enough to expose the Ku Klux Klan, and versatile enough to review the dancing of Pavlova. All the while Grandfather looked over his shoulder, and on the eve of the 1924 Republican Convention the old senator told editor Theodore J. Joslin: "I want Cabot to go to the Convention. I could, of course, take him with me, but I would prefer to have him go there as a working newspaperman. I make this personal request to you: Handle him as you would any other man. Be hard on him, for I want him to learn everything he possibly can there. Cabot thinks that he wants to be a newspaperman. He believes that some day he will have a newspaper of his own. That may be his calling, but I want to confide in you by saying that I hope the day may come when he will be sitting here where I am sitting. . . . My fondest hope is that the time will come when he will see his future as I believe that I foresee it."[73]

In 1926, now a Washington reporter for the New York *Herald Tribune*, Cabot married tall, blond Emily Sears. Her genealogy traced back to Richard Sears, "the Pilgrim," who arrived on Cape Cod in 1630, and, like the three previous generations of Lodge wives, she included in her pedigree a United States senator—Great-great-grandfather Jonathan Mason, whose career in politics was less auspicious than the role he played in developing Beacon Hill into the fashionable residential district of Boston in the year 1795.‡

The Sears-Lodge wedding was the social event of the year. They were married in Beverly, where the main street is named after George Cabot; the ushers included a Frelinghuysen; the reception was at the Cove, the Searses' summer home, and many of the guests came by yacht. Later the Searses would build the young Lodges their own French provincial villa on the estate. Although Bessie Lodge was to leave $900,000 to her three children, the infusion of Sears money could not have been unwelcome to a dynasty that had not engaged in trade for two generations.[74]

There was another fashionable Lodge wedding in 1929; also one less fashionable. In August, from her summer residence at Bar Harbor, Mrs. George Cabot Lodge announced the engagement of her daughter Helena to Edouard de Streel, first secretary of the Belgian Embassy. The next month the wedding was held at the former home of Senator Lodge on Massachusetts Avenue. Prince de Ligne, the Belgian ambassador, motored over to Washington from Gibson Island to act as best man.[75] Later Helena's husband was knighted.§

However, after John Davis Lodge's wedding the Cabots continued to converse with God but no longer exclusively. For his bride was Francesca Braggiotti, a beautiful blond dancer.

There has never been a family quite like the Braggiottis—unless it is the fictional Sangers in Margaret Kennedy's *The Constant Nymph*. When mezzo-soprano Lily Schlesinger wed tenor Isadore Braggiotti in 1900 they moved into a vanilla-colored stucco palazzo on a hill overlooking Florence and turned it into a *Scuola di Cante* for wealthy American debutantes. They also practiced Hindu philosophy, read aloud from the Bhagavad-Gita, became vegetarians, and raised eight children.

‡ Jonathan Mason (1752–1831), a Boston lawyer, studied under John Adams and Josiah Quincy. He served as a Federalist senator (1800–3) and as a member of the House of Representatives (1817–30). For the genealogy of the Sears family, see Ruth Lawrence, editor, *Colonial Families of America* (New York: National Americana Society, 1928), Vol. IV, pp. 58–71.

§ The Baron and Baroness de Streel now live in Brussels. After twenty years as equerry to Queen Elizabeth (widow of King Albert and mother of King Leopold), the baron went into business. They have three children: Jacqueline (who is married to a Belgian banker), Quentin (a sales representative in Norwalk, Connecticut), and Elizabeth (whose husband works for IBM in Belgium). Letter from Mrs. John Davis Lodge to author, August 4, 1964.

Every Saturday there would be a musicale presided over by Papa Braggiotti in a violet dinner jacket. The little ones sang, danced, played piano, violin, and cello. Since the parents believed that regimentation stifles a child's creative impulses, they also did other things, such as perform for a group of English ladies as "naked devils" with twigs sticking out of their "fannies."

The Braggiotti children, in advance of Sheldon's constitutional psychology, attached special significance to the shape of the body, specifically to people's behinds. These they carefully categorized: *culo ritto* (sturdy and firm), *culo dondola* (droopy), *culo piatto* (flat), *culo largo* (wide), and *culo da Joe* (swung in like that of a friend named Joe.)[76] By the Italians they were considered "those crazy Americans." By the Americans, after they arrived in Boston in 1919, they were considered "those crazy Italians."

Francesca and her sister Berta opened a dance studio over the firehouse in Brookline. For a public performance, sponsored by the exclusive Vincent Club, the mayor was asked to pass on the decency of their costumes, which, while much too scanty to be allowed on a public beach, were approved for educational purposes. Amy Lowell was so enchanted that she composed a poem in Francesca's honor; Isabella Stewart Gardner summoned them to a private audience at Fenway Court. Soon they had society girls dancing barefooted on the lawns of palatial estates.

The studio was the family's primary support; poor Papa had no head for business and preferred his hobbies—playing bridge, feeding the lions at the zoo, and sharpening pencils.

Francesca Braggiotti and John Davis Lodge met when she was invited to appear in a play given by the Cercle Français at Harvard, of which he was president. When he came to call he enjoyed roughhousing with his date's younger brothers and sisters. Cabot, however, was less able to enter into the spirit of the family. Having listened to Papa's stories at dinner, he turned to one of the younger Braggiottis and asked in evident irritation, "Gloria, why do you have to laugh so loud?"[77]

After John graduated from Harvard Law School he and Francesca were married. They then moved to New York, where he entered a Wall Street law firm and she entered a Broadway show, *The Vanderbilt Review.*¶

¶ Of John Davis Lodge's flamboyant in-laws, the best known is Mario Braggiotti, who with Jacques Fray created the duo-piano craze during the 1920s. Fray and Braggiotti claimed to be the first piano team to play both classical and jazz on the same program. Their radio performances featured Braggiotti's arrangement of "Yankee Doodle" in imitation of Bach, Beethoven, Chopin, Debussy, Gershwin, Mozart, Puccini, Schubert, Strauss, and Rachmaninoff. See New York *Times*, October 30, 1931, p. 27.

Of the other living Braggiottis, Sebastian is a retired actor who runs a gift

Newspaper assignments had taken Henry Cabot Lodge, Jr., from Boston City Hall to the London Naval Conference. He had covered three presidential conventions, interviewed Mussolini, and toured the Far East to report on colonial administrations. He wrote one book, *The Cult of Weakness*, an indifferent tract on the dangers of peace through unpreparedness. (Although the *Transcript* thought "it is an excellent book and every voter ought to read it," the sales were slight.[78]) Journalism, as his grandfather had told him, proved to be "at least the equal of the law as training for political life." So in 1932 he entered the race in Essex County for the Massachusetts House of Representatives, waged a door-to-door campaign, and was elected.

That year John Davis Lodge began his career as a movie actor.

Francesca had gone to Hollywood to be the Italian voice of Greta Garbo when one of the great Swede's pictures was being dubbed for export. Her husband came to visit, was given a screen test, and signed a contract with Paramount Pictures. "The news of Mr. Lodge's entry into motion pictures has caused considerable surprise here," reported the Boston *Herald*. "The Lodge family has so long been associated with the more orthodox professions. . . ."[79] Although it was predicted that the handsome newcomer would make his film debut opposite Mae West in *She Done Him Wrong*, the part went to Cary Grant, and Lodge settled for a Grade B thriller called *Murders in the Zoo*, in which he was strangled by "the Great Mamba," a giant serpent. He subsequently played a cattle rustler in *Under the Tonto Rim*, Shirley Temple's father in *The Little Colonel*, Frances Dee's boy friend in *Little Women*, and Marlene Dietrich's lover in *The Scarlet Empress*. But for most of his three years in Hollywood John Lodge (he dropped "Davis" for the screen) drew his salary and waited for parts that never came. Paramount had just too many he-man types around, stars like Gary Cooper and Randolph Scott. So in the summer of 1935 Lodge sailed for Europe and a new start in British films as "the Man Hollywood Forgot."

While Lodge was appearing in such cinema classics as *Bulldog Drummond at Bay* and *Queer Cargo*, his brother announced his candidacy for the United States Senate. It was 1936. Franklin D. Roosevelt was running for a second term, and the Republican leaders in Massachusetts were happy enough to have the thirty-four-year-old state legislator as a sacrificial lamb. The Democratic candidate was Governor James M. Curley, seasoned veteran of four decades of political fighting. Cabot Lodge soon found out that his opponent had not learned his politics at

shop of international novelties in Ogunquit, Maine; Gloria, a columnist for the Philadelphia *Inquirer*, is married to artist Emlen Etting; Rama is a free-lance cartoonist; and Chadwick is a retired U.S. foreign service officer, whose last post was as consul general at Bordeaux. Interview with Chadwick Braggiotti, October 13, 1965.

Harvard. Curley reminded Jewish groups that the Republican candidate's grandfather had opposed the confirmation of Louis D. Brandeis to the Supreme Court; he called Cabot "Little Boy Blue" and "Little Henry"; he told a Springfield rally, "You young Republicans have no more chance to join the Somerset Club than I have, if your ancestors didn't get rich in the first two or three generations by selling opium to the Chinese, rum to the Indians or getting in the slave racket."[80] Lodge ignored these attacks, traveled 43,000 miles, and made 680 speeches on national issues. When the ballots were counted Roosevelt carried Massachusetts by 174,000 votes; Henry Cabot Lodge, Jr., was elected by 136,000 votes, the only Republican to take a Democratic Senate seat. Curley claimed he had lost because of a third candidate in the race, supported by Father Coughlin, whom he had unsuccessfully offered $10,000 to withdraw. But his biographer credits his defeat to "his awful mistakes and excesses as governor" and to his being "completely out of touch with the rank and file."[81]

The nation discovered that the second Senator Henry Cabot Lodge was tall, a shade under six feet three, with as much the appearance of a virile leading man as his brother. As a politician he was a handshaker, but too much the Back Bay aristocrat to be a backslapper. Said a friend, "He's tried hard to be a regular fellow, but it just isn't in him. He'll never be mistaken for a common man."[82] Even when he became the first man to fall out of the presiding officer's chair in the Senate, he responded with an aplomb that would have pleased his ancestors. While Senator Reynolds of North Carolina was speaking against an anti-lynching bill in 1938, Cabot leaned too far backward and toppled over with a crash. After a pause Senator Lodge said, "The gentleman should not be so eloquent," and picked himself up.[83]

Yet, like his grandfather, he never forgot where the votes were, and increasingly they could be found in South Boston. His habit of never missing an important Irish funeral prompted President Truman's secretary, David K. Niles, to say, "You oughtn't to go to so many Irish funerals, Cabot, because it looks as if you just like to see dead Irishmen."[84] And even when he became ambassador to the United Nations Lodge continued to wear a green tie on St. Patrick's Day, a gesture that reporters covering the UN thought was carrying domestic political considerations too far.[85]

On domestic issues Senator Lodge was a middle-of-the-roader—sometimes liberal, sometimes conservative, sometimes evasive. In 1937 he was one of just two Republicans to vote for the Fair Labor Standards Act, which set minimum wages and maximum hours; but he also voted against the slum-clearance bill (1937), increased appropriations for public works projects to relieve unemployment (1939), and an amendment to the

Social Security Act to increase funds for the care of crippled children (1942).

He was a determined isolationist: against repeal of the Neutrality Act; against aid to Britain in May 1940. "The war in Europe is not our fight," he said in the fall of 1939. "If the British and French empires cannot stand without our help, they deserve to fall."[86] Yet he was also a proponent of a strong national defense. Since 1924 Lodge had been active in the army reserve. Each summer, as a cavalry officer, he pounded the trails with his unit. In 1952 he told a reporter, ". . . I'll always miss the maneuvers in Texas and New Mexico before the cavalry was mechanized. There's no more pleasant experience in life than waking up at first light and watching your horse's ears take shape against the far horizon."[87] A magazine profile described this army association as "actually the essence of Lodge."[88]

As Hitler massed his Panzer divisions for the attack on France, John Davis Lodge was in the little town of Romans-sur-Isère, fifty miles south of Lyons. Since going to Europe he had made fourteen films in England, France, and Italy. Mostly he had been cast in tough-guy roles—detectives, city editors, criminal lawyers, sea captains. "Heroes with a menace," he called them. But this time he was playing the ill-starred Archduke Franz Ferdinand in *Mayerling to Sarajevo*. As production began in June 1939 the newspapers were filled with articles noting that twenty-five years ago the Austrian's assassination had touched off a World War. Now Europe was on the brink of another war. From day to day the population of Romans-sur-Isère, who was being used as extras in the mob scenes, kept decreasing, as one class after another was called to the front. The film finally opened in May 1940 at the Marignan Theater on the Champs Elysées; in June the Nazis marched into Paris and destroyed all the prints they could find because of its Hapsburg sympathies.[89] By this time Lodge was back in the United States, having returned in February aboard the *Conte di Savoia* along with 550 refugees.

The actor bought a nine-and-a-half-acre estate at Westport, Connecticut, bordered on three sides by the Aspetuck River, with a small island, swimming pool, and waterfall. He starred on Broadway in a Shubert musical, *Night of Love*, which flopped after six nights, but his performance led to an important part in Lillian Hellman's *Watch on the Rhine*, the high point of his acting career. Then in the summer of 1942 he joined the navy as a lieutenant.

Though still a senator, Henry Cabot Lodge had also gone on active duty. After nine Stukas fired on him near Tobruk, he wrote, ". . . a ludicrous thought flashed through my mind. I was safe, but it certainly wasn't due to Senatorial immunity. It was luck and that handy slit trench."[90] His request for further service was turned down by the Secretary of War, and he returned to Washington.

In 1942 Lodge ran for re-election against Joseph Casey, the brightest of the young Irish New Dealers in the House of Representatives. It was a straight-out contest between a prewar isolationist and a strong interventionist. The Citizens Committee for Casey included four Cabots. But the defection was more than compensated for by the large number of Boston Irish whose isolationist convictions were stronger than their loyalty to the Democratic Party. Lodge won by 80,000 votes.[91]

Two years later Lodge resigned as a legislator, the first person to leave the Senate for military service since the Civil War. Wrote President Roosevelt, "Dear Cabot . . . I would do just what you are doing if I could. I missed the guns in 1917–18. It's too late now. I envy you the opportunity that is yours and I congratulate you on the decision you have made."[92] Lieutenant Colonel Lodge's record in the Mediterranean and European theaters earned him a Bronze Star, Legion of Merit, six battle stars, and France's Legion of Honor and Croix de Guerre with palm. John Davis Lodge's war years, though less heroic, included overseas assignments as censor during the invasion of Sicily, naval historian at the Salerno landing, and liaison officer with the French navy in the Toulon area. He too was decorated by General de Gaulle.

After the war Cabot ran for the Senate against David I. Walsh, who had been serving continuously in Washington since he had won the seat left vacant by the death of Grandfather Lodge. Like his younger opponent, Walsh had been a rabid pre-Pearl Harbor isolationist, a position he continued to maintain. But Cabot had changed. "I was 100 per cent wrong in believing we could stay out of World War II," he said. "I am now an older and a wiser man."[93] Cabot was overwhelmingly elected, winning sixty per cent of the vote.

The war also changed John Davis Lodge. Returning home, he got a research job in New York City, and a few months later, when Connecticut Congresswoman Clare Boothe Luce decided not to seek re-election, he threw his hat in the ring. Luck was with the former actor, who had never shown an interest in politics, had never made a political speech, and was unknown in the district where he had bought a house four years before. For various reasons the other three announced candidates for the Republican nomination were unacceptable to the party leaders. It went to Lodge by acclamation. With his black Homburg, his Bond Street suit, his Harvard accent, and his stage mannerisms, Lodge was an utterly new phenomenon to the industrial workers of Bridgeport, the district's principal city. Moreover, his Democratic opponent was Colonel Henry A. Mucci, Italian-American, Bridgeport-born, West Point-trained, the liberator of the Bataan death march survivors. When Mucci had returned home, the citizens of Bridgeport greeted him at the railroad station with a brass band; he campaigned for Congress in army uniform, his chest a dazzle of medals and campaign ribbons.

The turning point came when the two candidates addressed a Columbus Day rally of Italian-Americans at South Norwalk. Mucci spoke first, calling attention to his ancestry and humble origin. Lodge paid tribute to the colonel's war record and said some nice things about the Italians he had met when he fought in Italy. Then the amazing happened: Lodge suddenly switched languages and delivered the rest of his talk in purest Florentine Italian. Poor Mucci, it turned out, could not speak his parents' native tongue! The news of Lodge's achievement and Mucci's embarrassment quickly spread through the district. From then on the Lodge campaign resembled an Italian street carnival. Francesca appeared at rallies in a blue military cape of the Treviso Regiment, a unit that had been stationed at Florence during her childhood; she danced the tarantella, sang Italian folk songs, and lectured on beauty care. Lodge had been derisively called "the Carpetbagger from Massachusetts," but he won the election by 36,000 votes, the largest majority in any of the six congressional districts of Connecticut.

While Representative John Davis Lodge was serving two terms in the House of Representatives, his brother was coming to the fore at the other end of the Capitol. In 1949 Henry Cabot Lodge challenged Robert Taft for the leadership of the Republicans in the Senate. Taft overwhelmed him by a vote of 28 to 14. Noted Senator Arthur Vandenberg in his diary, "I deeply regretted that I could not vote for Lodge in this instance. He is one of my most precious friends. . . . I fully expect him to be a Republican President of the United States—and I hope I live long enough to have the chance to help put him in the White House."[94] (Ironically, columnist William S. White feels that, had not the 1949 rebellion driven a bitter wedge between the conservatives and liberals in the GOP, "Lodge might well have been nominated for President in 1964."[95])

Whether Lodge himself had such an ambition might be judged by an interview with a Boston *Post* reporter. "Nobody who knows the government would like to be President," said the senator. "Look at the pictures of Roosevelt since he first took office. You can see the lines in his face deepen, the sag of his chin, the look of weariness in his face." Mrs. Lodge shuddered, adding, "You know I just hate to talk about it. It's my nightmare."[96]

In 1950 John Davis Lodge challenged incumbent Chester Bowles for the governorship of Connecticut. Billboards proclaimed Lodge as "The Man You Can Believe." There was a record turnout for an off-year election, and as the early returns came in from the state's industrial areas,

Bowles piled up a commanding lead. The margin, however, was steadily whittled down as the small towns reported, and Lodge was finally elected by 17,000 votes. The voters had probably been more intent on defeating Bowles than on electing Lodge, for the governor had made many enemies within his own party and among powerful business and professional groups. Nonetheless, the result meant that there now was a Lodge governor of one state and a Lodge senator from another.

Senator Lodge went to Hartford to watch his brother inaugurated as the seventy-fifth governor of Connecticut. As has been the custom since 1771, the governor-elect was escorted to the State House by Foot Guard in colonial uniforms and saluted with swords and flintlocks. Then the colorful pageant ground to a halt. The Democratic-controlled state Senate found an excuse to delay the swearing-in ceremony for ten hours. Senator Lodge finally had to take a train back to Washington. At eight minutes to midnight his younger brother became governor and proceeded to read a long message on how he would get the state's financial house in order.*

For four years Lodge wrestled with the Democratic state Senate and with a faction of his own party. Except for construction of the Connecticut Turnpike, he ran an "austerity" administration. By clamping down on the personal use of state-owned cars alone he realized an annual savings of $200,000. When he left office he had turned an $11,000,000 deficit into a $17,000,000 surplus. "It is unfortunate that more of the people of Connecticut do not know this story," wrote his press agents. "It is not easy to dramatize plain devotion to duty and principle, but we have somehow got to show them the picture of this man Lodge, working 12 and 15 hours a day, staying up until 3 and 4 A.M., working on the budget—saving ten dollars here, a hundred dollars there, and more than a million in another place."[97]

On September 4, 1951, Senator Lodge visited Dwight Eisenhower at NATO headquarters in Paris. His mission was to convince the general that he should become a candidate for the Republican presidential nomination. Thinking to put the senator on the defensive, Eisenhower asked, "Why not run yourself?" "Because I cannot be elected," answered Lodge without a pause. This conversation, thought Eisenhower, marked the turning point in his career.[98]

Primarily because he was acceptable to both Governor Thomas Dewey

---

* Governor Lodge appointed a cousin as his administrative assistant. William Amory Gardner Minot (1916–63) was Constance Lodge Gardner's grandson. After Lodge left office Minot became deputy director of the U. S. Foreign Operation Administration in France. In 1958 he was elected to the Connecticut General Assembly and was Republican chairman of Greenwich at the time of his death. See New York *Times,* July 30, 1963, p. 30.

of New York and Pennsylvania's Senator James Duff, who distrusted each other, Lodge was named head of the "Draft Eisenhower" movement. Pulling no punches as campaign manager, he called the disputed Taft delegations "zombies," said they were employing "shyster methods," and were trying to turn the convention into a "kangaroo court." Eisenhower won the nomination, and Lodge won the deep enmity of the Taft partisans, which would haunt him in his own campaign for reelection to the Senate.†

The 1952 race between Congressman John Fitzgerald Kennedy and Senator Henry Cabot Lodge was the second confrontation between the two dynasties; Grandfather Fitzgerald had lost to Grandfather Lodge thirty-six years earlier. Besides their inherited place in politics, the two candidates bore other superficial similarities. They were both tall, handsome, and rich; both Harvard men with newspaper experience; both possessors of distinguished war records. Lodge was the distinct favorite, the winner of three previous state-wide campaigns against leading Irish Catholic politicians (Curley, Casey, and Walsh).

Yet there was one minor incident in Lodge's past that might have given him cause to reflect on the election's outcome. In 1938 Ambassador Joseph P. Kennedy had wanted to end the practice of presenting American debutantes at the Court of St. James's. Lodge agreed with him and the two decided that the action would be taken in a letter denying a request by Lodge for presentation of a Massachusetts girl. But when the letter was published Lodge was amazed to read in the newspapers that he had been "sharply turned down in his aristocratic attempt to present a Boston damsel of blue Back Bay blood by a sturdy red-haired Irish Bostonian of true democratic instincts . . . the Kennedys and the Fitzgeralds had shown the Cabots and the Lodges what real Americanism should be."[99] In a contest with the ambassador's son, could Lodge expect to maintain his carefully cultivated popularity with the state's Irish Catholic voters?

Basically it was not a battle of issues. In some areas, Kennedy's researchers pointed out, their candidate was actually closer to Taft's position than was their Republican opponent. It was a battle of charm. The senator's sister-in-law, Francesca Braggiotti Lodge, came to Massachusetts to address Italian-American audiences. But the Lodges were outnumbered and outcharmed. In one of the shortest known political speeches, Bobby Kennedy indicated the tremendous reservoir of family

† Though some attributed Lodge's subsequent defeat to the unreconstructed Taft men in Massachusetts, such as publisher Basil Brewer of the New Bedford *Standard-Times,* Taft himself backed Lodge, and sent letters to his followers in the state saying that the liberal Republican leader ought to be returned to the Senate for the good of the party. See William S. White, *The Taft Story* (New York: Harper, 1954), p. 182.

that could be thrown into a breech: "My brother Jack couldn't be here, my mother couldn't be here, my sister Eunice couldn't be here, my sister Pat couldn't be here, my sister Jean couldn't be here, but if my brother Jack were here, he'd tell you Lodge has a very bad voting record. Thank you."[100] Kennedy was elected by a 70,737-vote margin.

While Lodge lost, Eisenhower carried Massachusetts and the nation. One of the new President's first acts was to appoint his preconvention manager as American ambassador to the United Nations, with cabinet status and seniority just below the Secretary of State. Many found it ironic that the name most associated with the defeat of the League of Nations should now sit in the United Nations. Not so, thought the second Henry Cabot Lodge. In fact, he contended, a step-by-step analysis would show that all of Grandfather's reservations on the League Covenant had been incorporated in the UN Charter. ". . . it appears that my grandfather was essentially way ahead of his time."[101]

Much to the chagrin of professional diplomats, Lodge asserted his independence of the State Department, so that, in the opinion of veteran diplomat Robert Murphy, "our mission [to the UN] behaved less like an embassy than a second Foreign Office of the United States Government."[102] The Lodge policy was to offer instantaneous rebuttal to Communist charges. When Tsarapkin sought recognition at a Security Council meeting, Lodge asked, "For what purpose does the gentleman from the Soviet Union seek the floor?" Angrily Tsarapkin shouted, "I'm a delegate, not a gentleman!" Replied Lodge, "I had hoped that the two were not mutually exclusive."[103] This was the sort of talk that Americans came to expect of Lodge during his eight years at the United Nations; it became popular television entertainment. Rather like a Western movie, thought Marya Mannes of the *Reporter*—except that the saloon was made of glass, the bar was a curved table, and the battle between the good guys and the bad guys was with words instead of bullets. "In Henry Cabot Lodge, the American people have had a hero so exactly tailored to their dreams that no script writer could have improved on him."[104] Lodge's performance, however, was less popular among European diplomats, according to Joseph C. Harsch of NBC, who "felt that by attempting always to answer the Russians in kind, he succeeded only in annoying or antagonizing the friends of the West without having any effect on the Russians themselves. . . ."[105]

When Governor John Davis Lodge came up for re-election in 1954 his Democratic opponent was Congressman Abraham A. Ribicoff of Hartford. It was a quiet campaign until the last week. Lodge was running as "The Man Who Gets Things Done"; Ribicoff was appealing for economy in government. Then in the Hartford suburb of Berlin, before a rally of Italian-Americans, Ribicoff announced that the "American

Dream" would be fulfilled if he were elected—"Nowhere except in the Democratic party could a boy named Abe Ribicoff be nominated for governor of this state." The Republicans charged that this was a form of reverse bigotry; Ribicoff, in reply, justified his statement by citing some stories from New York newspapers as evidence that his opponents were conducting an undercover smear campaign against him; Lodge continued to talk exclusively on his record in office. The returns from Hartford, where Ribicoff piled up a margin of over 25,000 votes, decided the contest and Lodge lost by 3115.[106]

The Eisenhower Administration promptly shuffled its top diplomatic positions to make room for the defeated governor as ambassador to Spain. And the Senate quickly confirmed Lodge for the $25,000-a-year post with objections only from Senators Langer of North Dakota and Welker of Idaho, who were protesting that the small states had not got a fair share of major appointments.

The thirty-six Republican leaders whom Richard M. Nixon called together immediately after he had been made the 1960 Republican presidential nominee were agreed that Henry Cabot Lodge would add the most strength to the ticket. He was popular in the East, where Nixon considered himself weakest; he was a well-known personality, thanks to the televised debates at the United Nations; and he would help focus attention on international affairs. Nixon is reported to have told the meeting, "If you ever let them [the Democrats] campaign only on domestic issues, they'll beat us—our only hope is to keep it on foreign policy."[107]

While flying to Chicago to accept the nomination, Lodge told reporters that he was grateful to John F. Kennedy, the Democratic presidential candidate: "If I hadn't lost to Jack [in 1952], I never would have had eight years at the U.N., and I might not be running for Vice President." He added with a grin, "In fact, we're related, somehow. One of his cousins is related to a brother of one of my daughters-in-law." Remembering how Curley had called him "Little Boy Blue," Lodge promised, "Never, never, during this campaign will I refer to Jack's age. I know just how he feels."[108]

The Republican vice-presidential candidate campaigned with his wife Emily. Her sister, who is married to a prominent Democratic politician,‡ once told an interviewer, "I've never known anyone who enjoys life more. She's like a freshet of water springing out of the earth. . . . She is literally never bored. It's that delicious quality of her ridiculousness—

‡ Jean Sears is married to Archibald Stevens Alexander (1906–   ), Assistant and Under Secretary of the Army, 1949–52; unsuccessful Democratic candidate for U. S. Senate from New Jersey, 1948 and 1952; national director of Volunteers for Stevenson-Kefauver, 1956.

William Henry Harrison

1773-1841

Although he was elected President as the "log cabin" candidate, his father was a
wealthy Virginia plantation owner and a signer of the Declaration of Independence.

Benjamin Harrison
1833-1901
During his successful presidential campaign Harrison supporters sang, "Yes, Grandfather's hat fits Ben." They might also have added that his father was a congressman.

William Henry Harrison
1896-
The Harrisons continue to move westward. This grandson of President Benjamin Harrison represented Wyoming in Congress for four terms.

John Cabell Breckinridge

1821-1875

One of the best looking of a family known for its handsome men, he was the youngest Vice President of the United States and later Confederate Secretary of War.

William Campbell Preston Breckinridge

1837-1904

His promising congressional career was ended by a messy law suit which his former mistress won.

Israel Washburn, Jr.
1813-1883
Oldest of the four Washburn brothers in Congress, he also served as governor of Maine during the Civil War.

Elihu Benjamin Washburne
1816-1887
As chairman of the House Appropriations Committee he was the most politically powerful of the family.

Cadwallader Colden Washburn
1818-1882
Besides serving in Congress and as governor of Wisconsin, he was the first
millionaire in the dynasty.

*William Drew
Washburn*
1831-1912
He made a fortune in the Minnesota flour-
milling industry and was the only one of
the famous brothers to be elected to the
Senate.

Theodore Frelinghuysen
1787-1861

When he was the Whig candidate for Vice President in 1844 party publicists had difficulty fitting his surname into campaign slogans. They finally settled on "Hurah! Hurah! The country's risin'/For Henry Clay and Frelinghuysen."

Frederick Theodore Frelinghuysen
1817-1885

Through dynastic intermarriage this former Secretary of State became the great-grandfather of Henry Cabot Lodge, Jr., and John Davis Lodge.

Peter Hood Ballantine Frelinghuysen
1916-

This fifth Frelinghuysen in Congress represents the New Jersey district in which his family has lived for two and a half centuries.

Alphonso Taft

1810-1891

He settled in Cincinnati in 1839 and brought fame for the first time to the Taft family by serving in the Cabinet of President Grant.

William Howard Taft

1857-1930

His wife and brothers wanted him to be President; he preferred to be Chief Justice of the Supreme Court. Eventually he served in both positions—the only person in American history to have done so.

Robert Alphonso Taft
1889-1953
His party called him "Mr. Republican" yet thrice refused to give him the
presidential nomination.

Charles Phelps Taft
1897–

President Taft's youngest son has been mayor of Cincinnati and now heads a national organization of moderate Republicans. *(Carl Carlson photo.)*

David Sinton Ingalls
1899-

His Taft grandfather owned the Cincinnati *Times-Star,* which Ingalls sold in 1958. He was also a leading figure in his cousin Bob's attempts to be President. *(Photo by Halle-Spiegel Portrait Studios.)*

Robert Taft, Jr.
1917-

He has a reputation as a better "mixer" than his father, but he was defeated when he tried to go from the House of Representatives to the Senate in 1964.

Robert Field Stockton
1795-1866
Known as "Fighting Bob" or "the Navy's Problem Child," he later served in the Senate where he concerned himself with naval affairs.

John Potter Stockton
1826-1900
His support of President Andrew Johnson resulted in his expulsion from the Senate and may have changed the course of Reconstruction.

Russell Billiu Long
1918-

He is the only person in American history to have been preceded in the U.S. Senate by both his father and his mother.

Gillis William Long
1923-

Considered "cosmopolitan" by central Louisiana standards, he was defeated for reelection to the House of Representatives by cousin Speedy O. Long. *(Photo by Richard Townley)*

Speedy O. Long
1928–

Although the dynasty has been active in politics for only a half century, he is now the sixth Long to serve in Congress.

Henry Cabot Lodge, Sr.
1850-1924
The powerful chairman of the Senate Foreign Relations Committee expected his grandson and namesake to be a U.S. senator.

Henry Cabot Lodge, Jr.
1902-
Like his grandfather, he was extremely popular with the Boston Irish—until he was opposed by John F. Kennedy. *(Photo by Leo Rosenthal.)*

John Davis Lodge and Family
1903-

From left to right: daughter Beatrice Lodge de Oyarzabal, wife of a Spanish diplomat; Mrs. John Davis Lodge, the former Francesca Braggiotti; John Davis Lodge, ex-Governor of Connecticut; and daughter Lily Lodge Marcus, an actress before her marriage to a New York businessman.

George Cabot Lodge
1927-
He had the misfortune of being pitted against Edward M. Kennedy in his first race for elective office.

John F. Kennedy and Family
1917-1963
From left to right: Jacqueline Bouvier Kennedy; John F. Kennedy, Jr.; the President; and Caroline Kennedy.

Robert F. Kennedy and Family

1925-

Back row: Mary Courtney Kennedy; the New York Senator; Mary Kerry Kennedy; wife Ethel Skakel Kennedy holding Christopher Kennedy; Joseph Kennedy. Front row: Kathleen Kennedy; Michael Kennedy; David Kennedy; and Robert F. Kennedy, Jr. This photograph was taken in summer, 1964. On January 11, 1965, Mrs. Kennedy gave birth to her ninth child, Matthew Maxwell Taylor Kennedy.

Edward M. Kennedy
and Family
1932-
From left to right: Joan Bennett
Kennedy; Edward M. Kennedy, Jr.;
Kara Kennedy; and the Massachu-
setts senator.

R. Sargent Shriver
1915-
As director of the Peace Corps, President Kennedy's brother-in-law visits
a cooking class in Turkey. *(Photo by
Paul Conklin.)*

as though she loves life so much that she won't submit to bore-
dom. . . ."[109] Although she almost never made a speech, audiences
seemed to sense that Mrs. Lodge liked them, and they liked her.

Cabot, on the other hand, often struck reporters as being contemptuous
of the election proceedings, haughty, and quick to take offense. When,
for example, a reporter asked him for his position on the "religious
issue," he responded with smothered anger, "I do not want anybody
to vote for me on religious grounds. I refuse to accept the proposition
that my three Catholic grandchildren§ . . . are debarred from becoming
President because of religion . . . even for a journalist to bring it up
violates the spirit of the Constitution."[110] Yet he left with mass audiences
the feeling that he was the regular-guy-aristocrat who had fought their
battles. Lodge confined his pronouncements to one basic speech, which
reporters traveling with him soon knew by heart. He began, "I come
to you tonight after eight years at the United Nations, where I spoke
for all the nation—North and South, East and West, regardless of party."
He ended with thanks for listening to "a serious talk about foreign
affairs." It was a simple patriotic message, couched in generalities, and
its auditors cheered wildly. He rarely joked, except for a stock barb,
aimed at Kennedy's youth, to the effect that this is no time for "on-the-
job training" in the White House.[111]

Many were surprised that Lodge did not play a more prominent
part in the campaign. The only front-page news he made was to pledge
at a street-corner rally in East Harlem that Nixon, if elected, would
name a Negro to his Cabinet. "Whoever recommended that Harlem
speech," said a Virginia Republican, "should have been thrown out of
an airplane at 25,000 feet."[112] Nixon later wrote, "It hurt us in the
South unquestionably. And it did us no good in the North. To Negroes
as well as to other voters it appeared to be a crude attempt to woo
the support of Negroes without regard to the qualifications an individual
might have for high office—something that Lodge had never remotely
intended to suggest."[113]

It was not until long after the election, when Lodge was again
talked of as a candidate for national office, that it became apparent
that his performance in 1960 had left a bitter feeling in professional
Republican ranks. He was accused of having soldiered on the job, of
not having carried his share of the campaign burden. The story was
widely circulated that Lodge had taken two-hour naps in the afternoon.
One Western Republican told columnist Marquis Childs, "We didn't
mind his taking a nap after lunch every day. But why did he have

§ His son Henry Sears Lodge (1930–   ) was married in 1955 in a Roman
Catholic church to Elenita Zeigler, a great-great-granddaughter of piano manufacturer Henry E. Steinway. Their children are being raised in the Catholic
faith. See New York Times, July 28, 1955, p. 19; October 9, 1955, p. 91.

to put on his pajamas?"[114] To Lodge's defense came his former press secretary, Vincent O'Brien of the Lynn (Massachusetts) *Item:* "He thought it was a lot of nonsense to spend every waking hour shaking hands. To him Mr. Nixon and Mr. Kennedy and Mr. Johnson were all frenetic in their campaigning. He decided at the beginning that he would campaign mornings and afternoons, mornings and evenings, afternoons and evenings, but never all three on a given day. . . . But the two-hour nap in the middle of the afternoon is a myth."[115] Support for Lodge also came from an unexpected quarter. Conservative columnist William F. Buckley, Jr., wrote that if he took some of the frenzy out of presidential campaigning, "For this act of fortitude I honor him deeply."[116]

After the 1960 Republican defeat, former Ambassador Henry Cabot Lodge became director general of the Atlantic Institute, a private group to promote co-operation among Western nations, and former Ambassador John Davis Lodge became president of Junior Achievement, Inc.—showy jobs in which to display their inbred civic-mindedness until the opportunity again arose for governmental office.

For the younger brother it looked as if this would be in 1962. Senator Prescott Bush of Connecticut announced that he would not run for re-election, and John Davis Lodge was considered the heavy favorite to get the Republican nomination. After a bitter floor fight the state convention chose John Alsop as its candidate for governor.¶ Some delegates were already wearing "Lodge-Alsop" buttons. This unique ticket would have paired Theodore Roosevelt's grandnephew with his godson. But the convention suddenly rose in rebellion and nominated for senator Horace Seely-Brown, a former congressman and apple grower who campaigns by passing out pot holders.

Cabot Lodge, however, was back on the public payroll by mid-1963. He had told the new President that he was available for a tough diplomatic assignment, and on June 27, while touring in Ireland, John F. Kennedy announced that he was appointing his former opponent as ambassador to South Vietnam. Thirty-four years before, when Lodge was a reporter for the New York *Herald Tribune,* he had visited Indo-China and described its jungles as "the thickest, most persistent and most hopeless ones which I have seen in the Far Eastern tropics."[117] Now they were filled with the Communist Viet Cong, and in Saigon the Diem regime was in the midst of its Buddhist persecutions. Commented a Democratic politician on the appointment of the sixty-one-year-old Lodge: "If we're going to lose a country, we may as well have a Republican there."[118]

¶ See Roosevelt Dynasty, p. 207.

Thus was the ambassador eleven thousand miles away when there occurred what has been called "the Lodge Phenomenon." For a few remarkable months in early 1964 it looked as if he was to be politically resurrected. "Every presidential campaign seems to have a touch of the spectacular, the unbelievable, the fantastical," wrote the Washington *Post*. "This year the most amazing feat thus far must be credited to an Ambassador in a remote country who has not spoken a political syllable for public consumption—Henry Cabot Lodge."[119] Precluded by foreign service regulations from politicking, with his name not even on the ballot, Lodge decisively won the New Hampshire presidential primary.

The two announced candidates for the Republican nomination, Barry Goldwater and Nelson Rockefeller, had barnstormed through the early February snows, spending nearly a half million dollars between them. The Lodge forces, led by a tiny coterie of workers who looked to Cabot's son George as their leader, had a budget of $25,000, which they used for two state-wide mailings and thirty-nine television showings of a leftover Eisenhower endorsement from 1960 (with the Nixon plug snipped off). Some said later that the New Hampshire voters were merely being courteous to a Massachusetts neighbor; some said they were merely exhibiting the usual Yankee cussedness; some said they imagined similarities in Lodge to the martyred President Kennedy. But whatever the cause, this first primary of the year propelled Lodge into a commanding lead in every national public opinion poll. Suddenly the politician who had not won an election in eighteen years was the front runner for the 1964 Republican presidential nomination.

The "non-candidate" did nothing to encourage his supporters—neither did he do anything to discourage them. He had an opportunity to take himself out of the Oregon primary; he stayed in.[120] When Joseph Alsop flew to Saigon to talk politics, Lodge preferred to discuss the second volume of *The Adams Papers*.[121] Back home George Lodge spoke of a possible candidacy with a Gioconda smile. The last communication he had received from his father, he said at one point, was a letter "saying my mother had bought me a lamp. That could hardly be interpreted as having any political significance." Yet young Lodge seemed to turn up every place where voters were about to go to the polls. Quipped Democratic National Chairman John Bailey, "[Cabot Lodge's] Republican rivals keep asking him to come home and fight, but he is following the sensible motto of 'let George do it.'"[122]

The ambassador received sizable write-in votes in Pennsylvania, Illinois, New Jersey, and even Texas. His slate of convention delegates, including George Lodge, was elected in Massachusetts. Then the boom burst in the Oregon primary. And after William Scranton was substituted as the liberal Republican alternative to Goldwater, Ambassador Lodge announced that he was returning home.

During his ten months in Saigon the Diems had been deposed by a coup d'état and replaced by a military junta. Things were going better for the Vietnamese, he thought, than for his style of Republicanism. It was therefore his higher duty to campaign for Governor Scranton. This action was laudable but too late, commented the New York *Times*. "If he—and Governor Scranton, too—had spoken up earlier for moderate Republicanism, before Senator Goldwater had built up an almost insurmountable lead, the Republican party would be far better off today."[123] Lodge carried his belated campaign against Goldwaterism across the country. But did he do more harm than good? Bob Taft, Jr., thinks so. Perhaps recalling Lodge's role in defeating his father in 1952, young Taft said that Scranton committed "the most fatal mistake" by "injecting" Lodge into his campaign. He concludes, "This single step alone was enough to alienate and lose a great deal of potential support which might otherwise have remained available to Scranton. . . ."[124]

If Cabot Lodge had remained at San Francisco until the end of the convention he would have heard Brother John Davis Lodge, now candidate for the United States Senate, urge all Republicans to support Barry Goldwater, their party's nominee for President.

From Labor Day until the election, six days a week, John Davis Lodge left his Westport, Connecticut, home early in the morning, riding in the back of a white convertible with the top down. His driver, a retired state trooper, first took him to a train station, where he greeted departing commuters; then to a factory gate, where he shook hands with arriving workers; and so on to shopping centers, factories, political meetings. He dressed flamboyantly—plaid suit, pink shirt and blue bow tie, or hound's-tooth sports jacket and gray flannel slacks. Sometimes he was accompanied by Francesca. Their two daughters were now wives and mothers. The elder, Lily, after trying a career on the stage, was living in New York City with her husband, James Marcus, a promotion man; the younger, Beatrice Anna, was married to a Spanish diplomat and living in Madrid.*

His campaign was low-keyed. He supported the whole Republican ticket but avoided mentioning Goldwater's name. A right-wing group,

* Beatrice Anna Lodge married Antonio de Oyarzabal y Marchesi, now second secretary to the Spanish Foreign Minister, on July 6, 1961, at St. Brigid's Catholic Church in Peapack, New Jersey. (She had converted to Catholicism while a student in Spain.) The wedding reception was held at the home of Mathilde Frelinghuysen, a favorite cousin of the Lodges and aunt of Congressman Peter Frelinghuysen. See Maureen Daly, "A Connecticut Yankee Finds Her Destiny in Spain," *Ladies' Home Journal*, February 1965.

Youth for Goldwater, endorsed his opponent, Senator Thomas Dodd. Dodd attacked him for supporting Goldwater. The moderate Republican was trapped in an ideological cross fire. The New York *Times* gave Lodge a less than enthusiastic endorsement: he had been "a competent but uncreative Governor" and an ambassador to Spain who served "without incident although he exhibited an uncritical enthusiasm for the Franco regime."[125]

Cabot Lodge spent a day in Connecticut promoting his brother's candidacy. Otherwise he avoided politics by absenting himself from the country—on a diplomatic mission for President Johnson to inform the European nations of the U.S. position in South Vietnam.†

John Lodge lost his race for the Senate, though his margin of defeat was 80,000 less than Goldwater's. He had now failed in his last two election bids, as had his brother.

However, by 1965 it was clear that the Lodges were irrepressible. In June, John was elected to the Connecticut Constitutional Convention and subsequently became Republican assistant floor leader. In July, Cabot was renamed U.S. ambassador to Vietnam, and at an embassy party was soon heard entertaining Mary Martin of the visiting *Hello, Dolly!* troupe with his rendition of a racy little song called, "She's a Personal Friend of Mine." (He sang it in English, French, German, and Spanish.)[126]

But despite their youthful glands, the Lodge brothers had passed threescore years, and it was apparent that if the dynasty was to have a future it would rest in the capable hands of young George Lodge.

Cabot Lodge was said by a friend to be "an obsessive father." (This, thought the friend, was probably because Cabot's father had died when he was so young).[127] When his two sons were growing up Lodge devoted all his spare time to family activities. Dag Hammarskjold, after spending a weekend with the Lodge family at Beverly, remarked, "It's a clan, a tribe, where everyone is independent but still a part of the whole. . . ." An African delegate to the UN compared them to "a pride of lions."[128]

† The Cabots also deserted their usual Republicanism. Thomas D. Cabot (see p. 448n) and his cousin Paul Cabot publicly endorsed President Johnson. Paul Cabot is chairman of the board of the State Street Investment Corporation, a diversified investment company that he and two associates founded in 1924, and director of many major corporations (such as Ford, Continental Can, National Dairy, and B. F. Goodrich).

Thomas Cabot told a reporter that this was only the second time he had supported a Democrat for high office; the first was against Senator Henry Cabot Lodge in 1942. "He was still an isolationist at that point," said Mr. Cabot, "and I couldn't support that. He's changed his thinking since." See *Washington Post*, September 24, 1964, p. B2.

The younger son, Henry Sears Lodge, showed no interest in politics. (He is now an executive with an electronics firm.) But George has tried to parallel his father's career: from Harvard to newspaper work to government service.

In 1953, after interviewing Secretary of Labor Mitchell for the Boston *Herald,* George was offered a job in the Department's information office. And in early 1959 he was named Assistant Secretary of Labor for International Affairs.

When the Senate Committee on Labor and Public Welfare met to consider the nomination it was clear that the members were seeing George but thinking of Cabot. There was that striking physical resemblance; the Lodges have persistent genes. The young man was an inch under six and a half feet tall, with a towering forehead and the lean and darkly handsome Lodge face. There was the trace of Harvard in his speech, and the remnant of a childhood stutter. Senator Saltonstall, who had taken his father's seat in 1944, introduced George to the committee; Senator Kennedy, who had defeated his father in 1952, endorsed the nomination ("I have known [him] for a great many years . . . and I think he is admirably equipped for this job"); Chairman Lister Hill noted that Lodge is "carrying on in the tradition of his distinguished forebears, both on his father's side and his mother's side"; Senator Cooper recalled how he had served with the senior Lodge; Senator Randolph paid his respects to the "splendid tradition" of the family. Only Michigan's McNamara asked for any information. Was the nominee an active union member? George replied that he had been a member of Boston Local 32 of the American Newspaper Guild, though "not as active as I should have been."[129] The confirmation was made without dissent.

George remained as Assistant Secretary of Labor after the Kennedy Administration came to power. He had been elected to a year's term as chairman of the governing body of the International Labor Organization, and it would have been embarrassing to remove him from office. When he finally left government in 1962, with the thanks of the President for a job well done, it was to run for the Senate against the President's brother.

The Massachusetts campaign for John F. Kennedy's Senate seat was dynasticism run rampant. In the Democratic primary Edward M. Kennedy, youngest of Joseph Kennedy's children, was opposed by Edward J. McCormack, Jr., favorite nephew of the Speaker of the House of Representatives; George Lodge was entered in the Republican primary; and Professor H. Stuart Hughes of Harvard, grandson of onetime presidential candidate Charles Evans Hughes, was running as an independent. Said Lodge's Republican opponent, Congressman Laurence Curtis, "I am the only candidate running on his own name and own record of experience."[130] When *U. S. News & World Report* asked the contenders for their opinion on the "dynasty" issue, Ted Kennedy replied, "Anyone who suggests 'dynasty' suggests as well a system of succession. This is a failure to comprehend the democratic process in our country"; McCormack answered, "I wouldn't comment on the question of the 'dynasty' of the Kennedys . . . it has no part in my campaign strategy"; and Lodge said, "I have no dynasty. I have no brother in the White House, no brother who is Attorney General. I have no uncle who is Speaker of the House of Representatives. I have had no relative in high elective office for more than ten years. If anything, you might say that I belong to a dormant dynasty into which I am trying to inject some life."[131]

As expected, the primary winners were Ted Kennedy and George Lodge. The stage was set for the fourth contest between the clans. The Democratic candidate was thirty years old, the legal minimum for a United States senator; his Republican opponent was thirty-five. But then the Kennedys and Lodges have always been politically precocious: Cabot Lodge was thirty-four when first elected to the Senate; Jack Kennedy was thirty-five when he defeated Cabot. George could also contend that he had considerably more experience than his father had had in 1936. He was now a lecturer at the Harvard Business School and the author of a well-received book on the labor movement in developing countries, with nearly a decade of government service behind him.‡ Young Kennedy's credentials were less impressive. *Time* quoted George as saying in confidence, "I consider it a base impropriety that Teddy is so blatantly using his relationship with his brother for selfish purposes. What has he done to understand the world or Massachusetts? I first met Teddy in Nigeria during a meeting of the African region of the I.L.O. Teddy was there for a day and a half. He talks like that made him an expert on Nigeria. Well I know what he learned there because I briefed him. He does not know Nigeria. He pretends he does. It's a phony."[132]

Three white busses, with the name Lodge in huge red letters, carried the Republican candidate around Massachusetts. There was a circus atmosphere as the caravan pulled into a town and the zealous young campaigners passed out buttons and bumper stickers. Lodge made short, serious speeches, then answered questions with the scholarly regard for minute detail that characterized Jack Kennedy. He was scrupulously polite, in the Lodge manner, but without any of the family air of condescension. "If my father had been elected Vice President in 1960," said George, "I wouldn't be running for the Senate."[133] It was a subtle distinction. With a Lodge opposing a Kennedy the question of "dynasty" could hardly have been an exploitable issue.

‡ Lodge is the author of *Spearhead of Democracy* (New York: Harper, 1962). "A valuable and impressive study of the labor movement internationally," wrote R. M. Mallett, *Christian Science Monitor*, October 18, 1962, p. 16.

In young Kennedy, three years out of law school, Lodge surprisingly found himself up against the most natural politician of a family of natural politicians. Ted radiated a quality that academicians call charisma. "Charisma, hell," snapped a lady reporter. "It's just plain old sex appeal."[134] And against George's bubbling amateurs, Ted had the quietly efficient Kennedy organization, honed to a fine edge by six campaigns. There were no raised eyebrows when Ted Kennedy won by over a quarter of a million votes. "In another state, against another candidate," wrote Stewart Alsop, "George Lodge [would have been] an odds-on bet to win."[135]

Stripped of its colorful, though minor, figures, to date the dynasty has basically been the history of just two men—the Henry Cabot Lodges. Yet theirs has not been an inconsequential record: together they were three times elected to the House of Representatives, nine times to the United States Senate, played substantial roles in the making of two presidents, and in the making of American foreign policy after two World Wars.

In personality they bear a resemblance to the Adamses: their frosty demeanor has often erected a wall of ice between themselves and the voters who have held the key to the offices they have desired. But unlike the Adamses, whose political death was brought about by a failure to adapt, they have shown considerable ingenuity in relating to changing political realities.

The Lodges have been rooted in a region that reveres tradition. This has worked to their advantage. While the Kennedys have become national in character, it is less likely that their erstwhile opponents could be successfully transplanted. Although the Lodges have never been in the same financial category as the Kennedys, the acquisitive acumen of ancestors and in-laws has allowed them to devote themselves to public service. It is their calling; they have rarely been tempted by other pursuits. What one of Henry Cabot Lodge's sons said of his father in 1960 offers an explanation for four generations of a family that could well have spent their days smugly ensconced within the citadel of Boston. "We tease him about his nineteenth-century concept of public service," said the young Lodge. "But it's his whole life."[136]

The Kennedy Dynasty

"Joe [Junior] was supposed to be the politician. When he died, I took his place. If anything happened to me, Bobby would take my place. If something happened to Bobby, Teddy would take his place."

—John F. Kennedy[1]

A REMARKABLE family: the first Irish Catholics of great wealth in America, making most of their fortune in real estate; prominent in politics, having three members of the same generation in Congress and two members in Congress at the same time; outstanding in the affairs of their church, while socially advantaged enough to marry into English aristocracy.

Each of these achievements was shared later by the Kennedys, but this description, in fact, first fitted the Carrolls of Maryland.* These early Irish Catholic Brahmins were descended from an ancient family of Irish princes. Arriving in America a half century after the landing of the Pilgrims, the Carrolls came to Maryland under the patronage of Lord Baltimore during the reign of King James II.[2]

By the time of the American Revolution they owned most of the land on which the city of Washington was later built.[3] John Adams seems to have been particularly impressed by their wealth; having just arrived in Philadelphia for the opening of the first Continental Congress, he wrote in his ever present diary: "This day Mr. Chase introduced to us a Mr. Carroll, of Annapolis, a very sensible gentleman, a Roman Catholic, and of the first fortune in America. His income is ten thousand pounds sterling a year now, will be fourteen in two or three years, they say; besides, his father has a vast estate which will be his after his father."[4] Daniel

---

* The three Carrolls of the same generation in Congress were cousins: Charles Carroll "the Barrister" (1723–83), Charles Carroll of Carrollton (1737–1832), and Daniel Carroll (1730–96); the two Charles Carrolls were delegates to the Continental Congress in 1776; Daniel's brother John (1735–1815) was the first Roman Catholic bishop in the United States.

THE KENNEDY DYNASTY
(A Selective Genealogy)

Patrick Kennedy (1823–58)
Arrived America. 1848
m. Bridget Murphy (1821–88)
(4 children)

Patrick J. Kennedy ("P. J.")
(1858–1929)
State representative and state senator
m. Mary Hickey (d. 1923)
(3 children)

Joseph Patrick Kennedy (1888–   )
Ambassador to Great Britain
(9 children)

m.

John Francis Fitzgerald ("Honey Fitz")
(1863–1950)
HOUSE OF REPRESENTATIVES,
mayor of Boston
m. Josephine Hannon (1866–1964)
(6 children)

Rose Fitzgerald

Joseph Patrick
(1915–44)

John Fitzgerald
(1917–1963)
HOUSE OF REPRESENTATIVES,
SENATE, PRESIDENT
m. Jacqueline Bouvier
(3 children; 1 d.y.)

Robert Francis
(1925–)
Attorney General,
SENATE
m. Ethel Skakel
(9 children)

Edward Moore ("Ted")
(1932–)
SENATE
m. Joan Bennett
(2 children)

Rosemary

Kathleen
(1920–48)
m. Marquess of
Hartington (d. 1944)

Eunice
m. R. Sargent
Shriver (1915–)
Peace Corps director
(5 children)

Patricia
m. Peter Lawford
(1925–)
(divorced 1966)
(4 children)

Jean
m. Stephen Smith
(1927–)
(3 children)

Carroll signed the Articles of Confederation and his cousin Charles of Carrollton, Adams' friend, signed the Declaration of Independence. As he did so another delegate observed, "There go a few millions."[5]

Yet the influence of this first great Irish Catholic dynasty ended decades before the progenitor of the second great Irish Catholic dynasty—with its superficially similar record of achievement—arrived in the United States.

After the generation of the Founding Fathers, only two Carrolls were elected to high office.† The family preferred caste privilege to leadership. The granddaughters of Charles Carroll of Carrollton, anticipating the later flurry of matches between rich American ladies and titled Englishmen, became the Duchess of Leeds, the Marchioness of Wellesley, and the Baroness Stafford. For their beauty and charm the three were known in London as the "American Graces."

The Carrolls were part of a trickle of Irishmen who had been emigrating to America throughout the seventeenth and eighteenth centuries. Then in the late 1840s, with the sudden failure of the potato crop, it became a cascade, washing up to 216,000 immigrants a year into the ports of New York and Boston at the high-water mark. These new arrivals were unwelcome and, except for their brawn, unwanted. As the factory gates posted "No Irish Need Apply," the Irish applied themselves to politics, the one area in which their numbers were meaningful and their gregarious talents of value.

Prejudice channeled families like the Fitzgeralds and the Kennedys into public life by closing to them the more significant private life of the country, but this led in time to the election of the first Catholic President of the United States, an event which sociologist E. Digby Baltzell called "a turning point in our history and symbol of a trend toward ethnic aristocracy in America."[6]

It was not the blight of the potato, the legendary Great Hunger, that brought to America the great-grandfather of President Kennedy and his senator brothers.

He came from Dunganstown, County Wexford, in the southeast corner of Ireland, which was relatively prosperous and unaffected by the horror that was then sweeping other parts of the country. What probably caused Patrick Kennedy in October 1848 to travel the six miles from his home to the port of New Ross and board a ship for America was the fact that he was a youngest son. After the family had satisfied the demands of the landlord there would be little left over to start him on a farm of

† A great-grandson of Charles Carroll of Carrollton, John Lee Carroll (1830–1911), was governor of Maryland from 1875 to 1879, and a great-grandson of Daniel Carroll, Charles Hobart Carroll (1794–1865), served a term in Congress, 1843–47.

his own, even if land had been available. So he arrived in Boston, became a maker of whiskey barrels, and died of cholera fourteen years later—no richer than if he had remained in Ireland.[7]

Another young man from County Wexford arrived in Boston at about the same time. Thomas Fitzgerald became a farm laborer for six dollars a month and then the proprietor of a grocery and liquor store in the North End, not far from Paul Revere's house. He too died in his early thirties.

In the next generation the Fitzgeralds and the Kennedys would be alternately political enemies and allies in the constantly shifting mosaic of Boston politics; in the following generation they would permanently unite in marriage (though not always in politics); and in the fourth generation the Kennedy-Fitzgerald genes would change the contours of American political life.

John Francis Fitzgerald and Patrick Joseph Kennedy, the grandfathers who gave their names to a President, were very different types, as dissimilar as the nicknames by which they were known. Fitzgerald was "Honey Fitz"—an appellation that would have befitted a vaudeville song-and-dance man‡; Kennedy was simply "P.J." in the manner that imposing executives are referred to by underlings who would not think of addressing them familiarly by their first names.

Grandfather Kennedy, recalled the future President, "wouldn't let us cut up or even wink in his presence."[8] This austere and awesome figure was about five feet ten inches tall, weighed 185 pounds, and had sandy hair, blue eyes, and a luxuriously curled mustache. First a stevedore and longshoreman, he soon took over a saloon in Haymarket Square. But the barkeep rarely lifted a glass himself. Without cursing or raising his voice, he maintained order; brawlers, he made it understood, would not be tolerated. Eventually P.J. acquired an interest in three saloons, a wholesale liquor concern, a coal company, and a local bank. Joseph Kennedy, his only son, was not raised in a poor home; his father owned a sixty-foot cabin cruiser, the *Eleanor*.

In the Boston of the 1880s it was as predictable for an Irish saloon-keeper to go into politics as it had been for an earlier generation of Yankees to take to the sea or the countinghouse. P. J. Kennedy became a three-time member of Democratic presidential conventions and was six

‡ Several theories have been advanced as to the origin of the name "Honey Fitz." One is that an out-of-Boston journalist in 1907 mistakenly transformed "Little Johnny Fitz" into "Honey Fitz"; another is that he got the name as a boy from his habit of dipping into the sugar barrel in his father's store; a third is that the name refers to Fitzgerald's "hearts and flowers" style of oratory. See John Henry Cutler, *"Honey Fitz"* (Indianapolis: Bobbs-Merrill, 1962), pp. 82–83.

times elected to office, five as a member of the Massachusetts House of
Representatives and once as a state senator. But his overriding interest
was in East Boston, which he ran as a neighborly welfare state. Being its
boss, he was automatically a member of the four-man "Board of
Strategy," the "mayor-makers" who picked Democratic candidates for
city-wide office and ran Boston. Another member of the "board" was
John Francis Fitzgerald. Kennedy privately considered him insufferable.

For a man with P. J. Kennedy's sense of dignity, working with Honey
Fitz must have been unbearable indeed. Here was a bantam rooster of a
man—short, cocky, strutting, yet handsome, though his mouth was narrow and his eyes a little too close together; a study in perpetual motion, organizing dances, dancing with the wallflowers; an Irish chipmunk
with just a trace of brogue, chattering away at two hundred words a
minute; always turning up uninvited, always singing (except at wakes),
generally off key, always weeping—when it suited him; every inch the
charming rogue. The politicians despised him. The ladies adored him.

It suited Honey Fitz's purpose to recount a youth of hardship. But the
facts were otherwise. He graduated from the famed Boston Latin
School, a contemporary of Santayana and Berenson, captained a polo
team, and even attended Harvard Medical School until the death of his
father forced him to drop out in the first year. Next he took a civil service
examination, came out near the top of the list, and went to work as a
clerk at the customhouse under Leverett Saltonstall, grandfather of the
United States senator. Honey Fitz later founded a prosperous insurance
business, and in 1892 was elected to the state Senate. Reporters branded
him "the North End Napoleon." The name so pleased him that he
promptly adopted some of the mannerisms of the French Emperor. He
was now undisputed boss of the North End and one fourth of the "Board
of Strategy."

In 1894 Fitzgerald was elected to Congress (although opposed by
Kennedy). He was the only Democratic congressman from New England and the only Catholic in the House of Representatives. During his
six consecutive years in Washington he earned a reputation as an in-
sistent and irrelevant debater and an effective bread-and-butter fighter
for Boston Harbor. He won his third term despite his opponent's charge
that he was now a carpetbagger, since he had bought a home in respectable Concord, twenty-five miles removed from his North End constituents.

During this period Fitzgerald also became a newspaperman. He
bought the *Republic* for five hundred dollars and turned it into an
Irish-American social weekly. Readers didn't flock to it, but advertisers
who needed political favors did. The congressman-publisher was soon
netting $25,000 a year. (In 1914 when Walter Lippmann, Herbert Croly,
and Walter Weyl decided to found a journal of liberal opinion, they dis-

covered that an obscure Boston weekly already had their chosen title and were thus forced to name their magazine the *New Republic*.[9])

But Congress was only a curtain raiser for the job that really counted —mayor of Boston. In 1905 Honey Fitz became "His Honor, the Mayor" (again against the wishes of P. J. Kennedy). Fitzgerald was not the first Irishman to hold the post; two outstanding men, Hugh O'Brien and Patrick Collins, had preceded him. He was, however, the city's first Irish-American mayor to be born in this country, and, as James Michael Curley pointed out, he was the first Boston mayor without beard or mustache.

In the year that Fitzgerald was first elected mayor there were more persons of Irish extraction in Boston than in Dublin, an estimated sixty per cent of the city's population. The mayor's hold over his fellow Boston Irish was recounted by Curley, who was ten years younger than Honey Fitz and carved out of harder rock. Then teaching a class on naturalization for Irish immigrants, Curley asked a student to tell him who made the laws of the nation.

"John F. Fitzgerald," came the reply.

Who then, Curley wanted to know, made the laws of the state?

"John F. Fitzgerald," the young man answered again.

And who is the President of the United States?

"John F. Fitzgerald."

"If I hadn't stopped the man there," commented Curley, "I'm sure he would have gone on to tell me that John F. drove the snakes out of Ireland and discovered America."[10]

During his first two years in office Mayor Fitzgerald attended 1200 dinners, 1500 dances, 200 picnics, and 1000 meetings. He made 3000 speeches and danced with 5000 girls. If Honey Fitz were to be wakened in the dead of night and asked to speak on any subject under the sun, wrote a Boston *Post* reporter, "he will readily, not to say willingly, arise from his couch, slip his frock coat over his pajamas and speak eloquently for two hours and seventeen minutes on that subject."[11]

The Honey Fitz administration may have been an artistic success, but it did not please the city's good-government element. "Our present Mayor," said a Baptist minister from Roxbury, "has the distinction of appointing more saloonkeepers and bartenders to public office than any previous mayor."[12] A physician was removed from the Board of Health to make room for a saloonkeeper; liquor dealers were appointed as superintendent of public buildings and wire commissioner; a whitewasher became superintendent of sewers; a bartender who had been expelled from the legislature was named superintendent of streets. Civil service regulations were circumvented by the invention of such job categories as tea warmer, tree climber, rubber-boot repairers, and watchmen to watch the watchmen. Brother Henry Fitzgerald was put in charge of patronage; Brother Jim Fitzgerald was given a valuable liquor license; Brother Michael Fitzgerald, a Charlestown policeman, was paid $1100 a year to replace the U.S. mails as the conveyor of a daily traffic report from the Warren Avenue Bridge to City Hall, thus earning a reputation as "the human postage stamp."

The city discovered that under its charming mayor it had been defrauded of $200,000 by a single coal company; that it was paying sixty cents a barrel above the going price for cement; that bids and contracts for city work were often accepted verbally; that bills and vouchers had mysteriously disappeared; that there were dozens of strange land deals.

Meanwhile back at the *Republic* things were flourishing. Advertising rates in ratio to circulation were perhaps the highest in the country, while its advertisers, writes Francis Russell, "read like a summary of the Boston Stock Exchange."[13] In one issue of Honey Fitz's newspaper the Boston banks bought fourteen pages of advertising.

Mayor Fitzgerald was defeated in 1907.

The "better elements," made bold by their victory, doubled the mayoralty term to four years. So in 1909 Honey Fitz bounced back to beat a Beacon Street Yankee by 1402 votes.

The second term recorded some solid achievements (a City Hall annex, an aquarium, a zoo, a high school of commerce), as well as more of the same shenanigans. "Banned in Boston" became a legend. Honey Fitz outlawed the turkey trot and the tango as immoral, and *Salome* as sacrilegious. He also introduced a theme song, "Sweet Adeline," a popular hit of the day, which his daughter Rose had taught him. He became known as the only man who could sing the ballad when cold sober and get away with it. (Franklin D. Roosevelt once greeted him as "Dulce Adelina," claiming that after a Honey Fitz tour of South America the natives there thought it was the U.S. national anthem.)

For a man who was known to have made thirty speeches in one night there was little time left over for a normal family life. When Honey Fitz spent an evening with his wife and children because a magazine wanted to do a story on the mayor at home, Mrs. Fitzgerald told him, "John, it does indeed seem refreshing to have you here. I am not sorry you are to have photographs taken to mark the evening. I am going to frame one and place a card over it on which I will write: 'Taken on his evening at home.'" Mary Fitzgerald, a slender and erect woman, with fair hair and luminous brown eyes, a horror of ostentation and a fear of publicity, was in charge of bringing up the three boys and three girls. "I want my home to be a place of inspiration and encouragement to all my family," she told the magazine writer. "I am a home woman in every way. . . ."[14]

Since Mrs. Fitzgerald shrank from the public glare that her husband basked in, Honey Fitz drafted his pretty daughter Rose to act as his official hostess. Between his terms at City Hall she had been studying in a European convent. She was now a poised young lady with a deeply religious outlook and a command of music and foreign languages. She accompanied her father to political rallies, banquets, and wakes. At sixteen she presided over her first ship launching. She greeted President William Howard Taft and other celebrities. There was even a rumor that she was engaged to Sir Thomas Lipton.

At a dinner that Mayor Fitzgerald gave in 1912 for the City Council, James Michael Curley, uninvited, slipped into the room and used Honey Fitz's forum to announce his own candidacy for mayor. Under the constant, withering attack from the young challenger Fitzgerald withdrew from the race to succeed himself. He had no stomach for this sort of contest. Curley had developed a toughness from his slum youth that was totally lacking in Fitzgerald. Fitzgerald wanted to have fun and Curley wanted to have power. Curley's rise signified the end of the petty political barons like John F. Fitzgerald and P. J. Kennedy. He wanted to, and would, control the city; they only wanted their little shares, and had neither the cunning nor the ability to stem the class bitterness that he so adroitly manipulated.

After Fitzgerald left City Hall he would often run again for political office. But his luck and timing had run out.

The University of Notre Dame awarded Honey Fitz an honorary degree in 1915. And the next year "Dr. Fitzgerald," as he now liked to be called, ran for the United States Senate against Henry Cabot Lodge, Sr. He went down to Washington and sat in his august opponent's seat in the Senate chamber. "It feels natural," he declared.[15] But the New York *Times* thought the idea quite unnatural, editorializing that Fitzgerald was turning the election into a joke, and calling him ". . . this amiable kisser of the Blarney Stone, warbler of 'Sweet Adeline,' rider of Florida sharks, a butterfly flitting unconcerned around the solid men of Boston. . . ."[16] The electorate agreed, but by the surprisingly slim margin of 33,000 votes.§

He hoped to make a comeback by opposing Curley for mayor in 1917. The notion was short-lived, however. For the irrepressible James Michael announced that he planned a series of addresses, including one entitled, "Great Lovers: From Cleopatra to Toodles." Toodles, whose last name was Ryan, was a shapely blond cigarette girl at the Ferncroft Inn on the Newburyport Turnpike. Rumor had mentioned her in the same breath with Honey Fitz for a number of years and they were even linked in an anonymous limerick. The former mayor righteously insisted that there was no fire to match the smoke, but he nevertheless quickly backed out of the race. Curley's "Great Lovers" remained just a title of an undelivered speech.[17]

§ See Lodge Dynasty, pp. 458–59.

But Honey Fitz did make a comeback of sorts in 1918 when he was elected to the House of Representatives by 238 votes. His opponent's manager, Joe Kane, who was also Joseph P. Kennedy's first cousin (their mothers were sisters), carried the fight to Washington. He charged that Fitzgerald's election was "by means of the fraudulent votes of the liquor dealers, bartenders, and city job holders illegally registered in his ward, and in the padded returns of alleged residents in the cheap lodging houses."[18] A congressional committee agreed with the allegation and Honey Fitz was removed from office. Unfazed, he announced, "There are half a dozen men in the Senate now who were unseated in recent years, while Mr. McKinley, who was unseated in the 48th Congress, was afterwards elected President."[19]

Four years later Honey Fitz was defeated for governor of Massachusetts in a race that was of little significance except that it provided John Fitzgerald Kennedy with his earliest political memories; he toured the wards with his grandfather. In 1930 Fitzgerald's name was on the Democratic ballot for governor again, but he withdrew before the primary date. At seventy-nine years of age, in 1942, the old war horse was entered against Representative Joseph Casey in the primary for United States senator. The winner was to face Henry Cabot Lodge, Jr. Honey Fitz might have won the primary, thought Joe Kane, but Joseph P. Kennedy decided against putting up the $200,000 to $300,000 that would have been necessary to wage a successful campaign.

Twice, in 1933 and 1944, Honey Fitz was made president of the Massachusetts Electoral College, an honorary position, and for many years he served as an unsalaried member of the Boston Port Authority, whose development had always been one of his political loves. He was also a great booster of wearing long underwear, feeling that its use would revive his state's textile industry.

The ancient Hibernian lived long enough to sing *Sweet Adeline* at the celebration in honor of his grandson's first election to Congress in 1946. But he died in 1950, two years before John Fitzgerald Kennedy righted an old family score by defeating Henry Cabot Lodge, Jr., for the Senate. His wife, however, lived through the inauguration of her grandson as the first Catholic President. She was never told of the tragedy in Dallas. "I had a hunch she knew," said her son Thomas, "but we never talked about it."[20] She died on August 8, 1964, at the age of ninety-eight.

Honey Fitz was not pleased when Rose married Joseph P. Kennedy in 1914. He felt that the daughter of a famous mayor should do better than the son of a ward boss and saloon owner. His own candidate for son-in-law was a wealthy contractor.

The young man who had married into the Fitzgerald family was a graduate of Boston Latin and Harvard, Class of 1912. Robert Benchley, who shared the same college numerals, later described their class as having produced "only one Bishop of Albania," "only one member who caught a giant panda" (Kermit Roosevelt), and only one "village clerk of Hewlett Harbor, L.I."[21] Joe Kennedy didn't make the best clubs and Harvard later refused to recognize his existence with an honorary degree or a place on its Board of Overseers, but in its more than three hundred years he was its only self-made multimillionaire-ambassador-father of a President.

Nor did it take long to recognize the handsome redhead as a "comer." By the time he was twenty-five the newspapers were billing him as the youngest bank president in the nation—albeit a tiny Boston bank in which his father held substantial stock. It was Joe's ambition to be a millionaire by thirty-five, and it was an ambition that he easily realized. At the twentieth reunion of his Harvard class Kennedy listed his occupation as "capitalist." In a lifetime of money-making the capital came primarily from four sources: the movies, the stock market, liquor, and real estate.

The movies. In the mid-1920s Kennedy made an investment in a chain of New England theaters which eventually led him into the production side of the business. He moved himself (but not his family) to Hollywood in 1928 where three companies were each paying $2000 a week for his executive ability. He produced a series of films starring Gloria Swanson and arranged the merger that created RKO.[22] "After thirty-two months in the movies," writes his biographer, Richard J. Whalen, "he was more than thirty pounds underweight—and perhaps five million dollars richer."[23]

Stock market. In the roaring bull market of the late 1920s Joe Kennedy was a loner and a speculator. "He became a wizard of such tricky stock dodges as market rigging, matched orders, margin manipulation, and washed and short sales."[24] On one operation in Libbey-Owens-Ford stock Kennedy and others made a profit of $395,238 by spreading the rumor that the imminent repeal of Prohibition would make a fortune for LOF—though the facts were that the glassmaker did not manufacture whiskey bottles. Then suddenly in the summer of 1929 he left the market. He kept his huge movie profits in cash. Years later reporter Joseph Dinneen asked him why. "Very simply," answered Kennedy, "I dropped in at a shoeshine parlor on Wall Street. The boy who shined my shoes did not know me. . . . He looked up at me as he snapped the cloth over my shoes and told me what was going to happen to various stocks and offerings on the market that day. I listened as I looked down at him, and when I left the place I thought: 'When a time comes that a shoeshine boy knows as much as I do about what is going on in the stock market, tells me so and is entirely correct, there is something the matter either with me or with the market and it's time for me to get out,' and I did."[25] When the great crash came in October 1929 the Kennedy fortune was unaffected.

Liquor. It was apparent in 1933 that the amendment repealing Prohibition would soon become law, and the competition became intense for the rights to represent the British distillers in America. That September Mr. and Mrs. Joseph Kennedy went to Europe with Mr. and Mrs. James Roosevelt. The son of the American President and his friends were royally received by the English liquor interests. When they returned home Joe Kennedy was the U.S. agent for Haig and Haig, John Dewar, and Gordon's Gin. Three months before Prohibition ended his warehouses were overflowing with liquor that had been shipped into the country under "medicinal" licenses issued in Washington. "The British didn't select their agents haphazardly," said a rival distributor. "They felt Jimmy Roosevelt was a good connection, so they gave their lines to Kennedy." The story was told that Jimmy expected to go into the business as a partner. But when Kennedy's firm, Somerset Importers, was incorporated, Joe, as usual, had no partners. He replied to critics, "Kennedy was doing all right by himself before he ever met Jimmy Roosevelt."[26] The original Kennedy investment in the liquor business was $100,000. His annual net profit was estimated at a quarter of a million dollars. He sold out in 1946 for eight million dollars in cash.

Real estate. Ironically, when Joe Kennedy tried to play it safe he made more money than ever before. Expecting hard times, during World War II he started to put his money into real estate, primarily on the island of Manhattan. By the estimate of his agent he made one hundred million dollars. It was Joe's practice to move into a promising situation, exploit it, and then quickly move out. One property at Fifty-ninth Street and Lexington Avenue he bought for $1,900,000—only $100,000 in cash—and sold for $6,000,000. The one building that Kennedy held onto was Chicago's Merchandise Mart, which he bought in 1945 for $12,956,-516—approximately $1,000,000 down. It is now valued at $75,000,000 and produces annual rentals in excess of Kennedy's original purchase price.

These may not have been the ways that a "gentleman" would make his fortune, and Joe Kennedy was never accused of being gentlemanly in business. But the buccaneering founding father was also a time-honored tradition. Kennedy was possibly no more fastidiously ethical than Robert Livingston, First Lord of the Manor, or the privateering Cabots of the American Revolution. The difference was that he came later.

The *Fortune* magazine survey of America's multimillionaires in 1957 estimated the fortune of Joseph P. Kennedy at above $250,000,000. This put him in a class with Irenée and William Du Pont, Howard Hughes, and Sid Richardson. He was one of the few of the astronomically wealthy whose money didn't stem from inheritance or oil. In another way Joe Kennedy's fortune was different from most others. As one of his intimates said, "It isn't paper; it's real. Joe could write a check for nine million dollars just like that."[27]

Yet here was a capitalist who stood apart from the system. His wealth wasn't derived from finance, production, or distribution. His money wasn't used to create goods or pump them through the economic blood stream of the nation. No product bore the name Kennedy. And this standing apart from the business community—and generally holding it in low regard—was to play a significant role in the shaping of his children. For unlike many self-made men, who took pride in what they had created and wished their sons to perpetuate it, Kennedy led his sons away from his business and into public service.

Many could not see the man for the money. Those who tried often came away baffled and confused. Joseph P. Kennedy, above all, was a complex individual. He was by nature a pessimist, yet he held the most extraordinarily optimistic dream for his family; he was well educated, with refined taste in music, yet addicted to the crudest racial epithets; he could display the quickest, most infectious grin and the most explosive temper; he was a dictatorial executive and a maudlin emotionalist. He was openhanded and closefisted. He had an animal vitality.

At home during the children's youth he was the very model of a model Victorian paterfamilias: his word was law. But he wasn't home very often. It was not until a month after the birth of Patricia that Joe saw his new daughter. He was otherwise occupied at the Waldorf, stabilizing the stock of the Yellow Cab Company.

In 1915 Joe, Jr., was born. John was born two years later. Then came, during the twenties, in rapid succession: Rosemary, Kathleen, Eunice, Patricia, Robert, and Jean. The family named their sailboat *Tenofus*. But with the addition of Edward in 1932 they needed a bigger boat; it was christened *One More*.

In the absence of Father, there was Rose. Years later, when her sons held three of the highest offices in the land, Adlai Stevenson introduced her at a Washington banquet as "the woman who started it all, the head of the greatest employment agency in America. . . ."[28] But first she was a mother. "She was the glue," said her President son. And then he repeated himself for emphasis.[29] A petite brunette, with high cheekbones and a youthful figure ("Now I believe in the stork!" said F.D.R.'s son-in-law, John Boettiger, when he saw her at the White House), Rose Kennedy was the vivid presence in her children's first years. She took them sight-seeing, taught them the catechism, heard their prayers, kept a card index on their illnesses, saw them off to school—at least the oldest ones.¶ ("I told her that I had got up for the first six," Rose reported saying to the Queen of England, "but when seven, eight and nine came along I thought 'this can go on forever' and I rolled over and went to sleep. . . .")[30] Yet she was also tough-fibered and slightly aloof. "She was a little removed," recalled Jack, "which I think is the only way to survive when you have nine children."[31] When Joe was around he drove home his philosophy of competition: it's not how you play the game that counts, it's winning. Rose supported yet tempered her husband's drive. The combination, wrote Fletcher Knebel, was "just enough competitive father to keep them alert . . . just enough kindly mother to keep them from getting the shakes."[32]

There was also an important secondary influence on the younger children—Joe, Jr. Said Bobby Kennedy: "My brother Joe took the greatest interest in us. He taught us to sail, to swim, to play football and baseball." Added Jack Kennedy: "Joe made the task of bringing up a large family immeasurably easier for my father and mother, for what they taught him he passed on to us and their teachings were not diluted through him but strengthened."[33] This was part of the parents' philosophy of child rearing. "I always felt," said Mrs. Kennedy, "that if the older children are brought up right, the younger ones will follow their lead."[34] And young Joe was the leader. He had his mother's good looks and consideration for others; much of his father's drive and capacity for instant anger; his grandfather Honey Fitz's gift of banter. He was tall, well muscled, a natural athlete. He was a hail-fellow whom people automatically liked. "Joe had so much personality," his college roommate said, "that you could tell he'd entered a room if your back was to the door and he hadn't said a word."[35] Later he enjoyed smoking cigars, going to the race track, and talking about becoming the first Catholic President of the United States.

In the shadow of Joe, two years his junior, was Jack Kennedy. The two oldest boys fought constantly. They were altogether different, thought their father. Joe was "more dynamic, more sociable and easy going"; Jack "was rather shy, withdrawn and quiet."[36] His parents were sure that he would be a teacher or writer. Then came Bobby, eight years behind Jack. He was the smallest, with the poorest physical co-ordination and the least interest in intellectual pursuits. He was always scrambling to

¶ Commenting on Rose Kennedy's now famous card index, a reporter in 1939 wrote: "I picked out a bunch of the cards. They were Robert's. The date and hour of his birth were recorded, his weight day by day and then month by month. Every illness was there, the dates when he had chicken pox, mumps (both sides), mild scarlet fever, whooping cough, and when his tonsils and adenoids were removed." See Jerome Beatty, "Nine Kennedys and How They Grew," *Reader's Digest*, April 1939, p. 85.

catch up, to be included. As Ethel Kennedy was later to explain, "The major difference between Bobby and his brothers is that Bobby always had to fight for everything."[37] Teddy was seventeen years younger than his oldest brother, far too little to be considered an equal. He couldn't compete, but he rigged the sailboats for the others and worked hard at being liked.

The oldest of the girls was Rosemary. It was soon apparent that she was not like the other children. Her mother recalls: "She couldn't stay on a sled like the others. She couldn't balance herself on a bicycle. She was slow in school. I went to our family doctor, and then to specialists but there didn't seem to be any answer. . . . In Summer, the other youngsters would go out in the boat alone. She couldn't. And she couldn't understand why. It was the same at dancing school. She would come home and say, 'Mother, the boys danced with Eunice and Mary and Jean, but not with me.' "[38] Yet the family tried to include Rosemary in their activities to the extent of her ability. She was even formally presented to the Queen when Joe was ambassador to Great Britain. But in her twenty-third year she began to retrogress, to become irritable and difficult to manage. It was then decided, Eunice later wrote, "that she would be far happier in an institution, where competition was far less and where our numerous activities would not endanger her health. . . ."[39] So in 1941 Rosemary Kennedy was placed in St. Coletta's School at Jefferson, Wisconsin. For almost two decades after this the family would not say publicly that there was a retarded child. With the help of sympathetic writers they maintained the fiction that she was teaching at a Catholic school near Milwaukee.[40] Then in 1960 Joseph Kennedy revealed his daughter's misfortune and the family's substantial philanthropy in the field of mental retardation.

In the world of the Kennedy children the leadership of the girls was assumed by the next oldest, Kathleen. A Frenchman, who knew them when they lived in London, said, "Eunice is the most intellectual and Pat's the prettiest, but Kathleen is the one you remember."[41]

The Kennedy household was like a self-contained unit set in perpetual motion. It has also been described as an Oklahoma land grab, with everyone racing for his share. "I couldn't keep them straight," remembers novelist Gore Vidal. "They were always running around like so many wire-haired terriers."[42] They sustained each other. The world, as they saw it, consisted of two parts: Kennedys and others.

The family left Boston in the spring of 1926. They would still spend the summers at their rambling, eighteen-room house at Hyannis Port on Cape Cod, but Boston, said the father, was "no place to bring up Catholic children."[43] For the next decade they made their home in the Riverdale and Bronxville suburbs of New York City.

During this period Joe also set up trust funds for the children. With subsequent additions, the trusts would earmark upwards of ten million dollars for each child. This would one day make Jack Kennedy the richest President in American history. "I fixed it," Joe said, "so that any of my children, financially speaking, could look me in the eye and tell me to go to hell." But the future President considered his father's explanation for the trusts to be "a myth." ". . . that was in 1929, and he was speculating," said Jack. "It was very risky business. He was speculating pretty hard and his health was not too good at the time, and that was the reason he did it. There was no other reason for it."[44]

Yet despite Joe Kennedy's concentration on money-making, and the opulence with which he surrounded himself, he did not view wealth as an end in itself. For him it was a means to uplift his family, a foundation on which to build the next generation. "The measure of a man's success in life is not the money he has made," he said. "It's the kind of family he has raised." Or again: "My wife and I have given nine hostages to fortune. Our children . . . are more important than anything else in the world." This was a constant, recurring theme through all his life and all his public statements. Joe Kennedy, as his friend Arthur Krock said, "had a dynastic impulse."[45]

And the young Kennedys were just like any other nine competitive, combative, intelligent, articulate, athletic, attractive, multimillionaire kids.

Joe Kennedy first met Franklin D. Roosevelt during World War I when he was assistant manager of Bethlehem Steel's Fore River Shipyard in Quincy, Massachusetts, and F.D.R. was the Assistant Secretary of the Navy. Unlike so many others, Kennedy never underestimated the young Roosevelt. ". . . the hardest trader I'd ever run up against," said Joe.[46]

The two men were opposites in background—the son of an East Boston saloonkeeper and the son of a Hudson River aristocrat—opposites in outlook and style. Yet in 1932, when Honey Fitz and the Boston Irish politicians supported Al Smith for President—and considered it treason to do otherwise—Joe Kennedy became one of Roosevelt's staunchest backers. Why?

Because Kennedy, inherently pessimistic, feared the collapse of the economic system, and with it his fortune; and with the collapse of his fortune, the economic roof he had built over his family would collapse; and with its collapse, the end of his dream for his sons. The man who could prevent this was Roosevelt, "a man of action . . . [with] the capacity to get things done. . . ."[47]

So he gave $25,000 to the Roosevelt campaign, lent it another $50,000, and raised an additional $100,000. He helped get the nomination for Roosevelt in Chicago by using his influence with his friend William Randolph Hearst, who controlled the key California and Texas delegations, and he later traveled with Roosevelt on his campaign train.

And Roosevelt having been elected, and Kennedy being a practical man, Joe waited for his reward. He confidently expected to be named Secretary of the Treasury. Roosevelt had other ideas. Kennedy continued to wait. Finally, after more than a year, President Roosevelt appointed Joseph P. Kennedy to the new Securities and Exchange Commission, with the understanding that he would be its first chairman. The announcement was met with incredulity; the great stock market speculator was to be put in charge of the agency that was to police the stock market.* This was like "putting Peter Rabbit to work guarding the cabbage patch," said one Democrat.[48] But Kennedy did such a brilliant job at the SEC that when Roosevelt next called on him, to head the new Maritime Commission, Congress was so eager for him to accept that it passed an unprecedented resolution waiving the requirement that he sell his stock in Todd Shipyard, which would otherwise have been a conflict of interests.

Returning to Harvard that spring for his twenty-fifth reunion, Joe's classmates put on a skit, "In the Good Old Maritime," in which Commissioner Kennedy is heard telling his secretary, "Get me Frank at the White House." He picks up the phone. "I'm here, Frank. It's nine o'clock. Start the country."[49]

Then Joe Kennedy, the grandson of an Irish immigrant, was appointed United States ambassador to the Court of St. James's.

Old Honey Fitz, his barrel chest now swelling with pride, was introduced at a dinner of the Boston Chamber of Commerce by Charles Francis Adams. "I told Charley recently," announced Fitzgerald, "that I might go abroad pretty soon to meet the King and Queen, and Wallie and the rest of them, and asked him for some tips. You see, Charley Adams' great-grandfather and his grandfather were ambassadors to Great Britain in times of great stress, too."[50]

"The Ambassador," as he was from now on to be called, was at the height of his public career. The English were delighted and amused by the improper Bostonian, his lovely wife, and their nine children. "His bouncing offspring make the most politically ingratiating family since Theodore Roosevelt's," commented *Life* magazine. "Whether or not Franklin Roosevelt thought of it beforehand, it has turned out that when he appointed Mr. Kennedy to be Ambassador to Great Britain he got eleven Ambassadors for the price of one."[51]

* As Kennedy put it; "It was felt that the President had appointed me as Chairman of the SEC because he knew that I knew all the angles of trading, that I had studied pools and participated in them and was aware of all the intricacies and trickeries of market manipulation. This, it seems, made many people nervous." Joseph P. Kennedy as told to John B. Kennedy, "Shielding the Sheep," *Saturday Evening Post*, January 18, 1936, pp. 61 and 64.

The Kennedys were celebrities. They were even being satirized in a Broadway musical. Jack, a student at Harvard, had seen Victor Moore and Sophie Tucker in *Leave It to Me,* and reported to his parents that "the jokes about us got by far the biggest laughs whatever that signifies."[52]

Washington gossip was that Ambassador Kennedy had White House ambitions. The reasoning went that, since F.D.R. was barred by precedent from seeking a third term in 1940, Joe would emerge as a contender doubly blessed by Roosevelt and business. Ernest K. Lindley even wrote a magazine article entitled, "Will Kennedy Run for President?"†

Yet the man who stands on the political peak is often only one step removed from the precipice. As Hitler cast his net over Europe, Joe Kennedy took the fatal step. He threw his prestige behind the "peace at any price" policy of a former Birmingham hardware manufacturer with an umbrella, Neville Chamberlain. Never one to keep his opinions a secret, Joe announced: "It has long been a theory of mine that it is unproductive for both the democratic and dictator countries to widen the division now existing between them by emphasizing their difference . . . they could advantageously bend their energies toward solving their common problems by an attempt to re-establish good relations on a world basis."[53]

Kennedy's isolationism was based on a supposition and a desire, according to Harold Ickes, who was witness to an argument on the subject between Joe and Ambassador to France William Bullitt. Joe's supposition was that Germany was going to win the war; his desire was to save his children.[54]

Why did Roosevelt continue to retain an outspoken "appeaser" as his ambassador to Great Britain? The answer was probably supplied by columnists Joseph Alsop and Robert Kintner, who wrote, "The President regards Kennedy as likely to do less harm in London than in New York."[55]

But when Britain entered the war Kennedy's days in London were numbered. Roosevelt began by-passing his ambassador and dealing directly with Churchill, the new Prime Minister. Joe finally resigned his post after a Boston *Globe* interview, which he thought was off the record, revealed the extent of his isolationism as well as his comments on Churchill's fondness for brandy, the King's speech impediment, the Queen's housewifely appearance, and Eleanor Roosevelt's notes asking him "to have some little Susie Glotz to tea at the Embassy."[56]

Joseph P. Kennedy was never again to be a political force in his own right.

† His conclusion: "Professional political handicappers will give heavy odds against him at this stage. But a few connoisseurs of Presidential material are willing to make long-shot bets that the next Democratic nominee for President will be Joseph Patrick Kennedy." Ernest K. Lindley, "Will Kennedy Run for President?" *Liberty,* May 21, 1938, p. 15.

Nineteen-forty, the terminal year of Joe Kennedy's political career, was also the year of political awakening for his two oldest sons.

Two decades later Rose Kennedy would say that her sons were "rocked to political lullabies."[57] But the famous family dinner-table conversations (in later days pictured as almost a junior Algonquin round table) were primarily concerned with the men and moves of politics, not substantive issues. Young Jack could write his parents that "tonight is a big night in Boston as the Honorable John F. Fitzgerald is making a speech for his good friend, James Michael," and yet, at the same time, be so little aware of the great depression that he asked to be sent the *Literary Digest* "because I did not know about the Market Slump until a long time after. . . ."[58]‡

Jack Kennedy entered Harvard in 1936, the year Henry Cabot Lodge, Jr., was elected to the Senate, and as a scholar, in the opinion of one of his professors, was "reasonably inconspicuous."[59] He spent his junior year in Europe, partly working for his father at the embassy, and like another ambassador's son in the nineteenth century, the experience was revealing. (Jack Kennedy and Henry Adams were not so dissimilar at this period in their lives.) He returned to Harvard imbued with his father's view of the European situation and wrote a senior thesis entitled, "Appeasement at Munich: The Inevitable Result of the Slowness of the British Democracy to Change from a Disarmament Policy." Arthur Krock helped him get it published and suggested a new title, *Why England Slept*. It was an immediate success, selling 80,000 copies in the United States and England. As publisher Henry Luce wrote in the foreword, it was "a remarkable book" for two reasons: first, because of its "dispassionate" tone; and second, because it was written "by one so young."[60] For the first time the young man had become engaged in public issues, and, while the substance was still his father's, he was developing a style that was markedly his own.

In 1940 Joe, Jr., a twenty-five-year-old student at Harvard Law School, shared his father's isolationist views and bitterness toward F.D.R. As a Massachusetts delegate to the Democratic National Convention the young man pledged himself against a third term for the incumbent. The Roosevelt forces mercilessly beat on him to change his vote. But in this fiery baptism in national politics Joe stood firm. When the roll call ticked off the delegates' devotion to the President, he defiantly called out a protest vote for James A. Farley.[61]

‡ "In a recent interview," wrote Douglass Cater in 1959, "he [John F. Kennedy] was entirely prepared to admit that the coming of the New Deal had little intellectual or emotional impact on him. He cannot remember that it was the subject of much discussion around the family dinner table." See "The Cool Eye of John F. Kennedy," *Reporter*, December 10, 1959, p. 28.

After Pearl Harbor the Kennedys shed their isolationism and went to war. Young Joe became a navy pilot; Jack finally convinced the navy that he was serviceable despite a football injury to his back. He was given a desk job in Washington but used his father's influence to get transferred to PT boats. Even the ambassador wired Roosevelt that he wanted an assignment; the request was not granted.

Kathleen Kennedy returned to London to work in a Red Cross canteen and there fell in love with Billy Cavendish, Marquess of Hartington, son of the tenth Duke of Devonshire. The Cavendishes were among England's richest landholders. Their 180,000 acres included the estates of Chatsworth House, Hardwick Hall, Bolton Abbey, Compton Place, and Lismore Castle in Ireland. They were also militantly Protestant. Indeed the first Duke of Devonshire had withdrawn from the Privy Council of King Charles II in protest against Catholic influence, and the present duke was grand master of the Freemasons.

But Kathleen went ahead with the marriage despite her parents' protests. The wedding took place in May 1944 at the Chelsea Registry Office. Joe, Jr., then stationed in England, stood by his sister during the family crisis and gave the bride away. The bridegroom wore the uniform of the Coldstream Guards. Kathleen, as the future Duchess of Devonshire, could expect one day to be first lady in waiting to the Queen and mistress of the royal robes; the devout Rose could expect to be mother-in-law to the ranking Mason in the world. A London correspondent wrote, "One of England's oldest and loftiest family trees swayed perceptibly." In Boston Rose said she was "too sick to discuss the marriage."[62]

The young couple lived together for a little more than a month. Then the marquess went into combat in France and on September 10, while leading an infantry patrol, he was killed in action.

His death came only three weeks after young Joe Kennedy had been killed while performing a daring mission designed to destroy enemy submarine pens on the Belgian coast. Although eligible for rotation home, he had volunteered to fly a Liberator bomber loaded with 22,000 pounds of high explosives. The plan was for the pilot and co-pilot to parachute to safety when their plan neared the Channel coast, and for other planes to guide the Liberator to its target by remote control. For unknown reasons, before reaching the bail-out point Joe's plane suddenly exploded.

Within four years tragedy struck again. While flying to a reunion with her father on the Riviera, Kathleen's plane crashed into the Ardèche mountains. In the village of Privas, halfway between Lyons and Marseilles, Joseph Kennedy identified the body of his daughter.

"The thing about Kathleen and Joe was their tremendous vitality," Jack was to say. "Everything was moving in their direction . . . for someone who is living at their peak, then to get cut off—that's the shock."[63]

The untimely passing of the two young Kennedys, who had been marked by the family to lead their generation, acted as a catalyst on the others. It speeded up their motor reactions and geared them into an emotional overdrive. "The boys," said a friend in 1957, "are trying to live up to the image of Joe as they remember him. . . . The girls feel the same obligation to emulate Kathleen."[64]

After the war Jack Kennedy had to decide what to do with himself.

If he had taken inventory he would have found that, like Theodore Roosevelt, he had been trained for no profession; he was a war hero in peacetime, the savior of the crew of PT-109 after it had been rammed by a Japanese destroyer; his health was bad; he thought he might like to try his hand at newspaper reporting, but found it too passive; he had no interest in running his father's financial empire; yet neither did he have money worries or the necessity to administer his patrimony, since Joe Kennedy's office on New York's Park Avenue even took care of paying his personal bills.

The problem was solved for him in 1946 when Grandfather Honey Fitz's old nemesis, James Michael Curley, decided to give up his seat in the House of Representatives and try to become again mayor of Boston. Jack Kennedy ran for Congress.

Whether it was his idea or his father's is confused by contradictory quotations. "I got Jack into politics, I was the one," said Father Kennedy. "I told him Joe was dead and that it was therefore his responsibility to run for Congress. He didn't want to. . . . But I told him he had to." Jack then added: "It was like being drafted. My father wanted his eldest son in politics. 'Wanted' isn't the right word. He demanded it." But later, when he was a presidential contender and the ambassador was being sidelined for the duration, Jack explained, "I wanted to run and was glad I could."[65]

The Eleventh Congressional District was overwhelmingly Democratic. It included East Boston, Boston's North End and West End, Cambridge, Charlestown, and parts of Brighton and Somerville. The population was made up of Irish-Americans, Italian-Americans, and thirty-three other groups separated by hyphens. Of scenic interest was Bunker Hill, Harvard University, and some of the worst slums in the city. The district also contained the former strongholds of P. J. Kennedy and John F. Fitzgerald. When Curley heard that a candidate bore both names, he said, "He doesn't even need to campaign. He can go to Washington now and forget the primary and election."[66]

But the Kennedys took nothing for granted. Family friends came from as far away as Pittsburgh and San Francisco to work for Jack. A goodly number of Harvard students pitched in. Twenty-one-year-old Bobby, recently a seaman on the destroyer *Joseph P. Kennedy Jr.*, was put in charge of three East Cambridge wards. The Kennedy workers, according to Dave Powers, wore Eisenhower jackets on primary day—to remind voters that, besides a WAC major, Jack was the only veteran in the race. But there was little chance they would forget: the district had been saturated with John Hersey's *Reader's Digest* account of Kennedy's heroics. Neither effort nor money was spared. "Jokesters around the State House," reported Robert Bendiner in the *Nation,* "took to wearing twenty-dollar bills in their lapels as 'Kennedy campaign buttons.'"[67] Jack received nearly as many votes as his eight primary opponents combined; the general election was a mere formality. Kennedy became the Bay State's youngest congressman in over half a century; in fact, since his own grandfather was elected to the same seat in 1894.

It was the year of a new order in politics, 1946. In California another young naval veteran, Richard Nixon, unexpectedly won a seat in Congress; Henry Cabot Lodge, back from army service, regained his place in the Senate; a marine named Joe McCarthy ended the La Follette dynasty in Wisconsin. The Republicans, under the leadership of Robert A. Taft, captured the Congress for the first time in sixteen years. And twenty-nine-year-old John F. Kennedy began a career that had been reserved for his older brother, now dead, and for which he felt he was not equipped.§

The young congressman, who moved into a house in the fashionable Georgetown section of Washington with his sister Eunice, had an orderly, analytical mind (viz: *Why England Slept*), a high order of physical courage (viz: his wartime experiences), stamina and an attractive personality (viz: his campaign for Congress). The ladies particularly found him appealing. As columnist James Reston later wrote, "The effect he has on women voters is almost naughty."[68] But he had not yet developed a political philosophy, nor did he have a body of experience to prepare him to serve a disadvantaged urban district. He was Choate, Harvard, Palm Beach. He was socially secure enough to arrive at a formal dinner at Perle Mesta's wearing brown loafers; financially secure enough to deliver a check to the archbishop for one million dollars and not have the fare to pay the cabby.

The liberal-labor establishment of the Truman Administration and the ethnic politicians who ran his state party found him enigmatic. He had got elected primarily because he was Joe Kennedy's son and Honey Fitz's grandson; since he owed nothing to the pols, this made him suspect in their eyes. Moreover, they had never liked his father in the first place. ("Drink bourbon," Harry Truman is alleged to have said. "Every time you drink Scotch you make Joe Kennedy richer!"[69])

§ "After all," John F. Kennedy later said, "I wasn't equipped for it. I didn't plan to get into it, and when I started out as a congressman, there were lots of things I didn't know. . . ." See Ralph G. Martin and Ed Plaut, *Front Runner, Dark Horse* (Garden City, N.Y.: Doubleday, 1960), p. 148.

While Jack voted the straight Fair Deal line, as his constituency required, the liberals questioned the depth of his convictions. He, in turn, told a *Saturday Evening Post* writer, "I'd be very happy to tell them I'm not a liberal at all. . . . I never joined the Americans for Democratic Action or American Veterans Committee. I'm not comfortable with these people."[70] His attendance record was poor. He didn't have the herding instinct expected in a new House member.

After two years in Congress he began making speeches in all parts of Massachusetts. He didn't yet know what higher officer he was seeking. All he knew was that he was in a hurry and could not wait for seniority to catch up to ambition.

The opportunity presented itself in 1952, when Henry Cabot Lodge, Jr., came up for re-election. Kennedy may not have earned the nomination, but nobody else wanted it. The senator was formidable. Wrote Ralph Blagden in the *Reporter:* "It is difficult to see how Lodge deserves retirement. . . ."[71] Joe Kennedy urged his son to oppose Lodge. "When you've beaten him," he said, "you've beaten the best."[72]

One of Jack's problems was that the Lodges were in the midst of a half-century love affair with the Boston Irish. The elder Senator Lodge had been the first Brahmin politician to recognize their growing power; he and his grandson had acted accordingly. Said Joe Kennedy, with disgust: "All I ever heard when I was growing up in Boston was how Lodge's grandfather had helped to put the stained glass windows into the Gate of Heaven Church in South Boston and they were still talking about these same stained glass windows in 1952."[73]

But Lodge was met by a solid phalanx of Kennedys that would have pleased a Clausewitz. Besides the handsome senatorial candidate, there were:

—The ever present father, lavish with advice, contacts, and money. (One letter of solicitation began: "Believe it or not, Jack Kennedy needs money." But nobody took it seriously.) The powerful Boston *Post* broke with its Republican tradition to endorse Jack, and it was later revealed that Joe Kennedy had made a post-election loan of a half million dollars to the paper.[74]

—Brother Bobby, now a graduate of Harvard and the University of Virginia Law School, who gave up his job with the Justice Department to become Jack's campaign manager. He displayed the Kennedy dedication to family, combined with a super-Kennedian capacity for hard work and a rare organizational talent. "Let Jack be charming to them," he said.[75] Bobby, without complaint, would be the hatchet man. (Younger brother Teddy was then serving an army hitch in Germany.)

—The Kennedy women. Mother Rose and sisters Eunice, Pat, and Jean introduced tea as a political weapon: 8600 cups were consumed at one reception, and receptions were held in every corner of the state.

("It was those damn teas that licked me," Lodge was later reported to have said.[76]) Ethel, Bobby's wife, made a speech in Fall River, then drove to Boston and had a baby. ("When Archbishop Cushing baptized the baby . . . just before the election," said a Lodge aide, "that cut our hearts out."[77])

—Even ghosts of Kennedys past. A campaign tabloid featured a photograph of Joe, Jr., captioned: "John Fulfills Dream of Brother Joe Who Met Death in the Sky over the English Channel."[78]

Jack Kennedy told audiences that "my grandfather, the late John F. Fitzgerald, ran for the United States Senate thirty-six years ago against my opponent's grandfather, Henry Cabot Lodge, and he lost by only 30,000 votes in an election where women were not allowed to vote. I hope that by impressing the female electorate that I can more than take up the slack."[79] He did. Kennedy won by over 70,000 votes. "At last," said Rose Fitzgerald Kennedy, "the Fitzgeralds have evened the score with the Lodges!"[80]

Joseph Patrick III, born and christened at propitious times during his uncle Jack's successful campaign for the Senate in 1952, was the first male of a new generation of Kennedys. Ethel Kennedy had given birth to a girl, Kathleen Harrington, the year before. She would eventually have nine children—two, appropriately, on the Fourth of July—and, like her mother-in-law, would institute an index card system to keep track of their illnesses, vaccinations, and shots.

The young mother, slim, athletic, with brown eyes and sun-bleached hair, had no trouble adapting to the Kennedy clan. For she too was from a large and wealthy Catholic family. Her father, George Skakel, was a self-made millionaire who started as a railroad man, became a traffic expert in coal, and went on to control the Great Lakes Carbon Corporation, one of the largest privately owned companies in the United States.¶

Ethel Skakel had been Jean Kennedy's roommate at Manhattanville College of the Sacred Heart. She further prepped for life as a Kennedy by writing her senior thesis on *Why England Slept* and working in Jack's first congressional campaign in 1946.

She became known, in the Kennedy circle, as a fierce touch football player, even when pregnant; mistress of Hickory Hill, which abounded with pets (including a favorite sea lion), and the "only tree-house in the world that was designed by an architect"; a firm believer in the "method" school of living—whether it meant singing to Marian Anderson or spraying a member of European royalty from head to foot with an aerosol can

¶ Her three brothers—Rushton, James, and George Skakel, Jr.—now control the company, as well as its subsidiary, Great Lakes Properties, which bought 5000 acres in Camarillo, California, for an estimated twenty million dollars. See Los Angeles *Times*, February 13, 1965, p. 1.

of shaving cream. Ethel, in the opinion of one writer, is an "authentic American primitive—vivid, informal, artless, positive, happy and spontaneous."[81]

Very different was the shy, wide-eyed beauty whom Jack Kennedy was secretly courting during his 1952 senatorial campaign.

Jacqueline Lee Bouvier was descended on her father's side from a French soldier who fought at Yorktown, and on her mother's side distantly from the Lees of Virginia and Maryland. Arthur Krock remembers her father, John Vernon Bouvier III, a New York stockbroker, as "one of the most famously attractive men" who ever lived.[82] A society reporter in East Hampton thought "that he much resembles one of those handsome Egyptians you see careening along in their Rolls-Royce cars in Cairo, in the land of the Nile!"[83] He was known at Yale as "the Black Orchid." Jacqueline's mother, Janet Lee, was the child of a conservative New York banker, president of the Central Savings Bank, who gave his daughter a duplex apartment on Park Avenue when she was married in 1928.

Twelve years later, "with a hint of scandal in the air," they were divorced.[84] Jacqueline was then eleven and her sister Lee seven. Their Catholic father never remarried. But in 1942 their mother, an Episcopalian and not barred by religious conviction from a second marriage, became the wife of thrice-wed Hugh D. Auchincloss, a Washington stockbroker, whose winter estate in Virginia was called Merrywood and whose summer estate in Newport was called Hammersmith Farm. Auchincloss had three children by his previous unions, and would have two more by Jacqueline's mother. "It is a tribute to my mother," thought the future First Lady, "that though our family is steps and halfs, we don't feel like it. We are very close."[85]

Befitting her station, Jacqueline attended the most exclusive girls' schools—Chapin in New York, Holton Arms in Washington, and Miss Porter's School in Farmington, Connecticut, where she kept her own horse. She summered in East Hampton (with her father) and in Newport (with her stepfather). When she formally entered society, Hearst columnist Cholly Knickerbocker dubbed her "Queen Deb of the Year." She was then a student at Vassar. Later she spent her junior year at the Sorbonne. She won *Vogue* magazine's Prix de Paris, having submitted an essay, "People I Wish I Had Known." (They were Diaghilev, Oscar Wilde, and Baudelaire.) She finished her college education close to home at George Washington University.

Through Arthur Krock, whose avocation seems to have been manipulating the fortunes of the Kennedys, Jacqueline got a job on the Washington *Times-Herald* as the Inquiring Camera Girl. For $42.50 a week she asked such posers as: What do you think of wrestling as a sport for women? Would you like to crash high society? Do a candidate's looks influence your vote? What do you think of psychoanalysis? (One answer:

"Psychoanalysis is not natively American. It was brought in by foreigners and has never added one bit to this country's peace of mind.") She also went to Capitol Hill to find out what the solons thought of Senate page boys. (Richard M. Nixon: "I would predict that some future statesman will come from the ranks of the page corps. . . ." John F. Kennedy: "I've often thought that the country might be better off if we Senators and the pages traded jobs. . . ."[86]) Her biggest scoop, however, came when she waited outside a Washington public school to interview the ten- and eleven-year-old nieces of President-elect Eisenhower. The story appeared on page one, and the indignant mother called Jacqueline's editor to complain that her children's privacy had been invaded.

Congressman Kennedy's courtship of the Inquiring Camera Girl was a casual affair. He was away campaigning most of the time. Now and then he would call from some roadside pay phone "with a great clinking of coins." There were no love letters, just one postcard, "Wish you were here. Jack." When he proposed, the new senator said that he had decided to marry her a year before. "How *big* of you!" she replied.[87] The engagement was finally announced in June 1953. (It had been planned for an earlier date but was postponed so that the *Saturday Evening Post* could put out an article on Jack entitled, "The Senate's Gay Young Bachelor.")* They had a Newport wedding in September.

The new world of the Kennedys presented problems for a young lady whose sport was fox hunting ("it makes me feel clean and anonymous") rather than touch football. When she tried the latter, she broke an ankle. "Everybody tells the story as though the Kennedys roughed up a young bride," she said. "But it wasn't that way at all. I was running happily along by myself near the sideline when I slipped and fell. There wasn't a Kennedy within yards." Thus ended Jacqueline Kennedy's short career as a football player.[88]

There was also the problem of Joseph P. Kennedy. Early in her married life Jacqueline was late for lunch, a hitherto unpardonable sin in the patriarch's house. He started to needle her. But she cut him short, turning his slang and moralistic tales on him: "You ought to write a series of grandfather stories for children like The Duck with Moxie and The Donkey Who Couldn't Find His Way Out of a Telephone Booth."[89] Everyone waited for an explosion—instead Joe Kennedy broke out laughing. The bride had won her place in the dynasty. Later she would do water-color paintings especially for her father-in-law, such as one titled, "You Can't Take It with You, Dad's Got It All." The family's

---

* Said the article: "Many women have hopefully concluded that Kennedy needs looking after. In their opinion, he is, as a young millionaire senator, just about the most eligible bachelor in the United States—and the least justifiable one." Paul F. Healy, "The Senate's Gay Young Bachelor," *Saturday Evening Post*, June 13, 1953, p. 26.

judgment of Jacqueline was summed up by Bobby: "She's poetic, whimsical, provocative, independent, and yet very feminine. Jackie has always kept her own identity and been different. That's important in a
woman. What husband wants to come home at night and talk to another
version of himself? Jack knows she'll never greet him with 'What's new
in Laos?' "[90]

Two Kennedys were present when the 83rd Congress convened in
January 1953. Besides the new senator from Massachusetts, there was a
new associate counsel of the Senate Permanent Investigations Subcom-
mittee, Robert Francis Kennedy.

"Bobby is more direct than Jack. He resembles me much more than
any of the other children," thought their father. "He hates the same way
I do," Joe later added.[91] Unlike Jack, who tended to view issues as
an intricate variety of grays, there was in Bobby a tendency to see life
in contrasting blacks and whites. Jack had a cool grace; Bobby was emotional, sometimes explosive. The Puritan in him was accentuated by a
harsh, almost metallic voice. His speech was inelegant, as was his dress.

The Kennedys shared a preoccupation with power. But since Bobby
lacked Jack's finesse, it was more apparent in him. It was not the abstract idea that fascinated them—they had little patience with abstrac-
tions—but the men who had power and knew how to use it.

Here was a young man who had moved far and fast in the cause of
his brother. And he moved with a straight arm. Was it only that in the
sprint his more unattractive traits rose first to the surface? Those who
knew him best said he also had an appealing shyness, his mother's deep
religious convictions, and a sensitiveness to family, friends, and associates.
He was still a personality in transition.

By the time Bobby joined the McCarthy staff the Wisconsin senator
had already added an "ism" to the language. Three years before, in
Wheeling, West Virginia, he had announced the number of "known Communists" in the State Department and ushered in an incredible era. The
association with McCarthyism did not seem to concern Bobby. The
senator was known and liked by the Kennedys. The ambassador had
contributed to his campaign for re-election; Pat had dated him; Bobby
had invited him to speak at the University of Virginia. When, after six
months, Bobby resigned from the McCarthy Committee, it was not because of a disagreement with the chairman but because of a personality
clash with chief counsel Roy Cohn.

He then went to work for the Hoover Commission, which was proposing government reorganization, and of which Joe Kennedy was a member. Bobby found the work dull. Within eight months he was back on the
McCarthy Committee as the minority counsel to Democratic Senators
McClellan, Jackson, and Symington. In this capacity he wrote the Army-

McCarthy report, finding fault with both sides. But when the Watkins Committee voted to condemn McCarthy, Bobby was fishing in the Pacific Northwest.

Jack was also absent, in the hospital having surgery performed on his back. He was one of two senators who was not recorded on the McCarthy censure. In a speech that was not delivered, he said that he favored censure, but primarily because of the conduct of Roy Cohn. "I was rather in ill grace personally to be around hollering about what McCarthy had done in 1952 or 1951 when my brother had been on the staff in 1953," the senator told Professor James MacGregor Burns. "That is really the guts of the matter."[92]

After being close to death, Jack Kennedy slowly began to recover and, while his back was mending, he started to write another book. The idea came to him while reading about how Senator John Quincy Adams voted for Jefferson's embargo against the dictates of his own party. Why not a series of essays on political courage as displayed by American legislators? His list of subjects included Senators Daniel Webster (for supporting Clay's compromise between North and South), Edmund Ross (for voting against the impeachment of Andrew Johnson), George Norris (for backing Al Smith for President), and Robert Taft (for opposing the Nuremberg trials). *Profiles in Courage* was an instant success. There were critics, of course, such as Alfred Kazin, who felt that the book reminded him "of those little anecdotes from the lives of great men that are found in *Reader's Digest*, Sunday supplements, and the journal of the American Legion."[93] But the majority of readers were delighted to find that a U.S. senator was literate.

Kennedy was surprised that some cynics questioned his authorship. "The book isn't so good that it has to be ghosted," he said.[94] But despite the author's modesty, his book was awarded the Pulitzer Prize. (Again Arthur Krock was in the background. "I was on the Pulitzer board," said the New York *Times* columnist, "and I worked as hard as I could to get him that prize."[95])

In *Profiles in Courage* Jack Kennedy wrote, "Few, if any, face the same dread finality of decision that confronts a Senator facing an important call of the roll . . . when that roll is called he cannot hide, he cannot equivocate, he cannot delay. . . ."[96] Along with his failure to face the dread finality of the McCarthy issue, the handsome senator-author had to listen to innumerable word plays (including Eleanor Roosevelt's) about "showing less profile and more courage." The Washington Gridiron Club (to the tune of "Clementine") serenaded him with:

"Where were you, John—where were you, John,
When the Senate censored Joe?"

Though he ducked the McCarthy censure issue, Jack Kennedy also cast one vote during his first term in the Senate that could have qualified him for a place in a revised edition of *Profiles in Courage*. This was on the St. Lawrence Seaway. Feeling that its passage was of overriding national importance, he voted against the narrower interests of the port of Boston and his state. In 1960 he considered it the most difficult decision he had ever made. New England newspapers called him the "Suicide Senator."

"It was the turning point," said his assistant, Ted Sorensen, "between Jack as a Massachusetts senator and a national statesman."[97]

Between 1953 and 1956 the Kennedy family circle was increased by three as Eunice, Pat, and Jean were married.

Joe Kennedy paid daughter Eunice his highest compliment—she "has more drive than Jack or even Bobby," he said.[98] While all the girls were deeply involved in philanthropic and civic chores, Eunice was least inclined to choose the garden club variety. Once she spent a month inside a women's reformatory observing prison conditions.† She was then executive secretary to the National Conference on Juvenile Delinquency, and shared a Washington house with her bachelor congressman brother.

Eunice and Jack looked alike, both tall and heavily boned. They had the same mannerisms, even the same habit of stabbing the air with the index finger of the left hand; the same rapid-fire delivery, the same Boston accent, the same intellectual approach. Sargent Shriver said they were even subject to the same ailments. But Eunice could also be moody, outspoken, often tactless, sometimes rude, occasionally oblivious to the obvious. "Where was I yesterday?" she once inquired of Kennedy headquarters at 230 Park Avenue. "You were in Westbury, Long Island."[99]

The man Eunice married was from the Catholic branch of an old Maryland family. His parents were both Shrivers—second cousins—and maternal Grandfather Shriver had been a state senator, as well as roommate during a brief seminary period of a Baltimore youth named James Gibbons. (Cardinal Gibbons was to be Sargent Shriver's godfather.) Sarge's father, at one time a vice-president of the Baltimore Trust Company, was heavily hit by the stock market crash, causing the son to work while at Yale—as editor of the profit-making student newspaper—though he was still able to spend several college summers in Europe. Like the Kennedys, exposure to the European conflict turned young Shriver into an isolationist, but he too promptly enlisted as a submariner when the United States entered the war.

Returning from navy duty, the ruggedly handsome young veteran first

† Sargent Shriver, who was then courting her, said that she introduced him to "Machine Gun Kelly's wife, and other such interesting people." He was also surprised when Eunice invited some of the former inmates to their wedding reception. See Washington *Post*, February 18, 1965, p. E5.

joined a Wall Street law firm, found the work distasteful, then got a job on *Newsweek*, which his biographer felt was "slipping from under him" when Eunice introduced him to her father.[100] The chemistry was right. Joe liked the young man's competitive drive, frankness, religious convictions, and perhaps his prospects as a son-in-law. He gave him a job with the Merchandise Mart, where Sarge proved to be a supersalesman. In 1953, after a six-year courtship, Eunice Kennedy, thirty-one, and Sargent Shriver, thirty-seven, were married by Cardinal Spellman at St. Patrick's Cathedral. The groom's mother wasn't overly impressed by her son's famous in-laws. "We're nicer than the Kennedys," she said. "We've been here since the 1600s."[101]‡

Three years later St. Patrick's was the scene of another Kennedy wedding. Jack's favorite sister, Jean, the youngest, quietest, and least political, married Stephen E. Smith. After college she had tried working among juvenile delinquents with Eunice in Chicago but felt herself emotionally unsuited for it and joined the Christophers, a Catholic organization dedicated to fighting Communism and raising moral standards.

Her husband was a grandson of William E. Cleary, a run-of-the-mill Brooklyn congressman who opposed Prohibition and supported river and harbor improvements.[102] "Old Bill" also founded a sizable tugboat business, Cleary Brothers, for which Steve Smith worked after graduating from Georgetown University and serving as an air force officer. "My real job," he said, "was to see that the captains weren't drunk and to get the coal loaded."[103]

In appearance Smith has been compared to "a hard-boiled Freddy Bartholomew." He is handsome enough, wrote Tom Wicker of the New York *Times*, for one to imagine him "dashing onto a Broadway stage in flannels, shouting 'Tennis anyone?'"[104] Yet behind his fashion-plate dress, his shy manner, and his clipped, rapid, barely audible speech there lurks a "nerveless bandit." (So says a former aide when complimenting Smith's later political activities in behalf of his brothers-in-law.)

After marrying Jean he left the family firm to work for Joe Kennedy. Eventually he would supervise his in-laws' fortune. But Smith wished it understood: "My family had money before the Kennedys had money."[105]

Commenting on Jean's husband, Murray Kempton wrote in the *New Republic*, "For he is very like a Kennedy, even to the family intonations; and, since he gives the impression of having too much character to

‡ Mrs. Shriver overstated her case. The Schriebers—the name was later anglicized—came to America in the first great migration of Palatine Germans between 1709 and 1727. They settled in Union Mills, Maryland, in 1797. According to a family historian, a large number of them have been engaged in such manual occupations as plumbing, butchery, and carpentry. See Harry Clair Shriver, *A History of the Shriver Family* (Privately printed, 1962).

imitate an in-law, we may explain him as another example of the tendency of sisters in large families to marry young men who remind them of their brothers."[106] And Eunice, in a corollary to Kempton's Law, lifted a champagne glass at her wedding reception in a toast to her new husband: "I searched all my life for someone like my father," she said, "and Sarge came closest."[107]

Nobody, however, could have mistaken Pat's husband for a Kennedy.

When actor Peter Lawford was first presented to his future father-in-law he was wearing a blue blazer, white trousers, loafers, and bright red socks. "Mr. Kennedy," Lawford reported, "couldn't seem to take his eyes from the socks."[108]

But Pat, prettiest and most emotional of the Kennedy girls, always had liked "show biz." After graduating from Rosemont College she became a production assistant on Kate Smith's radio program and subsequently worked for "Father Peyton's Family Theatre" and the "Family Rosary Crusade" ("The Family That Prays Together Stays Together").

Peter was the only son of Lieutenant General Sir Sydney and Lady Lawford.§ For years he had been under contract to Metro-Goldwyn-Mayer and had appeared in a long string of mediocre films, playing such parts as Elizabeth Taylor's boy friend in *Julia Misbehaves*. But at age thirty he had outgrown the college-boy roles and his career was foundering. His major claim to fame was as part of Frank Sinatra's "Rat Pack," among whose members he was known as "Charley the Seal." (Sinatra and Lawford are now "estranged."[109])

Pat and Peter were married in 1954, after he converted to Catholicism. Said Lady Lawford, "I wasn't too happy about Peter marrying into the Kennedy family." Her view was apparently shared by Joe Kennedy, who told her son, "Peter, if there's anything I think I'd hate as a son-in-law, it's an actor; and if there's anything I think I'd hate worse than an actor as a son-in-law, it's an English actor."[110] The marriage lasted eleven years.

For Ted Sorensen the turning point between Jack Kennedy as a Massachusetts senator and a national statesman came with the vote on

§ Lieutenant General Sir Sydney Lawford (1865–1953), K.C.B., graduated from Sandhurst and joined the British army in 1885. He was cited for bravery in the Boer War and commanded a division in World War I. Commenting on his personal courage in France, Sir Jocelyn Lucas wrote, "When a shrapnel shell took his horse's head off as he was galloping along, he picked himself up, and having taken a signaller's mount rode on as if nothing had happened. . . ." Lawford retired in 1926, moved to the United States in 1938, and took minor parts in films, including the role of a British army general in *The Rogues' March*. See *The Times of London*, February 17, 1953, p. 11; February 20, 1953, p. 8.

the St. Lawrence Seaway, but to the more casual observer the turning point was the 1956 Democratic Convention.

When Jack Kennedy rose to place Adlai Stevenson's name in nomination for the presidency it was the first time that most Americans had seen the handsome young senator. And when Stevenson then threw the vice-presidential nomination up for grabs, there was an immediate ground swell for Kennedy.

Stevenson's decision caught the convention off guard; the Kennedys had only overnight to round up votes. "I'll never forget Bobby Kennedy during the balloting," said Quentin Burdick of North Dakota. "Standing in front of our delegation with tears in his eyes, he pleaded for our support."[111] Even Peter Lawford was pressed into service. From Los Angeles he called his friend Wilbur Clark, operator of the Desert Inn in Las Vegas and a Nevada delegate; on the second ballot Kennedy got thirteen of Nevada's fourteen votes. On the third ballot Kennedy climbed to within thirty-eight votes of the nomination, but then his vote total froze and Estes Kefauver was nominated. Calm, smiling, Jack Kennedy climbed to the rostrum and asked that the nomination be made by acclamation. The millions who had watched the cliff-hanging drama on television now applauded a good loser. At that moment Jack Kennedy became a national figure.

The defeat in 1956 had an unusual effect on Kennedy. It dispelled a cloud that he lived under—the curious belief that he was merely a shadowy substitute for his dead brother. As he told Bob Considine in 1957, "Joe was the star of our family. He did everything better than the rest of us. If he had lived he would have gone on in politics and he would have been elected to the House and to the Senate as I was. And, like me, he would have gone for the vice-presidential nomination at the 1956 convention, but, unlike me, he wouldn't have been beaten. Joe would have won the nomination." Jack paused and smiled. "And then he and Stevenson would have been beaten by Eisenhower, and today Joe's political career would be in shambles and he would be trying to pick up the pieces."[112]

Far from picking up pieces, by June of 1957 Jack Kennedy had become the most sought-after speaker on the Democratic Party circuit. He had engagements in nineteen states, and as a fellow senator said, "When you see a senator doing much speaking outside his own state, it means one of two things. He needs the money or he's got his eye on higher office. And Jack doesn't need the money."[113] Joseph Alsop casually said to him in the summer of 1958, "Of course, the vice-presidential nomination will be yours for the asking next time." Jack replied with a grin, "Let's not talk so much about vice. I'm against vice, in all forms."[114]

The presidency was a farfetched goal for a very young man and a

Catholic. Yet even beyond this was the fuzzy outline of something seemingly more preposterous. As early as 1957, Harold Martin wrote in the *Saturday Evening Post:*

Fervent admirers of the Kennedys profess to see in their rise to national prominence the flowering of another great political family, such as the Adamses, the Lodges and the La Follettes. They confidently look forward to the day when Jack [*then forty*] will be in the White House, Bobby [*then thirty-two*] will serve in the Cabinet as Attorney General, and Teddy [*then twenty-five*] will be the senator from Massachusetts.[115]

As Kennedys and their in-laws left homes in Boston, New York, Washington, Los Angeles, Chicago, and Palm Beach to join the family crusade for the presidency, Hubert Humphrey shook his head sadly and said he felt like an independent merchant running against a chain store.

Bobby, who had created a national reputation of his own as the counsel for the McClellan Rackets Committee, became his brother's campaign manager. Steve Smith came to Washington in January 1959 to open Jack's headquarters. He would be office manager, logistical expert, and administrator of finances and personnel. Teddy, best-looking of the family and as amiable as a big Irish cop, toured Wisconsin and West Virginia and was put in charge of corralling delegates in the Western states. Sarge Shriver, now a rising Illinois politician and president of the Chicago Board of Education, ran two districts in the Wisconsin primary. Even the widow of Honey Fitz, the candidate's ninety-five-year-old grandmother, was put to work; she spoke by telephone from Boston to a dinner meeting in West Virginia.

But what to do with Joe? His money, of course, would be necessary. An insider put the cost of the 1960 nomination drive at $1,150,000— and it can be assumed that most of it came from the family fortune.[116] (Jack, with his uncanny ability to turn a political liability into an asset, told a New York audience that he had received the following wire from his father: "Dear Jack: Don't buy one vote more than necessary. I'll be damned if I'll pay for a landslide."[117]) Joe would also use his contacts among old guard New York leaders. But the decision was made to keep the controversial ambassador under wraps. As an often-repeated couplet of the day went:

> Jack and Bob will run the show,
> While Ted's in charge of hiding Joe.¶

¶ Other Kennedy jokes:
—Joe Kennedy told Jack: "Don't worry, son, if you lose the election, I'll buy you a country." (Anonymous.)
—After the election: "Joe Kennedy hasn't lost a son, he's gained a country." (Mort Sahl.)

The show was masterfully run. Humorist Art Hoppe wrote that when a coffee machine in Kennedy headquarters went dry for three and a half minutes, "It was the first time in the memory of most observers that any machine remotely connected with Senator Kennedy's campaign for the Presidency had failed to function at peak efficiency."[118] The combination of Jack's attractiveness and Bobby's toughness—"a sort of sweet-and-sour brother act," said one politician—rolled to an easy first-ballot nomination.

"Of course, I'm voting for Nixon," was the caption of a *New Yorker* cartoon, "but I can't help wishing I could see what Jackie would do with the White House." Reporters speculated over whether the beautiful wife, a creature of *haute couture* and jet set, would be a political liability. Twenty Iowa housewives signed a letter to the New York *Times* saying, "We have better-looking floor mops" than Jacqueline's bouffant coiffure. She was uneasy with the strange characters who surrounded her husband. When Irish Patsy Mulkern told her, "Ya got to duke da pols," she was amazed to find he meant, "You must shake hands with the politicians."[119] Politics was the intruder in her home. Jack was always off campaigning; half of Caroline's first words (Daddy, airplane, car, shoe, hat, and thank you) had something to do with motion. Yet as her brother-in-law clearly perceived, Jacqueline Kennedy was a political asset. "We came out of that Los Angeles convention looking like a hard, tough family juggernaut," said Bobby, "but in her few gentle low-key TV appearances, Jackie softened that image and put the spotlight back where it belonged—on Jack and his family."[120]

Yet Jackie was not on the stump with her husband after the presidential convention. As the candidate told audiences, she was "otherwise committed." His sisters, particularly Eunice, filled in. And Jack drew laughs by saying, "My wife is going to have a boy in November." How did he know the child's sex? "My wife told me."[121]

However, Jackie's brother-in-law, Prince Stanislas Radziwill, was active in the cause. Lee Bouvier's second husband came from a family that had once been the richest in Poland. He numbered among his ancestors a member of royalty who had disappeared after a scandal involving the suicide of an English nurse, leaving a 100,000-acre estate, including forty-five lumber mills. "Stach" Radziwill came over from London to speak for Jack, and Bobby later told a cheering crowd in Cracow that his brother owed his election to the votes of the Polish-Americans.

(But the husband of Jackie's step-sister Nina was not so co-operative; Newton I. Steers, Jr., was a strong Nixon supporter, a self-styled "flaming moderate," and subsequently Republican state chairman of Maryland.)

The Kennedy strategy was to reconstitute F.D.R.'s winning formula— the coalition of urban politics, machines, Catholics, Jews, Negroes, and other minority groups, while relying on vice-presidential candidate Lyndon Johnson to hold onto the once solid Democratic South. As a veteran Democrat said, "I realized that the Kennedy people . . . were taking a calculated risk. They were going to talk about religion. They were the ones who brought up the religious issue and kept it alive. It wasn't the Republicans."[122] Said Bobby Kennedy at the opening of a headquarters in Cincinnati: "Did they ask my brother Joe whether he was a Catholic before he was shot down?"[123]

The major breakthrough with the Negro vote came after Sargent Shriver convinced the candidate that he should offer his sympathy to the wife of Martin Luther King, the jailed civil rights leader.

Yet probably the most important factor in the contest was the personality of the Democratic candidate. Nixon's attempt to brand his opponent as less mature was shattered by their first televised debate. Millions of viewers agreed that Jack Kennedy looked marvelous and sounded experienced. As Nixon's private pollster reported to him, "Kennedy . . . started the campaign as the less well-known candidate and with many of his adherents wondering about his maturity. He has done a good job [in the TV debates] of dissipating the immaturity label and . . . has succeeded in creating a victory psychology."[124]

The election was decided by two tenths of one per cent of the vote. Joe Kennedy had not paid for a landslide. As the returns came into the Kennedy compound at Hyannis Port, Jacqueline said to her husband, "Oh, Bunny, you're President now!"[125]

The addition of a President to a family brings inevitable changes. Shortly after the election Joe Kennedy determined that his children would go sailing, but Jack declined. Formerly this might have been considered insubordination. Now, however, the patriarch replied, "I don't think the President should have to go if he doesn't want to."[126]

While Joe Kennedy had not for some time been a major influence on his children in questions relating to public policy, he was still a dominant force in their career decisions. Joe had probably got Jack into politics in the first place, although the young man may have been eager to have the decision forced on him; Joe had influenced Bobby into going to work for the McCarthy Committee, while Jack had opposed the idea; Joe had played a major role in Jack's decision to run against Lodge in 1952 and in the subsequent campaign; and now he would once again guide his flock into an unprecedented decision.

Another President, Woodrow Wilson, had once rejected his own brother as a postmaster after a "struggle," he said, "against affection and temptation."[127] But then his brother had not been his campaign manager. Nor had there ever been such a relationship of dependency between a President and his brother. Speaking of Bobby, Dave Powers said, "He's first in Jack's needs, first in Jack's confidence, first in Jack's wants."[128] There was never any doubt that Robert F. Kennedy would be a part of the Administration of John F. Kennedy. The question was: In what job?

The President-elect first thought of making his brother Deputy Secretary of Defense. But their father felt he should be Attorney General, and Jack reluctantly agreed. Then when Bobby hesitated, Jack said, "We'll announce it in a whisper at midnight so no one will notice it." Later Jack told the Alfalfa Club, "I can't see that it's wrong to give him a little legal experience before he goes out to practice law." Bobby didn't think this was funny.[129]

The appointment drew an immediate outcry from those with accumulated complaints against the tough campaign manager. However, as columnist Robert Ruark pointed out, "A lot of people don't like Bobby, but nobody has to love an Attorney General." More serious were the objections of the legal profession. Wrote Yale law professor Alexander Bickel, "On the record, Robert F. Kennedy is not fit for the office."[130] Yet he was confirmed by the Senate with only one dissenting vote (Colorado Republican Gordon Allott). At thirty-five Bob Kennedy became the second youngest Attorney General in history—the youngest since thirty-three-year-old Richard Rush was appointed by James Madison in 1814.

Lawyers soon had to revise their estimates of the new Attorney General. Despite (or because of) his inexperience, Bobby picked top aides of rare distinction. Judged Columbia University law professor William L. Cary, "I can say truthfully that no Attorney General assembled a group of assistants of such extraordinarily first-rate quality since Francis Biddle."[131] Bobby displayed a gift for maintaining high morale. An insider, who has worked for all the Kennedys, said, "It is not generally known, but Bobby has always had better relations with his staff than his brothers. He is more interested in them." There were significant successes, notably in civil rights and fighting crime, as well as some failures, such as in civil liberties. But after two and a half years Washington correspondent Joseph Kraft concluded, "Justice has emerged as the most yeasty of all the Departments in the Administration."[132]

Moreover, Bobby's role in his brother's Administration ranged far beyond the confines of the Justice Department. He served as Jack's lightning rod, drawing the attack that would otherwise have been directed at the President; his inner ear, listening to rumblings that tend to be filtered out before they reach the White House; his most trusted adviser, flying to Indonesia to help settle the dispute over West New Guinea and to Brazil to discuss that country's economic crisis; and his comforter, such as when the Bay of Pigs invasion turned into a fiasco. Observing Bobby as he debated with Japanese Communists, arranged the Cuban prisoner ransom, and helped to plan a domestic Peace Corps,

Anthony Lewis of the New York *Times* reported, "Certainly there has never been an Attorney General like him."[133]

Perhaps also there has never been a presidential brother-in-law like Sargent Shriver. Late in the 1960 campaign Jack suggested creating a Peace Corps, almost as an afterthought, and when he became President he put Shriver in charge of nurturing the idea. The Peace Corps director later liked to say that since "everybody concerned" was convinced the project would fail, Jack appointed him—reasoning "it would be easier to fire a relative than a friend."[134]

He was the ideal choice. He had been president of the Chicago branch of the Catholic Interracial Council and was a devout adherent of the liberal wing of the Church, in the tradition of his godfather, Cardinal Gibbons. (This outlook, in fact, put him in conflict with Joe Kennedy, who was of the Church's conservative, Boston faction.) The Kennedy boys had been deliberately educated outside of the Catholic school system. Douglass Cater observed that when Cardinal Cushing was awarded an honorary degree by Harvard in 1959 all the Catholics present kissed his ring—except Jack Kennedy, who shook hands. (Murray Kempton even predicted that Jack would be the most anti-clerical President since Millard Fillmore.) The younger Kennedys, therefore, despite their regularity at religious observances, were basically secular in outlook. But Shriver was not. His religious conviction was a social commitment. And the idealistic Peace Corps would be his vehicle for applied Christianity; he would lead it in the footsteps of his hero, St. Paul —"Though I bestow all my goods to feed the poor . . . and have not love, it profiteth me nothing."[135]

At the Peace Corps Shriver lined his office with slogans by such philosophers as Horatio Alger and Leo Durocher—"There is No Place on This Club for Good Losers," "Nice Guys Don't Win Ball Games," et cetera. He was called "Mr. Clean" and "a Boy Scout." While his *modus operandi* as an administrator was to create inspired chaos, he was probably exactly what the infant organization needed as a parent—a supercharged, dedicated professional idealist with a Jimmy Stewart handsomeness that appealed to the program's young recruits. He built the Peace Corps into a monument to the Kennedy Administration.

"It's Ted's turn now," Joe Kennedy reportedly told his elder sons. "Whatever he wants, I'm going to see that he gets it."[136]

What Ted wanted in 1962 was Jack's old seat in the United States Senate.

Though such lofty ambition on the part of a thirty-year-old was generally regarded as the height of political cynicism and presumption, his brothers, the President of the United States and the Attorney General of the United States, reluctantly agreed. It was Joe Kennedy's last great decision in making his sons the most elevated family triumvirate in American history.

The youngest son hardly had impressive credentials to put before the electorate. He had been asked to leave Harvard at eighteen when it was discovered that he had induced another student to take a Spanish examination for him.* He then entered the army as a private, and two years later returned to Harvard and graduated. He was also a graduate of the University of Virginia Law School and had served a short time as an assistant district attorney of Suffolk County.

The finest hour in his brief career came quite by accident when he found himself at the top of a 180-foot ski jump during the 1960 Wisconsin primary. "Maybe if we give him a round of applause," said the announcer, "he will make his *first* jump." Teddy's initial reaction was to take off his skis, "but if I did, I was afraid my brother would hear of it. And if he heard of it, I knew I would be back in Washington licking stamps and addressing envelopes for the rest of the campaign."[137] He jumped. "Everybody I met after that," said Bobby, "wanted to know if I was Senator Kennedy, then if I was the fellow who went off the ski jump."[138] Teddy was later put in charge of winning the Western states; all but Hawaii went for Nixon.

Rose liked to tell audiences that "Teddy was the first American boy to receive his first Holy Communion from the Pope and I thought that with such a start he would become a priest or maybe a bishop but then one night he met a beautiful blonde and that was the end of that."[139] Teddy met Joan Bennett, the willowy and hazel-eyed daughter of a New York advertising executive,† when he dedicated a gymnasium that the family had given to Manhattanville College. Joan, a student there, decided to pass up the ceremony; she was a pianist, with little interest in gymnasia. However a friend convinced her that she had better attend the Kennedy tea "because if they miss you, you'll get demerits and you might be campused."[140] Teddy had no trouble spotting the young lady who had spent a college summer modeling for television commercials on the Eddie Fisher and Perry Como shows. Cardinal Spellman married

---

* The Republicans tried to make political capital out of this, e.g., "The quip currently making the rounds in Washington is that Teddy Kennedy is writing a book: 'How to Succeed at Harvard Without Really Trying.'" (*Republican Congressional Committee Newsletter*, April 13, 1962, p. 11). But Teddy's "confession" had been skillfully released to a friendly Boston reporter, and there was a sympathetic public response to the young man's mistake.

† Harry Wiggin Bennett, Jr. (1907–   ), has been a vice-president of a number of New York advertising agencies, most recently the Joseph Katz Company, and is now vice-president of a community antenna television company in Cocoa Beach, Florida. He is a Republican and a Protestant. However, his two daughters have always been devout Catholics, like their mother.

them the next year, 1958, during a ceremony in which the bride and groom were wired for sound movies.

While Teddy's achievements were few, he had absorbed the cumulative political wisdom of grandfathers, father, and brothers. And precept number one was "Start earlier and work harder than your opponent." On a Sunday in May 1961, more than a year before the Democratic state convention, a New York *Herald Tribune* reporter followed young Kennedy's footsteps. Beginning at 7 A.M., when Teddy got into a Cadillac Fleetwood in front of his Boston home, his day went as follows: 1) spoke to five hundred Knights of Columbus at a communion breakfast in North Easton; 2) made an afternoon speech in Winchester at a fund-raising rally for the Medical Missionaries of Mary; 3) appeared at a Polish-American veterans' dinner in Cambridge; 4) attended a reception for African students at Boston University; 5) spoke at a dinner of the Greater Boston Association for Retarded Children; 6) ended the day at St. Joseph's Church, Somerville, where a father-and-son program was being held. Teddy, nominally an assistant district attorney, was maintaining a personal staff of three secretaries and serving as chairman of the state cancer drive, chairman of the physical fitness program of Boston's United Fund, and president of the Joseph P. Kennedy Jr. Memorial Foundation. He was not at this time, or for some time to come, an avowed candidate for any public office.

What the Polish-American veterans and the parishioners of St. Joseph's Church were discovering was that Edward Moore Kennedy was the most enchanting politician in a family of political sorcerers. He was taller than his brothers (six feet two inches), handsomer (one reporter compared him to a model for the old Arrow-collar ads), and a better orator—after listening to him speak during the 1960 West Virginia primary, Jack told the audience, "I'd just like to remind Teddy that you can't be elected President till you're thirty-five." (He was then twenty-eight.)

And of course Teddy was a *Kennedy*, that easily recognizable brand name that the people of Massachusetts had used and liked. When one John F. Kennedy—unconnected with the famous product—ran for state treasurer, he was elected without campaigning. (State Treasurer John F. Kennedy was a stockroom foreman in South Boston with an evening high school education.)

Behind the name was the power. When the delegates to the Massachusetts Democratic Convention met in Springfield to decide whether they would give their senatorial endorsement to Teddy or to state Attorney General Edward McCormack, they also had to weigh factors other than the candidates' qualifications. "The patronage is being handled quite cleverly," wrote Paul Driscoll of the Worcester *Telegram and Gazette*. "There are, at this writing [June 4, 1962], fifteen vacant postmasterships in Massachusetts. For every vacancy, there must be at least six convention delegates who either want the job or have a friend who wants the job. Not one will go to a delegate who votes for McCormack, or to a friend of a delegate who votes for McCormack." While the Kennedy Administration in Washington officially proclaimed its neutrality, it was quite clear (as J.F.K. put it) that "We'd rather be Ted than Ed."[141]

Ted won the convention endorsement. Ed said he would win the primary on "the anti-*chutzpah* vote," but Ted defeated Ed by a two-to-one margin.[142] In round three, the general election, Ted faced George Lodge, son of the Henry Cabot Lodge who had lost to Jack Kennedy in 1952 and great-grandson of the Henry Cabot Lodge who had defeated Honey Fitz in 1916. Ted's campaign manager was brother-in-law Steve Smith, who now directed the Kennedy financial empire after brief service as a New Frontiersman with the State Department. Sensing an easy victory, Smith canceled many thousands of dollars' worth of television time. It was the sort of nervy judgment that the Kennedys respect—if it proves correct. Only George Lodge thought he had a chance. George was wrong.

"When the Kennedy administration becomes hereditary," wrote Malcolm Muggeridge for London's *New Statesman*, "the title of the heir, equivalent to our Prince of Wales, will presumably be the Senator for Massachusetts."[143] So a new Kennedy senator, ebullient and uncomplex, arrived in Washington. And in his first major address, before the Women's National Press Club, Teddy said: "I was down at the White House this afternoon with suggestions for the State of the Union address, but all I got from him was 'Are you still using that greasy kid stuff on your hair?'"[144]

In early 1963 the New York *Times* reported, "Within the last six weeks, several magazines have appeared on the newsstands *without* cover pictures of Mrs. Kennedy." But this was a respite, not a trend. For in the Kennedys two American dreams—political power and theatrical recognition—were being merged. It was as if the White House had become the Great Movie Set. And the semi-lurid magazines fanned the public's curiosity. "Jacqueline Kennedy—America's Newest Star. What You Should Know about Her Fears" (*Photoplay*); "Another Baby for Jackie. The Wonderful News All America Is Waiting For" (*Movie-TV Secrets*); "The Secret They're Keeping from Caroline Kennedy" (*Motion Picture*) —the "secret" was that she is a celebrity.

After two years on the New Frontier the President's wife said, "I think that people must be as sick of hearing about us . . . as I am."[145] Her thinking was wishful.

The public's fascination with the Kennedys was understandable. They

were fascinating. The First Lady gave glittering musicales, wore shimmering gowns, renovated the White House, spoke perfect French to
De Gaulle and Spanish to a group of farmers who gathered in a Venezuelan barnyard. Now she was seen water-skiing on the Riviera; now at
her Virginia retreat in the hunt country; now touring India or the Greek
isles with Princess Radziwill. The old Eleanor Roosevelt joke was dusted
off and reactivated: "Good night, Mrs. Kennedy, wherever you are."[146]
And the President, according to his friend Benjamin Bradlee of *Newsweek*, "could eat ten bowls of specially prepared fish chowder without
succumbing to either indigestion or embarrassment, and though he
smoked only rarely, he could chain-smoke three cigars when the spirit
moved him. His ability to devour the written word was legendary, and
he could unwrap presents faster than a five-year-old."[147] Out of such
stuff myths are made.

It was generally taken for granted that Jack would be re-elected in
1964. (Though the Kennedys took nothing for granted and Steve Smith,
who had been designated by the family as the President's campaign
manager, was already at work.) In the closing hours of Jack Kennedy's
first year in office, his father talked of him to a reporter. "I know nothing
can happen to him," said Joe. "I've stood by his deathbed four times. . . .
When you've been through something like that back, and the Pacific,
what can hurt you?"[148]

On November 22, 1963, John F. Kennedy, the youngest elected President of the United States, was murdered in Dallas.

There was an international shock wave, partly because of the senseless-
ness of the act, its brutality and suddenness; partly because a life of such
promise would now be unfulfilled; but also because of the impact this
young man of cool grace had already made on his world and time in the
two years, ten months, and two days of his presidency.

What sort of record?

Although he was the first Chief Executive since Andrew Johnson to
have served in both House and Senate he received little comfort
from his former colleagues. He did get confirmation of a test ban treaty
and a Trade Expansion Act, but at death his legislative program was in
disarray. The President was keenly aware of the thinness of his electoral
mandate; perhaps he was waiting for a more resounding vote of confidence in 1964 to push his proposals. Then too he felt hampered by the
generational difference between himself and the legislative leaders. He
had never been one of them; he didn't speak their language, which was
primarily of the rural South and Middle West. It remained for his successor, a former Senate Establishmentarian, to win approval for the
Kennedy program.

He reached his highest and lowest points in the handling of foreign policy. He gambled on overthrowing Castro by force, didn't commit the force necessary to succeed, and failed. But when Khrushchev moved missiles into Cuba he took the necessary steps to convince the Soviet Union that he would risk war to defend his nation's vital interests. The missiles were removed. "He assured his place in history by that single act," thought British Prime Minister Macmillan.[149] Yet on his death the Atlantic Alliance was decaying at the edges and his Alliance for Progress in Latin America was more dream than reality.

The future may well determine that the man, rather than his presidential acts, deserves special recognition.

The man John F. Kennedy was complex and paradoxical. Of robust elegance, he delighted in the biography of a little-known nineteenth-century English politician, in adolescent sports, in the polished style of Charles de Gaulle, in Ian Fleming's sex-and-intrigue stories. He felt operas should be performed in their original languages and listened to the records of Chubby Checker. He enjoyed the company of a Schlesinger and a Sinatra, Robert Frost and Oleg Cassini. He was immersed in the statistics of government, and could tell Peter Lawford about the box-office receipts for *Oceans Eleven* (a gangster film) in Manchester, England.

He was a politician—the only profession he had ever really practiced —who hated verbosity and pomposity. When William Attwood suggested during the 1960 campaign that he should "wave his arms the way other politicans did and give people a chance to get the cheers out of their throat," Kennedy borrowed a pencil (he was saving his voice for the day's speeches) and wrote, "I always swore one thing I'd never do is—" and he drew a picture of a man with his arms in the air.[150] He had a wry and irreverent wit, such as every campaign manual warns candidates against, yet he never lost an election. Kennedy was inordinately sensitive to manner, style, and how things were done. For this reason Sidney Hyman suggests that he made aesthetics rather than justice the chief object of politics.[151] And perhaps this may be how history will chiefly recall him. Except for one thing.

You must think of him as this little boy, sick so much of the time, reading in bed, reading history, reading the knights of the round table, reading Marlborough. For Jack, history was full of heroes. And if it made him this way— if it made him see the heroes—maybe other little boys will see.[152]

In this statement his widow perhaps sums up his greatness. For Jack Kennedy—the author of a collection of hero stories—believed that men could move mountains; given the right men—and as President he was certain he could recruit them—one could shape one's own destiny.[153] In the age of atom and automation he eloquently preached a man-centered universe. And this doctrine was enormously appealing to the young, the students, those starting careers. Many were attracted to government service, which now represented "doing" rather than red tape: many would be attracted after his death. This, in one opinion, was the legacy of John F. Kennedy.[154]

She was once described by her secretary as "the girl who has everything including the President of the United States."[155] She had been the third youngest First Lady; now, suddenly, she was the youngest presidential widow. Was there anything in her background to prepare the world for her majesty at her husband's grave? "She refused to be cheated of her right to this most terrible moment of her life," thought Katherine Anne Porter, "this long torment of farewell and relinquishment, of her wish to be conscious of every moment of her suffering: and this endurance did not fail her to the very end, and beyond. . . ."[156] Her job now would be to raise two small children and guard her husband in history. As celebrant of John F. Kennedy's memory she displayed a rare gift for the symbolic. She chose a grave site high up on a Virginia hillside overlooking the nation's capital and placed there an eternal light that flickers at night over the sleeping city. To the Kennedy crest she added a presidential motif—a fist clutching arrows, framed in olive branches.

By early summer of 1964 observers noticed that Bobby was finally emerging from the tragedy of Dallas. "There isn't that hollow look in the eyes," said a New York politician, "and the talk just doesn't turn automatically back to his brother the way it did a little while ago."[157]

His own loss had been compounded by his highly developed tribal sense of family. Joe was incapacitated by a stroke. Joe, Jr., was dead. Jack was dead. And Teddy, flying in an Aero-commander to the Massachusetts Democratic Convention, had crashed into an apple orchard. His administrative assistant and the pilot were killed. But Indiana Senator Birch Bayh had pulled young Kennedy from the wreckage, his back broken. Now Bobby was the oldest living son, leader of the dynasty, protector of his brother's widow and her children.‡

There were also political problems. "I don't want to become a retired elder statesman at thirty-eight," said Bobby.[158] But what to do? Teddy's election as a Massachusetts senator locked him out of the State in which the family was most closely identified.

The Democratic vice-presidential nomination shimmered before his

‡ There had always been a closeness between Bobby and Jackie. She once said: "I sometimes wish that Bobby, because he is so wonderful, had been an amoeba and then he could have mated with himself." (Thought Ethel: "That's just the kind of remark that Jackie's always coming up with.") See Marquis Childs, "Bobby and the President," *Good Housekeeping*, May 1962, p. 169.

eyes. Yet it is a political axiom that nobody runs for Vice-President; the choice is made by the presidential candidate, which in this case would be Lyndon B. Johnson. Bobby had not wanted Johnson to be on the ticket with his brother in 1960, and there was no love lost between the President-by-chance and the holdover Attorney General.[159] Bobby's strong showing in the New Hampshire primary (where he got more than 25,000 write-in votes) and in the Gallup polls fitted like a snug shirt on Lyndon Johnson's sunburn. It was even said that the President's buildup of Sargent Shriver was designed to deflate brother-in-law Bobby's political balloon.[160] (Shriver was sent to Jerusalem with a presidential letter for the Pope, asked to help reform the foreign-aid program, and appointed director of the War on Poverty.) Finally, in an artless move, the President announced that he would not consider choosing a running mate from the Cabinet. Cabinet member Kennedy replied that he planned to send notes to his colleagues: "I'm sorry I took so many nice fellows over the side with me."[161]

Then Robert Kennedy, who slept in Virginia, worked in Washington, and voted in Massachusetts, became the Democratic nominee for United States senator from New York. It was a marriage of convenience. New York was a Democratic state with a Republican governor and two Republican senators. The party leadership was shattered from years of internal feuding. "They don't give a damn where Bobby lives," said a Kennedy confidant, "they want to win."[162] So the state party without a winner and the winner without a state were wed. For better or for worse, in sickness and in health.

Bobby's campaign, as had been Jack's and Teddy's, became a call to arms for the entire Kennedy family. Steve Smith was again the campaign manager. (He was now being jokingly referred to as "Bobby Kennedy's Bobby Kennedy."[163]) Ethel, seven months pregnant with her ninth child, greeted voters in Brooklyn at the corner of Fulton and Pearl streets, and later gave three teas a week at her Long Island home. Her three oldest sons, ages twelve, ten, and nine, marched the entire length of the Columbus Day parade—from Forty-fourth Street to Eighty-sixth Street—wearing gigantic "Kennedy for Senator" buttons. Jacqueline appeared at the opening of her brother-in-law's headquarters. Nine volunteers, poring over transportation schedules and speaking requests, routed Eunice Shriver, Pat Lawford, and Jean Smith around the state. But the real star was Rose Kennedy. Sharing a speaking engagement with her, Bobby said, "You know my brother Jack and I never wanted to appear on a platform with her because she's the real campaigner. She's been campaigning for something like 72 years. . . . Was it in Grover Cleveland's Administration or maybe Lincoln's that you began, mother?"[164] (She had probably only been campaigning for sixty-four years; since William McKinley's Administration.) On some days she appeared in both New York for Bobby and Massachusetts for Teddy. Then she used her all-purpose speech, merely changing the name to fit the occasion. A Kennedy aide recalls that it went something like this:

The presidential days were cut short. Jack's enthusiasm, liveliness, ability, and faith are no longer with us. But he has bequeathed to us a wonderful legacy of purpose and of courage.

Now we have (Bob/Ted) to whom he entrusted his most ardent thoughts and ideals for which he worked so hard.

"Carpetbagger"—a word which had seen little circulation since Reconstruction—became the leading issue in 1964's most interesting political contest. Senator Kenneth Keating, the white-haired Republican incumbent, struck at his youthful opponent with ridicule. "Why, there are people who have been standing in line at the World's Fair longer than Bobby has been living in New York. . . . Bobby thinks the Gowanus Canal is part of the lower intestinal tract. . . . He thinks Tarrytown is a new brand of cigarette."[165] Kennedy reminded voters that he spent his early years in the state, and made a sentimental journey to his childhood home in Riverdale, accompanied by three-year-old John F. Kennedy, Jr. The Kennedys rented a thirty-room house on Long Island, and he now said, "This is a Glen Cove accent."[166]

But it was not the move to New York that bothered many New Yorkers so much as what was behind the move. As the *Times* said on September 2, Bobby is "a man in imperious pursuit of his star. . . ." Later, when the campaign became overheated, the newspaper dropped poetic niceties and announced, "His intense ambition, supported by adroit political acumen and all the power in the Kennedy name and fortune that can be brought to bear, suggests that he is interested in the Senatorial office not for itself but as a means to an end. . . ."[167] Bobby met the issue head on. "Let's assume that I'm using this as a power base . . . let's just assume the worst," he said. "I can't go any place in 1968; we have a President. He's going to be a good President until 1972. . . . I'm going to have to do an outstanding job in the Senate if the people all over the country [are going to] demand that I be the [1972 presidential] candidate. So I don't see how New York suffers."[168]

The electorate of New York is only thirty-five per cent white Anglo-Saxon Protestant—twelve per cent in New York City. The Jewish vote accounts for fifteen per cent, German fourteen per cent, Italian eleven per cent, Negro and Puerto Rican nine per cent, Polish five per cent. In no other state are minority groups so assiduously courted by the politicians. With no great ideological differences separating the candidates, the Kennedy-Keating race seemed to dissolve into which one could march and eat his way to the most ethnic support. "I do not campaign in search of a Jewish vote or a Catholic vote or a Negro vote," said Bobby.[169] Yet there he was (and his opponent too) marching with the Italians in honor of Columbus, with the Poles for Pulaski and the Germans for Steuben. He donned a *yamilke* to visit the Lubavitcher Rabbi and was photographed eating pizza in "Little Italy."

"The thing that's wrong with Bobby's campaign," said a campaign-watcher, "is that Bobby's not managing it."[170] It was disorganized and essentially formless. The candidate's flat voice and halting delivery seemed to come to life only when he was talking to young people. He constantly invoked the name of the martyred President. (To a group of Negro youth he said, "If you had any affection for President Kennedy, stay in school."[171]) His humor, a parody of the typical politician's, designed to set himself apart from them, was in itself a parody of his late brother's wit. ("I have eight children, and we eat fish every Friday," he told the fishmongers at Fulton Fish Market. "From now on, we'll eat fish twice a week. That's what we're going to do for the fishing industry of New York."[172]) He used his brother's technique of making a point through reference to ancient wisdom. (In one 1500-word statement he quoted from Andrew Jackson, Dante, Thomas Carlyle, Lord Tweedsmuir, Bonar Law, Francis Bacon, and John F. Kennedy.[173]) But the quotation marks stuck out awkwardly, like face cards shuffled into a deck of pedestrian thoughts.

What Bobby did have was star quality. At Jones Beach ten thousand bathers rushed forward to shake his hand; the helpless police told him that his presence would cause serious injuries and he managed to make an escape. Arriving at the quiet little upstate town of Glens Falls at one in the morning, four hours behind schedule, he found that four thousand persons (more than a fifth of the town's population) were waiting to greet him.

New Yorkers gave Lyndon Johnson a 2,500,000-vote majority; Bobby was elected by 800,000 votes. Had the President's huge mandate swept Bobby into office? Probably not. Careful students of election statistics feel that without the Johnson-Goldwater contest Bobby would have won by something over 300,000 votes—about what J.F.K. carried the state by in 1960. If Bobby had a victory ride, it was more likely on the coattails of his brother's memory. Even the cerebral Murray Kempton said, "I am for Robert Kennedy because he is a decent and talented young man terribly wounded whom I do not want to look upon wounded further. This is like being for Bonnie Prince Charlie; it has to do with commitment to a divine right and there are no reasonable arguments for a divine right." Many New Yorkers may have simply wanted to make amends for a presidential assassination.

While Bob Kennedy fought for his political life in New York his brother lay in a orthopedic-frame bed in New England Baptist Hospital. In the heavy evening fog of June 19, 1964, Teddy Kennedy, semiconscious, had been pulled out of the wreckage of a small private plane. He had injured five of the lower vertebrae of his backbone, three seriously, one crushed almost completely; he was in a deep state of shock, his blood pressure perilously low, at times he appeared almost without pulse; two middle ribs on his left side were broken; his left lung had been punctured and was partially collapsed. Some doctors thought he would never walk again.

Three days less than six months later Teddy Kennedy walked out of the hospital, in time for Christmas, as he had promised. His recovery was an amazing example of fortitude and determination.

While in the hospital he gathered a series of essays on his father, to be privately printed, much in the manner that his brother Jack had once put together reminiscences of Joe, Jr., while convalescing from the injury to his back. He also spoke to Bobby on the telephone from one to three times a day, giving advice and encouragement.

Meanwhile his wife Joan toured the state. Once Bobby had thought that she was "too beautiful to use" on the campaign hustings. But there could no longer be even this lighthearted caveat. As Rose Kennedy, the admiring matriarch, said: ". . . she stood in front of her audiences and completely charmed them with her simplicity and sincerity. She told them about the work Ted had been able to do for the state during his convalescence, the improvement he was making in his back injury. She related homey, amusing stories of the visits of the children to their father. She conveyed Ted's greetings and promised to convey to him their messages of affection and loyalty."[174] Joan Kennedy, the golden-haired politician, even managed to find time to fly to Iowa to assist her husband's former aide, John Culver, in his successful race for the U. S. House of Representatives.

While no Kennedy could have been defeated in the Bay State, Ted's victory was of unprecedented magnitude. Jack had won a second Senate term by a record margin of 874,608; Ted's margin was 1,129,245 votes. Besides the name and its magic memories, Ted Kennedy's election was a tribute to his personal popularity and his efforts within the Massachusetts Democratic organization. Unlike Jack, who had largely relied on his own following, Ted had worked constantly to solidify the regular party apparatus.[175]

At the opening ceremony of the 89th Congress, on January 4, 1965, Edward M. Kennedy of Massachusetts and Robert F. Kennedy of New York were sworn in as United States senators. Only once before, from 1800 to 1803, had two brothers served in the Senate at the same time.§ Never before had three brothers been senators.

§ Theodore Foster (1752–1828) was U.S. senator from Rhode Island, 1790–1803; his brother, Dwight Foster (1757–1803), was U.S. senator from Massachusetts, 1800–3.

In charting the future of the Kennedys, all who know them well agree that Teddy, despite Senate seniority, will defer to his older brother. The dynasty's hierarchy is rigid. But what will Bobby seek? After Jack won the presidential nomination he presented his campaign manager with a cigarette box. Inscribed across the lid:

ROBERT F. KENNEDY
When I'm Through, How About You?
Democratic National Convention
Los Angeles, 1960.[176]

A joke that made the rounds during the early days of the Kennedy Administration went: "We'll have Jack for eight years, Bobby for eight, and Teddy for eight. Then it'll be 1984." Such arithmetical tinkering was thrown out of balance by Jack Kennedy's death. Now there are many imponderables—Lyndon Johnson's health, his successes and failures as President, Hubert Humphrey's ambition, the mood of the country, war and peace, prosperity and recession, acts of God and man. But in any political timetable age weighs heavily in the Kennedys' favor. Most American presidents have been in their fifties. The precocious brothers Kennedy will be factors in politics for many years to come.

Presidential Election Years	Bob's Age	Ted's Age
1968	43	36
1972	47	40
1976	51	44
1980	55	48
1984	59	52
1988	63	56
1992	67	60

And in 1992 Joseph P. Kennedy III, Bobby's eldest son, will be forty, the age at which his uncle Jack started his drive for the presidency; John F. Kennedy, Jr., will be thirty, the same age as Uncle Teddy was when he entered the Senate.

Rose and Joe Kennedy have twenty-five grandchildren, thirteen named Kennedy. The youngsters are being raised in much the same manner as were their parents. Politics is bred into them. When Bobby's daughter Kathleen wanted to stop her younger brother from being naughty in a department store, she chose her words wisely. "Joe," she commanded, "do be quiet. You are losing votes acting like this!"[177]

Eunice Kennedy Shriver told a Chicago newspaperwoman in 1960, "All we talk about is winning." Then she picked up her infant son Timothy, held him aloft, and gently began his indoctrination: "Win, win, win."[178]

THE BEST BUTTER

1. Stewart Alsop, "What Made Teddy Run?" *Saturday Evening Post,* October 27, 1962, p. 20.

2. John Fischer, "The Editor's Easy Chair," *Harper's,* August 1957, p. 16.

3. Public service dynasties have not been limited to elective politics. In the related field of diplomacy, for instance, the late Secretary of State John Foster Dulles was the nephew and grandson of Secretaries of State. His brother Allen was director of the Central Intelligence Agency and his sister Eleanor was a high-ranking expert on Germany at the State Department.

4. Dynastically connected members of the U. S. Senate, 89th Congress: Quentin Burdick (D, N.D.)—son and brother-in-law of congressmen; Harry Flood Byrd (D, Va.)—nephew of two congressmen; Harry F. Byrd, Jr. (D, Va.)—son of the preceding; Frank Church (D, Ida.)—son-in-law of governor; Paul Douglas (D, Ill.)—husband of member of Congress; Sam Ervin (D, N.C.)—brother of congressman; Edward M. Kennedy (D, Mass.) and Robert F. Kennedy (D, N.Y.)—see Kennedy Dynasty; Russell B. Long (D, La.)—see Long Dynasty; Thruston B. Morton (R, Ky.)—brother of congressman; Maurine B. Neuberger (D, Ore.)—wife of senator; Claiborne Pell (D, R.I.)—son and great-grandson of congressmen, great-great-nephew of two congressmen; Leverett Saltonstall (R, Mass.)—great-grandson of congressman; George A. Smathers (D, Fla.)—nephew of senator; Margaret Chase Smith (R, Me.)—wife of congressman; Stuart Symington (D, Mo.)—son-in-law of senator; Herman Talmadge (D, Ga.)—son of governor; Joseph Tydings (D, Md.)—adopted son of senator. Harry Byrd, Jr., succeeded his father—they did not serve in the Senate at the same time.

In the U. S. House of Representatives, 89th Congress, there are eleven sons of congressmen (William H. Bates of Massachusetts, Paul G. Rogers of Florida, Compton I. White of Idaho, Andrew Jacobs of Indiana, John D. Dingell of Michigan, William J. Green of Pennsylvania, Robert E. Sweeney of Ohio, Clarence J. Brown of Ohio, Jed Johnson of Oklahoma, David E. Satterfield III of Virginia, and James Kee of West Virginia)—Mr. Johnson's father-in-law is a congressman and Mr. Kee's mother also served in Congress; two sons of senators (Jonathan B. Bingham of New York and David S. King of Utah); four who have had a brother in Congress (James Roosevelt of California, Rogers Morton of Maryland, Ed Edmundson of Oklahoma, and Morris Udall of Arizona); and three whose husbands were in Congress (Frances P. Bolton of Ohio, Leonor K. Sullivan of Missouri, and Lera Thomas of Texas)—Mrs. Bolton's son has also been in Congress. Others, such as Jack Edwards of Alabama, Peter Frelinghuysen of New Jersey, John Kunkel of Pennsylvania, Speedy O. Long of Louisiana, Thomas L. Ashley of Ohio, and William E. Brock III of Tennessee, have had more distant relations in Congress.

5. Arthur M. Schlesinger, Jr., "Two Years Later—The Roosevelt Family," *Life,* April 7, 1947, p. 113.

6. See Helen Taft Manning, "My Brother Bob Taft," *American Magazine,* January 1952, p. 104.

7. Although outside the scope of this study, there have been other political dynasties on the state and city levels. In Philadelphia there has even been a ward dynasty, with the 21st Ward under the control of the Hamilton family since the turn of the century.

8. The author is indebted to Scott D. Breckinridge, Jr., for the Bernadotte quotation.

9. The Rockefeller family is a notable example of the robber baron-politician relationship: John D. Rockefeller, Sr., founded Standard Oil; his son married the daughter of powerful U. S. Senator Nelson Aldrich; his grandsons sought elective office—Nelson Rockefeller being governor of New York and Winthrop having run unsuccessfully for governor of Arkansas in 1964.

10. The author is indebted to Richard M. Nixon for the story of Eisenhower's "common denominator."

11. See Karl Schriftgiesser, *Families* (New York: Howell, Soskin, 1940), p. 408.

12. See New York *Times,* June 23, 1965, p. 42.

13. See Edmund C. Stedman, editor, *An American Anthology, 1787–1900* (Cambridge: Riverside Press, 1900), 2 vols.

14. Clyde Kluckhohn and Henry A. Murray, *Personality in Nature, Society, and Culture* (New York: Knopf, 1948), p. 39.

15. See Charles Francis Adams, *Lee at Appomattox and Other Papers* (Boston and New York: Houghton Mifflin, 1902), p. 18.

16. An unusual example of the "Daddy's business factor" can be seen in the Park family. In this case, Daddy's business was administering women's higher education. Dr. J. Edgar Park was president of Wheaton College; his son William is president of Simmons College; his daughter Rosemary is president of Barnard College.

17. The author is indebted to Earl Mazo, a leading authority on political polling, for the information on Senator Gore's poll.

18. See New York *Times,* October 29, 1964, p. 22, and July 4, 1965, p. 15.

19. E. Digby Baltzell, *The Protestant Establishment* (New York: Random House, 1964), p. 76.

20. Quoted in Washington *Star,* July 11, 1962, p. B-12.

21. See Charles W. Eliot, *American Contributions to Civilization* (New York: Century, 1897), p. 136.

THE ADAMS DYNASTY

1. John F. Kennedy, "The Adams Papers," *American Historical Review,* LXVIII, No. 2 (January 1963), p. 479.

2. Henry Cabot Lodge, Sr., a memorial address, November 17, 1915, published with Charles Francis Adams, Jr., *An Autobiography* (Boston and New York: Houghton Mifflin, 1916), p. xiii.

3. Ibid., p. 30.

4. Quoted in Ferris Greenslet, *The Lowells and Their Seven Worlds* (Boston: Houghton Mifflin, 1946), p. 415.

5. John Quincy Adams, *Memoirs* (Philadelphia: J. B. Lippincott, 1874–77), Vol. IV, p. 388.

6. Quoted in Martin B. Duberman, *Charles Francis Adams* (Boston: Houghton Mifflin, 1961), p. 143.

7. Also see George W. Corner, editor, *The Autobiography of Benjamin Rush* (Princeton: Princeton University Press, 1948), pp. 255–56. Rush, a good friend of John Adams and a fellow signer of the Declaration of Independence, dined with John Quincy Adams on September 10, 1801, and wrote: "Mr. J. Q. Adams was very entertaining. [He said] that temperance in eating was very common [in Prussia], that 6 persons had died at table while he was in Berlin

of appoplexy, and one at a dance, a young man of 21, from too tight cloathes, especially a cravat tied round his neck by his servant."

8. John Quincy Adams, op. cit., Vol. VII, pp. 331–36.

9. Quoted in Samuel Flagg Bemis, *John Quincy Adams and the Union* (New York: Knopf, 1956), p. 139n.

10. Cleveland Amory, *The Proper Bostonians* (New York: Dutton, 1947), p. 144.

11. Henry Adams, *The Education of Henry Adams* (New York, 1931), p. 21 (Modern Library Edition).

12. The remark predates Charles Francis Adams. Charles II said of Prince George of Denmark: "I have tried George drunk and I have tried him sober, and drunk or sober, there is nothing in him!" See John A. Garraty, *Henry Cabot Lodge* (New York: Knopf, 1953), p. 14n.

13. During the presidential campaign of 1828 John Quincy Adams' opponents added up his compensations, salary, and allowance for eight years of diplomatic service. He had received about $12,500 a year, which proved conclusively that he had grown fat at the public trough. See Bemis, op. cit., p. 134.

14. In his diary Minister Adams suggests the cost of being accredited to the imperial court of Czar Alexander: "We have a maitre d'hotel, or steward; a cook, who has under him two scullions—mujiks; a Swiss, or porter; two footmen; a mujik to make the fires; a coachman and postillion; and Thomas, the black man, to be my valet-de-chambre; Martha Godfred, the maid we brought with us from America; a femme-de-chambre of Mrs. Adams, a housemaid and a laundry-maid. The Swiss, the cook, and one of the footmen are married, and their wives all live in the house. The steward has two children, and the washerwoman a daughter, all of whom are kept in the house. . . ." John Quincy Adams later fired the cook, engaged a caterer to furnish dinners, and somehow managed to live within his modest means. See John Quincy Adams, op. cit., Vol. II, p. 193.

15. Quoted in Arthur F. Beringause, *Brooks Adams* (New York: Knopf, 1955), pp. 189–90.

16. Quoted in Page Smith, *John Adams* (Garden City, N.Y.: Doubleday, 1962), p. 915.

17. Ibid., p. 857.

18. Quoted in Ernest Samuels, *The Young Henry Adams* (Cambridge: Harvard University Press, 1948), pp. 183, 184. Italics added.

19. Quoted in Bemis, op. cit., p. 136.

20. Henry Cabot Lodge, Sr., op. cit., p. xv.

21. Quoted in Bemis, op. cit., pp. 192–93n.

22. Quoted in Page Smith, op. cit., p. 992.

23. When the first Henry Cabot Lodge was a young man he visited the Adams home at Quincy and wrote in his diary: ". . . I mooned over a lovely portrait of J. Adams daughter. If she looked like her picture everyone must have fallen in love with her straightway. I did. Grew profoundly jealous of her husband Col. Smith on the opposite [wall] and longed to write verses to her. . . . I acquired a solid hate for Smith. Common name to give such a lovely woman." Quoted in Garraty, op. cit., pp. 39–40. Also see Lida Mayo, "Miss Adams in Love," *American Heritage,* February 1965, pp. 36–39, 80–89.

24. Quoted in Duberman, op. cit., p. 22.

25. Quoted in Samuel Flagg Bemis, *John Quincy Adams and the Foundations of American Foreign Policy* (New York: Knopf, 1949), p. 85.

26. Quoted in Bemis, *John Quincy Adams and the Union,* p. 116.

27. Ibid., p. 180.

28. Ibid., p. 183n.

29. Ibid., p. 189.

30. Quoted in Page Smith, op. cit., p. 850.

31. Ibid., p. 838.

32. Ibid., p. 298.

33. Ibid., p. 333.

34. Ibid., pp. 174–75.

35. Ibid., pp. 262–63.

36. Ibid., pp. 183–84.

37. Ibid., pp. 268–69.

38. Ibid., p. 966.

39. Quoted in James Truslow Adams, *The Adams Family* (Boston: Little, Brown, 1930), p. 85.

40. Quoted in Page Smith, op. cit., p. 844.

41. When John Quincy Adams was minister to Russia he took with him his sister Abby's son William Steuben Smith; in Great Britain, his assistant was another nephew, John Adams Smith. His own son John was his private secretary when he was President. In the next generation, Charles Francis Adams made his son Henry his secretary when he was a congressman and minister to Great Britain, and took son Brooks with him to Geneva for the *Alabama* claims arbitration.

42. Quoted in Bemis, *John Quincy Adams and the Foundations of American Foreign Policy,* p. 63.

43. Quoted in Frank Van Der Linden, *The Turning Point* (Washington: Luce, 1962), pp. 26–27.

44. Quoted in Bemis, *John Quincy Adams and the Foundations of American Foreign Policy,* pp. 88–89.

45. The President had John Quincy by-pass the Secretary of State and report directly to him on sensitive matters. "I wish you to continue the practice of writing freely to me, and cautiously to the office of State," he told his diplomat son. Ibid., p. 91.

46. Quoted in Van Der Linden, op. cit., p. 219.

47. Quoted in Page Smith, op. cit., p. 1057.

48. See Bemis, *John Quincy Adams and the Foundations of American Foreign Policy,* pp. 80–81. Mrs. John Quincy Adams' sister, Maria Johnson, married John Pope (1770–1845), a United States senator from Kentucky (1807–13), territorial governor of Arkansas (1829–35), and Democratic member of the House of Representatives (1837–43).

49. L. H. Butterfield, editor, *The Adams Papers* (Cambridge: Harvard University Press, 1961), Series I, Vol. 1, p. xx; Henry Adams, op. cit., pp. 16, 17, 18.

50. Quoted in Duberman, op. cit., pp. 3–4.

51. John Quincy Adams, op. cit., Vol. II, pp. 282–83.

52. Quoted in Bemis, *John Quincy Adams and the Union,* p. 301.

53. Quoted in John F. Kennedy, *Profiles in Courage* (New York: Harper, 1956), p. 41.

54. Also in the traveling party were John Quincy Adams' sister-in-law, Catherine Johnson, and his nephew, William Steuben Smith. Young Smith, who

acted as the envoy's private secretary, did not live up to the high family ideals, proving to be careless with money. But in the eyes of Catherine he apparently had other attributes. They were soon married, thus making Smith the brother-in-law as well as the nephew of John Quincy Adams.

55. Quoted in Page Smith, op. cit., p. 1096.

56. In Russia, Adams was an eyewitness to the scene that Tolstoy would immortalize. As his mother's faithful correspondent, the American envoy reported on the French Emperor's retreat from Moscow: "Of the immense host with which six months since he invaded Russia, nine-tenths at least are prisoners or food for worms. They have been surrendering by ten thousands at a time, and at this moment there are at least one hundred and fifty thousand of them in the power of the Emperor Alexander. From Moscow to Prussia, eight hundred miles of road have been strewed with his artillery, baggage wagons, ammunition chests, dead and dying men, whom he has forced to abandon their fate—pursued all the time by three large regular armies of a most embittered and exasperated enemy, and by an almost numberless militia of peasants, stung by the destruction of their harvests and cottages which he had carried before him, and spurred to revenge at once themselves, their country, and their religion. To complete his disasters the season itself during the greatest part of his retreat has been unusually rigorous, even for this northern climate; so that it has become a sort of by-word among the common people here that the two Russian generals who have conquered Napoleon and all his Marshals are *General Famine* and *General Frost*." Quoted in Bemis, *John Quincy Adams and the Foundations of American Foreign Policy*, p. 178. Italics in original.

57. The United States, however, was not Britain's prime concern in 1815, and its top diplomatists were undoubtedly reserved for the conference that was to open at Vienna. But of the American team at Ghent—Adams, Albert Gallatin, Henry Clay, James Bayard, and Jonathan Russell—only Russell was a second-rater. He was later to doctor some documents in an attempt to embarrass John Quincy Adams; but instead, Adams' savage counterattack wrecked Russell's political career.

58. Quoted in Bemis, *John Quincy Adams and the Foundations of American Foreign Policy*, p. 240.

59. Quoted in Charles Francis Adams, Jr., *Charles Francis Adams* (Boston and New York: Houghton Mifflin, 1900), p. 8.

60. Gallatin's liabilities were that he was foreign-born and had not supported Monroe's candidacy for President; while Clay, a Southerner, was from the same region of the country as the President.

61. Quoted in Beringause, op. cit., pp. 309–10.

62. Quoted in Bemis, *John Quincy Adams and the Foundations of American Foreign Policy*, p. 66n.

63. Henry Cabot Lodge, Sr., op. cit., p. l (Letter, not numeral).

64. Quoted in James Truslow Adams, op. cit., p. 176.

65. John Quincy Adams, op. cit., Vol. VI, pp. 457–58, 452–53. Italics added.

66. Margaret Bayard Smith, *Forty Years of Washington Society* (New York: Scribner's, 1906), p. 183.

67. Quoted in Samuels, op. cit., p. 78; Henry Adams, op. cit., p. 104.

68. John Quincy Adams, op. cit., Vol. VII, p. 163.

69. Quoted in James Truslow Adams, op. cit., p. 186.

70. Five years later another former President, James Monroe, would also die on July 4. At that time Henry Clay wrote to John Quincy Adams: "That

your fourth may be far distant I most sincerely wish." Quoted in Bemis, *John Quincy Adams and the Union*, p. 109n.

71. Comparing his Administration to Jefferson's, John Adams had said: "Mine, like Pope's woman, will have no character at all." Quoted in Page Smith, op. cit., p. 1111.

72. John Quincy Adams, op. cit., Vol. X, pp. 450–51.

73. Ralph Waldo Emerson, *Journals* (Boston and New York: Houghton Mifflin, 1909–14), Vol. XI, pp. 349–50.

74. Quoted in Bemis, *John Quincy Adams and the Union*, p. 258. Italics in original.

75. Quoted in Janet Whitney, *Abigail Adams* (Boston: Little, Brown, 1947), p. 93.

76. Quoted in J. J. Perling, *Presidents' Sons* (New York: Odyssey Press, 1947), pp. 18–19.

77. See Duberman, op. cit., pp. 27 and 430.

78. Quoted in Bemis, *John Quincy Adams and the Union*, pp. 95n, 192–93n.

79. Ibid., p. 480n.

80. Ibid., p. 524.

81. See Duberman, op. cit., p. 151.

82. Charles Francis Adams, Jr., *Charles Francis Adams*, pp. 95–97.

83. Quoted in Duberman, op. cit., p. 142.

84. Quoted in Charles Francis Adams, Jr., *Charles Francis Adams*, p. 133n.

85. Ibid., pp. 214–15.

86. Ibid., p. 401.

87. Quoted in Duberman, op. cit., p. 390.

88. Quoted in James Truslow Adams, op. cit., p. 326.

89. Quoted in Beringause, op. cit., p. 334.

90. See Charles Francis Adams, Jr., *Autobiography*, p. 16.

91. Henry Adams, op. cit., p. 27.

92. She continued: "His [Charles Francis Adams'] oldest son, John Quincy, is the leader of the Democratic party in Massachusetts and I shall not be surprised to see him elected governor before long. Charles Adams is a very forcible & brilliant writer in the North American Review & is just appointed Commissioner of railroads for Mass. He is not more than 33 years old. Henry Adams, still younger, writes financial & other articles for the Edinburg [sic] & other foreign reviews as well as for our own, & is rapidly rising as a clear & powerful thinker & writer . . . and Brooks, the youngest boy, is now a senior in Harvard where every male Adams since & including John, in his direct line has graduated. I doubt if any family in England or America can show such a history." See Theodore Clarke Smith, *The Life and Letters of James Abram Garfield* (New Haven: Yale University Press, 1925), Vol. II, p. 759.

93. Charles Francis Adams, Jr., *Autobiography*, p. 29.

94. Butterfield, op. cit., p. xxii.

95. Quoted in Mary Caroline Crawford, *Famous Families of Massachusetts* (Boston: Little, Brown, 1930), Vol. I, p. 36.

96. Worthington Chauncey Ford, editor, *Letters of Henry Adams* (Boston and New York: Houghton Mifflin, 1930–38), Vol. II, p. 55.

97. Charles Francis Adams, Jr., *Autobiography*, p. 190.

98. Quoted in Richard O'Connor, *Gould's Millions* (Garden City, N.Y.: Doubleday, 1962), p. 67.

99. Ford, op. cit., Vol. II, p. 271.

100. Quoted in Samuels, op. cit., p. 194.

101. Ibid., pp. 228 and 216.

102. Quoted in Elizabeth Stevenson, *Henry Adams* (New York: Macmillan, 1955), p. 103.

103. Quoted in Ernest Samuels, *Henry Adams, The Major Phase* (Cambridge: Harvard University Press, 1964), p. 604.

104. Theodore Roosevelt wrote to Henry Cabot Lodge, September 2, 1905: "The other day I was reading *Democracy*, that novel which made a great furore among the educated incompetents and the pessimists generally about twenty-five years ago. It had a superficial and rotten cleverness, but it was essentially false, essentially mean and base. . . ." Lodge replied, September 7, 1905: "I have not read *Democracy* for years, but I remember when it came out it impressed me as very clever, probably more clever than I should think it today, and also extremely sordid in the view it took. . . ." (They didn't know at the time that it was written by their friend Adams.) See *Selections from the Correspondence of Theodore Roosevelt and Henry Cabot Lodge* (New York: Scribner's, 1925), Vol. II, pp. 189 and 191.

105. Harold Dean Cater, editor, *Henry Adams and His Friends, A Collection of His Unpublished Letters* (Boston and New York: Houghton Mifflin, 1947), p. 158.

106. Samuels, *Henry Adams, The Major Phase*, p. 223. Elizabeth Cameron (1857–1944) was a niece of General William Tecumseh Sherman and Secretary of State John Sherman. Her husband Donald Cameron was senator from Pennsylvania (1877–97), and son of Simon Cameron, senator from Pennsylvania (1857–61, 1867–77). The Camerons, father and son, were also Secretaries of War.

107. Quoted in Beringause, op. cit., p. 25.

108. Quoted in Amory, op. cit., p. 166.

109. Immediately after the wedding Brooks turned to the bride's brother, Admiral Charles Henry ("Shakey") Davis, and said, "Mrs. Adams' name is Evelyn, not Daisy, and I expect her to be called that in the future." To which Davis replied, "My dear Brooks, you cannot expect me to change the habit of a lifetime for a comparative stranger." Mrs. Adams remained known as Daisy. Interview with John Davis Lodge, August 8, 1964, Washington, D.C. For the background of the Davis family, see Lodge Dynasty, pp. 445–80.

110. Quoted in Beringause, op. cit., pp. 95–96.

111. Ibid., pp. 160, 340, 358–59.

112. Ibid., pp. 182, 130, 111–12.

113. Ibid., pp. 328 and 359.

114. Ibid., pp. 312–13.

115. Ibid., pp. 370–72.

116. New York *Times*, February 22, 1929, p. 20.

117. "In personal appearance," wrote Herbert Hoover, "he was the image of his great ancestor, John Quincy Adams." *The Memoirs of Herbert Hoover* (New York: Macmillan, 1951–52), Vol. II, p. 220.

118. George Crowninshield (1766–1817), a noted sea captain and merchant, built the *Jefferson* in 1800. He was a brother of Charles Francis Adams' great-grandfather, Benjamin W. Crowninshield. George was also known for his unusual dress—bizarre waistcoat, shaggy beaver hat, and tasseled Hessian boots.

119. When the name of the dynastic Charles Francis Adams was proposed for membership in Boston's Tavern Club, the bulletin board identified him

as "the right one." See Amory, op. cit., p. 150; also Dixon Wecter, *The Saga of American Society* (New York: Scribner's, 1937), p. 52.

120. New York *Times*, June 21, 1929, p. 1.

121. New York *Times*, March 9, 1929, p. 3. After a session with Secretary of the Navy Adams, portrait artist S. J. Woolf commented, "He sees reporters, but declines to be interviewed; he issues statements, but does not talk for publication. . . . The wall of silence was impossible to scale." S. J. Woolf, "The Silent Man Who Directs Our Navy," *New York Times Magazine*, December 13, 1931, p. 8.

122. New York *Times*, March 26, 1930, p. 26.

123. See Irwin H. Hoover, *Forty-two Years in the White House* (Boston and New York: Houghton Mifflin, 1934), p. 189.

124. Herbert Hoover, op. cit., p. 220; New York *Times*, June 12, 1954, p. 15.

125. With the passage of the Federal Banking Act of 1933, J. P. Morgan & Co. had to choose between its security underwriting business and its private deposit banking. When it dropped the investment business Henry S. Morgan resigned from his father's company and with two partners formed a new investment firm, Morgan Stanley & Co., with which he is still associated. See John Gunther, *Inside U.S.A.* (New York: Harper, 1947), p. 571.

126. Letter from Charles F. Adams to author, May 11, 1964.

127. Quoted in John Henry Cutler, *"Honey Fitz"* (Indianapolis and New York: Bobbs-Merrill, 1962), p. 256.

128. Ford, op. cit., Vol. II, p. 55.

129. Quoted in James Truslow Adams, op. cit., p. 67.

130. Quoted in Beringause, op. cit., p. 380.

131. Brooks's view also fitted in with the popular theory of the day. See John F. Nisbet, *Marriage and Heredity* (London: Ward & Downey, 1889), p. 227: "Every family . . . is born with a certain measure of vitality, a given amount of physical and moral aptitudes. . . . The evolutionary process lasts until the family . . . has accomplished its destiny. . . . As soon as the stock of vitality is exhausted, the deterioriation of the family . . . sets in."

132. Quoted in Samuels, *Henry Adams, The Major Phase*, p. 154.

133. Francis Galton, *Hereditary Genius* (Cleveland and New York, 1962), pp. 170–71 (Meridian Books edition). First published in 1869.

134. Quoted in William Manchester, *Portrait of a President, John F. Kennedy in Profile* (Boston: Little, Brown, 1962), p. 218.

THE LEE DYNASTY

1. Quoted in Cleveland Amory, *Who Killed Society?* (New York: Harper, 1960), p. 304.

2. Franklin D. Roosevelt, "Foreword," to Ethel Armes, *Stratford Hall, the Great House of the Lees* (Richmond: Garrett & Massie, 1936), p. xxv.

3. See James Truslow Adams, *The Adams Family* (Boston: Little, Brown, 1930), p. 5.

4. For the most comprehensive account of the first American Lee, see Ludwell Lee Montague, "Richard Lee, the Emigrant," *Virginia Magazine of History and Biography*, LXII, No. 1 (January 1954).

5. Quoted in Karl Schriftgiesser, *The Amazing Roosevelt Family* (New York: Funk, 1942), p. 31.

6.

Hancock Lee (1652–1709)
m. Sarah Allerton (2 children)

Hancock (1709–62)
m. Mary Willis (7 children)

Elizabeth
m. Zachary Taylor (10 children)

John (1743–1802)
m. Elizabeth Bell (7 children)

Richard Taylor
m. Sarah Strather (8 children)

Lucinda
m. Dr. R. H. Call

Sarah
m. John J. Crittenden
(1787–1863)
SENATE

Zachary Taylor (1784–1850)
PRESIDENT
m. Margaret Smith
(3 children)

Wilkinson Call
(1834–1910)
SENATE

Richard Taylor
(1826–79)
Confederate
general

Sarah Knox Taylor
m. Jefferson Davis
(1808–89)
SENATE,
Confederate President

See Robert L. Preston, "Zachary Taylor," *Magazine of the Society of the Lees of Virginia*, IV, No. 1 (May 1926).

7. Quoted in Burton J. Hendrick, *The Lees of Virginia* (New York: Little, Brown, 1935), p. 32.

8. See Ethel Roby Hayden, "The Lees of Blenheim," *Maryland Historical Magazine*, XXXVII, No. 2 (June 1942).

9. Heinrich Ewald Buchholz, *Governors of Maryland* (Baltimore: Williams & Wilkins, 1908), p. 10.

10. See Walter W. Spooner, editor, *Historic Families of America* (New York: Historic Families Publishing Association, 1907), p. 343.

11. For Philip Ludwell Lee's arrogant treatment of a Williamsburg trades-man, see "The Narrative of George Fisher," *William and Mary Quarterly*, 1st Series, XVII, No. 2 (October 1908), pp. 135–37.

12. Quoted in Armes, op. cit., p. 92.

13. See Edmund Jennings Lee, *Lee of Virginia, 1642–1892* (Philadelphia: Franklin Printing, 1895), pp. 130–31.

14. See Agnes Rothery, *Houses Virginians Have Loved* (New York: Rine-hart, 1954), pp. 219–21.

15. See Richard H. Lee, *Memoir of the Life of Richard Henry Lee* (Phil-adelphia: H. C. Carey & I. Lea, 1825), Vol. I, pp. 17–19. The author was a grandson of his subject.

16.

> *Philip Ludwell I* (1640–c. 1723)
> Governor, North and
> South Carolina
> 1st m. *Lucy Higginson* (d. 1674)
> (2 children); 2nd m. *Lady Berkeley* (no issue)

> *Philip Ludwell II* (1672–1726)
> House of Burgesses, Council
> m. *Hannah Harrison* (1678–1731)

> *Hannah Ludwell*   *Philip Ludwell III* (1716–67)
> m. *Thomas Lee* (1690–1750)   Council
> Acting Governor of Virginia   m. *Frances Grymes*

> *William Lee* (1739–95) —— m. —— *Hannah Ludwell* (1737–84)
>   (4 children; 1 d.y.)

For an account of the children of Hannah Ludwell and William Lee, see Earl G. Swem, "The Lee Free School and the College of William and Mary," *William and Mary Quarterly*, 3d Series, XVI, No. 2 (April 1959), pp. 207–13.

17. Quoted in Hendrick, op. cit., p. 173.

18. Ibid., p. 212.

19. For an account that debunks Arthur Lee's part in the negotiations with Beaumarchais, questions his sanity and William Lee's patriotism, see Helen Augur, *The Secret War of Independence* (New York: Duell, Sloan & Pearce, 1955).

20. See Cazenove Gardner Lee, Jr., *Lee Chronicle* (New York: New York University Press, 1957), pp. 177 and 185.

21. For example, wrote Charles Carroll of Carrollton to William Carmichael: "The faction of the Lees is industriously propagating that their opponents are most of them engaged in mercantile connections with Deane and others. . . ." Quoted in Howard Swiggett, *The Extraordinary Mr. Morris* (Garden City, N.Y.: Doubleday, 1952), p. 69.

22. See L. H. Butterfield, editor, *Letters of Benjamin Rush* (Princeton: Princeton University Press, 1951), Vol. I, pp. 21–22, 248–49, 256–60; Vol. II, pp. 1122, 1204–5.

23. See Francis R. Packard, "William Shippen," *Dictionary of American Biography*, XVII, pp. 117–18.

24. See Nancy Shippen Livingston, *Nancy Shippen, Her Journal Book* (Philadelphia: Lippincott, 1935), p. 237.

25. See Page Smith, *John Adams* (Garden City, N.Y.: Doubleday, 1962), pp. 1011, 1015, 1064.

26. See Noble E. Cunningham, Jr., *The Jeffersonian Republicans* (Chapel Hill: University of North Carolina Press, 1957), p. 5.

27. Quoted in Armes, *Stratford Hall*, p. 277.

28. Hendrick, op. cit., p. 388.

29. Quoted in Armes, *Stratford Hall*, p. 308. Italics in original.

30. "The mother of General Lee, the well-known Confederate General in the American Civil War, was subject to trance seizures, and on one occasion was pronounced dead by the physician and 'buried.' Whilst, however, the sexton was filling in the grave, he heard loud crying and knocking, and Mrs. Lee was rescued from her perilous position and a horrible fate." William Tebb and Edward Perry Vollum; second edition by Walter R. Hadwen, *Premature Burial and How It May Be Prevented* (London: Swan Sonnerschein, 1905), p. 45.

31. See Armes, *Stratford Hall*, pp. 293–94; 546–47.

32. Quoted in Hendrick, op. cit., p. 401.

33. Quoted in James Parton, *Life of Andrew Jackson* (New York: Mason Brothers, 1861), Vol. III, pp. 297–98.

34. Quoted in Marshall W. Fishwick, *Lee After the War* (New York: Dodd, Mead, 1963), p. 153.

35. Quoted in Douglas Southall Freeman, *R. E. Lee* (New York: Scribner's, 1934), Vol. I, p. 365.

36. Quoted in Murray H. Nelligan, "American Nationalism on the Stage: The Plays of George Washington Parke Custis," *Virginia Magazine of History and Biography*, LVIII, No. 3 (July 1950), p. 317.

37. Henry Adams, *The Education of Henry Adams* (New York, 1931), p. 57 (Modern Library Edition).

38. Quoted in Philip Van Doren Stern, *Robert E. Lee, the Man and the Soldier* (New York: McGraw-Hill, 1963), p. 99.

39. See Virgil Carrington Jones, *The Civil War at Sea* (New York: Holt, Rinehart, Winston, 1961), Vol. II, pp. 252–53; Bern Anderson, *By Sea and by River, the Naval History of the Civil War* (New York: Knopf, 1962), p. 295.

40. For the Civil War correspondence between Admiral Samuel Phillips Lee and Assistant Secretary of the Navy Gustavus Vasa Fox, see Robert Means Thompson and Richard Wainwright, editors, *Confidential Correspondence of Gustavus Vasa Fox* (New York: Naval History Society, 1918–19), Vol. II, pp. 205ff.

41. See William Ernest Smith, *The Francis Preston Blair Family in Politics* (New York: Macmillan, 1933), Vol. I, p. 62.

42. Joseph Gales, Jr. (1786–1860), was the son of Joseph Gales, Sr. (1761–1841), a radical English editor, who came to America in 1795 and founded the Raleigh (North Carolina) *Register*. The paper was passed on to a son and a grandson, finally suspending operations about 1868.

The second Joseph Gales's wife Sarah was the daughter of Theodoric Lee (1766–1849), fourth son of Henry Lee and Lucy Grymes, "the Lowland Beauty."

43. Quoted in A. L. Long, *Memoirs of Robert E. Lee* (Philadelphia: J. M. Stoddart, 1887), p. 91.

44. Quoted in Edmund Jennings Lee, op. cit., pp. 490–91.

45. Quoted in Louise Pecquet du Bellet, *Some Prominent Virginia Families* (Lynchburg, Va., 1907?), Vol. II, pp. 265–66.

46. Quoted in Robert E. Lee, Jr., *My Father, General Lee* (Garden City, N.Y.: Doubleday, 1960), p. 77. Originally published as *Recollections and Letters of General Robert E. Lee* (1904).

47. Quoted in J. William Jones, *Virginia's Next Governor, Gen. Fitzhugh Lee* (New York: Cheap Publishing, 1885), pp. 11–12.

48. Quoted in Hendrick, op. cit., p. 436.

49. Robert E. Lee, Jr., op. cit., p. 333.

50. Ibid., p. 283.

51. Ibid., p. 245.

52. See New York *Times,* November 23, 1918, p. 11.

53. Mrs. Josephus Daniels, *Recollections of a Cabinet Minister's Wife, 1913–1921* (Raleigh, N.C.: Mitchell Printing, 1945), p. 78.

54. Quoted in Robert E. Lee, Jr., op. cit., p. 405.

55. Charles Francis Adams, *Lee's Centennial. An Address delivered at Lexington, Virginia, Saturday, January 19, 1907, on the Invitation of the President and Faculty of Washington and Lee University,* p. 21. Also see Charles Francis Adams, *Lee at Appomattox and Other Papers* (Boston and New York: Houghton Mifflin, 1902).

56. Of Robert E. Lee's sons:
    1. Custis Lee remained unmarried.
    2. William Henry Fitzhugh (Rooney) Lee first married Charlotte Wickham, who died while her husband was a prisoner of war, leaving no issue. By his second wife, Mary Tabb Bolling, he had two sons: Robert E. Lee III, a Washington lawyer, whose wife was a direct descendant of Arthur Middleton, a signer of the Declaration of Independence; and George Bolling Lee, the gynecologist, who married Helen Keeney of San Francisco, and had a son and a daughter. Letter from Robert E. Lee IV, June 15, 1965; New York *Times,* July 14, 1948, p. 23, and May 20, 1959, p. 35.
    3. Robert E. Lee, Jr., first married Charlotte Taylor Haxall, whose beauty was rhapsodized by the Virginia writer George W. Bagby. ("Her raven hair, her lips that burned with deep fire," etc.) See George W. Bagby, *The Old Virginia Gentleman and Other Sketches* (Richmond: Dietz, 1938), p. 220. She died in 1871 without issue. His second wife was a cousin, Juliet Hill Carter, by whom Lee had two daughters. Washington *Star,* October 20, 1914, p. 4, and New York *Times,* October 21, 1914, p. 11.

57. New York *Times,* April 29, 1905, p. 10.

58. General Fitzhugh Lee's oldest daughter Ellen married Major General James Rhea. Her daughter, Ellen B. Rhea, married Rear Admiral John Milton Opie. Interview with Mrs. Fitzhugh Lee Opie, June 25, 1965.

59. See Samuel Eliot Morison, "Leyte, June 1944–January 1945," Vol. XII in *History of United States Naval Operations in World War II* (Boston: Little, Brown, 1958), pp. 285–88; also New York *Times,* August 24, 1952, p. 64, and January 27, 1960, p. 13; letter from Vice Admiral Fitzhugh Lee, June 18, 1965.

60. Interview with Colonel E. Brooke Lee, June 25, 1965. Also New York *Times,* December 27, 1944, p. 19, and Washington *Post,* December 27, 1944, p. 10B.

61. See *Maryland Manual 1924,* pp. 197–98.

62. Colonel E. Brooke Lee's first wife was Elizabeth Somerville Wilson. Their three children are Blair Lee II, former member of the Maryland House of Delegates; E. Brooke Lee, Jr., a past treasurer of the Young Republicans of New Jersey and Republican finance chairman of Chester County, Pennsylva-

nia, who is now the $20,000-a-year fund raiser for Cafritz Memorial Hospital, Washington, D.C.; and Elizabeth Lee Scull, whose husband was the unsuccessful Republican candidate for the Maryland congressman at large seat in 1964. Mrs. Scull has been a member of the Montgomery County Human Relations Commission.

He second married Thelma Llewellyn Lawson, by whom he has one child, Bruce Lee, formerly a reporter with *Newsweek,* now on the staff of *Reader's Digest,* and author of *The Boy's Life of John F. Kennedy* (New York: Sterling, 1964).

The colonel has no issue by his third wife, Nina G. Lee.

63. Washington *Star,* May 13, 1962, p. C4.

64. Washington *Post,* August 1, 1965, p. E2.

65. Washington *Post,* May 2, 1962, p. B2.

66. Washington *Star,* May 9, 1962, p. B2.

67. Baltimore *Sun,* May 15, 1962, pp. 27 and 40.

68. See *Maryland Manual* 1963–4, p. 465.

69. Washington *Post,* October 23, 1964, p. D1.

70. Washington *Post,* August 24, 1964, p. A7.

71. Washington *Post,* May 14, 1965, p. B1.

72. See Washington *Star,* April 18, 1918, p. 14.

73. See Ralph Reppert, "Gen. Robert E. Lee: Always Ready for the Field," *Baltimore Sunday Sun Magazine,* February 10, 1963, pp. 10–11.

74. Washington *Post,* November 20, 1964, p. D2.

75. Photostats of all applications for membership in the Society of the Lees of Virginia are bound in two volumes in the Library of Congress.

THE LIVINGSTON DYNASTY

1. Theodore Roosevelt, *Gouverneur Morris* (Boston and New York: Houghton Mifflin, 1892), pp. 14–15.

2. Livingston paid: "To wit, three hundred guilders in zewant [wampum], eight blankets, and two children's blankets, five and twenty ells of duffels, and four garments of strouds, ten large shirts and ten small ditto, ten pairs of large stockings and ten pairs of small (ditto), six guns, fifty pounds of powder, fifty staves of lead, four caps, ten kettles, ten axes, ten adzes, two pounds of paint, twenty little scissors, twenty looking-glasses, one hundred fish hooks, awls and nails of each one hundred, four rolls of tobacco, one hundred pipes, ten bottles, three kegs of rum, one barrel of strong beer, and twenty knives, four stroud coats and two duffel coats, and four tin kettles."

See Edwin Brockholst Livingston, *The Livingstons of Callendar* (Edinburgh: Scott & Ferguson, 1887–92), Vol. I, pp. 364–65.

3. Joan Gordon, *The Livingstons of New York 1675–1860: Kinship and Class* (Unpublished Ph.D. dissertation, Columbia University, 1959), p. 11.

4. Lawrence H. Leder, *Robert Livingston 1654–1728 and the Politics of Colonial New York* (Chapel Hill: University of North Carolina Press, 1961), p. 35.

5. Gustavus Myers, *History of the Supreme Court of the United States* (Chicago: C. H. Keer, 1912), p. 139; George W. Schuyler, *Colonial New York, Philip Schuyler and His Family* (New York: Scribner's, 1885), Vol. I, p. 246; Thomas Allen Glenn, *Some Colonial Mansions and Those Who Lived in Them* (Philadelphia: H. T. Coates, 1898), p. 301-2.

6. Schuyler, op. cit., Vol. I, p. 259; quoted in John A. Krout, "Robert Livingston," *Dictionary of American Biography*, Vol. XI, p. 319.

7. The pre-American genealogy of the Livingstons:

William, 4th Lord Livingston of
Callendar (d. c. 1514)

Alexander (d. 1550)
5th Lord of Callendar

James
(d. prior to Oct. 13, 1547)

Reverend Alexander (d. c. 1598)
Rector of Monyabroch

Reverend William (1576–1641)
Minister of Lanark

Reverend John (1603–72)
of Ancrum

Robert (1654–1728)
1st Lord of Livingston Manor

The last male representative of the family in Scotland was Sir Thomas Livingstone, who died without issue in 1853.

Edwin Brockholst Livingston, *The Livingstons of Livingston Manor* (New York: Knickerbocker, 1910), pp. 6–9n.

8. Lawrence H. Leder, op. cit., p. 10; Thomas S. Clarkson, *A Biographical History of Clermont* (Clermont, N.Y.: Privately printed, 1869), p. 12.

9. Quoted in Lawrence H. Leder, op. cit., p. 5.

10. See James A. Padgett, "The Ancestry of Edward Livingston of Louisiana," *The Louisiana Historical Quarterly*, XIX, No. 4 (October 1936), p. 11.

11. Schuyler, op. cit., Vol. I, pp. 185–86, 206; Leder, op. cit., 21.

Philip Pieterse Schuyler (d. 1683)
Founder of the line; substantial
citizen of Albany. m. 1650 *Margarita
Van Slicklenhorst* (1628–1711), daughter
of resident director of Rensselaerwyck.

Gertrude (1654–1719) m. 1671 *Stephen Van Cortlandt* (1643–1700), 1st native-born mayor of New York City	*Alida* (1656–1729) 1st m. *Nicholas Van Rensselaer,* son of 1st Patroon of Rensselaerwyck. 2nd m. 1679 *Robert Livingston*

12. Quoted in Leder, op. cit., p. 93.

13. See Lawrence H. Leder, editor, *The Livingston Indian Records* (Gettysburg: Pennsylvania Historical Association, 1956), p. 7.

14. Quoted in Edwin B. Livingston, *The Livingstons of Callendar*, Vol. I, p. 329.

15. Lawrence H. Leder and Vincent P. Carosso, "Robert Livingston (1654–1728): Businessman of Colonial New York," *The Business History Review*, XXX, No. 1 (March 1956), p. 44.

16. John A. Krout, "Behind the Coat of Arms, a Phase of Prestige in Colonial New York," *New York History*, XVI, No. 1 (January 1935), p. 49.

17. *Representatives for Livingston Manor elected to the New York General Assembly, 1715–76:*

Date of Service	Name
1716–26	Robert Livingston (1654–1728), 1st Lord of the Manor.
1726–27	Robert Livingston of Clermont (1688–1775), son of 1st Lord.
1728–37	Gilbert Livingston (1690–1746), son of 1st Lord.
1737–58	Robert Livingston (1708–90), 3d Lord, grandson of 1st Lord.
1759–61	William Livingston (1723–90), grandson of 1st Lord, later governor of New Jersey.
1761–69	Peter R. Livingston (1737–94), son of 3d Lord and great-grandson of 1st Lord.
1769	Philip Livingston (1716–78), grandson of 1st Lord and later signer of Declaration of Independence.
1769–74	Judge Robert R. Livingston (1718–75), son of Robert of Clermont and grandson of 1st Lord.
1774–76	Peter R. Livingston (1737–94) (see above).

18. Quoted in Schuyler, op. cit., Vol. I, p. 289.

19.

19 Selected descendants of Robert the Nephew:

Robert Livingston (1663–1725), "The Nephew"
m. Margarita Schuyler (niece of Alida Livingston)

Angelica (1698–1747)
m. Johannes Van
Rensselaer (1708–83)

James (1701–63)
m. Maria Kierstede
(1704–62)

Janet (1703–24)
m. Henry Beekman
(b. 1688) 1st wife

John (1709–91)
m. Catharine
Ten Broeck, daughter
of mayor of Albany

Robert J.
(1725–71)
m. Susan
Smith,
sister of
William Smith, Jr.

Janet
(d. 1819)
m. William
Smith, Jr.
(1728–93)
Chief Justice
of Canada

Margaret
(1738–1809)
m. Peter R.
Livingston
(1737–94)
Manor line

Margaret Beekman
(1724–1800) m. Judge
Robert R. Livingston
Clermont, line

James
(1747–1832)
Revolutionary
Army hero

Catherine Van Rensselaer
m. General Philip Schuyler
(1733–1804) SENATE

Henrietta (b. 1776)
m. Jonathan Sewell
(1766–1839), Chief
Justice of Canada

Peter R.
(1766–1847)
m. Joanna
Livingston
(1759–1829)
Clermont line

Maturin
(1769–1847)
m. Margaret Lewis,
daughter of Governor
Morgan Lewis

Elizabeth (1757–1854)
m. Alexander Hamilton
(1755 or 1757–1804),
Secretary of Treasury

Margarita (b. 1758)
m. General Stephen Van
Rensselaer (1764–1839)

20. Quoted in Leder, *Robert Livingston and the Politics of Colonial New York*, p. 255.

21. See Lawrence H. Leder, editor, "Records of the Trials of Jacob Leisler and His Associates," *The New-York Historical Society Quarterly*, XXXVI, No. 4 (October 1952), pp. 431–57.

22. See Lawrence Leder, "Captain Kidd and the Leisler Rebellion," *The New-York Historical Society Quarterly*, XXXVIII, No. 1 (January 1954).

23. Quoted in Dunbar Maury Hinrichs, *The Fateful Voyage of Captain Kidd* (New York: Bookman Associates, 1955), p. 30.

24. See Morton Pennypacker, "Captain Kidd: Hung, Not for Piracy but for Causing the Death of a Rebellious Seaman Hit with a Toy Bucket," *New York History*, XXV, No. 4 (October 1944).

25. *John Winthrop* (1587–1649)
    Governor of Massachusetts, 1631–33, 1637–39, 1642–43
    |
    John Winthrop (1605–76)
    Governor of Connecticut, 1657–58, 1659–76
    |
    Fitz-John Winthrop (1638–1707)
    Governor of Connecticut, 1698–1707
    |
    Mary Winthrop (d. 1712/13)
    m. 1701 *John Livingston* (1680–1720)

26. Quoted in Leder, *Robert Livingston and the Politics of Colonial New York*, p. 229.

27. See Anson Titus, "Madam Sarah Knight, Her Diary and Her Times, 1666–1726," *The Bostonian Society Publications*, IX (Boston, 1912).

28. Geraldine Brooks, *Dames and Daughters of Colonial Days* (New York: T. Y. Crowell, 1900), p. 85.

29.

Anna (Stuyvesant) Bayard
Founder of the Bayard dynasty
in America.
Sister of Governor Peter Stuyvesant

Nicholas (1644–1707)   *Petrus* (d. 1699)
                                                 Founder of the
                                                 Delaware branch

Samuel (1669–1745)   *Margaret (Livingston) Vetch*
                                  (1681–1758)

Stephen ———— m. 1725 ———— *Alida*
(b. 1700)   (b. 1701)

William (1729–1804)
"The Loyalist"

30. Quoted in G. M. Waller, *Samuel Vetch, Colonial Enterpriser* (Chapel Hill: University of North Carolina Press, 1960), p. 252.

31. Mrs. Martha J. Lamb. Quoted in Edwin B. Livingston, *The Livingstons of Livingston Manor*, p. 138.

Philip married Catharine Van Brugh (1689–1756) in 1708. She was the daughter of Captain Peter Van Brugh (1666–1740), mayor of Albany, 1699 and 1721–23. See *Pennsylvania Magazine of History and Biography*, VII, No. 1 (1883), pp. 113–14.

32. Thomas Allen Glenn, op. cit., p. 310.

33. John Henry Livingston, *Livingston Manor* (New York, 1914?), p. 28.

34. Schuyler, op. cit., Vol. I, p. 203; also see Philip L. White, *The Beekmans of New York in Politics and Commerce, 1647–1877* (New York: New-York Historical Society, 1956), pp. 159–207.

35. Quoted in George Dangerfield, *Chancellor Robert R. Livingston, 1746–1813* (New York: Harcourt, Brace, 1960), p. 29.

36. See Edwin B. Livingston, *The Livingstons of Livingston Manor*, p. 149.

37. Ibid., p. 395.

38. Ibid., p. 527n.

39. Ibid., p. 199.

40. Quoted in John A. Krout, "William Livingston," *Dictionary of American Biography*, Vol. XI, p. 325.

41. Louis H. Patterson, "Governor William Livingston as Apprentice, Writer and Executive," *Proceedings of the New Jersey Historical Society*, IX, No. 2 (April 1924), p. 105–6.

42. Edwin B. Livingston, *The Livingstons of Livingston Manor*, p. 201; Dorothy R. Dillon, *The New York Triumvirate: A Study of the Legal and Political Careers of William Livingston, John Morin Scott, William Smith, Jr.* (New York: Columbia University Press, 1949), p. 16.

43. Quoted in Gordon, op. cit., p. 180.

44. See Theodore Sedgwick, Jr., *A Memoir of the Life of William Livingston* (New York: Harper, 1833), pp. 52–53. The author was Livingston's great-grandson.

45. James Alexander (1691–1756), born in Scotland, came to America in 1716 on the same ship as William Smith, with whom he gained fame as the counsel for Peter Zenger. Alexander's distinguished career included service as surveyor general of both New Jersey and New York, member of Council in both provinces, and attorney general of New Jersey.

Two of his children married children of the Second Lord of Livingston Manor: William Alexander married Sarah Livingston and Mary Alexander (1721–69) married Peter Van Brugh Livingston (1710–92), president of the New York Provincial Congress, 1775. See George Rose III, "James Alexander," *Dictionary of American Biography*, Vol. I, pp. 167–68.

46. Gordon, op. cit., pp. 128–29; Sedgwick, op. cit., pp. 58n–59n. William Smith, Sr. (1697–1769), joined James Alexander in the defense of Peter Zenger for libel in 1735. Both were disbarred, but readmitted to the bar two years later. Smith was a member of the Provincial Council, 1753–67, and an associate justice of New York from 1763 until his death. See Richard B. Morris, "William Smith," *Dictionary of American Biography*, Vol. XVII, pp. 352–53.

Two of Judge Smith's children, William, Jr. (1728–93), and Susan, married grandchildren of Robert Livingston, the Nephew.

William Smith, Jr., along with John Morin Scott and William Livingston, were called "the wicked triumvirate of New York" by Reverend Samuel Johnson, first president of King's College. But while Livingston became a Revolutionary leader, Smith remained loyal to the Crown and was rewarded by appointment as chief justice of New York (1779–83) and later Chief Justice of Canada (1786–93). See Richard B. Morris, "William Smith (Jr.)," *Dictionary of American Biography*, Vol. XVII, pp. 357–58; Hilda Neatby, "Chief Justice William Smith: An Eighteenth-Century Whig Imperialist," *The Canadian Historical Review*, XXVIII, No. 1 (March 1947); Hector L. Duff, *The Sewells in the New World* (Exeter: William Pollard, 1924).

47. Susanna French was the daughter of Susanna Brockholst and Philip French. Her paternal grandfather was mayor of New York and a Speaker of the New York Assembly; her maternal grandfather was a lieutenant governor of New York. Philip French lived well beyond his means and borrowed large sums from his Livingston son-in-law. See Milton Martin Klein, *The American Whig: William Livingston of New York* (Unpublished Ph.D. dissertation, Columbia University, 1954), pp. 123, 128–29.

48. Gordon, op. cit., pp. 171 and 201; Klein, op. cit., pp. 175–76.

49. Quoted in Sedgwick, op. cit., p. 75.

50. Ibid., pp. 63–64.

51. Gordon, op. cit., p. 172.

52. Quoted in Sedgwick, op. cit., p. 76n.

53. Ibid., pp. 88–89. The *Independent Reflector* ran from November 30, 1752, until November 22, 1753, when it was unable to get a printer because of pressure from the authorities. Dillon, op. cit., p. 34n.

54. Quoted in Peter H. B. Frelinghuysen, Jr., *Theodorus Jacobus Frelinghuysen* (Princeton: Privately printed, 1938), p. 77.

55. Quoted in Dillon, op. cit., p. 39.

56. *Philosophic Solitude* (Boston, 1762) was a series of rhymed couplets "obviously imitative of Pope." Despite its inferiority, the poem made Livingston the principal poet of colonial New York. See Klein, op. cit., pp. 103 and 106.

57. Quoted in Edwin B. Livingston, *The Livingstons of Livingston Manor*, pp. 457–58.

58. See Beverley W. Bond, Jr., editor, *The Intimate Letters of John Cleves Symmes and His Family* (Cincinnati: Historical and Philosophical Society of Ohio, 1956), pp. xvii, xxv, xxvi.

59. Harry Emerson Wildes, *Twin Rivers, the Raritan and the Passaic* (New York: Farrar & Rinehart, 1943), pp. 173–74.

60. Howard Swiggett, *The Extraordinary Mr. Morris* (Garden City, N.Y.: Doubleday, 1952), p. 352.

61. George Pellew, *John Jay* (Boston and New York: Houghton Mifflin, 1890), pp. 203–4.

62. Lois Hobart, *Patriot's Lady: The Life of Sarah Livingston Jay* (New York: Funk & Wagnalls, 1960), pp. 124–25.

63. John Jay (1745–1829) was the grandson of Augustus Jay, a French Huguenot exile who settled in New York about 1686 and married Anna Maria Bayard, a granddaughter of Anna Stuyvesant Bayard, the founder of the Bayard dynasty in America. See Mrs. Anson Phelps Atterbury, *The Bayard Family* (Baltimore, 1928), p. 11.

Jay's father was a rich merchant; his mother was a Van Cortlandt. An older brother, James (1732–1815), was knighted by George III in recognition of his work as a fund raiser for King's (Columbia) College. See Milton Halsey Thomas, "Sir James Jay," *Dictionary of American Biography*, Vol. X, pp. 4–5.

64. Kenneth B. Umbreit, *Our Eleven Chief Justices* (New York: Harper, 1938), pp. 14–15.

65. Quoted in Frank Monaghan, editor, "Unpublished Correspondence of William Livingston and John Jay," *Proceedings of the New Jersey Historical Society*, LII, No. 3 (July 1934), p. 143.

66. Quoted in Clarkson, op. cit., p. 265.

67. Thomas Tillotson (1752–1832) married Margaret Livingston (1749–1823) in 1779. He was surgeon general of the Northern Department of the army during the Revolutionary War; member of the New York Assembly (1788–90) and state Senate (1791–99); elected to the House of Representatives in 1800 but did not serve; and secretary of state of New York (1801–6, 1807–8). Gouverneur Morris said that Tillotson's birth and talents were nothing extraordinary. See *Biographical Directory of the American Congress, 1774–1961*, p. 1718; Dangerfield, op. cit., p. 189.

68. Freeborn Garrettson (1752–1827) married Catharine Livingston (1752–1849) in 1793. He was well to do, his grandfather being one of the most important early settlers in Maryland. Garrettson was raised as an Anglican, but mystical revelations led him into the Methodist Church, in which he became an itinerant minister. His earnestness was said to have more than made up for his lack of oratorical talents. Bishop Asbury commented, "Brother Garrettson will let no man escape a religious lecture that comes in his way." His aggressive opposition to slaveholding caused him in 1820 to write an important tract on the subject, "A Dialogue Between Do-Justice and Professing Christian." See Harris Elwood Starr, "Freeborn Garrettson," *Dictionary of American Biography*, Vol. VII, pp. 166–67.

69. Morgan Lewis (1754–1844) married Gertrude Livingston (1757–1833) in 1779. He was the son of Francis Lewis (1713–1803), who came to America from London in 1735, established prominent mercantile houses in New York and Philadelphia, and was a member of the Continental Congress (1774–79). The younger Lewis was chief of staff for General Gates at Ticonderoga and Saratoga; chief justice of the New York Supreme Court (1801–4); governor of the state (1804–7); and a major general in the War of 1812. He was "a respectable, dignified man, who prided himself on his aristocratic connections, [and] was quite unfit for the governorship." Dangerfield, op. cit., p. 399. Also see *Biographical Directory of the American Congress, 1774–1961*, pp. 1315–16, and Julia Delafield, *Biographies of Francis Lewis and Morgan Lewis* (New York: A. D. F. Randolph, 1877), 2 vols.

70. The son of an Irish immigrant who became a Revolutionary War general and a delegate to the Continental Congress, John Armstrong's career reflected a generous genius for intrigue. Among his many public offices were U.S. senator (1800–2, 1803–4), minister to France (1804–10), and Secretary of War (1813–14). He distinguished himself in none of these offices, but his service as the head of the War Department during the War of 1812 was particularly unfortunate.

Armstrong's daughter Margaret married William Backhouse Astor in 1818. John Jacob Astor, the German fur trader, was delighted by his son's union with the socially prominent Miss Armstrong, though he made sure, through a marriage settlement, that the bride would surrender her dower rights to the Astor fortune if anything happened to her husband. The younger Astor was the industrious assistant to his father, and later assumed his title of the "Richest Man in America."

Through this line, the Livingstons and the Roosevelts can claim a connection:

John Jacob Astor (1763–1848)

John Armstrong (1758–1843)
m. Alida Livingston (1761–1822)

William Backhouse Astor ——— m. —— Margaret Armstrong (1800–72)
(1792–1875)

John Jacob Astor
(1822–90)

William Astor
(1829–92)

William Waldorf Astor
(1848–1919)
U. S. minister to Rome,
1882–85
1st Viscount Astor

Helen Astor
(d. 1893)
m. James Roosevelt
Roosevelt (half brother
of F.D.R.)

See Freeman Cleaves, *Old Tippecanoe* (New York: Scribner's Sons, 1939), pp. 155–56; Julius W. Pratt, "John Armstrong," *Dictionary of American Biography*, pp. 355–58; *Biographical Directory of the American Congress, 1774–1961*, pp. 487–88; Kenneth Wiggins Porter, *John Jacob Astor, Business Man* (Cambridge: Harvard University Press, 1931), Vol. I, p. 563; Vol. II, p. 1039; Cleveland Amory, *Who Killed Society?* (New York: Harper, 1960), p. 471.

71. Quoted in J. M. LeMoine, *The Sword of Brigadier-General Richard Montgomery* (Quebec, 1870), p. 36. Also see James Truslow Adams, "Richard Montgomery," *Dictionary of American Biography*, Vol. XIII, pp. 98–99; John Armstrong, "Richard Montgomery," in Jared Sparks, editor, *American Biography* (New York and London: Harper and Brothers, 1902), Vol. XI.

72. Quoted in Charles Leonard Lundin, *Cockpit of the Revolution, the War for Independence in New Jersey* (Princeton: Princeton University Press, 1940), p. 90.

73. Quotations in Margaret Burnham Macmillan, *The War Governors in the American Revolution* (New York: Columbia University Press, 1943), pp. 254–55, and Lundin, op. cit., p. 89.

74. For a more favorable appraisal of Stirling as a soldier, see George H. Danforth, *The Rebel Earl* (Unpublished Ph.D. dissertation, Columbia Univer-

sity, 1955), p. 3 (abstract): "That he was the outstanding commander in the defense of Long Island is generally acknowledged; his superior role in other operations, such as the battles of Trenton and Germantown, is less well known. In the Battle of the Brandywine and at Monmouth he was unsurpassed by any other American officer."

When Stirling's daughter Catherine ("Lady Kitty") married William Duer in 1779, George Washington gave the bride away. Duer (1747–99) was a member of the Continental Congress, 1777–78, and Assistant Secretary of the Treasury under Hamilton, 1789–90. His later dealings helped to cause the first financial panic in New York history and sent him to debtor's prison, where he died. His son, William Alexander Duer (1780–1858), a New York jurist, wrote a highly laudatory biography of his maternal grandfather, *The Life of William Alexander, Earl of Stirling* (New York: Wiley and Putnam, 1847).

75. Colonel James Livingston (1747–1832), a grandson of Robert the Nephew, raised a regiment of Canadian refugees, including his two brothers, and fought with valor under Montgomery at Quebec. He resigned from the army in 1781, later serving as a member of the first Board of Regents of New York University, and as a state assemblyman (1786–87, 1789–91). He was the grandfather of Gerrit Smith (1797–1874), abolitionist leader and reformer for sundry causes, and Elizabeth Cady Stanton (1815–1902), first president of the National Woman Suffrage Association (1869–90). See James Thomas Flexner, *The Traitor and the Spy* (New York: Harcourt, Brace, 1953), p. 350; also Katharine Elizabeth Crane, "James Livingston," *Dictionary of American Biography*, Vol. XI, pp. 313–14.

76. Edwin B. Livingston, *The Livingstons of Livingston Manor*, pp. 511–12.

77. Quotations in Swiggett, op. cit., p. 56, and Edward P. Alexander, *A Revolutionary Conservative, James Duane of New York* (New York: Columbia University Press, 1938), p. 93.

78. Quoted in Nancy Shippen Livingston, *Nancy Shippen, Her Journal Book* (Philadelphia: Lippincott, 1935), p. 93.

79. Quoted in Alexander, op. cit., p. 148. A grandson, General James Chatham Duane (1824–97), was chief engineer of the Army of the Potomac during most of the Civil War, and later Chief of Engineers, U. S. Army. In 1850 he married Harriet W. Brewerton, daughter of General Henry Brewerton, then superintendent of the U. S. Military Academy. One of their three sons, Dr. Alexander Duane (1858–1926), was an important leader in the field of ophthalmology. See G. J. Fieberger, "James Chatham Duane," and John F. Fulton, "Alexander Duane," *Dictionary of American Biography*, Vol. V, pp. 464–67.

80. Quotations in Edwin B. Livingston, *The Livingstons of Livingston Manor*, p. 200, and George W. Corner, editor, *The Autobiography of Benjamin Rush* (Princeton: Princeton University Press, 1948), p. 146.

81. His estate in New York City was valued at £16,900, and he also owned 132,069 acres of rural land. See Gordon, op. cit., p. 160.

82. Quoted in John A. Krout, "Philip Livingston," *Dictionary of American Biography*, Vol. XI, p. 318.

83. See Richard P. McCormick, "The First Election of Governor William Livingston," *Proceedings of the New Jersey Historical Society*, LXV, No. 2 (April 1947).

84. Edwin B. Livingston, *The Livingstons of Livingston Manor*, p. 267.

85. Ibid., p. 266.

86. Quoted in Wildes, op. cit., pp. 175–76.

87. See Julia Delafield, op. cit., Vol. I, p. 150. This account was written by a great-granddaughter of Margaret Beekman Livingston. For the life of Mrs. Delafield (1801–82), who taught herself Greek after she was seventy so that "she might read the Gospels in the original," and her husband, Joseph Delafield (1790–1875), founder of Fieldston, New York, see John Ross Delafield, *Delafield, the Family History* (New York: Privately printed, 1945), Vol. I, pp. 261–62; Vol. II, p. 478.

88. Quoted in Clarkson, op. cit., p. 89.

89. Quoted in Dangerfield, op. cit., pp. 46–47. Italics in original.

90. Quoted in Elizabeth F. Ellet, *The Queens of American Society* (New York: Scribner, 1867), p. 54.

91. Quoted in Hobart, op. cit., p. 161.

92. Quoted in Hampton L. Carson, *The Supreme Court of the United States: Its History* (Philadelphia: P. W. Ziegler, 1892), Vol. I, pp. 230–31.

93. Frank Monaghan, *John Jay, Defender of Liberty* (New York and Indianapolis: Bobbs-Merrill, 1935), pp. 155–57.

94. Quoted in Edwin B. Livingston, *The Livingstons of Livingston Manor*, pp. 293–94.

95. Quoted in Pellew, op. cit., p. 223.

96. Quoted in Dangerfield, op. cit., p. 111.

97. Armes, op. cit., pp. 18–19.

98. Ibid., p. 107.

99. Ibid., p. 219.

100. Louis Otto married Elizabeth (1761–87), daughter of Mary Alexander and Peter Van Brugh Livingston, who was one of the founders of Princeton College. See Thomas J. Wertenbaker, *Princeton 1746–1896* (Princeton: Princeton University Press, 1946), pp. 14–16.

101. Gordon, op. cit., p. 146. Hardest hit by the war was Susan Livingston, widow of a grandson of Robert the Nephew, who was reduced to taking boarders into her Princeton home. However, this didn't solve her problem, for a son wrote: "Dr. Witherspoon, who was her landlord, by renting the house in which she lives over her head without previous notice, because he could get a little more from some other person, has entirely cut off her resources; and where she and her family will put their heads after the first of May next, God only knows!" Edwin B. Livingston, *The Livingstons of Livingston Manor*, pp. 275–76.

102. Quoted in Gordon, op. cit., p. 147.

103. John R. Livingston (1755–1851) was a younger brother of the Chancellor. Dangerfield, op. cit., p. 194, writes that he "devoted his energies to making what he called 'something clever' out of the Revolution in the way of business. . . ." Also see Gordon, op. cit., pp. 224–25.

104. Macmillan, op. cit., pp. 274, 285–86. The other top executives listed are Clinton of New York, Trumbull of Connecticut, Johnson of Maryland, Read and Rodney of Delaware, Rutledge of South Carolina, and Weare of New Hampshire. It is interesting that neither Patrick Henry nor Thomas Jefferson is on this list.

105. Quoted in Dillon, op. cit., p. 162.

106. Gordon, op. cit., pp. 296–98, 300, 302.

107. Ibid., pp. 303–4.

108. Dangerfield, op. cit., pp. 215–16, 240–41.

109. Quoted in William B. Hatcher, *Edward Livingston: Jeffersonian Republican and Jacksonian Democrat* (Baton Rouge: Louisiana State University Press, 1940), p. 14.

110. Quoted in Frank Monaghan, *John Jay*, p. 336.

111. Ibid., p. 328.

112. Dangerfield, op. cit., p. 260.

113. Of the 1795 gubernatorial contest between Livingston and Jay, Jay's son writes, "No competitor could probably have been selected with whom he [Jay] would have been more reluctant to contend than the Chancellor. Ancient friendship and ancient associations must have rendered it peculiarly painful to him to find in his old companion and fellow-labourer a voluntary rival. But whatever may have been his reflections on the occasion, they were confined in his own bosom; and nothing unkind towards his opponent escaped from his lips or his pen." William Jay, *The Life of John Jay, with Selections from His Correspondence and Miscellaneous Papers* (New York: Harper, 1833), Vol. I, pp. 400–1.

William Jay (1789–1858) was a New York judge and important figure in the abolitionist movement. His only surviving son, John Jay (1817–94), continued his work in the anti-slavery cause and later served as U.S. minister to Austria (1869–74), member of the New York Civil Service Commission (1884–87), and president of the American Historical Association (1890). See A. Everett Peterson, "William Jay" and "John Jay," *Dictionary of American Biography*, Vol. X, pp. 10–12.

114. Quoted in Milledge L. Bonham, Jr., "A Forgotten American Statesman," *American Mercury*, II, No. 8 (August 1924), p. 493.

115. William Howard Taft, *Our Chief Magistrate* (New York: Columbia University Press, 1925), p. 152.

116. Dangerfield, op. cit., p. 279.

117. Ibid., p. 278.

118. Edwin B. Livingston, *The Livingstons of Livingston Manor*, p. 397.

119. Ibid., p. 343. Seventy-five years later Livingston's speech was translated into Spanish and published in Mexico when a similar issue confronted that government. Bonham, op. cit., p. 494.

120. Quoted in Hatcher, op. cit., p. 70.

121. Ibid., pp. 68–69. Italics in original.

122. Quoted in Charles R. King, editor, *The Life and Correspondence of Rufus King* (New York: Putnam's, 1894–1900), Vol. III, p. 460.

123. Smith Thompson (1768–1843) married Sarah Livingston (1777–1833), a great-granddaughter of Gilbert, youngest son of the First Lord.

Thompson was a state judge, 1802–18, for the last four years serving as the chief justice of the New York Supreme Court. He was then appointed Secretary of the Navy by President Monroe and offered the U. S. Supreme Court seat left vacant by the death of Brockholst Livingston in 1823. He hesitated, feeling that he had some chance for the presidential nomination, but finally concluded that he could not defeat John Quincy Adams and accepted the court appointment. Although he remained on the bench until his death, he became the Republican nominee for governor of New York in

1828. His losing campaign against Martin Van Buren was one of the most bitter in the state's history, and he was sharply criticized for making the race without resigning from the court. At least one historian, Jabez D. Hammond, considered that "for legal acumen, clearness of perception, and logical power of mind, there are few if any men, in this or any other country, who can excel Judge Smith." See King, op. cit., Vol. VI, pp. 508–10 (for presidential ambitions); Robert Livingston Nicholson, *Material Relating to the Livingston, Nicholson, Clack, Wheelock, Hamilton, Steele, Roosevelt, and Schuyler Families* (Typewritten manuscript, 1939, Library of Congress), pages unnumbered (for genealogy); Jabez D. Hammond, *The History of Political Parties in the State of New York* (Cooperstown, N.Y.: H. and E. Phinney, 1846), Vol. I, pp. 180–81.

124. William S. Carpenter, "Edward Livingston," *Dictionary of American Biography*, Vol. XI, p. 309; Hatcher, op. cit., p. 185.

125. Quoted in King, op. cit., Vol. III, p. 459.

126. Quoted in Edwin B. Livingston, *The Livingstons of Livingston Manor*, p. 358. Italics in original.

When Morris was minister to France (1792–94) he took Henry Livingston with him as his private secretary. Besides the $1350 salary, the young man must have received a liberal education, for Morris and Talleyrand were having affairs with the novelist Adelaide de Flahaut at the same time. Swiggett, op. cit., p. 229; Charles Callan Tansill, *The Secret Loves of the Founding Fathers* (New York: Devin-Adair, 1964), pp. 123–64.

Henry Livingston (1768–1810), a grandson of the Third Lord of the Manor, later became the fifth of his dynasty to serve in the Congress, 1803–7. See *Biographical Directory of the American Congress, 1774–1961*, p. 1226.

127. The marriage of the Chancellor's daughter to Edward Philip Livingston gave the Livingston dynasty a second link to the Roosevelt dynasty:

Edward Philip Livingston (1779–1843)
m. 1799 *Elizabeth S. Livingston* (1780–1829)
|
Elizabeth Livingston (1813–96)
m. 1833 *Dr. Edward Hunter Ludlow* (1810–84)
|
Mary Livingston Ludlow (b. 1843)
m. 1861 *Valentine Gill Hall* (1834–80)
|
Anna Rebecca Hall (1863–92)
m. 1883 *Elliott Roosevelt* (1860–93)
|
Eleanor Roosevelt (1884–1962)
m. 1905 *Franklin Delano Roosevelt* (1882–1945)

128. His father was Walter Livingston (1740–97), ablest son of the Third Lord. He was a member of the Continental Congress, 1784–85, and a com-

missioner of the U. S. Treasury, 1785. Walter became involved in the financial manipulations of William Duer, having endorsed Duer's notes to the extent of $375,000, and came close to joining his associate in debtor's prison. See Dangerfield, op. cit., pp. 280–81; also *Biographical Directory of the American Congress, 1774–1961*, pp. 1226–27 (which incorrectly lists him as a son of Philip the Signer.)

129. Henry Adams, *History of the United States of America during the Administrations of Jefferson and Madison* (Boston and New York: Houghton Mifflin, 1947), Vol. II, p. 48.

130. Edward A. Parsons, editor, *The Original Letters of Robert R. Livingston, 1801–1803* (New Orleans: Louisiana Historical Society, 1953), p. 13.

131. Quoted in Edwin B. Livingston, *The Livingstons of Livingston Manor,* p. 276.

132. Quoted in Dangerfield, op. cit., p. 376.

133. Cleaves, op. cit., pp. 155–56.

134. Quoted in Edwin B. Livingston, *The Livingstons of Livingston Manor,* p. 382.

135.

John Stevens I (d. 1737)
Arrived America 1699
Real estate speculator

|

John II (1715–92)
CONTINENTAL CONGRESS

|

John III (1749–1838)
Brother-in-law of Chancellor
Livingston. Steamboat and
railroad innovator

Robert Livingston (1787–1856)   *Edwin Augustus* (1795–1868)

The brothers controlled the Camden & Amboy Railroad with the Stocktons.

Robert Livingston Stevens (1787–1856) assisted his father in the design and construction of the *Phoenix,* the first oceangoing steamboat in the world. He was considered the country's leading naval architect. Later, when he turned his attention to railroading, his designs included the T-rail (the standard section on all American railroads) and the "hook-headed spike" (substantially the railroad spike of today). See Carl W. Mitman, "Robert Livingston Stevens," *Dictionary of American Biography,* Vol. XVII, pp. 619–20.

Edwin Augustus Stevens (1795–1868) was also an inventor whose designs included the "two horse dump wagon," used extensively for many years to haul away refuse in New York. However, he primarily handled the business side of all Stevens family ventures. He left an estate of about eighteen million dollars, and founded the Stevens Institute of Technology, Hoboken, New Jersey. His marriage to Martha Bayard Dod linked the Stevens, Stockton, and Bayard families. His wife was a granddaughter of Samuel J. Bayard (the claims negotiator under the Jay Treaty) and a great-granddaughter of Susanna Stockton (the sister of Richard the Signer). See Carl W. Mitman, "Edwin Augustus Stevens," *Dictionary of American Biography*, Vol. XVII, pp. 608–9.

A daughter of Edwin A. Stevens married into the distinguished Garnett family of Virginia. Her husband was Muscoe Russell Hunter Garnett (1821–64), a strong defender of slavery, who left the U. S. House of Representatives in 1861 and later became a Confederate congressman. After Garnett's death Stevens ordered his daughter to return to New Jersey with her two small children. She refused. He then got President Lincoln to send a gunboat up the Rappahannock to bring his willful daughter back. Mary Stevens Garnett returned to her father's house, but only after the gunboat's commander had threatened to take her by force. See Agnes Rothery, *Houses Virginians Have Loved* (New York: Rinehart, 1954), pp. 210–11.

136. Dorothy Gregg, *The Exploitation of the Steamboat: The Case of Colonel John Stevens* (Unpublished Ph.D. dissertation, Columbia University, 1951), p. 37.

137. Talbot Hamlin, *Benjamin Henry Latrobe* (New York: Oxford University Press, 1955), pp. 188–89.

138. Dangerfield, op. cit., p. 287.

139. Ibid., pp. 50 and 415.

140. Ibid., p. 287.

141. Quoted in Hamlin, op. cit., p. 408.

142. H. W. Dickinson, *Robert Fulton, Engineer and Artist: His Life and Works* (London: John Lane, 1913), pp. 145–46.

143. Ibid., p. 270.

144. Quoted in Hamlin, op. cit., p. 376n.

145. James Thomas Flexner, *Inventors in Action, the Story of the Steamboat* (New York: Collier Books, 1962), p. 332. Originally published as *Steamboats Come True* (New York: Viking, 1944).

146. Archibald Douglas Turnbull, *John Stevens, an American Record* (New York: Century, 1928), p. 261.

147. Ibid., p. 331.

148. Quoted in Hamlin, op. cit., p. 372.

149. Quoted in Gordon, op. cit., p. 236.

150. Lyle Saxon, *Lafitte the Pirate* (New York: Century, 1930), pp. 119, 127–28; Also see William Bridgwater, "Jean Lafitte," *Dictionary of American Biography*, Vol. X, pp. 540–41.

151. Catharina V. R. Bonney, *A Legacy of Historical Gleanings* (Albany: J. Munsell, 1875), Vol. I, p. 86.

152. Howard Knott, "Auguste Genevieve Valentin D'Avezac," *Dictionary of American Biography*, Vol. V, p. 89.

153. Bonham, op. cit., p. 498.

154. Hatcher, op. cit., pp. 285–86.

155. Quoted in Roger Butterfield, *The American Past* (New York: Simon & Schuster, 1947), p. 37.

156. Quoted in Edwin B. Livingston, *The Livingstons of Livingston Manor*, pp. 436–37.

157. Quoted in Arthur M. Schlesinger, Jr., *The Age of Jackson* (Boston: Little, Brown, 1945), p. 64.

158. Quoted in Hatcher, op. cit., p. 383.

159. Quoted in Edwin B. Livingston, *The Livingstons of Livingston Manor*, p. 441.

160. Quoted in Louise Livingston Hunt, *Memoir of Mrs. Edward Livingston* (New York: Harper, 1886), p. 142.

161. Thomas Pennant Barton (1803–69) was the son of Benjamin Smith Barton (1766–1815), a famous physician and naturalist, who succeeded Benjamin Rush at the University of Pennsylvania and was the author of the first elementary botany written by an American.

162. Josiah Quincy, *Figures of the Past from the Leaves of Old Journals* (Boston: Little, Brown, 1926), p. 225. Italics in original.

163. Ibid., p. 227.

164.

Peter Van Brugh Livingston (1710–92)
President, New York Provincial Congress

|

Philip (1740–1810) ("Gentleman Phil")
A strong Tory

Peter Van Brugh (1792–1868)
U. S. minister to Ecuador, 1848

Charles Ludlow (d. 1873)
Speaker of the New York Assembly, 1832–33; state senate, 1834–37

165. John Henry Livingston (1848–1927) was the product of two generations of intra-family marriages. His parents were Clermont (of the Clermont line) and Cornelia Livingston (of the Manor line); his grandparents were Edward Philip (of the Manor line) and Elizabeth Stevens Livingston, the Chancellor's daughter (of the Clermont line).

166.

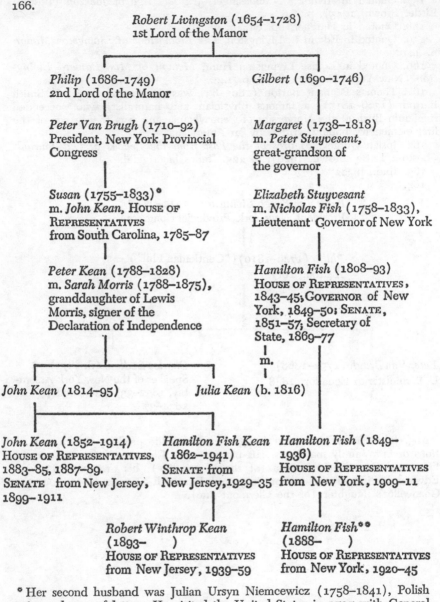

Robert Livingston (1654–1728)
1st Lord of the Manor

Philip (1686–1749)
2nd Lord of the Manor

Gilbert (1690–1746)

Peter Van Brugh (1710–92)
President, New York Provincial
Congress

Margaret (1738–1818)
m. *Peter Stuyvesant,*
great-grandson of
the governor

Susan (1755–1833)*
m. *John Kean,* HOUSE OF
REPRESENTATIVES
from South Carolina, 1785–87

Elizabeth Stuyvesant
m. *Nicholas Fish* (1758–1833),
Lieutenant Governor of New York

Peter Kean (1788–1828)
m. *Sarah Morris* (1788–1875),
granddaughter of Lewis
Morris, signer of the
Declaration of Independence

Hamilton Fish (1808–93)
HOUSE OF REPRESENTATIVES,
1843–45; GOVERNOR of New
York, 1849–50; SENATE,
1851–57; Secretary of
State, 1869–77

m.

John Kean (1814–95)

Julia Kean (b. 1816)

John Kean (1852–1914)
HOUSE OF REPRESENTATIVES,
1883–85, 1887–89.
SENATE from New Jersey,
1899–1911

Hamilton Fish Kean
(1862–1941)
SENATE from
New Jersey, 1929–35

Hamilton Fish (1849–
1936)
HOUSE OF REPRESENTATIVES
from New York, 1909–11

Robert Winthrop Kean
(1893–   )
HOUSE OF REPRESENTATIVES
from New Jersey, 1939–59

*Hamilton Fish**
(1888–   )
HOUSE OF REPRESENTATIVES
from New York, 1920–45

* Her second husband was Julian Ursyn Niemcewicz (1758–1841), Polish patriot and man of letters. He visited the United States in 1797 with General Kosciuszko after they had been released from a two-year imprisonment in St. Petersburg. The marriage to Mrs. Kean took place in 1800, after which they returned to Europe, where he was secretary to the Polish Senate until the 1830 insurrection. He continued to work for Polish independence but was never to return to his native land, and died in Paris. See Julian Ursyn Niemcewicz, *Under Their Vine and Fig Tree: Travels through America in 1797–1799* . . . (Elizabeth, N.J.: Grassman, 1965).

** His son, Hamilton Fish, Jr., declared his candidacy in 1964 for the House of Representatives from New York's 29th Congressional District, then withdrew from the race. In 1966 he announced his candidacy for the Republican nomination in the twenty-eighth Congressional District of New York.

See William B. Aitken, *Distinguished Families in America Descended from Wilhelmus Beekman and Jan Thomasse Van Dyke* (New York: Knickerbocker, 1912), pp. 13–14.

167. Quoted in Dangerfield, op. cit., p. 400.

168. There were three exceptions, grandsons of the wastrel Peter R. Livingston: Crawford (1811–47), Moncrieffe, Jr. (b. 1807), and William A. (1805–61). They were pioneers in the development of express companies, and their firms (Livingston, Wells & Co. and Livingston & Fargo) became the nuclei of the two giants in the field—the American Express Co. and Wells, Fargo & Co. See Edward Hungerford, *Wells Fargo* (New York: Random House, 1949), p. 5.

169. Myers, op. cit., p. 140.

170. Gordon, op. cit., p. 284.

171. Ibid., p. 277.

172. On the ban against Livingston males entering any profession other than law, there were two notable exceptions: John Henry Livingston (1746–1825), the famous clergyman-educator (see Frelinghuysen Dynasty), and Goodhue Livingston (1867–1951), a great-grandson of the Chancellor, an architect whose designs include the St. Regis Hotel, Hayden Planetarium, and Rikers Island Penitentiary in New York, and the state capitol of Oregon.

The architect's son, Goodhue Livingston, Jr. (1897–   ), had a distinguished career in New York municipal government. He was executive secretary to Mayor La Guardia (1943–45) and member of the City Planning Commission (1945–61). During 1942 he was in charge of American underground intelligence in South Africa. Now retired and living in Antigua, B.W.I., he still maintains an interest in public questions through the International Planned Parenthood Federation and the Committee for Collective Security, an organization that takes a liberal position on U.S. foreign policy. Letter from Goodhue Livingston, Jr., to author, March 27, 1964.

173. From the obituary of Robert Swift Livingston (1780–1867), a grandson of the Third Lord. *The Semi-Weekly Times* (New York), March 1, 1867. Quoted in Gordon, op. cit., pp. 248–49.

174. Ibid., p. 253.

THE WASHBURN DYNASTY

1. Quoted in Lilian Washburn, *My Seven Sons, the True and Amazing Story of the Seven Famous Washburn Brothers as told by the Old Grandsire, Israel, Sr., and Transcribed by his Granddaughter* (Portland, Me.: Falmouth, 1940), p. 11.

2. Quoted in William W. Folwell, *A History of Minnesota* (St. Paul: Minnesota Historical Society, 1926), Vol. III, p. 328.

3. Quoted in Gaillard Hunt, *Israel, Elihu and Cadwallader Washburn* (New York: Macmillan, 1925), p. 193.

4. See David Atwood, *Memorial Addresses on the Life and Character of Hon. C. C. Washburn* (Madison, Wis.: D. Atwood, 1883), p. 11.

5. George F. Hoar, *Autobiography of Seventy Years* (New York: Scribner's, 1903), Vol. I, p. 238.

6. "The Fight Over the Body of Keitt (A Fragment from the Great American Epic, the Washingtoniad)" *Punch or the London Charivari*, March 6, 1858, p. 100, including the memorable lines:

"Washburne stood with his brother—CADWALLADER stood with ELIHU; Broad Illinois sent the one, and woody Wisconsin the other."

7. Quoted in William C. Edgar, *The Medal of Gold* (Minneapolis: Bellman, 1925), p. 9.

8. Hunt, op. cit., p. 158.

9. Undated article from the Milwaukee *Sentinel* in the collection of Thomas D. Washburne of Baltimore.

10. Hunt, op. cit., p. 230.

11. Quoted in Lilian Washburn, op. cit., p. 24.

12. See Julia Chase Washburn, *Genealogical Notes of the Washburn Family* (Lewiston, Me.: Press of Journal Co., 1898); also letter from Elihu B. Washburne to Emory Washburn, June 24, 1859, Library of Congress.

13. Quoted in Lilian Washburn, op. cit., p. 64.

14. See Reginald H. Sturtevant, "Seven Sons," *Down East, the Magazine of Maine,* II, No. 8 (June 1956), p. 22.

15. Quoted in Hunt, op. cit., p. 172.

16. Quoted in Joseph Schafer, "Washburniana," *Wisconsin Magazine of History,* XIV, No. 3 (March 1931), p. 317.

17. Worthington Chauncey Ford, editor, *Letters of Henry Adams, 1858–1891* (Boston and New York: Houghton Mifflin, 1930), Vol. I, p. 63.

18. *Dedicatory Exercise of the Washburn Memorial Library* (Chicago, 1885), p. 39.

19. Grant to Elihu Washburne, February 21, 1862: "That portion of your letter which required immediate attention was replied to as soon as your letter was read. I mean that I telegraphed Col. C. C. Washburn, Milwaukee, Wis., asking him to accept a place on my staff." James Grant Wilson, editor, *General Grant's Letters to a Friend, 1861–1880* (New York and Boston: T. Y. Crowell, 1897), p. 4.

20. Lincoln to Elihu Washburne, October 26, 1863: "Inclosed I send the leave of absence for your brother [Cadwallader], in as good form as I think I can safely put it. Without knowing whether he would accept it, I have tendered the Collectorship at Portland, Me., to your other brother, the Governor [Israel]. . . . A second term would be a great honor and a great labor, which together, perhaps I would not decline, if tendered." From the Hempstead Washburne II Collection (transcripts in the possession of Thomas D. Washburne of Baltimore).

21. "It is not impossible that the appointment of Mr. Washburne's brother Charles, to be Commissioner to Paraguay and Minister to the same country, may have been influenced by the close bond between the President and the Congressman." Francis X. Gannon, *A Study of Elihu Benjamin Washburne: American Minister to France During the Franco-Prussian War and the Commune* (Unpublished Ph.D. dissertation, Georgetown University, 1950), pp. 9–10.

22. Elihu B. Washburne Papers, Library of Congress, Vol. 13.

23. Folwell, op. cit., Vol. III, p. 327.

24. See W. Burlie Brown, *The People's Choice* (Baton Rouge: Louisiana State University Press, 1960), p. 6.

25. See James G. Blaine, *Twenty Years of Congress* (Norwich, Conn: Henry Bill Publishing Co., 1884), Vol. I, pp. 509–10; *The Lake Forester* (Illinois), July 27, 1961, p. 78.

26. Robert Anderson, "A New Lincoln Letter," *Chicago Sunday Tribune Magazine,* January 14, 1962, pp. 44–45.

27. For example, Grant to Washburne, September 3, 1861: "In conclusion,

Mr. Washburne, allow me to thank you for the part you have taken in giving me my present position. I think I see your hand in it, and admit that I had no personal claims for your kind office in the matter." Wilson, op. cit., p. 2.

28. Washburne was an inveterate souvenir collector. He saved some chips from the apple tree under which Lee surrendered. Later in Paris, when he saw a small fragment fall off the Arc de Triomphe, he paid two francs to the soldier who had picked it up, and happily added the historic bit to his collection. See Hunt, op. cit., p. 223; Elihu B. Washburne, *Recollections of a Minister to France, 1869–1877* (New York: Scribner's, 1887), Vol. II, p. 97.

29. Hunt, op. cit., pp. 191–92, 194.

30. Quoted in Blaine, op. cit., Vol. II, p. 358.

31. *Diary of Gideon Welles* (Boston and New York: Houghton Mifflin, 1911), Vol. II, pp. 341–42.

32. Quoted in Folwell, op. cit., Vol. III, p. 329.

33. Welles, op. cit., Vol. II, p. 543.

34. Quoted in Charles A. Jellison, *Fessenden of Maine, Civil War Senator* (Syracuse: Syracuse University Press, 1962), p. 253.

35. The *Nation*, however, wasn't overly concerned about Washburne's appointment, because "Luckily there is no question of importance now pending between this country and France . . . and though we do not think the French, or any other mission, should be made a retreat for the President's invalid friends, no immediate mischief is likely to result from General Grant's choice in this instance." March 18, 1869, p. 204. But in an earlier editorial the *Nation* called Washburne "a very able and useful man," implying that he would have been a good Secretary of the Treasury. The magazine's complaint was that he was ill suited for a foreign policy post. March 11, 1869, p. 184.

36. Washburne, *Recollections of a Minister to France*, Vol. II, p. 67.

37. Ibid., Vol. I, pp. 272, 282, 235.

38. Ibid., Vol. I, pp. 286 and 289.

39. Quoted in Allan Nevins, *Hamilton Fish* (New York: Dodd, Mead, 1936), p. 406.

40. See Herbert J. Clancy, *The Presidential Election of 1880* (Chicago: Loyola University Press, 1958), p. 106n.

41. Charles A. Washburn, *Philip Thaxter* (New York: Rudd & Carleton, 1861), p. 243.

42. Charles A. Washburn, *Gomery of Montgomery* (New York: Carleton, 1865), Vol. II, p. 300.

43. Lilian Washburn, op. cit., p. 81.

44. Charles A. Washburn, *The History of Paraguay, with Notes of Personal Observations, and Reminiscences of Diplomacy under Difficulties* (Boston: Lee & Shepard, 1871), Vol. II, p. 460.

45. Ibid., Vol. II, p. 536.

46. Ibid., Vol. II, p. 523.

47. Lilian Washburn, op. cit., p. 126.

48. Charles A. Washburn, *The History of Paraguay*, Vol. II, p. 530; Vol. I, p. 243; Vol. II, p. 436.

49. Lilian Washburn, op. cit., p. 129.

50. Quoted in Edgar, op. cit., p. 64.

51. See Wilson, op. cit., p. 24.

52. Atwood, op. cit., p. 16.

53. Ibid., p. 16.

54. See Cyrus Woodman, *A Statement Relating to the Will of Hon. Cadwallader C. Washburn* (Cambridge, Mass.: Privately printed, 1884).

55. Quoted in Folwell, op. cit., Vol. III, pp. 494–95.

56. See *The Reminiscences of Stanley Washburn* (transcript in the Oral History Research Office, Columbia University), p. 4.

57. Arthur Wallace Dunn, *Gridiron Nights* (New York: Frederick A. Stokes, 1915), p. 38.

58. See Folwell, op. cit., Vol. III, pp. 389–99; Martin Ridge, *Ignatius Donnelly* (Chicago: University of Chicago Press, 1962), pp. 180–95.

59. See *Reminiscences of Stanley Washburn*, pp. 13–14.

60. Minneapolis *Journal*, January 25, 1895, p. 1. The newspaper agreed with the senator's assessment of his defeat. Its front-page cartoon, "Locking the Door after the Horse Is Stolen," was captioned: "In view of the notorious, scandalous employment of the patronage of the office of Governor by Knute Nelson to secure his election to the Senate, two members of the Legislature introduce bills to prevent this prostitution of public office to private advantage in the future."

61. See *Reminiscences of Stanley Washburn*, p. 17.

62. Folwell, op. cit., Vol. III, pp. 204–5.

63. See Graham H. Stuart, *The Department of State* (New York: Macmillan, 1949), pp. 153, 155–56.

64. See Minneapolis *Journal*, September 26, 1919, p. 1; New York *Times*, September 27, 1919, p. 13.

65. Stanley Washburn, *The Cable Game* (Boston: Sherman, French, 1912), p. 14.

66. See Stanley Washburn, *Trails, Trappers, and Tender-feet in the New Empire of Western Canada* (London: A. Melrose, 1912); Richard Barry, *The Events Man: Being an Account of the Adventures of Stanley Washburn, American War Correspondent* (New York: Moffat, Yard, 1907); New York *Times*, December 15, 1950, p. 31.

67. *Art Digest*, February 15, 1934, p. 21.

68. Lansing Lamont, "Washburn's Works," Washington *Evening Star* (typewritten copy in the collection of Reginald H. Sturtevant, president of the Livermore Falls [Maine] Trust Company.)

69. Ludwig A. Enge, "Cadwallader Washburn, Painter-Etcher" (typewritten copy in the collection of Mr. Sturtevant); also see *Art Digest*, November 6, 1937, p. 21; December 1, 1937, p. 19; April 1, 1934, p. 25.

70. Bessie Louise Pierce, *A History of Chicago* (New York: Knopf, 1957), Vol. III, p. 376.

71. See Charles B. Cheney, "Minnesota Politics," Minneapolis *Journal*, October 12, 1929, p. 4. For his strong views against the industry that made his father wealthy, see William D. Washburn, Jr., "Minnesota and the Railway Trust," *Outlook*, LIX, No. 5 (December 14, 1901), pp. 975–78.

72. Minneapolis *Journal*, October 10, 1929, p. 2.

THE MUHLENBERG DYNASTY

1. See *Document No. 249*, United States Senate, 77th Congress, 2nd Session, *Proceedings in Commemoration of the 200th Anniversary of the Landing of Henry Melchior Muhlenberg in Philadelphia, Pennsylvania, November 25, 1742* (Washington: Government Printing Office, 1942).

2. For the early German migration and the Germans' role in colonial America, see Louis Adamic, *A Nation of Nations* (New York: Harper, 1945), p. 168; Carl Wittke, *We Who Built America* (New York: Prentice-Hall, 1939), p. 66; Arthur D. Graeff, "Pennsylvania, the Colonial Melting Pot," in Ralph Wood, editor, *The Pennsylvania Germans* (Princeton: Princeton University Press, 1942); Albert Bernhardt Faust, *The German Element in the United*

States (Boston and New York: Houghton Mifflin, 1927), Vol. I; Andreas Dorpalen, "The Political Influence of the German Element in Colonial America," *Pennsylvania History*, VI, No. 3 (July 1939) and "The German Element in Early Pennsylvania Politics, 1789–1800," *Pennsylvania History*, IX, No. 3 (July 1942), p. 176.

3. See James Owen Knauss, *Social Conditions Among the Pennsylvania Germans in the Eighteenth Century, as Revealed in German Newspapers Published in America* (Lancaster, Pa.: New Era Printing, 1922), p. 73.

4. Quoted in Paul A. W. Wallace, *The Muhlenbergs of Pennsylvania* (Philadelphia: University of Pennsylvania Press, 1950), p. 267.

5. Quoted in Luther A. Weigle, *American Idealism* (New Haven: Yale University Press, 1928), p. 114.

6. See Theodore G. Tappert and John W. Doberstein, editors, *The Journals of Henry Melchior Muhlenberg* (Philadelphia: Evangelical Lutheran Ministerium of Pennsylvania, 1942), Vol. I, p. xvii.

7. See George Dangerfield, *Chancellor Robert R. Livingston of New York, 1746–1813* (New York: Harcourt, Brace, 1960), p. 15.

8. J. Bennett Nolan, *The Governor's Clock* (Reading, Pa., 1932), p. 7.

9. Quoted in Anne Ayres, *The Life and Works of William Augustus Muhlenberg* (New York: Harper, 1889), 4th edition, p. 7.

10. Quoted in Paul Wallace, *Conrad Weiser* (Philadelphia: University of Pennsylvania Press, 1945), p. 33; also P. C. Croll, "Ann Eve Weiser," in Gertrude B. Biddle and Sarah D. Lowrie, editors, *Notable Women of Pennsylvania* (Philadelphia: University of Pennsylvania Press, 1942), pp. 26–28.

11. See Henry A. Muhlenberg, *Life of Major-General Peter Muhlenberg of the Revolutionary Army* (Philadelphia: Carey and Hart, 1849), pp. 52–53. The biographer was a great-nephew of the general.

12. See James Grant Wilson, *Colonel John Bayard and the Bayard Family of America* (New York: Trow's Printing, 1885), p. 17; James Grant Wilson, "Andrew Kirkpatrick," *Proceedings of the New Jersey Historical Society*, 2nd Series, II (1872), p. 95.

13. Quoted in Otto A. Rothert, *History of Muhlenberg County* (Louisville: J. P. Morton, 1913), p. 6.

14. Wallace, *The Muhlenbergs of Pennsylvania*, p. 121.

15. *The Journals of Henry Melchior Muhlenberg*, Vol. II, p. 192.

16. Wallace, *The Muhlenbergs of Pennsylvania*, pp. 247–48.

17. Ibid., p. 107.

18. See Maldwyn Allen Jones, *American Immigration* (Chicago: University of Chicago Press, 1960), pp. 58–59.

19. See Herbert H. Beck, "Henry E. Muhlenberg, Botanist," *Papers Read Before the Lancaster County Historical Society*, XXXII, Nos. 7 and 8 (Lancaster, Pa., 1928); also Harry Baker Humphrey, *Makers of North American Botany* (New York: Ronald Press, 1961), pp. 185–86.

20. Quoted in Joseph Henry Dubbs, *History of Franklin and Marshall College* (Lancaster, Pa.: Franklin and Marshall College Alumni Association, 1903), pp. 8–9.

21. L. H. Butterfield, editor, *Letters of Benjamin Rush* (Princeton: Princeton University Press, 1951), Vol. I, pp. 421 and 424.

22. S. E. Ochsenford, editor, *Muhlenberg College, 1867–1892* (Allentown, Pa.: Muhlenberg College, 1892), p. 62.

23. See Armin George Weng, "The Language Problem in the Lutheran Church in Pennsylvania, 1742–1820," *Church History*, V, No. 4 (December 1936), p. 361.

24. See Dieter Cunz, *The Maryland Germans* (Princeton: Princeton University Press, 1948), pp. 66–67.

25. Quoted in Oswald Seidensticker, "Frederick Augustus Conrad Muhlenberg, Speaker of the House of Representatives in the First Congress, 1789," *Pennsylvania Magazine of History and Biography*, XIII, No. 2 (1889), p. 200.

26. Quoted in Weigle, op. cit., p. 157.

27. See Seidensticker, op. cit., pp. 196 and 198n.

28. See Allan Nevins, *The American States During and After the Revolution, 1775–1789* (New York: Macmillan, 1924), p. 184.

29. See George Adams Boyd, *Elias Boudinot, Patriot and Statesman* (Princeton: Princeton University Press, 1952), p. 156.

30. Quoted in Knauss, op. cit., p. 159.

31. See Mary P. Follett, *The Speaker of the House of Representatives* (New York: Longmans, Green, 1909), p. 65.

32. Quoted in Edward W. Hocker, *The Fighting Parson of the American Revolution* (Philadelphia: Published by the author, 1936), p. 143.

33. Quoted in Bernard Fay, "Early Party Machinery, Pennsylvania in the Elections of 1796," *Pennsylvania Magazine of History and Biography*, LX, No. 4 (October 1936), p. 386.

34. Quoted in Ayres, op. cit., pp. 6–7.

35. Quoted in Paul A. W. Wallace, *Pennsylvania, Seed of a Nation* (New York: Harper and Row, 1962), p. 131.

36. See Henry Melchior Muhlenberg Richards, "Governor Joseph Hiester," *The Pennsylvania-German Society, Proceedings and Addresses*, XVI (Lancaster, Pa., 1907), p. 38; William Frederick Worner, *Old Lancaster, Tales and Traditions* (Lancaster, Pa., 1927), p. 197.

37. See Mary Vernon Mish, *Jonathan Hager, Founder* (Hagerstown, Md.: Hagerstown Bookbinding, 1937), pp. 49–63.

38. See Philip S. Klein, "Early Lancaster County Politics," *Pennsylvania History*, III, No. 2 (April 1936), p. 106.

39. See Philip S. Klein, *Pennsylvania Politics, 1817–1832* (Philadelphia: Historical Society of Pennsylvania, 1940), p. 141.

40. See Frederic A. Godcharles, "Pennsylvania Statesmanship—At Home and Abroad," *Americana*, XXXVII, No. 4 (October 1943), pp. 606–7.

41. William Frederick Worner, editor, "Letters of James Buchanan," *Papers Read Before the Lancaster County Historical Society*, XXXVI, No. 8 (Lancaster, Pa., 1932), p. 205.

42. John Quincy Adams, *Memoirs* (Philadelphia: Lippincott, 1874–77), Vol. IX, pp. 491–92.

43. See Richard Vaux, *Sketch of the Life of Joseph Hiester* (Philadelphia: Allen, Lane and Scott, 1887), pp. 10–11.

44. George H. Genzmer, "William Augustus Muhlenberg," *Dictionary of American Biography*, Vol. XIII, pp. 313–14.

45. Quoted in E. Digby Baltzell, *Philadelphia Gentlemen* (Glencoe, Ill.: Free Press, 1958), p. 308.

46. Letter from Frederick A. Muhlenberg to author, July 9, 1963.

THE ROOSEVELT DYNASTY

1. Quoted in Arthur M. Schlesinger, Jr., *The Age of Roosevelt: The Crisis of the Old Order, 1919–1923* (Boston and New York: Houghton Mifflin, 1957), pp. 323–24.

2. See Eleanor Roosevelt, *This Is My Story* (New York: Harper, 1937), pp. 124–26.

3. Quoted in Nicholas Roosevelt, *A Front Row Seat* (Norman: University of Oklahoma Press, 1953), p. 40.

4. The relationship between Ulysses S. Grant and Franklin Delano Roosevelt:

Jonathan Delano
m. *Mercy Warren*

Susannah Delano	Thomas Delano
m. *Noah Grant*	m. *Jean Pecham*
Noah Grant	Ephraim Delano
m. *Rachel Kelly*	m. *Elizabeth Cushman*
Jesse R. Grant	Warren Delano
m. *Hannah Simpson*	m. *Deborah Church*
Ulysses S. Grant	Warren Delano
PRESIDENT	m. *Catherine Lyman*
	Sara Delano
	m. *James Roosevelt*
	Franklin Delano Roosevelt
	PRESIDENT

5. Bellamy Partridge, *An Imperial Saga, the Roosevelt Family in America* (New York: Hillman-Curl, 1936), p. 293.

6. Karl Schriftgiesser, *Families* (New York: Howell, Soskin, 1940), p. 408.

7. Paul Haber, *The House of Roosevelt* (Brooklyn, N.Y.: Author's Publishing Co., 1936), p. 11.

8. New York *Times*, March 15, 1935, p. 1.

9. Quoted in Allen Churchill, *The Roosevelts: American Aristocrats* (New York: Harper and Row, 1965), p. 39.

10. Eleanor Roosevelt, *On My Own* (New York: Harper, 1958), p. 12.

11. New York *Times*, November 3, 1936, p. 5.

12. Wrote Theodore Roosevelt, *Gouverneur Morris* (Boston and New York: Houghton Mifflin, 1898), p. 144: ". . . it needed all Hamilton's wonderful genius to force ratification of the [federal] Constitution [in New York State] in spite of the stupid selfishness of the Clintonian faction; as it was, he was only barely successful, although backed by all the best and ablest leaders in the community,—Jay, Livingston, Schuyler, Stephen Van Rensselaer, Isaac Roosevelt, James Duane, and a host of others."

13. Quoted in Karl Schriftgiesser, *The Amazing Roosevelt Family* (New York: Funk, 1942), p. 121.

14. Quoted in Nicholas Roosevelt, op. cit., p. 8.

15.

Heads of Roosevelt & Son:

James J. Roosevelt (1759–1840)
|
C.V.S. (1794–1871)

James A. (1825–98)   *Theodore* (1831–78)
| (father of President
W. Emlen (1857–1930)   Theodore Roosevelt)
|
George Emlen (1887–1963)
|
Julian (1924–   )

16. New York *Times*, September 4, 1963, p. 39. The correspondence with F.D.R. is also attributed to Philip J. Roosevelt, George Emlen's brother, in William T. Cobb, *The Strenuous Life. The "Oyster Bay" Roosevelts in Business and Finance* (New York: William E. Rudge's Sons, 1946), p. 1.

17. Roosevelts mentioned in this paragraph are in small capitals:

Jacobus Roosevelt (1692–1776)
Founder of Hyde Park Branch

Helena   *Isaac*   *Christopher*
(b. 1719)   (1726–94)   (1739–93)
m. *Andrew Barclay*   "The Patriot"
                  Great-great-
                  grandfather of F.D.R.

Charlotte Amelia   *James C.*
m. Richard Bayley   (b. 1770)

ELIZABETH ANN   *Richard*   JAMES H. (1800–63)
(Mother Seton)   Founder of
(1774–1820)   Roosevelt Hospital,
                             New York

JOHN ROOSEVELT
(1814–77)
Catholic archbishop

* Dr. Richard Bayley (1747–1801) was one of the most distinguished physicians of his era. His pathological studies helped cut the mortality of croup almost in half.

18. William D. Hassett, *Off the Record with F.D.R.* (New Brunswick: Rutgers University Press, 1958), p. 50.

19. Roosevelts mentioned on pages (174–75) are in small capitals:

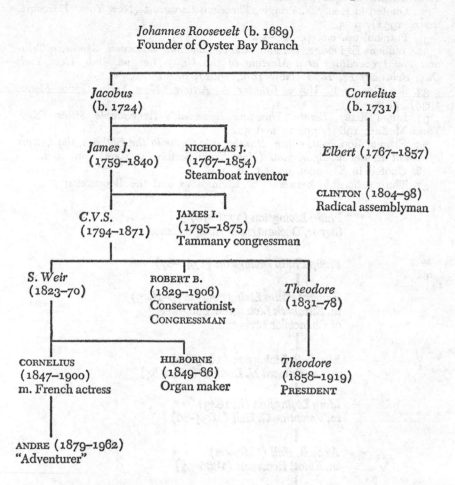

20. Quoted in Carleton Putnam, *Theodore Roosevelt, the Formative Years* (New York: Scribner's, 1958), p. 141.

21. Nicholas Roosevelt, op. cit., pp. 20–21.

22. New York *Times,* July 31, 1962, p. 27.

23. Hassett, op. cit., p. 124.

24. Quoted in Churchill, op. cit., p. 143.

25. Rita Halle Kleeman, *Gracious Lady, the Life of Sara Delano Roosevelt* (New York: Appleton-Century, 1935), p. 145.

26. Daniel W. Delano, Jr., *Franklin Roosevelt and the Delano Influence* (Pittsburgh: James W. Nudi, 1946), pp. 40–41.

F.D.R. was descended from Thomas Delano's brother Jonathan, husband of Mercy Warren, a granddaughter of the distinguished Richard Warren who came over on the *Mayflower.*

27. See Mrs. James Roosevelt as told to Isabel Leighton and Gabrielle Forbush, *My Boy Franklin* (New York: R. Long and R. R. Smith, 1933).

28. Delano, op. cit., p. 13.
29. Corinne Roosevelt Robinson, *My Brother Theodore Roosevelt* (New York: Scribner's, 1921), p. 18.
30. Quoted in Henry F. Pringle, *Theodore Roosevelt* (New York: Harcourt, Brace, 1931), p. 5.
31. Putnam, op. cit., pp. 48–49.
32. William E. Dodge, Jr., and others, *Theodore Roosevelt, Senior, a Tribute. The Proceedings at a Meeting of the Union League Club, New York City, February 14, 1878* (New York, 1902), p. 20.
33. See George F. Howe, *Chester A. Arthur* (New York: Dodd, Mead, 1934), p. 79.
34. Lilian Rixey, *Bamie, Theodore Roosevelt's Remarkable Sister* (New York: McKay, 1963), pp. 30 and 52.
35. Eleanor Roosevelt, editor, *Hunting Big Game in the Eighties, the Letters of Elliott Roosevelt, Sportsman* (New York: Scribner's, 1932), pp. ix–x.
36. Quoted in Kleeman, op. cit., p. 126.
37. The relationship between the Livingstons and the Roosevelts:

Philip Livingston (1716–78)
Signer, Declaration of Independence

Philip Philip Livingston (1741–87)

Edward Philip Livingston (1779–1843)
m. Elizabeth Livingston, daughter
of Chancellor Livingston

Elizabeth Livingston (1813–96)
m. Dr. Edward H. Ludlow (1810–84)

Mary Livingston (b. 1843)
m. Valentine G. Hall (1834–80)

Anna R. Hall (1863–92)
m. Elliott Roosevelt (1860–93)

Eleanor Roosevelt (1884–1962)
m. Franklin Delano Roosevelt (1882–1945)

See Robert Livingston Nicholson, *Material Relating to the Livingston, Nicholson, Clack, Wheelock, Hamilton, Steele, Roosevelt, and Schuyler Families* (typewritten manuscript, 1939, Library of Congress, pages unnumbered).
38. *In Loving Memory of Anna Hall Roosevelt by Three Friends* (New York, 1893), p. 24.
39. Eleanor Roosevelt, *Hunting Big Game in the Eighties,* pp. 145–46.
40. See Cleveland Amory, *The Proper Bostonians* (New York: Dutton, 1947), p. 20.
41. See Henry F. Pringle, ". . . Especially Pretty Alice," *American Heritage,* February 1958, p. 63.

42. Eleanor Roosevelt, *This Is My Story*, p. 79.

43. See Edith (Carow) Roosevelt and Kermit Roosevelt, *American Backlogs, the Story of Gertrude Tyler and Her Family* (New York: Scribner's 1928), pp. 30–41.

44. Quoted in Rixey, op. cit., p. 76.

45. Ibid., p. 88.

46. Ibid., p. 106.

47. Henry Adams, *The Education of Henry Adams* (New York, 1931), p. 417 (Modern Library edition).

48. Quoted in Partridge, op. cit., p. 218.

49. Quoted in Rixey, op. cit., p. 35. The editorial was by Carl Schruz.

50. Theodore Roosevelt, *An Autobiography*, Wayne Andrews, editor (New York: Scribner's, 1958), pp. 78–79.

51. Quoted in Pringle, *Theodore Roosevelt*, p. 81.

52. Henry Cabot Lodge, editor, *Selections from the Correspondence of Theodore Roosevelt and Henry Cabot Lodge* (New York: Scribner's, 1925), Vol. I, pp. 116 and 99.

53. Ibid., Vol. I, p. 87.

54. Corinne Roosevelt Robinson, op. cit., pp. 159–60; also see Walt McDougall, *This is the Life!* (New York: Knopf, 1926), pp. 130–31.

55. See Theodore Roosevelt, *The Rough Riders* (New York: Scribner's, 1899), pp. 9–26; Churchill, op. cit., p. 192.

56. *Selections from the Correspondence of Theodore Roosevelt and Henry Cabot Lodge*, Vol. I, p. 334. Italics in original.

57. Quoted in Pringle, op. cit., p. 114.

58. Ibid., p. 156.

59. Rixey, op. cit., pp. 160–61.

60. See Ernest Samuels, *Henry Adams, the Major Phase* (Cambridge: Harvard University Press, 1964), p. 247.

61. See Theodore Roosevelt, Jr., *All in the Family* (New York: Putnam's, 1929), p. 79; Joseph Bucklin Bishop, editor, *Theodore Roosevelt's Letters to His Children* (New York: Scribner's, 1919), p. 19; J. J. Perling, *Presidents' Sons* (New York: Odyssey, 1947), pp. 253–54.

62. *Theodore Roosevelt's Letters to His Children*, p. 104.

63. Irwin H. Hoover, *Forty-two Years in the White House* (New York and Boston: Houghton Mifflin, 1934), p. 28.

64. *Theodore Roosevelt's Letters to His Children*, p. 54; Stephen Gwynn, *The Letters and Friendships of Sir Cecil Spring-Rice* (London: Constable, 1929), Vol. I, p. 437.

65. Hermann Hagedorn, *The Roosevelt Family of Sagamore Hill* (New York: Macmillan, 1954), p. 186; *Town Topics*, October 20, 1904, p. 3.

66. Clara Longworth de Chambrun, *The Making of Nicholas Longworth* (New York: R. Long & R. R. Smith, 1933), p. 213. The author was Longworth's sister and a noted Shakespearean scholar. She was the wife of General Count Adalbert de Chambrun, a descendant of Lafayette, who was at one time commander of the French forces in Tunis.

67. Archibald W. Butt, *Taft and Roosevelt* (Garden City, N.Y.: Doubleday, 1930), Vol. II, p. 792.

68. Quoted in Rixey, op. cit., p. 262.

69. Quoted in William Howard Taft, *Our Chief Magistrate and His Powers* (New York: Columbia University Press, 1925), pp. 22–23.

70. See George E. Mowry, *Theodore Roosevelt and the Progressive Movement* (Madison: University of Wisconsin Press, 1947), pp. 15–16.

71. Quoted in Arthur Wallace Dunn, *Gridiron Nights* (New York: Frederick A. Stokes, 1915), pp. 229–30.

72. Worthington Chauncey Ford, editor, *Letters of Henry Adams* (Boston and New York: Houghton Mifflin, 1938), Vol. II, p. 515; Rixey, op. cit., p. 289.

73. See James MacGregor Burns, *Roosevelt: The Lion and the Fox* (New York: Harcourt, Brace, 1956), p. 25.

74. Quoted in Kleeman, op. cit., p. 244.

75. Ibid., p. 233.

76. Mrs. James Roosevelt, op. cit., p. 62.

77. Eleanor Roosevelt, *This I Remember* (New York: Harper, 1949), p. 16.

78. Quoted in Burns, op. cit., p. 32.

79. Quoted in Paul M. Angle, *Crossroads: 1913* (Chicago: Rand McNally, 1963), p. 80.

80. Quoted in John A. Garraty, *Henry Cabot Lodge* (New York: Knopf, 1953), p. 397.

81. Quoted in Ishbel Ross, *An American Family: The Tafts* (Cleveland and New York: World, 1964), p. 318.

82. Burns, op. cit., p. 76.

83. See Partridge, op. cit., p. 22; James Roosevelt and Sidney Shalett, *Affectionately, F.D.R.* (New York: Harcourt, Brace, 1959), p. 149; Rixey, op. cit., pp. 257–58.

84. Quoted in William L. Stidger, *These Amazing Roosevelts* (New York: Macfadden, 1938), p. 13.

85. Quoted in Bela Kornitzer, *American Fathers and Sons* (New York: Hermitage House, 1952), p. 260.

86. Quoted in Partridge, op. cit., p. 243. For another pre-election assessment of F.D.R., see Ray Thomas Tucker, *The Mirrors of 1932* (New York: Brewer, Warren & Putnam, 1931): "He lacks guts" (p. 77); "He is indecisive, indiscreet and impulsive" (p. 78); "He cannot concentrate" (p. 79); "He defies definition" (p. 80); "Just another politician" (p. 86).

87. *The Autobiography of William Allen White* (New York: Macmillan, 1946), p. 635.

88. Quoted in Rixey, op. cit., p. 228.

89. Adlai Stevenson, "She Was a Lady for All Seasons," Washington *Post*, August 30, 1964, p. E3.

90. Kermit Roosevelt, editor, *Quentin Roosevelt, a Sketch with Letters* (New York: Scribner's, 1922), pp. 232–33.

91. Ibid., p. 172.

92. Quoted in Pringle, op. cit., p. 601.

93. *Theodore Roosevelt's Letters to His Children*, p. 236.

94. See Harnett T. Kane, *Spies for the Blue and Gray* (Garden City, N.Y.: Hanover House, 1954), pp. 169–75.

95. Quoted in Perling, op. cit., p. 254.

96. Quoted in Hagedorn, op. cit., p. 145.

97. Mrs. Theodore Roosevelt, Jr., *Day Before Yesterday* (Garden City, N.Y.: Doubleday, 1959), p. 118.

98. Quoted in Perling, op. cit., p. 256.

99. See Frederick Lewis Allen, *Only Yesterday* (New York: Harper, 1931), p. 69.

100. Quoted in Churchill, op. cit., p. 271.

101. See Burl Noggle, *Teapot Dome: Oil and Politics in the 1920's* (Baton

Rouge: Louisiana State University Press, 1962), p. 19; M. R. Werner and John Starr, *Teapot Dome* (New York: Viking, 1959), p. 131.

102. Quoted in Perling, op. cit., p. 259.

103. Eleanor Roosevelt, *This I Remember*, pp. 31–32.

104. Quoted in Mrs. Theodore Roosevelt, Jr., op. cit., p. 304.

105.

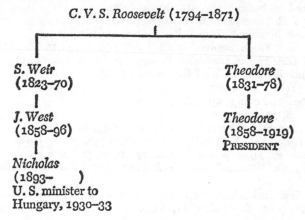

C. V. S. Roosevelt (1794–1871)

S. Weir
(1823–70)

J. West
(1858–96)

Nicholas
(1893–   )
U. S. minister to
Hungary, 1930–33

Theodore
(1831–78)

Theodore
(1858–1919)
PRESIDENT

106. Quoted in Mrs. Theodore Roosevelt, Jr., op. cit., p. 206.

107. New York *Times*, August 3, 1936, p. 8.

108. Alice Roosevelt Longworth, "What's the Matter with Bob Taft?" *Saturday Evening Post*, May 4, 1940, p. 29.

109. New York *Times*, October 26, 1936, p. 5.

110. See E. Digby Baltzell, *The Protestant Establishment* (New York: Random House, 1964), p. 234n.

111. Letter from Archibald Roosevelt to U.S. senators, June 28, 1963. Courtesy of the office of Senator Thomas H. Kuchel.

112. See Washington *Post*, October 8, 1964, p. C16.

113. Eleanor Roosevelt, *This I Remember*, p. 16.

114. Ibid., p. 26.

115. For example, see Anna, James, Franklin, Jr., and Elliott Roosevelt, "FDR As We Remember Him," *Saturday Evening Post*, April 10, 1965, pp. 38–50.

Anna Roosevelt is the only one who has been consistently frank about the difficulties of having a presidential father. See her "My Life with F.D.R.: How Polio Helped Father," *The Woman*, July 1949, p. 47; "My Life with F.D.R.: White House Vignettes," *The Woman*, October 1949, p. 44. Also interview with author, May 20, 1965.

116. Kornitzer, op. cit., p. 281. Three of the Roosevelt boys, James, Franklin, and John, also took a memorable two-week cruise with the President in July 1936. See *Log of the Cruise of President Franklin D. Roosevelt Aboard the Schooner Yacht Sewanna to Maine, Nova Scotia and New Brunswick, 14 July 1936–28 July 1936* (Washington: Government Printing Office, 1937) (copy in the library of Mrs. Anna Roosevelt Halsted).

117. Thomas Craven, editor, *Cartoon Cavalcade* (New York: Simon & Schuster, 1943), p. 249; Eleanor Roosevelt, *This I Remember*, p. 17.

118. Ibid., p. 17.

119. New York *Times*, May 14, 1938, p. 14.

120. Eleanor Roosevelt, *This I Remember,* p. 10.

121. Alva Johnston, "Jimmy's Got It," *Saturday Evening Post,* July 2, 1938, pp. 9 and 57.

122. New York *Times,* June 30, 1938, p. 18.

123. See Walter Davenport, "I'm Glad You Asked Me," *Collier's,* August 20, 1938.

124. Quoted in Perling, op. cit., pp. 318–19.

125. New York *Times,* March 16, 1933, p. 8.

126. Eleanor Roosevelt, *This I Remember,* p. 165.

127. New York *Times,* September 18, 1938, Sec. IV, p. 10.

128. New York *Times,* December 6, 1938, p. 22; Burns, op. cit., pp. 300–1.

129. Eleanor Roosevelt, *This I Remember,* p. 18.

130. New York *Times,* July 1, 1937, p. 22.

131. Quoted in Perling, op. cit., p. 323.

132. Ibid., p. 326.

133. See New York *Times,* February 13, 1945, p. 1.

134. See New York *Times,* December 28, 1942, p. 1; January 14, 1943, p. 1; February 27, 1944, p. 40; August 17, 1945, p. 12; S. J. Woolf, "F.D.R. Jr. Speaks for the Veteran," *New York Times Magazine,* September 1, 1946, p. 19.

135. See New York *Times,* February 29, 1940, p. 2; March 14, 1940, p. 3; May 1, 1940, p. 5; September 21, 1940, p. 4; September 5, 1942, p. 32; June 6, 1943, p. 42.

136. See New York *Times,* September 17, 1943, p. 9; July 14, 1944, p. 1; Cobb, op. cit., p. 90.

137. Drew Middleton, "The Battle Saga of a Tough Outfit," *New York Times Magazine,* April 8, 1945, p. 8.

138. New York *Times,* July 15, 1944, p. 12.

139. See *Who's Who in America, 1964–65,* p. 1712; New York *Times,* April 28, 1949, p. 5. General Theodore Roosevelt's other living children are Cornelius, a bachelor, who is an engineer working on secret navy research, and Grace, the wife of a Baltimore architect.

140. Letter from Mrs. Andrew M. (Edith Derby) Williams, November 2, 1964; Seattle *Post-Intelligencer,* July 28, 1960, p. B (Sunrise edition).

141. Letter from Mrs. Robert T. Gannett, November 10, 1964; Burlington (Vermont) *Free Press,* September 14, 1960, p. 1. Ethel Roosevelt Derby's third daughter, Judith, is married to Dr. Adelbert Ames of Concord, Massachusetts.

142. See David Wise and Thomas B. Ross, *The Invisible Government* (New York: Random House, 1964), pp. 110–17.

143. See Kermit Roosevelt, Jr., *A Sentimental Safari* (New York: Knopf, 1963).

144. New York *Times,* May 14, 1958, p. 67. Kermit Roosevelt's other child, Clochette, is the wife of John G. Palfrey, a former dean of Columbia College, who was appointed to the Atomic Energy Commission by President Kennedy in August 1962.

145. *Times* (London) *Literary Supplement,* October 22, 1954, p. 16; for a favorable comparison with Colette, see Gene Baro in New York *Herald Tribune Book Review,* April 25, 1954, p. 16. Mrs. Keogh's other novels include *Tattooed Heart* (1953), *The Fascinator* (1954), *My Name Is Rose* (1956), *Fetish* (1959), and *Gemini* (1961).

146. Alexander Barmine, chargé d'affaires at the Russian legation in Athens, became disgusted with the Soviet purges and escaped to Paris in

1937. Two years later he published his memoirs, *Vingt ans au service de l'U.R.S.S.* Edmund Wilson called it "the most illuminating document that had been published on the Soviet Union. . . ." The book, in a revised form, appeared in the United States as *One Who Survived: The Life Story of a Russian Under the Soviets* (New York: Putnam's, 1945). See *The New Yorker*, July 14, 1945, p. 65; *Time*, September 20, 1948, p. 93.

147. In 1960 Edith Kermit Roosevelt said, "I once read in a National Education Association tract that the day of the lone ranger is over except in folklore, but I decided to disprove this premise. Last August [1959] I began to syndicate my own column nationally. Having no capital except my newspaper salary on which to support myself and a family [daughter Margot], I could not afford promotion and advertising. I merely sent out my columns to newspapers selected at random from E & P [*Editor and Publisher*] Year Book." Among the papers now using the column are the Philadelphia *Bulletin*, the Denver *Post*, the Atlanta *Times*, and the Long Island *Press*. See Ray Erwin, "Another Roosevelt Syndicates Column," *Editor and Publisher*, February 6, 1960, p. 61; interview with Edith Kermit Roosevelt, October 20, 1964.

148. His only son, Theodore Robinson (1908–64), operated a pilot-training school and a dude ranch in Arizona; he first married the daughter of former Governor Nathan Miller of New York.

149. Arthur M. Schlesinger, Jr., "Two Years Later—The Roosevelt Family," *Life*, April 7, 1947, p. 129.

150. See *Time*, December 13, 1948, p. 45, and December 20, 1948, p. 38.

151. See New York *Times*, January 22, 1947, p. 12; May 1, 1947, p. 12; Perling, op. cit., p. 342.

152. See Franklin D. Roosevelt, Jr., "How We Won," *Collier's*, August 6, 1949; Robert G. Whalen, "Another Roosevelt Enters the Lists," *New York Times Magazine*, April 24, 1949; *The New Yorker*, May 7, 1949, p. 26; *Life*, May 9, 1949, p. 46; *Newsweek*, May 30, 1949, p. 17.

153. See *New Republic*, July 12, 1948, p. 16; Joe Alex Morris, "Another Roosevelt Makes His Pitch," *Saturday Evening Post*, October 7, 1950; Clarence Woodbury, "Will There Always Be a Roosevelt?" *American Magazine*, January 1953, p. 117; New York *Times*, November 10, 1950, p. 21, and February 17, 1954, p. 23.

154. See *The New Yorker*, November 1, 1952, p. 24; New York *Times*, August 16, 1953, p. 52; *Newsweek*, April 22, 1957, p. 27.

155. *Life*, February 15, 1954, p. 19; New York *Times*, January 19, 1954, p. 18; February 2, 1948, p. 48; June 10, 1954, p. 25; July 2, 1956, p. 45.

156. See Joseph and Stewart Alsop, "Can F.D.R., Jr., Get His Father's Old Job?" *Saturday Evening Post*, September 4, 1954; New York *Times*, November 3, 1954, p. 1; *Hearings Before the Committee on Commerce, United States Senate, 88th Congress, 1st Session, on the Nomination of Franklin D. Roosevelt, Jr., to be Under Secretary of Commerce* (Washington, 1963), p. 57.

157. Washington *Post*, February 5, 1963, p. A12, and February 6, 1963, p. A14; *New Republic*, February 16, 1963, pp. 5–6; *Hearings . . . on the Nomination of Franklin D. Roosevelt, Jr.*, p. 57.

158. Los Angeles *Times*, February 17, 1965, Part I, p. 1; New York *Times*, April 8, 1965, p. 24; Washington *Post*, September 20, 1965, p. A14, and August 26, 1965, p. A16.

159. Elliott Roosevelt campaign literature; also see Drew Pearson, "Washington Merry-Go-Round," Washington *Post*, May 26, 1965, p. D17.

160. Drew Pearson, "Junket Point System," Washington *Post*, June 6, 1965, p. E7.

161. Julius Duscha, "Roosevelt Showing Vigor as Mayor," Washington *Post*, June 20, 1965, p. A2.

162. New York *Times*, March 4, 1965, p. 28.

163. Jack Wilson, "Potomac Fever," Chicago *Sun-Times*, July 5, 1965, p. 46.

164. See Washington *Post*, March 14, 1965, p. F5.

165. See Washington *Star*, May 8, 1962, p. B1, and May 9, 1962, p. B1.

166. See Harold L. Ickes. *The Secret Diary of Harold L. Ickes* (New York: Simon & Schuster, 1954), Vol. II, p. 340.

167. Interview with Mrs. Anna Roosevelt Halsted, May 20, 1965.

THE HARRISON DYNASTY

1. Among the Harrison-Lee connections:

a)

Benjamin Harrison II (1645–1712)

Hannah Harrison (1678–1731)
m. Philip Ludwell II (1672–1726)

Hannah Ludwell (1701–49)
m. Thomas Lee (1690–1750)

Richard Henry Lee (1732–94)   Francis Lightfoot Lee (1734–97)
Signers of the Declaration of Independence

Hannah Harrison Ludwell, according to her tombstone, had "a most Exemplary Life/Spent in chearful Innocence." See Ethel Armes, *Stratford Hall* (Richmond: Garrett & Massie, 1936), p. 23.

b)

Robert ("King") Carter (1663–1732)

John Carter   Anne Carter
                   m. Benjamin Harrison IV (1700–44)

Charles Carter   Benjamin Harrison V (1726–91)
                   Signer, Declaration of Independence

Anne Hill Carter   William Henry Harrison (1773–1841)
m. "Light Horse Harry" Lee   PRESIDENT
(1756–1818)

For genealogical information, see Pauline Pearce Warner, *Benjamin Harrison of Berkeley, Walter Cocke of Surry, Family Records I* (Tappahannock, Va., 1962), mimeographed copy in Library of Congress; Charles P. Keith, *The Ancestry of Benjamin Harrison* (Philadelphia: Lippincott, 1893).

2. Among the Harrison-Randolph connections:

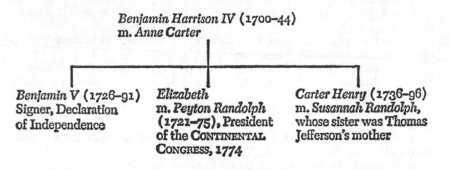

Benjamin Harrison IV (1700–44)
m. Anne Carter

Benjamin V (1726–91)   Elizabeth   Carter Henry (1736–96)
Signer, Declaration   m. Peyton Randolph   m. Susannah Randolph,
of Independence   (1721–75), President   whose sister was Thomas
                           of the CONTINENTAL   Jefferson's mother
                           CONGRESS, 1774

Peyton Randolph was the grandson of William Randolph (c. 1651–1711), who came to Virginia around 1673, and by 1705 was recognized as one of the leading planters in the colony. Peyton's father, Sir John Randolph (c. 1693–1737), served as Speaker of the House of Burgesses from 1734 until his death; Peyton's brother John (1727–84), a Virginia attorney general, remained loyal to the King and fled to England in 1775. Like his father and grandfather, Peyton Randolph was made Speaker of the House of Burgesses. In personality he much resembled his brother-in-law, Benjamin Harrison V, being portly and affable, though somewhat more liberal in his politics.

3. Sarah Harrison (1670–1713) married James Blair (1655–1743), a Scotsman, who came to Virginia as a missionary in 1685, founded William and Mary College in 1693, and was its first president. He also became a powerful politician, serving as president of the Council and acting governor in 1740–41. Governor Gooch considered him "a very vile old fellow," but marveled at his constitution. When he died in his eighty-eighth year, the governor wrote, "If his belly had been as sound as his head and breast, he might have lived many years longer." See Alf J. Mapp, Jr., *The Virginia Experiment* (Richmond: Dietz, 1957), pp. 185–87, 225–26.

But Blair, who had once been able to oust a lieutenant governor, apparently met his match in Miss Harrison. For at their wedding she three times refused to agree to that part of the ceremony which requires a wife to promise obedience to her husband. See Edmund S. Morgan, *Virginians at Home, Family Life in the Eighteenth Century* (Williamsburg: Colonial Williamsburg, 1952), pp. 47–48.

4. Ross F. Lockridge, Jr., "The Harrisons," *House Document No. 154,* 77th Congress, 1st Session, March 21, 1941, p. 30.

5. L. H. Butterfield, editor, *Letters of Benjamin Rush* (Princeton: Princeton University Press, 1951), Vol. II, p. 1090. A slightly different version of Harrison's remark to Gerry can be found in John Sanderson, editor, *Biography of the Signers of the Declaration of Independence* (Philadelphia: R. W. Pomeroy, 1823), Vol. VIII, p. 147.

6. See Clifford Dowdey, *The Great Plantation* (New York: Holt, Rinehart & Winston, 1957), p. 229.

7. Ibid., p. 209.

8. Beverley W. Bond, Jr., editor, *The Intimate Letters of John Cleves Symmes* (Cincinnati: Historical and Philosophical Society of Ohio, 1956), pp. 102–3.

9. Ibid., p. 82.

10. Lockridge, op. cit., p. 48.

11. See John Scott Harrison, *Pioneer Life at North Bend* (Cincinnati: R. Clarke, 1867), p. 10.

12. See George Adams Boyd, *Elias Boudinot, Patriot and Statesman* (Princeton: Princeton University Press, 1952), pp. 149–53.

13. Quoted in Dorothy B. Goebel, *William Henry Harrison* (Indianapolis: Historical Bureau of the Indiana Library and Historical Department, 1926), p. 244n.

14. Quoted in Freeman Cleaves, *Old Tippecanoe* (New York: Scribner's, 1939), p. 55.

15. See Dorothy B. Goebel and Julius Goebel, Jr., *Generals in the White House* (Garden City, N.Y.: Doubleday, 1952), p. 35.

16. Quoted in Goebel, *William Henry Harrison*, p. 218.

17. John Quincy Adams, *Memoirs* (Philadelphia: Lippincott, 1874–77), Vol. VII, p. 223.

18. Quoted in Cleaves, op. cit., p. 241.

19. Ibid., p. 263.

20. Adams, op. cit., Vol. VIII, pp. 189 and 212.

21. Quoted in Cleaves, op. cit., p. 264.

22. Quoted in J. J. Perling, *Presidents' Sons* (New York: Odyssey, 1947), p. 78.

23. Quoted in Percy W. Turrentine, *Life and Works of Nathaniel Beverley Tucker* (Unpublished Ph.D. dissertation, Harvard University, 1952), Vol. III, pp. 1171–72.

24. Quoted in Eugene H. Roseboom, *A History of Presidential Elections* (New York: Macmillan, 1957), p. 120.

25. Quoted in Cleaves, op. cit., p. 326.

26. Quoted in Robert Gray Gunderson, *The Log-Cabin Campaign* (Lexington: University of Kentucky Press, 1957), opposite p. 1 and p. 121.

27.

Benjamin Harrison VI (1755–99) ———(brothers)——— *William Henry Harrison*
  | (1773–1841) PRESIDENT.
Benjamin VII (1787–1842)
  |
 Henry (b. 1821)
 Secretary to the President

28. Peter Harvey, *Reminiscences and Anecdotes of Daniel Webster* (Boston: Little, Brown, 1877), pp. 160–63.

29. *Report of the Committee of Arrangements of the Common Council of New York, for the Funeral Obsequies in Memory of William H. Harrison, late President of the United States: With an oration by the Hon. Theodore Frelinghuysen* (New York, 1841), p. 94.

30. William Lewis Breckinridge, *Submission to the Will of God* (Louisville: Morton & Griswold, 1841), p. 6.

31. Quoted in Harry J. Sievers, *Benjamin Harrison, Hoosier Warrior* (Chicago: Regnery, 1952), p. 84.

32. Quoted in Lockridge, op. cit., p. 89.

33. Quoted in Sievers, op. cit., p. 121. Italics in original.

34. Quoted in Lockridge, op. cit., p. 90.

35. Quoted in J. J. Perling, op. cit., pp. 82 and 85.

36. W. H. Crook, *Memories of the White House* (Boston: Little, Brown, 1911), p. 211.

37. George F. Hoar, *Autobiography of Seventy Years* (New York: Scribner's, 1903), Vol. I, p. 414.

38. William Allen White, *The Autobiography of William Allen White* (New York: Macmillan, 1946), p. 358.

39. Quoted in Sievers, op. cit., p. 130.

40. Ibid., p. 150.

41. Quoted in Lockridge, op. cit., p. 154.

42. Quoted in Dorothy B. Goebel and Julius Goebel, Jr., op. cit., p. 228.

43. Quoted in Harry J. Sievers, *Benjamin Harrison, Hoosier Statesman* (New York: University Publishers, 1959), p. 83.

44. Ibid., p. 74.

45. Quoted in Oscar D. Lambert, *Stephen Benton Elkins: American Foursquare* (Pittsburgh: University of Pittsburgh Press, 1955), p. 120.

46. Quoted in Sievers, *Benjamin Harrison, Hoosier Statesman*, p. 343.

47. Ibid., p. 370.

48. Frank G. Carpenter, *Carp's Washington* (New York: McGraw-Hill, 1960), p. 299.

49. Ibid., p. 298.

50. See Irwin H. Hoover, *Forty-two Years in the White House* (Boston and New York: Houghton Mifflin, 1934), p. 8.

51. Quoted in O. O. Stealey, editor, *Twenty Years in the Press Gallery* (New York: Publishers Printing, 1906), pp. 297–98.

52. Quoted in Henry F. Pringle, *Theodore Roosevelt* (New York: Harcourt, Brace, 1931), p. 122.

53. Quoted in Harriet McIntire Foster, *Mrs. Benjamin Harrison* (Indianapolis, 1908), p. 27.

54. Henry Adams, *The Education of Henry Adams* (New York, 1931), p. 320 (Modern Library edition).

55. See John Wilson Townsend, "Carter Henry Harrison, Kentuckian," *Register of the Kentucky State Historical Society*, XXIV, No. 71 (1926), pp. 150–51; Alexander Brown, *The Cabells and Their Kin* (Boston and New York: Houghton Mifflin, 1895), pp. 257–60, 567–70; Willis John Abbot, *Carter Henry Harrison* (New York: Dodd, Mead, 1895), p. 7.

56. See Claudius O. Johnson, *Carter Henry Harrison I, Political Leader* (Chicago: University of Chicago Press, 1928), p. 75.

57. See Edward Wagenknecht, *Chicago* (Norman: University of Oklahoma Press, 1964), pp. 66–67.

58. See Frank K. Kelly, *The Fight for the White House, the Story of 1912* (New York: Crowell, 1961), pp. 92–93; Carter H. Harrison, *Stormy Years* (Indianapolis and New York: Bobbs-Merrill, 1935), p. 284; New York *Times*, December 26, 1953, p. 13.

59. See New York *Times*, January 6, 1948, p. 23.

60. See New York *Times*, October 31, 1920, p. 22; April 7, 1921, p. 15; December 26, 1955, p. 19.

61. See New York *Tribune*, September 22, 1891, p. 7.

62. Quoted in Perling, op. cit., p. 242.

63. See New York *Times*, December 14, 1936, p. 23.

64. See New York *Times*, October 4, 1964, p. 78; Rowland Evans and Robert Novak, "Goldwater Country?" Washington *Post*, October 27, 1964, p. A17.

65. Interview with William Henry Harrison, Washington, D.C., May 7, 1963.

THE BRECKINRIDGE DYNASTY

1. Quoted in John Gunther, *Inside U.S.A.* (New York: Harper, 1947), p. 644.

2. See William Hutchinson Vaughan, *Robert Jefferson Breckinridge as an Educational Administrator* (Nashville: George Peabody College for Teachers, 1937), p. 38.

3. Quoted in Samuel M. Wilson, *History of Kentucky from 1803 to 1928* (Chicago and Louisville: S. J. Clarke, 1928), p. 355.

4. Charles E. Hamlin, *The Life and Times of Hannibal Hamlin* (Cambridge: Riverside Press, 1899), p. 320.

5. Quoted in Lucille Stillwell, *John Cabell Breckinridge* (Caldwell, Idaho: Caxton, 1936), p. 182.

6. Edgar Dewitt Jones, *Lords of Speech* (Chicago and New York: Willett, Clark, 1937), p. 174.

7. See Lowell H. Harrison, "A Virginian Moves to Kentucky, 1793," *William and Mary Quarterly*, 3rd Series, XV, No. 2 (April 1958), p. 201.

8. Jane Buchanan Floyd's first husband was killed by Indians in Kentucky in 1783. Her son by this marriage was Dr. John Floyd (1783–1837), a governor of Virginia from 1830 to 1834.

9. See Philip Alexander Bruce, *History of the University of Virginia* (New York: Macmillan, 1920), Vol. I, pp. 210, 236, 290–91.

10. See Janie P. B. Lamb, "'Smithfield' Home of the Prestons, in Montgomery County, Virginia," *Virginia Magazine of History and Biography*, XLVII, No. 2 (April 1939).

11. See Lowell H. Harrison, "A Young Virginian: John Breckinridge," *Virginia Magazine of History and Biography*, LXXI, No. 1 (January 1963), p. 23n.

12. Lowell H. Harrison, "Young Mr. Breckinridge Experiences War, Pestilence and Inflation, 1781," *William and Mary Quarterly*, 3rd Series, IX, No. 2 (April 1952).

13. Lowell H. Harrison, "John Breckinridge: Western Statesman," *Journal of Southern History*, XVIII, No. 2 (May 1952), p. 139.

14. Ethelbert Dudley Warfield, *The Kentucky Resolutions of 1798* (New York: Putnam's, 1887), pp. 75–77.

15. See Dumas Malone, *Jefferson and the Ordeal of Liberty* (Boston: Little, Brown, 1962) p. 400.

16. Henry Adams, *The Formative Years: A History of the United States During the Administrations of Jefferson and Madison*, edited by Herbert Agar (New York and Boston: Houghton Mifflin, 1947), Vol. I, p. 127.

17. William Plumer, *Memorandum of Proceedings in the U. S. Senate* (New York, 1923), p. 13.

18. Vaughan, op. cit., p. 3. He gives as his source an interview with Desha Breckinridge in 1932.

19. H. Levin, editor, *The Lawyer and Lawmakers of Kentucky* (Chicago: Lewis Publishing, 1897), p. 616.

20. Margaret Bayard Smith, *Forty Years of Washington Society* (New York: Scribner's, 1906), pp. 274-75.

21. See Willard Thorp, editor, *The Lives of Eighteen from Princeton* (Princeton: Princeton University Press, 1948), pp. 100-1.

22. Joseph Cabell Breckinridge (1788-1823) had six children; one died in infancy. Among his daughters, Caroline Laurens (1813-67) married the Rev. Joseph J. Bullock, a chaplain of the U. S. Senate; Francis Ann (1812-37) married the Rev. John Young, the influential president of Centre College. "It is not extravagant to say," wrote a newspaperman of Young, "that as a fashioner of the mind and character of youth he has had few peers in our country." O. O. Stealey, editor, *Twenty Years in the Press Gallery* (New York: Publishers Printing, 1906), p. 217.

23. See Harris Elwood Starr, "John Breckinridge," *Dictionary of American Biography*, Vol. III, pp. 6-7.

24. See Edmund A. Moore, "Robert J. Breckinridge and the Slavery Aspects of the Presbyterian Schism of 1837," *Church History*, IV, No. 4 (December 1935), p. 283.

25. After meeting him at a party in 1829, the Washington socialite commented, "Oh what a zealous, saint-like man he is! He is indeed a burning and shining light but he is burning fast away, flesh and blood cannot sustain such exhausting and consuming labours. How I wish I could sit under his ministry. How cold and lifeless our Pastor seems, compared to him." Margaret Bayard Smith, op. cit., pp. 279-80.

26. Lewis Collins, *Historical Sketches of Kentucky* (Cincinnati: J. A. & V. P. James, 1847), p. 138.

27. Ibid., p. 139. John Breckinridge (1797-1841) first married Margaret Miller (1802-38), daughter of Professor Samuel Miller of the Princeton Theological Seminary, by whom he had four children. A son Samuel became a Missouri legislator, and a daughter Mary married the son of Letitia Breckinridge, Peter A. Porter, who was killed at Cold Harbor during the Civil War.

28. William Lewis Breckinridge (1803-76) was also president of Oakland College in Mississippi. His administration at Centre College was from 1863 to 1868. By his first wife, Frances C. Provost, whom he married in 1823, he had twelve children. Two of them were doctors in the Confederate Army and another was a Union Army doctor.

29. Cassius Marcellus Clay, *The Life of Cassius Marcellus Clay* (Cincinnati: J. F. Brennan, 1886), Vol. I, p. 219, and Hambleton Tapp, "Robert J. Breckinridge and the Year 1849," *Filson Club History Quarterly*, XII, No. 3 (July 1938), p. 130.

Cassius Clay (1810-1903), known as "The Lion of White Hall," became U.S. minister to Russia in 1861-62 and again in 1863-69.

30. The statement was made by John Wilson Townsend. Quoted in Samuel M. Wilson, op. cit., p. 480.

31. Clay, op. cit., Vol. I, p. 219.

32. Quoted in Clement Eaton, *Henry Clay and the Art of American Politics* (Boston: Little, Brown, 1957), p. 127.

33. Quoted in Tapp, op. cit., p. 129. The Kentucky meeting was in 1832. Robert Jefferson Breckinridge was also in the forefront of the fight that caused the Presbyterian schism of 1837, as he was in 1861 when the Church split into Northern and Southern wings.

34. Vaughan, op. cit., p. 25.

35. She was the widow of Alfred Shelby, son of Kentucky's first governor, Isaac Shelby. Her grandfather, Nathaniel Hart, had been killed by Indians at Boonesboro, Kentucky, in 1782, and her aunt, Chenoe Hart, was reputed to have been the first white child born in the state.

36. Vaughan, op. cit., p. 41.

37. See Luther H. Weigle, *American Idealism* (New Haven: Yale University Press, 1928), p. 284.

38. See Charleton Beals, *Brass-Knuckle Crusade* (New York: Hastings House, 1960), pp. 56 and 172.

39. Clay, op. cit., Vol. I, pp. 217–18.

40. See William H. Townsend, *Lincoln and the Bluegrass* (Lexington: University of Kentucky Press, 1955), pp. 207–10.

41. Quoted in Dorothy Garrett Melzer, "Mr. Breckinridge Accepts," *Register of the Kentucky Historical Society*, LVI, No. 3 (July 1958), p. 219.

42. Ibid., p. 220.

43. William H. Townsend, op. cit., p. 251.

44. Quoted in Mary Breckinridge, *Wide Neighborhoods* (New York: Harper, 1952), p. 117.

45. William H. Townsend, op. cit., p. 266; also see Margaret Leech, *Reveille in Washington* (New York, 1941), pp. 31–32 (Universal Library edition).

46. Wilson, op. cit., p. 356.

47. William H. Townsend, op. cit., p. 347.

48. John A. Joyce, *Jewels of Memory* (Washington: Gibson Brothers, 1895), p. 115.

49. See Basil W. Duke, *A History of Morgan's Cavalry* (Bloomington: Indiana University Press, 1960), pp. 550–51.

50. Quoted in A. D. Kirwan, editor, *Johnny Green of the Orphan Brigade* (Lexington: University of Kentucky Press, 1956), p. 10n; also see Ed. Porter Thompson, *History of the First Kentucky Brigade* (Cincinnati: Caxton, 1868), p. 307.

51. Hambleton Tapp, "Robert J. Breckinridge During the Civil War," *Filson Club History Quarterly*, II, No. 2 (April 1937), pp. 135 and 139; also see Frank Luther Mott, *A History of American Magazines, 1850–1865* (Cambridge: Harvard University Press, 1957), pp. 537–39.

52. Tapp, "Robert J. Breckinridge and the Civil War," p. 142. Italics added.

53. James G. Blaine, *Twenty Years of Congress* (Norwich, Conn.: Henry Bill Publishing, 1884), Vol. I, pp. 517–18.

54. See "The Civil War in Kentucky," Louisville *Courier-Journal*, November 20, 1960, p. 38.

55. See William H. Townsend, op. cit., p. 347; Levin, op. cit., p. 511.

56. He was named for his maternal uncle, William Campbell Preston (1794–1860), U.S. senator from South Carolina, 1833–42, a strong States' Rights advocate, and chief political correspondent of Beverley Tucker.

57. See "The Civil War in Kentucky," op. cit., p. 41; Ellis M. Coulter, "William Campbell Preston Breckinridge," *Dictionary of American Biography*, Vol. III, pp. 11–12.

58. William H. Townsend, op. cit., pp. 334–35.

59. Tapp, "Robert J. Breckinridge During the Civil War," p. 140n.

60. William H. Townsend, op. cit., p. 331.

61. Quoted in Stillwell, op. cit., pp. 131–32.

62. Joyce, op. cit., p. 114.

63. A. J. Hanna, *Flight into Oblivion* (Bloomington: Indiana University Press, 1959), p. 104.

64. Ibid., pp. 155–69.

65. Ibid., p. 233.

66. Clay, op. cit., Vol. I, p. 220.

67. Quoted in Ethelbert D. Warfield, *Joseph Cabell Breckinridge, Junior* (New York: Knickerbocker, 1898), p. 14.

68. William Eliot Knight, *The Wm. C. P. Breckinridge Defence* (Colfax, Iowa: Weekly Clipper, 1895), p. 20.

69. See Allan Nevins, *Grover Cleveland* (New York: Dodd, Mead, 1962), p. 340.

70. O. O. Stealey, editor, *Twenty Years in the Press Gallery* (New York: Publishers Printing, 1906), pp. 219–20.

71. Lloyd Bryce and A. Peniston, editors, *Both Sides of the Tariff Question* (New York: A. Peniston, 1890), p. 136.

72. Agnes Parker, . . . *The Real Madeleine Pollard* (New York, 1894), p. 33.

73. Anonymous, *The Celebrated Trial of Madeline Pollard vs. Breckinridge* . . . (no place of publication listed, 1894), pp. 68 and 77.

74. Ibid., pp. 168 and 172.

75. Quoted in Jones, op. cit., pp. 176–77.

76. John C. Breckinridge also had two daughters, one of whom, Frances, married a Kentucky legislator and bank president, John Andrew Steele. As a captain in Morgan's Cavalry, he had been wounded and taken prisoner. On Steele's death in 1921 all the Kentucky papers described him as a "venerable Southern Gentleman of the old school." See *Register of the Kentucky Historical Society*, XIX, No. 57 (1921), pp. 116–18.

77. Nevins, op. cit., p. 343.

78. Clay, op. cit., Vol. I, p. 219.

79. Mary Breckinridge, op. cit., p. 32.

80. *The Social Service Review*, XXII, No. 4 (December 1948), p. 427; also see *Who Was Who in America*, Vol. II, p. 78; New York *Times*, July 31, 1948, p. 15.

81. Quoted in Sophonisba Preston Breckinridge, *Madeline McDowell Breckinridge* (Chicago: University of Chicago Press, 1921), p. 239.

82. Ibid., p. 196.

83. Irving Dilliard, "Desha Breckinridge," *Dictionary of American Biography*, Vol. XXI, p. 115.

84. Quoted in Mary Breckinridge, op. cit., p. 282.

85. For a recent description of the work of the Frontier Nursing Service, see Louise Knight, "Kentucky Mountain Courier," *Wellesley Alumnae Magazine*, March 1965, pp. 168–69, 180.

86. Quoted in Ethelbert D. Warfield, *Joseph Cabell Breckinridge, Junior*, p. 58n.

87. See Arthur S. Link, *Wilson: The Struggle for Neutrality, 1914–1915* (Princeton: Princeton University Press, 1960), p. 75; also see *Document No. 1137*, House of Representatives, 63d Congress, 2d Session.

88. Josephus Daniels, *The Wilson Era: Years of Peace—1910–1917* (Chapel Hill: University of North Carolina Press, 1944), p. 446.

89. New York *Times*, May 7, 1936, p. 22.

90. *Current Biography*, 1954, pp. 114–16.

91. The Breckinridges were divorced in 1947. The same year Henry was married for the third time to Margaret Lucy Smith. They had one child, Madeline Houston Breckinridge.

92. See *Airship Investigation*. Report of Colonel Henry Breckinridge for the Joint Committee to Investigate Dirigible Disasters. 73d Congress, 1st Session.

93. See Kenneth S. Davis, *The Hero: Charles A. Lindbergh and the American Dream* (Garden City, N.Y.: Doubleday, 1959), pp. 270, 304, 313, 327.

94. New York *Times*, September 3, 1934, p. 1.

95. New York *Times*, September 4, 1934, p. 18.

96. Henry Breckinridge, *Excerpts, 1935–1936* (New York: Court Press, 1938), preface.

97. Ibid., pp. 13–14.

98. Henry Breckinridge, *Excerpts III, 1938–1941* (New York: Court Press, 1944), p. 10. His book was . . . *shall not perish* . . . (New York: Scribner Press, 1941).

99. Louisville *Courier-Journal*, August 20, 1961, Section 4, p. 1; Interview with Scott D. Breckinridge, Jr., August 31, 1963, and newspaper clippings provided by him; letter from John B. Breckinridge to author, August 29, 1963.

THE BAYARD DYNASTY

1. Quoted in Charles Callan Tansill, *The Congressional Career of Thomas Francis Bayard, 1869–1885* (Washington: Georgetown University Press, 1946), p. 24.

2. H. Clay Reed, editor, *Delaware: A History of the First State* (New York: Lewis Historical, 1947), p. 126.

3. Quoted in Henry H. Kessler and Eugene Rachlis, *Peter Stuyvesant and His New York* (New York: Random House, 1959), p. 204.

4. Ibid., p. 122. Also see Victor H. Paltsits, "Petrus Stuyvesant," *Dictionary of American Biography*, Vol. XVIII, pp. 187–88.

5. See Kessler and Rachlis, op. cit., p. 191.

6. Quoted in Mrs. Sarah Van Rensselaer, *Ancestral Sketches and Records of Olden Times* (New York: A. D. F. Randolph, 1882), p. 36. Italics in original.

7. Ibid., p. 37. Italics in original.

8. George W. Schuyler, *Colonial New York, Philip Schuyler and His Family* (New York: Scribner's 1885), Vol. I, p. 195.

9. A. Everett Peterson, "Nicholas Bayard," *Dictionary of American Biography*, Vol. II, pp. 68–69. Also see Lawrence H. Leder, *Robert Livingston and the Politics of Colonial New York* (Chapel Hill: University of North Carolina Press, 1961), pp. 59, 63, 75–76, 144, 174, 177.

10. See Archibald Douglas Turnbull, *John Stevens, an American Record* (New York and London: Century, 1928), p. 82, and Dorothy Gregg, *The Exploitation of the Steamboat: The Case of Colonel John Stevens* (Unpublished Ph.D. dissertation, Columbia University, 1951), p. 39.

11. See Charles Leonard Lundin, *Cockpit of the Revolution, the War for Independence in New Jersey* (Princeton: Princeton University Press, 1940), p. 7.

12. Quoted in George Pellew, *John Jay* (Boston and New York: Houghton Mifflin, 1890), p. 227.

13. The following is a genealogical chart of the New York branch of the Bayard family:

Samuel Bayard
m. Anna Stuyvesant

Balthazar (His eldest daughter married Augustus Jay, grandfather of John Jay.)	**Nicholas (1644–1707)** Mayor of New York, 1685–87 m. *Judith Verlet*	**Petrus** (Founder of the Delaware branch)

Samuel (1669–1745)
New York Assembly, 1713–15
m. *Margaret Van Cortlandt*

Stephen (b. 1700)
Mayor of New York, 1744–47
m. *Alida Vetch*, granddaughter
of Robert Livingston

William (1729–1804) ("Weeping Billy,")
N. Y. Assembly, 1761–68

William (1764–1826)
President, New York Savings Bank

Harriet Elizabeth (1799–1875)
m. *Stephen Van Rensselaer*

See Mrs. Anson Phelps Atterbury, *The Bayard Family* (Baltimore, 1928).

14. See Dieter Cunz, *The Maryland Germans* (Princeton: Princeton University Press, 1948), pp. 13–30; also Dieter Cunz, "Augustin Herrman, Origin and Early Events," *Tyler's Quarterly Historical and Genealogical Magazine,* XXIV, No. 1 (July 1942).

15. See George Armistead Leakin, "Labadists of Bohemia Manor," *Maryland Historical Magazine,* I, No. 4 (December 1906).

16. Bartlett Burleigh James and J. Franklin Jameson, editors, *Journals of Jasper Danckaerts, 1679–1680* (New York: Scribner's, 1913), p. 237.

17. See George Armistead Leakin, "A Visit to Bohemia Manor," *Maryland Historical Magazine,* II, No. 2 (1907).

18. Some of those who owned stock in the Hamilton-Bayard project to manufacture cotton at Paterson, N.J., were: Elias Boudinot, Judge Elisha Boudinot, Richard ("The Duke") Stockton, General Henry Knox, John Pintard, Henry Livingston, Brockholst Livingston, Philip Livingston, and Archibald Mercer. See William Nelson, "The Founding of Paterson," *Proceedings of the New Jersey Historical Society*, 2d Series, IX (1886–87), p. 182.

19. See A. Everett Peterson, "Samuel Bayard," *Dictionary of American Biography*, Vol. II, pp. 69–70; also James Grant Wilson, editor, "Judge Bayard of New Jersey and His London Diary of 1795–96," *Proceedings of the New Jersey Historical Society*, 2d Series, VIII, No. 4 (1885).

20. L. H. Butterfield, editor, *Letters of Benjamin Rush* (Princeton: Princeton University Press, 1951), Vol. I, p. 602.

21. William Blauvelt, a contemporary Presbyterian minister, wrote, "Chief Justice Kirkpatrick was as handsome a man as there was in the State of New Jersey, with a mellifluous tone of voice, but was considered vain." Quoted in "Notes on the Life of Rev. William Blauvelt," *Somerset County Historical Quarterly*, Vol. VII, p. 38.

22. Jane Eudora (Kirkpatrick) Cogswell, editor, *The Light of Other Days: Sketches of the Past, and Other Selections from the Writings of the Late Mrs. Jane Kirkpatrick* (New Brunswick: J. Terhune, 1856), p. vi.

23. The father of Samuel Harrison Smith was Jonathan Bayard Smith (1742–1812), delegate to the Continental Congress from Pennsylvania (1777–78); one of the founders of the University of the State of Pennsylvania (1779); and a trustee of Princeton College (1779–1808). See *Biographical Directory of the American Congress, 1774–1961*, p. 1620. He was also a close friend and Princeton classmate of Benjamin Rush, whose thesis for a medical degree at Edinburgh bore a secondary dedication to him. See George W. Corner, editor, *The Autobiography of Benjamin Rush* (Princeton: Princeton University Press, 1948), p. 43.

24. Quoted in Frank Van Der Linden, *The Turning Point* (Washington: Luce, 1962), pp. 116–17. Italics in original.

25. Gaillard Hunt, editor, *Forty Years of Washington Society, Portrayed by the Family Letters of Mrs. Samuel Harrison Smith* (New York: Scribner's, 1906).

26. Margaret Bayard Smith, *What is Gentility? A Moral Tale* (Washington: P. Thompson, 1828), p. 4. Italics in original.

27. Morton Borden, *The Federalism of James A. Bayard* (New York: Columbia University Press, 1955), p. 21.

28. Quoted in John A. Munroe, editor, "William Plumer's Biographical Sketches of James A. Bayard, Caesar A. Rodney, and Samuel White," *Delaware History*, IV, No. 4 (September 1951), p. 367.

29. William Pierce of Georgia. Quoted in Saul K. Padover, *The Living U. S. Constitution* (New York: Praeger, 1953), p. 37.

30. Quoted in Robert E. Pattison, "The Life and Character of Richard Bassett," *Papers of the Historical Society of Delaware*, XXIX (Wilmington, 1900), p. 9.

31. Munroe, op. cit., p. 367.

32. Elizabeth Donnan, editor, "Papers of James A. Bayard, 1796–1815," *Annual Report of the American Historical Association for the Year 1913*, II (Washington, 1915), pp. 110–11n.

33. Ibid., p. 94.

34. Ibid., p. 115.

35. Ibid., p. 124.

36. Quoted in George Tucker, *The Life of Thomas Jefferson, Third President of the United States* (Philadelphia: Carey, Lea & Blanchard, 1837), Vol. II, p. 509.

37. Donnan, op. cit., p. 128.

38. Ibid., p. 127.

39. Ibid., pp. 128–29.

40. *National Intelligencer*, February 18, 1801, p. 3.

41. Donnan, op. cit., p. 131.

42. Ibid., p. 132.

43. Ibid., p. 152.

44. Henry C. Conrad, editor, "Letters of James Asheton Bayard, 1802–1814," *Papers of the Historical Society of Delaware*, XXXI (Wilmington, 1901), p. 12.

45. Munroe, op. cit., p. 366.

46. Ibid., p. 366n.

47. H. Clay Reed, op.cit., p. 134.

48. Conrad, op. cit., p. 6.

49. Ibid., p. 7. Caesar A. Rodney (1772–1824) was the son and nephew of members of the Continental Congress from Delaware. His uncle Caesar was also a signer of the Declaration of Independence. Rodney was appointed Attorney General of the United States by Jefferson, and served from 1807 to 1811, when he resigned because of being passed over for a seat on the Supreme Court. He was later a U.S. senator (1822–23), and died in Buenos Aires, where he was serving as U.S. minister to Argentina.

50. John Quincy Adams, *Memoirs* (Philadelphia: Lippincott, 1874–77), Vol. I, pp. 500–1.

51. Quoted in Samuel Flagg Bemis, *John Quincy Adams and the Foundations of American Foreign Policy* (New York: Knopf, 1949), p. 190.

52. Quoted in John A. Munroe, "James A. Bayard and the Milligans," *Delaware History*, VIII, No. 2 (September 1958), p. 148.

53. Ibid., p. 154.

54. Quoted in Borden, op. cit., p. 95.

55. Quoted in Harold Bell Hancock, "The Campaign and Election of 1860," *Delaware History*, VII, No. 2 (September 1956), p. 119.

56. See William B. Hesseltine, editor, *Three Against Lincoln, Murat Halstead Reports the Caucuses of 1860* (Baton Rouge: Louisiana State University Press, 1960), p. 266.

57. The fight in the Delaware Democratic Convention was more organizational than philosophical. Throughout this period the Bayards were opposed by the Saulsburys, called "the party of the three brothers." Williard Saulsbury was a U.S. senator (1859–71), but his drinking habits attracted notice, and his brother-in-law, who was governor, appointed him chancellor, the state's highest judicial officer; Eli Saulsbury was also a U.S. senator (1871–89), and their brother Gove Saulsbury was a governor.

58. Hancock, op. cit., p. 128.

59. Harold Bell Hancock, "The Coming of the War," *Delaware History*, VII, No. 3 (March 1957), pp. 246–48.

60. *Congressional Globe*, 38th Congress, 1st Session, pp. 31–37.

61. See John F. Kennedy, "Let's Get Rid of College Loyalty Oaths!" in Lewis W. Gillenson, editor, *Fabulous Yesterday* (New York: Harper, 1961), p. 144. (Reprinted from *Coronet* magazine, April 1960.)

62. Harold Bell Hancock, "The Political History of Delaware During the Civil War: A Divided House," *Delaware History*, VII, No. 4 (September 1957), p. 356.

63. New York *World*, July 11, 1872, p. 1.

64. Quoted in Charles H. Dennis, *Eugene Field's Creative Years* (Garden City, N.Y.: Doubleday, 1924), pp. 29–30.

65. George F. Hoar, *Autobiography of Seventy Years* (New York: Scribner's, 1903), Vol. II, p. 69.

66. O. O. Stealey, editor, *Twenty Years in the Press Gallery* (New York: Publishers Printing, 1906), p. 203.

67. Quoted in Harry J. Sievers, *Benjamin Harrison, Hoosier Statesman* (New York: University Publishers, 1959), p. 214.

68. *Congressional Globe*, 42nd Congress, 2nd Session, May 9, 1872, pp. 3260–61.

69. Quoted in Tansill, op. cit., p. 246.

70. Ibid., p. 274.

71. Frank G. Carpenter, *Carp's Washington* (New York: McGraw-Hill, 1960), p. 32.

72. See Edward Spencer, *An Outline of the Public Life and Services of Thomas F. Bayard* (New York: Appleton, 1880).

73. Quoted in Tansill, op. cit., p. 239.

74. Ibid., p. 325.

75. Ibid., p. 123.

76. See Allan Nevins, *Grover Cleveland* (New York: Dodd, Mead, 1962), pp. 314–15.

77. Carpenter, op. cit., p. 80.

78. Quoted in Charles Callan Tansill, *The Foreign Policy of Thomas F. Bayard, 1885–1897* (New York: Fordham University Press, 1940), pp. xxv and xxiii.

79. Quoted in Samuel Flagg Bemis, editor, *The American Secretaries of State and Their Diplomacy* (New York: Knopf, 1927–29), Vol. VIII, p. 63.

80. Quoted in Graham H. Stuart, *The Department of State* (New York: Macmillan, 1949), p. 171.

81. Tansill, *The Foreign Policy of Thomas F. Bayard*, p. 733n.

82. Ibid., p. 720.

83. Quoted in John A. Garraty, *Henry Cabot Lodge* (New York: Knopf, 1953), p. 159; for other examples of Lodge's dislike of Bayard, see *Selections from the Correspondence of Theodore Roosevelt and Henry Cabot Lodge* (New York: Scribner's, 1925), Vol. I, pp. 31 and 170.

84. Tansill, *The Foreign Policy of Thomas F. Bayard*, pp. 652–53.

85. Ibid., p. 780n.

86. See New York *Times*, June 12, 1954, p. 15; Wilmington *Journal-Every Evening*, June 11, 1954, pp. 1 and 4, and June 12, 1954, p. 21.

87. Stewart H. Holbrook, *The Age of the Moguls* (Garden City, N.Y.: Doubleday, 1953), p. 269.

88. New York *Times*, December 3, 1922, Sec. IX, p. 4.

89. New York *Times*, November 18, 1922, p. 16.

90. New York *Times*, April 19, 1925, p. 1.

91. New York *Times*, November 8, 1928, p. 28.

92. Wilmington *Journal-Every Evening*, October 7, 1948, p. 4.

93. *Delaware State News* (Dover), October 30, 1952, p. 6.

94. Wilmington *Journal-Every Evening*, August 27, 1952, p. 1.

95. Wilmington *Journal-Every Evening*, November 3, 1952, p. 11.

96. Wilmington *Journal-Every Evening*, October 14, 1952, p. 4.

97. New York *Times*, October 22, 1952, p. 21.

98. *Mardindale-Hubbell Law Directory* (Summit, N.J., 1964), p. 1114.

99. Letter from Alexis I. Du Pont Bayard, February 28, 1964; New York *Times*, February 25, 1965, p. 23 (AP).

100. James Grant Wilson, *Colonel John Bayard and the Bayard Family in America* (New York: Trow's Printing, 1885), p. 16.

THE TAFT DYNASTY

1. Quoted in Ishbel Ross, *An American Family, The Tafts—1678 to 1964* (Cleveland and New York: World, 1964), p. 188.

2. Quoted in Alvin F. Harlow, *The Serene Cincinnatians* (New York: Dutton, 1950), p. 18.

3. Henry W. Taft, *Opinions: Literary and Otherwise* (New York: Macmillan, 1934), p. 14.

4. Ibid., pp. 4–5.

5. *Look*, November 22, 1960, p. 120.

6. Alphonso Taft, "The Tafts of Yesterday," in Lewis Alexander Leonard, *Life of Alphonso Taft* (New York: Hawke, 1920), pp. 238 and 256.

7. The pre-Ohio Taft family genealogy:

Robert Taft (c. 1640–1725)
Arrived in America before 1678
m. *Sarah* (d. 1725)

|

Joseph (1680–1747)
m. *Elizabeth Emerson* (1687–1760)
(of the same family as Ralph Waldo Emerson)

|

Peter (b. 1715)
m. *Elizabeth Cheney* (b. 1707)

|

Aaron (1743–1808)
m. *Rhoda Rawson* (d. 1827)

|

Peter Rawson (1785–1867)
m. *Sylvia Howard* (d. 1867)

|

Alphonso (1810–91)
Moved to Ohio, 1839

See Mabel Thacher Rosemary Washburn, *Ancestry of William Howard Taft* (New York: Frank Allaben, 1908).

8. "The Living Taft Legend," *Newsweek*, August 22, 1955, p. 25.

9. Quoted in Ross, op. cit., p. 78.

10. Henry W. Taft, *Legal Miscellanies* (New York: Macmillan, 1941), p. 3.

11. Horace Dutton Taft, *Memories and Opinions* (New York: Macmillan, 1942), p. 16.

12. Henry W. Taft, *Legal Miscellanies*, p. 3n.

13. Wrote Rutherford B. Hayes in his diary: "3d June, 1875.—I was nominated for Governor yesterday at Columbus. I persisted in declining to the last. The leading other Candidate before the Convention, Judge Taft of Cincinnati, is an able and good man. But he had such a record on the Bible question in the Schools, that his nomination was impossible. I did all I could to remove the prejudice against him, and to aid his nomination. . . ." For Hayes, the Ohio governorship was the steppingstone to the White House. See T. Harry Williams, editor, *Hayes, the Diary of a President, 1875–1881* (New York: McKay, 1964), p. 4.

14. Quoted in Leonard, op. cit., p. 159.

15. When the newly appointed diplomat wrote on official stationary to inquire of an English Taft about that branch of the family, the reply came back: "There is nothing I can say about the Tafts which could possibly be of interest to an Envoy Extraordinary and a Minister Plenipotentiary. Very truly yours," Quoted in Phyllis Robbins, *Robert A. Taft, Boy and Man* (Cambridge: Dresser, Chapman & Grimes, 1963), p. 15.

16. Quoted in Ross, op. cit., p. 71.

17. Quoted in Joseph Alsop and Robert Kintner, "Taft & Taft," *Life*, March 18, 1940, p. 92. Alphonso also wrote to Delia: "The trouble with us Americans is that we can never get it out of our heads that we are just as good as anybody in the same company." Quoted in Ross, op. cit., p. 74.

18. Horace Dutton Taft, op. cit., p. 41.

19. Quoted in *Newsweek*, August 22, 1955, p. 25.

20. Quoted in Ross, op. cit., p. 71.

21. Ibid., p. 67.

22. Ibid., p. 50.

23. Archibald W. Butt, *Taft and Roosevelt* (Garden City, N.Y.: Doubleday, 1930), Vol. I, p. 175.

24. See Helen Taft Manning, "My Brother Bob Taft," *American Magazine*, January 1952, p. 102.

25. Quoted in John T. Dallas, *Mr. Taft* (Littleton, N.H.: Courier Printing, 1949), pp. 36 and 33.

26. Andrew D. McIntosh, quoted in Pauline Helen Isaacson, *Robert Alphonso Taft, an Assessment of a Persuader* (Unpublished Ph.D. dissertation, University of Minnesota, 1956), p. 62.

27. Dallas, op. cit., p. 96.

28. Butt, op. cit., Vol. I, p. 235.

29. Herbert S. Duffy, *William Howard Taft* (New York: Minton, Balch, 1930), pp. 76–77.

30. Henry F. Pringle, *The Life and Times of William Howard Taft* (New York: Farrar & Rinehart, 1939), Vol. I, p. 237.

31. See New York *Times*, May 23, 1943, p. 43 (UP).

32. Frederick C. Hicks, *William Howard Taft, Yale Professor of Law and New Haven Citizen* (New Haven: Yale University Press, 1945), p. 112.

33. Pringle, op. cit., Vol. I, p. 367.

34. Ellen Maury Slayden, *Washington Wife* (New York: Harper & Row, 1963), pp. 357–58.

35. Charles Franklin Thwing, *Friends of Men* (New York: Macmillan, 1933), p. 83.

36. William Allen White, *The Autobiography of William Allen White* (New York: Macmillan, 1946), p. 426.

37. Butt, op. cit., Vol. I, p. 38.

38. Mrs. William Howard Taft, *Recollections of Full Years* (New York: Dodd, Mead, 1914), pp. 25–26.

39. Quoted in Pringle, op. cit., Vol. I, pp. 57–58.

40. Quoted in Bela Kornitzer, *American Fathers and Sons* (New York: Hermitage House, 1952), p. 29.

41. Quoted in Noel George Rapp, *The Political Speaking of Senator Robert A. Taft, 1939 to 1953* (Unpublished Ph.D. dissertation, Purdue University, 1955), p. 19.

42. Theodore Roosevelt, "Governor William H. Taft," *Outlook,* September 21, 1901, p. 166.

43. Carlos P. Romulo, *I Walked with Heroes* (New York: Holt, Rinehart & Winston, 1961), p. 139.

44. Mrs. William Howard Taft, op. cit., p. 125.

45. Charles P. Taft, *Democracy in Politics and Economics* (New York: Farrar, Straus, 1950), p. 40.

46. Quoted in Robbins, op. cit., p. 62.

47. Manning, op. cit., p. 99.

48. Quoted in *Time,* January 29, 1940, p. 21.

49. Manning, op. cit., p. 102.

50. Ibid., p. 100.

51. See Earle Looker, *The White House Gang* (New York: Revell, 1929), pp. 14, 16–19. Looker, who was also a member of the "gang," writes that Charlie, or "Taffy" as his friends called him, "was remarkable for his calmness, slowness to anger, good humor, and steadfast determination when roused."

52. Isaacson, op. cit., p. 66.

53. Quoted in Darrah Dunham Wunder, "My Most Unforgettable Character," *Reader's Digest,* June 1962, p. 84.

54. Quoted in Robbins, op. cit., p. 116.

55. Quoted in Ross, op. cit., p. 227.

56. Ibid., p. 119.

57. See Forrest Crissey, *Theodore E. Burton, American Statesman* (Cleveland & New York: World, 1956), pp. 174–78.

58. Arthur Wallace Dunn, *Gridiron Nights* (New York: Frederick A. Stokes, 1915), p. 222.

59. Butt, op. cit., Vol. II, p. 791.

60. Quoted in Robbins, op. cit., p. 133.

61. Ibid., p. 134.

62. *Newsweek,* August 22, 1955, p. 25.

63. Manning, op. cit., p. 100.

64. Mrs. William Howard Taft, op. cit., p. 331.

65. David Grayson, *American Chronicle, the Autobiography of Ray Stannard Baker* (New York: Scribner's, 1945), p. 255.

66. Butt, op. cit., Vol. I, p. 110.

67. William Howard Taft, *Our Chief Magistrate and His Powers* (New York: Columbia University Press, 1925), pp. 139–40.

68. Wayne Andrews, editor, *The Autobiography of Theodore Roosevelt* (New York: Scribner's, 1958), pp. 197–98.

69. William Howard Taft, op. cit., p. 144.

70. Charles Willis Thompson, *Presidents I've Known* (Indianapolis: Bobbs-Merrill, 1929), p. 213.

71. Quoted in Pringle, op. cit., Vol. I, p. 535.

72. Henry L. Stimson and McGeorge Bundy, *On Active Service in Peace and War* (New York: Harper, 1948), p. 26.

73. Charles E. Barker, *With President Taft in the White House* (Chicago: Krock, 1947), pp. 36–37.

74. Manning, op. cit., p. 99.

75. Butt, op. cit., Vol. I, p. 174.

76. See Lilian Rogers Parks, *My Thirty Years Backstairs at the White House* (New York: Fleet, 1961), p. 111; also Irwin H. Hoover, *Forty-two Years in the White House* (Boston and New York: Houghton Mifflin, 1934), p. 45.

77. Butt, op. cit., Vol. II, p. 680.

78. Alice Roosevelt Longworth, however, was unconcerned by the crowd, the crudity, or the damp grass. She appeared at the Tafts' party in a blue satin gown, flesh-colored stockings, and gold slippers. According to Mrs. Slayden, "She held the very scant skirt quite high, and when the band played, kicked about and moved her body sinuously like a shining leopard cat. . . ." Slayden, op. cit., pp. 156–57.

79. Isaacson, op. cit., p. 80.

80. Ibid., p. 456.

81. Alsop and Kintner, op. cit., p. 92; also Frances S. Philbrick, "Lloyd Wheaton Bowers," *Dictionary of American Biography*, Vol. II, p. 508.

82. John Gunther, *Inside U.S.A.* (New York: Harper, 1947), p. 432.

83. Duffy, op. cit., p. 219.

84. Butt, op. cit., Vol. II, p. 804.

85. Stimson and Bundy, op. cit., p. 53.

86. Parks, op. cit., p. 127.

87. Quoted in Frank K. Kelly, *The Fight for the White House, the Story of 1912* (New York: Crowell, 1961), p. 144.

88. Thompson, op. cit., p. 216.

89. Dunn, op. cit., p. 277.

90. Quoted in Hicks, op. cit., p. 30.

91. Ibid., pp. 79–80.

92. Ibid., p. 10.

93. Quoted in Pringle, op. cit., Vol. II, p. 906.

94. Ibid., Vol. II, p. 858.

95. See Lewis L. Strauss, *Men and Decisions* (Garden City, N.Y.: Doubleday, 1962), p. 19. For the work of the U. S. Food Administration, see *The Memoirs of Herbert Hoover: Years of Adventure, 1874–1920* (New York: Macmillan, 1951), pp. 240–430.

96. Edward G. Lowry, *Washington Close-ups* (New York and Boston: Houghton Mifflin, 1921), p. 264.

97. Quotations in Pringle, op. cit., Vol. II, pp. 960 and 964.

98. As Chief Justice, Taft also lobbied with considerable success for increasing the number of federal judges, constructing a separate building for the Supreme Court, tightening the administrative machinery of the federal judiciary, and for procedural changes that would increase the Court's efficiency. See Alpheus Thomas Mason, *William Howard Taft: Chief Justice* (New York: Simon & Schuster, 1965), pp. 271 ff.

99. Pringle, op. cit., Vol. II, p. 1079.

100. Donald Day, editor, *The Autobiography of Will Rogers* (Boston: Houghton Mifflin, 1949), p. 224. Italics in original.

101. Quoted in Caroline Thomas Harnsberger, *A Man of Courage, Robert A. Taft* (Chicago: Wilcox & Follett, 1952), p. 142.

102. Alice Roosevelt Longworth, "What's the Matter with Bob Taft?" *Saturday Evening Post,* May 4, 1940, p. 91.

103. Quoted in "Charlie Taft's Big Chance," *Fortune,* August 1947, p. 162.

104. See Charles P. Taft, *City Management, the Cincinnati Experiment* (New York: Farrar & Rinehart, 1933), pp. 167–69; also Jerome Beatty, "The Other Taft," *American Magazine,* July 1947, p. 88.

105. See Ross, op. cit., p. 349.

106. Gunther, op. cit., p. 450.

107. Quoted in *Editor & Publisher,* September 30, 1950, p. 18; also see New York *Times,* January 20, 1959, p. 35 (AP).

108. See New York *Times,* July 21, 1958, p. 14 (AP), and October 20, 1959, p. 48 (AP).

109. Charles P. Taft, *You and I—and Roosevelt* (New York: Farrar & Rinehart, 1936), p. 7.

110. Ibid., p. 4.

111. Alsop and Kintner, op. cit., p. 90.

112. Quoted in Frank Gervasi, "Bob Taft's Martha," *Collier's,* April 3, 1948, p. 63.

113. Longworth, op. cit., p. 91.

114. New York *Times,* October 3, 1958, p. 29; *Newsweek,* October 13, 1958, p. 90; Gervasi, op. cit., p. 64.

115. *Time,* January 29, 1940, p. 22.

116. *Time,* October 6, 1947, p. 25.

117. Harold L. Ickes, *The Secret Diary of Harold L. Ickes* (New York: Simon & Schuster, 1955), Vol. II, p. 201.

118. *Time,* January 29, 1940, p. 22.

119. J. J. Perling, *Presidents' Sons* (New York: Odyssey, 1947), p. 279.

120. *Fortune,* August 1947, p. 164.

121. Arthur H. Vandenberg, Jr., editor, *The Private Papers of Senator Vandenberg* (Boston and New York: Houghton Mifflin, 1952), p. 164.

122. *Fortune,* August 1947, p. 165.

123. Elmo Roper, *You and Your Leaders* (New York: Morrow, 1957), p. 198.

124. Quoted in Harnsberger, op. cit., p. 136.

125. Ibid., p. 123.

126. See William S. White, *The Taft Story* (New York: Harper, 1954), pp. 49–50.

127. John F. Kennedy, *Profiles in Courage* (New York: Harper, 1956), p. 211.

128. Ibid., p. 215.

129. Butt, op. cit., Vol. II, p. 749.

130. Henry W. Taft, *Japan and America, a Journey and a Political Survey* (New York: Macmillan, 1932), p. v.

131. "Even the obscure Einstein theory of relativity," wrote Henry Taft, "may be the subject of social conversation." He recalled that General Sherman was "among the best conversationalists I ever met," and even his father's old boss, President Grant, "could converse well when he had to express some-

thing. . . ." Henry W. Taft, *Kindred Arts, Conversation and Public Speaking* (New York: Macmillan, 1929), pp. 32, 68, 64.

132. Robert A. Taft, "Reply by Senator Taft," *American Mercury*, June 1948, p. 655.

133. Marvin C. Harrison, *Robert A. Taft, Our Illustrious Dunderhead* (Cleveland: No publisher listed, 1944), p. 3.

134. Quoted in Harnsberger, op. cit., p. 173.

135. See Isaacson, op. cit., pp. 261–66.

136. Quoted in Harnsberger, op. cit., p. 175.

137. Ibid., p. 187.

138. *Newsweek*, October 18, 1954, p. 28.

139. Wunder, op. cit., p. 86.

140. Holmes Alexander, *The Famous Five* (New York: Bookmailer, 1958), p. 168.

141. See James Reichley, *States in Crisis* (Chapel Hill: University of North Carolina Press, 1964), p. 128; Joseph and Stewart Alsop, *The Reporter's Trade* (New York: Reynal, 1958), pp. 158–60; New York *Times*, November 8, 1950, p. 5; November 9, 1950, p. 1.

142. *Newsweek*, May 19, 1952, p. 29.

143. *Time*, January 12, 1948, p. 17.

144. *Newsweek*, November 19, 1951, p. 29.

145. Quoted in Paul T. David, Malcolm Moos, Ralph M. Goldman, editors, *Presidential Nominating Politics in 1952* (Baltimore: Johns Hopkins Press, 1954), Vol. I, p. 70.

For Lodge's tactics in 1952, see Lodge Dynasty, p. 470. Taft's campaign manager, David Ingalls, however, was no less outspoken. He called Eisenhower "a pig in a poke . . . a good-looking mortician to preside over the funeral rites." Quoted in Henry A. Zeiger, *The Remarkable Henry Cabot Lodge* (New York: Popular Library, 1964), p. 103.

146. Quoted in David, Moos, and Goldman, op. cit., p. 76.

147. Richard L. Maher, "Political Paradox," *Nation*, October 4, 1952, p. 300.

148. *Fortune*, August 1947, p. 86.

149. Ibid., p. 165.

150. See White, op. cit., p. 227; also see Dwight D. Eisenhower, *Mandate for Change* (Garden City, N.Y.: Doubleday, 1963), pp. 218–22.

151. Quoted in Jhan and June Robbins, *Eight Weeks to Live, the Last Chapter in the Life of Senator Robert A. Taft* (Garden City, N.Y.: Doubleday, 1954), p. 23.

152. Quoted in Malcolm Moos, *The Republicans* (New York: Random House, 1956), p. 430.

153. Quoted in *Newsweek*, October 18, 1954, p. 27.

154. Interview with William Howard Taft III, February 4, 1965, Washington.

155. See William H. Hessler, "Taft vs. Kennedy in Ohio," *Reporter*, October 25, 1962, pp. 40–42.

156. Quoted in Richard Armstrong, "A New Taft and a Young Kennedy Go to Washington," *Saturday Evening Post*, January 19, 1963, p. 54.

157. Quoted in *Time*, May 15, 1964, p. 37.

158. Quoted in New York *Times*, April 5, 1964, p. 80.

159. Ibid., October 20, 1964, p. 27.

160. Marquis Childs, "The Newest Taft on the Horizon," Washington *Post*, February 27, 1963, p. A16.

Another syndicated columnist now claims that Taft's "master plan" calls for him to get elected to the House of Representatives in 1966, to the Senate in 1970, and to run for the presidency against Robert F. Kennedy in 1972. See Leslie Carpenter, "1972: Taft vs. Kennedy?" Atlantic City *Press*, September 29, 1965, p. 4.

THE FRELINGHUYSEN DYNASTY

1. Quoted in Felix James Schrag, *Pietism in Colonial America* (Part of Ph.D. dissertation, University of Chicago, 1948), p. 87.

2. See *The Journals of Henry Melchior Muhlenberg* (Philadelphia: Evangelical Lutheran Ministerium of Pennsylvania, 1942), Vol. I, pp. 108, 199–200.

3. Peter H. B. Frelinghuysen, Jr., *Theodorus Jacobus Frelinghuysen* (Princeton: Privately printed, 1938), p. 27.

4. Harry Emerson Wildes, *Twin Rivers, the Raritan and the Passaic* (New York: Farrar & Rinehart, 1943), p. 84.

5. Anne MacVicar Grant, *Memoirs of an American Lady* (Albany: J. Munsell, 1876), pp. 204 and 197. First Published in London, 1808.

6. Ibid., p. 201.

7. Frelinghuysen, op. cit., pp. 74–75.

8. Grant, op. cit., p. 205.

9. Andrew D. Mellick, Jr., *The Story of an Old Farm, or Life in New Jersey in the Eighteenth Century* (Somerville, N.J.: Unionist-Gazette, 1889), pp. 255–59; see version edited by Hubert G. Schmidt, *Lesser Crossroads* (New Brunswick: Rutgers University Press, 1948), pp. 131–36. Also see Charles Hartshorn Maxson, *The Great Awakening in the Middle Colonies* (Chicago: University of Chicago Press, 1920), pp. 121n and 123n.

10. See Joan Gordon, *The Livingstons of New York 1675–1860: Kinship and Class* (Unpublished Ph.D. dissertation, Columbia University, 1959), p. 102.

11. William H. S. Demarest, *A History of Rutgers College, 1766–1924* (New Brunswick: Rutgers College, 1924), pp. 84–85.

12. See John De Witt, *A Funeral Discourse, Pronounced in the Reformed Dutch Church of New-Brunswick, Occasioned by the Decease of the Rev. John H. Livingston* (New Brunswick: William Myer, 1825); also see Tobias Van Zandt (pseud.), *Eulogy on the Life and Character of the Reverend John H. Livingston* (New York: Hopkins & Morris, 1825).

13. The Princeton-Rutgers merger committee included John Bubenheim Bayard, Elias Boudinot (Richard Stockton's brother-in-law), Frederick Frelinghuysen, Archibald Mercer (whose daughter married Frederick Frelinghuysen's son), and Andrew Kirkpatrick (John Bayard's son-in-law). See John Mclean, *History of the College of New Jersey* (Philadelphia: Lippincott, 1877), Vol. I, pp. 352–53.

14. The lottery was then a common device to raise funds for such purposes as bridge and church building and paying Indian claims. There were also lotteries for the relief of private creditors, such as the one held on the default of John Hardenbergh, sheriff of Somerset County and son of the president of Rutgers. See Oscar M. Voorhees, "Some Somerset County Lotteries," *Somerset County Historical Quarterly*, Vol. III, pp. 88–89; Vol. IV, pp. 155–56.

15. See Charles Leonard Lundin, *Cockpit of the Revolution, the War for Independence in New Jersey* (Princeton: Princeton University Press, 1940), p. 99; Demarest, op. cit., pp. 114–15.

16. Quoted in Robert V. Hoffman, *The Revolutionary Scene in New Jersey* (New York: American Historical Co., 1942), pp. 80–81.

17. Quoted in Edwin Mark Norris, *The Story of Princeton* (Boston: Little, Brown, 1917), p. 76.

18. Among those who were fellow students with Frelinghuysen at Princeton were James Madison (President), Aaron Burr (Vice-President), William Bradford (Attorney General), Gunning Bedford (governor of Delaware), "Light Horse Harry" Lee (governor of Virginia), Morgan Lewis (governor of New York), Aaron Ogden (governor of New Jersey), Henry Brockholst Livingston (justice of the Supreme Court), Philip Freneau ("Poet of the Revolution"), John Ewing Colhoun (senator from South Carolina), and Samuel Stanhope Smith (president of Princeton). See Samuel Davies Alexander, *Princeton College During the Eighteenth Century* (New York: A. D. F. Randolph, 1872).

19. Talbot W. Chambers, *Memoirs of the Life and Character of the Late Hon. Theo. Frelinghuysen* (New York: Harper, 1863), p. 23; A. Van Doren Honeyman, "Early Career of Governor William Paterson," *Somerset County Historical Quarterly*, Vol. I, p. 242.

20. *Selections from the Correspondence of the Executive of New Jersey, from 1776 to 1786* (Newark: Daily Advertiser, 1848), pp. 141–42.

21. Ibid., pp. 155–56; Also in Francis Bazley Lee, *Genealogical and Memorial History of the State of New Jersey* (New York: Lewis Historical, 1910), Vol. I, pp. 9–10.

22. Quoted in Walter R. Fee, *The Transition from Aristocracy to Democracy in New Jersey, 1789–1829* (Somerville, N.J.: Somerset Press, 1933), p. 82n. Italics in original.

23. Quoted in Leland D. Baldwin, *Whiskey Rebels* (Pittsburgh: University of Pittsburgh Press, 1939), p. 223.

24. Quoted in Henry P. Thompson, *History of the Reformed Church, at Readington, New Jersey* (New York: Board of Publication of the Reformed Church in America, 1882), p. 54.

25. See Chambers, op. cit., pp. 137, 138–39, 140.
The Rev. Talbot W. Chambers (1819–96), who wrote the biography of Theodore Frelinghuysen, was married to the senator's niece, Louisa Mercer Frelinghuysen (daughter of Theodore's brother John). Chambers, one of the great biblical scholars of his day, had been raised as a Presbyterian but became a Dutch Reformed minister when he differed with his family over the Old School-New School controversy in the church of his birth.

26. Quoted in Ebernezer C. Tracy, *Memoir of the Life of Jeremiah Evarts* (Boston: Crocker & Brewster, 1845), p. 369.

27. Quoted in Chambers, op. cit., p. 69.

28. Thomas H. Benton, *Thirty Years' View* (New York: Appleton, 1854), Vol. I, p. 166.

29. Quoted in Chambers, op. cit., pp. 70–71.

30. Bayard Tuckerman, editor, *The Diary of Philip Hone, 1828–1851* (New York: Dodd, Mead, 1889), Vol. I, pp. 113–14.

31. Louis Clinton Hatch, *A History of the Vice-Presidency of the United States* (New York: American Historical Society, 1934), pp. 178, 195–97,

206–7. Hatch also suggests that "financial considerations may have played a part in the nomination" of Frelinghuysen, p. 305.

32. Ibid., p. 198.

33. Allan Nevins and Milton Halsey Thomas, editors, *The Diary of George Templeton Strong* (New York: Macmillan, 1952), Vol. I, p. 232.

34. See Allan Nevins and Frank Weitenkampf, *A Century of Political Cartoons* (New York: Scribner's, 1944), pp. 58–59.

35. Chambers, op. cit., pp. 174–81.

36. Ibid., p. 177.

37. Hatch, op. cit., p. 210; also Eugene H. Roseboom, *A History of Presidential Elections* (New York: Macmillan, 1957), p. 132.

38. "Notes on the Life of Rev. William Blauvelt," *Somerset County Historical Quarterly*, Vol. VII, p. 37. When Frelinghuysen left the legal profession a former student of his who became president of the American Bar Association said it was "the greatest mistake of his life." See Cortlandt Parker, *The Essex Bar* (Newark: Ward & Tickenor, 1874), pp. 8–9.

39. Quoted in Chambers, op. cit., pp. 99–100. The professor was Taylor Lewis.

40. Joshua L. Chamberlain, *New York University* (Boston: R. Herndon, 1901), p. 102.

The chairman of the board who opposed Frelinghuysen was James Tallmadge (1778–1853), a former Democratic congressman (1817–19) and lieutenant governor of New York (1824–26).

41. Theodore Frelinghuysen married Charlotte Mercer (1784–1854), the daughter of Archibald Mercer (1747–1814), a judge of the Court of Common Pleas for Somerset County, who had served on the board of trustees of Rutgers with Theodore's father.

Besides Frederick, Theodore also adopted Frederick's sister, Gertrude Ann (1814–86), and Mrs. Frelinghuysen's nephew, William T. Mercer (1812–86). William, who became a physician and established a drug business, married Gertrude Ann Frelinghuysen in 1835.

42. Howard K. Beale, editor, *Diary of Gideon Welles* (New York: Norton, 1960), Vol. III, p. 348.

43. John F. Hageman, "The Life, Character and Services of Frederick T. Frelinghuysen," *Proceedings of the New Jersey Historical Society*, 2nd series, IX (1886–87), pp. 58–59.

44. William E. Sackett, *Modern Battles of Trenton* (Trenton: J. L. Murphy, 1895), Vol. I, pp. 29–30.

45. Charles Callan Tansill, *The Congressional Career of Thomas Francis Bayard, 1869–1885* (Washington: Georgetown University Press, 1946), pp. 180–81.

46. Quoted in Philip Marshall Brown, "Frederick Theodore Frelinghuysen," *The American Secretaries of State and Their Diplomacy*, Samuel Flagg Bemis, editor (New York: Knopf, 1927–29), Vol. VIII, p. 3.

47. George Frederick Howe, *Chester A. Arthur* (New York: Dodd, Mead, 1934), p. 161; also see Thomas A. Bailey, *A Diplomatic History of the American People* (New York: Crofts, 1942), p. 436.

48. Graham H. Stuart, *The Department of State* (New York: Macmillan, 1949), pp. 160–61.

49. See Russel B. Nye, *George Bancroft, Brahmin Rebel* (New York: Knopf, 1944), pp. 125 and 127.

50. Howe, op. cit., p. 175.

51. Irwin H. Hoover, *Forty-two Years in the White House* (Boston and New York: Houghton Mifflin, 1934), p. 30.

52. See New York *Times*, April 30, 1935, p. 17; February 20, 1939, p. 17.

53. Walter Evans Edge, *A Jerseyman's Journal* (Princeton: Princeton University Press, 1948), p. 85.

54. "The Reminiscences of Boris Bakhmeteff," p. 460, Oral History Research Office, Columbia University.

55. New York *Times*, June 15, 1920, p. 2.

56. New York *Times*, February 3, 1921, p. 3; February 4, 1921, p. 2; February 8, 1921, p. 1.

57. Samuel Hopkins Adams, *Incredible Era, the Life and Times of Warren Gamaliel Harding* (Boston: Houghton Mifflin, 1939), p. 212.

58. New York *Times*, July 3, 1921, p. 1.

59. New York *Times*, June 18, 1922, p. 2; October 17, 1922, p. 3.

60. New York *Times*, September 28, 1922, p. 20.

61. New York *Times*, November 7, 1922, p. 1.

62. New York *Times*, May 23, 1928, p. 24; also see June 5, 1928, p. 5; and June 14, 1928, p. 8.

63. New York *Times*, May 2, 1930, p. 17; May 14, 1930, p. 29; June 18, 1930, pp. 1 and 13.

64. See Peter Frelinghuysen, Jr., "The 10-Year Record of Peter Frelinghuysen, Jr.," *Congressional Record*, 87th Congress, 2d Session, October 3, 1962.

65. New York *Times*, October 10, 1964, p. 26.

66. See Drew Pearson, "Why War on Poverty Is Lagging," Washington *Post*, May 21, 1964, p. H13, and "Squabble Behind Arends' Victory," January 19, 1965, p. C23.

67. Washington *Post*, January 15, 1965, p. A1; Rowland Evans and Robert Novak, "Again the Southern Strategy," Washington *Post*, January 19, 1965, p. A17.

68. Washington *Post*, January 13, 1965, p. A1; New York *Times*, January 13, 1965, p. 38; January 15, 1965, p. 16.

69. Robert N. Burnett, "Henry Osborne Havemeyer," *Cosmopolitan*, April 1903, p. 704.

70. See Aline B. Saarinen, *The Proud Possessors* (New York: Random House, 1958), pp. 144–73; Louisine W. Havemeyer, "Memories of a Militant," *Scribner's Magazine*, May 1922, pp. 528–39, and June 1922, pp. 661–76; New York *Times*, February 11, 1919, p. 5.

71. See *National Cyclopaedia of American Biography*, Vol. XLIII, pp. 511–12.

72. Quoted in Cleveland Amory, *The Last Resorts* (New York: Harper, 1952), p. 46.

73. *The New Yorker*, October 9, 1948, pp. 21–22.

THE TUCKER DYNASTY

1. Mrs. George P. (Mary H.) Coleman, editor, "Randolph and Tucker Letters," *Virginia Magazine of History and Biography*, XLII, No. 3 (July 1934), p. 222.

2. Quoted in John William Kaye, *The Life and Correspondence of Henry St. George Tucker, Late Accountant-General of Bengal, and Chairman of the East India Company* (London: R. Bentley, 1854), p. 4.

3. In 1774 Colonel Tucker wrote to a son: "I don't know any one undertaking for the last seven years that has succeeded with me." Quoted in Wil-

fred Brenton Kerr, *Bermuda and the American Revolution: 1760–1783* (Princeton: Princeton University Press, 1936), p. 14.

4. Quoted in Percy Winfield Turrentine, *Life and Works of Nathaniel Beverley Tucker* (Unpublished Ph.D. dissertation, Harvard University, 1952), Vol. I, p. 19.

5. On sending him to William and Mary College, St. George's sister wrote him that their father was impressed with "the Cheapness of it . . . the students are boarded, Lodged and have the best Masters for the inconsiderable sum of 13 pounds ten shillings per Annum." Quoted in Mrs. George P. (Mary H.) Coleman, *St. George Tucker: Citizen of No Mean City* (Richmond: Dietz, 1938), p. 12.

6. Quoted in Beverley Randolph Tucker, *Tales of the Tuckers* (Richmond: Dietz, 1942), p. 115. The author, a fifth-generation Tucker, was a professor of neurology and psychiatry at the Medical College of Virginia, a Richmond physician, and a prolific writer, whose books include *Nervous Children* (Boston: Badger, 1916), *The Gift of Genius* (Boston: Stratford, 1930), and *Narna Darrell* (Boston: Stratford, 1936). The latter is a novel which recounts several centuries of love between various characters named Lucius and various characters named Narna from the time that Lucius, a Roman centurion who lands in the British Isles with Caesar, meets Narna, a "silver—gold"—tressed Druid, until sometime in the future.

7. Lewis Leary, *The Literary Career of Nathaniel Tucker, 1750–1807* (Durham: Duke University Press, 1951), pp. vii-viii.

8. Ibid., p. 91.

9. See Mrs. George P. (Mary H.) Coleman, editor, "Letters from Old Trunks," *Virginia Magazine of History and Biography*, XLIV, No. 1 (January 1936), pp. 25–34.

10. Mrs. George P. (Mary H.) Coleman, editor, "Randolph and Tucker Letters," *Virginia Magazine of History and Biography*, XLII, No. 1 (January 1934), p. 50.

11. Quoted in Turrentine, op. cit., Vol. I, pp. 334–35.

12. See letter from Patrick Henry to William Livingston, February 23, 1786, in *Selections from the Correspondence of the Executive of New Jersey, from 1776–1781* (Newark: Daily Advertiser, 1848), p. 360.

13. The poem was called "On General [Benedict] Arnold." It includes the lines, "Thy crime succeeding ages shall proclaim,/And Judas be forgot, in Arnold's name!" See David Manning White, "Franklin Applauds the Muse," *William and Mary Quarterly*, 3d Series, IV, No. 2 (April 1947), p. 226.

14. Mrs. George P. (Mary H.) Coleman, editor, "Randolph and Tucker Letters," *Virginia Magazine of History and Biography*, XLII, No. 2 (April 1934), p. 130.

15. Days of my youth,
          Ye have glided away;
      Hairs of my youth,
          Ye are frosted and gray;
      Eyes of my youth,
          Your keen sight is no more;
      Cheeks of my youth,
          Ye are furrowed all o'er;
      Strength of my youth,
          All your vigor is gone;
      Thoughts of my youth,
          Your gay visions are flown.

> Days of my youth,
>   I wish not your recall;
> Hairs of my youth,
>   I'm content ye should fall;
> Eyes of my youth,
>   You much evil have seen;
> Cheeks of my youth,
>   Bathed in tears you have been;
> Thoughts of my youth,
>   You have led me astray;
> Strength of my youth,
>   Why lament your decay?
>
> Days of my age,
>   Ye will shortly be past;
> Pains of my age,
>   Yet awhile ye can last;
> Joys of my age,
>   In true wisdom delight;
> Eyes of my age,
>   Be religion your light;
> Thoughts of my age,
>   Dread ye not the cold sod;
> Hopes of my age,
>   Be ye fixed on your God.

Edmund C. Stedman, editor, *An American Anthology, 1787–1900* (Cambridge: Riverside Press, 1900), Vol. I, p. 10.

16. Henry St. George Tucker, "Patrick Henry and St. George Tucker," *University of Pennsylvania Law Review,* LXVII, No. 1 (January 1919), p. 72.

17. William Wirt, Patrick Henry's first biographer, wrote St. George Tucker, August 16, 1815: "I have taken almost entirely, Mr. Henry's speech in the convention of '75 from you, as well as your description of its effect on you verbatim." See "William Wirt's Life of Patrick Henry," *William and Mary Quarterly,* 1st Series, XXII, No. 4 (April 1914), p. 252.

18. See Turrentine, op. cit., Vol. I, p. 89. Tucker's diaries give perhaps the most meticulously accurate account of the Yorktown siege. See Edward M. Riley, "St. George Tucker's Journal of the Siege of Yorktown, 1781," *William and Mary Quarterly,* 3d Series, V, No. 3 (July 1948), pp. 375–95.

19. Mrs. George P. (Mary H.) Coleman, editor, *A Williamsburg Scrap Book* (Richmond: Dietz, 1932), p. 27.

20. See Mrs. George P. (Mary H.) Coleman, editor, *Virginia Silhouettes, Contemporary Letters Concerning Negro Slavery in the State of Virginia* (Richmond: Dietz, 1934), pp. 3–4.

21. Tucker resigned from the Virginia Court of Appeals in 1811 and was appointed to the federal District Court by President Madison in 1813. His resignation from the state court was ostensibly because of an increase in judicial sessions, which would have necessitated his being away from home for long periods. However, there is some evidence that his real reason was a personality conflict with Spencer Roane, an irascible fellow judge, who was also the political boss of the state. See Rex Beach, "Spencer Roane and the Richmond Junto," *William and Mary Quarterly,* 2d Series, XXII, No. 1 (January 1942), pp. 13–16.

22. Quoted in Elizabeth K. Bauer, *Commentaries on the Constitution, 1790–1860* (New York: Columbia University Press, 1952), p. 176.

23. Francis Biddle, *A Casual Past* (Garden City, N.Y.: Doubleday, 1961), p. 34.

24. L. H. Butterfield, editor, *Letters of Benjamin Rush* (Princeton: Princeton University Press, 1951), Vol. II, p. 1042.

25. Quoted in Anna Robeson Burr, *Weir Mitchell, His Life and Letters* (New York: Duffield, 1929), pp. 19–20.

26. Quoted in William Cabell Bruce, *John Randolph of Roanoke* (New York: Putnam's, 1922), Vol. II, p. 267. Mr. Bruce (1860–1946), a Virginian by birth, and a Democratic senator from Maryland between 1923 and 1929, is almost as biased in Randolph's favor as the Henry Adams biography is against him.

27. Judith Randolph's mother wisely objected to her marriage. See letter from Mrs. Anne Randolph to St. George Tucker, September 23, 1788, in "Randolph and Tucker Letters," *Virginia Magazine of History and Biography*, XLII, No. 1 (January 1934), pp. 49–50.

28. See Jay and Audrey Walz, *The Bizarre Sisters* (New York: Duell, Sloan & Pearce, 1950). Bizarre was the name of Richard Randolph's plantation.

29. See William Macfarlane Jones, "Will of Richard Randolph, Jr., of 'Bizarre,'" *Virginia Magazine of History and Biography*, XXXIV, No. 1 (January 1926), pp. 22–26.

30. Quoted in Turrentine, op. cit., Vol. II, p. 484.

31. Quoted in William C. Bruce, op. cit., Vol. II, p. 517.

32. See *Virginia Magazine of History and Biography*, XLVIII, No. 3 (July 1940), p. 241.

33. Quoted in Jay B. Hubbell, "William Wirt and the Familiar Essay in Virginia," *William and Mary Quarterly*, 2d Series, XXIII, No. 2 (April 1943), p. 139.

34. Quoted in Edward Younger, editor, "A Yankee Reports on Virginia, 1842–1843, Letters of John Adams Kasson," *Virginia Magazine of History and Biography*, LVI, No. 4 (October 1948), pp. 415–16. The young student became a noted diplomat and Iowa congressman.

35. See Robert Colin McLean, *George Tucker, Moral Philosopher and Man of Letters* (Chapel Hill: University of North Carolina Press, 1961), p. 22.

36. Vernon L. Parrington, *Main Currents in American Thought* (New York: Harcourt, Brace, 1927–30), Vol. II, p. 35, and letter from Henry St. George Tucker to Nathaniel Beverley Tucker, January 20, 1833, in "Correspondence of Judge Tucker," *William and Mary Quarterly*, 1st Series, XII, No. 2 (October 1903), pp. 89–91.

37. Quoted in William C. Bruce, op. cit., Vol. I, p. 441.

38. See Turrentine, op. cit., Vol. II, pp. 470 and 600.

39. See John Randolph Tucker, "The Judges Tucker of the Court of Appeals of Virginia," *Virginia Law Register*, I, No. 11 (March 1896), p. 802.

40. Quoted in William C. Bruce, op. cit., Vol. I, p. 506.

41. See G. MacLaren Brydon, "The Antiecclesiastical Laws of Virginia," *Virginia Magazine of History and Biography*, LXIV, No. 3 (July 1956), pp. 259–85.

42. See letter from Henry St. George Tucker (1853–1932) in Ephraim Tucker, *Genealogy of the Tucker Family* (Worcester, Mass.: F. S. Blanchard, 1895), p. 326.

43. Quoted in Turrentine, op. cit., Vol. I, p. 424.

44. Ibid., Vol. III, p. 1202.

45. Ibid., Vol. II, p. 537.

46. Quoted in Beverley Randolph Tucker, op. cit., p. 19.

47. See Turrentine, op. cit., Vol. II, p. 961.

48. See Philip Alexander Bruce, *History of the University of Virginia* (New York: Macmillan, 1920), Vol. II, p. 310. The student assassin, Joseph E. Semmes, was released on $25,000 bail. He jumped bail and was never brought to trial.

49. Quoted in Turrentine, op. cit., Vol. II, p. 1262.

50. William C. Bruce, op. cit., Vol. II, pp. 203–4, and Carl Bridenbaugh, "Introduction," Nathaniel Beverley Tucker, *The Partisan Leader* (New York: Knopf, 1933), p xxvi.

51. See John Francis McDermott, "Nathaniel Beverley Tucker in Missouri," *William and Mary Quarterly*, 2d Series, XX, No. 4 (October 1940), p. 507.

52. Quoted in Mary C. Simms Oliphant, Alfred Taylor Odell, and T. C. Duncan Eaves, editors, *The Letters of William Gilmore Simms* (Columbia: University of South Carolina Press, 1952–56), Vol. II, p. 505.

53. See Beverley Randolph Tucker, *S. Weir Mitchell* (Boston: Badger, 1914), pp. 42–43.

54. See Ernest E. Leisy, *The American Historical Novel* (Norman: University of Oklahoma Press, 1950), p. 29, and Bertha Monica Stearns, "The Literary Treatment of Bacon's Rebellion in Virginia," *Virginia Magazine of History and Biography*, LII, No. 3 (July 1944), pp. 173–75.

Tucker's daughter Anne married Lyon G. Tyler (1853–1935) a son of the U. S. President by his second wife; president of William and Mary College, 1888–1919; author, *The Letters and Times of the Tylers* (Richmond: Whillet & Shipperson, 1884–96), and other historical works; and founder, *Tyler's Quarterly Historical and Genealogical Magazine*. See James Southall Wilson, "Lyon Gardiner Tyler," *William and Mary Quarterly*, 2d Series, XV, No. 4 (October 1935), pp. 319–22.

55. See John Beauchamp Jones, *A Rebel War Clerk's Diary*, Howard Swiggett, editor (New York: Old Hickory Bookshop, 1935), Vol. II, pp. 319–20.

56. See Theodore Roscoe, *The Web of Conspiracy, the Complete Story of the Men Who Murdered Abraham Lincoln* (Englewood Cliffs, N.J.: Prentice-Hall, 1959), pp. 449–51.

57. Quoted in Jane Ellis Tucker, *Beverley Tucker, a Memoir by His Wife* (Richmond: Frank Baptist Printing, 1893?), p. 56.

58. See Francis Wilson, *John Wilkes Booth, Fact and Fiction of Lincoln's Assassination* (Boston and New York: Houghton Mifflin, 1929), p. 251.

59. Quoted in Marshall W. Fishwick, *Lee after the War* (New York: Dodd, Mead, 1963), pp. 75–76.

60. Quoted in Jane Ellis Tucker, op. cit., p. 57.

61. Ibid., pp. 48–49.

62. Quoted in Beverley Randolph Tucker, *Tales of the Tuckers*, p. 59.

63. See John W. Davis, "John Randolph Tucker: The Man and His Work," *John Randolph Tucker Lectures* (Lexington, Va., 1952), p. 22.

64. See Beverley Randolph Tucker, *Tales of the Tuckers*, p. 68.

65. See Walter Edward Harris, "John Randolph Tucker," in O. O. Stealey, editor, *Twenty Years in the Press Gallery* (New York: Publishers Printing, 1906), p. 448.

66. See William Alexander MacCorkle, *The Recollections of Fifty Years of West Virginia* (New York: Putnam's, 1928), pp. 473–75.

67. *Report of the Twentieth Annual Meeting of the American Bar Association* (Philadelphia, 1897), p. 555.

68. Quoted in Davis, op. cit., pp. 15–16.

69. See Theodore Clarke Smith, *The Life and Letters of James Abram Garfield* (New Haven: Yale University Press, 1925), Vol. I, p. 589; Beverley Randolph Tucker, *Tales of the Tuckers,* p. 65.

70. Quoted in Davis, op. cit., p. 19.

71. "Industrial Vocational Rehabilitation," *Report No. 164,* U. S. House of Representatives, 68th Congress, 1st Session, February 7, 1924.

72. See Allan Nevins, *Grover Cleveland* (New York: Dodd, Mead, 1962), p. 693; "Memorial Services Held in the House of Representatives of the United States, Together with Remarks Presented in Eulogy of Henry St. George Tucker," *House Document No. 570,* U. S. House of Representatives, 72d Congress, 2d Session, p. 45.

73. Robert T. Taylor, "The Jamestown Tercentennial Exposition of 1907," *Virginia Magazine of History and Biography,* LXV, No. 2 (April 1957), p. 186.

Tucker succeeded General Fitzhugh Lee, the former Virginia governor, who died suddenly in 1905.

74. Quoted in Beverley Randolph Tucker, *Tales of the Tuckers,* pp. 150–51.

75. Quoted in Paschal Reeves. "Thomas S. Martin: Committee Statesman," *Virginia Magazine of History and Biography,* LXVIII, No. 31 (July 1960), p. 363n; also see Virginius Dabney, *Dry Messiah, the Life of Bishop Cannon* (New York: Knopf, 1949), pp. 54–56.

76. Quoted in New York *Times,* July 24, 1932, p. 23.

77. Quoted in Beverley Randolph Tucker, *Tales of the Tuckers,* p. 152.

78. Quoted in Turrentine, op. cit., Vol. I, p. 38.

79. Ibid., Vol. II, pp. 808–9.

80. Ibid., Vol. III, p. 1401n.

81. Quoted in Beverley Randolph Tucker, *Tales of the Tuckers,* p. 121.

82. Beverley Dandridge Tucker, *My Three Loves* (New York and Washington: Neagle, 1910), pp. 74–75. His other volume, *Confederate Memorial Verses* (Norfolk: United Daughters of the Confederacy, 1904), contains a poem in honor of his uncle Ran, John Randolph Tucker.

83. Beverley Randolph Tucker, *Tales of the Tuckers,* pp. 126–27. A slightly different version of this story appears in Cleveland Amory, *The Last Resorts* (New York: Harper, 1952), pp. 54–55.

84. See *Current Biography,* 1943, pp. 774–76; also New York *Times,* February 4, 1948, p. 19; August 9, 1959, p. 88.

85. Quoted in *William and Mary Quarterly,* 1st Series, XVI, No. 2 (October 1907), p. 113.

86. Homer S. Cummings, *Address . . . Delivered at the Dedication of the New Law School Building Erected in Honor of John Randolph Tucker at the Washington and Lee University, Lexington, Virginia, June 11, 1936* (Washington, 1938), p. 6.

THE STOCKTON DYNASTY

1. Quoted in Frank Luther Mott, *A History of American Magazines, 1865–1885* (Cambridge: Harvard University Press, 1957), p. 462.

2. Quoted in Alfred Hoyt Bill, *A House Called Morven* (Princeton: Princeton University Press, 1954), p. 19.

3. See C. H. Hunter, "Morven—The Princeton Home of the Stockton Fam-

ily," *Proceedings of the New Jersey Historical Society*, IX, No. 2 (April 1924), pp. 124–37.

4. L. H. Butterfield, "Annis and the General," *Princeton University Library Chronicle*, VII, No. 1 (November 1945), p. 32.

5. Quoted in L. H. Butterfield, "Morven: A Colonial Outpost of Sensibility," *Princeton University Library Chronicle*, VI, No. 1 (November 1944), p. 13.

6. The compiler of Washington's papers says of the general's last note, "On May 4, 1789 Washington wrote to Mrs. Annis Boudinot Stockton, thanking her, quite briefly, for another of her poems." John C. Fitzpatrick, editor, *The Writings of George Washington* (Washington: Government Printing Office, 1939), XXX, p. 308n.

7. Quoted in Bill, op. cit., p. 27. The letter was from Governor William Franklin of New Jersey.

8. See Richard P. McCormick, "The First Election of Governor William Livingston," *Proceedings of the New Jersey Historical Society*, LXV, No. 2 (April 1947), pp. 92–100.

9. Quoted in Frederick W. Ricord and William Nelson, editors, "Documents Relating to the Colonial History of the State of New Jersey," *Archives of the State of New Jersey* (Newark: Daily Advertiser, 1886), 1st Series, X, p. 429.

10. Quoted in J. J. Boudinot, editor, *The Life, Public Services, Addresses and Letters of Elias Boudinot* (Boston and New York: Houghton Mifflin, 1896), Vol. I, p. 89.

11. L. H. Butterfield, editor, *Letters of Benjamin Rush* (Princeton: Princeton University Press, 1951), Vol. I, p. 123.

12. The Act of Congress, January 3, 1777, reads:

"*Whereas*, Congress hath received information that the honorable Richard Stockton, Esq. of New Jersey, and a member of this Congress, hath been made a prisoner by the enemy, and that he has been ignominiously thrown into a common gaol, and there detained;

"*Resolved*, That General Washington be directed to make immediate inquiry into the truth of this report, and if he finds reason to believe it well founded, that he send a flag of truce to General Howe, remonstrating against this departure from humane procedure that has marked the conduct of these states to prisoners, who have fallen into their hands; and to know of General Howe, whether he chuses that this shall be the future rule for treating all such, on both sides, as the fortune of war may place in the hands of either party."

Quoted in Thomas C. Stockton, *The Stockton Family of New Jersey and Other Stocktons* (Washington: Carnahan Press, 1911), pp. 38–39.

13. Bill, op. cit., p. 41; also see Charles Leonard Lundin, *Cockpit of the Revolution, the War for Independence in New Jersey* (Princeton: Princeton University Press, 1940), p. 161.

14. *Letters of Benjamin Rush*, Vol. I, p. 126.

15. Quoted in L. H. Butterfield, "Morven: Colonial Outpost of Sensibility," op. cit., p. 5.

16. George W. Corner, editor, *The Autobiography of Benjamin Rush* (Princeton: Princeton University Press, 1948), p. 147.

17. Bill, op. cit., p. 67.

18. See Robert C. Hallock, "Historic Old Tennent," *Proceedings of the New Jersey Historical Society*, 2d Series, IX (1886–87), pp. 235–43.

19. Mabel Lorenz Ives, *Home of Richard Stockton* (Upper Montclair, N.J.: Lucy Fortune, 1932), p. 4; also George Adams Boyd, *Elias Boudinot,*

Patriot and Statesman, 1740–1821 (Princeton: Princeton University Press, 1952), p. 253.

20. Elias Boudinot, *Memoirs to the Life of the Rev. William Tennent* (New York: W. Alexander, 1822), pp. 25 and 31. Later Tennent claimed another divine intercession. While he was standing trial for perjury, two witnesses suddenly showed up with evidence to acquit him: both stating that they had been directed to the courthouse by a vision in their dreams. However, Richard Stockton Field, a distinguished lawyer, looked into the case and concluded that there was a more natural cause for their appearance. See Richard Stockton Field, "Review of the Trial of the Rev. Wm. Tennent for Perjury in 1742," *Proceedings of the New Jersey Historical Society*, VI (1853).

21. Susanna Stockton Pintard was also the grandmother of George Dashiell Bayard (1835–62), the Civil War general killed in action at the battle of Fredericksburg. See Bayard Dynasty, pp. 273–98.

22. Boyd, op. cit., p. 110; also see Robert V. Hoffman, *The Revolutionary Scene in New Jersey* (New York: American Historical Co., 1942), p. 21.

23. Boyd, op. cit., p. 90.

24. J. J. Boudinot, op. cit., Vol. I, p. 180. For some of Boudinot's espionage exploits, see John Bakeless, *Turncoats, Traitors and Heroes* (Philadelphia: Lippincott, 1959), Chapter XIII.

25. See Milton Halsey Thomas, editor, *Elias Boudinot's Journey to Boston in 1809* (Princeton: Princeton University Library, 1955), p. x.

26. The following is the genealogy of the Bradford family (not related to William Bradford, the Pilgrim Father):

William Bradford (1663–1752)
Arrived in America, 1685; began
the first newspaper in New York, 1725

|

Andrew Bradford (1686–1742)
Began the first newspaper in
Philadelphia, 1719

|

(adopted son)

|

William Bradford (1722–91)
Known as the "patriot printer of 1776";
at fifty-six years of age he enlisted in the
Revolutionary Army; severely wounded at
the battle of Princeton

Thomas (1745–1838)
Innovator of the financial
page and the book page in
modern journalism

William (1755–95)
Attorney General of
Pennsylvania at 25;
U.S. Attorney General,
1794–95
m. *Susan Boudinot*
(1764–1854)
(no issue)

Rachel (1764–1805)
m. *Judge Elisha
Boudinot* (1749–1819),
brother of Elias
Boudinot

For an account of the Bradfords' publishing careers before the Revolution, see Arthur M. Schlesinger, *Prelude to Independence: The Newspaper War on Britain, 1764–1776* (New York: Knopf, 1958).

27. Quoted in James Grant Wilson, "Andrew Kirkpatrick," *Proceedings of the New Jersey Historical Society,* 2d Series, II (1870–72), p. 95.

28. *Letters of Benjamin Rush,* Vol. I, p. 328.

29. Ibid., Vol. I, p. 327.

30. Ibid., Vol. II, p. 1215. Italics in original.

31. Ibid., Vol. I, p. 513.

32. Ibid., Vol. II, p. 797. The treasurer of the Mint was little more than a bookkeeper; an assistant signed most of the receipts for Rush.

33. Ibid., Vol. II, pp. 1211–12.

34. Quoted in Boyd, op. cit., p. 247.

35. *Letters of Benjamin Rush,* Vol. II, pp. 1041–42.

36. *The Autobiography of Benjamin Rush,* p. 162.

37. Quoted in William Cabell Bruce, *John Randolph of Roanoke* (New York: Putnam's, 1922), Vol. II, p. 200.

38. See Gertrude B. Biddle and Sarah D. Lowrie, editors, *Notable Women of Pennsylvania* (Philadelphia: University of Pennsylvania Press, 1942), pp. 131–32.

39. Elizabeth Ellet, *The Queens of American Society* (New York: Scribner's, 1867), p. 363.

40. Ibid., pp. 365–69.

41. Quoted in *Dictionary of American Biography,* Vol. XVI, p. 231. In 1964 the Ridgway branch of the Philadelphia Library Company, at Broad and Christian streets, was purchased by the city to be redeveloped as a recreational facility.

42. Richard Stockton (1764–1828) married Mary Field, the sister of his brother-in-law Robert Field.

43. See Walter R. Fee, *The Transition from Aristocracy to Democracy in New Jersey, 1789–1829* (Somerville, N.J.: Somerset Press, 1933), p. 130.

44. Bill, op. cit., p. 74.

45. Ibid., p. 85.

46. Josiah Quincy, *Figures of the Past from the Leaves of Old Journals* (Boston: Little, Brown, 1926), p. 192. This Josiah Quincy (1802–82) was mayor of Boston from 1845 to 1849; his father, Josiah Quincy (1772–1862), was mayor of Boston (1823–28) and president of Harvard (1829–45); and his grandson, Josiah Quincy (1859–1919), was also mayor of Boston (1895–99).

47. Writes Frank R. Stockton, "It is said that at one time he [Commodore Stockton] challenged all the [British] officers in Gibraltar to meet him in single combat, one after another, and he actually did engage in duels with several of them." *Stories of New Jersey* (New Brunswick: Rutgers University Press, 1961), p. 247.

48. Quincy, op. cit., p. 193.

49. The explosion on the U.S.S. *Princeton,* while cruising on the Potomac River, February 15, 1844, also injured Senator Thomas Hart Benton of Missouri. The injury, thought Andrew Jackson, affected the senator's mind. See Eugene H. Roseboom, *A History of Presidential Elections* (New York: Macmillan, 1957), p. 129.

50. J. Elfreth Watkins. *The Camden and Amboy Railroad* (Washington: Gedney & Roberts, 1892), p. 20.

51. The most careful student of the Camden and Amboy Railroad does not

believe that this meeting took place. However, he adds: "This is not questioning the fact that quid pro quo agreement was secured. . . ." George L. A. Reilly, *The Camden and Amboy Railroad in New Jersey Politics, 1830–1871* (Unpublished Ph.D. dissertation, Columbia University, 1952), p. 21.

52. Ibid., p. 35.

53. Ibid., p. 37.

54. Ibid., p. 194.

55. Samuel J. Bayard, *A Sketch of the Life of Com. Robert F. Stockton* (New York: Derby and Jackson, 1856), p. 206; also see Robert Field Stockton, *Speech . . . on the Past, Present and Future of the American Party* (Camden: J. H. Jones, 1859).

56. Irving S. Kull, editor, *New Jersey, a History* (New York: American Historical Society, 1930–32), Vol. III, p. 757.

57. Reilly, op. cit., p. 97.

58. Quoted in Eric L. McKitrick, *Andrew Johnson and Reconstruction* (Chicago: University of Chicago Press, 1960), p. 321n.

59. Ibid., p. 323.

60. Ibid., p. 323n.

61. Quoted in George H. Haynes, *The Senate of the United States* (Boston: Houghton Mifflin, 1938), Vol. I, p. 32n. "The Stockton law" specified that "on the second Tuesday after organization of a legislature when a Senator from that State is to be elected, the two houses shall meet separately, and by a *viva-voce* name a person for Senator. On the following day, the two houses shall meet in joint assembly, and the results of the voting shall be canvassed. If each house has given a majority vote to the same candidate, he shall be declared elected; if not, 'the joint assembly shall meet at twelve o'clock, meridian, of each succeeding day during the session of the legislature, and take at least one vote until a Senator shall be elected.'"

62. Edward Spencer, *An Outline of the Public Life and Services of Thomas F. Bayard* (New York: Appleton, 1880), p. 41.

63. Quoted in Reilly, op. cit., p. 232.

64. The Stocktons continued their tradition of public service on a minor scale in the twentieth century. A grandson of the commodore, Bayard Stockton (1853–1928), served as Mercer County prosecutor for two terms; his son Richard (1885–1943) was an assistant attorney general of New Jersey for many years. But the latter's son, Bayard Stockton III (1912–   ), writes, "I was never interested in politics and even if I was I didn't have the education or enough public speaking to carry it out." (He is a liquor company executive, who served at one time as coach of the Princeton junior varsity football team.) See New York *Times*, May 19, 1928, p. 13; letter from Bayard Stockton III, June 3, 1965; *Who's Who in the East, 1962–63*, p. 879.

65. One's signature on the Declaration of Independence has had a way of blotting out less attractive qualities. For example, see Dorothy Horton McGee, *Famous Signers of the Declaration* (New York: Dodd, Mead, 1956), pp. 121–28, and Grace C. Gallaher, "New Jersey Signers of the Declaration of Independence," *Daughters of the American Revolution Magazine*, August–September 1964, pp. 685, 688, 723, 737.

THE LONG DYNASTY

1. Quoted in Carleton Beals, *The Story of Huey P. Long* (Philadelphia: Lippincott, 1935), p. 218.

2. Quoted in Stan Opotowsky, *The Longs of Louisiana* (New York: Dutton, 1960), p. 232.

3. Quoted in Thomas Martin, *Dynasty: The Longs of Louisiana* (New York: Putnam's, 1960), p. 193.

4. Quoted in *Real America*, October 1933, p. 52.

5. Harnett T. Kane, *Louisiana Hayride, the American Rehearsal for Dictatorship, 1928–1940* (New York: Morrow, 1941), p. 36.

6. Hugh Mercer Blain, editor, *Favorite Huey Long Stories* (Baton Rouge: O. Claitor, 1937), pp. 26–27.

7. Huey P. Long, *Every Man a King* (New Orleans: National Book Co., 1933), p. 3.
This "autobiography," according to Hermann B. Deutsch, columnist for the New Orleans *Times-Picayune*, was written by Huey in collaboration with John Klorer, then editor of Long's weekly *American Progress*. See Deutsch, *The Huey Long Murder Case* (Garden City, N.Y.: Doubleday, 1963), pp. 8–9.

8. T. Harry Williams, "The Gentleman from Louisiana: Demagogue or Democrat," *Journal of Southern History*, XXVI, No. 1 (February 1960), p. 6.

9. Fred Hamlin, *Land of Liberty, Being an Informal History of the Common People and Their Heroes* (New York: Crowell, 1947), p. 265.

10. Hilda Phelps Hammond, *Let Freedom Ring* (New York: Farrar and Rinehart, 1936), pp. 38–39.

11. Quoted in James Rorty, "Callie Long's Boy Huey," *Forum*, August 1935, p. 78.

12. A. J. Liebling, *The Earl of Louisiana* (New York: Simon & Schuster, 1961), p. 8.

13. See Hodding Carter, "Huey Long: American Dictator," in Isabel Leighton, editor, *The Aspirin Age, 1919–1941* (New York: Simon & Schuster, 1949), p. 347. (Originally published as "Huey Long's Louisiana Hayride," *American Mercury*, LXVIII, No. 304 [April 1949], pp. 435–47); also see Kane, op. cit., p. 48.

14. (John Franklin Carter), *American Messiahs by the Unofficial Observer* (New York: Simon & Schuster, 1935), p. 28.

15. Beals, op. cit., p. 14.

16. John Gunther, *Inside U.S.A.*, Revised edition (New York: Harper, 1951), pp. 893–95.

17. See Williams, op. cit., p. 21. It is interesting that generally it has been the journalists who have taken the "dictator" view of Long, while part of the academic community is now viewing him as the "social reformer." Professor Williams' thesis, which goes furthest toward sanitizing Long, was given as his presidential address before the Southern Historical Association, meeting at Atlanta, Georgia, November 12, 1959.

18. See V. O. Key, Jr., *Southern Politics* (New York: Knopf, 1949), p. 164 (Vintage Books edition).

19. Kane, op. cit., p. 33.

20. Ibid., p. 62.

21. Long, op. cit., opposite title page.

22. Hamilton Basso, *Mainstream* (New York: Reynal and Hitchcock, 1943), pp. 191–92.

23. Kane, op. cit., p. 40.

24. Long, op. cit., p. 77.

25. Allan P. Sindler, *Huey Long's Louisiana* (Baltimore: Johns Hopkins

Press, 1956), pp. 49–50, states that Long was defeated not by weather but by the religious issue—two Protestants were competing against one Catholic.

26. Beals, op. cit., p. 205: Opotowsky, op. cit., p. 93.

27. Opotowsky, op. cit., p. 96.

28. Kane, op. cit., p. 81.

29. Long, op. cit., p. 195.

30. Beals, op. cit., pp. 176–77.

31. See Long, op. cit., pp. 264–65; Beals, op. cit., p. 209; Kane, op. cit., p. 80.

32. Martin, op. cit., p. 45.

33. Reinhard H. Luthin, *American Demagogues* (Boston: Beacon, 1954), pp. 224–25.

34. Edward J. Flynn, *You're the Boss* (New York: Viking, 1947), p. 96.

35. John Franklin Carter, op. cit., p. 18.

36. Raymond Moley, *27 Masters of Politics* (New York: Funk and Wagnalls, 1949), p. 221.

37. Kane, op. cit., p. 137.

38. Long, op. cit., p. 201.

39. For a summary of the charges, see Opotowsky, op. cit., pp. 48–49.

40. Sindler, op. cit., p. 65.

41. Long, op. cit., p. 172.

42. For the Constitutional League's list of Huey Long's relatives on the state payroll, see Webster Smith, *The Kingfish, a Biography of Huey P. Long* (New York: Putnam's, 1933), pp. 182–84.

43. Beals, op. cit., p. 195.

44. Martin, op. cit., p. 48.

45. *Time*, February 2, 1948, p. 13.

46. Opotowsky, op. cit., pp. 231–32.

47. Martin, op. cit., p. 115.

48. Burton K. Wheeler with Paul F. Healy, *Yankee from the West* (Garden City, N.Y.: Doubleday, 1962), p. 285; Flynn, op. cit., p. 101.

49. Martin, op. cit., p. 138.

50. Alice Roosevelt Longworth, "Strange Bedfellows," *Ladies' Home Journal*, October 1935, p. 44. Later she wrote, "Huey Long had charm. No matter how despicable and dangerous you knew him to be, there it was, something to be reckoned with." Alice Roosevelt Longworth, "What's the Matter with Bob Taft?" *Saturday Evening Post*, May 4, 1940, p. 89.

51. Luthin, op. cit., p. 254; Edwin P. Hoyt, *The Tempering Years* (New York: Scribner's, 1963), p. 200; quoted in Deutsch, op. cit., p. 34.

52. Kane, op. cit., p. 101; Hodding Carter, op. cit., p. 353; Williams, op. cit., p. 18.

53. Kane, op. cit., p. 128.

54. John Franklin Carter, op. cit., p. 22; James J. A. Fortier, editor, *Huey Pierce Long, "The Martyr of the Age"* (New Orleans: T. J. Moran's, 1937), p. 35; David H. Zinman, *The Day Huey Long Was Shot* (New York: Obolensky, 1963), p. 37; Opotowsky, op. cit., p. 74.

55. Huey P. Long, *My First Days in the White House* (Harrisburg, Pa.: Telegraph Press, 1935), p. 18.

56. See Donald R. McCoy, *Angry Voices, Left-of-Center Politics in the New Deal Era* (Lawrence: University of Kansas Press, 1958), p. 70; James A. Farley, *Jim Farley's Story* (New York: Whittlesey House, 1948), p. 51; also

see Harold L. Ickes, *The Secret Diary of Harold L. Ickes* (New York: Simon and Schuster, 1953), Vol. I, p. 462.

57. Hodding Carter, op. cit., p. 343.

58. Quoted in Luthin, op. cit., p. 259.

59. Senate Document No. 59, 88th Congress, 2d Session, *Memorial Addresses in the Congress of the United States and Tributes in Eulogy of John Fitzgerald Kennedy* (Washington, 1964), p. 199.

60. Luthin, op. cit., p. 262; Martin, op. cit., p. 86.

61. House Document No. 480, 74th Congress, 2d Session, *Memorial Services Held in the House of Representatives of the United States, Together with Remarks Presented in Eulogy of Huey Pierce Long* (Washington, 1936), p. 50. Russell Long later said of Smith's oration, "It was a political speech to himself." Zinman, op. cit., p. 190.

62. Forrest Davis, *Huey Long, a Candid Biography* (New York: Dodge, 1935), postscript p. 1.

63. Zinman, op. cit., after title page.

64. Sindler, op. cit., p. 86n.

65. Davis, op. cit., postscript p. 3.

66. Deutsch, op. cit., p. 177.

67. See Frank J. Wilson as told to Howard Whitman, "The Kingfish Gets Hooked," *Collier's*, May 17, 1947, p. 92; Elmer L. Irey and William J. Slocum, "The End of the Kingfish," in Lewis W. Gillenson, editor, *Fabulous Yesterday* (New York: Harper, 1961), p. 217. (Reprinted from *Coronet*, January 1948.)

68. Deutsch, op. cit., p. 178.

69. Kane, op. cit., p. 140.

70. Julius T. Long, "What I Know About My Brother, Senator Huey P. Long," *Real America*, September 1933, p. 39.

71. John Franklin Carter, op. cit., p. 6.

72. Opotowsky, op. cit., p. 237.

73. Kane, op. cit., p. 153.

74. Martin, op. cit., p. 153.

75. Ibid., p. 190.

76. Sindler, op. cit., p. 122.

77. Deutsch, op. cit., p. 138.

78. Sindler, op. cit., p. 128.

79. Martin, op. cit., p. 161.

80. Sindler, op. cit., p. 136.

81. Kane, op. cit., p. 261.

82. *Time*, August 30, 1948, p. 16.

83. See Liebling, op. cit., p. 122; Kane, op. cit., p. 290; Opotowsky, op. cit., pp. 154 and 140. "He [Earl] is motivated partly by a rivalry with Huey's ghost," writes Irving Ferman, "Louisiana Side-Show," *New Republic*, January 21, 1952, p. 14.

84. Sindler, op. cit., p. 144.

85. Opotowsky, op. cit., p. 128.

86. Sindler, op. cit., p. 137.

87. Kane, op. cit., p. 288.

88. Ibid., p. 434.

89. Sindler, op. cit., p. 148.

90. Kane, op. cit., p. 430; *Time*, January 29, 1940, p. 24: "Governor Earl Long wrapped the mantle of Huey around him, with some opponents saying he had no right to wear it and some saying it was no mantle."

91. Opotowsky, op. cit., p. 195.

92. *Time*, August 30, 1948, p. 16.

93. Liebling, op. cit., p. 191.

94. Quoted in Martin, op. cit., p. 194.

95. Opotowsky, op. cit., p. 233.

96. See George M. Leppert, "Long Live the Kingfishes!" *American Mercury*, LXXXIII, No. 393 (October 1956), p. 99.

97. *Memorial Services Held in the House of Representatives and Senate of the United States, Together with Remarks Presented in Eulogy of George Shannon Long* (Washington, 1958), pp. 42 and 40.

98. Opotowsky, op. cit., p. 233.

99. Martin, op. cit., p. 288.

100. *Time*, July 13, 1959, p. 16.

101. Rorty, op. cit., p. 78.

102. Martin, op. cit., p. 201.

103. Harnett T. Kane, "Louisiana Story: End of a Chapter," *New York Times Magazine*, September 27, 1959, p. 32; also see Thomas B. Morgan, "Blaze Starr in Nighttown," *Esquire*, July 1964, p. 62.

104. Blanche Long, "His Wife's Story of the Commitment," *Life*, June 15, 1959, p. 36.

105. Martin, op. cit., p. 283.

106. Earl Mazo, "Louisiana's Latest Long," New York *Herald Tribune*, March 11, 1962, Sec. 2, p. 3.

107. Washington *Post*, December 9, 1963, p. A4 (UPI).

108. Interview with Gillis Long, April 14, 1964, Washington, D.C.

109. Quoted in Wesley Pruden, Jr., "The Longs of Louisiana," *National Observer*, December 7, 1964, p. 18.

110. Ibid., p. 1.

111. Interview with Speedy Long, January 8, 1965, Washington, D.C.

112. Quoted in Opotowsky, op. cit., p. 235.

113. *Congressman Gillis Long Reports*, July 1964, p. 1.

114. Interview with Gillis Long, August 10, 1964, Washington, D.C.

115. Quoted in Emile Comar, "Speedy Long, the Redneck Spellbinder," New Orleans *Clarion Herald*, July 30, 1964.

116. Quoted in Cabell Phillips, "The Lengthening Shadow of Huey Long," *New York Times Magazine*, November 7, 1948, p. 14.

117. Ibid, p. 79.

118. Quoted in *Time*, February 8, 1963, p. 17.

119. Quoted in Jerome S. Cahill, "How Sen. Long Engineered the Tax Bill to Victory," Philadelphia *Inquirer*, February 16, 1964, "Today's World" section, p. 2.

120. The majority whip is the assistant leader, ranking next to the majority leader in the party's Senate hierarchy. He serves as acting majority leader when the majority leader is absent, keeps track of his colleagues' positions on issues, lines up support for party programs, and tries to assure that party members will be on the Senate floor when critical votes are taken.

121. Washington *Post*, December 12, 1964, p. A1.

122. See William S. White, "Democrats' Whip," Washington *Post*, December 16, 1964, p. A27.

123. See Rowland Evans and Robert Novak, "Kingfish Jr.," Washington *Post*, January 11, p. A13.

124. See New York *Times*, April 28, 1964, p. 36.

THE LODGE DYNASTY

1. The original cod-Cabot-God quatrain was given as a toast in 1905 at the twenty-fifth reunion of the Harvard Class of 1880:

> Here's to old Massachusetts,
> The home of the sacred cod,
> Where the Adamses vote for Douglas,
> And the Cabots walk with God.

Five years later John Collins Bossidy read the verse's most famous variant before a Midwestern dinner of the Holy Cross College alumni. And a later Boston court decision, allowing a man name Kabotznick to change his name to Cabot, inspired a new batch of parodies:

> And this is good old Boston,
> The home of the bean and the cod,
> Where the Lowells have no one to talk to,
> 'Cause the Cabots talk Yiddish, by God!
> > (anonymous newspaper poet)

> Then here's to the city of Boston,
> The town of the cries and the groans,
> Where the Cabots can't see the Kabotschniks,
> And the Cabots won't speak to the Cohns.
> > (Franklin P. Adams)

See Karl Schriftgiesser, *The Gentleman from Massachusetts: Henry Cabot Lodge* (Boston: Little, Brown, 1944), pp. 199n–200n; Cleveland Amory, *The Proper Bostonians* (New York: Dutton, 1947), p. 35; Leigh White, "He Runs the Show for Ike," *Saturday Evening Post*, May 31, 1952, p. 18.

2. John A. Garraty, *Henry Cabot Lodge* (New York: Knopf, 1953), p. 61.

3. James Michael Curley, *I'd Do It Again* (Englewood Cliffs, N.J.: Prentice-Hall, 1957), p. 298.

4. Mary Caroline Crawford, *Famous Families of Massachusetts* (Boston: Little, Brown, 1930), Vol. I, p. 157n.

5. Quoted in Schriftgiesser, op. cit., p. 7.

6. Samuel Griswold Goodrich, *Recollections of a Lifetime* (New York: Miller, Orton and Mulligan, 1856), Vol. II, p. 37. Goodrich (1793–1860), writing under the name of Peter Parley, was a prolific author of children's stories, whose books sold seven million copies. He met Cabot in 1814 at the Hartford Convention to which Cabot and Goodrich's uncle were delegates.

7. "His firm and many others in Massachusetts, benefited by an act which he framed and put through Congress, in February, 1797, granting a bounty . . . to vessels engaging in the codfish industry. . . ." Crawford, op. cit., Vol. I, p. 164n.

8. Henry Adams, "Lodge's Cabot," *Nation*, July 5, 1877, p. 13.

9. Henry Cabot Lodge, Sr., *Life and Letters of George Cabot* (Boston: Little, Brown, 1877), p. 302.

10. Quoted in Page Smith, *John Adams* (Garden City, N.Y.: Doubleday, 1962), p. 913.

11. Quoted in Henry Adams, *History of the United States During the Administrations of Jefferson and Madison* (Englewood Cliffs, N.J.: Prentice-

Hall, 1963), abridged by George Dangerfield and Otey M. Scruggs, Vol. II, p. 144.

12. Ibid., p. 137.

13. See Samuel Flagg Bemis, *John Quincy Adams and the Union* (New York: Knopf, 1956), p. 95.

14. (Clinton W. Gilbert), *The Mirrors of Washington* (New York: Putnam's, 1921), p. 131.

15. William Lawrence, *Henry Cabot Lodge* (Boston and New York: Houghton Mifflin, 1925), pp. 15–16. Lawrence, who was a Harvard classmate and lifelong friend of Lodge, became Episcopal bishop of Massachusetts.

16. See John A. Garraty, "Spoiled Child of American Politics," *American Heritage*, August 1955, pp. 55–59.

17. See Charles H. Davis, Jr., *Life of Charles Henry Davis, Rear Admiral, 1807–1877*, (Boston and New York: Houghton Mifflin, 1899). The biography was written by his son.

Mrs. Lodge had another sister, Louisa Minot Davis (1860–1907), who married the son of Admiral Stephen Bleecker Luce (1827–1917), a commandant of the Naval Academy, first president of the Naval War College, and a strong supporter of the theories of A. T. Mahon.

18. Mrs. Winthrop Chanler, *Roman Spring* (Boston: Little, Brown, 1935), p. 192–93.

19. Arthur Wallace Dunn, *Gridiron Nights* (New York: Frederick A. Stokes, 1915), p. 277.

20. Garraty, *Henry Cabot Lodge*, p. 101.

21. Charles S. Groves, *Henry Cabot Lodge, the Statesman* (Boston: Small, Maynard, 1925), pp. 137–38.

22. See Worthington Chauncey Ford, editor, *Letters of Henry Adams* (Boston and New York: Houghton Mifflin, 1930), Vol. I, p. 228; Henry Cabot Lodge, Sr., *Early Memories* (New York: Scribner's, 1913), p. 241.

23. *Letters of Henry Adams*, Vol. II, p. 77.

24. See Ernest Samuels, *Henry Adams, the Major Phase* (Cambridge: Harvard University Press, 1964), p. 240.

25. Groves, op. cit., pp. 136–37.

26. Lawrence, op. cit., p. 39.

27. Henry Cabot Lodge, Sr., editor, *Selections from the Correspondence of Theodore Roosevelt and Henry Cabot Lodge* (New York: Scribner's, 1925), Vol. I, p. 179.

28. Ibid., Vol. I, p. 25.

29. Edward G. Lowry, *Washington Close-ups* (Boston and New York: Houghton Mifflin, 1921), p. 184; also see Van Wyck Brooks, *New England: Indian Summer* (New York: Dutton, 1940), pp. 423–24.

30. Henry Adams, *The Education of Henry Adams* (New York, 1931), p. 420. (Modern Library edition.)

31. Crawford, op. cit., p. 83n.

32. Harold Dean Cater, editor, *Henry Adams and His Friends; a Collection of Unpublished Letters* (Boston and New York: Houghton Mifflin, 1947), p. 579.

33. See Aline B. Saarinen, *The Proud Possessors* (New York: Random House, 1958), pp. 25–55; Amory, op. cit., pp. 129–38; Mrs. Winthrop Chanler, *Autumn in the Valley* (Boston: Little, Brown, 1936), pp. 35–42; Morris Carter, *Isabella Stewart Gardner and Fenway Court* (Boston and New York: Houghton Mifflin, 1925), pp. 48–49.

34. Mrs. Constance (Lodge) Gardner, *Augustus Peabody Gardner* (Cambridge: Privately printed, 1919), p. 20.

35. *Reception and Dinner in Honor of the Fifth-sixth Birthday of Augustus Peabody Gardner, a Pioneer for Preparedness, by the Roosevelt Club* (Boston, 1921), p. 6.

36. *Letters of Henry Adams*, Vol. II, p. 398.

37. "The Reminiscences of Robert Lincoln O'Brien," pp. 104 and 107. Oral History Research Office, Columbia University. O'Brien was Washington correspondent for the Boston *Transcript*, 1895–1906; editor, 1906–10; editor and publisher of the Boston *Herald*, 1910–28.

38. James W. Wadsworth, "Henry Cabot Lodge, a Massachusetts Institution," in Albert Bushnell Hart, editor, *American History Told by Contemporaries* (New York: Macmillan, 1929), Vol. V, p. 528. Wadsworth was a U.S. senator from New York at the time this was written.

39. Quoted in Clara Longworth de Chambrun, *The Making of Nicholas Longworth* (New York: Ray Long and Richard R. Smith, 1933), p. 198.

40. *Selections from the Correspondence of Theodore Roosevelt and Henry Cabot Lodge*, Vol. I, p. 142. Italics in original.

41. "The Reminiscences of Robert Lincoln O'Brien," op. cit., p. 107.

42. Chanler, *Autumn in the Valley*, pp. 279–80; also see New York *Times*, December 31, 1942, p. 15, and *National Cyclopedia of American Biography*, Vol. XXXII, p. 409.

43. Edith Wharton, *A Backward Glance* (New York: Scribner's, 1964), p. 149.

44. "The Reminiscences of Robert Lincoln O'Brien," op. cit., p. 107.

45. Edmund Wilson, *The Shock of Recognition* (New York: Farrar, Straus and Cudahy, 1955), p. 742; Brooks, op. cit., p. 458.

46. Quoted in Garraty, *Henry Cabot Lodge*, pp. 271–72.

47. Quoted in *Letters of Henry Adams*, Vol. II, p. 552n; Chanler, *Roman Spring*, pp. 292–93.

48. Quoted in Henry Adams, *The Life of George Cabot Lodge* (Boston and New York: Houghton Mifflin, 1911), p. 96.

49. See *contra*, Samuels, op. cit., p. 510: "Adams did his young friend the justice to take his work seriously and he tried to explicate its major achievements with critical penetration. . . . The reader of the memoir cannot help but come away with a sense of the true magnitude of the young poet's achievement."

50. Cater, op. cit., pp. 760–61; also p. 767.

51. Interview with John Davis Lodge, August 8, 1964, Washington, D.C.

52. See Kenneth W. Hechler, *Insurgency, Personalities and Politics of the Taft Era* (New York: Russell & Russell, 1964), p. 196.

53. Quoted in Alice Roosevelt Longworth, *Crowded Hours* (New York: Scribner's, 1934), p. 239.

54. Gardner, op. cit., p. 24.

55. Ibid., p. 22.

56. Quoted in Garraty, *Henry Cabot Lodge*, p. 328.

57. Quoted in John Henry Cutler, *"Honey Fitz"* (Indianapolis: Bobbs-Merrill, 1962), p. 210.

58. See Garraty, *Henry Cabot Lodge*, pp. 329–32.

59. Henry Cabot Lodge, Jr., "Lessons from a Historic Debate," *New York Times Magazine*, January 30, 1944, p. 38; also see Henry Cabot Lodge, Jr., "Grandson Backs His Elder," *Life*, September 14, 1953, pp. 181–82.

60. Quoted in Gene Smith, *When the Cheering Stopped* (New York: Morrow, 1964), p. 59.

61. Quoted in Schriftgiesser, op. cit., p. 351. When Senator Watson of Indiana told Lodge that he didn't think the League could be defeated, Lodge replied, "Ah, my dear James, I do not propose to try to beat it by direct frontal attack, but by the indirect method of reservations." Quoted in Gene Smith, op. cit., p. 118; also see Alice Roosevelt Longworth, op. cit., p. 295.

62. L. Vernon Briggs, *History and Genealogy of the Cabot Family, 1475–1927* (Boston: C. E. Goodspeed, 1927), Vol. II, p. 649; Crawford, op. cit., Vol. I, p. 193n.

63. H. L. Mencken, *A Mencken Chrestomathy* (New York: Knopf, 1949), p. 408. (Reprinted from the Baltimore *Evening Sun,* June 15, 1920.)

64. H. L. Mencken, *A Carnival of Buncombe,* Malcolm Moos, editor, (Baltimore: Johns Hopkins Press, 1956), p. 19. (Reprinted from the Baltimore *Evening Sun,* September 13, 1920.)

Senator Wadsworth, however, stoutly denied that Lodge and the "senatorial cabal" picked Harding. "I know positively that they never got together on anything in the way of a program for the nomination of a President or a Vice President," he said. "If there ever was a crowd of men who behaved like a bunch of chickens with their heads off it was these alleged conspirators who gathered in this smoke filled room." "The Reminiscences of James W. Wadsworth," pp. 271 and 277. Oral History Research Office, Columbia University. See *contra,* Francis Russell, *The Great Interlude* (New York: McGraw-Hill, 1964), p. 56.

65. See Joe Martin as told to Robert Donovan, *My First Fifty Years in Politics* (New York: McGraw-Hill, 1960), p. 44.

66. See Schriftgiesser, op. cit., p. 218n.

67. Quoted in Garraty, *Henry Cabot Lodge,* p. 422.

68. See Henry A. Zeiger, *The Remarkable Henry Cabot Lodge* (New York: Popular Library, 1964), p. 23.

69. John Mason Brown, *Through These Men* (New York: Harper, 1956), pp. 153 and 143. (Reprinted from *Saturday Review,* July 11 and July 18, 1953.)

70. Gloria Braggiotti, *Born in a Crowd* (New York: Crowell, 1957), p. 239.

71. "The Reminiscences of Robert Lincoln O'Brien," op. cit., pp. 109–10.

72. Bill Davidson, "Brother Act," *Collier's,* January 18, 1947, p. 65.

73. Quoted in Garraty, *Henry Cabot Lodge,* pp. 422–23.

74. See New York *Times,* July 23, 1960, p. 38.

75. New York *Times,* August 20, 1929, p. 20; September 15, 1929, p. 30.

76. See Braggiotti, op. cit., p. 56.

77. Ibid., p. 239.

78. Boston *Transcript,* December 10, 1932, p. 2.

79. Quoted in Rufus Jarman, "You Can't Beat a Lodge," *Saturday Evening Post,* March 15, 1947, p. 140.

80. Curley, op. cit., pp. 297–98.

81. Joseph F. Dinneen, *The Purple Shamrock* (New York: Norton, 1949), p. 245.

82. Quoted in Leigh White, op. cit., p. 19.

83. New York *Times,* January 7, 1938, p. 5.

84. Quoted in Davidson, op. cit., p. 63.

85. Marya Mannes, "Candidate from the U.N.," *Reporter,* October 27, 1960, p. 25.

86. Quoted in Leigh White, op. cit., p. 19.

87. Ibid., p. 49.

88. Clay Blair, Jr., "The Evolution of Cabot Lodge," *Saturday Evening Post*, October 22, 1960, p. 113.

89. New York *Times*, October 27, 1940, IX, p. 6.

90. Quoted in Zeiger, op. cit., pp. 71–72.

91. See William V. Shannon, *The American Irish* (New York: Macmillan, 1963), pp. 339–42, 358–59.

92. Quoted in Brown, op. cit., p. 152.

93. Quoted in John Hohenberg, "Ambassador Lodge: Our UN Salesman," *Coronet*, February 1954, pp. 119–20.

94. Arthur H. Vandenberg, Jr., editor, *The Private Papers of Senator Vandenberg* (Boston: Houghton Mifflin, 1952), p. 467; also see p. 428 for Lodge's role as Platform Committee chairman in getting the 1948 Republican Convention to adopt a liberal foreign policy plank.

95. William S. White, "Verdict on Halleck," Washington *Post*, December 23, 1964, p. A22.

96. Quoted in Davidson, op. cit., p. 65.

97. Mimeographed statement, "Accomplishments of Lodge Administration," Part 2, p. 9. Received from John Davis Lodge, September 9, 1964.

98. See Dwight D. Eisenhower, *Mandate for Change, 1953–1956* (Garden City, N.Y.: Doubleday, 1963), pp. 16–18.

99. See New York *Times*, April 12, 1938, p. 22.

100. Quoted in Paul F. Healy, "The Senate's Gay Young Bachelor," *Saturday Evening Post*, June 13, 1953, p. 27.

101. Henry Cabot Lodge, Jr., *Life*, September 14, 1953, p. 182.

102. Robert Murphy, *Diplomat Among Warriors* (Garden City, N.Y.: Doubleday, 1964), p. 368.

103. Quoted in Stanley Karnow, "The Quandary of Henry Cabot Lodge," *Saturday Evening Post*, February 8, 1964, pp. 71–72; also see *Congressional Quarterly*, Part II, Weekly Report No. 33, August 12, 1960, p. 1421.

104. Mannes, op. cit., p. 23.

105. "Ambassador Lodge," *New Republic*, October 24, 1960, p. 6.

106. See New York *Times*, November 3, 1954, pp. 1 and 16; November 10, 1954, p. 34.

107. Quoted in Theodore H. White, *The Making of the President 1960* (New York: Atheneum, 1961), p. 206; also see Richard M. Nixon, *Six Crises* (Garden City, N.Y.: Doubleday, 1962), pp. 317–18.

108. Quoted in *Newsweek*, August 8, 1960, p. 18.

109. Quoted in Elsie Lee, *Henry Cabot Lodge, Man and Statesman* (New York: Lancer, 1964), pp. 92 and 103.

110. Quoted in Blair, op. cit., p. 113.

111. See Tom Wicker, "The Bostonian vs. the Texan," *New York Times Magazine*, October 23, 1960, pp. 19 and 114–16.

112. Quoted in Theodore H. White, op. cit., p. 297.

113. Nixon, op. cit., p. 351.

114. Marquis Childs, "How to Win and Not Really Try," Washington *Post*, April 15, 1964, p. A22; also see *Time*, May 15, 1964, p. 34.

115. Bruce Biossat, "Lodge's Nap Myth Gets a Rude Awakening," Washington *Daily News*, April 16, 1964, p. 39.

116. William F. Buckley, Jr., "Oregon Holds Answer to Lodge," Washington *Daily News*, April 20, 1964, p. 17.

117. Quoted in Peter Grose, "Portrait of the Distant 'Candidate,'" *New York Times Magazine,* May 10, 1964, p. 102.

118. Quoted in Karnow, op. cit., p. 72. Walter Lippmann commented that Lodge's appointment "was in line with his [John F. Kennedy's] regular practice, to neutralize public issues by looking for a Republican whom he could appoint to the controversial offices." Washington *Post,* April 7, 1964, p. A17.

119. "Lodge Phenomenon," Washington *Post,* April 14, 1964, p. A16.

120. See Robert Novak, *The Agony of the G.O.P. 1964* (New York: Macmillan, 1965), pp. 371–72.

121. See Joseph Alsop, "Lodge-Watching," Washington *Post,* May 13, 1964, p. A17.

122. New York *Times,* February 27, 1964, p. 17.

123. New York *Times,* June 24, 1964, p. 36.

124. Robert Taft, Jr., "A Challenge to the Republican Party," speech to the Cincinnati Junior Chamber of Commerce, January 18, 1965, p. 7 (mimeographed text).

125. New York *Times,* September 29, 1964, p. 40.

126. Washington *Post,* October 13, 1965, p. A18.

127. Blair, op. cit., p. 115.

128. Elsie Lee, op. cit., p. 96.

129. See *Hearings Before the Committee on Labor and Public Welfare, United States Senate, 86th Congress, 1st Session, on George C. Lodge to be Assistant Secretary of Labor for International Affairs, January 27, 1959* (Washington: Government Printing Office, 1959), pp. 2–5.

130. Quoted in *Time,* September 28, 1962, p. 17.

131. *U. S. News & World Report,* July 30, 1962, pp. 51–54.

132. *Time,* September 28, 1962, p. 17.

133. Quoted in Joe McCarthy, "One Election JFK Can't Win," *Look,* November 6, 1962, p. 26.

134. Quoted in Stewart Alsop, "What Made Teddy Run?" *Saturday Evening Post,* October 27, 1962, p. 18.

135. Ibid., p. 20.

136. Quoted in Blair, op. cit., p. 116.

THE KENNEDY DYNASTY

1. Quoted in Robert Curran, *The Kennedy Women* (New York: Lancer, 1964), p. 2.

2. See *National Cyclopaedia of American Biography,* Vol. VII, p. 441; also Vol. I, pp. 480–82; Vol. II, pp. 389–90.

3. See *Library of Congress Information Bulletin,* XXIII, No. 7 (February 17, 1964), p. 78.

4. Quoted in James Truslow Adams, *The Adams Family* (Boston: Little, Brown, 1930), p. 47.

5. Quoted in Arthur Bernon Tourtellet, "We Mutually Pledge to Each Other Our Lives, Our Fortunes and Our Sacred Honor," *American Heitage,* December 1962, p. 39.

6. E. Digby Baltzell, *The Protestant Establishment* (New York: Random House, 1964), p. 81.

7. See Tim Pat Coogan, "Sure, and It's County Kennedy Now," *New York Times Magazine,* June 23, 1963, pp. 7 and 32.

8. Quoted in James MacGregor Burns, *John Kennedy: A Political Profile* (New York: Harcourt, Brace, 1960), p. 23.

9. "Lippmann Tells 'Inside Story' at New Republic's Birthday Party," Washington *Post*, March 6, 1964, p. B9.

10. James Michael Curley, *I'd Do It Again* (Englewood Cliffs, N.J.: Prentice-Hall, 1957), p. 62.

11. Quoted in John Henry Cutler, *"Honey Fitz"* (Indianapolis: Bobbs-Merrill, 1962), p. 57.

12. Ibid., pp. 103–4.

13. Francis Russell, *The Great Interlude* (New York: McGraw-Hill, 1964), p. 177.

14. Cutler, op. cit., pp. 173 and 170–71.

15. Ibid., p. 207.

16. Ibid., p. 209.

17. Ibid., p. 216.

18. Ibid., p. 228.

19. Ibid., p. 229.

20. New York *Times*, August 9, 1964, p. 77.

21. Quoted in William V. Shannon, *The American Irish* (New York: Macmillan, 1963), p. 347.

22. Writes Hollywood columnist Hedda Hopper: "She [Gloria Swanson] . . . found a friend, patron saint, and bank roll all in one and the same person —Joseph P. Kennedy.

"Soon after this lucky meeting Gloria accompanied Mr. and Mrs. Kennedy on a trip to Europe. It must have been a mighty trying trip for Mrs. Kennedy. I often wondered how she weathered it.

". . . Joe Kennedy's father-in-law, the legendary 'Honey Fitz,' onetime mayor of Boston, ordered Joe to wind up his film affairs and get out of Hollywood by a given date or certain secrets—still secret except to a few—would burst into the open. Joe always was a lucky Irishman. He sold out his Hollywood holdings at the peak, took a profit of six million dollars, and wound up as our Ambassador to Great Britain. . . ." Hedda Hopper, *From Under My Hat* (Garden City, N.Y.: Doubleday, 1952), p. 168.

23. Richard J. Whalen, *The Founding Father: The Story of Joseph P. Kennedy* (New York: New American Library, 1964), p. 99.

24. William Manchester, *Portrait of a President* (Boston: Little, Brown, 1962), p. 69.

25. Quoted in Joseph F. Dinneen, *The Kennedy Family* (Boston: Little, Brown, 1960), pp. 34–5.

26. Quoted in Whalen, op. cit., p. 136.

27. Ibid., p. 411.

28. Quoted in Stanley P. Friedman, *The Magnificent Kennedy Women* (Derby, Conn.: Monarch, 1964), p. 5.

29. Quoted in Ralph G. Martin and Ed Plaut, *Front Runner, Dark Horse* (Garden City, N.Y.: Doubleday, 1960), p. 122.

30. Quoted in Curran, op. cit., p. 23.

31. Quoted in Burns, op. cit., p. 21.

32. Eric Sevareid, editor, *Candidates 1960* (New York: Basic Books, 1959), pp. 188–89.

33. Quoted in Robert E. Thompson and Hortense Myers, *Robert F. Kennedy: The Brother Within* (New York: Macmillan, 1962), p. 64; Joe McCarthy, *The Remarkable Kennedys* (New York: Dial, 1960), p. 56.

34. Quoted in Dinneen, op. cit., p. 37.

35. Quoted in Eleanor Harris, "The Senator Is in a Hurry," *McCall's*, August 1957, p. 119.

36. Quoted in McCarthy, op. cit., p. 19.

37. Quoted in Thompson and Myers, op. cit., p. 45.

38. Quoted in Curran, op. cit., p. 33.

39. Eunice Kennedy Shriver, "Hope for Retarded Children," *Saturday Evening Post*, September 22, 1962, pp. 71–72.

40. For example, see Dinneen, op. cit., p. 60; McCarthy, op. cit., p. 14; Burns, op. cit., p. 129.

41. Quoted in McCarthy, op. cit., p. 15.

42. Quoted in Manchester, op. cit., p. 181.

43. Quoted in Cutler, op. cit., p. 249.

44. Harold H. Martin, "The Amazing Kennedys," *Saturday Evening Post*, September 7, 1957, p. 20; Martin and Plaut, op. cit., p. 121.

45. Harold H. Martin, op. cit., p. 48; Whalen, op. cit., p. 336; Manchester, op. cit., p. 172.

46. Quoted in Ernest K. Lindley, "Will Kennedy Run for President?" *Liberty*, May 21, 1938, p. 16.

47. See Joseph P. Kennedy, *I'm for Roosevelt* (New York: Reynal & Hitchcock, 1936), p. 3.

48. Quoted in Deane and David Heller, *Jacqueline Kennedy* (Derby, Conn.: Monarch, 1961), p. 98.

49. Quoted in Cutler, op. cit., p. 268.

50. Ibid., p. 281.

51. Ibid., p. 279.

52. Quoted in Burns, op. cit., p. 37.

53. Quoted in McCarthy, op. cit., p. 79.

54. See Harold L. Ickes, *The Secret Diary of Harold L. Ickes* (New York: Simon & Schuster, 1955), Vol. III, p. 147.

55. Quoted in McCarthy, op. cit., p. 85.

56. Quoted in Cutler, op. cit., p. 286.

57. Quoted in Victor Lasky, *J.F.K. the Man and the Myth* (New York: Macmillan, 1963), p. 400.

58. Cutler, op. cit., p. 275; Whalen, op. cit., p. 112.

59. Quoted in Lasky, op. cit., p. 73.

60. John F. Kennedy, *Why England Slept* (New York: Funk, 1961), pp. xv–xvi.

61. See James A. Farley, *Jim Farley's Story* (New York: Whittlesey House, 1948), p. 264.

62. Quotations in McCarthy, op. cit., pp. 110 and 112.

63. Quoted in Burns, op. cit., p. 54.

64. Quoted in Harold H. Martin, op. cit., p. 20.

65. Whalen, op. cit., p. 392; Sevareid, op. cit., p. 20.

66. Quoted in Dinneen, op. cit., p. 123.

67. Robert Bendiner, "Bay State Prospects," *Nation*, October 12, 1946, p. 402.

68. Quoted in Joan Younger, "Jack Kennedy, Democratic Dynamo," *Ladies' Home Journal*, March 1960, p. 148.

69. Quoted in Heller, op. cit., p. 97.

70. Quoted in Paul F. Healy, "The Senate's Gay Young Bachelor," *Saturday Evening Post*, June 13, 1953, p. 127.

71. Ralph M. Blagden, "Cabot Lodge's Toughest Fight," *Reporter*, September 30, 1952, p. 13.

72. Quoted in Manchester, op. cit., p. 184.

73. Quoted in McCarthy, op. cit., p. 25.

74. See Martin and Plaut, op. cit., p. 172; Whalen, op. cit., p. 430.

75. Quoted in Thompson and Myers, op. cit., p. 58.

76. Quoted in Cutler, op. cit., p. 11.

77. Quoted in Martin and Plaut, op. cit., p. 184.

78. Ibid., p. 167.

79. Ibid., pp. 169–70.

80. Quoted in Ruth Montgomery, "She's Not Ready for JFK's Rocker," Washington *Post*, May 5, 1963, p. F1.

81. Quoted in Friedman, op. cit., p. 72.

82. Quoted in Curran, op. cit., p. 48.

83. Quoted in Mary Van Rensselaer Thayer, *Jacqueline Bouvier Kennedy* (Garden City, N.Y.: Doubleday, 1961), p. 14.

84. See Friedman, op. cit., p. 116.

85. Quoted in Younger, op. cit., p. 150.

86. Quoted in Mini Rhea with Frances Spatz Leighton, *I Was Jacqueline Kennedy's Dressmaker* (New York: Fleet, 1962), p. 60; Thayer, op. cit., p. 85.

87. Manchester, op. cit., pp. 167 and 64–65.

88. Quoted in Curran, op. cit., p. 44; Heller, op. cit., p. 103.

89. Quoted in Curran, op. cit., p. 63.

90. Ibid., p. 64.

91. Quoted in Whalen, op. cit., p. 457.

92. Burns, op. cit., p. 152.

93. Alfred Kazin, "The President and Other Intellectuals," *American Scholar*, Autumn 1961, p. 504.

94. Quoted in Martin and Plaut, op. cit., p. 199.

95. Quoted in Manchester, op. cit., p. 112.

96. John F. Kennedy, *Profiles in Courage* (New York: Harper, 1956), p. 8.

97. Quoted in Martin and Plaut, op. cit., p. 193.

98. Quoted in Manchester, op. cit., p. 177.

99. Quoted in Friedman, op. cit., p. 44.

100. Robert A. Liston, *Sargent Shriver: A Candid Portrait* (New York: Farrar, Straus, 1964), p. 47.

101. Quoted in *Time*, July 5, 1963, p. 20.

102. See New York *Times*, November 19, 1922, Sec. 8, p. 12; December 21, 1932, p. 19.

103. Quoted in Curran, op. cit., p. 143.

104. Tom Wicker, "The Name Is Smith," *New York Times Magazine*, July 28, 1963, p. 11.

105. Quoted in Friedman, op. cit., p. 64.

106. Murray Kempton, "Stephen E. Smith," *New Republic*, March 9, 1963, p. 15.

107. Quoted in Liston, op. cit., p. 59.

108. Peter Lawford, as told to Vernon Scott, "The White House Is Still Wondering What to Do with Me," *McCall's*, January 1963, p. 110.

109. See New York *Times*, April 18, 1965, Sec. 2, p. 9.

110. Friedman, op. cit., p. 53; Harold H. Martin, op. cit., p. 47; Curran, op. cit., p. 109; Whalen, op. cit., p. 440.

111. Quoted in Lasky, op. cit., p. 191.

112. Quoted in McCarthy, op. cit., pp. 103–4.

113. Quoted in Harold H. Martin, op. cit., p. 48.

114. Joseph Alsop, "The Legacy of John F. Kennedy," *Saturday Evening Post*, November 21, 1964, p. 17.

115. Harold H. Martin, op. cit., p. 48.

116. See Stewart Alsop, "Kennedy's Magic Formula," *Saturday Evening Post*, August 13, 1960, p. 60. Whalen, op. cit., p. 453, puts Joe Kennedy's investment in his son's preconvention campaign at $1,500,000.

117. Quoted in Theodore H. White, "Perspective/1960," *Saturday Review*, March 26, 1960, p. 14.

118. Quoted in Lasky, op. cit., p. 382.

119. Quoted in Friedman, op. cit., p. 122; Martin and Plaut, op. cit., p. 143.

120. Quoted in Curran, op. cit., p. 56.

121. Quoted in Theodore H. White, *The Making of the President 1960* (New York: Atheneum, 1961), p. 256.

122. Quoted in Thompson and Myers, op. cit., p. 209.

123. Quoted in Lasky, op. cit., p. 430.

124. Quoted in Earl Mazo, *The Great Debate, an Occasional Paper of the Fund for the Republic*, 1962, p. 4.

125. Quoted in White, *The Making of the President 1960*, p. 18.

126. Quoted in Lasky, op. cit., p. 540.

127. Quoted in Stan Opotowsky, *The Kennedy Government* (New York: Dutton, 1961), p. 78.

128. Quoted in Thompson and Myers, op. cit., p. 43.

129. See Manchester, op. cit., p. 160.

130. Alexander M. Bickel, "Robert F. Kennedy: The Case Against Him for Attorney General," *New Republic*, January 9, 1961, p. 19.

131. New York *Times*, October 12, 1964, p. 28.

132. Joseph Kraft, "Riot Squad for the New Frontier," *Harper's*, August 1963, p. 69. Arthur M. Schlesinger, Jr., although in a partisan context, called Bobby Kennedy "the best Attorney General the country has had for a generation." See New York *Times*, September 2, 1964, p. 34.

133. Anthony Lewis, "What Drives Bobby Kennedy?" *New York Times Magazine*, April 7, 1963, p. 34.

134. Quoted in Liston, op. cit., p. 111.

135. See Sargent Shriver, *Point of the Lance* (New York: Harper & Row, 1964), particularly "The Roots of Racism," pp. 142–46, a speech given to the First National Catholic Conference for Interracial Justice, August 29, 1958.

136. Quoted in Stewart Alsop, "What Made Teddy Run?" *Saturday Evening Post*, October 27, 1962, p. 16; also see Whalen, op. cit., p. 475.

137. Quoted in Tom O'Hara, "Teddy Out to 'Win' Massachusetts," New York *Herald Tribune*, May 16, 1961, p. 4.

138. Quoted in Thompson and Myers, op. cit., p. 62.

139. Quoted in Curran, op. cit., p. 23.

140. Quoted in Betty Hannah Hoffman, "What It's Like to Marry a Kennedy," *Ladies' Home Journal*, October 1962, p. 97.

141. Paul Driscoll, "Jack Was Asking About You," *New Republic*, June 4, 1962, p. 8; Manchester, op. cit., p. 161.

142. See John L. Saltonstall, Jr., "First Round for Brother Ted," *New Republic*, June 18, 1962, p. 7.

143. Quoted in Lasky, op. cit., pp. 580–81.

144. Quoted in Friedman, op. cit., p. 98.

145. Quoted in Alistair Cooke, "The Public Face of John F. Kennedy," *Show,* April 1963, p. 70.

146. Quoted in Hugh Sidey, *John F. Kennedy, President* (New York: Atheneum, 1963), p. 95.

147. Benjamin Bradlee, *That Special Grace* (Philadelphia: Lippincott, 1964), pages unnumbered.

148. Quoted in Manchester, op. cit., p. 237.

149. Quoted in James Reston, "What Was Killed Was Not Only the President but the Promise," *New York Times Magazine,* November 15, 1964, p. 126.

150. See William Attwood, "In Memory of John F. Kennedy," *Look,* December 31, 1963, p. 11.

151. See Karl E. Meyer, "The Myth Is Swallowing the Man," Washington *Post,* November 22, 1964, p. E4.

152. Quoted in Theodore H. White, "For One Shining Moment There Was Camelot," *Life,* December 6, 1963, p. 159.

153. Ironically his experience as President seems to have somewhat shaken his faith in the great-man theory of history. See John F. Kennedy, "Foreword," in Theodore C. Sorenson, *Decision-Making in the White House* (New York: Columbia University Press, 1963), p. xii.

154. See *contra,* Donald N. Michael, *The Next Generation* (New York: Random House, 1965), pp. 163–65.

155. Quoted in Curran, op. cit., p. 44.

156. Katherine Anne Porter, "Jacqueline Kennedy: Her Legend Will Live," *Ladies' Home Journal,* March 1964, p. 59.

157. Quoted in Murray Kempton, "Will Bobby Kennedy Run in New York?" *New Republic,* June 6, 1964, p. 8.

158. Quoted in *Newsweek,* August 24, 1964, p. 27.

159. See Theodore H. White, *The Making of the President 1964* (New York: Atheneum, 1965), p. 259.

160. See *U.S. News & World Report,* March 23, 1964, p. 44.

161. New York *Times,* August 7, 1964, p. 1.

162. Quoted in *Newsweek,* August 24, 1964, p. 23.

163. See New York *Times,* November 5, 1964, p. 38.

164. Quoted in Marquis Childs, "If Keating Loses So Does the GOP," Washington *Post,* October 28, 1964, p. A20.

165. Quoted in *Time,* October 30, 1964, p. 33.

166. Quoted in *Newsweek,* October 12, 1964, p. 36.

167. New York *Times,* September 2, 1964, p. 34; October 27, 1964, p. 36.

168. Quoted in *Newsweek,* October 12, 1964, p. 36.

169. Quoted in *Time,* October 30, 1964, p. 33.

170. Quoted in New York *Times,* October 26, 1964, p. 27.

171. Quoted in New York *Times,* October 11, 1964, p. 46.

172. Quoted in New York *Times,* September 3, 1964, p. 1.

173. See "Robert Kennedy's Tribute to JFK," *Look,* February 25, 1964, pp. 37–42.

174. Quoted in Christine Sadler, "The Coming of Age of Joan Kennedy," *McCall's,* February 1965, p. 160.

175. For example, see Robert Massie, "A New Taft and a Young Kennedy Go to Washington," *Saturday Evening Post,* January 19, 1963, p. 55.

176. When a reporter asked Bobby about the inscription, he replied, ". . . that sentence did not mean literally 'take my place.' He [Jack] had it

engraved immediately following the [1960] election campaign, and its meaning was more in the nature of: What will you do when I have finished . . . you as a human being?" See Oriana Fallaci, "Robert Kennedy Answers Some Blunt Questions," *Look*, March 9, 1965, p. 64.

177. Quoted in Friedman, op. cit., p. 76.
178. Quoted in Lasky, op. cit., p. 457.

PUBLIC OFFICES HELD BY POLITICAL DYNASTIES

THE ADAMSES

Samuel Adams (1722–1803)
Continental Congress, 1774–82; Massachusetts constitutional conventions, 1779 and 1788; president, state Senate, 1781; lieutenant governor, 1789–94; governor, 1794–97.

John Adams (1735–1826)
Continental Congress, 1774–78; diplomat in Holland and France, 1778–85; U.S. minister to England, 1785–88; Vice-President, 1789–97; President, 1797–1801.

John Quincy Adams (1767–1848)
U.S. minister to the Netherlands and later to Berlin, 1795–1801; Massachusetts State Senate, 1802; U. S. Senate, 1803–8; U.S. minister to Russia, 1809–14; U.S. minister to England, 1815–17; Secretary of State, 1817–25; President, 1825–29; U. S. House of Representatives, 1831–48.

Charles Francis Adams (1807–86)
Massachusetts House of Representatives, 1840–43; state Senate, 1843–45; U. S. House of Representatives, 1859–61; U.S. minister to England, 1861–68.

Charles Francis Adams (1835–1915)
Chairman, Massachusetts Board of Railroad Commissioners, 1872–79.

Brooks Adams (1848–1927)
Delegate, Massachusetts Constitutional Convention, 1917.

Charles Francis Adams (1866–1954)
U. S. Secretary of the Navy, 1929–33.

In-laws and Collateral Relations

Thomas Johnson (1732–1819)
Uncle of *Mrs. John Quincy Adams* (1775–1852). Continental Congress from Maryland, 1774–77; governor, 1777–79; state House of Delegates, 1780, 1786, 1787; chief judge, General Court of Maryland, 1790–91; Justice of U. S. Supreme Court, 1791–93.

Nathaniel Gorham (1738–96)
Grandfather of *Mrs. Charles Francis Adams* (1808–89). Massachusetts State Senate, 1780–81; Continental Congress, 1782–83, 1785–87.

Joseph Allen (1749–1827)
Nephew of *Samuel Adams* (1722–1803). Massachusetts Constitutional Convention, 1788; U. S. House of Representatives, 1810–11; State councilor, 1815–18.

William Stephens Smith (1755–1816)
Husband of *Abigail Adams* (1765–1813). Secretary to the U. S. Legation at London, 1784–88; U.S. marshal for the district of New York, 1789; surveyor of the port of New York, 1800; U. S. House of Representatives, 1813–15.

Peter Chardon Brooks (1767–1849)
Father-in-law of *Charles Francis Adams* (1807–86). Massachusetts State Senate, 1806–14; Massachusetts Council, 1817–19.

William Cranch (1769–1855)
Nephew of *Mrs. John Adams* (1744–1818). Chief justice, U. S. Circuit Court for the District of Columbia, 1806–55.

John Pope (1770–1845)
Brother-in-law of *Mrs. John Quincy Adams* (1775–1852). Kentucky House of Representatives, 1802, 1806, 1807; U. S. Senate, 1807–13; state Senate, 1825–29; territorial governor of Arkansas, 1829–35; U. S. House of Representatives, 1837–43.

Benjamin W. Crowninshield (1772–1851)
Grandfather of *Mrs. John Quincy Adams II*. Massachusetts House of Representatives, 1811, 1821, 1833; state Senate, 1812; U. S. Secretary of the Navy, 1814–18; U. S. House of Representatives, 1823–31.

Benjamin Gorham (1775–1855)
Uncle of *Mrs. Charles Francis Adams* (1808–89). Massachusetts House of Representatives, 1814–18; state Senate, 1819–21, 1823; 1841; U. S. House of Representatives, 1820–23, 1827–31, 1833–35.

Edward Everett (1794–1865)
Brother-in-law of *Mrs. Charles Francis Adams* (1808–89). U. S. House of Representatives from Massachusetts, 1825–35; governor, 1836–40; U.S. minister to Great Britain, 1841–45; U. S. Secretary of State, 1852–53; U. S. Senate, 1853–54.

Charles Allen (1797–1869)
Grandson of *Samuel Adams* (1722–1803). Massachusetts House of Representatives, 1830, 1833, 1835, 1840; state Senate, 1836, 1837; U. S. House of Representatives, 1849–53; chief judge of the Suffolk County Superior Court, 1859–67.

William C. Lovering (1835–1910)
Father-in-law of *Charles Francis Adams* (1866–1954). Massachusetts State Senate, 1874, 1875; U. S. House of Representatives, 1897–1910.

William Everett (1839–1910)
Nephew of *Mrs. Charles Francis Adams* (1808–89). U. S. House of Representatives from Massachusetts, 1893–95.

Henry Cabot Lodge (1850–1924)
Brother-in-law of *Mrs. Brooks Adams* (d. 1927). See Lodge Dynasty.

THE BAYARDS

Nicholas Bayard (1644–1707)
Mayor of New York City, 1685–87.

Samuel Bayard (1669–1745)
New York State Assembly, 1713–15.

Stephen Bayard (b. 1700)
Mayor of New York City, 1744–47.

William Bayard (1729–1804)
New York State Assembly, 1761–68.

John Bubenheim Bayard (1738–1807)
Pennsylvania General Assembly, 1776–79, 1784; Continental Congress, 1785–87; mayor of New Brunswick, New Jersey, 1790.

Samuel Bayard (1767–1840)
Agent for U.S. claims under the Jay Treaty, 1795–99; *post* 1806, judge, Westchester County, New York; judge, Court of Common Pleas for Somerset County, New Jersey; New Jersey House of Representatives.

James Asheton Bayard (1767–1815)

U. S. House of Representatives from Delaware, 1797–1803; U. S. Senate, 1804–13; U.S. commission to Ghent, 1814.

Richard Henry Bayard (1796–1868)
Mayor of Wilmington, Delaware, 1832; U. S. Senate, 1836–39, 1841–45; chief justice of Delaware, 1839–41; U.S. chargé d'affaires to Belgium, 1850–53.

James Asheton Bayard (1799–1880)
U.S. district attorney for Delaware, 1838–43; U. S. Senate, 1851–64, 1867–69.

Thomas Francis Bayard (1828–98)
U.S. district attorney for Delaware, 1853–54; U. S. Senate, 1869–85; U. S. Secretary of State, 1885–89; U.S. ambassador to Great Britain, 1893–97.

Thomas Francis Bayard (1868–1942)
City solicitor of Wilmington, Delaware, 1917–19; U. S. Senate, 1922–29.

Alexis I. Du Pont Bayard (1918–   )
Lieutenant governor of Delaware, 1949–53; member of Delaware River and Bay Authority, 1965–(present).

In-laws and Collateral Relations

Samuel Vetch (1668–1732)
Father-in-law of *Stephen Bayard* (b. 1700). See Livingston Dynasty.

Lewis Pintard (1732–1818)
Father-in-law of *Samuel Bayard* (1767–1840). See Stockton Dynasty.

Arthur St. Clair (1734–1818)
Husband of *Phebe Bayard*. Pennsylvania Council of Censors, 1783; Continental Congress, 1785–87; governor, Northwest Territory, 1789–1802.

Charles Carroll of Carrollton (1737–1832)
Grandfather of *Mrs. Richard H. Bayard*. See Lee Dynasty.

Jonathan Bayard Smith (1742–1812)
Father-in-law of *Margaret Bayard* (1778–1844). Continental Congress from Pennsylvania, 1777–78; Philadelphia alderman, 1792–94; auditor general of Pennsylvania, 1794.

Richard Bassett (1745–1815)
Father-in-law of *James A. Bayard* (1767–1815). Delaware State Senate, 1782; state House of Representatives, 1786; U. S. Constitutional Convention, 1787; Delaware convention that ratified the federal Constitution, 1787; U. S. Senate, 1789–93; chief justice of Delaware, 1793–99; governor, 1799–1801.

William Paterson (1745–1806)
Brother-in-law of *John Bubenheim Bayard* (1738–1807). New Jersey Provincial Congress, 1775, 1776; state Senate, 1776, 1777; attorney general of New Jersey, 1776–83; U. S. Constitutional Convention, 1787; Continental Congress, 1780–81, 1787; U. S. Senate, 1789–90; governor, 1790–93; U. S. Supreme Court, 1793–1806.

Andrew Kirkpatrick (1756–1831)
Husband of *Jane Bayard* (1772–1851). New Jersey State Assembly, 1797; judge of state Supreme Court, 1797–1824.

Stephen Van Rensselaer (1764–1839)
Father-in-law of *Harriet Elizabeth Bayard* (1799–1875). New York State Assembly, 1789–91, 1798, 1818; state Senate, 1791–96; lieutenant governor, 1795; U. S. House of Representatives, 1822–29.

Samuel Harrison Smith (1772–1845)
Husband of *Margaret Bayard*. U. S. Commissioner of Revenue, 1813.

Littleton Kirkpatrick (1797–1859)
Son of *Jane Bayard Kirkpatrick* (1772–1851). Mayor of New Brunswick, New Jersey, 1841, 1842; U. S. House of Representatives, 1843–45.

Henry Bell Van Rensselaer (1810–64)
Brother-in-law of *Harriet Elizabeth Bayard*. U. S. House of Representatives from New York, 1841–43.

THE BRECKINRIDGES

Robert Breckinridge (1754–1833)
Virginia House of Delegates, 1788; Kentucky House of Representatives, 1792–95.

John Breckinridge (1760–1806)
Virginia House of Burgesses, 1780–85; attorney general of Kentucky, 1795–97; Kentucky House of Representatives, 1798–1800; U. S. Senate, 1801–5; U. S. Attorney General, 1805–6.

James Breckinridge (1763–1833)
Virginia House of Delegates, 1789–1802, 1806–8, 1820, 1821, 1823, 1824; U. S. House of Representatives, 1809–17.

James Douglas Breckinridge (d. 1849)
Kentucky House of Representatives, 1809–11; U. S. House of Representatives, 1821–23.

Joseph Cabell Breckinridge (1788–1823)
Speaker, Kentucky House of Representatives, 1817–18; Kentucky Secretary of State, 1818–23.

Robert Jefferson Breckinridge (1800–71)
Superintendent of public instruction, Kentucky, 1847–53; Kentucky House of Representatives, 1825.

John Cabell Breckinridge (1821–75)
U. S. House of Representatives, 1851–55; Vice President, 1857–61; U. S. Senate, 1861.

Robert Jefferson Breckinridge (1833–1915)
Attorney general of Kentucky, 1900–2.

William Campbell Preston Breckinridge (1837–1904)
U. S. House of Representatives from Kentucky, 1885–95.

Clifton Rodes Breckinridge (1846–1932)
U. S. House of Representatives from Arkansas, 1883–94; U.S. minister to Russia, 1894–97; commissioner, Indian Territory, 1900–5.

Henry Breckinridge (1886–1960)
Assistant Secretary of War, 1913–16.

John Bayne Breckinridge (1913–   )
Kentucky House of Representatives, 1956–59; State attorney general, 1960–64.

In-laws and Collateral Relations

John Witherspoon (1723–94)
Grandfather of *Mrs. Joseph Cabell Breckinridge*. Provincial Congress of New Jersey, 1776; Continental Congress, 1776–79, 1780–81, 1782.

Joseph Cabell (1732–98)
Father-in-law of *John Breckinridge* (1760–1806). Virginia House of Burgesses, 1764–75; House of Delegates, 1776–81, 1788–90; state Senate, 1781–85.

Francis Preston (1765–1836)
Father-in-law of *Robert Jefferson Breckinridge* (1800–71). Virginia House of Delegates, 1788–89, 1812–14; U. S. House of Representatives, 1793–97; state Senate, 1816–20.

Joseph Desha (1768–1842)
Grandfather of *Issa Desha* [*Mrs. William C. P. Breckinridge*]. Kentucky House of Representatives, 1797, 1799–1802; state Senate, 1803–7; U. S. House of Representatives, 1807–19; governor, 1824–28.

Peter Buell Porter (1773–1844)
Husband of *Letitia Preston Breckinridge* (1786–1831). New York State Assembly, 1802, 1828; U. S. House of Representatives, 1809–13, 1815–16; secretary of state of New York, 1815, 1816; U. S. Secretary of War, 1828–29.

Henry Clay (1777–1852)
Grandfather of *Lucretia Hart Clay* (1836–60). [*Mrs. William C. P. Breckinridge*]. Kentucky House of Representatives, 1803, 1808–9; U. S. Senate, 1806–7, 1810–11, 1831–42, 1849–52; U. S. House of Representatives, 1811–14, 1815–21, 1823–25; U. S. Secretary of State, 1825–29.

William Campbell Preston (1794–1860)
Brother-in-law of *Robert Jefferson Breckinridge* (1800–71). South Carolina House of Representatives, 1828–34; U. S. Senate, 1833–42.

Thomas Hart Clay (1803–71)
Father-in-law of *William C. P. Breckinridge*. U.S. minister to Nicaragua, 1862–63.

Robert Ward Johnson (1814–79)
Father-in-law of *Joseph Cabell Breckinridge* (b. 1844). U. S. House of Representatives from Arkansas, 1847–53; U. S. Senate, 1853–61.

Levin Irving Handy (1861–1921)
Son of *Marie L. P. Breckinridge Handy* (b. 1836). U. S. House of Representatives from Delaware, 1897–99.

John S. Graham (1905–   )
Husband of *Elizabeth Breckinridge*. Assistant Secretary of the Treasury, 1948–53; Atomic Energy Commissioner, 1957–62.

THE FRELINGHUYSENS

Frederick Frelinghuysen (1753–1804)
Provincial Congress of New Jersey, 1775, 1776; Continental Congress, 1778, 1779, 1782, 1783; New Jersey General Assembly, 1784, 1800–4; New Jersey convention that ratified the federal Constitution, 1787; State Council, 1790–92; U. S. Senate, 1793–96.

Theodore Frelinghuysen (1787–1862)
Attorney general of New Jersey, 1817–29; U. S. Senate, 1829–35; mayor of Newark, New Jersey, 1837, 1838.

Frederick Theodore Frelinghuysen (1817–85)
City attorney of Newark, New Jersey, 1849; City Council, 1850; attorney general of New Jersey, 1861–66; U. S. Senate, 1866–69, 1871–77; U. S. Secretary of State, 1881–85.

Joseph Sherman Frelinghuysen (1869–1948)
New Jersey State Senate, 1906–12; president State Board of Agriculture, 1912–25; president, State Board of Education, 1915–19; U. S. Senate, 1917–23.

Peter Hood Ballantine Frelinghuysen (1916–)
U. S. House of Representatives from New Jersey, 1953–(present).
Henry O. H. Frelinghuysen (1916–)
Coroner of Morris County, New Jersey, 1938.

In-laws

Peter D. Vroom (1791–1873)
Brother-in-law of *Frederick Frelinghuysen* (1788–1820). New Jersey General
Assembly, 1826–27, 1829; governor, 1829–31, 1833–36; U. S. House of
Representatives, 1839–41; U.S. minister to Prussia, 1853–57.
John Davis (1851–1902)
Husband of *Sarah Helen Frelinghuysen* (c. 1854–1939). Assistant Secretary
of State, 1882–84; judge of U. S. Court of Claims, 1885–1902.

THE HARRISONS

Benjamin Harrison I (d. 1645)
Virginia House of Burgesses, 1642.
Benjamin Harrison II (1645–1712)
Virginia House of Burgesses, 1676–77, 1680, 1682, 1691, 1692, 1696, 1698;
Council, 1698–1712.
Benjamin Harrison III (1673–1710)
Speaker, Virginia House of Burgesses, 1704.
Benjamin Harrison IV (1700–44)
Virginia House of Burgesses.
Benjamin Harrison V (1726–91)
Virginia House of Burgesses, 1749–75; Continental Congress, 1774–78; Vir-
ginia House of Delegates, 1776–82, 1787–91; governor, 1782–84.
William Henry Harrison (1773–1841)
Delegate to U. S. House of Representatives from Northwest Territory, 1798–99;
territorial governor of Indiana, 1801–13; U. S. House of Representatives from
Ohio, 1816–19; state Senate, 1819–21; U. S. Senate, 1825–28; U.S. minister
to Colombia, 1828–29; President, 1841.
Carter Bassett Harrison (d. 1808)
Virginia House of Delegates, 1784–86, 1805–8; U. S. House of Representatives,
1793–99.
John Scott Harrison (1804–78)
U. S. House of Representatives from Ohio, 1853–57.
Carter Henry Harrison (1825–93)
U. S. House of Representatives from Illinois, 1875–79; mayor of Chicago,
1879–87, 1893.
Benjamin Harrison (1833–1901)
U. S. Senate from Indiana, 1881–87; President, 1889–93.
Russell Harrison (1854–1936)
Indiana House of Representatives, 1921–23; state Senate, 1925–29.
Carter Henry Harrison (1860–1953)
Mayor of Chicago, 1897–1905, 1911–15.
William Henry Harrison (1896–)
Indiana House of Representatives, 1927–29; Wyoming House of Representa-
tives, 1945–50; U. S. House of Representatives, 1951–55, 1961–65.

In-laws and Collateral Relations

Philip Ludwell (1640–c. 1723)
Father-in-law of *Hannah Harrison* (1678–1731). Governor of North Carolina, 1690–93; governor of North and South Carolina, 1693.

James Blair (1655–1743)
Husband of *Sarah Harrison* (1670–1713). President, Virginia Council; acting governor, 1740–41.

Robert Carter (1663–1732)
Father-in-law of *Benjamin Harrison IV* (1700–44). Virginia House of Burgesses, 1691–92, 1695–99; Council, 1699–1732.

Philip Ludwell II (1672–1726)
Husband of *Hannah Harrison* (1678–1731). Speaker, Virginia House of Burgesses; Council.

Sir John Randolph (1693–1737)
Father-in-law of *Elizabeth Harrison*. Speaker, Virginia House of Burgesses, 1734–37.

Philip Ludwell III (1716–67)
Son of *Hannah Harrison* (1678–1731). Virginia Council, 1751–55.

Peyton Randolph (1721–75)
Brother-in-law of *Benjamin Harrison V* (1726–91). Virginia House of Burgesses, 1764–74; Continental Congress, 1774, 1775.

John Randolph (1727–84)
Brother-in-law of *Elizabeth Harrison*. Attorney general of Virginia, 1766.

John Cleves Symmes (1742–1814)
Father-in-law of *William Henry Harrison* (1773–1841). New Jersey Council, 1778; chief judge, New Jersey Supreme Court, 1777–87; Continental Congress, 1785–86; judge, Northwest Territory, 1788–1802.

John Breckinridge (1760–1806)
Brother-in-law of *Robert Carter Harrison* (1765–1840). See Breckinridge Dynasty.

James Findlay (1770–1835)
Uncle of *Mrs. William Henry Harrison* (1804–46). Ohio House of Representatives, 1803; mayor of Cincinnati, 1805, 1806, 1810, 1811; U. S. House of Representatives, 1825–33.

Alvin Saunders (1817–99)
Father-in-law of *Russell Harrison* (1854–1936). Iowa State Senate, 1854–56, 1858–60; governor, Territory of Nebraska, 1861–67; U.S. senator from Nebraska, 1877–83.

THE KENNEDYS

Patrick J. Kennedy (1858–1929)
Massachusetts House of Representatives, 1886–90; state Senate, 1892–93; Boston wire commissioner, 1902–5; Boston fire commissioner, 1905.

Joseph Patrick Kennedy (1888–   )
Chairman, Securities and Exchange Commission, 1934–35; chairman, U. S. Maritime Commission, 1937; U.S. ambassador to Great Britain, 1937–40.

John Fitzgerald Kennedy (1917–63)
U. S. House of Representatives from Massachusetts, 1947–53; U. S. Senate, 1953–60; President, 1961–63.

Robert Francis Kennedy (1925–   )
U. S. Attorney General, 1961–64; U. S. Senate from New York, 1965–(present).

Edward Moore Kennedy (1932–   )
U. S. Senate from Massachusetts, 1963–(present).

In-laws and Collateral Relations

William Edward Cleary (1849–1932)
Grandfather-in-law of *Jean Kennedy Smith*. U. S. House of Representatives from New York, 1918–21, 1923–27.

John Francis Fitzgerald (1863–1950)
Father-in-law of *Joseph Patrick Kennedy*. Boston Common Council, 1892; Massachusetts State Senate, 1893, 1894; U. S. House of Representatives, 1895–1901, 1919; mayor of Boston, 1906, 1907, 1910–14; Port of Boston Authority, 1934–48.

R. Sargent Shriver (1915–   )
Husband of *Eunice Kennedy*. President, Chicago Board of Education, 1955–60; director of the Peace Corps, 1961–66; director, Office of Economic Opportunity, 1964–(present).

THE LEES

Richard Lee (c. 1613–64)
Clerk of the Quarter Court of Virginia, 1640–43; attorney general of Virginia, 1643–49; high sheriff, York County, Virginia, 1646; House of Burgesses, 1647; secretary of state of Virginia, 1649; Council, 1651–52, 1660.

Richard Lee (1646–1714)
Virginia Council, 1676, 1680–88, 1692–98; House of Burgesses, 1677.

Hancock Lee (1652–1709)
Virginia House of Burgesses, 1699.

Thomas Lee (1690–1750)
Virginia House of Burgesses, 1720–32; Council, 1732–49; acting governor, 1749–50.

John Lee (1724–67)
Virginia House of Burgesses, 1762–65.

Philip Ludwell Lee (1726–75)
Virginia House of Burgesses, 1756; Council, 1757.

Richard Lee (1726–95)
Virginia House of Burgesses, 1757–74; Virginia House of Delegates, 1777–93.

Henry Lee (1729–87)
Virginia House of Burgesses, 1758–72; state Senate, 1780.

Richard Henry Lee (1732–94)
Virginia House of Burgesses, 1758–75; Continental Congress, 1774–80, 1784–87; Virginia House of Delegates, 1777, 1780, 1785; U. S. Senate, 1789–92.

Francis Lightfoot Lee (1734–97)
Virginia House of Burgesses, 1758–75; Continental Congress, 1775–80; Virginia House of Delegates, 1780–81; state Senate, 1778–82.

William Lee (1739–95)
Sheriff of London, 1773–74; alderman of London, 1775–77; U.S. commercial agent at Nantes, France, 1777; commissioner to the courts of Vienna and Berlin, 1777–79.

Arthur Lee (1740–92)
U.S. commissioner to France and Spain, 1776–80; Virginia House of Delegates, 1781–83, 1785–86; Continental Congress, 1781–84; U. S. Treasury Board, 1785–89.

Thomas Sim Lee (1745–1819)
Maryland Provincial Council, 1777–78; governor, 1779–83, 1792–94; Continental Congress, 1783–84; Maryland House of Delegates, 1787.

Henry Lee (1756–1818)
Continental Congress from Virginia, 1785–88; governor, 1791–94; U. S. House of Representatives, 1799–1801.

Charles Lee (1758–1815)
U. S. Attorney General, 1795–1801.

Richard Bland Lee (1761–1827)
Virginia House of Delegates, 1784–88, 1796, 1799–1806; U. S. House of Representatives, 1789–95; judge, Orphans' Court of the District of Columbia, 1819–27.

Henry Lee (1787–1837)
Virginia House of Delegates, 1810–13; Assistant Postmaster General.

John Lee (1788–1871)
U. S. House of Representatives from Maryland, 1823–25; Maryland House of Delegates and state Senate.

Fitzhugh Lee (1835–1905)
Governor of Virginia, 1886–90.

William Henry Fitzhugh Lee (1837–91)
Virginia Senate, 1875–78; U. S. House of Representatives, 1887–91.

Blair Lee (1857–1944)
Maryland State Senate, 1905–13; U. S. Senate, 1913–17.

E. Brooke Lee (1892–   )
Comptroller of the Treasury of Maryland, 1920–22; secretary of state of Maryland, 1923–25; House of Delegates, 1928–31.

P. Blair Lee (1895–   )
Chairman, Philadelphia Housing Authority, 1950–62.

Blair Lee III (1916–   )
Maryland House of Delegates, 1955–62.

In-laws and Collateral Relations

Philip Ludwell I (1640–c. 1723)
Grandfather-in-law of *Thomas Lee* (1690–1750). See Harrison Dynasty.

Philip Ludwell II (1672–1726)
Father-in-law of *Thomas Lee* (1690–1750). See Harrison Dynasty.

William Shippen (1712–1801)
Father-in-law of *Alice Lee* (1736–1818). Continental Congress from Pennsylvania, 1778–80.

Philip Ludwell III (1716–67)
Father-in-law of *William Lee* (1739–1818); brother-in-law of *Thomas Lee* (1690–1750). See Harrison Dynasty.

George Mason (1725–92)
Grandfather-in-law of *Sydney Smith Lee* (1802–69). Virginia Constitutional Convention, 1776; Federal Constitutional Convention, 1787.

Charles Carroll of Carrollton (1737–1832)
Grandfather-in-law of *John Lee* (1788–1832) and *Mary Digges Lee* (b. 1800). Continental Congress from Maryland, 1776–78; state Senate, 1777–80; U. S. Senate, 1789–92.

William Fitzhugh (1741–1809)
Uncle of *Mrs. Robert E. Lee* (1808–73). Virginia House of Delegates, 1776–77, 1780–81, 1787–88; Continental Congress, 1779–80; state Senate, 1781–85.

John Marshall (1755–1835)
Uncle-in-law of *Anne Kinloch Lee* (1800–64). Virginia House of Burgesses, 1780, 1782–88; U. S. House of Representatives, 1799–1800; U. S. Secretary of War, 1800–1; Chief Justice, U. S. Supreme Court, 1801–35.

George William Smith (1762–1811)
Son of *Alice Lee;* grandson of *Philip Lee* (1681–1744). Virginia House of Delegates, 1794, 1802–8; Council, 1810–11; governor, 1811.

Outerbridge Horsey (1777–1842)
Husband of *Eliza Lee* (1783–1862). Delaware House of Representatives, 1801–2; attorney general of Delaware, 1806–10; U. S. Senate, 1810–21.

Zachary Taylor (1784–1850)
Grandson of *Elizabeth Lee*. President, 1849–50.

Joseph Gales, Jr. (1786–1860)
Husband of *Sarah J. M. Lee;* son-in-law of *Theodoric Lee* (1766–1849). Mayor of Washington, D.C., 1827–30.

John J. Crittenden (1787–1863)
Husband of *Sarah Lee;* son-in-law of *John Lee* (1743–1802). Attorney general of Illinois Territory, 1809–10; Kentucky House of Representatives, 1811–17, 1825, 1829–32; U. S. Senate, 1817–19, 1835–41, 1842–48, 1855–61; U. S. Attorney General, 1841, 1850–53; governor, 1848–50; U. S. House of Representatives, 1861–63.

James Murray Mason (1798–1871)
Brother-in-law of *Sydney Smith Lee* (1802–69). Virginia House of Delegates, 1826–32; U. S. House of Representatives, 1837–39; U. S. Senate, 1847–61; Confederate commissioner to Great Britain and France, 1861–65.

Montgomery Blair (1813–83)
Brother-in-law of *Samuel Phillips Lee* (1812–97). U. S. Postmaster General, 1861–64.

Francis Preston Blair, Jr. (1821–75)
Brother-in-law of *Samuel Phillips Lee* (1812–97). Missouri House of Representatives, 1852–56, 1870; U. S. House of Representatives, 1857–59, 1860, 1861–62, 1863–64; U. S. Senate, 1871–73.

John Lee Carroll (1830–1911)
Son of *Mary Digges Lee* (b. 1800): Maryland State Senate, 1867–72; governor, 1875–79.

Wilkinson Call (1834–1910)
Son of *Lucinda Lee;* grandson of *John Lee* (1743–1802). U. S. Senate from Florida, 1879–97.

William Atkinson Jones (1849–1918)
Grandson of *Mary Lee* (1790–1848). U. S. House of Representatives from Virginia, 1891–1918.

THE LIVINGSTONS

Robert Livingston (1654–1728)
New York General Assembly, 1716–26.

Philip Livingston (1686–1749)
New York Council.

Robert Livingston (1688–1775)
New York General Assembly, 1726–27.

Gilbert Livingston (1690–1746)
New York General Assembly, 1728–37.

Robert Livingston (1708–90)
New York General Assembly, 1737–58.

Peter Van Brugh Livingston (1710–92)
Speaker, New York Provincial Congress, 1775.

Henry Livingston (1714–99)
New York General Assembly, 1759–68.

Philip Livingston (1716–78)
New York City Board of Aldermen, 1754–62; New York General Assembly, 1763–69; Continental Congress, 1774–78; New York State Senate, 1777.

Robert R. Livingston (1718–75)
New York General Assembly, 1769–74; judge, New York Supreme Court, 1763–75.

William Livingston (1723–90)
New York General Assembly, 1759–61; Continental Congress from New Jersey, 1774–76; governor, 1776–90.

Peter R. Livingston (1737–94)
New York General Assembly, 1761–69, 1774–76.

Walter Livingston (1740–97)
New York State Assembly, 1777–79; Continental Congress, 1784–85.

Gilbert Livingston (1742–1800)
New York Provincial Congress, 1775–77; New York State Assembly, 1777, 1778, 1788.

Robert R. Livingston (1746–1813)
Continental Congress from New York, 1775–77, 1779–81; Secretary of Foreign Affairs, 1781–83; Chancellor of New York, 1777–1801; U.S. minister to France, 1801–4.

James Livingston (1747–1832)
New York State Assembly, 1786–87, 1789–91.

Edward Livingston (1764–1836)
U. S. House of Representatives from New York, 1795–1801; mayor of New York City, 1801–3; Louisiana House of Representatives, 1820; U. S. House of Representatives from Louisiana, 1823–29; U. S. Senate, 1829–31; U. S. Secretary of State, 1831–33; U.S. minister to France, 1833–35.

Henry Brockholst Livingston (1757–1823)
Judge, New York Supreme Court, 1802–6; justice, U. S. Supreme Court, 1806–23.

Henry Walter Livingston, (1768–1810)
New York State Assembly, 1802, 1810; U. S. House of Representatives, 1803–7.

Henry Alexander Livingston (1776–1849)
New York State Assembly, 1827; state Senate, 1838–41.

Edward Philip Livingston (1779–1843)
New York State Senate, 1808–12; 1822–24, 1838–39; lieutenant governor, 1830.

Peter Van Brugh Livingston (1792–1868)
U.S. minister to Ecuador, 1848.

Robert Le Roy Livingston (b. 1784)
U. S. House of Representatives from New York, 1809–12.

Charles Ludlow Livingston (d. 1873)
Speaker, New York State Assembly, 1832–33; state Senate, 1834–37.

Goodhue Livingston, Jr. (1897–   )
Executive secretary to mayor of New York City, 1943–45; New York City Planning Commission, 1945–61.

In-laws and Collateral Relations

Fitz-John Winthrop (1638–1707)
Father-in-law of *John Livingston* (1680–1720). Governor of Connecticut, 1698–1707.

Peter Van Brugh (1666–1740)
Father-in-law of *Philip Livingston* (1686–1749). Mayor of Albany, New York, 1699, 1721–23.

Samuel Vetch (1668–1732)
Husband of *Margaret Livingston* (1681–1758). Military governor of Nova Scotia, 1710–14; civil governor, 1715–17.

James Alexander (1691–1756)
Father-in-law of *Peter Van Brugh Livingston* (1710–92) and *Sarah Livingston* (1725–1804). Attorney general of New Jersey, 1723–27; Council of New Jersey, 1723–35; Council of New York, 1721–32.

William Smith, Sr. (1697–1769)
Father-in-law of *Janet Livingston* (d. 1819) and *Robert J. Livingston* (1725–71). New York Provincial Council, 1753–67; associate justice of New York Supreme Court, 1763–69.

Francis Lewis (1713–1803)
Father-in-law of *Gertrude Livingston* (1757–1833). Continental Congress from New York, 1774–79.

John Armstrong (1717–95)
Father-in-law of *Alida Livingston* (1761–1822). Continental Congress from Pennsylvania, 1778–80, 1787–88.

Pierre Van Courtlandt (1721–1814)
Husband of *Joanna Livingston* (1722–1808). Lieutenant governor of New York.

William Smith, Jr. (1728–93)
Husband of *Janet Livingston* (d. 1819). New York Council, 1753–67; chief justice of New York Supreme Court, 1763–69, 1779–83; Chief Justice of Canada, 1786–93.

Philip Schuyler (1733–1804)
Son-in-law of *Angelica Livingston* (1698–1747). Continental Congress from New York, 1775–77; 1778–81; state Senate, 1780–84, 1786–90, 1792–97; U. S. Senate, 1789–91, 1797–98.

James Duane (1733–97)
Husband of *Mary Livingston* (1738–1821). Attorney general of New York, 1767; state Indian commissioner, 1774; Continental Congress, 1774–84; state Senate, 1782–85, 1788–90; mayor of New York City, 1784–89; U. S. District Court judge, 1789–94.

Richard Montgomery (1738–1775)
Husband of *Janet Livingston* (1743–1828). New York Provincial Congress, 1775.

John Cleves Symmes (1742–1814)
Husband of *Susannah Livingston* (b. 1748). See Harrison Dynasty.

John Jay (1745–1829)
Husband of *Sarah Livingston* (1756–1802). Continental Congress from New York, 1774–77, 1778, 1779; U.S. minister to Spain, 1779–84; Secretary of Foreign Affairs, 1784–89; Chief Justice of U.S., 1789–95; U.S. minister to Great Britain, 1794–95; governor of New York, 1795–1801.

William Duer (1747–99)
Son-in-law of *Sarah Livingston* (1725–1804). New York State Senate, 1777; Continental Congress, 1777–78; New York State Assembly, 1786.

James Armstrong (1748–1828)
Brother-in-law of *Alida Livingston* (1761–1822). U. S. House of Representatives from Pennsylvania, 1793–95.

Thomas Tillotson (1752–1832)
Husband of *Margaret Livingston* (1749–1823). New York State Assembly, 1788–90; state Senate, 1791–99; secretary of state of New York, 1801–6, 1807–8.

Morgan Lewis (1754–1844)
Husband of *Gertrude Livingston* (1757–1833). Chief justice, New York Supreme Court, 1801–4; governor, 1804–7.

John Armstrong (1755–1843)
Husband of *Alida Livingston* (1761–1822). U. S. Senate from New York, 1800–2, 1803–4; U.S. minister to France, 1804–10; U. S. Secretary of War, 1813–14.

John Kean (1756–95)
Husband of *Susan Livingston* (1755–1833). Continental Congress from South Carolina, 1785–87.

Smith Thompson (1768–1843)
Husband of *Sarah Livingston* (1777–1833). Judge, New York Supreme Court, 1802–18; U. S. Secretary of the Navy, 1819–23; justice, U. S. Supreme Court, 1823–33.

Auguste Genevieve Valentin d'Avezac (1780–1851)
Brother-in-law of *Edward Livingston* (1764–1836). U.S. chargé d'affaires to the Netherlands, 1829–39, 1845–50; New York State Assembly, 1843.

THE LODGES

Henry Cabot Lodge, Sr. (1850–1924)
Massachusetts House of Representatives, 1880–81; U. S. House of Representatives, 1887–93; U. S. Senate, 1893–1924.

Henry Cabot Lodge, Jr. (1902–   )
Massachusetts House of Representatives, 1933–36; U. S. Senate, 1937–44,

1947–53; U.S. ambassador to the United Nations, 1953–60; U.S. ambassador to South Vietnam, 1963–64, 1965–(present).

John Davis Lodge (1903–   )
U. S. House of Representatives from Connecticut, 1947–51; governor, 1951–55; U.S. ambassador to Spain, 1955–61; Connecticut Constitutional Convention, 1965.

George Cabot Lodge (1927–   )
Assistant Secretary of Labor, 1959–62.

In-laws and Collateral Relations

George Cabot (1752–1823)
Grandfather of *Mrs. John Ellerton Lodge* (1821–1900). Massachusetts Provincial Congress, 1775; convention that ratified the federal Constitution, 1787; U. S. Senate, 1791–96.

Elijah Hunt Mills (1776–1829)
Grandfather of *Mrs. Henry Cabot Lodge, Sr.* (1850–1915). Massachusetts State Senate, 1811; U. S. House of Representatives, 1815–19; U. S. Senate, 1820–27.

Frederick T. Frelinghuysen (1817–85)
Grandfather of *Mrs. George Cabot Lodge* (c. 1877–1960). See Frelinghuysen Dynasty.

John Davis (1851–1902)
Father-in-law of *George Cabot Lodge* (1873–1909). See Frelinghuysen Dynasty.

Augustus Peabody Gardner (1865–1918)
Husband of *Constance Lodge* (1872–1941). Massachusetts State Senate, 1900, 1901; U. S. House of Representatives, 1902–17.

Archibald S. Alexander (1906–   )
Brother-in-law of *Mrs. Henry Cabot Lodge, Jr.* Assistant and Under Secretary of the Army, 1949–52.

THE LONGS

Julius Long (1879–1965)
District attorney, Winn Parish, Louisiana, 1912–20.

George Shannon Long (1883–1958)
Oklahoma House of Representatives, 1920–22; U. S. House of Representatives from Louisiana, 1953–58.

Huey Pierce Long (1893–1935)
Railroad commissioner of Louisiana, 1918–28; governor, 1928–32; U. S. Senate, 1932–35.

Earl Kemp Long (1895–1960)
Lieutenant governor of Louisiana, 1936–39; governor, 1939–40, 1948–52, 1956–60.

Rose McConnell Long [*Mrs. Huey P. Long*].
U. S. Senate from Louisiana, 1936–37.

Blanche Revere Long [*Mrs. Earl K. Long*].
Louisiana Tax Commission, 1964–(present).

Russell Billiu Long (1918–   )
U. S. Senate from Louisiana, 1948–(present).

Gillis W. Long (1923–)
U. S. House of Representatives from Louisiana, 1963–65; assistant director, U. S. Office of Economic Opportunity, 1965.

Speedy O. Long (1928–)
Louisiana Senate, 1956–64; U. S. House of Representatives, 1965–(present).

THE MUHLENBERGS

John Peter Gabriel Muhlenberg (1746–1807)
Supreme Executive Council of Pennsylvania, 1784–87; U. S. House of Representatives, 1789–91, 1793–95; 1799–1801; U. S. Senate, 1801; U.S. supervisor of revenue for Pennsylvania, 1801; U.S. collector of customs at Philadelphia, 1802–7.

Frederick Augustus Conrad Muhlenberg (1750–1801)
Continental Congress, 1779–80; Pennsylvania House of Representatives, 1780–83; president, Pennsylvania convention to ratify the federal Constitution, 1787; U. S. House of Representatives, 1789–97; Speaker, U. S. House of Representatives, 1789–91, 1793–95.

Henry Augustus Philip Muhlenberg (1782–1844)
U. S. House of Representatives, 1829–38; U.S. minister to Austria, 1838–40.

Francis Swaine Muhlenberg (1795–1831)
Ohio House of Representatives, 1827; U. S. House of Representatives, 1828–29.

Henry Augustus Muhlenberg (1823–54)
Pennsylvania Senate, 1849–52; U. S. House of Representatives, 1853–54.

Frederick Augustus Muhlenberg (1887–)
U. S. House of Representatives, 1947–49.

In-laws and Collateral Relations

Conrad Weiser (1696–1760)
Father-in-law of *Henry Melchior Muhlenberg* (1711–87). Justice of the peace for Lancaster County, Pennsylvania, 1741; justice of the peace for Berks County, Pennsylvania, 1752; president-judge of Berks County, 1752–60.

Joseph Hiester (1752–1832)
Father-in-law of *Henry Augustus Muhlenberg* (1782–1844). Pennsylvania convention that ratified the federal Constitution, 1787; state House of Representatives, 1787–90; state Senate, 1790–94; U. S. House of Representatives, 1797–1805, 1815–20; governor, 1820–24.

John Richards (1753–1822)
Brother-in-law of *Maria Salome Muhlenberg* (1766–1827). Judge of the Court of Common Pleas for Montgomery County, Pennsylvania, 1784; federal Constitutional Convention, 1787; U. S. House of Representatives, 1795–97; state Senate, 1801–7.

Matthias Richards (1758–1830)
Husband of *Maria Salome Muhlenberg*. Judge of Berks County (Pennsylvania) Court, 1791–97; U. S. House of Representatives, 1807–11.

John Andrew Schulze (1775–1852)
Son of *Eve Elizabeth Muhlenberg Schulze* (1748–1808). Pennsylvania House of Representatives, 1806–9, 1821; state Senate, 1822–23; governor, 1824–32.

THE ROOSEVELTS

Nicholas Roosevelt (1658–1742)
New York State Assembly, 1700.

Isaac Roosevelt (1726–94)
New York Provincial Congress, 1775; state Senate.

James I. Roosevelt (1795–1875)
New York State Assembly, 1835, 1840; U. S. House of Representatives, 1841–43; justice, New York Supreme Court, 1851–59; U.S. district attorney for Southern New York, 1860–61.

Clinton Roosevelt (1804–98)
New York State Assembly, 1835.

Robert Barnwell Roosevelt (1829–1906)
New York State fish commissioner, 1868–88; U. S. House of Representatives, 1871–73; U.S. minister to Holland, 1888–90.

Theodore Roosevelt (1858–1919)
New York State Assembly, 1882–84; U.S. civil service commissioner, 1889–95; New York City police commissioner, 1895–97; Assistant Secretary of the Navy, 1897–98; governor, 1899–1900; Vice-President, 1901; President, 1901–9.

Henry Latrobe Roosevelt (1879–1936)
Assistant Secretary of the Navy, 1933–36.

Franklin D. Roosevelt (1882–1945)
New York State Senate, 1910–13; Assistant Secretary of the Navy, 1913–20; governor, 1928–32; President, 1933–45.

Eleanor Roosevelt (1884–1962)
U.S. representative to the United Nations General Assembly, 1945, 1949–52; chairman, Commission on Human Rights, UN Economic and Social Council, 1946.

Theodore Roosevelt, Jr. (1887–1944)
New York State Assembly, 1919–21; Assistant Secretary of the Navy, 1921–24; governor of Puerto Rico, 1929–32; governor general of the Philippines, 1932–33.

Nicholas Roosevelt (1893–   )
Vice-governor, Philippine Islands, 1930; U.S. minister to Hungary, 1930–33; deputy director, Office of War Information, 1942–43.

James Roosevelt (1907–   )
Secretary to the President, 1937–38; U. S. House of Representatives from California, 1955–65; U.S. representative to the UN Economic and Social Council, 1965–(present).

Elliott Roosevelt (1910–   )
Mayor of Miami Beach, Florida, 1965–(present).

Theodore Roosevelt III (1914–   )
Secretary of Commerce of Pennsylvania, 1949–51.

Franklin D. Roosevelt, Jr. (1914–   )
U. S. House of Representatives from New York, 1949–55; Under Secretary of Commerce, 1963–65; chairman, Equal Employment Opportunities Commission, 1965–(present).

John Roosevelt (1916–   )
Member, President's Commission on Government Contracts, 1953–61.

In-laws and Collateral Relations

William Sheffield Cowles (1846–1923)
Husband of *Anna* ("*Bamie*") *Roosevelt* (1855–1931). Connecticut House of Representatives, 1916.

Joseph Willard (1865–1924)
Father-in-law of *Kermit Roosevelt* (1889–1943). Virginia House of Delegates, 1893–1901; lieutenant governor, 1901–5; state corporation commissioner, 1906–10; U.S. ambassador to Spain, 1913–21.

Nicholas Longworth (1869–1931)
Husband of *Alice Roosevelt*. Ohio House of Representatives, 1899–1900; state Senate, 1901–3; U. S. House of Representatives, 1903–13, 1915–31.

Joseph Wright Alsop (1876–1953)
Son-in-law of *Corinne Roosevelt Robinson* (1861–1933). Connecticut House of Representatives, 1907–9; state Senate, 1909–13; state public utilities commissioner, 1917–43.

Theodore Douglas Robinson (1883–1934)
Son of *Corinne Roosevelt Robinson*. New York State Assembly, 1911; state Senate, 1916–18, 1920–24; Assistant Secretary of the Navy, 1924–29.

THE STOCKTONS

John Stockton (1701–58)
Judge, Somerset (New Jersey) Court of Common Pleas.

Richard Stockton (1730–81)
Executive Council of New Jersey, 1768–76; judge of New Jersey Supreme Court, 1774–76; Continental Congress, 1776.

Samuel Witham Stockton (1751–95)
Secretary to the American Commission to Austria and Germany, 1774–79; secretary to New Jersey convention that ratified the federal Constitution, 1787; secretary of state of New Jersey, 1794.

Richard Stockton (1764–1828)
U. S. Senate from New Jersey, 1796–99; state General Assembly, 1813–15; U. S. House of Representatives, 1813–15.

Lucius Horatio Stockton (d. 1835)
Prosecuting attorney for Mercer County, New Jersey.

Richard Stockton (1791–1827)
Attorney general of Mississippi.

Robert Field Stockton (1795–1866)
U. S. Senate from New Jersey, 1851–53.

John Potter Stockton (1826–1900)
U.S. minister to Italy, 1857–61; U. S. Senate from New Jersey, 1856–66, 1869–75; attorney general of New Jersey, 1877–92.

Robert Field Stockton (1832–98)
Adjutant general of New Jersey, 1858–67; comptroller of New Jersey, 1877–80.

In-laws and Collateral Relations

Lewis Pintard (1732–1818)
Husband of *Susanna Stockton* (b. 1742). Deputy commissary of prisoners during the Revolutionary War, 1776–79.

Elias Boudinot (1740–1821)
Husband of *Hannah Stockton* (1736–1808). Continental Congress from New Jersey, 1777, 1778, 1781–83; commissary general of prisoners during the Revolutionary War, 1777–79; U. S. House of Representatives, 1789–95; director of the U. S. Mint, 1795–1805.

Benjamin Rush (1745–1813)
Husband of *Julia Stockton* (1758–1848). Continental Congress from Pennsylvania, 1776, 1777; Pennsylvania convention that ratified the federal Constitution, 1787; treasurer of the U. S. Mint, 1799–1813.

William Bradford (1755–95)
Son-in-law of *Hannah Stockton Boudinot*. Attorney general of Pennsylvania, 1780–91; U. S. Attorney General, 1794–95.

John Pintard (1759–1844)
Adopted son of *Susanna Stockton Pintard*. New York City Council, 1788–89; New York State Assembly, 1790.

Erastus Root (1773–1846)
Husband of *Elizabeth Stockton* (d. 1871). New York State Assembly, 1798–1802, 1818–22, 1826–28, 1830; U. S. House of Representatives, 1803–5, 1809–11, 1815–17, 1831–33; state Senate, 1812–15, 1840–44; lieutenant governor, 1822–24.

Richard Rush (1780–1859)
Son of *Julia Stockton Rush*. Attorney general of Pennsylvania, 1811; comptroller of the U. S. Treasury, 1811; U. S. Attorney General, 1814–17; U.S. minister to Great Britain, 1817–25; U. S. Secretary of the Treasury, 1825–28; U.S. minister to France, 1847–49.

Selah Reeve Hobbie (1797–1854)
Son-in-law of Elizabeth Stockton (d. 1871). New York State Assembly, 1827–29; U. S. House of Representatives, 1827–29; U. S. Assistant Postmaster General, 1829–51, 1853–54.

John Renshaw Thomson (1800–62)
Husband of *Annis Stockton* (b. 1804). U.S. consul at Canton, China, 1823–25; U. S. Senate from New Jersey, 1853–62.

Richard Stockton Field (1803–70)
Son of *Abigail Stockton Field*. New Jersey House of Representatives, 1837; New Jersey attorney general, 1838–41; U. S. Senate, 1862–63; federal District Court judge, 1863–70.

THE TAFTS

Alphonso Taft (1810–91)
Cincinnati City Council; judge, Cincinnati Superior Court, 1865–72; U. S. Secretary of War, 1876; U. S. Attorney General, 1876–77; U.S. minister to Austria-Hungary, 1882–84; U.S. minister to Russia, 1884–85.

Charles Phelps Taft (1843–1929)
Ohio House of Representatives, 1871–73; U. S. House of Representatives, 1895–97.

William Howard Taft (1857–1930)
Judge, Superior Court of Ohio, 1887–90; U. S. Solicitor General, 1890–92; Federal Circuit Court judge, 1892–1900; president of Philippine Commission and governor general of Philippine Islands, 1900–4; U. S. Secretary of War,

1904–8; President of the U.S., 1909–13; Chief Justice, U. S. Supreme Court, 1921–30.

Robert Alphonso Taft (1889–1953)
Assistant counsel, U. S. Food Administration, 1917–18; counsel, American Relief Administration, 1919; Ohio House of Representatives, 1921–26; Ohio Senate, 1931–32; U. S. Senate, 1939–53.

Charles Phelps Taft (1897–   )
Prosecuting attorney, Hamilton County, Ohio, 1927–28; Cincinnati City Council, 1938–42, 1948–51, 1955–present; mayor of Cincinnati, 1955–57.

William Howard Taft III (1915–   )
U.S. ambassador to Ireland, 1953–57.

Robert Taft, Jr. (1917–   )
Ohio House of Representatives, 1955–62; U. S. House of Representatives, 1963–65.

In-laws and Collateral Relations

Eli Collins (1786–1848)
Grandfather of *Mrs. William Howard Taft* (1861–1943). New York State Assembly, 1815; U. S. House of Representatives, 1823–25.

William Collins (1818–78)
Uncle of *Mrs. William Howard Taft*. U. S. House of Representatives from New York, 1847–49.

Henry Frederick Lippitt (1856–1933)
Brother-in-law of *Mrs. William Howard Taft*. U. S. Senate from Rhode Island, 1911–17.

Lloyd W. Bowers (1859–1910)
Father-in-law of *Robert A. Taft* (1889–1953). U. S. Solicitor General, 1909–10.

David Sinton Ingalls (1899–   )
Grandson of *Charles Phelps Taft* (1843–1929). Assistant Secretary of the Navy, 1929–32.

THE TUCKERS

Thomas Tudor Tucker (1745–1828)
Continental Congress from South Carolina, 1887, 1888; U. S. House of Representatives, 1789–93; U. S. Treasurer, 1801–28.

St. George Tucker (1752–1827)
Judge, General Court of Virginia, 1788–1800; president, Supreme Court of Appeals of Virginia, 1803–11; federal district judge, 1813–27.

George Tucker (1775–1861)
Virginia House of Delegates, 1815; U. S. House of Representatives, 1819–25.

Henry St. George Tucker (1780–1848)
Virginia House of Delegates, 1807–8; U. S. House of Representatives, 1815–19; state Senate, 1819–23; Virginia chancery judge, 1824–31; president, Supreme Court of Appeals of Virginia, 1831–41.

Nathaniel Beverly Tucker (1784–1851)
Missouri Circuit Court judge, 1818–26.

Nathaniel Beverley Tucker (1820–90)
U.S. consul at Liverpool, England, 1857–61.

John Randolph Tucker (1823–97)
Attorney general of Virginia, 1857–65; U. S. House of Representatives, 1875–87.

Henry St. George Tucker (1828–63)
Clerk of the Virginia Senate, 1851–52; clerk of the Virginia House of Delegates, 1853–59.

Henry St. George Tucker (1853–1932)
U. S. House of Representatives from Virginia, 1889–97, 1922–32.

In-laws and Collateral Relations

Theodorick Bland (1718–84)
Father-in-law of *St. George Tucker* (1752–1827). Virginia Senate, 1777–79.

Theodorick Bland (1742–90)
Brother-in-law of *St. George Tucker* (1752–1827). U. S. House of Representatives from Virginia, 1789–90.

John Coalter (1769–1838)
Husband of *Frances Tucker* (1769–1813). Virginia Supreme Court of Appeals, 1811–31.

Hugh Lawson White (1773–1840)
Uncle of *Lucy Ann Smith* (1812–67) [*Mrs. Nathaniel Beverley Tucker*]. Tennessee Senate, 1807–9, 1817–25; U. S. Senate, 1825–40.

John Randolph of Roanoke (1773–1833)
Stepson of *St. George Tucker* (1752–1827). U. S. House of Representatives from Virginia, 1799–1813, 1815–17, 1819–25, 1827–29, 1833; U. S. Senate, 1825–27; U.S. minister to Russia, 1830.

John Tyler (1790–1862)
Father-in-law of *Anne Tucker*. President, 1841–45, and other offices.

George Mifflin Dallas (1792–1864)
Father-in-law of *David Hunter Tucker* (1815–71). Mayor of Philadelphia, 1829; U. S. Senate from Pennsylvania, 1831–33; state attorney general, 1833–35; U.S. minister to Russia, 1837–39; Vice-President of the United States, 1845–49; U.S. minister to Great Britain, 1856–61.

William Cabell Rives (1792–1868)
Brother-in-law of *Maria Tucker*. Virginia House of Delegates, 1817–20, 1822–23; U. S. House of Representatives, 1823–29; U.S. minister to France, 1829–32, 1849–53; U. S. Senate, 1832–34, 1836–45.

Thomas Walker Gilmer (1802–44)
Father-in-law of *Henry St. George Tucker* (1828–63). Virginia House of Delegates, 1829–36, 1839–40; governor, 1840–41; U. S. House of Representatives, 1841–44; U. S. Secretary of the Navy, 1844.

THE WASHBURNS

Israel Washburn (1718–96)
Massachusetts Constitutional Convention, 1780; state House of Representatives, 1780.

Israel Washburn (1755–1841)
Massachusetts House of Representatives, 1804–10.

Israel Washburn (1784–1876)
Massachusetts House of Representatives, 1815, 1816, 1818, 1819.

Reuel Washburn (1793–1878)
Maine State Senate, 1827–28; judge of probate for Androscoggin County, 1857–59.

Israel Washburn (1813–83)
Maine House of Representatives, 1842–43; U. S. House of Representatives, 1851–61; governor, 1861–62; collector of port of Portland, Maine, 1863–77.

Elihu Benjamin Washburne (1816–87)
U. S. House of Representatives from Illinois, 1853–69; Secretary of State, 1869; U.S. minister to France, 1869–77.

Cadwallader Colden Washburn (1818–82)
U. S. House of Representatives from Wisconsin, 1855–61, 1867–71; governor, 1872–74.

Charles Ames Washburn (1822–89)
U.S. minister to Paraguay, 1861–68.

William Drew Washburn (1831–1912)
Minnesota House of Representatives, 1861–65, 1871, 1874, 1880, 1882; U. S. House of Representatives, 1879–85; U. S. Senate, 1889–95.

Hempstead Washburne (1851–1918)
Chicago city attorney, 1885–89; mayor of Chicago, 1891–93; Chicago Civil Service Commission, 1898.

William Drew Washburn (1863–1929)
Minnesota House of Representatives, 1901, 1905, 1909, 1911, 1917, 1921, 1923, 1925.

OTHER FAMILIES
IN WHICH THREE OR MORE MEMBERS
HAVE SERVED IN CONGRESS

Symbols: Pres.   President of the United States
V.P.   Vice-President of the United States
Gov.   Governor
U.S.S.   Member, United Stated Senate
H.R.   Member, U. S. House of Representatives
C.C.   Delegate, Continental Congress

ADAMS et al

Samuel Adams (1722–1803). See the Adams Dynasty. Massachusetts; C.C. 1774–82; Gov. 1794–97.

Joseph Allen (1749–1827), nephew of Samuel Adams. Massachusetts; H.R. 1810–11.

Charles Allen (1797–1869), grandson of Samuel Adams. Massachusetts; H.R. 1849–53.

AIKEN

William Aiken (1806–87). South Carolina; H.R. 1851–57.

David Wyatt Aiken (1828–87), cousin of William Aiken. South Carolina; H.R. 1877–87.

Wyatt Aiken (1863–1923), son of David W. Aiken. South Carolina; H.R. 1903–17.

ALDRICH et al

William Aldrich (1820–85). Illinois; H.R. 1877–83.

Nelson Wilmarth Aldrich (1841–1915), cousin of William Aldrich. Rhode Island; H.R. 1879–81, U.S.S. 1881–1911.

James Franklin Aldrich (1853–1933), son of William Aldrich. Illinois; H.R. 1893–97.

Richard Steere Aldrich (1884–1941), son of Nelson Wilmarth Aldrich. Rhode Island; H.R. 1923–33.

Nelson Aldrich Rockefeller (1908–   ), grandson of Nelson Wilmarth Aldrich. New York; Gov. 1959–(present).

ALEXANDER et al. Also see Williams.

Sydenham Benoni Alexander (1840–1921). North Carolina; H.R. 1891–95.

John Sharp Williams (1854–1932), cousin of Sydenham B. Alexander; grandson of Christopher H. Williams. Mississippi; H.R. 1893–1909; U.S.S. 1911–23.

Adlai Ewing Stevenson[†] (1835–1914), cousin of Sydenham B. Alexander. Illinois; H.R. 1875–77, 1879–81; V.P. 1893–97.

---

[*] The source for most information through 1961 is *Biographical Directory of the American Congress 1774–1961* (Washington: Government Printing Office, 1961).

[†] Grandfather of Adlai E. Stevenson (1900–65), 1952 and 1956 Democratic presidential candidate.

ALLEN. See Adams.

ALLEN. See Rose.

ALSTON. See Macon.

AMES *et al*

Benjamin Franklin Butler (1818–93). Massachusetts; H.R. 1867–75, 1877–79.

Adelbert Ames (1835–1933). Mississippi; U.S.S. 1870–74.

Butler Ames (1871–1954), grandson of Benjamin F. Butler; son of Adelbert Ames. Massachusetts; H.R. 1903–13.

ANDERSON *et al*

Simeon H. Anderson (1802–40). Kentucky; H.R. 1839–40.

Albert Gallatin Tabott (1808–87). Kentucky; H.R. 1855–59.

William Clayton Anderson (1826–61), son of Simeon H. Anderson; nephew of Albert G. Tabott. Kentucky; H.R. 1859–61.

ARMSTRONG

John Armstrong I‡ (1717–95). Pennsylvania; C.C. 1778–80, 1787, 1788.

James Armstrong (1748–1828), son of John Armstrong I. Pennsylvania; H.R. 1793–95.

John Armstrong II (1755–1843), son of John Armstrong I. New York; U.S.S. 1800–2, 1803–4.

ARNOLD. See Green.

ASHE

John Baptista Ashe I (1748–1802). North Carolina; C.C. 1787; H.R. 1789–93; Gov. 1802.

Thomas Samuel Ashe (1812–87), nephew of John B. Ashe. North Carolina; H.R. 1873–77.

John Baptista Ashe II (1810–57), nephew of John B. Ashe; brother of William S. Ashe, Tennessee; H.R. 1843–45.

William Shepperd Ashe (1813–62), nephew of John B. Ashe I; brother of John B. Ashe II. North Carolina; H.R. 1849–55.

BACON

John Bacon (1735–1820). Massachusetts; H.R. 1801–3.

Ezekiel Bacon (1776–1870), son of John Bacon. Massachusetts; H.R. 1807–13.

William Johnson Bacon (1803–89), son of Ezekiel Bacon. New York; H.R. 1877–79.

BANKHEAD

John Hollis Bankhead I (1842–1920). Alabama; H.R. 1887–1907; U.S.S. 1907–20.

John Hollis Bankhead II (1872–1946), son of John Hollis Bankhead I. Alabama; U.S.S. 1931–46.

‡ All numerals after names have been added for identification purposes.

William Brockman Bankhead§ (1874–1940), son of John Hollis Bankhead I. Alabama; H.R. 1917–40.

Walter Will Bankhead (1897–   ), son of John Hollis Bankhead II. Alabama; H.R. 1941.

BARBER. See Morgan.

BARBOUR

James Barbour (1775–1842). Virginia; U.S.S. 1815–25.

Philip Pendleton Barbour (1783–1841), brother of James Barbour. Virginia; H.R. 1814–25, 1827–30.

John Strode Barbour I (1790–1855), cousin of James Barbour and Philip P. Barbour. Virginia; H.R. 1823–33.

John Strode Barbour II (1820–92), son of John S. Barbour I. Virginia; H.R. 1881–87; U.S.S. 1889–92.

BECKHAM. See Wickliffe.

BELL

Samuel Bell (1770–1834). New Hampshire; U.S.S. 1823–35; Gov. 1819–23.

James Bell (1804–57), son of Samuel Bell. New Hampshire; U.S.S. 1855–57.

Charles Henry Bell (1823–93), nephew of Samuel Bell; cousin of James Bell. New Hampshire; U.S.S. 1879; Gov. 1881–83.

Samuel Newell Bell (1829–89), grandson of Samuel Bell; nephew of James Bell. New Hamphire; H.R. 1871–73, 1875–77.

BIDDLE

Edward Biddle (1738–79). Pennsylvania; C.C. 1774–76, 1778–79.

Richard Biddle (1796–1847), nephew of Edward Biddle. Pennsylvania; H.R. 1837–40.

Charles John Biddle (1819–73), nephew of Richard Biddle. Pennsylvania; H.R. 1861–63.

BLAND. See Jackson.

BLOUNT

William Blount (1749–1800). North Carolina; C.C. 1782–83, 1786–87. Tennessee; U.S.S. 1796–97.

Thomas Blount (1759–1812), brother of William Blount. North Carolina; H.R. 1793–99, 1805–9, 1811–12.

William Grainger Blount (1784–1827), son of William Blount. Tennessee; H.R. 1815–19.

BOLTON *et al*

Henry B. Payne (1810–96). Ohio; H.R. 1875–77; U.S.S. 1885–91.

Frances Payne Bolton (1885–   ), granddaughter of Henry B. Payne. Ohio; H.R. 1940–(present).

Chester Castle Bolton (1882–1939), husband of Frances P. Bolton. Ohio; H.R. 1929–37, 1939.

§ Father of Tallulah Bankhead, the actress.

Oliver Payne Bolton (1917–   ), son of Chester and Frances P. Bolton. Ohio; H.R. 1953–57, 1963–65.

BOWEN *et al.* Also see Johnston.

Rees Tate Bowen (1809–79). Virginia; H.R. 1873–75.

Henry Bowen (1841–1915), son of Rees T. Bowen; nephew of John W. Johnston. Virginia; H.R. 1883–85, 1887–89.

William Bowen Campbell (1807–67), cousin of Henry Bowen. Tennessee; H.R. 1837–43, 1866–67; Gov. 1851–53.

BOWIE *et al*

Walter Bowie (1748–1810). Maryland; H.R. 1802–5.

Thomas Fielder Bowie (1808–69), grandnephew of Walter Bowie. Maryland; H.R. 1855–59.

Reverdy Johnson (1796–1876), brother-in-law of Thomas F. Bowie. Maryland; U.S.S. 1845–49, 1863–68.

BRANCH

John Branch (1782–1863). North Carolina; U.S.S. 1823–29; H.R. 1831–33; Gov. 1817–20. Florida; Gov. 1844–45.

Lawrence O'Bryan Branch (1820–62), nephew of John Branch. North Carolina; H.R. 1855–61.

William Augustus Blount Branch (1847–1910), son of Lawrence O'B. Branch. North Carolina; H.R. 1891–95.

BRAWLEY. See Hemphill.

BRENT. See Carroll.

BRODERICK *et al*

Case Broderick (1839–1920). Kansas; H.R. 1891–99.

Andrew Kennedy (1810–47), cousin of Case Broderick and David C. Broderick. Indiana; H.R. 1841–47.

David Colbreth Broderick (1820–59), cousin of Case Broderick and Andrew Kennedy. California; U.S.S. 1857–59.

BROWN. See Young.

BROWN

John Brown (1757–1837). Virginia; C.C. 1787–88; H.R. 1789–92. Kentucky; U.S.S. 1792–1805.

James Brown (1776–1835), brother of John Brown. Louisiana; U.S.S. 1813–17, 1819–23.

Benjamin Gratz Brown (1826–85), grandson of John Brown. Missouri; U.S.S. 1863–67; Gov. 1871.

BROWN *et al*

John Brown (1736–1803). Rhode Island; H.R. 1799–1801.

Benjamin Brown (1756–1831), nephew of John Brown. Massachusetts; H.R. 1815–17.

John Brown Francis (1791–1864), grandson of John Brown. Rhode Island; U.S.S. 1844–45; Gov. 1833–38.

BUCK. See Clayton.

BUCKNER. See Hawes.

BULLOCH *et al*
Archibald Bulloch (c. 1730–77). Georgia; C.C. 1775–76.
William Bellinger Bulloch (1777–1852), son of Archibald Bulloch. Georgia; U.S.S. 1813.
Theodore Roosevelt (1858–1919), great-great-grandson of Archibald Bulloch. See Roosevelt Dynasty.

BURDICK *et al*
Usher Lloyd Burdick (1879–1960). North Dakota; H.R. 1935–45, 1949–59.
Quentin Northrop Burdick (1908–   ), son of Usher L. Burdick. North Dakota; H.R. 1959–60; U.S.S. 1960–(present).
Robert Woodrow Levering (1914–   ), son-in-law of Usher L. Burdick. Ohio; H.R. 1959–61.

BURGES. See Green.

BURRILL. See Green.

BUTLER. See Ames.

BUTLER
William Butler I (1759–1821). South Carolina; H.R. 1801–13.
William Butler II (1790–1850), son of William Butler. South Carolina; H.R. 1841–43.
Andrew Pickens Butler (1796–1857), son of William Butler I. South Carolina; U.S.S. 1846–57.
Matthew Calbraith Butler (1836–1909), son of William Butler II. South Carolina; U.S.S. 1877–95.

BYRD. See Flood.

CALHOUN *et al*
Joseph Calhoun (1750–1817). South Carolina; H.R. 1807–11.
John Ewing Colhoun (1750–1802), cousin of Joseph Calhoun and John C. Calhoun. South Carolina; U.S.S. 1801–2.
John Caldwell Calhoun (1782–1850), cousin of John E. Colhoun and Joseph Calhoun. South Carolina; H.R. 1811–17; U.S.S. 1832–43, 1845–50; V.P. 1825–32.

CALL *et al.* Also see Walker.
Richard Keith Call (1792–1862). Florida; H.R. 1823–25; Gov. 1835–40, 1841–44.
James David Walker (1830–1906). Arkansas; U.S.S. 1879–85.

Wilkinson Call (1834–1910), nephew of Richard K. Call; cousin of James D. Walker. Florida; U.S.S. 1879–97.

CANDLER

Allen Daniel Candler (1834–1910). Georgia; H.R. 1883–91; Gov. 1898–1902.

Milton Anthony Candler (1837–1909), cousin of Allen D. Candler. Georgia; H.R. 1875–79.

Ezekiel Samuel Candler, Jr. (1862–1944), nephew of Milton A. Candler. Mississippi; H.R. 1901–21.

CARROLL *et al*

Charles Carroll "the Barrister" (1723–83), cousin of Charles Carroll of Carrollton and Daniel Carroll. Maryland; C.C. 1776.

Daniel Carroll (1730–96), cousin of Charles Carroll "the Barrister" and Charles Carroll of Carrollton. Maryland; C.C. 1780–84; H.R. 1789–91.

Charles Carroll of Carrollton (1737–1832), cousin of Charles Carroll "the Barrister" and Daniel Carroll. Maryland; C.C. 1776–78, 1780; U.S.S. 1789–92.

Richard Brent (1757–1814), nephew of Daniel Carroll. Virginia; H.R. 1795–99, 1801–3; U.S.S. 1809–14.

Charles Hobart Carroll (1794–1865), great-grandson of Daniel Carroll. New York; H.R. 1843–47.

John Lee Carroll (1830–1911), great-grandson of Charles Carroll of Carrollton. Maryland; Gov. 1875–79.

CHANDLER *et al*. Also see Hale.

John Chandler (1762–1841). Massachusetts; H.R. 1805–9. Maine; U.S.S. 1820–29.

Thomas Chandler (1772–1866), brother of John Chandler. New Hampshire; H.R. 1829–33.

Zachariah Chandler (1813–79), nephew of John Chandler and Thomas Chandler. Michigan; U.S.S. 1857–75, 1879.

Frederick Hale (1874–1963), grandson of Zachariah Chandler. Maine; U.S.S. 1917–41.

CHAPPELL. See Lamar.

CHASE *et al*

Dudley Chase (1771–1846). Virginia; U.S.S. 1813–17, 1825–31.

Salmon Portland Chase (1808–73), nephew of Dudley Chase; cousin of Dudley C. Denison. Ohio; U.S.S. 1849–55, 1861; Gov. 1855–59.

Dudley Chase Denison (1819–1905), nephew of Dudley Chase; cousin of Salmon P. Chase. Vermont; H.R. 1875–79.

CHIPMAN

Nathaniel Chipman (1752–1843). Vermont; U.S.S. 1797–1803.

Daniel Chipman (1765–1850), brother of Nathaniel Chipman. Vermont; H.R. 1815–16.

John Logan Chipman (1830–93), grandson of Nathaniel Chipman. Michigan; H.R. 1887–93.

CILLEY

Bradbury Cilley (1760–1831). New Hampshire; H.R. 1813–17.

Joseph Cilley (1791–1887), nephew of Bradbury Cilley; brother of Jonathan Cilley. New Hampshire; U.S.S. 1846–47.

Jonathan Cilley (1802–38), nephew of Bradbury Cilley; brother of Joseph Cilley. Maine; H.R. 1837–38.

CLAIBORNE

Thomas Claiborne I (1749–1805). Virginia; H.R. 1793–99, 1801–5.

John Claiborne (1777–1808), son of Thomas Claiborne I. Virginia; H.R. 1808.

Thomas Claiborne II (1780–1856), son of Thomas Claiborne I. Tennessee; H.R. 1817–19.

CLAIBORNE *et al*

William Charles Cole Claiborne (1775–1817). Tennessee; H.R. 1797–1801. Louisiana; Gov. 1812–17; U.S.S. 1817.

Nathaniel Herbert Claiborne (1777–1859), brother of William Charles Cole Claiborne. Virginia; H.R. 1825–37.

John Francis Hamtramck Claiborne (1809–84), nephew of William Charles Cole Claiborne and Nathaniel Herbert Claiborne. Mississippi; H.R. 1835–38.

Herbert Claiborne Pell, Jr. (1884–1961), great-grandson of John Francis Hamtramck Claiborne. New York; H.R. 1919–21.

Clairborne De Borda Pell (1918–   ), son of Herbert Claiborne Pell, Jr. Rhode Island; U.S.S. 1961–(present).

CLARK

Christopher Henderson Clark (1767–1828). Virginia; H.R. 1804–6.

James Clark (1770–1839), brother of Christopher H. Clark. Kentucky; H.R. 1813–16, 1825–31.

John Bullock Clark (1802–85), nephew of Christopher H. Clark and James Clark. Missouri; H.R. 1857–61.

John Bullock Clark, Jr. (1831–1903), son of John B. Clark. Missouri; H.R. 1873–83.

CLAYPOOL *et al*

Horatio Clifford Claypool (1859–1921). Ohio; H.R. 1911–15, 1917–19.

John Barney Peterson (1850–1944), cousin of Horatio C. Claypool. Indiana; H.R. 1913–15.

Harold Kile Claypool (1886–1958), son of Horatio C. Claypool. Ohio; H.R. 1937–43.

CLAYTON *et al*

Joshua Clayton (1744–98). Delaware; U.S.S. 1798; Gov. 1793–98.

Thomas Clayton (1778–1854), son of Joshua Clayton. Delaware; H.R. 1815–17; U.S.S. 1824–27, 1837–47.

John Middleton Clayton (1796–1856), nephew of Joshua Clayton. Delaware; U.S.S. 1829–36, 1845–49, 1850–56.

Clayton Douglass Buck (1890–1965), great-grandnephew of John M. Clayton. Delaware; U.S.S. 1943–49; Gov. 1929–37.

Thomas Coleman Du Pont (1863–1930), father-in-law of Clayton Douglass Buck. Delaware; U.S.S. 1921–22, 1925–28.

CLINTON

George Clinton I (1739–1812). New York; C.C. 1775–76; Gov. 1777–95; V.P. 1804–12.

George Clinton II (1771–1809), son of George Clinton I. New York; H.R. 1805–9.

De Witt Clinton (1769–1828), nephew of George Clinton I. New York; U.S.S. 1802–3; Gov. 1817–21, 1825–28.

James Graham Clinton (1804–49), nephew of George Clinton I; half brother of De Witt Clinton. New York; H.R. 1841–45.

COCHRANE. See Hazelton.

COCKE

William Cocke (1747–1828). Tennessee; U.S.S. 1796–97, 1799–1805.

John Cocke (1772–1854), son of William Cocke. Tennessee; H.R. 1819–27.

William Michael Cocke (1815–96), grandson of William Cocke; nephew of John Cocke. Tennessee; H.R. 1845–49.

COLES *et al*

Isaac Coles (1747–1813). Virginia; H.R. 1789–91, 1793–97.

Patrick Henry (1736–99), cousin of Isaac Coles. Virginia; C.C. 1774–76; Gov. 1776–79, 1784–86.

Walter Coles (1790–1857), son of Isaac Coles. Virginia; H.R. 1835–45.

COLHOUN. See Calhoun.

COMPTON. See Key.

CONDICT *et al*

Silas Condict (1738–1801). New Jersey; C.C. 1781–84.

Lewis Condict (1772–1862), nephew of Silas Condict. New Jersey; H.R. 1811–17, 1821–33.

Augustus William Cutler (1827–97), great-grandson of Silas Condict. New Jersey; H.R. 1875–79.

CONKLING

Alfred Conkling (1789–1874). New York; H.R. 1821–23.

Frederick Augustus Conkling (1816–91), son of Alfred Conkling. New York; H.R. 1861–63.

Roscoe Conkling (1829–88), son of Alfred Conkling. New York; H.R. 1859–63, 1865–67; U.S.S. 1867–81.

CONTEE. See Hanson.

CORWIN

Moses Bledso Corwin (1790–1872). Ohio; H.R. 1849–51, 1853–55.

Thomas Corwin (1794–1865), brother of Moses B. Corwin. Ohio; H.R. 1831–40, 1859–61; U.S.S. 1845–50; Gov. 1840–42.

DENISON. See Chase.

DENNIS

John Dennis I (1771–1806). Maryland; H.R. 1797–1805.

Littleton Purnell Dennis (1786–1834), nephew of John Dennis I. Maryland; H.R. 1833–34.

John Dennis II (1807–59), son of John Dennis I. Maryland; H.R. 1837–41.

DIXON

Nathan Fellows Dixon I (1774–1842). Rhode Island; U.S.S. 1839–42.

Nathan Fellows Dixon II (1812–81), son of Nathan F. Dixon I. Rhode Island; H.R. 1849–51, 1863–71.

Nathan Fellows Dixon III (1847–97), son of Nathan F. Dixon II. Rhode Island; H.R. 1885; U.S.S. 1889–95.

DONNELL. See Spaight.

DOX. See Nicholas.

DU PONT. See Clayton.

EARLE *et al*

Elias Earle (1762–1823). South Carolina; H.R. 1805–7, 1811–15, 1817–21.

Samuel Earle (1760–1833), nephew of Elias Earle. South Carolina; H.R. 1795–97.

John Baylis Earle (1766–1863), nephew of Elias Earle; cousin of Samuel Earle. South Carolina; H.R. 1803–5.

William Lowndes Yancey (1814–63), uncle of Joseph Haynsworth Earle. Alabama; H.R. 1844–46.

Joseph Haynsworth Earle (1847–97), great-grandson of Elias Earle; nephew of William L. Yancey; cousin of John L. M. Irby. South Carolina; U.S.S. 1897.

John Laurens Manning Irby (1854–1900), great-grandson of Elias Earle; cousin of Joseph Haynsworth Earle. South Carolina; U.S.S. 1891–97.

EDWARDS *et al*

Benjamin Edwards (1753–1829). Maryland; H.R. 1795.

Ninian Edwards (1775–1855), son of Benjamin Edwards. Illinois; U.S.S. 1818–24; Gov. 1826–31.

Benjamin Edwards Grey, grandson of Benjamin Edwards. Kentucky; H.R. 1851–55.

ELKINS. See Davis.

ELMER

Jonathan Elmer (1745–1817). New Jersey; C.C. 1776–78, 1781–84, 1787, 1788; U.S.S. 1789–91.

Ebenezer Elmer (1752–1843), brother of Jonathan Elmer. New Jersey; H.R. 1801–7.

Lucius Quintius Cincinnatus Elmer (1793–1883), son of Ebenezer Elmer. New Jersey; H.R. 1843–45.

Franklin Corwin (1818–79), nephew of Moses B. Corwin and Thomas Corwin. Illinois; H.R. 1873–75.

CRAVENS

Jordan Edgar Cravens (1830–1914). Arkansas; H.R. 1877–83.

William Ben Cravens (1872–1939), cousin of Jordan E. Cravens. Arkansas; H.R. 1907–13, 1933–39.

William Fadjo Cravens (1899–   ), son of William B. Cravens. Arkansas; H.R. 1939–49.

CRUMPACKER

Edgar Dean Crumpacker (1851–1920). Indiana; H.R. 1897–1913.

Maurice Edgar Crumpacker (1886–1927), son of Edgar D. Crumpacker. Oregon; H.R. 1925–27.

Shepard J. Crumpacker, Jr. (1917–   ), cousin of Edgar D. Crumpacker and Maurice E. Crumpacker. Indiana; H.R. 1951–57.

CULLOM

Alvan Cullom (1797–1877). Tennessee; H.R. 1843–47.

William Cullom (1810–96), brother of Alvan Cullom. Tennessee; H.R. 1851–55.

Shelby Moore Cullom (1829–1914), nephew of Alvan Cullom and William Cullom. Illinois; H.R. 1865–71; U.S.S. 1883–1913; Gov. 1877–83.

CUTLER. See Condict.

DARLINGTON

Isaac Darlington (1781–1839). Pennsylvania; H.R. 1817–19.

William Darlington (1782–1863), cousin of Isaac Darlington and Edward Darlington. Pennsylvania; H.R. 1815–17, 1819–23.

Edward Darlington (1795–1884), cousin of Isaac Darlington and William Darlington. Pennsylvania; H.R. 1833–39.

Smedley Darlington (1827–99), second cousin of Isaac Darlington, William Darlington, and Edward Darlington. Pennsylvania; H.R. 1887–91.

DAVIS *et al*

Henry Gassaway Davis (1823–1916). West Virginia; U.S.S. 1871–83.

Thomas Beall Davis (1828–1911), brother of Henry G. Davis. West Virginia; H.R. 1905–7.

Stephen Benton Elkins (1841–1911), son-in-law of Henry G. Davis. New Mexico; H.R. 1873–77. West Virginia; U.S.S. 1895–1911.

Davis Elkins (1876–1959), grandson of Henry G. Davis; son of Stephen B. Elkins. West Virginia; U.S.S. 1911, 1919–25.

DAWES

Rufus Dawes (1838–99). Ohio; H.R. 1881–83.

Charles Gates Dawes (1865–1951), son of Rufus Dawes. Illinois; V.P. 1925–29.

Beman Gates Dawes (1870–1953), son of Rufus Dawes. Ohio; H.R. 1905–9.

EPES *et al*

James Fletcher Epes (1842–1910). Virginia; H.R. 1891–95.

Sydney Parham Epes (1865–1900), cousin of James F. Epes. Virginia; H.R. 1897–98, 1899–1900.

William Bacon Oliver (1867–1948), cousin of Sydney P. Epes. Alabama; H.R. 1915–37.

FESSENDEN

William Pitt Fessenden (1806–69). Maine; H.R. 1841–43; U.S.S. 1854–64.

Samuel Clement Fessenden (1815–82), brother of William P. Fessenden and Thomas A. D. Fessenden. Maine; H.R. 1861–63.

Thomas Amory Deblois Fessenden (1826–68), brother of William P. Fessenden and Samuel C. Fessenden. Maine; H.R. 1862–63.

FINDLAY

John Findlay (1766–1838). Pennsylvania; H.R. 1821–27.

William Findlay (1768–1840), brother of John Findlay and James Findlay. Pennsylvania; U.S.S. 1821–27.

James Findlay (1770–1835), brother of John Findlay and William Findlay. Ohio; H.R. 1825–33.

FISH

Hamilton Fish I (1808–93). New York; H.R. 1843–45; U.S.S. 1851–57; Gov. 1849–50.

Hamilton Fish II (1849–1936), son of Hamilton Fish I. New York; H.R. 1909–11.

Hamilton Fish III (1888–   ), son of Hamilton Fish II. New York; H.R. 1920–45.

FISHBURNE. See Maverick.

FLOOD *et al*

Henry De La Warr Flood (1865–1921). Virginia; H.R. 1901–21.

Joel West Flood (1894–   ), brother of Henry De La Warr Flood. Virginia; H.R. 1932–33.

Harry Flood Byrd (1887–   ), nephew of Henry De La Warr Flood and Joel W. Flood. Virginia; Gov. 1926–30; U.S.S. 1933–65.

Harry Flood Byrd, Jr. (1915–   ). Virginia; U.S.S. 1966–(present).

FLOYD. See Preston.

FORNEY

Peter Forney (1756–1834). North Carolina; H.R. 1813–15.

Daniel Munroe Forney (1784–1847), son of Peter Forney. North Carolina; H.R. 1815–18.

William Henry Forney (1823–94), grandson of Peter Forney. Alabama; H.R. 1875–93.

FRANCIS. See Brown.

FRANK. See Patterson.

GAILLARD. See Hunt.

GAMBLE

John Rankin Gamble (1848–91). South Dakota; H.R. 1891.

Robert Jackson Gamble (1851–1924), brother of John R. Gamble. South Dakota; H.R. 1895–97, 1899–1901; U.S.S. 1901–13.

Ralph Abernethy Gamble (1885–1959), son of Robert J. Gamble. New York; H.R. 1937–57.

GARNETT *et al*

James Mercer Garnett (1770–1843). Virginia; H.R. 1805–9.

Robert Selden Garnett (1789–1840), brother of James M. Garnett. Virginia; H.R. 1817–27.

Charles Fenton Mercer (1778–1858), cousin of Robert S. Garnett. Virginia; H.R. 1817–39.

Muscoe Russell Hunter Garnett (1821–64), grandson of James M. Garnett. Virginia; H.R. 1856–61.

GERRY

Elbridge Gerry I (1744–1814). Massachusetts; C.C. 1776–81, 1782–85; H.R. 1789–93; Gov. 1810–11; V.P. 1813–14.

Elbridge Gerry II (1813–86), grandson of Elbridge Gerry I. Maine; H.R. 1849–51.

Peter Goelet Gerry (1879–1957), great-grandson of Elbridge Gerry I. Rhode Island; H.R. 1913–15; U.S.S. 1917–29, 1935–47.

GILMAN

John Taylor Gilman (1753–1828). New Hampshire; C.C. 1782, 1783; Gov. 1794–1805, 1813–16.

Nicholas Gilman (1755–1814), brother of John T. Gilman. New Hampshire; C.C. 1786–88; H.R. 1789–97; U.S.S. 1805–14.

Charles Jervis Gilman (1824–1901), grandnephew of John T. Gilman and Nicholas Gilman. Maine; H.R. 1857–59.

GOFF *et al*

Nathan Goff (1843–1920). West Virginia; H.R. 1883–89; U.S.S. 1913–19.

Guy Despard Goff (1866–1933), son of Nathan Goff. West Virginia; U.S.S. 1925–31.

Brazilla Carroll Reece (1889–1961), son-in-law of Guy D. Goff. Tennessee; H.R. 1921–31, 1933–47, 1951–61.

Louise Goff Reece, wife of Carroll Reece; daughter of Guy D. Goff. Tennessee; H.R. 1961–62.

GOLDSBOROUGH *et al*

Robert Goldsborough (1733–88). Maryland; C.C. 1774–75.

Charles Goldsborough (1765–1834). Maryland; H.R. 1805–17; Gov. 1818–19.

Robert Henry Goldsborough (1779–1836). Maryland; U.S.S. 1813–19, 1835–36.

Winder Laird Henry (1864–1940), great-grandson of Charles Goldsborough and Robert Henry Goldsborough. Maryland; H.R. 1894–95.

Thomas Alan Goldsborough (1877–1951), great-great-great-grandson of Robert Goldsborough; great-grandson of Charles Goldsborough. Maryland; H.R. 1921–39.

GRAYSON *et al*

William Grayson (1740–90). Virginia; C.C. 1784–87; U.S.S. 1789–90.

Alexander Dalrymple Orr (1761–1835), nephew of William Grayson. Kentucky; H.R. 1792–97.

William John Grayson (1788–1863), son of William Grayson. South Carolina; H.R. 1833–37.

GREEN. See Wharton.

GREEN *et al*

Jonathan Arnold (1741–93), father of Lemuel Hastings Arnold; great-great-grandfather of Theodore Francis Green. Rhode Island; C.C. 1782–84.

Lemuel Hastings Arnold (1792–1852), son of Jonathan Arnold; great-great-uncle of Theodore F. Green. Rhode Island; H.R. 1845–47; Gov. 1831–32.

James Burrill, Jr. (1772–1820), great-grandfather of Theodore F. Green. Rhode Island; U.S.S. 1817–20.

Tristam Burges (1770–1853), great-great-uncle of Theodore F. Green. Rhode Island; H.R. 1825–35.

Samuel Greene Arnold (1821–80), great-uncle of Theodore F. Green. Rhode Island; H.R. 1862–63.

Theodore Francis Green (1867–1966). Rhode Island; U.S.S. 1937–61.

GREY. See Edwards.

GRIFFIN. See Wilson.

GUDGER *et al*

James Madison Gudger, Jr. (1855–1920). North Carolina; H.R. 1903–7, 1911–15.

John Wesley Langley (1868–1932), son-in-law of James M. Gudger, Jr. Kentucky; H.R. 1907–26.

Katherine Gudger Langley (1888–1948), daughter of James M. Gudger, Jr.; wife of John W. Langley. Kentucky; H.R. 1927–31.

HABERSHAM

Joseph Habersham (1751–1815). Georgia; C.C. 1783, 1784.

John Habersham (1754–99), brother of Joseph Habersham. Georgia; C.C. 1785, 1786.

Richard Wylly Habersham (1786–1842), nephew of Joseph Habersham and John Habersham. Georgia; H.R. 1839–42.

HALE. Also see Chandler.

Eugene Hale (1836–1918). Maine; H.R. 1869–79; U.S.S. 1881–1911.

Frederick Hale (1874–1963), grandson of Zachariah Chandler; son of Eugene Hale. Maine; U.S.S. 1917–41.

Robert Hale (1889–   ), cousin of Frederick Hale. Maine; H.R. 1943–59.

HALL

William Augustus Hall (1815–88). Missouri; H.R. 1862-65.

Willard Preble Hall (1820–82), brother of William A. Hall. Missouri; H.R. 1847–53; Gov. 1864, 1865.

Ariel Sebree Hall (1852–1932), son of William A. Hall. Missouri; H.R. 1893–97.

HALSEY

Silas Halsey (1743–1832). New York; H.R. 1805-7.

Nicoll Halsey (1782–1865), son of Silas Halsey. New York; H.R. 1833–35.

Jehiel Howell Halsey (1788–1867), son of Silas Halsey. New York; H.R. 1829–31.

HAMPTON *et al*

Wade Hampton I (1752–1835). South Carolina; H.R. 1795–97, 1803–5.

Francis Preston (1765–1836), father-in-law of Wade Hampton II. Virginia; H.R. 1793–97.

Wade Hampton II (1818–1902), grandson of Wade Hampton I; son-in-law of Francis Preston. South Carolina; Gov. 1876–79; U.S.S. 1879–91.

HANNA *et al*

Marcus Alonzo Hanna (1837–1904). Ohio; U.S.S. 1897–1904.

Ruth Hanna (1880–1944), daughter of Marcus A. Hanna. Illinois; H.R. 1929–31.

Joseph Medill McCormick (1877–1925), first husband of Ruth Hanna. Illinois; H.R. 1917–19; U.S.S. 1919–25.

Albert Gallatin Simms (1882–1964), second husband of Ruth Hanna. New Mexico; H.R. 1929–31.

HANSON *et al*

John Hanson (1715–83). Maryland; C.C. 1780–83.

Benjamin Contee (1755–1815). Maryland; C.C. 1787–88; H.R. 1789–91.

Alexander Contee Hanson (1786–1819), grandson of John Hanson; grand-nephew of Benjamin Contee. Maryland; H.R. 1813–16; U.S.S. 1816–19.

HARDIN

Martin Davis Hardin (1780–1823). Kentucky; U.S.S. 1816–17.

Benjamin Hardin (1784–1852), cousin of Martin D. Hardin. Kentucky; H.R. 1815–17, 1819–23, 1833–37.

John J. Hardin (1810–47), son of Martin D. Hardin. Illinois; H.R. 1843–45.

HAWES *et al*

Aylett Hawes (1768–1833). Virginia; H.R. 1811–17.

Richard Hawes (1797–1877), nephew of Aylett Hawes; brother of Albert G. Hawes; cousin of Aylett H. Buckner. Kentucky; H.R. 1837–41.

Albert Gallatin Hawes (1804–49), nephew of Aylett Hawes; brother of Richard Hawes; cousin of Aylett H. Buckner. Kentucky; H.R. 1831–37.

Aylett Hawes Buckner (1816–94), nephew of Aylett Hawes; cousin of Richard Hawes and Albert G. Hawes. Missouri; H.R. 1873–85.

Harry Barton Hawes (1869–1947), grandnephew of Richard Hawes and Albert G. Hawes. Missouri; H.R. 1921–26; U.S.S. 1926–33.

HAWKINS *et al.* Also see Macon.

Benjamin Hawkins (1754–1816). North Carolina; C.C. 1781–84, 1786–87; U.S.S. 1789–95.

Nathaniel Macon (1757–1837). North Carolina; H.R. 1791–1815; U.S.S. 1815–28.

Micajah Thomas Hawkins (1790–1858), nephew of Benjamin Hawkins; nephew of Nathaniel Macon. North Carolina; H.R. 1831–41.

HAZELTON *et al*

Clark Belton Cochrane (1815–67). New York; H.R. 1857–61.

Gerry Whiting Hazelton (1829–1920), nephew of Clark B. Cochrane; brother of George C. Hazelton. Wisconsin; H.R. 1871–75.

George Cochrane Hazelton (1832–1922), nephew of Clark B. Cochrane; brother of Gerry W. Hazelton. Wisconsin; H.R. 1877–83.

HEMPHILL *et at*

Robert Witherspoon (1767–1837). South Carolina; H.R. 1809–11.

John Hemphill (1803–62). Texas; U.S.S. 1859–61.

John James Hemphill (1849–1912), nephew of John Hemphill. South Carolina; H.R. 1883–93.

William Huggins Brawley (1841–1916), cousin of John James Hemphill. South Carolina; H.R. 1891–94.

Robert Witherspoon Hemphill (1915–   ), great-great-nephew of John Hemphill; grandnephew of John James Hemphill; great-great-grandson of Robert Witherspoon. South Carolina; H.R. 1957–65.

HENRY. See Goldsborough.

HENRY *et al*

Patrick Henry (1736–99). Virginia; C.C. 1774–76; Gov. 1776–79, 1784–86.

William Henry Roane (1787–1845), grandson of Patrick Henry. Virginia; H.R. 1815–17; U.S.S. 1837–41.

Robert Lee Henry (1864–1931), great-great-great-grandson of Patrick Henry. Texas; H.R. 1897–1917.

HEPBURN. See Lyon.

HERLONG. See Johnson.

HIESTER

John Hiester (1745–1821). Pennsylvania; H.R. 1807–9.

Daniel Hiester I (1747–1804), brother of John Hiester; cousin of Joseph Hiester. Pennsylvania; H.R. 1789–96. Maryland; H.R. 1801–4.

Joseph Hiester (1752–1832), cousin of John Hiester and Daniel Hiester. Pennsylvania; H.R. 1797–1805, 1815–20; Gov. 1820–24.

Daniel Hiester II (1774–1834), son of John Hiester. Pennsylvania; H.R. 1809–11.

William Hiester (1790–1853), nephew of John Hiester and Daniel Hiester I. Pennsylvania; H.R. 1831–37.

Henry Augustus Muhlenberg (1823–54), grandson of Joseph Hiester. Pennsylvania; H.R. 1853–54.

Isaac Ellmaker Hiester (1824–71), son of William Hiester. Pennsylvania; H.R. 1853–55.

Hiester Clymer (1827–84), nephew of William Hiester. Pennsylvania; H.R. 1873–81.

HOAR

Samuel Hoar (1778–1856). Massachusetts; H.R. 1835–37.

Ebenezer Rockwood Hoar (1816–95), son of Samuel Hoar. Massachusetts; 1873–75.

George Frisbie Hoar (1826–1904), son of Samuel Hoar. Massachusetts; H.R. 1869–77; U.S.S. 1877–1904.

Rockwood Hoar (1855–1906), son of George Frisbie Hoar. Massachusetts; H.R. 1905–6.

Sherman Hoar (1860–98), son of Ebenezer Rockwood Hoar. Massachusetts; H.R. 1891–93.

HOUSTON *et al*

David Hubbard (1792–1874). Alabama; H.R. 1839–41, 1849–51.

Samuel Houston (1793–1863), cousin of David Hubbard. Tennessee; H.R. 1823–27; Gov. 1827–29. Texas; U.S.S. 1846–59; Gov. 1859–61.

Andrew Jackson Houston (1854–1941), son of Samuel Houston. Texas; U.S.S. 1941.

HUBBARD. See Houston.

HUNT *et al*

John Gaillard (1765–1826). South Carolina; U.S.S. 1804–26.

Theodore Gaillard Hunt (1805–93), nephew of John Gaillard. Louisiana; H.R. 1853–55.

Carleton Hunt (1836–1921), nephew of Theodore Gaillard Hunt. Louisiana; H.R. 1883–85.

INGERSOLL

Jared Ingersoll (1749–1822). Pennsylvania; C.C. 1780, 1781.

Charles Jared Ingersoll (1782–1862), son of Jared Ingersoll. Pennsylvania; H.R. 1813–15, 1841–49.

Joseph Reed Ingersoll (1786–1868), son of Jared Ingersoll. Pennsylvania; H.R. 1835–37, 1841–49.

IRBY. See Earle.

JACKSON *et al*

George Jackson (1757–1831). Virginia; H.R. 1795–97, 1799–1803.

John George Jackson (1777–1825), son of George Jackson. Virginia; H.R. 1803–10, 1813–17.

Edward Brake Jackson (1793–1826), son of George Jackson. Virginia; H.R. 1820–23.

William Thomas Bland (1861–1928), grandson of John G. Jackson. Missouri; H.R. 1919–21.

James Monroe Jackson (1825–1901), cousin of William T. Bland. West Virginia; H.R. 1889–90.

JACKSON

James Jackson I (1757–1806). Georgia; H.R. 1789–91; U.S.S. 1793–95, 1801–6; Gov. 1798–1801.

Jabez Young Jackson (1790–1839), son of James Jackson I. Georgia; H.R. 1835–39.

James Jackson II (1819–87), grandson of James Jackson I; nephew of Jabez Y. Jackson. Georgia; H.R. 1857–61.

JOHNSON. See Bowie.

JOHNSON

James Johnson (1774–1826). Kentucky; H.R. 1825–26.

Richard Menton Johnson (1781–1850), brother of James Johnson and John T. Johnson. Kentucky; H.R. 1807–19, 1829–37; U.S.S. 1819–29; V.P. 1837–41.

John Telemachus Johnson (1788–1856), brother of James Johnson and Richard M. Johnson. Kentucky; H.R. 1821–25.

Robert Ward Johnson (1814–79), nephew of James Johnson, Richard M. Johnson, and John T. Johnson. Arkansas; H.R. 1847–53; U.S.S. 1853–61.

JOHNSON *et al*

Jed Johnson, Sr. (1888–1963). Oklahoma; H.R. 1927–47.

Albert Sydney Herlong, Jr. (1909–   ), father-in-law of Jed Johnson, Jr. Florida; H.R. 1949–(present).

Jed Johnson, Jr. (1939–   ), son of Jed Johnson, Sr. Oklahoma; H.R. 1965–(present).

JOHNSTON *et al.* Also see Bowen.

Charles Clement Johnston (1795–1832). Virginia; H.R. 1831–32.

Joseph Eggleston Johnston (1807–91), brother of Charles C. Johnston. Virginia; H.R. 1879–81.

John Warfield Johnston (1818–89), nephew of Charles C. Johnston and Joseph E. Johnston. Virginia; U.S.S. 1870–83.

Henry Bowen (1841–1915), nephew of John W. Johnston. Virginia; H.R. 1883–85, 1887–89.

JONES. See Monroe.

KEAN

John Kean I (1756–95). South Carolina; C.C. 1785–87.

John Kean II (1852–1914), great-grandson of John Kean I. New Jersey; H.R. 1883–85, 1887–89; U.S.S. 1899–1911.

Hamilton Fish Kean (1862–1941), great-grandson of John Kean I. New Jersey; U.S.S. 1929–35.

Robert Winthrop Kean (1893–   ), son of Hamilton F. Kean; nephew of John Kean II. New Jersey; H.R. 1939–59.

KENNEDY. See Broderick.

KERR et al

John Kerr I (1782–1836). Virginia; H.R. 1813–15, 1815–17.

Bartlett Yancey (1785–1828), cousin of John Kerr. North Carolina; H.R. 1813–17.

John Kerr II (1811–79), son of John Kerr. North Carolina; H.R. 1853–55.

John Hosan Kerr (1873–1958), grandnephew of John Kerr I. North Carolina; H.R. 1923–53.

KEY et al

Philip Key (1750–1820). Maryland; H.R. 1791–93.

Philip Barton Key (1757–1815), cousin of Philip Key. Maryland; H.R. 1807–13.

Barnes Compton (1830–98), great-grandson of Philip Key. Maryland; H.R. 1885–89, 1889–90, 1891–94.

KING

Rufus King (1755–1827). Massachusetts; C.C. 1784–87. New York; U.S.S. 1789–96, 1813–25.

Cyrus King (1772–1817), half brother of Rufus King. Massachusetts; H.R. 1813–17.

John Alsop King (1788–1867), son of Rufus King; brother of James G. King. New York; H.R. 1849–51.

James Gore King (1791–1853), son of Rufus King; brother of John A. King. New Jersey; H.R. 1849–51.

KITCHIN

William Hodges Kitchin (1837–1901). North Carolina; H.R. 1879–81.

William Walton Kitchin (1866–1924), son of William H. Kitchin; brother of Claude Kitchin. North Carolina; H.R. 1897–1909; Gov. 1909–13.

Claude Kitchin (1869–1923), son of William H. Kitchin; brother of William W. Kitchin. North Carolina; H.R. 1901–23.

Alvin Paul Kitchin (1908–   ), grandson of William H. Kitchin; nephew of William W. Kitchin and Claude Kitchin. North Carolina; H.R. 1957–63.

KUNKEL et al. Also see Sergeant.

John Sergeant (1779–1852), great-grandfather of John Crain Kunkel; grandfather of John S. Wise. Pennsylvania; H.R. 1815–23, 1827–29, 1837–41.

John Christian Kunkel (1816–70). Pennsylvania; H.R. 1855–59.

John Crain Kunkel (1898–   ), great-grandson of John Sergeant; grandson of John Christian Kunkel. Pennsylvania; H.R. 1939–51, 1961–(present).

LAMAR et al

Absalom Harris Chappell (1801–78). Georgia; H.R. 1843–45.

Lucius Quintus Cincinnatus Lamar (1825–94), cousin of Absalom H. Chappell. Mississippi; H.R. 1857–61; U.S.S. 1877–85.

William Barley Lamar (1853–1928), nephew of L. Q. C. Lamar, Florida; H.R. 1903–9.

LANE

Joseph Lane (1801–60). Oregon; H.R. 1851–59; U.S.S. 1859–60.

La Fayette Lane (1842–96), son of Joseph Lane. Oregon; H.R. 1875–77.

Harry Lane (1855–1917), grandson of Joseph Lane; nephew of La Fayette Lane. Oregon; U.S.S. 1913–17.

LANGLEY. See Gudger.

LEVERING. See Burdick.

LINCOLN

Levi Lincoln I (1749–1820). Massachusetts; H.R. 1800–1; Gov. 1808–9.

Levi Lincoln II (1782–1868), son of Levi Lincoln I. Massachusetts; H.R. 1834–41; Gov. 1825–34.

Enoch Lincoln (1788–1829), son of Levi Lincoln I; brother of Levi Lincoln II. Massachusetts; H.R. 1818–21. Maine; H.R. 1821–26; Gov. 1827–29.

LOCKE *et al*

Matthew Locke (1730–1801). North Carolina; H.R. 1793–99.

Francis Locke (1776–1823), nephew of Matthew Locke. North Carolina; U.S.S. 1814–15.

Effiegene Locke Wingo (1883–   ), great-granddaughter of Matthew Locke. Arkansas; H.R. 1930–33.

Otis Theodore Wingo (1877–1930), husband of Effiegene Locke Wingo. Arkansas; H.R. 1913–30.

LONGWORTH. See Storer.

LYON *et al*

Matthew Lyon (1746–1833). Vermont; H.R. 1797–1801. Kentucky; H.R. 1803–11.

Chittenden Lyon (1787–1842), son of Matthew Lyon. Kentucky; H.R. 1827–35.

William Peters Hepburn (1833–1916), great-grandson of Matthew Lyon. Iowa; H.R. 1881–87, 1893–1909.

McARTHUR. See Nesmith.

McCORMICK. See Hanna.

McDOWELL. See Preston.

McDOWELL

Joseph McDowell (1756–1801). North Carolina; H.R. 1797–99.

Joseph (P. G.) McDowell (1758–99), cousin of Joseph McDowell. North Carolina; H.R. 1793–95.

Joseph Jefferson McDowell (1800–77), son of Joseph McDowell. Ohio; H.R. 1843–47.

MACLAY

William Maclay (1737–1804). Pennsylvania; U.S.S. 1789–91.

Samuel Maclay (1741–1811), brother of William Maclay. Pennsylvania; H.R. 1795–97; U.S.S. 1803–9.

William Plunkett Maclay (1774–1842), son of Samuel Maclay. Pennsylvania; H.R. 1816–21.

McLEAN *et al*. Also see Walker.

John McLean (1791–1830). Illinois; H.R. 1818–19; U.S.S. 1824–25.

William McLean (1794–1863), brother of John McLean. Ohio; H.R. 1823–29.

James David Walker (1830–1906), nephew of John McLean; grandson of David Walker; cousin of Wilkinson Call. Arkansas; U.S.S. 1879–85.

MACON *et al*. Also see Hawkins.

Nathaniel Macon (1757–1837). North Carolina; H.R. 1791–1815, U.S.S. 1815–28.

Willis Alston (1769–1837), nephew of Nathaniel Macon. North Carolina; H.R. 1799–1815, 1825–31.

Micajah Thomas Hawkins (1790–1858), nephew of Nathaniel Macon; nephew of Benjamin Hawkins. North Carolina; H.R. 1831–41.

Charles Henry Martin (1848–1931), great-grandson of Nathaniel Macon. North Carolina; H.R. 1896–99.

MARTIN. See Macon.

MATTHEWS. See Watterson.

MAURY. See Maverick.

MAVERICK *et al*

James Luther Slayden (1853–1924). Texas; H.R. 1897–1919.

Abram Poindexter Maury (1801–48). Tennessee; H.R. 1835–39.

John Word Fishburne (1868–1937). Virginia; H.R. 1931–37.

Fontaine Maury Maverick (1895–1954), nephew of James L. Slayden; cousin of Abram P. Maury and John W. Fishburne. Texas; H.R. 1935–39.

MERCER. See Garnett.

MIDDLETON.

Henry Middleton I (1717–84). South Carolina; C.C. 1774–76.

Arthur Middleton (1742–87), son of Henry Middleton I. South Carolina; C.C. 1776–78, 1781–83.

Henry Middleton II (1770–1846), son of Arthur Middleton. South Carolina; H.R. 1815–19; Gov. 1810–12.

MONROE *et al*

Joseph Jones (1727–1805). Virginia; C.C. 1777, 1778, 1780–83.

James Monroe I (1758–1831), nephew of Joseph Jones. Virginia; C.C. 1783–86; U.S.S. 1790–94; Gov. 1799–1802; Pres. 1817–25.

James Monroe II (1799–1870), nephew of James Monroe I. New York; H.R. 1839–41.

MORGAN *et al*

Noyes Barber (1781–1836). Connecticut; H.R. 1821–35.

Edwin Barbour Morgan (1806–81), nephew of Noyes Barber; brother of Christopher Morgan. New York; H.R. 1853–59.

Christopher Morgan (1808–77), nephew of Noyes Barber; brother of Edwin B. Morgan. New York: H.R. 1839–43.

MORRIS

Lewis Morris (1726–98). New York; C.C. 1775–77.

Gouverneur Morris (1752–1816), half brother of Lewis Morris. New York; C.C. 1777–78; U.S.S. 1800–3.

Lewis Robert Morris (1760–1825), nephew of Lewis Morris and Gouverneur Morris. Vermont; H.R. 1797–1803.

NESMITH *et al*

James Willis Nesmith (1820–85). Oregon; U.S.S. 1861–67; H.R. 1873–75.

Joseph Gardner Wilson (1826–73), cousin of James W. Nesmith. Oregon; H.R. 1873.

Clifton Nesmith McArthur (1879–1923), grandson of James W. Nesmith. Oregon; H.R. 1915–23.

NICHOLAS *et al*

John Nicholas (1757–1819). Virginia; H.R. 1793–1801.

William Cary Nicholas (1761–1820), brother of John Nicholas. Virginia; U.S.S. 1799–1804; H.R. 1807–9; Gov. 1814–17.

Robert Carter Nicholas (1793–1857), nephew of John Nicholas and William C. Nicholas. Louisiana; U.S.S. 1836–41.

Peter Myndert Dox (1813–91), grandson of John Nicholas. Alabama; H.R. 1869–73.

OLIVER. See Epes.

ORR. See Grayson.

PATTERSON *et al*

William Patterson (1789–1839). New York; H.R. 1837–39.

George Washington Patterson (1799–1879), brother of William Patterson. New York; H.R. 1877–79.

Augustus Frank (1826–95), nephew of William Patterson. New York; H.R. 1859–65.

PATTON *et al*

John Patton (1823–97). Pennsylvania; H.R. 1861–63, 1887–89.

John Patton, Jr. (1850–1907), son of John Patton; brother of Charles E. Patton. Michigan; U.S.S. 1894–95.

Charles Emory Patton (1859–1937), son of John Patton; brother of John Patton, Jr. Pennsylvania; H.R. 1911–15.

William Irvin Swoope (1862–1930), nephew of John Patton. Pennsylvania; H.R. 1923–27.

PELL. See Claiborne

PENDLETON *et al*

Edmund Pendleton (1721–1803). Virginia; C.C. 1774, 1775.

John Penn (1741–88), nephew of Edmund Pendleton; cousin of Nathaniel Pendleton. North Carolina; C.C. 1775–80.

Nathaniel Pendleton (1756–1821), nephew of Edmund Pendleton; cousin of John Penn. North Carolina; C.C. 1789.

PENN. See Pendleton.

PETERSON. See Claypool.

PRESTON *et al*

Francis Preston (1765–1836). Virginia; H.R. 1793–97.

James Patton Preston (1774–1843), brother of Francis Preston. Virginia; Gov. 1816–19.

John Floyd (1783–1837), brother-in-law of Francis Preston and James Patton Preston. Virginia; H.R. 1817–29; Gov. 1830–34.

William Campbell Preston (1794–1860), son of Francis Preston; nephew of James Patton Preston. South Carolina; U.S.S. 1833–42.

James McDowell (1796–1851), nephew of Francis Preston and James Patton Preston. Virginia; Gov. 1842–46; H.R. 1846–51.

William Ballard Preston (1805–62), son of James Patton Preston; nephew of Francis Preston. Virginia; H.R. 1847–49.

William Preston (1816–87), nephew of Francis Preston and James Patton Preston. Kentucky; H.R. 1852–55.

Wade Hampton (1818–1902), son-in-law of Francis Preston; brother-in-law of William Campbell Preston. South Carolina; Gov. 1876–79; U.S.S. 1879–91.

RANSOM. See Wharton.

REECE. See Goff.

REID. See Settle.

ROANE. See Henry.

ROCKEFELLER. See Aldrich.

RODNEY

Caesar Rodney (1728–84). Delaware; C.C. 1774–76, 1777, 1778; Gov. 1778–82.

Thomas Rodney (1744–1811), brother of Caesar Rodney. Delaware; C.C. 1781–83, 1785–87.

Caesar Augustus Rodney (1772–1824), son of Thomas Rodney. Delaware; H.R. 1803–5, 1821–22; U.S.S. 1822–23.

George Brydges Rodney (1803–83), cousin of Caesar Rodney, Thomas Rodney, and Caesar A. Rodney. Delaware; H.R. 1841–45.

ROOSEVELT. See Bulloch.

ROSE et al

Robert Selden Rose (1774–1835). New York; H.R. 1823–27, 1829–31.
Nathaniel Allen (1780–1832). New York; H.R. 1819–21.
Robert Lawson Rose (1804–77), son of Robert S. Rose; son-in-law of Nathaniel Allen. New York; H.R. 1847–51.

RUTLEDGE

John Rutledge (1739–1800). South Carolina; C.C. 1774–76, 1782–83; Gov. 1779–82.
Edward Rutledge (1749–1800), brother of John Rutledge. South Carolina; C.C. 1774–77; Gov. 1798–1800.
John Rutledge, Jr. (1766–1819), son of John Rutledge. South Carolina; H.R. 1797–1803.

SANFORD

John Sanford I (1803–57). New York; H.R. 1841–43.
Stephen Sanford (1826–1913), son of John Sanford. New York; H.R. 1869–71.
John Sanford II (1851–1939), son of Stephen Sanford. New York; H.R. 1889–93.

SAULSBURY

Eli Saulsbury (1817–93). Delaware; U.S.S. 1871–89.
Willard Saulsbury I (1820–92), brother of Eli Saulsbury. Delaware; U.S.S. 1859–71.
Willard Saulsbury II (1861–1927), son of Willard Saulsbury I. Delaware; U.S.S. 1913–19.

SERGEANT et al. Also see Kunkel and Wise.

Jonathan Dickinson Sergeant (1746–93). New Jersey; C.C. 1776, 1777.
John Sergeant (1779–1852), son of Jonathan D. Sergeant. Pennsylvania; H.R. 1815–23, 1827–29, 1837–41.
John Sergeant Wise (1846–1913), grandson of John Sergeant; son of Henry A. Wise. Virginia; H.R. 1883–85.
John Crain Kunkel (1898–   ), great-grandson of John Sergeant; grandson of John Christian Kunkel. Pennsylvania; H.R. 1939–51, 1961–(present).

SETTLE et al

Thomas Settle I (1789–1857). North Carolina; H.R. 1817–21.
David Settle Reid (1813–91), nephew of Thomas Settle I. North Carolina; H.R. 1843–47; Gov. 1850–52; U.S.S. 1854–59.
Thomas Settle II (1865–1919), grandson of Thomas Settle I. North Carolina; H.R. 1893–97.

SEYMOUR

Horatio Seymour (1778–1857). Vermont; U.S.S. 1821–33.
Origen Storrs Seymour (1804–81), nephew of Horatio Seymour. Connecticut; H.R. 1851–55.
Edward Woodruff Seymour (1832–92), son of Origen S. Seymour. Connecticut; H.R. 1883–87.

SIMMS. See Hanna.

SINNICKSON

Thomas Sinnickson I (1744–1817). New Jersey; H.R. 1789–91, 1797–99.

Thomas Sinnickson II (1786–1873), nephew of Thomas Sinnickson I. New Jersey; H.R. 1828–29.

Clement Hall Sinnickson (1834–1919), grandnephew of Thomas Sinnickson I. New Jersey; H.R. 1875–79.

SLAYTON. See Maverick.

SMITH

Jeremiah Smith (1759–1842). New Hampshire; H.R. 1791–97; Gov. 1809–10.

Samuel Smith (1765–1842), brother of Jeremiah Smith. New Hampshire; H.R. 1813–15.

Robert Smith (1802–67), nephew of Jeremiah Smith and Samuel Smith. Illinois; H.R. 1843–49, 1857–59.

SMITH

Nathaniel Smith (1762–1822). Connecticut; H.R. 1795–99.

Nathan Smith (1770–1835), brother of Nathaniel Smith. Connecticut; U.S.S. 1833–35.

Truman Smith (1791–1884), nephew of Nathaniel Smith and Nathan Smith. Connecticut; H.R. 1839–43, 1845–49; U.S.S. 1849–54.

SOUTHARD

Henry Southard (1747–1842). New Jersey; H.R. 1801–11, 1815–21.

Isaac Southard (1783–1850), son of Henry Southard; brother of Samuel L. Southard. New Jersey; H.R. 1831–33.

Samuel Lewis Southard (1787–1842), son of Henry Southard; brother of Isaac Southard. New Jersey; U.S.S. 1821–23, 1833–42; Gov. 1832–33.

SPAIGHT *et al*

Richard Dobbs Spaight (1758–1802). North Carolina; C.C. 1782–85; H.R. 1798–1801; Gov. 1792–95.

Richard Dobbs Spaight, Jr. (1796–1850), son of Richard D. Spaight. North Carolina; H.R. 1823–25; Gov. 1835–37.

Richard Spaight Donnell (1820–67), grandson of Richard D. Spaight. North Carolina; H.R. 1847–49.

STEVENS

Charles Abbot Stevens (1816–92). Massachusetts; H.R. 1875.

Moses Tyler Stevens (1825–1907), brother of Charles A. Stevens. Massachusetts; H.R. 1891–95.

Isaac Ingalls Stevens (1818–62), cousin of Charles A. Stevens and Moses T. Stevens. Washington; Gov. 1853–57; H.R. 1857–61.

STEVENSON. See Alexander.

STONE

Thomas Stone (1743–87). Maryland; C.C. 1775, 1779, 1784–85.

Michael Jenifer Stone (1747–1812), brother of Thomas Stone. Maryland; H.R. 1789–91.

Frederick Stone (1820–99), grandson of Michael J. Stone. Maryland; H.R. 1867–71.

STORER *et al*

Bellamy Storer I (1796–1875). Ohio; H.R. 1835–37.

Bellamy Storer II (1847–1922), son of Bellamy Storer I. Ohio; H.R. 1891–95.

Nicholas Longworth (1869–1931), nephew of Bellamy Storer II; also son-in-law of Theodore Roosevelt. Ohio; H.R. 1903–13, 1915–31.

STROTHER

George French Strother (1783–1840). Virginia; H.R. 1817–20.

James French Strother I (1811–60), son of George F. Strother. Virginia; H.R. 1851–53.

James French Strother II (1868–1930), grandson of James F. Strother I. West Virginia; H.R. 1925–29.

SULLIVAN

John Sullivan (1740–95). New Hampshire; C.C. 1774–75, 1780–81; Gov. 1786–87.

James Sullivan (1744–1808), brother of John Sullivan. Massachusetts; C.C. 1782; Gov. 1807–8.

George Sullivan (1771–1838), son of John Sullivan. New Hampshire; H.R. 1811–13.

SWOOPE. See Patton.

SYMINGTON. See Wadsworth.

TABOTT. See Anderson.

TAYLOR

Nathaniel Green Taylor (1819–87). Tennessee; H.R. 1854–55, 1866–67.

Alfred Alexander Taylor (1848–1931), son of Nathaniel G. Taylor; brother of Robert L. Taylor. Tennessee; H.R. 1889–95; Gov. 1921–23.

Robert Love Taylor (1850–1912), son of Nathaniel G. Taylor; brother of Alfred A. Taylor. Tennessee; H.R. 1879–81; U.S.S. 1907–12; Gov. 1887–91, 1897–99.

UNDERWOOD

Joseph Rogers Underwood (1791–1876). Kentucky; H.R. 1835–43; U.S.S. 1847–53.

Warner Lewis Underwood (1808–72), brother of Joseph R. Underwood. Kentucky; H.R. 1855–59.

Oscar Wilder Underwood (1862–1929), grandson of Joseph R. Underwood. Alabama; H.R. 1895–96, 1897–1915; U.S.S. 1915–27.

VAN RENSSELAER

Jeremiah Van Rensselaer (1738–1810). New York; H.R. 1789–91.

Killian Killian Van Rensselaer (1763–1845), cousin of Jeremiah Van Rensselaer. New York; H.R. 1801–11.

Solomon Van Vechten Van Rensselaer (1774–1852), son of Jeremiah Van Rensselaer and nephew of Killian K. Van Rensselaer. New York; H.R. 1819–22.

WADSWORTH *et al*

James Wolcott Wadsworth I (1846–1926). New York; H.R. 1881–85, 1891–1907.

James Wolcott Wadsworth II¶ (1877–1952), son of James W. Wadsworth I. New York; U.S.S. 1915–27; H.R. 1933–51.

[William] Stuart Symington* (1901–   ), son-in-law of James W. Wadsworth II. Missouri; U.S.S. 1953–(present).

WALKER. Also see Call and McLean.

George Walker (1763–1819). Kentucky; U.S.S. 1814.

David Walker (d. 1820), brother of George Walker. Kentucky; H.R. 1817–20.

James David Walker (1830–1906), grandson of David Walker; nephew of John McLean; cousin of Wilkinson Call. Arkansas; U.S.S. 1879–85.

WALTON

John Walton (1738–83). Georgia; C.C. 1778.

George Walton (1750–1848), brother of John Walton. Georgia; C.C. 1776–78, 1780–81, 1787–88; U.S.S. 1795–96; Gov. 1779–89.

Matthew Walton (d. 1819), cousin of John Walton and George Walton. Kentucky; H.R. 1803–7.

WATTERSON *et al*

Harvey Magee Watterson (1811–91). Tennessee; H.R. 1839–43.

Stanley Matthews (1824–89). Ohio; U.S.S. 1877–79.

Henry Watterson (1840–1921), son of Harvey M. Watterson; nephew of Stanley Matthews. Kentucky; H.R. 1876–77.

WEEKS

John Wingate Weeks I (1781–1853). New Hampshire; H.R. 1829–33.

John Wingate Weeks II (1860–1926), grandnephew of John W. Weeks I. Massachusetts; H.R. 1905–13; U.S.S. 1913–19.

Edgar Weeks (1839–1904), cousin of John W. Weeks II. Michigan; H.R. 1899–1903.

Sinclair Weeks (1893–   ), son of John W. Weeks II. Massachusetts; U.S.S. 1944.

¶ Son-in-law of John Hay (1838–1905), U. S. Secretary of State; father of James J. Wadsworth (1905–   ), U. S. Ambassador to UN 1953–61, and Federal Communications Commission, 1965–(present).

* Father of James Wadsworth Symington (1928–   ), Chief of Protocol, U. S. Department of State 1966–(present).

WHARTON et al
Jesse Wharton (1782–1833). Tennessee; H.R. 1807–9; U.S.S. 1814–15.
Wharton Jackson Green (1831–1910), grandson of Jesse Wharton. North Carolina; H.R. 1883–87.
Matt Whitaker Ransom (1826–1904), cousin of Wharton J. Green. North Carolina; U.S.S. 1872–95.

WHITE
James White (1749–1809). North Carolina; H.R. 1786–88. Tennessee; H.R. 1794–96.
Edward Douglas White I (1795–1847), son of James White. Louisiana; H.R. 1829–34, 1839–43; Gov. 1834–38.
Edward Douglas White II (1845–1921), son of Edward D. White I. Louisiana; U.S.S. 1891–94.

WHITE
John White (1802–45). Kentucky; H.R. 1835–45.
Addison White (1824–1909), cousin of John White. Kentucky; H.R. 1851–53.
John Daugherty White (1849–1920), nephew of John White. Kentucky; H.R. 1875–77, 1881–85.

WHITEHILL
John Whitehill (1729–1815). Pennsylvania; H.R. 1803–7.
Robert Whitehill (1738–1813), brother of John Whitehill. Pennsylvania; H.R. 1805–13.
James Whitehill (1762–1822), son of John Whitehill. Pennsylvania; H.R. 1813–14.

WHITTLESEY
Elisha Whittlesey (1783–1863). Ohio; H.R. 1823–38.
Frederick Whittlesey (1799–1851), cousin of Elisha Whittlesey and Thomas T. Whittlesey. New York; H.R. 1831–35.
Thomas Tucker Whittlesey (1798–1868), cousin of Elisha Whittlesey and Frederick Whittlesey. Connecticut; H.R. 1836–39.
William Augustus Whittlesey (1796–1866), nephew of Elisha Whittlesey. Ohio; H.R. 1849–51.

WICKLIFFE et al
Charles Anderson Wickliffe (1788–1869). Kentucky; H.R. 1823–33, 1861–63; Gov. 1839–40.
John Crepps Wickliffe Beckham (1869–1940), grandson of Charles A. Wickliffe; cousin of Robert C. Wickliffe. Kentucky; U.S.S. 1915–21; Gov. 1900–7.
Robert Charles Wickliffe (1874–1912), grandson of Charles A. Wickliffe; cousin of John C. W. Beckham. Louisiana; H.R. 1909–12.

WILLIAMS et al. Also see Alexander.
Christopher Harris Williams (1798–1857). Tennessee; H.R. 1837–43, 1849–53.
John Sharp Williams (1854–1932), grandson of Christopher H. Williams. Mississippi; H.R. 1893–1909; U.S.S. 1911–23.

Sydenham Benoni Alexander (1840–1921), cousin of John S. Williams; cousin of Adlai E. Stevenson. North Carolina; H.R. 1891–95.

WILLIAMS

Robert Williams (1773–1836). North Carolina; H.R. 1797–1803.

John Williams (1778–1837), brother of Robert Williams and Lewis Williams. Tennessee; U.S.S. 1815–23.

Lewis Williams (1782–1842), brother of Robert Williams and John Williams. North Carolina; H.R. 1815–42.

Marmaduke Williams (1774–1850), cousin of Robert Williams, John Williams, and Lewis Williams. North Carolina; H.R. 1803–9.

John Lanier Williams (1810–65), son of John Williams. Tennessee; H.R. 1837–43.

WILSON. See Nesmith.

WILSON *et al*

Isaac Griffin (1756–1827), great-grandfather of Eugene McL. Wilson. Pennsylvania; H.R. 1813–17.

Thomas Wilson (1765–1826). Virginia; H.R. 1811–13.

Edgar Campbell Wilson (1800–60), son of Thomas Wilson. Virginia; H.R. 1833–35.

Eugene McLanohan Wilson (1833–90), son of Edgar C. Wilson; grandson of Thomas Wilson and Isaac Griffin. Minnesota; H.R. 1869–71.

WINGO. See Locke.

WISE. Also see Sergeant

Henry Alexander Wise (1806–76). Virginia; H.R. 1833–44; Gov. 1856–60.

Richard Alsop Wise (1843–1900), son of Henry A. Wise; brother of John S. Wise; cousin of George D. Wise. Virginia; H.R. 1898–99, 1900.

John Sergeant Wise (1846–1913), grandson of John Sergeant; son of Henry A. Wise; brother of Richard A. Wise; cousin of George D. Wise. Virginia; H.R. 1883–85.

George Douglas Wise (1831–98), nephew of Henry A. Wise; cousin of Richard A. Wise and John S. Wise. Virginia; H.R. 1881–89, 1889–90, 1891–95.

WITHERSPOON. See Hemphill.

YANCEY. See Kerr.

YOUNG *et al*

William Singleton Young (1790–1827). Kentucky; H.R. 1825–27.

Bryan Rust Young (1800–82), brother of William S. Young. Kentucky; H.R. 1845–47.

John Young Brown (1835–1904), nephew of William S. Young and Bryan R. Young. Kentucky; H.R. 1859–61, 1873–77; Gov. 1891–95.

ACKNOWLEDGMENTS

No book that attempts to tell the story of so many could possibly have been written without the generous help of the current members of America's political dynasties and those who know them. The author expresses his deep indebtedness to the following:

Charles Francis Adams, Mrs. Hugh D. Auchincloss, Geoffrey V. Azoy, Mrs. Elbert Baldwin, Alexis I. Du Pont Bayard, D. Chadwick Braggiotti, John B. Breckinridge, Mr. and Mrs. Scott D. Breckinridge, Jr., Mrs. George P. Coleman, Henry O. H. Frelinghuysen, Peter H. B. Frelinghuysen, Mrs. Robert T. Gannett, Milton S. Gwirtzman, Anna Roosevelt Halsted, William Henry Harrison, Fred Holborn, and David S. Ingalls.

Also Edward M. Kennedy, Robert F. Kennedy, Bruce Lee, E. Brooke Lee, Mrs. Fitzhugh Lee II, Fitzhugh Lee III, P. Blair Lee, Robert E. Lee IV, Goodhue Livingston, George Cabot Lodge, Henry Cabot Lodge, Jr., Mr. and Mrs. John Davis Lodge, Gillis Long, Russell B. Long, Speedy O. Long, Cynthia Taft Morris, Frederick A. Muhlenberg, Mr. and Mrs. Fitzhugh Lee Opie, and Belle Roosevelt Palfrey.

Also Archibald B. Roosevelt, Edith Kermit Roosevelt, Elliott Roosevelt, Franklin D. Roosevelt, Jr., James Roosevelt, Kermit Roosevelt, R. Sargent Shriver, Bayard Stockton III, Reginald H. Sturtevant, Charles P. Taft, Peter Taft, Robert Taft, Jr., William Howard Taft III, C. Langhorne Washburn, Mrs. I. H. Washburn, Thomas Washburne, and Mrs. Andrew M. Williams.

Most of the research for *America's Political Dynasties* was done at the Library of Congress and the District of Columbia Public Library, whose staffs were invariably kind and helpful. At the Library of Congress the author is under particular obligation to those who man the Thomas Jefferson Room, Local History and Genealogy, Rare Book Collection, Manuscript Division, Microfilm Reading Room, Newspaper Section, and Law Library. Thanks also to the staff of the Oral History Collection of Columbia University and to Edward R. Riley, director of research, Colonial Williamsburg.

On Capitol Hill, two charming ladies, Fran Cochran and Helen Cannen, respectively of the staffs of Senators Joseph S. Clark and Thomas H. Kuchel, served as the author's personal monitoring system.

The photographs in this volume were either contributed by those pictured or are from the collection of the Library of Congress, where Milton Kaplan, curator of prints and photographs, has once again allowed the author to exploit a valued friendship.

A number of good friends, whose services fit into no exact category, but whose unfailing thoughtfulness has been invaluable, deserve special mention. Among them: Alvin Deutsch, Irving Ferman, André Maillard, Mr. and Mrs. William Mason, Earl Mazo, and John C. Whitaker.

Miss Rose Winters typed almost all of the manuscript, a labor whose magnitude was matched only by her cheerfulness. Kathryn Tebbel was copyreader *par excellence*.

And finally, the author's deepest gratitude is reserved for the two ladies who made this book possible, his wife, Elena Shayne Hess, to whom this work is dedicated, and Ellin K. Roberts, an editor of rare insight and good will.

To all of these people goes much credit for any new light that is thrown on the subject; for the book's shortcomings, the author bears full responsibility.

STEPHEN HESS

Washington, D.C.
November 5, 1965

BIBLIOGRAPHY*

A) *Autobiographies, Memoirs, and Published Collections of Letters, Speeches, and Writings*

Adams, Charles Francis, Jr. *An Autobiography.* Boston and New York: Houghton Mifflin, 1916.

Adams, Henry. *The Education of Henry Adams.* Boston and New York: Houghton Mifflin, 1918.

——*Henry Adams and His Friends; a Collection of His Unpublished Letters.* Harold Dean Cater, editor. Boston and New York: Houghton Mifflin, 1947.

——*Letters of Henry Adams, 1858–1891.* 2 vols. Worthington Chauncey Ford, editor. Boston and New York: Houghton Mifflin, 1930–38.

——*The Selected Letters of Henry Adams.* Newton Arvin, editor. New York: Farrar, Straus & Young, 1951.

Adams, John. *Diary and Autobiography of John Adams.* (*The Adams Papers,* Series I.) 4 vols. L. H. Butterfield, editor. Cambridge: Harvard University Press, 1961.

Adams, John Quincy. *Memoirs.* 12 vols. Charles Francis Adams, editor. Philadelphia: J. B. Lippincott, 1874–77.

Alsop, Joseph and Stewart. *The Reporter's Trade.* New York: Reynal, 1958.

Baker, Ray Stannard. *American Chronicle.* New York: Charles Scribner's Sons, 1945.

Barker, Charles E. *With President Taft in the White House.* Chicago: A. Krock, 1947.

Bayard, James A. "Letters of James Asheton Bayard, 1802–1814." Henry C. Conrad, editor. *Papers of the Historical Society of Delaware.* XXXI. Wilmington, 1901.

——"Papers of James A. Bayard, 1796–1815." Elizabeth Donnan, editor. *Annual Report of the American Historical Association for the Year 1913.* II. Washington, 1915.

Bayard, Samuel. "Judge Bayard of New Jersey and His London Diary of 1795–96." James Grant Wilson, editor. *Proceedings of the New Jersey Historical Society.* 2d Series, VIII, No. 4 (1885).

Benton, Thomas H. *Thirty Years' View.* 2 vols. New York: D. Appleton, 1854–56.

Biddle, Francis. *A Casual Past.* Garden City, New York: Doubleday, 1961.

Blaine, James G. *Twenty Years of Congress.* 2 vols. Norwich, Connecticut: Henry Bill Publishing Company, 1884–86.

Boudinot, Elias. *Elias Boudinot's Journey to Boston in 1809.* Milton Halsey Thomas, editor. Princeton: Princeton University Library, 1955.

——*The Life, Public Services, Addresses and Letters of Elias Boudinot.* 2 vols. J. J. Boudinot, editor. Boston and New York: Houghton Mifflin, 1896.

Braggiotti, Gloria. *Born in a Crowd.* New York: Crowell, 1957.

Breckinridge, Henry. *Excerpts, 1935–1936.* New York: Court Press, 1938.

——*Excerpts III, 1938–41.* New York: Court Press, 1944.

Breckinridge, Mary. *Wide Neighborhoods.* New York: Harper & Brothers, 1952.

---

* Private collections of manuscripts and memorabilia, as well as printed sources of more limited use, are indicated in the footnotes.

Breckinridge, William L. *A Christian College: Its Instruction and Its Government*. Cincinnati: Moore, Wilstach & Baldwin, 1864.
——*Submission to the Will of God*. Louisville: Morton & Griswold, 1841.
Buchanan, James. "Letters of James Buchanan." William Frederic Worner, editor. *Papers Read Before the Lancaster County Historical Society*. XXXVI, No. 8. Lancaster, Pennsylvania, 1932.
Butt, Archibald W. *Taft and Roosevelt*. 2 vols. Garden City, New York: Doubleday, 1930.
Carpenter, Frank G. *Carp's Washington*. New York: McGraw-Hill, 1960.
Chanler, Mrs. Winthrop. *Autumn in the Valley*. Boston: Little, Brown, 1936.
——*Roman Spring*. Boston: Little, Brown, 1935.
Clay, Cassius Marcellus. *The Life of Cassius Marcellus Clay*. 2 vols. Cincinnati: J. F. Brennan, 1886.
Clay, Henry. *The Papers of Henry Clay*. 3 vols. James F. Hopkins, editor. Lexington: University of Kentucky Press, 1959–63.
Curley, James Michael. *I'd Do It Again*. Englewood Cliffs, New Jersey: Prentice-Hall, 1957.
Danckaerts, Jasper. *Journals of Jasper Danckaerts, 1679–1680*. Bartlett Burleigh James and J. Franklin Jameson, editors. New York: Charles Scribner's Sons, 1913.
Daniels, Mrs. Josephus. *Recollections of a Cabinet Minister's Wife, 1913–1921*. Raleigh: Presses of Mitchell Printing Company, 1945.
Edge, Walter Evans. *A Jerseyman's Journal, Fifty Years of American Business and Politics*. Princeton: Princeton University Press, 1948.
Eisenhower, Dwight D. *Mandate for Change, 1953–1956*. Garden City, New York: Doubleday, 1963.
Farley, James A. *Jim Farley's Story, the Roosevelt Years*. New York: Whittlesey House, 1948.
Flynn, Edward J. *You're the Boss*. New York: Viking Press, 1947.
Fox, Gustavus Vasa. *Confidential Correspondence of Gustavus Vasa Fox, Assistant Secretary of the Navy, 1861–1865*. 2 vols. Robert Means Thompson and Richard Wainwright, editors. New York: Naval History Society, 1918–19.
Goodrich, Samuel Griswold. *Recollections of a Lifetime*. 2 vols. New York: Miller, Orton & Mulligan, 1856.
Grant, Anne MacVicar. *Memoirs of an American Lady*. London: Longman, Hurst, Rees & Orme, 1808.
Grant, Ulysses Simpson. *General Grant's Letters to a Friend, 1861–1880*. James Grant Wilson, editor. New York and Boston: T. Y. Crowell, 1897.
Green, Johnny. *Johnny Green of the Orphan Brigade*. A. D. Kirwan, editor. Lexington: University of Kentucky Press, 1956.
Griscom, Lloyd C. *Diplomatically Speaking*. Boston: Little, Brown, 1940.
——*The Reminiscences of Lloyd C. Griscom*. Transcript in Oral History Research Office, Columbia University.
Harrison, Carter H. *Stormy Years*. Indianapolis and New York: Bobbs-Merrill, 1935.
Harrison, John Scott. *Pioneer Life at North Bend*. Cincinnati: R. Clarke, 1867.
Harrison, Mary Lord, *Pension to*. Hearings before the Committee on Pensions, United States Senate, 75th Congress, 1st Session, Washington: Government Printing Office, 1937.
Hassett, William D. *Off the Record with F.D.R.* New Brunswick: Rutgers University Press, 1958.

Havemeyer, Louisine W. "The Suffrage Torch, Memories of a Militant." *Scribner's Magazine*, LXXI, No. 5 (May 1922).

——"The Prison Special, Memories of a Militant." *Scribner's Magazine*, LXXI, No. 6 (June 1922).

Hayes, Rutherford B. *Hayes, the Diary of a President*. T. Harry Williams, editor. New York: D. McKay, 1964.

Hoar, George F. *Autobiography of Seventy Years*. 2 vols. New York: Charles Scribner's Sons, 1903.

Hone, Philip. *The Diary of Philip Hone, 1828–1851*. 2 vols. Bayard Tuckerman, editor. New York: Dodd, Mead, 1889.

Hoover, Herbert. *The Memoirs of Herbert Hoover*. 3 vols. New York: Macmillan, 1951–52.

Hoover, Irwin H. *Forty-two Years in the White House*. Boston and New York: Houghton Mifflin, 1934.

Ickes, Harold L. *The Secret Diary of Harold L. Ickes*. 3 vols. New York: Simon & Schuster, 1953–55.

Irby, Sam. *Kidnapped by the Kingfish*. New Orleans: Orleans Publishing Company, 1932.

Jay, John. *The Correspondence and Public Papers of John Jay*. Henry P. Johnston, editor. New York: G. P. Putnam's Sons, 1890–93.

Joyce, John A. *Jewels of Memory*. Washington: Gibson Brothers, 1895.

Kennedy, John F. *The Kennedy Wit*. Bill Adler, editor. New York: Citadel Press, 1964.

King, Rufus. *The Life and Correspondence of Rufus King*. 6 vols. Charles R. King, editor. New York: G. P. Putnam's Sons, 1894–1900.

Kirkpatrick, Mrs. Jane. *The Light of Other Days: Sketches of the Past, and Other Selections from the Writings of the Late Mrs. Jane Kirkpatrick*. Janes Eudora Cogswell, editor. New Brunswick: Press of J. Terhune, 1856.

Knight, Sarah. "Madam Sarah Knight, Her Diary and Her Times, 1666–1726." Anson Titus, editor. *The Bostonian Society Publications*. IX. Boston, 1912.

Lee, Richard Henry. *The Letters of Richard Henry Lee*. 2 vols. James Curtis Ballagh, editor. New York: Macmillan, 1911–14.

Lee, Robert E., Jr. *My Father, General Lee*. Garden City, New York: Doubleday, 1960.

Lee, William. *Letters of William Lee, 1766–1783*. 3 vols. Worthington Chauncey Ford, editor. New York: Historical Printing Club, 1891.

Livingston, Nancy Shippen. *Nancy Shippen, Her Journal Book*. Ethel Armes, editor. Philadelphia: J. B. Lippincott, 1935.

Livingston, Robert. *The Livingston Indian Records, 1666–1723*. Lawrence W. Leder, editor. Gettysburg: Pennsylvania Historical Association, 1956.

Livingston, Robert R. *The Original Letters of Robert R. Livingston, 1801–1803*. Edward A. Parsons, editor. New Orleans: Louisiana Historical Society, 1953.

Livingston, William. *Selections from the Correspondence of the Executive of New Jersey, from 1776 to 1786*. Newark, 1848.

——"Unpublished Correspondence of William Livingston and John Jay." Frank Monaghan, editor. *Proceedings of the New Jersey Historical Society*. LII, No. 3 (July 1934).

Lodge, George C., *to be Assistant Secretary of Labor for International Affairs, Nomination of*. Hearings before the Committee on Labor and Public

Welfare, United States Senate, 86th Congress, 1st Session. Washington: Government Printing Office, 1959.

Lodge, Henry Cabot. *Early Memories.* New York: Charles Scribner's Sons, 1913.

Long, Huey P. *Every Man a King.* New Orleans: National Book Company, 1933.

——*My First Days in the White House.* Harrisburg: The Telegraph Press, 1935.

Longworth, Alice Roosevelt. *Crowded Hours.* New York: Charles Scribner's Sons, 1934.

Looker, Earle. *The White House Gang.* New York: Fleming H. Revell, 1929.

Maclay, William. *The Journal of William Maclay.* New York: D. Appleton, 1890.

Manning, Helen Taft. "My Brother Bob Taft." *American Magazine.* January 1952.

Martin, Joe, as told to Robert J. Donovan. *My First Fifty Years in Politics.* New York: McGraw-Hill, 1960.

Mencken, H. L. *A Carnival of Buncombe.* Malcolm Moos, editor. Baltimore: Johns Hopkins Press, 1956.

——*A Mencken Chrestomathy.* New York: Alfred A. Knopf, 1949.

Muhlenberg, Henry Melchior. *The Journals of Henry Melchior Muhlenberg.* 2 vols. Philadelphia: The Evangelical Lutheran Ministerium of Pennsylvania and Adjacent States and the Muhlenberg Press, 1942.

Murphy, Robert. *Diplomat Among Warriors.* Garden City, New York: Doubleday, 1964.

Nixon, Richard M. *Six Crises.* Garden City, New York: Doubleday, 1962.

O'Brien, Robert Lincoln. *The Reminiscences of Robert Lincoln O'Brien.* Transcript in Oral History Office, Columbia University.

Parker, Agnes. *The Real Madeleine Pollard, a Diary of Ten Weeks' Association with the Plaintiff in the Famous Breckinridge-Pollard Suit.* New York: G. W. Dillingham, 1894.

Parks, Lilian Rogers, with Frances Spatz Leighton. *My Thirty Years Backstairs at the White House.* New York: Fleet, 1961.

Paterson, William. *Glimpses of Colonial Society and the Life at Princeton College, 1766–1773.* W. Jay Mills, editor. Philadelphia: J. B. Lippincott, 1903.

Quincy, Josiah. *Figures of the Past from the Leaves of Old Journals.* Boston: Roberts Brothers, 1883.

Rhea, Mini, with Frances Spatz Leighton. *I Was Jacqueline Kennedy's Dressmaker.* New York: Fleet, 1962.

Robinson, Corinne Roosevelt. *My Brother Theodore Roosevelt.* New York: Charles Scribner's Sons, 1921.

Rogers, Will. *The Autobiography of Will Rogers.* Donald Day, editor. Boston: Houghton Mifflin, 1949.

Roosevelt, Anna. "My Life with F.D.R." *Woman,* May–November 1949.

Roosevelt, Eleanor. *On My Own.* New York: Harper & Brothers, 1958.

——*This I Remember.* New York: Harper & Brothers, 1949.

——*This Is My Story.* New York: Harper & Brothers, 1937.

Roosevelt, Elliott (1860–93). *Hunting Big Game in the Eighties; The Letters of Elliott Roosevelt, Sportsman.* Eleanor Roosevelt, editor. New York: Charles Scribner's Sons, 1932.

Roosevelt, Elliott (1910–   ). *As He Saw It.* New York: Duell, Sloan & Pearce, 1946.

Roosevelt, Franklin D., Jr. "How We Won," *Collier's*, August 6, 1949.

——*Franklin D. Roosevelt, Jr., to be Under Secretary of Commerce, Nomination of.* Hearings before the Committee on Commerce, United States Senate, 88th Congress, 1st Session. Washington: Government Printing Office, 1963.

Roosevelt, James, and Sidney Shalett. *Affectionately, F.D.R.* New York: Harcourt, Brace, 1959.

Roosevelt, Nicholas. *A Front Row Seat.* Norman, Oklahoma: University of Oklahoma Press, 1953.

Roosevelt, Sara Delano, as told to Isabel Leighton and Gabrielle Forbush. *My Boy Franklin.* New York: R. Long & R. R. Smith, 1933.

Roosevelt, Quentin. *Quentin Roosevelt, A Sketch with Letters.* Kermit Roosevelt, editor. New York: Charles Scribner's Sons, 1922.

Roosevelt, Theodore. *An Autobiography.* Wayne Andrews, editor. New York: Charles Scribner's Sons, 1958.

——*The Rough Riders.* New York: Charles Scribner's Sons, 1899.

——*Selections from the Correspondence of Theodore Roosevelt and Henry Cabot Lodge.* 2 vols. Henry Cabot Lodge, editor. New York: Charles Scribner's Sons, 1925.

——*Theodore Roosevelt's Letters to His Children.* Joseph Bucklin Bishop, editor. New York: Charles Scribner's Sons, 1919.

Roosevelt, Theodore, Jr., *All in the Family.* New York: G. P. Putnam's Sons, 1929.

Roosevelt, Mrs. Theodore, Jr. *Day Before Yesterday.* Garden City, New York: Doubleday, 1959.

Rosenman, Samuel I. *Working with Roosevelt.* New York: Harper & Brothers, 1952.

Rush, Benjamin. *The Autobiography of Benjamin Rush.* George W. Corner, editor. Princeton: Princeton University Press, 1948.

——*Letters of Benjamin Rush.* 2 vols. L. H. Butterfield, editor. Princeton: Princeton University Press, 1951.

Shriver, R. Sargent. *Point of the Lance.* New York: Harper & Row, 1964.

Simms, William Gilmore. *The Letters of William Gilmore Simms.* 5 vols. Mary C. Simms Oliphant, Alfred Taylor Odell, and T. C. Duncan Eaves, editors. Columbia: University of South Carolina Press, 1952–56.

Slayden, Ellen Maury. *Washington Wife.* New York: Harper & Row, 1963.

Smith, Margaret Bayard. *Forty Years of Washington Society, Portrayed by the Family Letters of Mrs. Samuel Harrison Smith.* Gaillard Hunt, editor. New York: Charles Scribner's Sons, 1906.

Stealey, O. O. *Twenty Years in the Press Gallery.* New York: Publishers Printing Company, 1906.

Stimson, Henry L., and McGeorge Bundy. *On Active Service in Peace and War.* New York: Harper & Brothers, 1948.

Stockton, Richard. "Letters from Richard Stockton to John Rutherford, Senators from New Jersey, in 1798." *Proceedings of the New Jersey Historical Society*, 2d Series, III, Newark, 1874.

Stockton, Robert Field. *Speech of Commodore Robert F. Stockton, on the Past, Present and Future of the American Party.* Camden: J. H. Jones, 1859.

Strauss, Lewis L. *Men and Decisions.* Garden City, New York: Doubleday, 1962.

Strong, George Templeton. *The Diary of George Templeton Strong.* 4 vols. Allan Nevins and Milton Halsey Thomas, editors. New York: Macmillan, 1952.

Symmes, John Cleves. *The Intimate Letters of John Cleves Symmes and His Family.* Beverley W. Bond, Jr., editor. Cincinnati: Historical and Philosophical Society of Ohio, 1956.

Taft, Charles P. *City Management, the Cincinnati Experiment.* New York: Farrar & Rinehart, 1933.

Taft, Henry W. *Opinions: Literary and Otherwise.* New York: Macmillan, 1934.

Taft, Horace Dutton. *Memories and Opinions.* New York: Macmillan, 1942.

Taft, Mrs. William Howard. *Recollections of Full Years.* New York: Dodd, Mead, 1914.

Taft, Mrs. William Howard, III. "The Tafts in Ireland," *McCall's,* January 1954.

Tucker, Jane Ellis. *Beverley Tucker, a Memoir by His Wife.* Richmond: The Frank Baptist Printing Company, 1893.

Tucker, Nathaniel Beverley. "Correspondence of Judge Tucker." *William and Mary Quarterly,* 1st Series, XII, No. 2 (October 1903).

Vandenberg, Arthur H. *The Private Papers of Senator Vandenberg.* Arthur H. Vandenberg, Jr., editor. Boston: Houghton Mifflin, 1952.

Wadsworth, James W. *The Reminiscenses of James W. Wadsworth.* Transcript in Oral History Research Office, Columbia University.

Washburn, Charles A. *The History of Paraguay, with Notes of Personal Observations, and Reminiscences of Diplomacy Under Difficulties.* 2 vols. Boston: Lee & Shepard, 1871.

Washburne, Elihu B. *Recollections of a Minister to France, 1869–1877.* 2 vols. New York: Charles Scribner's Sons, 1887.

——and others. *Dedicatory Exercises of the Washburn Memorial Library.*

Washburn, Stanley. *The Cable Game.* Boston: Sherman, French, 1912.

——*Field Notes from the Russian Front.* 3 vols. London: A. Melrose, 1915–17.

——*The Reminiscences of Stanley Washburn.* Transcript in Oral History Research Office, Columbia University.

——*Trails, Trappers, and Tender-feet in the New Empire of Western Canada.* London: A. Melrose, 1912.

Chicago: Fergus Printing Company, 1885.

Welles, Gideon. *Diary of Gideon Welles.* 3 vols. Howard K. Beale, editor. New York: W. W. Norton, 1960.

Wharton, Edith. *A Backward Glance.* New York: Charles Scribner's Sons, 1964.

Wheeler, Burton K., with Paul F. Healy. *Yankee from the West.* Garden City, New York: Doubleday, 1962.

White, William Allen. *The Autobiography of William Allen White.* New York: Macmillan, 1946.

Wunder, Darrah Dunham. "My Most Unforgettable Character." (Robert A. Taft) *Reader's Digest,* June 1962.

B) *Genealogical Works and Family Histories*

Adams, James Truslow. *The Adams Family.* Boston: Little, Brown, 1930.

Aitken, William B. *Distinguished Families in America Descended from Wilhelmus Beekman and Jan Thomasse Van Dyke.* New York and London: Knickerbocker Press, 1912.

Armes, Ethel. *Stratford Hall, the Great House of the Lees*. Richmond: Garrett & Massie, 1936.

Atterbury, Mrs. Anson Phelps. *The Bayard Family*. Baltimore, 1928.

Bill, Alfred Hoyt. *A House Called Morven*. Princeton: Princeton University Press, 1954.

Briggs, Lloyd Vernon. *History and Genealogy of the Cabot Family, 1475–1927*. 2 vols. Boston: C. E. Goodspeed, 1927.

Brown, Alexander. *The Cabells and Their Kin*. Boston and New York: Houghton Mifflin, 1895.

Brown, John Mason. *Memoranda of the Preston Family*. Frankfort, Kentucky: S. I. M. Major, 1870.

Churchill, Allen. *The Roosevelts: American Aristocrats*. New York: Harper & Row, 1965.

Clarkson, Thomas S. *A Biographical History of Clermont*. Clermont, New York: Privately printed, 1869.

Clemens, William M. *The Ancestry of Theodore Roosevelt*. New York: W. M. Clemens, 1914.

Cobb, William T. *The Strenuous Life. The "Oyster Bay" Roosevelts in Business and Finance*. New York: William E. Rudge's Sons, 1946.

Comstock, Helen. "The Lees of Virginia." *American Collector*, June 1946.

Crawford, Mary Caroline. *Famous Families of Massachusetts*. 2 vols. Boston: Little, Brown, 1930.

Delafield, John Ross. *Delafield, The Family History*. 2 vols. New York: Privately printed, 1945.

Delano, Daniel W., Jr. *Franklin Roosevelt and the Delano Influence*. Pittsburgh: James W. Nudi, 1946.

Dinneen, Joseph F. *The Kennedy Family*. Boston: Little, Brown, 1960.

Dowdey, Clifford, *The Great Plantation*. New York: Holt, Rinehart & Winston, 1957.

Du Bellet, Louise Pecquet. *Some Prominent Virginia Families*. 4 vols. Lynchburg, Virginia: J. P. Bell Company, 1907?

Duff, Hector L. *The Sewells in the New World*. Exeter, England: William Pollard, 1924.

Fister, Gordon B., editor. *For God and Country, the Epic Story of the Heroic Muhlenberg Family*. Allentown, Pennsylvania: The Muhlenberg Bicentennial Celebration, Inc., 1942.

Glenn, Thomas Allen. *Some Colonial Mansions and Those Who Lived in Them*. Philadelphia: H. T. Coates, 1898.

Gordon, Joan. *The Livingstons of New York 1675–1860: Kinship and Class*. Unpublished Ph.D. dissertation, Columbia University, 1959.

Green, Thomas Marshall. *Historic Families of Kentucky*. Cincinnati: R. Clarke, 1889.

——*A Sketch of the Breckinridge Family*. Unpublished manuscript, Library of Congress.

Greenslet, Ferris. *The Lowells and Their Seven Worlds*. Boston: Houghton Mifflin, 1946.

Hagedorn, Hermann. *The Roosevelt Family of Sagamore Hill*. New York: Macmillan, 1954.

Benjamin Harrison Memorial Commission, Report of. House Document No. 154, 77th Congress, 1st Session. Washington: Government Printing Office, 1941.

Hayden, Ethel Roby. "The Lees of Blenheim." *Maryland Historical Magazine*, XXXVII, No. 2 (June 1942).

Hendrick, Burton J. *The Lees of Virginia*. Boston: Little, Brown, 1935.

Hill, Valeria E. C. *A Genealogy of the Hiester Family*. Reading: Reading Eagle Press, 1941.

Hunter, C. H. "Morven—The Princeton Home of the Stockton Family." *Proceedings of the New Jersey Historical Society*, New Series, IX, No. 2 (April 1924).

Ives, Mabel L. *Home of Richard Stockton*. Upper Montclair, New Jersey: Lucy Fortune, 1932.

Keith, Charles P. *The Ancestry of Benjamin Harrison*. Philadelphia: J. B. Lippincott, 1893.

Kennedy, Mary Selden. *The Seldens of Virginia and Allied Families*. 2 vols. New York: Frank Allaben Genealogical Company, 1911.

Lamb, Janie P. B. "'Smithfield,' Home of the Prestons, in Montgomery County, Virginia." *Virginia Magazine of History and Biography*, XLVII, No. 2 (April 1939).

Leakin, George Armistead. "A Visit to Bohemia Manor." *Maryland Historical Magazine*, II, No. 2 (1907).

Lee, Cazenove Gardner, Jr. *Lee Chronicle*. New York: New York University Press, 1957.

Lee, Edmund Jennings. *Lee of Virginia, 1642–1892*. Philadelphia: Press of Franklin Printing Company, 1895.

Lee, Francis Bazley. *Genealogical and Memorial History of the State of New Jersey*. 4 vols. New York: Lewis Historical Publishing Company, 1910.

Livingston, Edwin Brockholst. *The Livingstons of Callendar*. 5 vols. Edinburgh: Scott & Ferguson, 1887–92.

——*The Livingstons of Livingston Manor*. New York: Knickerbocker Press, 1910.

McCarthy, Joe. *The Remarkable Kennedys*. New York: Dial Press, 1960.

Mackenzie, George Norbury. *Colonial Families of the United States of America*. 7 vols. New York and Boston: Grafton Press, 1907–15.

Mallery, Charles P. "Ancient Families of Bohemia Manor." *Papers of the Historical Society of Delaware*, VII. Wilmington, 1888.

Martin, Thomas. *Dynasty: The Longs of Louisiana*. New York: G. P. Putnam's Sons, 1960.

Proceedings in Commemoration of the 200th Anniversary of the Landing of Henry Melchior Muhlenberg in Philadelphia, Pennsylvania, November 25, 1742. Senate Document No. 249, 77th Congress, 2d Session. Washington: Government Printing Office, 1942.

Opotowsky, Stan. *The Longs of Louisiana*. New York: E. P. Dutton, 1960.

Padgett, James A. "The Ancestry of Edward Livingston of Louisiana." *The Louisiana Historical Quarterly*, XIX, No. 4 (October 1936).

Partridge, Bellamy. *An Imperial Saga, the Roosevelt Family in America*. New York: Hillman-Curl, 1936.

Philoon, James E. "Livermore's Famed Washburn Family." *Lewiston* (Maine) *Evening Journal Magazine*, August 24 and 31, 1957.

Reichmann, Felix. *The Muhlenberg Family, a Bibliography*. Philadelphia: Carl Schurz Memorial Foundation, 1943.

Richards, Henry Melchior Muhlenberg. "The Hiester Family." *Pennsylvania-German Society, Proceedings and Addresses*, XVI (1907).

Roosevelt, Hall. *Odyssey of an American Family*. New York: Harper & Brothers, 1939.

Roosevelt, Mrs. Theodore, and Kermit Roosevelt. *American Backlogs. The Story of Gertrude Tyler and Her Family.* New York: Charles Scribner's Sons, 1928.

Ross, Ishbel. *An American Family: The Tafts, 1678 to 1964.* Cleveland and New York: World Publishing, 1964.

Schriftgiesser, Karl. *The Amazing Roosevelt Family.* New York: Wilfred Funk, 1942.

——*Families.* New York: Howell, Soskin, 1940.

Schuyler, George W. *Colonial New York, Philip Schuyler and His Family.* 2 vols. New York: Charles Scribner's Sons, 1885.

Shriver, Harry Clair. *A History of the Shriver Family.* Privately printed, 1962.

Smith, William Ernest. *The Francis Preston Blair Family in Politics.* 2 vols. New York: Macmillan, 1933.

Smith, Zachary F., and Mary Rogers Clay. *The Clay Family.* Louisville: J. P. Morton, 1899.

Spooner, Walter W., editor. *Historic Families of America.* New York: Historic Families Publishing Association, 1907.

Stidger, William L. *These Amazing Roosevelts.* New York: Macfadden, 1938.

Stockton, John W. *A History of the Stockton Family.* Philadelphia: Press of Patterson & White, 1881.

Stockton, Thomas Coates. *The Stockton Family of New Jersey and Other Stocktons.* Washington: Carnahan Press, 1911.

Sturtevant, Reginald H. "Seven Sons" (the Washburns). *Down East,* June 1956.

Tucker, Beverley Randolph. *Tales of the Tuckers.* Richmond: Dietz, 1942.

Tucker, Ephraim. *Genealogy of the Tucker Family.* Worcester, Mass.: Press of F. S. Blanchard & Company, 1895.

Van Rensselaer, Florence. *Lines Composing the Pedigree of Master John Livingston, D.D. (1603–1673).* 1945. Photocopy of manuscript in Library of Congress.

Wallace, Paul A. W. *The Muhlenbergs of Pennsylvania.* Philadelphia: University of Pennsylvania Press, 1950.

Warner, Pauline Pearce. *Benjamin Harrison of Berkeley, Walter Cocke of Surry, Family Records I.* Tappahannock, Virginia: Privately printed, 1962.

Washburn, Julia Chase. *Genealogical Notes of the Washburn Family.* Lewiston: Press of Journal Company, 1898.

Washburn, Lilian. *My Seven Sons, the True and Amazing Story of the Seven Famous Washburn Brothers, as told by the Old Grandsire, Israel, Sr., and Transcribed by his Granddaughter.* Portland: Falmouth Publishing House, 1940.

Washburn, Mabel Thacher Rosemary. *Ancestry of William Howard Taft.* New York: Frank Allaben Genealogical Company, 1908.

White, Philip L. *The Beekmans of New York in Politics and Commerce, 1647–1877.* New York: New-York Historical Society, 1956.

Whitney, Emma St. Clair. *Michael Hillegas and His Descendants.* Pottsville, Pennsylvania: Press of M. E. Miller, 1891.

Wilson, James Grant. *Colonel John Bayard and the Bayard Family of America.* New York: Trow's Printing and Bookbinding Co., 1885.

Zorn, Walter Lewis. *The Descendants of the Presidents of the United States of America.* Monroe, Michigan: Privately printed, 1955.

C) *Biographies*

Abbot, Willis John. *Carter Henry Harrison*. New York: Dodd, Mead, 1895.

Abbott, Edith, and others. "Sophonisba Preston Breckinridge, 1866–1948." *Social Service Review*, XXII, No. 4 (December 1948).

Adams, Charles Francis, Jr. *Charles Francis Adams*. Boston and New York: Houghton Mifflin, 1900.

Adams, Henry. *The Life of George Cabot Lodge*. Boston and New York: Houghton Mifflin, 1911.

——*John Randolph*. Boston and New York: Houghton Mifflin, 1882.

Adams, Samuel Hopkins. *Incredible Era, the Life and Times of Warren Gamaliel Harding*. Boston: Houghton Mifflin, 1939.

Ainley, Leslie G. *Boston Mahatma* (Martin Lomasney). Boston?: W. M. Prendible, 1949.

Alexander, Edward P. *A Revolutionary Conservative, James Duane of New York*. New York: Columbia University Press, 1938.

Anthony, Robert Warren. *Philip Livingston, a Tribute*. Albany: Fort Orange Press, 1924.

Atwood, David, and others. *Memorial Addresses on the Life and Character of Hon. C. C. Washburn*. Madison, Wisconsin: D. Atwood, 1883.

Ayres, Anne. *The Life and Works of William Augustus Muhlenberg*. New York: Harper & Brothers, 1880.

Barry, Richard. *The Events Man: Being an Account of the Adventures of Stanley Washburn, American War Correspondent*. New York: Moffat, Yard, 1907.

Bayard, Samuel J. *A Short History of the Life and Services of Gen. William Henry Harrison*. Seneca Falls, New York: Fuller & Bloomer, 1840.

——*A Sketch of the Life of Com. Robert F. Stockton*. New York: Derby & Jackson, 1856.

Beals, Carleton. *The Story of Huey P. Long*. Philadelphia: J. B. Lippincott, 1935.

Beatty, Jerome. "The Other Taft." (Charles P. Taft) *American Magazine*, July 1947.

Beck, Herbert H. "Henry E. Muhlenberg, Botanist." *Papers Read Before the Lancaster County Historical Society*, XXXXII, 1928.

Bemis, Samuel Flagg. *John Quincy Adams and the Foundations of American Foreign Policy*. New York: Alfred A. Knopf, 1949.

——*John Quincy Adams and the Union*. New York: Alfred A. Knopf, 1956.

Beringause, Arthur F. *Brooks Adams*. New York: Alfred A. Knopf, 1955.

Blair, Clay, Jr. "The Evolution of Cabot Lodge." *Saturday Evening Post*, October 22, 1960.

Bolles, Blair. "The Political Education of James Roosevelt." *New York Times Magazine*, March 6, 1938.

Bonham, Milledge L., Jr. "A Forgotten American Statesman." (Edward Livingston) *American Mercury*, II, No. 8 (August 1924).

Borden, Morton. *The Federalism of James A. Bayard*. New York: Columbia University Press, 1955.

Boudinot, Elias. *Memoirs to the Life of the Rev. William Tennent*. New York: W. Alexander & Son, 1822.

Boyd, George Adams. *Elias Boudinot, Patriot and Statesman, 1740–1821*. Princeton: Princeton University Press, 1952.

Bradlee, Benjamin. *That Special Grace.* (John F. Kennedy) Philadelphia: Lippincott, 1964.

Breckinridge, Sophonisba Preston. *Madeline McDowell Breckinridge, a Leader in the New South.* Chicago: University of Chicago Press, 1921.

Bruce, William Cabell. *John Randolph of Roanoke.* 2 vols. New York: G. P. Putnam's Sons, 1922.

Burnett, Robert N. "Henry Osborne Havemeyer." *Cosmopolitan,* XXXIV, No. 6 (April 1903).

Burns, James MacGregor. *John Kennedy: A Political Profile.* New York: Harcourt, Brace, 1960.

——*Roosevelt: The Lion and the Fox.* New York: Harcourt, Brace, 1956.

Burr, Anna Robeson. *Weir Mitchell, His Life and Letters.* New York: Duffield, 1929.

Carter, Morris. *Isabella Stewart Gardner and Fenway Court.* Boston and New York: Houghton Mifflin, 1925.

Chambers, Talbot W. *Memoir of the Life and Character of the Late Hon. Theo. Frelinghuysen.* New York: Harper & Brothers, 1863.

Cleaves, Freeman. *Old Tippecanoe* (William Henry Harrison). New York: Charles Scribner's Sons, 1939.

Coleman, Mary Haldane (Mrs. George P.) *St. George Tucker, Citizen of No Mean City.* Richmond: Dietz Press, 1938.

Crippen, Lee F. *Simon Cameron, Ante-Bellum Years.* Oxford, Ohio: The Mississippi Valley Press, 1942.

Crissey, Forrest. *Theodore E. Burton, American Statesman.* Cleveland and New York: World, 1956.

Cutler, John Henry. *"Honey Fitz"* (John F. Fitzgerald). Indianapolis: Bobbs-Merrill, 1962.

Dabney, Virginius. *Dry Messiah, the Life of Bishop Cannon.* New York: Alfred A. Knopf, 1949.

Dallas, John T. *Mr. Taft* (Horace Dutton Taft). Littleton, New Hampshire: Courier Printing Co., 1949.

Danforth, George H. *The Rebel Earl* (William Alexander). Unpublished Ph.D. dissertation, Columbia University, 1955.

Dangerfield, George. *Chancellor Robert R. Livingston of New York, 1746–1813.* New York: Harcourt, Brace, 1960.

Davis, Charles H., Jr. *Life of Charles Henry Davis, Rear Admiral, 1807–1877.* Boston and New York: Houghton Mifflin, 1899.

Davis, Forrest. *Huey Long, a Candid Biography.* New York: Dodge, 1935.

Davis, John W. "John Randolph Tucker: The Man and His Work." *John Randolph Tucker Lectures,* Lexington, Virginia, 1952.

de Chambrun, Clara Longworth. *The Making of Nicholas Longworth.* New York: Ray Long and Richard R. Smith, 1933.

Delafield, Julia. *Biographies of Francis Lewis and Morgan Lewis.* 2 vols. New York: A. D. F. Randolph, 1877.

Dickinson, Henry W. *Robert Fulton, Engineer and Artist: His Life and Works.* London: John Lane, 1913.

Dinneen, Joseph F. *The Purple Shamrock: The Hon. James Michael Curley of Boston.* New York: W. W. Norton, 1949.

Dodge, William E., Jr., and others. *Theodore Roosevelt, Senior, A Tribute. The Proceedings at a Meeting of the Union League Club, New York City, February 14, 1878.* New York, 1902.

Duberman, Martin B. *Charles Francis Adams, 1807–1886.* Boston: Houghton Mifflin, 1961.

Duer, William Alexander. *The Life of William Alexander, Earl of Stirling.* New York: Wiley & Putnam, 1847.

Duffy, Herbert S. *William Howard Taft.* New York: Minton, Balch, 1930.

Fineran, John Kingston. *The Career of a Tinpot Napoleon, a Political Biography of Huey P. Long.* New Orleans: J. K. Fineran, 1932.

Fishwick, Marshall W. *Lee After the War.* New York: Dodd, Mead, 1963.

Fortier, James J. A., editor. *Huey Pierce Long, "The Martyr of the Age."* New Orleans: Press of T. J. Moran's Sons, 1937.

Foster, Harriet McIntire. *Mrs. Benjamin Harrison.* Indianapolis, 1908.

Freeman, Douglas Southall. *R. E. Lee, A Biography.* 4 vols. New York and London: Charles Scribner's Sons, 1934–35.

Frelinghuysen, Peter H. B., Jr. *Theodorus Jacobus Frelinghuysen.* Princeton: Privately printed, 1938.

Frick, William K. *Henry Melchior Muhlenberg.* Philadelphia: Lutheran Publication Society, 1902.

Furman, Bess. "Candidate's Wife" (Mrs. Robert A. Taft). *New York Times Magazine,* November 2, 1947.

Gannon, Francis X. *A Study of Elihu Benjamin Washburne: American Minister to France During the Franco-Prussian War and the Commune.* Unpublished Ph.D. dissertation, Georgetown University, 1950.

Gardner, Mrs. Constance (Lodge). *Augustus Peabody Gardner.* Cambridge: Privately printed, 1919.

Garraty, John A. *Henry Cabot Lodge.* New York: Alfred A. Knopf, 1953.

Gervasi, Frank. "Bob Taft's Martha." *Collier's,* April 3, 1948.

Giberne, Agnes. *A Lady of England, the Life and Letters of Charlotte Maria Tucker.* New York: A. C. Armstrong & Son, 1895.

Gilpin, Henry D. *Biographical Notice of Edward Livingston.* Philadelphia: J. C. Clark, 1843.

Goebel, Dorothy Burne. *William Henry Harrison.* Indianapolis: Historical Bureau of the Indiana Library and Historical Department, 1926.

Grose, Peter. "Portrait of the Distant 'Candidate.'" (Henry Cabot Lodge, Jr.) *New York Times Magazine,* May 10, 1964.

Groves, Charles S. *Henry Cabot Lodge, the Statesman.* Boston: Small, Maynard, 1925.

Hageman, John F. "The Life, Character and Services of Frederick T. Frelinghuysen," *Proceedings of the New Jersey Historical Society,* 2d Series, IX (1886–87).

Hamilton, Alexander. *Memorial of Hon. John Randolph Tucker, Presented and Read at the Ninth Annual Meeting of the Virginia State Bar Association.* Richmond: James E. Goode Printing Co., 1897.

Hamlin, Charles E. *The Life and Times of Hannibal Hamlin.* Cambridge: Riverside Press, 1899.

Hamlin, Talbot. *Benjamin Henry Latrobe.* New York: Oxford University Press, 1955.

Harnsberger, Caroline T. *A Man of Courage, Robert A. Taft.* Chicago: Wilcox & Follett, 1952.

Harris, Eleanor. "The Senator Is in a Hurry" (John F. Kennedy). *McCall's,* August 1957.

Harris, Thomas O. *The Kingfish—Huey P. Long, Dictator.* New Orleans: Pelican Publishing Co., 1938.

Harrison, Lowell H. "John Breckinridge: Western Statesman." *Journal of Southern History*, XVIII, No. 2 (May 1952).

——"A Young Virginian: John Breckinridge." *Virginia Magazine of History and Biography*, LXXI, No. 1 (January 1963).

Harrison, Marvin C. *Robert A. Taft, Our Illustrious Dunderhead*. Cleveland, 1944.

Hart, Charles Henry. *A Necrological Notice of the Hon. Richard Stockton Field*. Philadelphia: C. B. Collins, 1870.

Hatcher, William B. *Edward Livingston: Jeffersonian Republican and Jacksonian Democrat*. Baton Rouge: Louisiana State University Press, 1940.

Healy, Paul F. "The Senate's Gay Young Bachelor" (John F. Kennedy). *Saturday Evening Post*, June 13, 1953.

Heller, Deane and David. *Jacqueline Kennedy*. Derby, Conn.: Monarch Books, 1961.

Hicks, Frederick C. *William Howard Taft, Yale Professor of Law and New Haven Citizen*. New Haven: Yale University Press, 1945.

Higgins, Marguerite. "Rose Fitzgerald Kennedy." *McCall's*, May 1961.

Hobart, Lois. *Patriot's Lady: The Life of Sarah Livingston Jay*. New York: Funk & Wagnalls, 1960.

Hocker, Edward W. *The Fighting Parson of the American Revolution: A Biography of General Peter Muhlenberg*. Philadelphia: Published by the author, 1936.

Hohenberg, John. "Ambassador Lodge: Our UN Salesman." *Coronet*, February 1954.

Howe, George Frederick. *Chester A. Arthur*. New York: Dodd, Mead, 1934.

Hunt, Gaillard. *Israel, Elihu and Cadwallader Washburn*. New York: Macmillan, 1925.

Hunt, Louise Livingston. *Memoir of Mrs. Edward Livingston*. New York: Harper & Brothers, 1886.

Isaacson, Pauline Helen. *Robert Alphonso Taft, an Assessment of a Persuader*. Unpublished Ph.D. dissertation, University of Minnesota, 1956.

Jellison, Charles A. *Fessenden of Maine, Civil War Senator*. Syracuse: Syracuse University Press, 1962.

Johnson, Claudius O. *Carter Henry Harrison I, Political Leader*. Chicago: University of Chicago Press, 1928.

Jones, J. William. *Virginia's Next Governor, Gen. Fitzhugh Lee*. New York: Cheap Publishing Co., 1885.

Kaye, John William. *The Life and Correspondence of Henry St. George Tucker, Late Accountant-General of Bengal, and Chairman of the East India Company*. London: R. Bentley, 1854.

Keasbey, Anthony Q. "Memoir of the Hon. Richard S. Field." *Proceedings of the New Jersey Historical Society*, 2d Series, II (1872).

Kempton, Murray. "Stephen E. Smith." *New Republic*, March 9, 1963.

Memorial Addresses in the Congress of the United States and Tributes in Eulogy of John Fitzgerald Kennedy. Senate Document No. 59, 88th Congress, 2d Session. Washington: Government Printing Office, 1964.

Kessler, Henry H., and Eugene Rachlis. *Peter Stuyvesant and His New York*. New York: Random House, 1959.

Kleeman, Rita Halle. *Gracious Lady, the Life of Sara Delano Roosevelt*. New York: D. Appleton-Century, 1935.

Klein, Milton Martin. *The American Whig: William Livingston of New York*. Unpublished Ph.D. dissertation, Columbia University, 1954.

Lambert, Oscar Doane. *Stephen Benton Elkins, American Foursquare.* Pittsburgh: University of Pittsburgh Press, 1955.

Lasky, Victor. *J.F.K., the Man and the Myth.* New York: Macmillan, 1963.

Lawrence, William. *Henry Cabot Lodge, a Biographical Sketch.* Boston and New York: Houghton Mifflin, 1925.

Leary, Lewis. *The Literary Career of Nathaniel Tucker, 1750–1807.* Durham: Duke University Press, 1950.

Leder, Lawrence H. *Robert Livingston, 1654–1728, and the Politics of Colonial New York.* Chapel Hill: University of North Carolina Press, 1961.

——and Vincent P. Carosso. "Robert Livingston (1654–1728): Businessman of Colonial New York." *The Business History Review,* XXX, No. 1 (March 1956).

Lee, Elsie. *Henry Cabot Lodge, Man and Statesman.* New York: Lancer Books, 1964.

Lee, Richard Henry. *Life of Arthur Lee.* 2 vols. Boston: Wells & Lilly, 1829.

——*Memoir of the Life of Richard Henry Lee.* 2 vols. Philadelphia: H. C. Carey & I. Lea, 1825.

Leonard, Lewis Alexander. *Life of Alphonso Taft.* New York: Hawke Publishing Co., 1920.

——*Life of Charles Carroll of Carrollton.* New York: Moffat, Yard, 1918.

Lewis, Anthony. "Shriver Moves into the Front Rank." *New York Times Magazine,* March 15, 1964.

——"What Drives Bobby Kennedy?" *New York Times Magazine,* April 7, 1963.

Liebling, A. J. *The Earl of Louisiana* (Earl Long). New York: Simon & Schuster, 1961.

Link, Arthur S. *Wilson.* 4 vols. Princeton: Princeton University Press, 1947–64.

Lisagor, Peter. "Portrait of a Man Emerging from Shadows" (Robert F. Kennedy). *New York Times Magazine,* July 19, 1964.

Liston, Robert A. *Sargent Shriver: A Candid Portrait.* New York: Farrar, Straus, 1964.

Lodge, Henry Cabot. *Life and Letters of George Cabot.* Boston: Little, Brown, 1877.

Memorial Services Held in the House of Representatives of the United States, Together with Remarks Presented in Eulogy of George Shannon Long. Washington: Government Printing Office, 1958.

Memorial Services Held in the House of Representatives of the United States, Together with Remarks Presented in Eulogy of Huey Pierce Long. House Document No. 480, 74th Congress, 2d Session, Washington: Government Printing Office, 1936.

McLean, Robert Colin. *George Tucker, Moral Philosopher and Man of Letters.* Chapel Hill: University of North Carolina Press, 1961.

Manchester, William. *Portrait of a President, John F. Kennedy.* Boston: Little, Brown, 1962.

Mann, William J. *Life and Times of Henry Melchior Muhlenberg.* Philadelphia: G. W. Frederick, 1887.

Mannes, Marya. "Candidate from the U.N." (Henry Cabot Lodge, Jr.) *Reporter,* October 27, 1960.

Mason, Alpheus Thomas. *William Howard Taft: Chief Justice.* New York: Simon & Schuster, 1965.

Mish, Mary Vernon. *Jonathan Hager, Founder*. Hagerstown, Maryland: Hagerstown Bookbinding and Printing Co., 1937.

Monaghan, Frank. *John Jay, Defender of Liberty*. New York and Indianapolis: Bobbs-Merrill, 1935.

Montague, Ludwell Lee. "Richard Lee, the Emigrant." *Virginia Magazine of History and Biography*, LXII, No. 1 (January 1954).

Muhlenberg, Henry A. *The Life of Major-General Peter Muhlenberg of the Revolutionary Army*. Philadelphia: Carey & Hart, 1849.

Neatby, Hilda. "Chief Justice William Smith: An Eighteenth-Century Whig Imperialist." *The Canadian Historical Review*, XXVIII, No. 1 (March 1947).

Nevins, Allan. *Grover Cleveland*. New York: Dodd, Mead, 1932.

——*Hamilton Fish*. New York: Dodd, Mead, 1936.

Newton, William W. *Dr. Muhlenberg* (William Augustus Muhlenberg). Boston and New York: Houghton Mifflin, 1890.

Nye, Russel B. *George Bancroft, Brahmin Rebel*. New York: Alfred A. Knopf, 1944.

Parton, James. *Life of Andrew Jackson*. 3 vols. New York: Mason Brothers, 1861.

Patterson, Louis H. "Governor William Livingston as Apprentice, Writer and Executive." *Proceedings of the New Jersey Historical Society*, IX, No. 2 (April 1924).

Pattison, Robert E. "The Life and Character of Richard Bassett." *Papers of the Historical Society of Delaware*, XXIX (Wilmington, 1900).

Pellew, George. *John Jay*. Boston and New York: Houghton Mifflin, 1890.

Porter, Katherine Anne. "Jacqueline Kennedy." *Ladies' Home Journal*, March 1964.

Porter, Kenneth Wiggins. *John Jacob Astor, Business Man*. 2 vols. Cambridge: Harvard University Press, 1931.

Pringle, Henry F. *The Life and Times of William Howard Taft*, 2 vols. New York: Farrar & Rinehart, 1939.

——*Theodore Roosevelt*. New York: Harcourt, Brace, 1931.

Putnam, Carleton. *Theodore Roosevelt, the Formative Years*. New York: Scribner's, 1958.

Raskin, A. H. "Generalissimo of the War on Poverty" (Sargent Shriver). *New York Times Magazine*, November 22, 1964.

Reeves, Paschal. "Thomas S. Martin: Committee Statesman," *Virginia Magazine of History and Biography*, LXVIII, No. 3 (July 1960).

Ridge, Martin. *Ignatius Donnelly*. Chicago: University of Chicago Press, 1962.

Rixey, Lilian. *Bamie, Theodore Roosevelt's Remarkable Sister*. New York: D. McKay, 1963.

Robbins, Phyllis. *Robert A. Taft, Boy and Man*. Cambridge: Dresser, Chapman & Grimes, 1963.

In Loving Memory of Anna Hall Roosevelt by Three Friends. New York, 1893.

Roosevelt, Theodore. "Governor William H. Taft." *Outlook*, LXIX, No. 3 (September 21, 1901.)

——*Gouverneur Morris*. Boston and New York: Houghton Mifflin, 1892.

Rorty, James. "Callie Long's Boy Huey." *Forum*, August 1935.

Sadler, Christine. "The Coming of Age of Joan Kennedy." *McCall's*, February 1965.

Samuels, Ernest. *Henry Adams, the Major Phase.* Cambridge: Harvard University Press, 1964.
——*Henry Adams, the Middle Years.* Cambridge: Harvard University Press, 1958.
——*The Young Henry Adams.* Cambridge: Harvard University Press, 1948.
Schachner, Nathan. *Thomas Jefferson.* New York: T. Yoseloff, 1957.
Schriftgiesser, Karl. *The Gentleman from Massachusetts: Henry Cabot Lodge.* Boston: Little, Brown, 1944.
Sedgwick, Theodore, Jr. *A Memoir of the Life of William Livingston.* New York: J & J Harper, 1833.
Seidensticker, Oswald. "Frederick Augustus Conrad Muhlenberg, Speaker of the House of Representatives in the First Congress, 1789." *Pennsylvania Magazine of History and Biography,* XIII, No. 2 (1889).
Sidey, Hugh. *John F. Kennedy, President.* New York: Atheneum, 1963.
Sievers, Harry J. *Benjamin Harrison, Hoosier Statesman.* New York: University Publishers, Inc., 1959.
——*Benjamin Harrison, Hoosier Warrior.* Chicago: Henry Regnery, 1952.
Smith, Page. *John Adams.* 2 vols. Garden City, New York: Doubleday, 1962.
Smith, Theodore Clarke. *The Life and Letters of James Abram Garfield.* 2 vols. New Haven: Yale University Press, 1925.
Smith, Webster (pseudonym). *The Kingfish, a Biography of Huey P. Long.* New York and London: G. P. Putnam's Sons, 1933.
Spencer, Edward. *An Outline of the Public Life and Services of Thomas F. Bayard.* New York: D. Appleton, 1880.
Stern, Philip Van Doren. *Robert E. Lee, the Man and the Soldier.* New York: McGraw-Hill, 1963.
Stevenson, Elizabeth. *Henry Adams.* New York: Macmillan, 1955.
Stillwell, Lucille. *John Cabell Breckinridge.* Caldwell, Idaho: Caxton, 1936.
Stoever, M. L. *Memoir of the Life and Times of Henry Melchior Muhlenberg.* Philadelphia: Lindsay & Blakiston, 1856.
Stryker, Helen Boudinot. "Elias Boudinot." *Pennsylvania Magazine of History and Biography,* III, No. 2 (1879).
Swiggett, Howard. *The Extraordinary Mr. Morris* (Gouverneur Morris). Garden City, New York: Doubleday, 1952.
Tansill, Charles Callan. *The Congressional Career of Thomas Francis Bayard, 1869–1885.* Washington: Georgetown University Press, 1946.
——*The Foreign Policy of Thomas F. Bayard, 1885–1897.* New York: Fordham University Press, 1940.
Thayer, Mary Van Rennselaer. *Jacqueline Bouvier Kennedy.* Garden City, New York: Doubleday, 1961.
Thompson, Robert E., and Hortense Myers. *Robert F. Kennedy: The Brother Within.* New York: Macmillan, 1962.
Townsend, John Wilson. "Carter Henry Harrison, Kentuckian." *Register of the Kentucky State Historical Society,* XXIV, No. 71 (1926).
Memorial Services held in the House of Representatives of the United States, Together with Remarks Presented in Eulogy of Henry St. George Tucker. House Document No. 570, 72d Congress, 2d Session. Washington: Government Printing Office, 1933.
Tucker, John Randolph. "The Judges Tucker of the Court of Appeals of Virginia." *Virginia Law Register,* I, No. 11 (March 1896).
Turnbull, Archibald Douglas. *John Stevens, an American Record.* New York and London: Century, 1928.

Turner, Russell. "Senator Kennedy: The Perfect Politician." *American Mercury,* March 1957.

Turrentine, Percy Winfield. *Life and Works of Nathaniel Beverley Tucker.* Unpublished Ph.D. dissertation, Harvard University, 1952.

Van Zandt, Tobias (pseudonym). *Eulogy on the Life and Character of the Reverend John H. Livingston.* New York: Hopkins & Morris, 1825.

Vaux, Richard. *Sketch of the Life of Joseph Hiester.* Philadelphia: Allen, Lane & Scott, 1887.

Wallace, Lew. *Life of Gen. Ben Harrison.* Philadelphia: Hubbard Brothers, 1888.

Wallace, Paul A. W. *Conrad Weiser.* Philadelphia: University of Pennsylvania Press, 1945.

Waller, G. M. *Samuel Vetch, Colonial Enterpriser.* Chapel Hill: University of North Carolina Press, 1960.

Warfield, Ethelbert D. *Joseph Cabell Breckinridge, Junior.* New York: Knickerbocker Press, 1898.

Whalen, Richard J. *The Founding Father: The Story of Joseph P. Kennedy.* New York: New American Library, 1964.

Whalen, Robert G. "Another Roosevelt Enters the Lists" (Franklin D. Roosevelt, Jr.) *New York Times Magazine,* April 24, 1949.

White, Leigh. "He Runs the Show for Ike" (Henry Cabot Lodge, Jr.) *Saturday Evening Post,* May 31, 1952.

White, William S. *The Taft Story* (Robert A. Taft). New York: Harper & Brothers, 1954.

Whitehead, W. A. "Sketch of the Life of Richard Stockton." *Proceedings of the New Jersey Historical Society,* 2d Series, IV (1877).

Whitney, Janet. *Abigail Adams.* Boston: Little, Brown, 1947.

Wicker, Tom. "Kennedy without Tears" (John F. Kennedy). *Esquire,* June 1964.

——"The Name Is Smith" (Stephen E. Smith). *New York Times Magazine,* July 28, 1963.

——"The Son of the Kingfish" (Russell B. Long). *New York Times Magazine,* April 4, 1965.

Wilson, James Grant. "Andrew Kirkpatrick." *Proceedings of the New Jersey Historical Society,* 2d Series, II (1872).

Wilson, James Southall. "Lyon Gardiner Tyler." *William and Mary Quarterly,* 2d Series, XV, No. 4 (October 1935).

Woolf, S. J. "The Silent Man Who Directs Our Navy" (Charles Francis Adams). *New York Times Magazine,* December 13, 1931.

Wright, Marcus J. "A Sketch of the Life of General John Peter Gabriel Muhlenberg." *Publications of the Southern Historical Association,* V, No. 3 (May 1901).

Younger, Joan. "Jack Kennedy, Democratic Dynamo." *Ladies' Home Journal,* March 1960.

Zeiger, Henry A. *The Remarkable Henry Cabot Lodge.* New York: Popular Library, 1964.

D) *Reference Works*

Amory, Cleveland, editor. *International Celebrity Register.* New York: Harper & Row, 1959.

Barber, John W., and Henry Howe. *Historical Collections of the State of New Jersey.* New York: S. Tuttle, 1844.

Biddle, Gertrude Bosler, and Sarah Dickinson Lowrie, editors. *Notable Women of Pennsylvania*. Philadelphia: University of Pennsylvania Press, 1942.

Biographical Cyclopaedia of American Women.

Biographical Directory of the American Congress, 1774–1961.

Biography Index (1946–64).

Britannica Book of the Year (various editions).

Buchholz, Heinrich Ewald. *Governors of Maryland.* Baltimore: Williams & Wilkins, 1908.

Congressional Directory (various editions).

Congressional Record (various editions).

Current Biography (various editions).

Daughters of the American Revolution Lineage Book (various editions).

Dictionary of American Biography.

Dictionary of National Biography.

Dodson, E. Griffith. *The General Assembly of the Commonwealth of Virginia, 1919–1939.* Richmond: State Publication, 1939.

Heitman, Francis B. *Historical Register and Dictionary of the United States Army.* 2 vols. Washington: Government Printing Office, 1903.

Maryland Manual (various editions).

National Cyclopaedia of American Biography.

New York Times Index (various editions).

Smith, Margaret Vowell. *Virginia, 1492–1892, a History of the Executives.* 2 vols. Washington: W. H. Lowdermilk, 1893.

Society of the Lees of Virginia. *Application Forms.*

Stanard, William G., and Mary Newton. *The Colonial Virginia Register.* Albany, New York: Joel Munsell's Sons, 1902.

Who Was Who in America.

Who's Who in America (various editions; also regional editions).

Who's Who in Delaware (1939).

Who's Who in Maryland (1939).

Who's Who in New Jersey (1939).

Who's Who of American Women (various editions).

E) *Newspapers and Periodicals*

American Heritage

American Historical Review

American Magazine

American Mercury

Americana (*American Historical Magazine*)

Art Digest

Baltimore *Sunpapers* (*Sun* and *Evening Sun*)

Boston *Transcript*

Burlington (Vermont) *Free Press*

Business History Review

Canadian Historical Review

Chicago *Sun-Times*

Christian Science Monitor

Church History

Collier's

Congressional Quarterly

Coronet

Cosmopolitan

Daughters of the American Revolution Magazine
Delaware History
Delaware State News (Dover)
Editor & Publisher
Esquire
Filson Club History Quarterly
Fortune
Forum
Good Housekeeping
Harper's
Journal of Southern History
Journal of Southern Politics
Ladies' Home Journal
Liberty
Life
Look
Los Angeles *Times*
Louisiana Historical Quarterly
Louisville *Courier-Journal*
Lutheran Church Review
McCall's
Magazine of the Society of the Lees of Virginia
Maryland Historical Magazine
Minneapolis *Journal*
Minnesota History Bulletin
Muhlenberg College Alumni Magazine
Nation
National Intelligencer (Washington, D.C.)
National Observer
New England Historical and Genealogical Register
New Orleans *Times-Picayune*
New Republic
Newsweek
New York *Herald Tribune*
New-York Historical Society Quarterly
New York History
New York *Times*
New York *Tribune*
New York *World*
Outlook
Papers Read Before the Lancaster County Historical Society
Pennsylvania History
Pennsylvania Magazine of History and Biography
Philadelphia *Inquirer*
Princeton University Library Chronicle
Proceedings of the New Jersey Historical Society
Reader's Digest
Real America
Register of the Kentucky Historical Society
Republican Congressional Committee Newsletter
Saturday Evening Post
Saturday Review

Scribner's Magazine
Seattle *Post-Intelligencer*
Social Service Review
Somerset County (New Jersey) *Historical Quarterly*
Time
The Times of London
Tyler's Quarterly Historical and Genealogical Magazine
University of Pennsylvania Law Review
U.S. News & World Report
Virginia Cavalcade
Virginia Law Register
Virginia Magazine of History and Biography
Washington *Afro-American*
Washington *Daily News*
Washington *Post*
Washington *Star*
William and Mary Quarterly
Wilmington *Journal-Every Evening*
Wisconsin Magazine of History
Woman
Yale Law Report

F) *Secondary Sources: Books*

Adams, Charles Francis, Jr. *Lee at Appomattox and Other Papers.* Boston and New York: Houghton Mifflin, 1902.
——*Lee's Centennial.* Lexington, Virginia, 1907.
Adams, Henry. *The Formative Years: A History of the United States During the Administrations of Jefferson and Madison.* 2 vols. Herbert Agar, editor. Boston: Houghton Mifflin, 1947.
Alexander, Holmes. *The Famous Five.* New York: Bookmailer, 1958.
Alexander, Samuel Davies. *Princeton College During the Eighteenth Century.* New York: A. D. F. Randolph, 1872.
Allen, Frederick Lewis. *Only Yesterday, an Informal History of the Nineteen-twenties.* New York: Harper & Brothers, 1931.
Amory, Cleveland. *The Last Resorts.* New York: Harper & Brothers, 1952.
——*The Proper Bostonians.* New York: E. P. Dutton, 1947.
——*Who Killed Society?* New York: Harper & Brothers, 1960.
Anderson, Bern. *By Sea and by River, the Naval History of the Civil War.* New York: Alfred A. Knopf, 1962.
Anonymous. *The Celebrated Trial, Madeline Pollard vs. Breckinridge.* 1894.
Augur, Helen. *The Secret War of Independence.* New York: Duell, Sloan & Pearce, 1955.
Bagby, George W. *The Old Virginia Gentleman and Other Sketches.* Richmond: Dietz Press, 1938.
Bakeless, John. *Turncoats, Traitors and Heroes.* Philadelphia: J. B. Lippincott, 1959.
Baldwin, Leland D. *Whiskey Rebels.* Pittsburgh: University of Pittsburgh Press, 1939.
Baltzell, E. Digby. *Philadelphia Gentlemen.* Glencoe, Illinois: Free Press, 1958.
——*The Protestant Establishment.* New York: Random House, 1964.
Basso, Hamilton. *Mainstream.* New York: Reynal & Hitchcock, 1943.

Bauer, Elizabeth K. *Commentaries on the Constitution, 1790–1860.* New York: Columbia University Press, 1952.

Beals, Carleton. *Brass-Knuckle Crusade.* New York: Hastings House, 1960.

Bemis, Samuel Flagg, editor. *The American Secretaries of State and Their Diplomacy.* 10 vols. New York: Alfred A. Knopf, 1927–29.

Binkley, Wilfred E. *American Political Parties.* New York: Alfred A. Knopf, 1943.

Blain, Hugh Mercer, editor. *Favorite Huey Long Stories.* Baton Rouge: O. Claitor, 1937.

Bodley, Temple. *History of Kentucky before the Louisiana Purchase in 1803.* Chicago and Louisville: S. J. Clarke Publishing Co., 1928.

Bonney, Catharina V. R. *A Legacy of Historical Gleanings.* 2 vols. Albany: J. Munsell, 1875.

Bradley, Glenn D. *Winning the Southwest.* Chicago: A. C. McClurg, 1912.

Bridenbaugh, Carl. *Seat of Empire, the Political Role of Eighteenth Century Williamsburg.* Williamsburg: Colonial Williamsburg, 1950.

Briley, Richard, III. *Death of the Kingfish! Who Did Kill Huey Long?* Dallas: Triangle Publishing, 1960.

Brooks, Geraldine. *Dames and Daughters of Colonial Days.* New York: T. Y. Crowell, 1900.

Brooks, Van Wyck. *New England: Indian Summer.* New York: E. P. Dutton, 1940.

Brown, John Mason. *Through These Men.* New York: Harper & Brothers, 1956.

Brown, William Burlie. *The People's Choice: The Presidential Image in the Campaign Biography.* Baton Rouge: Louisiana State University Press, 1960.

Bruce, Philip Alexander. *History of the University of Virginia.* 5 vols. New York: Macmillan, 1920–22.

Carson, Hampton L. *The Supreme Court of the United States: Its History.* 2 vols. Philadelphia: P. W. Ziegler, 1892.

Carter, John Franklin. *American Messiahs by the Unofficial Observer.* New York: Simon & Schuster, 1935.

Case, Carleton B. *Good Stories about Roosevelt.* Chicago: Shrewesbury Publishing, 1920.

Chamberlain, Joshua L. *New York University.* Boston: R. Herndon, 1901.

Clancy, Herbert J. *The Presidential Election of 1880.* Chicago: Loyola University Press, 1958.

Clark, Mary Sherrerd. *In the Olden Days, Papers Colonial and Revolutionary.* Greenwich, Connecticut: Literary Collector Press, 1905.

Cleland, Robert Glass. *A History of California: The American Period.* New York: Macmillan, 1922.

Coleman, Mary Haldane (Mrs. George P.). *Story of a Portrait.* Richmond: Dietz Press, 1935.

——, editor. *A Williamsburg Scrap Book.* Richmond: Dietz Press, 1932.

Collins, Lewis. *Historical Sketches of Kentucky.* Cincinnati: J. A. & V. P. James, 1847.

Cunningham, Noble E., Jr. *The Jeffersonian Republicans.* Chapel Hill: University of North Carolina Press, 1957.

Cunz, Dieter. *The Maryland Germans.* Princeton: Princeton University Press, 1948.

Curran, Robert. *The Kennedy Women.* New York: Lancer Books, 1964.

Daniels, Josephus. *The Wilson Era: Years of Peace, 1910–1917.* Chapel Hill: University of North Carolina Press, 1944.

David, Paul T., Malcolm Moos and Ralph M. Goldman, editors. *Presidential Nominating Politics in 1952.* 5 vols. Baltimore: Johns Hopkins Press, 1954.

Demarest, William H. S. *A History of Rutgers College, 1766–1924.* New Brunswick: Rutgers College, 1924.

Deutsch, Hermann B. *The Huey Long Murder Case.* Garden City, New York: Doubleday, 1963.

De Witt, John. *The Path of the Just as the Shining Light: A Funeral Discourse, Pronounced in the Reformed Dutch Church of New-Brunswick, Occasioned by the Decease of the Rev. John H. Livingston.* New Brunswick: William Myer, 1825.

Dillon, Dorothy Rita. *The New York Triumvirate: A Study of the Legal and Political Careers of William Livingston, John Morin Scott, William Smith, Jr.* New York: Columbia University Press, 1949.

Dorris, Jonathan Truman. *Pardon and Amnesty Under Lincoln and Johnson.* Chapel Hill: University of North Carolina Press, 1953.

Dubbs, Joseph Henry. *History of Franklin and Marshall College.* Lancaster: Franklin and Marshall College Alumni Association, 1903.

Duke, Basil W. *A History of Morgan's Cavalry.* Bloomington: Indiana University Press, 1960.

Dunn, Arthur Wallace. *Gridiron Nights.* New York: Frederick A. Stokes, 1915.

Eaton, Clement. *Henry Clay and the Art of American Politics.* Boston: Little, Brown, 1957.

Edgar, William C. *The Medal of Gold.* Minneapolis: Bellman, 1925.

Ellet, Elizabeth F. *The Queens of American Society.* New York: C. Scribner, 1867.

——*The Women of the American Revolution.* 2 vols. New York: Baker & Scribner, 1848–50.

Faust, Albert Bernhardt. *The German Element in the United States.* 2 vols. Boston and New York: Houghton Mifflin, 1927.

Fee, Walter R. *The Transition from Aristocracy to Democracy in New Jersey, 1789–1829.* Somerville, New Jersey: Somerset Press, 1933.

Flexner, James Thomas. *Steamboats Come True; American Inventors in Action.* New York: Viking Press, 1944.

——*The Traitor and the Spy, Benedict Arnold and John André.* New York: Harcourt, Brace, 1953.

Follett, Mary P. *The Speaker of the House of Representatives.* New York: Longmans, Green, 1896.

Folwell, William W. *A History of Minnesota.* 4 vols. St. Paul: Minnesota Historical Society, 1921–30.

Friedman, Stanley P. *The Magnificent Kennedy Women.* Derby, Connecticut: Monarch Books, 1964.

Fuller, Helen. *Year of Trial: Kennedy's Crucial Decisions.* New York: Harcourt, Brace and World, 1962.

Galloway, George B. *History of the House of Representatives.* New York: Crowell, 1962.

Galton, Francis. *Hereditary Genius.* London: Macmillan, 1869.

Gilbert, Clinton W. *The Mirrors of Washington.* New York: G. P. Putnam's Sons, 1921.

Goebel, Dorothy Burne, and Julius Goebel, Jr. *Generals in the White House*. Garden City, New York: Doubleday, 1952.

Gordon, Thomas F. *The History of New Jersey*. Trenton: D. Fenton, 1834.

Greene, Le Roy. *Shelter for His Excellency, the Story of Pennsylvania's Executive Mansion and the One Hundred Governors of the Commonwealth*. Harrisburg: Stackpole, 1951.

Gregg, Dorothy. *The Exploitation of the Steamboat: The Case of Colonel John Stevens*. Unpublished Ph.D. dissertation, Columbia University, 1951.

Gunderson, Robert Gray. *The Log-Cabin Campaign*. Lexington: University of Kentucky Press, 1957.

Gunther, John. *Inside U.S.A.* New York: Harper & Brothers, 1947. Revised edition, 1951.

Hammond, Hilda Phelps. *Let Freedom Ring*. New York: Farrar & Rinehart, 1936.

Hanna, Alfred J. *Flight into Oblivion*. Richmond: Johnson Publishing, 1938.

Hatch, Louis Clinton. *A History of the Vice-Presidency of the United States*. New York: American Historical Society, 1934.

Haynes, George H. *The Senate of the United States*. 2 vols. Boston: Houghton Mifflin, 1938.

Hechler, Kenneth W. *Insurgency, Personalities and Politics of the Taft Era*. New York: Russell & Russell, 1964.

Hendrick, Burton J. *Statesmen of the Lost Cause*. Boston: Little, Brown, 1939.

Hesseltine, William B., editor. *Three Against Lincoln, Murat Halstead Reports the Caucuses of 1860*. Baton Rouge: Louisiana State University Press, 1960.

Hoffman, Robert V. *The Revolutionary Scene in New Jersey*. New York: American Historical Co., 1942.

Holbrook, Stewart H. *The Age of the Moguls*. Garden City, New York: Doubleday, 1953.

Jones, Edgar Dewitt. *Lords of Speech*. Chicago and New York: Willett, Clark, 1937.

Jones, Maldwyn Allen. *American Immigration*. Chicago: University of Chicago Press, 1960.

Jones, Virgil Carrington. *The Civil War at Sea*. 3 vols. New York: Holt, Rinehart, Winston, 1960–62.

Judson, L. Carroll. *A Biography of the Signers of the Declaration of Independence*. Philadelphia: J. Dodson & Thomas, Cowperthwait, 1839.

Kane, Harnett T. *Louisiana Hayride, the American Rehearsal for Dictatorship, 1928–1940*. New York: W. Morrow, 1941.

——*Spies for the Blue and Gray*. Garden City, New York: Hanover House, 1954.

Kelly, Frank K. *The Fight for the White House, the Story of 1912*. New York: Crowell, 1961.

Kennedy, John F. *Profiles in Courage*. New York: Harper & Brothers, 1956.

——*Why England Slept*. New York: W. Funk, 1940.

Kennedy, Joseph P. *I'm for Roosevelt*. New York: Reynal & Hitchcock, 1936.

Kerr, Wilfred Brenton. *Bermuda and the American Revolution: 1760–1783*. Princeton: Princeton University Press, 1936.

Key, V. O., Jr. *Southern Politics in State and Nation*. New York: Alfred A. Knopf, 1949.

Klein, Philip S. *Pennsylvania Politics, 1817–1832.* Philadelphia: Historical Society of Pennsylvania, 1940.

Knapp, Charles Merriam. *New Jersey Politics During the Period of the Civil War and Reconstruction.* New York: W. F. Humphrey, 1924.

Knauss, James Owen. *Social Conditions Among the Pennsylvania Germans in the Eighteenth Century, as Revealed in German Newspapers Published in America.* Lancaster: Press of the New Era Printing Co., 1922.

Knight, William Eliot. *The Wm. C. P. Breckinridge Defence.* Colfax, Iowa: Weekly Clipper, 1895.

Kornitzer, Bela. *American Fathers and Sons.* New York: Hermitage House, 1952.

Kuhlmann, Charles B. *The Development of the Flour-Milling Industry in the United States.* Boston and New York: Houghton Mifflin, 1929.

Kull, Irving S., editor. *New Jersey, a History.* 6 vols. New York: American Historical Society, 1930–32.

Leisy, Ernest E. *The American Historical Novel.* Norman: University of Oklahoma Press, 1950.

Levin, H., editor. *The Lawyers and Lawmakers of Kentucky.* Chicago: Lewis Publishing, 1897.

Lomask, Milton. *Andrew Johnson: President on Trial.* New York: Farrar, Straus, 1960.

Longworth, Nicholas, and others. *Reception and Dinner in Honor of the 56th Birthday of Augustus Peabody Gardner, a Pioneer for Preparedness, by the Roosevelt Club, Hotel Westminster, Boston, November 5, 1921.* Boston: The Roosevelt Club, 1921.

Lowry, Edward G. *Washington Close-ups.* Boston and New York: Houghton Mifflin, 1921.

Lundin, Charles Leonard. *Cockpit of the Revolution, the War for Independence in New Jersey.* Princeton: Princeton University Press, 1940.

Luthin, Reinhard H. *American Demagogues.* Boston: Beacon Press, 1954.

Maclean, John. *History of the College of New Jersey.* 2 vols. Philadelphia: J. B. Lippincott, 1877.

Macmillan, Margaret Burnham. *The War Governors in the American Revolution.* New York: Columbia University Press, 1943.

MacNeil, Neil. *Forge of Democracy, the House of Representatives.* New York: D. McKay, 1963.

Malone, Dumas. *Jefferson and the Ordeal of Liberty.* Boston: Little, Brown, 1962.

Martin, Ralph G., and Ed Plaut. *Front Runner, Dark Horse.* Garden City, New York: Doubleday, 1960.

Maxson, Charles Hartshorn. *The Great Awakening in the Middle Colonies.* Chicago: University of Chicago Press, 1920.

McCormick, Richard P. *Experiment in Independence, New Jersey in the Critical Period, 1781–1789.* New Brunswick: Rutgers University Press, 1950.

McCoy, Donald R. *Angry Voices, Left-of-Center Politics in the New Deal Era.* Lawrence: University of Kansas Press, 1958.

McKitrick, Eric L. *Andrew Johnson and Reconstruction.* Chicago: University of Chicago Press, 1960.

Moley, Raymond. *27 Masters of Politics.* New York: Funk & Wagnalls, 1949.

Moos, Malcolm. *The Republicans, a History of Their Party.* New York: Random House, 1956.

Morgan, Edmund S. *Virginians at Home, Family Life in the Eighteenth Century.* Williamsburg: Colonial Williamsburg, 1952.

Mowry, George E. *Theodore Roosevelt and the Progressive Movement.* Madison: University of Wisconsin Press, 1947.

Myers, Gustavus. *History of the Supreme Court of the United States.* Chicago: C. H. Keer, 1912.

Nead, Daniel Wunderlich. *The Pennsylvania-German in the Settlement of Maryland.* Lancaster: Press of the New Era Publishing Co., 1914.

Nevins, Allan. *The American States During and After the Revolution, 1775–1789.* New York: Macmillan, 1924.

Noggle, Burl. *Teapot Dome: Oil and Politics in the 1920's.* Baton Rouge: Louisiana State University, 1962.

Novak, Robert D. *The Agony of the G.O.P. 1964.* New York: Macmillan, 1965.

Ochsenford, S. E., editor. *Muhlenberg College, 1867–1892.* Allentown: Muhlenberg College, 1892.

Opotowsky, Stan. *The Kennedy Government.* New York: E. P. Dutton, 1961.

Parker, Cortlandt. *The Essex Bar.* Newark: Ward & Tichenor, 1874.

Parrington, Vernon Louis, Jr. *American Dreams, a Study of American Utopias.* Providence: Brown University, 1947.

Perling, J. J. *Presidents' Sons.* New York: Odyssey Press, 1947.

Pierce, Bessie Louise. *A History of Chicago.* 3 vols. New York: Alfred A. Knopf, 1937–57.

Rapp, Noel George. *The Political Speaking of Senator Robert A. Taft, 1939 to 1953.* Unpublished Ph.D. dissertation, Purdue University, 1955.

Reed, H. Clay, editor. *Delaware: A History of the First State.* 3 vols. New York: Lewis Historical Publishing, 1947.

Reichley, James. *States in Crisis.* Chapel Hill: University of North Carolina Press, 1964.

Reilly, George L. A. *The Camden and Amboy Railroad in New Jersey Politics, 1830–1871.* Unpublished Ph.D. dissertation, Columbia University, 1952.

Report of the Twentieth Annual Meeting of the American Bar Association. Philadelphia, 1897.

Robbins, Jhan and June. *Eight Weeks to Live, the Last Chapter in the Life of Senator Robert A. Taft.* Garden City, New York: Doubleday, 1954.

Robinson, Corinne Roosevelt. *Service and Sacrifice.* New York: Charles Scribner's Sons, 1919.

Roper, Elmo. *You and Your Leaders.* New York: Morrow, 1957.

Roscoe, Theodore. *The Web of Conspiracy, the Complete Story of the Men Who Murdered Abraham Lincoln.* Englewood Cliffs, New Jersey: Prentice-Hall, 1959.

Roseboom, Eugene H. *A History of Presidential Elections.* New York: Macmillan, 1957.

Rothery, Agnes. *Houses Virginians Have Loved.* New York: Rinehart, 1954.

Russell, Francis. *The Great Interlude.* New York: McGraw-Hill, 1964.

Saarinen, Aline B. *The Proud Possessors.* New York: Random House, 1958.

Sabine, Lorenzo. *Biographical Sketches of Loyalists of the American Revolution.* 2 vols. Boston: Little, Brown, 1864.

Sackett, William Edgar. *Modern Battles of Trenton.* 2 vols. Trenton: J. L. Murphy, 1895–1914.

Salinger, Pierre, and Sander Vanocur, editors. *A Tribute to John F. Kennedy.* Chicago: Encyclopaedia Britannica, 1964.

Sanderson, John, editor. *Biography of the Signers of the Declaration of Independence.* 9 vols. Philadelphia: R. W. Pomeroy, 1820–27.

Scharf, J. Thomas. *History of Delaware, 1609–1888.* 2 vols. Philadelphia: L. J. Richards, 1888.

Schlesinger, Arthur M., Jr. *The Age of Jackson.* Boston: Little, Brown, 1945.

——*The Age of Roosevelt: The Crisis of the Old Order, 1919–1923.* Boston: Houghton Mifflin, 1957.

Schrag, Felix James, *Pietism in Colonial America.* Part of a Ph.D. Dissertation, University of Chicago, 1948.

Sevareid, Eric, editor. *Candidates 1960.* New York: Basic Books, 1959.

Shannon, William V. *The American Irish.* New York: Macmillan, 1963.

Sindler, Allan P. *Huey Long's Louisiana.* Baltimore: Johns Hopkins Press, 1956.

Smith, Gene. *When the Cheering Stopped.* New York: Morrow, 1964.

Smith, Margaret Bayard. *What is Gentility? A Moral Tale.* Washington: P. Thompson, 1828.

——*A Winter in Washington; or, Memoirs of the Seymour Family.* 2 vols. New York: E. Bliss & E. White, 1824.

Smith, William Henry. *Speakers of the House of Representatives of the United States.* Baltimore: S. J. Gaeng, 1928.

Stockton, Frank R. *Stories of New Jersey.* New Brunswick: Rutgers University Press, 1961.

Stuart, Graham H. *The Department of State, a History of Its Organization, Procedure, and Personnel.* New York: Macmillan, 1949.

Taft, Charles P. *Democracy in Politics and Economics.* New York: Farrar, Straus, 1950.

——*Trade Barriers and the National Interest.* Dallas: Southern Methodist University Press, 1955.

Taft, Charles P. *You and I—and Roosevelt.* New York: Farrar & Rinehart, 1936.

Taft, Henry W. *Kindred Arts, Conversation and Public Speaking.* New York: Macmillan, 1929.

——*Legal Miscellanies.* New York: Macmillan, 1941.

Taft, Robert A. *A Foreign Policy for Americans.* Garden City, New York: Doubleday, 1951.

Taft, William Howard. *Our Chief Magistrate and His Powers.* New York: Columbia University Press, 1916.

Tanzer, Lester, editor. *The Kennedy Circle.* Washington: Luce, 1961.

Thatcher, Harold Wesley. *The Social Philosophy of William Livingston.* Chicago, 1938.

Thompson, Ed. Porter. *History of the First Kentucky Brigade.* Cincinnati: Caxton Publishing, 1868.

Thompson, Henry P. *History of the Reformed Church, at Readington, New Jersey.* New York: Board of Publication of the Reformed Church in America, 1882.

Thorp, Willard, editor. *The Lives of Eighteen from Princeton.* Princeton: Princeton University Press, 1946.

Thwing, Charles Franklin. *Friends of Men.* New York: Macmillan, 1933.

Tiffany, Charles C. *A History of the Protestant Episcopal Church in the United States of America.* New York: Christian Literature Co., 1895.

Townsend, William H. *Lincoln and the Bluegrass*. Lexington: University of Kentucky Press, 1955.

Tucker, Beverley Dandridge. *Confederate Memorial Verses*. Norfolk: United Daughters of the Confederacy, 1904.

——*My Three Loves*. New York and Washington: Neagle Publishing, 1910.

Tucker, Nathaniel Beverley. *The Partisan Leader*. Carl Bridenbaugh, editor. New York: Alfred A. Knopf, 1933.

Tucker, St. George. *Hansford: A Tale of Bacon's Rebellion*. Richmond: G. M. West, 1857.

Umbreit, Kenneth Bernard. *Our Eleven Chief Justices, a History of the Supreme Court in Terms of Their Personalities*. New York: Harper & Brothers, 1938.

Van Der Linden, Frank. *The Turning Point, Jefferson's Battle for the Presidency*. Washington: Robert B. Luce, 1962.

Van Rensselaer, Mrs. Sarah. *Ancestral Sketches and Records of Olden Times*. New York: A. D. F. Randolph, 1882.

Vaughan, William Hutchinson. *Robert Jefferson Breckinridge as an Educational Administrator*. Nashville: George Peabody College for Teachers, 1937.

Wagenknecht, Edward. *Chicago*. Norman: University of Oklahoma Press, 1964.

Ward, William Rankin. *Down the Years, a History of the Mutual Benefit Life Insurance Company, 1845–1932*. Camden: Haddon Craftsmen, 1932.

Warfield, Ethelbert Dudley. *The Kentucky Resolutions of 1798*. New York: G. P. Putnam's Sons, 1887.

Washburn, Charles A. *From Poverty to Competence*. Philadelphia: J. B. Lippincott, 1887.

——*Gomery of Montgomery*. 2 vols. New York: Carleton, 1865.

——*Philip Thaxter*. New York: Rudd & Carleton, 1861.

Washburn, Israel, Jr. *Notes, Historical, Descriptive, and Personal, of Livermore*. Portland: Bailey & Noyes, 1874.

Washburn, William D., Jr. *Some Rejected Verse*. New York: Knickerbocker Press, 1902.

Watkins, J. Elfreth. *The Camden and Amboy Railroad*. Washington: Press of Gedney & Roberts, 1892.

Wecter, Dixon. *The Saga of American Society*. New York: Charles Scribner's Sons, 1937.

Weigle, Luther A. *American Idealism*. New Haven: Yale University Press, 1928.

Werner, M. R., and John Starr. *Teapot Dome*. New York: Viking Press, 1959.

Wertenbaker, Thomas Jefferson. *Princeton 1746–1896*. Princeton: Princeton University Press, 1946.

White, Theodore H. *The Making of the President 1960*. New York: Atheneum, 1961.

——*The Making of the President 1964*. New York: Atheneum, 1965.

Wildes, Harry Emerson. *Twin Rivers, the Raritan and the Passaic*. New York: Farrar & Rinehart, 1943.

Wilson, Edmund, editor. *The Shock of Recognition*. New York: Farrar, Straus & Cudahy, 1955.

Wilson, Francis. *John Wilkes Booth, Fact and Fiction of Lincoln's Assassination*. Boston and New York: Houghton Mifflin, 1929.

Wilson, Samuel M. *History of Kentucky from 1803 to 1928.* Chicago and Louisville: S. J. Clarke, 1928.

Wood, Ralph, editor. *The Pennsylvania Germans.* Princeton: Princeton University Press, 1942.

Woodman, Cyrus. *A Statement Relating to the Will of Hon. Cadwallader C. Washburn.* Cambridge: Privately printed, 1884.

Zinman, David H. *The Day Huey Long Was Shot.* New York: I. Obolensky, 1963.

G) *Secondary Sources: Articles*

Adams, Henry. "Lodge's Cabot." *Nation,* July 5, 1877.

Adams, Mildred. "Roosevelts and Du Ponts: Both Molders of History." *New York Times Magazine,* June 27, 1937.

Alsop, Joseph, and Stewart. "Can F.D.R., Jr., Get His Father's Old Job?" *Saturday Evening Post,* September 4, 1954.

Alsop, Joseph. "The Legacy of John F. Kennedy." *Saturday Evening Post,* November 21, 1964.

Alsop, Stewart. "Kennedy's Magic Formula." *Saturday Evening Post,* August 13, 1960.

——"What Made Teddy Run?" *Saturday Evening Post,* October 27, 1962.

Armstrong, Richard, and Robert Massie. "A New Taft and a Young Kennedy Go to Washington." *Saturday Evening Post,* January 19, 1963.

Beach, Rex. "Spencer Roane and the Richmond Junto." *William and Mary Quarterly,* 2d Series, XXII, No. 1 (January 1942).

Beatty, Jerome. "Nine Kennedys and How They Grew." *Reader's Digest,* April 1939.

Bendiner, Robert. "Bay State Prospects." *Nation,* October 12, 1946.

Blagden, Ralph M. "Cabot Lodge's Toughest Fight." *Reporter,* September 30, 1952.

Brydon, G. MacLaren. "The Antiecclesiastical Laws of Virginia." *Virginia Magazine of History and Biography,* LXIV, No. 3 (July 1956).

Butterfield, L. H. "Annis and the General: Mrs. Stockton's Poetic Eulogies of George Washington." *Princeton University Library Chronicle,* VII, No. 1 (November 1945).

——"Morven: A Colonial Outpost of Sensibility. With Some Hitherto Unpublished Poems by Annis Boudinot Stockton." *Princeton University Library Chronicle,* VI, No. 1 (November 1944).

Cater, Douglass. "The Cool Eye of John F. Kennedy." *Reporter,* December 10, 1959.

Coleman, Charles W. "Glimpses of Old College Life." *William and Mary Quarterly,* 1st Series, VIII, No. 3 (January 1900).

Coleman, Mary Haldane (Mrs. George P.) "Letters from Old Trunks." *Virginia Magazine of History and Biography,* XLIV, No. 1 (January 1936).

——"Randolph and Tucker Letters." *Virginia Magazine of History and Biography,* XLII, No. 1 (January 1934) and No. 3 (July 1934).

Coogan, Tim Pat. "Sure, and It's County Kennedy Now." *New York Times Magazine,* June 23, 1963.

Cooke, Allistair. "The Public Face of John F. Kennedy." *Show,* April 1963.

Cooke, Jacob E. "Chats with Henry Adams." *American Heritage,* December 1955.

Cunz, Dieter. "Augustin Herrman, Origin and Early Events." *Tyler's Quarterly Historical and Genealogical Magazine,* XXIV, No. 1 (July 1942).

Davidson, Bill. "Brother Act." (Henry Cabot Lodge, Jr., and John Davis Lodge). *Collier's,* January 18, 1947.

Dorpalen, Andreas. "The German Element in Early Pennsylvania Politics, 1789–1800." *Pennsylvania History,* IX, No. 3 (July 1942).

——"The Political Influence of the German Element in Colonial America." *Pennsylvania History,* VI, No. 3 (July 1939) and VI, No. 4 (October 1939).

Fallaci, Oriana. "Robert Kennedy Answers Some Blunt Questions." *Look,* March 9, 1965.

Fay, Bernard. "Early Party Machinery in the United States, Pennsylvania in the Election of 1796." *Pennsylvania Magazine of History and Biography,* LX, No. 4 (October 1936).

Ferman, Irving. "Louisiana Side-Show." *New Republic,* January 21, 1952.

Field, Richard Stockton. "The Provincial Courts of New Jersey." *Collections of the New Jersey Historical Society,* III (1849).

——"Review of the Trial of the Rev. Wm. Tennent for Perjury in 1742." *Proceedings of the New Jersey Historical Society,* VI (1853).

Godcharles, Frederic A. "Pennsylvania Statesmanship—At Home and Abroad." *Americana,* XXXVII, No. 4 (October 1943).

Hancock, Harold Bell. "The Campaign and Election of 1860." *Delaware History,* VII, No. 2 (September 1956).

——"The Coming of the War." *Delaware History,* VII, No. 3 (March 1957).

——"The Political History of Delaware During the Civil War." *Delaware History,* VII, No. 4 (September 1957).

Harrison, Lowell H. "A Virginian Moves to Kentucky, 1793." *William and Mary Quarterly,* 3d Series, XV, No. 2 (April 1958).

——"Young Mr. Breckinridge Experiences War, Pestilence and Inflation, 1781." *William and Mary Quarterly,* 3d Series, IX, No. 2 (April 1952).

Hessler, William H. "Taft vs. Kennedy in Ohio." *Reporter,* October 25, 1962.

Hoffman, Betty Hannah. "What It's Like to Marry a Kennedy." *Ladies' Home Journal,* October 1962.

Jarman, Rufus. "You Can't Beat a Lodge." *Saturday Evening Post,* March 15, 1947.

Jones, William Macfarlane. "Will of Richard Randolph, Jr., of 'Bizarre.'" *Virginia Magazine of History and Biography,* XXXIV, No. 1 (January 1926).

Kane, Harnett T. "Louisiana Story: End of a Chapter." *New York Times Magazine,* September 27, 1959.

Karnow, Stanley. "The Quandary of Henry Cabot Lodge." *Saturday Evening Post,* February 8, 1964.

Kempton, Murray. "Will Bobby Kennedy Run in New York?" *New Republic,* June 6, 1964.

Kennedy, Joseph P., as told to John B. Kennedy. "Shielding the Sheep." *Saturday Evening Post,* January 18, 1936.

Kennedy, Robert F. "Tribute to JFK." *Look,* February 25, 1964.

Klein, Philip S. "Early Lancaster County Politics." *Pennsylvania History,* III, No. 2 (April 1936).

Kraft, Joseph, "Riot Squad for the New Frontier." *Harper's,* August 1963.

Krout, John A. "Behind the Coat of Arms, a Phase of Prestige in Colonial New York." *New York History,* XVI, No. 1 (January 1935).

Leakin, George Armistead. "Labadists of Bohemia Manor." *Maryland Historical Magazine,* I, No. 4 (December 1906).

——"A Visit to Bohemia Manor." *Maryland Historical Magazine*, II, No. 2 (June 1907).

Leary, Lewis. "St. George Tucker Attends the Theatre." *William and Mary Quarterly*, 3d Series, V, No. 3 (July 1948).

Leder, Lawrence. "Captain Kidd and the Leisler Rebellion." *New-York Historical Society Quarterly*, XXXVIII, No. 1 (January 1954).

——, editor. "Records of the Trials of Jacob Leisler and His Associates." *New-York Historical Society Quarterly*, XXXVI, No. 4 (October 1952).

——"Robert Livingston's Voyage to England." *New York History*, XXXVI, No. 1 (January 1955).

Lindley, Ernest K. "Will Kennedy Run for President?" *Liberty*, May 21, 1938.

Lodge, Henry Cabot, Jr. "Grandson Backs His Elder." *Life*, September 14, 1953.

——"Lessons from a Historic Debate." *New York Times Magazine*, June 30, 1944.

Longworth, Alice Roosevelt. "Strange Bedfellows." *Ladies' Home Journal*, October 1935.

——"What's the Matter with Bob Taft?" *Saturday Evening Post*, May 4, 1940.

McCarthy, Joe. "One Election JFK Can't Win." *Look*, November 6, 1962.

McCormick, Richard P. "The First Election of Governor William Livingston." *Proceedings of the New Jersey Historical Society*, LXV, No. 2 (April 1947).

McDermott, John Francis. "Nathaniel Beverley Tucker in Missouri." *William and Mary Quarterly*, 2d Series, XX, No. 4 (October 1940).

Matthews, Brander. "Senator Lodge as a Man of Letters." *New York Times Book Review and Magazine*, June 19, 1921.

Mayo, Lida. "Miss Adams in Love." *American Heritage*, February 1965.

Meade, Robert D. "John Randolph of Roanoke, Some New Information." *William and Mary Quarterly*, 2d Series, XIII, No. 4 (October 1933).

Melzer, Dorothy Garrett. "Mr. Breckinridge Accepts." *Register of the Kentucky Historical Society*, LVI, No. 3 (July 1958).

Michelson, Edward J. "Lodge Dislodged?" *Nation*, October 4, 1952.

Moore, Edmund Arthur. "Robert J. Breckinridge and the Slavery Aspects of the Presbyterian Schism of 1837." *Church History*, IV, No. 4 (December 1935).

Morley, Felix. "The Case for Taft." *Life*, February 9, 1948.

Morris, Joe Alex. "Another Roosevelt Makes His Pitch." *Saturday Evening Post*, October 7, 1950.

Munroe, John A. "James A. Bayard and the Milligans." *Delaware History*, VIII, No. 2 (September 1958).

——, editor. "William Plumer's Biographical Sketches of James A. Bayard, Caesar A. Rodney, and Samuel White." *Delaware History*, IV, No. 4 (September 1951).

Nelligan, Murray H. "American Nationalism on the Stage: The Plays of George Washington Parke Custis." *Virginia Magazine of History and Biography*, LVIII, No. 3 (July 1950).

Pennypacker, Morton. "Captain Kidd: Hung, Not for Piracy but for Causing the Death of a Rebellious Seaman Hit with a Toy Bucket." *New York History*, XXV, No. 4 (October 1944).

Reston, James. "What Was Killed Was Not Only the President but the Promise." *New York Times Magazine*, November 15, 1964.

Riley, Edward M. "St. George Tucker's Journal of the Siege of Yorktown, 1781." *William and Mary Quarterly*, 3d Series, V, (July 1948).

Schafer, Joseph. "Washburniana." *Wisconsin Magazine of History*, XIV, No. 3 (March 1931).

Schlesinger, Arthur M., Jr. "Two Years Later—The Roosevelt Family." *Life*, April 7, 1947.

Seyfert, A. G. "Members of Congress Who Represented Lancaster County in the United States Congress from 1789 to the Present Time." *Papers Read Before the Lancaster County Historical Society*, XXXIV, No. 3 (1930).

Skow, John. "Lodge Faces His Big Test in Oregon." *Saturday Evening Post*, May 16, 1964.

Stearns, Bertha Monica. "The Literary Treatment of Bacon's Rebellion in Virginia." *Virginia Magazine of History and Biography*, LII, No. 3 (July 1944).

Tapp, Hambleton. "Robert J. Breckinridge and the Year 1849." *Filson Club History Quarterly*, XII, No. 3 (July 1938).

——"Robert J. Breckinridge During the Civil War." *Filson Club History Quarterly*, XI, No. 2 (April 1937).

Tucker, Henry St. George. "Patrick Henry and St. George Tucker." *University of Pennsylvania Law Review*, LXVII, No. 1 (January 1919).

Vidal, Gore. "The Best Man 1968." *Esquire*, March 1963.

White, David Manning. "Franklin Applauds the Muse." *William and Mary Quarterly*, 3d Series, IV, No. 2 (April 1947).

Wicker, Tom. "The Bostonian vs. the Texan." *New York Times Magazine*, October 23, 1960.

Williams, T. Harry. "The Gentleman from Louisiana: Demagogue or Democrat." *Journal of Southern History*, XXVI, No. 1 (February 1960).

Woodbury, Clarence. "Will There Always Be a Roosevelt?" *American Magazine*, January 1953.

Woolf, S. J. "F.D.R. Jr. Speaks for the Veteran." *New York Times Magazine*, September 1, 1946.

INDEX

1

Dear George,
Dear Mary

Mary Calvi

St. Martin's Press ♏ New York

DEAR GEORGE, DEAR MARY. Copyright © 2019 by Mary Calvi. All rights reserved. Printed in the United States of America. For information, address St. Martin's Press, 175 Fifth Avenue, New York, NY 10010.

www.stmartins.com

Endpapers: Timothy Scandal Adjutant, "A Return of the State of Capt. Polly Philips's Dependant Compny, with the Kill'd, Wounded, Deserted, and Discharg'd &c, during the Campaigns 1756 & 1756 (sic)," December 25, 1756, LO 6475, Huntington Library, San Marino, California.

Illustration on page xi: *Philipse Manor Hall,* unknown artist "D.R." Probably New York, post-1783, ink wash on paper. Gift of La Duchesse de Talleyrand. Historic Hudson Valley, Pocantico Hills, New York (PM.65.866).

Designed by Donna Sinisgalli Noetzel

Library of Congress Cataloging-in-Publication Data

Names: Calvi, Mary – author.
Title: Dear George, Dear Mary / Mary Calvi.
Description: First edition. | New York : St. Martin's Press, 2019.
Identifiers: LCCN 2018037733 | ISBN 9781250162946 (hardcover) | ISBN 9781250162939 (ebook)
Subjects: LCSH: Washington, George, 1732–1799—Fiction. | Philipse, Mary, 1730–1825—Fiction. | GSAFD: Biographical fiction.
Classification: LCC PS3603.A44639 D43 2019 | DDC 813/.6—dc23
LC record available at https://lccn.loc.gov/2018037733

Our books may be purchased in bulk for promotional, educational, or business use. Please contact your local bookseller or the Macmillan Corporate and Premium Sales Department at 1-800-221-7945, extension 5442, or by email at MacmillanSpecialMarkets@macmillan.com.

First Edition: February 2019

10 9 8 7 6 5 4 3 2 1

To my husband, my children, my family,
and our hometown

Contents

Note to the Reader

AS A JOURNALIST, I search for untold stories. I never would have imagined I'd find one hidden away for centuries in my hometown. This novel has been crafted from thousands of letters, journal entries, witness accounts, publications, and other sources related to George Washington, Mary Eliza Philipse, and historical figures, known and unknown to the modern-day public, who influenced their world and the birth of a nation in the eighteenth century. Maybe history wanted their romance hidden. I do not know. What I do know is that during my research in libraries, museums, church basements, and through digital archives, document after document pieced together like a puzzle until I was awestruck by the theory it revealed. Throughout, I've used the written or spoken words of Washington and those figures whose records have been preserved. I chose to present Mary and George's story as a novel rather than nonfiction because, despite relying on historical documents, I wanted to write what captivated me most: imagining their lives and picturing the lives and habits of real flesh-and-blood young Americans in the 1700s.

A person can live or die,
no matter the breath on one's lips.

A person can be rich or poor,
no matter the pence in one's pocket.

A person can love or hate,
no matter the devotion within one's heart.

A person can be hero or traitor, no matter the will
of one's mind.

On the 14th of February, 1756,
no matter the choice,
destiny became sealed as if etched into metal.

Part I

The Encounter

Chapter One

—◆◈◆—

Guardian's Wall

Love is said to be an involuntary passion and it is
therefore contended that it cannot be resisted.

—GEORGE WASHINGTON

YONKERS-ON-HUDSON
FEBRUARY 14, 1756

Mary Eliza lay upon cold leaves whose color had washed away a season ago, wishing she could bring back the living. Dead things surrounded her; every flower bud hung shriveled. The dull winter had brought only a few flakes. Spring, when fragrance emerged from its cocoon, was her favorite time of year. That was not this time. Today nature emitted not even a scent to smell.

Wan light peeked through the dark cloud hovering above her. She'd been here at Hudson's Hook since sunrise, writing poetry in her head:

Here I lie,
As mine eyes, my heart, wait,
So close art thou and I.
Here I lie,
Where the ravens fly,
And the guardian's wall, my gate.

Here I lie,
As mine eyes, my heart, wait.

The gallop of approaching stallions echoed. She attempted to rise, but alas, guilt confined her limbs like a fetter. The horses halted. She knew who had arrived. Boots crunching across hardened grasses came next. His silly chain clinked louder as he drew closer. She expected her brother to holler. She assumed that was coming. Instead, he just stood there, glaring at her. His murmuring sounded as if impatience was boiling in a kettle.

A long silence followed. She heard another audible exhalation from him. Frederick lay down, leaving just inches between them. "Polly." He never used her birth name. "I have a great inclination to take you back by force!" Agitation combined with steam in his threat.

She added a few more inches between them.

A deep groan released from his lips. His body shifted sideways. "This trial of my patience . . . ends now." He spoke through teeth clenched.

She didn't respond. What would she even say? Worrying thoughts had taken up much of the space in her head, for no ordinary winter's day was before them. This night, as the sun found its repose, the Philipse family would welcome the hero of the South to a grand banquet and pleasure ball with beaux dressed in princely garments and belles adorned in royal costumes. For most hosts, it would be reason for celebration. For Mary, it was reason for tumult. In the midst of such crowds, the noisomeness of hair powder lingered like a fog, bringing back the image that forever haunted her: the little boy's eyes filled with horror, filled with fear. The memory caused her to cringe.

She would rather have remained here with her disquiet fading into the season's emptiness. But with her brother about to snatch her from her stillness, she closed her eyes and repeated to herself the words she promised Papa she would say each day: You are capable of the impossible, for you have survived the unthinkable.

Slowly, she rose and retied her riding dress's silk sash into a proper bow. Throughout, she envisioned the man of honor of the evening,

the most celebrated colonel of the colonies, riding more than five hundred miles to be in attendance. His name was George Washington.

THE TRIP BACK to the manor was quiet, except for the clank of the chain Frederick was wearing. Then he began lecturing her. "Two hundred and twenty of the highest-ranking citizens will converge on our home, each of them viewing each of us, including you, Polly."

Mary could not even acknowledge him, not with the confusion of emotions affecting her spirit. Certainly she would want to meet the hero. She already knew more about Colonel Washington than she was comfortable talking about. He was a brave one, unlike her. But the number of guests—220—it sat like a weight upon her chest.

If she made the decision, she would be riding Willoughby back to the Yonkers manor. This four-wheeled, horse-drawn, covered carriage was the kind people of quality rode in, always moving at a leisurely pace to make the journey comfortable. She didn't need comfort. She needed air.

The carriage was conveying them along the dirt roads that belonged to her and Frederick and their sister Susannah. Theirs was an immense treasure of land along the Hudson River, stretching from the center of Manhattan Island to parts north in the Highlands, 390 square miles in total. As she looked upon it now, she could see only winter's barrenness instead of a season of torpid inaction when even love's embrace could not force a flower's bloom out of a dormant state.

Mary's brother waved to the elderly fellow with a pile of white hair upon his face and head who was keeping order at the bridge they needed to cross. Other travelers, including farmers with livestock and merchants with their wagons full of goods, formed a long, chaotic line. But the Philipses never needed to wait nor pay the three-pence toll, unlike every other man or animal to cross. They had inherited this, too—a toll bridge twenty-four feet in width, with a draw, the first and only link connecting the metropolis to the mainland. They called it King's Bridge. The franchise had been granted to their great-grandfather by British charter.

Frederick turned back to her and bumped upward as they crossed

over the bridge's wooden planks, "As for your attendance, Polly, what is your answer?"

Mary attempted to sit up straight. "You summon these men to our home, Frederick, and expect I should open the door to let a stranger in."

"You speak as if I've brought commoners."

"You are well aware that titles are of no consequence to me."

"Do you not realize who *you* are?"

"I am a woman who knows a good fortune does not necessitate the yearning for a husband." She tried to keep her head from bouncing up and down.

"These are accomplished men. The sheriff is a fine gentleman with a superior estate."

Mary had to cover her mouth, for the beginning of a giggle almost came from her lips. The previous attempt at a suitor left Frederick waiting alone with the sheriff for nearly an entire teatime.

"Colonel Washington is trekking from Virginia on horseback to be here!" Frederick's nostrils flared when he raised his voice to her. "Polly, you will attend!"

"Will you be wearing this accoutrement about your neck?" She pointed to the ridiculous pendant she knew he enjoyed displaying.

Frederick's eyes shifted down. "Do you not like it?" The hefty gold chain with a jeweled badge signified his role as Keeper of the Deer Forests. The ancestral office had been passed down through generations of the Philipses.

Mary only shrugged.

They arrived at Philipse Manor. The Georgian-style mansion, covered in brick and accented with ivory moldings, was the most exquisite example of refinement that could be found anywhere in the colony. It overlooked the immense Hudson River and provided a view of the Palisades' earth formation, cliffs across the water that appeared as outstretched hands reaching for the heavens. A guardian's wall is how she thought of it. She often wished she could climb to the top and embrace those who had been taken too soon.

She was glad of the weather's crispness as she exited the carriage, for she was in desperate need of cooling off. The moment Mary entered the manor, she smelled its warmth. Baking. Fresh loaves. Bread made her mouth water.

Up the grand staircase she went and entered her bedchamber that had not changed her entire life. A gilded four-poster bed with a lofty canopy sat opposite a hearth framed with blue-and-white Delft tiles. An intricately carved desk and chair paired with a massively sized bookcase climbing high to the ceiling. A tall mahogany chest took up another wall. In the closet hid a space for washing.

The morning's muted rays made the silver softly sparkle on the wall's ornate fabric covering and cast faint shadows through silk draperies over the dark wood floor. The abigails rushed over to help Mary remove her riding clothes, until she was dressed in only a laced shift. A gaze at her reflection in a mosaic-framed mirror showed a figure that looked every bit of a woman, yet acted as an awkward lassie. Poise had never been her forte. If she brought back her shoulders, that might do it, but it didn't feel quite right, as if she was pretending to be regal when she was really just Mary Eliza. Beautiful? Others had described her as such. Her sister Susannah—yes, she was definitively beautiful. Many admired her for her fair skin, her hair of light amber waves, and her feet; she had the prettiest little feet. Susannah carried herself with natural grace.

As for Mary, she was of a shy disposition when surrounded by strangers in dressy clothing. Guests weren't fond of reticence. They responded to cheerfulness, to vivaciousness. They adored the social adroitness of Susannah, who spoke of all that was in vogue.

After the lady's maids departed, Mary practiced smiling. She had to rely on the art of distraction; a dimple formed on her right cheek, providing a diversion when she had little to say. Tonight would be one of those times when she most missed her younger sister. The white plague slowly robbed Margaret of her vitality, until there was nothing left. Margaret was the free one, a madcap, the one who laughed her way through any crowd encircling Mary, taking her far from the

frenzy. With Margaret now gone, Mary felt even more trepidation, imagining the crush of people who would enter the house, especially the presence of one of them. She did not like to think about him, and worked to banish him from her thoughts. At the last banquet she attended, he pointed his deformed finger at her and whispered something that nearly made her collapse: "As goes the mother, so, too, the daughter."

The sound of a horn interrupted her thinking. One long sound was followed by a pause, and proceeded by two in quicker succession. She practically leapt toward the window overlooking the river. The usual disturbance tried to make its way into her being, as it did each time she looked out over the Hudson. She needed to put that aside now. She breathed in deeply and exhaled, leaving a cloud on the pane of glass. The water was tranquil, the sole movement coming from the ship with its lofty white sails carrying it toward the family's dock. With her ear to the chilled window, she listened. The horn of the vessel sounded again—one slow, two fast. This was the signal she had waited weeks to hear. With a squint, she could see sea captain Garvan Rous at the wheel of the *Gabriel*.

Mary had little time to fuss. She was too anxious to learn the particulars. She raced to her high mahogany chest and pulled out a woolen Brunswick. She felt its heaviness when she placed it over herself. She quickly picked a ruffled cap from her collection. Slipping on her burgundy walking shoes, she rushed down the stairwell and into the kitchen. As she moved, she set her loose chestnut-brown hair under the head covering.

Mary grabbed the basket she had asked to have prepared. She counted six glass jars, five of them containing pickled ingredients: fennel, onion, white plums, lemons, and walnuts. A jar of twenty-year catsup was filled to the brim. In the center of the jars was a silver spoon. She placed above the jars a steaming loaf that was a bit too hot to the touch. The delicious aroma excited her appetite. She knocked her hip against the back door to open it and moved as quickly as possible onto the porch, pinching her cheeks with her avail-

able hand as she went. Through the boxwood-lined gardens and down the stone path she went, dashing toward the family's dock at the Hudson River's edge, arriving just as the vessel was being secured.

"A miracle, Mary!" cheered Captain Garvan as he tucked his rumpled white linen shirt into his breeches. "A miracle has happened!"

She hurried faster, while carefully keeping her shoes from slipping off the path and into the mud nearest the dock. She put the basket down on the wooden planks. "Tell me! Tell me!"

Swiftly, he moved to greet her. His days at sea were apparent from his bronzed skin and sun-weathered wavy hair. "He is alive, Mary! My son lives . . . because of *you*." He enveloped her in an embrace that wrapped her in the essence of an ocean breeze.

Elation poured over Mary. Concern for the child had given her such worry.

"He even took a step on his own without my help." His eyes became watered. "The apothecary you sent to my home, Mary, he saved my boy's life. What you have done for me . . ."

"Your wife would have been proud of all you have accomplished with him."

"I wish she could have lived to see him. . . ." He took some time before continuing. "She would have loved his great flop of golden hair." A tear trailed down his cheek.

Mary stepped back and held his hands in hers. "He will make a fine mariner, your William Rous, just like his father and his father before him."

She made the prediction with confidence, knowing full well the fabric of which Rous men were made. It was a confidence established when she was just a child. Captain Garvan, then a lad in his teenage years, swept her right out of death's door.

———◦———

THAT EVENING, *one cloaked in a deep red sunset, Mary's world went dark. In the midst of a refined affair at the manor, a fright came over*

the little girl, causing her to run as fast as she could. She found herself outside, alone on the south porch, steps away from the smaller Neperhan River, which flowed into the Hudson. She was not by herself for long that evening. Young Elbert Peck came to ease her worry, walking out of his cottage that sat near the mansion on the property. He was the head gardener's son, a playful, freckle-cheeked boy with ginger hair always in disarray.

Elbert's head tilted. "Are you crying?"

She could not answer. Her hands covered a face full of tears.

"I will show you something. It will make you happy." Elbert started to skip in the direction of the river. "I shall get it for you by the water."

"No, Elbert. Mama says it is dangerous by the river."

But Elbert had already begun to run along the garden path.

"No. No, Elbert." Mary started after him. She cried out, "Mama says no! Mama says no!"

She reached him at the water's edge just as he picked a stem of forget-me-nots.

"They are the color of your dress." His stance became wobbly as he stretched his arm to hand the flowers to her. "They are blue." His little black shoe was covered in mud. She knew Mama wouldn't like that. No, Mama wouldn't like muddy shoes. She stood still, not moving an inch. He reached farther toward her, trying to keep his balance to give her the blossoms, but the slippery earth forced him down. His body shifted ever nearer to the ancient, unyielding river. Mary lurched forward, her shoes now sinking into the mud. Her little hand got ahold of his, and she began to cry out as his body made a splash. His green eyes turned toward the unstoppable waters behind him. Then he stared back at her.

Without words, she knew; in his eyes, she saw desperation and terror.

Despite using every ounce of her strength, she could not bring him close enough to grab hold of the long grasses that lined the bank. Her right hand held on as mightily as she could to his right hand, which still held the flowers. Her wee voice yelled out for help. A wave pulled

him, plunging Elbert under the water. Refusing to let him go, she, too, went into the river.

The current moved her to and fro. She could no longer feel Elbert's hand in hers. As Mary frantically threw her head back to find breath, she caught a glimpse of Mama; Mama was coming. She looked scared.

"I am here!" Lady Joanna did not stop at the shoreline. "I am coming for you!"

Mary's heart screamed out—It is dangerous, Mama.

Mama's red dress with the pretty flowers spread out wide as she jumped into the water and tried to swim toward Mary. Mary could see her getting closer, calling out to her.

It was dark.

A chill overtook her body.

She was cold, so very cold.

THEN ALL *she could see was light.*

As if heaven wrapped her in its embrace, Mary felt strong arms lift her from a wet grave. Cradled to a young man's chest, she could hear a voice commanding, "Breathe, child. Breathe." She remained in this angel's arms, bundled in a quilted blanket embroidered with blue flowers. Her hand held tightly to wilted forget-me-nots as pandemonium swirled around them.

She watched as they carried Mama out of the river with her pretty red dress dragging upon the ground. Papa laid her mother's body on the porch. Lantern light shone upon her pale face. Mary saw her father's hands tremble. He was crying.

Papa placed a kiss upon the forehead and closed its eyes.

———◦———

MARY'S ANGUISH OVER the loss never ceased. Why did they perish? Why did she survive? Why didn't she immediately reach for the flowers? If only she had held on tighter to little Elbert's hand.

Though years passed, the trauma never left her. With certainty, though, she knew what she needed to do. Papa helped her find her

purpose. "Protect. Save. As a beacon in the darkness, be the light," he told her. Every year on the anniversary of that fateful day, he would take her to light a tall lantern at Hudson's Hook.

Now a woman, Mary stood here near the shore. The lad who rescued her a grown man, Captain Garvan gave her a quick peck on the forehead. "I am forever in your service, my dear Mary."

"As I am in yours."

As the two spoke, the sailors transferred crates aplenty of goods and liquors from the *Gabriel* to the dock.

"They have not much time. Hasten your walk!" He pointed his men toward the cases of Madeira. His face turned back to Mary's. "This man they call a hero—I understand he arrives here this night."

Mary felt a breeze blowing from the water. "At sundown, yes." She lowered her eyes to her arms, crossed.

"He comes to see you, Mary."

She lifted a wayward curl off her face and tucked it behind her ear.

"With my own eyes I have seen it. Washington is the best chap in the regiment, riding the most splendid horse. A fitting choice." Never before had the captain offered praise for one of her potential suitors. He knew them or of them all, as gossip flowed freely on board his ship. "I believe it in your benefit to meet the major."

"Colonel." Mary corrected him. "He is now Colonel Washington."

"Seems you know of this fine fellow and his unparalleled reputation."

Yes.

She listened carefully to each detail spoken about him. His auburn hair fell below his shoulders. His face carried a square jaw, a nose that was large and straight, and penetrating eyes. Not a week earlier, her cousin Eva Van Cortlandt quoted the poet John Dryden when describing him: "a temple Sacred by birth, and built by hands divine." And Mary read Washington's journal over and over. As she stood here now, she tried to think of how many times. Ten? Fifteen? Could it be twenty times, maybe more?

To fill the moment's quiet, which lasted a heartbeat too long, she

picked up the basket and placed it in Captain Garvan's hands as she told him her wish for young William: "A wind to steer the course to true happiness."

The captain responded with a wide grin. Those were his words to her on her twenty-first birthday. "And my wish for you always, Mary."

With his farewell kiss upon her cheek, Mary turned to the manor, which bustled with preparations for the affair. The nervous excitement that now filled her whole being could hardly be contained. The words "I believe it in your benefit to meet the major" replayed in her head. In equal parts, she eagerly anticipated and dreaded this night. She wished she could meet the colonel under different circumstances than a ball, which, like so many others, brought back memories of the day her world changed. It was not her decision. She should have fought her siblings on this matter; she did not, thinking it would never come to pass. Colonel Washington agreed to travel five hundred miles to see her! This surprised her completely.

As she entered the manor and walked up the back steps behind the East Hall, she heard Frederick's voice.

"Drag her out myself! I shall do it!"

Mary rolled her eyes and made sure to stay behind a wall, out of his view.

"Oh, Frederick. Every belle blooms in her own way, at her own time." Her sister spoke softly between sighs. "Tonight will be glorious."

"Just as you said about the last reception and the one before that."

"Dearest Frederick, like a jewel being polished to an utmost shine, so will our sister be. You must be patient."

"Our family's reputation is at stake. I've invited every royal justice of the colony, the barons of New York, the Speaker of the House, the members of the Assembly, the newly installed mayor, the sheriff, the aldermen, and the lords of the manors. Susannah, we have a colonel traveling from Virginia to be here."

"She will be glad to be in Colonel Washington's presence."

"Are you certain of this?"

An empty moment in the conversation lingered.

"If it takes force, then so be it!" Frederick declared like his usual scolding self.

"Curing what ails her cannot be done with coercion. We have learned tenderness is the only path to sensibility."

Mary caught a whiff of plum pudding and knew the conversation about finding her a mate would soon come to a close. The aroma would most certainly draw Frederick's substantially sized nose to the kitchen. Thankfully, she was correct. She did not want to listen to her brother again this morning. She had had enough of his persistence and felt a tinge of irritation over the first line of the invitation, clearly written as a message to her:

> *While we live, let us LIVE*
> *Your company is desired to dine with*
> *Lord Frederick Philipse and the family of Philipse*
> *At the Manor of Philipse*
> *On the second month, 14th day,*
> *Of the seventeen hundred and fifty-sixth year*
> *Dinner to be on the table at six o'clock*
> *Musical Entertainment at eight o'clock*
> *Dancing to commence at nine o'clock*

A group of select guests received these special invitations which included the private banquet ahead of the dancing. Expected to be welcomed in stately manner was Washington. The colonel was becoming one of only a few so highly esteemed in the military.

Hanging in an ornate frame beside the invitation on the second-floor landing of the manor was a diagram of the guests' placement. Mary walked over to it. The principal guest of the evening, Washington, would be seated at the head of the long refectory table, flanked on his right by her brother and on the left by Susannah with her true. Next to Frederick would be Mary.

She took a breath. So close.

Mary was involved with each of the stages of the elaborate event,

as her brother and sister requested. For the past month, she worked with a dancing master of her own choosing for another part of the evening that made her feel ill at ease. Even after intensive instruction, she wasn't sure of her readiness. This was not due to his coaching. Dancing was an area for which the gift of natural talent was not afforded her. Whenever she pushed herself to try before at previous balls, dames around her muttered the words—"inelegant," "untaught," "unready."

Mary heard delicate footsteps climb the stairs. Her sister leaned against a banister, elegantly posed. Mary wasn't sure she knew any other way to stand.

"The time is drawing near," Susannah chimed. "Your dancing lesson commences in one hour's time, and we depart for your final fitting immediately afterward, my sister."

"What if there's a chill? The gown seems too open to be worn on a night like tonight."

"You may find a gentleman's arms to warm you, Polly. Quite a few will be attending tonight's ball and certainly one in particular."

The evening had been conjured up by Susannah. She had found love in Major Beverley Robinson. His brother, the Honorable John Robinson, carried the title of Speaker of the Virginia House of Burgesses. It was John Robinson who was in communication via letter with Colonel Washington. Beverley and John had spent many afternoons in childish play with George while growing up as neighbors and young schoolmates in Virginia.

At Susannah's urging, an invitation to Washington was delivered directly to the colonel, inviting him to stay at the Philipse family estate. "The ball comes at a perfect time of year, Polly." Mary knew to what she was referring. "'For this was on Saint Valentine's Day,'" said Susannah.

"'When every bird cometh there to chose his mate.'" The sisters recited in unison a line from Geoffrey Chaucer.

"I believe I have the perfect mate for the colonel to choose."

"There will be many belles from whom the colonel may choose."

"Correct you are. Many a lady in New York has found the stories of the hero intriguing, especially as he has evaded the capture of matrimony. But there stands none so beautiful as you, Miss Polly Philipse."

"What if—"

"There are no what ifs." Susannah folded her arms. "There will be no what ifs. Not tonight, my sister, not tonight. Now, change into your practice clothes."

Mary headed into her bedchamber. This night would be the first time the sisters would meet the gentleman whom Major Robinson often praised. The major was not alone in his opinion of the newly appointed colonel. Commanders and laymen alike spoke of George Washington as a man guided by Providence. Mary knew this from her reading of *The New-York Mercury*. Nearly every newspaper in the colonies and in London had printed the *Journal of Major George Washington*. The edition of the *Mercury* was neatly placed at perfect eye level on a shelf of her bookcase. She'd read Washington's firsthand account of his exposure to peril on the frontier, engrossed by his escapes from death. The hardships he survived through his acts of bravery were far from the comforts of polite life in New York.

For more than two years, the newspaper remained here. She would always place the publication back again on the same shelf in the same position after reading it. Mary picked it up, feeling the linen paper on her fingers. She moved toward the window's light and turned to the page that displayed his writings, in wonderment that on this night, if she found the fortitude, she would meet the man described as having the courage of a hundred men.

He began simply:

I WAS COMMISSIONED and appointed by the Honourable Robert Dinwiddie, Esq; Governor, &c of Virginia, to visit and deliver a Letter to the Commandant of the French Forces on the Ohio, and set out on the intended Journey the same Day . . .

Tension welled up inside her. She knew well the feelings that overwhelmed her at every other lavish gathering. Mary wanted to attend, but what if . . .

This time, she hoped it would be different . . . that *she* would be different.

She read on.

Chapter Two

——◄•►——

George's Journal

*. . . was I to live more retired from young Women I might
in some measure eliviate my sorrows . . .*

—GEORGE WASHINGTON

FREDERICKSBURG, VIRGINIA
OCTOBER 31, 1753

Under heathery gray skies, the air holding the odor of pine, and
with the sugar maples putting on a fiery display of reds, golds, and
yellows, George Washington walked out of his home and into the
wilderness—alone. He was used to that.

'Tis better to be alone than in bad company.

As a boy, he had written down 110 rules from a prominent book
on correct behavior. George strove to incorporate each of them into
his conduct. Anything he learned, he had to do on his own. Without
a father in his home, 110 rules were, at least, a start.

This was the day of his intended journey to deliver the letter to
the commandant of the French forces on the Ohio. He set out on the
intended journey within hours of receiving the order from the
governor.

Covered in a leather match coat belted at the waist and falling past
the knee, the twenty-one-year-old carried a few days' provisions on
his back with necessaries for his travels, including a small tent, a sleep-

ing blanket, dried meats, a drum canteen that he filled with a quart of water, strings of wampum, the governor's letter to the enemy, his leather journal with hand-stitching at the binding, as well as an ink-well with ink he made from blackberries and a quill from a white goose feather with a tip he cut at a precise forty-five-degree angle; he planned to keep rough minutes along the way.

His mission was clear. Ride into the fortress of the French, deliver the governor's letter, and demand surrender.

Cease. Desist. Depart.

That was, in essence, what the governor was asking George to do—singlehandedly force the French from the continent. How was this young man qualified to handle such a mission? He wasn't and he knew it. Military experience, diplomatic experience, for-mal education—he had none of these. What he did have was the resolve to become a man worthy of respect, which is why he ac-cepted this mission as a volunteer, putting aside money for a higher purpose.

ONE DAY INTO the mission, rain fell fast. His coat was soggy, his hair dripping. Glad of his hood, George disembarked from the ferry, which crossed the Rappahannock River. The boat pulled into the wharf, beyond which a tiny town greeted him. It was perfectly situ-ated along the river, with establishments for a smith, a tailor, and an ordinary keeper. A coffeehouse with a stone front was first. He en-tered to get out of the rain. He removed his soaked hat with both hands.

"Walk in, gentle man." A round-faced woman with a ruffled cap carried a coffeepot in her right hand and a plate of biscuits in her left. He breathed deeply, inhaling flavors that reminded him of home. "Rest at your ease. Pay for what you call for and call for what you please."

He needed to inquire the whereabouts of a man he once knew well. "May I ask your assistance in finding a villager, a friend by the name of Jacobus Vanbraam?"

"Ah. You are in need of a mercenary."

"I am in need of an interpreter of the French language, as I've been asked to deliver a letter to the commandant of the French forces."

She put down the pot. "Indeed, Jacobus is a French speaker . . . as he is a master of the blade. We shall find him." She pointed George toward seating by the fire.

George moved to a wide tree stump of a table that appeared as if it had grown right through the flooring. He sat down on one of the stools around it and began his work. He was determined to put quill to paper to map out the excursion into enemy territory. The journey would be long, he surmised, nearly one thousand miles. Part of it would be through forests he knew well, having worked as a land surveyor of these backwoods. He assessed the need for six men to assist him.

"THE MERCENARY'S IN sight!" shouted the woman.

George headed to the entrance to greet his old companion, who had taught him everything he knew about fighting with a sword and who had served in the British Navy with George's older half brother, Lawrence. Clean-shaven, with long, wet, black hair neatly thrown away from the face, Jacobus steadied the saber with a curved blade attached to a scabbard at his belt as he stepped along Sophia Street with a lady in tow, the two speaking in loud-enough voices for him to hear.

"You mean to enter enemy territory," she groaned to Jacobus. Her hair and dress were damp from the rain. "And then what? Banish an army of Frenchmen with one who is barely a man?"

"Aye." Jacobus didn't even turn to her.

She slapped his arm. "Five years since you have had an exercise in arms with this boy. How can you be assured he is prepared for the roar of battle?"

"This is a mission of diplomacy, not a fight to the death." He kept his steady pace.

"Diplomacy with this enemy?" she scoffed, now in a full rage.

"You underestimate the man who has come for me."

"If he is without sword, you will see me protest this preposterous mission."

"The cutlass, the foil, the claymore, the saber—the boy mastered each under my tutelage."

"How will you safeguard him?"

"Safeguard him? Ha! The man guided by divine Providence will safeguard me." Jacobus looked toward George, whose body filled the doorway. "Drea Vanbraam, may I acquaint you with George Washington. This giant of a man was struck by lightning while still in the womb, guarded by the heavens from before his birth."

She stared long and hard at George and at his commanding height, which caused his head to reach the top of the entryway. "'Tis true?" she asked of Jacobus.

"Have you ever known me to tell an untruth?" replied Jacobus. "The fork and knife at the table where his mother was eating fused together from the bolt."

She looked down at George's waist, from which Lawrence's sword, one uncommonly broad at the base, hung. Drea swung around to her husband. She pushed a satchel into his chest. "You have my blessing."

As the two men entered the coffeehouse, Jacobus raised his hand to reach George's shoulder. "If I remember correctly, the young lady did not survive the bolt?"

George nodded, knowing to what he was referring. He was asked to tell the story more times than he desired. On a stormy Sunday afternoon after church services, lightning struck his family's cottage. The electric bolt came through the chimney, knocking over a guest invited to supper, taking the life right out of her as she sat at the table with Mary Washington. The tragedy left his mother forever fearful of storms and worry-filled that she might never be blessed with motherhood. When her first child was born, she carried him everywhere, announcing that George Washington was protected by the Almighty.

"Truly remarkable. And pay no mind to the wife. *Une chieuse.*"

Jacobus's mouth tipped into a smile as he wiped droplets from his sleeves. "And what of you? Have you selected a flower from the *jardin* or is the fortress of a military man's heart impenetrable?"

"I pass the time." He signaled to the woman with the pot.

"With the man you've become, I'm sure of it." They found seats at the stump.

"In truth, I am trying to forget a lady." A difficult task, is what he didn't say. George could still feel the silkiness of his Affa's flowing black hair in his hands.

"And where might we find this lady?"

"The lowlands."

"A beauty of the lowlands. Hard to banish from the heart, I'm sure. But fear not. We will find other such lovelies on our journey."

"That would only add fuel to fire, making me the more uneasy." That woman—Affa—had crushed his spirit. Had he been wealthier, more educated . . . Clearly, he was not enough. "Was I to live more retired from young women, I might in some measure eliviate my sorrows . . . burying passion in eternal forgetfulness."

Jacobus laughed aloud. "I guarantee you this: Before long, another passion will emerge, lifting you from such a grave of oblivion."

The round-faced woman brought brewed coffee and sweet bread to the stump. George's stomach noted their arrival, but he did not immediately partake. He thought of one of the rules he followed: *Drink not nor talk with your mouth full.*

"Lieutenant Vanbraam, my thanks for the personal respect you showed my family."

"My condolences on the distressing event that has befallen you. Your late brother was a good man. I am proud to have served with him."

"Lawrence is the reason I took up this mission." The white plague robbed George of his half brother, who had been fourteen years his senior and who had been his mentor and closest companion. With a successful mission as this, he could bring honor to Lawrence's memory and, perhaps, become a bit more like him. George and Lawrence were different. Lawrence was a product of George's father's first

marriage and had received a formal education in London and vast military experience. When his father died, so went George's chances of a similar path—life among the landed gentry as his brother; there would be no moneys for that.

George spoke about what motivated him to deliver the letter of ultimatum. "Lawrence believed strongly that if the French take possession of the Ohio, they might easily invade Virginia. Our mountains are not so formidable to protect us."

"Wherever they come, they destroy. Your brother would have been glad to see you take up this mission. When the sword of war threatens, we must strike."

THAT AFTERNOON, GEORGE hired his party, following another of his rules: *Associate with men of good quality if you esteem your own reputation.* He engaged a servitor, along with frontiersman Christopher Gist. If anyone could pilot them out, it would be Gist, haughty, brooding in his outward appearance, with a ruddy face covered by a full beard, the only explorer with precise knowledge of the Ohio country.

With baggage and horses, they traveled to the mouth of Turtle Creek at the Monongahela. George kept track of each detail in the land they traversed.

"Our leader's heart is fixed," Jacobus said to Gist as they trekked through marshlands, "to a beauty of the lowlands."

"I would find a woman in the highlands." Gist spoke with a slow drawl.

"Where the ladies can read and write," added Jacobus.

"Aye," replied Gist, "especially the rich ones."

George did not want to speak on the subject. He believed that if he tried such a thing again, he would receive a rejection which would only add to his agony. He halted. "Gentlemen, more pertinent matters are before us."

A scalp was staked into an elm.

Jacobus raised his eyes to it. "Such as pray they do not kill the messenger."

Positioned above the scalp was a sizable copper plate bearing France's royal arms.

"The blood is fresh. Scalping parties are near." Gist examined the clean incision from the forehead to the back of the neck. "The enemy pays thirty francs in trading goods for each scalp. The pounding of stakes has become a common sound—the French claiming the territory as theirs."

"*Vive le roi* is their call." Jacobus looked to George. "Shall we take shelter from the enemy?"

"Waiting here is very contrary to my inclinations," said George. "We must make all possible dispatch."

———◈———

MARY WONDERED WHAT bravery looked like in the flesh. She might learn that this night. She imagined the colonel a gallant warrior, rough-hewn, with a brawny physique, and a strong jaw that, when clenched, would display defined muscles at the sides of his face.

Washington's writings continued on to the most perilous part of the journey. In order to deliver his letter to the enemy, he had first to cross through the natives' trading post, without invitation, and get past guards staying close to their weapons, men who didn't take kindly to strangers.

Susannah would soon be calling out for her, but Mary refused to put down the newspaper. Her delicate fingers turned the page.

———◈———

DAY 27

The stars told George the time reached nine o'clock in the evening. The flame of a torch guided him down a dirt path. One guard in war paint walked in front of him, the other behind. He could hear chanting in the distance.

This was the natives' trading post, a place called Logstown.

Calm and composed, George convinced those at the gate to let his company through. After agreeing, guards took him alone to a

narrow dwelling built among the trees. He requested a meeting with the elders to obtain permission to continue through their lands and ask for assistance in the journey.

Upon entrance, a gamy smell greeted him. Skinned hides hung across bark-covered walls. Three glowing hearths ran down the center, with gray wisps dancing to smoke holes that opened to the night sky. Seated around the second hearth were men George believed to be the chiefs of the Six Nations of Iroquois, Seneca, Onondaga, Oneida, Cayuga, Mohawk, and Tuscorona. Without a word, one of them, Chief Tanacharison, tall and strong, with a fox fur upon his head—a man whom George heard was called "Half King"—motioned for him to address the sachems.

Every action done in Company, ought to be with Some Sign of Respect, to those that are Present—rule number one. With no time to prepare, and having never given a speech of diplomatic importance, or one of any significance, he accomplished this with one word, the first:

Brothers,

I have called you together in Council, by Order of your Brother the Governor of Virginia, to acquaint you that I am sent, with all possible Dispatch, to visit, and deliver a Letter to the French Commandant, of very great Importance to your Brothers the English; and I dare say, to you their Friends and Allies.

I was desired, Brothers, by your Brother the Governor, to call upon you, the Sachems of the Nations, to inform you of it, and to ask your Advice and Assistance to proceed the nearest and best Road to the French. You see, Brothers, I have got thus far on my Journey.

His Honour likewise desired me to apply to you for some of your young Men, to conduct and provide Provisions for us

on our Way; and be a Safeguard against those French Indians who have taken up the Hatchet against us. I have spoke this particularly to you, Brothers, because his Honour our Governor treats you as good Friends and Allies, and holds you in great Esteem. To confirm what I have said, I give you this String of Wampum.

Half King accepted the offering. George ended his speech there. *Let your discourse with men of business be short and comprehensive.* Success. Provisions and passage granted. Three guides provided.

DAY 46

Nearly seven weeks into the most fatiguing journey as is possible to conceive, George pushed the men onward. He could feel nothing from his fingertips. As for his toes, he knew not whether they were still connected to his feet.

They lit fires to keep warm. George made a forked stick to cook his food, hunted from the woods. He had no dish, using instead a piece of bark for a plate.

They slept on whatever natural cover they could find, right on the wilderness floor.

Then they came upon a dead end.

Before him was a creek with waters so high and rapid, any chance at rafting or fording was impossible. They were obliged to pass through this place, somehow. Only one other way was possible, Gist informed him: a swamp downstream.

George had no choice. He and his men advanced through the stench. Without the ability to see much of what was in front of him, he led the men, keeping himself upright as his horse carried him through.

THE WEATHER PROVED more arduous every mile the company crossed, until finally the enemy was before them. A handful of men

against an army. Never before in his lifetime had George suffered such anxiety as he did in this moment. French guards swarmed them upon approach. A strikingly regal lot quickly surrounded him in the middle of the forest. The soldiers wore ornate uniforms of white coats with bright blue lapels. Frilled lace flowed from the cuffs. His focus, though, was more on the weapons they were pointing at him and his men.

Scars crossed the face of the man for whom the French soldiers cleared a path, the commandant, George surmised. *Gaze not on the marks or blemishes of others.* He had all signs of a battlefield veteran, yet he dressed as a knight, with not a wrinkle in his uniform, and he carried himself with the deportment of royalty. A black patch sat over his right eye. Through interpreter Jacobus, Captain Jacques Legardeur de Saint-Pierre demanded to know the reason for this invasion.

George stood tall and cleared his throat. His mind remained focused. *Think before you speak. Pronounce not imperfectly nor bring out your words too hastily, but orderly and distinctly.* He pulled out the letter to the enemy from the Governor, which Jacobus interpreted:

Sir,

The lands upon the River Ohio, in the western parts of the Colony of Virginia, are so notoriously known to be the property of the Crown of Great Britain that it is a matter of equal concern and surprise to me, to hear that a body of French forces are erecting fortresses and making settlements upon that river, within His Majesty's dominions.

The many and repeated complaints I have received of these acts of hostility lay me under the necessity of sending, in the name of the King, my master, the bearer hereof, George Washington, Esq., one of the Adjutants-General of the forces of this dominion,

to complain to you of the encroachments thus made,
and of the injuries done to the subjects of Great Britain,
in violation of the law of nations, and the treaties now
subsisting between the two Crowns. If these facts be true,
and you think fit to justify your proceedings, I must
desire you to acquaint me by whose authority and instructions
you have lately marched from Canada with an armed force,
and invaded the King of Great Britain's territories, in the
manner complained of; that according to the purport and
resolution of your answer I may act agreeably to the
commission I am honored with from the King, my master.

However, sir, in obedience to my instructions, it
becomes my duty to require your peaceable departure;
and that you would forbear prosecuting a purpose so
interruptive of the harmony and good understanding,
which His Majesty is desirous to continue and cultivate
with the Most Christian King.

I persuade myself you will receive and entertain Major
Washington with the candor and politeness natural to your
nation; and it will give me the greatest satisfaction if you
return him with an answer suitable to my wishes for a very
long and lasting peace between us.

I have the honor to be,
Sir,
Your very humble,
Robert Dinwiddie

Silence.
Washington watched an eye stare at him with a guarded look.
   The commandant's soldiers with their heavy weaponry took a step
forward now. George sensed Jacobus reach for his saber. An endless

number of the enemy's men moved in closer. He could feel the cold breath of one of them at his neck.

It may have been seconds, but it felt like hours as George tried to remain as still as possible. He realized that this might have been the worst decision of his life. Who was he to step onto enemy territory and make such a demand? He was only an adjutant general! And in name only. A volunteer is all, and an ill-advised one at that. How could he have ever believed such an inexperienced person as he could negotiate a matter of such great importance? Moreover, how could the governor! The moment of clarity that struck George in that second left him scared for his life.

He watched Legardeur scan his clothing from hat to shoe; he was wearing little more than hunter's garb. He eyed George's delegation with a smirk, seemingly looking upon them as a motley sort.

"As to the summons you send me to retire, I do not think myself obliged to obey it." Legardeur's French was interpreted for George.

George moved not a muscle.

"We refuse to acquiesce," the commandant said with certainty.

The guards moved in closer. George believed this the end. He swallowed hard.

The commandant raised his hand to stop his guards' movement. "Monsieur Washington." Legardeur motioned to George to follow him into a private room and offered him a seat at a heavy table. He spoke to him through his interpreter. "You are a brave man for coming to this place."

George nodded his appreciation, although he rather would have left this place by now, for the guards again surrounded him, too close for his comfort.

The commandant put quill to paper for a response to the Colonial governor of Virginia and had his interpreter say the words aloud: "Whatever may be your instructions, mine bring me here by my general's order; and I entreat you, sir, to be assured that I shall attempt to follow them with all the exactness and determination which can

be expected from a good officer. I have made it my particular care to receive Mr. Washington with a distinction suitable to your dignity, as well as his own quality and great merit, and I flatter myself, sir, that he will do me the justice to be my witness for it with you, as well as the evidences of deep respect with which . . . I have the honor to be, your very humble and very obedient servant, Jacques Legardeur de Saint-Pierre."

One guard melted gold wax. Legardeur himself sealed the paper with the mark of the French. A guard handed it to George. With the commandant's letter of refusal in hand, George and his band of men departed the enemy's fort with urgency.

The blackest night was before them, brightness coming only from the moon's light reflecting on the heavily falling snow. They did not welcome sleep this night nor for many more. Danger was too close.

DAY 54

Frost reached his skin through stiff clothing. Exhaustion left George without any ability to continue. Eight days had passed since he left the commandant. This was the longest of those days. George refused any stoppage. He nearly collapsed on whatever ground was below him. He found respite seated against a naked maple. Fierce, howling winds stripped trees of their white coats. George wished for warmth. He wished for her. He imagined Affa in his embrace, the silkiness of her hair, the way its softness would feel with his hand through it.

If he were wealthier or more educated, maybe then he would be enough for her. She never responded to his letters. He forced the thought from his mind and closed his eyes to allow sleep in.

AT DAYBREAK, THE company continued. For days more, they traveled. He wrote in his journal the trials of the journey:

Our Horses were now so weak and feeble, and the
Baggage heavy (as we here obliged to provide all the
Necessaries that the Journey would require) that we
doubted much their performing it: therefore
myself and others (except for the Drivers who were
obliged to ride) gave up our Horses for Packs, to
assist along with the Baggage. I put myself in an
Indian walking Dress, and continued with them three
Days, till I found there was no Probability of their
getting home in any reasonable Time. The Horses
grew less able to travel every Day.

Therefore as I was uneasy to get back, to make Report
of my Proceedings to his Honour the Governor,
I determined to prosecute my Journey the nearest
Way through the Woods, on Foot.

Accordingly, I left Mr. Vanbraam in Charge of
our Baggage; with Money and Directions, to
provide Necessaries from Place to Place for themselves
and Horses, and to make the most convenient
Dispatch in.

George chose only Gist to travel with him now. They moved quickly,
completing eighteen miles in one day. Each had his reasons for a swift
return. George was in a hurry to return a response to the governor.

As for Gist: "My child, George, my first, is about to be born. I have
no time to waste in this godforsaken spot."

They arrived at the place others told George about. What he saw
explained why it was called "Murdering Town."

Their fast pace came to a halt as they heard the sound of a stranger's
feet racing in the white powder. A warrior with his face covered in
paint came from behind a big standing oak, pointed a pistol at them;
he fired.

Gist crouched down.

George raced to Gist's side. "Have you been shot?"

"No," he replied and began to run toward the man behind the tree.

George hurried to the left to stop the assailant. The man was attempting to reload. George grabbed him.

"You will die today!" Gist shouted at the man.

George, with a length of rope he'd carried at his side, tied the shooter's hands behind his back. "Do not take his life, Gist. I forbid it. We shall keep him in custody. Be sure he has no other weapons." George searched the area to see if another enemy was lurking. Nearby, he discovered newly set traps and footprints. Worry set in that they could be scalped if they stayed any longer.

"Make the man build us a fire," George advised Gist. "When darkness falls, we shall let him go."

"We must get away from this place."

"We shall travel through the night. If the enemy is watching, they will believe we stayed encamped by the fire."

Hours later, they freed him and listened until he was out of earshot.

The two ran for miles through the threatening wilderness, only pausing to set their compass to lead them toward the Allegheny River, hoping to find the river frozen, which would allow them to walk over it.

Instead of an icy sheet, they found ferocious currents breaking apart whatever blocks of ice remained.

The next day was spent building a makeshift raft to cross the river. When they completed this task, they placed the raft in the water, setting their sights on the other side. It was not to be:

before we were Half Way over, we were jammed
in the Ice, in such a Manner that we expected every
Moment our Raft to sink, and ourselves to perish,
I put-out my setting Pole to try to stop the Raft, that the
Ice might pass by; when the Rapidity of the Stream threw
it with so much Violence against the Pole, that it jirked
me out into ten Feet Water: But I fortunately saved myself

by catching hold of one of the Raft Logs. Notwithstanding all
our Efforts we could not get the Raft to either Shore; but
were obliged, as we were near an Island, to quit our Raft
and make to it.

A numbing chill penetrated George's body. He felt ground below his feet. They waded in the water through the dead of night,
continuing to cross. George placed the knapsack above his head,
tying the handles about his neck to keep the French commandant's
letter secure. The struggle left them fighting against rushing hunks
of ice.

Land brushed George's hand. A small island was before them in
the middle of the river. George pulled himself up onto it and assisted
Gist. A great sense of relief led to a deep exhale that looked like a frozen mist in the night.

Without a raft or access to food, George believed they could be
doomed. The cold turned even more severe. Gist's fingers and some
of his toes became frostbitten.

MORNING ARRIVED.

George awoke to a silence emerging like a loud boom through ominous lands. His bleary eyes opened wide after seeing an unexpected
occurrence of fortune. He told Gist to arise, to view the miracle before them. No longer were they in a life-or-death situation. The water
had completely frozen over.

The survivors of winter's fury crossed the Allegheny on foot and
headed home, battered but alive.

———◄•►———

MARY REACHED THE end of Colonel Washington's journal. She never
put the publication down without reading every last word, as if he
would not survive if she didn't finish. She knew how he must have felt
in that water, the fear of being one breath away from your last. This
one moment in his life she shared with him.

She looked up, trying to imagine how far her eyes would have to rise

to look into his. Carefully, she folded the newspaper and placed it on the shelf, always on the same shelf in the same position with the writing away from her. Best to keep him away from the cursed. That is how she viewed herself. She felt responsible for the deaths of a little boy, her mother, her father, her Margaret. She was the cursed one.

Chapter Three

——❖——

Charming Miss Polly

. . . the passions of your sex are easier roused than allayed. Do not therefore boast too soon, nor too strongly, of your insensibility to, or resistance of its powers.

——GEORGE WASHINGTON

YONKERS-ON-HUDSON
FEBRUARY 14, 1756

The grand Banneker in the hall struck ten o'clock—time for her lesson. Mary found the dancing master already in movement on the makeshift dance floor on the second level of the manor. With finesse, Michael Tenoe, a picture of masculinity, leaped into a split in the air. When his arms extended, he reached high, appearing as if his life depended on it.

Mary never asked about the scar on his face that shone clear when angled in the light. The first time she saw it, a fright came over her. She didn't need to know. She could only imagine the trials he must have been through.

Now he greeted her. She assumed her first stance.

"In a delicate manner." His voice sounded pleasant even when correcting her. "The placing of your heel must be in gentle fashion."

She tried to perfect her posture as Tenoe directed: "Imagine a

string running from the bottom of your back to the top of your head and to the ceiling."

Mary knew she was not quite balanced. "If grace could choose her dancer, I would be left at the wall."

"Free yourself." Tenoe shifted her shoulders back. "Without words, communicate what lies deep within your soul. The only limit to your possibility is the limitation you've made possible. This is your time."

Truth be told, it was also his. Mary meant to see him released from the indentured servitude out of which her family temporarily hired him, and planned to take the necessary steps to make it so. "What will you do when you're pronounced free?"

"Oh, what will I not do."

"You will make the world your dance floor."

"Each time my feet are on the floor, I am no longer servant, but sir." He reached for her hand. "This is why I dance."

She placed her hand in his and curtsied. "Henceforth, Sir Tenoe is what I shall call you."

Like nearly everyone else, she read what was printed in an advertisement in the *New York Weekly Journal* about him:

> Michael Tenoe is my servant, and hath been for
> near seven years past; and all sums of money due for
> teaching are due and payable to me. And I do hereby
> forewarn all persons from paying him any money,
> giving him credit or dealing with him,
> on any account whatever, until he has discharg'd
> himself from all obligations due to me; which shall
> be publickly advertised, when accomplished.

Tenoe himself told her his story. Poor and without shelter at the age of fourteen, he sold himself to a ship's captain for passage to the New World. He confided in her the rumors that drew him across the Atlantic: bountiful feasts and limitless moneys. Those were not to be his fate, for his life dues were immediately purchased by Jones Irwin. Mary asked Tenoe to bring the contract papers with him this day.

"You will not only impress the crowd but intimidate it," Tenoe encouraged her.

The sounds of someone racing up the stairs stopped them. Eric Arthur Angevine rushed into the room.

Tenoe showed disappointment in his face. "Your expected time of arrival was a quarter of an hour ago."

Mary thought Eric Arthur the perfect choice for a dance partner. His father served as estate steward for the Philipses, loyal, efficient, and at the constant side of her brother. Eric was a working lad, helping his father, but also elected to a position at the town's church. The occupation of sexton sounded prestigious. Mary had heard Eric wanted the young females in town to know his title. While some boys turned away from girls like Saint Vitus' dance, not Eric. He gave the girls tours of the church, showing them the secret passage to the bell tower, and he always had enough coins to crowd his pockets. Mary knew, as sexton, Eric was really just the town grave digger, shoveling out an adult person's grave for eight shillings, four shillings for children. Being practically a child himself, Eric complained about that part of the job, but about shillings in his pocket he did not.

With pockets stuffed with coins, Eric took his position apart from her on the expansive floor. They began their practice of the baroque steps of the flirtatious minuet. She became nervous as she imagined a dance with the colonel and made a failing attempt to punctuate the complex nature of the dance with the Z figure sequence of steps. Right foot. Left foot. Right again. Left toe points. Three taps. Left hands touch.

"Again." Tenoe had them join hands. Eric, with his weighty pockets, reached out his right hand to hold her left one. Coins jingled. They retreated to both touch right hands. The quick change that followed to touch left hands did not go according to Tenoe's instruction. Instead, Eric's breeches fell around his feet. His undergarment made an appearance. Tenoe howled. Mary giggled. Eric hurried to tug up his waistband. "I will never be caught with my breeches down again!"

Mary completed her lesson with glee.

Before leaving, she requested from Tenoe his contractual papers and moved to the privacy of her study to read through each detail:

> This INDENTURE witnessed that Michael Tenoe
> doth Voluntarily put himself as servant to Jones Irwin,
> for and during the full Space, Time and Term of 10 years
> from the first Day of the arrival of the Ship; during which
> time, or term, the Master shall and will feed and supply
> Michael Tenoe with sufficient meat, drink, apparel,
> lodging and all other necessaries befitting such a servant;
> and at the end and expiration of the said term;
> Michael Tenoe is to be made Free, and receive
> according to the Custom of the Country. If the servant,
> Michael Tenoe, shall pay Jones Irwin 15 pounds
> British with twenty percent interest before that time,
> he shall be free. In Witness whereof the parties have
> hereunto interchangeably put their Hands and Seals.

Mary secretly tallied the amount with interest and marched to the library to make her demands. There, she informed her brother of the sum to be paid for Tenoe's services once the pleasure ball ended.

"Eighteen pounds!" Frederick shouted. "I have already settled with Mr. Irwin for a smidgeon of that amount."

"Mr. Tenoe has developed a number of new dances for the ball. I believe he deserves compensation. Besides, he is a master of dance!"

"A self-taught dancing master?" Frederick grimaced. "It is unheard of."

She knew the total was exorbitantly higher than what should be required for one evening of work. But she also meant to see him freed. "If he is not paid properly . . . you will not see my feet upon that floor."

"Eighteen pounds for a dancing man . . . absurd! Eight is all. Not a shilling more."

"Then, Frederick, I expect a fee"—she stomped her feet—"for my attendance!"

His eyebrows lifted high. "A fee?"

She raised her hands in front of him with fingers outstretched. "Ten British pounds."

"An outrage!" His nostrils flared.

"Ten."

"Eight."

"Ten."

"I will make my decision tonight."

"Fine . . . eight. If you find the evening a success, I expect the full amount." Here she was negotiating terms for an event she wasn't even confident she would attend. If Frederick allowed her to handle her own money, this would be completed already, but Papa had written that upon his death, Frederick would remain in charge of the estate.

Susannah marched in. "We will be late." Clutching her arm, she led Mary toward the door. "Frederick, our sister has her final fitting. Now leave her be." She walked Mary out of the room, the manor, and straight into the coach awaiting them.

MARY STOOD ATOP a wooden stand inside a little yellow box of a house on a hill, a stone's throw from the manor. The cottage belonged to the Sherwoods. Rosie, with pointed spectacles hanging from her neck and a bun never quite neat atop her head, created the finest gowns in the Hudson Valley. Susannah and cousin Eva joined her for the fitting.

Throbbing started squarely between Mary's eyes and an ache moved patiently through her midsection. Did she position the newspaper on the shelf correctly with the words away from her, words always away from the cursed? She didn't have time to double-check. Clamminess on her palms was the first sign of trouble. She tried to remain calm through the pulling and tugging. She needed to take her mind off the publication and instead concentrate fully on the details of the gown or maybe on the man who would see her in it tonight. She just had to go, or at least peek out a door to see him. This was the hero of the South who charged into enemy territory with

nothing more than a knapsack. Just months ago, they lauded him again for saving an army from defeat on the battlefield. This was the same person coming to her home in just a matter of hours.

She felt flushed. She took in a deep breath. What is that lingering reek overwhelming my nose? Mary wondered. At least it provided a distraction.

Susannah and their cousin, seated near Mary, kept up a bombardment of adulation. "Nature exhausted its charming stock in her creation. Every belle will stand in envy."

"Polly's beauty is beyond compare!" Her cousin added a theatrical emphasis with the flailing of her arms. Mary knew her unrelenting onslaught of flummery was nothing more than a mummery. Mary was envious of how Eva was so at ease in her own skin. She had large brown eyes, a full face, and a chuckle that was infectious. Mary called Eva her cousin, but in truth she was related via adoption; two generations earlier, Eva's grandmother had been taken in by the Philipse family. "You do look lovely," added Eva with sincerity this time, slouching comfortably in the chair.

Mary's mind would not be calmed until she got back to that shelf. Yes, she believed she placed the newspaper correctly. At least she thought so. Mary stood nervously, looking at her reflection as she wore a shimmering gold silk dress made up of three pieces. The first was the bodice, which was corseted at the back and had an opening at the front that fell too low for Mary's comfort. She pulled it higher.

Rosie removed the needle and thread from its holding spot between her lips. "Miss Polly, we must emphasize your apple dumplin' shop, dear."

Eva broke into sounds halfway between giggling and cackling.

Mary would rather cover her full bosom than put it on display.

The skirt was conical to show off her elongated waist. The train, which could be removed for dancing, was made of a highly decorative cloth with rich embroidery in pure gold thread. The ball gown had frilling at the hem so as to allow her ivory silk shoes to show

through the bottom. They were highly embellished with floral embroidery in delightful colors of blues and plums.

Rosie lowered the gown below Mary's shoulders.

"Each gentleman shall behold our charming Miss Polly with love's eye," Susannah said, continuing her near exaltation.

"A sight so amiable and lovely." Eva fluttered her eyelashes.

"Even deformity is pleasing, I suppose, if there is some good food and drink." Mary had quite enough of the encomiums.

Eva smiled. "And beauty, hideous, if there is none."

Rosie adjusted the lace at the bottom of the gown's sleeves. "Nary a thing, not even a hogshead of rum, can help a gentleman of three outs."

Mary knew exactly what she meant.

"Three outs?" inquired Susannah.

"The raucous rogues about town, men of the three outs." She lifted a middle finger. "Out of money." She raised a pointer finger. "Out of wit." And she added her thumb. "Out of manners. They're not worth a farthing of ye time."

"And what do you make of the sheriff, Rosie?" asked Eva.

"That man again," said Mary. He was the suitor who shared tea with Frederick when Mary refused to come out of her bedchamber.

"He's as divine a young fella as nature could form, plus I appreciate a belly that's fulla money."

"He's of the mind that his purse can seduce any woman to fall in love with him. He's employed every talent against the female persuasion. Each has fallen, except for one, of course." Eva stared Mary's way.

"Stay aside, ladies, from a gilly gaupus, like the man with the head that flares like a bell, Timothy Scandal, or whate'er he calls himself today." Rosie made a bell shape with her hands around her head.

"I take offense! Yes, he's a bit of an awkward fellow, but using a sobriquet is quite romantic, Rosie, and I admire his hairstyle. He's a fine writer, you know. Tell them, Polly, what the poet sent over to you." The grin on Eva's face grew larger.

"What did the scandalous one write to you this time?" Susannah appeared none too pleased.

Mary stayed quiet for a moment but relented and recited the lines he had written. "'So desirous I felt from only a light touch . . .'"

"Oh my." Susannah huffed.

"'Unaffected thy were, and I too much!/ How is this, that few gains move me thus, and my love reigns?'"

"Please keep going. Keep going," urged Eva.

Mary did so. "'I grin, then sigh, I shake to and fro; / Such a fleeting moment to cause me to flutter so.'"

"'A Touch of the Petticoat,' he entitled it." Eva was hardly able to contain her amusement. "A touch of the petticoat."

"Did he touch your petticoat?" Susannah asked abruptly.

"Absolutely . . . not. No. No. Certainly not."

"He is a superior writer." Eva always defended the man. "I've read his elegantly styled essays with their Latin phrasing. Not many men can quote a philosopher quite like he can."

"A philosopher? Better to choose a gollumpus," Rosie muttered. "He may be clumsy, but properly fat. And if you see an owl in an ivy bush run the other way, the same goes for the nick ninny, the niffynaffy, and the nickumpoop."

"Tell us the difference, Rosie," Eva pressed her.

"The nick ninny is too simple a man. The niffynaffy is too trifling a man."

A low titter from Mary soon turned into a chorus of unrestrained merriment between her and Eva.

"And the nickumpoop is too foolish a fellow to have ever even seen his wife's . . ." She gave a cough to fill in the missing word.

Eva burst into a cachinnation.

Susannah nearly spit out her tea. She grabbed hold of her gown for the evening and left the room. Eva followed her, folded over in laughter.

Mary regained her composure, turned to Rosie, and spoke quietly. "And how is your little Lulu feeling today?"

"Praise the heavens she's out of danger. She prayed for you before her rest today. She is sleeping with the pillow doll you sent over for her."

"Oh, how precious."

"That thing woulda eaten her whole. That bloody wolf! It took the life out of her right leg." She helped Mary down from the wooden stand, walked her to the hall, and pointed to the animal head at the other end of it, hanging on the wall with her husband's initials, J.E., written in blood beneath it. "My beloved hunted that devil down."

Mary had heard the girl's screams a week prior. The sound of Willoughby's galloping caused the wolf to let go of the child's leg as it was dragging her away. The wolf turned back into the trees.

"Has she regained her strength to walk?"

"Her leg on the right drags quite a bit." Rosie dragged her own right leg to show Mary. "Don't think she'll ever be able to dance again."

"Oh, let's not even think such things. We'll be sure she receives the very best care. Why don't you bring her tonight? I'll carry her around with me if I have to."

"Your brother would run us out of the place! But I'll bring her for the costuming."

"If you care to stay, you will be my guests." Mary caught notice of Rosie's little boy, Jeffrey, peeking from the doorway. "Good day, Master Sherwood."

"Bring in some eggs, would you, son?"

Jeffrey nodded kindly.

"And be sure your father is not drinking ale before his meal?"

Only the top of Jeffrey's head could be seen around the doorway. It nodded.

THE PAYERS OF compliments soon returned: Susannah and Eva in elegant gowns.

"Let the rogues move aside, for only one man stands with the stature of a king." Eva carried in both of her hands a highly ornate box tied in a glorious red satin bow.

"My true tells me Colonel Washington's height towers over that of his fellow officers." Susannah followed beside Eva.

"This is a man of commanding presence with a body hard of

muscle," said Eva. "There is not a prince in any part of the world who would not appear a *valet de chambre* next to him."

"A favorite of heaven, you know," Susannah added. "A man who can never die in battle."

"Ne'er die?" Rosie rolled a golden thread around its spool. "I've heard a great spirit can protect a person so not even a bullet will get 'im."

The words "can never die" stayed with Mary. For a woman whose heart had an indifference toward the most elite of men, she wondered how she could have such admiration for one she had not ever met.

"Each of Polly's potential suitors is of the finest quality. Half of the officers in New York stand with mouths agape as my sister rides by. Nearly all of them have asked for interviews. Frederick is quite finicky as to whom he will allow. I am in agreement. Our Polly should not be with just any man."

For all of those desiring to be close to Mary, none received a return glance.

A bright-eyed smile flashed across Eva's face as she handed the box to Mary. "It's for you, Polly. Open it."

Mary slowly lifted the lid.

Chapter Four

—◦◦◦—

Miracle of Monongahela

... I have been protected beyond all human probability &
expectation ...

—GEORGE WASHINGTON

PRINCETON, NEW JERSEY
FEBRUARY 14, 1756

The tailor was no beanpole. Hence, standing atop a crate, with eyes
helped by round spectacles and morning's light peeking through a
high window, old Gerald Vincent sized the cravat around George's
neck at the rear of his millinery shop on Old Fish Street in Princeton. George and his personal secretary stood in one room. In another, a group of officers who traveled north with them awaited a
transformation befitting an English gentleman.

This would be the first time George would wear a neckerchief
made of fine fabric. Twice, Vincent added another inch of silk. He
would have to add one more.

It was the final hour before they were to continue their journey to
the New York Colony. On this day, the cavalcade would arrive before
sunset, just as the banquet being given in George's honor was to
begin.

Put not off your clothes in the presence of others, nor go out your

chamber half dressed. Behind a privacy curtain, he removed his hunter's shirt and worn breeches. He stood bare-skinned. "Have you sent the correspondence?" George looked out with one eye.

His personal secretary, John Kirkpatrick, took a seat on a bench of worked oak nearest the hearth. "Yes, Colonel. The letter to Captain Roger Morris regarding the Braddock incident has been delivered. We await his response." The secretary began reviewing the list George had written for the tailor. "The colonel prefers the cloaks laced."

"As for the trimmings?" Vincent laid out a garment on a working table.

"Silver. Are you content with silver, Colonel?"

"I like that fashion best." George remained without a stitch of clothing.

"As for the coats, they've been faced and cuffed with scarlet, as you requested."

"My profound gratitude for your expedited service, as we are excessively hurried." George watched as Vincent scurried away, leaving the two in private.

Keep to the fashion of your equals. His equals were no longer volunteers in the military. He was now a commander. After his brave conduct in the expedition into enemy territory to deliver the letter of ultimatum to the French, his military status rose from nothing to one level above nothing. This was followed, though, by a show of courage in the field of battle, one which almost didn't happen because he was stricken with a sickness. He had served as a major under British general Edward Braddock of His Majesty's Army. The road to get here had not been an easy one.

Today he was the newly promoted colonel of the Virginia Regiment and commander in chief of all forces of the colony.

This elevation in fashion was a necessity due to the circles in which he would find himself, especially the one beginning this night. He accepted an invitation from his childhood friend Beverley for a first visit to New York. Major Robinson became a man of great wealth and

influence upon marriage. And Mrs. Robinson's sister had not yet pledged herself to another. George had heard plenty about the belle of the North.

"A ravishing beauty awaits your arrival, Colonel. If I may be allowed to offer some advice now, since I will not be accompanying you . . . Move quickly, for others intend to batter down the virgin gates."

"I shall labor to keep alive in my breast that little spark of celestial fire called conscience." In truth, George buried his passions for women in that grave of oblivion. He was certain that might very well be the only way. The antidote, the remedy, the cure was to stay away from any one thing that brought that other woman's silky hair back into his mind.

"Ah, his love reigns with gentle sway. It is a rarity in this age, especially when a robust fortune is the consequence."

"Happiness depends more upon the internal frame of a person's own mind than on the externals in the world."

"I shall be confident in this, Colonel. After becoming acquainted with you, her heart will find warmth beyond the common degree of fondness."

Yes, George had risen to a higher rank. He was finally receiving the respect he deserved. Still, he was not convinced.

The talk of the heiress extended to the officers who would join Washington. He listened as they swooned over her; their voices came through the open door.

"A fair-faced vision who carries the scent of wildflowers," George heard Captain Robert Stewart say. Stewart was a plain, honest fellow and a brave man—he witnessed this on the battlefield.

George covered his bareness and moved closer to the doorway. He wanted to learn particulars of this beauty.

"My eyes were blessed with the sight of her," added Stewart, who had spent some time in New York.

"Does she carry a softened shape?" One junior officer motioned a woman's shape. "Parts are in proportion?"

"Sweet breath?" asked another.

"Those and one other," acknowledged Stewart. "Purity."

"Finally!" Captain George Mercer exclaimed. Mercer was of a different type than Stewart. "I've grown tired of the great imperfections we've seen along the way. The bad figures of the ladies." He shuffled with back arched and head drooping. "Many of them have a crooked shape and a very bad air." Mercer waved his hand in front of his mouth.

George quickly regretted the decision to bring Mercer. He was recommended due to his experience as a surveyor of these parts to help make the journey faster. He also had served in the Virginia Regiment before Washington took over command.

Mercer drew laughs from the group. "When she sees us dressed in regal nature"—Mercer walked with bravado to the window—"we shall introduce ourselves as captains of the finest army, as heroes."

"Think before you speak, gentlemen," Washington advised. George could take the discourteousness no longer, and beyond that, he did not favor vanity, believing it unbecoming of a gentleman. "And Captain Mercer, a man ought not to value himself of his achievements." Even on a day like this, self-admiration would not be on display, neither for himself nor for those traveling with him.

The young military officers nodded to him and remained with mouths shut as they removed their battle-worn garb to be outfitted with regimentals of scarlet superfine woolen broadcloth coats with silver lace at the arms, blue breeches, and all topped with silver-laced hats. George had ordered the garments himself. He wanted his company to look proper for the occassion. The colonel assigned five well-mounted men, in addition to two body servants, to accompany him on this trek. The servants were more vivaciously dressed. Complete livery suits in a cream color with gold accents had even been ordered.

IN FULL COSTUME, George approached a mirror that showed his whole body—well-groomed and elegant without being ostentatious. He adjusted the ruffled cambric about his neck. A blue coat with

scarlet accents lined in gold silk fabric and adorned with two rows of ten golden buttons down the front and simple gold tassels at the shoulders was appropriate, he thought, for a night like tonight. He pulled his hair back and tied it. He placed a gold-laced hat upon his head. *To be a gentleman, act a gentleman.* Yes, this was fitting.

The body servants busily prepared a trunk next to him, removing the garb within to make room for a new, refined wardrobe. "What shall be done with your coat, Colonel?" One of them held up the garment George had worn on that doomful day. "Four clear holes right through." The servant placed his finger through each of the openings.

George hadn't noticed it before, but the gold metal seal with his family's coat of arms was missing from the coat, replaced with a bullet hole right through to where his heart would be. The tricorn hat, which they pulled from the trunk, had another two shots through it. The battle, still fresh in his mind, had been brutal. In a span of three hours, two out of every three British and Colonial officers lost their lives in the backwoods of the Monongahela. George not only managed to survive, he became a hero, a legend, a man who couldn't die.

"Protected by above." The servant raised his eyes upward in reverence, his finger still in one of the holes. "The direction of Providence."

MONTHS EARLIER
GREAT CROSSING OF THE YOUGHIOGHENY, PENNSYLVANIA

For ten days, George had been in quarantine, seized with a vile illness. The shooting pain that started around his eyes stretched its way to the back of his head. Excessive weakness made it difficult for him even to count out the prescribed small grains of fever powder. He was advised that taking one more granule of Doctor James's powder than absolutely necessary could kill a man.

The sickness confined him to a bed in a covered wagon on the side of a dirt road. His fevers were at a near-crisis level—an experience he was all too familiar with. Name a disease, and George suffered through it at one point in his life. Violent pleurisy. Diphtheria. Dysentery. Smallpox—that disease left faded pockmarks on his face. Congestive fever. Lung fever. White plague—he had watched Lawrence waste away from the same disease; the image never left his mind.

This time, bloody flux invaded George's body. The doctor forbade him to move, warning that his life would be endangered if he did so. Frustration overwhelmed him as he awaited better health.

He would have gotten here, to camp, earlier if not for his mother. She had stopped him from leaving—stopped him right at the doorway—alarmed by his decision to enlist. He could still hear her keys jangling—the ones she always wore on a large metal ring looped into the sash around her waist. He needed to convince her. There was a farm to manage, she insisted. But this was for his future. Serve king and country, certainly, and he had other reasons, selfish considerations. Learn the specifics of the British tactical battlefield maneuvers. Write each of the details into his personal journal. Secure a post of high rank. Become a man of distinction. No better opportunity would present itself than this to educate himself in the military arts. He was invited to serve as an aide-de-camp under General Braddock. These reasons contributed to his decision to join up without pay. What else was he to do? Stay on Ferry Farm forever? He sat his mother down that day to speak with her about his choice. "The God to whom you commended me, madam, when I set out upon a more perilous errand, defended me from harm, and I trust He will do so now. Do not you?"

This changed her mind. "Go, George, fulfill the high destinies which Heaven appears to have intended you for," she had told him.

The mission was not turning out as he hoped. His plan to keep a detailed journal was fading. George attended only one council of

war before the weakness set in. He sent a letter to fellow aide-de-camp Captain Roger Morris, asking him to provide a copy of all of the general's orders by the first safe conveyance.

Now, a day later, a wagon arrived, driven by a scrappy lad, a couple of years his junior, with a tongue that never lay still. He walked with a spring in his step and always wore that same coonskin hat. Daniel Boone approached. He offered no salutation before his assertions began. "Sir, I must tell you . . . they believe it a joke."

"A good day to you, Boone," George said.

"Yes, good day. They reckon it a battle ill-planned in England, and ill-concerted in America. It was said and I heard it: 'We have not a single Indian on our side or the least fear of being trapped by ambush.'" Boone adjusted his hat. It had become askew. "Doomed. We are doomed. Even one of the general's own aides, not Morris, of course, believes your theory of warfare of the wilderness. He says, 'The general is in a place more adapted than any in the world to face an enemy who can fight from the woods, and yet we continue the tradition of the old in our maneuvers.'"

In his only formal council of war with the general, George laid out the maps that he had drawn of the land the enemy occupied in the backcountry, and he advised the general that these forces would find a way to conceal themselves in the brush. George knew the charts were imperfect, since they were roughly sketched for want of proper utensils, but they offered a clear indication of the dangers of the wild. Braddock marked his planned maneuvers with standard lines onto George's map with an adherence to rows of soldiers. They would never depart from the conventional linear British-style warfare. George insisted that would not suffice, keeping to his rules of civility. *Strive not with your superiors in argument, but always submit your judgment to others with modesty.*

Braddock pontificated: "The savages may have proven formidable to your raw American soldiers; however, faced with the king's troops, they will hardly make the least of effects."

The general ignored George's continued opposition.

"They will fight from the trees, General," George told him fervently. But it was to no avail. The general would not listen, even when George suggested they hurry. "If we could credit our intelligence. The French are weak at the forks but hourly expect reinforcements, which to my certain knowledge could not arrive with provisions or any supplies in time. I urge our regiment to push on with only the artillery and such other things as absolutely necessary."

Braddock scoffed at him. "We shall take our entire contingent, wagons, horses, troops, and all other supplies we see fit." His soldiers had gone on to level every molehill in their way, which decelerated the pace of troop movement. Braddock wouldn't listen to any of George's recommendations, calling him "a young hand," "a beardless boy."

It wasn't as if he was unaccustomed to that. George often heard insults directed at him—"illiterate," "unlearned," "unread."

Boone kept up his chatter. "In private, our Indian ally told us he believes the general looks upon the natives as dogs. They believe Braddock sees this country as empty of integrity and fidelity." Boone removed a scroll from his backpack. "A letter for you, sir, from Captain Morris. I'm told you should read it and offer a response to his reply if you care to." Boone stepped back to provide privacy.

Read no letters, books, or papers in company. George lifted the seal and unrolled the letter.

Dear Washington,

It is the Desire of every particular in the Family, & the Generals positive Commands to you, not to stirr, but by the Advice of the Person under whose Care you are, till you are better, which we all hope will be very soon — This I can personally assure you, that you may follow the Advice of the surgeon to whom I know you are recommended as a proper Man.

Yours &c.
Roger Morris
Monday five o'Clock in the Afternoon

George motioned for Boone to return. He would have no answer to the letter, infuriated as he was. Morris provided nothing he requested. No details of the military orders, not even the supply lists.

"And Captain Morris," Boone continued, "'tis but assured his promotion to lieutenant colonel upon victory at Duquesne. You know the other getting what they want? That woman layered in jewels. The general's been overheard bragging about how he will take her into battle for it will be a swift victory. He's wasted months of our time as he feasts with her. Do you know what I transported to him on the evening last? Cases and cases of eatables—hams, cheeses, loaves of sugar. Sugar! Eight kegs of biscuits, sturgeon, herring, a barrel of potatoes, tubs of butter, and kegs of spirit . . . and they were set aside just for the general's table!"

George turned to Boone with astonishment at those words. *Let your judgment always be balanced. Where there is no occasion for expressing an opinion, it is best to be silent.*

"He says, Captain Stewart does, that without Washington, we cannot win."

THE DAY OF BATTLE
FORKS OF THE OHIO

George placed a hand on his brother's sword; he was glad to have it at his side. A field abloom in pristine white lay before him. The shade contrasted strikingly against a sea of brilliant red tunics worn by the British soldiers. The men were lined up in strict formation as far as the eye could see. George wore blue, not having had an opportunity to receive his uniform, since he rejoined the company only hours beforehand with a paleness in his face and a

pain at his bottom that forced him to mount his horse on a couple of cushions.

Glancing one row in front, he watched a graceful woman riding a horse. Her black hair, straight and long to her waist, bounced in synchrony with the horse's gallop. She reminded him of the woman of the lowlands. That hair's length. Its shine. It was like hers—his Affa's. This woman beside the general wore a bright orange dress ornamented with pure gold bracelets about her arms. She stood out against so many red coats.

"We will strike fear in the enemy!" Braddock exclaimed. George noticed his hair, surprised a general would style it for battle. A high puff carried over his noggin from ear to ear and fell in a tail of false white curls. "Expel the French from the continent!"

For the British to take control of the Ohio country, this fort built by the French at the Forks of the Ohio would need to be captured. Here at Fort Duquesne, both the Monongahela and Allegheny Rivers came together to form the Ohio River, which was essential for trade and movement of the military.

The area appeared abandoned. The general marched the officers forth. They were lined in English tradition. The silvery lace of their uniforms glistened in the sun. With what appeared a clear path to victory on level land, despite two ravines covered with trees and high grass surrounding the final open field, the general signaled the boys to begin to play. George moved aside as the line of young fifers and drummers, just children, passed by him. The smallest of the group played the fife. The eldest carried the drum; he appeared to be beginning to show signs of manhood from the few hairs upon his face. It was he who struck the first beat.

The marching song of the British Grenadiers played.

The men began to sing.

Captain Morris, who wore a boutonniere of white clover as if on parade, was loudest of all.

Some talk of Alexander, and some of Hercules,
Of Hector and Lysander, and such great names as these,

But of all the world's great heroes, there's none that can compare
With a tow, row, row, row, row, row, to the British Grenadiers.

Those heroes of antiquity ne'er saw a cannon ball,
Nor knew the force of powder to slay their foes with all,
But our brave boys do know it, and banish all their fears,
With a tow, row, row, row, row, row, for the British Grenadiers.

When e'er we are commanded to storm the palisades,
Our leaders march with fuses, and we with hand grenades;
We throw them from the glacis about the enemies' ears.
Sing tow, row, row, row, row, row, for the British Grenadiers.

Just as the last words were sung, George heard the first bullets whistle, coming from an invisible enemy among the trees. The first fire was fatal. A boy's drum fell to the ground. Blood seeped from his neck as his thin frame collapsed. The little fifer was next to fall.

A terrible carnage began. The enemy overwhelmed the soldiers with a horseshoe attack, trapping them like animals in a pen. An endless barrage came from the brush. A blur of violence faded into a cloud of chaos. The rapid discharge of musketry did not obscure the screams of injured men, dying men.

The deadly siege was exactly what George had warned against, exactly what he presaged would be the outcome of the Battle of Monongahela. His prediction of warfare in the wild was coming true.

The force of the French with their native allies aimed at the officers on horseback, and next at the officers on the ground, leaving the British force doomed. The enemy struck the first flank; every soldier was killed or wounded. Over and over again, the general ordered his men to form their proper line and march forward. Hundreds more officers advanced in British formation, an open target for the warriors firing from nature's camouflage. Before long, those officers, too, were shot and killed.

"Ye enemy! They are hidden behind the trees!" Daniel Boone

shouted to George above the gunfire. "They slaughtered the men! They scalped 'em! I saw it myself."

George raced on horseback to Braddock.

"General, allow me to enter into tree fighting! We must change course." Everywhere he looked, the bodies of his comrades had fallen—were falling—all around him.

"I swear, Washington, I've a mind to run you through the body!"

"Alter the fight. Allow me to use three hundred of your men. They are in the trees, General!"

"Washington, this is my battle!"

"I implore you."

"We'll sup today in Fort Duquesne or else in hell!"

The sting of annihilation struck. A massacre unfolded before George's eyes. Morris fell to the ground. The general's lady, drenched in red, dropped from her horse. Braddock had five horses shot from under him, yet he remained in the center of the fight. A bullet struck the general in the back of his shoulder. A second shot to the breast dropped him.

With no other leader standing, George had no choice but to take control. He could have retreated; instead, he chose to reload. He could have been fearful; instead, he chose to be fearless. Leadership was thrust upon him during this dire fight. He answered the call. Refusing to let his surviving band of brothers fall, he rode in every direction, rallying the men. They took to the trees. They rushed the brush. Unlike the general, who had told the men to charge, George led the charge, with his men following.

Twice, George's horse was hit. It collapsed.

Four times, bullets pierced George's coat.

But he continued to stand. He would not go down.

Two shots struck his hat.

George's blood did not spill. He ordered cannons to fire and, with furor, grabbed his rifle, planted one hand on the muzzle, situated the other on the breach, and controlled the weapon as if it were weightless.

Gunfire directed toward him grew even more intense.

Fire after fire.

He did not fall.

He remained in the battle, sustaining not even a wound. Desperate to save the lives of the living, he continued the fight to protect his officers.

Suddenly, the bombardment from the enemy ceased.

The bullets fell silent. George was left bewildered by the quiet.

"We have General Braddock!" Captain Stewart cried out to him. Washington rushed to the general's side, hearing him murmur that he wished to be left to die with his men. Together, they placed Braddock in a tumbrel. They carried him off as he begged them to leave him there.

"The woman?" asked George of Stewart.

"Scalped and dragged off."

His focus turned to the field of clover, those white blossoms trampled and stained red. The cries of the dying pierced his heart. The stink of death surrounded him. Gloom and horror everywhere.

George saw Morris at a distance of a dozen or more yards, stumbling, seeming near collapse. He rushed to his fellow aide-de-camp and found him with hands over a bloodied face, the silver lace on his sleeve stained red. "A bullet." Morris gasped. "A bullet took my nose." He ducked under Morris's left arm and, carrying him, led him away from that meadow of death.

Four hundred and twenty-one. George, with Stewart's assistance, counted the injured lying on the ground. The two of them helped transport the wounded to a safe campsite. Each name Stewart wrote down. The last of the injured was a young boy with a small flute still across his chest, who slowly turned his desperate eyes to George when he asked his name.

"Miles Brown," he said, his voice weak. His little face resembled that of his father, a slave by the name of Billy Brown, who was in the fight and now knelt by his son's side. With George beside them, the elder Brown rose and, with rage in his voice and tears in his eyes, began to speak loudly enough for the others to hear.

"I've been given the name Billy Brown. In God's name, I tell you now. I saw the truth on that field." A great number of men turned to hear him. "Washington, he came up to the general during the fight and asked permission to take to the trees with his men." It seemed the whole camp, every wounded and the few whole, listened to his words. "The general, he screamed at him, cursed him! He said to him—and I will remember these words for the rest of my life—the general said to him, 'I've mind to run you through the body!' He swore at this man. He used these words: 'We'll sup today in Fort Duquesne or else in hell!'"

Cheers and assents erupted among the officers.

"This is the truth!" Brown yelled. "I tell you, this is the truth!" He knelt again by his young son.

From a distance, an officer's voice could be heard, reading the names of the missing and the killed on the banks of the Monongahela.

The list seemed to go on indefinitely. The force of fifteen hundred men shattered by a party of what could have been no more than a few hundred of the enemy. After the final name was read, George spoke quietly to Stewart: "The horrific scenes which showed themselves on this day are unspeakable, sickening."

"We have suffered an incomprehensible defeat." Stewart moved with him behind a large oak, away from the injured.

"The dead—the dying—the groans—lamentations—and cries along the road of the wounded for help . . . were enough to pierce the heart."

Both stood, each with a hand over his heart, face bowed.

A voice interrupted. It was Dr. James. "Washington. The general has made a request for your presence. A bullet pierced the general's lung. We have not much time."

George walked with the doctor, passing rows upon rows of the wounded, including Captain Morris. Still bleeding about the nose, the bandaged captain jumped to his feet, appearing flabbergasted that it was Washington about to enter General Braddock's private cabin.

Morris questioned the doctor as to whether it was he the general requested.

Speak not injurious words neither in jest nor earnest scoff at none although they give occasion. George stayed silent.

The doctor gave him a firm "Nay."

In the corner of the one-room structure, light pierced through a dusty window, its rays hitting the face of the general, whose skin appeared almost grayish. "The blue," Braddock muttered in a shaky voice. "The blue saved us."

When another speaks be attentive your self and disturb not the audience if any hesitate in his words help him not nor prompt him without desired, interrupt him not, nor answer him till his speech be ended. He waited until the general finished his words.

The general turned his eyes toward George. "Who would have thought it?"

George sat on a stool next to him. Dr. James stood a few feet back.

"We shall better know how to deal with them another time." Braddock's breathing was coming short and shallow.

He nodded to the dying man. The general pointed to a small trunk near his bedside. George lifted it to him. As Braddock's shaky hands grabbed hold of it, he whispered, "For not taking your guidance, I must apologize." His fingers weakly fumbled with the latch. Inside was the commander's sash, colored in brilliant British red and stained with the general's blood, as he had worn it in the battle. "It is yours," Braddock said, as he feebly handed over the sash. "George Washington, you are the next in command."

As the only aide uninjured in the fight and the man who saved an army from utter annihilation, the raw volunteer from the Virginia woods was now commander. *Undertake not what you cannot perform but be careful to keep your promise.* Knowing this edict, George pledged his commitment to serve.

A rattling noise came from the back of the general's throat. His eyes became glassy as he stared into a distance above him. The doctor

rushed over as Edward Braddock took his final breath. A blue color presenting itself upon his lips.

BY THE LIGHT of a torch, a group of men gathered to choose the general's resting place. With a bandage covering nearly his whole face, Morris interrupted, requesting that he perform the obsequies, noting his close ties with Braddock, having signed his allegiance to the general and having traveled with him from Britain. None would have it. To the utter agitation of Morris, they turned to the new commander to determine not only the burial details but also the movement of the entire company.

The decision George made was to have Braddock buried in the middle of the high road cut for wagons. In order not to arouse any suspicion on the part of the enemy, he planned for no fanfare; not even a volley would be fired. If the enemy forces had any idea of the burial site's location, they would surely dig up the corpse and carry his scalp as a trophy.

WRAPPED IN two blankets, the general's body was lowered into a shallow grave. George read a devotion from the Book of Common Prayer, which Dr. James had carried with him:

Forasmuch as it hath pleased Almighty God
of his great mercy to take unto himself the soul of our
dear brother here departed, we therefore commit his
body to the ground, earth to earth, ashes to ashes,
dust to dust, in sure and certain hope of the Resurrection
to eternal life, through our Lord Jesus Christ, who
shall change our vile body that it may be like unto
his glorious body, according to the mighty working,
whereby he is able to subdue all things to himself.

"His attachments were warm," George noted upon completion of a moment of silence. "His enmities were strong, and having no disguise about him, both appeared in full force."

He signaled for the soldiers to travel on. He ordered the wagon drivers to roll over the dirt above the general's resting place and the men to march over it. He wanted to obliterate any trace of the unmarked grave, any trace of the past.

Chapter Five

———◆◆◆———

Gooch's Kitchen

*. . . when once the Woman has tempted us, & we have
tasted the forbidden fruit, there is no such thing as
checking our appetites, whatever the consequences may be.*
—GEORGE WASHINGTON

YONKERS-ON-HUDSON
FEBRUARY 14, 1756

Lured by the scent of almonds, Mary's appetite was calling her to the
kitchen after the return from the dressmaker's cottage. For the feast
welcoming the hero and his Southern officers, Mary's brother hired
an army of culinarians. From confectioners to cooks to additional
dairy and scullery maids, they joined an already large staff. The Clerk
of the kitchen, the ever neat and well-kempt Temperance Gooch,
ruled like a crowned head; not even a drop of gravy dare land on her
apron. Mary found it amusing, the disdain Temperance showed for
the others her brother hired, many of whom were French. Frederick
never cared much for taking sides in war, or in anything else for that
matter.

Down to the kitchen Mary went, where an eruption was shaking
the pots.

"A gallimaufry"—Temperance pushed aside the French cook's
completed creation of *crème croquante*—"and nothing more!"

"Mademoiselle, to taste *une crème croquante*, one must pause to find *la delicatese* of each layer of flavor." This was Chef François, one of those new hires, enunciating between his curled mustache and chin beard. "This is how I create."

Mary, watching the two through the half-opened door, did not interrupt.

"Create? Imitate would be more proper a term." Temperance, Mary knew, despised the French way of cooking. "Chef d'Anjou, I shall not fill my table with such nonsense." A cook's daughter, Temperance had grown up in the manor. She began working in the kitchen when she became old enough. And now, at twenty-four years of age, she demanded certain pay for her work, to which Frederick agreed. On a day like today, Temperance would not be outprepared, especially by a French cook who was in the middle of a serenade over his pot.

"*Vous insulte ma creation, Mademoiselle Gooch!*" The chef walked closer to Temperance and pointed to a silver tray. "You yourself make a dessert of snowballs." His nose scrunched up, as if it had been assaulted by putrescence.

"A dish that is a creation, not an imitation," snapped Temperance. Over the balls made of boiled rice, apples, and a touch of cinnamon, she drizzled a sauce that combined butter, white wine, and nutmeg. "It is to the liking of the lady of the house."

"Mademoiselle, never has a snowflake fallen to the south"—he picked up the tray—"just as never has a snowball had a place at a banquet."

"I am aware it would not be French to show praise to a good cook," Temperance declared, storming past him. "As for your crème, it is more dull than divine."

"I am at your pleasure, Mademoiselle." He leaned near her. "As for my crème, I shall be sure to dulcify it for you."

It seemed to Mary that the chef found Temperance's superciliousness quite engaging, while Temperance nearly winced at the close proximity.

She interrupted for Temperance's sake and looked right at the

dessert in François's hand. "Splendid! As we await snowfall outside, you have brought a touch of radiant frost inside."

"A day for celebration, Mademoiselle Philipse!" François happily responded, still holding the tray of snowballs.

"Miss Polly, good day." Temperance approached her with a long dish holding small sampling bowls. "Just for you, I have created an orange pudding, as well as a lemon pudding, a millet pudding, carrot pudding, quince pudding, apricot pudding, white pear and plum-apple pudding."

"The sweetness that brings me to the kitchen every time." Mary noticed Temperance's nervousness around François. Naming each pudding—it wasn't like her to do that.

"Rice pudding, custard pudding, bread pudding, chestnut pudding, prune pudding," added Temperance. For the last, she handed Mary a specially crafted blue-and-white Canton bowl containing Mary's favorite. "For our Miss Polly, the pretty almond pudding."

"They've arrived!" The heiress examined the porcelain she suggested be ordered for the special occasion from Ching-te-chen. With the family's influence, the East India Trading Company shipped with urgency the entire table set for the banquet. "And without breakage?"

"Not a one, Miss Polly."

"If you please," said François, bringing over additional samples of his own. "For you, *crème au chocolat, crème de café, crème au zeste d'orange, crème de vin du Rhin, crème croquante, crème à la fleur de vanille.*"

"*Merci beaucoup. Je suis impatiente de tous deguster.* At present, the pretty almond pudding will do my stomach just fine."

"Then all of them we shall display. A fine table it shall be!" François returned to his pot as well as to his serenade.

Temperance walked with Mary as she enjoyed the sample of pretty almond pudding.

"Your admirer's eyes remain on you," whispered Mary.

"He is impossible."

"Impossibly handsome."

"Impossibly French."

Temperance walked Mary through the many dishes that would be served during dinner, beginning with Mary's special request, the salamongundy—a salad dish of edible flowers, herbs, small onions, string beans, boiled eggs, grapes, and lemon-roasted chicken with an oil dressing beaten with vinegar, salt, and pepper.

The guests would be treated to a culinary extravaganza this night. For years, Mary helped Temperance write and rewrite recipes to attain the perfect combination of flavors. Now Mary reviewed the menu, hopeful the dishes would be to Colonel Washington's liking.

"Scotch collops, leg of lamb, rump of beef, roasted duck, and loaf of oysters," Temperance added. "The French influence for Lord Frederick will be in the *lapereaux aux truffes* and the *côtes de boeuf à la Sainte Menoux*. Your brother has asked that catsup be served as well."

"Catsup?" Mary could see that Temperance was pleased with her work. "A perfect choice. Papa, too, would have enjoyed that." The offerings were more than Mary could have imagined. This was the first time in longer than she could remember that the home was so filled with activity. Since the devastating loss of Mary's sister Margaret, her father, and, of course, her mother, the manor had never been so alive. "Everyone would have relished in this glorious feast."

Tenderly, Temperance took hold of Mary's hand. "Miss Polly, a proud night is before you." Temperance knew more than most about the Philipses, their joys and their grief.

Trying to regain her composure, trying to find her calm, her eyes began to fill. "I find it difficult to rejoice when we have been through much sorrow." Her whole being was thrust into an anxious state. She exited the kitchen. Her pace quickened as she moved into the hall. Furniture was being moved out of the foyer to make space.

Those crowds! She thought of the poking and prodding, the bumping of shoulders, the accidental and intentional brushing of a hand here, a hip there, the hollow chatter, meaningless queries, and the hall stifling from the fetor of hair powder. She knew scores of eyes would

be on her on a night like tonight. The questions would be endless: Why had she not attended any recent balls or banquets? A crush of people would soon fill the room. The barrage she imagined made her feel dizzy.

Her legs grew weak. She pictured her shoes slipping through muddy ground. A chill ran through her. That night—the one when she lost her mother—plunged her spirit into a depth so deep, she had never recovered. It didn't matter that one of the guests was the hero of the South. It didn't matter that the dancing master's freedom might depend on her. Her brother's wishes were inconsequential. What occupied her thinking was the horde, her unease, and especially the disquieting presence of the man of her nightmares; just the smell of him triggered her return to the torment.

She needed to run. Hide. Get away. The same as she had done time and time again.

PALE BLUE.

She liked that color best.

Mary often lost track of the hours when she was in here, painting. She came to this room in the cellar when she needed to escape. It was a place to hide from the distress that often disturbed her countenance.

She delicately dried nature and gently glossed over death with the color on her paintbrush. This was madness; she knew that. Blossoms bereft of life she brought back to brightness with the stroke of her brush.

"Every flower must emerge from the darkness to bathe in the light," she remembered her mother often telling her on those mornings they gathered blooms at Hudson's Hook and tied them into a bunch with a red satin ribbon. Spring was her mother's favorite time of year. And Mary fondly recalled her younger sister with them, vivacious and exuberant, frolicking about with her bare feet on tender grasses.

Years later, Mary cut wildflowers to be placed at Margaret's bedside when the sickness took hold of her. Day after day, Mary held a handkerchief, careful to conceal her emotion, while sitting outside the

door of the bedchamber, the one Mary was ordered not to enter. Every day, she would sing her sister a melody. She sang it now:

If to me as true thou art
As I am true to thee, sweetheart
We'll hear one, two, three, four, five, six
From the bells of Aberdovey.
Hear one, two, three, four, five, six
Hear one, two, three, four, five and six
From the bells of Aberdovey.

Margaret would clap along—one, two, three, four, five, six— albeit feebly. Until one day there was silence. A deafening emptiness fell upon the home.

"I remember that song." Mary hadn't heard Frederick come into the cellar room. As he spoke, he crouched to avoid garlands of dried autumn leaves she'd placed above the entry. A few leaves fell loose. "You wouldn't leave her door until you heard Margaret clap her hands to six with you. On a night like tonight, the little rascal would have been dancing till the sun rose. What of the time she pulled the peruke right off of Lord Livingston?"

The moment came clear in her mind.

"Robert the Elder ran from the center of the room, chasing after her for it," she said.

"Right in the middle of the minuet."

"On his face was dread, with not a hair upon his head."

His rhyme about the curmudgeon always made her laugh.

Frederick placed his hands in his pockets. "You are aware, Polly, that you cannot remain hidden away forever."

She turned back to her brushstrokes. He did not understand her. How could he? How could anyone? She felt as if her soul had been shattered, and its broken shards with their jagged edges piercing her heart. Over the years, Mary attempted to carry on by building an impenetrable wall to block her emotions. Many times her brother tried to relieve her misery. And for that she was grateful. He always

told her their deaths—Elbert's, Mother's, Father's, Margaret's—were not her fault. Mary knew the truth. She could have reached for the flower from Elbert. She could have stayed away from her father and from Margaret. Mary knew she was not just the cursed one; she was the one damned to stay alive.

"I know I'm not Father. I would do more for you if I knew how."

The woe that gripped her had remained for so long.

For too long.

She arose.

In the distance, the bells of St. John's Church sounded. Eric Arthur pledged he would watch for the hero's arrival. His signal to her would be one lasting chime, give it time to echo, and follow that with two more in quicker succession.

"Come, Polly, your tomorrow awaits you," said Frederick. "First, however, we may need to remove this nature from your hair."

"Mine? Wait until you see the mess you've made of yours."

The bells sounded again.

One slow followed by two fast.

Colonel George Washington had arrived.

Chapter Six

———◆◆◆———

The Hero Washington

. . . I do not think vanity is a trait of my character.

—GEORGE WASHINGTON

George's horse left the dirt and moved onto the cobblestones of Albany Post Road in the town of Yonkers. The colonel rode atop a superb chestnut bay. The coaches following behind him were elegantly covered with an embroidered coat of arms on the material. The crest displayed a bird that looked like an eagle sitting atop a white shield of stars and stripes, and beneath the shield, the name George Washington was hand-stitched.

Trailing pine from a line of evergreens welcomed George to the New York Colony.

He listened to the clangs coming from the belfry of an enormous stone church. One slow followed by two fast.

"He comes. He comes." George could hardly believe his ears, until he heard the townspeople shout his name clearly. "The hero Washington, he comes!" The hero *Washington*. He never would have expected to be recognized in such a way. Quite a site of pageantry it

was. George watched what seemed to be hundreds of people lining the path to greet him.

The cheers grew louder. "The hero Washington has arrived!" Throngs of people applauded him and those riding with him, including Mercer and Stewart. Mercer seemed more interested in gazing at the belles. George reminded him of a rule he himself followed: *Play not the peacock, looking everywhere about you to see if you be well deck't.*

"He comes! The hero, he comes!" Young ladies threw flower petals before him.

A lady with pointed spectacles hanging on a chain loudly shouted from just feet away.

"The most handsome man mine eyes have ever beheld!"

"One touch of him!" exclaimed another lady with hair piled high above her head as she pushed through the crowd. "I must have just one touch!" Her actions became so intense that at one point a child in her path, a little girl with ginger hair, fell to the ground. In a panic, others hollered at the woman. George stopped the cavalcade until the child was upright. Without hesitation, the girl raced with one leg limping to embrace the woman with the pointed glasses, and cried out, "Huzza!"

Before him now lay the handsome estate of the Philipse family, surrounded by massive mills with cascading water. The powerful rushes fell to the grand Hudson River. A Georgian-style mansion by the water's edge looked even more impressive as he drew closer. It exuded wealth from its symmetrical design and classic detail. Two formal entries were accented with pilasters. Three floors high, the house had eight windows across the front and five windows at the side of the second floor. Large chimneys reached into the sky. A viewing rail sat upon the roof.

The cavalcade stopped before the path that led to the mansion. A bronze tablet, polished to perfection, caught George's attention. It was situated to the left of the walkway, engraved with the family's coat of arms, a crowned lion issuing from a coronet. Today George felt polished to perfection as well. Refined. A man of honor. It had taken

him years of hard work to achieve this. New Yorkers, he thought, were a fine people indeed.

George dismounted. A kindly fellow received him. "We are honored with your arrival at the town of Yonkers-on-Hudson, Colonel Washington. Joseph Chew's the name. I shall tend to your horses. If I might further assist, please make me aware."

As he was about to answer, someone with a familiar face approached. George quickly tipped his hat to Chew before greeting Major Beverley Robinson. Fifteen years it had been since seeing his good friend.

"Colonel Washington, my congratulations on your success with command of the Virginia Regiment."

"We've certainly come a long way, friend, from throwing rocks across the Rappahannock." George could recall clearly the days they spent on the farm together, riding horses, and trying not to get into too much trouble with George's mother.

"If I remember correctly, it was only you who got them straight away to the other side of the river." Beverley pretended to toss one in the air.

"A long wait for the ferry will do that."

"It was rocks then. Today we could use silver dollars." Beverley patted his coat pocket.

"Silver dollars? Those would remain safe in my pocket."

A grinning Robinson escorted George to the dignitaries lined up to greet him. As George approached them, he followed his rule for meeting the dignified classes: *In pulling off your hat to persons of distinction, as noblemen, justices, churchmen and company, make a reverence, bowing more or less according to the custom of the better bred, and quality of the person.*

"May I introduce Colonel George Washington. A man of such strength that I've witnessed him throw . . . a silver dollar across . . . the Potomac River."

Before George were the distinguished gentlemen of the town. He could tell this from their voices, which were as sophisticated as their costume. They seemed to take Beverley's story as truth. The Potomac

was twice as wide as the Rappahannock. George tried to correct him, but the major wouldn't have it and continued on with introductions to the heads of the Livingston, Jay, Van Cortlandt, and Delancey families. George took note as he approached a Delancey, who was announced as the town's sheriff. He gave George no greeting whatsoever.

Chapter Seven

———◆◆◆———

The Pleasure Ball

'*Tis true I profess myself a votary of love . . .*

—GEORGE WASHINGTON

Mary could hear the revelry downstairs and it made her worry. What if her spirit failed her? What if she ran off in the middle of a minuet? What if the fog of hair powders enveloped her, dragged her down, and choked her? Please, Mary, no, she told herself. The last thing she wanted was to embarrass her family again. She'd done enough of that.

She shut her eyes and begged her mind to go blank as the sounds of instrumentalists playing Johann Pachelbel's Canon in D Major reached her room. She stood as still as possible while the abigails tightened her corset. She found this difficult, for she was trembling inside. With her swift transformation under way, she took in the *Chaenomeles speciosa*. It must have been Susannah who had placed the flowering quince branches in her bedchamber. The pink blooms combined sweet and fresh and sultry in one bold fragrance.

The swoosh of her door swinging open startled her.

Dressmaker Rosie hurried into the room. "Pull it tighter!" She

carried precious Lulu on her hip. "He's a vision, Miss Polly!" Rosie's bun sat even more disheveled than usual. "A vision!" She tried to catch her breath. "Colonel Washington. The chap came close 'nough for me to 'bout touch him. Almost got ahold of his big paws." She had a jolly laugh. "We saw the hero. Didn't we, darlin'?"

Lulu nodded feverishly, hanging on to her mother tightly. The little girl's hair was in crooked pigtails, one high, one low.

Rosie made her way to the gown and placed Lulu down. The child hopped on one foot to Mary and threw her arms around her, which caused Mary's hair to come loose from the waterfall braid being completed. All of this caused a scramble not just among the lady's maids but also in Mary's conflicted spirits. A vision. Mary always knew he would be. She tried to calm her nerves by taking a moment to fix the little girl's pigtails.

Rosie removed Lulu from the gown, sat her on a stool, and placed herself on the floor. Her hands adjusted the hem. "The dress gots to be below the shoulders. Shine 'em up with cream!" Rosie looked up with a large grin. "We want our angel to shimmer."

Two ladies followed the instructions, while another continued working on her hair; she placed the curling iron into the fire and twisted Mary's hair around the heated rod. Mary liked this style, for the subtle waves fell loosely from the braid that pulled her hair away from her face. A fourth lady added a red pomade to Mary's lips and a light rouge to her cheeks. Mary wondered whether she should have them add more paint to her face, or use less. How could she even know? She'd never worn any before. In the end, she decided to ask that no paint be added to her eyes.

Rosie slid back to look at her. "A vision. *You* are the vision."

She assumed Rosie was just being kind. She only hoped that, at the least, she would be presentable.

"We've not time!" Susannah sounded frantic as she rushed into the room sideways. Her sister's dress was so wide that she could not get through the door any other way. "Colonel Washington is here. He's walking into the manor!" Luxuriously dressed from crown to silk shoe, Susannah, wearing a silvery cerulean-colored gown, held out the boxed

gift for Mary to open, the same one Eva presented her at the fitting at the Sherwood house.

Her cousin knew Mary well—too well. Mary lifted the lid to reveal the diadem. Made of pure gold, the half crown had hand-carved silhouettes in ivory at its points, representing women of the Philipse and Van Cortlandt families. Lady Joanna was at its center with her face carved in perfect detail. Mary felt a sense of peace knowing her mama would be with her tonight. The group carefully adjusted the decorative on her head and secured it.

"You look like a princess, my dear Polly." Susannah's face brightened. "You remind me of Princess Florine awaiting her charming."

"Miss Polly! Miss Polly!" little Lulu piped. Mary turned toward her. "You told me that fairy's tale."

Mary reached over and gently tapped her on the top of her head. "Lulu, you remembered."

"Prince Charmin' don't care 'bout no curses." The girl motioned a swat with her hand.

Mary adored the child. "Would you like me to read it again to you on my next visit?"

Lulu's whole face smiled, even her freckled nose.

It was one of Mary's favorite stories. The tale by Madame d'Aulnoy told of a handsome Prince Charming who had been cursed and transformed into a bluebird because of his love for a sweet-hearted princess who had been hidden away from the world. He traveled in flight for years in search of his true love.

"'Bird, with wings of heaven's blue,'" Susannah began, reciting the tale. "'Haste to where I wait for you.' My sister, your charming is dressed in heaven's blue."

"Please tell me he arrives not covered in feathers," Mary replied.

Susannah laughed. Lulu covered her mouth so as not to let out giggles, but a few high-pitched ones escaped.

"Come. Look at the beauty you've become." Susannah helped her sister to the mirror. The gentle rustling of gowns could be heard. "Impossible it will be for him to have eyes for anyone else than so captivating a belle."

Mary stood staring into a full-length mirror. Her reflection presented a dewy face in a glimmering dress. Her cheeks were rosy, her hair fancy, her shoulders shiny, her shoes colorful, her posture in proper position. Today she most certainly looked like Florine coming out of hiding. She knew what she really was—madness in elegant clothing.

Susannah moved her to the doorway to exit her chamber. As Mary approached the stairwell, she could hear Frederick one floor below, making one toast too many. She was well aware this was on account of her being delayed to greet the guests.

"To Colonel Washington. May you continue to show greatness against our enemy combatants."

"To the officers of the South. May you continue to commit your service for all."

"To the New York dignitaries. May your work continue to make our colony a symbol of greatness."

"For the weather—"

When he started a toast to the temperature, the guests began to sound restive, seemingly anxious to enter the dining room, where Temperance's feast awaited.

"May winter continue to remain mild and dry in our Yonkers to allow for safe and comfortable travel."

As he started one more toast, Mary hurriedly moved to the staircase. She heard a loud gasp coming from the guests. The musicians stopped playing. She took a deep breath, kept her shoulders back, and pinched the front of her dress to keep it from catching on her shoes. She placed one foot slowly below the other. She could feel a man's gaze upon her, his eyes slaying her, as if sending an arrow straight to her heart. A glimpse of him was all she could handle. He stood strong and tall, a striking figure in his azure coat with its golden accents at the shoulders. His hair, untouched by powder, was neatly pulled back, showing the strength of his features. The color of his eyes she did not see. What are the color of his eyes? she wondered. The view of him was ever so quick. She had a desire for another look, but she wouldn't dare look again.

"Ladies and gentlemen, Miss Polly Philipse," Frederick announced. She recognized that smile of his. She'd made her brother proud. The room resounded with a burst of applause. Tonight she quite liked that Frederick was introducing her. It had been years. Had it been since that affair when she was just a child? Yes. She remembered. Her brother announced her that day . . . at the banquet. Her mother told her to stay put. Why did she run? Her brother, yes, he was the one to say her name. She could remember it now. He was young then. That was before. Before the hour that changed everything.

Like a storm cloud rolling in, the odor of hair powdering—the mix of wheat flour and fine white clay—ignited an inner upheaval. She paused on the third step.

Please, Mary, don't collapse, her mind begged her.

A sea of eyes was upon her. The images that she feared most re-emerged. She was afraid. The waves. The slippery earth. If she had only reached for the flower . . .

She drew quick breaths.

Not again. Not tonight. "There will be no what-ifs." She heard her sister's voice in her head.

"Protect. Save." She remembered what her father had told her. "As a beacon in the darkness. Be the light."

The bright and lively interlude of "The Arrival of the Queen of Sheba" by Handel began to play. Sir Tenoe's face—she could see the dancing master at the back of the crowd. He stood there looking proudly at her. His scar shone clear from the light of the window. At least do this for *him*. Mary focused on Tenoe's scar as she continued her descent to the grand foyer. Not a person's face turned from her, including the hero's. She could see him looking, out of the corner of her eye. She hoped her expression did not give away too much of her inner struggle. Her brother received her at the base of the stairs and walked her to the man of honor this evening.

There he was, the hero of the South before her. How handsome he looked. How brave.

"Colonel George Washington, may I introduce you to my dear sister."

"Miss Mary Eliza Philipse." The colonel used her birth name as few ever did.

Her eyes remained on his shoes. Not a speck of mud.

He placed his hand below hers, rugged to dainty. She felt him bring her hand to his lips. She raised her eyes to his.

"Your presence affords me unspeakable pleasure."

Blue.

His eyes were blue, with a hint of gray.

The feel of his lips was upon her right hand. How thankful she was that in her haste she had forgotten to slip on her lace gloves. With his warm breath on her bare skin, she decided if she could remain here in this very position for her entire life, she would be contented.

She realized she would have to respond to his greeting with words, if she could find them. She hadn't thought of a response. She knew much about him from reading his journal over and over. She could have recited every line of his writings. A plan should have been made for this moment. There was not. So, with dimpled cheek, she curtsied unhurriedly, trying to regain some type of composure.

You must say something, she thought. Her eyes shifted to the ground. If they had done justice to her state of mind, they would have revealed abounding passions. "And it is my presence to be in your pleasure, Colonel Washington."

Teeth. He had a wide mouth and his eyes smiled along with his lips. Like a prince, a charming prince. Her charming: Had he arrived? Maybe it was the sweet music, or perhaps it was his blue eyes locked on her, or maybe his strength—which gave her the feeling that he could protect her for an eternity—that made her tingly.

The two, side by side, began their walk to the dining room as the bells were rung for the banquet.

"Mary." His face, she noticed, carried a square jaw, as she had imagined. "What a charming name."

The tingle stretched from the top of her head down to her toes when he used the word *charming*.

"It is the name of my mother," he went on. "The most beautiful woman I've ever known."

She wondered if the surprise showed on her face, because she was surprised that a military commander would speak of his mother with such praise. "How fortunate I am to carry the same name."

"The sum of who I am I owe to my mother. I attribute my success in life to the moral, intellectual, and physical education I received from her."

"My mother's presence is always close to my heart," said Mary. "I hold her memory with the greatest affection." They walked a few more steps in quiet, until Mary felt the need to speak to break the momentary silence. She looked down. "My mother would have admired your shoes."

AN HEIRESS STANDING before him. The belle of the North. Glorious as love. George paused to take in her delightful face, her tender voice, her pleasant manner, her delicate hands, the gentleness of her dark eyes. It seemed she had no idea how lovely she was. How could it be that she carried not a hint of coquetry?

Mary Eliza Philipse.

He decided right then and there that he had never met a lady like her before. He wondered if men lost portions of their hearts to women like her. "A fair-faced vision who carries the scent of wildflowers"— Captain Stewart was correct in his assessment. She smelled as if she had been lying in a garden of lavender blooms. He enjoyed the thought of it. Her complexion, fair and smooth, glowed. Her lips carried a luster of reddish tone. Shiny waves tumbled over her round and quite shimmery shoulders. She carried a softened shape, just as his men described, which looked as if nature had formed it from a perfect mold. Her waist was so small, it seemed his fingers would touch if he wrapped his hands around it. Her gown was highly ornamented, though she needed no embellishment. Her natural grace alone was enough.

George gazed at her once more, trying not to let his eyes linger on

her face for longer than appropriate. He realized he did not know of her mother's passing. His secretary, Kirkpatrick, had assured him he provided every detail—her education level, her circle of friends, her properties. Clearly, he had not learned enough.

The banquet room was masterly appointed for the occasion, decorated with deep red and blue flower bouquets and with affluence displayed in every direction he looked. The beauteous one stepped in first and motioned to a chair at the head of the table, to where his back would be to the hearth. It would not have been his choice of a seat, as he always followed his rule: *Set not yourself at the upper of the table; but if it be your due or that the master of the house will have it so, contend not, lest you should trouble the company.*

His eyes remained on her as he was seated in a fancifully carved mahogany chair with such an extreme polish that it appeared wet. Then he faced the table, which was so laden with dishes, it was impossible to see a square inch of the table covering. Set in the most orderly fashion were blue-and-white porcelain plates with gold lining the rims. Each was filled with extravagant fare. Small dishes—there must have been more than fifty of them—covered the table. The loaf of oysters grabbed his attention.

How his life had changed. Tonight he was dining with the most well-to-do family in New York, quite possibly the wealthiest family across all of the colonies. It was not long ago that dining meant using a forked stick to cook food hunted from the woods and a large chip of bark acted as his plate.

"Are you comfortable in your seating by the fire?" Beverley asked, taking his seat.

"Humbled and quite appreciative." George moved his chair closer to the table. "Happy's he that gets the berth nearest the flame."

"Have your other hosts not treated you with polite attention?" Frederick's brow furrowed as he sat down.

"My journey has been an arduous one."

"Arduous?" inquired Frederick.

"At times I had not slept above three nights or four in succession

in a bed. I would lay down upon a little hay straw fodder or bearskin whichever was to be had . . ."

Frederick raised his glass of Madeira to make another toast. "Let your days ahead be filled with hospitality and friendship. To the hero of the South!"

"Hear! Hear!" The guests raised their glasses to salute him. The heiress, sitting next to Frederick, did so as well. George's thoughts turned to the feel of her smooth skin on his lips.

"Let us enjoy the banquet before us," announced Frederick.

The mix of delicious aromas whetted his appetite. George had not eaten since the journey began at dawn. He was eager to satisfy his hunger. As he brought oysters to his tongue, one rule of civility proved challenging: *Put not another bite into your mouth till the former be swallowed. Let not your morsels be too big for the jowls.* Bite by bite, each magnificent taste finally settled his cravings. Tonight, though, he hoped hunger would be appeased not just in his stomach; it had been so long since he felt a woman's touch.

This night 'twas truly a feast for his senses.

The sounds of tinkling crystal interrupted his thinking. His glass was filled to the rim immediately after each sip. The dishes were cleared. To his astonishment, new plates of blue-and-white porcelain were set down. He'd believed dinner was completed. A suckling pig was placed at the head of the table, a dressed goose at the foot, and along the table's edges sat four roasted chickens. In the center were trays of crayfish, shrimp, and stewed dishes of hare, duck, boar, and lamb. Add to those, additional plates of pickled mackerel, mashed potatoes topped with a ragoo, partridges with truffles, and breads of many kinds. George was urged by Frederick to try the catsup.

"May we add our congratulations on your promotion, Colonel Washington," said Frederick. "We are glad to hear of your accolades in His Majesty's Army."

"Your success and good fortune are the toasts of every table, Colonel," Beverley added. "Every officer, I hear, is willing to venture under your command."

"Be not deceived," said George. "I do not believe myself equal to such an appointment."

"Is there a place for you and your companies to feast?" Frederick took a buttered biscuit.

"The men must prepare their meals in their barracks. Each is equipped with a kettle and not much more for cooking."

The heiress appeared astonished by his comment.

"Where have they set your post?" questioned Frederick.

"In Winchester. I have been honored to form a regiment made up of sixteen companies there."

The color of rose juxtaposed against ivory as a gentle blush bloomed on the belle's cheeks.

"Where have you arrived from this day?" she asked.

He listened to how she pronounced each word, with a sweet inflection at the end of the question. "We were stopped at Laurel Hill."

"Laurel Hill?" Her radiant face tilted.

"Of New Jersey," he replied, "but not to gather laurels, except of the kind which cover the mountains." It was a pun, and not a very good one at that. Still, Mary Eliza Philipse smiled.

THE DINNER PLATES were cleared away, as was the tablecloth. A new fabric that sent up a scent of mint replaced it. Then came dessert. Trumpets led a procession. A chef wearing a toque and sporting a curled mustache entered with cooks carrying plate after plate of confections. Three dozen types of sugary eatables, maybe more, were presented for the guests to try. Tipsy cakes, pies of gooseberry, orangeado, plum, cherry, and every type of pudding made their way into the dining room.

The chef then explained in a French accent the next dish he was carrying—enticing snowballs. George ate not one but two. He made note, as well, of the numerous French-speaking attendants. It seemed the family paid no mind to the war. In addition, every race was represented in the household; a female cook entered and walked directly to the heiress, with a small bowl of pudding.

Mary Eliza Philipse gave her an appreciative look.

George watched closely as the heiress kindly smiled and whispered, "I thank you. The desserts, the feast, all divine."

"As is the company," the lady quietly responded.

The guests arose upon completion of their feast and, led by Frederick, were escorted out of the room. Mary Eliza Philipse waited in her chair. George, with belly full and spirit soaring, approached her. With a shy smile, she placed her hand inside his arm, which he had outstretched to receive her.

GEORGE'S SMILE PIERCED Mary like a fork into sugar cake. Not a hint of vanity was demonstrated in his countenance.

Colonel George Washington.

She realized she had never met another man like him in all her life.

Her favorite aria from Handel's opera *Radamisto* was being performed in the music room.

"Do you play?" she asked.

"An instrument?"

She found this funny. She nodded.

"I cannot raise a single note on any one of them."

How honest of him, she thought. "And there is not a tutor in New York who would feel pride in naming me a student under his tutelage." She would be truthful as well. "Of this, I am confident."

The aria was reaching its apex. As the countertenor lingered over the words *la vendetta*, he seemed to unleash a revenge on the song itself. In overemotional fashion, a tear came to the singer's eye as he presented the chorus in a sensational manner.

"Nothing is more agreeable, and ornamental, than good music. Of what is he singing?"

"The name of it is 'Ombra Cara,'" she answered. "An enchanting woman survives death after being thrown into furious waters. She tries to escape a tyrannical ruler who desires to possess her as a city is burned to the ground in a war over her affection."

"Quite a tale."

"In the end, the strings intertwine and suddenly, her first love, her true, returns for her. "

"The power of melody. It is enough to soothe even the ferocity of the wild beast."

"Love, too, can wash away the dust of the soul with just one note." What was she saying? Why would you twice use the word love? she questioned herself. It must have been the wine. Mary had already had more than a glassful while dining.

She was thankful for her cousins walking toward her. Eva carried herself in an attractive blue-green gown that outspread wide below the waist. Silk bows lined the top of it. Her hair was worn in a tuck-and-cover style, where the thin floral crown showed in the front but was wrapped with her dark hair around the back. The rest of her waves hung down. Their cousin Margaret appeared exquisite with her blond, almost white, loose curls, some placed atop her head, the others flowing down her back. Her ivory skin was as flawless as her choice of a silk gown in a pale pink fabric with hand-embroidered bleeding heart flowers throughout.

"Colonel, my cousins Miss Eva Van Cortlandt and Miss Margaret Kemble."

"Pleased to make your acquaintances," he said, after which he politely excused himself and moved toward his officers.

Eva's big eyes opened wide. She leaned toward Mary's ear. "Oh, he is lost in adoration. Unable to surrender the view that is our charming Polly."

"He still looks this way?" Mary asked without turning toward him.

"As if trapped in intoxication." Eva then took their hands and formed a circle. "It is true, is it not, Polly, that he is a temple sacred by birth?"

"He is quite delicious, isn't he?" Mary welled up with excitement.

Eva peeked past her. "Built by hands divine."

Margaret's head tilted slightly toward him. Her ringlets followed suit. "And it doesn't appear he thinks of himself as such."

"One of the very few men of such caliber." Eva sighed.

"Polly, are you aware of how dazzling you look tonight?" Margaret gave her a broad smile.

"What I am aware of is the desperate need to take a breath. I am ever so tightly squeezed up in this gown."

The three burst into laughter as Mary separated from them and walked toward the doorway. In need of detaching her train for dancing and wanting a bit of air, she moved through the banquet room, where the dining coverings were being removed. Exquisite mahogany wood with a heavily shined surface was displayed. Silver trays of fruit were placed upon it.

Around the table, three little boys, the children of the elite, raced in a competition of sorts. "Good evening, gentlemen," Mary greeted them.

They halted, appearing frightened of a scolding, but then grinned wide. "Good evening to you, Miss Philipse," Robert and Henry Livingston, along with John Jay, announced in something like unison.

Henry broke from the group and ran over to her. "Tonight is a night to delight and not fight."

Mary reached down to hug him. "My poet Henry—that is a handsome rhyme. One day your poetry will be known around the world. I'm certain of it. And yes, boys, no fights tonight."

"Yes, Miss Philipse." They quickly recommenced their races in the parlor.

As she rounded the corner toward the powder room, she noticed the faint smell of mud. This stopped her. A forceful jerk tugged her backward. A man's arm grabbed her about the waist like a snake capturing its prey. The other arm wrapped around her neck, pressing her face against his moistened cheek. Each of his fingers, even the crooked one, was covered in metal rings.

"Your allure shakes me." The voice sounded sharp as a razor's edge. "Had you forgotten to send me an invitation, dearest Polly?"

She caught a glimpse of raven black hair covered in hair powder; the clay dust emitted a foulness that forced her into a motionless state.

Her mouth suddenly went dry. She did not scream. She could not say a word.

"Have you not read the many correspondences I have sent to you? You are the one I desire to possess, merchandise more precious than rubies, finer than gold."

She detested every word that came from the man's loathsome tongue.

"You leave me always aching for more of you. I will remain here until I hear thy word. *Yes* will be the only one I will accept."

No one would have believed it. James Jay—the physician, a member of polite society, his father, the esteemed Peter Jay. But Mary knew the real James. The signs of his rage. His erratic behavior. The twitch in his eye.

Her eyes shifted downward to see his boots, which were specked with dried mud. The heels had long gilt spurs attached to them. They made jangling sounds when he took three steps back to force her into the corner of a storage room. She was desperate for release. With his hand upon her chin, he pressed the side of her face onto his lips.

"*Laissez-la partir!*" A shout came from the north-side doorway.

Jay's hands held on tightly to her. "A threat from a French cook? Go back to your kettle!"

She could feel the movement of muscles in his wet face.

A plate shattered across the floor at the doorway. It was Temperance who'd thrown it, and who now appeared with fury upon her face. François grabbed a broken piece of the porcelain up from the floor and leveled it at James Jay.

"Let her go!" Temperance shrieked.

"*Je vous egorge!*" François shook the shard. "I will cut you!"

"Your kind, I detest." James's obsession with the wine cup was evident from his breath. "Nothing more can you take from me and my family."

"You talk of nonsense," François said, moving closer to him.

Temperance yelled, "Let her go!"

"You, the French, you stole everything. You think we don't remem-

ber your kind's Edict of Fontainebleau, confiscating my family's land, forcing them to run from your evil country. Now you wish to take my love from me. I will not have it." James's hands wrapped around Mary's neck.

François lunged, drawing blood from James's arm.

He writhed in pain, long enough to allow Mary to wrangle from his tight grip.

With blood dripping onto his sleeve, James looked up in a rage. "I will have my revenge!"

Frederick raced in. "What have you done?"

James raised a fist in the air, red trailing down his arm. "Your cook cut me!"

Frederick placed his body in between Mary and James. "Leave at once!" he shouted at James.

"Leave? Lord Philipse, that will never happen," countered James. "I am family, your cousin. Did you not know?"

"You will never be part of this family. You will never, never be one of us."

"Your dear little sister agreed to be mine long ago."

'Twas true, she was only a child then. Mary remembered feeling pain. He wouldn't let go. She couldn't scream. "You will be my queen, and I your king" were his words to her. She finally agreed to marry him so he would release her.

"I proposed myself a partner for life to her. And, my love, my Polly, you agreed."

"Never will you have her, James." Frederick moved Mary farther away, using his body to block her. "You have been rejected many times."

"Address me with the proper title. I am Doctor James Jay, a student of medicine."

"You shame the name of your family, you insolent drunkard, mutton-headed schemer. Poison spills from your being."

"Your family stole from mine what rightfully belongs to the family of Jay. This house, your land, the whole of your belongings—they are mine!"

"Your words excite a hateful passion. I tell you, leave now or I will bring in the guards."

James staggered toward the door. As he moved past Mary, he leaned into her. "I want all of it, including you, Polly."

She felt unsteady as the door closed behind James. A sensation took hold of her; it felt as if the room were moving, spinning about her head. She could barely hear Frederick's words. Her sight blurred.

"We will be sure to assign guards at the door," her brother's words echoed. "He will never get near her again. He will never get any of our attention ever again."

Blackness overcame her.

"LIKE SILENT POETRY," announced the dancing master to the assembled in the ballroom. "Let your dance be a captivating sight as the musicians play to your ears' delight. Strong charms, each gentleman will soon impart as he makes a passage straight to each belle's heart."

"My hope is that you enjoy the evening," Beverley said to George. "I wouldn't have suggested a ball to welcome you to Philipse Manor, Colonel, if I was not aware of your prowess with the minuet."

"I shall let others lead the way." George did feel at ease on the dance floor. The minuet was one he knew well. He had experience with high society in Virginia, it was true, and he patterned his models and refined his sentiments among that colony's elite men and women. While not one of them, he spent enough time with them to understand what was needed to elevate one's position. His late half brother, Lawrence, had married Anne Fairfax. She welcomed George into her family, which was of the superior class.

Many a night she would take to the piano and encourage him to learn to dance. Anne's brother, George William Fairfax, became a dear friend, and Fairfax's wife, Sally, would serve as partner to the new dancer. On a night like tonight, George was glad of the many dances he shared with her. "A man who cannot dance is a man who

cannot desire a place in polite society," she would say to him. Tonight, unlike the simple piano that played in the Fairfax house, there were a dozen instrumentalists and a dancing master.

Tonight nearly fifty couples would fill the dance floor. Moving through the crowd proved difficult, especially past the belles who seemed to be vying for his attention. George felt a woman's hand brush along his back as he stood with his officers. "A touch of him. I got a touch of him!" that woman exclaimed to her female companions. He recognized her. He noticed her hair before, off the side of the cobblestone street as he entered the town. It climbed higher now. Prodigiously powdered, the pile was white and spotted with pearls. There was even a white feather sticking out.

"We have invited fine beauties on your account, gentlemen." Beverley addressed Stewart and Mercer, who were standing by George.

"I believe one looked my way." Stewart sighed. "Which one to choose?"

"I'll take them all." Mercer winked at the females. "Oh, ladies of easy virtue, be mine. I'd like to tip the velvet of that one." He pointed to the woman with the highest pile of hair. Mercer and Stewart walked away from George and Beverley.

"Encouraging looks given for no other purpose than to draw men to make overtures that the women may then reject," remarked Beverley. "They are pretty pictures, best kept suspended in frames."

George looked around the room, not at the coquettes, but for the heiress. She was nowhere in sight.

MARY FELT COOL dampness on her forehead. She opened her eyes slowly to Temperance's face, which was upside down from hers and looking at her with concern. Mary lay on the floor with a rag on her head, which was nestled into Temperance's lap.

"Cancel the pleasure ball." Frederick was speaking with urgency to the estate steward, Leonard Angevine. "Alert the dancing master and have him make the announcement."

"What shall we have him announce, Lord Philipse?" asked Angevine.

"Due to an unforeseen family matter, we must cancel—no, no, we must delay the ball due to an emergency of unexpected nature."

"Please, Frederick," Mary pleaded.

"Polly!" Frederick rushed over to her.

She took his hand in hers. "I beg you, do not. Not tonight. Not again will I be the cause of embarrassment for our family." Mary wiped her own tears. She inhaled deeply to calm herself. She stood up, straighter than she ever had before, and looked directly at her brother. "Tonight, Frederick, we dance."

"DANCING THE MINUET will commence." The dancing master in his fanciful cap struck up the orchestra. "We welcome to the dance floor our hero of the South, our man of honor, Colonel George Washington."

George, knowing correct manners, bowed to him. The positioning of first of the ball was a heavy responsibility. Customarily, the best dancer was granted this position in order to lead dances throughout the evening. He knew he was certainly not the best of this group, but confident he could get by. As he awaited the announcement of his dance partner, he kept in mind another rule: *The gestures of the body must be suited to the discourse you are upon.* He knew those well, having studied not only the rules of motion but also the rules of standing: *The weight of each foot resting equally to the other and substantially separated; straight must the knees be; there must be a moderate bend at the wrist as the hands fall freely; the head must be slightly turned to the right to complete a gallant deportment.*

"And Miss Mary Eliza Philipse," announced the dancing master.

The grand doors of the ballroom opened. Mary's brother escorted the belle into the room, and she moved delicately beside him.

APPEAR DELICATE IN your walk, she reminded herself as she moved through the throng of guests. This was a mocking age she lived in,

and ne'er did a day pass that the other ladies did not take advantage of it.

"They've placed Polly as the first to dance with him?" She heard the angry whispers from bigheaded Bernadette Clara Belle.

Be poised, Mary reminded herself.

"One step and he will skip to his next dancer," Bernadette sneered.

Pay no mind to all the eyes watching, she kept telling herself.

"An heiress who dances with the grave digger."

Their insults on this night did not linger. She brushed past them, standing regal, refined. She wanted to be brave, strong, fearless, just like the hero in the pages of the *Journal of Major George Washington*.

"Sir Tenoe." She curtsied in a show of respect to him. He reciprocated with a bend at the waist. She knew the rules of walking: *Carry a genteel attitude. The hands shall hold the petticoat with the fingers slightly apart; there shall be no stiffness about the body, while the motion shall have a minor swing to it to avoid the appearance of stiffness, and the foot shall always move ahead of the body, the whole of your being carried with ease.*

The beaux and belles who crowded the floor parted to allow her to the center. Her charming was before her with a gallant deportment. George faced her from the middle of the floor. She had to look down for a moment. Her nerves were getting the best of her. His polished shoes. No mud. She raised her eyes to his face. Then she saw them: faded scars on George's cheeks—from sickness, she surmised. She hadn't noticed them earlier.

He was wounded, she thought. Just like me.

The two turned toward Frederick to show the outward sign of respect to the host. George bowed. Mary curtsied. She turned to George and curtsied to him; his lips curved as he bowed to her. The music commenced. His eyes fixed a stare on her. A tingle reached from the top of her head to the tips of her toes, for she knew what was coming next: her left hand was upon his right hand and his touch made her quiver as the music took them into its alluring wave, with eyes on each other, hands touching, hands releasing, stepping in close, stepping back in three-quarters time, right foot, left foot, right again, left

toe points, three taps, lefts hands touch. The rhythm took her to a place far from the crowds; she even had to glance at her feet, for she sensed she could be floating.

Joyous applause followed as the instrumentalists finished the song. Broad and proud smiles emerged on the faces of her siblings.

"In honor of our Virginia officers," the dancing master trumpeted. "Strike up the Sir Roger de Coverley!"

The excitement was palpable as the crowd rushed to form two lines, gentlemen in one, ladies in the other.

As they waited for the beats to begin, Mary grabbed hold of Eva's hand, and Eva grabbed hold of Margaret's.

"Is that a quill in that woman's head?" asked Margaret as she leaned over to look at Mary.

"The ink must have landed on her face," added Eva.

Bernadette couldn't have added any more paint to her eyes, nor any more white powder to her face. Red rouge applied in large round circles covered her entire cheeks. Her eyebrows were daubed in a black color.

"It's just a feather," said Mary. "I think."

Mary stood opposite George as they formed the beginning of the lines. They would not come together for this dance. Instead, she met the gentleman from the back of the line, Sheriff Delancey, who danced his way to her. As the sheriff moved to meet her at the center of the two lines, she directed her sights to George, desiring another look into his eyes of blue with a touch of gray.

George, at the head of the gentlemen's line, met the heap of hair above a painted face at the center. The dance continued, with couples swinging at the center and adding a dos-à-dos.

Bernadette was so giddy around George, it made Mary cross.

The last couple formed an arch and the dancing couples moved through it. A roar continued in the ballroom as Tenoe carried to the center of the dance floor a chapeau bras. The dancing master presented it to Mary. She knew just what to do. The dance was called "the Magic Hat." She asked the female dancers to remove a personal

article to deposit into it. Susannah added a glove; Eva, a handkerchief. Bernadette pulled that feather item from her hair and placed it into the hat. Mary noticed a bit of ink at the tip. It was a quill! Then Mary walked over to a woman who was standing by herself near the wall, Elizabeth Rutgers, a handsome woman who tragically became a widow a year prior, this being her first outing since her husband's passing. Dressed in a plain blue gown, she kindly looked at Mary and dropped in her fan. By the time each of the ladies had provided an item, the hat was filled to the top. Mary now asked the beaux to remove one article from the hat and dance with the lady to whom it belonged. Captain Stewart chose the handkerchief. He smiled as he met Eva, who reciprocated with a grin.

Mary stepped over to Frederick, who stood guard at the door, flanked by half a dozen footmen to his left and right, and offered the hat to him. His expression showed that he was not pleased to be asked to take to the dance floor. "You know the rules, brother. The dance's leader is to be obeyed, with no refusal permitted." She watched as he began to lift the fan from the hat. "Elizabeth Rutgers!" Mary was elated he did not pick the quill.

As he traipsed over to the woman, Mary noticed a bit of nature with its stem caught in the ribbon of his peruke. A dried maple leaf. Had it been on his head all night? she wondered. Since he went to see her in the cellar and said to her, "I want to see the you that used to be"? He tried for so long with her. She plucked the leaf and, not knowing where to put it, quickly tucked it below the items in the hat.

The dance exhilarated the guests, which is what Tenoe told her he expected. He urged her to allow him to try something new and attractive. This was one of the dances he suggested. "Every dancing master wishes to have the honor of promulgating that which is unique," he had told her. "If appreciated by guests, a dance becomes copied time and time again, and that is what we strive for." It seemed he was correct, as the ladies stood anxiously awaiting their item to be chosen.

Mary made sure the men turned their heads aside as their hand

reached in. Mercer got a bit of ink on his when he chose Bernadette's item. George, she approached last.

Only a leaf was left. George inspected the hat thoroughly, which made her laugh. He placed it into his hand and reached out for hers as the dancing master called out the allemande. Mary tried to remember each of the steps of the Baroque dance as the orchestra played Bach's Magnificat in D Major. She relaxed as she stood near George. As the two danced, the leaf remained in his hand until it settled between their palms as they whirled about the room. Their bodies approached each other's ever so closely.

WHEREVER SHE MOVED, a trace of wildflowers trailed behind her, calling him to follow. It seemed there could have been no others in attendance, for the heiress occupied his attention completely. They danced the English minuet with its sink and rise steps in the form of a bourée and a half coupé. George knew this version, distinct from the other forms of this dance. He enjoyed watching redness appear on the heiress's cheeks when she circled instead of stepped. He wondered if she had any idea how prettily she moved, even when she made a misstep.

His enjoyment was ne'er interrupted. The hours passed in delight. The courante, the sarabande, the gigue, and half a score of additional minuets were danced between the two, followed by country dances. Even after the clock struck midnight, their feet remained on the floor, each dance taking them into and out of each other's touch.

"The Serpent will now be danced," announced Tenoe. "Colonel Washington, will you lead the way?"

George nodded to him. "Will you kindly follow me, Mary Eliza Philipse?"

"It would be my pleasure, Colonel." Such a gaiety appeared in her countenance.

He strolled with her to the corner of the room, gently set his hands on her bare shoulders. Her skin was smoother than he ever thought skin could be. He slowly turned her toward the wall. He lined the other women behind her, leaving space between each one. The gen-

tlemen, formed into a loose chain, moved quickly between the ladies in a serpent's pattern until he reached Mary. A clap of Tenoe's hands had each of the men dance with the lady closest to him.

George knew the heiress must have had numerous offers from these men. He noticed Sheriff Delancey twice had the pleasure of dancing with her, but now he seemed much chagrined. George heard the displeased sheriff growl within close proximity to him as they were lined up in the chain. "Is there not a time this dancing master gives us a chance to dance with her for longer than a refrain?"

"Does the left cheek dimple?" asked a man with hair that flared out like a bell, who was standing with Delancey. "I must know the answer to a question so simple."

To this, George moved his thoughts to her dimple. Does her left cheek dimple as well as the right? he wondered.

The final dance was upon them. George asked Mary Eliza to join him for one last minuet as the instrumentalists played Vivaldi's "Spring" from *The Four Seasons* with vigor.

AFTER BEING ENCHANTED by him all evening, Mary surmised she knew what passion must feel like. His polite manner, handsome air, and cheerful demeanor—she had never seen this before in a man, or maybe had never noticed. It seemed he was ever grateful for the chance to dance with her. If only he knew how very grateful she was to dance with him, the charming prince, her charming. If the night could have gone any better, she did not know how.

She leaned into him and whispered, "Your feet have not left this dance floor." She let her hands fall upon his ever so lightly.

"I'm honored to have shared this night with you. I am hopeful I may be blessed to increase our friendship."

Mary curtsied to her hero of the South as the song came to an end.

Hurriedly, Frederick stepped toward her. "Polly, may I have your attention for a moment?" The two walked toward the doorway. "Jones Irwin is at the door. I told the guards to have him return tomorrow, but he has shown us a letter written by you that required his arrival here at this time."

"This is correct."

"Polly, it is four o'clock in the morning."

"Precisely. A payment is required of you, Frederick. I shall meet you in the library." She moved quickly out of the banquet hall, through the foyers, into the parlor, through a doorway and into the library, where she had placed the paperwork inside a closet on the north side of the room. She had been careful with the document and had made sure to have a quill at the ready on the desk.

A man of medium height with a bald, heavy head, and swollen eyelids, walked in the room alongside Frederick with a look of ire upon his shriveled face. A grimace spoiled the verbal greeting he gave Mary. As Mary placed down the papers, she spoke into Frederick's ear: "I expect the full amount."

Frederick read the contract. He cast a stern glance at her.

Mary heard a huff from Irwin before she left them alone. She headed into the ballroom,

She passed George and kindly nodded, but at this moment she could not give him any more of her time. She asked Tenoe for his assistance in the parlor. As they neared the library together, loud voices could be heard. Angevine, who had been guarding the door, opened it to allow the dancing master to enter.

With arms crossed, Mary paced. Her finger went into the air, calculating the numbers again. She hoped she had tallied the amount correctly. She was quite anxious to see if her ruse had worked. She instructed Angevine to open the door a bit as she put her ear close to it.

"Mr. Michael Tenoe, the Philipse family has fulfilled your obligations in total," she heard Frederick announce. "This day, I can say, you are a free man."

Not a word came from Tenoe in response. A pause followed. She could hear footsteps briskly moving closer to her. The double doors swiftly opened as Sir Tenoe rushed out. He stopped in front of her. In that very spot, he fell to his knees.

"You have given me life!" Tenoe reached out for Mary's hands.

"You have given me life!" Without any ability to control his emotion, Mary bent down to meet him and soon was also on her knees, embracing him. "Miss Philipse," he cried out. "I am forever in your debt!"

Teardrops flowed down his scarred cheek.

She cried, too. A healing rain to her soul.

Be the light, Mary Eliza.

Yes, Papa.

Part II

—◆◆◆—

The Courtship

Chapter Eight

⬦•⬦

An Heiress's Prayer

For be assured a sensible woman can never be happy with a fool.

—GEORGE WASHINGTON

The chain hanging from Mary's arm tugged a bit, leaving an indented mark upon her skin. She paid no mind to that, for she adored what it held. Connected to the silver links was a small psalmbook covered in blue velvet and smelling of dried flowers. Lady Joanna had carried it with her to services every Sunday. Few possessions did Mary treasure as much as this one. Today she let it dangle as she set herself upon the dark wood kneeling board inside St. John's Church. Although the years had passed, the memories, the moments she had shared with her mother, she kept close to her heart. Mary closed her eyes to remember her mother's lyrical voice. "Every daughter is her own kind of flower," Mama used to say. "What kind of flower am I?" she remembered asking her.

The reverend's prayer broke her thoughts: "'For before the harvest, as soon as the bud blossoms/And the flower becomes a ripening grape,/Then He will cut off the sprigs with pruning knives/

And remove and cut away the spreading branches/They will be left together for mountain birds of prey,/And for the beasts of the earth;/And the birds of prey will spend the summer feeding on them,/And all the beasts of the earth will spend harvest time on them.'"

Light came through the stained-glass windows, bathing the altar in a prismatic glow. Mary beheld the lofty space. The Philipse siblings built this church. Each of them offered ideas for its interior. Frederick asked that vast semicircle arches be designed at the entrance between the large wooden Ionic columns to welcome visitors. Mary suggested the chamber organ with tall pipes and huge bellows; she loved the heavenly sounds that came from it. Susannah was quite specific that carvings of angels must be holding painted flowers to help introduce the altar's grandeur.

Of course, there was the family's other house of worship, which sat twelve miles north of the manor, at the place where the Pocantico River flowed into the Hudson. "The oldest ecclesiastical edifice in all of the New York Colony" is how Papa used to describe it. As a girl, Mary would clutch his hand tightly as he provided tours to guests. In 1697, her great-grandfather laid the pulpit with his own hands. The first Frederick's initials were engraved into it. And Mary always admired the shape of the little chapel with its gambrel roof that spread out at the bottom. The words *Si Deus Pro Nobis, Quis Contra Nos?* could be found etched inside a bell in the belfry. It meant "If God be for us, who can be against us?" Papa showed this to her to help her find strength.

Mary adored the small church. As she grew older, though, her deep devotion could not help her overcome the hollowness she felt each Lord's Day, for next to the chapel was the ground where they buried her mother, her father, and her sister Margaret. It was her brother who made the decision to build a new church, a grander one, that would allow Mary to worship free of heartache bathed in silent tears.

As she knelt this day, she opened to the back of the book, placed

her hand on the pressed forget-me-not painted pale blue, and privately prayed:

> Lord, I am shattered and I am frayed,
> I pray what's dead inside me can breathe again,
> I pray to know when my struggle will cease,
> I pray to know when my spirit can rise from the ashes,
> Use me, Lord, to be a beacon in the darkness,
> Let me, Lord, be the light.

Mary leaned forward to gaze across the aisle past Susannah and Beverley. George was there. Even kneeling, he could almost look Frederick, standing, in the eye.

"Polly, Polly." Susannah tugged at her sleeve. "We must go. The service has concluded."

Ariose singers raised their voices in song from under the cupola. Mary closed the psalmbook and adjusted the clasp, careful to keep the delicate flowers secure.

Following Susannah and Beverley, Mary, dressed in a deep red woolen cape, made her way down the long aisle and out the front door and onto the stone path. With one hand, Mary placed the hood over her head as she stood by her sister, who was complimenting ladies on the majestic costumes they had worn to the ball. She hardly heard the words, for she felt George's eyes fixed on her. She clutched her hands inside a red feathered muff as she turned toward him. George stood at a distance, with a backdrop of the church's elegant stone facade, appearing like nobility. She peeked around, thinking he must be staring at someone else. A state of uncertainty about his intentions remained, for they had not even bid each other good night.

Susannah disturbed her moment. "I have a word to tell you. Something that I have not heard from my true, since he forbade me to utter a breath about the conversation."

"Regarding the colonel?"

"Yes, my dear Polly, about your George."

Your George. Susannah's reference ushered in that same tingle that she had experienced the night before. Just as her sister was to reveal information that Mary desperately wanted to hear, a man startled her.

"Such a radiant day is before us, Miss Polly." Sheriff Delancey's belly strained against the buttons of his tight vest.

"Mr. Delancey, a good day to you." She hoped the conversation would be short.

His chin rose a bit higher as he spoke, looking down his nose to address her. "If I may, in correction, I carry the rank of captain." He grabbed hold of one of the many medals he was wearing—there were far too many around his neck. "Upon my return from private studies abroad at Eton, then in Cambridge at my father's alma mater, as you know, Corpus Christi College, I was admitted to the esteemed Lincoln's Inn." He showed her another medal. "Following my studies of law there, the army saw fit to have me named to the prestigious position of captain." He lifted a different medal. "And, of course, the assignment of sheriff of our town was inevitable."

Mary wondered when this conversation would end.

He continued after a brief pause. "And I'm sure you are well apprised that my father has granted a charter for the creation of a fine institution. King's College is the name."

"I've read the news." She was thrilled to hear of the new institution being formed; however, she needed to turn away from him or else be fixated by his one raised eyebrow. She wondered if it was permanently lifted, or was it voluntary, like a pretentious move of some sort? Did he think it made him appear more refined?

"King's College, established to enlarge the mind, improve the understanding, polish the whole man, and qualify him to support the brightest characters in all the elevated stations of life. The first of such kind in all of New York. King George the Second has looked favorably upon our colony."

The eyebrow kept her focus.

"Do you know what is now positioned next to the educational building?"

It seemed he might go on forever.

"The finest racetrack in the entire of America." He answered his own question.

Racetrack. Yes, she had heard this.

"It is my understanding you have a fondness for horses."

"I ride a lovely horse, a fairly spirited one named Willoughby."

"A stable full of them are in my possession. They are English Thoroughbreds that I purchased, the first imported into our colony. You must get a glimpse of them, if your spirit will allow you to be among the crowds of New York City. I will have an invitation sent over to you for the inaugural Subscription Plate taking place on my track, the first horse race in the colony. I acquired a sporting taste for racing while overseas. I get such amusement from watching them run. They are fine specimens."

"Specimens?" She suddenly became miffed—both by his reference to horses and to her spirit. The Delanceys. She was sure they knew everything about her and her past.

"The finest anywhere in our New York."

Mary could take no more of his puffery or his brow. She excused herself, moved away from him, and found Susannah, who was in deep conversation with Beverley. Mary lifted her face upward; a white snowflake landed gently on the tip of her nose, like a kiss from the sky.

Susannah tapped her on the shoulder. "He's asked Beverley for an extended stay."

"He?"

"Your George will be staying another night at the manor and will then ride with us to New York for days more, and, Polly, he just asked Frederick to be granted a proposal to wait upon you. I hope you are not disagreeable to it, since I've already confirmed your agreement to such an interview. What type of tea should be served?"

Mary had not gotten past the word *proposal*. It would be the first

such interview she had granted in quite some time. "I am fond of ambrosia." She could hardly even breathe.

"The food of the gods. Ambrosia and equal parts nectar. That will do. And Polly, I suggested the interview be held this afternoon."

Chapter Nine

—◄•►—

The Interview

I can't say that ever in my Life I suffer'd so much Anxiety as I did in this affair.

—GEORGE WASHINGTON

George waited in the west parlor inside Philipse Manor. He held his black tricorn hat in his hand as he sat alone. He was offered a seat on a hand-carved mahogany bench with a comfortable tapestry pouf. It faced the windowsill, which had a built-in long wooden bench and was also topped with a cushion. Through the opening of the sheer curtains, the sun's rays hit him in the eyes.

That anyone pictured him a suitable match for the heiress, he little anticipated. Doubt flooded his mind. Her attention to him the prior evening justly left him with a glimmer of optimism. She seemed to be fond of dancing with him, or was it just for display? This he had not ascertained. He knew for certain that Mary Eliza Philipse was beset with admiration from a great many men. This morning outside the church left him muddled, for her time was taken up by the sheriff, a man of significant wealth, who undoubtedly meant to seize her surrender.

George was costumed in the most resplendent way he knew possible: a navy and bright red coat, red breeches, white silk stockings, and black shoes with large gold buckles. He was not comfortable in these clothes. The shirt fit tolerably well, yet he would have had the wristbands made narrower, the ruffles deeper by half an inch, and the collar larger by possibly three-quarters of an inch for proper bigness. Whether it was the measurement taken or the fault of the tailor's hands in quick sewing, he did not know. Next time, he would get the measurement himself to be sure.

He followed one of his rules of civility as he checked that he had not a speck of dust on him. *Wear not your clothes foul, ripped, or dusty, but see they be brushed once every day at least and take heed that you approach not to any uncleanness.*

From the music room, a tune with sweet modulation was being played by a trio of instrumentalists. Its melody slowed into a feathery innocence.

He rose as he heard soft footsteps upon the rug. Mary Eliza Philipse arrived in an ivory gown embroidered with cherry-colored flowers throughout. At the bottom of her sleeves hung long laced accents. Around her neck, she wore a thin black velvet ribbon.

"Miss Mary Eliza Philipse. A pleasure to see you again."

"And you, Colonel Washington." Her hair was lifted demurely with a small lace veil to cover the upsweep.

"George." The vision before him nearly took his breath away. "George would be fine."

As she neared him, her pace quickened, causing her to stumble and fall . . . into him. He enjoyed this moment that her shoulder kissed his chest and his hands wrapped around her. This, plus the scent of lavender from her skin, left him feeling weak in her presence.

She straightened and arrived at the window seat, where she gently placed herself. "Colonel George, my apologies."

A throbbing in his heart. George tried not to stare at her. He realized he was as he found his seat.

Tea steeped in a silver pot embossed with the seal of the Philipse family, a lion emerging from a coronet, with its tongue sticking out of its mouth. A delicious hint of citrus combined with coconut emerged as his cup was filled three-quarters. The wisps of steam rose and curled in the sunlight coming through the window.

The conversation lulled before it even began.

He watched as she placed a cloth napkin between the porcelain and her hand. The cup was blue and white and depicted a leaping deer.

"Have you seen the family of fawn by the river?" She began with a nervous twitch in her voice.

He motioned a nay with his head.

"I understand Frederick took you on a tour of the manor property."

The lands seemed to go on infinitely. Lord Philipse gave him much of his time after the church service, providing him a tour of the property, which had taken generations of Philipses and nearly a century to amass through purchase agreements with the Iroquois and Ottawa tribes and good standing with the British Empire. Under their proprietorship were businesses of commercial trade and milling. On the estate were located great revolving wheels and milldams for the growing flour industry, as well as the largest of greenhouses. At the family's dock, he was shown where the sloops brought goods from East India for trade. On the empty parcels, young farmers leased acres, benefiting from the fertile soil. George, too, owned a small parcel in Virginia—his mother's land is how he always thought of it—but few options for farming. It was certainly nothing compared to the Philipses'.

"They just arrived this week." A quaver in her voice emerged. "The deer."

"I did have a view of your library." The sheer volume alone impressed him. Without a formal education, he relied on books. "It seems for all of us a knowledge of books is the basis upon which other knowledge is to be built."

And off she went, articulating her feelings about the literary

genius of the classic authors. "I look upon their writings as fine art." She told him how she spent a significant part of her time in her library. She conversed without hesitation, much different from her first greeting: "It is my presence to be in your pleasure." A darling beginning.

He admired her lips while watching them move as she conveyed details of Herodotus's legend of the Phoenix. "Out of the ashes. Out of nothing comes life," she told him. He listened carefully to the rhythm of her cadence. While her eyes under lengthy lashes fell to her tea, he found himself taken by her voice, which had a melody to it. "According to one of my favorite playwrights, Joseph Addison, 'Reading is to the mind what exercise is to the body,' and I agree."

Her face expressed such serenity, her composure was of the majestic sort, and yes, her frame was exquisite, but it was her mind that strengthened his affection for her. Education perfects what nature's hand creates. Thus distracted in her precious company, George forgot that tea is hot. He cowered after feeling a burn on his lip, almost spilling the beverage.

"Colonel!" Her eyes opened wide. She reached over, touching his knee. "George!" She shook her head. "Was the tea brewed too hot?"

With her hand upon him, he wasn't sure he remembered what pain felt like. "I am fine."

"I will have another pot made."

"This is fine." The concern she showed for him was quite apart from what he was used to. "Please continue."

She moved her hand back to her teacup. Her voice had a flutter to it as she began to speak again. "If I may say, it may be your writing that I have found most profound."

"Mine?"

"Your journal . . . *The Journal of Major George Washington*. I have read it several times."

At no time had he thought anyone would read his scrawl.

"*You've* read my journal?" He had expected only a quick review by Virginia's Colonial governor. "I did not in the least conceive . . . that it ever would be published, or even have more than a cursory reading."

"It was printed in its entirety in our *New-York Mercury*. And not only published here in New York. An acquaintance of mine in London wrote me that she, too, had read it."

Mary Eliza Philipse read his journal! He was informed in a meeting of the General Assembly that it was published. Now he was learning this was not just in Virginia. In no way was the writing prepared for print. "I can do no less than apologize . . . for the numberless imperfections of it. There intervened but one day . . . for me to prepare and transcribe from the rough minutes I had taken."

"I found no imperfection."

She read it. That was done. How could he even offer an explanation? It was printed without his consent, without even time to correct its flaws. "I had no time to offer it in a more proper form or to correct or amend the diction of old."

"I felt quite anxious for your well-being as I read it." She sat quietly listening, her head tilting at times as he began speaking of the wearying journey down one creek where they were obliged to carry their canoes to get over the shoals.

"We remained in the water half an hour or more."

"I was captivated by your bravery through your travails."

This surprised him, that she would have any interest in the journey to the French commandant. He went on about how the horses grew less able to travel every day, with the cold increasing fast and the roads becoming much worse due to the deep snow. She seemed absorbed by his account. "After completing that journey," he added, "I feel I have a strong enough constitution to survive the most difficult of trials." He never had such a long conversation with a woman about such.

"Had you been educated in skills of survival?"

If only he had had such an opportunity. He preferred not to discuss his lack of education in any area. "I saw that every stratagem that the most fruitful brain could invent was practiced. I can't say that ever in my life I suffered so much anxiety as I did in this affair."

She continued to have queries for him as to what he ate, where he slept. She asked specific details about whether there was a heavy current in the river, whether it was dark, and whether he was afraid in the water. He answered each of her questions honestly.

"And as for you, Miss Mary Eliza Philipse, I would imagine you an esteemed writer."

A dimple on her cheek appeared. "I would be honored to offer an affirmation on that account; however, I have written nothing more than a few lines of poetry."

A dimple only on the right. Whether there was one on the left, he still did not know.

"I would enjoy much satisfaction in hearing these lines."

"It would be my honor to share one with you, George, but from what I see behind you, there is a footman awaiting your presence in the foyer."

The time was a few minutes after five o'clock, and the agreeable interview between the pair had gone on for more than one hour. A coach was awaiting the colonel's presence for a meeting scheduled at King's Arms Tavern.

His heart was succumbing to a tender passion. Could it be the infancy of a courtship? He hoped it so.

GEORGE AND BEVERLEY approached the front of the two-story building at the southeast corner of Whitehall and Bridge streets. A sign with a lion and a bird battling for the crown was affixed to the heavy door they opened. The great hall released a scented medley of smoke, rye whiskey, and roasted beans.

It sounded as if the place was serving up a meal of high-volumed swearing inside. The noise helped distract George from his thoughts, which were completely engrossed with the interview with the belle.

The journal. She read it! Without his knowledge, it was printed. He wrote it for the governor's perusal only. He would be sure that type of thing would never happen again. Every word from this point forward would be fit for print. And even with that, their discourse seemed to move in a pleasurable fashion. He wondered if their time together went too well. Affairs of the heart had not ended well for him up to this point. He recalled what he had come to believe—there is no truth more certain, than that all our enjoyments fall short of our expectations; and to none does it apply with more force, than to the gratification of the passions. He believed this firmly . . . up until now.

"How d'ye," said a white-swelled woman in greeting. She was holding a tray of jumballs shaped into an intricate knot. George's stomach jumped. He was fond of spiced shortbread.

"Mrs. Baron, good day." Beverley led the way.

"I've already filled your bumpers at the far corner, gentlemen."

"The first coffeehouse in the New World, Colonel," Beverley said, turning to him, "right here in our New York Colony, dating to the last century."

In a booth sat Mary's brother, who introduced another Delancey, the sheriff's uncle, Oliver. They exchanged mutual salutations. George took a seat next to Oliver.

"Oliver, I must tell you." Frederick sipped his drink. "The colonel can dance better than the finest of gentlemen."

"You're very kind," replied George. "Trained by your friend Fairfax."

"The good governor?" asked Frederick.

"His nephew, George William Fairfax."

"We had the honor of hosting Governor Fairfax, along with George William and his lovely wife, Sally. They spent a number of merry days with us upon the governor's return from the Indian Council at Albany. Sally and Mary got along swimmingly."

A green velvet privacy curtain enclosed the booth.

"George William?" Oliver put down his drink. "The West Indian boy?"

They looked to George.

Frederick added, "His visage appears to indicate a Creole parentage."

"Yes," George stated. "His grandfather served as chief justice of the Bahamas."

Outside of this, not a drop of serious talk ensued during the "meeting" Frederick asked him to attend. Instead, Mrs. Baron brought in a game board, and they took in a hit at backgammon. Frederick beat Oliver twice, and George won two games against Beverley.

"You see this antique." Frederick pointed to Oliver. "He needs your fashion sense, Colonel. A dandy he is not."

"Do you not favor my frock?" Oliver held up a sleeve.

"'Tis pitiful with its trolly lolly upon the arms. Just wretched."

"At least it is made of domestics," Beverley pointed out.

George felt the need to say something witty. "I might add that I do not conceive that fine clothes make fine men, any more than fine feathers make fine birds."

"'Tis true. Take the alarming appearance of the raven," said Frederick. "Yet a bird of valor."

"The raven indeed." Beverley pulled on the bell rope. "Fill up the bumpers!"

Trifling chat continued. George kept in mind the edict from his discipline book: *Drink not too leisurely nor yet too hastily. Before and after drinking, wipe your lips.* A hearty bowl of oysters arrived at the table. Manhattan Island was a seaport with a steady flow of small trade, he was told. The oysters were considered some of the best in the colonies. Another heaping bowl arrived, and then another. *It's unbecoming to stoop much to ones meat, keep your fingers clean and when foul, wipe them on a corner of your table napkin.* He denied himself the pleasure of more than just a few. This was not an occasion for indulging, and certainly not one for slurping oysters from shells. This was an evening to form a proper impression on a family wealthier and more educated. He did not want to appear an unrefined man, especially with the considerable matter still to be discussed.

The night went on without a bit of conversation upon the subject at the forefront of George's mind. 'Twas a meeting that did not satisfy his doubts. Their conversation, yes, was pleasant, however trivial. George wasn't expecting to sleep well this night.

Chapter Ten

———◈◈◈———

A Morning's Light

*The day seems now to dawn upon us, but Clouds and
tempests may yet arise to endanger our Bark . . .*
—GEORGE WASHINGTON

Now, being the morning afterward, Mary felt anxious. She heard
her brother's coach return; it was well into the night, too late to ask
about the particulars of the meeting. Her brother and George—
what was said? Had he even mentioned her? She was so very eager to
find out, but it was only dawn.

"What shall become of me?" Mary spoke the words aloud while
alone in her bedchamber. The Prelude and Fugue No. 2 in C Minor
by Bach was playing in her head. Thoughts of the prior afternoon
swirled about. She attempted as delicate a walk toward him as she
could, wanting to appear genteel. She hoped her footsteps did
not echo too loudly as she was often told they did. She even practiced a sashay with Susannah beforehand. "Step softly," her sister had
advised.

Embarrassment filled her mind as she reflected on the moment
she tripped on the rug. She rushed, for she knew she needed to take her

seat quickly before the tune's up-tempo returned. Her nerves took over. She stumbled left. Her shoulder hit his chest, which did give her a touch of his solidity. Built by hands divine for certain.

Then the moment lasting too long. Could she think of nothing better to ask about than deer? Why not ask about his military position? His expertise in field command? His home in Virginia? No, instead she brings up deer! A thousand and one times she pictured him. Any sense became ruffled in his presence. Just his physical mass appeared as if it could wrap around her and protect her from the world.

She was overly gregarious about literature. She was sure of it. While often her greatest deficiency was conversation, sometimes without the ability to articulate a syllable, she went on without hesitation with him. He hardly said a word on the subject. He just looked at her with a heavy eyelid in a romantic sort of way. Blue with a touch of gray. She sighed at the memory.

She placed her hands on the ornate wallpaper next to the fireplace. The fire from the birch logs rose to warm her hands. Watching the flame, she let her fingers move along the wall as she imagined what it would be like to place her hands around George and feel his lips on hers. Oh heavens! His lips. The tea was too hot. She should have let it cool before it was poured. She hoped he did not suffer a burn.

The stove plate on the floor at the front of her hearth caught her eye. The engraving, an Old Testament passage with no spaces between letters, cast in relief in a slab of iron, was created long ago to ease her mind when sorrow roused a maelstrom of emotion within:

ICHHABEDENRABENBEFOLENDICHZWERS
DIBD   K17C

Today she did not want to give thought to the seventeenth chapter of the Book of Kings and the passage "I have commanded the ravens to feed thee." It reminded her of her broken will and the shrill call of the raven. If it weren't for those birds, she might not have

been rescued those years ago—the day Elbert vanished in the river's current. If not for the raven, she would have been left to die, as she should have been. She didn't like ravens.

She stared at the words for a time. Her eyes moved to a cleanly cut piece of birchwood that she reached down to pick up and used her strength to place over each of the letters in the metal. When the letter *I* was still peering out, she looked upon it with disgust. Heat struck her hands as she maneuvered another log to cover the letters on the metal slab completely.

She was tired of rereading these mournful chapters of her life. Tired of being afraid, of crying herself to sleep, of the nightmares. She wanted to think of the mingling of sweetness and gallantry, of generosity combined with charm, of the man who was helping to restore her one heartbeat at a time. George did not look upon her face with pity, as did so many others. It seemed he might know nothing of her past. When his eyes gazed into hers, she felt alive with the hope of a destiny still to be discovered.

With a newfound breath within, Mary walked toward the window. Her feet stopped at the shelf. She checked the position of the newspaper, the one that had printed George's journal. Relief. The paper was neatly placed, with writing away from the cursed.

Glancing out the window, she espied something unexpected. Temperance and François. What a splendorous sight! This was the first time she ever saw Temperance holding a man's hand. She was always so busy in the kitchen, she seemed to have little time for beaux. Temperance smiled widely as she bid him farewell; she looked happy. So happy. Mary was happy for her. Love. Everyone needs more of it in their lives.

FOOTSTEPS IN PERFECT even tempo sounded from the stairs. A knock at the door. It was Temperance. "Mr. Angevine has asked me to advise you that five articles of correspondence have arrived for you. Ten more arrived yesterday, one of them an invitation delivered by the sheriff himself, which requires a response. He is a persistent one, that Mr. Delancey."

"Captain Delancey." Mary rolled her eyes. "He's made certain I know of his title." The constant requests from him—she paid no mind to them. "Temperance?"

"Yes, Miss Polly."

Mary desperately wanted to ask her about *son petit ami*, but she refrained. "The banquet was more than any of us could have asked for."

"The evening was my pleasure. The food that remained was placed in packages, as you suggested, and taken to the church for distribution to the need-filled." Temperance's face had a beautiful glow to it.

"My gratitude for all you've done."

THE MORNING WAS chilly, requiring Mary to put on a woolen riding coat. Around her waist, the brown fabric fit snugly and fell wide at the hips. She wrapped herself up with a silk scarf. She put on leather gloves and a riding hat. "You are capable of the impossible, Mary Eliza, for you have survived the unthinkable," she murmured, remembering how her father said it with such inspiration. She had promised Papa she would say it each day.

She hurried down the stairs and out to the back porch. The winter air enveloped her in its coolness. The sun was low on a clear horizon. A soft wind blew from the northwest, bringing with it a trace of hay. She practically skipped toward the stables. Riding always made her feel alive. Her breath left a trail a smoke. She could hear Mr. Chew speaking loudly.

"She has a pretty large swelling under her belly."

"In foal, you suppose?" Was that George she could hear with him in the stable?

"I suppose, or occasioned by the buckling of the girths too tight," responded Chew.

George's voice alone made her feel giddy. She regained her composure as she entered.

"Gentlemen, a good day to you both."

"Miss Philipse, good day. Would you kindly take a look at Colonel Washington's horse? I believe her in foal."

Mary was glad of the request, for it kept her from wanting to stare at the commanding presence before her. "May I ask the name of this fine mare of yours?"

For a moment, George seemed incapable of an utterance. After a hesitation, he spoke. "Diamond."

Mary looked at him quizzically.

"Her name. Diamond."

"A lovely name." Mary gently placed her hand on the filly. "Diamond. Shall we place her with the gentle mares on the hill at the north, Mr. Chew?"

"I will see to it. He's named every one of his horses, Miss Polly." Chew pointed to them. "Each of them hath a name."

He names each of his horses, how endearing, she thought.

Mary approached another one of George's horses, a chestnut bay.

"This is Woodfin." George followed her. "A horse that carries the English crown upon his shoulder . . . and my Jack, spotted like a fawn upon the side of his neck. This horse has come a long way after being injured in a fall."

"Oh, the poor creature."

"How did he recover, Colonel?" asked Chew.

George patted the horse. "I followed Gervase Markham's directions as near as I could."

"Markham has the surest ways to cure a horse's malady in the known world," added Chew.

Mary smoothed her hand across its hide. "Which remedy was used to effect a cure, Colonel?"

"I had the horse slung upon canvas and his leg fresh-set—walked him on three legs, with the sound leg tied up very sure with a garget, to require him to put weight on the lame leg. When I let down the lame leg and let it stand on the ground, I heated a little water and clapped it onto the swelling that remained. I then tied up the lame leg again and repeated the same."

"What about the bloodletting, Colonel? Tell her about the bloodletting."

She saw George signal with his hand to Chew to discontinue that conversation.

"Let me introduce you to the rest of the team." He walked with her to the next horse. "Rock was bred in Pennsylvania. Not a spot of white on his dark brown coating, standing strong and fourteen and a half hands high. Prince is near a twin to Rock. This here is Buck. Crab belongs to Captain Mercer. This fine bright bay is the largest horse of the group and has not been named as of yet."

Mary enjoyed his introductions.

"What do you think of the name Bale?"

"That will suit him just fine with his coloring." Mary replied. "A rather tall horse."

"Fifteen hands high, yes," he responded.

He paid such kind attention to his horses, unlike the sheriff, calling them "specimens." How ludicrous!

"And a remarkably large hind, wouldn't you say?" asserted Chew.

"Mr. Chew tells me not to dare ride with the finest equestrian of the colony."

"And who might that be, Mr. Chew?" she asked coyly.

"I must apologize for telling the colonel of your prowess on horseback."

"Very kind of you, Mr. Chew." Mary added another blanket on the horse before lifting herself up to sit sidesaddle. "You're welcome to join me, George."

Not even a second passed before George mounted Woodfin. His buff wool riding coat trimmed in a light green silk was quite elegant with its coattails down the back. She quite liked his fashionable boots, black at the bottoms with brown turn-over tops. She also could not help but notice the outline of a coin in his left-hand pocket and his leg's strength through his buff-colored buckskin breeches, which fit like a second skin on him.

The pair moved the horses in a sedate walk out of the stables. 1W was branded on his horse. W for Washington, she was certain. 1W— the same as Willoughby, but for a different reason. Her father gifted

her this mare. She recalled his words that day: "I have branded her with a one and a *W,* for I have only *one wish* for my Mary Eliza," Papa had said to her. "My wish for you is freedom . . . to let go and allow love to find its way to your heart."

"Would you care to see the deer park?" she blurted out to George. Not again, she thought, after the word was already out of her mouth—deer!

He nodded, not taking his stare off of her.

"Quite easy in hand is your Woodfin," she said to fill the quiet.

"As is your Willoughby."

"I believe in caring for him with tenderness."

"I experienced the tragic loss of a horse in my youth." A sympathetic tone surfaced in his voice. "Now I treat all with a discipline of proper care and a good amount of exercise."

Arriving at the park within minutes, Mary pulled back the reins. They dismounted. Westward, upon a sloping path to the river, the family of deer was before them. "Not a person is allowed near them. Frederick takes fine care of them. Never has one been hunted on our property. They are in their first year. They still carry the light yellowish brown tone."

"And I would imagine the younger they are taken, the easier they are raised." He looked directly into her eyes. "The view adds a romantic and picturesque appearance to the whole."

The use of the word *romantic* impaired her rational thinking.

He began to speak again, thankfully. "And what of the deer distinguishable by the darkness of their color?"

She shook her head to clear her mind. She knew this answer. "From England. Near a dozen have been brought here from different parts of the world. Frederick holds the office of Keeper of the Deer Forests. It's been passed down for generations in our family. He formed our deer park himself, yet he often laments the damage to the gardens."

"At a loss, I would be, in determining whether to give up the shrubs or the deer!"

As she laughed, a ringlet fell to the front of her face. George reached

over, placed his fingers upon it, and took time in moving it away from her cheek.

Happy emotions spun around inside her head. She searched for something to say to him. "Would you care for some dirty chocolate, George?"

She watched him cock his head before he answered yes.

He placed his hands around her waist to assist her in mounting Willoughby. Her lips let out a sigh. After he mounted, she prodded her horse into a canter. The two rode to the manor.

GEORGE WHISPERED TO her after they had dismounted. "I hope you have not forgotten my request."

"What would that be?"

He spoke into her ear. "To hear your lines of verse."

Jitters simmered up inside. She responded the only way she knew how—by moving quickly past him. She walked to the nearest door. It was the one to the lower level. They entered from the side entrance into the dim cellar, which extended under the southern portion of the manor below the west parlor.

What she noticed caught George's attention with light from a small window shining onto them—columns of ten-shilling and ten-pence pieces in neat linear formation, filling the rectangular working tables.

"The counting of toll moneys begins in about an hour from now," she said. "Much work needs to be done, for King's Bridge is the only crossing to the mainland."

George was silent, staring behind the tables at the canvas bags filled with coin piled on top of one another.

She felt the need to explain. "Charity and humility. That is where true worth comes, not from coin."

He took a moment before responding. "One thing is more envied than wealth."

"And what might that be?"

"The circle of an amiable family . . . in a situation free from cares."

His words, "free from cares"—that is how she felt in his presence. She guided him up the stairwell. "If you would, please follow me, George."

"A demand I so ardently wish for."

She tiptoed up the stairs. He copied her manner of walking, which made her chuckle. They quietly made their way to the first floor of the manor.

"If you would kindly find a seat in the parlor. I will be in the kitchen to have our beverage made." Mary hurried to see Temperance, who quickly answered her request. She measured a pint of milk and brought it to a boil with a stick of cinnamon in a chocolate pot. When the liquid was hot, Mary sweetened it with Lisbon sugar and added cocoa pieces. The mixture emitted the most pleasing of scents. She watched Temperance pour this into cups with two handles, one on each side. Mary hoped this might offer more protection for the colonel, as she didn't want to have another burning incident.

To the second floor, Mary scurried to get out of her riding clothes and find a poem. Which could she choose? Most of them harped on sorrow, on gloom. Might there be one? Please let there be one, she thought. One that would be acceptable, maybe one of no measurable importance, of a jovial nature.

Had she even written a poem like that? She shuffled through the papers on her desk. Was there not a moment of merriment in her world she could have made the subject? Each focused on guilt, on regret. He did not need to know the truth about her, not now. If he knew she was cursed, he would certainly run from this place.

Chapter Eleven

---◆◇◆---

Poetry's Intimacy

I feel the force of her amiable beauties in the recollection of a thousand tender passages . . .

—GEORGE WASHINGTON

George stood by the window, holding his two-handled porcelain cup. Although tempting his nose and tongue, he hadn't touched the dirty chocolate. He focused now on the view across the Hudson to New Jersey. Like stoned fingers, a rock wall rose more than one hundred feet from the ground. What a strong encampment that place would make, he envisioned. War had not come to this place. If it did, troops would be protected by nature's camouflage and by the rushing river. And if units were stationed on this side of the river as well, not an enemy's boat would get north of this town.

The steam rose in a swirl from the surface of his drink, reminding him of the incident with the last hot beverage he drank with her. A bit of a burn lingered on his lip. He did enjoy how her hand felt on his knee. Her touch was gentle and her expression of concern sincere.

Now he could hear Mary Eliza's voice from just outside the entryway. She began to read verse aloud. Her poem? It must be. About a

bluebird. She arrived. Her soft pink gown revealed the skin below her neck. She had changed out of her riding clothes. He smiled at the thought. She would look lovely, he fancied, in anything she wore, or didn't wear.

She read from a linen paper with a whimsical tone to her voice.

Alas! The bluebird to a sill arrives,
Into his reflection he peered to see whether still alive,
In his breast, the pit-a-pat of his heart yielded delight,
For a beauty in the fairest form which had enchanted his sight,
With an adjustment to his peruke he designed,
To yield an affirmation if the divine creature was so inclined.

"And that, George, must clearly be the finest piece of literature you have ever heard."

For an instant, he couldn't decide which was lovelier, the poem or its author. Then her eyelashes fluttered and she curtsied, and he knew.

"The finest, yes, regarding a bird and his peruke." He laughed, which astonished him. It wasn't like him to laugh aloud.

As he laughed, she laughed with him, adding, "Possibly the only one written upon that account."

"Your poem is very acceptable, as it not only displays your genius but exhibits sentiments . . . expressive of the benevolence of your heart."

"In truth, it is pure fiction," she said with a smile so wide it revealed the truth. The left. Yes. One dimple on her right cheek. Another on the left.

A new opportunity presented itself for him to speak eloquently, unlike his morning with her. He wasn't even able to voice a greeting in the stable. Diamond? This was all he could utter to her! A simple "Good day" would have sufficed. He was not going to let another chance go by with the heiress. "Fiction is, to be sure, the very life and soul of poetry—all poets and poetesses have been indulged in the free and indisputable use of it. To oblige you to make such an excellent poem, on such a subject, without any materials but those of simple

reality, would be as cruel as the edict of the pharaoh which compelled the children of Israel to manufacture bricks without the necessary ingredients."

"If only I knew a hero who could provide the subject for literary greatness."

He took a sip of the chocolate, careful of the heat touching his lips this time. "Heroes have made poets, and poets heroes." He noticed a blush surface on her cheeks. "You could choose Alexander the Great. He is said to have been enraptured with the poems of Homer."

"If only I had lived in such an age." She picked up the cup with both hands.

"An age proverbial for intellectual refinement and elegance in composition, where the harvest of laurels and bays was wonderfully mingled together."

"We still have great poets in this age who have brought intimacy to their work, as the Countess of Winchilsea does." Mary recited a stanza of her "Letter to the Same Person":

Love without Poetry's refining Aid
Is a dull Bargain, and but coarsely made;
Nor e'er Poetry successful prove,
Or touch the Soul, be when the Sense was Love.
    Oh! Cou'd they both in Absence now impart
Skill to my Hand, but to describe my Heart . . .

Savoring the last sip of the beverage, he took her in—all of her, even the trace of bashfulness she seemed to carry about her own beauty. He glanced around briefly, taking in the luster of this place and the sweets of domestic enjoyments. What more could a man ask for than to reside in a pleasing country seat with an enchanter who had regard for him? Many other suitors would revel in the opportunity to be in his place. The affluence of the family. The influence in society. And yet here she was alone with him, reciting poetry.

"I believe it's time to hear your writing, George."

Mary Eliza Philipse—he was enamored of her. No paper was

necessary for his poetry. He started to speak. "From your . . ." He stopped himself. Being that he was feeling confident that he had piqued her interest, he rose from his chair and sauntered over to her. She seemed near startled when he placed himself in close proximity to her on the long cushion. His thigh grazed hers. She drew a quick breath and rustled her gown. He removed the cup from her palm and placed it down onto its saucer. Porcelain clinked porcelain.

Shifting his body toward her, he took both of her hands in his and relished the softness of her skin. He'd written the poem long ago, but now was the first time it was fitting to recite to someone:

From your bright sparkling Eyes, I was undone;
Rays, you have, more transparent than the sun,
Amidst its glory in the rising Day,
None can you equal in your bright arrays;
Constant in your calm and unspotted Mind;
Equal to all, but will to none Prove kind,
So knowing, seldom one so Young, you'l Find.
Ah! woe's me, that I should Love and conceal,
Long have I wish'd, but never dare reveal,
Even though severely Loves Pains I feel;
Xerxes that great, was't free from Cupids Dart,
And all the greatest Heroes, felt the smart.

Her face brightened in this very moment as a flower emerging from the darkness to bathe in the light. "George, you are a true gentleman."

To be a gentleman, act a gentleman.
Finally.
Affirmation.

Chapter Twelve

The Winner's Cup

*. . . I consider storms and victory under the direction of a
wise providence . . .*

—GEORGE WASHINGTON

NEW YORK CITY

At precisely five minutes after four, tensions ran high. Voices rose
into a frantic roar with shouts of elation and worry—"Run!" "Hurry!"
"They're coming!" Any vestige of refined manner vanished in the one
moment the dirt began to fly and a beat erupted like the thunderous
roll of drums. Speed and endurance were the only way to survive the
heat—three of them, to be precise.

Just off the riverfront, with a cold breeze leaving a chill, a spectacle never before seen in the colony was unfolding at a sanctuary,
not produced for a peace but for a rush.

A six-horse race was under way on Delancey's newly built private
track, the first in New York, positioned west of Broadway at Church
Farm, near Trinity Church. The track was surrounded by oak fencing. The crowd standing behind it stood at least ten deep.

An unusually large wager was set for today: three hundred pounds.
The winner's award was the silver cup, a double-handled presentation
vessel with a dome cover and engraving. The race would match

Delancey's newest Thoroughbred, Cub, to the rest of the lot, including the most revered of New Jersey's horses, Old Tenor. This was the inaugural race. The announcement was published in the *New-York Gazette*:

> On the 18th of February, the New York Subscription
> Plate will be run for any Horse, Mare or Gelding,
> carrying eight Stone Weight, Saddle and Bridle
> included, the best in three Heats, two Miles in each
> Heat.

In the crisp air, refined fellows who donned cocked hats and rich greatcoats, as well as common folk attempting correct fashion, completely lost themselves. Mary was surrounded by polite society—as they called themselves—emitting not only a whiff of tobacco but also one of mendacity.

The shouts grew louder as the first lap was completed in two minutes, the third in just over the same. Out of the fifth, the winner was still in question. Which one would capture the treasured prize?

Mary remained still. She was flanked on every side. She didn't like crowds, but she had no other choice but to come, if she had hopes of finding her hero. For two days since their time together, her head filled entirely with thoughts of him. If George was in the crowd, she'd not yet seen him.

The number of other men attempting to attract Mary's attention was endless, each outdoing the other with their salutations. The poet, Scandal, offered her a rose along with a greeting in rhyme. Another fellow, Daniel Webb, asked Susannah to beg Mary for a moment of her time. The third, Colin Dufresne, got on tiptoe to reach over the crowd to give her an invitation to dine with him. Her reactions to them were pleasant, except to the one with the raised eyebrow, the sheriff. His self-admiration irritated her.

The vision before her was captivating. It was hard to take her eyes off the horses with the extreme slope in their shoulders. They raced in a cluster. The roar of hooves thundered. One mare of strong muscling and significant bone structure launched, capturing the lead.

"Onto victory!" she heard Scandal shout. "Into history!"

"Triumph be yours!" Bernadette Clara Belle, standing by Mary, cried out, When Bernadette lifted her arms to cheer for the Delancey mare, her petticoat, already with a hem inches short of appropriate, rose above her knee. Bernadette never missed an occasion where finery was displayed. Her head was quite comically adorned with a tremendous headdress created of yellow ribbons with vivid red accents that glistened like rubies—Mary surmised they were only colored glass. Oh, and that feather, too, was in her hair, the same one from the ball, Mary assumed.

"Cub's in the lead!" exclaimed Bernadette.

In the lead by a mile, it seemed, the English mare bore the Delancey coat of arms, bright red with a lion and a shield of three spears. As for Old Tenor, he was nowhere.

The shouts grew more intense—"Cub!" "She's coming." "Cub will be victorious!"

Delancey lost all sense of himself as he screeched, "She's mine. All mine! The plate is mine!"

Mary watched as Cub sped with ease to the finish. This was not the end. As onlookers erupted in applause, the animal became startled and took off. The horse bolted through the gate with the rider still on its back.

Bedlam ensued.

She watched the sheriff's usual air of importance dissolve into chaos. He darted from his position, climbed over the oak fencing, and hotfooted it down the course. His hair, always in perfect order, was instead representative of the moment.

Mary bit her lip to avoid a grin. Gentlemen scrambled to the outside field, where the mare galloped in wild circles. For quite a time, Delancey himself was run amok, chasing the tail. The rider jumped off. Scandal practically grabbed the horse a few times before the mare won this game of cat and mouse, leaving them in the dust.

After a few minutes' time, a riderless Cub returned on her own to the track and stopped in the center of it, as if to take a bow and await a bouquet before the guests. The crowd roared.

This was followed by a dreadfully long ceremony, in which the sheriff waxed grandiloquent about his influence on horse racing, "Triumph is clearly in the hands of the just. Earth hath provided us her abundant favor—this has led to the defeat over the bulwarks of the foe. I take the greatest satisfaction in this day, for I have received the most favorable outcome. We have cut down the hand of the spoiler and ruined his rise. We have become heirs to an eternal achievement." His speech finally ended as the sun found its repose, but not before he called himself "Father of the American Turf."

The winning audience made its way to the Horse and Cart Inn. It was near nightfall when Mary and her family arrived after a short walk. Bold red bunting lined the balconies of the second and third floor of the club, while below hundreds of guests stood awaiting entry. This is where the elite converged with alacrity to enjoy handsome entertainment. The Philipses were escorted around the crowd, in through the rear door and up the stairs to the second floor. The inn was owned by the Delanceys. This caused Mary's spirits to rise.

That touch of a kiss lingered upon her hand; George had taken his time in saying farewell. He had been whisked away from her just moments after reciting his poetry. Brother Frederick and the sheriff's father, Lieutenant Governor James Delancey, had invited him to meet the dignitaries of the town. She hoped to again hear those words, "From your bright sparkling eyes, I was undone," but alas, his belongings were removed from the manor and carried to the Robinson town house on Pearl Street on the island. He'd tour New York with the Delanceys by day was what she was told.

Mary had waited her entire life, not for someone like him, but *him*. In the pages of her mind, she had envisioned his strong chin and broad shoulders—even his voice sounded familiar. When his lids lowered slightly in a most romantic way, she felt as if she had seen that endearing expression before. She was more surprised she hadn't known him than she was by the profound impression he was leaving on her heart.

As the thoughts of him whirled about, a soothing voice spoke to her from behind. "Miss Mary Eliza Philipse. Neither time nor absence can impair the warmth of fondness I feel in your presence."

His words left her without any of her own. George turned her around, clutched her bare hand, and lifted it to his lips. The now-familiar tingle shot through her.

In place of a greeting, she settled her hand into his folded elbow, his strength feeling like chiseled rock and savoring of manliness—soap combined perfectly with brawn. Her nose stayed close to him as she escorted him in a slow walk to the balcony overlooking the Hudson, where they could be alone. Twilight's reflection rippled upon the river. Above them twinkled a dome of lights. Her hip leaned against an ornate French wrought-iron railing. "Do you believe"—she shifted her gaze upward—"anything can endure longer than the stars in the sky?"

Before answering, he moved within a space of her. He gently took her chin into his hand. "The chain of sincere love." His lids dipped. "If strong and lasting, it will endure while sun and stars give light."

At this, his face came nearer to hers, so near as to almost touch. Her own eyelids closed as she felt his breath on her lips. The hairs on her arms stood up. She could feel the beating of her heart as the flame grew larger and, in its bright splendor, the sound stronger. Was it a choir she was hearing? Music sounded its rhythm in the fast-approaching moment that Cupid's feathered dart was striking.

The loud booming of drums struck a distracting chord, interrupting her bliss. A band in formation marched directly below the balcony, bringing Mary back into proper position. Musicians on celebratory parade traveled by. Mary became flustered.

George seemed to pay no attention. His face lifted to the cluster of lights above. His finger pointed to a pattern of stars. "Andromeda."

She looked up at the constellation. "The chained maiden of mythology."

His hand fell on her waist, causing her to stir. "Stars aligned in a perfect sequence."

"As the legend goes, she was saved from death by the bravery of her hero."

He brought her body nearer to him. "She is in perfect view this night."

"Andromeda is displayed in 'The World in Miniature,' I've read.

The entire universe is represented in the exhibit. It's made the transatlantic journey from England. It is now here in our New York."

George led her farther away from the door and the noise of the crowd inside. His hand latched on to her waist.

"A transatlantic journey . . . it is one I could never take." She felt comfortable talking with him. "I have a rather delicate makeup when it comes to capacious waters. The only place I have a desire to travel to is Barbados, where my father was born and his grandfather served as governor."

"My brother, Lawrence, and I were graciously received on the island of Barbados."

"Oh? My father would often speak of the rough seas in getting there."

"Rough seas indeed. During the thirty-seven-day passage, we experienced hard squalls of wind and rain, with a fomented sea jostling in heaps. Pretty large swells made the ship roll much and me . . . very sick."

She always pictured in her mind what the trip might be like from beginning to end.

"Upon our departure from Virginia, we found clear and pleasant weather for a sail, with fresh gales of wind, even saw a great many fish, including dolphin."

"A dolphin!" Her palm grabbed hold of the outer part of his arm. "I've never had the pleasure of seeing one." She didn't want to let go.

"But soon, even the seamen confessed that they had never seen such weather before. It was surmised there had been a violent hurricane not far distant."

"How did you make it to the island?"

"We were greatly alarmed with the cry of 'Land' at four o'clock one morning. We quitted our beds with surprise and found the land plainly appearing about three leagues distant. We weighed anchor and arrived in Carlisle Bay."

"That is quite a journey to take. Why, George, did you make such a trip? For trade? Or for repose?"

His eyes shifted down before answering. "We hoped the warm air would benefit my brother's health at the time."

She touched his hand with hers.

"The doctors, they had hoped time in the islands, the fresh air, might bring a cure. The white plague claimed him in the summer of 'fifty-two."

"My deepest condolences for your loss."

"No one entertained a higher opinion of his worth than I."

She wished that year, 1752, never happened. Devastation struck the Philipse family, too, during that summer. Both the father who held her like a treasure and her Margaret were taken from her. "I, too, George, experienced a deepest loss during that same time of that same year. My sister, my Margaret . . ." She tried to hold back tears. "She died of that same terrible disease in the summer of 'fifty-two."

George grabbed hold of her right hand and held it tightly.

"She was so young, so good and just, with a warm heart." She inhaled deeply. "And Lawrence?"

"He was a captain and a well-respected member of the legislature. He left behind a widow, Anne. His death left us both numb."

"George, my sister, she died alone . . . all alone." The memories rushed in of how she would sing outside Margaret's door and wait for her to clap—one, two, three, four, five, six. "They would not let me near her. They would not let anyone near her. She left this world all alone." She could not speak further, as grief overcame her.

"I understand the pain in bidding adieu to those we love," he said gently.

"It is my fault, George." She had never spoken about this with anyone outside of the family. "I was the first to get the fevers. If only . . . I had stayed away from them. If only . . . I had kept them back."

He wrapped his arms around her.

She leaned her head upon his chest. "The hurt is so deep, I feel I will not be able to take another day without her. I wait for the day when . . . I can let go of the pain."

Melancholy seeped into her spirit. Mary's eyes watered.

Their quiet was a deep quiet.

He kept her in his embrace.

. . .

THE EVENING'S AFFAIR was a protracted one. The longer the evening went on, the more unintelligible sounds from the bumper men reached George and Mary. The aroma of the claret was formidable.

The two of them reentered the gaming room as Delancey yelled, "To Satan with morality and ethics. Bumpers for all of the guests!"

This was answered by drunken laughter.

"A toast to the possessor of the most valued mare," said Scandal. "Now, take your standing as turf's king with flair."

Delancey bowed with great flamboyance and hollered, "More wine! Bring out the cards! Bring out the dice! The evening is becoming dead. Let's hope for comedy or dread, something of consequence to happen."

Mary could hear the scraping of spurs. Could it be? The man with the raven hair covered in powder seemed to come from nowhere and made his way to the center of the crowd. James Jay's voice was thick with anger. "If you should witness a prized racehorse surrender the cup to a lackey, would you not presume deception by a cheat?"

This caused an eruption from the Delancey brigade.

"Look at this fool, stubborn as a mule!" Scandal mocked him. "Dare you enter uninvited?"

"Leave him be," answered Delancey. "When a man is as drunk as he, how can we expect reason? I pity you, Jay."

"I will not be indifferent to the treatment I have received," shouted James, "by the likes of those who have sold their souls to the king."

"Dr. Jay, you heathen. You've spent too much time with experiments in the dungeon. The work has clouded your mind." Delancey spun a finger around his head.

"Your obsession with the lion disgusts me." James stumbled forward.

"Jay, your obsession with the glass disgusts us all!" Scandal snickered.

"If you have anything, even a suspicion to allege against me, you will candidly declare it, in order that I may vindicate myself to you."

Frederick and Beverley rushed toward Mary.

"The time for departure has come." Frederick took hold of her arm.

"Colonel Washington, we must be leaving with Polly. A carriage for you is awaiting your departure when you are ready."

They did not say another word. Frederick and Beverley flanked Mary on each side, moved her swiftly through the crowd and out the door. Not a good-bye was said between her and George.

Mary could hear the sliding of the spurs as she was helped out the front door and moved swiftly into an awaiting carriage. The face of her nightmares glared out the window watching her every move.

"As goes the mother, so, too, the daughter."

She would never forget his threat.

Chapter Thirteen

A Hundred Eyes

Silence . . . speaks more Intelligably than the sweetest Eloquence.

.—GEORGE WASHINGTON

From the windows above, soothing sunlight flooded the rotunda. Here, clove mingled with spice to fill the air. *Matthiola incana* blooms stood tall in a high metal vase on top of an ornately carved wooden table in the center of the room. The Robinsons' town home on Pearl Street on Manhattan Island was appointed with care throughout.

As each hour passed, uncertainty remained as to whether Mary Eliza Philipse would receive him today. A pain in her head was the explanation, the reason she did not leave her bedchamber this day. She, as well, stayed at the residence. George knew there must have been other reasons. The abrupt departure the evening before yielded questions.

George walked past an extensive array of portraits that hung on walls ornately covered in rich silver and gold fabric coverings. He clasped his hands behind his back. George felt eyes on him, faces in frames judging him as he moved with a steady pace.

Beverly was with him. "The painting of your mother, does it still hang in the entryway?"

"The one by the hand of Captain Middleton?"

Beverley nodded.

"It does." George's late father, Augustine, had commissioned the portrait of her. The artist used subtle tones and feathery strokes on a dark background. The painting caught her likeness, yet it conveyed a softness rarely seen in her. More often, the business of managing the family's small farm weighed on his mother's head. "Middleton is the only artist for whom she sat."

Beverley paused and turned to him. "You missed it, Colonel; the sheriff ran about like a madman at his own race!"

"My absence was on account of a tour reviewing the lands of the Hudson."

"He would have kept you longer if you hadn't insisted on returning." Beverley moved him through the spacious gallery, where a number of paintings of the majestic Hudson hung. They separated the portraits of those lost from those still alive. "I hear Delancey's aide brought you very near the estuary."

"I saw the strong current of the river up close."

"Very close, from what I understand."

"The pointed fin. Have you seen it yourself?" George asked.

"Only once, and in the distance. The shark was enormous. Did he mention that the creature took a man in the very spot you visited? The fish lurched forth and grabbed a fellow at the leg and brought him below the waves, near the great rocks in the town of Yonkers. The man disappeared, never seen again, taken by the devil himself. And now you have survived the area we call 'Spiting Devil.'"

George pretended to wipe his brow.

Beverley pointed to a trio of portraits as the paintings moved to depictions of the living. "The hand of John Wollaston. Susannah's father commissioned the portraits when the three sisters were in their blooming years—chosen as the artist's first sitters in the Americas. We keep Margaret next to her sisters. Susannah refuses to move her

to the other part of the gallery, for she is 'alive in us,' Susannah says. The critics reviewed Polly's painting. 'Nature and we must bless the hand that can such heavenly charms portray and save the beauty of this land from envious obscurity' is what was written of hers."

How glorious Mary Eliza would look painted with the brush of Captain Middleton, George thought. He analyzed Wollaston's portrait further. Her expression displayed something more, something that instantly moved him, mixing admiration with concern. She had laid her heart before him on that balcony.

In her painted expression, he could see genuine and deep sorrow.

Elegance weaved with torment.

Grace intertwined with heartache.

Beauty combined with anguish.

"There is sadness in her eyes," remarked George.

"Polly has suffered through tragic times. A devastating illness took the life of their father and their Margaret. She's felt responsible for their deaths, you know . . . and the others."

Be not Curious to Know the Affairs of Others. This was an edict George followed. Her mother—he still did not know the circumstances of her death.

"She has a brave spirit. The guilt of losing her mother seems to live in every fiber of her being. The passage across the Hudson River is a precarious one," Beverley explained. "When our Polly was only a child, she tried to save a little boy, the gardener's son. Precocious, he was. The child jumped into the water leading to the Hudson River by the Yonkers manor and Polly ran after him. They tell me she tried with all her might to swim to him, to rescue him. She has never been able to wipe the tragedy from her mind."

"The young boy?"

"His body never surfaced. The night became even more tragic for the family. Lady Joanna Philipse heard her little girl's screams and jumped into the water. It is believed the fine lady swam to her daughter and gave her a push that prevented her end."

George felt a lump in throat. "Such a tragedy for a young girl."

"The Hudson, Colonel, chooses whom it takes. I have heard many

stories of that horrific night. If not for the raven, I'm told, our Polly might have died there, too, in the night. Their shrill call from above her nearly breathless body alerted a rescuer to her whereabouts. He found her lying, half-submerged, in tall grasses at the water's edge. And now we will do anything and everything to protect her, to keep her safe."

Now George understood the emptiness he saw in her. A genuine soul untouched by airs and honest about her own limitations. She truly was one of the most exceptional women he'd ever known.

As he took in Beverley's words, George felt a strong need to bring Mary Eliza Philipse into his embrace, to protect her, to surround her mind with peace.

Chapter Fourteen

——◄•►——

The World in Miniature

The Mind of Man is fond of Novelty.

—GEORGE WASHINGTON

A faint sound coming from under her chamber door startled her. Mary quieted her breath. She remained still, though her heart pounded. A man's footsteps sounded in the hall. Had she locked the door?

She had kept the covers over her head since her arrival here last night. The bed was her solace, sleep her escape. She didn't want to see anyone today. Her spirit forbade her from rising. It had been a difficult end to the night. Deep feelings buried inside her were roused, leaving her emotionally spent. And seeing that man brought back the anxiety she so desperately wanted to rid herself of.

Papers slid below the oak door. She allowed one eye to peek out from under the quilt. The paper on top appeared to be an advertisement cut from *The New-York Mercury*. Curiosity lifted her from bed. She tiptoed and her bare feet felt the touch of the cool wood below her feet. What she read wiped away her fright and made her mood dance:

To be seen at the New Exchange, that elaborate and
celebrated piece of mechanism, called the Microcosm,
of the World in Miniature. Built in the form of a Roman
Temple, after twenty-two years close study and application
by the late ingenious Mr. Henry Bridges of London.
It will be shown every day beginning at ten in the morning.

George. He must have been the one at her door. He, too, slept at
the town house of Beverley and Susannah. She hadn't seen him
since her departure from the inn.

On a second paper, in the most beautiful hand, with script displaying thin upstrokes and wide downstrokes of loops and curves,
was written:

Mean-time the Song went round; and Dance, and Sport,
Wisdom, and friendly Talk successive stole
Their Hours away. While in the rosy Vale
Love breath'd his Infant Sighs, from Anguish free,
Fragrant with Bliss, and only wept for Joy.

Had George placed heavier pressure on the nib as he wrote the
word *Love*? Mary stared at the deeper, larger strokes on that particular word. She closed her eyes. She fell to pieces in his arms the prior
evening. He put her back together and helped her see she was not
alone in grief. He understood her and her frailty, which she was never
comfortable revealing to anyone.

"'Love breath'd his Infant Sighs,'" she whispered.

She brought the written words closer to her heart. The thought of
him looking at her in that tender way made her feel so special, so
loved. She raced to the door and unlocked it. No one was in the hall
when she opened it. She couldn't wait another minute. She made her
way to the upper floor. She tapped at the door. "It is I," she said in a
quiet voice.

The door swung open and she leapt into the room, falling on
her knees in front of her sister with papers still in hand. "He's

written me the words of the poet Thomson. 'Love breath'd his Infant Sighs . . .'"

"Truly?" Susannah knelt down next to her.

"'Love breath'd his Infant Sighs, from Anguish free,/Fragrant with Bliss, and only wept for Joy.' He's written me the words of the poem 'Spring.' Susannah, I am without words over this, over this man. It is not to be believed the impression he is leaving on my heart."

Susannah hugged her. "It may be you who also holds him in gentle sway."

"Susannah, I feel as though I've been restored." Mary felt so much changed in her in such a short time, yet she was more herself than ever before.

AS BEVERLEY ASSISTED the sisters in exiting the chaise outside the exhibit hall, statues greeted them. Mary almost became one herself from embarrassment. The merchants appeared frozen in place as she placed her feet, in jewel-embellished shoes, upon the path leading to the exhibit hall. She carried a parasol adorned with feathers to shield her from the sun. That was Susannah's idea. It is the fashion of the day, she insisted.

Mary wore her hair braided, with each braid carried over to the opposite side, and upon her nape a swath of hair hung low in the form of a snood. She chose a costume with a soft hue that reflected her delight. The peach-colored taffeta dress embroidered with tiny gray swirled designs was paired with a white petticoat. Upon the sleeves hung white silk frill. Mary felt flushed, not because of the strangers' glares, but because of the man who was leaving a profound impression on her.

With a pleasant, dignified air, George neared her. "Miss Mary Eliza Philipse, it is an honor to see you this day." He was wearing a most fashionable suit of silvery gray silk. She couldn't tell for sure, but she thought there was a lining in a salmon color. The suit's opulent buttons shimmered in the afternoon light. Their outfits matched, as if they'd purposely coordinated them.

She took in his clean scent. "My deepest gratitude for the invita-

tion, George." She laid her hand upon his offered arm. The feel of him set her insides aflame. They approached the New Exchange, which sat right in the middle of wide Broadway. It was considered the center of commercial importance. The place for the public to rendezvous bore unique architecture. The rectangular enclosed part of it sat high in the air, supported by grand arches. Below them, merchants traded their goods with their carts moving to and fro between the curvatures.

A sprightly, talkative fellow greeted the four of them near a stairwell to the exhibition house. "Your passage into the World in Miniature!" He handed them highly designed tickets embossed on silver metal. "My name is Mr. Bridges, but my father often called me 'Genius.'"

She found this "genius" amusing, with his hearty greeting and spectacles that enlarged his eyes to double a normal size.

Mr. Bridges practically marched up the outdoor spiral staircase. Mary followed behind him as George's hands held her waist. Glee overtook her as she went around and around. She never climbed like this before, feeling as if life were turning her from the end of one journey to the start of another.

"Welcome to an astronomical phenomena that has traveled the globe," Bridges announced as he opened a grand door. "You join an elite company of those who have stood in its presence, including the royal family of Britain and Sir Isaac Newton, who spent time with my father's creation while checking the mechanisms." His arms spread out wide as he walked to the center of the space. "Ladies and gentlemen, our world in miniature!"

The golden display stood twelve feet high and ran along the walls of the room: an intricate composition of sculpture, paintings, and metalwork—filled with a visual and musical extravaganza—a representation of the known universe. An amazing variety of scenes moved in exact time to several pieces of music.

"Open your ears to hear the harp and the hautbois." Bridges placed his hands behind his oversized ears. "The organ, the spinet, and flageolet combine to produce the music of Signor Corelli and Mr. Handel. Inside the great Microcosm, the mechanisms are carefully

constructed to gratify the ear while accompanying each moving scene. The music is coordinated to match with great exactness the vision before you."

On tiny instruments, sculptured Muses positioned in a Roman temple played Mary's favorite aria from *Radamisto* in perfect tempo. "Our song," she whispered to George, "'Ombra Cara.'" She hardly knew where to fix her eyes. Mostly, she wanted to set them upon George.

The pleasing images were just shy of innumerable. She leaned in for a closer view. Miniature gardens in metal with an orchard of trees and vines in full bloom caught her attention. She imagined sitting with George in such a lively, green, and luxurious place. She thought of him taking her in his arms.

George spoke quietly to her and she felt his lips gently brush her neck. "To sit under your own vine, your own fig tree . . ." She adored how the wisps of his hair tickled her cheek as he spoke. "The enjoyment of peace and freedom combined." Every word he said sounded to her like elegant prose. "I would rather be on my own farm than be emperor of the world."

She settled her hand in the bend of his arm again as they viewed the exhibit and its wonderland. Orpheus played his lyre in the forest. Lilliputian horses pulled a golden chariot fit for a king. A whimsical land emerged with birds of fantastical variety, each moving in harmony to the music being played.

George guided her to the three-dimensional models of the solar system. They watched Jupiter and his four satellites, in exact proportion, completing their proper revolutions.

"George, look!" She pointed. "Andromeda."

"'But happy they! the happiest of their Kind! / Whom gentle stars unite . . .'"

She recited the next lines of the poem. "'. . . and in one Fate/their Hearts, their Fortunes, and their Beings blend.' James Thomson's 'Spring' is a favorite of mine." Just as the planets abounded, she felt her heart follow, performing its own dance to the diurnal motion. Together, they studied the next piece of art. Two miniaturized wooden

ships sailed closer and closer to each other. "It's been said, 'How vast the sea proves no obstacle when two ships are destined to meet.'" Her eyes met his. They remained here for a few heartbeats.

"Shall I show you the most exceptional part?" announced Mr. Bridges. "Ladies and gentlemen, the inner genius of the World in Miniature." The maker's son unlocked the sides of the exhibits to show the internal mechanisms: wheels of minute size whirling in synchronic time. Each of the scenes' pinions cranked and spun and pumped. "The clockwork of the exhibit is so exact that the orbits complete their mutual transits while following the velocity of ten months' motion in ten minutes. My father spent his life creating this marvelous structure. And when it was finished. exceeding his expectations, he continued making considerable improvements. Twelve hundred wheels and pinions in unison. In harmony."

Mary stood amazed by the work and the word harmony. It felt right—the two of them together—Mary and George. Their thinking, their doing, their being, in sync . . . in perfect harmony. As they walked toward the exit, her spirit teemed with enthusiasm.

They departed the exhibit and started down the spiral staircase. The aide to Lieutenant Governor Delancey was standing at the bottom with what appeared to be letters in hand. For the first time she could see what she had pictured in her mind; well-defined muscles at the sides of George's face clenched along his jawline.

"Colonel, my apologies for this interruption. I've been requested to deliver these to you with expediency."

George was given two scrolls of correspondence. "If you'll excuse me," he said to Mary and her family. "My attendance on a matter is necessary. I must settle some important business."

Mary's emotions sank. The worried look that appeared on his face distressed her. What is in those letters? she wondered.

Chapter Fifteen

——◆◆◆——

The Defiant One

*There is nothing more necessary than good intelligence to
frustrate a designing enemy.*

—GEORGE WASHINGTON

Insubordination. Or worse. The letter infuriated him. George gave
a specific command to Captain Roger Morris; he refused to comply.
First, George asked as a fellow aide-de-camp. Then he asked as a
colonel. Both times, Morris acted injurious to the cause, denying
George access to the journals concerning the military's movement
leading up to the Battle of Monongahela.

George would have written the details himself if not for the bloody
flux. He had volunteered to serve in the Braddock expedition, yes, to
serve king and country, but in truth, he had a selfish motivation, to
gain knowledge of the military arts. He was very clear to the parties
involved that this was his desire. Yet now he remained with nothing
tangible.

He unrolled the letter from Morris to reread it:

Dear Washington

I own, I am at a loss what to say in answer to some
particulars in your Letter; & shall only appeal to your
Judgment, from what I say.

My orderly Books, being lost I could not gett an authentick,
one that was proper, & therefore was obligd from Necessity,
to omit, what I would have complyd with, with Pleasure, if
I had had it in my Power.

I must now conclude to desire you to forbear your Judgment,
till I am convicted by Proof, or very strong Presumption, of
what I am sure at present I am innocent of —

I am as I always was Your very well Wisher, & obedt Sert

Roger Morris

George's temper flared. Morris! He remembered how colorfully
the Brit sang before sending those men to their deaths. The soldier
with the floral boutonniere! George rolled the letter.

Who was in charge—a British officer of lower rank, or a soldier of
the Americas of higher standing? A meeting with the commander in
chief should answer his questions of whether he had justifiable
command over British officers. George needed to deal with the matter
immediately. The second letter granted his request to meet with the
general in person in Boston to answer the question once and for all.

Chapter Sixteen

——◄•►——

He Cannot Tell a Lie

*. . . I hope I shall always possess firmness and virtue
enough to maintain (what I consider the most enviable of
all titles) the character of an honest man.*

—GEORGE WASHINGTON

The coach was conveying them to the Yonkers manor—Mary sat
next to Frederick, Susannah nestled close to Beverley.

"About the town with a Southern officer," Frederick said in a teasing manner.

Mary wanted to pay no attention to him.

"The Delanceys tell me there was quite a scene in front of the New
Exchange."

She tried to take her mind off her discontent with Frederick's prying by thinking of George. Her feelings for him were becoming inexpressible.

"How is it that you conduct yourself in such manner?" her brother
continued. "I appreciate being informed."

A deep sigh came from her lips. "Frederick, the colonel traveled
five hundred miles on horseback to be here. The least I could do was
accept an invitation from him."

Her brother turned to Susannah and Beverley, "The Delanceys believe him to be phlegmatic in his address."

Susannah sat up straight, with hands folded. "I believe his countenance is marked by caution and watchfulness."

Mary copied her sister's seated position. "The faculty of concealing one's own sentiments is a requisite of a statesman, is it not?"

"It is a common feature in commanders of the military," Susannah backed her.

Beverley affirmed with a nod and added, "He is an honest man. To this, I can attest."

"Are you certain?" asked Frederick.

"If I may offer an example from our childhood, one involving a sorrel beloved by his mother, but of a fierce nature, which resisted any attempt to be reined."

"His mother's horse?" inquired Frederick.

"What is she like?" Susannah leaned on her true. "His mother."

"Compared to my own parents, of her, I was a thirteen times more fearful."

"How else would we expect her to be?" Mary felt the need to defend the woman.

"She is a lady who demands discipline and morality from her children," said Beverley.

"I hear she is a beautiful woman," Mary noted.

"And what of the horse?" prodded Frederick.

"It was believed there was not a person who could ride this furor of an animal. Of course, George was of a different opinion. Upon his request, my brother, John, and I assisted in trapping the animal into a closed space and pushing a bit into its mouth. With that, Washington sprung upon its back and tore off into the fields. The power of George's strength could tame even its grandsires. He held on to the wild steed with all his might. The conflict went on for longer than our comfort could have imagined. We soon regretted taking any part in this enterprise, for the struggle between man and horse became near terrifying as the horse used all of its

energy in one forceful effort that resulted in a violent plunge to the ground."

"What of George?" Mary burst out.

"Unharmed and without even a bruise," Beverley told them.

"And the horse?" Mary was completely engrossed in every detail.

"Died right there before us."

The sisters gasped.

"George was devastated," Beverley asserted. "Never again did he treat a horse with less than extreme tenderness and care."

Mary adored how he named each one of his horses. So this was why.

"What tale did you tell to his mother?" Frederick leaned back.

"We planned out several stratagems."

"I would suspect." Frederick folded his arms.

"Though George had little interest in our lie making. At breakfast the next morn, Mrs. Washington asked us if we had seen her favorite steed. When there was no answer, she asked it again. George replied, 'Your sorrel is dead.'"

Mary leaned forward, truly fascinated. Strong and brave and honest. This man was gaining possession of every part of her heart.

"A look of shock appeared upon his mother's face. 'Dead!' she snapped. 'How could this be?' George went on to tell her the whole story, how the horse had been beyond controllable, how he had asked us to aid him, and how in his fight for mastery of the horse, the sorrel fell to the ground in a violent fit and died right there."

Susannah brought her hands to the sides of her cheeks. "And what was the mother's reaction?"

"She turned red as a beet. After a minute's time, she spoke, saying she regretted losing her favorite horse but rejoiced in knowing her son always spoke the truth. My brother and I can attest to this: George Washington cannot tell a lie."

"Hmm. I wonder whether I should test this theory," countered Frederick.

Mary rolled her eyes. The last thing she needed was for Frederick to interrogate George.

Frederick shifted his eyes to look out the window. "It's unfortunate that his military position requires him to journey to Boston."

"George is leaving us?" Mary's heart dropped like a lump of lead. "When?"

He kept his focus outdoors. "The Delanceys tell me the colonel received a letter, requiring him to leave for New England on the twenty-third."

"Of this month?" She felt a queasiness well up.

"Yes, Polly."

"Beverley, is not his birthday the day prior, on the twenty-second?" asked Susannah. "Is this not true, my true?"

"The twenty-second, yes. Well, this is according to the Gregorian calendar. His authentic date of birth, I believe, is on the tenth or the eleventh."

"This calls for a celebration, Frederick." Susannah's eyes lit up. "A ball."

"Another ball?" Frederick turned to look at her. "It would not be appropriate on the heels of the other."

"There must be dancing on his final night, Frederick," chimed Susannah.

"I cannot approve."

"We could invite a select group for a small private affair of kind entertainment without the show of ceremony," Susannah suggested.

Mary tried to hold back the thrill that raced through her, knowing George might be in the manor once more. Would he kiss her hand again? Might she feel his lips upon her own? It was almost too much. She had to get a yes from Frederick. She just had to. She knew just what to say.

"And, Frederick, we could send an invitation to Mrs. Rutgers." Mary knew Frederick had grown fond of the woman. She saw his eyes linger as his dance with Elizabeth ended the night of the ball. "Elizabeth."

Was that redness she saw flash on Frederick's cheeks? She knew an affirmative answer was coming.

"Very well."

Chapter Seventeen

—◄•►—

Bread and Butter Ball

Oh Ye Gods why should my Poor Resistless Heart
Stand to oppose thy might and Power
At Last surrender to cupids feather'd Dart.

—GEORGE WASHINGTON

YONKERS-ON-HUDSON

For his birthday of his twenty-fourth year, he could think of no better way to mark it than with Mary Eliza Philipse. He would put aside military matters at least for today. So, wearing a brilliant red woolen coat accentuated with a turned-up collar, he looked the part of a man on the precipice of greatness in his red-and-ivory-striped waistcoat, a white silk cravat about his neck. His breeches were ivory, with vertically lined gold buttons down the sides.

George arrived at Philipse Manor just past five o'clock in the afternoon. Each day spent with her he relished. Her ease in conversation. Her intelligence. Her humility. For these and so many other reasons, he was succumbing to love's passion. His fortune, he knew, was not sufficient to maintain her in the manner to which she was accustomed. He needed to be assured his devotion was enjoyed by her. Without such, if feelings are not reciprocated, the heart struggles. He learned this once before and pledged he would never again. The lowland beauty, she tore apart his spirit.

With Mary Eliza, he felt something more. She seemed to truly enjoy being with him, even dancing with him, and hearing his mediocre poetry; he'd never recited a poem to anyone before. His lack of education and his lack of wealth did not seem to matter to her; maybe she didn't know. Either way, he realized he'd never felt this way before about himself. Confident. Accepted. Yes, with her, he felt he was enough. With Mary Eliza Philipse, the dawn shined bright and propitious.

IN MARY'S BEDCHAMBER, the ladies dabbed perfume of lavender-steeped water to her neck just before the dressmaker, Rosie Sherwood, added a sheer white mull fichu with a ruffle to the bodice of Mary's dress—a last-minute request. Mary believed the neckline was too plunging without it.

Music was playing one floor below the bedchamber. Sir Tenoe had made the request of Mary that only joyous songs be played this night. She had agreed. This would be Tenoe's first ball since being declared free. He would also be introducing a new dance to the colony, one that he taught her. "The Waltzen," it was called.

Singers burst into the chorus of Handel's *Messiah*. "Hallelujah, Hallelujah, Hallelujah, Hallelujah." Little Lulu, sitting on a stool, hummed along to the muffled music, not knowing the words of the verses in the least, but "Hallellujah" she sang out perfectly.

The young girl stared at Mary with eyes wide. "Are you's getting married today?" Lulu asked, interrupting her mother's work.

Rosie's eyes peered over pointed spectacles at Mary, the corners of her eyes wrinkled from smiling. "He is a tall, handsome-bodied, manly man, isn't he, Miss Polly?"

"That he is," Mary agreed. A nervous excitement came over her. "And Lulu, today's not the day." Just the thought of a wedding caused Mary to want to spin around with her arms out wide. "When I do get married . . ." She paused. "Well, if I get married, we will dress you up, Lulu, as a princess for the banquet."

Mrs. George Washington. What would that be like? Mary wondered. Euphoria wrapped in bliss, she imagined. Mary never pictured

herself a bride before meeting him. He would, of course, have to choose her. That would have to come first. He would have to ask her brother to negotiate a settlement, then ask her to be his. Negotiations! Those took time. She remembered how long it took before Beverley and Susannah signed an agreement. Maybe time a colonel leading a regiment of the South did not have, if he even wanted to propose, if he even wanted her to be his true. But if he did, and if she said, "Yes! Yes! Yes!," well, she would walk down the aisle into the arms of her Prince Charming. Mary was so elated to see George, she felt her heart could jump out of her skin.

GEORGE VIEWED THE belle as she walked rather quickly down the staircase to greet him. The fabric of her gown matched the tones of his costume, red-and-white shimmery striped silk. As the light of a sun's ray through the window landed on her, her décolletage was visible to him.

When she reached him, dimples on her left and right cheeks greeted him. He realized, here and now, that the time apart from her had pained him. "Mary Eliza Philipse." He slowly kissed one hand and the other.

She sighed. "The days have been dreadfully long without you."

He followed her through the foyer. She wore her hair up in a style that displayed her smooth neck and shoulders. Her upswept waves wrapped around a floral crown that he was admiring as she turned toward him.

"Do you like it?"

George nodded.

"The *Myosotis*." Mary lightly touched the small blue flower buds. "Legend states that the wearer of the forget-me-not will never be forgotten."

Forgotten she would never be, he thought.

She smiled with a blush and continued into the parlor, where a fire burned brightly in the hearth. Her aroma lingered as she walked, so redolent of what beauty should smell like.

Frederick approached with a woman standing close by him.

"Colonel Washington." Frederick reached over and gave him a firm grip. "Have you been acquainted with Mrs. Elizabeth Rutgers?"

George greeted her politely.

"Would you care for a beverage, Colonel? Ale? Wine?" asked Frederick.

"Wine and bitters, please."

Frederick hesitated. His brows lifted. "Together?"

George didn't think much of his drink choice. He often combined Madeira with lemon juice, nutmeg, and a sprinkle of sugar.

Frederick shrugged his shoulders and turned to a man George recognized from the other night at the banquet, the French chef who had worn a toque. He wore it still.

"François, if you would, wine and bitters for the colonel. For you, Polly, as well?"

She said yes. Both of her hands were wrapped around George's bent elbow.

"Colonel, you bring us a new way of thinking," Frederick acknowledged. "Wine and bitters, interesting."

The drinks were delivered with a stirrer made of a feather with its bottom half cleared.

"'Tis a peacock's tail?" asked Frederick.

François handed the beverages to George and Mary. "Do you not approve, Lord Philipse?"

"My thanks for the cock tail." George gave the chef a nod.

"A cock tail for me, as well," said Frederick. "And one for Beverley. Beverley, would you care for a cock tail?"

Beverley looked perplexed but nodded in agreement.

After they received the cocktails, Frederick beckoned them and the few other invited guests to gather: "A toast to our guest of honor," declared Frederick. "On this, your birthday of the twenty-fourth year. We wish you success in your endeavors! And now, we shall partake in the games of the evening." Frederick led the group into the drawing room, where tables were set up.

George offered Mary a chair. He couldn't pull his eyes away from her as he watched her frame delicately take a seat by a kindling

fire. It appeared her heart was growing attached to him. True devotion. This is what he wished for. In the composition of his own heart, he knew, there lay a great deal of inflammable matter. Dormant. Asleep. Now, with the torch put to it, it might burst into a blaze.

George and Mary were teamed up against Susannah and Beverley. The four of them sat before the walnut gaming table with their hands atop it, settling in for the long haul. The wells were filled with gaming chips.

"It is about time I can take revenge for the losses of my boyhood." Beverley dealt out fifty-two cards, facedown, each player getting thirteen.

George hadn't played cards with Beverley since their days at Ferry Farm. Friendship with the Robinson brothers, as he saw it, was like a slow-growing plant that withstood the shocks of adversity. George knew well to be courteous to all but intimate with only a few, and to let those few be well tried before you gave them your confidence.

Beverley revealed the trump card—the suit of clubs. "I believe I will have to make up for John's losses as well."

"Your brother is a gentleman for whom I entertain the highest respect and greatest friendship." George noticed Beverley's ante. George was not fond of gambling; moreover, at this table, the stakes were high: Five shillings equaled ten days' military pay.

The card game went on in white-knuckle fashion, with wins for one team and then the other.

Each took a turn in winning a trick by showing the highest card. George had a heart. He won this trick. Mary grabbed George's arm. "Tied! Three tricks for them. Three for us!"

"This must be the tensest game of whist we've ever played, Polly," Susannah exclaimed.

The play went on. Twelve tricks were completed. "Who shall be the grand winner of this measly prize?" quipped Beverley. It came down to the last round.

Measly. Not so for George. He turned the last card faceup. The heart would be the trump card for this round. Play continued. Mary

nearly jumped out of her seat with excitement at her card. Victory was theirs. "I've never enjoyed a game of whist as much as this!"

"It seems Providence protects you again, my friend." Beverley reached his hand out to George. They shook hands.

"It is infinitely wise and kind."

The dancing master, Sir Tenoe, entered the parlor. "Let the dancing begin!"

The musicians were playing brilliantly, the sounds echoing through the manor.

George and Mary walked through to the dining room, where the banquet table was set for a royal gathering. George had no appetite for viands, instead choosing just a piece of bread with butter.

"Are you not hungry for supper, George?"

Tonight, he was not, although his nose enjoyed the feast. What he desired most was to take Mary Eliza Philipse into his arms. "I appreciate an evening where music and dancing are the chief entertainment."

"At the least, we can share a bit of bread." Mary broke off a piece of the upper crust from his hand. She reached into George's breast pocket and pulled out his handkerchief, and in it she wrapped the bread. "There is no need for formality"—her brown eyes under raised brows shot him a look—"among intimate acquaintances."

George wanted to plant his lips on hers right then and there.

Mary led him to the foyer, away from the others.

"Be it remembered that pocket handkerchiefs served the purposes of tablecloths and napkins and that no apologies would be made for either." He took a bite of the bread in her hand. "Shall we therefore distinguish this night by the style and title of . . . the Bread and Butter Ball?" He spoke with his mouth full.

"I am fond of both." She twirled to the doorway of the dance floor, motioning for him to follow. "And, of course, fond of one of the guests, as well."

The dancing master called out, "Tonight we introduce to the colony the most graceful of dances: the Waltzen."

"May I have this dance, Mary Eliza Philipse?"

A dimple on the right cheek and one on the left.

All his eyes could see was her. All her eyes could see was him.

HIS BREATH TOUCHED her lips as their bodies came ever so close. His left hand settled at her waist. His right hand took her left hand into his. The instrumentalists struck the first chords of "Air on the G String." Her body pressed against his. The form of lyrical movement in the dance had her in a dreamy state, and her heart was swaying toward him even further, giving wings to reciprocal endearment.

Following the three-quarter time, they moved continuously on the floor with a whirl that propelled her into constant motion. Their feet moved in three beats in a perpetual flight. It left Mary dizzy, not as much from the turns as from the proximity of her lips to George's neck. She had never known how handsome a gentleman's neck could be. He had a fine one, muscular. She wished she could place her lips upon it, just to confirm her thoughts; she wouldn't dare.

His powderless chestnut hair was pulled back. She was glad of her evening shoes with their raised heels, which brought her lips closer to his. She inhaled him—clean, manful, with a hint of bergamot, combined into one scent. She could never tire of dancing with him.

SHE COULDN'T TELL how long they had been hand in hand, body against body. With him, time could not be counted in any rational sequence, but melded into one big beautiful moment. They soon found themselves on the outside of the northern doors, still moving to the music of the instrumentalists. Even the coolness of the air did not lower her body's temperature.

Her brother also was there, and he quickly moved toward the two of them. "Colonel Washington, I must ask you this. I've been told you cannot tell a lie." Frederick might have had a glass too many. "This is the truth?"

Mary near leaped in between the two of them. She couldn't believe her brother's audacity.

George answered politely. "I hold the maxim no less applicable to public than to private affairs, that honesty is the best policy."

"Does it not concern you that others may have an unfair advantage, knowing of this attribute?"

"I believe that worry is the interest paid by those who borrow trouble."

Before Frederick could ask another meaningless question, Mary quickly led George away, rushing him toward the staircase. It must have been her heel that caught a plank on the floor, for suddenly she found her herself tripping and falling *up* the stairs.

"It is the first time I have ever seen a person fall up the stairs!"

She burst into giggles from his remark. Normally, she would have been flustered by her clumsiness. She needn't bother with airs around this man.

George joined her in her mirth. They both laughed to the point where her belly hurt. Mary took his hand in hers and guided him onto the second-level staircase. They soon found themselves up another flight, still laughing, until they were outdoors on the roof balcony of the manor.

The stillness of night would have been glorious for most with the moonlight shining upon a calm river. But the sound of a raven in the distance disrupted her thoughts, making her feel an anxious chill. As the pitch began its descent into her bones, George stepped nearer to her and gently placed her body in front of his and wrapped his arms completely around her.

He brought her close to him, protecting her. They remained quiet, taking in each other and the view before them.

"What is it that will make you a happy man, George?"

"More evenings like this one." His voice sounded soft in her ear.

She was absorbed by his loving tone and there, in the night, became lost in his arms. In his strength, her fear dissipated. His cheek touched her temple, and she could feel the roughness of his skin. "And what would make you truly happy, Mary Eliza Philipse?" Her name sounded divine when he said it.

She adored him. "Hearing more of your poetry."

"My mediocre poetry?"

"I wouldn't say mediocre, more like poetry on the verge of distinction."

He covered the side of her face in light kisses. "More like on the verge of extinction." His lips found her dimple. "Very well, 'What will make a life truly blessed? . . . A good estate on a healthy soil, not got by vice, nor yet by toil.'"

"Ah. He gifts me with rhymes."

"'Round a warm fire, a pleasant joke, with chimney ever free from smoke. A strength entire, a sparkling bowl, a quiet wife . . .'"

"A quiet wife—where might you find one?"

"'A quiet soul, a mind as well as body whole.'"

She sighed.

"'Prudent simplicity, constant friends, a diet which no art commends.'"

"If an evening like this, 'tis a diet where no eating commences."

He laughed and continued. "'A merry night without much drinking, a happy thought without much thinking. Each night by quiet sleep made short, a will to be but what thou art.'" His voice sounded more tender. "'Possessed of these, all else defy, and neither wish nor fear to die.'" He turned her shoulder so that she would now be face-to-face with him. "'These are things which once possessed will make a life that's truly blessed.'"

Her lower back tingled as his left hand caressed it, his right through her hair, and she let her head fall back. George placed small kisses at her neck as he spoke to her. "The charms of your person, and the beauties of your mind, have a powerful operation."

"George . . ." She turned her face away from him. "I am undeserving of your kind attention to me. There are things you should know about me—scars that live deep within me that I may never erase."

He cupped her face in his hands. "These have endeared you to me."

Her world changed as his lips found hers. The intensity set her thoughts on fire, her heart into a rapture, her body toward a heavenly serenity.

With earnest ardor, his mouth parted her lips, sending delicious

shivers down her spine. Love's radiant luster shone ever bright, awakening in her a new passion she had not known was within her.

"How do you affect me so?" she whispered to him.

His cheek brushed against hers. "Everything which partakes of your nature has a claim to my affections."

She treasured this man, everything he stood for, everything he was. In his arms, she let go, until their hearts were beating as one. She remained in her blanket of protection as he took her will and breathed it back to life.

With George in her world, she felt whole.

——⋙•⋘——

Chapter Eighteen

Cromwell's Head

There is a Destiny which has the control of our actions, not to be resisted by the strongest efforts of Human Nature.

—GEORGE WASHINGTON

BOSTON

If only he had more time with her. Another week. A year. A lifetime. Instead, he left the manor the morning after the tantalizing grip of affection devoured them on the roof's balcony. He might have asked her right then to be his forever . . . if they weren't interrupted.

Now, more than two weeks later, George was spending his final night in Boston. He journeyed here to Massachusetts where there was business to attend to. He also used a few hours to visit a jeweler, one highly recommended, who melted metal into the shape of a ring.

George's journey to meet the commander in chief of the British forces in North America was only partially successful. George hoped to be granted a royal commission in the British Army, but that was not to be. The general did establish a level of respect for him. British officers had previously refused George's command, claiming that a Virginia officer did not outrank a British officer of lower rank. The

commander in chief ordered that that form of disrespect would no longer be acceptable.

Tonight George found himself at the Cromwell's Head Inn, a musty and dusty old place that looked as if it hadn't been tidied up since the turn of the century. On a wall, a whale's jaw opened wide, and on shelves were displayed the trophies of hunts at sea.

George lowered his head when he entered. The ceiling planks hung low. He was also in need of a larger seat. The small stool was hardly big enough for him, nor was the table, which he towered over. Still, he followed his edict: *When you sit down, keep your feet firm and even, without putting one on the other or crossing them.*

Captains Mercer and Stewart sat at the table with him, leaning over to read his instructions. They traveled with him to the northern colony.

George was writing with his quill. "Blood-warm?"

"Little more than blood-warm, Colonel," advised the inn's owner, Anthony Brackett, a short, stout man with bulging eyes. He offered George and his contingent lodging during their stay in Massachusetts. When they first entered the center of town, Captain Stewart knocked his head right into the tavern's low-hanging swing sign as they walked by it, causing him to need a moment to recover.

"Then put in a quart of yeast," Brackett instructed.

George read the recipe aloud, wanting to double-check his transcibing of it: "To make small beer, take a large sifter full of bran hops to your taste, boil these three hours; strain out thirty gallons into a cooler and put in three gallons of molasses while the beer is scalding hot. Let this stand till it is little more than blood-warm. Put in a quart of yeast. Bottle it the day it is brewed."

"Aye," answered Brackett. "If the weather is very cold, cover it with a blanket and let it work in the cooler twenty-four hours; put it into the cask and leave the bung open till it is almost done working." Brackett placed wooden trenchers of a dark meat and a dish of porridge in front of the men, for what would be their final dinner in the colony.

Stewart and Mercer watched out the window as nearly every

person showed respect in front of that low-hanging tavern sign. "Are they bowing to the sign?" Stewart still had an obvious red mark on his forehead.

"I've hung the sign for Cromwell's Head low to force each passerby to make a reverence to our Lord Protector. We pay homage to a man whose design was not dominion. His judges were the traitors. They were the enemies. Oliver Cromwell was a man who refused the title of king."

"'Tis true, Cromwell's head was put upon a stick?" Mercer prodded him.

"Carried about like a trophy," Brackett grumbled with disgust in his voice as he walked away.

"Was he hero or traitor?" Stewart turned toward George. "Oliver Cromwell. Was he a hero or traitor, Colonel?"

George could have been very clear about his feelings regarding the Lord Protector of the Commonwealth of England, Scotland, and Ireland. It was during the usurpation of Oliver Cromwell in the mid-1600s that George's family had emigrated from one of the northern counties of England, but whether from Lancashire, Yorkshire, or one still more northerly, he did not know precisely. "Hero?" He showed one palm. He turned the other hand over. "Traitor? One's character is rarely drawn until decades, even centuries, after the sphere of action has long come to a conclusion."

George watched as Brackett lumbered to the table with a small sculpted head on a stick and placed it right in the center of the table with a thump. "They should exhume his judges and behead THEM!" Brackett said. "The wretches humiliated the legacy of an honorable man by removing his body from the grave, dragging his corpse through the streets, and taking off his head."

"But what of his body?" Mercer interrupted him.

"His daughter, Mary, removed it from the burial site, protecting it from harm," Brackett replied.

"'Tis a memorable name, Mary." Mercer looked at George.

The name was memorable indeed; however, George felt a bit of irritation when Mercer uttered it.

Mercer's attention was quickly taken by the belles outside the front window of the tavern. "A man who hopes to retain control of his heart should never venture to the north. The ladies are beyond lovely."

"Magnificent," emphasized Stewart. "Our north country is made of beauties."

"Better than those other ladies we've seen, with their bad air and bad shape, like crooked boards." Mercer continued his diatribe, yet again, contorting his body to show a sloping of the back. "Quite different from the enticing, heaving, throbbing, alluring, exciting, plump breasts common with our northern belles."

Let your recreations be manful not sinful. George was careful in this, and hence, he could hold back no longer. "In forming a connection, many considerations besides the mere gratification of the passions are essential to happiness."

"Aye." Stewart nodded.

Mercer puffed, clearly irritated.

"Do we soon return to New York, Colonel?" asked Stewart.

George had learned the answer from a letter he received from stable master Joseph Chew. In it, Chew wrote on a number of matters. He added a postscript on the back of the letter, stating, "I have this moment a Letter from our Worthy friend B. Robinson. He, Mrs. Robinson, and the agreeable Miss Polly and all his family are Very well."

This was the answer to his request that he had desired to hear: agreeable.

George reached down to feel the small box from the jeweler in his pocket. "We leave in the morning."

Chapter Nineteen

———◄•►———

A Soldier and a Lover

*. . . know my good friend that no distance can keep
anxious lovers long asunder . . .*

—GEORGE WASHINGTON

YONKERS-ON-HUDSON

Mary wished George had stayed longer. Another hour. Another day. Forever. He asked for a return visit. She said she was agreeable to it. Of course she was agreeable to it.

Here on the hills' northern pasture, Mary stood alone, her only company the mare named Diamond and her foal. The horse gave birth while George was away in Boston. Mary bore witness to the miracle. Her tears flowed when the filly emerged after a trying delivery. No matter how many times Mary saw the birthing process in the stable, each was a wondrously emotional event.

Today, in the open air, she watched the foal—a young one experiencing life with a mother to help guide the way, a bonding, an intimacy that would remain for a lifetime. Infancy is a splendid thing, she thought, a masterpiece of the heavens, when is born a destiny that, if allowed to flourish, will see its bestowed graces realized.

Taking in the chorus of robins in the trees, she listened for their

whistles proclaiming the approach of the new season. Their melody was leading her into the throes of a wistful embrace. Mary found the harbingers of spring exhilarating. Her mother had been right: This time of year offered great possibility as the day followed a more capacious circuit in the hemisphere; even the shriveled bud began to break through winter's tomb—nature on the threshold of glory. The grass displayed its wee blades. The new shoots upon the weeping cherry tree emerged. Their fragrance wafted on a mellow breeze.

"Each flower must emerge from the darkness to bathe in the light." Mary recalled her mother's words, as well as the emotional inflection she had used to express them. Mama had always sounded as if she were singing. If her voice had been a season, it would have been spring, for there had been such hope in Mama's words.

Mary squinted to see as far as she could. From this highest point of Yonkers, she could canvass the fine landscapes stretched out before her—valleys and hills and waterways; the Hudson and the rivers to the east of it were in view.

She found the entire picture breathtaking—hope in its inception.

For so long, she refused it entry. She turned hope away. Those times she did try to find a light within her, her spirit blocked this vision, chained it and shut it down. Despair always defeated her, dragging her into its abyss.

Mary found a place to lay her heavy blanket and put her quill to paper:

How came you to this place
Where virtue and vice hide
With ardor in your embrace?
Shall I allow you to be my guide,
Or remain behind the guardian's wall?
Let me succumb to dreams of sweet delight.
Into your arms, allow me a fall,
But, alas, a cursed star only lives in the night,
And destiny must be allowed to bloom.

For what I am, I may never know,
There was such grief and gloom.
That was long ago.
Today, grant me release from my cry,
On Cupid's wings, let me fly.

If only she had reached for the flower that day. If only . . .

Regret is not a pretty thing.

The sadness of that day and the many other sadnesses that followed remained for so long. She was tired of the torment. She was tired of living in the past.

George, my love. Without him even knowing it, he was showing her the way.

As she peered about, she thought she could see an image of him, moving quickly. She rubbed her eyes to clear her mind's confusion. When she opened them, she saw with clarity. It was George. In the distance, her hero, her charming. George was coming! With the most perfect posture, he rode with exact rhythm to the stride of his Woodfin. She watched him coming closer.

Without caution, she arose, took one step and another. Soon she was allowing her feet to hit whatever ground was beneath them. One foot leaped in front of the other. Her legs were flying free, for she adored how his eyes gazed into hers, how her heart trembled each time he neared her. She loved the way he touched her without even touching her. If joy could be writ upon her chest, it would be inscribed in capitals. Cupid's feathered dart struck her hard. Today she was ready to surrender to sweet dream's delight. Had she felt this way before? Never.

The belle of the North was in flight on love's wings. Mary Eliza Philipse was running to *him*. She was a dream—pleasing, beautiful, captivating, with a hundred pure charms. He longed to bring her into his arms as he watched the morning sun and its majesty of light glimmer in her long waves, which came undone, flowing up and down with her graceful movement. She didn't try to cover herself, though

her breasts pressed against the fabric of her dress. As he dismounted and laid his feet upon the fertile ground of her land, he moved to meet her, knowing the season had now come.

Love refused to take pity on her as she reached him. Mary, overpowered by emotions, threw herself into his arms. She laid her head upon his chest. She felt his heartbeat on her temple and listened as he released heavy breaths. "I worried you wouldn't come," she said as she sank into his arms. She never wanted to let go.

He stroked the side of her face. He felt her shiver. He placed his other hand into the back of her hair, feeling silkiness through his fingers. He felt her relax in his arms, soften. "Mary Eliza Philipse, my fond heart overflows with joy to see you." She smiled and her lips trembled. A thrill ran through him as he took in her smell: lavender.

How perfect her name sounded coming from his lips. This left her in ecstasy. She couldn't say a word, for there were no words to express the feelings of her heart. First she felt anxious to greet this man. Then she feared kissing him. Now that she knew she adored him, she was afraid to lose him. She realized that she had fallen for him the first moment her name came from his lips.

Sensing her comfort, he felt at ease to make known his sentiments. "If my expression was equal to the feelings of my heart . . ."

His lips were calling her to where warm kisses play. She shyly turned her face from him, for the intimacy of the moment was too much for her to take in. "How did you find me?"

"Mr. Chew directed me to Diamond and the foal. He tells me of the trials you had to bear in helping to deliver her. How brave of you."

"She is beautiful and bears the most lovely patch of white, shaped as a heart. She hath not a name, George."

"What do you suggest we call her?"

We. What a beautiful sound that word carried. She had never known it to be so glorious until he said it. We. "Shall we call her Valentine?"

He brought her close to where her body was against his. "I find

that name entirely perfect." He was beginning to feel such a deep attachment to this woman. He wondered if it was the sort of devotion that belonged to a man who loves only once in a lifetime. He prayed it would be so. "My poor heart. How will it stand to oppose thy might and power?"

She cherished his words and the way he said them, sounding like love in perfect rhythm.

He placed his face against hers and began to take in her breath. "And now lies bleeding every hour, for she will not take pity on me." He removed his long red greatcoat and laid it on the ground. He knelt on it and guided her down to him. Both faced each other, their bodies close, near close enough to touch.

"I believe it is you who should take pity on my heart." Her voice was tender.

He wanted to carry a kiss to her and give her assurances of his fond regard. He took both of her hands in his. "I'll sleep among my most inveterate foes and with gladness never wish to wake."

At this very moment, a realization came clear—one that she never imagined, for she never knew romance in real life, always thinking it a matter of fiction that played out in a poem or a song, but now, as she thought of the wonders of what it would be like to share his bed, as her one hand let go of his and her fingers threaded through his loose hair while staring into his blue-with-a-touch-of-gray eyes, as she fought to keep her lips from reaching up to devour his, as she shifted her gaze to her riding dress, which had slipped off her shoulder, as she lifted her dress back in place, and as she watched him move it back off her shoulder, a truth emerged from the deepest depths of her heart: Mary Eliza Philipse was in love with George Washington.

Her cheek grazed his hand and her creamy skin lingered there—the feel of loveliness in the flesh. His adoration grew fierce at her touch. A light wind moved her hair just so. He moved his fingers to the loose strands and put them back in place. She closed her eyes at this. She looked blissful. He spoke to her quietly. "'Twas perfect love before, but how I do adore." She was completely still, despite the curve of her lips, which ushered in an angelic smile. He placed a kiss

upon her dimpled right cheek. Another kiss he laid upon the left dimple. Gently, he kissed every part of her face.

Again and again, softly his lips touched her skin, leaving a sensation each place he lingered, until she dissolved into his tender passion.

Her lips parted to meet his.

Below the brightness of the meridian sun, two breaths became one.

Part III

The Deception

Chapter Twenty

◈◈◈

Friend or Fiend?

*The turning points of lives are not the great moments.
The real crises are often concealed in occurrences so
trivial in appearance that they pass unobserved.*

—GEORGE WASHINGTON

WINCHESTER, VIRGINIA

George paced the floor of the room he rented at Cocke's Tavern.
For four pounds a month, he could lay his head amid the clamor of
the evening's bumper men playing fives and the odor of bumbo
and ale seeping through the walls. In the day, he conducted his business here.

His personal secretary had accompanied him on his return to
Virginia. "You know nearly every military man is resolved to serve
under the new general and finding every stratagem possible to journey to New York to do so." John Kirkpatrick laid a new scroll flat to
transcribe a letter.

George would have liked to do the same—journey to New York.
His British superiors turned his requests down. Months passed since
the day his treasured one shed tears upon their parting at that place
he fondly remembered as Valentine's Hill. His mind filled with
thoughts of her, every detail of her, down to the softness of her skin
at the nape of her neck. Little time was possible for good-byes. He

yearned to be back in that northern colony to visit his lovely. He wished he had something to remember her by. A miniature—wouldn't that be fine—a portrait miniature that he could place in his pocket and carry with him everywhere he went.

His confidant, stable master Joseph Chew, had pledged he would keep the colonel abreast of Mary Eliza's comings and goings. George wished he could have waited on her for days more; however, an order from the British forces required his return to Virginia. The decision was made to build a fort. "Barbarities daily committed by the French and their Indian allies" is how the crisis was described. George was placed in charge of the construction in the "town of Winchester, in the County of Frederick, Be it Enacted, by the authority aforesaid, That the commander in chief of this colony, is hereby impowered and desired to order a fort to be built with all possible dispatch in the aforesaid Town of Winchester, and that his honor do give such orders and instructions for the immediate erecting and garrisoning."

George began the work the day he arrived in Winchester. Now, months into the mission, he knew that just one fort would not be sufficient. This was dangerous territory. The enemy lurked within miles of this place. George proposed a chain of fortifications to be built on the frontiers, in Augusta and Bedford, and one in Hampshire. George also pleaded for additional men as well as additional supplies.

Even more crucial was getting approval to march against the enemy and stop the incursions once and for all. The prospects for this improved: A new British commander arrived in the colonies to replace the prior general, who refused George's request for an offensive maneuver. It was this new commander to whom George now wrote.

"Must we include the full title, Colonel?" Kirkpatrick was seated at a small desk by the window. He dipped his quill in an inkwell and waited.

"It is expected." George's heels made even-tempoed thumps as he walked with his hands clasped behind his back.

"'The Right Honourable, John, Earl of Loudoun—General and Commander in Chief of all His Majesty's Forces in North America

and Governor and Commander in Chief of His Majesty's Most ancient Colony and Dominion of Virginia'?" Kirkpatrick waited for a reply. "I shall add 'the most pretentiously recrementitious holder of titles of Great Britain.'"

George held back a grin as he asked Kirkpatrick to read back what he'd written in a first draft. Kirkpatrick cleared his throat and began, first reading Loudoun's title in its entirety again, with a smirk, followed by the body of the letter:

> We the Officers of the Virginia Regiment beg Leave to congratulate Your Lordship on your safe Arrival in America: And to express the deep Sense We have of His Majesty's great Wisdom and paternal Care for his Colonies in sending your Lordship to their Protection at this critical Juncture.
>
> Full of Hopes that a perfect Union of the Colonies will be brought about by Your Lordship's Wisdom and Authority, and big with Expectations of seeing the extravagant Insolence of an Insulting Subtle and Inhuman Enemy restrained, and of having it in our Power to take our desired Revenge: We humbly represent to your Lordship, that We were the first Troops in Action on the Continent on Occasion of the present Broils, And that by several Engagements and continual Skirmishes with the Enemy, We have to our Cost acquired a Knowledge of Them, and of their crafty and cruel Practices, which We are ready to testify with the greatest Chearfulness and Resolution whenever We are so happy as to be honoured with the Execution of your Lordship's Commands.

Kirkpatrick drew a breath. "What would you like as the final salutation?" he asked. "'Your most obedient Servant'?"

George signed most letters that way. "If I could have a moment on that matter."

Kirkpatrick rose from his seat. "Take time, then. Decision making,

like coffee, needs a cooling process, as you always say. I'll pour myself a cup of George in the meantime. Would you care for one, Colonel?"

While most Virginians began the day with a mug of ale or beer, Washington favored coffee. "Black, please." *Cup of George*. George knew he never said that, but just shook his head. Kirkpatrick was indeed a card.

George pondered the various possible endings for the letter to Lord Loudoun. "Obedient servant" didn't seem the most appropriate. Instead, he told Kirkpatrick, "'In behalf of the Corps, George Washington, Colo.'"

Chapter Twenty-One

———◆•◆———

Andromeda

. . . to this hour I am held in darkness . . .
—GEORGE WASHINGTON

YONKERS-ON-HUDSON

The portrait artist placed a bouquet of roses on Mary's lap as she sat in the west parlor with autumn's golden light seeping though the window. "Every daughter is her own kind of flower." She thought of her mama. "What kind of flower am I?" she recalled asking her mother as Mary's nose settled into a bloom to inhale its perfume. "Oh, my Polly, you are a beautiful rose."

Out of all the flowers she could be, did she have to be a rose? The rose is a diabolical bit of nature, Mary had come to realize, a complicated flower—much like the charms of life that entice and betray. The rose's alluring perfume draws one in, only to have sharp thorns puncture the skin.

The lace around her neck made her skin itch. Mary tried to keep still. She scratched quickly, put her hair back full in front of her, and made sure not to cover the lovely lily of the valley that was affixed to a brooch at the bustline of her gold gown.

Three hours crawled by with the painter stroking the canvas, stepping back, asking Mary to sit still, sit up straight, adjust the roses. He painted for another hour.

Susannah's lips pursed. "Wilting will commence if you have her sit much longer."

Mary wasn't sure if she was speaking of the flowers on the brooch, those in her lap, or maybe Mary herself. "May I see it?"

The painter nodded. Mary rose from her seat. She shook her foot several times, for it had taken a nap. She carried the roses with care. She planned to place them into an arrangement to deliver to Lulu, Rosie's little girl.

Susannah smiled, her full teeth showing as she stared at the canvas. "Captain Middleton. She is breathtaking!"

Mary leaned her head around to view the canvas. Odd. She didn't remember smiling during the sitting, yet he painted dimples on both her right and left cheeks. The dimples had been passed down to her from her mother, her wavy chestnut hair as well. The painting before her displayed a radiant, blushing beauty. She had to look at it twice, for she could hardly believe it was a likeness of her.

Maybe she *was* beautiful? Or—more likely—it was the result of a fine brush in talented hands. She never heard of James Godsell Middleton before. In fact, the only other portrait she knew he painted was of the mother of the man Mary tried not to think about every minute of every day. This was the information, at least, that Susannah learned from her true.

It was George, she believed, who commissioned Middleton. The painter, though, would not confirm the payer's name. "A gift from an admirer" is how he put it. She hoped George would smile, too, when he saw it. The moment when they would be together again filled her thoughts entirely.

She examined the portrait more closely. On her brooch, the painter stroked tiny buds into the shape of the constellation of Andromeda. Mary walked away to hide her giddiness.

Andromeda!

She came back to the painting again to be sure. Yes. Painted specks in the shape of the chained maiden. First the dimples, then the constellation. She was certain the portrait was commissioned by George. And the artist was beginning a portrait miniature from the large painting. He would say only that it was customary to have a miniature made from the same. She wondered if he would deliver that to her George. Six months now passed since she had seen him in the flesh. She would wait for him to return. Theirs was a perfect felicity.

"*The New-York Mercury* has arrived!" Temperance called out to the sisters.

"The wedding announcement is expected to be printed today!" exclaimed an elated Susannah as she received the two publications from Temperance. One of them, she placed to the side. As for the other, she turned the pages until settling on one of them. Susannah read aloud:

Last Thursday night, Colonel Frederick Philipse, Esq.,
of Philipsburg, in this Province, was married to
Mrs. Elizabeth Rutgers, Widow of the late Anthony Rutgers, Esq.,
and Daughter of Charles Williams, Esq., Naval Officer for the
Port of New York; a very agreeable Lady and possessed of
every Virtue and Accomplishment that can adorn her Sex
and make the Marriage State truly happy.

"How lovely for them! I wish you would have danced on that night." Susannah's disappointment with Mary was clear.

Mary danced—one dance—with her brother on his wedding night. She refused to dance with the other men who asked, many of them military officers.

"Just because you dance with someone doesn't mean you are ruining yourself for Colonel Washington, my sister."

"I danced. Did you not see my minuet with our dear brother?"

"It seemed every bachelor was waiting for a chance to waltz with you."

That would not be. The feelings of her heart were unalterably fixed. Mary caught a glimpse of the other newspaper brought into the parlor. The *Virginia Gazette*. How perplexing, she thought. "Who delivered this to the manor?"

Susannah shrugged.

"May I see that other publication?" requested Mary, knowing the colonel who captured her heart commanded the Virginia Regiment.

Susannah carried it over to her. Mary placed down the roses, and took the publication to the light of the window. Nearly the entire front page was taken up by one article:

An effeminate Creature, that spent all his Time in the
Company of Women, Feasting, Rioting. Certainly,
Censure cannot be silence; nor can the Public receive much
Advantage from a Regiment of such dastardly Debauchees.

They employed themselves in nothing but Banquets, Games,
Parties of Pleasure and Carousals. Public Rewards were
bestowed on those, who gave the most magnificent Entertainments; and even to such Cooks of Genius, as were best skilled in
the important Arts of inventing new Refreshments to tickle the
Palate.

Mary realized the author was comparing the commander of the Virginia Regiment to the most scurrilous military leaders in history. An assault on George? Her George? How could it be! She couldn't believe what else was written about him: "Sensual Indulgencies were his daily Employ," she read. "Their Country calls; and see! the Hero runs to save her." Save *her*? Could they have been speaking . . . of *her*? Written anonymously, signed L. & V. An anonymous cow-ard! It had to be . . . or someone else. The article continued with a passage from Virgil:

Quis metus, o numquam dolituri, o semper inertes
Tyrrheni, quae tanta animis ignauia venit?
Femina palantis agit, atque haec agmina uertit?
Quo ferrum, quidue haec gerimus tela inrita dextris?
At non in Venerem segnes nocturnaque bella,
Aut, ubi curua choros indixit tibia Bacchi,
Exspectare dapes et plenae pocula mensae—
Hic amor, hoc studium—

She translated the passage in her head as best she could. She moved herself to her bedchamber to be alone. Feelings of dread creeped through her. She looked again at the passage. Mary covered her mouth with her hand to stop a scream and rushed to her shelf for a book with an English translation of the *Aeneid*. After swiftly turning page after page, she found it:

What fear, what cowardice has filled your hearts,
O, sluggish Tuscans, O you, who are never ashamed?
Can a woman drive you to scatter and turn your ranks?
Why bear our hand with useless swords and spears, steel not
    made to fight?
But you are not slow to love or for battles of the night, nor when
the curved pipe proclaims Bacchus' dance.
Wait then for the feast and cups on the plenteous table,
Your passion, your pleasure is there.

Was she to blame? Others might have taken her attention to him—and his to her—and turned it into salacious gossip. She stepped back from the newspaper and remained still. An esteemed colonel reduced to this with the stroke of an evil pen. Hatred in ink. He must be devastated to have read such an offensive article, she thought.

She knew better than to believe any of it. Not George.

She looked down to see her laced glove stained red. Blood. The sight made her queasy. She tried to shake her head to clear it of its

dizzy feeling. A thorn must have punctured her skin. This reaffirmed what she already knew.

A rose has thorns.

Could it be her curse beginning to defeat him? Censure George? She prayed it would not be so. She knew she should have shunned him. That would have kept him protected. The newspaper—she neatly folded it and quickly moved to place it on the shelf of her bookcase above the other, words away from her.

A disturbance overwhelmed her and she felt faint. She dropped her body into a chair. She looked again at the publication to be sure it was in proper position on the shelf—writing away from the cursed.

Right there, she fell down to her knees in prayer:

Please, angels, take up my fight. Protect him. Keep him safe. Please, angels, listen to my prayer. Protect George from the enemy. I've hurt too many. I am the one who deserves to be punished. Don't let him be cursed by the cursed. Please, angels, don't give up on his plight; don't leave him alone, for a rose . . . for a rose has thorns.

Worry, when it got ahold of her, caused her mind to begin playing its tricks. Inner demons, they weaken your faith. They put strange thoughts into your mind. Inner demons don't fight fairly. Like a nightmare, they strike even in waking hours. She was trembling. Think of nothing. Empty your mind, she told herself. Terrifying images would often haunt her when she lost herself in despair. She had gotten glimpses of the frightening pictures in her head throughout her life. Lately, they were darker than ever, clouding her rationality. Drag me. Punish me. Leave me to rot. She should have been the one taken.

A thick white fog rolled toward her, turning dark as it crept over filthy ground. From it, a little hand emerged, reaching for her in desperation. She couldn't get to him. She couldn't save him. A beast with a crooked finger pulled her away, covered her mouth until her throat closed from the dust, her air taken away, plunging her into nothingness.

The night that changed her days was becoming clearer. She was remembering what happened, why she ran outside when her mother said to stay put, why she was always terrified when the man of her nightmares came near her.

She rose from her kneeling place, walked downstairs to the kitchen, grabbed hold of a knife, and entered the darkness of the cellar.

Chapter Twenty-Two

---◄•►---

The Invisible Enemy

I hate deception . . .

—GEORGE WASHINGTON

WINCHESTER

George wanted to take the author by the neck. Infuriating! Two thousand words on the front page of the *Virginia Gazette,* each one driving a dagger through his reputation, inch by inch. How dare someone write such lies, and with identity concealed! Who would dare accuse him of such inordinate depravity? Signed anonymous with a pseudonym—L. & V. Washington slammed the paper down onto his desk.

In black and white were printed accusations of drunkenness and profanity in his regiment:

No Profession in the World can secure from Contempt and Indignation a Character made up of Vice and Debauchery; and no Man is obliged to treat such a character as sacred. When raw Novices . . . never used to command or have been found insufficient for the Management of their own private Affairs are honored with Commissions in the Army.

Kirkpatrick charged into the room, holding a copy. "Vain babbling! Worthless—malicious—envious sycophants!" Kirkpatrick became angry in the face and stomped his foot. "Colonel, these assertions are utter nonsense. Insanity. Who dares write such slander?"

Never express anything unbecoming, nor act against the rules moral before your inferiors. George chose civility in Kirkpatrick's presence, although he wanted to utter coarse words against the article's author.

"Ill-natured slander!" asserted Kirkpatrick. "Two, three, four men gathered together to propagate lies and lay them onto paper."

Let your conversation be without malice. George tried to remain calm. He made clear that he wasn't interested in discussing this with Kirkpatrick.

His secretary seemed to get his message and walked toward the doorway. "Remember what Alexander Pope says—'Envy will merit, as its shade, pursue, but like a shadow, proves the substance true. . . .'"

George also knew what else Pope had written: "Be silent always when you doubt your sense." He read through the article once more. The most scathing denunciation of his ability was printed in the paper.

> . . . Soldiers differ; some will shed their *Blood,*
> And some drink *Bumbo*—for their Country's Good.
> Some in the Field will nobly risque their Lives;
> Some Hero like, will *swear,* or play at *Fives.*
> Some show themselves the genuine Sons of *Mars*:
> Some brave in *Venus'* or *Bacchus'* Wars,
> Can show their *lecherous* and *drunken* Scars.

> . . . when the Officers give their Men an Example
> of all Manner of Debauchery, Vice and Idleness,
> When this is the Case, how wretchedly helpless
> must a Nation be? What useless Lumber, what an
> Encumbrance is the Soldiery.

Men of Virtue and true Courage can have
no Heart to enlist, and mingle in such a Crowd. And the
few of that Character, that may be among them, are in
Danger of catching the general Contagion; of being
damped and mortified at the Sight of such Scenes of
Vice, Extravagance and Oppression.

The article continued with a final strike at his reputation, with a quote from Shakespeare that the writer used to defame him.

Men's Flesh preserv'd so whole but seldom win.

George's jaw muscles clenched. He could nearly feel his blood getting hot. If there was a person who believed him incapable of command or, more seriously, in need of censure, he wanted to know who it was. No one would endeavor to act more in the interests of the military than George.

Certainly his inexperience had led to some mistakes in his leadership, but his first principle in every move he made in the military was a deep love to serve. He was sensible enough to know that some in his contingent were idle. He was far from exonerating the traits of his officers, but to compare him to a prince who destroyed his empire—this was blasphemy.

A heavy knock at the door of his room at Cocke's Tavern drew his attention. He answered it, still holding the publication, to find the Honorable John Robinson, Beverley's brother. George had asked him to come. He was glad to see him for a number of reasons, one being affirmation, the other a personal favor.

"A vile and ignorant scribbler!"

George needed that confirmation.

"To be aspersed in such a way!" Robinson found himself a seat and grunted before his muttering continued. "To whom shall we give credit for the malicious reflections in that scandalous libel?"

George's pacing was emphatic as he stepped toward the window of the room, hesitated, and turned back. "I do not know."

"I have never heard any man of honor or reputation speak the least disrespectfully of you or censure your conduct in the least."

"I have followed the strictest dictates of honor." George placed himself on a bench near the one window in the room. He opened it with his right hand; he needed some air.

"No man can blame you for showing a proper resentment at it."

"I assure you my conduct will remain honorable so long as I am able to distinguish between good and evil."

"I hope you will allow your ruling passion, the love of your country, to stifle your resentment. At least await the arrival of Loudoun in Virginia."

George glanced around at the four walls of his small room. He had to gain control of his emotions. An utter attack on his character from an anonymous writer! He walked to the hall for a moment's escape from the confines of the space. He called for food and drink for his guest. *Be not angry at table whatever happens and if you have reason to be so, show it not but on a cheerful countenance.* Then he returned for a discussion on the subject that would be dear to the heart of any man. "May we speak on another matter?" George cleared his throat. "The personal one."

Chapter Twenty-Three

—◈—

Lord Loudoun's Banquet

. . . it is uncertain how far the Enemy may attempt to pursue their Victory.

—GEORGE WASHINGTON

YONKERS-ON-HUDSON
DECEMBER 24, 1756

Ten months had gone by since George swept Mary into his arms and she felt, for the first time in her life, whole. Now her eyes welled up. Sitting on a wooden stool feeling distraught, she slouched. The only light came from the window in her painting room in the cellar.

Live or die?

What would be the choice?

Mary begged herself to close the door on what had been, to say good-bye to the dark. She had grown tired of hiding herself away, of losing herself in loneliness. She wanted to finally put an end to the demons, put an end to the memories of that beast, before they put an end to her. She placed her fingers on the knife's hilt and grasped it tightly. A primal anguish screamed out from the base of her soul.

"Die!"

The blade made its incision.

She pictured the powerful imagery in that story she read many times about the legend of the Phoenix. In the myth, the grand bird builds a nest of death and, with a clap of its wings, sets fire to itself, and burns in flames in the midst of an inferno.

Death was not the end, but the beginning.

From the ashes, the Phoenix rises, brilliantly rises. Feathers in the boldest peacock blue, eyes sparkling sapphire, the magical bird takes flight, illuminating the night sky in newfound life, one that is brighter, more radiant than before.

Renewal.

Rebirth.

With the paring knife, she tore into a rose, and into another and another, lashing the pile of flowers before her; they were bloodred, as were her fingers from the nicks of their thorns. The deepest red roses she chopped down to where only the blossom with a short stem survived. The stems with their thorns, she tossed away.

She arranged the roses in a radial fashion to make a full base in the low Delft vase. Bright blue irises, twenty in total, emerged from the center—tall, reflective of the rise to a new beginning.

She wished she could experience the same.

She heard footsteps.

She put down the knife.

She assumed it was Frederick coming to negotiate her surrender. Her siblings wanted her to attend the banquet hosted by Lord Loudoun. She hadn't been to a gala since George left. Every day, he was in her thoughts. Every day, she waited for word from him. The only letter that arrived was to Beverley, from Beverley's brother, asking whether Frederick would consider negotiation through letters, for Colonel Washington's physical presence was not possible at this time. Mary was elated, for negotiation could lead to nuptials. Frederick balked, saying such was unheard of. "Any such discussion has to be done face-to-face," he told her. She fought him on this, but in the end she relented, for she believed with certainty that George would return for her. He promised he would return to her.

She wiped her eyes as her visitor entered.

Sir Tenoe. He was silent. The first thing she noticed was the scar on his face, which looked even deeper in this light. She cast her eyes to the ground as she tried to regain some type of composure. Blood on her hands. Slits, small ones, covered her fingers.

"Sir Tenoe." She used the fabric of her dress to cover them. "Forgive me. I knew not of your visit." He was hired to serve as dancing master for the night's grand banquet. She was glad of this. It was the only reason she even considered attending. Why he was here left her perplexed. "Was it Frederick who sent for you?" She blew out of her mouth to get the hair away from her eyes. It wasn't like him not to speak. She wondered what it was that he wanted to say. From his long silence, she surmised it wasn't something she wanted to hear.

He reached out to touch the floral garlands that lined the walls of the cellar room and his fingers lingered on the dried petals painted blue. "Each of us has a scar."

That was not what she expected.

"Mine"—he gestured to his face—"mine is on display for everyone to see."

Mary remained quiet as she listened to him.

"This wound, it is who I am."

With her head, Mary motioned for him to take a seat at the empty stool in front of her.

He followed her direction and took to staring out the window as he spoke. "I had just turned thirteen. I was poor, without a father. The day that left me branded I had scraped food for supper when I saw them—a group of men. They smelled of whiskey; they stumbled, with a little girl in their grip. She was no more than eleven, twelve, no more. I'd never seen her before. They slammed her down to the ground. They hollered things, horrible things, at her. 'Pay no attention, boy. Move on,' they ordered." Tenoe spoke slowly. "Leaving would not be my option." A rhythm of short quick breaths followed. "One of them put his hands over her mouth. Another held her down. I charged into their circle in the alley. 'Release her!' I shouted. I was

enraged. I'd never been so angry in my life. I heard them snickering. That little girl's eyes stared at me in fierce desperation." Tenoe's eyes shut tight. "My mother . . . she had faced that same fate; for her, I stayed; for her, I fought. One punch. Then another. I stayed. The six of them, they beat me bloody. I stayed. I fell down. I rose. I stayed. The child got up. She ran. I wouldn't move until that girl was clear out of sight. I saw the broken bottle coming. A man struck me across the face with it. I stayed . . . until that girl was clear out of my sight." Tenoe looked right into Mary's eyes. "I wear this scar with pride."

Tears burst from Mary's eyes.

"Fate put me there that day, just like it puts me here today." He reached out for her hand. She could see him looking at the bloody pricks on her fingers. "Destiny doesn't care that we're wounded. Destiny sees through scars. All that destiny sees is light."

AN AWKWARD FIFTH wheel, that's what Mary felt like in the carriage as Frederick and his new bride made goggle eyes at each other on one side. Beverley, whispering to Susannah, who giggled, sat next to Mary; the three of them were positioned quite close. Beverley was nearly covered in the fabric of their bell-shaped gowns, which spread out wide. Mary looked out of the window past the leafless elm trees, hoping to find a light to guide her destiny. Not a brightness flickered anywhere.

Her brother's periwig took an unexpected bounce as the carriage moved off of the central thoroughfare of Broadway and onto Whitehall Street, where the banquet was to take place on the southernmost point at the tip of Manhattan Island.

Within the walls of the massive fort curtained in stone, inside the fort's residential mansion lived the new general and commander in chief of all His Majesty's Forces in North America, the governor and commander in chief of His Majesty's Most ancient Colony and Dominion of Virginia. Why he had the longest of titles, Mary could only surmise. She wondered, too, why he decided to take up residency in New York rather than in Virginia.

As she stepped from the carriage to the ground, Mary could hear

her brother say to Susannah, "Do you not think she should have worn a piece with her gown?"

Her brother was dressed in holiday ostentation from head to toe: a fully woolen greatcoat of a deep purple adorned with velvet trimmings and nearly thirty gold buttons down the front. His chain marking him Keeper of the Deer Forests was on proud display.

Mary didn't answer him. She refused to wear anything fancy to the banquet, especially gems. Rosie made a last moment's choice of a simple gown made of deep green Spitalfields damask, with an added brooch of a yellow flower; the costume was certainly less fancy than the usual wear for such an event. Her hair was wrapped above her head, high, but not high enough to be considered gaudy.

She was here for one person only. She promised Sir Tenoe that she would attend. How could she not? Here she was.

Mary relaxed a bit when she saw two belles approaching her. Cousins Eva and Margaret arrived at the same time. Not just the Van Cortlandts and the Kembles would be in attendance; the Livingstons, the Delanceys, and every other polite family in the colony were expected.

"Have you seen Lord Loudoun's chariot?" Margaret appeared elated to be attending. "'Tis black and pure gold!" She did look lovely in her bold red gown, her blond ringlets flowing. "I hear he even brought from England his personal *valet de chambre* and *maître d'hôtel*. Groomsmen, coachman, footmen, postilion, as well!"

"We know. We know." Eva stayed close to Mary's side as they walked through the enormous entry door. "And who needs to import nineteen horses? Every one with green velvet housing embroidered with the coat of arms of the Loudoun family. I hear they filled an entire ship."

Mary was glad she was arriving with these ladies. They took her mind off her worries. The crowds would be enormous. She could already smell them.

"What will be the reaction when the British officers see Miss Polly

Philipse in attendance?" Eva took Mary by the arm. "Every military man will be wanting to join the regiment of your admirers."

"Eva Van Cortlandt, you are aware I have no desire to meet a man this evening," Mary muttered.

"Her heart is fixed," replied Eva. "Any gentlemen who have demands on our Captain Polly are desired to apply immediately, as we have great reason to imagine the company will soon be broke!"

They placed themselves on either side of her as they entered. Mary took one last breath of fresh, chilled air. As the large doors opened, pine smacked with cinnamon welcomed her.

Everything in view was red. Red flowers were everywhere she looked. Upon pillar stands in every corner were vases filled with forced red blossoms. Long-needled garlands, with cinnamon sticks and red ribbons as decoratives, traveled about the winding stairwell's balustrade in the center foyer. On the doors hung wreaths made from winter's greenery with red-ribboned bows at their tops. The assemblage of redcoats parted to give the belles room to approach the host of the evening.

"Could that be London?" Margaret asked with burgeoning excitement.

"Loudoun," Eva groaned. "Must be. I can tell by how high his chin is lifted."

The gentleman of high rank seemed to hasten his conversation with the sheriff's father, Lieutenant Governor Delancey, as they neared him. Costumed in bright red velvet with shimmering gold tassels, Loudoun stood high on his heel.

"The Dutch millionaire's family," Mary thought she heard an aide say as the man she assumed to be Lord Loudoun moved from his position to greet her.

"How is it that I may sufficiently thank you, Miss Philipse, for not only your polite acceptance of my invitation but also for the agreeable gift of your flowers?"

"The Philipse family wishes you a splended holiday," she responded in an amiable manner. The floral arrangement of the Phoenix design clearly arrived.

"I am abundantly honored to have your presence at my gala this evening. You are welcome in my humble abode at any hour, always." His voice was higher in pitch than Mary would have thought for a person in his position, his face so pale, it seemed he must have been powdered white. "And may I add all the compliments of the season to you, Miss Philipse." His pure white hand, decorated with a ruby ring, brought her gloved hand up to his lips. He kissed it. She flinched.

The ladies escorted her to the reception line, where the salutations were endless, with one officer after the next awaiting Mary's arrival. Her hands were kissed far too many times.

One colonel hastily licked his palm and smoothed thinning gray hair over his baldness as she drew near. He mumbled a few lines to her, which she forgot to listen to. She did catch his name: Colonel John Stanwix.

Then another colonel, Thomas Hickey, greeted her, followed by a lieutenant colonel, Hugh Mercer.

"Are you a relation of Captain George Mercer?" asked Mary.

"I've been asked the question before," replied Mercer. "My family hails from Scotland, while the other Mercer hails from Virginia. However, as I understand it, I'll be headed there in a week's time and hope to finally meet the captain I am connected to, though in name only."

"Pray be so kind as to present my regards to Captain Mercer . . . and Colonel Washington." Just saying his name sent shivers down her spine. She felt a warmth on her cheeks.

"'Twould be my pleasure, Miss Philipse. My wish for a merry Christmas to you and your family."

Mary noticed Margaret adjust her hair ringlets as they approached a strapping Englishman with dark eyebrows that stood out against his powdered hair. Thomas Gage was his name.

Eva's face filled with giddy anticipation as they approached the next man. Mary always found him to be an interesting-looking fellow with waved hair that flared like a bell.

"It is he! It's Scandal," whispered Eva.

He spoke to them in rhythmic verse. "Let me sigh, for nothing can be more delightful to the eye, nothing more penetrating to the heart than seeing the glorious women of this colony from whom I'll never desire to part."

After Eva's hand was sufficiently kissed, Mary had to pick her up from a curtsy that lasted longer than necessary.

"I understand congratulations are in order, Mr. Pownall," Mary said to him.

"Lord Loudoun has been gracious to add Secretary Extraordinaire to my title," he bragged.

This greeting was followed by one with Delancey, who was dressed in a showy and gay manner for the evening. Mary tried to move past him quickly or else be caught up in his stare, accompanied by a single lifted eyebrow.

The next officer was quite fashionable, buttoned up, light brown hair combed neatly and tied back, and smelling significantly scrubbed. His nose was large, shifted to the left, and had a serious mark on it. "In this moment, my heart takes flight." He flashed his ivory. He fell to his knees, saying, "*Genista triquetra*," with an animated expression as he merrily kissed her gloved hand not once but three times.

Mary winced and pulled her hand away. "Sir, please."

He rose and spoke with a British accent. "When a lady possesses every grace and beauty as is possible to attain, do you not believe she should be praised for such a fine choice in flowers?"

Mary's brooch—a yellow flower whose formal Latin name was *Genista triquetra*. The fellow was right. *Genu*, from the Latin word meaning of the knee. She was quite surprised he knew of it, but now she understood his reason for kneeling.

"Your charm alone affects me so." Loudly he made this proclamation. "I do declare, here and now, if you deny me the pleasure of one dance with you this evening, you will send me to the grave."

"Sir, I must present a nay in that regard, for I hardly know you."

"My name is Roger Morris, captain in His Majesty's Army and at the service of the finest belle of the ball."

"It does not become me to bear witness to such public proclamations." Mary hurriedly moved past him and right into Bernadette Clara Belle's towering structure erected at the apex of her head. The entire circle of maidens by Bernadette's side, including Emily Joyce and Elle Cole, was on a parade of pretension, showing off the mountainous monstrosities that called their heads home. If Mary could measure Bernadette's hair, she presumed it would equal a yard high, being that it was buttressed with gauze, ribbons, and that feathered quill again. She had seen garish fashions before, but these heaps might very well take the cakes. She stood in amazement, gazing at the bigness that literally stood up on its own.

"You never afforded me a correspondence in response to my letter to you." Bernadette emphasized the *s* sound in her speech with her usual coquettish tone. For years—it seemed forever—Bernadette had not had a kind word to say to Mary. Now, suddenly, she decided to attempt a connection.

Mary delayed a response, for she was still astonished by how such a pile could remain balanced upon Bernadette's head. The letter, she had never read, assuming it a disingenuous attempt at friendship. She wondered whether Bernadette used the feather on her head to write it. "Yes, while my spirit had a willingness to write, the flesh would not guide my quill," said Mary.

Eva and Margaret faked a smile to Bernadette and moved Mary into the hall. Once they were away from the crowd, Eva began to joke about the military men they met in the reception line.

"I surmise none of these lads has made an impression on our Captain Polly Philipse. Therefore, we shall now determine those killed, wounded, deserted, and discharged from Captain Polly's regiment during this, the Campaign of 1756." Eva pretended to write upon an imaginary scroll. "And what shall we make of that valiant nobleman who bows before his captain?"

"The Morris fellow's forehead was nicely sized," added Margaret. "I believe a sign of distinction."

Mary laughed. She was surprised they didn't comment on his nose.

"Our Earl of Loudoun?"

Mary shook her head.

"Very well. Although I believe he would be interested in mustering occasionally. He did offer you an invite to the mansion . . . at any hour. I shall give, now, the conditions of the others, and if you disagree, please acknowledge." The two of them listened to Eva's silliness. "What of Colonel Stanwix?"

"He nearly looked devastated by Polly's reaction to him."

"What was my reaction to this Stanwix fellow?"

"You hardly noticed him," noted Margaret.

"I didn't hear a word the man said to me."

"I would say wounded and taken by surprise," offered Margaret.

"And what of our sheriff, Captain Delancey?" Eva looked at Mary.

"Outlawed!" Mary couldn't help but offer her assessment of him.

"Tell me where the charmer is on the list." Margaret stared at the officers' line.

"Colonel Gage?" inquired Mary.

"Colonel Gage. Just the name affects me so."

"Let us place him in the regiment of Captain Margaret," suggested Mary.

"There is no doubt he will have you on the dance floor this evening," Eva assured her and turned to look at Mary.

"Pownall?" asked Eva with a glint in her eye. "Or shall we go by his pseudonym, Timothy Scandal. He is a Secretary Extraordinaire, indeed. The finest writer in all of the colonies. He is the scholarly author of the political letters printed in our newspapers. He's proficient in Latin, as well, which clearly I am not, even in the English language."

"Yes, but after seeing your minuet, Eva, he is 'likely to desert' the Captain Polly regiment and for certain join that of Captain Eva."

"I only hope of it. And now we return to the condition of our Captain Roger Morris."

"Discharged," asserted Margaret. "No, no. Wounded."

"Ah, yes, but the one who kneels, it seems, has an adoration for

her which runs deep." Eva's lips went crooked as she put on her thinking face. "I will mark him down as 'shot through the heart.'"

Shot through the nose would be more appropriate, thought Mary.

Attention was being drawn to the grand staircase as the Delanceys called for the crowd to enter the foyer.

The lieutenant governor, with his son the sheriff at his side, made the announcement. "May I introduce our Lord and Victor, John, Earl of Loudoun, our general, our commander in chief over all our forces, regular and provincial, and governor general of Virginia."

"How many titles does one man need?" Eva whispered.

Mary tried to prevent a guffaw from being released from her mouth as Loudoun walked to the center of the room. After polite yet dull applause, he began to drone on about his dominions. He spoke in a patronizing tone.

Before Loudoun uttered his final word, the kneeler approached Mary. "I would be the most crestfallen officer in the world if you should not allow me one dance this night."

The first chord was struck. She saw Sir Tenoe on the floor, leading as dancing master.

Mary found herself with Captain Morris in a moment's time as the crowd moved them to the center of the room. She tried to separate from him; however, he became more emphatic with his requests. "You shall plunge me into a evening of wretchedness! I shall cry aloud as you banish me into a dismal abyss!" exclaimed Morris.

In order to not make the awkward situation worse, especially with the importance of the event for Sir Tenoe, she reluctantly began to move with him, although resisting conversation. His teeth were fully on display. The singer erupted into "Love's but a Frailty of the Mind."

"My first opportunity," Captain Morris practically sang out, "to dance with the one on whom is fixed the chief happiness I wish to enjoy in this world."

At least he wore no hair powder. She felt thankful for that. She caught Sir Tenoe's eye; he nodded his approval.

She kept a distance between herself and the captain as the two of them moved about the dance floor. He had a gaiety to his step. Her

eyes kept falling on his pinned flower. She didn't recognize the species. She was curious to ask about it, but to question this fellow might lead to further conversation, which she wanted to avoid.

"If there's delight in love," the singer crooned, "'tis when I see that heart which others bleed for, bleed for me." The final verse.

Mary decided to speak. "Please, give me leave to acquaint you with the fact that I have no intention of courtship. I am quite content with my present situation." She hastily made her escape; the moment of release was liberating.

It wasn't even a minute's time that passed before a group of little boys grabbed hold of her. "Miss Philipse! Miss Philipse!"

What a pleasant surprise it was to find her young friends at the ball. She recognized the boys one at a time, nodding to each. "Mr. Livingston, Mr. Livingston, Mr. Jay, how do you do this evening?"

Henry Livingston Jr., with cute chubby red cheeks and hair so blond that it could be considered white, darted toward an adjacent parlor with his hand still in hers and sat her down on a bench near the fire. "'Tis the night before Christmas!" he said.

"Oh, Henry, it certainly is."

"My cousins, Robert and John, have tired of listening to my rhymes."

"Of what subject are you composing? Something that makes you happy?"

"Tonight. Tonight makes me happy, 'Tis the night before Christmas." She could see his mind working hard. "And all through the house," he continued, "nothing was astir. Not even a horse."

"That doesn't rhyme at all," Robert interrupted.

"I find your rhyme thoroughly enjoyable," Mary encouraged Henry.

"I am now eleven years of age, Miss Philipse," announced John.

"Mr. Jay, you just had a birthday?"

"I did."

"And what do you want to be when you grow up?"

"A justice of the peace, just like your father, Miss Philipse." John Jay stood up straighter.

"Me, as well." Robert's posture followed suit.

"A noble profession, sirs. I shall call you by different names from henceforth: the Honorable Robert Livingston, the Honorable John Jay, and the poet Livingston."

"Thank you, Miss Philipse," they chimed in unison.

"Have you seen my brother this evening?" asked John. "He has been looking for you."

A shudder came over her. She turned quickly to look over her shoulder, scanning the room for the beast with the green eyes hard as glass. Her throat went dry as she turned back toward the boys. The day had come. She had to confront him. She had to bring herself out of this darkness. This was the only way. She knew now what had happened that night, the one that marked her life before and her life after. James Jay was responsible. Address him. Find a release from the weight of it, she encouraged herself. There was no other way forward. She thought of how Sir Tenoe fought and fought when evil confronted him. She had to do the same . . . for herself. With that, she got up and straightened her stance. "And I am looking for him as well."

It didn't take long for her to find the subject of her fears. He was standing alone in the corner of a hallway just outside the room where she had been with the boys. Her hands trembled. She clasped them together to stop them from shaking. She remembered the pain of that day so long ago, in the room of the cellar at the manor, as he pulled her hair and wouldn't let go. "You will be my queen, and I your king" had been his words to her. The smell of his hair powder—she could never get his stench out of her. She was just a little girl at the time. She remembered running from him, his spurs sounding as he chased her. She had closed the door to the cellar, holding tightly to the knob. He fought from the other side of the door.

Now she approached him with purpose in her walk, and she pointed her finger into his face."YOU! It was YOU who caused the nightmare that lives with me every day of my life," Mary cried out to him. She finally found the voice to put an end to his tyranny over her.

"You who made me fear the water, fear the dark, fear the unknown. It was you. You tormented me over and over again. I was just a little girl. Then, the day you dragged me into the room in the cellar. Held my face into the floor for so long I could not breathe. I had to run for my life, until I found myself outside, alone on the south porch. You caused me to run. My mother would be alive if not for you. I lost her because of you."

"Oh, my dear Polly, I am deaf to your words, for I hear only a yearning in your voice." James Jay lifted a hand to her face, and with the other, he placed a tight grip about her waist. His hair powder was thick and crusty at his scalp as he grabbed her and pushed her into a darkened room. "You affirmed it, my darling."

———<•>———

IT HAD BEEN dark then, too. So dark. She was scared. Her little arm hurt when he pinched her. She held the doorknob as tightly as she could. Keep him away. He was coming for her. The door pulled open. She tried to close it. He won. He grabbed her and dragged her down the cellar stairs, into the tiny room with the small window. He pushed her down. She covered her eyes. She wanted him to disappear. He yanked her hair back as he held her down into the hard ground and repeated the words to her: "You will be my queen, and I your king." She was too scared to yell. He said it again, then screamed at her, "Affirm it! Affirm it!" His face covered her face. She breathed in his hair powder. She gasped for breath, taking in dust; it covered her tongue and throat. She couldn't yell. "You will be my queen, and I your king. Affirm it!" "Yes," she whispered. He let her go. She ran outside, where Elbert found her, and by the river he picked a flower to make her happy.

———<•>———

NOW A FOG BEGAN to envelop her. Her body shuddered. She struggled to get free. Tears flooded her eyes and shut her throat. Her vision blurred. Her hand fought him, pushing him from her. She fought

until she couldn't breathe. His hand was over her face. The darkness won. The drag of his spur upon the floor followed as she felt him lift her up. The shutting of the door was the next sound she heard, until he spoke in a wet whisper close to her face. "Whether it be in life or in death, you are mine and always will be."

Chapter Twenty-Four

—◄•►—

Doubtful Spring

I am left like a wanderer in a wilderness.

—GEORGE WASHINGTON

WINCHESTER

The temperature dropped near twenty degrees, leaving the air miserably raw, much like his mood, since he spent the Christmas season in near desolation. His reputation had been damaged by a still-unknown scribbler and his hopes of a holiday in the North dashed. George stood at the edge of a six-foot-wide hole in the ground, glaring into its empty depths. It seemed a lost cause.

"Can't say there will be any likelihood of a spring," Lieutenant Charles Smith said as he placed down an empty bucket. He'd been digging for water for months now. He was one of the few officers who didn't complain over lack of money, lack of clothes, or lack of protection. Smith continued to serve at the fort for another reason: His military status would likely keep him from conviction.

"How many feet?" George designed the well on paper and figured Smith's oversize hands were strong enough to use the hand tool to create holes in the limestone. After all, Smith's fist killed a man with just one punch; the fellow died on the spot.

"The hole is near ninety feet deep." Captain Stewart was overseeing Smith's project.

Not a drop of water in it.

"Fill it with gunpowder and detonate. Continue to one hundred feet," George instructed them.

The only drop came from above. A misty rain fell for days, making everything damp, like his optimism. His mouth was dry.

Not reaching water added to his troubles at this fort. The other more pressing issue was war. Twenty people were killed just twelve miles from the garrison. George sent a detachment to find the savages—without success. How could he secure a frontier of more than 350 miles with minimal manpower? He was using every means in his power, but the effort was in vain.

Even protection of the fort itself was unacceptable. George was in need of twenty-four cannons. Twelve-pounders protected it now, and only a few. As he looked up to the bastions, he knew they were nearly defenseless. An attack with a half-pounder could destroy it and destroy them. Maybe he was capable of an hour's defense. Maybe.

The blank sky was welcoming deep, dark clouds. George headed back to his space inside the partially built fort. Sweeping winds picked up quickly, pushing the rain against the single window of the room. He felt choked by these four walls, so tight, and by his circumstances. On his desk, he rolled out the designs for the fort. Fully constructed, it would include four bastions and barracks for 450 men. But now, even the mission itself he questioned. Why did this place exist other than to keep a colonel and his men trapped in a barren and dangerous frontier with ambiguous orders?

Adding to that frustration, the announcement of the name change a day earlier; it nearly infuriated him to be stationed at Fort *Loudoun*. This Loudoun—this newly appointed governor of Virginia—never responded to George's welcome letter six months prior nor stepped foot in Virginia! How could Loudoun protect a colony when he knew nothing of its defenses or its terrain?

George moved to a small table by the fire to eat the last of the pick-

led white plums Mary Eliza had sent to him in a hand-carved trunk with a brass lock. Her gift of preserves, tipsy cakes, and catsup of different flavorings—including mushroom catsup—provided the only enjoyment in the months that passed in winter's cold.

He felt an unease as his fork entered the last slice of plum and he lifted it to his mouth. Over the time away from Mary, he had collected any information he could about her. The assessment presented by Captain Hugh Mercer was more than any man with dignity could take. A banquet was hosted by Loudoun, where officers gawked at the woman who held his heart. "I will wait for you" is what she had said to him. He knew she was true to her word. He placed his elbow upon his desk and let his forehead fall on his hand.

Loudoun! The man who called Virginia his dominion! Throwing banquets was more important to that man. George knew he himself had sacrificed much, risked even more for a position in the military and a chance at a better life not only for him but for the colonists, who ought to have days of peace. He wanted to fight. He wanted to protect. He wanted to save a people! Many of them suffered at the hands of the enemy, and now this!

George took out his quill for a second letter to this Lord Loudoun. It irked him even to write his location—Fort Loudoun. In page after page of rage, George presented his bitterness and frustration like a malcontent. He got to the end:

> . . . if, under all these concomitant Evils I shoud be sickened in a Service that promises so little of a Soldiers reward.

> I have long since been satisfied of the impossibility of continueing in this Service without loss of Honour . . .

> Althô I have not the Honour to be known to Your Lordship: Yet, Your Lordship's Name was familiar to my Ear, on account of the Important Services performed to His

Majesty in other parts of the World — don't think My Lord I am going to flatter. I have exalted Sentiments of Your Lordships Character, and revere Your Rank; yet, mean not this, (coud I believe it acceptable), my nature is honest, and Free from Guile.

We have my Lord, ever since our Defence at the Meadows, and behaviour under His Excellency General Braddock been tantalized; nay, bid expect most sanguinely, a better Establishment; and have waited in tedious expectation of seeing this accomplished. The Assembly it is true, have, I believe, done every thing in their Power to bring this about, first, by Sollicitting His Honour the Lieutenant Governor to Address His Majesty: and next, addressing His Majesty themselves in favour of their Regiment, what Sucess these Addresses have met with I am yet a stranger to.

In regard to myself, I must beg leave to say, Had His Excellency General Braddock survived his unfortunate Defeat, I should have met with preferment equal to my Wishes: I had His Promise to that purpose, and I believe that Gentleman was too sincere and generous to make unmeaning offers, where none were ask'd.

And now before I sum up the whole, I must beg leave to add — my unwearied endeavours are inadequately rewarded — The Orders I receive are full of ambiguity: I am left like a wanderer in the wilderness, to proceed at hazard — I am answerable for consequences, and blamed, without the privilege of Defence!

He continued on a page more. He exhaled. It was done. He folded the fifteen pages and put them aside. He would read them through before sending them to New York.

Another letter needed to be written. He would return for her, so

he had told her before his swift departure when their moment upon Valentine's Hill was interrupted by a cavalry of British officers rushing to present him the memorandum from the assembly requiring his immediate departure on account of a fort needing to be built.

If only he had refused the order and chosen love instead. If only he had reached out for her hand and asked her then to be his and only his for all time. Happiness, moral duty, they should be able to be connected, inseparably connected.

George brought out the gift he'd purchased in Boston, which he so desperately wanted to take to her. He imagined her eyes looking at him in that loving way and how they would react as she opened the box. He then pulled out the last letter he had received from Yonkers. Joseph Chew had kept his pledge to keep George abreast of her situation, "Pretty Miss Polly," wrote Mr. Chew, "is in the same condition and situation as you last saw her." She was waiting for him, just as she promised. George, too, was in the same condition. This frustrated him. He and she should be moving forward, not remaining in stasis.

Chapter Twenty-Five

——◆◆——

Genu

But alas! we are not to expect that the path will be strewed with flowers.

—GEORGE WASHINGTON

YONKERS-ON-HUDSON

Mary didn't want to do what Frederick told her must be done. Her stomach felt sick over it. He was right, but that didn't mean she should be happy about it. She would quickly thank Captain Roger Morris and be done with it. It took her this long to finally agree. Months had gone by since the banquet. Her world had gone silent that night.

It had been Captain Morris who discovered her lying alone in the dark in that room where that scoundrel left her. She had little knowledge of what happened. An image flashed in the back of her mind; she forced the thought into hiding, for she wanted to keep its awfulness from even herself.

She would keep the conversation with the captain short. More than anything, she wanted the guards assigned to her by Lord Loudoun gone. The protection began after the banquet. They followed her each time she set foot outside, each time she rode on horseback. She wanted to get fresh air alone; instead, she had to deal with officers

trailing her. Valentine, the horse born to George's mare, outsped the guards every time. George would be proud. She wrote to him numerous times to keep him abreast of the young horse, which, although small, was still a fine mare. She hoped he received these letters, but how was she to know? He never wrote back, not a word. She understood, for he was a colonel fighting a war. There would be little time, she surmised, for writing letters.

She heard the clip-clop of hooves hitting the cobblestone path leading to the front door of the manor. Through the window to the right of the doorway, she saw the arrival of an ostentatious chariot. It looked as if a sheet of ice covered the exterior, for the black color had an extreme gloss. A golden lion shimmered upon its door. Green velvet housing covered the livery.

Dressed in a yellow suit, the man Eva had taken to calling "Genu," Captain Morris, stepped onto the path. He wasn't particularly tall. He was close to her height if she wore a satin heel. He held something sizable concealed behind his back. The last thing she wanted was a gift from him.

The captain had a spring in his step as he walked to the manor's front door. He appeared to her as a summer's garden in bloom, with embroidered flowers on the fabric of his coat that were large enough to see from a distance.

She planned to answer the door herself. No attendant for this. She needed the greeting to be over before it even started. She moved back from the window as he drew closer. The sound of his heels could be heard near the doorway. A quiet moment followed. Maybe he decided to turn around. She did not hear his heels click again. The lightest tap at the door came next. He must have seen her at the window. How humiliating, she thought. She waited before opening the top portion. If she looked only from the top, this affair would be done with sooner. Otherwise, he would expect to be invited in.

She undid the latch and opened it. Before she could get out the sentence she planned to say to him, he took off his tricorn hat and brought his hand from behind his back to reveal giant-sized flowers—with faces like the sun.

"For you, the *Helianthus verticillatus*."

An awkward lull followed. She peered out the top of the door but could not see the stems. She undid the latch to open the bottom half. "These flowers are known to grow double this size."

"Where do they come from?"

"They are native to France, Italy, and Spain. There are other species of this genus, as well—of the smaller variety." He pointed to the seeds at the center of the flower. "If planted at the correct time of year, your gardeners will find they can be propagated quite easily, especially in the greenhouse."

"The flower heads appear to be tilting."

"I surmise due to their flexibility . . . or for reasons of kneeling before beauty." With these words, he knelt before her. "Without flowers, you might as well live out of this world." He handed her the bouquet. He stood back up, said a brief farewell, and strolled off.

Mary was left holding a bouquet of sunflowers that carried a scent of musky earthiness. She realized she never thanked him for what he had done. She would hear of it from her brother.

Chapter Twenty-Six

—◆◆◆—

State of Denial

I am become in a manner an exile . . .

—GEORGE WASHINGTON

FORT LOUDOUN

Dullness ruled. George could do no more than acknowledge its power. The days dragged on. The months dragged on. Fifteen months passed.

He wiped his brow; the heat was sweltering. He smelled of sweat and he didn't like it. He sat at the slant-front desk he recently obtained and opened the prospect door to expose the interior drawers. He did his correspondence here. The desk was plain but neat and not very large—spacious enough to store his papers.

Today he shuffled through the letters he kept aside for personal matters. He tried continually to get leave to make his travels, to take care of the personal business he should have addressed when he was in New York with Mary Eliza in his arms. Now he was trapped in this lonely place, protecting a frontier with an inadequate force and dealing with skirmishes from a crafty enemy. Left nearly defenseless. Still alive, until the time the savages decided to attack.

He organized the letters from his superiors again. He put those next to the ones he sent; George transcribed every letter he wrote, so that he could review any one of them at a later time.

To Colonel John Stanwix in New York, he had written:

> I should be much obliged, cou'd I obtain your permission
> to be absent about 10 days to settle some private affairs of
> very great consequence to me — You may be assured, Sir,
> I shall make no ungenerous use of your indulgence if my
> request is granted; and that I shall not quit my post if there
> is even an appearance of danger.

His commanders denied every such request, writing back to him:

> I hope Col. Washington has not been upon the Cerimony of not
> going for ten days on his private affairs without my leave, hope
> he will always take this upon himself, being well assured of your
> not being Absent from your Command where your presence is so
> very necessary . . .

George made additional requests. Each one of them was denied: "yr Absence on that Account from Ld Loudoun must be suspended till our affrs gives a better prospect . . ."

How could the affairs give a better prospect if they never bolstered the number of troops or arms? Instead, he waited in a fort not yet complete for want of moneys and materials. He looked over his letter in response:

> I did not purpose when I asked leave, nor ever intended to be
> answered, but at some favorable time, when the Service could
> admit of it without any detriment.

Why was it only he was refused personal leave? It seemed every other officer but him had such an opportunity. He again wrote to Stanwix:

I took the liberty in a letter to ask leave
to be absent about 12 or 14 days, if circumstances
in this quarter would permit; but having heard nothing
from you since, I am inclined to address you again
on that head.

The response to his request, he reviewed:

tis more than a fortnight ago that I answer'd your
letter when you mention'd its being convenient to
your private affairs to attend them . . . in
wch letter I express'd my Concern that you should
think such a thing necessary to mention to me as I
am sure you would not choose to be out of call should
the service require your immediate attendance . . .

As he sat, frustrated, he heard a knock at the door. The post rider
had mail for him. "Colonel Washington, for you," said the messenger.

George opened the packet and was pleasantly surprised by a letter from Chew. He quickly sat down and opened it. Washington had
written him to inquire about the subject so dear to his heart. This
was Chew's reply:

Dear Sir

I hope the Conclusion of the Summer may bring forth
something at Present Every thing look dark & Gloomy.
I find no fault with the measures taken and the scripture
forbids us to speak Evil of the Rulers of the Land . . .

as to the Latter part of your Letter what shall I say,
I often had the Pleasure of Breakfasting
with the Charming Polly, Roger Morris was there

George stopped here for a moment as shock struck him. Roger Morris! It couldn't be.

(dont be startled) but not always, you know him he is a Ladys man, always something to say, the Town talk't of it as a sure & settled Affair.

George slumped back in his seat, devastated to hear such news.

I can't say I think so and that I much doubt it, but assure you had Little Acquaintance with Mr. Morris and only slightly hinted it to Miss Polly; but how can you be Excused to Continue so long . . . I think I should have made a kind of Flying march of it if it had been only to have seen whether the Works were sufficient to withstand a Vigorous Attack, you a Soldier and a Lover. Mind I have been arguing for my own Interest now for had you taken this method then I should have had the Pleasure of seeing you — my Paper is almost full and I am Convinced you will be heartily tyred in Reading it — however will just add that I intend to set out tomorrow for New York where I will not be wanting to let Miss Polly know the sincere Regard you h a Friend of mine has for her. and I am sure if she had my Eyes to see thro she would Prefer him to all others.

now my Dear Friend I wish you Eternall Happiness and Content and assure you that I am with sincere Esteem Your most Obedt Servt.

Jos Chew

Chapter Twenty-Seven

⫸•⫷

The Games They Play

The game, whether well or ill played hitherto, seems now to be verging fast . . .

—GEORGE WASHINGTON

YONKERS-ON-HUDSON

Mary nearly burst into an uproar. She stormed into Frederick's library. "They stole him!" She shut the door hard, turned to her brother, and waxed impassioned. "Right off the street!" Frederick quickly shifted his eyes to the left. She hadn't realized they were in the company of Beverley. "My apologies, Beverley."

"Polly, I know what you're here to discuss," said Frederick. "I have been told that the dressmaker's husband willingly signed the contract to serve."

"Leaving a tavern at midnight is not a time to sign up for Britain's army. J. E. Sherwood has a wife, a son, and a daughter who is not well. He must be allowed to return home. Rosie is alone."

"I cannot assert myself into every predicament your townspeople find themselves in," her brother declared. "Influence ceases to exist if not used prudently."

"They have nowhere else to turn, Frederick."

"Beverley, what do we know of this situation?"

"Lord Loudoun has assigned a recruiting captain who has lugged many a man right off the street. The colony is a paradise for recruiters. A captain offers ale, flashes gold before their eyes, and can twist a nay into an affirmation from any chub."

"Frederick, please. Mr. Sherwood is a good, hardworking man."

Beverley continued. "Not only here, in the colonies of Maryland and Pennsylvania, they've even signed up indentured servants to enlist, offering them freedom after their service. The same for slaves in the South. Of course, the masters, they see these recruiting officers as thieves. However, those seeking freedom have signed up in plentiful numbers. They've made the best soldiers in America, from what I understand."

"And Frederick?"

"Yes, Polly."

"Rosie fears British soldiers will move into her home on order of Lord Loudoun. They've taken over homes in New York City."

"'Tis true," Beverley said. "Loudoun is demanding colonials quarter the troops under the Mutiny Act."

"An Act of England—extended to America?" asked Frederick.

"Aye. Lord Loudoun has used one enacted in Scotland to allow for troops to be housed in private homes. And one separately enacted in England, forcing the allowance of incidentals."

"Thirty companies have arrived in the last month." Frederick's brow furrowed. "I never considered where they would be sheltered."

"And there is no legal redress!" Mary added.

"Calls have been made elsewhere for the Crown to put an end to quartering any man in America—but to no avail. We should negotiate to prevent their use of the manor and of the church. They've turned churches into hospitals elsewhere in the colonies."

"Our St. John's?" Frederick looked anxious. "They would not dare. And the manor?"

For a moment, no one spoke.

Frederick rose from his seat, stepped to the window, pushed aside the curtain, and peered out. "Polly, I believe now is the time to allow a visit."

"A visit? What does one have to do with the other? The visit already occurred."

"A chance meeting at the entryway will not do. Captain Morris lives in Lord Loudoun's mansion and is an aide to him. How can we ask for help if you still haven't thanked him? This has gone on too long."

"Frederick, a visit is not necessary. Since the last visit, this captain has been near me every time I leave this place."

"And you've spoken not a word to him."

"You say he is one of my two guards now; however, there must be gossip, for he follows too close. He even came inside the manor one morning while I was breakfasting!"

"This captain in His Majesty's Army is a well-respected one. Polly, I expect you to keep your pledge."

"I have not affirmed anything." She turned her back to Frederick.

"One for the other."

HER HEAD ACHED with a dull throbbing that did not stop its constant beat for the two days since she agreed to a visit from the kneeler. Today Mary was attempting to create a French dessert. Being surrounded by sweetness helped take her mind off of the day's miserable task.

Mary watched as Temperance carefully removed a lovely ring from her finger, a gift from François, and placed it into a box on the shelf above her. It was a posy ring, the kind with a secret inscription hidden inside, that it may touch the skin. She adored the inscription inside Temperance's ring: *Retrouvons-nous à minuit.* Mary knew the translation: "Let us meet at midnight." Mary's eyes shifted to her own hands. There was no posy ring. She couldn't even imagine the feeling of receiving such a ring. Mary often imagined what romance would be like. Find a love that makes you feel free. She believed she had found this in George. And yet she waited still for his return.

"We have not time for silliness, François." Temperance laughed at his serenade over his pot. "Please tell him, Miss Polly." Temperance gave her hands over to a full-force kneading in a bowl of dough.

"*Ma chère petite amie.* I sing to my pot for to awaken the flavors. And I suggest *le pain* you are making will need a half pound of butter."

"More butter! The French style is excessive." Temperance rolled her eyes.

Mary should have been entertaining the guests, but this was, for certain, more enjoyable.

"François," Mary asked, "have the clove gilliflowers been steeping for long enough in the lemon's juice?" Mary wanted to create a perfect marbling effect on the fruit wafers she made from his instruction. François suggested taking the pulp from plums, putting it through a hair sieve, adding three ounces of that to six ounces of fine sugar. Both were heated on the fire until almost boiling. Mary poured the mixture onto glass and let it almost dry.

"*Parfait,*" he said.

With his help, she added the coloring from the steeped cloves, which gently maneuvered through the wafers to add the red effect.

"Miss Polly, we are fond of you in the kitchen, but should you not be attending the garden party?" asked Temperance. "François will take the dessert wafers out to you when they are ready."

TODAY WAS THE day she was to thank Captain Morris for his gallantry those months ago. "One for the other," as Frederick had put it. This would bring J.E. home to Rosie and Lulu and Jeffrey. Mary had no choice, though it seemed too long after that Christmas Eve banquet. And it wasn't as if she hadn't seen the man. Not only did he follow her as a guard nearly every day, he sent a new species of flower to the manor each morning with a note explaining its origin and a note requesting an interview. Genu. She thought of how Eva got down on her knees as she said the name.

Mary, of course, never responded to Morris. Her heart was fixed. But would George come back for her? Not receiving any word from him was sowing doubt as to whether he would return for her. Sixteen months passed. She reminded herself he was fighting a war.

Mary walked out to see the battledore feathers flying in an utterly

confused fashion. Three women—Bernadette Clara Belle, Emily Joyce, and Elle Cole—stood in a circle, playing with the paddles on the velvety lawn near the slope that led to the water.

Before she could reach them, she was stopped by the sprightly captain.

"Miss Philipse, if I may," Captain Morris said. "Might there be a day we could ride together?"

Mary looked at him, hoping silence would imply indifference.

"I could ask the other guard to hold back."

She didn't answer.

"If, in fact, you cared to ride alone, I would be sure to give you that space."

She didn't want him to be kind to her. She wanted to dislike him. But not having the guards would give her a chance to finally ride fast without stopping or riding sidesaddle. It would finally give her freedom. So, she turned to the answer she and Susannah had conjured up for any request from Captain Morris. "Apply to my brother, for he, and only he, will provide you with a response."

He smiled wide and buckled, falling an inch short of having his knees touch the lawn. "Alas, the spark of hopeful attention I so desperately desire!"

"Polly, join us!" called out Bernadette, who was wearing a dress too low at the top for such a game and the same feather in her high hair.

'Twas true that Mary was not fond of these ladies, but she felt thankful now for an excuse to move away from him. She had good reason for inviting the belles.

"And Captain Morris, thank you for your assistance the night of the banquet," she said quickly with a small smile. She walked toward the ladies. She didn't look back.

Play stopped as Mary came into the circle.

"He's handsome, Polly, and magnetic!" Bernadette offered the captain a flirtatious smile and wave. "Don't you agree, Emily?"

Emily gave a wink to the other officers near Morris. "I will need a moment to admire the dapper fellows before us."

"Is it true none of them has presented a ring as of yet?" Elle asked.

Bernadette, Emily, and Elle giggled. Mary was having difficulty masking her distaste.

"If any of these men asked, I would give them my hand," Bernadette said, "immediately."

"Solely your hand?" Emily lifted her bosom higher.

Bernadette shifted her dress lower at the top.

Mary was miffed. "Ladies, would you consider joining hands with a man who does not possess the whole heart?"

Elle appeared surprised by the question. "With any of these men, certainly, except for Captain Morris, of course. He has his eyes on someone else."

"Should not the state of marriage be accepted with only the most honest intentions?" Mary wasn't sure why she was even debating the topic.

"If you find a man willing, you should immediately seize the opportunity, Miss Polly," said Bernadette with a smirk. "Act up quickly to the nuptial vows, especially true for one who is past the age of prudence."

Mary could have fired back a retort. In truth, she knew Bernadette was right.

Mary needed to end the discussion. "Let us play."

With wooden paddles in hand, the four of them, three of them giddy, played the game. Back and forth they went, with one winning, then the other. Bernadette was in a frenzy, trying to hit each feathered birdie. Mary couldn't have cared less who was winning, but Bernadette was playing as if a laurel-wreath crown were at stake. They played in a round-robin style, two against two, then Elle versus Emily, and finally, Bernadette versus Mary. Bernadette's eyes narrowed; her face became stern, more serious than Mary thought it capable. Mary found this quite amusing. The birdie flew back and forth in the air and back again.

The officers began to cheer as the match went on longer than Mary would have expected. Bernadette's hair flew high in the air, left to right. Bernadette was quick, but Mary was strong, so strong that she

at last hit the birdie hard, too hard; it went high, so high and far, they had to look up at it.

Hair fanning behind her, Bernadette raced for the birdie. She was headed for the slope. Mary ran after her, shouting, "No, Bernadette! No!"

She wouldn't listen.

"Please, leave it be!"

She didn't stop.

"You're too close." Mary rushed after her. "Bernadette, no!"

But Bernadette kept going and leaped. Her hair unwound from the mass atop her head. The feather came loose and launched into the air.

"Be careful of the rocks!" Mary yelled.

Bernadette hit the birdie. A shout of triumph emerged from her smiling lips. The grin was quickly wiped away. Her body hit the ground with such force they felt the ground shake. She tumbled and tumbled down the hill. She neared the edge, the one that led to the water, off the stubby cliff.

Mary screamed louder and picked up her pace. "Please, no!"

Her heart screamed out: Mama says it's dangerous.

Chapter Twenty-Eight

———◆◆◆———

Melancholy Things

I shall be anxious till I am relieved from the Suspence
I am in . . .

—GEORGE WASHINGTON

FAIRFAX, VIRGINIA

Sunset's reflection rocked gently on the calm waves of the Potomac River. Some of the happiest times of George's young life had been spent with the Fairfaxes in this very place—Belvoir. The family had given him hope of a firm position in a society otherwise elusive to him.

He was out of Fort Loudoun, where he felt like an exile. He wished his quick visit were taking place under better circumstances. His late brother's widow reached her hand up high, placing the backside of it onto his forehead. "You look pale," Anne Washington said to him. She was wearing all black.

Speak not of melancholy things, and if others mention them change if you can the discourse. "'Tis truly one of the most beautiful seats on the river." The air breathed purer for him here.

They stood on the manicured grounds of the estate. The gardens with tamed bushes in geometric symmetry displayed not a leaf out of place. The property had belonged to Anne's father, Colonel Fairfax, who died the week prior. The service took place the prior afternoon.

The last time George had seen Colonel Fairfax, he made one request of George; it was the same as Lawrence's desire: "Keep the enemy far from Virginia." George wasn't sure he could fulfill their wish—not with an incomplete fort, an insufficient number of officers, and the British commanders remaining mute to George's many requests.

Now George and Anne were joined by her brother, George William, who motioned for a servant to bring closer a tray with wine glasses and a carafe. "Your name was never far from my father's lips, 'George Washington's good health and fortune is the toast at every table,' my father would say." He handed a glass to George. "So now we toast you, Colonel Washington. Glad we are to have you here."

Anne interrupted, "He is not well, brother. The best drink for him is pure water."

"The best drink for him . . . sister . . . is a red Burgundy."

A rush of chills spread through George's body.

"Are you sick?" Anne asked George.

"Of course he is sick." George William's wife, Sally, approached. She was also wearing black, but with a laced collar that showed skin along the neckline. "When love seizes the heart, separation causes a fever stronger than any medication will cure."

George knew there was truth in her words. He hadn't seen Mary Eliza in a very long time. When he would be able to, he did not know. Every request for an extended leave had been denied. He would need ten days, at the least, to make the journey.

"Drinks, whether water or wine, cannot cure heartache," added Sally. "May we discuss the personal matter at hand?"

"When did Robinson last contact you?" George William took a sip of red.

"Is this an appropriate time for such a discussion?" George did not drink.

"Father would want to see you married, see you happy." Anne turned to the servant and asked for pure water.

"On July tenth. I had thought they had quite forgotten me."

"Have you asked for leave, George?" Anne took the glass of wine from George's hand.

"I have. Multiple times. I've offered to take the time whenever the service could admit without any detriment."

George William took the glass from Anne and gave it back to George. "What was the response?"

"The colonel, John Stanwix, expressed concern that I should think such a thing necessary, that I would choose to be out of call. After additional requests, I was told no orders from him, nor Lord Loudoun, will move me from my present station."

"And any news from New York?" George William asked.

"Just two weeks ago, a friend wrote to tell me Miss Philipse has had a pain in her face."

Sally placed her hand over her heart. "Oh, the heiress waits for her George. Of course she would have a pain in her face. Imagine her longing. Look at you, the handsome and brave colonel of His Majesty's Army."

"The only way to learn the truth is to journey there yourself," George William added. "You must arrive in person. This type of negotiation must be done . . . in person."

Sally motioned to a servant for a quill and paper. "Darling, certain gifts must be presented on such a visit. We must place an order for you with Captain Dick."

George William continued. "There must be conversation with the elders, discussion of your worth, in regard to your estate. Her worth and estate must be discussed. There must be guarantees."

"You shall try again." Anne handed George a glass of water. "It makes no sense to keep you away so long."

George knew differently. Nearly every officer in New York and beyond had his eyes set on Mary Eliza. George was coming to the realization that a scheme must be in the works. A letter from a colonel whom he had served alongside in the Braddock expedition made this clear when he wrote that "a very considerable regular force is now in New York, but what they will be employed in is more, by far, than I can inform you." The letter's author, Colonel Thomas Gage, was working on the hand of heiress Margaret Kemble. George recalled meeting her at the Yonkers manor; she was Mary Eliza's cousin.

"You must try again," Anne said kindly.

"Write this down, darling." Sally waited a moment for her husband to prepare the paper, and began to list the items of necessity:

A Compleat sett fine Image China
2 dozn fine wine glasses Ingravd
Fine Oblong China dishes
Tureen
Two dozen Fine Plates
One dozen ditto soop
1 ps. Huccabuck Towelling
1 ps. 9/4 Irish Sheeting 74 yards
5 10/4 Damask Table Cloths
1 dozn damask Napkins

"This must be sent with the utmost expediency," she added.

"And I will speak privately with Captain Stewart." George William looked up from writing, turned and gave a wave to Stewart, who had journeyed with Washington here. "He and I shall discuss a next step. We shall inform you at the proper time. This must be done."

He motioned for George to drink.

George chose the wine.

Chapter Twenty-Nine

---◆◆◆---

A Weakened State

*Hence it follows that love may and therefore that it ought
to be under the guidance of reason. For although we
cannot avoid first impressions, we may assuredly place
them under guard.*

—GEORGE WASHINGTON

YONKERS-ON-HUDSON

Mary's head hit the rocks hard. She sensed a bloody warmth on her skin. Droplets fell, one, then another, until her yellow dress was colored red. She ran after Bernadette, watching her body tumble down the slope. When Mary reached her, she clutched onto Bernadette's arm, but the force of the fall defeated Mary's strength, the downward thrust too great, causing Mary to lose her balance. Bernadette plunged off the rocky edge, taking Mary with her.

The screams and muffled shrieks echoed as if they were coming through a cloud. Ladies melted into a woeful mass of sorrow. Officers flooded them. Mary remembered how Captain Morris raced over, ripped off the shirt he was wearing, and wrapped it around her head. The men carried a bloodied Bernadette into the manor. They laid the body in the east parlor. The belles pulled twigs from her hair in between their echoing wails.

. . .

IN THE MONTHS that followed, not an ounce of joy emerged in Mary's spirit. Guilt clenched her in its wretched grip. That day reminded her of what she already knew: She was the cursed one. The letter, the one Bernadette had written her months ago, well, she finally read it after they buried Bernadette in the dirt:

Dearest Polly,

You and I share vast amiable qualities,
blooming beauties, highly accomplished with qualities
that captivate every man who nears us. What we both
don't have is the same, as well — our mothers. This is why
I wear her feather in my hair, the same quill she used to
write letters to your mother, her dearest friend.

When shall our correspondence finally begin?

'Tis what our mothers would have wanted. My wait has been
far too long.

Humbly,
Bernadette Clara

Riding Valentine helped bring some peace to Mary's nerves. The farther she rode, the calmer she became; the air cleared her mind, giving her a chance to breathe. Susannah had urged her to ride, reminded her that she was capable of the impossible, for she had survived the unthinkable.

Today the wind blasted Mary's cheeks as she nudged the mare into a bright trot on this late-October afternoon. She sensed the mare's willingness to pick up her pace, so she let her move into a long, bounding stride. They moved fast, as fast as Valentine's legs would take her. Nearly fifty miles they covered.

She looked to her left and a little behind. He was there: Captain Morris, keeping up no matter how fast Valentine galloped. It had been discussed—a match between the two of them. The captain had met with her brother on a number of occasions; Frederick did discuss these meetings with her, letting her know the captain guaranteed to maintain her high sphere of society and make her more content than any other woman could hope to be.

Riches do not ensure happiness. Of this fact, she was certain.

Her brother tried to convince her that there was much to consider: security of the manor, the church, the milling business, the trade business. Becoming linked with the British in New York would protect their property and protect the townspeople.

The requests for visits from Captain Morris grew constant. Their British counterparts bombarded her brother with stories of George. "Don't be fooled," they told him. "Washington is nothing more than a spendthrift, a debaucher, a gambler. He has no money of his own. No land." Mary already knew his worth. He was brave and strong and on the verge of greatness—that's what she truly believed. He wouldn't be a commander for long, they said, for he had already been censured. Hadn't she read what was written about him? Of course she had. She wouldn't believe it; she couldn't. But for George not to write to her for so long . . . Maybe there was some truth in what they were telling her.

Valentine took her to the grove of quince trees. This place reminded Mary of happier times. They had spoken about love, planned their lives with their trues—the three sisters, back in childhood, Susannah, Mary, and Margaret. She recalled the moment as she rode near the manor gardens that, at their best, flowered with buds of every color. Hours had been spent together sitting in the grasses, the paths lined with flowers, emitting fragrance that invited summer into each breath. The three young girls would gather a blanket and a basket of cakes to delight in the afternoon's warmth, while listening to the gentle murmurs of the rivulet. Margaret played her mandolin. Susannah sang. Mary attempted to dance to their music.

The afternoon of arias descended into levity as they imagined their

future loves. Mary and her younger sister would blush as Susannah serenaded the two with verse from Dryden;

Love has in store for me one happy minute,
And She will end my pain who did begin it;
Then no day void of bliss, or pleasure leaving,
Ages shall slide away without perceiving.

One happy minute.

Maybe that is all that love had in store for her.

Her moment of bliss. Had it already passed? She adored the time she had spent with George. The days she was in his arms, she had felt brave and free. Her thoughts became murky without word from him. Did he even want her? Nineteen months without him had crawled by. Layers of ache found a permanent place in her heart. George, she believed, might be better without her by his side. He had more to do. In him was a bright hope. She had seen it in his eyes.

Captain Morris, astride his white horse, reached her and Valentine. They rode side by side now. Each day brought new pressure on her to find a match; she was beyond the usual matrimonial age. Twenty-seven years old. "Past the age of prudence." Bernadette had been correct. Mary shook her head to get the thoughts of that day out of her mind. The tumble. The muffled screams. The bloody hem of Bernadette's dress dragging in the mud. The cursed one had returned.

Living in the manor with Frederick and his bride? Mary couldn't do that much longer. As for a single woman living in New York alone? Unheard of, her brother told her—unacceptable.

She reluctantly took the visits from the captain, starting with one a week, then two, and now three a week. He assured her that his ambitions were solely felicitous and his views honorable.

The horses slowed by a row of oak trees that had moss drooping lazily from their branches. "If curled properly, 'twould make a tolerable periwig," the captain joked.

She found that amusing. She had become weary.

Mary thought of the letters Captain Morris had sent her. Each

came with a new floral bouquet. Most of the notes were silly words of love. She hardly paid any mind to them. Then she read one that made her question how she had become so bitter.

My Dearest Flower

Upon my departure from you, I frequently
search deep within for the reason why I cannot make
you the happiest creature on the Earth, for you give me
the greatest delight I can imagine having.

When you announced love was nothing more than
a jest, I could hardly think of how to respond. I will
therefore try again to find the way to your heart.

Roger Morris

Captain Morris helped Mary dismount. They arrived back at Philipse Manor.

He fell to his knees before her, clasped his hands together, practically pleading with her. "Miss Polly, suffer me not to be in woebegone want for just one smile, one spark of hope. My adoration for thee cannot be exceeded by another. I feel such deep affection for you. I ask that you offer me one spark of hope."

She said nothing.

"I give you my honesty that if you choose another, I will be undone. My affection is for you and only you."

Her spirit was weak. She reached out and allowed her hand to settle into Captain Morris's.

'Twas true love is nothing more than a jest.

Chapter Thirty

—◆◆◆—

A Night's Ride

To guard against this evil, let us take a review of the
ground upon which we now stand.

—GEORGE WASHINGTON

STATEN ISLAND, NEW YORK

A light snow fell on the close of a winter evening with a purple-hued
sky. The sun was setting not only on the day but on George's spirit.
A sharp wind bit his face. The freeze clung to his nose. He charged
along frost-heaved roads lined with trees that had lost their dress
months ago. Woodfin under him galloped as if knowing the necessity
of finding a faster pace. Hooves thundering over the dirt released the
sound of steady speed. George bounced his heels back to take further command of the horse. At least the horse bent freely to George's
will. If only his life acquiesced with the same ease.

He disembarked from the ferry that brought him from Perth
Amboy, New Jersey, to Staten Island, New York, at five in the evening.
Nearly fourteen miles still lay ahead of him. He hadn't much time to
board the next. York Ferry would take him to Pearl Street by nine in
the evening.

He wanted to turn off his thinking and stop his brain from analyzing the evil he surmised had transpired. After leaving Belvoir

and returning to Fort Loudoun, he had again asked for leave. George made numerous requests to Colonel Stanwix, even to the governor. The responses were the same as they had been since the beginning:

> I cannot Agree to allow you Leave.
> You know the Fort is to be finish'd & I fear in Your
> Absence Little will be done.

The denials swam in his head as he rode faster.

> Surely the Commanding Officer Should not be Absent when
> daily Alarm'd with the Enemys Intents.
> I think you are in the wrong to ask it.

He hoped the letter he had written to Beverley had been received. For a year and ten months, George had remained trapped. How much longer did he have to wait? He picked up speed. He was traveling solely in the company of his horse. The gifts Sally had ordered for him never arrived. The order for items had been sent in September!

George would rather have not read what Captain Stewart's hand had written months later, from Fort Loudoun—addressed to Colonel John Stanwix. He remembered every word of Stewart's letter, having committed it to memory:

> Sir

> For near Four Months past Colo. Washington has
> Labour'd under a Bloudy Flux which till of late he
> did not conceive could be productive of those bad
> consequences it now too probably will terminate in,
> at least he would not be prevail'd upon in any Degree
> to abate the exertion of that steady Zeal for the Interest
> of the Service he in so emenent a manner has always been
> remarkable for, however about two weeks ago his Disorder
> greatly encreas'd and at same time was Seiz'd with Stitches

& violent Plueretick Pains under that Complication of
Disorders his Strength & viguour diminish'd so fast that
in a few days he was hardly able to Walk and was (by the
Docr) at length prevail'd upon to leave this place as change
of air & quietness (which he could not possibly enjoy here)
was the best chance that remain'd for his Recovery . . .

. . . he expresses much concern for his omission of not giving
you previous Notice of the necessity he was under of leaving
this place and as he's not in condition to write himself desires
me to inform you of the reasons of it which I have now the
honr to do . . .

George traveled without stopping.

Chapter Thirty-One

—◆◆◆—

His Visit

. . . our Hearts are fired with Love and Affection . . .
—GEORGE WASHINGTON

Mary's hand trembled as she sat at a highly polished carved desk in the drawing room of Susannah and Beverley's town house on the corner of Broad and Pearl streets, with a quill in her hand. A crowd of esquires whose names she did not care to know glared at her as she fidgeted with the unfurled linen scroll in front of her. Frederick and Beverley stood nearby. She put the quill down a third time without a signature. A lady's maid rushed a glass of water to her. Mary took a sip. Her eyes returned to the document and she carefully read it, as if she hadn't quite understood each line the first or second time through.

> This Joint agreement made on this day between
> Roger Morris of Yorkshire, England, on the one part
> and Mary Eliza Philipse of Yonkers, New York, on
> the Other part, Witnesseth that Whereas there is a
> Marriage Intended between the said Morris and

said Philipse. When said marriage Shall take place
and be Consummated, it is the intent of the
agreement that said Philipse will maintain all of the
property, share in the Philipse family milling and trade
business, household furniture, Clothing and Ornamentals
brot to the said Morris at the time of their intermarriage.

In Confirmation of the foregoing agreement the
parties do hereby bind themselves, and their heirs
Executors & administrators to the faithful
performance thereof according to their true
intent and meaning of said agreement. In Witness
whereof the parties have hereunto Set their hands
& Seals.

Signed, Sealed & Delivered to each other.

She held her breath and wrote "Mary Eliza Philipse" next to Roger
Morris's signature. He had signed it earlier in the day without hesitation. The ante-nuptial contract came with the solemn pledge of accompanying Captain Morris to the altar; the vows would be celebrated at
the expiration of one week.

It was done.

She jumped out of the chair and rushed from the room. Overwhelming feelings of confusion, guilt, and fear compounded into
such a mixed-up mess, she wanted to not be seen by anyone. She
raced up the stairwell, into the bedchamber, shut the door, and fell
to the floor.

Was Roger Morris an awful man? No. He was a respectable
man of good breeding who never failed to declare his sincerity
with the best of intentions. Had he kept his word? He had. He protected the town, kept her family from the awful scenes of war. The
order to quarter troops in the Sherwood house was reversed and
J.E.'s enlistment voided, allowing Rosie's husband to return home.

Still, Mary shuddered at her answer. Polite society told her that

what she was about to do was for the best. George was never coming back for her.

THE HORSE RIDE from the port to the Robinson town house proved difficult; George could hardly see ahead of him with the heavy fall of snow driving thickly. Still, he kept up his pace, for it had been so long since he heard her speak the words, "You are a true gentleman."

Through the tumult of the winter's night, George could make out the image of a lion on a shiny black-and-gold chariot. He arrived, dismounted, and walked through the white-covered path, leaving his large footprints, each nearly twelve inches in length. The time was late, too late to make a call upon a lady. He knew the rules of civility. It was not good manners to do so. He paused for a moment by the door.

Forget rules, he thought. His lovely had already waited too long.

He removed his riding gloves and knocked at the door. He waited for a long minute. He knocked again. The door was answered by Susannah. He had forgotten how much she resembled Mary Eliza Philipse. He was glad to see her. She, on the other hand, appeared stunned to see him. He had no opportunity to offer a greeting.

"Miss Philipse is indisposed," she blurted out to him. "Please wait here." She walked away with an elegant, straight posture yet scampering footsteps.

So George stood, brushing snow from his tricorn hat as he waited outside the front door. Snow continued to fall on him. The door remained open. He could hear a conversation coming from a room at the end of the hallway. A man in a red coat emerged from it and quickly marched toward him. A messenger, he assumed. George stopped him and peered at a packet in the person's hand. "What are you delivering from this place?"

"They are the nuptial papers, sir," was his answer.

"Nuptial papers?" George's heart sank. "Where are they to be delivered?"

"I've been ordered to take them directly to the residence of our commander in chief, Lord and Victor, John, Earl of Loudoun."

"POLLY. POLLY. YOU must rise!" Susannah raced into the bedchamber with her voice breaking as she whispered.

Mary lifted her head from the bed pillow. Her sister looked as if she'd seen a ghost.

"HE . . . is . . . here," Susannah said slowly, deliberately.

"*He?*"

"Colonel Washington is in our entryway." She ran through the words and threw her hand over her mouth.

Mary shook her head. "It cannot be."

Susannah nodded frantically, with her hand still over her mouth. "No! No!"

"Shall I have Beverley—"

"Please no!" Mary climbed out of the quilt. "Do not turn him away!" She looked to the window. It was late, too late for a visit, and the weather treacherous. How did he arrive here? Why today? Why not any other one prior to this? She near couldn't believe it until she peered out the second-floor window.

George.

She could see him walking away on the snow-covered path into the night. He was leaving. Passion told her to throw out caution and papers and pledges. Reason told her to remain in place. What was she to do?

"Oh, for heaven's love, what are you waiting for?" Mary said aloud.

WHEN ALL IS lost, only silence remains. Stilled emptiness surrounded him. He could see only darkness, blank air that even the white of snow could not brighten. George walked alone into a trail of wood smoke, the scent that made known it was warming those who had loves to comfort them.

He was alone. He was used to that.

Why had she chosen that man, the insubordinate one? He was certain their marriage was the subject of the nuptial papers.

In the snow-muffled quiet, he heard a voice, her voice, the voice that had a melody to it. She cried out his name. He turned toward the sound and raised his hand to block the snow from his vision. The ache of missing Mary Eliza Philipse struck like a dagger to the core.

Through the flakes, appearing like diamonds shimmering their luster in the moonlight, *she* was running toward him. Mary Eliza was coming.

Before he could find words to say, his arms opened to envelop her. She leapted onto him. He lifted her from the cold, raw ground and both of his arms wrapped tightly around her, and she pressed her whole body against his. He felt her wholeness melting into his arms as if she and he were one and the same. "Words cannot express—" He held himself from speaking, realizing words would only diminish the intimacy of this moment in time. His face found hers and gently he laid a kiss on her forehead and on her right dimpled cheek and on the left.

Mary could not speak. No letters put together into sounds could explain the deep feelings she had for him. She placed her hands into his snow-covered hair and brought his lips close to hers. She wondered, was it fate that brought him here this night, for the snow blanketed them and the world around them, hiding them from its prying eyes. Just the two of them alone, with not a soul to see their yearning for each other.

George felt her lips just a breath away from his. He touched his nose to hers. He caressed her cheek with his cheek. Their lips nearly touched. Her eyes gently closed.

Quiet surrounded them in an alluring peace. It seemed to Mary that nature was bowing in deference to them. Then a beautiful swoosh emitted a sound. Had it been the wind, or had the world released a sigh? She thought the latter.

No longer able to wait for minds to reason, their lips found heaven.

Enthralled by her, George came to realize a simple truth: She was his; he was hers. What had come before, what would come after mattered not.

Together, they were *one*.

The clarity that revealed itself allowed him to reognize that one knows no place; the two of them could have been anywhere in the universe, together or separate, and he realized one knows no time; they could have been in the past or the future, for one exists not only for the present but for eternity, and through these truths George opened his heart to fall in love, in the middle of a storm, in the middle of a street, in the middle of a night, because with her in his embrace, he felt complete, understood, worthy; with Mary Eliza, he felt free.

Their kiss did not have an end. It endured even when their lips parted. Keeping her protected in his arms, he carefully walked through the cover of freshly fallen snow. One set of prints made an impression upon the cobblestone path as they approached the doorway. He carried her over the threshold. He had her now and he would not allow anything to disturb this time with her. He moved toward the fireplace in the parlor. He approached a settee by the hearth. Its bright hue welcomed them like warm rays of sun. Upon his lap she lay, his hands cradling her head to his chest.

In his arms, with his fingertips smoothing her hair, deep feelings stirred inside of her. Heat flooded through from the tippy top of her head down to her toes. Blue eyes with a hint of gray studied her. She bit her lip to stop herself from panting. Blue eyes gazing at her with such adoration. Why hadn't she waited for him? Every ounce of her being had told her to wait. If only George had written to her— at least a letter expressing his feelings—she would have waited and waited. Her face leaned against his hard chest, the beat of his heart on her skin. The pounding. Even-tempoed. Strong. Her ears became buried in the throbbing of it. If she could have remained here in this position forever, she would have been contented, listening, feeling the beat.

She never asked why there had not been word from him, why he had not returned for her.

Many questions he wanted to ask her. Why hadn't she waited for him? Why hadn't she responded to his letters? He wanted to ask her all of it, but his love was in his arms, and if this was the last time he would be with her, he would not let conversation interrupt. Heat reached every inch of his body. Her tears flowed. She never moved from within his arms.

He held her closer, as if he understood. Maybe it was true. Maybe he was protected. She would keep it that way. Keep him away from the cursed.

He breathed in her breath. He knew from her tears. She didn't have to explain. The enemy had won.

NIGHT TURNED TO dawn.

She had fallen asleep in his arms. The last small flame was burning out in the hearth. George rose and gently placed his precious onto the sofa and covered her in a quilt. He walked over to the fireplace, placed white birch logs into it, and waited to be assured the glow did not go dark. From his pocket, he removed a small box. He set the gift on the table before her.

He left this place.

Neither a sad ending nor a happy ending would come to pass.

For them, there was no ending.

Chapter Thirty-Two

———◆·◆———

The Prophecy

*I have always considered Marriage as the most interesting
event of ones life. The foundation of happiness or misery.*

—GEORGE WASHINGTON

YONKERS-ON-HUDSON

She chose to wear Mama's dress. Mary laid her hands on the simple
mull fabric with a color on the verge of ivory. Embroidered flowers
decorated the base. The neckline was square. The sleeves came out
full, then sat tight at the elbow. She tied her hair simply and placed it
behind her shoulders. She wore no crown on her head or decorative
around her neck.

Brilliance described everything else around her. Three sleighing
parties carried her and her bridal attendants up Albany Road to the
manor. Mary resided with her dearest cousin for the days leading up
to this one. Bells jingled all the way from Van Cortlandt Manor. The
sun was shining. The weather was brisk, requiring a heavy cape of
white satin lined in fur.

Eva sat up close to Mary in the open sleigh. "At any time, my
hand will be ready to whisk you away from this." Eva placed her gloved
hand atop Mary's.

Mary kept seeing him in the crowd, though it wasn't him; it

couldn't be. She glanced at the people moving about and thought she saw George. Auburn hair falling past the shoulders of a tall man standing on a corner with his back to her. The sleigh kept going. The same vision flashed before her eyes. Auburn hair. Tall. It wasn't him. It couldn't be.

What else could she have done on the morning after that night? Run after him? She certainly thought about it. Where would she have gone to find him? He left without saying good-bye, left without even a note of farewell. He didn't want her. She could understand why. But the way she felt falling into a dreamy sleep in his arms, she would never forget, like being wrapped in a cloud of warm sunshine, and, of course, there was the kiss. . . .

Mrs. George Washington. It was not to be.

She wondered how she had come to this place in life.

"She comes! Here comes the bride!" Loud cheers erupted as the sleigh, with an immensely-sized red ribbon at the front and horses in red velvet furnishings, rushed past the townspeople, who ran toward the street to wave to her. Auburn hair in the crowd. She needed to stop looking.

The bells of St. John's Church chimed. She smiled as she looked to the bell tower. Eric Arthur Angevine pulled the ropes wildly, jumping and waving his arms to her. Mary nearly cried when she saw him. My prayers are answered, she thought. Be the light. Keep George away from the cursed. Keep him protected. Blessed. Yes. She knew she was blessed this day. Why, then, was such heaviness weighing on her heart?

The colony's great social event was planned by Frederick and Susannah. Every leading family would be in attendance, as well as the elite members of the British Army. Her brother and sister thought of everything. Garlands made up of flowers of the Holy Night wrapped around lanterns. White bunting hung from cottage windows. The white blanket of snow at the front path of Philipse Manor was cleared, replaced with crimson-colored carpeting to welcome her and the guests into the manor.

Mary had no role in the preparations for this day, except for one demand: Townspeople would have a seat at the banquet. "Guests, high and low" is how Captain Morris put it when speaking of them. The "low" should be seated at a separate feast, he said. She disapproved of this sort of talk, so he agreed to end it. Everyone would be invited to one space.

A hush fell over the crowd as the sleigh carrying Mary arrived. The only sounds were precious squeaks from the lively Lulu. Her crown of forget-me-nots went crooked on her head as she ran in her tilted way to Mary. Ginger ringlets fell down over her freckled face, covering one of her bright green eyes. She looked as darling as a flower girl could in her tiny gown of crimson velvet.

"Do you like me dress?" She spun around and buried her face into the base of the wedding gown. Mary crouched down to hug her tight and straighten the headdress that was askew.

"Today, Lulu, you look like a princess."

Lulu did her best at a curtsy. "I'm 'posed to walk through the people, but I'm not very good at walking, Miss Polly."

"One step after another. You will get there when you are meant to arrive."

THE BRIDAL ATTENDANTS led the way, each appearing exquisite in their deep crimson gowns and white gloves. Lulu followed them into the manor, carrying a basket of sunflower petals that she had been instructed to throw as she walked down the aisle. It seemed she didn't make it a step into the room before darting back outside to Mary with a nervous expression upon her face.

"I forgot what I'm 'posed to do."

Mary got down next to her small friend and spoke to her. "Let a petal land everywhere you take a step. It will show me the way." Mary gently tapped Lulu's nose with her finger and kissed her freckled forehead. "Be brave, little one."

With that, the girl gave her a lopsided curtsy, turned around, stood as tall as her little body would allow, and began to walk into the

manor with a drag on the right. She turned to toss single petals at the spots where her steps had been. She started before she entered the front door.

A hand signaled for Mary to enter the foyer. She breathed in and closed her eyes. She took one last fresh breath before stepping inside. She worried the smell of the crowd would cause her usual fainting feeling. Susannah, in a golden gown and with burgundy flowers elegantly placed in her hair, met her at the doorway.

Susannah looked at her with a lovely smile. "You look beautiful, my sister." She handed her a bundle of white, red, and yellow flowers tied with a red satin ribbon. "The stephanotis for good luck. The amaryllis for worth beyond beauty. The goldfields for strength. The ivy for fidelity. These are for you to carry."

"Down the aisle?"

"If your day becomes overwhelming, remember to breathe in the bloom."

"Susannah, thank you. I've been nothing more than a burden to you."

"You are my sister and that's the most special gift of all."

Frederick, who was wearing his jeweled deer badge, offered her his arm. He began his walk. She didn't move. He gave her the most bewildered look.

"I cannot go farther," she said to him.

"Polly, hundreds of the highest-ranking citizens have converged on our home."

'Twas true, the parlor was so full, there wasn't an inch for another person.

"Life brings us many predicaments, Polly—"

"I am stuck."

"Today yours is to get to the front of this aisle."

Mary lifted her dress to reveal her pale blue shoe. "No, truly. I am stuck." The heel was caught between two floorboards. She twisted it several times but failed to find its release.

Frederick called the footmen to assist. They got down to free her

shoe, one of them lying on the ground. Mary covered her face in disbelief. They finally yanked hard, and the shoe came free.

The walk continued. The guests were staring. Frederick led her forward. She tried not to look at the crowd, instead breathing in the fragrance of her flowers. Ahead of her, at the front of the aisle, was a maroon canopy emblazoned with the crest of the Philipse family, the gold lion emerging from the coronet. The bridal altar was adorned by a tall arch of deep red and bright yellow flowers.

And there, awaiting her, was Captain Morris. Mary never saw so many teeth before; his mouth was spread out so wide. He was fancifully dressed in a most spirited ensemble. Sparkling golden metallic thread ran in a bright zigzag pattern along the edges of his red wool coat, lace exploding from his arms and neck. Were those golden yellow shoes he was wearing? It looked as if he had grown right out of her bouquet.

The rector of Trinity Church, the Reverend Henry Barclay, officiated the service. "Dearly beloved, we are gathered together here in the sight of God, and in the face of this company, to join together this Man and this Woman in holy Matrimony, which is an honourable estate, instituted of God, signifying unto us the mystical union that is betwixt Christ and his Church: which holy state Christ adorned and beautified with his presence and first miracle that he wrought in Cana of Galilee, and is commended of Saint Paul to be honourable among all men, and therefore is not to be entered into unadvisedly or lightly, to satisfy men's carnal lusts and appetites, like brute beasts that have no understanding; but reverently, discretely, advisedly, soberly, and in the fear of God."

The chill first started in her feet and slowly ran up her body. She watched the minister continue to speak. Fog wrapped its ugly hand around her. The words did not have clarity. She heard the words beasts and fear. All else was fuzzy.

The minister continued: "I require and charge you both, as ye will answer at the dreadful day of judgment when the secrets of all hearts shall be disclosed, that if either of you do know any impediment, why

ye may not be lawfully joined together in Matrimony, ye do now confess it."

Mary looked back to the foyer. Was that auburn hair? Hard to tell, since there were so many guards blocking the entryway to the parlor. Besides, she couldn't see clearly. She squinted to get a better view.

"Into this holy estate Mary Eliza Philipse and Roger Morris come now to be joined. If any man can show just cause, why they may not lawfully be joined together, let him speak, or else hereafter forever hold his peace."

She felt all eyes on her at this very moment; even the captain stared at her as if words would escape her mouth. If she wanted to say something, the Reverend Barclay allowed only seconds before moving on.

He turned to the groom. "Wilt thou have this Woman to thy wedded wife, to live together after God's ordinance in the holy estate of Matrimony? Wilt thou love her, comfort her, honour, and keep her in sickness and in health; and, forsaking all others, keep thee only unto her, so long as ye both shall live?"

Morris practically sang out his response, loudly exclaiming, "I will!"

The Reverend Barclay turned to Mary. She looked down.

"Wilt thou have this Man to thy wedded husband, to live together after God's ordinance in the holy estate of Matrimony? Wilt thou love him, comfort him, honour, and keep him in sickness and in health; and, forsaking all others, keep thee only unto him, so long as ye both shall live?"

The fog got thicker. Her head grew hot. She felt as if she might faint right there in front of the hundreds of guests. Darkness enveloped her. Wet darkness. Breathe, child. Breathe. She looked around. Where was he? Where was Captain Garvan when she needed him? He hadn't passed the manor in his sailing ship in longer than she could remember. She needed to escape from this place. She was confused. She glanced over at her brother. With a miffed expression on his face, he appeared as if he was about to scold her. He looked so old and silly with a peruke on his head. She let out a giggle.

"Mary . . ." A voice, she could hear a voice. "Mary, are you well?" Captain Morris whispered.

"I am," she replied.

"O Eternal God," continued the minister, "Creator and Preserver of all mankind, Giver of all spiritual grace, the Author of everlasting life; Send thy blessing upon these thy servants, this man and this woman, whom we bless in thy Name, that they, living faithfully together, may surely perform and keep the vow and covenant betwixt them made, whereof this Ring given and received is a token and pledge, and may ever remain in perfect love and peace together, and live according to thy laws, through Jesus Christ our Lord. Amen."

He joined their right hands together.

Clouds filled every space between her ears. She breathed in the bloom. Mary noticed a wedding ring on her finger. She wasn't sure how it got there.

"Those whom God hath joined together let no man put asunder."

TEMPERANCE AND FRANÇOIS combined their talents for the grandest of feasts, although Mrs. Roger Morris didn't eat a thing. She remained by her husband's side and greeted every person in the manor, even the "humbler folk," as he called them. She didn't correct him; there would be other times for that. The festivities included fine music and a bit of dancing where people could find the room. The crowd was deep. She couldn't even smell them today, for she held the flowers near her nose the entire night. She was glad everyone was with her, joining in the wedding feast. Eric Arthur, wearing pants tightly cinched about his waist, danced encircled by a group of young belles. J.E. held his glass of ale. Rosie's smile never left her face. Her hair was in a beautiful coiffure for the occasion and she held Lulu's hands to "dance fancy," as the little girl described it. The mother and daughter never looked so pretty and aglow.

Before Mary stepped one foot into the dancing circle in the parlor by the foyer, the top half of the grand front door swung open. A howling gust swished through the room, coating the guests in winter's chill.

The music stopped.

Stillness hovered over the crowd.

Captain Morris raced over to the door to shut it. The wind buffeted him. An echo murmured through the crowd. Startled, Mary froze.

The bottom half of the door flew open, nearly striking him.

"Fear not," the captain yelled over the bold gust of air.

Mary didn't believe it. She knew too well that once a door to darkness is opened, it cannot be closed.

A haunting shadow covered the door.

"'Tis the devil!" Rosie shrieked.

A large hand stopped the door from closing. A tall man, so tall, with the fur of a fox atop his head, met the ceiling. A grave expression marked his countenance. His face was covered in paint, like a native warrior ready for battle. His hair, black as night, fell long over the scarlet-colored blanket draped around him.

The crowd stared upon this mystery of a man.

The light of the candelabra struck him, casting a long shadow now onto the manor's floor. The man made no movement. His hair lifted with the wind. He didn't speak. His eyes looked straight ahead with an expression on his face that looked as if he would slay any man who came near him. None did.

In a deep, coarse voice, prophecy spoke: "Your possessions shall pass from you when the Eagle shall despoil the Lion of his mane."

Chapter Thirty-Three

——◆◦◆——

Awakening

... the World has no business to know the object of my Love ...

—GEORGE WASHINGTON

MOUNT VERNON, VIRGINIA

The ink flowed. Word after word poured onto the paper, relieving the burden on George's soul. He wrote what was a simple fact, an obvious one to anyone who knew him intimately. His true feelings were as fervent as ever and not in doubt. His honest confession he laid out to a receiver who would never expose it. He trusted Sally and her husband, George William. They were lifelong friends. They had written to him many times on the subject. Now he responded, first with a letter to George William.

In the other letter, the one to Sally, he released his heart's despair on paper:

'Tis true, I profess myself a Votary to Love —
I acknowledge that a Lady is in the Case — and further
I confess, that this Lady is known to you.

I feel the force of her amiable beauties
in the recollection of a thousand tender passages that
I coud wish to obliterate, till I am bid to revive them.
— but experience alas! sadly reminds me how Impossible
this is. — and evinces an Opinion which I have long
entertaind, that there is a Destiny, which has the Sovereign
controul of our Actions — not to be resisted by the strongest
efforts of Human Nature.

You have drawn me my dear Madam, or rather have I drawn
myself, into an honest confession of a Simple Fact —
misconstrue not my meaning — 'tis obvious — doubt it not,
nor expose it — the World has no business to know the
object of my Love, declard in this manner to you — when I
want to conceal it — One thing, above all things in this
World I wish to know, and only one person of your
Acquaintance can solve me that, or guess my meaning.
— but adieu to this, till happier times, if I ever shall see
them. — the hours at present are melancholy dull.
— neither the rugged Toils of War, nor the gentler conflict
of A — B — s is in my choice. — I dare believe you are as
happy as you say — I wish I was happy also —

George signed his name after a word of closing and neatly folded
the letter. As he placed the letters to husband and wife together in the
same packet, he became distracted by the thumping of a wagon's
wheels as they rumbled over the cobblestone path. He'd been staying
at the Mount Vernon estate of his late brother, Lawrence, since leaving New York. Lawrence's widow had found another to love. So here
George remained alone in this expanse of a house. He had hoped
there'd be someone to share it with. It was not to be.

Thuds coming from the circle in front of the west side of the dwelling house drew him to the window in the first-floor study. He
watched as proprietor Captain Dick brought the wagon to a stop. Anger
boiled in every vein of George's body at the sight. Dick exited the coach

and retrieved a crate. George couldn't believe what he was seeing. Boxes. The fine china arrived, late. Too late.

George exited the study with heaviness in his gait. He stomped into a small hallway, through the richly decorated dining room with its bold green color on the walls, into the central passageway to reach the entry, opened the door, and stood glaring at the man and his box. "I suppose I should not have received them at all!" George's hands clasped behind his back.

The captain's eyebrows shot up to his hairline. "Colonel, my sincerest apology for the delay."

George flew into a fit of rage. So unaccountably indolent is Captain Dick! he thought. "Was it carelessness that prevented their coming to my hand till near six weeks after arrival at port?"

"The vessel with your goods was sent to several different ports, without grant to dock." He set down the crate near George. "We were refused the ability to remove the goods from the vessel, even after being docked one month and a half."

"By whom?"

Captain Dick shrugged as he turned away with quick steps back to retrieve additional crates.

George's jaw muscles clenched. He reached down to carry the merchandise into the house. Captain Dick carried another crate through to the study. They set them down.

"I will be sure to make this up to you on the next journey," Captain Dick said. He thanked George again for his patience and quickly walked out.

Just the sight of these boxes made George angrier. He untied the rope at the top and lifted the lid on one of the crates. He removed what looked like a teapot wrapped tightly in newspaper. He slowly unwrapped it and held the china in one hand, the newsprint in the other.

What was he to do with all these goods now? He set the teapot down delicately upon his desk. He noticed something on the page of the printed paper. The *Virginia Gazette*? Each piece of newspaper print that he removed from the fine china made him more enraged. The china was wrapped in salacious falsities. The very publication that

printed lies about him. The very article that defamed him—it covered the teapot!

They condemned him, blasphemed him, claimed debauchery, gambling. He was a spendthrift, a drunkard, it said.

They.

They were responsible.

They were the ones. The article was written by the anonymous L & V. The truth sickened George. It infuriated him. He recalled the words of the messenger as he left with the nuptial papers; he was delivering them to the "commander in chief, Lord and Victor, John, Earl of Loudoun." Lord and Victor. L & V.

Keep him away from Mary Eliza Philipse so another could seize her surrender.

He rushed over to the trunk containing his necessary papers. He pulled out the letters of denial: "yr Absence on that Account from Ld Loudoun must be suspended till our affrs gives a better prospect." Their dastardly behavior kept him trapped, until it was done.

Colonel Stanwix followed the guidance of Lord Loudoun, whose aide was Roger Morris. The writer of the article, likely Loudoun's secretary extraordinaire, Thomas Pownall, he of the ridiculous pseudonyms. George learned of the whole diabolical cast from Hugh Mercer.

George raised his head for guidance. Before him were his brother's eyes. The portrait of Lawrence was the only painting in the study. The only one he needed. George decided right then. He would quit his command. He would retire from all public business. The British took her from him. George would leave his military post to be filled by others who had their endeavors crowned with better success than he.

Back and forth he paced over the creaking floor. George walked into the central passageway, heading toward the double doors on the east side of the house. He opened them with force, catching a cold breeze. Before him was the grand Potomac River. This sight had always made him feel hopeful. Not today. That appearance of glory once in view—that hope—that laudable ambition of serving, and meriting applause, was now no more.

George followed the path through the gardens, down the south lane, and finally arrived at the burial place—Lawrence's tomb.

All is lost, George thought as he shut his eyes. "All is lost."

He placed himself on a half brick wall to the left of the tomb. He gritted his teeth. "We are acting under an evil Geni. For we who view the actions of great men at a distance can only form conjectures agreeable to the small extent of our knowledge—ignorant of the comprehensive schemes intended. The conduct of our leaders is tempered with something—I don't care to give a name." Arising from his seated position, George paced back and forth, feeling heat rising to the muscles in his jaw. "Indeed. I will go further, and say they are d—" He stopped himself from saying the word aloud, "Or something worse."

Yes. It was clear now.

They were the enemy.

Part IV

The Reprisal

Chapter Thirty-Four

—◂•▸—

Note to Self

. . . woe's me, that I should Love and conceal . . .
—GEORGE WASHINGTON

HARLEM HEIGHTS, NEW YORK
JUNE 1776

Ambrosia and nectar found her nose; the scent reminded her of him. Still, after twenty years, it reminded her of him. She forced the steam away with a quick blow to prevent a burn on her lips. She let a small sip of warmth in.

The curtain in daylight shimmered pink, tinting the portico where she stood. Upon the highest point of Harlem Heights, on the northern end of Manhattan Island, her mansion, with its Tuscan columns from ground to roof, emerged like a white palace squarely in the middle of the land between rivers. From here, they'd be able to see the enemy coming.

With her at the mansion was a guest, a friend, Lasthenia Sherwood.

"My pa told me the tale once—of the giants hollering 'Fee Faw Fum.'" The girl who'd grown into a young woman fidgeted with the delicate handle of the gold-embossed porcelain cup. Big green eyes

with short ginger lashes swiveled toward Mary. "'Ne'er be spooked by them giants,' he told me." She gulped the tea.

Looking past the cornfields and grove of white-blossomed trees, they could see them far in the distance. Like predators about to attack the sheep, the ships of the Royal Navy practically covered the surface of the ocean. A tax on tea—that's what many colonists thought this war was over. Mary was of a different opinion.

Mount Morris was prepared—Mary had seen to it—with large supplies of food, enough to feed an army.

"Would you care for something? You must be hungry, Lulu." Mary worried about her.

Lasthenia shook her head. "I'd best get back to my's reading." Her hair—red and long enough to reach her waist—shifted gently as she turned her slim, small frame back to the foyer's doorway. Her muslin dressed billowed. "I ne'er read 'The Blue Bird' by myself, up tills now."

Mary let her be. She'd have the kitchen prepare her something anyhow.

Below her, the yanking and pulling had been going on all day. Mary knew the timing was odd, being that the colony lay on the precipice of war, but she couldn't stand the invasive species any longer. Her groundskeepers removed the tendrils that had attached to the walls in thatches and climbed until their dead feet surrounded her; ivy is stubborn like that.

So here, alone on the balcony, Mary remained. She'd gotten used to being alone. She looked out—the Hudson to her right, the Harlem River and East River beyond it, to her left. Colonel Morris had wanted to build on this land because of those views. She bought the estate after they married and after he retired from military life. The land had been advertised in the *New York-Gazette*:

A Pleasant situated farm on the Road leading to King's Bridge, in the Township of Harlem of York Island, containing about 100 Acres; about 30 Acres of which is Wood Land, a fine Piece of Meadow Ground, and more may easily be made;

and commands the finest Prospect in the whole country; the
Land runs from River to River.

They argued before he left—she and her husband. He was gone—
escaped to England a year prior. He hailed from Britain, but he
hadn't left to fight on behalf of his native land. He departed because
he was afraid. He had made this clear to her that last day, erupting
into a frantic soliloquy about a crime from long ago. No matter
what she did or how she asked, he would not reveal what it was that
he had done or to whom.

The argument centered around not that, but Lulu. Lulu was not a
low guest! His snobbery irritated Mary. What was she to do? Leave
Lulu in the street? No one could understand better the feeling of
witnessing the last breaths of your mother and your father. Poor
Rosie, dying of heartache after Jeffrey took a bullet to the head while
lighting the lantern at Hudson's Hook, fired from a ship in the river,
certainly not aimed at him, but hitting him square between the
eyes nonetheless. Mary and Lulu planted forget-me-not flowers and
Mary renamed the site Jeffrey's Hook in his honor. Lulu's father
didn't stay alive for long after that.

Yes, Lulu could stay with her for as much time as she needed.

MARY DID NOT want war. She was not the only one. Other heads of
elite families from the New York Colony were of the same opinion.
A letter—an olive branch, a last effort to avert bloodshed—had been
drafted and signed by several of those families, pleading with the citizens of England. She had hosted the group at her estate. The Honorable Robert Livingston—the boy who long ago had told Mary he
wanted to be a chief justice—had achieved success. Now judge of the
Court of General Sessions, he was the letter's author:

Friends, Countrymen and Brethren!

Give us leave most solemnly to assure you, that we have not
yet lost sight of the object we have ever had in view, a

reconciliation with you on constitutional principles, and a restoration of that friendly intercourse, which, to the advantage of both, we till lately maintained.

A cloud hangs over your heads and ours; e'er this reaches you, it may probably burst upon us; let us then (before the remembrance of former kindness is obliterated) once more repeat those appellations which are ever grateful in our ears; let us entreat heaven to avert our ruin, and the destruction that threatens our friends, brethren, and countrymen, on the other side of the Atlantic.

Colonel Morris was furious, not about the letter, but about the gathering. He wrote her from England: "I can easily conceive your disagreeable situation, but I did not imagine you would have thought yourself safer under the protection of the chief justice." In her letter in return, she explained that she'd known Robert since he was a little boy—that he needed a neutral place to meet. This did her no good, nor did the letter. The British responded to the peace offering by calling the signers rebellious.

Spirited by the conviction to independence, common folk across the colonies took up arms against the mother country. Hatred moved from ink to blood. First in Boston. New York was next.

To think! George Washington had gained the position of general to defend the colonists in the War of Independence. She couldn't deny that when he walked into a room, he had a commanding presence—a man of authority, a man guided by Providence, the man who couldn't die. No, there was no one better to command than George.

When she closed her eyes, she could recall the day her world changed on a balcony. "Everything which partakes of your nature has a claim to my affections." His whisper in her ear, she remembered it clearly. But that was long ago, long before he left without saying goodbye. George had married well, an older woman, a wealthy widow with

a plantation in Virginia, a lady who didn't dance—at least that was the word from Sir Tenoe. Tenoe often wrote to Mary from there and elsewhere, wherever his travels took him to teach the waltz to children of the privileged.

Now George had arrived here in New York, headquartered at the southern end of the island. She peered out as far as she could see. He was out there somewhere. She could feel him.

Mary walked toward the north wing of the house, treading upon the wide-planked floor, and passed through a narrower hall in order to get to the study. She needed to write a letter of her own. It had been on her mind for quite some time.

She squinted as she entered the study. The cornices and moldings were painted extremely bright, a scarlet red. Colonel Morris had been particular about this color; he had demanded an extremely vivid tone with a hint of orange to match the military uniform he had once worn. He despised the coloring on the wall that Mary had chosen—dull gray, with *Helianthus verticillatus* painted in a lighter shade of gray.

Mary placed herself at the intricately carved mahogany desk that once belonged to her mother. She thought of her every day. Mary began a note to her younger self:

Dearest Mary Eliza Philipse,

I know what you're feeling. Cursed one. Rose with thorns.
This is who you are. Open your eyes. Awaken to the
realization that you are nothing. Blame yourself
for their deaths. Take that in. Feel the guilt. Hate yourself.
Find the emptiness that the power of words cannot fix.

Does this make you uncomfortable? I'm glad. Now, go deeper
into the abyss, into your darkest days, into your deepest fears,
and grab your inner demons and choke them until they stop
breathing, because until you destroy the fear, the little hand

that reaches out to you from the cold darkness of your
nightmares, until you let that go, you will forever be
encompassed by fear.

Become nothing.

Like a Phoenix, start again. Be strong
like the sharp rocks that don't budge even when waves
slam against them time after time. When all is gone, there
will only be Mary Eliza left. This is when you will BE.

These years have passed and you still hold on to what
should have been. If only. Yes, if only. Release yourself of
it. Find life beyond the guardian's wall. The battle cannot be
won without faith and belief that there is a destiny in our lives,
one that even with the most fervent action against it has control
of our actions.

So I ask you in your youth to set your sight to the heavens
and ask for assistance. Life has not been fair to you. I know
this. The path is a long one that leaves you lost without a
direction. Sorrow is painful. Unsettledness is lonely. I know
what's it's like to be encompassed by both.

Move your focus to love. Love out loud. Love with no fear.
Love the love that is right in front of you. Why have you
fallen asleep to him? He is right there, holding you in his
embrace. In his arms, you feel whole for the first time in
your life — the only time in your life. You believe you have
no right to him. The mistakes, the loss left you scattered and
frail. Don't hide. Don't be afraid. Cease the battle with
your conscience. It has consumed you for so long, for too long.
Even when you wish to let it go, it instead holds like mud on
a shoe.

Remember the words of your father: "Be the light, Mary Eliza. You are capable of the impossible, for you have survived the unthinkable."

Her hand trembled as it did every time her signature was required. "Mrs. Roger Morris," she wrote.

Chapter Thirty-Five

———◄•►———

Hail to the Chief

. . . the wound often irritated and never healed, may at length become incurable.

—GEORGE WASHINGTON

NEW YORK CITY
JUNE 1776

George knew this was best, to send his wife back to Virginia. The journey would carry her far from the toil of what was expected: an invasion on New York. Placing a kiss atop the white bonnet on her head, George thought of the many disagreeable sensations resulting from his command of the troops of the United Provinces of North America: One being, that for her, it was a cutting stroke.

"As life is always uncertain"—he bent down to reach her. Martha was a full foot and two inches shorter than him—"I have asked that a will be drafted."

As he opened the carriage door to let her inside, she turned and offered a meek smile through narrow lips. "The shades below are far from your reach." Her voice was thin, sounding hardly above the level of a whisper. She adjusted her frilled headgear and used his hand to assist her in climbing in. "Besides, you have entered into an engagement, not to quit the theater of this world before the year 1800." She

tapped on his hand with her other. "I rely upon your pledge of no breach of contract on that account."

George married the widow Martha Custis in a simple ceremony, one year after Mary Eliza Philipse changed her name. He met the widow Custis on her plantation in Virginia. He proposed quickly. The couple never had children together. Martha had a son and daughter from a previous marriage. Her first husband had passed away eight months before she met George.

"You may believe me, my dear Patsy," said George to her, "when I assure you, in the most solemn manner, that, so far from seeking this appointment, I have used every endeavor in my power to avoid it-—not only from my unwillingness to part with you and the family but from a consciousness of its being a trust too great for my capacity."

His wife was afraid of war. For the short time they were here in New York, he had watched her shudder and shake when she heard the sound of a gun firing. She despised it all, thinking the preparations terrible indeed, she told him privately.

His large hand settled on her knee. "I shall feel no pain from the toil or the danger of the campaign. My unhappiness will flow from the uneasiness I know you will feel being left alone. I beg of you to pass your time as agreeably as possible."

AS THE HORSES took her carriage out of his sight, George lingered to scan the lands and the shoreline. The sea power of the enemy waited beyond the river, in the Atlantic, staring back at him. Every day, the two sides were seemingly doing nothing more than observing each other's movements from a mile's distance. Waves on the Hudson River moved turbulently, but not as passionately as what was to come.

His mind considered the great task ahead. The powerful fleet of the naval force of the kingdom threatened. Whether this be a place to rendezvous or to facilitate operations, he did not know. Whether they would go north by land or water, and whether they would pay their compliments to him beforehand, he was uncertain.

Experience taught him that it is easier to stop an enemy from entering than it is to dislodge him after he's taken possession. For this reason, he ordered his forces to repair to this city with all possible expediency.

Nothing seemed of greater importance.

Protect the Hudson.

Possess the Hudson.

He would do whatever necessary to prevent the mighty British from sailing up the river. Lines of defense would be all he could establish, for he had only a hastily formed navy, made up of just private vessels. And as for George's army, his contingents consisted of undisciplined bands of common folk, volunteers of a motley sort, oftentimes half-starved, half-dressed, and now going up against a behemoth.

A YEAR PRIOR at a meeting in Philadelphia, the dispirited colonies chose George to lead—voted in by a unanimous voice. Representative John Adams, out of Massachusetts, nominated him: "I have but one gentleman in my mind for that important command, and that is a gentleman from Virginia who is among us and very well known to all of us, a gentleman whose skill and experience as an officer, whose independent fortune, great talents and excellent universal character would command the approbation of all America, and unite the cordial exertions of all the colonies better than any other person in the union."

George left the room when he heard this. He had been sitting near the exit. Although the cause of freedom from the oppressor was emblazoned in his heart, he was certain he had neither the expertise nor the skill for such a position.

Destiny was of a different opinion.

A STEADY gait carried him into a temporary headquarters established in a grand two-floor mansion on a high hill, on the corner of Varick and Vandam streets. The white house with an Ionic portico

held columns from floor to roof. It sat on the southern tip of Manhattan Island. A series of meetings awaited him inside.

After he entered, George acknowledged both the British deserter, Sergeant Thomas Hickey Jr., now a personal guard assigned to him, and a young housekeeper tiptoeing in the hall.

"Fair day to you, General," the man said to him with the accent of a Brit who'd spent a bit of time in New York.

In the parlor, George offered proper salutations to a sachem, whose name was Chief Red Hawk. The native warrior had sought out council with him for some time. He'd traveled from the Great Kanawha River, near the Ohio, to offer support to his army—the same man who claimed to have shot at George multiple times at the Battle of Monongahela. The brutal battle all those years ago had been seared into George's memory.

The chief carried himself as one whose maturity in life could be sensed from the grave manner in which he spoke. "I am a chief and ruler over my tribes. My influence extends to the waters of the great lakes and to the far blue mountains. I have traveled a long and weary path, that I might see the warrior of the great battle."

These were surprising words from a man who was once George's rival on the field of war. The chief never took a seat, standing in upright position, with a slight tilt to his back. "It was on the day when the white man's blood mixed with the streams of our forests that I first beheld this chief." He pointed his whole hand in George's direction. "I called to my young men and said, 'Mark yon tall and daring warrior.'"

George realized this daring warrior he spoke of was himself; he recalled the endless gunfire coming at him from the invisible enemy in the trees.

The chief spoke of his own prowess with weapons and how he never missed his targets. Firing at George proved fruitless, he told him; he had shot at him seventeen times. Not a one spilled his blood.

Seventeen times. George had never known this.

"'Quick,' I told them. 'Let your aim be certain, and he dies.' Our

rifles were leveled, rifles that, but for him, knew not how to miss—'twas all in vain; a power mightier far than we shielded you from harm."

George recollected the blur of the day, the screams of the dying, and the stink of death. He recalled falling as his horse was shot. He had four holes in his coat. Two bullets hit his hat.

Then the enemy's weapons went silent.

"'He is not of the redcoat tribe; he hath an Indian's wisdom. He cannot die in battle,' I professed to my warriors." The chief seemed to want to let out what had been hidden inside him for decades. "I am old, and soon shall be gathered to the great council fire of my fathers in the land of shades, but ere I go, there is something bids me speak in the voice of prophecy."

George leaned forward as the chief spoke in a quieter voice.

"Listen! The Great Spirit protects you." His eyes shut. He raised his head high. "It guides your destiny." The chief pointed his finger into George's chest, directly at his heart. "You . . . you will become the chief of nations, and a people yet unborn will hail you as the founder of a mighty empire."

With this, the chief offered his farewell, the allegiance of his tribe, and left.

GEORGE DID NOT move from where he was standing for some time as he absorbed the native's prophecy. George fully put his trust in Providence, which preserved him up until this point. In it, he had a great reliance. In the past, it befriended him, protected him, bestowed graces upon him. His beliefs went far back to his childhood, to his mother. She always believed the heavens would shield him from harm.

Bullet holes in his coat and his hat. No wound. He should not have survived. The work of Providence, he thought. George remembered well the battle and the field of red clover and carrying the wounded from that meadow of death.

This cause would yield its protection again. It would have to. It would be the only way to defeat an empire.

George walked with certain stride into the war room to review

his military plan for New York. He picked up a large scroll and unfurled it onto a heavy table at the center of the room. The survey of the Hudson was drawn on a map with detailed diagrams of the planned defenses. The Mount Morris estate sat at the northernmost end of the island, squarely in the middle of the land between rivers— high up on a hill, the highest point in the city, offering views of the waterways. This place, Harlem Heights, was the key to the northern country.

George's desire was to prevent any Brit from marching onto that property. He'd set up batteries south of the mansion's location to prevent forces from moving north by land.

On the water, he planned for a chain across the Hudson to New Jersey's Palisades. George marked the spot with his finger along the shoreline near King's Bridge. Here. At Jeffrey's Hook is where the links would begin on this side of the river.

George studied the other defensive structure on paper; a cheval-de-frise would be sunk in the same spot.

THE CAPTAIN OF the New York Artillery Company arrived for a meeting with the general to provide his account of ammunitions and weaponry.

George acknowledged him as he entered. "I must commend you, Captain Hamilton, for the masterly manner of executing your work." George knew of the young man, recently commissioned as a captain, who had led a militia of students from King's College that stole—or, as it had been reported to him, liberated—British cannons at the Battery.

"I thank you, General." Alexander Hamilton was youthful in appearance and replied in a firm voice with a twinge of coarseness to it. His name had become known for another reason. He had authored an essay defending the colonists' rights. Hamilton moved to the maps that George was surveying. "The North River. Aye. If we can get there before them, all will be well." His head cocked to one side as he peered over the defensive strategy.

"The Hudson. If lost, it will be of the most fatal consequence."

"We little imagined it would come to this, General. How ridiculous is their assumption that we are quarreling for the trifling sum of three pence a pound on tea."

"They are practicing such low and dirty tricks that men of sentiment and honor must blush for their villainy. They meant to drive us into what they termed *rebellion,* then stripped us of the rights and privileges of Englishmen. If they were actuated by principles of justice, why did they refuse, indignantly, to accede to the terms which were humbly supplicated before hostilities commenced?"

"Jealousy." Hamilton placed his hands in the pockets of his coat. "Wars oftener proceed from angry and perverse passions than from cool calculations of interest. Jealousy is a source of the greatest evils. Give me the steady, uniform, unshaken security of constitutional freedom; give me the right to be tried by a jury of my own neighbors, and to be taxed by my own representatives only."

George became furious just thinking about what the British had done. "We are now embarked on a tempestuous ocean from whence, perhaps, no friendly harbor is to be found. Arms alone must decide it."

A knock on the door interrupted their meeting. Samuel Fraunces entered, holding glasses of ale. He offered to feed the men during their stay, as they were located just doors from his tavern.

"General Washington, Sam took a hole to the roof of his tavern for us!" exclaimed Hamilton as he clapped Sam on the back. "The Brits fired a cannonball in retaliation for our liberation of their cannons."

"For the cause of freedom!" Sam cheered as he distributed the ale. He announced food would be served in the dining area.

GEORGE FOUND A seat on a wide tapestried chair at a polished mahogany table. Roasted turkey wafted in the air. Hunger set in. The day had been too busy to make time for food until this hour. The dish of meat looked appetizing, but George's teeth had been giving him trouble in the form of a shooting pain through his gums. He settled on starting with the side portion of peas on his dinner plate.

George forked a few of them. He lifted them to his mouth.

The young housekeeper, whom he greeted in the hall earlier, ran toward him with her face appearing alarmed. "Poison! Poison!" she shrieked. "The peas is poisoned!"

Chapter Thirty-Six

———◄•►———

A Traitor Among Us

. . . guard against the impostures of pretended patriotism . . .

—GEORGE WASHINGTON

YONKERS-ON-HUDSON
JULY 1776

Lulu, all freckled innocence and pure cream skin, sat up straight on a cushioned bench. She appeared quite graceful in an ivory floral gown that Mary had made for her. An unexpected picture, considering her choice of language: "Dastardly maggot of a fella. Mum woulda spit on him as he hung from the gallows." She feigned expectorating from her lips.

Mary would have her act more in accordance with her place in high society now; however, in truth she agreed with such an action, and about Rosie—yes, she would have spit on him.

Lulu continued reading aloud, albeit slowly, pronouncing each syllable, from the *New-York Gazette:*

In the forenoon was executed in the field, near the
Bowry Lane (in the presence of near twenty
thousand spectators) soldier Thomas Hickey, belonging to his

Excellency General Washington's guards, for mutiny
and conspiracy; being one of those who formed and
was soon to have put in execution, that horrid plot of
assassination.

Mary let out a deep breath. The Hickey plot—it could have killed
him, she thought.

"Peas! I ne'er liked those bum vegetables anyhows." Lulu turned
the page to continue her pronouncing; Mary had her do this each
day to improve her reading. She was advancing quickly, as she
worked through the sounds of each word:

This day the CONTINENTAL CONGRESS declared
the UNITED COLONIES FREE and INDEPENDENT
STATES.

"What's it mean?" asked Lulu.

"Why, it means that freedom . . . true freedom is soon to come."

"To your birthday!" exclaimed Susannah, raising a glass in a toast
as she entered the east parlor. A footman carried in a tray with three
drinks, each glass with the family's engraved silver medal seal—a lion
emerging from a coronet.

"Must we still celebrate when reaching my stage in life?" replied
Mary, picking up a glass of Madeira and handing one to Lulu.

"Sluice your gob," Lulu said loudly.

Susannah looked dumbfounded.

Mary laughed.

Lulu gulped. "I woulda chosen calibogus if it was me choosin'."

"You drink rum, girl?" asked a perplexed-looking Susannah.

"Who else will be joining us?" Mary asked this question coyly,
knowing full well whom they planned to introduce to Lulu.

Susannah looked at Mary with a gleam in her eye as a strapping
young fellow walked through the doorway. "Lulu Sherwood, may I
introduce you to Nathaniel Gist."

"Is he a beard splitter?" whispered Lulu to Mary.

"No, he is not a ladies' man," Mary quietly responded. "He's a gentleman. We wouldn't introduce you to him if we didn't think so."

"May I stay in this spot? Youse know I don't walk so good."

"Lulu, you can do whatever you like. But please know, no one is perfect."

The rugged dark-haired lad came closer. The Philipse family had offered him a place to stay just northeast of the manor, at one of their outer cottages. Mary approved of him. He was just as Mary had pictured his father, Christopher Gist, the frontiersman who had charged into enemy territory with George all those years ago. She had read about their journey many times in the newspaper that she still kept on the shelf in her bedchamber at Philipse Manor, its writing away from her, always away from her.

The four of them sat and toasted Mary's day. After a few minutes, the sisters gave Lulu and Nathaniel privacy as the siblings moved to the dining room of the manor.

"SHE APPEARS A child." Susannah glanced back at her as they walked away.

"Hard to believe, but Lasthenia is an adult now. She's asked to be treated as such, yet I, too, still see her as that little girl with crooked pigtails."

Mary was drawn to an appetizing scent as she entered the dining room. Temperance approached. Except for the faint fine lines around her eyes, she hadn't aged a bit in all these years. She wore her hair the same way as she always had, placed neatly into a bun. "*Mes filles* helped with the icing." Temperance smiled as she spoke.

Mary looked over the chef's shoulder to see her twin girls peeking out from behind the door. They were neatly dressed, with their hair pinned back perfectly in buns, replicas of their mother. "We've made your favorite, a great cake with almonds," added Temperance.

"I thank you, and please offer my gratitude to François. The table setting is spectacular."

The table looked glorious, set with a blue-and-white porcelain set-ting and white flowers. The chairs were wrapped in wide white satin ribbon. The decorated cake sat at the center. The darling setup was in stark contrast to the ugliness of the conversation.

Beverley, Frederick, and Elizabeth were already seated.

"James Jay is the author of it." Beverley sipped his tea.

Just the sound of his name made Mary feel anxious as she took her seat.

"He calls himself a patriot. Nonsense!" Frederick picked up a French biscuit. Elizabeth quickly called over her lady's maid to butter it for him. "Dr. Jay has no such power." Frederick shifted in his seat, for his corpulence was greater than the chair could accom-modate.

"If he becomes a member of the New York Senate, he will," added Beverley with a grunt.

"The honorable Philip Livingston is in charge. He would never al-low that man to become a member." Frederick ate the biscuit in one bite.

"Robert the elder?" Susannah took her seat, as did Mary.

"Yes, my true," replied Beverley.

"What is that man the author of?" Mary needed to know. Ner-vousness welled up inside her.

"It means nothing, even if the law were to pass." Frederick spoke with his mouth full.

"Rumor is that an act of attainder is being proposed by Dr. Jay to the new legislature formed by a group of colonists."

"An attainder?" Mary launched out of her chair. "An attainder! Like Fontainebleau?"

They gave her a bewildered look.

"The Edict of Fontainebleau." Mary raised her hands as she stared at Frederick.

Frederick shrugged. "One has nothing to do with the other."

Mary moved about the room. "James threatened this long ago." She paced back and forth. "Under Fontainebleau, the Jay family

property was confiscated, their possessions taken, and the family condemned to death if caught in the province. Father told us the story. This is why they arrived here from France . . . with nothing." Mary had always known the beast would return to take revenge. "Do we not believe he would do the same to *us*?"

"Our great-grandfather was kind enough to adopt Jay's grandmother into this family. That should have been enough. She had no rights to the manor." Frederick's lips pursed as he spoke in disgust. A crumb clung to his cheek.

"Where does the senior Jay stand on this?" asked Beverley.

"James was disowned by his father years ago." Frederick nodded as Elizabeth handed him a piece of cake. "Mr. Jay even cut his scoundrel son from the will."

"His brother?" Beverley inquired.

"The Honorable John Jay is a man of justice," replied Frederick. "He would disown his brother, too, if this should come to pass."

"Why would they attaint us, my true?" Susannah sat with a straight posture, as if a board were behind her.

"They've asked the head of every elite family to sign a pledge in person to be considered a friend to the American cause," Beverley replied glumly. "The declaration for independence has now been signed by the colonies."

"Whichever side James is on, find this family on the opposite." Frederick forked into the dessert. "What is Roger's opinion on the matter?"

"Roger?" Mary was confused.

He motioned for her to sit. "Yes, your espoused."

She placed herself back onto the velvet-cushioned, hand-carved chair. "He's written me saying we have only to pray to God to put an end to the unhappy and unnatural situation of affairs. He dreads the miseries that will befall both countries."

Elizabeth had additional pieces of cake cut.

"What of the other families?" asked Frederick.

"The Van Cortlandts have signed the colonists' pledge," Beverley said.

Elizabeth handed a plate with a cut of cake to Mary, who accepted it from her.

"Eva's husband has not signed it, though." Mary couldn't even think about eating.

Susannah sipped tea gracefully. "How is her life on Long Island?"

This is not a time for light talk, Mary thought. "She's written me that all is fine," she replied anxiously.

"The Kembles have signed, staunchly loyal to the Crown," said Beverley.

"I ponder whether Margaret's enjoying life in Boston with Thomas Gage," remarked Susannah.

More polite remarks, thought Mary. "Margaret's allegiance is torn," she said.

"Oh!" exclaimed her sister.

"She's written me that she prays her husband will not be the instrument that sacrifices countrymen's lives. He is general of the British forces, Susannah."

"The Gage wedding was a lovely wedding," Susannah said.

"The Delanceys?" Beverley asked of Frederick.

"Sheriff James sailed to England six months ago. Oliver and his family remain; he is considering forming his own brigade to protect his property. He has no faith in either side."

"Brother, if we don't formally choose a side, each will believe we support the other," said Susannah.

The prophecy from the night of her nuptials kept repeating in Mary's head. *Your possessions shall pass from you when the Eagle shall despoil the Lion of his mane. Your possessions shall pass from you when the Eagle shall despoil the Lion of his mane.* She had never forgotten it. "An attainder is without judicial process, correct?" asked Mary as she once again began to get up from her chair. Frederick placed his hand on her shoulder to keep her put.

"If passed, those attainted would be declared guilty. You are correct, Polly, and with no judicial process allowed." Beverley had a nervous twitch now in his voice. "Anyone attainted and caught would suffer death."

"And what if the act of attainder finds its way to a vote?" Susannah's eyebrows surged upward.

"We will defend ourselves at trial." Frederick eyes began to close in readiness of a nap.

"Would anyone care for more tea?" Elizabeth chimed in, appearing anxious.

"Unfortunately, Frederick, there would be no trial. Enemies of the state are convicted without proof," said Beverley, "without a chance to defend. If attainted, we would be banished, our lands confiscated, all of our lands, including those in your name." He glanced at Mary and then at his wife. "As well as yours, my true."

"It cannot be!" Susannah cried out in horror.

Mary let it settle in. She knew all along vengeance would find her. "We would be condemned to death as traitors."

"They wouldn't dare!" shouted Susannah.

"Condemned to death, Susannah, if they get to us"—Mary tried to calm a shaky breath—"they could capture and kill us."

"Nonsense! Traitors?" The color drained from her sister's face. She looked as if she would faint right there at the table.

The stench of hair powder attacked Mary's nose. A sick feeling began to swirl in her stomach. "James Jay has no fortune of his own." There was not a touch of powder in anyone's hair in the room. She could still smell it. She felt nearly overpowered by it, like a fog rolling in. She took a deep breath to find composure and asked the question that jolted her back into focus. "That man is distressed of money. Is it beyond the realm of possibility that he could gain commission in a forfeiture sale of our confiscated land?"

"Absurdity—that's what this is. Philip would never allow it." Frederick grunted. "The Honorable Philip Livingston would have to die first."

Chapter Thirty-Seven

———◦•◦———

Cheval-de-frise

. . . it must be known, that we are at all times ready
for war.

—GEORGE WASHINGTON

HARLEM HEIGHTS

If it weren't wartime, this would make a charming picture. From the river's edge, just south of Spiting Devil, George peered across the Hudson at the grandeur of the steep precipice—the Palisades. A slight breeze carried with it a breath of lavender; it reminded him of her. Still, after all these years, it reminded him of her.

Mount Morris, as some called it, had fields blanketed in wildflowers stretching all the way from the Hudson River to the east end of the island. Upon the highest ground, beyond the cornfields, sat the mansion that belonged to her . . . and the insubordinate one—the man who had taken off for England when George was named general.

George appeared as a commander should, wearing a blue coat equipped with a rise-and-fall collar, breeches, and underdress in matching buff: That shade, buff, was the same as the uniform for his soldiers. George decided on hunting shirts for the men; no dress

would be cheaper, or more convenient. He also remembered the look on the French commandant's face when he, Gist, and his crew of a motley sort arrived in enemy territory in no more than hunter's garb. Even George's expert marksmen would be dressed in such garb. As he looked at them gathered in front of him, he knew it was the right decision. Surprise the enemy. Besides, there was no money for anything more.

General Washington spoke before his men. "The hour is fast approaching, on which the honor and success of this army, and the safety of our bleeding country, depend." He spoke loudly, firmly, clearly. "Let it never be said, that in a day of action, you turned your backs on the foe—let the enemy no longer triumph—They brand you with ignominious epithets—Will you patiently endure that reproach? Will you suffer the wounds given to your Country to go unrevenged? Every motive that can touch the human breast calls us to the most vigorous exertions—Our dearest rights—our dearest friends—our own lives—honor—glory, and even shame, urge us to the fight—And, my fellow soldiers! when an opportunity presents, be firm, be brave, show yourselves men, and victory is yours!" His soldiers applauded him.

TODAY GEORGE WOULD begin to fortify this property. He believed these grounds about King's Bridge well calculated for a defense. Obstructions placed from one side of the river to the other would prevent a British incursion. These would stop the enemy's movement north from Manhattan Island. He would have his troops prepared to defend with a minute's warning. Lookouts would be established at the highest points of Harlem Heights. Every regiment posted in this place, from Morris's house to camp, needed to be furnished with guards to prevent any surprises. George's entire army had pushed northward after the British landed their ships on the southern tip and after they tried to kill him.

His forces would be ready. He would be ready.

A man George considered a fast friend to the colonies approached and spoke to him. "This, General Washington, I guarantee, will stop

the enemy from entering Hudson's River. I call this a marine cheval-de-frise." Inventor and master ironworker Robert Erskine had developed defenses never before seen. One of them was an enormous medieval-style defensive weapon with a steel center frame and long iron spikes projecting outward. It was moving closer to them, carried on a flat cart with wheels, sluggishly led by eight horses. "The consequence of a ship's running against it must either be that she will stake upon it or overset it, in which case the other horns will rise and take her in the bottom, and either overset her or go through her; or else she must break it with her weight, thereby rendering her unfit for further service."

George assigned nearly a hundred men to assist in its launch. He had only eighteen hundred soldiers at his disposal in this place. "Let it be sunk in the darkness," he told Erskine.

George presumed the British would make several attempts at an attack. Their troops lay encamped about two miles south. Their weaponry was being transported from Long Island, he had learned. The signs were clear: They would make an attack soon. By land. By water. He had to put the forces in the best defensive position that time and circumstance would allow.

"As for the chain?" asked George.

"The chain is being completed—twelve hundred links of iron to allow it to reach seventeen hundred feet in length. It will be installed here at Jeffrey's Hook."

"It is of the utmost importance that the greatest diligence should be used to complete and render the defense effectual," added George.

"Aye. Our Benedict Arnold has offered assurance he will oversee the installation of the second chain north in the Highlands, at the shoreline of the Beverley Robinson estate."

George heard Beverley built a fine estate on Susannah's property in the Highlands along the Hudson River. Robinson not only allowed for the installation but also offered residency to Arnold or any other commander, including George.

"And the turtle is complete, General. We needed seven hundred pounds of lead."

"The submersible? And it is operational?"

"Aye, General. The device is completed with a brass oar for rowing forward and backward. It will be sunk by letting in water via a spring near the bottom. It's watertight, General. It will make its attempt below the water upon the British warship *Eagle*. Explosives will be affixed to the sides of the ship and provide enough time to allow for the officers' escape."

PUTTING HIS SPYGLASS to his eye, George looked south. What to do with the southern tip of Manhattan Island still remained a question. Till of late, he had no doubt about defending it, but the British had infiltrated with thousands more troops than he could take down. He had to move his soldiers from that place. Now he wondered whether the enemy should have rights to its comforts and conveniences. Could he go so far as to make their encampment useless? Possibly level it, if necessary? Burn it down? Destroy the southern tip? Yes, he believed that was the only way. He would leave the matter to Congress to decide.

The enemy, he feared, planned to enclose his army. If the British filled southern Manhattan Island and obtained control of King's Bridge to the north of his present location, his armed forces would be trapped in the middle, then cut to pieces.

Brigadier General Hugh Mercer rode up to him. He'd become a close confidant of George's over the twenty years they had known each other. George needed to discuss another location with him.

"Mercer, as I look to the west," George viewed the Palisades across the Hudson, "it appears to me of the utmost importance to have a strong encampment at the post on the Jersey side of the North River, opposite our post. I think it advisable that you detach such a force from Amboy."

"Certainly, General," Mercer responded. "I will see to it. And General, there is news on the subject of government." His Scottish accent was detectable. "The honorable Philip Livingston—"

"Yes?"

"He is dead, General. Fainted from a dizzy spell in chambers. He died right there on his desk. There is word that the medical doctor,

James Jay, will replace him as a representative of the Southern District in the New York Senate."

A crushing sound interrupted their discussion, for the massively long cart rolling the cheval flattened a large wooden post on the property. The engraved marker with the words *Mount Morris* was flattened below its wheels. As the cart moved past it, splintered pieces lay on the ground, any trace of the words obliterated.

Chapter Thirty-Eight

---·◦·---

By Order of George Washington

. . . I have nothing further to add, except a Wish, that the measures I have taken to dissipate a Storm, which had gathered so suddenly & unexpectedly, may be acceptable . . .

—GEORGE WASHINGTON

HARLEM HEIGHTS

"Philip Livingston would have to die first," her brother had said. He was right. There was no telling what Senator James Jay would do to her and to her family.

Standing on the balcony of her mansion, she believed she was shielded from him, for now. She watched the military men pitching tents on her property. The general must be there among them, she thought. She searched as carefully as she could for auburn hair. She wondered what he looked like after all these years.

"He's a tall, handsome-bodied, manly man," said Lulu as she arrived, carrying a rolled paper. "Just like Mum always said."

"Are you certain?"

"About my mum?"

"Well, no, that is what she always said. Are you for certain it was General George Washington?" Saying his name gave her a slight tingle.

"'Twas him. But I was a wee girl last I seen 'im. Looked like the same to me."

She remembered that day when Lulu, such a sweet little child, standing at her mother's side, talked about the tale of the bluebird before Mary's first encounter with her charming.

Lulu handed her the packet she was holding. "I invited him, just like you asked. His cub asked me to bring this to you."

"His aide?"

"Sort of a dumplin' kind of fella—a bit of a short, thick man. Hugh Mercer was the name."

Hugh Mercer? Mary wondered if it could be the man she greeted long ago at that forsaken banquet on Christmas Eve. She had heard a Mercer was in New York. "Well, thank you, Lulu. You are very kind to do that for me."

"After all you's did for me? I'm forevers in your debt."

Mary smiled as she opened the correspondence. She immediately recognized the hand in which it was written—its slim upstrokes and larger downstrokes, made up of elegant loops and curves:

By order of George Washington:

Whereas a Bombardment and Attack upon the City of
New York by our cruel and inveterate Enemy, may be
hourly expected: And as there are great Numbers of Women,
Children, and infirm Persons, yet remaining in the City,
whose Continuance will rather be prejudicial than advantageous
to the Army, and their Persons exposed to great Danger and
Hazard: I Do therefore recommend it to all such Persons, as
they value their own safety and Preservation, to remove with
all expedition, out of the said Town, at this critical Period—
trusting, that with the Blessing of Heaven upon the American
Arms, they may soon return to it in perfect Security. And I
do enjoin and require, all the Officers and Soldiers in the Army,

under my Command, to forward and assist such Persons in their Compliance with this Recommendation.

A bombardment? An attack south of her mansion in the city could certainly leave one of her most prized possessions damaged or destroyed. She needed to depart at once to retrieve it from her town home on the southern tip of the island on Stone Street. She quickly made her way out of the mansion and toward the coach. She got in the driver's seat with her fine mare, Valentine, in front of her.

Chapter Thirty-Nine

———◄•►———

Mary's Mansion

*. . . evils of this nature work their own cure; tho' the
remedy comes slower . . .*

—GEORGE WASHINGTON

MOUNT WASHINGTON

He made a headquarters of Mary's Mansion. From here on the
widow's walk, George could look out to monitor the movements of
his forces. The massive estate in Harlem Heights offered a perfect view
of each of the waterways around the island of New York City as well as
the woods and fields. From the southern tip to this place, only one
road was large enough for an army's wagons to travel. For the British,
no other way was possible by land. They would have to pass through
here to get to points north. George ordered impediments along the
route. "Fell trees across the roads. Dig deep pits," he ordered his men.
"Have it broken up and destroyed in such a manner as to render it utterly
impassable."

Other defensive maneuvers were under way. The cheval was sunk
into the Hudson. On land, the troops positioned themselves properly
in preparation for an attack. The building of a fort at Jeffrey's Hook
was under way.

Still, at this point, George's fear of failure exceeded his expectations

of success. Nearly thirty thousand men made up the British lines. Add to that, they were fighting troops regularly trained, superior in arms and with battle experience. His were men who dragged themselves out of domestic life, not used to living encamped, inexperienced in arms, and without confidence. Would they be frightened by their own shadows when confronted? George believed it possible.

His numbers were insufficient. Even if he collected his divided army from Long Island, Governors Island, Powles Hook, Red Hook, and Horn's Hook into one body, it would still be wholly inferior against the enemy.

The months leading up to this point had been a failure militarily. The night before, the attack on the Royal Navy, underwater with the submersible, had failed to sink the *Eagle*.

At the battle across from the river on Long Island, the British had outflanked his men. He would have lost Brooklyn, too, if the dense fog hadn't rolled in during a nighttime retreat across the river. In great secrecy, they evacuated on any seagoing vessels they could find. Most were just rowboats. They were slow and small, but Providence sent a wind. They tarried until every last man crossed the East River. George left the fires burning and moved thousands of troops in silence across the water through the fog.

George turned to the doorway and moved to a gray-walled study with its moldings painted in a red as bold as the color of the British uniforms. George took a seat at the desk to write to Congress. He needed to tell them that the power of words could not even describe the impossible task before him. His army, as he looked at it, was broken. George began composing a letter to the president of Congress, John Hancock, in the forenoon.

We are now encamped with the Main body of the Army on the Heights of Harlem, where I should hope the Enemy would meet with a defeat in case of an Attack, If the Generality of our Troops would behave with tolerable bravery, but experience to my extreme affliction has convinced me that this is rather to be wished for than expected;

However I trust, that there are many who will act like men,
and shew themselves worthy of the blessings of Freedom.
I have sent out some reconoitring parties to gain Intelligence
If possible of the disposition of the Enemy and shall inform
Congress of every material event by the earliest Opportunity.

A voice cried out from the hall: "Redcoats! Redcoats in the fields!"

George rushed out to the portico and looked through his spyglass. The British were advancing northward. George hurried to mount his stallion.

He found his colonels and ordered them to take 150 of the Rangers to investigate. He headed to the advanced posts, moving straight toward the enemy. He needed to assess the situation properly. For about two miles he rode, from the northernmost end of the camp to the southernmost. They had arrived. Thousands of them. The enemy was before him in large bodies of troops, moving from the southern tip to Harlem Heights. How this event would end, only God knew. The bullets whistled through the air.

Exchanges of gunfire erupted between the British advance parties and the detachment that George sent out to investigate. A colonel raced up to him on horseback. "The advance party is in a skirmish, General. There's more of the enemy concealed."

One brigade was in a confused, disorderly jumble. His greatest fears of defeat were being realized. "Good God, have I got such troops as those!" shouted George. Men with no experience, no expertise, no willingness to take orders made up his ranks. George threw his hat to the ground in a furor. "Are these the men with which I am to defend America!"

George felt the ground shake below him.

"The redcoats are in hot pursuit, moving northward!" yelled a colonel.

That's when George heard them, the pounding of hooves. The enemy rushed downhill. This was followed by bugle calls—a quick series of pulsating double notes. The British were playing "Gone Away." The fox has left its refuge. The hunt is on. A mocking gesture to George.

George ordered a contingent from the New England regiments, volunteers who'd been farmers up until now, to face the enemy with him. They set out bravely, heroically. He wanted to draw the whole of the British units into the open field, cut them off from hiding in the extremity of the wooded areas. A feint attack at the front forced them out. He ordered another contingent to take to the trees. To George's surprise, the plan was working. The gunfire of his sharpshooters from nature's camouflage was easily hitting its targets. The British were falling in huge numbers.

Their forces wanted to entrap him. He entrapped them with a horseshoe offensive.

He ordered three companies of riflemen from Virginia to get to the rear of the enemy's lines. A larger force of additional Rangers reinforced by riflemen, this one led by Captain Hamilton, moved to the left. Another contingent took the right.

The enemy was trapped.

"Take the cornfield!" the general ordered.

His crew of a motley sort was winning.

Yes, the hunt *is* on.

Chapter Forty

—◄◦►—

Burn It Down

*Tho this place is under a cloud at present, I have no
doubt but that it will Phoenix like again rise into
consequence out of its own ashes—*

—GEORGE WASHINGTON

NEW YORK CITY

The little hand reached out to her. Mary grabbed it tightly, so tightly
that she was nearly amazed at her strength. No mud spotted her shoes;
Elbert's were polished to a shine. "There's no mud, Elbert." The boy
smiled wide. The dirt could not touch them. The child's feet were above
the ground. No way could he slip. No way could he fall into the river.
The two of them turned their eyes to the water, so clear and glorious
and blue. She could see all the way to the bottom. Across the still surface moved a reflection of black birds, ravens flying high, soaring, away
from her, far away, even past the guardian's wall. Elbert's sparkling eyes
turned back to her; they were aglow like an angel's before her.

A loud pounding distracted her. Mary wanted to get back to Elbert. The knocking grew heavier, more intense. "Please, let me go back
to him," she whispered. Something was burning. She coughed to clear
her throat. She jumped from her bed, awakened from her deep slumber by fire. She slipped on shoes, rushed out of her bedchamber with

whatever gown she had on, and raced down the stairwell. Someone was knocking. She answered the door.

A stunned face looked back at her. "I saw a coach at your front." The soldier spoke to her calmly but with intensity. "Why are you here, madame?"

"It is my home."

"The city's on fire. We've been ordered to take you out of here."

"By whom?"

"Please, madame, we must go!"

Before leaving, Mary raced back into the parlor, grabbed a painting off the wall, wrapped it in a table covering, and left.

The scorching air smacked her in the face. The burning odor seeped into her nose. Her eyes stung. She shielded them with one hand. With the other, she clutched the covered canvas. She placed the painting in the coach and tried to climb on Valentine while covering her mouth to stop the taste of ash. The soldier told her to enter, that he would be her driver.

She refused this. He made way for her.

"An officer will lead you out."

"Your name?"

He jumped on a horse, headed in a southern direction. "Nathan Hale," he replied from a distance.

Her mare charged ahead, veering around the hellfire. The mighty inferno swallowed the homes across the road. Smoke poured out onto Stone Street. The wind carried flames toward her. The odor of charred wood was everywhere. On each road she passed, another home quartering British troops burned to ash.

As she rode on Broadway toward the northern end of Manhattan Island, the heat was intense. She watched as the British soldiers tried to put down the flames with Newsham engines. She'd seen them operate before—how they streamed water nearly 150 feet. This time, they appeared dry. No fire bells sounded. Not a fireman could be found anywhere.

Valentine never galloped this fast before. She looked back and saw the city behind her glowing orange, engulfed in flames.

She rode her way out of the ruins.

Hatred, indeed, moved to blood in New York. Was it the work of human hands? George must have known. The timing of his order. The broken engines. No firemen anywhere. How could he allow this to happen? Burn a city down. What kind of man would do such a thing! Yes, maybe they were right about him. How dare he! Burn it to the ground, she thought. She knew where he was. She would find him and speak her mind! "Make way! " She'd charge in. She wouldn't pay his guards any mind. "Where's the general?" She wouldn't wait for an answer. She'd demand his attention. "I have been disillusioned all these years by an idea of a man. Now I know what has been in my mind is distant from reality. You retreat and you burn!" He would return only a cold stare. "How do you not feel a deep sense of sympathy for a city that is now in ruins? Fire burned a third of this metropolis down! Who is responsible for this?"

"Providence—or some good honest fellow," he would say, "has done more for us than we were disposed to do for ourselves."

"And you will let this go without justice served!"

"Had I been left to the dictates of my own judgment, New York should have been laid in ashes before I quitted it!"

"It's been burned to the ground!"

"Ah, yes, a new town is fast rising out of the ashes of the old."

SHE PULLED THE reins to stop Valentine where the road was blocked by a cluster of cannon. Ominous clouds rolled closer and looked ready to burst their storm upon her. A man in a hunting shirt and tricorn hat approached.

"By order of the general, the road to Mount Washington is not passable for a coach's travel. You must turn the other way," he commanded her.

"Mount Washington?"

"Yes, ma'am."

Had he changed the name of the estate from Mount Morris to Mount Washington? she wondered. "And where is this general, so that I may make a request personally?"

"Ma'am, he is in the mansion on Mount Washington. I'm ordering you to turn the other way."

"Mount Washington! This is my property! You turn the other way." She had never been so angry. "Let me through!"

Another man interceded. "Wait, please, madame." Both rushed to speak to another officer, who appeared to be of a higher rank.

For a time she waited and watched. Dark clouds that appeared ready to release their burden cast a shadow over Harlem Heights. Mount Washington? Is there no other land in all of the colonies he could have named his? Mount Washington. Revenge? Could it be? Questions swirled through her mind. She had sent him an invitation for tea, only.

In front of her, soldiers piled logs into stacks. A fort? Were they building a fort on her estate? Here? Yes, she would have plenty to say to him. She couldn't wait to see the general. He named her property Mount Washington! Now he was building a fort on it.

A soldier of higher rank approached her. "Oh." He stopped in his tracks. "Mary Eliza Philipse, my apologies."

"Mrs. Roger Morris," she said, correcting him.

"My name is Captain Hamilton. I will see to it that you are escorted safely to your home."

"I thank you, Captain Hamilton." She wanted to say more, but instead, she stayed quiet. She knew he was there—George.

SHE RODE AS fast as she could, trying to race past her escort; however, obstructions lay in the way. Trees. Deep pits. The road to her home was completely destroyed. She needed to follow the captain. She had no other choice. Thunder sounded. Drops, light ones, fell on her. She would tell the general her mind today!

She dismounted outside the portico of her mansion. Captain Hamilton was there to receive her horse. Six soldiers guarded the entrance. Mary grabbed the painting from the coach, adjusted the covering, and moved toward them with a quick step, shielding the canvas from the wetness. She was seething.

Inhaling a deep breath, Mary readied herself to fight for entrance into her own house.

Those guarding the entrance made way for her, greeting her kindly. No one stopped her. She found Lulu standing in the foyer; she helped her with the painting, which was almost bigger than Lulu.

"It near knocked me straight over."

"What did?"

"Shot right through the roof! Those redcoats!" hollered Lulu. "The cannonball. It came straight through the house. Left a hole right in the ceiling."

"A cannonball? You are all right, Lulu?"

"I told them the redcoats were comin'. I saw them, 'cause I was standin' on the porch. They went straight out and stopped those coats from getting here, but the reds—they fired and fired and fired. Anyhows, it's in the basement—the cannonball—and they's covered the hole with wood and things."

"Thank God you are all right."

"We's won. The British went running from this place. We's won. Soldiers told me we brought them good luck. The general had his men protect me."

"General Washington?"

"Yes, the manly man."

"Where will I find him?"

Lulu pointed to the stairwell.

Mary swallowed hard and suddenly felt nervous. "I'll take the painting upstairs. We leave soon for Yonkers, Lulu. It's not safe for us to stay much longer." Mary checked her heart with her hand to be assured it hadn't leapt from her body. It was pounding hard now.

She climbed the steps to the second floor ever so slowly. A sensation ran from the very top of her head down to her toes. She expected a war meeting and loud, boisterous officers to be shouting orders at one another. Instead, only steady raindrops hitting the window made noise. The door to her study was partially open. She'd store the painting here. She walked in quickly.

She nearly lost her breath. General George Washington was seated right there in front of her, alone at her desk near the window. His hair, now cinnamon mixed with salt, fell carelessly over his broad shoulders. She scanned down his loose ivory linen shirt; it was tucked into his breeches, fitting snugly. His calves looked like tree trunks relative to the chair's slender wooden legs. Black shoes with gold buckles covered his large feet. Her eyes rose then to his sizable hands. It somehow felt so intimate, knowing her hands had been on the same wooden surface his now touched.

His writing hand stopped. He calmly placed down the quill and raised his head from the paper.

She got her mind to stay focused and willed away her desire. "You have taken on a Goliath." She spoke quietly.

Slowly, his face, with those familiar strong features, turned toward her. His eyes opened wide. He made no other move.

"Have you lost your mind? A fight against an empire?" As the words came out of her mouth, she didn't believe them herself. Only one man could defeat the British forces, and he was sitting right in front of her.

He was silent.

The pounding in her chest beat faster, in harmony with the drops outside the window, falling harder.

His immense frame lifted from the chair—a tall, handsome-bodied, manly man.

"All that is dear is at stake." His voice was gentle and sincere as he spoke.

A deep shooting pain in her core emerged; the ache that had been buried so long finally found the power to be felt.

"The spirit of freedom beat too high in me. The British nation deprived us of the most sacred and invaluable privileges . . . *justice* . . . *truth* . . . And to execute their scheme . . ." He paused. A hint of hardness took over his tone. "Nothing else would satisfy a tyrant and his diabolical ministry."

"And *you* will single-handedly force the English from the continent?" Indignation emerged in her voice.

His teeth clenched. She could tell from the muscles appearing at his jawline. He took a moment. She heard him exhale. Then he spoke. "Listen well to what I tell you and let it sink deep into your heart. We have punished the English and made them sorry for all the wicked things they had in their hearts to do. We have sworn to take vengeance on our enemies. We were determined to shake off all connections with a state so unjust, and unnatural."

She had to turn her face away from him. The two of them were standing feet apart, yet she could feel him as if he were pressed up against her.

"There can be no doubt that success will crown our efforts, if we firmly and resolutely determine to conquer . . . or to *die*!" His voice was firm.

Death, no, not death. Please. Not death, her mind yelled out. "To die?" Tears begged to be shed, but she turned them away. "To die?" She stared straight into him.

"I'll die on my feet before I'll live on my knees! I am a *warrior*!"

She recalled the daily prayers she said for him: Keep him alive. Angels, protect him. Don't let the curse find its way to him. Save him from me. Here he was in the flesh before her. Strong. Alive. Should she run the other way? Should she run as fast as she could into his arms? Something inside begged her: Love out loud. Love with no fear. Love the love that is right in front of you.

The storm intensified now, becoming furious. A rumble of thunder sounded.

She could sense him analyzing her. The painting gave her a moment to think. She clumsily tried to keep it from falling over, but she couldn't seem to calm the quivering of her hands. The covering fell away. She steadied the portrait finally, leaning it against a wall. She could say nothing. She feared her face flushed crimson, for the heat rushed to her cheeks. To think how the years passed, and still she felt the same for him.

George moved his gaze to the painting. He took his time with it. His eyelids lowered in a most romantic way. His mouth tilted into a half smile.

What lay hidden in the shadows of her soul now surfaced. "At what cost?" Honesty poured out of her. "At what cost, not to you, but to *me*. I've spent my life pained that I lost your heart. I've hardly been able to bear it." She could hold back her tears no longer. "Still now, decades later, I'm hardly able to bear it. Now you tell me that you are willing to give *your life*! And General Washington, I tell you, nothing else would satisfy 'a tyrant and his diabolical ministry' more than that."

He approached her, walking ever so slowly. "George." His shirt buttons, two of them, were open at his neck. It could have been seconds, but each step felt like an eternity. With his fingers, he moved his long hair back, away from his face.

"George." She spoke in hushed tone, with her tears trailing. "For me, losing you entirely, that I could not endure."

He was a step away from her now. He reached over and moved a wet wave of hair to behind her shoulder, his hand touching her cheek as he did so. She caught a glimpse of his sun-burnished, exposed forearm. He smelled of soap mixed with brawn, perfectly combined. She recalled his words to her so long ago: "'Twas perfect love before, but how I do adore." Had she said this aloud? She hoped it was not so.

All she could see was him.

All he could see was her.

The woman who still appeared the belle of the North was before him. The woman who had fallen asleep in his arms those years ago. The shadows of age had not reached her. Her warm, sweet breath fanned the skin on his arm. The blush on her cheeks tugged at his heart. She still smelled the same: lavender. Her damp hair fell free. Her dark eyes shone love, true love, the same as before. The thoughts of Mary Eliza, and the desire for her, were never quenched.

Everything about her was the same as before, everything except for her choice of clothing. As she peered down at herself, in only a nightdress, with moistened fabric from the rain clinging to her skin, a panicked look appeared on her face. Her beautifully arched eyebrows rose high. She stepped back from him and shook her head. An embarrassed tilt appeared on her mouth. Mary turned and walked away from him, toward the door.

The sound of thunder pierced the room. George turned toward the window. Lightning flashed. When he turned back, her eyes with those slightly tilted eyelashes were staring at him, scanning every inch of him. Her hand touched the doorknob.

Alone with George. She had waited so long for this moment. Envisioned what he would look like. What he would feel like. Every detail of him she had stored in her mind. Nothing had changed. The same hero of the South was before her. Their years apart mattered not. Nothing felt so right as this. She never let go of her affection for him, never let go of the kiss that had no end. Even now, she felt a oneness between them. His caress upon the nape of her neck—she wanted to experience it again. His lips placing soft kisses on her cheeks, his strength lifting her from the ground. She wanted more. More of him. More of them. She closed the door.

They remained gazing at each other. It was long ago that he had come to realize a simple truth—she was his and he was hers. Then a soft smile appeared on her face—one dimple on the right, one on the left. He watched her turn the key to lock the door.

"The world can never know," she whispered wistfully.

Mary Eliza returned to him.

Chapter Forty-One

—◄•►—

The Heart of Neutral Ground

You know the value of secrecy in an expedition circum-stanced like this.

—GEORGE WASHINGTON

VALENTINE'S HILL, YONKERS

Never could George remember a time in his life when he was in such a divided state. The war moved George to Yonkers. George made his headquarters on Valentine's Hill, on the northern pasture of the Philipse property, where he once enjoyed time with Mary Eliza under a meridian sun.

George stood atop this highest point of town. From here, he viewed Philipse Manor; she was there, safe. He would keep it that way, order his men to safeguard this property, consider it the heart of neutral ground.

Earlier this day, George traveled with Blueskin along the main roads leading here to make an inspection of them. He ordered they be lined with stone fences. The adjacent fields needed to be divided off with stone as well. He had good reason. Narrow paths would make it impossible for British wagons of ammunition and artillery to pass or would at least slow their pace. He remembered how all those years ago General Braddock had leveled every molehill to allow his wagons

to pass. George surmised the British would do the same now—make the roads proper for travel.

Every other route, he entrenched with a line of camps and ordered troops to slaughter any redcoat who passed.

The preceding days proved chaotic. Enemies don't succumb easily. On the Hudson River, the unthinkable transpired nights before. In the waters off Philipse Manor, four British warships, including the *Phoenix* and the *Rose*, fired their cannons. George ordered vessels, including one sloop of a hundred tons, the other packed with combustibles, a small craft, and two galleys, to face them—nowhere near the immensity of their warships. It was the best he had. The forces grappled for hours. Conflagration laid waste to two of the Royal Navy's warships. One sank. The other disentangled itself. The warships retreated. The British dropped down the river, headed for New York Harbor.

Without any true warships of their own, the American forces proved victorious in this battle, one of the first solely aquatic engagements of the war, here off Mary's property in Yonkers. His first victory on land, that, too, took place on her property in Harlem Heights. It was as if the finger of Providence had a hand in both, blinding the eyes of the enemy. The British were closing in fast. A few days would determine the course of this war. What became abundantly clear to him was that this contest would not be easy nor swift. How long the duration, he did not know.

Now George gripped the hilt of his brother's sword. What the British had done to him, to them, to the colonies, this needed to be rectified. How could a man of virtue hesitate in the least in making the choice to lead this fight? He was more determined than ever to end their hold.

What he did know for certain was that he was up against an empire whose resources were nothing short of inexhaustible, a force whose fleets covered the ocean's waters. Soldiers who had harvested laurels across the globe were his opponents. What did he have?

No preparation.

No money.

Not nearly enough men or supplies.

What he did have was the resolve to win.

Here on Valentine's Hill, with a sunrise emitting bold colors of hope, George removed Lawrence's sword from its sheath. Untrodden ground was beneath his feet. Destiny was calling him to a greater purpose. Where it would take him, he was not certain.

George placed a knee to the ground and prayed aloud. "The Lord God of Gods, the Lord God of Gods, He Knoweth, and Israel. He shall know; if it be in rebellion, or if in transgression against the Lord, save us not this day."

George rose with an unconquerable spirit. Revolution was calling him. He stood ready to fulfill the high destinies that Heaven appeared to have intended for him, and for all of America.

Freedom was in his grasp.

Chapter Forty-Two

—◦◦◦—

Let Freedom Ring

. . . truth will ultimately prevail where pains is taken to bring it to light.

—GEORGE WASHINGTON

HUDSON RIVER

Cry out. Throw yourself into the water. Shed a tear.

Nothing.

Mary just stood there unsteadily, letting herself be rocked by the currents. Her pale fingertips grasped the side of the sailing vessel. She felt the worn, dry wood scraping against her hands. Leaning over the rail, she took a hesitant breath of sea air. Her body did not violently protest as she supposed it would. You fear the water, she thought. On this morning, she stared straight down into the dark vastness, watching a single wave as it rose and as it fell.

Along the shoreline of what was her home, the autumn tones of the leaves looked like a necklace of gold, curving up and down rolling hills. She never viewed the land like this before, by boat. The property carried farther than the eye could see. She wondered whether she had explored every acre. Nevermore could she place her feet upon the fresh, tender grasses that tickled her toes or put her nose into the fragrant, curved petals that effloresced her hope.

The days passed now. George moved north of Yonkers. He hadn't left without a promise. "Not a battle scar will this place see," his aide told her. "It will remain the heart of neutral ground."

Mary escaped alone when the ship's horn blew—one long sound, followed by two in quicker succession. She knew the day had come. Her entire family scrambled for their lives, not because of the war, but because of the beast. She would not dare name him. She would not give him the dignity. Beverley and Susannah rushed to their estate in the Highlands, where Benedict Arnold was encamped, and pledged to protect them; Beverley planned to start his own regiment, made up of indentured servants and slaves. Sir Tenoe would return to New York to join and wrote Mary that he'd have *Liberty to Slaves!* embroidered on the uniforms. Frederick would soon be headed east toward Long Island. Temperance and François vowed they would care for the manor as best they could, believing firmly the Philipse family would return. Lulu stayed with Nathaniel Gist, who gave his word that he would keep her safe inside the Sherwood house. This disappointed Mary; however, she had no time to convince Lulu otherwise. Men, radicals, were coming for Mary, coming for the traitors.

The Act of Attainder would not remain in place, the general's aide told her. A captain in George's army, Alexander Hamilton, already spoke out against the New York legislation, which with one vote charged, tried, and convicted her and her family of treason, without proof. Maybe this law, the harshest ever passed in any colony, would one day be reversed.

Or maybe all was lost.

She might have stayed a day or so longer, if not for George's letter to the family. One simple, cordial line was written to her. She interpreted this as his signal to her to make an immediate escape. If they found her in the colony, the attainder ordered that she be put to death. But leaving this place, how could she leave, leave her mother? Mary remained by the Hudson for this very reason. In the waves is where she left her. In the same waves, she was leaving her again.

Before her, sunset's reflection of oranges and pinks set the river on fire. The flames lobbed to and fro.

What would her father think of everything that had happened? She couldn't imagine he would have ever let this come to pass. "Be the light, Mary Eliza," he had told her. Papa, I tried my best. My best wasn't good enough, she thought. Every day, she recited the pledge she promised him she would say: "You are capable of the impossible, for you have survived the unthinkable." Maybe Papa was wrong.

She saw the legal notices, stating judicial recourse was forbidden. Everything would be confiscated—the manors, the land, the mills, the bridge, the barns. Auctioned off to the highest bidder, and just like that, all these would vanish from their hands. The confiscations began with the animals. The sheep fetched thirty-one shillings each. Mary, with her head covered by her cape, nearly ran onto the stage to protest when they were accepting only three shillings for poor Valentine. She was weak and old, yes, but a good horse, solid in physique and gentle in temperament. Mary always felt safe with Valentine, just as she had in the embrace of the one who had given her the mare.

Wind moved the *Gabriel*, faster, farther.

She felt too heartbroken to think further about Valentine or her valentine today. She would put those out of her mind. She closed her eyes, hoping the darkness would wash away the treacherous label forced upon her.

"Traitor! Traitor!"

The words repeated in her head. What had she done wrong?

Nothing.

Take her home. Take her property. Take every last one of her possessions. With everything gone, maybe she could finally let go.

Nothing.

That is what she was. No longer an heiress. No longer a landowner. No longer the belle of the colony. She was nothing. During her entire life, she had always tried to hide from it, shoo it away, ignore it, fight it. None of that mattered; fate is foreordained.

Forget.

She wanted to tear pages out of her memory and watch them sink in the depths of the river.

A sudden breeze sent a chill through her. The hairs on her arms stood up. She was cold. Captain Garvan rushed over to her. Such kindness from a man who knew she could offer him no compensation. Here he was saving her again. In the decades she had known him, he had never asked anything from her.

Another man never asked for anything but her love. The moments with him she treasured. Would she have to forget even George? How could she not cherish the tender passions that rendered her whole in his arms? No, these pages of her life she would remember and protect. They would not see the river's floor, nor would the world discover what she desperately wanted to conceal. Not today. Centuries should pass without the truth's being revealed.

What she wanted now was in her trunk. She refused to leave the item behind. The captain helped her over to the chest crafted from the land's robust oaks. He had wrapped the trunk in canvas and secured it with rope to be sure no harm would come to it. Trying to keep her balance, she knelt down next to it, watching him unravel the protective covering. She undid the silver latch.

She opened it and removed the quilt with frayed edges that lay inside. Mary had kept this safe for decades. The captain smiled. He remembered. He wrapped her in the blanket of blue flowers when he rescued her as a little girl.

Taking the blanket from her, he opened it wide and waited to embrace her in it.

About to close the trunk, curiosity begged her to look deeper. Below were her beloved things: her mother's psalmbook and the diadem with her mother's face in ivory, which Mary had quickly wrapped in silk. Beneath that was the wooden box Frederick handed to her moments before she made her escape. She hadn't had time to examine the contents. Within it she expected there to be currency. Instead,

she found a pile of folded papers. Dozens of letters. She carefully removed one. As she straightened the folds, she recognized the writing
immediately. The script displayed thin upstrokes and wide downstrokes of loops and curves.

Her mind began to race.

Papers from George. They were dated 1756. Had they been written then and never delivered to her? She watched as her deep breath
dissipated in the air. Had he held these from her—Frederick? She
worked her brain hard, trying to remember the details. Mary recalled the heartache as she had waited for George to return, without
any word, not a note, that he was alive, that he would return. Negotiations had to be done in person; she remembered her brother remaining
firm on this, clearly firm on this. Then Captain Morris, playing guard,
staying close. They had deceived her. They had defamed George, vili-
fied him. They had kept them apart so that another could possess her.
The truth was clear now. She wanted to turn the boat around and
release a fury on her brother. She wanted to race after George and tell
him . . . tell him the truth of what had happened! And what? Stop a
revolution?

Mary's eyes fell to the writing before her. He'd written the lines
from Thomson's "Spring":

'Tis Love creates their Melody, and all
This Waste of Music is the Voice of Love;
That even to Birds, and Beasts, the tender Arts
Of pleasing teaches. . . .

But now the feather'd Youth their former Bounds,
Ardent, disdain; and, weighing oft their Wings,
Demand the free Possession of the Sky. . . .

On Ground
Alighted, bolder up again they lead,
Farther and farther on, the lengthening Flight;

Till vanish'd every Fear, and every Power
Rouz'd into Life and Action, light in Air
Th' acquitted Parents see their soaring Race,
And once rejoicing never know them more.

Her eyes opened to see them—ravens soaring above. They were flying away, past the Palisades, beyond the earth formation that she had always considered her protector—the guardian's wall.

A power greater than her took control. She had to accept this. Accept everything.

George. He had more to do. Providence, she was sure, had him marked for a great purpose.

Garvan got down next to her. "Breathe, Mary. Breathe." He covered her in the quilt.

The sun's rays shone brightly on the water ahead. She watched them, the birds, taking possession of the sky, flying far into the light, flying free. This was her chance, maybe for the first time. Yes, the first time. When you are nothing . . . this is when you will be like a Phoenix rising from the ashes. A new beginning.

They called her traitor. She'd refuse the title.

They showed her hatred. She'd find love.

They took everything, leaving her not even a pence in her pocket, but she knew that no being can be poor who is rich in spirit.

Underneath the papers was something more. A smaller box, decorated as a gift. Her fingers fumbled with it. This must have been from him. As she lifted the lid, her breath stopped. Inside was the softest of velvet bags tied at the top with a satin string. Carefully, with a trembling hand, she undid the bow. One hand cradled the bag; two fingers reached within. She removed a posy ring. She brought it into the light. Her eyes focused closely to read the inscription along the interior rim. The hidden message came through with clarity—words that touched her deeply. She reread the line as the weight that had held her down for so long, for too long, finally released her.

She realized her truth and finally knew who she really was. She was *Mary Eliza*, and she was enough.

As long as there was breath on her lips, she decided right then, she would live.

In her hands, destiny was etched into metal: *Where there is love, there is freedom.*

Acknowlegments

First and foremost, I would like to thank the power of curiosity, for this is what propelled me to search, physically and digitally, through dusty basements and attics, as well as storage units in libraries, museums, historic sites, and churches. Words cannot express my gratitude to the lovers of history who for centuries have kept the records. Through these thousands of documents, this story emerged. Special thanks to the University of Virginia for the comprehensive collection of the Papers of George Washington, the Library of Congress, the New York Public Library, the New-York Historical Society, George Washington's Mount Vernon, Harvard University's Houghton Library, the Huntington Library, the Morris-Jumel Mansion, the Philipse Manor Hall State Historic Site, the Costume Institute at the Metropolitan Museum of Art, from which fashion throughout the manuscript was drawn, Yonkers City Hall, the Sherwood House Museum, St. John's Episcopal Church, the Historic Hudson Valley, the Boston Public Library, the Fraunces Tavern Museum, Jeffrey's Hook Lighthouse, the Hudson River Museum, Old Dutch Church, St. Joseph's Seminary, the Van Cortland Manor House Museum, and countless others.

Boundless thank-yous to my wise and brilliant editor, Elizabeth Beier. If not for you and publisher extraordinaire Steve Cohen, this story may have never made it into ink. To the whole team at St. Martin's Press—Paul Hochman, Michelle Cashman, Leah Johanson, Clare Maurer, Meg Drislane, Donna Sinisgalli Noetzel, Kerri Resnick, Jennifer Donovan, Carol Edwards, Carly Sommerstein, and Laura Starrett—my gratitude. Over the years, numerous individuals have had a profound impact on my career, most especially my longtime agent and dear friend, Sandy Montag. Thanks also to Peter Dunn, David Friend, Tony Petitti, and Janine Rose.

My sanity might have been lost somewhere between the first and second page if not for my family. To my husband, Michael, if not for your inauguration as mayor of Yonkers. New York, this story may never have been discovered. Thank you for believing in me, encouraging me, and motivating me. It's meant the world to me. To my writing and research assistants, otherwise known as my children, Michael, Alexandra, and Christopher, you are our everything. To the great bunch of relatives who read and read and offered suggestions and propped me up, and even found the title for this novel over Sunday dinner, my gratitude to the Calvi family, the Spano family, the Ragone family, and the Circosta family—thank you for your suggestions, your research, and your patience. I adored our readings by the bay and our laughs over wine and cheese.

To my dear friends Alexandrea Denis and Andrea Smyth, your joy is infectious—thank you for joining with me on this adventure and helping to bring this story to life. To the many, many others, including Josyane Colwell, Danielle Parker, Dana Tyler, Nancy Montag, and Michael Downs, thank you from the bottom of my heart.

To all of you in my hometown of Yonkers, New York, I am forever in your debt.

Resources

Custis, George Washington Parke, 1781–1857. *Recollections and Private Memoirs of Washington*. New York: Derby & Jackson, 1860.

Flick, Alexander Clarence, 1869–1942. *Loyalism in New York During the American Revolution*. New York: Columbia University Press, 1901.

Glasse, Hannah, 1708–1770. *The Art of Cookery Made Plain and Easy*. London: Prospect Books, 1983.

Grose, Francis, 1731?–1791. *A Classical Dictionary of the Vulgar Tongue*. London: S. Hooper, 1785.

Hall, Edward Hagaman, 1858–1936. *Philipse Manor Hall at Yonkers, N.Y.: The Site, the Building and Its Occupants*. New York: American Scenic and Historic Preservation Society, 1912.

Irving, Washington, 1783–1859. *The Life of Washington*. New York: John W. Lovell, 1855.

Jefferys, Charles W. (Charles William), 1869–1951, Gerhard Richard Lomer, and Allen Johnson. *The Chronicles of America Series*. Roosevelt, ed. New Haven: Yale University Press, 1919.

L. & V., "The Virginia-Centinel. No. X." *The Maryland Gazette*, November, 25, 1756: 1. Print.

Manuscripts and Archives Division, The New York Public Library. "George Washington notebook as a Virginia colonel," The New York Public Library Digital Collections. 1757. http://digitalcollections.nypl.org/items /18d75990-8319-0132-56d7-58d385a7bbd0.

———. "Lawrence Washington letter to unknown person," The New York Public Library Digital Collections. 1749. http://digitalcollections.nypl .org/items/f13a2b90-e23d-0133-0b0f-00505686a51c.

Morris, Rogers. Letters to Mary Philipse Morris, 1775–1777, Morris Jumel Archives, New York.

Pargellis, Stanley McCrory, 1898–1968. *Lord Loudoun in North America.* New Haven, Conn.: Yale University Press, 1933.

Parkman, Francis, 1788–1852. *Montcalm and Wolfe.* Boston: Little, Brown and Company, 1884.

Sargent, Winthrop, 1825–1870. *The History of an Expedition Against Fort Du Quesne, In 1755: Under Major-General Edward Braddock.* Philadelphia: For the Historical Society of Pennsylvania, 1856.

Sparks, Jared, 1789–1866. *The Life of George Washington.* New York: Miller, Orton & Mulligan, 1856.

Timothy Scandal Adjutant, "A Return of the State of Capt. Polly Philips's Dependant Compny, with the Kill'd, Wounded, Deserted, and Discharg'd &c, during the Campaigns 1756 & 1756 (sic)," December 25, 1756, LO 6475, Huntington Library, San Marino, California.

Washington, George, 1732–1799. *The Journal of Major George Washington: Sent by the Hon. Robert Dinwiddie to the Commandant of the French Forces in Ohio.* New York: Reprinted for J. Sabin, 1865.

———. *The Writings of George Washington from the Original Manuscript Sources, 1745–1799.* Washington, D.C.: U.S. Government Printing Office, 193144.

———. *The Writings of George Washington: Being His Correspondence, Addresses, Messages, and Other Papers, Official and Private.* Boston: Little, Brown, 1858.

———. *Washington's Rules of Civility and Decent Behavior in Company and Conversation: A Paper Found Among the Early Writings of George Washington. Copied from the Original with Literal Exactness.* Washington, D.C.: W. H. Morrison, 1888.

———. George Washington Papers, Series 1, Exercise Books, Diaries, and Surveys -99, Subseries 1A, Exercise Books -1747: School Copy Book, Volume 1. 1745. Manuscript/Mixed Material. Retrieved from the Library of Congress, www.loc.gov/item/mgw1a.002/.

———. A.L.s.to [Sally Cary Fairfax]; Camp at Fort Cumberland, 12 Sep 1758., 1758. Susan Dwight Bliss autograph collection, MS Fr 167 (57). Houghton Library, Harvard College Library.

Washington, George, and William W. Abbot. *The Papers of George Washington, Colonial Series,* vol. 1–10. Charlottesville: University Press of Virginia, 1993.

Watson, John F., 1779–1860. *Annals of Philadelphia and Pennsylvania, in the Olden Time: Being a Collection of Memoirs, Anecdotes, and Incidents of the City and Its Inhabitants, and of the . . . Inland Part of Pennsylvania from the Days of the Founders*, 2d ed. Philadelphia: Penington, 1844–1843.

Whipple, Wayne, 1856–1942. *The Story of Young George Washington.* Philadelphia: H. Altemus, Co., 1918.

Wilson, Woodrow. "Colonel Washington." *Harper's New Monthly Magazine*, no. 550, March 1896.

Further Reading

Aulnoy, Madame d', 1650 or 1651–1705. *The Fairy Tales of Madame D'Aulnoy*. New ed., with additional illustrations. London: Lawrence and Bullen, 1898.

Chaucer, Geoffrey, d. 1400. *The Complete Works of Geoffrey Chaucer*. Oxford [Oxfordshire]: Clarendon Press, 1894–1900.

Dryden, John, 1631–1700. *The Poems of John Dryden*. London: Oxford University Press, 1935.

Hemstreet, Charles, b. 1866. *The Story of Manhattan*. New York: Charles Scribner's Sons, 1901.

Hoyle, Edmond, 1672–1769. *A Short Treatise on the Game of Whist: Containing the Laws of the Game, and Also Some Rules . . . Bath*. For W. Webster, 1743.

Johnson, Samuel, 1709–1784. *A Dictionary of the English Language: In Which the Words Are Deduced from Their Originals, and Illustrated in Their Different Significations by Examples from the Best Writers, to Which Are Prefixed, a History of the Language, and an English Grammar*. London: Printed by W. Strahan, 1755.

Jones, Thomas, 1731–1792. *History of New York During the Revolutionary War: And of the Leading Events in the Other Colonies at That Period*. New York: Printed for the New-York Historical Society, 1879.

Kirkwood, Agnes E. *Church and Sunday-school Work in Yonkers: Its Origin and Progress*. New York: G. L. Shearer, 1889.

La Chapelle, Vincent. *Le Cuisinier Moderne: Qui Apprend à Donner Toutes Sortes De Repas, en Gras & En Maigre, D'une Manière Plus Délicate Que Ce Qui en a été écrit Jusqu'à Présent: Divisé en Cinq Volumes, avec de Nouveaux Modéles de Vaiselle, & des Desseins de Table dans Le Grand*

Goût D'aujourd'hui, Gravez en Taille-douce, 2d ed., rev., corr. & augm. La Haye: V. La Chapelle, 1742.

Markham, Gervase, 1568?–1637. *Markham's Master-piece Revived: Containing All Knowledge Belonging to the Smith, Farrier, or Horse-leach, Touching the Curing All Diseases in Horses*. London: Printed for John Wright and Thomas Passinger (12th printing), 1681.

Morris, Richard. *Flora Conspicua*. London: Printed for Longman, Rees, Orme, Brown and Green, 1826.

Tomlinson, Kellom, 1690–1753. *The Art of Dancing explained by reading and figures whereby the manner of performing the steps is made easy by a new and familiar method*. London: Printed for the author, 1735.

Thomson, James, 1700–1748. *The Seasons: A Poem*. Boston: Crosby and Nichols, 1862.

Winchilsea, Anne (Kingsmill) Finch, countess of, 1661–1720. [from old catalog]. *The Poems of Anne, Countess of Winchilsea*. Chicago: University of Chicago Press, 1903.